CALDWELL COLLEGE LIBRARY
NEW JERSEY 07006

INTERNATIONAL MARKETING MANAGEMENT

5TH EDITION

SUBHASH C. JAIN
THE UNIVERSITY OF CONNECTICUT

SOUTH-WESTERN College Publishing

An International Thomson Publishing Company

CALDWELL COLLEGE LIBRARY
CALDWELL, NEW JERSEY 07006

Sponsor: Crystal Chapin
Production Editor: Karen L. Truman
Production House: Ambos Company
Internal Design: Craig LaGesse Ramsdell
Marketing Manager: Stephen E. Momper

Copyright © 1996
by South-Western College Publishing
Cincinnati, Ohio

All Rights Reserved
The text of this publication, or any part thereof, may not be reproduced or transmitted in any form or by any means, electronic or mechanical, including photocopying, recording, storage in an information retrieval system, or otherwise, without the prior written permission from the publisher.

1 2 3 4 5 6 7 8 9 0 D1 4 3 2 1 0 9 8 7 6 5
Printed in the United States of America

Library of Congress Cataloging-in-Publication Data:
Jain, Subhash C.,
    International marketing management / Subhash C. Jain - 5th ed.
      p. cm.
    Includes bibliographical references (p.) and indexes.
    ISBN 0-538-85281-X
    1. Export marketing—Management.   I. Title
    HF1416.J35 1996
    658.8'48—dc20   95-21360
                                              CIP

I(T)P
International Thomson Publishing
South-Western College Publishing is an ITP Company. The trademark ITP is used under license.

To Aarti and Amit

Brief Contents

PART ONE *Framework of International Marketing* — 1
- 1 Aspects of International Marketing — 2
- 2 Economic Rationale of Multinational Trade and Business — 29
- — Part 1 Cases — 57

PART TWO *The Field of International Business* — 101
- 3 International Monetary System — 102
- 4 International Finance and Accounting — 122
- 5 Regional Market Agreements — 140
- — Part 2 Cases — 163

PART THREE *Environmental Factors Affecting International Marketing* — 187
- 6 Economic Environment — 188
- 7 Cultural Environment — 214
- 8 Political Environment — 245
- 9 Legal Environment — 273
- — Part 3 Cases — 301

PART FOUR *Perspectives of International Markets* — 333
- 10 International Marketing Research — 334
- 11 Global Marketplace — 365
- — Part 4 Cases — 395

PART FIVE *International Marketing Decisions* — 441
- 12 Product Policy and Planning — 442
- 13 International Pricing Strategy — 481
- 14 International Channels of Distribution — 508
- 15 International Advertising — 548
- 16 Multinational Sales Management and Foreign Sales Promotion — 583
- 17 Export Marketing — 605
- — Part 5 Cases — 639

PART SIX *Planning and Control* — 671
- 18 Organization and Control in International Marketing — 672
- 19 Marketing Planning and Strategy for International Business — 702
- — Part 6 Cases — 729
- Subject Index — 777
- Name Index — 789

Contents

PART ONE *Framework of International Marketing*   1

   1   **Aspects of International Marketing**   2
Overview of the Book 5   International Business 5   International Marketing and Its Growing Importance 13   Framework of International Marketing 17   Multinational Corporations 18   Entry Strategies 21   Conclusion 25   Summary 26   Review Questions 26   Creative Questions 27   Endnotes 27

   2   **Economic Rationale of Multinational Trade and Business**   29
Theory of Comparative Advantage 30   Product Life Cycle and International Trade 36   Production Sharing 37   Internalization Theory 38   Trade Barriers and Trade Liberalization 39   U.S. Trade Liberalization 47   MNCs and World Markets 49   Summary 54   Review Questions 55   Creative Questions 55   Endnotes 55

Cases   Case 1: Xerox and Fuji Xerox 57
Case 2: Curtis Automotive Hoist 80
Case 3: Metro Corporation 87
Case 4: Marks and Spencer 92
Case 5: Hatfield Graphics, Inc 94
Case 6: Protective Devices Division 98

PART TWO *The Field of International Business*   101

   3   **International Monetary System**   102
The Development of Today's International Monetary System 103   Foreign Exchange 108   Balance of Payments 113   Eurodollars 117   Current and Emerging Issues 118   Summary 119   Review Questions 120   Creative Questions 121   Endnotes 121

   4   **International Finance and Accounting**   122
Implications of Financial Decisions on Marketing 123   Multinational Financial Management 125   Making International Investments 131   International Accounting 134   Summary 137   Review Questions 138   Creative Questions 139   Endnotes 139

   5   **Regional Market Agreements**   140
Effects of Market Agreements on Marketing 141   Early Attempts at Regional Economic Integration 143   Types of Market Agreements 144   Market

Agreements in Force 146   Summary 159   Review Questions 160   Creative Questions 160   Endnotes 161

Cases

Case 7: Shanghai Volkswagen Corp. 163
Case 8: Hillebrand Estates Winery Limited: Competing Against the World on the Basis of Unique Quality 169
Case 9: EQ Bank 177
Case 10: International Machine Corporation 180
Case 11: Sperry/MacLennan 182

PART THREE   *Environmental Factors Affecting International Marketing*   187

6   Economic Environment   188
Macroeconomic Environment 189   Microeconomic Environment 195   Economic Environment and Marketing Strategy 198   Analysis of Economic Environments 200   Opportunities in the Developing World 210   Summary 211   Review Questions 212   Creative Questions 213   Endnotes 213

7   Cultural Environment   214
The Concept of Culture 215   Cultural Field 217   Culture and Marketing 222   Cultural Analysis—The Primacy of Host Country Viewpoint 231   Cultural Adaptation 234   Cultural Change 238   Summary 240   Review Questions 241   Creative Questions 242   Endnotes 242

8   Political Environment   245
Politics and Marketing 246   Sources of Political Problems 248   Political Intervention 251   Political Perspectives 256   Political Risk Assessment 263   Strategic Response 266   Summary 269   Review Questions 270   Creative Questions 270   Endnotes 271

9   Legal Environment   273
International Legal Perspectives 274   Host Country Laws 276   U.S. Laws 282   Arbitration 295   Summary 297   Review Questions 298   Creative Questions 298   Endnotes 298

Cases

Case 12: Collision Course in Commercial Aircraft: Boeing–Airbus–McDonnell Douglas—1991 301
Case 13: El Norte Chemicals, Ltd. 317
Case 14: Kellogg In Europe 324
Case 15: The Clondike Works 328
Case 16: All Shave in Saudi Arabia 330

PART FOUR   *Perspectives of International Markets*   333

10   International Marketing Research   334
Meaning of Marketing Research 336   Framework for International Marketing Research 338   Information Requirements of International Marketers 341   Gathering Secondary Data at Home 345   Secondary Research at Home 350

Primary Data Collection 355   Organization for International Marketing Research 358   International Marketing Information System 359   Summary 362   Review Questions 362   Creative Questions 363   Endnotes 363

11 Global Marketplace 365
Global Market 366   Dimensions of the Global Market 375   Segmenting the Global Market 377   Segmentation Process 380   Criteria for Grouping Countries 381   In-Country Segmentation 390   Summary 392   Review Questions 392   Creative Questions 393   Endnotes 393

Cases
Case 17: McIlhenny Company: Japan 395
Case 18: Currency Concepts International 410
Case 19: Mondetta Everywear 416
Case 20: Idéale Imprimerie 429
Case 21 California Foods Corporation 433
Case 22: Chivaly International 437

PART FIVE *International Marketing Decisions* 441

12 Product Policy and Planning 442
Meaning of Product 443   International Product Planning 444   Product Design Strategy 447   Developing an International Product Line 453   Product Elimination 461   Adoption and Diffusion of New Products 462   Foreign Product Diversification 465   Brand Strategy 466   International Packaging 472   International Warranties and Services 474   Summary 476   Review Questions 477   Creative Questions 477   Endnotes 478

13 International Pricing Strategy 481
Importance of Pricing 482   Parent Company's Role in Pricing 482   Pricing Factors 485   International Price Setting 490   Transfer Pricing 498   Dumping 501   Leasing 504   Summary 505   Review Questions 506   Creative Questions 507   Endnotes 507

14 International Channels of Distribution 508
Alternative Distribution Channels 509   International Channel Members 514   Channel Management 525   Wholesaling in Foreign Environments 533   Retailing in Overseas Markets 535   International Franchising 540   International Physical Distribution 541   Summary 544   Review Questions 545   Creative Questions 546   Endnotes 546

15 International Advertising 548
Perspectives of International Advertising 549   Determining Advertising Strategy: Standardization Versus Localization 553   Media 563   International Advertising Program 570   Global Advertising Regulations 575   Industry Self-Regulation 578   Advertising Agencies 578   Summary 579   Review Questions 580   Creative Questions 580   Endnotes 581

16 Multinational Sales Management and Foreign Sales Promotion 583

Sales Personnel and Personal Selling Abroad 584 Formulating Policy Guidelines 590 Implementing Policy Guidelines 591 Repatriation and Reassignment 594 International Sales Negotiations 597 Foreign Sales Promotion 599 Public Relations Overseas 601 Summary 603 Review Questions 603 Creative Questions 604 Endnotes 604

17 Export Marketing 605

U.S. Export Trade 606 U.S. Government Encouragement of Exports 612 U.S. Government Hindrance of Exports 621 Export Management 622 Choosing Attractive Markets 622 Export Procedure 627 Duty-Free Zones 633 Barter 634 Summary 635 Review Questions 636 Creative Questions 637 Endnotes 637

Cases

Case 23: Schweppes Drinks—Export Light 639
Case 24: Ulker Biscuits, Inc. 649
Case 25: Toys "R" Us 655
Case 26: The Kellogg Company 662
Case 27: Avon Products, S.A. de C.V. 664
Case 28: Connecticut Corporation (Japan) 667

PART SIX Planning and Control 671

18 Organization and Control in International Marketing 672

Alternative Organizational Designs 673 Choosing an Appropriate Organizational Structure 681 Seeking Organizational Changes 682 Delegating Decision-Making Authority to Foreign Subsidiaries 686 Performance Evaluation and Control of Foreign Operations 691 Conflicts and Their Resolution 695 Summary 698 Review Questions 699 Creative Questions 700 Endnotes 700

19 Marketing Planning and Strategy for International Business 702

Dimensions of International Planning and Strategy 703 Planning at a Subsidiary Level 704 Marketing Planning at the Corporate Level 710 Information Scanning and Monitoring 719 Achieving Planning Effectiveness 719 Epilogue 720 Summary 724 Review Questions 726 Creative Questions 726 Endnotes 726

Cases

Case 29: Logitech 729
Case 30: Barossa Winery 740
Case 31: Federal Express Goes Global 753
Case 32: Mubarak Dairies Limited 765
Case 33: MacDermid, Inc. 771
Case 34: American Express International, Inc. 773

Subject Index 777

Name Index 789

Preface

The United States plays a leading role in world trade. In recent years, however, the international business environment has been marked by far-reaching changes that have challenged U.S. business. In the context of these changes, international marketing as a discipline of study achieves greater significance than ever before.

After decades of resting comfortably at the top, American business has awakened to a fiercely competitive world. As more countries become industrial powerhouses and their companies seek larger marketplaces, the United States faces more and stronger competitors. Japan, the most potent of them all, is pushing into such American strongholds as biotechnology and supercomputers. Western Europe is coming up fast in aeronautics and office equipment. The newly industrialized countries—China, Taiwan, South Korea, Malaysia, Singapore, India, Brazil—are establishing themselves as low-cost producers of everything from steel to television sets. In addition, the United States may face new competition in Canada and Mexico as a result of the North American Free Trade Agreement (NAFTA).

After many years, U.S. export performance is finally improving. A variety of forces are establishing an export culture among U.S. companies that should endure. Americans are now low-cost manufacturers after a long decline in both labor costs and the dollar and a rise in productivity. They also find themselves with a wealth of high-quality products that are often known around the world. English has spread as the *lingua franca* of global business, which lowers language barriers. Yet it is safe to say that America's leadership in some industries is probably gone for good. The United States may never be able to make a significant comeback in mass-manufactured commodities; among them, textiles, shoes, consumer electronics, and machine tools. But the more complex the product, the more likely America can hold its edge. The United States is still strong in such products as semiconductors (world market share: 40 percent), personal computers (70 percent) and jet engines (90 percent). Moreover, the United States remains the leading force in health care, entertainment, and financial services. To take on the world, however, U.S. industry must continue to fight hard to regain its prowess in the marketplace.

At the same time that American supremacy is being challenged, the powerful force of technology is driving the world toward a converging commonality: the emergence of global markets. Millions worldwide want all the things they have heard about, seen, or experienced via new communication technologies. To capitalize on this trend, American companies must learn to operate and compete globally, as if the world were one large market, ignoring superficial regional and national differences. Global markets offer unlimited opportunities. Corporations geared to this new reality can benefit from enormous economies of scale in production, distribution, marketing, and management. By translating these benefits into reduced world prices, they can dislodge competitors who still operate with the perspectives of the 1970s and 1980s. Today, only companies capable of changing their perspective and becoming global will achieve long-term success.

As more business battles cross borders, managers must broaden their view of markets and competition. Doing business in a global economy requires a lot of new learning—including how to find the right country in which to build a plant, how to coordinate production schedules across borders, and how to absorb research wherever it occurs. They must learn what sort of people to hire, how to inculcate a global mentality in the ranks, and when to sell standardized products instead of customizing them for local markets.

Only a few managers are capable of handling the competitive rigors of the new global marketplace. Companies, even those long accustomed to doing business overseas, find it difficult to make their managers look beyond their own domain to consider the capabilities and needs of the company as a whole to serve the global marketplace. They struggle to reorient their managers to be global strategists.

Business schools across the country face a similar problem. They must focus on the development of business education programs that produce graduates able to understand and function effectively in today's global business environment.

For over a decade, the American Assembly of Collegiate Schools of Business (AACSB) has been offering seminars emphasizing how business schools may internationalize their curriculum. The U.S. Department of Education continues to provide funding for enhancing international business education. These kinds of support have helped many schools in adding international components to their existing courses, and in developing new international courses. Despite these efforts, in most business education programs insufficient attention is paid to the international dimension of business. A recent study[1] commissioned by AACSB on the future of management education and development summarizes the problem:

> International business is an area of the curriculum where we found a considerable amount of, at worst, lip service, and, at best, serious concern on the part of deans and faculty (but, we should point out, *not* on the part of most corporate-sector respondents). It was one of the four specific areas most often mentioned in both interviews and on the surveys as needing more emphasis in the curriculum. The problem, as most acknowledged, is how to implement this—whether to do it through adding more specific courses on international business, international finance, international marketing and the like, or by putting more emphasis on international issues in courses already in the curriculum. This whole area has been the object of much discussion within the business school community, and we probably cannot shed much additional light on the curriculum aspects of the matter except to say this: Although there seems to be an increasing awareness among business school deans and faculty that more ought to be done to emphasize this area, this awareness of sensitivity so far does not appear to us to have been translated into a great deal of action. More is being done now than ten years ago, and this seems clearly demonstrable by an examination of curricula and in interviews with knowledgeable observers, but much more needs to be done.

As business schools globalize their curriculum, a variety of specific international courses are being added to give students a worldwide perspective. Because of the deep

---

[1] Lyman W. Porter and Lawrence E. McKibbin, *Management Education and Development: Drift or Thrust into the 21st Century?* (New York: McGraw-Hill Book Co., 1988), p. 85.

impact of local customs and business practices on marketing, marketing requires separate exposure in the international context, more so than any other area of business. Many business schools now have international marketing courses at the undergraduate level, and some even at the graduate level. Many more schools are rapidly adding such courses.

This book is designed to enable readers to develop skills to make marketing decisions in the global context: how to find new markets to replace saturated markets, how to customize products for the demands of new markets, which products world customers want, how to best reach the customers, what pricing strategies are most appropriate, what distribution channels are adequate to serve the world customers, how to overcome barriers that hinder implementation of marketing programs, and so on. National marketing boundaries are gradually dissolving. Marketers must monitor and evaluate emerging developments in a holistic and systematic way to define the opportunity for globalized marketing. Successful monitoring requires close communication and cooperation within and between organizations. The successful marketer should "think globally, act locally."

In addition to covering all important frameworks of marketing, the book briefly touches upon those concepts from other disciplines (for example, finance and accounting) that must be grasped to understand fully the perspective of conducting marketing across national boundaries. Throughout the book, a variety of examples are used to illustrate the points made. Important frameworks and theories are explained with quotes from original sources. The learning objectives are summarized at the beginning of each chapter. Included at the end of each part are cases that describe unique decision-making situations in international marketing. The cases provide adequate information for an intelligent and lively discussion, and should enhance the learning experience.

The following objectives guided preparation of the fifth edition: (a) to incorporate material on new developments (e.g., the finalization of the Uruguay Round and the North American Free-Trade Agreement); (b) to rearrange the material within the chapters for a better flow of ideas; (c) to include new cases reflecting a variety of international marketing situations; (d) to collapse material to keep it a semester-length book without compromising on complete coverage; (e) to strengthen the discussion on such topics as entry strategies, international trade, U.S. exports, and marketing planning and strategy; and (f) to update concepts, illustrations, and statistics. Accomplishment of the above objectives leads to the following distinguishing features of the fifth edition: (a) new and expanded material on various concepts, theories, and frameworks; (b) an in-depth look at the role played by international agreements and institutions in formulating global marketing strategies, including discussion of the progress of the Europe 1992 program; (c) spread throughout the book, International Marketing Highlights, describing interesting ideas, stories, and factual information relevant to marketing decisions; (d) new and interesting examples, both from industrialized and developing nations, to illustrate the underlying concepts; (e) a stand-alone book suitable for students with relatively little background in marketing; (f) discussion of the latest round of GATT talks (i.e., the Uruguay Round) and NAFTA; (g) substantial revision of chapters on economic analysis of multinational trade and business, multinational sales management and foreign sales promotion, export management, and marketing planning and strategy for international business; (h) updating of statistics, illustrations, and references to provide the most current perspectives on the subject; (i) increase in the number of cases from thirty to thirty-four, ten of which are comprehensive; (j) an *Instructor's Manual* with a variety of pedagogical aids: answers to the end-of-chapter discussion questions, true-false and multiple choice examination questions, a computerized test bank, transparency masters, solutions to cases, suggestions for further reading, and a listing of additional cases.

A new feature of the fifth edition is the inclusion of creative questions for class discussion. Positioned at the end of each chapter, the creative questions challenge the students on their understanding of concepts and theories presented in the text and lead to lively discussion.

The book has been developed based on the methodological and theoretical underpinnings developed in various social sciences. It also attempts to integrate major marketing paradigms and frameworks. In each case, the cultural, legal, political, and institutional implications of international operations are properly analyzed. The book successfully makes the reader an "informed observer" of the global marketplace.

A project like this cannot be completed without help and advice from different sources. I have been fortunate in having the counsel of many scholars who have contributed comments and criticism on previous editions. While it many not be feasible to recognize them all here, I would like to thank Catherine N. Axinn, *Syracuse University*; S. Tamer Cavusgil, *Michigan State University*; Claude Cellich, *International Trade Center (UNCTAD/GATT)*, Geneva; Rajan Chandran, *Temple University*; John R. Darling, *Louisiana State University at Shreveport*; Gary N. Dicer, *University of Tennessee*; Louis V. Dominguez, *University of Miami*; Roberto Friedman, *University of Georgia*; Thomas Greer, *University of Maryland*; Sandra M. Huszagh, *University of Georgia*; Hugh E. Kramer, *University of Hawaii at Manoa*; Ravi Parameswaran, *Oakland University*; Ronald J. Patten, *DePaul University*; Samuel Rabino, *Northeastern University*; Ram Rao, *Cleveland State University*; John K. Ryans, Jr., *Kent State University*; and Attila Yaprak, *Wayne State University*.

My special thanks are due to Andrew Forman, *Hofstra University*; William Lesch, *Illinois State University*; Marilyn Liebrenz-Himes, *George Washington University*; and Gerald Parkhouse, *Elmira College*, for meticulously reviewing the fourth edition and making useful comments. The fifth edition has been much improved because of their inputs.

I owe a great debt to my students at the University of Connecticut and the Graduate School of Business Administration Zurich, for their patience and enthusiasm in working with the ideas and helping me clarify my thinking in innumerable ways.

I also want to thank the following individuals for their permission to include cases written by them: Mohammed Ali Alireza, *University of San Diego*; Lyn S. Amine, *St. Louis University*; Robert Ballinger, *Siena College*; Vinod Bavishi, *University of Connecticut*; Mary R. Brooks, *Dalhousie University*; Grady D. Bruce, *California State University, Fullerton*; David W. Conklin, *University of Western Ontario*; Farok J. Contractor, *Rutgers University*; Ellen Cook, *University of San Diego*; Paul W. Farris, *University of Virginia*; Benjamin Gomes-Casseres, *Harvard Business School*; John F. Graham, *University of Western Ontario*; Philip Hunsaker, *University of San Diego*; Madhav P. Kacker, *Texas Graduate School of International Management*; Erdener

Kaynak, *Pennsylvania State University at Harrisburg*; M. G. Mostafa Khan, *University of Bahrain*; Mohammed Ishaq Khan, *St. Louis University*; Kwangsu Kim, *University of Connecticut*; Han Li, *Old Dominion University*; Leena Malik, *University of Western Ontario*; Gordon H. G. McDougall, *Wilfrid Laurier University*; Krista McQuade, *Harvard Business School*; C. P. Rao, *Old Dominion University*; Adrian B. Rayans, *University of Western Ontario*; Harry A. Shawky, *State University of New York at Albany*; Brook Smith, *University of Western Ontario*; David K. Smith, *Michigan State University*; Theodore F. Smith, *Old Dominion University*; William Van Doren, *University of Virginia*; Eric J. Vayle, *Harvard Business School*; and David B. Yoffie, *Harvard Business School*.

I am indebted to Stephen M. Walsh, State University of New York College at Oneonta, for contributing 125 objective questions to the *Instructor's Manual*.

A special mention of appreciation must go to my graduate assistant Monika Thiel, and especially to Melissa Pember of our word processing center, for coordinating various revision chores and for typing portions of the manuscript. I would like to thank our departmental secretary, Mary Palmer, and student helper, Lisa Bald, for their administrative support. I also acknowledge the assistance of Norma Holmquist at the University of Connecticut's Trecker Library in Hartford. I am thankful to many writers and publishers for granting me the permission to include excerpts from their works. Acknowledgment is due to John O'Connor, State Director, Connecticut Small Business Development Center, for his support and administrative help.

The talented staff at South-Western College Publishing Company deserves praise for their role in shaping the fifth edition. My editor, Crystal Chapin, offered excellent advice and direction on the structure of the fifth edition. My production editor, Karen Truman did an excellent job of managing the manuscript to completion. Thanks are due to Robert G. Ambos, Ambos Company, for the fine job of production.

I want to thank my dean, Thomas G. Gutteridge, for his encouragement and support in this endeavor, and my former professor, Stuart U. Rich of the University of Oregon, who continues to influence my thinking through his writings.

Finally, my thanks go to my wife and our children, Aarti and Amit, who have put up with me through the hectic times of book revision. They provided the time, support, and inspiration so necessary to complete a project of this nature.

Subhash C. Jain
Storrs, Connecticut

PART · I

Framework of International Marketing

Aspects of International Marketing

CHAPTER FOCUS

After studying this chapter you should be able to:

- Explain the growing importance of international business

- Describe how international marketing differs from domestic marketing

- Discuss the significant role of multinational corporations in the expansion of business on an international scale

- Compare alternative entry routes into foreign markets

One of the most significant economic developments since World War II is the increasing internationalization of business. Although business has been conducted across national boundaries for centuries, during the last four decades business dealings have escalated on a global scale. Leading corporations around the world have increasingly turned their attention to international business in order to maintain a competitive edge in today's dynamic economic scene.[1]

This global increase of international business affects the world economic order profoundly. It is a change with an impact comparable to that of the Industrial Revolution. In fact, today's global activity has been described as the second Industrial Revolution. Today's market provides not only a multiplicity of goods, but goods from many places. It is not surprising if your shirt comes from Taiwan, your jeans from Mexico, and your shoes from Italy. You may drive a Japanese car equipped with tires manufactured in France, nuts and bolts manufactured in India, and paint from a U.S. manufacturer (see International Marketing Highlight 1.1).

Gucci bags, Sony Walkmans, and McDonald's golden arches are seen on the streets of Tokyo, London, Paris, and New York. Thai goods wind up on U.S. grocery shelves as Dole canned pineapple and on French farms as livestock feed.

International Marketing Highlight 1.1

Do You Know Where Your Ford Was Made?

The 1992 Ford cars get controllers for their antilock brakes from Germany, engine computers from Spain, shock absorbers from Japan, and key axle parts from England. Windshields, instrument panels, seats, and fuel tanks are made in Mexico.

Source: Fortune, June 17, 1992, p. 53.

Briefly, worldwide consumers, particularly those in the developed countries, live in a global village. For example, young Europeans, Americans, and Japanese alike sport Benetton sweaters made in Italy, covet Japanese compact disc players, and haunt similar hangouts (see International Marketing Highlight 1.2).

America is irrevocably enmeshed in global business. We export some 20 percent of our industrial production, and we sell 2 out of 5 acres of our farm produce abroad.

In 1992, U.S. exports of goods and services supported a total of 10.5 million U.S. jobs. From 1989 to 1991, exports accounted for approximately 90 percent of U.S. real economic growth. The U.S. Department of Commerce estimates that over 37,000 U.S. manufacturing companies export, slightly more than one-third of all U.S. firms.[2] Almost one-third of U.S. corporate profit derives from international trade and foreign investment. The share of trade in the gross national product has more than doubled in the past decade. Considering our potential exposure to import penetration, more than three-fourths of U.S. goods are now effectively in international competition and more than half the supplies of twenty-four important raw materials, ranging from petroleum to cobalt, come from foreign sources.

International Marketing Highlight 1.2

Americanization of the World

Fifteen years ago, Japanese slept on mats in cotton quilts, shopped daily, grabbed a quick meal at a noodle shop, and drank green tea at breaks. Now they sleep in beds under sheets, shop once a week to fill their freezers, hit McDonald's for fast food, and have coffee and doughnuts at teatime.

Source: Kenichi Omhae, *Beyond National Borders* (Homewood, IL: Dow Jones-Irwin, 1987).

The internationalization of marketing and manufacturing activity has become irreversible even for relatively small companies. A conference board study showed that a commitment to international marketplace is important to sustained growth and superior profitability. Sales for firms with no foreign activities grow at half the average. Firms with international activities grow faster in every industry and in most size categories than those without. Profitability also rises for firms with a broad global scope. Companies with foreign plants in all three major global regions (i.e., North America, Europe, and the Pacific Rim) significantly outperform companies with more restricted international activities—both in return on assets and return on equity.[3]

Briefly, a world view based on outmoded concepts of nationality and traditional antagonisms between nations and ethnic groups is not useful in today's environment. In fact, to dismiss such a view outright and consider the inhabitants of such countries as Japan, the European nations, and the U.S. as a single race of consumers with shared needs and aspirations is the first conceptual leap toward a pragmatic and productive businessperson's world view. This is critical, because recognition of new opportunities requires an awareness of new realities.

Doing business is a creative enterprise. Doing business outside one's own country is a much more demanding, complicated enterprise. Setting aside other difficulties, consider briefly the simple fact that business environments of countries are different. Consider advertising. In the U.S., television advertising of consumer products is taken for granted. However, in many countries such as the Netherlands commercials are not permitted on television. In some countries, television advertising is permitted, but only on a limited scale. In Switzerland, commercials are broadcast between 6:30 A.M. and 8:00 A.M. on weekdays.

Similarly, the retailing industry structure varies dramatically across Europe. In the U.K., an ever-increasing percentage of total retail sales are made through large national retailing chains; while in Italy and Spain, the retail industry is made up essentially of independent "mom and pop" stores. Other countries have strong cooperative retailing or buying groups.

Just from this limited consideration of marketing perspectives, it is clear that international business necessitates an awareness of the clash of cultural standards among countries. These differences require international marketers to have good analytical abilities and sound business acumen in order to make viable decisions and operate successfully.

Overview of the Book

In this chapter we will examine what international marketing is, how it differs from domestic marketing, and why international marketing must be studied as a separate subject. Chapter 2 analyzes the rationale behind worldwide economic activity.

Chapters 3 through 5 in Part Two review the international institutions and agreements that continually create the conditions of the worldwide economic scene in which international marketing is conducted. Part Three, Chapter 6 through 9, explores the economic, cultural, political, and legal environments that affect business decisions. Chapters 10 and 11 provide the perspectives of the international marketplace. Chapters 12 through 16 are devoted to marketing decisions about products and their price, distribution, and promotion. Chapter 17 examines exporting.

The two final chapters deal with marketing planning and control. Chapter 18 discusses corporate organizational arrangements for international marketing management. Chapter 19 introduces the formulation of marketing strategy within the context of international business and provides a foundation for the advanced study of international marketing.

First, however, we must have an understanding of the state of the art of international business. Then we will discuss the crucial role of the marketing function in conducting business across national boundaries, a framework for making international marketing decisions, the reasons firms engage in foreign business, and the various modes of entry. Finally, we will consider the pivotal importance of the multinational corporation in global business.

International Business

The term *international business* refers to a wide range of activities involved in conducting business transactions across national boundaries. International business suggests a comprehensive approach to operations of both large and small firms engaged in business overseas. It is from this perspective that we will consider international marketing as it has developed and as it must, in the author's opinion, change in the future.

Perspectives of U.S. Business Overseas

Although many U.S. firms had long engaged in international business ventures, greater impetus to overseas expansion came after World War II. While the U.S. government helped to reconstruct war-torn economies through the Marshall Plan by providing financial assistance to European countries, the postwar American economy emerged as the strongest in the world. America's economic assistance programs, in the absence of competition, stimulated extensive U.S. corporate interest overseas.

In recent years, overseas business has become a matter of necessity from the viewpoint of both U.S. corporations and the U.S. government. Many U.S. industries face increasing foreign competition. Take the shoe industry, for example. The share of U.S. producers plunged from 50 percent in 1981 to 28 percent in 1985 to 21 percent in 1990.[4] The bicycle industry proves another example: the import share of bike sales jumped to 60 percent in 1990 from 42 percent in 1984.[5]

Faced with saturated markets at home, U.S. corporations have been forced to look for new markets. The flat growth rate of the beer industry in the early 1980s necessitated Anheuser-Busch's exploration of the huge overseas beer market. The company estimates that by the year 2000, foreign operations will account for almost one-fourth of its earnings.[6]

In brief, whereas in the 1950s and 1960s international business was a means of capitalizing on new opportunity, today's changing economic environment has made international business dealings vital for survival.

Essentially, there are two aspects of international business: direct investment and trade. At the end of 1993, according to a U.S. Department of Commerce report, the U.S. direct investment abroad stood at $450 billion, up from $314.3 billion in 1987.[7]

Over 75 percent of U.S. investments overseas have traditionally been in developed countries. However, as many *less-developed countries (LDCs)* gained political freedom after the war, their governments sought U.S. help to modernize their economies and improve their living standards. Thus, LDCs provided additional investment opportunities for U.S. corporations, especially in the more politically stable countries. However, it is interesting that, while for cultural, political, and economic reasons the more viable opportunities were found in Western Europe, Canada, and to a lesser extent, Japan, many developing countries provided a better return on direct U.S. investments.[8]

Direct foreign investment in the United States has come traditionally from Europe and Canada. Almost $344 billion of the $408 billion in book value of direct foreign investment in the U.S. at the end of 1993 came from the Netherlands, the U.K., Canada, Germany, Japan, and Switzerland. By contrast, direct investment in the U.S. by the 13 nations of the Organization of Petroleum Exporting Countries (OPEC) in 1991 was about 1.6 billion.[9]

Foreign investments in the U.S. have taken the form of both wholly owned subsidiaries and stock ownership. For example, Bic Pen Corporation (a French company), BMW (a German company), Lever Brothers (an English company), and Nestlé S.A. (a Swiss company) operated U.S. subsidiaries as part of their worldwide operations; that is, they are owned by the parent corporations. Other foreign investments are in the form of stock ownership in U.S. corporations. In 1989, for example, a Swiss-Swedish company, ASEA Brown Boveri (Holding) Ltd., bought a controlling interest in Combustion Engineering Inc. and Westinghouse Electric Corp's smaller electrical-transmission equipment unit. Likewise, a German group maintains about one-third ownership in A & P (Great Atlantic and Pacific Tea Co.), a large food chain.

In 1990, Matsushita Electric Industrial Co. of Japan, the world's largest maker of television sets and twelfth-largest corporation, bought MCA Inc. (the entertainment giant) for around $6.8 billion. In 1994, Sandoz AG of Switzerland acquired Gerber Products Company for $3.7 billion. In 1993, Cadbury Schweppes PLC, a British company, spent $334 million for A & W Brands Inc.

The other aspect of international business is trade. In 1994 the U.S. exported an estimated $503 billion in goods and services. Imports during the same year amounted to $669 billion, resulting in a balance-of-trade deficit of $166 billion. While the subject of trade will be explored in detail in Chapter 17, it is important to note that the U.S. share of the world exports in 1993 for manufactured goods—measured by value—comes to about 12.3 percent, slightly higher than it was in the 1980s.[10]

The traditional view of foreign trade as an exchange of tangible goods is increasingly giving way to the more balanced view that trade encompasses both goods and services. As the economies of more and more countries have become service oriented, foreign sales of engineering, consulting, banking, transportation, motion pictures, insurance, tourism, franchising, construction, advertising, and computer services are gaining recognition as significant factors in the foreign trade position of many nations. The importance of such exported U.S. services is borne out by the fact that deficits in merchandise trade have been partially balanced by growing services and investment income from abroad. Services exports and their income from overseas U.S. affiliates reached an estimated $174 billion in 1993, compared with $120 billion in 1990. Services imports in 1993 were estimated at $116 billion, giving a favorable balance of $58 billion.[11]

Why Go International?

There are several reasons for U.S. firms to seek business opportunities elsewhere in the world. Traditionally, the major focus of U.S. business has been on its large and expanding domestic market. In recent years, however, new factors have made international business the more desirable alternative for growth. These factors are expected to persist and to have even greater impact through the remainder of the 1990s and beyond.

Even if a company does not conduct international business, its competitors are likely to hail from all over and challenge its position in its own home market. For example, foreign manufacturers, including many from the Third World, created problems for such established U.S. firms as USX, LTV, and other stay-at-home steelmakers.

Market Saturation Markets for a variety of goods in the U.S. are becoming saturated far faster than new markets are being found. Staple consumer goods such as cars, radios, and TVs already outnumber US. households, and other products are fast approaching the same level. The slowing growth of the U.S. population means that the number of households is likely to grow at less than 1.8 percent per year to the year 2,000, and demand for consumer goods is unlikely to grow any faster.[12]

This point may be illustrated with reference to the baby food market in which Gerber Products Company has 70 percent of the U.S. market. Nonetheless, the company has trouble growing—it loses 10,000 customers a day as tots start taking grownup's food. The U.S. birth rate is declining, making it harder to replace them. Moreover, infants are eating less baby food on average these days.[13]

Thus, companies in many industries must develop new markets to continue to operate successfully. International markets, especially those where market saturation is a distant threat, provide an attractive alternative. Take the case of the cigarette industry. While sales have stagnated in the U.S., Third World countries offer rich markets. In Indonesia, per capita cigarette consumption quadrupled in the last ten years. Kenya's consumption has been rising 10 percent annually. Further, Third World markets are unburdened by many of the restraints imposed in the U.S. and other industrialized nations. Firms generally can advertise freely on radio and television, and packages don't have to carry health warnings.[14]

To transform global challenges into new opportunities, smart companies seek markets across national borders (see International Marketing Highlight 1.3). For

International Marketing Highlight 1.3

Coors Brews Big Plans for Korea

Coors is going where the growth is. With Korean beer sales expanding 15 percent a year, compared with a puny 2 percent in the U.S., Coors Brewing Co. is forming a joint venture with Jinro, Korea's largest producer of alcoholic beverages, to build a 1.8 million-barrel brewery in Seoul to produce Coors beer. Coors is aiming to capture 20 percent of the Korean market before long.

The plant is scheduled to come on line in 1995. It will be Coors's first plant outside the U.S. and is part of an international expansion program for America's third-largest brewer, which wants to be in 20 markets outside the U.S. by 1995. Coors beer is now for sale in seven countries outside the U.S.

Source: Business Week, December 9, 1991, p. 44.

---

example, Disney's theme park in France, following its entry in Japan, shows how important it is for a company to expand overseas in the wake of market saturation at home. Some U.S. hospitals, facing tighter health care budgets and dwindling occupancy rates, have started seeking foreign patients.[15]

United States Trade Deficit American industry grew up accustomed to a climate of private enterprise—nationwide markets without trade barriers to hamper the full development of economic efficiency. Most decisions could be made without considering how they would affect world market position. This is no longer true. U.S. business faces a declining share of world manufactured exports, and a continuing trade deficit, which means living beyond one's means. Just as an individual family should not, and cannot in the long run, live beyond its means, neither should a nation do so on a continuing basis. Therefore, the staggering U.S. trade deficit has to be balanced—the U.S. must make all attempts to increase exports.

Foreign Competition In many industries, U.S. firms face fierce and intense competition from foreign manufacturers. Consider, for example, the copying machine business. Currently, foreign competitors are offering low-priced, high-quality machines and are invading what was once Xerox Corporation's undisputed turf. Xerox no longer can take industry leadership for granted. In a crowded field with some 14 competitors from Japan alone, the battle resembles the one being fought by U.S. automakers against foreign importers. Another example is the $70 billion textile industry. Garment imports increased three-fold between 1980 and 1990 to $30 billion a year. Some 300 textile mills have been closed since 1980, and over 200,000 jobs have vanished. Industry experts think that textile apparel imports will continue to grow 15 percent annually. At this pace, imports will have 80 percent of the U.S. market by the year 2000.[16] The Japanese invasion of the U.S. auto market shows how foreign competition can harm the local industry (see International Marketing Highlight 1.4).

International Marketing Highlight 1.4

How Japanese Automakers Invaded the U.S. Market

During the late 1960s, Japanese car manufacturers wanting to enter the U.S. market looked for a niche and found one at the low end of the market: students and other consumers who wanted no-frills transportation. The small-and-cheap car market, as it so happened, was a niche that did not interest the Detroit auto companies. (Even relatively small American-made cars, such as Ford's Falcon and Fairlane, were essentially family cars.) The only formidable presence in this market was Volkswagen. Even so, VW could not fill the wide-open, small-car market fast enough. The Japanese companies responded by following a time-tested military strategy: taking uncontested ground first.

Datsun and Honda first began to introduce their cars into the U.S. around 1967. U.S. automakers paid little attention to the newcomers; they derided the Japanese cars as cheap models suitable only for a market that did not interest them in the first place. Essentially, the American automakers' attitude was to let Volkswagen fight it out with Datsun and Honda. Meanwhile, the Japanese focused on providing low-cost products, built up a following (and, more important still, a low-cost, high-quality manufacturing base), then gradually introduced larger, better, higher-priced models.

Now Toyota, Datsun, Honda, Mitsubishi, and other major Japanese manufacturers have established themselves as a permanent, formidable presence in the U.S. automobile market. These companies have moved beyond their initial niche to satisfy America's demands for a wide variety of high-quality cars. The Detroit automakers have had an increasingly difficult time competing effectively against them.

The truth of the matter is that the United States' ability to compete in the world market has eroded significantly during the past two decades. Most of this decline has occurred in such traditional industries as steel, automobiles, consumer electronics, apparel, and machine tools. Recently, even high-tech industries have become susceptible. Competition has forced some companies to shift their consumer electronics manufacturing to the Far East, which explains why the high-tech industry is losing its edge.[17] Even this measure did not succeed for General Electric, which in 1986 sold 80 percent of its consumer electronics business (including the RCA brand acquired in late 1985) to Thomson, France's state-owned leading electronics manufacturer. Thus in the color television business the U.S. becomes a minor player, yielding the market to Japanese and European companies. Japan leads with over 18 million units, while Europe accounts for 15 million units. The U.S. share is limited to 2 million sets.[18]

The declining international position of the U.S. in the high-tech area is a matter of serious concern. Additionally, the U.S. has been losing market position in a number of product areas. For example, the American manufacturers' share of the world semiconductor market declined from 44 percent in 1980 to less than 6 percent in 1993.[19] In the commercial aircraft business, Europe's Airbus Industrié has become a threat to Boeing and McDonnell Douglas.[20]

All the more troubling is the fact that many of these high-tech products derive from technology developed in the U.S. Phonographs, color TVs, audiotape recorders, and videotape recorders were all invented in the U.S., yet U.S. companies have practically no business left in these products (see International Marketing Highlight 1.5).

One way for U.S. companies to meet the challenge from foreign companies is to enter the home markets of their foreign competitors. While Japanese automakers had a leeway with American consumers in the early 1980s, there may be Japanese car buyers interested in U.S. cars now and in the future, but not if these cars have their steering wheels on the wrong side.

International Marketing Highlight 1.

There Goes Another One

In recent years, U.S. companies have conceded one homegrown industry after another to more aggressive and competitive foreign rivals. First came cameras, then televisions, tape recorders, stereo equipment, and semiconductors. In September 1990, Cincinnati Milacron, the last independent U.S. producer of heavy industrial robots, agreed to sell the business to a subsidiary of Switzerland's Asea Brown Boveri.

Milacron retreated from the $4 billion market after 13 years because its share of the business had dwindled from a commanding 75 percent to just 10 percent, and its losses from robotics had been mounting since the mid 1980s. The company will concentrate on its traditional lines of machine tools and other industrial products.

Source: Business Week, September 24, 1990, p. 71.

Emergence of New Markets The world is changing fast resulting in the emergence of new markets. In the 1990s, new business opportunities will flow from the European Community, enhanced by the reunification of Germany, the thriving economies in the Pacific Rim countries, efforts to curb inflation in Latin America, and the emerging market-based economies in Eastern Europe (see International Marketing Highlight 1.6). Elsewhere in developing countries, momentum toward privatization (i.e., transfer of business ownership from government to private citizens and/or institutions) and liberal policies promise new opportunities (see International Marketing Highlight 1.7).

International Marketing Highlight 1.6

Quick Shave

A few years ago, Gillette Co. discovered that only 8 percent of Mexican men who shave use shaving cream. Sensing an opportunity, Gillette in 1975 introduced plastic tubes of shaving cream in Guadalajara, Mexico, that sold for half the price of its aerosol. In a year's time 13 percent of Guadalajaran men began to use shaving cream. Gillette is planning to sell its new product, Prestobarba (Spanish for "quick shave"), in the rest of Mexico, Colombia, and Brazil.

Source: David Wessel, "Gillette Keys Sales to Third World Tastes," *The Wall Street Journal*, January 23, 1986, p. 35.

International Marketing Highlight 1.7

Gerber Locates a Niche in India

Gerber Products Company has undertaken extensive market research in India. Despite India's predominantly poor population, the country has a prosperous middle class and a small but wealthy upper class that Gerber considers a promising market.

Until recently, most Indians have been unlikely to show any interest in Western-style baby foods. Lately, though, the convenience of such products, plus their status appeal, has heightened consumers' curiosity and openness. Initial focus groups show that baby foods have high potential for success in certain areas of the subcontinent.

For U.S. marketers, rising Pacific power holds great promise. There is the emergence of a market of more than two billion potential consumers. In the last 25 years, as the Pacific region began its time-bending leap into the 20th century, millions of Asians began an equally rapid transition from rural to urban, from agrarian to industrial, from feudal to contemporary society. With more of the Pacific region's rural population traveling to the cities to shop every day, the demand for goods and services—from the most basic household commodities to sophisticated technical devices—is soaring (see International Marketing Highlight 1.8). The growing importance of Asia for the U.S. is supported by the fact that the share of America's exports that goes to Europe has fallen from 31 percent to 20 percent over the past 20 years, while the share going to Asia has risen from 20 percent to 30 percent.[21]

International Marketing Highlight 1.8

PepsiCo Inc. Plans China Investment

PepsiCo Inc. plans to invest $350 million in China in the next 5 years, matching equally bullish efforts by Coca-Cola Co. in the largely untapped market. PepsiCo received government approval to build 10 bottling plants in China, which will result in a $350 million investment by the company and a $250 million investment by its local joint-venture partners. PepsiCo already owns 8 bottling plants in China and has invested $100 million there.

According to PepsiCo, early in the next century, China is expected to be the second-largest market after the U.S.

The Chinese soft-drink market accounted for just 700 million cases last year, or about 13 servings a person, compared with about 8 billion cases, or nearly 800 servings a person, in the U.S.

Source: The Wall Street Journal, January 27, 1994, p. 1.

The emerging markets in less-developed countries (LDCs) can help many U.S. corporations to counter the results of demographic changes in the Western nations. In most advanced nations of the world, birth rates are declining while population in the Third World countries is growing. Consider the automobile industry. The people-per-car ratio in China is 680; Philippines, 131; Thailand, 70; Brazil, 14; Mexico, 12.5; South Korea, 7; and Poland, 6. In the U.S., Europe, and Japan, the respective figures are 1.7, 2.5, and 3, showing the tremendous potential in the developing countries.[22]

Globalization of Markets Theodore Levitt asserts that technology has homogenized worldwide markets; therefore, companies should produce globally standardized products and market them in the same way to people everywhere.[23] All the principal barriers to the growth of such markets have weakened in the last decade. Tariffs have been reduced by the General Agreement on Tariffs and Trade (GATT). Transportation costs have declined with the use of containerization and larger-capacity ships. Many products have emerged that pack very high value into very small packages. Consumer needs in the industrialized nations have become increasingly similar, and purchasing power in many countries has increased sharply. In consequence, a multitude of distinct national markets is beginning to coalesce into a true world market for a number of products in different industries. This development can be a source of competitive advantage for companies that plan their strategies accordingly.

A few examples will suggest how extensive the global product phenomenon has already become. Kids everywhere are playing on Nintendo and bounding along the streets to the sound of a Sony Walkman. The videocassette recorder market took off simultaneously in Japan, Europe, and the U.S., but the most extensive use of videocassette recorders today is probably in places like Riyadh and Caracas. Shopping centers from Dusseldorf to Rio sell Gucci shoes, Yves St. Laurent suits, and Gloria Vanderbilt jeans. Siemens and International Telephone & Telegraph (ITT) telephones can be found almost everywhere in the world. Mercedes-Benz and the Toyota Corolla are as much objects of passion in Manila as in California.

Just about every gas turbine sold in the world has some General Electric technology or component in it, and what country doesn't need gas turbines? How many airlines around the world could survive without Boeing or Airbus equipment? Third World markets for high-voltage transmission equipment and diesel-electric locomotives are bigger than those in the developed countries. Today's new industries—robotics, videodiscs, fiber optics, satellite networks, high-technology plastics, and artificial diamonds—seem to be global at birth.

Opportunities via Foreign Aid Programs Although in recent years U.S. foreign aid programs for developing countries have declined gradually, in the 1950s and 1960s they provided billions of dollars to developing countries to undertake programs of economic buildup. Most of these programs required that aid recipients spend U.S. money on goods and services from U.S. corporations, except in cases where the desired goods were available only from non-U.S. sources. In either circumstance, the aid money created new markets in developing countries. Even more recent aid programs, small as they were ($17.4 billion in 1993, $10.6 billion in economic support, and $6.8 billion for military hardware), provided opportunities for some businesses to go abroad.

Other Reasons A variety of other reasons make conducting business across national boundaries profitable and attractive.

> In industries where economies of scale are feasible, a large market is essential. However, if the home market is not large enough to absorb the entire output of an industry, entering foreign markets may be an attractive alternative. Polaroid Corporation, a dominant force in the U.S. photographic industry, claims to have achieved economies of scale by entering foreign markets.[24]

International business provides a safety net during business downturns. Usually a recession starts in one country and takes several quarters to move into other countries. It is said that European economies are affected by a U.S. recessionary trend after about six months. Thus, firms that do business internationally can shift their emphasis from U.S. to foreign markets during the recession. For example, during the U.S. recession of 1991, multinational companies were able to shift their marketing focus to Europe and Asia, where an economic boom was in progress.[25]

In many industries, labor constitutes a major proportion of costs. Since labor cost in Third World countries is much lower than in the U.S., it is economically attractive for the companies to expand foreign operations. For example, electronics companies depend on hundreds, sometimes thousand, of young women to do the painstaking job of assembling tiny parts that are shipped to the US. for use in computers and other products. Labor sometimes represents as much as half of the cost of these parts, so the cheaper the labor, the higher the profit. Thus, a number of U.S. companies—Hewlett-Packard, Intel, National Semiconductor, and ITT, among a dozen others—have gone as far as Malaysia to save on labor cost.

Some nations offer tax incentives to attract foreign businesses to their countries. An important motive for extending such tax incentives is to increase scarce foreign exchange and create jobs at home. Typically, a company finding such tax concessions viable will establish a plant in the low-tax country and then sell the manufactured goods locally, as well as export from there to its primary markets.

Many companies find it more desirable to develop and/or test new products outside the U.S. This avoids exposure to competitors and, to some extent, keeps new development information secret until the product is ready for full introduction. Ford Motor Company, for example, did much of its world-car development in Germany.

Many international markets are less competitive than the U.S. market; several are still in an embryonic stage. Further, in some instances, governments will give companies a monopoly or quasi-monopoly position if they assemble and produce their products there.

Finally, international presence provides expanded access to advances in technology, worldwide raw materials, and diverse international economic groups. For example, European auto manufacturers led the way in fuel injection technology. Active U.S. auto company presence in Europe would have provided earlier insights into this technology. Some countries have easier access to certain markets that are difficult for U.S. companies to enter because of bilateral agreements.

International Marketing and Its Growing Importance

Stage of International Involvement

The term *international marketing* refers to exchanges across national boundaries for the satisfaction of human needs and wants. The extent of a firm's involvement abroad is a function of its commitment to the pursuit of foreign markets. A firm's overseas involvement may fall into one of several categories:

1. *Domestic*: Operate exclusively within a single country.

2. *Regional exporter*: Operate within a geographically defined region that crosses national boundaries. Markets served are economically and culturally homogeneous. If activity occurs outside the home region, it is opportunistic.
3. *Exporter*: Run operations from a central office in the home region, exporting finished goods to a variety of countries; some marketing, sales, and distribution outside the home region.
4. *International*: Regional operations are somewhat autonomous, but key decisions are made and coordinated from the central office in the home region. Manufacturing and assembly, marketing, and sales are decentralized beyond the home region. Both finished goods and intermediate products are exported outside the home region.
5. *International to global*: Run independent and mainly self-sufficient subsidiaries in a range of countries. While some key functions (R&D, sourcing, financing) are decentralized, the home region is still the primary base for many functions.
6. *Global*: Highly decentralized organization operating across a broad range of countries. No geographic area (including the home region) is assumed a priori to be the primary base for any functional area. Each function including R&D, sourcing, manufacturing, marketing, and sales is performed in the location(s) around the world most suitable for that function.

Typically, the journey begins at home. Companies operating exclusively within a single country reach the limits to growth in their home market and face the need to expand to achieve further growth.[26] The time that it takes to reach this outer growth limit depends almost entirely on the size of the home market. Thus, North American companies will take longer to reach the outer limit than will companies in Singapore, South Korea, Taiwan, and Japan, whose home markets are substantially smaller and provide less room to grow. Once the domestic barrier is reached, companies evolve into an export modality, either on a limited, regional basis where markets are still economically and culturally homogeneous, or on a broader basis where finished goods are exported to a variety of countries. Regional exporters and export companies continue to run operations from a central office in the home market, though some marketing, sales, and distribution functions begin to crop up elsewhere.

As companies become more successful in their export operations, they reach that critical point where the need to achieve greater proximity to overseas markets becomes paramount.[27] At this point, such companies begin to replicate their business systems in new markets by creating relatively autonomous regional operations. Manufacturing and assembly, marketing, and sales are decentralized and both finished goods and intermediate products are exported outside the home region, but key decisions are made, or at least coordinated, by a head office in the home region. Companies that have reached this stage of evolution may be characterized as international companies. The replication of a company's business system in various locations around the world does not, however, represent a long-term formula for profitable growth and, ultimately, international companies face the need to optimize their businesses globally by adopting a global model of operation. For global companies, no one geographic area is assumed to be the primary base for any function—research and development, sourcing, and manufacturing are situated in the most suitable locations world-wide.[28]

Why Study International Marketing?

We have already examined the factors that make international business an important field of endeavor from the viewpoint of a businessperson. How does this importance extend to marketing? Marketing is more significant, both for doing business abroad and for analyzing the impact of international happenings on business in the U.S., than other functions of a business—such as manufacturing, finance, and research and development—because marketing responds to the local culture and businesses' multiple interrelationships with the local environment. Growing internationalization of business brings about changes in the positioning of competitors and the appropriate competitive strategies. You can't sell what people won't buy is a truism. Consumers overseas have different needs and expectations than they do in America.

The only way to guarantee long-term competitive success is by providing better value to customers. Consider the Japanese market. American companies and U.S. government agencies began to complain that restrictions, in the form of tariffs and visible (and invisible) non-tariff barriers and constraints, excluded much U.S. business from Japanese markets. However, an unbiased analysis showed that American business had not made a great effort to enter the Japanese market. As has been remarked:

> Americans still are going to have to practice the marketing methods they preach if they are going to exploit the opportunities that are opening up in Japanese markets. In short, U.S. businesses still must find out what the Japanese consumers want, tailor products to fit the Japanese market, and put these products into suitable distribution channels.[29]

A U.S. Chamber of Commerce report indicated that U.S. business had fallen short of success in Japan because it failed to keep track of changes in Japan's marketing environment. Certain U.S. consumer goods such as automobiles, watches, cigarette lighters, and whiskey had been regarded in Japan as status symbols and were consumed by a limited number of wealthy buyers. Distribution of such products had been organized emphasizing the exclusiveness of the products and brand prestige. This traditional mode of marketing luxury items was inadequate to substantially increase exports to Japan or to develop a mass market. In brief, if imports were to become a part of Japanese daily life, rather than just status symbols, U.S. manufacturers had to reexamine pricing policies and distribution channels and then develop products that better fit Japanese consumers' needs.[30]

Briefly, U.S. companies frequently fumble overseas because they fail to respond to the peculiarities of the markets. Apple Computer, Inc., had the market to itself when it became the first company to sell a personal computer in Japan. But the company began to lose ground for failing to do the right things. Apple didn't provide Japanese manuals. The computers arrived with keyboards that didn't work, and the packaging was shoddy.[31] Like the English, the Japanese drive on the left. American automakers would like the Japanese to buy their cars, but they do not manufacture cars with steering on the right side.

In the developing world also, U.S. corporations have not been on target in marketing.[32] Most firms pursue short-term strategies on the international scene by attempting to sell luxury goods to the affluent classes. Instead, an orientation toward developing and securing mass markets would provide lasting, long-term benefits. For example, malnutrition is a common problem in LDCs. Therefore, vitamin pills are important. But U.S. firms sell the same vitamin at about the same price in poor countries as they do in the U.S. Obviously, the two markets cannot afford the same pills.

Mass markets are ready for U.S. products, but American businesses have not responded to the opportunities with responsible marketing. To cash in effectively on the opportunities these markets represent, in LDCs and elsewhere, U.S. corporations must become more sophisticated marketers.[33]

Domestic Versus International Marketing

The basic nature of marketing does not change from domestic to international marketing, but marketing outside national boundaries poses special problems. International marketing, unlike domestic marketing, requires operating simultaneously in more than one kind of environment, coordinating these operations, and using the experience gained in one country for making decisions in another country. The demands are tough and the stakes are high. International marketers not only must be sensitive to different marketing environments internationally, but also must be able to balance marketing moves worldwide to seek optimum results for the company.

The impact of environment on international business can be illustrated by the watch industry. New technology, falling trade barriers, and changing cost relationships have affected the competitive patterns of the industry worldwide. Only companies with global perspective are operating successfully. A few *world companies* sell *world product*s to increasingly brand-conscious consumers. This multinationalization of the watch industry has made four producers—Switzerland, Japan, Hong Kong, and the U.S.—dominate the scene by emphasizing brand names. Manufacturing operations are specialized by country according to costs of specific processes, components, and subassemblies.

To successfully compete globally, rather than simply operate domestically, companies should emphasize: (1) Global *configuration* of marketing activities (i.e., where activities such as new product development, advertising, sales promotion, channel selection, marketing research, and other functions should be performed), (2) *global coordination* of marketing activities (i.e., how global marketing activities performed in different countries should be coordinated); and (3) *linkage* of marketing activities (i.e., how marketing activities should be linked with other activities of the firm).[34]

Many marketing activities, unlike those in other functional areas, must be dispersed in each host country to make an adequate response to the local environment. Not all marketing activities need to be performed on a dispersed basis, however. In many cases, competitive advantage is gained, in the form of lower cost or enhanced differentiation, if selected activities are performed centrally as a result of technological changes, buyer shifts, and evolution of marketing media. These activities include production of promotional materials, sales force and service support organization training, and advertising. Further, international marketing activities dispersed in different countries should be properly coordinated to gain competitive advantage. Such coordination can be achieved by (1) performing marketing activities using similar methods across countries; (2) transferring marketing know-how and skills from country to country; (3) sequencing marketing programs across countries; and (4) integrating the efforts of various marketing groups in different countries.

Finally, a global view of international marketing permits linking marketing to upstream and support activities of the firm, which could lead to advantages in various ways. For example, marketing can unlock economies of scale and learning in production and/or R&D by (1) supporting the development of universal products by providing the information necessary to develop a physical product design that can be sold worldwide; (2) creating demand for more universal products even if historical demand has been for more varied products in different countries; (3) identifying and penetrating segments in many countries to allow the sale of universal products; and (4) providing services and/or local accessories that effectively tailor the standard physical product to the local needs.

Framework of International Marketing

Marketing decisions relative to product, price, promotion, and distribution must be made whether business is conducted in the U.S., France, Japan, or Mexico. But the environment within which these decisions are made is unique to each country. This differential of environment distinguishes international marketing from domestic marketing.

Typically, a firm should make domestic marketing decisions only after considering internal and external environments. *Internal environment factors* primarily refers to corporate objectives, corporate organization, and resource availability. *External environment factors* include competition, technological change, the economic climate, political influences, social and cultural changes, pertinent legal requirements, current ethical business standards, consumerism, and changes among marketing channels.

A U.S. firm interested in doing business in a foreign country would face the same internal and external factors it would face domestically, but from an entirely different environmental perspective. Economic conditions vary from one country to another. The anti-trust laws in the U.S. are much tougher than those in Japan. The U.S. has a two-party political system, Mexico does not. Women have an important decision-making role as consumers in the U.S. and in other Western countries, but this is not the situation among the Muslims. As a matter of fact, business environments vary tremendously even among countries that are geographically in the same region, or that have the same cultural heritage. For instance, it would be wrong to assume that the U.S. and England have common marketing environments. There may be some similarities, but overall the two are very different.

Figure 1.1 depicts the marketing decisions and environments of international marketing. The nature of decision making in international business is essentially the same as in domestic business. Consideration of environment, however, is more philosophically abstract. In addition to the internal and external environmental aspects listed previously, the environment of each individual country has a combined environmental reality that the international marketer must perceive. The international marketer can sort out and combine these realities using four general categories: economic, cultural, political, and legal environments. In addition, an understanding of international economic institutions (for example, the International Monetary Fund) and an understanding of agreements (for example, the General Agreement on Tariffs and Trade) among nations are essential, even though it may not be strictly correct to label these as a part of the country's marketing environment.

Further, an international marketer must be sensitive to certain aspects of the domestic U.S. environment, such as competition and technological changes, included in Figure 1.1 under other types of environments. Marketing decisions to serve the

FIGURE 1.1 Decisions and Environments of International Marketing

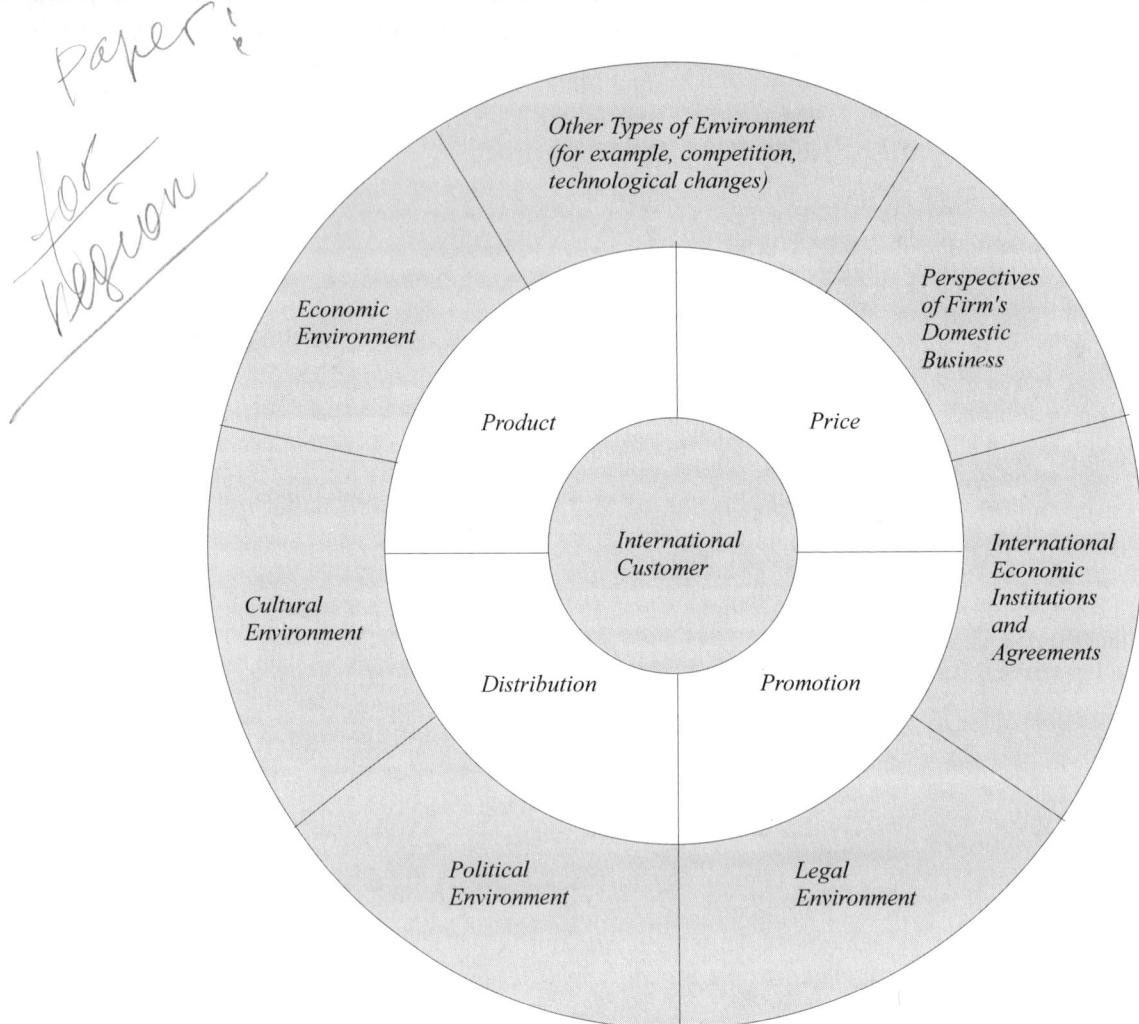

international customer also require consideration of the firm's domestic business—its objectives and strategies, commitments and resources, and organization structure.

Multinational Corporations

The *multinational corporation (MNC)* is the principal instrument in the expansion of business on an international scale. In barely four decades, it has become, by all accounts, the most formidable single factor in world trade and investment. The MNC plays a decisive role in the allocation and use of the world's resources by conceiving new products and services, by creating or stimulating demand for them, and by developing new modes of manufacturing and distribution. Current rates of energy consumption,

Dimension of MNCs

for example, would be unthinkable without the role of MNCs in the development and expansion of the automobile and electrical appliance industries. Indeed, MNCs largely set the patterns and pace of industrialization in today's capitalist economies.

The MNC represents the highest level of overseas involvement and is characterized by a global strategy of investment, production, and distribution. According to a UN estimate, at least 37,000 MNCs were in operation in the early 1990s, controlling more than 200,000 foreign affiliates. Worldwide assets accumulated from past foreign direct investment (FDI) stood at $2.1 trillion at the end of 1993. The largest 100 MNCs controlled over 60 percent of these assets and accounted for about 30 percent of all new FDI in 1993. Most of these large companies were in a handful of industries: 26 percent of their foreign assets were in electronics, followed by petroleum and mining (24 percent), motor vehicles (19 percent), and chemicals and pharmaceuticals (15 percent).

An important dimension of MNCs is the predominance of large firms. Typically, an MNC's annual sales run into hundreds of millions of dollars. In fact, more than 500 MNCs have annual sales of over $1 billion. The largest 80 MNCs have sales ranging between $10 billion and $125 billion.[35]

Many MNCs derive a substantial portion of their net income and sales from overseas operations. As shown in Table 1.1, the non-U.S. earnings of American Standard, Avon, Caterpillar, Coca-Cola, Colgate-Palmolive, Dow Chemical, Gillette, Hewlett-Packard, and IBM exceed 50 percent. Similarly, international business accounts for over 40 percent of sales of all but W. R. Grace and Xerox.

TABLE 1.1
Nondomestic Earnings, Sales, and Assets of Selected U.S. Firms (1993)

	PERCENT OF NET EARNINGS	PERCENT OF SALES	PERCENT OF ASSETS
American Standard	64	50	18
Avon	52	45	34
Black & Decker	49	51	56
Caterpillar	58	59	31
Coca-Cola	56	46	34
Colgate-Palmolive	55	62	34
Dow Chemical	53	59	52
Gillette	68	68	70
W.R. Grace	50	36	35
H.J. Heinz	43	44	46
Hewlett-Packard	52	58	27
IBM	65	58	56
ITT	48	47	48
Johnson & Johnson	42	43	41
Xerox	35	39	27

Source: Compiled by the author from the various companies' annual reports

The economic strength of these corporations as compared with other economic entities, including the economies of many nations, suggests an important source of global power. Table 1.2 shows that many MNCs have a higher annual revenue than the GNP of various countries. For example, General Motors generates more revenue annually than the GNP of Denmark, Greece, or Colombia. Similarly, IBM's annual sales exceed the GNP of New Zealand or Singapore.

TABLE 1.2
GNP of Various Countries Ranked with Sales of Selected Corporations—1993.

Switzerland	$248.7*
Sweden	233.2
Argentina	200.3
Austria	174.8
General Motors	138.2
Denmark	133.9
Exxon	111.2
Ford Motor Co.	108.5
Greece	75.1
Mobil	64.0
IBM	62.7
General Electric	60.6
Sears Roebuck	50.8
Colombia	44.6
Singapore	44.3
New Zealand	41.2
Dupont	37.1
Chevron	37.1
Texaco	34.1

*Figures in billions of U.S. dollars.

Source: GNP—The World Bank, 1994. Sales figures of corporations taken from the various companies' annual reports.

Another important feature of MNCs is their predominantly oligopolistic character; that is, they operate in markets that are dominated by a few sellers. Further, their technological leads, their special skills, and their ability to differentiate their products through advertising are all factors that help to sustain or reinforce their oligopolistic nature. Most MNCs have a sizeable number of foreign branches and affiliates. Two hundred MNCs, among the largest in the world, have affiliates in 25 or more countries.

Multinational corporations are mainly the product of developed countries. However, the relative importance of MNCs from different home countries has changed in the last 15 years—that of Japanese and Western European companies has increased and that of U.S. companies has declined. The available evidence suggests that these shifts are due primarily to changes in the international competitiveness of companies based in different home countries.[36]

Multinationals from the Third World

MNCs belonging to the developing countries are a new source of competition in the world markets. The Birla Group of India, United Laboratories from the Philippines, and Autlan of Mexico are among the several hundred multinationals from the Third World whose overseas subsidiaries have increased from dozens around 1960 to a few thousand today. They are successfully competing for a share of world markets.

These multinationals have gone abroad following the international product life cycle concept (see Chapter 2). They began by seeking export markets. When tariffs, quotas, or other barriers threatened overseas markets, these companies started assembling abroad. Their initial move, and greatest impact so far, has been in neighboring developing countries.

The strength of Third World MNCs comes from their special experience with manufacturing for small home markets. Using low technology and local raw material, running job-shop kinds of plants, and making effective use of semiskilled labor, they are able to custom-design products best suited to host countries. For example, a Philippines paper company has managed projects in countries ranging from Indonesia to Nigeria. Its managers have drawn on their ability to make paper from inexpensive, locally available materials. In addition, they run a very efficient job-shop operation with printing, folding, and cutting machinery selected or built in-house to make very short runs of a wide range of cigarette, candy, and other packages. These are skills that the Western multinationals have usually forgotten.[37]

While small-scale manufacturing remains their unique strength, these companies also are moving in other areas that are particularly suited to local conditions. For example, a Thai company uses rice stalks for paper and plantain products for glue. A Brazilian company has developed sunfast dyes and household appliances that resist high humidity and can survive the fluctuating voltages common in the developing world.

The rapid growth of Third World multinationals provides both a threat and an opportunity to the multinationals from the advanced countries. The Third World MNCs can be tough competitors in seeking contract work in building plants that do not require high technology such as steel plants and chemical complexes. But these MNCs also offer profitable opportunities to Western companies for joint operations. Lacking in marketing skills, for example, they may share their special know-how with traditional multinationals in exchange for brand names and skills in promoting new lines.[38] Further, as Third World MNCs become visible and viable economic entities, their governments may well become more sympathetic to the needs of MNCs from the developed world.

Entry Strategies

Four different modes of business offer a company entry into foreign markets: (1) exporting, (2) contractual agreement, (3) joint venture, and (4) manufacturing.

Exporting

A company may minimize the risk of dealing internationally by exporting domestically manufactured products either by minimal response to inquiries or by systematic development of demand in foreign markets. Exporting requires minimal capital and is easy to initiate. Exporting is also a good way to gain international experience. A major part of the overseas involvement of large U.S. firms is through export trade.

Contractual Agreement

There are several types of contractual agreements:

Patent Licensing Agreement This is based on either a fixed-fee or a royalty basis and includes managerial training.

Turnkey Operation This is based on a fixed-fee or cost-plus arrangement and includes plant construction, personnel training, and initial production runs.

Coproduction Agreement This is most common in the socialist countries, where plants are built and then paid for with part of the output.

Management Contract Currently widely used in the Middle East, this requires that a multinational corporation provides key personnel to operate the foreign enterprise for a fee until local people acquire the ability to manage the business independently. For example, Whittaker Corp. of Los Angeles operates government-owned hospitals in several cities in Saudi Arabia.

Licensing This works as a viable alternative in some contractual agreement situations where risk of expropriation and resistance to foreign investments create uncertainty. *Licensing* encompasses a variety of contractual agreements whereby a multinational marketer makes available intangible assets such as patents, trade secrets, know-how, trademarks, and company name to foreign companies in return for royalties or other forms of payment. Transfer of these assets usually is accompanied by technical services to ensure proper use. Licensing, however, has some advantages and disadvantages as summarized below.[39]

Some of the advantages of licensing are as follows:

1. Licensing requires little capital and serves as a quick and easy entry to foreign markets.
2. In some countries licensing is the only way to tap the market.
3. Licensing provides life extension for products in the maturity stage of their life cycles.
4. Licensing is a good alternative to foreign production and marketing in an environment where there is worldwide inflation, skilled-labor shortages, increasing domestic and foreign governmental regulation and restriction, and tough international competition.
5. Licensing royalties are guaranteed and periodic, whereas shared income from investment fluctuates and is risky.
6. Domestically based firms can benefit from product development abroad without research expense through technical feedback arrangements.
7. When exports no longer are profitable because of intense competition, licensing provides an alternative.
8. Licensing can overcome high transportation costs, which make some exports noncompetitive in the target markets.
9. Licensing is immune to expropriation.
10. In some countries, manufacturers of military equipment or any product deemed critical to the national interest (including communication equipment) may be compelled to enter licensing agreements.

Some disadvantages of licensing are as follows:

1. To attract licensees, a firm must possess distinctive technology, a trademark, and a company or brand name that is attractive to potential foreign users.
2. The licensor has no control over production and marketing by the licensee.
3. Licensing royalties are negligible compared with equity investment potential. Royalty rates seldom exceed 5 percent of gross sales because of host government restrictions.
4. The licensee may lose interest in renewing the contract unless the licensor holds interest through innovation and new technology.
5. There is a danger of creating competition in third, or even home, markets if the licensee violates territorial agreements. Going to court in these situations is expensive and time consuming and no international adjudicatory body exists.

Joint Venture

Joint venture represents a higher-risk alternative because it requires various levels of direct investment. A joint venture between a U.S. firm and a native operation abroad involves sharing risks to accomplish mutual enterprise. Joint ventures, incidentally, are the next most common form of entry once a firm moves beyond the exporting stage to a more regular overseas involvement. One example of a joint venture is General Motors Corporation's partnership with Egypt's state-owned Nasar Car Company to establish a plant to assemble trucks and diesel engines. Another example of a joint venture is between Matsushita of Japan and IBM to manufacture small computers. The alliance between Coca-Cola Co. and Nestlé S.A. to develop and sell ready-to-drink coffees and teas is still another example of a joint venture. Joint ventures normally are designed to take advantage of the strong functions of the partners and supplement their weak functions, be they management, research, or marketing.

Joint ventures provide a mutually beneficial opportunity for domestic and foreign businesses to join forces. For both parties, the ventures are a means to share both capital and risk and make use of each other's technical strength. Japanese companies, for example, prefer entering into joint ventures with U.S. firms because such arrangements help ensure against possible American trade barriers. American firms, on the other hand, like the opportunity to enter a previously forbidden market, to utilize established channels, to link American product innovation with low-cost Japanese manufacturing technology, and to curb a potentially tough competitor.

As a case in point, General Foods Corporation tried for more than a decade to succeed in Japan on its own and watched the market share of its instant coffee (Maxwell House) drop from 20 to 14 percent. Then, in 1975, the firm established a joint venture with Ajinomoto, a food manufacturer, to use the full power of the Japanese partner's product distribution system and personnel and managerial capabilities. Within two years, Maxwell House's share of the Japanese instant coffee market had recovered and in 1982 was close to 25 percent.[40]

Joint ventures, however, are not an unmixed blessing. The major problem in managing joint ventures stems from one cause: there is more than one partner and one of the partners must play the key, dominant role to steer the business to success.

Joint ventures should be designed to supplement each partner's shortcomings, and not to exploit each other's strengths and weaknesses.[41] It takes as much effort to make a joint venture a success as to start a grass-roots operation and eventually bring it up to a successful level. In both cases, each partner must be fully prepared to expend the effort necessary to understand customers, competitors, and himself. A joint venture is a means of resource appropriation and of easing a foreign business's entry into a new terrain.[42] It should not be viewed as a handy vehicle to reap money without effort, interest, and/or additional resources.

Joint ventures are a popular mode to seek entry in a foreign country. There is hardly a Fortune 1000 company, active overseas, that does not have at least one joint venture. Widespread interest in joint ventures is related to:

1. *Seeking market opportunities.* Companies in mature industries in the U.S. find joint venture a desirable entry mode to attractive new markets overseas.
2. *Dealing with rising economic nationalism.* Often host governments are more receptive to or require joint ventures.
3. *Preempting raw materials.* Countries with raw materials such as petroleum or extractable material usually do not allow foreign firms to be active there other than through joint venture.
4. *Sharing risk.* Rather than taking the entire risk, a joint venture allows the risk to be shared with a partner, which can be especially important in politically sensitive areas.
5. *Developing an export base.* In areas where economic blocs play a significant role, joint venture with a local firm smoothes the entry into the entire region, such as entry into the EC market through a joint venture with an English company.
6. *Selling technology.* Selling technology to developing countries becomes easier through joint ventures.

Although joint venture is an attractive entry mode, firms considering such an arrangement should be realistic about potential failure.[43] When either partner in a joint venture concludes that the venture is a failure, there are five alternatives to resolve the problem. First, the joint venture may be continued even if it is seen as a failure if the circumstances force the partners to do so. Both partners may be temporarily dependent on the venture for some critical resource, or one party may have legal basis for forcing continuation. Second, one partner may be temporarily dependent on the venture for some critical resource, or one party may have legal basis for forcing continuation. Second, one partner may be much more dependent on the joint venture than the other and may want to continue the business. Third, another entity may acquire all or a major portion of the joint venture. Fourth, a new organization independent of the original partners is created to run the business. This option is usually relevant for joint ventures that have achieved some measure of success but that are no longer useful to the founding partners. Finally, the joint venture may be liquidated.

The choice of which termination strategy to use depends on a number of factors. If either partner is dependent on the joint venture for some critical resource, the preservation of that resource will be a critical consideration in selecting a strategy. Another factor is whether the joint venture could survive as an independent entity. If the joint venture is not dependent specifically on the founding partners, it may be able to shift its association to some other business organization.

If the owners decide not to continue a joint venture, the outcome will depend on whether the venture is worth more as a going concern than its liquidation value. New joint ventures will be less visible and less attractive to potential buyers than old ones. Small joint ventures are unlikely to have the necessary resources to survive as independent organizations. All of these factors suggest that new and small ventures will be liquidated. Larger and longer-established ventures have a greater opportunity for survival.

In recent years, a new type of collaborative strategy in international business has gained popularity. Commonly called **strategic alliance**s, leading firms, particularly in high-tech industries, have used this route for their mutual benefit. Strategic alliances are short of complete merger, but deeper than arm's length market exchanges. They involve mutual dependence and shared decision making between two or more separate firms. Strategic alliances differ from joint ventures in that they encompass select activities and, often, are formed for a specific period. Strategic goals pursued through strategic alliances are product exchange or supply alliances (aimed to reduce transaction costs by establishing a mutual commitment between the supplying and buying firms); learning alliances (aimed to develop new capabilities through technology transfer or joint research); and market positioning alliances (aimed to develop demand for a product, spread technology, or develop a dominant standard in the market).

Manufacturing

A multinational corporation may also establish itself in an overseas market by direct investment in a manufacturing and/or assembly subsidiary. Because of the volatility of worldwide economic, social, and political conditions, this form of involvement is most risky. An example of a direct investment situation is Chesebrough-Pond's operation of overseas manufacturing plants in Japan, England, and Monte Carlo.

Manufacturing around the world is riskier, as illustrated by India's Bhopal disaster, in which a poisonous gas leak in a Union Carbide Corp. plant killed over 2,000 people and permanently disabled thousands (in the worst industrial accident that has ever occurred). It is suggested that MNCs should not manufacture overseas where the risk of a mishap may jeopardize the survival of the whole company. As a matter of fact, in the wake of the Bhopal accident, many host countries tightened safety and environmental regulations. For example, Brazil, the world's fourth-largest user of agricultural chemicals, restricted the use of the deadly methyl isocyanate.[44]

Conclusion

A firm interested in entering the international market must evaluate the risk and commitment involved with each entry and choose the entry mode that best fits the company's objectives and resources.[45] Entry risk and commitment can be examined by considering the following five factors:

1. Characteristics of the product.
2. The market's external macroenvironment—particularly economic and political factors, and the demand and buying pattern characteristics of potential customers.
3. The firm's competitive position—especially the product's life cycle stage as well as various corporate strengths and weaknesses.
4. Capital budgeting considerations including resource costs and availabilities.
5. Internal corporate perceptions, which affect corporate selection of information and the psychic distance between a firm's decision makers and its target customers, as well as control and risk-taking preferences.

These five factors combined indicate the risk to be reviewed vis-à-vis a company's resources before determining a mode of entry.[46]

Computerized simulation models can be employed to determine the desired entry route by simultaneously evaluating such factors as environmental opportunity, risk index, competitive risk index, corporate strength index, product channel direction index, comparative cost index, and corporate policy and perception index.[47]

It is useful to remember that a company may use different modes of entry in different countries. For example, McDonald's Corporation deemed it sufficient to license three restaurants on the small Caribbean island of Aruba, but in Japan it has had a joint venture since 1971. The local partner helped McDonald's blanket the Japanese market to such an extent that there are now over 600 outlets across the country, the largest number of McDonald's restaurants in any country outside the U.S.

Summary

In today's environment even firms that do not seek to do business outside their national boundaries have no choice but to be aware of the international business scene. The U.S. economy in particular is so intricately linked to international economics that even strictly domestic business is affected by what takes place in other countries. The far-reaching impact of international business necessitates that students of business be thoroughly informed about the perspectives of international business.

International marketing instruction in particular is required because, of all the functional areas of a business, marketing problems are the most fundamental and the most frequent. While basic marketing decisions do not change as marketers expand their business from the domestic field to the international field, the environments they must consider while making those decisions can be profoundly different. The major aspects of the international marketing environment include the economic, cultural, and legal and political environments.

International marketing is also affected by international institutional arrangements such as the international monetary system vis-à-vis the International Monetary Fund and multinational agreements such as the European Community (EC).

A firm aspiring to enter the international scene may choose from the various entry modes—exporting, contractual agreement, joint venture, and manufacturing. Each entry mode provides different opportunities and risks.

Today's thrust for growth in international business comes from MNCs (multinational corporations). In recent years, the tactics of the MNCs, however, have become a subject of intense discussion, particularly with reference to their operations in LDCs (less-developed countries). While the MNC will continue to be an institution of great significance, the environment in the future will require a greater awareness of the needs of host countries.

Review Questions

1. Why should a business operating entirely in the U.S. domestic market be concerned with happenings in the international business environment?

2. Why should international marketing be considered as a separate field of study even though marketing decisions in both domestic and international markets are basically the same?
3. What do you recommend that MNCs do to become more acceptable in LDCs?
4. What are the different modes of entry into the international market? What are the relative advantages and disadvantages of each mode?
5. How can a firm's overseas involvement be categorized?
6. Why do a very large proportion of U.S. firms confine themselves to domestic markets?
7. Why should a firm enter international business? Explain the reasons with illustrations.

Creative Questions

1. Usually, MNCs are associated with a particular country such as U.S. multinationals, Japanese multinations, etc. In as much as MNCs do business globally, and their stockholders are spread all over the world, is it conceivable that MNCs in the future would be characterized under the authority of an international agency and become stateless? What are the pros and cons of such a move?
2. What is the difference between a joint venture and a strategic alliance? What are the key issues in the successful management of strategic alliances?

Endnotes

1. *See* Andrew Kupfer, "How to Be a Global Manager," *Fortune*, March 14, 1988, p. 52.
2. "U.S. Trade Facts," *Business America*, April 1994, p. 40.
3. *U.S. Manufacturers in the Global Marketplace* (New York: The Conference Board, Inc., 1994.
4. U.S. Department of Commerce. *Also see*: Lynda Schuster, "Brazil Captures a Big Share of the U.S. Shoe Market," *The Wall Street Journal*, August 27, 1985.
5. U.S. Department of Commerce.
6. *See*: Subhash C. Jain, "Global Competitiveness in the Beer Industry: A Case Study," Working Paper (Storrs, CT: Food Policy Center, The University of Connecticut, 1994).
7. The direct investment position is the net book value of U.S. companies and other investors' equity in and outstanding loans to foreign affiliates.
8. *The Global Century: A Source Book on U.S. Business and the Third World* (Washington, D.C.: National Cooperative Business Association, 1989).
9. *Statistical Abstract of the United States: 1994* (Washington, D.C.: U.S. Department of Commerce, 1994), p. 684.
10. "U.S. Trade Facts," *Business America*, April 1994, p. 40.
11. *Ibid.*
12. Ken Dychtwald and Grey Gable, "American Diversity," *American Demographics*, July 1991, pp. 75–77.
13. Richard Gibson, "Gerber Missed the Boat in Quest to Go Global, So It Turned to Sandoz," *The Wall Street Journal*, March 1, 1994, p.1.
14. *See* "No Smoking Sweeps America," *Business Week*, July 27, 1987, p. 40. *Also see* James S. Hirsch, "U.S. Liquor Makers Seek Tonic in Foreign Markets," *The Wall Street Journal*, October 24, 1989, p.B1.
15. *See Business Week*, February 29, 1988, p. 74.
16. *See* Edmund Faltermayer, "Is 'Made in U.S.A.' Fading Away," *Fortune*, September 24, 1990, p. 62.
17. "America's High-Tech Crisis," *Business Week*, March 11, 1985, p. 56. *Also see* Bernard Wysocki, Jr., "American Firms Send Office Work Abroad to Use Cheaper Labor," *The Wall Street Journal*, August 14, 1991, p. 1.
18. *Also see* Robert L. Rose, "Zenith Sells a 5% Stake to Goldstar," *The Wall Street Journal*, February 26, 1991, p. A3.
19. *The Economist*, April 2, 1994, p. 79.
20. Kenneth Labich, "Airbus Takes Off," *Fortune*, June 1, 1992, p. 51.

21. *The Economist*, Februrary 19, 1994, p. 21.

22. "New Worlds to Conquer," *Business Week*, February 28, 1994, p. 51.

23. Theodore Levitt, "The Globalization of Markets," *Harvard Business Review*, May–June 1983, pp. 92–102.

24. Adapted from Douglass C. Norvell and Sion Raveed, "Eleven Reasons for Firms to Go International," *Marketing News*, October 17, 1980, p. 1.

25. Neal Templin, "Beleaguered at Home, U.S. Car Makers Get a Boost From New Customers Abroad," *The Wall Street Journal*, November 8, 1991, p. B1.

26. *The International Dimension of Management Education*, a report by a Special Brookings Panel (Washington, D.C.: The Brookings Institution, 1975), p. 10.

27. *A Special Report on Globalization* (New York: Booz, Allen & Hamilton, 1991), pp. 10–11.

28. Frederick W. Gluck, "Meeting the Challenge of Global Competition," *The McKinsey Quarterly*, Autumn 1982, p.10

29. Frank Meissner, "Americans Must Practice the Marketing They Preach to Succeed in Japan's Mass Markets," *Marketing News*, October 17, 1980, p.5.

30. *See* Kenichi Ohmae, *Beyond National Borders* (Homewood, IL: Dow Jones-Irwin, 1987), Chapter 3.

31. Stephen K. Yoder, "Apple, Loser in Japan Computer Market, Tries to Recoup by Redesigning Its Models," *The Wall Street Journal*, June 21, 1985, p. 30.

32. *Business and International Education*, a report of the Task Force on Business and International Education (Washington, D.C.: American Council on Education, 1977), p. 3.

33. David A. Ricks, *Big Business Blunders* (Homewood, IL: Dow Jones-Irwin, 1983).

34. Hirotaka Takeuchi and Michael E. Porter, "Three Roles of International Marketing in Global Strategy," in Michael Porter, ed., *Competition in Global Industries*, (Boston: Harvard Business School Press, 1986), pp. 111–46.

35. Factual information in this section is mainly from David Gold, "World Investment Report 1993: Transnational Corporations and Integrated International Production—An Executive Summary," *Transnational Corporations*, Vol. 2, No. 2, August 1993, pp. 99–123.

36. *Ibid.*

37. *See* Heidi Vernon-Wortzel and Lawrence H. Wortzel, "Globalizing Strategies for Multinationals from Developing Countries," *Columbia Journal of World Business*, Spring 1988, pp. 27–36.

38. Francis H. Ulgado, Chwo-Ming J. Yu, and Anant R. Negandhi, "Multinational Enterprises from Asian Developing Countries: Management and Organizational Characteristics," *International Business Review*, Vol. 3, No. 2, 1994, pp. 123–34.

39. Allan C. Reddy, "International Licensing May Be Best Bet for Companies Seeking Foreign Markets," *Marketing News*, November 12, 1982, p. 6. *Also see* Farok J. Contractor, "Technology Licensing Practice in U.S. Companies: Corporate & Public Policy Implications," *Columbia Journal of World Business*, Fall 1983, pp. 80–88.

40. Kenichi Ohmae, *Triad Power* (New York: The Free Press, 1985), p. 116.

41. "The Partners," *Business Week*, February 10, 1992, p. 102.

42. F. Kingston Berlew, "The Joint Venture: A Way into Foreign Markets," *Harvard Business Review*, July–August 1984, p. 48. *Also see* Farok Contractor, "A Generalized Theorem of Joint-Venture and Licensing Negotiations," *Journal of International Business Studies*, Summer 1985, pp. 23–49.

43. Wilbur Moulton, "International Joint Ventures: What to Do When Things Go Wrong," *Global Perspective*, Fall 1990, p. 1.

44. "For Multinationals It Will Never Be the Same," *Business Week*, December 24, 1984, p. 57. *Also see* M. Krishna Erramillli and C. P. Rao, "Choice of Foreign Market Entry Modes by Service Firms," 1988 Educators' Conference Proceedings (Chicago: American Marketing Association, 1988), p. 20.

45. Yang-Chul Kwon and Leonard J. Konopa, "Impact of Host Country Market Characteristics on the Choice of Foreign Market Entry Mode," *International Market Review*, Vol. 10, No. 2, 1993, pp. 60–76.

46. *See*: Sanjeer Agarnwal and Sridhar N. Ramaswami, "Choice of Foreign Market Entry Mode: Impact of Ownership, Location and Internationalization Factors," *Journal of International Business Studies*, Vol. 23, No. 1, 1992, pp. 1–28.

47. James D. Goodnow, "Development of Personal Computer Software for International Mode of Entry Decision," a paper presented at the 1985 Annual Meeting of the Academy of International Business, New York, October 1985.

CHAPTER · 2

Economic Rationale of Multinational Trade and Business

CHAPTER FOCUS

After studying this chapter, you should be able to:

- Discuss the rationale for multinational trade and business

- Describe the barriers that nations impose to restrict free trade

- Examine the role of the General Agreement on Tariffs and Trade (GATT) in liberalizing world trade

- Describe the U.S. trade liberalization endeavors

- Discuss how a multinational corporation participates in global markets

Commerce is older than recorded history. Archaeological discoveries provide us with evidence of the antiquity of trade. Thousands of ancient commercial documents indicate that a considerable commercial class existed many centuries before any European or Mediterranean city attained a high degree of civilization. In the ancient world, there had even developed a system of payment of precious objects for traded goods—a forerunner of the modern system.

Trading has evolved through the ages in response to altering needs spurred by changes in technology and philosophy. Growth in trade was particularly stimulated by the discovery and use of metals and by the global horizons provided by advances first in transportation and later in communication. Trade has evolved from exchanges between isolated peoples, to trade through conquest, to trade among friendly neighbors, to a system of silent barter among both adversaries and friends. In brief, world trade as we know it today is not a new phenomenon. Groups of people have always traded.

As civilization progressed around the world, however, trading became more organized and productive. For example, ancient seaborne commerce was inefficient and, proportionately, insignificant. Piracy and raiding of ships were commonplace. Such hazards discouraged trade expansion and required that harbors be fortified for protection. In modern times, although nations still go to war, piracy and raiding have been virtually eliminated by a variety of treaties, arrangements, and other international laws.

World trade requires that nations be willing to cooperate with each other. Countries naturally trade with those nations with whom they are on friendly terms. Nonetheless, trading often goes on among nations even when political relations are not amicable. For example, the U.S. and China are on many issues politically opposed, yet the two nations trade with each other. The mutual benefits, or economic advantages, of U.S.–China trade outweigh political differences. Economic advantage has historically been the most important consideration that trading nations share. This chapter examines and discusses the nature of this advantage and also deals with the political and economic hindrances that produce economic disadvantage and tend to discourage trade, particularly among developed and developing countries.

In the post-World War II period, world trade has multiplied tremendously and has added new dimensions to global economic activity. An example is presented here to depict the emergence of the MNC as the basic institution of present international economic activity. Current international economic activity is much wider in both scope and activity than the traditional importing and exporting trade described by classical economists.

Theory of Comparative Advantage

The classical economists—Adam Smith, David Ricardo, and John Stuart Mill—are credited with providing the theoretical economic justification for international trade.

In simple terms, modern trade takes place because a foreign country is able to provide a material or product cheaper than native industry can. For example, if the landed cost of a Japanese-made TV is less than the cost of an America-made TV, it makes economic sense to import TVs from Japan. Likewise, if U.S. computers can be sold cheaper in Japan than computers manufactured in Japan, Japanese businesses would find it economically desirable to import U.S. computers.

Theory of Comparative Advantage

Ricardo advanced the concept of *relative or comparative costs* as the basis of international trade. Ricardo emphasized labor costs more than other aspects of production. He thought such aspects as land and capital either were of no significance or were so evenly distributed overall that they always operated in a fixed proportion, whereas labor did not. In sum, the *theory of comparative advantage* states that even if a country is able to produce all its goods at lower costs than another country can, trade still benefits both countries, based on comparative, not absolute, costs. In other words, countries should concentrate efforts on producing goods that have a *comparative* advantage compared to other countries, and then export those goods in exchange for goods that command advantage in their native countries (see International Marketing Highlight 2.1).

To illustrate this point, let us assume the following information about the U.S. and Italy:

COUNTRY	LABOR COSTS PER UNIT (IN HOURS)	
	Hand Calculators	Bottles of Wine
United States	6	8
Italy	30	15

Suppose the cost of both manufacturing hand calculators and producing wine is lower in the United States than in Italy. Despite that, according to the theory of comparative advantage, the United States will be better off by specializing in hand calculators and exchanging them for Italian wine. In this way, the United States will be able to obtain from Italy a bottle of wine, which requires eight hours of effort at home, in exchange for a hand calculator, requiring only six hours for its manufacture. In other words, the wine is obtained for six hours of labor instead of the eight hours it would have required if it were produced in the United States. Italy would also gain from the exchange by concentrating on producing wine and exchanging it for hand calculators at the cost of 15 instead of 30 hours of labor. As has been said:

> The key to the concept is in the word "comparative"—which implies that each and every country has both definite "advantage" in some goods and definite "disadvantage" in other goods.[1]

The following example quantitatively demonstrates the benefits derived from free trade. Consider two countries, Japonia and Latinia. Japonia has a clear competitive advantage over Latinia in producing both radios and TVs, as follows:

	WORKER HOURS REQUIRED FOR ONE UNIT	
	Japonia	Latinia
RADIO	1	4
TV	4	8

It follows that 48 worker hours of production results in 24 radios and 6 TVs in Japonia. The same number of worker hours produces six radios and three TVs in Latinia. Therefore, the 2 countries can produce a total of 30 radios and 9 TVs with 96 worker hours of effort.

International Marketing Highlight 2.1

How the U.S. Pressed Managed Trade on the Japanese

On his January 1992 trip to Japan, U.S. President George Bush chose to match Japan's producer lobbies with a set of his own, led by the heads of General Motors, Ford, and Chrysler. These industrial leaders complained the Japanese did not buy enough of their cars. Japanese carmakers obligingly promised to help out by buying American car parts and displaying American cars in their dealerships.

This approach can hardly be called trade. After all, it is an odd sort of trade in which a firm asks its competitors to sell its goods for it. It is also odd to claim that because Japan does not import large quantities of the same things as it exports, such trade is "adversarial," a term generally contrasted to the sort of trade that is "mutually beneficial." This conflicts with what trade is all about.

The point of trade is to allow an economy to specialize. If a country is better at making ships than sealing wax, it makes sense to put more resources into shipbuilding and to export some of the ships to pay for imports of sealing wax. This is true even if that country is the world's best maker of sealing wax, for it will still prosper by making ships instead—which, in turn, is why countries can trade successfully even if they are not the best at anything. This is what David Ricardo, a British economist in the early nineteenth century, meant when he coined the term *comparative advantage*. That phrase is now one of the most misused of economic ideas, since it is often wrongly assumed to mean an advantage compared with other countries, as in, "Soon America will not have a comparative advantage in anything." This matters for more than merely semantic reasons, for Ricardo's insight was a powerful one.

Source: The Economist, January 11, 1992, p. 11.

Suddenly, Japonia and Latinia choose free trade and tear down the barriers they had erected against each other's products. With the same worker hour requirement per unit and the same number of worker hours devoted to production, their combined output now changes to 32 radios and 10 TVs.

This is not really a miracle; it simply is division of labor based on comparative advantage. Under free trade, Latinia is induced to withdraw resources it had devoted to radio production and concentrate entirely on TVs. Now Latinia produces 6 TVs and no radios in 48 hours.

Japonia is induced to reallocate some resources. It devotes 32 worker hours to radios, where its comparative advantage is greatest, and the remaining 16 hours to TVs, enabling it to turn out 32 radios and 4 TVs with every 48 worker hours of effort.

The world has more product, but are Japonia and Latinia better off individually? To find out, we have to introduce the price system. In doing that, one thing needs emphasis: it isn't prices per se that count, but price relationships. Differences in price relationships are what people act upon.

Here is the lineup of prices (we'll use the same prices both before and after free trade):

Theory of Comparative Advantage

	JAPONIA	LATINIA
RADIO	24,000 yen	600 pesos
TV	96,000 yen	1,200 pesos

After free trade, the Japonian retailer can choose a TV at 96,000 yen or 1,200 pesos, corresponding to an exchange ratio of 80:1. The retailer will want to buy pesos whenever they can be obtained for less than 80 yen apiece. The Latinian retailer can choose a radio at 24,000 yen or 600 pesos, corresponding to a ratio of 40:1. This retailer will be in the market for yen whenever more than 40 yen can be exchanged for a peso.

The differential in price relationships between TVs and radios in the two countries has created an entrepreneurial opportunity: buying and selling currencies. Price differentials on many products in addition to radios and TVs, and many other factors including people's expectations concerning the relative economic outlook of the countries involved, play a part in establishing exchange rates. But the Japonian and Latinian radio and TV marketers should be satisfied if the yen/peso rate falls somewhere between 40:1 and 80:1.

We could choose any number, but let us say that the exchange rate becomes 60:1—right in the middle. Before free trade, a Japonian retailer could buy a shipment of 20 radios and 5 TVs for 960,000 yen. A Latinian retailer could buy the same shipment for 18,000 pesos. After free trade, the Japonian and Latinian retailers, each acting in his or her own self-interest, do their buying. Here is the result:

JAPONIAN RETAILER	
20 radios × 24,000 yen	= 480,000 yen
5 TVs × 1,200 pesos × 60 yen	= 360,000 yen
Shipment	840,000 yen
Savings: 120,000 yen	

LATINIAN RETAILER	
20 radios × 24,000 yen ÷ 60 pesos	= 8,000 pesos
4 TVs × 1,200 pesos	= 6,000 pesos
Shipment	14,000 pesos
Savings: 4,000 pesos	

In both countries, purchasing power has been increased. Both can afford to buy more of the same things or to buy new things they could not afford before. Both are wealthier.

Possibly you aren't convinced until you can see it "in dollars and cents." So why not create a world price in dollars for radios and TVs and redo the arithmetic? At a 60:1 yen/peso exchange rate, the dollar price of a TV is $240, since 300 yen equals 5 pesos equals $1. You will find that Japonia will have enough extra radios to sell at $80 each to buy from Latinia the TVs it stopped producing, and it will still have some dollars to spare. Latinia will have dollars left over after selling extra TVs to buy all of the radios it no longer makes.

Rationale for Seeking Comparative Advantage

Every nation seeks to increase the material standard of living of its people; living standards increase as a function of productivity. With greater productivity, the same amount of labor yields more goods and services. As productivity increases, greater material wealth results.

Different countries enjoy productivity gains in different ways. Sweden has made a choice of longer vacations; the U.S. prefers increased material possessions. Whatever the eventual choice, increased productivity affords a wider range of choice.

Another ingredient of productivity is the specialization of production, whereby countries do not try to produce all the goods they require. Specialization is more efficient and, in effect, raises the standard of living by providing certain goods through import while providing certain goods and services nationally. These *sheltered* businesses include the provision of services such as health care, government administration, and goods distribution, as well as the production of special goods such as pharmaceuticals and essential military goods.

Businesses included in the sheltered category are influenced by consideration of economic feasibility, national security, and self-sufficiency. Sheltered manufacturing businesses include those in which increased production scale is not great enough to offset the costs of distributing the product to a larger geographic area. This category includes products that, for one reason or another, are expensive to transport such as milk or sulfuric acid.

For a nation to have a high standard of living, it must export enough goods to balance the import of the goods it cannot efficiently produce itself. Exports are especially important for maintaining the living standard in a country whose resources are limited and whose imports, in balance, are relatively high. Consider Japan, which built a viable export market and in return developed an invulnerable position in many industries. South Korea, Taiwan, and Brazil appear to be following Japan's example by developing export markets.[2]

Table 2.1 presents a hypothetical comparison of two countries whose only export is oil. If the market absorbs the production of both countries, the price is usually set according to the cost of the labor hours required by the least efficient producer, in this case Country B. Country A may set a price slightly lower in order to guarantee the sale of all its output. Regardless, Country A's per-hour income will be much higher than that of Country B. This greater income can be used for higher wages, for reinvestment to support a free health care system for everyone in the country, or for whatever the country desires. In brief, specialization profits Country A and leads it to a higher standard of living.

TABLE 2.1 Relative Productivity: A Hypothetical Example

	LABOR HOURS PER BARREL	
	Country A	Country B
Operating	1	3
Capital cost amortization	1	2
Total	2	5
World price (in labor-hour equivalents)	5.0	5.5
Income (per labor hour)	2.5	1.1

Business Specialization and Trade

The *economic law of comparative advantage* states that every nation benefits when specialization and trade take place. Even when one nation cannot produce any good more efficiently than another can, it is still in the economic interest of both nations for each to specialize. Regardless of its productivity relative to other suppliers, every nation has comparative advantages in producing certain goods rather than others. The specialization and the advantage are achieved on the basis of one or more production factors—natural resources, technology, capital, managerial know-how, and labor.[3]

Classical economists considered labor the chief delineating factor of comparative advantage between two trading nations. In modern days, however, other factors besides labor may be more important in equipping a country for specialization. As a matter of fact, wage levels for blue-collar workers are becoming increasingly irrelevant in world competition. This is because blue-collar labor no longer accounts for enough of total costs to give low wages much competitive advantage. For example, blue-collar costs in U.S. manufacturing account for 18 percent of total costs, but they are down from 23 percent only a few years ago, and they are dropping fast.[4]

In addition to being influenced by the preceding production factors, a country's leverage may change with time and changes in the political, social, cultural, and economic environment. For example, Japan has a comparative advantage relative to the U.S. in producing steel. Japan's leverage in steel is based on managerial ability and technology. Even though Japan has to import the raw material of iron ore, other factors provide enough leeway to ensure comparative advantage. This does not mean that its current comparative advantage in steel is everlasting. The supplier of Japan's iron ore could stop supplying for political reasons, or another country could develop a technology superior to Japan's and supersede its advantage. Thus, leverage must be not only developed but also maintained for long-term gains.

Natural Resources. Nature randomly endowed different regions of the world with natural resources. The natural riches of a place bestow upon it unique economic advantages. But nations are groups of communities arbitrarily organized, usually without regard to such economic considerations as the abundance or lack of natural resources.

The most outstanding example of the possession of a resource providing economic leverage is the abundance of oil in the Middle East. In raw material exchanges based on natural resources, even if both nations have the same natural resource, one country may be better off than the other because of various physical characteristics of the resource. For example, certain economic considerations—such as seam thickness, depth, and purity of ore bodies or the number of hours required to pump a barrel of oil—come into play. Saudi Arabian oil from a shallow well is a richer resource than Iranian oil from a deep well.

Mineral trade is based on the natural availability of minerals in different countries. The aircraft industry is crucially dependent on cobalt, which is used in jet engine blades. Zambia and Zaire produce two-thirds of the world's cobalt and thus have a natural advantage in this area. Since the metal is important for an essential industry, the random distribution of the natural resource leads to world trade. In brief, the natural resources of a country can permit it to engage in international trade from an advantageous position.

Technology. Manufacturers in different countries have different production costs as a result of the unevenness of technological advances. Differences in production scale, run lengths, distribution structure, product mix, and technological development capability, among other things, often determine productivity differences among producers. For example, some Japanese companies can assemble a TV in one-third the time required by their European or American competitors. This advantage is derived from product designs that use fewer components, machines that automate some of the board assembly, and equipment that reduces labor in the handling of materials. Japan's technological advantage in manufacturing steel leads it to surpass India in the world markets. This happens despite the fact that Japan imports iron ore from India and Indian labor is much less expensive than Japanese labor.

Managerial Know-How. People who bring capital, labor, and resources together to fashion them into a productive organization that must face the risks of an uncertain world occupy strategic positions. Thus, given the same inputs, presumably a country with superior management will do better than one with weak management. The importance of managerial know-how can be illustrated by the airlines industry. Most airlines of the Free World use the same planes and offer essentially the same services while charging common prices. Yet some carriers outperform others. For example, Singapore Airlines does better than any other airline, partly because of its lower labor costs, but mainly because of superior management.[5]

Obviously, an explanation of world business involves many elements. However, with a basic understanding of the few elements covered so far—comparative advantage and specialization—we can now consider other reasons for nations to engage in international business.

Product Life Cycle and International Trade

The theory of comparative advantage is a classic explanation of world trade. In the late 1960s, researchers at the Harvard Business School provided a new explanation of international trade and investment patterns.[6] The new approach uses the concept of product life cycle in marketing and gives a significant insight into how multinational corporations evolve.

The *product life cycle model* states that products go through the following four stages:[7]

Phase I	U.S. export strength builds
Phase II	Foreign production starts
Phase III	Foreign production becomes competitive in export markets
Phase IV	Import competition begins in domestic U.S. markets

During Phase I, the product is manufactured in the U.S. for a high-income market and afterward introduced into foreign markets through exports. At that point, the U.S. usually holds a monopoly position as the only country able to supply the product. The product continues to be manufactured only in the U.S. since business acumen suggests locating operations close to markets where the demand exists. Overseas customers, however, import the U.S. product in response to their own market demands and thus create a program of export of the U.S. product.

During Phase II, as the product becomes popular, entrepreneurs in other advanced countries, perhaps in Western Europe, venture into producing the same product. The technology involved is by then fairly routine and easily transferred from the U.S. Subsequently, the overseas-manufactured product begins to outsell the U.S. export in selected markets because the overseas product benefits from lower labor costs and savings in transportation. The stage where overseas manufacturers are able to compete effectively against U.S. exports has been reached.

In the third phase, the foreign producers begin to compete against the U.S. exports in Third World countries. This further adds to the declining market for the U.S. exports. Between Phases I and II, the U.S. firms begin to consider making direct investments abroad to sustain or regain their original market position.

Phase IV occurs when the foreign firms, strong in their home and export markets, achieve economies of scale and then begin to invade the U.S. home markets. Presumably, the foreign firms have lower costs so that, despite ocean freight and U.S. customs costs, they are able to compete effectively against the domestically produced U.S. products.

These four phases complete the product life cycle and describe how American firms that once commanded a monopoly position in a product find themselves being pushed out of their home market.

The product life cycle theory of world trade holds that advanced countries like the U.S. play the innovative role in product development. Later on, other relatively advanced countries such as Japan or Western European countries take over the market position held by the innovative country.[8] The second-stage countries would go through the same cycle as did the innovative country and, in turn, would lose their markets to the next group of countries, say Third World countries. In other words, a product initially produced in the U.S. could eventually be produced only in less-developed countries (LDCs), with the result that the U.S., Western Europe, and Japan would meet their needs for that product through import from LDCs.

The product life cycle model has been helpful in explaining the history of a number of products, particularly textiles, shoes, bicycles, radios, TVs, industrial fasteners, and standardized components for different uses.[9] These products, available in the U.S., Western Europe, and Japan, are being imported from Korea, Taiwan, Hong Kong, Brazil, Mexico, Malaysia, India, and other emerging countries. For example, South Korea has made enormous strides out-competing Japan in a number of consumer products. Thus, abandoning years of prejudice, Japanese are snatching up low-priced goods from newly industrialized countries. For example, in 1988, an imported 20-inch color TV was available for $375 while a similar Japanese-made TV was priced at $617.[10] Despite its apparent validity in the manufacturing field, the product life cycle model does not provide a complete answer to the growth activities of multinational enterprises.[11]

Production Sharing

In the late 1970s, Peter Drucker introduced a new concept of international business and trade. He labeled this concept *production sharing* and described it as the newest world economic trend. Although production sharing is neither "export" nor "import" in the traditional sense, this is how it is still shown in our trade figures and treated in economic and political discussions. Yet it is actually economic integration by stages of the productive process.[12]

The production-sharing concept describes an economic reality existing in developed countries where higher levels of education create higher levels of personal expectation. There then follows a gradual disappearance of semiskilled and unskilled labor, so necessary to labor-intensive manufacturing. Production sharing suggests that developed countries will turn to developing countries where the availability of labor is a major asset. This concept also covers the U.S. tariff-schedule advantage to U.S. companies whereby American components made by American labor can be further processed or assembled abroad and then returned to the U.S. market for further work or sale with duty paid only on the value added.

Drucker describes the process as follows:

> Men's shoes sold in the United States usually start out as the hide on the American cow. As a rule the hide is not tanned, however, in the United States, but shipped to a place like Brazil for tanning—highly labor-intensive work. The leather is then shipped—perhaps through the intermediary of a Japanese trading company—to the Caribbean. Part of it may be worked up into uppers in the British Virgin Islands, part into soles in Haiti. And then uppers and soles are shipped to islands like Barbados or Jamaica, the products of which have access to Britain, to the European Common Market, and to Puerto Rico, where they are worked up into shoes that enter the United States under the American tariff umbrella.
>
> Surely these are truly transnational shoes. The hide, though it's the largest single-cost element, still constitutes no more than one quarter of the manufacturer's cost of the shoe. By labor content these are "imported shoes." By skill content they are "American-made." Raising the cow, which is capital-intensive, heavily automated, and requires the greatest skill and advanced management, is done in a developed country, which has the skill, the knowledge and the equipment. The management of the entire process, the design of the shoes, their quality control and their marketing are also done entirely in developed countries where the manpower and the skills needed for these tasks are available.[13]

Currently, production sharing seems to be quite prevalent, and growing at a rapid pace. It is a new phenomenon for which there are no classic or neoclassic explanatory theories. Strictly speaking, production sharing is different from the traditional idea of international trade. It is a transnational business integration—a new relationship made possible by technological and business forces. Production sharing offers both the developed and developing countries of the world a chance to share their resources and strengths for the mutual benefit.

Internalization Theory

A multinational firm can serve a market across national boundaries either by exporting from a production facility located in the country of the parent company, or from a third country subsidiary, or it can set up production facilities in the market itself. The sourcing policy of the firm is the result of the firm's decisions as to which of its production facilities will service its various final markets. Thus, the firm establishes an international network linking production to markets. Such a network enables the firm to grow by eliminating external markets in intermediate goods and subsequently by *internalizing* those markets within the firm. When international markets are internalized, the internal transfers of goods and services are transferred. The incentives to internalize intermediate-goods markets are strongest in areas where research inputs and proprietary technology are an important part of the manufacturing process.[14]

Many intermediate-product markets, particularly for types of knowledge and expertise embodied in patents and human capital, are difficult to organize and costly to use. In such cases, the firm has an incentive to create internal markets whenever transactions can be carried out at a lower cost within the firm than through external markets. This internalization involves extending the direct operations of the firm and bringing under common ownership and control the activities by the market.

The creation of an internal market permits the firm to transform an intangible piece of research into a valuable property specific to the firm. The firm can exploit its advantage in all available markets and still keep the use of the information internal to the firm in order to recoup its initial expenditures on research and knowledge generation.[15]

The internalization theory assumes that the firm has a global horizon, and it recognizes that the enterprise needs a competitive advantage or a unique asset to expand. However, the underlying thesis of internalization is the firm's desire to extend its own direct operations rather than use external markets. The internalization approach rests on two general axioms: (a) firms choose the least-cost location for each activity they perform; and (b) firms grow by internalizing markets up to the point where the benefits of further internalization are outweighed by the costs.[16]

The internalization theory provides an economic rationale for the existence of MNCs. The sourcing decision rests on the costs and benefits to the firm, taking into consideration industry-specific factors (e.g., nature of the product), region-specific factors (e.g., geographic location), nation-specific factors (e.g., political climate), and firm-specific factors (e.g., managerial ability to internalize).

The internalization theory primarily focuses on the motives and decision processes within the multinational firm but pays little attention to the host country policies and other external factors that may affect internalization cost/benefit.[17]

Trade Barriers and Trade Liberation

We have discussed different theories and frameworks that describe the economic rationale for international trade and business. No matter how we look at it, the internationalization of business and trade appears to perpetuate worldwide prosperity. Despite that fact, no one country permits international business dealings at will. Governments impose all sorts of barriers to restrict trade and business across national boundaries. But there are reasons for trade barriers and for the efforts that have been made internationally to liberate trade. The U.S. effort to promote free trade is particularly interesting.

Trade Barriers   There are two types of trade barriers: tariff and nontariff barriers.

Tariff Barriers   *Tariffs* refer to taxes levied on goods moved between nations. The most important of these is the tax usually called the *customs duty* that is levied by the importing nation. But a tax may also be imposed by the exporting nation, and that is called an *export tax*. Even a country through which goods pass on their way to their destination may impose a *transit tariff*. The real purpose behind trade barriers is to protect national interest. Exhibit 2.1 lists the major reasons that countries advance for such protection.

Different nations handle tariff barriers differently. A country may have a single tariff system for all goods from all sources. This is called a *unilinear or single-column tariff*. Another type of tariff is the *general-conventional tariff*. This tariff applies to all nations except those that have tariff treaties (or a convention to that effect) with a particular country. A tariff may be worked out on the basis of a tax permit, called *specific duty*, or as a percentage of the value of the item, which is referred to as *ad valorem* duty. Sometimes both specific and ad valorem duty may be levied on the same item as a combined duty.

EXHIBIT 2.1   Arguments for Protection

Keep-money-at-home argument: To prevent national wealth from being transferred in exchange with another nation for goods.

Home-market argument: To encourage home industry to perpetuate.

Equalization-of-costs-of-production argument: To make local goods compete fairly against imports, which otherwise may be cheaper because of technological advantages or other similar reasons.

Low-wage argument: To protect home industry from imports from low-wage countries.

Prevention-of-injury argument: To safeguard against potential trade concessions that may have to be made in response to multinational trade agreements.

Employment argument: To prevent level of home employment.

Antidumping argument: To prevent dumping of foreign products.

Bargaining-and-retaliation argument: To seek reduction of tariffs by other countries or to retaliate against another country.

National security argument: To be on one's own for national security reasons such as war or natural calamities.

Infant-industry argument: To encourage new industry in the country.

Diversification argument: To promote a broad spectrum of industries in the country.

Terms-of-trade argument and the optimum tariff: To compensate the country for loss in revenue when price elasticity of import demand is greater than zero.

The theory of the second-best: This argument is based on the fact that free trade, while the best alternative, cannot be pursued optimally due to a variety of distortions. As an alternative, new distortions of tariffs may be utilized to neutralize the existing distortions.

Source: Franklin R. Root, *International Trade & Investment*, 3rd ed. (Cincinnati, OH: South-Western Publishing Co., 1983), pp. 306–322

Nontariff Barriers *Nontariff barriers* include quotas, import equalization taxes, road taxes, laws giving preferential treatment to domestic suppliers, administration of antidumping measures, exchange controls, and a variety of "invisible" tariffs that impede trade. Cao has summarized the principal nontariff barriers in the following categories:[18]

1. *Specific limitation on trade.* This category includes the measures that limit the allowable amount of imports, such as *quotas*, referring to quantity or value allowed for specific imported products during a specific period; *licensing requirements*, which obligate exporters and/or importers of specific products to obtain licenses before trading; *proportion restrictions of foreign to domestic goods*, which limit the quantity of imports to a specified proportion of domestic production; *minimum import price limits*, requiring adjustment of import prices to equal or surpass domestic prices; and *embargoes*, prohibiting import of specific products from specific origins.
2. *Customs and administrative entry procedures.* This category includes procedural requirements comprising *valuation of imports* (i.e., enforcing a varying valuation process on imported goods that is often left at the discretion of customs officials and is highly arbitrary and discriminatory); *antidumping practices* (i.e., measures against imported goods sold at prices below those in the home market of the exporting country to injure the importing country industry); *tariff classifications* (i.e., arbitrary classification of imported products into a high-tariff category); *documentation requirements* (i.e., enforcing unnecessary and time-consuming bureaucratic requirements); and *fees* (i.e., imposing fees for different services to boost the price of imported goods).
3. *Standards.* This category includes unduly discriminatory health, safety, and quality standards such as *standard disparities* (i.e., imposing higher standards on imported goods than on domestic products); *intergovernmental acceptance of testing methods* (i.e., using tougher testing methods than those used for domestic products to determine the wholesomeness of products); and applying *packaging, labeling, and marketing standards* of the country to imported goods in an unduly stringent and discriminatory way (see International Marketing Highlight 2.2).
4. *Government participation in trade.* This category includes government involvement in trade through *procurement policies* favoring domestic products over the imported ones; *export subsidies* (i.e., providing tax incentives, export credit terms, or direct subsidies to domestic firms); *countervailing duties* (i.e., taxes levied to protect domestic products from the imported products that had been given export subsidy by the exporting country's government); and *domestic assistance programs* (i.e., other forms of assistance given to domestic products to strengthen their position against the imports).
5. *Charges on imports.* This category consists of various types of charges levied on imports to make them less competitive against the domestic goods, including *prior import deposit requirements* (i.e., requiring domestic importers to deposit a percentage of import value with the government before importing); *border tax adjustment* (i.e., levying various taxes on imported products that have been charged to domestic products); *administrative fees* (i.e., making an extra charge for processing import-related requirements); *special supplementary duties* (i.e., unusual

charges levied on imports); *import credit discriminations* (i.e., providing credit accommodation to domestic producers); and *variable levies* (i.e., taxing imports at a higher rate than domestic goods).

6. *Other categories*. These categories include recent measures employed by importing countries to discourage imports such as *voluntary export restraints*, whereby an exporting country, often at the request of the importing country, agrees to limit its exports of a specific product to a particular level, and *orderly marketing agreements*, which refers to explicit and formal agreements negotiated between exporting and importing countries to restrict imports.

Among the nontariff barriers, subsidies, quotas, and monetary barriers are the most common. Many nations provide direct payments to select industries to enable them to compete effectively against the imports. For example, since 1980 the U.S. government has been providing a kind of subsidy for the steel industry to strengthen its position against Japanese imports. Quotas impose a limit on the quantity of one kind of good

---

International Marketing Highlight 2.2

Nontariff Barriers in Japan

Japanese standards are said to be written in a way that often excludes foreign products from the Japanese market. The Japanese standards-setting process is not easily understood, making participation—and even access to information—by foreigners difficult. Other problems include nonacceptance of foreign test data, lack of approval for product ingredients generally recognized as safe worldwide, and the nontransferability of product approval.

America's food processing industry, for example, maintains that these standards are deliberately discriminatory. Unlike the U.S. and most other countries whose governments issue lists of additives generally safe for human consumption and a comparable list of substances banned, the Japanese have only one list. A specific additive can only be used for a specific purpose and only in a prescribed amount. Foods containing additives not on the so-called "positive" list may not be imported into Japan, even if those additives are not considered unsafe. The explicit policy of the Ministry of Health and Welfare is not to add ingredients to the positive list.

Regarded as an even more exasperating problem is the fact that Japan does not accept the results of certain testing and certification procedures conducted outside Japan for certain products such as drugs. The U.S., on the other hand, generally accepts foreign data from testing done in accordance with appropriate U.S. standards and test procedures.

Furthermore, foreign manufacturers cannot apply directly to Japanese ministries for product approval. Only an approved Japanese entity can hold approval rights. Until recently, if foreign exporters wanted to change agents, their new agents had to reapply for product approval unless their formerly "approved" agents were wiling to give up their rights. Of course American firms could circumvent this constraint by establishing a subsidiary in Japan, but this option is not necessarily open to all manufacturers.

that a country permits to be imported. A quota may be applied on a specific country basis or on a global basis without reference to exporting countries.[19] The U.S., for example, has established quotas for textile imports from particular countries.

Monetary barriers are exchange controls of which there are three widespread types: blocked currency, differential exchange rate, and government approval to secure foreign exchange. Blockage of currency totally cuts importing by completely restricting the availability of foreign exchange. This barrier is often used politically against one or more nations. For example, in 1979, Iran used blockage of currency to avoid trading with the U.S. The differential exchange-rate barrier describes setting different rates for converting local currencies into the foreign currency needed to import goods from overseas. A government can set higher conversion rates for items whose import it wishes to restrict, and vice versa. Finally, a country may require specific government approval before allowing the import of any goods. Most developing countries working toward maintaining a secure foreign exchange position not only strictly enforce, but also grudgingly grant, specific approval accompanied by a variety of hindrances and bureaucratic headaches.

Tariff Reduction Programs

Internationally, systematic tariff reduction programs started after World War II. In 1947, the U.S. and 22 other major trading countries got together in Geneva to find ways to reduce tariffs and remove trade barriers. The *General Agreement on Tariffs and Trade (GATT)* resulted.[20] Since then, eight major efforts to reduce trade barriers have been undertaken under GATT's auspices (see Table 2.2).

The first two rounds, Geneva 1947 and Annecy (France) 1949, are considered significant, both for tariff reduction and for structuring GATT's organization. The Torquay (England) 1951 and Geneva 1956 rounds are regarded as less significant. Insurmountable differences arose among nations over the issue of tariff disparities, that is, the difference between the high tariff of one country and low tariff of another. Next, the Dillon Round in 1962 resulted in further reduction of average world tariff rates. But it fell short of its goals: an across-the-board 20 percent reduction of tariffs and the settlement of problems unresolved since the 1956 meeting, especially those involving trade agreements with less-developed countries.

The Kennedy Round, sixth in the negotiation series, was the most comprehensive round of negotiations in terms of the number of participating countries, the value of the world trade involved, and the size of tariff reductions. The negotiations were concluded in 1972 with tariffs reduced on some 60,000 commodities valued at $40 billion in world trade. Despite its success, the Kennedy Round did not quite meet all the ambitious goals set for it. A major goal of the Kennedy Round was a 50 percent across-the-board reduction in tariffs on industrial products. However, overriding national interests forced exceptions to such a reduction for such commodities as chemicals, steel, aluminum, pulp, and paper. The question of tariff disparities, linked with the 50 percent goal, also yielded to exceptions because many Western European countries raised objections. Overall, the Kennedy Round negotiators agreed to tariff cuts on industrial products that averaged about 35 percent. The round was also meant to resolve the problem of nontariff barriers, but the results were rather modest except for the adoption of an antidumping code.

TABLE 2.2 Dimensions of Agreements Under GATT

MAJOR AGREEMENTS	NUMBER OF CONTRACTING PARTIES	VALUE OF WORLD TRADE INVOLVED (BILLIONS OF DOLLARS)	PERCENT OF AVERAGE TARIFF REDUCTION
1947 Geneva	23	$10.0	n.a.*
1949 Annecy, France	33	n.a.*	n.a.*
1951 Torquay, England	37	n.a.*	n.a.*
1956 Geneva	35	2.5	4
1962 Geneva (Dillon Round)	40	4.9	7
1967 Geneva (Kennedy Round)	70	40.0	35
1973 Tokyo (Tokyo Round)	85	115.0	50
1986 Punta del Este (Uruguay Round)	117	n.a.*	n.a.*

n.a.: not available

The principal objective of the Tokyo Round in 1973, seventh in the negotiation series, was the expansion and ever-greater liberalization of world trade. The Tokyo Round recognized that the scope of exceptions should be limited and supported the general feeling that the special interests of the developing countries should be borne in mind in the tariff negotiations. The Tokyo Round, concluding in 1978, was the most complex and comprehensive trade negotiating effort attempted to date. It tried to develop a substantially freer world trading system with balanced opportunities for countries with different economic and political systems and needs. While the actual achievements fell short of the goals, the overall results of the Tokyo Round were very encouraging.

In November 1985, 90 countries unanimously agreed to a U.S. proposal to launch a new round of global trade talks, eighth in the negotiation series, in September 1986 in Punta del Este, Uruguay, named the Uruguay Round. The focus of this round was on agricultural exports, services, intellectual properties, and voluntary trade limits.

The timing for another round of trade talks could not be more appropriate. Protectionist forces had been gaining momentum, particularly in the U.S. In Europe, where half of all economic activity relates to trade, America's protectionist sentiments had created uneasiness. The Europeans had warned that they would retaliate if the U.S. adopted protective measures. The developing economies did not know what to do, since the Western nations constituted a big market for their limited exportable products. Individual efforts of different nations to meet the protectionist threat did not succeed. One of the achievements of 50 years of trade liberalization had been the expansion of world trade, which was being challenged in the 1980s. What countries could not accomplish unilaterally, however, they might be able to accomplish under the GATT umbrella.

In the 40 years of its existence, GATT can claim some successes; average tariffs in industrial countries have tumbled to around 5 percent today from an average of 40 percent in 1947. The volume of trade in manufactured goods has multiplied twentyfold. GATT's membership has increased five fold. But the growing protectionism nurtured by the economic difficulties that beset the world in the 1970s has served to undermine the credibility of GATT and threaten the open trading system it upholds.

Trade Barriers and Trade Liberation

Cars, steel, videos, semiconductors, and shoes have followed textiles and clothing into "managed trade" (see International Marketing Highlight 2.3). In agriculture, where the U.S., the EC, and Japan are spending a total of $70 billion a year on subsidies, GATT rules have proved unworkable. GATT did not cover services (nearly 30 percent of all world trade) or investment abroad or intellectual property (patents, copyrights, and so on), which are of growing importance to the rich countries as the centers of manufacturing increasingly shift to the Third World.

International Marketing Highlight 2.3

Costs of Trade Protection

Restrictions on Japanese car imports have forced British and American buyers to pay much higher prices; and restrictions on imports of textiles and clothing cost a typical family $200–$420 a year in America, $220 a year in Canada, and up to $130 a year in Britain. Because trade-policy taxes fall most heavily on goods such as basic foods and cheap clothing, they are regressive. In Canada, one study showed that the tax-rate levied by barriers to imports of clothes was three times higher for poor families than for rich ones.

Source: From a GATT pamphlet entitled "Trade, the Uruguay Round and the Consumer," August 1993.

The Uruguay Round had generally been acknowledged to be a make-or-break affair for GATT. The intention was to strengthen GATT rules in its traditional areas, especially in agriculture where the rules were ambiguous; improve its enforcement powers; and extend its scope of neglected areas such as services. But after four years of talks, the Uruguay Round was suspended in December 1990 without an agreement. The talks stumbled over the refusal of different nations to make concessions demanded by others.

Finally, in December 1993, after tortuous negotiations, trade officials from 117 nations wrapped up a trade pact that slashed tariffs and reduced subsidies globally. It was intended to reduce barriers to trade in goods, including tariffs and such nontariff barriers as quotas, export subsidies, and anti-import regulations. It also was intended to extend the 47-year-old General Agreement on Tariffs and Trade, the rule book for international trade, to agriculture, financial, and other services and protection of intellectual property such as patents. The Uruguay Round Agreement met some of these goals, but negotiators jettisoned several controversial issues at the last minute.

The following are the key results of the Uruguay Round.[21]

Tariff: The U.S., Europe, and other major industrial powers agreed to eliminate tariffs altogether on pharmaceuticals, construction equipment, medical equipment, paper, and steel. In all, the share of goods imported by developed countries without tariffs will more than double to 43 percent from 20 percent; for developing countries it will rise to 45 percent from 22 percent. Tariffs also are to be cut substantially on chemicals, wood, and aluminum. Most tariffs on microprocessors would remain at zero, but those on memory chips and others would drop to 7 percent from 14 percent. Industrial tariffs, which now average 4.7 percent of the value of the products traded, would be reduced to an average of 3 percent.

Dumping: The agreement provides for tougher and quicker GATT actions to resolve disputes over use of antidumping laws, invoked by the U.S. and Europe to impose penalties on foreign producers that sell goods abroad below cost. Developing nations, often the subject of such antidumping laws, sought to curtail their use. Nonetheless, the final compromise is closer to the U.S. and European position.

Textiles and Apparel: Textiles and clothing are the most important export for many developing countries, accounting for nearly a quarter of their industrial exports. A system of quotas that limits imports of textiles and apparel to the U.S. and other developed countries, the Multi-Fiber Arrangement, will be phased out over 10 years. Most U.S. textile tariffs would be reduced by about 25 percent.

Intellectual Property: The pact provides for 20-year protection of patents, trademarks, and copyrights. However, it allows developing countries at least 10 years to phase in patent protection for pharmaceuticals, and patent protection for biotechnology products is also weak.

Agriculture: Countries that export farm goods will reduce the volume of subsidized exports by 21 percent over 6 years. Bans on rice imports in Japan and South Korea will be lifted. Quotas for imports of sugar, dairy, and peanuts to the U.S. will be phased out and replaced by tariffs. Initial access to previously closed markets would equal at least 3 percent of domestic consumption; Japan agreed to allow the share of imported rice to increase to 4 percent in 1995 and 8 percent over six years. The largest tariff cuts are for cut flowers; the smallest for dairy products.

Service: Trade in services among GATT members amounts to more than $900 billion a year but hasn't previously been covered by GATT rules. Developing countries agreed to open their markets in legal services, accounting, and software. However, U.S. negotiators failed to secure access to foreign markets that are largely closed to U.S. banks and securities firms such as Japan, several Southeast Asian nations, and many developing countries. The U.S. agreed to open its doors to foreign financial-services firms but asserted the right to limit access after January 1996 to firms from nations that don't reciprocate.

Audio-Visual Services: Among the very last remaining issues was a dispute between the U.S. and the European Union, France especially, over European limits on foreign programming shown on European television and the use of taxes on movie tickets and blank videocassettes to subsidize the French film industry. Unable to resolve this thorny issue, negotiators agreed to drop it altogether.

Subsidies: The agreement limits government subsidies for research in such goods as computer chips to 50 percent of applied research (that which leads to the first prototype) and 75 percent of basic research, and allows governments to average the limits for research that is a combination of the two.

Multilateral Trade Organization: The agreement creates a World Trading Organization (WTO) to replace the GATT secretariat, but details of the new organization's powers remain unclear. The WTO would, however, have more authority to oversee trade in services and agriculture than GATT now does.

Estimates by the World Bank and the Organization for Economic Cooperation and Development (OECD) suggest that the Uruguay Round Agreement could eventually be worth some $213 billion–$274 billion each year to the world economy.[22] Such numbers, at best sophisticated conjecture, are almost certainly conservative because they do not take into account benefits from strengthening GATT's rules and from liberalizing investment and trade in services. The gains are likely to accrue as follows: EU, $82 billion; China, $38 billion; Japan, $29 billion; U.S., $25 billion; EFTA, $15 billion; Latin America, $9 billion; Other Asia, $6 billion; and other nations, $8 billion (see International Marketing Highlight 2.4).

■■■■■■■■■■ **International Marketing Highlight 2.4** ■■■■■■■■■■

GATT's Payoffs

Trade barricaded American consumers $70 billion in higher prices in 1990: The Uruguay Round Agreement will reduce that "tax" by 47 percent or more, i.e., $32.8 billion a year in 1990. Of those savings, $17 billion will come from liberalization of the highly protected textile and apparel industries. Consumers will save another $1.2 billion from reduced agricultural protection.

Source: Fortune, February 7, 1994, p. 28.

U.S. Trade Liberalization

Liberalization of U.S. foreign trade began with the enactment of the Reciprocal Trade Agreement Act of 1934. With that act, Congress authorized the president to reduce then-existing tariff duties by 50 percent. A noteworthy aspect of the act was the inclusion of the *most-favored-nation clause*, which limited discrimination in trade by extending to third parties the same terms provided to contracting parties. This clause has become a fundamental principle of U.S. trade policy.

The Reciprocal Trade Agreement Act of 1934 encouraged bilateral agreements that would increase U.S. exports, as long as the exports did not adversely affect domestic industry. In effect, the injury to domestic industry could not take place because of highly protective tariff rates and an item-by-item approach to negotiations, which allowed certain commodities to be excluded if a decrease in rates would result in an increase in imports.

The act was extended every three years, and by 1945 the U.S. had concluded negotiations with 29 countries. Overall, the act helped in reducing the average rate of tariffs on taxable imports into the U.S. from 47 percent in 1934 to 28 percent in 1945. In 1945, Congress authorized the president to cut rates by an additional 50 percent. While the act has been successful in reducing tariff barriers, it did little to reduce such nontariff barriers as quotas and internal taxes.

The second phase in U.S. trade liberalization efforts came in 1947. At that time the U.S. and 22 other major trading nations negotiated simultaneously for both reduction of tariffs and removal of trade barriers. These efforts, as previously discussed, resulted in the establishment of GATT.

GATT institutionalized multilateral tariff negotiations by promoting the unconditional most-favored-nation principle, i.e., a tariff reduction given to one trading nation had to apply to all other trading nations that were signatures to the GATT.

The Trade Expansion Act of 1962 marks another phase in U.S. foreign trade policy. This act authorized the president to: (1) reduce tariffs up to 50 percent of the rates existing as of July 1, 1962; (2) eliminate tariffs on products in which the U.S. and Common Market countries together accounted for at least 50 percent of world trade; and (3) eliminate rates that did not exceed 5 percent.[23]

The act empowered the president to negotiate across-the-board tariff reductions (rather than item-by-item reductions) and modify the safeguard provisions of the old trade agreements program. As a matter of fact, this act was designed to stimulate not only U.S. exports, but also world trade in general, so that benefits would accrue to all nations as a result of international specialization and trade. When the U.S. entered trade negotiations for the Kennedy Round, the authority of the Trade Expansion Act of 1962 was in effect.

In the 1970s, despite the urgency for a new international trade perspective, no effective trade legislation was passed by Congress. As a matter of fact, in the 1970s, a variety of U.S. government measures hindered rather than helped trade. The Trade Act of 1974 barred export-import credit via the Export-Import Bank, which was established to finance "big-ticket" item exports like aircraft or nuclear power technology. The Foreign Corrupt Practices Act of 1977 imposed jail terms and fines for overseas payoffs by U.S. companies. The Carter administration's human rights legislation denied export-import credit to rights violators. Loans were withheld from South Africa, Uruguay, and Chile. U.S. trade embargoes banned exports to Cuba, Vietnam, Rhodesia, and other countries.

In the 1980s, the Reagan administration took a variety of ad hoc measures in response to emerging problems and crises. In 1982, President Reagan signed the Export Trading Company Act, which was designed to attract manufacturers, export-management companies, banks, freight forwarders, and other export services into joint efforts to gain foreign markets (see Chapter 17). In the fall of 1985, to avert a possible trade war stemming from mounting protectionist pressures in the Congress and the nation, the Reagan administration committed itself to join England, France, Germany, and Japan in intervening heavily on the world's financial markets to lower the dollar's value. This was planned to help the U.S. reduce its trade deficit. The U.S. government also unveiled a "fair trade" program built around the threat of retaliation against nations that refused to chop barriers to U.S. goods.

A hallmark of the Reagan era was the passage of the 1988 trade bill. To seek a long-term solution to the problem of the U.S. trade deficit, the U.S. government enacted the Omnibus Trade and Competitiveness Act of 1988. This act was the product of a three-year effort involving Congress, the administration, and the business community. The act maintained the U.S. commitment to free trade. It did, however, provide better trade-remedy tools for judicious use in opening foreign markets.

During the Bush administration, the major emphasis had been on extending the U.S.–Canada Free Trade Agreement into a truly North American Free Trade Agreement, and on helping Eastern Europe, the former Soviet States, and Latin America toward greater reliance on market forces. Progress continued to be made in implementing the U.S.–Canada Free Trade Agreement that went into force in 1989, and Congress authorized the president to pursue a similar agreement with Mexico.

Early in his administration, President Clinton announced a new export strategy to massively upgrade the U.S. government's trade promotion efforts. The strategy comprised creating one-stop shops for consolidating federal programs traditionally handled by 19 different agencies, developing a strategic plan for each major country, providing higher-level U.S. government support for foreign government procurement (for example, wooing Saudi Arabia into buying $6 billion worth of Boeing and McDonnell civilian aircraft); increasing Overseas Private Investment Corporation (OPIC) project limit from $50 million to $200 million (for providing insurance coverage for U.S. companies in developing countries), liberalizing high-tech exports (previously restricted in many nations), and tying foreign aid to American exports.[24]

In putting together the National Export Strategy, the administration had several assumptions in mind. First, in looking ahead at the American economy, it became clear that no national priority, with the exception of military security, would rank higher than the creation of more and better jobs. To realize this goal, we must sell more into the marketplace beyond our shores. Second, competition for markets abroad was increasingly brutal. The U.S. needed to be aggressive and strategic. Traditional competitors such as Japan, France, and Germany, as well as newcomers such as South Korea and Taiwan, have actively and skillfully been seeding new markets and cementing their role as the main supplier of goods and services to countries around the globe. Third, many dramatic new opportunities have been opening in the world marketplace. In Asia and Latin America, economic growth is healthy and everywhere governments are turning to open markets, making them significant for U.S. sales. Fourth, as a nation, we were performing far below our potential. Some 50 firms in the U.S. account for nearly half of all our exports of goods. Ten states account for 64 percent of our merchandise exports. There seemed to be tremendous room for export expansion merely if more firms began to think globally.

MNCs and World Markets

Multinational corporations (MNCs) are among the most, if not the most, influential factors in global economic life today. Within the last 30 years they have become the most formidable single factor in world trade and investment. MNCs play a decisive role in the allocation and use of the world's resources. They conceive new products and services, create and stimulate demand for them, and develop new modes of manufacture and distribution (see International Marketing Highlight 2.5). Consider the example of Gillette and how it participates in world markets as a MNC.

The Gillette Company

Gillette is the leading manufacturer of blades and safety razors in the world. Gillette's products are sold in more than 200 countries and territories throughout the world. While the company's market position varies from country to country, Gillette plays an important role in most blade/razor markets.

International Marketing Highlight 2.5

How to Become a Global Company

There is no handy formula for going global, but any company serious about joining the race will have do most or all of the following:

Make yourself at home in all three of the world's most important markets—North America, Europe, and Asia.

Develop new products for the whole world.

Replace profit centers based on countries or regions with ones based on product lines.

"Glocalize," as the Japanese call it: Make global decisions on strategic questions about products, capital, and research, but let local units decide tactical questions about packaging, marketing, and advertising.

Overcome parochial attitudes such as the "not-invented-here" syndrome. Train people to think internationally, send them off on frequent trips, and give them the latest communications technology such as teleconferencing.

Open the senior ranks to foreign employees.

Do whatever seems best wherever it seems best, even if people at home lose jobs or responsibilities.

In markets that you cannot penetrate on your own, find allies.

Source: Jeremy Main, "How to Go Global and Why," *Fortune*, August 28, 1989, p. 76.

The company so dominates shaving worldwide that its name has come to mean a razor blade in some countries. It is the leader in Europe with a 70 percent market share and in Latin America with 80 percent. (In the U.S., the company holds a 64 percent share of the net shaving market compared with 13 percent at No. 2 rival Shick.[25]) Indeed, for every blade it sells at home, it sells five abroad, a figure likely to grow as recent joint ventures in China, Russia, and India expand. As a matter of fact, the company holds a dominant position in many markets. In select markets, this dominance extends to its other product lines as well, such as grooming aids, toiletries, and writing instruments. According to company management, its success in international markets is based on continual efforts at product innovation and improvement, strict quality control, aggressive marketing, and able management worldwide.

In addition to U.S. and Canadian plants, Gillette has manufacturing plants in a number of countries abroad. Shaving products plants are located in Isleworth (U.K.), Berlin, Annecy (France), Rio de Janeiro, Buenos Aires, Cali (Colombia), Mexico City, Melbourne, and Seville. These plants serve the host country as well as other countries in the region.

During 1993, Gillette derived over 68 percent of its sales and 71 percent of its income from markets outside the U.S. (excluding Canada). This statistic reveals the importance of its international operations. Gillette concentrates on three main product areas: shaving, stationery, and small electrical appliances. Razors and blades account for one-third of the company's sales, but two-thirds of its operating profits.[26]

Organization   Traditionally, Gillette International, a division of Gillette Company, was responsible for overseas manufacturing and marketing, which affects almost all of Gillette products including blades and razors, toiletries and grooming aids, and writing instruments.[26] In 1986, the company restructured its international operations. The company is divided into two groups: Gillette North Atlantic and Gillette International. Gillette North Atlantic integrates the U.S., Canadian, and most of the European operations. Gillette International is responsible for the rest of the world.

Gillette North Atlantic's organization structure integrates European and U.S. operations by different product groups: blade and razor group, personal care group, and stationery products group. Each group has a North American Division and a European Division, the latter organized into five areas each under the leadership of a general manager as follows: Northern Europe, Western Europe, Southeast Europe, Central Europe, and Iberia.

The integration of European operations within the U.S. organization indicates Gillette's move toward becoming a true global company. This should also help the company to take advantage of the European Market integration program.

Gillette International, located at company headquarters in Boston, is organized into three groups: (1) Latin American, (2) Asian-Pacific, and (3) African, Middle Eastern, and Eastern European. Each of the three groups is headed by a group general manager. In addition, there is a staff group called the Gillette International Marketing Department (GIMD), located in Boston, led by a marketing director, assisted by individual specialists in each product field and international coordinators in market research and advertising. These specialists give advice to marketing personnel worldwide. The organization in each country consists of a general manager to whom heads of manufacturing, marketing, personnel, and accounting report. The marketing organization employs people in sales, market research, sales promotion, and brand management. The Gillette salesforce in each country handles a wide range of Gillette products including shaving products, toiletries, and writing instruments. It is organized along the same line in each country and follows essentially the same selling technique.

Decision Making   Gillette's global decision-making system is mostly centralized. The recommendations of executives based overseas are sought and considered, but major marketing decisions, including those that concern strategic goals, the price structure, and global advertising, are made in Boston. However, both Gillette International and Gillette North Atlantic are responsible for operational decision making in their own regions.

Within Gillette International, key marketing decisions are generally made at the headquarters level in Boston, where management of the three component regions is also based. Implementation decisions, such as advertising placement and local distribution, are made at the country level.

Subsidiary executives have the authority to set their own prices as long as they stay within the centrally planned positioning strategy. Distribution strategy is similarly planned centrally and adjusted, when necessary, by the subsidiaries.

Advertising campaigns are sometimes fine-tuned at the local level. Promotion campaigns, although developed locally, must also support marketing goals established by headquarters.

Most of Gillette North Atlantic's significant marketing decisions are made in Boston by the product division at the general manager's level. Like Gillette International, most strategic decisions are also centralized in Boston. Overseas executives are mainly involved in moving products through the distribution system to the final consumer, and in designing and implementing local store promotions, coupon campaigns, and so on.

Desired price relationships vis-à-vis competing brands and products are defined by product executives at headquarters. Within these parameters, subsidiary executives are responsible for setting prices in their own markets.

As part of its preparation for the post-1992 EC, Gillette North Atlantic recently switched to a pan-European packaging strategy, that relies less on words and more on symbols to make the same packaging usable in many countries.

Advertising Gillette International's advertising strategy is formulated at the regional level, and Gillette North Atlantic's at the product group level. Each uses a single, though different, advertising agency to create and coordinate its global campaigns. International retains McCann Erickson, while North Atlantic primarily uses BBDO Worldwide Advertising Agency.

The decision not to use one agency throughout the world follows logically from the two-region organizational structure Gillette has adopted. Moreover, the company's senior management believes it is unwise to put all its international advertising eggs in one basket. These two agencies were chosen because they were deemed to be particularly strong in the operating region of the respective Gillette entity each is to serve.

Both North Atlantic and International centralize virtually all aspects of advertising. This usually means simply dubbing foreign languages into ads created by headquarters. Typically, ads are made with only music on the basic soundtrack. Then the various messages to be used in the different countries are dubbed in with voice-overs. This approach is designed to make ads easily transferable from one market to the next.

In rare instances, when mandated by official regulation, overseas subsidiaries use local actors in locally shot commercials. Even then, however, the creative aspects, including the dialogue, theme, and slogan, are developed in Boston. The Gillette Sensor campaign, "Gillette, the best a man can get," is a good example of the company's global approach.

Foreign Staffing Gillette is firmly committed to staffing foreign subsidiaries with local citizens and third-country nationals. It attributes much of its international success to the strength of its overseas companies and management organizations. The company strives to be perceived as a local company in foreign markets rather than a locally established global company. For this reason, Gillette avoids filling executive openings at its subsidiaries, including those in marketing, with American expatriates.

Within Gillette International, no Americans hold group vice president positions. Latin America is headed by an Argentinean, the Africa/Middle East/Eastern Europe region by a Spaniard, and Asia/Pacific by a Briton. Most general managers are also local nationals or third-country nationals. Within Latin America, six of the seven key general managers are local nationals. Moreover, none of the eight general managers in the Asia/Pacific region is an American.

Gillette North Atlantic is similarly ethnically diverse: The general managers of the company's subsidiaries in Italy, Spain/Portugal, and Northern Europe are Italian, South African, and British, respectively.

Growth Strategy Tailoring its marketing to Third World budgets and tastes—from packaging blades so they can be sold one at a time, to educating the unshaven about the joys of a smooth face—has become an important part of Gillette's growth strategy.[28] The company sells its pens, toiletries, toothbrushes, and other products in developing countries.

The market for blades in developed countries is stagnant. In the Third World, there is a very high proportion of people under 15 years old who will be in the shaving population in a very short time.

Few U.S. consumer-products companies that compete in the Third World expended as much energy or made as many inroads as Gillette, which draws more than 60 percent of its sales from abroad. Since the company targeted the developing world in 1969, the proportion of its sales that come from Latin America, Asia, Africa, and the Middle East has doubled to 25 percent and the dollar volume has risen eightfold.

Gillette has had a strong business in Latin America since it began building plants there in the 1940s. Fidel Castro once told television interviewer Barbara Walters that he grew a beard during the Cuban revolution because he could not get Gillette blades while fighting in the mountains.

The company's push in to Asia, Africa, and the Middle East dates to 1969, when Gillette dropped a policy of investing only where it could have wholly owned subsidiaries. That year, it formed a joint venture in Malaysia, which was threatening to bar imports of Gillette products. The company has added one foreign plant nearly every year in such countries as China, Egypt, Thailand, and India.

The company always starts with a factory that makes double-edged blades— still popular in the Third World—and, if all goes well, expands later into production of pens, deodorants, shampoo, or toothbrushes. Only a few ventures have failed: A Yugoslav project never got off the ground, and Gillette had to sell its interests in Iran to its local partners.

In a few markets, Gillette has developed products exclusively for Third World buyers. The low-cost shaving cream is one. Another is Black Silk, a hair relaxer developed for sale to blacks in South Africa and now being sold in Kenya, Nigeria, and other African countries.

More often, Gillette sells familiar products in different packages or smaller sizes. Because many Latin American consumers cannot afford a seven-ounce bottle of Silkience shampoo, for instance, Gillette sells it in half-ounce plastic bubbles. In Brazil, Gillette sells Right Guard deodorant in plastic squeeze bottles instead of metal cans (see International Marketing Highlight 2.6).

As is evident in the Gillette case, MNCs capitalize on opportunities far and wide the world over. In strictly theoretical terms, MNCs acquire raw materials and capital where they are most abundant, manufacture products where wages and other costs are lowest, and sell in the most profitable markets. In other words, MNCs seek to follow the economic law of comparative advantage—everyone benefits if each does its best work, *no matter where* the work is performed.

■■■■■■■■■■■■■■■■ **International Marketing Highlight 2.6** ■■■■■■■■■■■■■■■■

How to Convince People to Shave

The hardest task for Gillette is convincing Third World men to shave. The company recently began dispatching portable theaters to remote villages to show movies and commercials that tout daily shaving.

In South African and Indonesian versions, a bewildered bearded man enters a locker room where clean-shaven friends show him how to shave. In the Mexican version, a handsome sheriff, tracking bandits who have kidnapped a woman, pauses on the trail to shave every morning. The camera lingers as he snaps a double-edged blade into his razor. In the end, of course, the smooth-faced sheriff gets the woman.

In other places, Gillette agents with an oversized shaving brush and a mug of shaving cream lather up and shave a villager while others watch. Plastic razors are then distributed free and blades—which, of course, must be bought—are left with the local storekeeper. Such campaigns have a lasting impact.

Source: David Wessel, "Gillette Keys Sales to Third World Tastes," *The Wall Street Journal,* January 23, 1986, p. 35.

Summary

We have examined the rationale for world trade and business activity. The classic explanation of world trade is provided by the theory of comparative advantage. When one country has an advantage over another, not only in the production of one product but of all products, and its advantage in the production of the one product is greater than its advantage in the production of the other products, that country, according to the theory, has a comparative advantage in the production of the first product. To follow the theory of comparative advantage, each country should figure out which products have a comparative advantage and concentrate its productive efforts on those; other products should be imported in exchange.

Significant world trade and investment patterns in recent years have been examined in various other ways. We have also discussed three particular approaches to international business and trade activity. Using the concept of product life cycle, Harvard researchers Raymond Vernon and Louis Wells have hypothesized that products are first manufactured in the most developed countries like the U.S. and exported to other advanced countries like Japan and those of Western Europe. The advanced countries soon adapt the product and begin to manufacture it in their own countries. Then, the first manufacturer faces tough competition from the advanced countries not only in its home market but also in the Third World countries as well, where cheaper labor is available. This leads the first country to make direct investments in manufacturing in the second countries and thus counter their advantage. Despite this defensive measure, however, the first country may find it difficult to compete. This cycle continues with the result that the developing countries may eventually command the market everywhere.

In response to the limitations of the product life cycle theory, other concepts have been formulated. Peter Drucker has advanced the concept of production sharing. Production sharing postulates splitting manufacturing into stages undertaken in different countries.

Finally, according to the internalization theory, a firm establishes an international network linking production to its various markets. Such a network enables the firm to grow by eliminating external markets in intermediate goods and thus internalizing those markets within the firm.

We have also examined trade barriers and the international efforts that have been made to liberalize trade. Two types of barriers were mentioned: tariff and nontariff barriers. Efforts at liberalization of international trade in a systematic fashion began after World War II with the establishment of GATT. In all, eight rounds of multilateral negotiations have been held under GATT toward this end. The U.S. has made legislative efforts that have both encouraged and hindered liberal trade with other nations.

Unquestionably, the MNC is the agent of modern day international business. The global business practices of the Gillette Company are illustrative of multinational trade and business in the 1990s and beyond.

Review Questions

1. Differentiate between absolute and relative advantage. Illustrate, with the help of an example, how comparative (relative) advantage encourages trade.
2. Despite the comparative advantage argument, nations continue to opt for self-sufficiency. How would you explain this behavior?
3. What are the limitations of the product life cycle theory of international trade?
4. Use an example to explain the concept of production sharing.
5. What factors lead countries to seek protection against imports?
6. What are the major types of tariffs that nations use against imports?
7. Discuss major types of nontariff barriers.
8. What role have GATT agreements played in reducing trade barriers?
9. How did the Kennedy Round negotiations differ from the Tokyo Round negotiations?

Creative Questions

1. Nontariff barriers continue to be a major deterrent to world trade. Could the forerunner of GATT, the Multilateral Trade Organization (MTO), be entrusted the task of enforcing the implementation of agreed upon rules to eliminate nontariff barriers? Will nations agree to specific rules relative to nontariff barriers? Will they let the MTO punish countries that break the rules?
2. What is the function of the U.S. trade representative's office? How does it differ from what the U.S. International Trade Commission does? For more effective trade policy, should these two organizations be merged?

Endnotes

1. Paul Samuelson, *Economics* (New York: McGraw-Hill Book Company, 1981), p. 669. *Also see* David H. Blake, *The Politics of Global Economic Relations* (Englewood Cliffs, NJ: Prentice-Hall, 1983); Ian M.D. Little, *Economic Development: Theory, Policy and International Relations* (New York: Basic Books, 1982).

2. Value can sometimes be uncoupled from production hours, but typically only in cases of long-term scarcity (as with some precious metals) or when the quality of one producer's manufactured products is not matched by other suppliers. In these circumstances, virtual monopolies can develop.

3. *See*: William W. Lewis, Hans Gersbach, Tom Jansen, and Koji Sakate, "The Secret to Competitivenes—Competition," *The McKinsey Quarterly*, November 4, 1993, pp. 29–44.

4. Peter F. Drucker, "Low Wages No Longer Give Competitive Edge," *The Wall Street Journal*, March 16, 1988, p. 23.

5. G. Todd Russell, "Business Travelers Rate Asia's Airlines as the World's Best," *The Asian Wall Street Journal Weekly*, November 18, 1985, p. 1. *Also see* Louis Kraar, "Flying High with the Singapore Girls," *Fortune*, June 18, 1979, pp. 132–39.

6. Raymond Vernon, "International Investment and International Trade in the Product Cycle," *Quarterly Journal of Economics*, May 1966, pp. 190–207. *Also see* Raymond Vernon, *Sovereignty at Bay* (New York: Basic Books, 1971), pp. 65–112; Louis T. Wells, Jr., "Test of a Product Cycle Model of International Trade," *Quarterly Journal of Economics*, February 1969, pp. 152–62.

7. Louis T. Wells, Jr., "A Product Life Cycle for International Trade?," *Journal of Marketing*, July 1968, pp. 1–6. *Also see* J. F. Hennart, *A Theory of Multinational Enterprise* (Ann Arbor: University of Michigan Press, 1982).

8. Damon Darlin, "Japanese Learn Thrills of Bargain Shopping from Mentors Abroad," *The Wall Street Journal*, March 11, 1988, p. 1.

9. Raymond Vernon, *Sovereignty at Bay* (New York: Basic Books, 1971), p. 107.

10. James M. Lutz and Robert T. Green. "The Product Life Cycle and the Export Position of the United States," *Journal of International Business Studies*, Winter 1983, pp. 77–94. *Also see* Sak Onkvisit and John J. Shaw, "An Examination of the International Product Life Cycle and Its Application Within Marketing," *Columbia Journal of World Business*, Fall 1983, pp. 73–78.

11. Alicia Mullor-Sebastian, "The Product Life Cycle Theory: Empirical Evidence," *Journal of International Business Studies*, Winter 1983, pp. 95–106.

12. Peter F. Drucker, "The Rise of Production Sharing," *The Wall Street Journal*, March 15, 1977, p. 24. *Also see* Martin K. Starr, "Global Production and Operations Strategy," *Columbia Journal of World Business*, Winter 1984, pp. 17–22.

13. Peter F. Drucker, "Economics Erases National Boundaries," excerpt ad from *Managing in Turbulent Times* by Peter F. Drucker (New York: Harper & Row, 1979), in *Industry Week*, April 28, 1980, pp. 63–64.

14. Alan M. Rugman and Michael Gestrin, "The Strategic Response of Multinational Enterprises to NAFTA," *Columbia Journal of World Business*, Winter 1993, pp. 18–29.

15. Peter J. Buckley, *Multinational Enterprises and Economic Analysis* (Cambridge, England: Cambridge University Press, 1982).

16. Peter J. Buckley and R. D. Pierce, "Overseas Production and Exporting by the World's Largest Enterprises: A Study in Sourcing Policy," *Journal of International Business Studies*, Spring/Summer 1979, pp. 9–20.

17. Robert Grosse and Jack N. Behrman, "Theory in International Business," *Transnational Corporations*, February 1992, pp. 93–126.

18. A. D. Cao, "Non-tariff Barriers to U.S. Manufactured Exports," *Columbia Journal of World Business*, Summer 1980, pp. 93–102. *Also see* Alan Bauerschmidt, Daniel Sullivan, and Kate Gillespie, "Common Factors Underlying Barriers to Export: Studies in the U.S. Paper Industry," *Journal of International Business Studies*, Fall 1985, pp. 111–24.

19. *See*: Tacho Bark and Jaime de Melo, "Export Quota Allocations, Export Earnings, and Market Diversification," *The World Bank Economic Review*, Vol. 2, No. 3, pp. 341–48.

20. At the time of the GATT negotiations, nations were also working toward setting up an international trade organization (ITO), but the matter was dropped since the participating nations failed to come to an agreement.

21. Bob Davis and Lawrence Ingrassia, "After Years of Talks, GATT is at Last Ready to Sign Off on a Pact," *The Wall Street Journal*, December 15, 1993, p. 1. *See also*: Louis S. Richman, "What is Next After GATT's Victory?," *Fortune*, January 10, 1994, p. 66.

22. "The Eleventh Hour," *The Economist*, December 4, 1993, p. 23.

23. *Future United States Foreign Trade Policy*, report to the President, submitted by the Special Representative for Trade Negotiations (Washington, D.C.: U.S. Government Printing Office, 1969). *Also see* Gordon O. Weil, *Trade Policy in the 70s* (New York: The Twentieth Century Fund, 1969).

24. "The National Export Strategy," *Business America*, April 1994, pp. 5–10.

25. Lawrence Ingrassia, "Gillette Holds its Edge by Endlessly Searching for a Better Shave." *The Wall Street Journal.*, December 10, 1992, p. 1.

26 "Blade Runner." *The Economist*, April 10,1993, p. 65.

27. Information on Gillette Company was obtained through a personal interview with a company executive and from the Company's Annual Report for 1987.

28. David Wessel, "Gillette Keys Sales to Third World Tastes." *The Wall Street Journal,* January 23, 1986, p. 35. Also see "Gillette Inches Closer to the Razor's Edge." *Business Week*, February 19, 1988, p. 36.

PART · I

Cases

Case 1: Xerox and Fuji Xerox

> *We are committed to strengthening the strategic and functional coordination of Xerox and Fuji Xerox so that we will compete effectively against strong and unified global competitors.*
>
> —Paul Allaire, President and CEO of Xerox Corporation
> —Yotaro Kobayashi, President and CEO of Fuji Xerox

Fuji Xerox, the joint venture between Xerox and Fuji Photo Film, was at a pivotal point in its 28-year history in 1990. Many considered it the most successful joint venture in history between an American and a Japanese company. Originally a sales organization for Xerox products in Japan, Fuji Xerox had evolved into a fully integrated operation with strong research, development, and manufacturing capabilities. As its sales and capabilities evolved, so did its importance within the Xerox Group: its 1989 revenues of $3.6 billion represented 22% of the Xerox Group's worldwide revenue.[1] Furthermore, Fuji Xerox supplied the rest of the Xerox Group with low-to mid-range copiers. In Japan, the home country of Xerox's major competitors, Fuji Xerox held 22% of the installed base of copiers and 30% of revenues in the industry.

Yotaro "Tony" Kobayashi, Fuji Xerox's president and CEO, ascribed a good deal of the company's success to the autonomy that the joint venture had enjoyed from the beginning. Fuji Xerox was not "the norm" for joint ventures, he contended, adding that "the degree to which Xerox let us run was very unusual." Yet, paradoxically, as the company grew to represent a larger portion of Xerox's worldwide business (**Exhibit 1**), this situation seemed to be changing. "We have to begin to pay more attention to what our actions mean to Xerox," explained Kobayashi.

Paul Allaire, Xerox's president and CEO, added that Fuji Xerox's autonomy had been an important factor not only in its own success, but also in its growing contribution to the Xerox Group:

> The fact that we had this strong company in Japan was of extraordinary importance when other Japanese companies started coming after us. Fuji Xerox was able to see them coming earlier, and understood their development and manufacturing techniques.
>
> We have excellent relationships with Fuji Xerox at the research, development, manufacturing, and manage-

---

Copyright©1991 by the President and Fellows of Harvard College. Harvard Business School case 9-391-156, Rev 12/8/92
Research Associate Krista McQuade and Professor Benjamin Gomes-Cassers prepared this case as the basis for class discussion rather than to illustrate either effective or ineffective handling of an administrative situation. Reprinted by permission of the Harvard Business School.

1. The Xerox Corporation (XC) is referred to in this case simply as Xerox. The combination of Rank Xerox (RX), Fuji Xerox (FX), and the Xerox Corporation is referred to as the Xerox Group. The revenues of Rank Xerox were consolidated into those of Xerox Corporation, but Fuji Xerox revenues were not. As described below, Xerox Corporation received 66% of RX earnings, which in turn included half of FX earnings.

EXHIBIT 1 Growth of Xerox Corporation and Fuji Xerox, 1968–1989

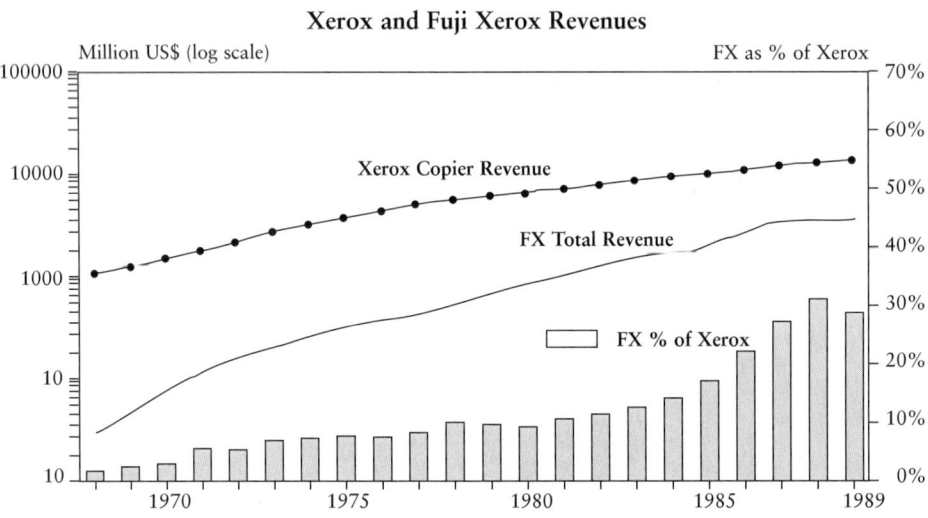

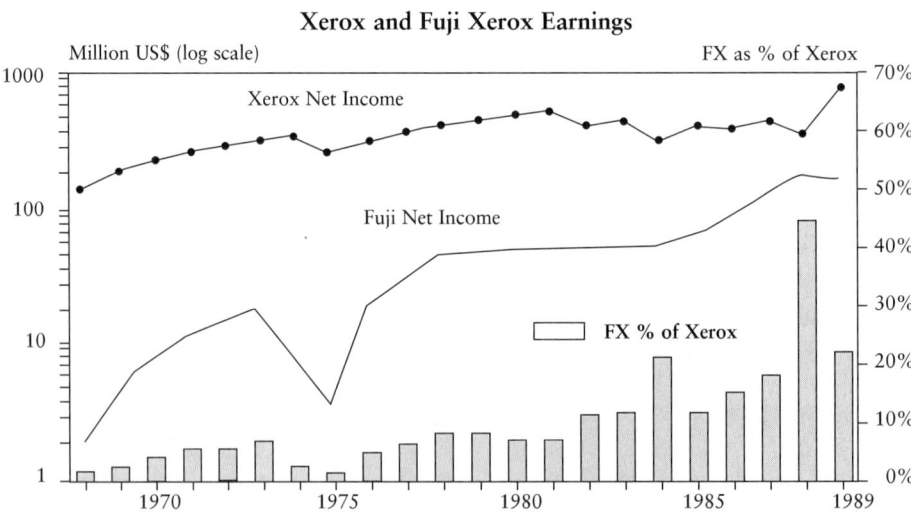

Source: Xerox and Fuji Xerox annual reports

Notes: Top: The Xerox revenues shown include Rank Xerox but not Fuji Xerox.
Bottom: Xerox earnings include 33% of FX earnings

rial levels. Yet, because of this close relationship, there is a greater potential for conflict. If Fuji Xerox were within our organization, it would be easier, but then we would lose certain benefits. They have always had a reasonable amount of autonomy. I can't take that away from them, and I wouldn't want to.

Over the years, Fuji Xerox saw its local competitors grow rapidly through exports. The terms of its technology licensing agreements with Xerox, however, limited Fuji Xerox's sales to Japan and certain Far Eastern territories. As Canon, in particular, grew to challenge Xerox worldwide in low-end copiers, laser printers, and color copiers, Fuji Xerox began to feel constrained by the relationship. "Fuji Xerox has aspirations to be a global company in marketing, manufacturing, and research," explained Jeff Kennard, who had managed the relationship between Xerox and Fuji Xerox since 1977. Kobayashi elaborated:

> The goals of Xerox and Fuji Xerox can be described as mostly compatible and partly conflicting. There *are* serious issues facing us. We often compare our situation with that of Canon or Ricoh, companies that have a single management organization in Japan. Are we as efficient and effective in the worldwide management of our business as we could be?
>
> Some of Fuji Xerox's products, such as facsimile machines, are managed like Canon's—with single-point design and manufacturing. But now there are external conditions in the United States and Europe that call for local manufacturing and development. Rank Xerox and Xerox are able to reach efficient volumes in their marketplaces. If Fuji Xerox manufactures only for Japan and adjacent markets, our volume will be too small, but Xerox is insisting on this. It is a tough challenge that we have to face together.

How should Fuji Xerox's aspirations be managed within the context of the Xerox Group? This was one of the questions facing the Codestiny Task Force commissioned in 1989 to review the capabilities and goals of Xerox and Fuji Xerox. Composed of senior managers from both companies, the task force would seek ways to enhance the strategic relationship between Xerox and Fuji Xerox for the 1990s. This was the third such review; Codestiny I (1982) and Codestiny II (1984) had both resulted in changes in contracts and agreements between the firms. With the basic technology licensing contract between Xerox and Fuji Xerox due to be renegotiated in 1993, participants in Codestiny III knew that their analysis could well lead to a substantial restructuring of the strategic relationship between the companies.

Xerox's International Expansion

When Chester Carlson tried to sell the rights to the revolutionary xerographic technology that he invented in 1939, GE, IBM, RCA, and Kodak all turned him down. Instead, the Haloid Corporation—a small photographic paper firm in Rochester, NY—agreed in 1946 to fund further research, and 10 years later acquired the full rights to the technology. By the time the company introduced its legendary 914 copier in 1959, xerographic products had come to dominate its business; in 1961 Haloid's name was changed to Xerox Corporation. The 914 was the world's first automatic plain paper copier (PPC), and produced high-quality copies four times faster than any other copier on the market. These advantages, coupled with an innovative machine rental scheme, led Xerox to dominate the industry for nearly 20 years. Company revenues rose from $40 million in 1960 to nearly $549 million in 1965, and to $1.2 billion in 1968, breaking the American record for the fastest company to reach $1 billion in sales. Net income grew from $2.6 million in 1960 to $129 million in 1968. In a mere decade, the name Xerox had become synonymous with copying.

Xerox moved quickly to establish an international network. Lacking the funds to expand alone, it formed a 50/50 joint venture in 1956 with the Rank Organization of Britain. Xerox would be entitled to about 66% of the profits of Rank Xerox. Rank operated a lucrative motion picture business and was seeking opportunities for diversification. Rank Xerox (RX), the new joint venture, was to manufacture xerographic products developed by Xerox and market them exclusively worldwide, except in the United States and Canada. By the early 1960s, Rank Xerox had established subsidiaries in Mexico, Italy, Germany, France, and Australia. In 1964, Xerox bought back the right to market xerographic products in the Western hemisphere.

Japanese firms immediately inquired about obtaining xerography licenses from Rank Xerox, but they were refused on the grounds that the technology was not commercially mature. By 1958, however, RX executives had turned their sights to the Japanese market. Aware of Japanese government regulations that required foreign firms to sell through local licensees or joint ventures, they sought a strong partner. Twenty-seven Japanese firms jockeyed for the position; Fuji Photo Film (FPF) was the only nonelectronics firm in this group. Still, the company was chosen, partly because of the personal relationship and trust that had developed between RX President Thomas Law and FPF Chairman Setsutaro Kobayashi.

Fuji Photo Film was a manufacturer of photographic film since the early 1930s and second only to Kodak in that field. The company was trying to diversify its business away from silver-based photography, and was convinced that its technical expertise was well suited to the requirements of xerography. Under the direction of Nobuo Shono, the company had already begun experimenting with xerography; by 1958, it had invested six million yen in research and manufacturing facilities for the copiers that it hoped to license from Rank Xerox. As negotiations between the two companies intensified, Rank Xerox insisted on a joint venture instead of simply a license to Fuji Photo Film.

The Establishment of Fuji Xerox

Fuji Xerox, the 50/50 joint venture established by Fuji Photo Film and Rank Xerox in 1962, was originally intended to be a marketing organization to sell xerographic products manufactured by Fuji Photo Film. When the Japanese government refused to approve a joint venture intended solely as sales company, however, the agreement was revised to give Fuji Xerox manufacturing rights. Fuji Xerox—not Fuji Photo Film—then became the contracting party with Rank Xerox, and received exclusive rights to xerographic patents in Japan. Fuji Xerox, in turn, subcontracted Fuji Photo Film to manufacture the products. As part of its technology licensing agreements with Rank Xerox, Fuji Xerox had exclusive rights to sell the machines in Japan, Indonesia, South Korea, the Philippines, Taiwan, Thailand, and Indochina. In return, Fuji Xerox would pay Rank Xerox a royalty of 5% on revenues from the sale of xerographic products. Rank Xerox would also be entitled to 50% of Fuji Xerox's profits.

Nobuo Shono became Fuji Xerox's first senior managing director, and Setsutaro Kobayashi, its president. Shono and Kobayashi drew their core executive staff, later known as the "Seven Samurai," from the ranks of Fuji Photo Film. A board of directors consisting of representatives from Rank Xerox and Fuji Photo Film was established to decide policy matters, while day-to-day operations were left to the Japanese management. The Xerox Corporation itself was to have no direct relationship with Fuji Xerox, and would participate in the profits of the joint venture only through its share in Rank Xerox.

Although Fuji Xerox adopted a number of business practices from Xerox, including organizational structure and the rental system, it remained distinctly Japanese throughout its history. Hideki Kaihatsu, managing director and chief staff officer at Fuji Xerox, explained:

> Employees are typically rotated through many functions before rising to the level of general management, and compensation and lifetime employment practices are similar to those of other Japanese firms. We emphasize long-term planning, teamwork, and we follow bottom-up decision making, including the "ringi" system. Furthermore, in procuring parts we follow the Japanese practice of qualifying a small group of vendors and working closely with them.

The Development of Fuji Xerox's Capabilities

Well before negotiations for the joint venture were finalized, engineers at Fuji Photo Film geared up for the production of Xerox copiers. Xerox machines were disassembled and studied to determine the equipment and supplies necessary for production. Three FPF engineers spent two months touring Xerox and Rank Xerox production facilities. At the establishment of the joint venture, a specific schedule was agreed upon, calling first for the sale of imported machines, then the assembly of imported knocked-down kits, and finally the domestic production of copiers. Import restrictions in Japan and government pressure to source locally accelerated this schedule, and the first Japanese-produced Xerox 914 was completed in September 1962; by 1965, 90% of the parts for the 914 came from local suppliers.

Fuji Xerox's first sales plan targeted financial institutions, large manufacturing corporations, and central government agencies. At the time of the introduction of the 914, 85% of the market was held by the inexpensive diazo type of copier. Although these copiers were difficult to operate and produced poor quality copies, they had been enormously successful in Japan, as the large number of characters in the Japanese language made typewriters difficult to use, and made copiers essential even for small offices. Ricoh, Copyer, and Mita had sold diazo copiers since the 1940s. By the early 1960s, Ricoh held an estimated 75% share of the market. A diazo copy was often referred to as a "Ricopy" in Japan.

Though Fuji Xerox had intended to sell the 914 copier outright, at Rank Xerox's insistence it implemented Xerox's trademark rental system. Within a year, the back-order list for the copier was five months' long. Output rose fivefold in five years, and Fuji Photo Film soon built a second production facility. In 1967, Fuji Xerox's sales passed those of Rank Xerox's French and German subsidiaries. Fuji Xerox's product line expanded to include other models, including a faster version of the 914, and a smaller, desktop model. The 2400, capable of making 40 copies per minute (cpm),[2] was introduced in 1967. Sales subsidiaries were established throughout Fuji Xerox's licensed territory.

By the late 1960s, Fuji Xerox dominated the high-volume segment of the Japanese copier market. Ricoh, however, had made great inroads into the middle segment with an electrostatic copier based on an RCA technology, and was squeezing Fuji Xerox's market from below. In addition to the threat of substitute technologies, Fuji Xerox faced the end of its monopoly in plain paper copying; some of Xerox's core patents were scheduled to expire between 1968 and 1973. FX managers were already aware of efforts by several Japanese firms to develop plain paper copiers. In response to these pressures, Peter McColough, Xerox's president and CEO at the time, proposed to transfer the manufacture of copiers from Fuji Photo Film to Fuji Xerox, and in this way combine manufacturing and marketing activities under one roof. McColough described the rationale for the decision:

> Fuji Xerox had to develop its own manufacturing capability. It had built up a good marketing organization, but had no assured source of supply. That left the company vulnerable. Fuji Photo Film initially resisted this idea because it would lose manufacturing volume and product revenues. They realized in the end that the issue went to the heart of the joint venture. Looking back, that was the most difficult period in our relationship.

In 1971, Fuji Photo Film transferred its copier plants to Fuji Xerox. That same year, Fuji Xerox completed the construction of a 160,000 square-foot manufacturing and engineering facility. From then on, Fuji Photo Film had little direct role in Fuji Xerox's operations. Yoichi Ogawa, senior managing director at Fuji Xerox in 1989 and one of the Seven Samurai, explained why Fuji Photo Film remained a passive partner after 1971:

> According to Fuji Photo Film's agreement with Xerox, the company, as a shareholder, could collect information from Fuji Xerox, but it could not use it in its own operations. In addition, a technology agreement between Fuji Xerox and Xerox provided that any technology acquired by Fuji Xerox from outside sources (including from Fuji Photo Film) could be freely passed on to Xerox.

In a separate development, Rank Xerox also lost much of its direct role in Fuji Xerox's operations. In December 1969, Xerox bought an additional 1% share of Rank Xerox from the Rank Organization, giving it 51% control of that joint venture. From then on, Rank Xerox would be managed as a Xerox subsidiary. Moto Sakamoto, an FX resident at Rank Xerox at the time, noticed an immediate change: "Things changed instantly as the Americans started coming in . . . gone was the old British style of management."

---

2. The copier market was typically divided into low-, mid-, and high-volume segments. In the 1960s, the 2400 was considered a high-volume model; the original 914 copier made seven copies per minute. In the 1980s, copiers making less than 25 cpm were generally considered low-volume, whole those making over 90 cpm were considered high-volume.

Sakamoto was transferred to Xerox's main facility in Rochester, NY, as Fuji Xerox began to deal directly with Xerox. Rank Xerox's ownership share in Fuji Xerox remained at 50%, and the Xerox Corporation continued to receive 66% of Rank Xerox's profits, and therefore 33% of Fuji Xerox's.

Product Development at Fuji Xerox

The transfer of production facilities to Fuji Xerox and the direct relationship established between Fuji Xerox and Xerox contributed to a continued strengthening of FX technical capabilities. Fuji Photo Film engineers had already been making modifications to Xerox designs in order to adapt the copiers to the local market; Japanese offices, for example, used different sized paper than American offices. Nobuo Shono, however, advocated the development of long-term R&D capabilities that would enable the company to develop its own products. In particular, he envisioned a high-performance, inexpensive, compact machine that could copy books. At the time, Xerox's priorities were different. Tony Kobayashi explained:

> We had been insisting that the Xerox Group needed to develop small copiers as an integral part of its worldwide strategy. However, Xerox's attitude was that the low end of the market was not a priority.... On the other hand, we were seeing rising demand for small copiers in Japan.[3]

Shono's development group produced four experimental copiers, each with projected manufacturing costs approximately half those of Xerox's smallest machine. When they first heard of the effort, engineers at Rank Xerox and Xerox doubted that these models could become commercially viable. Shono persisted, and in 1970 took a working prototype to London, where its performance amazed Rank Xerox executives. The machine was slow (5 cpm), but substantially smaller and lighter than comparable Xerox models. This demonstration immediately boosted Fuji Xerox's technical reputation within the Xerox Group, and for the first time Xerox allowed Fuji Xerox a small budget for R&D. In 1973, the FX2200—the world's smallest copier—was introduced in Japan with the slogan: "It's small, but it's a Xerox." The speed of the FX2200 was doubled in 1977 by the FX2202, and the basic model was improved further by the FX2300 and the FX2305.

Mushrooming Competition

The FX2200 appeared just in time to face an avalanche of new and serious competition. Canon was the first Japanese company to enter the plain paper copier market, introducing its low end "New Process" copiers in 1970; these machines were developed in-house and did not infringe on any Xerox patent. Ricoh and Konica, Fuji Photo Film's chief Japanese rivals in film, followed with their own technologies. In 1972, Canon made another major move by introducing copiers using liquid instead of dry toner. This technology was later licensed to Saxon, Ricoh, and Copyer. Liquid-toner copiers had the advantage of being smaller and less expensive to manufacture than dry-toner copiers like Xerox's, but they were cumbersome to use. They were introduced as a cheap alternative to Xerox dry copiers. Minolta, Copia, Mita, Sharp, and Toshiba also entered the plain paper copier industry; by 1975, eleven companies competed in the Japanese market.

In addition to developing small machines for its local market, Fuji Xerox tried to stem the competitive onslaught with more aggressive sales strategies. The company began to offer two-and three-year rental contracts as well as its standard one-year contract, and provided price incentives that were tied to contract length. It also began to offer three of its new low-priced copiers for outright sale, as the competition had been doing. Matazo Terada, one of the Seven Samurai, recalled that when the company tried to sell copiers before, Xerox management resisted:

> Xerox insisted on uniform policies—every country had to be managed like the U.S. firm. That was successful only while we were protected from competitors because of our monopoly. If Xerox had been more flexible from the beginning, we might have captured a larger market. That was a lost opportunity.

By 1977, Ricoh accounted for 34% of the number of copiers installed in Japan. Fuji Xerox followed with

---

3. Quoted in "Fuji Xerox Company, Ltd." Translation of a case study prepared by the Nomura School of Advanced Management in Tokyo.

25%, Canon with 15%, and Konica with 10%. In terms of copy volume, however, Fuji Xerox led the competition with more than 50% of the market, followed by Ricoh with 20%, and Canon and Konica with 10% each. In the low end of the market, Ricoh accounted for 50% of copy volume, compared to 10% for Fuji Xerox.

Fuji Xerox's TQC Movement

Partly as a response to the new competition of the 1970s, as well as the oil shock and recession of 1973-1975, Fuji Xerox launched a Total Quality Control (TQC) program. Fuji Photo Film had operated a successful statistical quality control program, and in 1956 won the prestigious Deming Prize, awarded to companies that had shown outstanding quality management throughout their organization. Fuji Xerox's New Xerox Movement had three primary aims: to speed up the development of products that matched customer needs; to reduce costs and eliminate waste; and to adopt aggressively the latest technologies.

The focal point of the campaign was the development of "dantotsu," roughly translated as the "Absolute No. 1 Product." Company executives challenged the marketing and engineering departments to develop a product fitting this description in less time and at a lower cost than the competition. For six months, project proposals were turned down until the basic concept for the new product emerged in 1976: a compact, 40 cpm machine manufactured for half the price of any comparable machine, with half the number of parts of previous models, and developed in two years, compared to Xerox's typical four. Setsutaro's son, Tony Kobayashi, who became FX president in 1978 after his father died, explained:

> This was the first time Fuji Xerox had developed a copier based on our own design concept. The FX2200 copier we previously developed was an improved adaptation of a model developed in the United States. The American system of development was well established in our company. However, the U.S. way of developing new products on a step-by-step basis was too time consuming for our dynamic environment. The competition in the Japanese market required us to study the development systems of our rivals.... We found that we had been spending too much time in development. That is why we formulated the design concept for the new model and committed the entire company's resources to its development within a very limited timetable.[4]

The FX3500 was indeed introduced two years later, and by 1979, it had broken the Japanese record for the number of copiers sold in one year. Ricoh and Canon rushed to develop copiers that could compete in the FX3500's market segment. Largely because of Fuji Xerox's effort to develop the FX3500, the company won the Deming Prize in 1980. In addition, the FX3500 firmly established Fuji Xerox as a technologically competent member of the Xerox Group. David Kearns, who would become Xerox's president in 1977, was amazed when he first saw a demonstration of the FX3500 prototype, and spontaneously broke out in applause.

Later, some observers labeled the FX3500 Fuji Xerox's "declaration of independence." The FX3500 project came after Xerox canceled a series of low-to mid-volume copiers on which Fuji Xerox was depending. Code-named SAM, Moses, Mohawk, Elf, Peter, Paul, and Mary, they were each canceled in mid-development, even though Fuji Xerox had gaps in its product range in the Japanese market. Jeff Kennard remembered that when Tony Kobayashi was told about the cancellation of Moses, he was also asked to stop work on the FX3500 project. "Tony refused," Kennard recalled, adding that Kobayashi said, in effect, "As long as I am responsible for the survival of this company, I can no longer be totally dependent on you for developing products. We are going to have to develop our own."

Xerox's Lost Decade

During the 1970s, competition in the U.S. and European copier markets changed radically. Prior to that period, Xerox had a virtual monopoly because of its xerography patents. But beginning in 1970, one competitor after another entered the industry, often with

---

4. Quoted in "Fuji Xerox Company, Ltd."

EXHIBIT 2 Copier Sales of Leading Vendors Worldwide, 1975–1985 (in millions of US$)

	1975	1980	1985
Xerox Group	$3,967	$7,409	$8,903
U.S. and Americas	2,340	3,866	4,770
Rank Xerox	1,350	2,856	2,400
Fuji Xerox	277	687	1,733
Canon	87	732	2,178
Ricoh	290	1,092	1,926
Kodak	1	300	900
IBM	310	680	700
Minolta	25	387	743
3M	380	575	400
Oce	178	680	600
Savin	52	430	448
Konishiroku	85	302	470
Nashua	155	401	278
Agfa	115	268	200
Pitney Bowes	52	129	204
A.B. Dick	35	55	60
Saxon	56	127	20
AM International	59	23	10
Other Japanese	155	1,220	2,846
Other	596	792	1,115
Total	$6,598	$15,602	$22,001

Shares of Leading Firms in World Market

	1975	1980	1985
Xerox Group	60%	47%	40%
Americas	35	25	22
Rank Xerox	20	18	11
Fuji Xerox	4	4	8
Canon	1	5	10
Ricoh	4	7	9
Kodak	0	2	4
IBM	5	4	3
Minolta	0	2	3

Source: Donaldson, Lufkin & Jenrette, Inc.

new and improved PPC technologies. The Xerox Group share of worldwide PPC revenues fell from 93% in 1971 to 60% in 1975, and 40% in 1985 (**Exhibit 2**). This was Xerox's "lost decade"—an era of increasing competition, stagnating product development, and costly litigation.

New Competition High and Low

The proliferation of PPC vendors that started in Japan in the early 1970s soon appeared in the United States and Europe. By 1975, approximately 20 PPC manufacturers operated worldwide, including reprographic companies (Xerox, Ricoh, Mita, Copyer, A.B. Dick, AM, and 3M), paper companies (Dennison, Nashua, and Saxon), office equipment companies (IBM, SCM, Litton, and Pitney Bowes), photographic equipment companies (Canon, Konica, Kodak, and Minolta), and consumer electronics companies (Sharp and Toshiba).

Canon's New Process copiers were the first to hit the U.S. market, followed by a wave of liquid-toner copiers. The new Japanese machines were priced aggressively, and sold outright through independent dealers. On average, these machines broke down half as often as Xerox copiers. Canon sold under its own brand name, taking advantage of its reputation for quality photographic products, and supported its dealers through extensive financing, and sales and service training. Ricoh sold its machines through Savin Business Machines and the Nashua Corporation. Savin, primarily a marketing company, had funded the Stanford Research Institute's development of a liquid-toner copier, and subsequently had licensed Ricoh to manufacture the machines. The first Ricoh machines using this new technology were introduced in 1975 and were an instant success. Konica, Toshiba, Sharp, and Minolta, entered the U.S. market through OEM relationships, as well as with their own brands.

Despite the entrance of so many Japanese competitors into the U.S. market, Xerox initially did little to respond to them. These competitors targeted the low end of the market, leaving Xerox's most important segments seemingly unaffected. Furthermore, Xerox continued to dominate the world copier market, with revenues that rose each year by more than Savin's total copier sales. Xerox executives were more concerned by the entrance of IBM and Eastman Kodak into the copier industry, as these companies targeted the mid- and high-volume segments. (See **Exhibit 3**.)

IBM's introduction of its Copier I in 1970 signaled the end of Xerox's monopoly in its home market. Although IBM's first model was not successful because of a combination of high and performance problems, the Copier II, introduced in 1972, began to take market share away from Xerox. These machines were marketed by IBM's office products sales force on a rental basis, supported by heavy advertising. IBM introduced the Copier II in Europe and Japan in 1975, and by 1976 had installed 80,000 copiers worldwide, against Xerox's estimated 926,000. IBM's high-volume Copier III came out in 1976, but was withdrawn because of reliability problems. It was reintroduced as a mid-volume machine early in 1978, but IBM's copier business suffered permanently from the setback.

Eastman Kodak's main facilities were located across town from Xerox's in Rochester, NY. Kodak's success as a high-technology, chemistry-based, American firm had been a model for Xerox's founders and early leaders. When Kodak introduced the high-end Ektaprint 100 copier in 1975, however, admiration quickly turned to intense rivalry. Unlike the IBM Copier I, Kodak's first machine was extremely innovative. In particular, it featured a microcomputer that monitored the performance of the copier and alerted operators to problems through a digital display. A central computer at Kodak monitored the trouble signals and dispatched service people to a machine before breakdown. The machines were also capable of excellent reproduction. The Ektaprint series was well accepted in the marketplace, and quickly gained a reputation for the highest-quality image reproduction in the field.

Xerox's Stagnation

In its first competitive actions against IBM, Kodak, and the Japanese entrants, Xerox could not come up with a winning strategy. It focused R&D on developing a super high-speed copier and field-tested its first

---

5. David T. Kearns, "Leadership Through Quality," *Academy of Management Executive*, vol. 4 (1990): 86–89.

Cases

EXHIBIT 3 Copier Unit Placements of Xerox and Major Competitors

		Thousand of Units placed by market segment (net)[a]					Share of net placements in each market segment				
		PCs	Low	Mid	High	Total	PCs	Low	Mid	High	Total
In the United States:											
Xerox	1975	—	9	-8[b]	1	2	—	29%	—	100%	6%
	1980	—	34	6	6	46	—	11%	22%	52%	13%
	1985	—	66	27	15	108	0%	10%	21%	53%	10%
	1989	12	101	53	13	179	5%	14%	27%	45%	15%
Kodak and IBM	1975	—	—	10	—	10	—	0%	213%	0%	27%
	1980	—	—	5	5	11	—	0%	20%	48%	3%
	1985	—	—	2	13	14	0%	0%	2%	46%	1%
	1989	—	—	5	9	13	0%	0%	2%	31%	1%
Canon	1975	—	3	—	—	3	—	10%	0%	0%	8%
	1980	—	46	4	—	50	—	15%	14%	0%	14%
	1985	176	107	17	—	300	86%	16%	13%	0%	29%
	1989	141	106	19	4	270	62%	15%	10%	13%	23%
Others	1975	—	19	3	—	22	—	61%	55%	0%	59%
	1980	—	237	12	—	249	—	75%	44%	0%	70%
	1985	30	514	81	—	625	14%	75%	64%	0%	60%
	1989	75	513	123	3	714	33%	71%	61%	11%	61%
Total for All Vendors	1975	—	31	5	1	37					
	1980	—	317	27	11	355					
	1985	206	687	126	28	1,047					
	1989	227	710	200	29	1,176					
In Western Europe:											
Rank Xerox	1980	—	40	4	4	48	—	11	22%	100%	13%
	1984	—	54	19	9	82	0%	9%	25%	74%	10%
	1989	18	73	49	4	144	7%	10%	29%	34%	12%
Kodak	1980	—	—	4	—	4	—	0%	22%	0%	1%
	1984	—	—	—	3	3	0%	0%	0%	26%	0%
	1989	—	—	2	2	3	0%	0%	1%	13%	0%
Canon	1980	—	36	4	—	40	—	10%	21%	0%	11%
	1984	115	81	8	—	204	90%	15%	10%	0%	26%
	1989	130	110	25	3	268	49%	15%	15%	26%	22%
Total for all Vendors	1980	—	351	19	4	374					
	1984	128	578	76	12	794					
	1989	268	752	168	11	1,199					
In Japan											
Fuji Xerox	1986					112					20%
	1989					142					21%
Canon	1986					138					25%
	1989					195					28%
Others	1986					311					55%
	1989					354					51%
Total for All Vendors											

Source: Dataquest Incorporated. [a] "Net Placements" are sales and new rentals minus old rentals returned to the vendor. Volume segments are defined as follow: PC = less than 12 cpm (average price about $1,000), Low = 12 to 30 cpm (average price about $3,000), Mid = 31 to 69 cpm (average price about $8,500), and High = over 70 cpm (average price about $55,000). [b] Indicates that on balance, 8,000 rental units were returned. [c] Ricoh was particularly strong in Japan, with a 32% share in 1989.

color copier in 1971; neither became a commercial success. Xerox's mid-volume 4000 and 3100 series, introduced in the early 1970s, suffered from reliability problems and were also commercial failures. Even when the price of the 3100 was slashed from $12,000 to $4,400, it did not sell well. Ricoh/Savin became the top seller in the U.S. market in 1976, and Xerox's market share in the United States continued to fall. However, the seriousness of Xerox's situation was slow to sink in, according to David Kearns:

> ...we dominated the industry we had created. We were convinced that we were providing the world with high-quality machines, and our convictions were reinforced by the broad acceptance of Xerox products by our customers. We had always been successful, and we assumed that we would continue to be successful. Our success was so overwhelming that we became complacent.[5]

About 1978, Fuji Xerox offered to sell its FX2202 copier to Xerox and Rank Xerox to help them counter Japanese competition in the United States and Europe. Rank Xerox purchased 25,000 of the machines, but Xerox Corporation refused to buy any.[6] Bill Glavin, the managing director at Rank Xerox at that time, noted:

> We had never placed such a large order before and expected to sell them in 12 months. Two thousand machines per month was an incredible rate of sales, but we did it. For Tony Kobayashi, that order must have represented a substantial part of his production that year. We worked closely with them, and they gave us top-notch support.

This first successful cooperation led Rank Xerox to import more of the FX machines. In addition, Kodak had delayed its entry into Europe by two years, giving Rank Xerox time to formulate a defensive marketing strategy for the high end. As for IBM, its excellent distribution network and reputation in Europe could not make up for a generally inferior product. As Wayland Hicks, the general manager of Rank Xerox's U.K. operating company in the late 1970s, noted, "If IBM had Kodak's product, Xerox would have been dead." Rank Xerox was able to defend its market share while Xerox's U.S. share continued to decline.

In 1979, largely because of Rank Xerox's success with the FX product, Xerox began to import the FX2202, and later the FX2300 and the FX2350. Typically, in the year that the products were introduced in the U.S. market, the machines were assembled by Fuji Xerox before export. Then, acceding to union demands in the United States, Fuji Xerox exported them as knock-down units to be assembled at Xerox. "Some of our people had been reluctant to import FX machines," recalled Peter McColough. "Our engineers felt that they had developed xerography, and that the first FX machines weren't good enough."

Courtroom Battles

Xerox became involved in the 1970s in a series of courtroom battles. Immediately after IBM came out with its Copier I in 1970, Xerox sued for patent infringement, and IBM countersued. The companies argued 12 separate counts in the United States and Canada. Xerox won some of these suits and the rest were settled in 1978, when the firms agreed to an exchange of patents covering all information-handling products and to a $25 million payment to Xerox. Two other American firms, the SCM Corporation and Van Dyk Research, sued Xerox for alleged antitrust violations in 1973 and 1975, respectively, each claiming $1.5 billion in damages. Both lost their suits in 1978–1979.

More damaging still, the Federal Trade Commission (FTC) initiated action against Xerox in 1973, charging that the firm controlled 95% of the plain paper copier industry, and that its pricing, leasing, and patent-licensing practices violated the Sherman Antitrust Act. The FTC demanded that Xerox offer unrestricted, royalty-free licenses on all its copier patents, that it divest itself of Rank Xerox and Fuji Xerox, and that it allow third parties to service, maintain, and repair copiers leased from Xerox. In 1975, Xerox settled out of court by signing a consent decree with the FTC, in which it agreed to license more than 1,700 past and future patents for a period

---

[6] Although Xerox had acquired equity control of Rank Xerox in 1969, the line operations of the two firms were not integrated until 1978. Rank Xerox could thus make this decision in relative autonomy.

of 10 years. Competitors were permitted to license up to three patents free of royalties, to pay 0.5% of revenues on the next three, and to license additional patents royalty free. Xerox also agreed to forgive past patent infringements, to cease offering package-pricing plans on machines and supplies, and to begin outright sales of machines.

Kodak, IBM, Canon, Ricoh, and other Japanese firms were among the firms to secure Xerox licenses under this arrangement. At this point, the Japanese firms that had entered the market with liquid-toner copiers switched to Xerox's dry-toner process.

Adjusting the Relationship between Xerox and Fuji Xerox

As Fuji Xerox's business grew and Xerox's came under increasing pressure at home, the relationship between the two companies changed. The original joint venture and technology assistance agreements of the early 1960s were updated in 1976 and in 1983, and numerous interim agreements were signed to adjust policies on such issues as procurement and relations to third parties (**Exhibit 4**). Bob Meredith, a lawyer by training and Xerox's resident director in Tokyo, described the role of these contracts:

> The legal contracts are flexible. We don't follow an adversarial, arm's-length approach, where you might try to gain short-term advantage or act opportunistically. The equity commitment focuses our relationship on one main objective: What is the profit-maximizing thing to do?

Technology agreements and other contracts between Xerox and Fuji Xerox provided guidelines for the relationship. In addition, the contracts specified royalties and transfer pricing procedures. In 1976, a Technology Assistance Contract (TAC) had been signed by Xerox and Fuji Xerox, which maintained the 5% royalty that Xerox received from Fuji Xerox's xerographic sales, and that was to last 10 years. During the Codestiny I discussions, however, the royalty structure of the contract was revised. The 1983 TAA established a basic royalty on Fuji Xerox's total sales, representing Fuji Xerox's right to use the Xerox tradename and technology in its licensed territory. The royalty on xerographic sales, however, was set to decline annually between 1983 and 1993. In addition, for the first time Fuji Xerox would begin receiving a manufacturing license fee (MLF), designed to compensate it for its development and manufacturing investments. In particular, an MLF of up to 20% could be added to the unit costs of FX machines exported in knocked-down form and assembled and sold by Xerox.

These and other subtle changes in the relationship between the two firms tended to reinforce Fuji Xerox's autonomy. David Kearns recalled how he worked to "unfetter" Fuji Xerox in the late 1970s:

> Xerox was attempting to control so many aspects of Fuji Xerox's operations. We were reviewing their marketing strategies, what products they were going to develop, and so on. But it didn't make sense to me to try to run the business from thousands of miles away. So, I encouraged them to pursue their own strategies and develop their own products. Of course, they were moving in that direction anyway.

Turning Around Xerox

In 1979, Xerox began to formalize a strategy based on the reality of its declining position in the copier industry. Kearns recalled the initial shock of the necessity to do so:

> The Japanese were selling products in the United States for what it cost us to *make* them. We were losing market share rapidly, but didn't have the cost structure to do anything about it. I was not sure if Xerox would make it out of the 1980s.

One of Xerox's strategies was to diversify out of copiers by acquiring a number of financial services companies between 1983 and 1988. Financial services, Kearns believed, would provide "an anchor in a nonmanufacturing business, and one in which Japanese companies were not active overseas." Before the financial services industry went sour at the end of the decade, this line of business was a steady source of earnings for Xerox, providing more than $2 billion in profits in five years. In 1989, however, financial services' earnings declined significantly and substantial assets were written off.

Kearns also began to take a closer look at the strategies of Fuji Xerox and other Japanese compa-

EXHIBIT 4 Major Agreements Between Xerox and Fuji Xerox

1960 Joint Enterprise Contract and Articles of Incorporation (1962)

- Established equal ownership of FX by Rank Xerox and Fuji Photo Film
- Defined Fx's exclusive license to Xerography in its territory: Japan, Taiwan, Philippines, the Koreas, Indonesia, Indochina
- FX nonexclusive license to nonxerographic products in territory
- Specifies terms of technology assistance: Royalty due Rank Xerox: 5% of net sales of xerographic products

1976 Joint Enterprise Contract (JEC)

- Agreement between Rank Xerox and Fuji Photo Film, updating 1960 JEC
- Specified Board of Directors composition
- FX Management to be appointed by Fuji Photo Film
- Agreements on technology transfer, royalties, and transfer pricing
- Identified matters requiring Xerox concurrence, including
  - Financial policy, including major capital expenditures
  - Business and operating plans
  - Relationships with third parties
  - Sales outside of FX licensed territory

1976 Technological Assistance Contract (TAC)

- 10-year agreement between Xerox and Fuji Xerox
- Revised technology assistance agreements of 1960, 1968, and 1971
- Maintained 5% royalty on xerographic products

1978 R&D Reimbursement Agreement

- Defines reimbursement to FX for R&D on FX products marketed by Xerox = 100% to 120% of design cost

1983 Technology Assistance Agreement (TAA)

- 10-year agreement between Xerox and Fuji Xerox
- Replaced 1976 technology transfer agreements
- Revised royalty rates
  - Basic Royalty on total FX revenue plus
  - Royalty on xerographic revenues to decline annually from 1983 to 1993

1983 Product Acquisition Policy

- Provides guidelines for intercompany transfer pricing
- Established concept of reciprocal Manufacturing License Fee (MLF), designed to reimburse FX for development and manufacturing costs:
  - up to 25% mark-up on assembled machines supplied by Fiji
  - Up to 20% mark-up on unit cost for FX machines assembled by XC
  - Specific designs and service required by Xerox reimbursed 100%

1985 Procurement Policy

- Provides guidelines for Xerox procurement in FX licensed territory:
- FX right to bid first
- Procurement from third party to be coordinated with FX

1986 Arrangements Strategy Agreement

- Defined parameters for negotiating alliances with third parties

Source: Compiled from Xerox Corporation documents

nies. Upon importing the first FX products, Xerox engineers had been amazed by a reject rate for parts that was a mere fraction of the American rate, and by substantially lower manufacturing costs. Visits to FX facilities introduced Xerox executives to the practice of "benchmarking," or systematically tracking costs and performance in all areas of operations against those of the best in the field. The findings from Xerox's own benchmarking efforts helped fuel Kearns's efforts to infuse his organization with new vision and determination.

In 1981, Kearns announced a companywide initiative for "business effectiveness," and two years later formally launched Xerox's Leadership Through Quality Program. Xerox's program was based on the experience of Fuji Xerox, and throughout the effort, Kearns called upon Kobayashi and others at Fuji Xerox for help. Xerox hired Japanese consultants recommended by Fuji Xerox, and some 200 high-level Xerox and Rank Xerox managers visited Fuji Xerox in later years to learn first-hand about its TQC management and philosophy. The Leadership Through Quality program emphasized high employee involvement in attaining five major goals: (1) increased market research and competitive benchmarking; (2) just-in-time manufacturing to decrease costs; (3) faster product development; (4) development of state-of-the-art technology; and (5) a devotion to quality in all areas.

The rallying point for Xerox's quality movement was the development of the 10 Series, a new family of copiers. Wayland Hicks, in charge of this development effort, stated: "The Xerox turnaround started on September 22, 1982, at the announcement of the 1075 in New York." Led by this mid-volume machines, the 10 Series became the most successful line of copiers in Xerox history, and served to restore the company's finances and morale. The series—dubbed the "Marathon" family of copiers—represented a new generation of machines aimed primarily at the mid-volume segment of the market. Altogether, some fourteen models were introduced between 1982 and 1986, six of which were still sold in 1990. Fuji Xerox designed and produced the low end models in the 10 Series—the 1020, 1035, and the 1055, the latter drawing on basic technologies developed for the FX3500. The 1075 became the first American-made product to win Japan's Grand Prize for Good Design. Because at that time Xerox's Japanese competitors were not strong in mid-volume copiers, the 10 Series forestalled their move into that segment of the market and helped Xerox win back market share. The company regained 2-3 percentage points in 1983, and 12 points in 1984. By the end of 1985, more than 750,000 10 Series machines had been rented or sold, accounting for nearly 38% of Xerox's worldwide installed base.

Throughout the 1980s, Xerox continued to change the way it did business. For example, over 100,000 employees went through three days of off-site training to unite the entire organization behind the quality effort. The program achieved significant improvements in Xerox operations. After reducing its supplier base, the company reduced its purchased parts' costs by 45% and their quality was improved dramatically. Xerox's average manufacturing costs were reduced by 20% and the time-to-market for new products was cut by 60%. Xerox's progress was recognized by the U.S. Commerce Department in 1989, when the company's Business Products and Systems division received the Malcolm Baldrige National Quality Award for its "preeminent quality leadership." (Xerox's 1980s financial results are in **Exhibit 5**.)

Xerox and Fuji Xerox in the 1990s

The Canon Challenge

A number of factors were expected to continue to draw Fuji Xerox and Xerox closer to each other in the 1990s. One was the continuously rising capabilities of the Xerox Group's competitors, particularly Canon. While Xerox's precipitous decline in the 1970s had been stemmed and many of the competitors from that decade had faded away, Canon's copier business continued to expand. From 1980 to 1989, Canon's total sales grew from $2.9 billion to $9.4 billion, a growth rate of 14% per year. Canon's R&D spending grew even more rapidly at 24% per year, from $77 million to $525 million. By 1989, Canon was no longer primarily a camera company—40% of its revenues came from copiers, and 20% from laser

EXHIBIT 5 Key Financial Data for Xerox and Fuji Photo Film (in millions of dollars)

	1971	1976	1981	1982	1983	1984	1985	1986	1987	1988	1989
XEROX CORPORATION											
Total Revenue	1,954	4,515	8,180	8,073	10,463	11,400	11,994	13,287	15,108	16,441	17,635
Document processing			8,013	7,895	8,223	8,714	9,068	9,744	10,834	11,688	12,431
Financial services			167	178	2,240	2,686	2,926	3,543	4,274	4,753	5,204
Operating income	785	1,486	2,071	1,654	1,444	1,557	1,502	1,327	1,376	2,154	2,031
Net income	213	365	598	424	466	291	475	465	578	388	704
Total assets	2,250	4,959	7,674	7,668	14,064	15,154	16,838	19,050	22,450	26,441	30,088
Long-term debt	425	1,000	870	850	1,461	1,614	1,583	1,730	1,539	5,379	7,511
Stockholders' equity	1,052	2,179	3,728	3,724	4,664	4,543	4,828	5,129	5,547	5,667	6,116
R&D expenses	96	226	511	541	529	555	597	650	722	794	809
Employees (millions)	66	100	112	103	108	111	113	112	112	113	111
Earnings/Share ($)	2.85	4.35	6.25	4.06	4.5	3.26	3.42	4.48	5.3	3.49	6.56
Dividend/Share ($)	0.80	1.10	3.00	3.00	3.00	3.00	3.00	3.00	3.00	3.00	3.00
Document processing revenues (as share of total)	a	a	98%	98%	79%	76%	76%	73%	72%	71%	70%
Operating income/Revenue	40%	33%	25%	20%	14%	14%	13%	10%	9%	13%	12%
Operating income/Assets	35	30	27	22	10	10	9	7	6	8	7
Operating income/Equity	75	68	56	44	31	34	31	26	25	38	33
Net income/Revenue	10.9%	8.1%	7.3%	5.3%	4.5%	2.6%	4.0%	3.5%	3.8%	2.4%	4.0%
Net income/Assets	9.5	7.4	7.8	5.5	3.3	1.9	2.8	2.4	2.6	1.5	2.3
Net income/Equity	20.2	16.8	16.0	11.4	10.0	6.4	9.8	9.1	10.4	6.8	11.5
R&D expense/Revenue	4.9%	5.0%	6.2%	6.7%	5.1%	4.9%	5.0%	4.9%	4.8%	4.8%	4.6%
Long-term debt/Assets	19%	20%	11%	11%	10%	11%	9%	9%	7%	20%	25%
Equity/Assets	47	44	49	49	33	30	29	27	25	21	20
Dividends/Earnings	28	25	48	74	67	92	88	67	57	86	46
FUJI PHOTO FILM											
Total revenue							3,136	4,504	5,636	6,833	6,732
Net income							600	801	1,030	1,217	1210
Dividends							21	30	35	41	36
Net income/Revenue							19%	18%	18%	18%	18%
Dividends/Earnings							3.5%	3.7%	3.4%	3.4%	3.0%

Source: Company annual reports
a Practically 100%

printers.

In the second half of the 1980s, Canon developed a dominating presence in the low end laser printers that were becoming ubiquitous companions to microcomputers. Laser printing technology was closely related to plain paper copying technology, and as digital copying systems were introduced, the importance of laser printing in the PPC market was bound to increase. Canon's laser printing engines were the core of the highly successful Hewlett-Packard Laserprinter series, which accounted for about 50% of laser printer sales in the United States. This OEM business was thought to yield Canon some $1 billion in revenues. In the rest of the world, Canon sold printers under its own brand name.

In copiers, Canon was strong in the low end of the market, and had recently developed a growing business in color copiers, where it held 50% of the market by 1989. Analysts pointed out that Canon was introducing twice as many products as the Xerox Group, although it spent less than $600 million on R&D annually, compared to Xerox's $800 million and Fuji Xerox's $300 million. Canon's goal was to become a $70 billion company by the year 2000, implying a 22% annual growth rate in the 1990s. A significant portion of this growth was projected to come from Xerox's heartland—high- and mid-volume copiers and printers.

Xerox, however, was determined to be aggressive in its response. Hicks, who in 1989 had become the executive vice president for worldwide marketing at Xerox, hung a framed blow-up of a 1984 *Fortune* article on Canon in his office. It was entitled "And Then We Will Attack;" below it Hicks hung a sign that read: "And Then They Will Lose."

Xerox Group strategists saw the relationship between Xerox and Fuji Xerox as a critical element in competing worldwide against Canon. Canon had a strong presence in all major world markets, as did the Xerox companies (**Exhibit 6**). But Xerox CEO Paul Allaire highlighted a major difference in the two firms' global networks: "When we negotiate with Fuji Xerox, we can't just represent ourselves. We need to find what is fair and equitable to essentially three partners. Canon is 100% owned by one company."

The Fuji Xerox Challenge

Another trend drawing Fuji Xerox and Xerox closer was the growth of Fuji Xerox itself (**Exhibit 7**). Fuji Xerox's dollar revenues grew faster than Xerox's in the 1980s, and represented a more significant portion of the Xerox Group's worldwide revenues than it had previously. Fuji Xerox's financial contribution to Xerox's net earnings in the form of royalties and profits had also grown sharply—from 5% in 1981 to 22% in 1988. And throughout the decade, Fuji Xerox had been an important source of low end copiers for Xerox. Between 1980 and 1988, Fuji Xerox's sales to Xerox and Rank Xerox grew from $32 million to $620 million (**Exhibit 8**). "Fuji Xerox is a critical asset of Xerox," concluded Allaire.

Fuji Xerox developed its technological capabilities further in the 1980s, investing heavily in R&D (**Exhibit 9**). While it continued to rely on Xerox for basic research on new technologies, by the late 1980s very few of the models sold by Fuji Xerox in Japan had been designed by Xerox (**Exhibit 10**). For the most part, they were high-end models, working at speeds of above 120 cpm. Heavy investment by Fuji Xerox during the late 1980s had produced many low-end models, and even a few in the 60-90 cpm range. Many of these were exported to or manufactured by Xerox and Rank Xerox. In 1980, 70% of the low-volume units sold by Xerox and Rank Xerox were of their own design, and 30% were of Fuji Xerox design; by 1987, 94% were of Fuji Xerox design. Even in 1989, however, all of Xerox and Rank Xerox's mid- and high-volume copiers were of their own design.

All these factors led Fuji Xerox and Xerox to intensify their cooperation on research, product development, manufacturing, and planning in the 1980s. Bill Glavin and Jeff Kennard worked together to launch "strategy summits." Glavin described why:

> We needed the senior management of research, engineering, manufacturing, and planning from both companies to come together, and begin discussing the issues that affected them jointly. The talks included people from all product lines—copiers, printers, and systems. We tried to agree on common strategies and allocate who should do what.

These top management summits were held about twice a year during the 1980s, and led to further

EXHIBIT 6 Global Configuration of Xerox Group and Canon in 1989

	United States	Japan	Western Europe	Other
Share of world GNP	26%	14%	21% (4 largest countries)	39%
Share of world PPC market (units)	33%	20%	34%	14%

XEROX GROUP

	United States	Japan	Western Europe	Other
Revenue	$6.6 billion	$3.5 billion	$4.0 billion	$1.7 billion
Employees	54,000	19,600	29,000	16,000
Production				
PPC	149,000	180,000	176,400	39,000
Printers	15,000	60,000	15,700	—
Systems	8,000	18,000	1,900	—
Faxes	—	95,000	—	—
% of Market (units)				
PPCs	15%	22%	12%	
R&D centers	2	1	1	1
Alliances	—	Fuji Photo Film	Rank Organization	

CANON

	North America	Japan	Europe	Other
Revenue	$2.9 billion	$2.9 billion	$2.9 billion	
Employees	4,500	27,500	6,500	
Production				
PPC	60,000	700,000	370,000	
Other	Laser printers and engines	Cameras, printers		Cameras in China
% of Market (units)				
PPCs	23%	26%	23%	
Laserprinting	70			
Color PPCs	50			
R&D centers	0	1	0	
Alliances	HP ($1B OEM) Kodak, NeXT		Olivetti	

Source: Xerox and industry sources

EXHIBIT 7 Key Financial Data for Fuji Xerox (in millions of US$) (at yearly average exchange rates)

	1971	1976	1981	1982	1983	1984	1985	1986	1987	1988	1989
Revenues	107	307	872	962	1,111	1,282	1,456	2,303	2,955	3,570	3,554
Operating Expenses	79	259	754	813	970	1,125	1,304	2,093	2,673	3,197	3,180
R&D	—	13	49	47	84	109	117	151	194	242	292
S, G, and A	38	119	308	333	399	443	507	801	1,041	1,296	1,324
Operating income	27	47	117	150	141	157	152	210	282	373	374
Net income	10	17	46	50	56	61	59	71	106	173	162
Total assets	176	405	897	931	1,046	1,199	1,276	1,883	2,457	3,186	3,093
Total equity	49	121	324	325	388	440	487	744	959	1,237	1,285
Retained earnings	33	84	270	277	338	390	439	680	885	1,154	1,131
Depreciation and amortization	16	63	131	113	130	155	153	218	266	271	278
Capital expenditures	65	64	196	178	230	217	244	296	284	297	512
Employees (thousands)	4.9	7.7	9.8	11.3	12.6	13.9	15.1	16.5	17.2	18.0	19.6
Dividends paid out	1	7	9	8	8	8	8	12	14	18	30
FINANCIAL RATIOS											
Operating income/Revenue	25%	15%	13%	16%	13%	12%	10%	9%	10%	10%	11%
Operating income/Assets	15	12	13	16	13	13	12	11	11	12	12
Net income/Revenue	9.1%	5.6%	5.3%	5.2%	9.1%	4.8%	4.1%	3.1%	3.1%	4.9%	4.5%
Net income/Assets	5.5	4.3	5.1	5.3	5.4	5.1	4.6	3.7	4.3	5.4	5.2
Net income/Equity	19.9	14.3	14.2	15.3	14.6	13.8	12.2	9.5	11.1	14.0	12.6
R&D expense/Revenue	—	4.4%	5.6%	4.9%	7.6%	8.5%	8.0%	6.5%	6.6%	6.8%	8.2%
Capital expenditures/Revenue	61.2%	20.9%	22.5%	18.5%	20.7%	16.9%	16.8%	12.9%	9.6%	8.3%	14.4%
Total equity/Assets	28%	30%	36%	35%	37%	37%	38%	40%	39%	39%	42%
Dividends paid/Total equity	1.6%	6%	3%	2%	2%	2%	2%	2%	1%	1%	2%
Dividends/Earnings	8.2%	41%	20%	16%	14%	13%	14%	17%	13%	10%	19%
Average exchange rate (yen per US$)	348	297	221	249	238	238	239	169	145	128	138

Source: Fuji Xerox annual reports; exchange rate from the IMF

Note: FY ending October 20

EXHIBIT 8 Intra-Firm and Bilateral Trade in Copiers

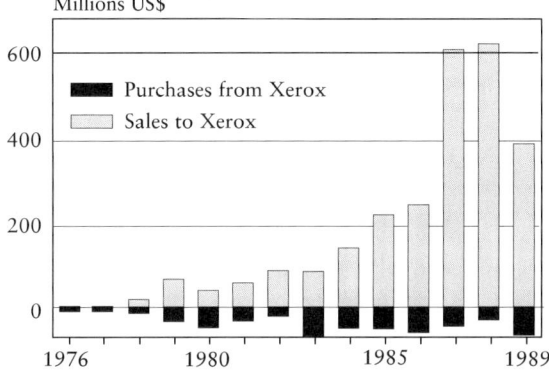

Fuji Xerox Trade with Xerox Group

Japan-US Trade in Copiers

Source: Fuji Xerox annual report and United Nations, *SITC Trade Data Base*
Notes: Top: Includes finished machines, parts, and knock-down kits.
         Bottom: Includes copiers (SITC 75182) and copier parts and accessories (SITC 75919).

harder to implement in development and manufacturing; there was no coordination at all between marketing groups, as each had a different licensed territory. Of course, there was some tendency to protect traditional turfs. "On both sides you cannot totally the NIH syndrome," commented Tony Kobayshi. "It is another form of parochialism." Still, where the incentives for collaboration were high, the companies launched joint projects, agreeing on who would take "lead" and "support" roles and eliminating overlapping activities. Bill Spencer, Xerox vice president of technology at the time, described the rationale behind one of these joint research projects:

> It is an attempt to combine American ingenuity with the manufacturing skills of the Japanese. Xerox has excellent basic research and software capabilities, and Fuji Xerox is good at development and hardware design. Together, we should be able to develop better products quicker than alone.

The functional collaboration between the companies was reinforced by exchanges of personnel and by an evolving communication process. Since the 1970s, personnel from Fuji Xerox had spent time as residents at Xerox and engineers from both companies had frequently crossed the Pacific to provide on-the-spot

EXHIBIT 9 Fuji Xerox Technology Spending and Receipts, 1968–1989

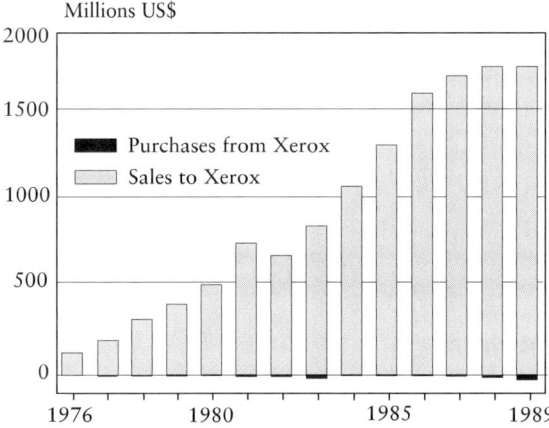

FX Technology Spending and Receipts
Share of Total FX Revenue

Source: Fuji Xerox annual report
Note: Technology receipts represent reimbursement to Fuji Xerox for special design and customization work on machines sold by XC and RX.

meetings between the functional organizations on each side. Fuji Xerox's organization mirrored Xerox's: a corporate research group did basic and applied research; machines were designed and built by the development and manufacturing organization; and products were sold and serviced by the marketing organization. Collaboration between Xerox and Fuji Xerox seemed to be most successful in research, and

EXHIBIT 10 Growth of Fuji Xerox Technical Capabilities, 1970–1989

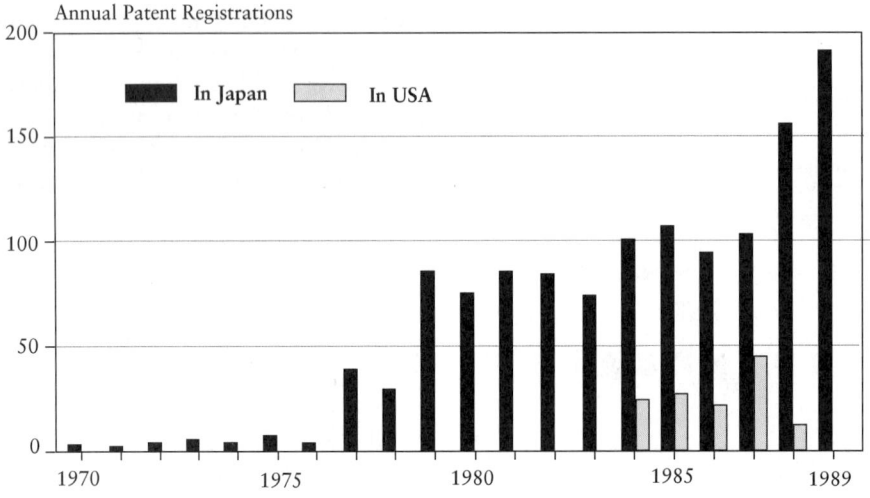

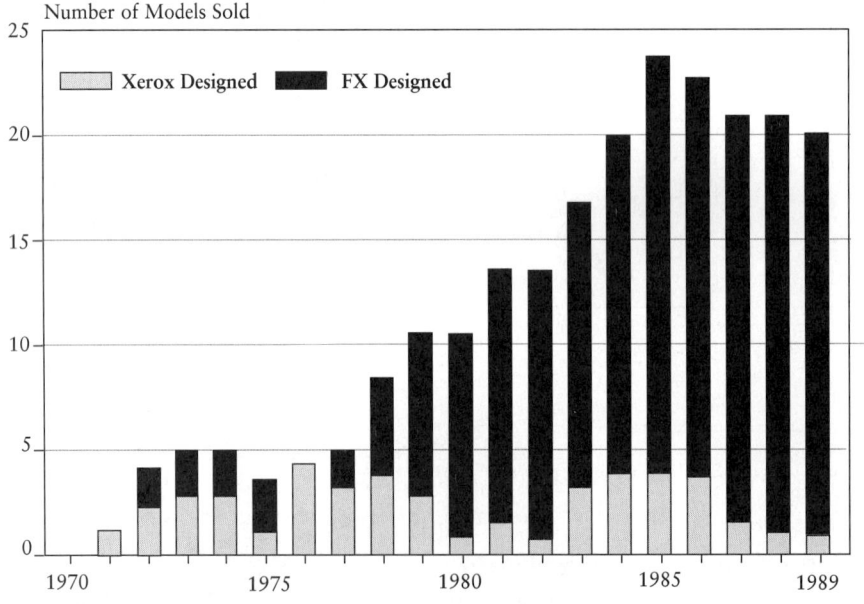

Source: Fuji Xerox
Notes: Top: Utility models included in Japan.
Bottom: Based on product introductions, assuming that every product has a commercial life of four years.

assistance. These personnel exchanges had, in fact, been an important channel for the transfer of technology from Xerox to Fuji Xerox. By 1989, an estimated 1000 young, high-potential FX employees had spent three years each as residents at Xerox, and some 150 Xerox people had done this at Fuji Xerox. These residents were directly involved in the work of their host companies. Every year there also some 1000 shorter visits by engineers and managers. These exchanges and the summit meetings contributed to a constructive relationship. "Whenever a problem came up, we established a process to manage it," explained Jeff Kennard. "The trust built up between the companies has been a key factor in the success of this relationship. It enables one to take on short-term costs in the interest of long-term gains for the group."

By the mid-1980s, most Xerox managers also had mixed feelings of challenge and admiration toward Fuji Xerox, which were echoed by Kennard:

> It seems that every time Xerox blinks and retracts, Fuji Xerox forges ahead. Fuji Xerox continues to be the agent for change. They have great corporate vision and they target what is strategically important. Then they take tough decisions and make the needed investment.

The Management Challenge

In this context, Allaire and Kobayashi commissioned the Codestiny III Task Force, charging it with developing a framework for cooperation between the two companies in the 1990s. The task force consisted of top planners in each company and was to report to the two CEOS within a year of its formation. Roger Levien, Xerox's vice president for strategy and head of the Codestiny III talks, described the motivation for the project:

> Fuji Xerox had certain issues they wanted to discuss, and we agreed to do so in the Codestiny process. One of their desires was to get the worldwide market for the low end. They also wanted to develop a more symmetric relationship with us. We wanted to spell everything out, identify all of the alternatives, and leave the final decision to top management.

One of the issues to be addressed by the Codestiny team was Fuji Xerox's aspiration to expand its markets in Asia. Under the existing technology licensing contracts, Fuji Xerox had the right to sell in Indonesia, South Korea, the Philippines, Taiwan, and Thailand (total GDP in 1989: $570 billion), and it had indeed established sales subsidiaries in each of these markets. But Rank Xerox in London was responsible for managing sales in what it called the South Pacific Operations—Australia (1989 GDP: $280 billion), New Zealand ($45 billion), Singapore ($28 billion), Malaysia ($37 billion), China ($420 billion), and Hong Kong ($63 billion). Since the early 1980s, Fuji Xerox had argued that this arrangement led to inefficiencies in serving the South Pacific markets. At that time, knock-down kits were sometimes shipped from Fuji Xerox to Britain for assembly, and then shipped back to Asia for sale. Furthermore, Rank Xerox followed a very different marketing strategy in these markets than Fuji Xerox did in its neighboring Asian markets. Rank Xerox emphasized high profit margins and sales of high-end machines, whereas Fuji Xerox put greater emphasis on market share and low-end products. As a result, when Fuji Xerox urged Rank Xerox in the late 1970s to adopt a more aggressive sales strategy in Australia before Canon entered that market, Rank Xerox refused. Although Rank Xerox managed the South Pacific countries out of a regional office in Hong Kong, Fuji Xerox's sales subsidiaries were usually joint ventures with local partners, and so drew more on local management talent.

Another key issue for the Codestiny team was how the Xerox Group should manage the low-end laser printer business in the United States. This market segment was receiving renewed attention in 1989, following the appointment of Bill Lowe as Xerox's executive vice president for development and manufacturing. Lowe came to Xerox from IBM, where he had been in charge of the personal computer business. Soon after arriving at Xerox, he began to focus on the problems in the low-end copier and printer businesses, where Fuji Xerox typically developed and manufactured products sold by Xerox.

> Both companies were trying to get full profit out of it, even though the margins were slim. Fuji Xerox's policy was to mark up costs; Xerox's was to get an acceptable gross profit. Furthermore, each product had a different mark-up scheme, and many sideline deals confounded the issues. This fostered sharp dealings between the

partners. So, most of our energy was focused on each other, not on Canon. We were pointing fingers and frustrating ourselves.

The Codestiny team analyzed these specific issues within a broad framework, and began by outlining the various options available for cooperation in marketing, research, and development and manufacturing (**Exhibit 11**). The team considered the advantages and disadvantages of each of these options and began to develop possible strategies for the South Pacific Operations and for the low-end printer business in the United States.

But there was much more at stake than decisions in these two areas. The central question facing Xerox and Fuji Xerox was: How should the relationship between the two companies be structured and managed in the new global environment of the 1990s?

EXHIBIT 11 Relationship Options Identified by Codestiny Task Force

MARKETING

A	Independent and Overlapping	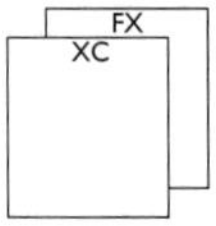 [XC/FX overlapping boxes]	Act as two separate companies serving the world market, with some coordination on business direction and strategy. No geographic constraints.
B	Independent and Separate	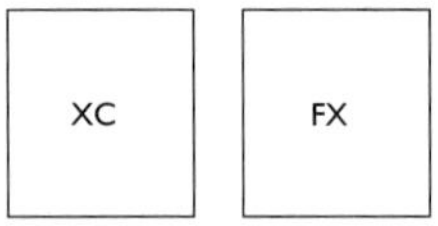 [XC and FX separate boxes]	Concentrate efforts on licensed territories for core products, with multinational business as required.
C	Separate with exception	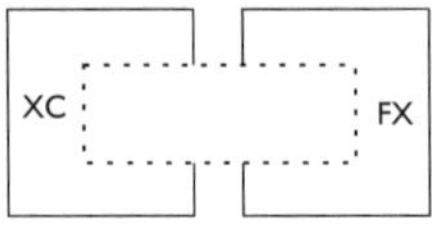 [XC and FX boxes with dashed connection]	Same as B, but with joint or overlapping activities across territorial boundaries on case by case basis.
D	Coordinated global product mandates	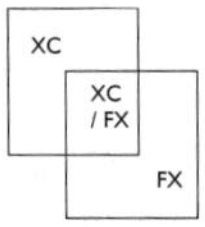 [XC, XC/FX, FX overlapping boxes]	Worldwide and exclusive responsibility for products or product ranges manufactured under special licenses.

(Continued)

Case 1: Xerox and Fuji Xerox

EXHIBIT 11 Relationship Options Identified by Codestiny Task Force (continued)

RESEARCH

A Independent — Each pursues own interest and becomes self-sufficient

B Coordinated — Coordinated group research program of XC and FX, with both self-sufficiency and overlap

C Joint — Single research organization without overlap

D Complementary — Separate organizations operating on exclusive projects

DEVELOPMENT AND MANUFACTURING

A Independent — Each development and manufacturing (D&M) organization supplies its own marketing organization (MCD)

B Complementary without overlap — Assign development roles to each organization, with no overlap allowed in development projects

C Complementary with overlap — Same as B, but with overlap in development projects

D Joint — Single development and manufacturing organization with individual project targeted to needs of separate marketing organizations

Source: Compiled from Xerox documents

Case 2: Curtis Automotive Hoist

In September 1990, Mark Curtis, president of Curtis Automotive Hoist (CAH), had just finished reading a feasibility report on entering the European market in 1991. CAH manufactured surface automotive hoists, a product used by garages, service stations, and other repair shops to lift cars for servicing. The report, prepared by CAH's marketing manager, Pierre Gagnon, outlines the opportunities in the European Economic Community and the entry options available.

Mr. Curtis was not sure if CAH was ready for this move. While the company had been successful in expanding sales into the United States market, Mr. Curtis wondered if this success could be repeated in Europe. He thought that with more effort, sales could be increased in the United States. On the other hand, there were some positive aspects to the European idea. He began reviewing the information in preparation for the meeting the following day with Mr. Gagnon.

Curtis Automotive Hoist

Mr. Curtis, a design engineer, had worked for eight years for the Canadian subsidiary of a U.S. automotive hoist manufacturer. During those years, he had spent considerable time designing an above-ground (or surface) automotive hoist. Although Mr. Curtis was very enthusiastic about the unique aspects of the hoist, including a scissor lift and wheel alignment pads, senior management expressed no interest in the idea. In 1980, Mr. Curtis left the company to start his own business with the express purpose of designing and manufacturing the hoist. He left with the good wishes of his previous employer who had no objections to his plans to start a new business.

Over the next three years, Mr. Curtis obtained financing from a venture capital firm, opened a plant in Lachine, Québec, and began manufacturing and marketing the hoist, called the Curtis Lift.

From the beginning, Mr. Curtis had taken considerable pride in the development and marketing of the Curtis Lift. The original design included a scissor lift and a safety locking mechanism that allowed the hoist to be raised to any level and locked in place. As well, the scissor lift offered easy access for the mechanic to work on the raised vehicle. Because the hoist was fully hydraulic and had no chains or pulleys, it required little maintenance. Another key feature was the alignment turn plates that were an integral part of the lift. The turn plates meant that mechanics could accurately and easily perform wheel alignment jobs. Because it was a surface lift, it could be installed in a garage in less than a day.

Mr. Curtis continually made improvements to the product, including adding more safety features. In fact, the Curtis Lift was considered a leader in automotive lift safety. Safety was an important factor in the automotive hoist market. Although hoists seldom malfunctioned, when they did, it often resulted in a serious accident.

The Curtis Lift developed a reputation in the industry as the "Cadillac" of hoists; the unit was judged by many as superior to competitive offerings because of its design, the quality of the workmanship, the safety features, the ease of installation, and the five-year warranty. Mr. Curtis held four patents on the Curtis Lift, including the lifting mechanism on the scissor design and a safety locking mechanism. A number of versions of the product were designed that made the Curtis Lift suitable (depending on the model) for a variety of tasks, including rustproofing, muffler repairs, and general mechanical repairs.

In 1981, CAH sold twenty-three hoists and had sales of $172,500. During the early years, the majority of sales were to independent service stations and garages specializing in wheel alignment in the Québec and Ontario market. Most of the units were sold by Mr. Gagnon, who was hired in 1982 to handle the marketing side of the operation. In 1984, Mr. Gagnon began using distributors to sell the hoist to a wider geographic market in Canada. In 1986, he signed an agreement with a large automotive wholesaler to represent CAH in the U.S. market. By 1989, the company sold 1,054 hoists and had sales of $9,708,000 (Exhibit 1). In 1989, about 60 percent of

---

This case is printed here with the permission of the author, Gordon H. G. McDougall of Wilfrid Laurier University, Québec.

sales were to the United States with the remaining 40 percent to the Canadian market.

Industry

Approximately 49,000 hoists were sold each year in North America. Typically hoists were purchased by an automotive outlet that serviced or repaired cars, including new car dealers, used car dealers, specialty shops (for example, muffler shops, transmission, wheel alignment), chains (for example, Firestone, Goodyear, Canadian Tire), and independent garages. It was estimated that new car dealers purchased 30 percent of all units sold in a given year. In general, the specialty shops focus on one type of repair, such as mufflers or rustproofing, while "nonspecialty" outlets handle a variety of repairs. While there was some crossover, in general, CAH competed in the specialty shop segment and, in particular, those shops that dealt with wheel alignment. This included chains, such as Firestone and Canadian Tire as well as new car dealers (for example, Ford) who devote a certain percentage of their lifts to the wheel alignment business, and independent garages who specialized in wheel alignment.

The purpose of a hoist was to lift an automobile into a position where a mechanic or service person could easily work on the car. Because different repairs required different positions, a wide variety of hoists had been developed to meet specific needs. For example, a muffler repair shop required a hoist that allowed the mechanic to gain easy access to the underside of the car. Similarly, a wheel alignment job required a hoist that offered a level platform where the wheels could be adjusted as well as providing easy access for the mechanic. Mr. Gagnon estimated that 85 percent of CAH's sales were to the wheel alignment market to service centers such as Firestone, Goodyear, and Canadian Tire and to independent garages that specialized in wheel alignment. About 15 percent of sales were made to customers who used the hoist for general mechanical repairs.

Firms purchasing hoists were part of an industry called the automobile aftermarket. This industry was involved in supplying parts and service for new and used cars and was worth over $54 billion at retail in 1989, while servicing the approximately 11 million cars on the road in Canada. The industry was large and diverse; there were over 4,000 new car dealers in Canada, over 400 Canadian Tire stores, over 100 stores in each of the Firestone and Goodyear chains, and over 200 stores in the Rust Check chain.

The purchase of an automotive hoist was often an important decision for the service station owner or

EXHIBIT 1 Curtis Automotive Hoist—Selected Financial Statistics (1987 to 1989)

	1989	1988	1987
Sales	$9,708,000	$7,454,000	$6,218,000
Cost of Sales	6,990,000	5,541,000	4,540,000
Contribution	2,718,000	1,913,000	1,678,000
Marketing expenses*	530,000	510,000	507,000
Administrative expenses	840,000	820,000	810,000
Earnings before tax	1,348,000	583,000	361,000
Units sold	1,054	847	723

*Marketing expenses in 1989 included advertising ($70,000), four salespeople ($240,000), marketing manager and three sales support staff ($220,000).
Source: Company records.

dealer. Because the price of hoists ranged from $3,000 to $15,000, it was a capital expense for most businesses.

For the owner/operator of a new service center or car dealership the decision involved determining what type of hoist was required, then what brand would best suit the company. Most new service centers or car dealerships had multiple bays for servicing cars. In these cases, the decision would involve what types of hoists were required (for example, in-ground, surface). Often, more than one type of hoist was purchased, depending on the service center/dealership needs.

Experienced garage owners seeking a replacement hoist (the typical hoist had a useful life of ten to thirteen years) would usually determine what products were available and then make a decision. If the garage owners were also mechanics, they would probably be aware of two or three types of hoists but would not be very knowledgeable about the brands or products currently available. Garage owners or dealers who were not mechanics probably knew very little about hoists. The owners of car or service dealerships often bought the product that was recommended and/or approved by the parent company.

Competition

Sixteen companies competed in the automotive lift market in North America: four Canadian and twelve United States firms. Hoists were subject to import duties. Duties on hoists entering the U.S. market from Canada were 2.4 percent of the selling price; from the U.S. entering Canada the import duty was 7.9 percent. With the advent of the Free Trade Agreement in 1989, the duties between the two countries would be phased out over a ten-year period. For Mr. Curtis, the import duties had never played a part in any decisions: the fluctuating exchange rates between the two countries had a far greater impact on selling prices.

A wide variety of hoists were manufactured in the industry. The two basic types of hoists were in-ground and surface. As the names imply, in-ground hoists required that a pit be dug "in-ground" where the piston that raised the hoist was installed. In-ground hoists were either single-post or multiple-post, were permanent, and obviously could not be moved. In-ground lifts constituted approximately 21 percent of total lift sales in 1989 (Exhibit 2). Surface lifts were installed on a flat surface, usually concrete. Surface lifts, compared to in-ground lifts, were easier to install and could be moved, if necessary. Surface lifts constituted 79 percent of total lift sales in 1989. Within each type of hoist (for example, post-lift surface hoists), there were numerous variations in terms of size, shape, and lifting capacity.

The industry was dominated by two large U.S. firms, AHV Lifts and Berne Manufacturing, who together held approximately 60 percent of the market. AHV Lifts, the largest firm with approximately 40 percent of the market and annual sales of about $60 million, offered a complete line of hoists (that is, in-ground and surface) but focused primarily on the in-ground market and the two-post surface market. AHV Lifts was the only company that had its own direct sales force; all other companies used (1) only wholesalers or (2) a combination of wholesalers and company sales force. AHV Lifts offered standard hoists with few extra features and competed primarily on price. Berne Manufacturing, with a market share of approximately 20 percent, also competed in the in-ground and two-post surface markets. It used a combination of wholesalers and company salespeople and, like AHV Lifts, competed primarily on price.

Most of the remaining firms in the industry were companies that operated in a regional market (for example, California or British Columbia) and/or offered a limited product line (for example, four-post surface hoist).

Curtis had two competitors that manufactured scissor lifts. AHV Lift marketed a scissor hoist that had a different lifting mechanism and did not include the safety locking features of the Curtis Lift. On average, the AHV scissor lift sold for about 20 percent less than the Curtis Lift. The second competitor, Mete Lift, was a small regional company with sales in California and Oregon. It had a design that was very similar to the Curtis Lift but lacked some of its safety features. The Mete Lift, regarded as a well-manufactured product, sold for about 5 percent less than the Curtis Lift.

Marketing Strategy

As of early 1990, CAH had developed a reputation for a quality product backed by good service in the hoist lift market, primarily in the wheel alignment segment.

The distribution system employed by CAH reflected the need to engage in extensive personal selling. Three types of distributors were used: a company sales force, Canadian distributors, and a U.S. automotive wholesaler. The company sales force consisted of four salespeople and Mr. Gagnon. Their main task was to service large "direct" accounts. The initial step was to get the Curtis Lift approved by large chains and manufacturers and then, having received the approval, to sell to individual dealers or operators. For example, if General Motors approved the hoist, then CAH could sell it to individual General Motors dealers. CAH sold directly to the individual dealers of a number of large accounts including General Motors, Ford, Chrysler, Petro-Canada, Firestone, and Goodyear. CAH had been successful in obtaining manufacturer approval from the big three automobile manufacturers in both Canada and the United States. CAH had been successful in obtaining manufacturer approval from the big three automobile manufacturers in both Canada and the United States. CAH had also received approval from service companies such as Canadian Tire and Goodyear. To date, CAH had not been rejected by any major account but, in some cases, the approval process had taken over four years.

In total, the company sales force generated about 25 percent of the unit sales each year. Sales to the large "direct" accounts in the United States went through CAH's U.S. wholesaler.

The Canadian distributors sold, installed, and serviced units across Canada. These distributors handled the Curtis Lift and carried a line of noncompetitive automotive equipment products (for example, engine diagnostic equipment, wheel balancing equipment) and noncompetitive lifts. These distributors focused on the smaller chains and the independent service stations and garages.

The U.S. wholesaler sold a complete product line to service stations as well as manufacturing some equipment. The Curtis Lift was one of five different types of lifts that the wholesaler sold. Although the wholesaler provided CAH with extensive distribution in the United States, the Curtis Lift was a minor product within the wholesaler's total line. While Mr. Gagnon did not have any actual figures, he thought that the Curtis Lift probably accounted for less than

EXHIBIT 2 North America Automotive Lift Sales, by Type (1987 to 1989)

	1987	1988	1989
In-ground			
Single-post	5,885	5,772	5,518
Multiple-post	4,812	6,625	5,075
Surface			
Two-post	27,019	28,757	28,923
Four-post	3,892	3,162	3,745
Scissor	2,170	2,258	2,316
Other	4,486	3,613	3,695
Total	48,234	50,187	49,272

Source: Company records.

20 percent of the total lift sales of the U.S. wholesaler.

Both Mr. Curtis and Mr. Gagnon felt that the U.S. market had unrealized potential. With a population of 248 million people and over 140 million registered vehicles, the U.S. market was over ten times the size of the Canadian market (population of 26 million, approximately 11 million vehicles). Mr. Gagnon noted that the six New England states (population over 13 million), the three largest mid-Atlantic states (population over 32 million), and the three largest mid-Eastern states (population over 32 million) were all within a day's drive of the factory in Lachine. Mr. Curtis and Mr. Gagnon had considered setting up a sales office in New York to service these states, but they were concerned that the U.S. wholesaler would not be willing to relinquish any of its territory. They had also considered working more closely with the wholesaler to encourage it to "push" the Curtis Lift. It appeared that the wholesaler's major objective was to sell a hoist, not necessarily the Curtis Lift.

CAH distributed a catalog-type package with products, uses, prices, and other required information for both distributors and users. In addition, CAH advertised in trade publications (for example, *Service Station & Garage Management*), and Mr. Gagnon traveled to trade shows in Canada and the U.S. to promote the Curtis Lift.

In 1989, Curtis Lifts sold for an average retail price of $10,990 and CAH received, on average, $9,210 for each unit sold. This average reflected the mix of sales through the three distribution channels: (1) direct (where CAH received 100 percent of the selling price), (2) Canadian distributors (where CAH received 80 percent of the selling price), and (3) the U.S. wholesaler (where CAH received 78 percent of the selling price).

Both Mr. Curtis and Mr. Gagnon felt that the company's success to date was based on a strategy of offering a superior product that was primarily targeted to the needs of specific customers. The strategy stressed continual product improvement, quality workmanship, and service. Personal selling was a key aspect of the strategy; salespeople could show customers the benefits of the Curtis Lift over competing products.

The European Market

Against this background, Mr. Curtis had been thinking of ways to continue the rapid growth of the company. One possibility that kept coming up was the promise and potential of the European market. The fact that Europe would become a single market in 1992 suggested that it was an opportunity that should at least be explored. With this in mind, Mr. Curtis asked Mr. Gagnon to prepare a report on the possibility of CAH entering the European market. The highlights of Mr. Gagnon's report follow.

History of the European Community

The European Community (EC) stemmed from the 1953 Treaty of Rome in which five countries decided it would be in their best interest to form an internal market. These countries were France, Spain, Italy, West Germany, and Luxembourg. By 1990, the EC consisted of twelve countries (the additional seven were Belgium, Denmark, Greece, Ireland, the Netherlands, Portugal, and the United Kingdom) with a population of over 325 million people.* In 1992, virtually all barriers (physical, technical, and fiscal) in the EC were scheduled to be removed for companies located within the EC. This would allow the free movement of goods, persons, services, and capital.

In the last five years many North American and Japanese firms had established themselves in the EC. The reasoning for this was twofold. First, these companies regarded the community as an opportunity to increase global market share and profits. The market was attractive because of its sheer size and lack of internal barriers. Second, in 1992, companies that were established within the community were subject to protection from external competition via EC protectionism tariffs, local contender, and reciprocity requirements. EC protectionism tariffs were only temporary and would be removed at a later date. It would be possible for companies to export to or establish in the community after 1992, but there was some risk attached.

---

* As of September 1990, West Germany and East Germany were in the process of unification. East Germany had a population of approximately 17 million people.

Market Potential

The key indicator of the potential market for the Curtis Lift hoist was the number of passenger cars and commercial vehicles in use in a particular country. Four countries in Europe had more than 20 million vehicles in use, with West Germany having the largest domestic fleet of 30 million vehicles, followed in order by France, Italy, and the United Kingdom (Exhibit 3). The number of vehicles was an important indicator because the more vehicles in use meant a greater number of service and repair facilities that needed vehicle hoists and potentially the Curtis Lift.

An indicator of the future vehicle repair and service market was the number of new vehicle registrations. The registration of new vehicles was important as this maintained the number of vehicles in use by replacing cars that had been retired. Again, West Germany had the most new cars registered in 1988 and was followed in order by France, the United Kingdom, and Italy.

Based primarily on the fact that a large domestic market was important for initial growth, the selection of a European country should be limited to the "Big Four" industrialized nations: West Germany, France, the United Kingdom, or Italy. In an international survey companies from North America and Europe ranked European countries on a scale of 10 to 100 on market potential and investment site potential. The results showed that West Germany was favored for both market potential and investment site opportunities while France, the United Kingdom, and Spain place second, third, and fourth, respectively. Italy did not place in the top four in either market or investment site potential. However, Italy had a large number of vehicles in use, had the second-largest population in Europe, and was an acknowledged leader in car technology and production.

Little information was available on the competition within Europe. There was, as yet, no dominant manufacturer, as was the case in North America. At this time, there was one firm in Germany that manufactured a scissor-type lift. The firm sold most of its units within the German market. The only other available information was that twenty-two firms in Italy manufactured vehicle lifts.

Investment Options

Mr. Gagnon felt that CAH had three options for expansion into the European market: licensing option was a real possibility as a French firm had expressed an interest in manufacturing the Curtis Lift.

In June 1990, Mr. Gagnon had attended a trade show in Detroit to promote the Curtis Lift. At the show, he met Phillipe Beaupre, the marketing manager for Bar Maisse, a French manufacturer of wheel alignment equipment. The firm, located in Chelles, France, sold a range of wheel alignment equipment throughout Europe. The best-selling product was an electronic modular aligner that enabled a mechanic to utilize a sophisticated computer system to align the wheels of a car. Mr. Beaupre was seeking a North American distributor for the modular aligner and other products manufactured by Bar Maisse.

At the show, Mr. Gagnon and Mr. Beaupre had a casual conversation in which each explained what

EXHIBIT 3 Number of Vehicles (1988) and Population (1989)

Country	Vehicles in Use (Thousands)		New Vehicle Registrations (Thousands)	Population (Thousands)
	Passenger	Commercial		
West Germany	28,304	1,814	2,960	60,900
France	29,970	4,223	2,635	56,000
Italy	22,500	1,897	2,308	57,400
United Kingdom	20,605	2,915	2,531	57,500
Spain	9,750	1,750	1,172	39,400

their respective companies manufactured; they exchanged company brochures and business cards, and both went on to other exhibits. The next day, Mr. Beaupre sought out Mr. Gagnon and asked if he might be interested in having Bar Maisse manufacture and market the Curtis Lift in Europe. Mr. Beaupre felt the lift would complement Bar Maisse's product line and the licensing would be of mutual benefit to both parties. They agreed to pursue the idea. Upon his return to Lachine, Mr. Gagnon told Mr. Curtis about these discussions, and they agreed to explore this possibility.

Mr. Gagnon called a number of colleagues in the industry and asked them what they knew about Bar Maisse. About half had not heard of the company, but those who had commented favorably on the quality of its products. One colleague, with European experience, knew the company well and said that Bar Maisse's management had integrity and would make a good partner. In July, Mr. Gagnon sent a letter to Mr. Beaupre stating that CAH was interested in further discussions and enclosed various company brochures including price lists and technical information on the Curtis Lift. In late August, Mr. Beaupre responded stating that Bar Maisse would like to enter a three-year licensing agreement with CAH to manufacture the Curtis Lift in Europe. In exchange for the manufacturing rights, Bar Maisse was prepared to pay a royalty rate of 5 percent of gross sales. Mr. Gagnon had not yet responded to this proposal.

A second possibility was a joint venture. Mr. Gagnon had wondered if it might not be better for CAH to offer a counter proposal to Bar Maisse for a joint venture. He had not worked out any details, but Mr. Gagnon felt that CAH would learn more about the European market and probably make more money if they were an active partner in Europe. Mr. Gagnon's idea was a 50—50 proposal where the two parties shared the investment and the profits. He envisaged a situation where Bar Maisse would manufacture the Curtis Lift in their plant with technical assistance from CAH. Mr. Gagnon also thought that CAH could get involved in the marketing of the lift through the Bar Maisse distribution system. Further, he thought that the Curtis Lift, with proper marketing, could gain a reasonable share of the European market. If that happened, Mr. Gagnon felt that CAH was likely to make greater returns with a joint venture.

The third option was direct investment where CAH would establish a manufacturing facility and set up a management group to market the lift. Mr. Gagnon had contacted a business acquaintance who had recently been involved in manufacturing fabricated steel sheds in Germany. On the basis of discussions with his acquaintance, Mr. Gagnon estimated the costs involved in setting up a plant in Europe at: (1) $250,000 for capital equipment (welding machines, cranes, other equipment), (2) $200,000 in incremental costs to set the plant up, and (3) carrying costs to cover $1,000,000 in inventory and accounts receivable. While the actual costs of renting a building for the factory would depend on the site location, he estimated that annual building rent including heat, light, and insurance would be about $80,000. Mr. Gagnon recognized these estimates were guidelines but he felt that the estimates were probably within 20 percent of actual costs.

The Decision

As Mr. Curtis considered the contents of the report, a number of thoughts crossed his mind. He began making notes concerning the European possibility and the future of the company.

- If CAH decided to enter Europe, Mr. Gagnon would be the obvious choice to head up the direct investment option or the joint venture option. Mr. Curtis felt that Mr. Gagnon had been instrumental in the success of the company to date.
- While CAH had the financial resources to go ahead with the direct investment option, the joint venture would spread the risk (and the returns) over the two companies.
- CAH had built its reputation on designing and manufacturing a quality product. Regardless of the option chosen, Mr. Curtis wanted the firm's reputation to be maintained.
- Either the licensing agreement or the joint venture appeared to build on the two companies' strengths; Bar Maisse had knowledge of the market and CAH had the product. What troubled Mr. Curtis was

whether this apparent synergy would work or whether Bar Maisse would seek to control the operation.
- It was difficult to estimate sales under any of the options. With the first two (licensing and joint venture), it would depend on the effort and expertise of Bar Maisse: with the third option, it would depend on Mr. Gagnon.
- CAH's sales in the U.S. market could be increased if the U.S. wholesaler would "push" the Curtis Lift.

Alternatively, the establishment of a sales office in New York to cover the eastern states could also increase sales.

As Mr. Curtis reflected on the situation he knew he should probably get additional information—but it wasn't obvious exactly what information would help him make a "yes" or "no" decision. He knew one thing for sure—he was going to keep his company on a "fast growth" track—and at tomorrow's meeting he and Mr. Gagnon would decide how to do it.

Case 3: Metro Corporation

In the fall of 1979, Metro Corporation entered into a licensing agreement with Impecina, a Peruvian company. The negotiations went smoothly. In the aftermath, however, the management wondered what lessons the Peruvian deal offered for future technology transfer opportunities to other developing countries.

All Metro's licensing is handled by its international division, International Construction and Engineering (ICE), which is beginning to develop a reputation in Western Europe and Latin America as a good source for specialized construction technology.

The Licensor Firm

Metro Corporation is a diversified steel rolling, fabricating, and construction company based in the Midwest and considers itself to be in a mature industry. Innovations are few and far between. With transport and tariff barriers, and the support given by many governments to their own companies, exporting as a means of doing foreign business is rather limited. Similarly, given the large investment, modest return, and political sensitivity of the industry, direct foreign investment is all but a closed option. In a global strategic sense then, Metro Corporation has far more frequently focused on licensing as a market entry method, with technologies confined to (1) processes and engineering peripheral to the basic steel making process, e.g., mining methods, coke oven door designs, galvanizing, etc., and (2) applications of steel in construction and other industries, e.g., petroleum tank design, welding methods, thermo-adhesion, etc.

The Proposed Licensee

Impecina, a private firm, is the largest construction company in Peru and operates throughout Latin America. Impecina has a broad range of interests including residential and commercial buildings, hydraulic works, transportation, and maritime works. Employing several thousand personnel, engineers, and technicians, its sales had doubled in the last five years. It was still primarily a Peruvian business with most turnover in Peru but was in the process of expanding into Colombia, the North African Mediterranean countries, and Argentina, Brazil, and Venezuela. Impecina has advanced computer capacity with a large IBM and other computers at its branches. In oil storage tanks, Impecina's experience was limited to the smaller fixed-cone roof designs under 150 feet in diameter.

This case is printed here with the permission of the author, Farok J. Contractor, of the State University of New Jersey, Rutgers.

The Technology

National Tank Inc., a fabrication division of Metro, had designed a computerized design procedure for floating-roof oil storage tanks that minimized the use of steel within American Petroleum Institute or any other oil industry standards. Particularly for the larger tanks, for instance 150 in diameter and above, this design procedure would give the bidding contractor a significant cost advantage. National Tank had spent one man-year, at a direct cost of $225,000, to write the computer program alone. Patents were involved in an incidental manner, only for the seals of the floating roof. Metro had only filed for this patent in the U.S.

The Market

Peru's indigenous oil output is very low, but it imports and refines annually 50 million tons, mostly for domestic demand. Following the escalation of oil prices and tightening of supplies in 1973, the Peruvian government determinedly set about to formulate a program to augment Peru's oil storage capacity. Impecina's representatives, at a preliminary meeting with ICE in the U.S. headquarters, said their government planned $200 million in expenditures on oil storage facilities over the next three years (mostly in large tanks). Of this, Impecina's "ambition" was to capture a one-third market share. That this appeared to be a credible target was illustrated by their existing 30 percent share of the "fixed-cone type under 150 feet in diameter." Additionally, they estimated private-sector construction value over the next three years to total $40 million.

Approximately half of a storage system's construction cost goes for the tank alone; the remainder for excavation, foundation, piping, instrumentation, and other ancillary equipment, all of which Impecina's engineers were very familiar with.

Neighboring Colombia was building a 12 million ton refinery but, according to the Impecina representative, the tank installation plans of other Latin American nations were not known.

Each of Impecina's competitors in Peru was affiliated with a prominent company: Umbertomas with Jefferson Inc. in the United States, Zapa with Philadelphia Iron & Steel, Cosmas with Peoria-Duluth Construction Inc., and so on. Thus association with Metro would help Impecina in bidding.

The First Meeting

National Tank division had in the past year bid jointly with Impecina on a project in southern Peru. Though that bid was unsuccessful, Impecina had learned about Metro's computerized design capabilities and initiated a formal first round of negotiations that were to lead to a licensing agreement. The meeting took place in the United States. Two Impecina executives of subdirector rank were accompanied by an American consultant. Metro was represented by the vice president of ICE, the ICE attorney, and an executive from National Tank Division.

Minutes of this meeting show it was exploratory; both genuine and rhetorical questions were asked. Important information and perceptions were exchanged, and the groundwork laid for concluding negotiations. Following is a bare summary of important issues gleaned from the somewhat circular discussion.

a. *License Market Coverage:* Impecina tried to represent itself as an essentially Peruvian firm. They reviewed their government's expenditure plans and their hoped-for market share. Yet throughout the meeting, the issue of the license also covering Libya, Algeria, Morocco, Colombia, Argentina, Brazil, and Venezuela kept cropping up.

b. *Exclusivity:* For Peru, Metro negotiators had no difficulty conceding exclusivity. They mentioned that granting exclusivity to a licensee for any territory was agreeable in principle, provided a minimum performance guarantee was given. At this, the question was deferred for future discussion. At one point a Metro executive remarked, "We could give Impecina a nonexclusive—and say, for example, we wouldn't give another [licensee] a license for one year [in those nations]" proposing the idea of a trial period for Impecina to generate business in a territory.

c. *Agreement Life:* Impecina very quickly agreed to a ten-year term, payment in U.S. dollars, and other minor issues.
d. *Trade Name:* The Impecina negotiators placed great emphasis on their ability to use Metro's name in bidding, explaining how their competition in Peru had technical collaboration with three U.S. companies (see above). "Did that mean Metro's National Tank Division could compete with Impecina in Peru?" they were asked rhetorically. (Actually, both sides seem to have tacitly agreed that it was not possible for Metro to do business directly in Peru.)
e. *Licensee Market Size:* Attention turned to the dollar value of the future large (floating-roof) tank market in Peru. Impecina threw out an estimate of $200 million government expenditures and $40 million private-sector spending, over the coming three years, of which they targeted a one-third share. Later, a lower market size estimate of $150 million (government *and* private), with a share of $50 million received by Impecina over three years, was arrived at (memories are not clear on how the estimates were revised). The question "Will Impecina guarantee us they will obtain one-third of the market?" brought the response "That's an optimistic figure but we hope we can realize [it]." Impecina offered as evidence their existing one-third share of the "fixed-roof under 150 feet" market, an impressive achievement.
f. *Product Mix Covered by Licensee:* It became clear that Impecina wanted floating-roof technology for *all* sizes, *and* fixed-roof over 100 feet diameter. They suggested the agreement cover tanks over 100 feet in size. "Would Impecina pay on all tanks [of any size]?" to simplify royalty calculation and monitoring? After considerable discussion, Metro seems to have acceded to Impecina's proposal (to cover both types, only over 100 feet) based on consensus over three points.
   1. The competition probably does not pay (their licensors) on small tanks, and therefore Impecina would be at a disadvantage if they had to pay on small tanks also.
   2. The market in floating-roof tanks was over 100 feet anyway, usually.
   3. Impecina claimed that customers normally dictate the dimensions of the tanks, so Impecina cannot vary them in order to avoid paying a royalty to Metro.
g. *Compensation Formula.* Metro proposed an initial lump-sum payment (in two installments, one when the agreement is signed, the second on delivery of the computer program and designs), *plus* engineers and executives for bid assistance on a per-diem rate, *plus* a royalty on successful bids based on the barrel capacity installed by Impecina. Impecina's American consultant countered with the idea of royalties on a sliding scale, lower with larger capacity tanks, indicating talk about "one million barrel capacity tanks." The (rhetorical?) question "What is Peru's oil capacity?" seems to have brought the discussion down to earth and veered it off on a tangent, while both sides mentally regrouped.

   On returning to this topic, Impecina executives ventured that as a rule of thumb, their profit markup on a turnkey job was 6 percent. (However, on excluding the more price-sensitive portions such as excavation, piping, and ancillary equipment, which typically constitute half the value, Impecina conceded that on the tank alone they might mark up as much as 12 percent, although they kept insisting 5 to 6 percent was enough.)

   Impecina executives later offered only royalties (preferably sliding) *and* per-diem fees for bid assistance from Metro executives and engineers. Metro countered by pointing out that per-diem fees of, say, $225 plus travel costs amounted at to recovering costs, not profit.

   At this stage, the compensation design question was deferred for later negotiation, the broad outlines having been laid. Metro's starting formal offer, which would mention specific numbers, was to be telexed to Lima in a week.
h. *The Royalty Basis:* Metro considered the fact that Impecina engineers were very familiar with excavation, piping wiring, and other ancillary equip-

ment. Metro was transferring technology *for the tank alone*, which typically composed half of overall installed value.

i. *Government Intervention.* Toward the end of the discussions, Impecina brought up the question of the Peruvian government having to approve of the agreement. This led to their retreat from the idea of a ten-year term, agreed to earlier, and Impecina then mentioned five years. No agreement was reached. (Incidentally, Peru had in the last two years passed legislation indicating a "guideline" of five years for foreign licenses.)

Internal Discussion in Metro Leading to the Formal Offer

The advantages derived by the licensee would be acquisition of floating-roof technology, time and money saved in attempting to generate the computerized design procedure in-house, somewhat of a cost and efficiency advantage in bidding on larger tanks, and finally, the use of Metro's name.

a. It was estimated that National Tank division had spent $225,000 (one man-year = two executives for six months, plus other costs) in developing the computer program. Additionally, it may cost $40,000 (three-quarters of a man-year) to convert the program into Spanish and the metric system, and to adapt it to the material availability and labor cost factors peculiar to Peru. Simultaneously, there would be semiformal instruction of Impecina engineers in the use of the program, petroleum industry codes, and Metro fabrication methods. All this had to be done before the licensee would be ready for a single bid.

b. It was visualized that Metro would then assist Impecina for two man-weeks for each bid preparation and four man-weeks on successful receipt of a contract award. Additionally, if Metro's specialized construction equipment were used, three man-months of on-site training would be needed.

As the licensee's personnel moved along their learning curve, assistance of the type described in paragraph b would diminish until it was no longer needed after a few successful bids.

Additional considerations that went into a determination of the initial offer:

1. Metro obligations (and sunk costs) under paragraph a were fairly determinate, whereas their obligations under b depended on the technical sophistication and absorptive capacity of the licensee's engineers, their success rate in bidding, and so on.
2. If Impecina's market estimates were used, they would generate large tank orders worth $50 million, on which they would make a profit of $3 million (at 6 percent on $50 million or 12 percent on half the amount) over the next three years.
3. The market beyond three years was an unknown.
4. Exclusive rights might be given to Impecina in Peru and Colombia, with perhaps ICE reserving the right of conversion to nonexclusive if minimum market share was not captured.
5. While Impecina's multinational expansion plans were unknown, their business in other nations was too small to justify granting them exclusivity. They may be satisfied with a vague promise of future consideration as exclusive licensees in those territories.
6. Metro would try for an agreement term of ten years. It was felt that Impecina computer and engineering capability was strong enough so they would not need Metro assistance after a few bids.

Surprisingly, the discussions reveal no explicit consideration given to the idea that Impecina may emerge someday as a multinational competitor.

In view of the uncertainty about how successful the licensee would actually be in securing orders and the uncertainty surrounding the Peruvian government's attitude, a safe strategy seemed to be to try and get as large a front-end fee as possible. Almost arbitrarily, a figure of $400,000 was proposed. (This was roughly 150 percent of the development costs plus the initial cost of transferring the technology to the licensee.) There would be sufficient margin for negotiations and to cover uncertainties. In order that the licensee's competitiveness not be diminished by the large lump-sum fee, a formula may be devised whereby the first five years' royalties could be reduced (see the following material).

The Formal Offer

The formal offer communicated in a telex a week later called for the following payment terms:

- A $400,000 lump-sum fee payable in two installments.
- A 2 percent royalty on any tanks constructed of a size over 100 feet in diameter, with up to one half of royalties owed in each of the first five years reduced by an amount up to $40,000 each year, without carryovers from year to year. The royalty percentage would apply to the total contract value less excavation, foundation, dikes, piping, instrumentation, and pumps.
- Agreement life of ten years.
- Metro to provide services to Impecina described in paragraph a (page 90) in consideration of the lump-sum and royalty fees.
- For additional services, described in paragraph b (page 90), Metro would provide personnel at up to $225 per day on request, plus travel and living costs while away from their place of business. The per-diem rates would be subject to escalation based on a representative cost index. There would be a ceiling placed on the number of man-days Impecina could request in any year.
- All payments to be made in U.S. dollars, net after all local, withholding, and other taxes.
- Impecina would receive exclusive rights for Peru and Colombia only, and nonexclusive rights for Morocco, Libya, Algeria, Argentina, Venezuela, Brazil, and Colombia. These could be converted to an exclusive basis on demonstration of sufficient business, in the future. For Peru and Colombia, Metro reserves the right to treat the agreement as nonexclusive if Impecina fails to get at least 30 percent of installed capacity of a type covered by the agreement.
- Impecina would have the right to sublicense only to any of its controlled subsidiaries.
- Impecina would supply free of charge to ICE all improvements made by it on the technology during the term of the agreement.
- Impecina would be entitled to advertise its association with Metro in assigned territories, on prior approval of ICE as to wording, form, and content.

The Final Agreement

ICE executives report that the Peruvians "did not bat an eyelash" at their demands and that an agreement was soon reached in a matter of weeks. The only significant change was Metro agreeing to take a lump sum of $300,000 (still a large margin over costs). Other changes were minor: Impecina to continue to receive benefit of further R&D; ICE to provide, at cost, construction engineer if specialized welding equipment was used; the per-diem fee fixed $200 per day (indexed by an average hourly wage escalation factor used by the U.S. Department of Labor); and the $300,000 lump-sum fee to be paid in installments over the first year.

In other respects, such as territory, royalty rate, exclusivity, travel allowances, etc., the agreement conformed with Metro's initial offer.

An Upset

The Peruvian government disallowed a ten-year agreement life. By then, both parties had gone too far to want to reopen the entire negotiations and Metro appears to have resigned itself to an agreement life of five years, with a further extension of another five years subject to mutual consent. Given Impecina's in-house engineering and computer capability, extension of the agreement life was a very open question.

Case 4: Marks and Spencer

J. Edward Sieff, president of Marks and Spencer, Ltd., sat in his office after a weekly meeting with his staff. He pondered about the future of his company and more specifically how it could maintain its growth and dominate the retail industry. During the staff meeting the major topic of discussion was the expansion of M & S to foreign markets. The United States retail market looked most favorable to many of the staff but Sieff had his reservations. During the mid-1970s the company had a lackluster experience in the Canadian retail market compared to the home market and this was still fresh on his mind.

Sieff was also aware of the French Printemps corporation's attempt to franchise into the U.S. market. Printemps had opened a store in Denver and had been struggling. The dominant French retailer was seeing powerful U.S. retailers opening stores in better locations near its fledgling, which squeezed the already weak operation.

M & S learned from these attempts by other companies, and from its own experience, that the U.S. market is tough to break into. On April 12, 1987, M & S sent a team to the U.S. to study the different entry possibilities open to the company. It is now July 10, 1987, and the pressing problem on Edward Sieff's mind is how to be competitive in this new foreign market. Will the company's current marketing strategy and other policies be effective in the U.S. or should they be altered? Should M & S try, as they did in Canada, to expand the current M & S company under a different name (D'Allaird's, Peoples) directly to the U.S., should they franchise as Printemps tried, or should they just acquire their way into the U.S. markets?

Company Background

In 1884, a Polish immigrant named Michael Marks began visiting town markets in northern England. There he set up stalls that featured a sign that read, "Don't ask the price—it's a penny." This slogan became so popular he began to open more shops that featured goods that cost a penny. High turnover overcame the low margins, and the business began to flourish. In 1894 Marks took Thomas Spencer as a partner. By 1903 the company had forty branches, and it was in this year that Marks and Spencer, Ltd. was formed with headquarters in Manchester.

By 1908, both Marks and his partner Spencer had passed away and the business temporarily left the family control. In 1914, the founder's son Simon Marks regained control of the company with its then-140 branches. After that time the family maintained a tight lock on the company control. In fact, in 1974 there were no outside members on the board of directors. Currently three of seventeen board members are from the family.

M & S was founded and run with the strong personal values of its founders. There was a strong commitment to the customer and to the employees of the company. There was also a deep concern for the society in general that had made the company very popular. In 1924 Simon Marks visited the U.S. and saw the "super stores" that were prevalent here. He returned to England committed to making M & S a chain of super stores with continuous merchandise flow and a central organization sensitive to customer needs. In 1926, M & S went public, and by 1936 it was present in every major town in England.

In 1933 a welfare department was established to look after the employees' needs. In 1936 a pension fund was initiated for employees. Benefits of employment included dental and medical coverage as well as special treatment for chiropody (prevalent among people who stand a lot). The stores had special rooms for the staff to eat and relax.

In 1928 M & S had its own brand name (St. Michael) and was committed to selling only brand name products at moderate prices. Quality was also critical to the M & S way. To help maintain quality, M & S began to work very closely with its suppliers. Since the suppliers were generally small firms they were anxious to cooperate, M & S made sure that suppliers used the newest technology and continually managed to keep their costs down. This created quality products at the best margins possible. M & S has worked with some of its suppliers for over thirty years.

After WW II, M & S experienced phenomenal growth. The St. Michael brand name became synonymous with quality and value. M & S became the dominant force in its market and began a modernization and expansion strategy. In 1956 there was large concern over the increase of overhead as the company grew. This concern resulted in a plan to reduce the bureaucracy and paperwork at the company. This plan was called "Operation Simplification." The emphasis management was to increase sales while not increasing overhead. M & S began to look everywhere to improve the efficiency of operation. The company eliminated 120 tons of paperwork each year. The number of company staff declined from 32,000 to 22,000. Managers were freed to personally get involved with their departments. Since that time, the company has been leery of statistics and has counted on the "seeing eyes" and "critical minds" to make correct decisions.

The efficiency emphasis has become a part of the corporate culture. Through the 1970s, the officers literally ate, slept, and dressed M & S All executives wore only M & S clothing and worked about sixty hours a week. On their way home and on Saturdays they would drop in on stores to see how things had been going. This attitude was prevalent not only for management but also for all employees.

The employees of M & S were deeply committed to their jobs because the company was committed to them. M & S paid good wages and provided good benefits to its employees. The company sponsored social and recreational clubs for employees and the higher-level needs of the employees were met by listening to suggestions and providing challenging responsibilities. The company provided lunch rooms and meals for workers even during retirement. Some other important factors that promoted employee performance were teamwork and cross training.

The marketing at M & S was all based on the customer. Edward Sieff said: "The future of the business depends on quick imaginative study of what the people need, not on what the public can be persuaded to buy." M & S was committed to supplying the customers' needs for the long term. M & S offered a selective and streamlined range of products that turned over inventory very quickly. The company used the 80/20 rule that states 80 percent of revenue comes from 20 percent of their products. They prioritized their stock to the fastest-moving items. The company sold about 3,000 textile items and 700 food-related items. High quality at moderate prices was considered by customers to be "value for money." M & S originated with just one mark-up percentage for all items but has since allowed several different mark-up percentages depending on the items. M & S never held sales and only reduced slow-selling items for clearance. M & S also did very little advertising. They averaged about 0.3 percent of dollar sales spent on advertising as compared to 2–3 percent in the U.S. Advertising was limited to information on new product lines and other changes made to a store. The executives at M & S believed that the items sold themselves and most publicity for the stores was passed by word of mouth. M & S did not in the past sponsor credit cards for purchases. It is only recently that credit cards can be used at M & S stores. One other M & S strength was the optimum locations they had for each of their stores.

M & S also had to work within strict government regulations and tax structures in England. Many officers at M & S spoke out against the government's "misguided interference."

M & S had a good financial position. They paid high dividends and had low equity. They also had low debt. M & S was the only retail store in the world that had a triple A Standard and Poors bond rating.

Company Statistics

M & S has been called by many the most successful retail chain in the world, with 269 stores in the U.K., nine others in Europe, and 230 stores in Canada. In the U.K., M & S controls a hefty 16 percent of the clothing market. The profit margins that M & S enjoys are some 20 percent higher than the U.S. industry average. For the year ending March 31, 1987, M & S earned $812 million before taxes on sales of $7.9 billion. This was a 16 percent increase from the previous year. Food by now represented 37 percent of sales but expansion in this area was slowing.

The Canadian Experience

M & S has not always enjoyed good planning, as their Canadian expansion proved. They have stores under the names Peoples, D'Allaird's, and M & S. The Canadian operation lost money for ten of its first fourteen years. Analysts say that M & S was a slow to read the Canadian customer and this resulted in most of the problems. For example, the stores in the U.K. do not have dressing rooms to try on clothing before purchasing it. This policy was a security measure adopted due to the shoplifting that was prevalent. In Canada, however, not having dressing rooms was a major deterrent to the customer.

Competition

The competition for M & S has always been stiff but they have been able to be dominant in all of their markets. In the U.K. they have intense customer loyalty and their competitors have difficulty creating this same commitment in their customers. The U.S. market is one of the most brutal retail markets in the world. The competition is powerful and difficult to dominate. U.S. competitors are very much in tune with their customers and are not afraid to spend ten time the amount M & S currently spends on advertising as a percentage of sales.

Case Considerations

The main consideration of the case is choosing the best way for M & S to enter the U.S. retail market. How should their current policies be adjusted, if at all, so they can be successful in this foreign market? Thought should be given to the best route to take for entering the market: franchise, acquisition, or building stores from scratch? What name should be used in the U.S. market? The reaction of powerful competitors in the U.S. must be examined if M & S is to make the U.S. a new growth market. How do U.S. customers and their preferences compare to U.K. customers?

Case 5: Hatfield Graphics, Inc.

In the spring of 1990, Mark Hunt, senior vice president of marketing at Hatfield Graphics, Inc. (HGI), was preparing an evaluation of the corporation's progress in penetrating overseas markets. While Hatfield's sales had been very respectable in their well-established European subsidiaries, Hunt was anxious to see the firm evaluate, penetrate, and develop some of the previously ignored markets in other parts of the world. He was particularly interested in China and the Eastern European countries, because he believed that these countries represented potentially large untapped markets for Hatfield products, especially in light of the lack of competition there. Hunt began to review the possible strategies the company could adopt to capture these markets.

Company Background

Hatfield Graphics, Inc., was organized in 1945. Headquartered in New Haven, Connecticut, it conducted its business through two principal subsidiaries: (1) the Hatfield Scientific Instrument Company, a manufacturer of computer-controlled drafting and plotting systems and turnkey interactive computer graphic design (IDS) and data management systems (DMS), and (2) Hatfield Garment Technology, Inc., a manufacturer of computer-controlled fabric cutting systems. In addition, the company owned about 54 percent interest in Ashi Engineering Development, Ltd., of Beersheba, Israel, whose principal products were electronic medical and dental instruments. The company's total sales in 1989 amounted to $148 million.

	1985	1986	1987	1988	1989
Drafting Systems	58%	55%	59%	54%	42%
Cutting Systems	30	22	30	25	32
IDS and DMS	8	18	7	17	23
Other	4	5	4	4	3
Total	100%	100%	100%	100%	100%

HGI's Businesses

Hatfield designed, manufactured, marketed, and serviced different computer-controlled drafting and cutting systems and provided software for its systems. Its principal businesses fell into three categories: drafting systems, cutting systems, and IDS and DMS. Following is the sales history of the company for five years.

Drafting Systems Hatfield's computer-controlled drafting systems were used primarily to produce finished engineering drawings and graphic artwork many times faster and more accurately than a draftsman could do the same work. A drafting system was composed of a control unit and a plotter. The control unit was computer programmed to receive instructions from an input device, such as a magnetic tape reader, and to process the information and issue commands to drive the plotter. The plotter was an electromechanical device that moved the drafting tool over the drafting medium. Hatfield produced a variety of plotters of different sizes, speeds, and accuracy. Computer-controlled drafting systems were used to produce engineering drawings in an array of industries including the automotive, aerospace, shipbuilding, mapmaking, garment, and electronic industries. The price of such drafting systems, including control software and various accessories, ranged from $50,000 to $500,000. Hatfield had been engaged in the production of computer-controlled drafting systems for fifteen years.

Cutting Systems Hatfield produced computer-controlled cutting systems that provided quick and accurate cutting of a wide variety of fabrics for different industries. Multiple layers of material spread on a long table and compressed by a patented vacuum system were cut to the desired shape by a computer-controlled cutterhead containing a reciprocating knife. Depending on the particular application, the user realized significant savings in materials and cutting and sewing operations, and there was a significant improvement in productivity. A typical cutter system was priced anywhere from $325,000 to $550,000.

Interactive Design and Data Management Systems A typical IDS consisted of a mini-computer, a keyboard, a cathode ray tube display, and other devices such as a plotter and applications software. A primary function of an IDS was the preparation and recording of data involved in the design process. In manufacturing industries, a design begins with the creation of a mathematical model of a tangible item, such as a mechanical part. The IDS provided the means for a design engineer to construct a mathematical model of the part easily and quickly, to view the part in the form of a graphic display, and to make engineering changes. From this design data, an IDS could produce documents, such as engineering drawings and layouts, on microfilm, paper, or vellum, as well as generate bills for materials. Using the final design data, manufacturing engineers could use the IDS to generate numerical control tapes for automatic operation of the machine tools used to produce the part.

The IDS could be used by all industries and businesses requiring graphic design. In addition to designing mechanical products such as those found in the aerospace and automotive industries, IDS could be used in architectural design, mapmaking, design of printed circuit boards, electrical schematics, tooling design, plant layout, and various other applications.

Hatfield's DMS provided flexibility by linking several IDS into a single "distributed" interactive graphics system. This networking, which used the DMS computer, permitted different engineering and manufacturing groups to share a common design data base as well as the computing and data storage resources. The DMS also could be linked together and to large mainframe computers, thus providing very large storage and data management capacity and computer power to run complex analysis programs for an IDS. The software of Hatfield's DMS provided full security of the design data, so that only persons with appropriate clearance had access to the data.

Hatfield's IDS and DMS were available in a large number of configurations, permitting each system to be tailored to a customer's particular requirements.

Research and Development

Hatfield had major research and development programs in effect, in both hardware and software. The objective of these programs was to create new products and improve, as well as modify, existing products for Hatfield's present customers. Research and development expenditures amounted to $3,270,000 in 1989. The company held more than 200 U.S. and more than 150 foreign patents.

Marketing

Hatfield's products were sold to end-users primarily through Hatfield's direct salesforce in the United States, through wholly owned subsidiaries in Western Europe, and through independent sales representatives in other areas. The Western European subsidiaries were headquartered in Belgium, Germany, and the United Kingdom, with sales personnel in other significant European countries. The subsidiaries served as sales representatives on a commission basis. Hatfield also had 54 percent interest in an Israeli company. In 1988, the company entered into agreements with Yokogawa Electric Works Ltd., Tokyo, which gave Yokogawa the exclusive right to manufacture and sell Hatfield's IDS and DMS in Japan, Korea, and Singapore.

Hatfield first began foreign sales and support activities through a combination of foreign sales agents and sales representatives. This gave Hatfield fast inroads into foreign markets because of its agents' and representatives' familiarity with the language, local industry, and business customs. Technical support and service for each sale, however, were handled by domestic personnel until local people could be trained as service personnel, usually employees of a subsidiary.

The first overseas offices, located in the United Kingdom and Brussels, were designed along the lines of the domestic sales organization. Each office operated independently and had both sales and service responsibility for its respective territory. Office staff were primarily composed of home nationals. Unfortunately, it was not long before serious personnel problems developed. Many employees complained of ambiguity in the channels of command and were unclear as to whether their loyalties were to the home office or the parent.

In view of these problems, Hatfield established wholly owned subsidiaries totally staffed by locals. The nationals naturally spoke the local language and were thought to be much more skilled in local sales techniques. They were also expected to have a competitive advantage over other foreign manufacturers because of their ability to deal on a local manufacturer to local customer basis.

Each overseas subsidiary was designed to support full sales, service, and manufacturing activities. Despite these capabilities, Hatfield conducted all manufacturing in the United States. Hunt explained:

> Back when we set up our subsidiaries, the cost of manufacturing overseas was lower due to a rather depressed wage scale. In addition, the U.S. dollar was overvalued relative to other currencies. However, the forecasts were for overseas wage rates to eventually climb beyond those in the United States and for the dollar to realign itself at a much lower level. For example, the average hourly wage rates in the United States were currently $17 to $18 with associated fringe benefits of 30 to 40 percent of total salary. Average hourly wages in Germany, by comparison, were $19 to $19.50 with fringe benefits amounting to 50 to 60 percent of salary.

Competition

Hatfield competed with a variety of companies, some of which were larger and had greater monetary resources. In the computer-controlled drafting systems, however, Hatfield was the major supplier in the United States, and one of the major suppliers in the Western European market. In other businesses, the company' position was among the major competitors. Approximately twelve companies offered turnkey interactive computer graphic design systems. Of those, Applican, Inc., Autotrol Technology Corporation, Calma Company, and ComputerVision Corporation were the formidable competitors.

Expansion into International Markets

According to Hunt, three ingredients are essential in marketing products overseas:

1. The entire corporation must make a commitment to export the product overseas. Exports of your product must be recognized as a vital part of your business and as a major growth area in the future. Anything less than a full, long-term emotional commitment to overseas markets will not be profitable for the company.
2. The product must offer something useful to the market you are entering. It must either be seriously looking for the product you are offering or be developed by proving to the end-user the benefits of the product.
3. The product must be adapted to its target market. Environmental differences, such as the different power requirements in Europe, require that the product be modified in order to be accepted by the user.

Hatfield first became involved in foreign markets through unsolicited orders from large European electronics firms looking to acquire the high-technology products that Hatfield manufactured and that were not available in their own countries. As these orders became a more significant part of Hatfield's total sales revenue, the company began to develop aggressively a sales and service organization to address the needs of these foreign customers.

The prospect of an established overseas market for Hatfield's products had many attractive characteristics. One of the most appealing of these was the potential for effectively lowering its per-unit research and development costs through increased unit sales.

Since Hatfield's products were highly specialized and required the most exact engineering, development costs were high and represented a substantial initial investment. An overseas market would allow the company to increase substantially their return on this investment.

The overseas market also offered an avenue by which they could increase the sales life expectancy of their products. "Many countries have not experienced the rapid advances in technology that we have in the United States," Hunt commented. "Some products considered nearly obsolete by our standards are thought to be state-of-the-art in foreign markets."

Finally, many industries that were the prime users of Hatfield products were growing at a much faster rate overseas than in the United States. The European market for so-called systems products, for example, was estimated to be growing at 20 percent per year.

Future International Markets for Hatfield Products

Hunt discussed the possibilities for future expansion of Hatfield's sales overseas. Continued growth could be expected in the well-established European market, although at a declining rate. With this forecast, Hatfield was considering the possibilities for development of a number of new markets, particularly those in China and the Eastern European countries.

Chinese Market China, as described by Hunt, would provide Hatfield with an outlet for his company's software and marketing systems within the nation's large garment industry. The Chinese garment industry, unlike its European counterparts, did not have a need for Hatfield's fast, accurate garment cutters because of China' abundant, cheap labor resource. Materials, however, were in constantly short supply and very expensive, accounting for 85 percent of the total cost of each garment. The China market, therefore, seemed a likely candidate for Hatfield's AM-1 marker grading systems. which automatically arranged and marked materials for manual cutting operations. In addition, Mr. Hunt felt that the market offered great potential when viewed against several other criteria.

A primary consideration was the overall size of the Chinese marketplace. The country, with a population of approximately one billion people (the largest in the world), had a workforce that increased by 20 million annually. The Chinese government was also supporting a national modernization program for specific industries. The garment industry, while not an immediate high priority in that program, hoped to gain increased government support over the next three to ten years. Hunt, therefore, foresaw an overall increase in demand for Hatfield products in China over the long term.

Eastern European Countries The Eastern European countries offered rich potential markets for Hatfield's products. Romania, in particular, had expressed interest in Hatfield equipment. United States and Romanian government regulations and red tape, however, caused extremely long and frustrating sales transactions. In a previous sale in 1981, the Romanian and United States governments delayed a signed order for three years. When the order was finally approved, Hatfield was obligated to manufacture a then-obsolete piece of equipment at great expense and little profit. Despite these admitted difficulties, Hunt felt that Hatfield was in a strong financial position to explore possibilities in the post-communist Eastern European countries, which promised a vast potential in the coming years.

How to Proceed

While the China and Eastern European markets appeared attractive, Hunt was not sure what entry strategy would be most desirable to make inroads into these markets. In addition, he wondered what information should be gathered to determine entry routes.

Case 6: Protective Devices Division

My name is Steve Ball. This story is true but all the names in it have been changed.

My job was Assistant Marketing Manager of the Protective Devices Division of Electronic Systems, Inc. (ESI). ESI was an electronics manufacturer whose major markets were in the aerospace industry. Protective Devices Division (PDD) was an acquisition in a fairly unrelated business, the intrusion alarm industry.

ESI's products were custom-engineered and required an electronics engineer to sell them. In contrast, PDD's products were sold in a commercial market. Although PDD's products were electronic, PDD's customers were fairly unsophisticated in electronics. Thus, PDD's markets were quite unlike any with which its parent corporation, ESI, had any experience.

ESI's sales were in the $80 million dollar range and PDD's were in the two million dollar range. PDD had about seventy-five employees.

My story begins one sunny, hot day in August when I was on vacation.

The phone rang. My General Manager, Andy Smith (see the Organizational Chart), was on the phone.

"Steve, this is Andy. Is your passport up-to-date?"

"Yes, it is, Andy."

"Good, something has come up here. I won't be able to take that European trip I had planned, so I want you to go in my place. Is that okay with you?"

"Oh sure Andy, I'll start planning for it right away."

When I hung up, I really had mixed feelings. It would be fun to go to Europe again. The itinerary included Germany, France, Sweden, and England. It

---

This case is printed here with the permission of the author, Robert M. Ballinger of Siena College, Loudonville, New York.

would be in September, so the weather should be pleasant. But, I also knew that now I would have to negotiate with our French distributor's manager, who was really upset with us. I'd hoped that since Andy got us in this mess that he would have the "pleasure" of dealing with Monsieur Dupuis. Also, I wondered why Andy skipped my immediate boss, Tom Daniels.

Two years before I had convinced Andy that we should exhibit at the Security Equipment Trade Show sponsored by the U.S. Department of Commerce at the U.S. Trade Center in Milan, Italy. At that time, we had not exported any products. I had recently joined PDD after having been employed by a competitor in the alarm manufacturing business in international marketing.

Although we did not find a distributor in Italy, we did obtain a good lead in France. I visited our prospective distributor, Systems de Securité (SDS), which placed a substantial trial order for ultrasonic intrusion detection systems. SDS asked for the usual exclusive agreement to market our products in France. Because ESI's corporate policy did not permit exclusive distributorships, I was not able to accept SDS' request. I was able to resolve this difficulty by promising to refer any inquiries to SDS that we received from France. This I did on a number of occasions. SDS was pleased with our equipment and re-ordered several times. Eventually we became so comfortable with SDS that we no longer required our sight drafts to be secured by SDS' letters of credit. The next year, SDS was our third largest customer, following two of the largest intrusion alarm installation companies in the United States.

About a year and a half after appointing SDS, the Telex rattled with a message from Paris. It was from another distributor which wished to import our products into France. In fact, they were sending a Bob Peters over to visit us in a week. I wanted to refer

EXHIBIT I Organizational Chart for Protective Devices Division

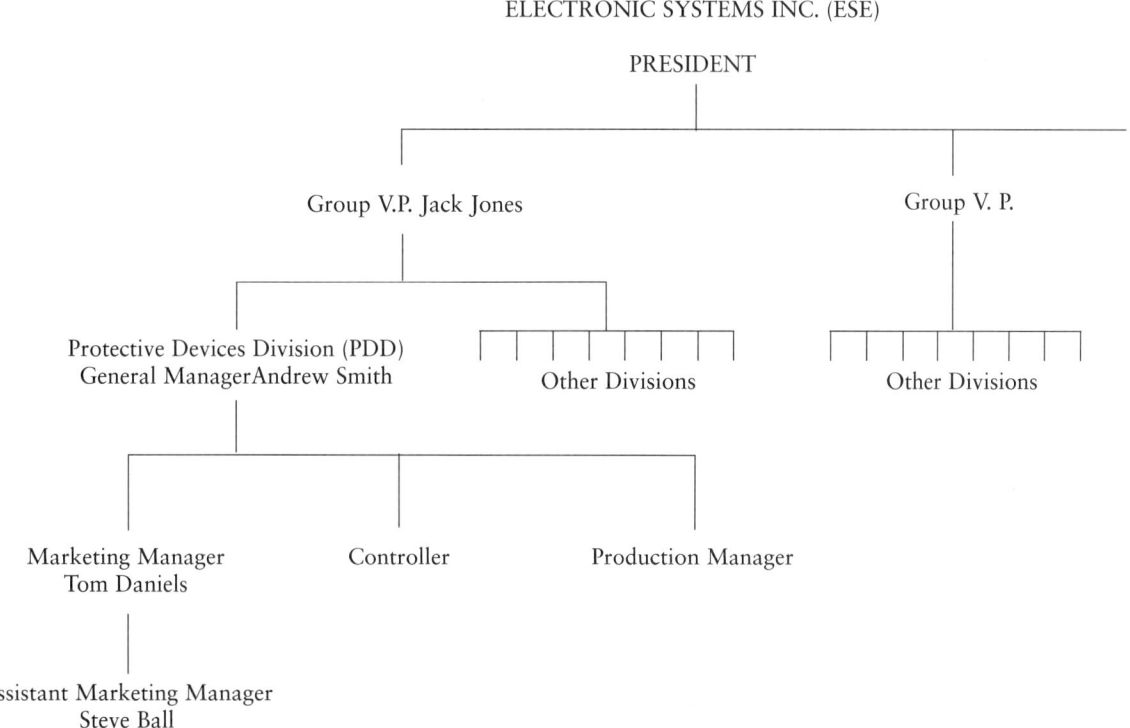

Peters to SDS but was overruled by Andy Smith.

> "Remember, Steve, ESI's Group Vice President, Jack Jones, was really adamant. He said there would be no exclusive distributorships and that means we have to talk to Bob Peters.
>
> "Well, Andy, I can tell you right now that the SDS people are going to be very upset if they see us going behind their back.
>
> "Oh heck, Steve, if they like our products, they'll continue to buy. Don't worry about it. We'll work something out."

Bob Peters visited the next week. He was an expatriate American who had lived in Paris for a number of years. He represented some wealthy businessmen who wanted to enter the alarm business. He claimed that the French market "had not yet been scratched." Bob made a good impression on everyone at PDD, even me. He placed a fairly significant order for some $30,000. At this time, SDS was purchasing about $100,000 of our products annually.

Although I later tried to get SDS to serve Peters' company, Peters continued to order directly from PDD. Meanwhile, our relations with SDS deteriorated.

First, SDS fell behind in paying their sight drafts. Second, they complained that some new PDD microwave intrusion detection systems they ordered did not work properly. In fact, the new system "false-alarmed." (It signaled the police that a protected building was being burglarized, but when the police responded, no evidence was found to indicate that a burglary had taken place. A few such occurrences are acceptable, but our new system was doing this much too often.)

At this time, we were no longer sure that SDS would continue to be a good distributor. Maybe Peters' group would be better, we thought. At least, it was easier to communicate with Peters than it was to communicate with SDS.

We then learned that another Security Equipment Show was to be held at the U.S. Trade Center in Paris. It seemed like a good idea to exhibit at this show to attract sales leads for our French distributors. Also, we could resolve the French distributor problem and perhaps find distributors for the other European countries.

Andy Smith decided to represent us in Paris, to visit ESI's subsidiary in England and to visit a German and a Swedish prospect. Although disappointed that I was not to make this trip, I also was gleeful that Andy would "have to work something out" with SDS.

This brings my story up to the point where the phone rang during my vacation.

I went to Europe as requested. First, I visited a German prospect near Frankfurt. Then, I took the Trans-European Express to Paris. Upon arrival, I attempted to contact Monsieur Dupuis. "He was not available." Bob Peters, however, welcomed me and I was taken around to see the sights of Paris by Peters and his French associates.

I then made sure that the exhibit was correctly installed at the U.S. Trade Center. After I repeatedly phoned Dupuis' office, he showed up at the exhibition without notice. He was furious.

> "Ball, you assured me that you would refer all your inquiries to SDS. But you have been dealing with this upstart Peters behind my back."
>
> "Now wait a minute, Monsieur Dupuis," I responded, "We did refer Peters to you but you chose not to deal with him. Furthermore, SDS has been delinquent in paying for about $50,000 on orders we shipped. What are you going to do about that?"

PART · 2

The Field of International Business

CHAPTER · 3

International Monetary System

CHAPTER FOCUS

After studying this chapter, you should be able to:

- Describe the development of today's international monetary system

- Explain how foreign exchange transactions are conducted

- Identify the problems associated with exchange rate fluctuations

- Discuss the balance of payments perspectives of the United States

- Explain the creation of Eurodollars and its monetary effect

This chapter examines the subject of international trade in monetary terms. Trade settlements involve topics such as determination of foreign exchange rates, balance of payments, foreign exchange transactions, international financial flows, and international financial and trade institutions.

Each country has its own currency through which it expresses the value of its goods. For international trade settlements, however, the various currencies of the world must be transformed from one into the other. This task is accomplished through foreign exchange markets.

Periodically, a country must review the status of its economic relations with the rest of the world in terms of its exports and imports, its exchange of various kinds of services, and its purchase and sale of different types of assets and other international payments or receipts and transfers. Such an overall review is necessary to ascertain if the country has a favorable or unfavorable monetary balance in relation to the rest of the world. In the post-World War II period, a number of institutions came into existence to monitor and assist countries, as necessary, in keeping their international financial commitments in order. As a result of the establishment of these institutions, a new system of international monetary relations emerged in the late 1950s. This institutional framework went a long way toward increasing international trade in the 1950s and 1960s. In the early 1970s, however, the weakening of the U.S. dollar caused the system to falter. The all-important commitment of the U.S. deserves mention here. In order to encourage worldwide monetary stability, the U.S. government agreed to exchange the dollar at the fixed price of $35 for an ounce of gold. With the value of the dollar stabilized, countries could deal in dollars without being constrained by currency fluctuations. Thus, the dollar became the common denominator in world trade. Because of the weakening of the dollar and other related issues, the monetary stability of the world was disturbed and remained unsettled into the 1970s and early 1980s. As the 1980s advanced, the U.S. economy stabilized and the value of the dollar, against other currencies, climbed to an all-time high, adversely affecting the U.S. trade balance. In the fall of 1985, leading industrialized countries joined in the U.S. effort to intervene in the foreign exchange markets to decrease the value of the dollar. The dollar continued to stay weak in the remaining years of the 1980s and in the early 1990s. It appears that the value of the dollar is unlikely to appreciate much to the year 2000.

The Development of Today's International Monetary System

Post-World War II financial developments had long-range effects on international financial arrangements, the role of gold, and the problems of adjustment of balance of payments disequilibria. Following World War II, a keen awareness of the need to achieve economic prosperity grew among nations. The war years had shattered Europe and Japan. They needed reconstruction. A number of countries were wresting political freedom from colonial rulers, particularly from Britain. It did not take long for these countries to realize that political freedom alone was not sufficient. Economic prosperity was not only necessary for existence but mandatory for long-term survival and growth. Countries realized that planned international cooperation fostered economic development and prosperity. Thus, immediately after the war, nations agreed to a framework of international rules—a code of behavior—to maintain monetary discipline and to ensure that dissenting nations did not frustrate economic development efforts through counteractions.

The Bretton Woods Conference

The negotiations to establish the postwar international monetary system took place at Bretton Woods, New Hampshire, in 1944. There was a general feeling at that time that the economically disastrous interwar period and, to an extent, the precipitation of World War II resulted from the failure to include economic factors as a major consideration in post–World War I planning. Thus, there was a strong determination to avoid the mistakes of the past and to adhere to goals that would bring economic prosperity.

The negotiators at Bretton Woods made certain recommendations in 1944:

- Each nation should be at liberty to use macroeconomic policies for full employment. (This tenet ruled out a return to the gold standard.)

- Free-floating exchange rates could not work. Their ineffectiveness had been demonstrated during the 1920s and 1930s. The extremes of both permanently fixed and free-floating rates should be avoided.

- A monetary system was needed that would recognize that exchange rates were both a national and an international concern.

The International Monetary Fund

After long and careful deliberations, a monetary system was agreed upon at Bretton Woods. Member countries agreed to control the limits of their exchange rates in a predetermined way. Under the original agreement, exchange rates were permitted to vary by one percent above or below par. As a country's rate of exchange attained or approached either limit, called "arbitrage support points," its central bank intervened in the market to prevent the rate from passing the limit. Market intervention required a nation to accumulate international reserves, composed of gold and foreign currencies, above normal trading requirements. An institution called the *International Monetary Fund (IMF)* was established at Bretton Woods to oversee the newly agreed upon monetary system. (See the appendix to this chapter for a more detailed discussion of the IMF.)

More and more nations joined the original 55 IMF signatories, so that today there are over 150 members. With the passage of time, various changes were made in the IMF system to ameliorate the difficulties that nations faced. For example, if a nation's fixed parity ceases to be realistic, it may therefore either overvalue or devalue its currency. In such cases, the IMF agreed on orderly and reasonable changes in parity based upon the initiative of the country concerned. Such a system of alterable pass is often termed "the adjustable peg."

There are several major accomplishments to the credit of the International Monetary System. For example, it:

- Sustained a rapidly increasing volume of trade and investment.

- Displayed flexibility in adapting to changes in international commerce.

- Proved to be efficient (even when there were decreasing percentages of reserves to trade).

- Proved to be hardy (it survived a number of pre-1971 crises, speculative and otherwise, and the down-and-up swings of several business cycles).
- Allowed a growing degree of international cooperation.
- Established a capacity to accommodate reforms and improvements.[1]

To an extent the fund served as an international central bank to help countries during periods of temporary balance-of-payments difficulties, by protecting their rates of exchange. Because of that, countries did not need to resort to exchange controls and other barriers to restrict world trade.

As time passed, it became evident that the fund's resources for providing short-term accommodation to countries in monetary difficulties were not sufficient. To resolve the situation, the fund, after much debate and long deliberations, created special drawing rights in 1969. *Special drawing rights (SDRs)*, sometimes called *paper gold*, are special account entries on the IMF books designed to provide additional liquidity to support growing world commerce. Although SDRs are a form of fiat money not convertible to gold, their gold value is guaranteed, which helps to ensure their acceptability. Initially SDRs worth $9.5 billion were created. By the end of 1992, $21.4 billion SDRs had been issued to member countries.[2]

Participant nations may use SDRs in a variety of ways: as a source of currency in a spot transaction, as a loan for clearing a financial obligation, as security for a loan, as a swap against currency, or in a forward exchange operation. A nation with a balance-of-payments need may use its SDRs to obtain usable currency from another nation designated by the fund. A participant also may use SDRs to make payments to the fund, such as repurchases. The fund itself may transfer SDRs to a participant for various purposes, including the transfer of SDRs instead of currency to a member using the fund's resources.

By providing a mechanism for international monetary cooperation, working to reduce restrictions to trade and capital flows, and helping members with their short-term balance-of-payments difficulties, the IMF makes a significant and unique contribution to human welfare and improved living standards throughout the world.

In the post–World War II period, in addition to IMF, a variety of other institutions came into existence to strengthen global trade and business and to promote economic development. The General Agreement on Tariffs and Trade (GATT), Organization for Economic Cooperation and Development (OECD), and Multilateral Development Banks (consisting of the World Bank family, i. e., International Bank for Reconstruction and Development, International Development Association, and the International Finance Corporation; the Inter-American Development Bank, the Asian Development Bank, and the African Development Bank). GATT (replaced by a new World Trading Organization) governed the trade of its member countries. OECD was organized for mutual cooperation in implementing the Marshall Plan, and now promotes economic growth of its member countries. The MDBs assist the growth of LDCs around the globe.

The IMF and the Debt Crisis

In the 1970s, developing nations all over the world found their efforts to manage their economic affairs swamped by a unique combination of adverse circumstances—dramatically increased oil prices followed by worldwide inflation, a collapse in commodity prices, the worst world recession since the 1930s, and historically high interest rates.

When oil prices shot up, these countries borrowed heavily at high interest rates to stave off economic dislocation.

Between 1974 and 1982, the two oil price shocks created a temporary savings surplus in high-income oil-exporting countries. Their surplus funds were recycled to developing countries. This process is now well understood. In addition to increasing their development aid, high-income oil-exporting countries placed much of their surplus oil revenue with international commercial banks in the form of short-term deposits. This contributed to raising liquidity in the international banking system because credit demand in the industrial countries had been depressed by the oil price shocks. Liquidity and monetary expansion in the industrial countries drove real interest rates down. It also prompted banks to compensate for the slack in their traditional markets by lending more to developing countries.

Commercial lending to developing countries—along with official lending and aid—grew very rapidly during this period. As a result, the total medium- and long-term debt of developing countries rose fourfold in nominal terms, from about $140 billion at the end of 1974 to about $560 billion in 1982. By the end of 1992, their indebtedness had reached $1.9 trillion.[3] Developing countries were happy to take advantage of this unaccustomed access to cheap loans with few strings attached. They stepped up their commercial borrowing. This enabled them to maintain domestic growth and to finance major public investment programs, especially in the energy sector. With hindsight, it is clear that lending and borrowing decisions were often imprudent and resulted in excessive indebtedness in a number of countries. New funds were often channeled into low-yielding investments. In a number of countries, borrowings fueled a flight of capital that drained the pool of resources for investment even as the burden of foreign debt mounted.

The debt crisis has had a profound impact on the economic performance of developing countries. One of the most urgent tasks facing the international community is to find ways of reducing the drag exerted by the continuing debt overhang on economic growth in the developing world.

There can be no simple, single solution to the debt problem; a comprehensive framework is needed. Its main objectives should be, first, to enable debtor countries to allocate more resources to investment and consumption and, second, to strengthen their creditworthiness, thus eventually permitting a resumption of voluntary commercial lending. Debtors and creditors alike stand to gain from such an approach.[4] As creditworthiness is restored, the secondary-market discounts on outstanding debt—which exceed 50 percent for many of the highly indebted countries—would drop. Moreover, the debtors' improving growth prospects would enable them to import more from the industrial countries. That would assist in the global correction of external imbalances.

A framework to reduce the burden of debt must have two elements. First, the debtors need to grow faster and export more. Second, the cost of debt service must fall. With the right policies in both industrial and developing countries, these elements can go hand in hand.

While long-term solutions to the debt crisis are being examined, most countries have sought IMF assistance for debt relief. In the debt crisis, the fund assumed a new role as financial organizer for the troubled debtor nations. For example, the fund worked out a two-year program of austerity, currency devaluations, and domestic economic restructuring designed to produce sustained economic restructuring designed to produce sustained economic health for Brazil in 1982. It helped Brazil emerge from a $16 billion balance-of-payments deficit in 1982 to a $530 million surplus in 1984. The devaluations stopped capital flight and spurred exports, mainly of steel, shoes, textiles, and alcohol. In addition, steps to conserve energy slashed oil imports. Since then, Brazil has been able to service its over $100 billion debt.[5]

International Monetary Crisis in the 1970s

Toward the end of the 1960s, the American economy began to deteriorate. Inflation continued to increase, and unemployment became widespread. Subsequently, President Nixon announced on August 15, 1971, that the U.S. would not redeem dollars officially held in gold. In addition, the dollar was devalued in 1971 and again in 1973. Thus, starting with 1971, the dollar's link with gold was broken. The U.S. dollar began to float without any attachment to gold. The U.S. hoped this would force its trading partners to revalue their currencies. It was commonly held that many strong foreign currencies were undervalued, which gave them a substantial advantage against the dollar. Revaluation would have the effect of making the exports of revaluing countries like Japan and the then West Germany more expensive and their imports less expensive, thus working to reduce the U.S. balance-of-payments deficits.

Fixed Versus Floating Rates

In the 1960s, most monetarists considered fixed exchange rates to be the backbone of international financial cooperation and the stability of the international monetary system. Floating or "flexible" exchange rates were considered impractical. Today, however, all major nations have floating currencies.

In 1976, at an IMF meeting in Kingston, Jamaica, over 100 member nations reached consensus on amendments to the IMF Articles of Agreement that in effect accepted floating rates as the basis for the international monetary system.[6]

The amended agreement, while reaffirming the importance of international cooperation and exchange rate stability, recognized that such rate stability can only be achieved as the result of the stability in underlying economic and financial conditions. Exchange rate stability of any lasting duration cannot be imposed externally by adoption of the pegged exchange rates and heavy official intervention in the foreign exchange market.[7]

However, the merits attributed to floating exchange rates were not borne out. For example:

- When the floating exchange rates were introduced, it was said that balance-of-payments adjustments would be facilitated, but not only have imbalances not disappeared, they have become worse.

- It was thought that speculation would be curtailed. On the contrary, never has it assumed such proportions nor had such destabilizing effects.

- It was believed that market forces, left at last to their own devices, would determine the correct exchange-rate balance. But never have imbalances been so great, nor fluctuations so wide and erratic and so little justified by economic fundamentals.

- It was hoped that autonomy in economic and monetary policy would be preserved, allowing each country free choice of its monetary policy and rate of inflation. Facts have completely belied this illusion.

In the mid 1980s, the countries with primary responsibility for the world economy recognized the need for renewed international cooperation on monetary matters. Subsequently, in early 1987, the U.S., Japan, France, Britain, the then West Germany, Canada, and Italy concluded an accord, called the Louvre Agreements, on two complementary aspects: coordination of economic policy and more stable exchange rates. The seven signatories agreed to policies aimed at reducing their internal and external imbalances. For example, they agreed to intervene on exchange markets, if necessary.

Since then, the Louvre Agreements have been reconfirmed and adjusted as required by economic and market developments. Economic policy commitments have been adapted and strengthened, including those of central banks. Thus, a first milestone has been reached on the road to rebuilding an international monetary order, though it rests on the will and ability of governments to impose self-discipline. Beyond this stage, how might one envisage a true international monetary system with a standard unit of value, automatic mechanisms, and sanctions that would be beyond the control of the countries involved? The time is ripe for dispassionate consideration of this issue, since inflation has receded and the Louvre Agreements are at present working well.[8]

A new international monetary system, based on the spirit of the Louvre Agreements, may emerge in the latter half of the 1990s. In their 1991 annual meeting in Bangkok, the IMF members reaffirmed their commitment to exchange rate stability. The members called for the creation of a representative committee of ministers from developing and industrial countries to consider the reform and improvement of the international monetary system.

The world is undergoing tremendous changes in its economic and political spheres. In the midst of such changes, further adjustments and amendments will be necessary to reform the international monetary system in future years (see International Marketing Highlight 3.1).

Foreign Exchange

An international marketer needs to transact financial transfers across national lines in order to close deals. The financial transfers from one country to another are made through the medium of foreign exchange. This section examines the framework for dealing in foreign exchange and reviews problems and complexities associated with the foreign exchange system.

The Meaning of Foreign Exchange

Foreign exchange is the monetary mechanism by which transactions involving two or more currencies take place. Assume a Mexican representative imports a machine from Cincinnati Milacron, a U.S. manufacturer. The machine costs 1.2 million U.S. dollars. Commercial exchanges take place in the U.S. in dollars, in Mexico in pesos. But Cincinnati Milacron wants to be paid in U.S. dollars, not pesos. The Mexican importer, therefore, must buy U.S. dollars against pesos, that is, obtain foreign exchange or, more specifically, dollar exchange to pay Milacron. Thus, *foreign exchange* refers to the exchange of one country's money for another country's money.

International Marketing Highlight 3.1

Cooperation Remains the Watchword

The Louvre Accord may constitute the most important watershed in the post–Bretton Woods era. The major industrialized countries agreed not only to cooperate closely in foreign exchange markets but also to coordinate their macroeconomic policies toward commonly agreed goals—sustainable noninflationary growth and the elimination of external imbalances.

Monetary policy has been managed broadly within the framework of such international policy coordination. Fiscal policy, however, has been managed more independently, owing partly to domestic political constraints. As a result, monetary policy has been overburdened and its independence called into question.

We are confronted with a most difficult policy problem: how to incorporate fiscal policy discipline within the framework of international macroeconomic policy coordination. We have not solved this problem under either the Bretton Woods regime or the managed floating system.

Here, we should consider the issue of structural adjustment. It is, of course, important to promote more efficient resource allocation through structural reform, which may in turn contribute to achieving the aims of macroeconomic policy. At the same time, however, we should keep in mind that structural reforms are basically support measures, and not a substitute, for demand management policy. It is also important to understand that such reforms take time. This is what Japan has told the U.S. repeatedly in recent meetings and on other occasions. There may be no policymakers nowadays who have not become keen advocates of international policy coordination. We should be prepared to subordinate national interests to international objectives when necessary.

Source: Takeshi Ohta, "Beyond Bretton Woods," *Speaking of Japan*, March 1990, p. 18.

Related Terms   Transacting foreign exchange deals presents two problems. First, each country has its own methods and procedures for effecting foreign exchanges—usually developed by its central bank. The transactions themselves, however, take place through the banking system. Thus, both the methods and procedures of the central bank and commercial banking constraints must be thoroughly understood and followed to complete a foreign exchange transaction.

The second problem involves the fluctuation of the rates of exchange. Fluctuations in exchange rates are based on the supply and demand of different currencies. For example, back in the 1960s, a U.S. dollar could be exchanged for about five Swiss francs. In the early 1990s, this rate of exchange went down to as low as 1.3 Swiss francs for a U.S. dollar. Thus, a U.S. businessperson interested in Swiss currency has to pay much more today than in the 1960s. As a matter of fact, the rate of exchange between two countries can fluctuate from day to day. This produces a great deal of uncertainty since a businessperson cannot know the exact value of foreign obligations and claims.

To appreciate fully the complexities of foreign exchange, a few terms must be understood. Their understanding also will provide a historical perspective on the making of payments across national boundaries. The terms are gold standard, gold exchange standard, gold bullion standard, inconvertible currencies, and hard and soft currencies.

Gold standard refers to using gold as the medium of exchange for effecting foreign commercial transactions. Before World War I, most countries followed the gold standard. Private citizens were permitted to own gold, and it could be shipped in and out of the country by individuals or banks without government interference. After World War I, the gold standard was abandoned because gold holdings were concentrated in a few countries, which made international trade difficult to manage.

After the gold standard, many countries adopted the *gold exchange standard*, which means that the foreign exchange rate of a currency is set in relation to that country's gold holdings. The country on the gold exchange standard is able to buy in the free market its own currency when it falls in value and to sell it when it increases beyond a predetermined point. This mechanism facilitates minimizing fluctuations in foreign exchange value. Another way of maintaining a parity with gold is to be on the *gold bullion standard*, which amounts to holding an adequate quantity of gold in reserve in bar or bullion form to settle international transactions at the level of government. Under the gold bullion standard, private individuals are prohibited from possessing gold and it is no longer in coinage, but a government may deal in gold by buying and selling it. After World War II, most nations prohibited conversion of currency into gold. The phrase *inconvertible currencies* also refers to currencies that cannot be conveniently exchanged for other currencies. For example, currencies of a number of developing countries are inconvertible to U.S. dollars. Currencies may also be labeled as *hard and soft currencies: hard* are those in great demand; *soft* are relatively easily available. The currencies of the majority of developing countries are described as soft currencies as far as international transactions are concerned, while those of developed nations are hard currencies.

Exchange Rates

When countries were on the gold standard, the value of two currencies was determined on the basis of the gold content of each currency. (The technical term used to describe this procedure of determining relationship between two currencies is *par of exchange*.) For example, in the 1920s, a U.S. dollar had 23.22 grains of pure gold, while the British pound sterling had 113.0016 grains. Since the latter currency had 4.8665 times more fine gold than the American dollar, it was worth $4.8665.

For those countries off the gold standard, exchange rates are regulated by the central banks. Most countries, however, attempt to maintain a steady exchange rate. This is necessary to promote foreign trade. The base price of a currency is determined by the supply and demand of a currency.

The supply and demand of a currency is influenced by a variety of factors. For example, if a country continues to buy, year after year, more from other nations than it exports, the supply of its currency increases. Likewise, if a country spends overseas—say, to fight a war—its currency supply increases. Such increases adversely affect currency value, the base or market price.[9] (Table 3.1 lists the factors affecting the supply and demand of the U.S. dollar.)

The base or market price, however, may not be the real value of a currency since the central bank may set a different price in order to realize a stated set of objectives. For example, the value of the U.S. dollar was slowly deteriorating in the market in the 1960s, but President Johnson refused to devalue it.

Many countries set a lower value on their currency to encourage exports and/or to seek balance-of-payment adjustments. In other words, long-term objectives may lead a country to set a different value on its currency than the current market value. Incidentally, the IMF assists nations in arriving at a realistic value for their currency in relation to long- and short-term goals. Frequently, the fund pressures a country to value its currency at what seems to be an unacceptable level. For example, the IMF persuaded the Philippines to devalue its currency, the peso, in 1986, and India to devalue its rupee in 1991.

Conducting Foreign Exchange Transactions

Foreign exchange transactions may be conducted by governments via their central bank, brokers, commercial banks, or business corporations. Described here is the process that corporations follow to conduct foreign exchange dealings. Let us assume Boeing wishes to buy $300 million worth of Rolls Royce (British) jet engines for use in its new series of airplanes. Boeing needs to buy the equivalent of $300 million in British pound sterling to pay Rolls Royce for the engines. Boeing may buy the British currency either on the spot or in a forward market. In the spot transaction, the purchase is effected right away; forward buying is finalized at a predetermined future date. If the payment is to be made right away, Boeing will have no choice but to buy British pound sterling on the spot. However, if payment is to be made at a future date, Boeing may transact a forward deal. A forward deal will be preferable if British currency is currently available at a rate that is expected to increase by the time the payment is due. The forward deal will enable Boeing to buy British pound sterling at a future date at a currently agreed upon price.

TABLE 3.1 Factors Affecting the Supply and Demand of U.S. Dollars

THE FOLLOWING FACTORS INCREASE THE SUPPLY OF U.S. DOLLARS IN WORLD MARKETS	THE FOLLOWING FACTORS INCREASE THE DEMAND FOR U.S. DOLLARS IN WORLD MARKETS
1. Imports of merchandise	1. Exports of merchandise
2. Imports of gold and silver	2. Exports of gold and silver
3. Payments to foreign ships for freight and passenger service	3. Foreign payments to U.S. shippers
4. American tourist expenditures abroad	4. Foreign tourist expenditures in the U.S.
5. Banking and all other financial charges payable to foreigners	5. Banking and other financial charges receivable from foreigners
6. Interest and dividends due on American securities held abroad	6. Interest and dividends due on foreign securities held here
7. New purchases of foreign securities	7. New sale of American securities abroad
8. Repurchase and redemption of American securities held abroad	8. Repurchase and redemption of foreign securities held here
9. Transfer of American balances to foreign banks	9. Transfer of foreign balances to American banks
10. U.S. government grants and loans	

Whether the purchase is to be made on the spot or in the future, Boeing Company will contact a number of commercial banks to seek price quotations for British pound sterling in terms of the U.S. dollar. Usually, different banks will quote different prices. For example, a multinational bank like Citicorp might have acquired British pound sterling balances when British currency was priced very low. That bank would be able to offer a better price to Boeing than, say, Bank of America, which might not have British pound sterling on hand and would then have to buy it on the open market to satisfy Boeing's needs. The market might contain customers interested in exchanging British pound sterling for another currency, or a British bank might be willing to lend the local currency. Even when the British pound sterling must be bought from the market, one bank might quote a better price than the other. It all depends on the size of the transaction, the importance of the customer to the bank, the direction of the currency market, future prospects of the currency, and the bank's present financial position.[10] Other things being equal, Boeing would choose the bank providing the best price.

Many MNCs pointedly seek the foreign currencies of the countries in which they are active by making deals at advantageous times.[11] For example, if a currency is declining, a corporation would buy for future use. A U.S. corporation with excess cash on hand might buy a currency whose price is low in expectation of the price going up when the corporation would need U.S. dollars again. In this way, a corporation, through astute money management, can make money dealing in foreign exchange transactions (see International Marketing Highlight 3.2).

International Marketing Highlight 3.2

Shock from the Rise in Yen's Value

Sony's annual report for 1986 published an enviable listing of business achievements—new products, sales gains in major ranges, production and distribution rationalization, and strong performances by overseas subsidiaries. Yet the same report broke the bad news that net sales were down 7 percent, operating income had plummeted 75 percent, and net income had fallen 43 percent.

Where did the shock come from? Why the miserable results? Sony was the victim of a 40 percent rise in the yen's value against the dollar. Business excellence—doing all the right things, including protecting the value of revenues through forward currency contracts—had failed to shield the company from the ravages of foreign exchange rate turbulence.

Sony is not alone in having to inform its shareholders of disastrous results following adverse movements in exchange rates. Many other companies that are heavily dependent on international markets are also at the mercy of exchange rates. The auto industry is an obvious example. In 1987, Honda reported that "the strong yen . . . [made] it impossible to raise prices sufficiently to keep pace with currency movements . . . leading to significant declines in earnings." In 1986, Swedish forest products group MoDo cited the falling dollar's lead role in inducing a severe displacement of competitiveness in North American pulp markets. Volvo, Sanyo, Nissan, Matsushita, Philips, and Porsche have all suffered. Losses can come quickly and be painful.

Source: Staffan Hertzell and Christian Caspar, "Coping with Unpredictable Currencies," *The McKinsey Quarterly*, Summer 1988, p. 12.

Balance of Payments

The *balance of payments* of a country summarizes all the transactions that have taken place between its residents and foreigners in a given period, usually a year. The word *transactions* refers to exports and imports of goods and services, lending and borrowing of funds, remittances, and government aid and military expenditures. The term *residents* includes all individuals and business enterprises, including financial institutions, that are permanently residing within a country's borders, as well as government agencies at all levels. In other words, the balance of payments reflects the totality of a country's economic relations with the rest of the world: its trade in goods, its exchange of services, its purchase and sale of financial assets, and such important governmental transactions as foreign aid, military expenditures abroad, and the payment of reparation. Certain forces determine the volume of these transactions, how they are brought into balance, what problems arise when they fail to balance, and what policies are available to deal with those problems.

Recording Balance-of-Payments Transactions

Table 3.2 highlights the U.S. balance-of-payments position for the year 1993. The transactions are recorded in three categories: current account, capital account, and addendum. The balance-of-payments record is made on the basis of rules of debit and credit, similar to those in business accounting. For example, receipts are entered as credits, and payments as debits. Thus, exports, like sales, are entered as credits; imports, like purchases, are debits. All transactions affecting increases in assets, like direct investment abroad, or decreases in indebtedness, like the repayment of external debts, are recorded as credits. However, decreases in assets, like liquidation of foreign securities, and increases in liabilities, like borrowing abroad, are treated as debits.

The *current account* section shows U.S. trade in currently produced goods and services. The positive or negative sign preceding each figure indicates whether the transaction represents a gain (+) or a loss (−) of foreign currency. In merchandise transactions, there was a negative balance (of trade) in 1993, meaning the import of goods exceeded the export of goods by $84.3 billion. Line 4 shows the net effect of expenditures incurred by U.S. military installations abroad and the amount of foreign currency earned by selling armaments. Line 5 shows that in 1993 America spent $32.0 billion less on services (tourism, shipping, other) than foreigners spent in the U.S. Line 6 focuses on another major source of our foreign earnings, return on U.S. investments abroad.

The net result of all trading in goods and services is shown on Line 7. Lines 8–10 describe *unilateral transfers,* comprising private gifts to foreigners and official foreign aid. The current account balance ($76.0 billion in 1993) is shown on Line 11.

Lines 12–18 summarize the *capital* transactions. Line 12 shows that, on balance, Americans bought $31.3 billion more in assets abroad than private foreign investors bought in the U.S. (see the difference of Lines 13 and 14).

The whopping current account deficit combined with the surplus in the capital account left the U.S. with a fairly large balance-of-payments deficit (see Line 19).

Since the two accounts together should balance as a simple matter of arithmetic, the difference is considered a *statistical discrepancy* (Line 20). While part of this discrepancy is attributable to errors in data collection and computation, the major portion reflects the U.S. balance-of-payments deficit.

TABLE 3.2
U.S. Balance of Payments Accounts, 1993*

CURRENT ACCOUNT		
(1) Balance of trade		−$84.3
(2) Merchandise exports	+$448.2	
(3) Merchandise imports	−532.5	
(4) Net military transactions		−2.5
(5) Net services		+32.0
(6) Net income from investments		+10.1
(7) Balance on goods and services (Lines 1 plus 4 plus 5 plus 6)		−44.7
(8) Unilateral transfers		−31.3
(9) Private	−13.8	
(10) U.S. government (nonmilitary)	−17.5	
(11) Balance on current account (Lines 7 plus 8)		−76.0
CAPITAL ACCOUNT		
(12) Net private capital flows		+31.3
(13) Change in U.S. assets abroad	−48.8	
(14) Change in foreign assets in the U.S.	+80.1	
(15) Net governmental capital flows		+39.4
(16) Change in U.S. government assets	+0.9	
(17) Change in foreign official assets in the U.S.	+38.5	
(18) Balance on capital account (Lines 12 plus 15)		+70.7
ADDENDUM		
(19) Sum of Lines (11) and (18)		−5.3
(20) Statistical discrepancy		+5.3

*Figures in billions of dollars
Source: *Statistical Abstract of the United States: 1994* (Washington, D.C.: U.S. Department of Commerce), pp 794–95.

The balance-of-payments record may not strictly follow double-entry bookkeeping in that not every transaction gives rise to equal and offsetting debit and credit entries. Discrepancies will occur when particular balance-of-payments entries do not represent the movement of funds, but rather the movement of a document or other proof of obligation. Further, some international payments are unilateral or one-sided such as gifts, grants, and transfer payments. Payments of this type are entered as debits, and receipts as credits. Finally, instead of using the "T" account, the U.S. Department of Commerce posts all balance-of-payments transactions in a single column with debits preceded by minus signs and credits by no sign at all.

"Surplus" or "Deficit" Balance-of-Payments

In Table 3.2, with the help of the statistical discrepancy item, the entries added up to zero. This is the usual way of striking the balance. But if the balance adds up to zero, what determines whether a country has a payments deficit or payments surplus? The answer is somewhat complex: the "deficit" or "surplus" is worked out based not on the aggregate of all transactions in the balance-of-payments accounts, but on the net balance in certain selected categories.

Here is another way of explaining the determination of balance-of-payments status:

> The identification of a "surplus" or "deficit" therefore involves the segregation of certain items from the main body of the balance of payments as being different in some significant respect from the rest. The question of presenting and measuring the balance of payments can, thus, be posed in terms of the search for a suitable distinguishing principle or organizing concept for determining which items are to be placed in the main body of the balance of payments (above the line) and which are to be placed outside (below the line). Account being taken of errors and omissions..., both groups of items will net out to the same figure with opposite signs.
>
> Under such an "organizing concept," a negative balance (or an excess of debits over credits) for the transactions grouped above the line represents a balance-of-payments deficit, while a positive for the same group of transactions constitutes a balance-of-payments surplus.[12]

The fact that select transactions are included for determining the balance of payments raises the issue of which of the transactions should be considered. The IMF recommends that transactions be divided between regular and settlement (below-the-line) transactions. The regular transactions represent overseas involvement on a perpetual basis such as trade and service transactions. The settlement transactions are meant to settle the deficit or surplus that may be said to have been caused or produced by the above-the-line items—that is, transactions directed toward bringing about a balance.

In the case of the U.S., however, the distinction between the "regular" and the "settlement" items is quite difficult to make, for two reasons. First, the U.S. dollar plays a key role in international trade and finance even after its devaluation. For this reason, a number of transactions take place in U.S. dollars between other nations exclusive of the US. Second, foreign central banks, as well as the IMF, hold U.S. dollars as investments and as working balances to finance international trade and payments. With the complexities produced by these numbers, no single number can adequately describe the international position of the U.S. during any given period.

To illustrate the difficulty involved in compiling the "true" balance-of-payments figure for the U.S., consider the following case. Based on the balance-of-payments data, the dollar commonly was held to be overvalued in the 1980s. Rational analysis, however, shows that these data are suspect.[13] Official government statistics reveal that the U.S. has had continuous trade deficits since 1977. The trade deficit for 1985, for example, reached $150 billion. Further, with the exception of a very small surplus in 1980, the current account, a broader measure, has also been in deficit since 1977. Traditionally, nations with continuing balance-of-trade and current account deficits experience a drop in the international value of their currencies. Indeed, this is the basic adjustment mechanism in a floating exchange rate system. Yet, the U.S. until 1985 enjoyed a "strong" dollar. (In 1985, the United States' major trading partners agreed to bring the value of the dollar down.)

Balance-of-payments data are drawn from diverse sources, and serious gaps exist. Since debit and credit totals do not balance, statistical discrepancy is used as a residual, a balancing entry. If the account almost always had the same sign, and the dollar values were fairly consistent and relatively small, one could embrace the data with a strong degree of confidence. During the 1950s and most of the 1960s the statistical discrepancy was very small. From 1951 to 1959, the account bore a positive sign every year and the high/low values spanned roughly $1 billion. From 1960 to 1969, the entries all had negative signs and sparred some $2 billion.

During the 1970s, however, there were six years with negative signs and four with positive signs. Further, very large numbers began to appear. For example, the trade deficit of $25.5 billion in 1980 was accompanied by a statistical discrepancy entry of $29.5 billion. The $36 billion deficit in 1982 was accompanied by an error factor of $41.3 billion. Statistical discrepancy as a percentage of the trade balance ranged from 6.5 percent to 115.7 percent over the 1977–1983 period. Absolute annual swings in this account have been as high as $32 billion. These are huge sums, and the fluctuations are erratic. If, for example, one divides the statistical discrepancy figure by the current account balance, the results range from lows of 14 percent (1977) and 22 percent (1983) to less modest figures of 81 percent (1978) and 369 percent (1982) to a staggering 2,635 percent (1979). Consider how you might react to an accountant's report warranting a company's income statement as "accurate within 702 percent" (the ratio for 1980).

When statistical discrepancy fell by $32 billion during 1982–1983, some economists heaved a sigh of relief, maintaining that the $9.3 billion entry for 1983 was a much more "manageable" figure. Actually, such a fluctuation is hardly comforting, but instead reinforces the unreliability of the data. The U.S. deficits, for instance, could be far worse than they reportedly are or perhaps not as bad as they seem to be. We really do not know. To be sure, we need a better handle on the facts before initiating policy changes.

The United States Balance-of-Payments Position

Since World War II, the international transactions of the U.S. have shown enormous growth. In 1950, total receipts came to $10,203 million. Such transactions in 1960 amounted to $19,650 million; in 1970 to $42,969 million; and in 1992 to an estimated $148,000 million. Even after adjusting for inflation, this reflects a vast growth in international dealings by the U.S. with the rest of the world. This phenomenon is reflected in the upsurge in U.S. private foreign investment, the rise in U.S. government expenditures abroad, and the emergence of the U.S. dollar as the world's principal reserve and trading currency.

Another interesting development is the gradually growing deficit in the international accounts of the U.S. Historically, the U.S. has run a deficit in the international accounts in every year but two, 1957 and 1968. But in the 1950s, the deficits aroused no concern. As a matter of fact, these deficits (averaging about $1.3 billion annually) during 1950–1957 were characterized as "purposeful," for those were the days of dollar shortages. In 1958, the situation changed. That year, the deficit amounted to $3.4 billion and the U.S. had to provide gold worth $2.3 billion to offset part of the deficit. During 1957–1967, the deficits averaged $2.7 billion a year and the gold outflow averaged $1.1 billion a year. The 1970s saw a drastic worsening of the situation. The deficit on merchandise trade alone shot up from $2.3 billion in 1971 to about $144.3

billion in 1985. Since then, the situation has significantly improved. The deficit in 1993 was $116 billion (for further discussion on this topic, see Chapter 17).

In recent years, the U.S. government began to adopt a variety of measures to improve the balance-of-payments position. For example, U.S. exports have been encouraged at all levels. Further, as the U.S. economy is restructured via new investments and technology, the productivity has risen to make U.S. products competitive abroad. Similarly, efforts have been made through persuasion and negotiations to limit Japanese exports to the U.S. Finally, the efforts to bring the value of U.S. dollar down by intervening in the financial markets has made U.S. products competitive in the export markets.[14]

Eurodollars

The term *Eurodollars* refers to U.S. dollars accumulated over the years by European banks and other banks outside the US. Since these dollars are outside the jurisdiction of the U.S. government, the European banks are free to deal in them without any restriction.

In addition to the U.S. dollars acquired by banks with their own or foreign currency, Eurodollars also come into existence when a domestic or foreign holder of dollar demand deposits in the U.S. places them on deposit in a bank outside the U.S.

Usually banks are supposed to maintain certain reserves in some proportion to their deposits to protect their depositors. But dollar borrowing and lending can be done anywhere in the world without being subject to certain costly regulation imposed by the U.S. authorities on banks at home, particularly reserve requirements.

The Eurodollars reached a substantial amount in early 1970. The total deposits were greater than the total gold reserves held by governments. It is estimated that in 1995, Eurodollars, or "stateless money" as they are sometimes called, will increase from $1.2 trillion to $1.5 trillion.[15] The size of this amount can only be considered by relating it to the fact that total gold reserves held by governments are about $40 billion.

While the "offshore market" initially was created in U.S. dollars, today a number of other currencies are freely deposited and borrowed outside their home bases. These are the German mark, the Swiss Franc, the British pound sterling, and the French franc. As time passes, monetary authorities see the problem related not to the Eurodollar alone, but the *Eurocurrencies*.

The prefix "Euro," incidentally, does not limit the dealings in Eurodollars (or Eurocurrencies) to Europe alone. It just happens that the market for the expatriate U.S. dollar grew up in Europe and that most of the dealing in Eurodollars was done by banks in London or in other European financial centers. Thus, the term *Eurodollar* has been loosely applied to deposits in Toronto, Rio de Janeiro, Hong Kong, Singapore, and Kuala Lumpur.

The market in "Asian dollars" is really only an offshoot of the Eurodollar market. The Asian market deals in U.S. dollars (and other leading currencies) deposited in local banks, and then lends them to Asian borrowers. Pioneered by the Bank of America in Singapore in 1968, the Asian market has since grown rapidly because of the deliberate relaxation of banking regulation and reserve requirements by the governments of Singapore and Malaysia.

Monetary Effect of Eurodollars

Eurodollars often have been blamed for U.S. inflation and in part for the decline in the value of the U.S. dollar. Further, the Eurodollar has been thought to represent "loose" money that could lead to the collapse of worldwide money markets.[16]

While opinions differ, the problems attributed to Eurodollars are not fully documented. From the vantage point of the U.S., however, the Eurodollar affects domestic monetary arrangements in two ways. First, the Eurodollar leads to a shift in the U.S. deposit structure. To resolve this problem the U.S. government in 1969 regulated reserve requirements on U.S. demand deposits held by both foreign branches of domestic banks and foreign banks. Thus, the first effect has been partially mitigated. Second, competition between U.S. banks can cause one bank to lose reserves to another as the result of Eurodollar activity. Since regulated interest ceilings prevent direct competition, a bank must compete aggressively through the provision of monetary services. This tends to increase the cost of funds for U.S. banks.

Overall, the Eurodollar market augments the world money supply, which increases the price of traded goods. It is difficult, however, to estimate the net addition of Eurodollars to the world money supply. Portions of the reserve balances of foreign countries, as well as that of the U.S., support the operations of Eurodollar banks. Although the Eurodollar market lowers the effective ratio of reserves to deposits, the base assets support a substantial volume of conventional bank liabilities—which would cause difficulty were the Eurodollar market to vanish. The implication is that inflationary forces emanate not from institutional weakness in the Eurodollar market but from the combined policies of central banks worldwide.

Current and Emerging Issues

This section briefly examines the current strains on the world monetary system and attempts to project forthcoming events in the 1990s and beyond. Although the world has overcome the crisis created by the 1973–1974 oil price increase, new trends seem pertinent to the future.

In recent years, OPEC has shown a decline in its surplus. OPEC may take measures in the 1990s to prevent a recurrence of the erosion. This may lead to a further increase in the price of oil and a continuing need to recycle funds from oil exporters to the rest of the world. On the other hand, if the price of oil continues to decline, many oil-producing countries, Nigeria and Mexico, for example, may face new difficulties.

A large number of countries lived through the 1970s by means of heavy borrowing. At the same time, their ability to repay debts declined. International bankers in the last few years were stunned by the inability of these countries to service and repay their debts. Although IMF assistance has helped many nations in meeting the immediate crisis, the debt problem is likely to linger on for many years.

The private international bankers are already overcommitted, especially in developing countries. These institutions may be unwilling to go much further in accommodating the growing needs of the LDCs in the 1990s.

Persistently high U.S. trade and budget deficits, and the growing concern about them at both governmental and public levels, could lead to moderate growth in the economies of LDCs in the 1990s. This eventually would result in less-buoyant export markets for the developing countries.

The Vulnerability of the International Financial System

Since the first oil crisis in 1973, international banking has become a dominant force in the international monetary and financial structure. This evolution has occurred in the following manner. The unspent surplus balances of the oil producers were mainly deposited in U.S. and European banks, while the banks played a crucial role in meeting the increasing financial needs of non-oil developing countries. The volume of international bank loans increased from $320 billion at the end of 1973 to $1,148 billion at the end of 1983, and to $2,143 billion at the end of 1993.

The vital role that private banks played in salvaging the developing countries in the 1970s has had the following consequences.[17]

1. The banks find it difficult to meet their normal obligations with short-term maturity funds.
2. Inflation has caused their capital ratios to decline.
3. They are rapidly running up against countries' borrowing limits, which were legally imposed or internally set for the containment of risks.
4. A large proportion of the loans are concentrated in potentially vulnerable countries like Zaire and Peru.
5. The profitability of international lending is declining.

The people involved with international banking are aware of the problems of the international financial system, and discussions have taken place in recent years about how to reduce international lending and liquidity risk. For example, it has been proposed that a *private safety net* be organized for individual banks to resort to in case of an emergency in terms of liquidity. Such an arrangement would ensure the stability of the system by an injection of liquidity, if, for some reason, the deposits were to dry up. The idea of a safety net, however, has been opposed by representatives of Third World countries. They fear such a measure would scare private banks that deal with the developing countries. In the future, however, under the umbrella of IMF, some sort of multilateral agreement—a standby swap agreement between the IMF and each of the 20 or so major international banks—could be effected. Since a liquidity crisis very probably would be accompanied by an exchange crisis in which many banks of different nationalities might be involved, an international swap network would offer an adequate degree of security.

Summary

After World War II, an important realization about the future occurred among nations. For a secure future, national economies would have to be rebuilt and/or developed, and such a feat could only be accomplished through worldwide cooperation. Subsequently, a historic meeting of 55 nations took place at Bretton Woods, New Hampshire, to develop a monetary system that would ensure stable conditions for a healthy growth of the world economy. The International Monetary Fund (IMF) was originated to oversee the system. Essentially, the system controlled the limits on exchange rate movements in its member countries in a predetermined way. The exchange rates were permitted to vary by 1 percent above and below par. As a country's rate of exchange attained or approached either limit, the country's central bank intervened in the market to prevent the rate from passing the limits.

The IMF not only reviews the status of different economies, but also gives advice on how a nation can achieve monetary stability.

In times of temporary balance-of-payments deficits, countries can approach the IMF for short-term loans to weather the difficult period. The IMF's short-term accommodation, however, proved insufficient, and, therefore, special drawing rights (SDRs) have been created to provide additional liquidity.

Along with the IMF system, the U.S. used to guarantee to convert the U.S. dollar into gold at a fixed rate of $35 per ounce of gold. This guarantee helped countries to trade. As a matter of fact, many countries linked their national currencies to the U.S. dollar. In the early 1970s, however, the value of the U.S. dollar began to decline. Finally, the U.S. devalued its dollar twice and abandoned the fixed parity between its dollar and gold. Since then, all currencies have floated free, and their values fluctuate on the basis of supply and demand.

This chapter also examined the framework for transacting payments in foreign trade. When people import something, they must make payment to the exporter for it. Since the exporting country ordinarily has a different currency than the one used in the importing country, the importer must obtain the exporter's currency in order to pay for the imported good. The importer obtains the exporter's currency from a central bank. The central bank of the country sets an exchange value on its currency for the other currency. In this way, it is possible to determine how much the importer needs, in local currency, to pay the bank in order to receive the requisite amount of the exporter's currency.

Also discussed was the balance-of-payments concept. This term refers to a systematic record of the economic transactions of a nation during a given period between its residents and the rest of the world. In general, if a nation exports more than it imports, it will have a favorable balance of payment; if the reverse is true, the nation will have an unfavorable balance of payment.

This chapter also examined the accumulation of U.S. dollars in another form outside the U.S., i.e., Eurodollars. Eurodollars are U.S. dollars accumulated in Europe and in other parts of the world that are outside the regulatory jurisdiction of the U.S. government. Thus, their circulation becomes a matter of concern, since unlimited dealings in Eurodollars can lead to inflation.

Review Questions

1. What reasons led nations to seek international monetary stability? How does such stability help promote world trade?
2. How did the Bretton Woods agreement provide a stable monetary environment?
3. What are special drawing rights? Why were they created?
4. What led the U.S. to devalue its dollar?
5. Why is it desirable for a country to maintain a stable foreign exchange rate for its currency?
6. Define *balance of payment*. How does it differ from balance of trade? How accurate are the U.S. balance-of-payment records?
7. What difficulties do Eurodollars present? What steps have been taken by the U.S. to restrict the free flow of Eurodollars?

Creative Questions

1. Since its birth at the Bretton Woods Conference, has the role of the IMF in the world economy become less important? (For example, maintenance of fixed exchange rates.) What new role may the IMF play to continue to be a viable institution?
2. In the interest of increasing its exports, can a country devalue its currency indiscriminately? Is there a limit beyond which it may be counter-productive to devalue the currency? Why? Why don't the Japanese devalue the yen to help Japanese companies keep their export tempo?

Endnotes

1. *The Role and Function of the International Monetary Fund* (Washington, D.C.: International Monetary Fund, 1985), p. 2.
2. David D. Driscoll, *The IMF and the World Bank: How Do They Differ*. (Washington, D.C.: IMF, 1993), p. 8.
3. "To Fix or Float Exchange Rates," *The Economist*, August 7, 1993, p. 70. *Also see:* "Third World Debt," *Business Week*, January 23, 1988, p. 57.
4. John A. C. Congbeare, "On the Repudiation of Sovereign Debt: Sources of Stability and Risk," *Columbia Journal of World Business*, Summer/Spring 1990, pp. 46–52.
5. *See World Development Report 1993* (Washington, D.C.: The World Bank. 1993).
6. "Sisters in the Wood: A Survey of the IMF and the World Bank," *The Economist*, October 12, 1991, pp. 5–48.
7. *See* R. Bryant, *Money and Monetary Policy in Independent Nations* (Washington, D.C.: Brookings Institution, 1980).
8. *See* Edward Balladur, "Rebuilding an International Monetary System," *The Economist*, February 23, 1988, p. 28.
9. Robert G. Ruland and Timothy S. Doupink, "Foreign Currency Translation and the Behavior of Exchange Rates," *Journal of International Business Studies*, Fall 1988, pp. 461–76.
10. Arvind D. Jain and Douglas Nigh, "Politics and the International Lending Decisions of Banks," *Journal of International Business Studies*, Summer 1989, pp. 349–59.
11. Timothy A. Luehrman, "Exchange Rate Changes and the Distribution of Industry Value," *Journal of International Business Studies*, Fourth Quarter 1991, pp. 619–49.
12. Andrew Crockett, "Issues in the Use of Fund Resources," *Finance & Development*, June 1982, pp. 24–27.
13. See various issues of *Survey of Current Business*.
14. "Exports: 'This Show Has Legs,'" *Business Week*, September 19, 1994, p. 48.
15. "Sisters in the Wood: A Survey of the IMF and the World Bank," *Op. Cit.*
16. Ian H. Griddy, "Why Eurodollars Grow," *Columbia Journal of World Business*, Fall 1979, pp. 54–60.
17. Rainaldo Ossola, "The Vulnerability of the International Financial System: International Lending and Liquidity Risk," *Review of International Economics*, January 1980, pp. 292–305

CHAPTER 4

International Finance and Accounting

CHAPTER FOCUS

After studying this chapter, you should be able to:

■ Explain the implications of financial decisions on international marketing strategy

■ Describe the perspectives of international money management

■ Discuss how international investment decisions are made

■ Compare U.S. accounting practices with those followed in other nations

Today's multinational enterprises must deal with an international monetary system full of complexities, challenges, and risks. Finance managers and treasurers in particular play a key role in managing worldwide money matters. It is important for future marketing managers to possess insight into multinational finance and accounting functions. An international marketer must have an understanding and appreciation of the financial side of international business in order to make wise marketing-related decisions. For example, without such understanding, a marketing manager for an airplane manufacturer that is supplying 10 planes to a Mexican airline might accept routine negotiation for payment over 3 years in Mexican pesos. But a manager with international financial insight might foresee the depreciation of Mexican currency and opt for payment in U.S. dollars. The impact of the finance function on international marketing decisions can spell success or failure with each decision.

The financial objectives of a corporation typically constrain the latitude of a marketing manager. Marketers are affected by their companies' money management—the raising of money, the investing of money, the maintenance of liquidity, even lesser factors like the repatriation of funds from subsidiaries to parent corporations. The decisions of marketing managers also are affected by accounting considerations.

Implications of Financial Decisions on Marketing

A discussion of the financial aspects of multinational business in a marketing text may appear odd. But the fact is, an enterprise ultimately ventures across national boundaries for the enhancement of its long-term profitability. Therefore, financial commitments and their results deeply affect the marketing perspective of a business. While the relationship between finance and marketing functions is nothing new, in the realm of international business, financial considerations can bear more heavily on marketing decisions.

Marketing is affected both directly and indirectly by the international financial policies of the parent corporation. Transfer pricing policy, for example, has a significant, direct impact on marketing. While *transfer pricing* will be discussed thoroughly in Chapter 13, it means, in brief, setting prices for the transfer of goods, services, and technology between related affiliates in different countries. Such intrafirm transfer pricing is affected by many considerations such as fund positioning, income taxes, tariffs, and quotas; managerial incentives and evaluation; antitrust prosecution; the interest of joint-venture partners; and corporate bargaining power with suppliers and/or financial institutions. Many of these conflicting considerations have financial underpinnings.

Eventually, all marketing decisions that involve capital investment and/or other types of long-term financial commitment on the part of the parent corporation must be reviewed in the context of corporate international financial policy. For example, marketing wisdom might suggest improving the provision of after-sale services, which might entail manufacturing parts locally. But the latter could require substantial investment and transfer of technology. Considered in the context of overall financial goals, the parent may find it undesirable to invest in manufacturing spare parts and supplies in a host country. Or the parent may learn that another affiliate recently expanded capacity to manufacture the same parts may learn that another affiliate recently expanded capacity to manufacture the same parts, or that the political situation in the host country is discouraging to additional investments, and so on. In the end, the decision, which appeared potentially desirable based on marketing considerations, may be postponed or dropped when reviewed from the financial angle.

The financial strength of a company deeply affects marketing, particularly in the company's ability to maintain inventories. Making timely deliveries to customers could provide important competitive leverage in international business, particularly if inventory replenishment involves great distances and time. Similarly, marketing is affected by the company's ability to make economical bulk purchases of merchandise. The company's capacity to undertake promotion in the mass media to strengthen the brand, to commit resources to research and development for the timely introduction of new and improved products, or to make investment in developing cordial relationships with channels of distribution are all influenced by financial decisions. This intimate relationship between the two functions of finance and marketing requires basic knowledge of financial matters to conduct international marketing with expertise (see International Marketing Highlight 4.1).

Few companies, small or large, today can afford to disregard the growing importance of overseas markets as a source of corporate growth. Increasingly interdependent trade flows and growing government involvement in economic affairs make financial management a difficult function. The volatility of exchange rates further adds to the difficulty. Quite clearly, given these difficulties and the turbulent world environment of the 1990s, setting marketing strategies for a global corporation without the benefit of financial inputs is like looking through a pair of binoculars with one eye closed (see International Marketing Highlight 4.2).

International Marketing Highlight 4.1

How Volkswagen Lost It All

To illustrate the impact of exchange rate changes, a financial perspective on marketing, consider the case of Volkswagen. In the 1960s, VW experienced phenomenal growth. During 1960–1970, its annual sales increased from DM (deutsche mark) 4 billion to DM 15 billion and its exports increased manyfold. In the early 1960s, exports represented half of total sales; toward the end of the decade, exports had become two-thirds of its total sales. VW emerged as the largest automobile exporter in the world.

Volkswagen's success in the U.S. market was highly remarkable. Since their introduction in the U.S. market in the early 1950s, VW's vehicles (particularly the Beetle) had filled an important market niche, catering to price-sensitive consumers. To many Americans, the Beetle was the ideal economy vehicle.

Volkswagen's commitment to the U.S. market was never in doubt. With service support and corporate commitment, annual sales increased from 200,000 vehicles in 1960 to 600,000 vehicles by the end of the decade. In the early 1960s, the U.S. was VW's largest foreign customer—accounting for 30 percent of VW's exports—the U.S. market for imported cars was increasing and VW was getting an increasing share of a growing market. By 1970, when imported cars constituted 14 percent of the U.S. car market, VW's market share in the U.S. was 6 percent, compared with 3 percent in 1960.

Then came the decline, and by 1973 the losses were huge. In October 1969 the DM was revalued, and its full effect was felt in 1970. The revaluation of the DM weakened the competitive position of VW in all the export markets. Volkswagen's net earnings dropped from DM 330 million in 1969 to DM 190 million in 1970. In some European countries, considerable losses in market share were experienced. The DM was again revalued in 1971 and 1972, and by 1972 the DM's revaluation amounted to 40 percent over the 1969 figure. To partially offset currency change effects, VW prices were increased in the U.S., and as a result VW lost its market share. In 1971 alone, the losses in the U.S. due to currency changes were estimated to be DM 200 million.

The early 1970s saw the gradual and regular strengthening of the DM and, with it, the weakening of VW's position. VW's fortunes were inextricably linked with those of the DM: as the DM rose, VW's profits fell. A strong currency clearly weakens the position of the country's exporters; this is particularly true if they are catering to price-sensitive markets. As its annual report of 1972 poignantly recorded, "Exports account for more than two-thirds of the Volkswagen AG's total sales. Of all the world's leading automobile manufacturers, VW is therefore the one most affected by variations in exchange rates."

Stuart Perkins, the chief executive of VW's American subsidiary, was so frustrated and exasperated by the havoc currency changes were playing on his sales that he exploded: "I used to call the sales people and ask how sales were doing. Last quarter, my first move was to call the financial people and ask how the D-mark-to-dollar exchange rate was doing."

The final collapse came in 1973, when VW incurred a loss of DM 807 million. Cash flow plunged from DM 1,671 million in 1972 to DM 618 million in 1973. Equity dropped to 24 percent of assets, from 31 percent the previous year. There was a steady decline in sales in the U.S. market, from a high of 570,000 vehicles in 1968 to 200,000 vehicles in 1976. VW ended 1975 in the red, with losses of DM 160 million.

Currency changes affected VW in three ways. First, the DM revaluation vis-à-vis the dollar made VW's position very uncompetitive in the U.S., its biggest market. Second, the DM's revaluation in relation to other Western European currencies such as the pound sterling, the lira, and the French franc resulted in similar effects in those markets. VW found it increasingly difficult to compete in the U.K., France, and Italy. Third, within the [former] West German market, VW had to face increasing import competition, especially from Renault and Fiat. Because of the weakening of the French and Italian currencies, these automobiles became very competitive on the German market.

Source: Based on S. L. Srinivasulu, "Strategic Response to Foreign Exchange Risks," *Columbia Journal of World Business,* Spring 1981, pp. 13–24. Copyright 1981. Reprinted with permission.

Multinational Financial Management

The finance function has two principal aspects: (1) to provide the monetary wherewithal to do business and (2) to ensure an adequate financial return on the assets of the company commensurate with its objectives. Even in a strictly domestic business, the able management of funds and investment poses all sorts of problems. The problems relate to issues such as: What financial return is adequate? How should the return be

International Marketing Highlight 4.2

Marketing Transaction Example

Suppose that J.T. Enterprises, a small manufacturer of wooden block sets, discovers an opportunity to sell 1,000 cases of blocks to a toy company in France. Under the terms of the sale agreement, the company will export the blocks to France and receive payment in French francs in approximately 60 days. The company must then sell the francs in exchange for U.S. dollars.

The French company has agreed to pay all shipping costs as well as the going rate of $100 per case of blocks. On the day of the sale agreement (September 4, 1992) the exchange rate between U.S. dollars and French francs is .20777, which means that one franc is worth 20.777 cents U.S. Or, put another way, it takes 1/.20777 or 4.813 francs to equal one dollar. Thus, the French toy company agrees to pay J.T. Enterprises 481.3 francs per case (4.813 x 100) or 481,300 francs for the entire order (481.3 x 1,000).

The company enters into the agreement with great confidence. The actual cost of manufacturing and packing the blocks for sale is $75 per case. Thus, the company expects to realize a profit of $25,000 ($100 − $75 x 1,000). But, will the company actually realize this amount? Three possible situations could occur. First, the exchange rate may hold for the next 60 days. Second, the dollar could "weaken" in relation to the French franc within the next 60 days. And third, the dollar could "strengthen" in relation to the French franc in the next 60 days.

1. If the exchange rate between U.S. dollars and French francs holds at .20777, the company will indeed realize a profit of nearly $25,000. When it receives payment for the order, it can exchange 481,300 francs for $100,000 U.S. (with a slight amount of transaction costs).
2. If the dollar weakens relative to the French franc, then it takes less French francs to equal one US. dollar. This situation would be favorable to J.T. Enterprises. If, for example, the exchange rate was .26316 in 60 days, it would take only 1/.26316 or 3.800 francs to equal one U.S. dollar. Thus, the company could exchange 481,300 francs for $126,658 (481,300/3.800) and the profit realized would be approximately $51,658.
3. If, however, the dollar grows stronger relative to the French franc in the next 60 days, there will be a negative impact on the profit realized by J.T. Enterprises. For example, if the exchange rate fluctuates to .17241 on the day that the company receives its payment for the shipment, it will take 1/.17241 or 5.800 francs to equal one U.S. dollar. Thus, when the company makes the currency exchange it will receive only $82,983 (481,300/5.800) and profit realized will be approximately $7,893.

Given these examples it seems prudent for the company to take measures that will protect its anticipated profitability of $25,000 on the transaction. When a company fails to protect its profitability, it has what is known as an "open" position, that is, it's open or exposed to exchange rate risk. If, however, a company insures that it will receive the profit anticipated at the time of the sale agreement, it's said to have "covered" the exchange risk of the transaction.

Source: Nebraska Business Development Center Report, June 1993, p. 1.

defined? What sources of funds should be tapped? When should funds be raised? Where should funds be used? In the international arena, the problems multiply. Finance management must not only deal with different currencies and their fluctuating rates, but also allow for the vagaries of the economic and political environments of nations with varying perspectives. This section briefly examines various facets of the finance function and relates them to conducting business across national boundaries.

Financial Objectives

Consider the financial objectives of a MNC that manufactures different types of parts and accessories for the automotive industry and related markets.

Financial Goals

The corporation's measure of performance is the return on capital employed. Capital employed is the sum of all assets plus the accumulated reserves for depreciation.

It is recognized that not all operations are directly comparable, and targets for individual profit centers and operations will be set taking into account the nature of the operation, its performance plans, and its record of achievement against them.

Target profit performance shall consist of:

1. A competitive return on capital employed with a basic minimum pretax return of 15 percent, which shall be inflation adjusted from time to time.
2. An annual growth rate of pretax profits of at least 12 percent.

New projects and further capital commitments shall be subject to a minimum hurdle rate of 25 percent return on capital unless deemed otherwise necessary or desirable by the corporation in view of legal requirements or in the corporation's best long-term interest.

Emphasis on asset management at all levels will include annual targets for cash generation, capital expenditures, and balance sheet items, including inventory and receivables management.

Particular attention is drawn to the differences between actual cash-generating capacity and book results. Each group and profit center is expected to develop not only net cash-generating capacity for its own requirements, but also sufficient funds for the corporation to meet its high-priority investment commitments and opportunities.

In the corporation's international borders, differing tax treatments and currency-exchange matters make cash self-sufficiency even more important.

It is intended to repatriate surplus funds for redeployment by the corporation as required. As a guideline, the corporation intends each of its non-U.S.-dollar organizations to remit as dividends, or otherwise, an amount of its annual after-tax earnings equal to the same percentage that the corporation is currently paying from its consolidated after-tax income to its stockholders. Deviations from this policy may be expected when international restrictions exist or when it is in the corporation's best long-term interest.

Financial Limitations

1. Investment in net working capital of less than 35 percent of annual sales; investment in net fixed assets of less than 25 percent of annual sales.

2. Dividend payments of approximately 40 percent of earnings.
3. No significant dilution of shareholders' ownership.

This company has nicely blended the financial objectives for both domestic and international business. From every business deal it expects a minimum inflation-adjusted pretax return of 15 percent, a minimum annual growth of 12 percent in pretax profits, and a 25 percent return on capital from new projects—the hurdle rate. The company intends to regularly repatriate profits and duly provide for exchange rate fluctuations. The objectives clearly recognize the legal/political constraints that may be imposed by host governments, and the company is willing to accept deviations from its objectives to comply with the local environment.

The financial limitations, stated as a part of the objectives, provide guides for sources and uses of funds. The company wants to make rather substantial, regular dividend payments of approximately 40 percent. This means internal funds in the form of retained earnings will be limited for investment in growth. Also the company wants no significant dilution of shareholder's equity. It is possible then that equity capital will have to be considered as a last resort for raising money.

The objectives, as stated above, constitute the foundation for making financial decisions for that company. For example, in order to protect itself against exchange rate fluctuations, it might require managers in overseas subsidiaries to forecast regularly the exchange rates month-by-month for the upcoming six months. On the basis of those forecasts, corporate funds in a currency likely to be substantially depreciated would be utilized before funds in stronger currencies. To illustrate the point, in early 1990 the U.S. dollar continued to decline, and all indications pointed toward a further depreciation of the U.S. currency. At the same time, the Japanese yen continued to strengthen. Thus, in 1991 international financial managers had good reason to spend their dollar accumulations and save yen.

Likewise, the goal to repatriate profits suggests that a financial manager in a foreign subsidiary can only plan in part on meeting future investment needs from retained earnings. According to the financial objectives, a new project proposed in a subsidiary outside the U.S. need not be put through the channels for final approval by the corporate management if it does not expect to meet the hurdle rate. Thus, financial objectives affect investment decisions as well.[1]

Money Management

Money management deals with sources and uses of funds. Money management involves such considerations as how funds should be obtained (equity versus debt); in which currency a corporation or subsidiary should be responsible for raising funds; how the transfer of funds from one subsidiary to another or between a subsidiary and corporation should be handled; and in which financial instrument the funds should be invested and in which market. Prudent international money management requires minimizing the cost of funds and maximizing the return on investment over time by means of the best combination of currency of denomination and maturity characteristics of financial assets and liabilities. Such money management requirements are very complex in the international context. They require the formulation and revision of capital structure decisions for different entities, and budgets for intracompany funds transfer.[2]

Typically, a multinational enterprise is susceptible to three risks related to money management[3]: (1) the political risk of assets being taken over by the host country; (2)

the exchange risk whereby the value of the U.S. dollar changes with reference to the host-country currency; and (3) the translation risk whereby the corporate financial statements are required by SEC (United States Securities and Exchange Commission) regulations to be based on historical costs rather than current value.

The goal of an international money manager is to obtain finances for foreign projects in a way that minimizes after-tax interest costs and foreign exchange losses. The exchange rate parity theory suggests that international differentials in interest costs are offset by changes in foreign exchange rates; that is, the expected value for net financing costs will be equal for all currencies over any given time period, provided foreign exchange markets are efficient. Thus, it makes no difference which currency is used to finance a foreign project.

Assuming the exchange rate parity theory holds, a number of considerations such as tax policies favor the use of host-country financing. Many countries—Australia, Indonesia, South Africa, and Germany, for example—have no taxes on gains or losses arising from most long-term exchange transactions.[4] In some countries, gains and losses from long-term exchange transactions are subject to preferential capital gains tax rates or reserves treatment.[5] Furthermore, most countries apply some kind of surtax on foreign interest payments. These taxes are generally of the withholding sort and are usually available for rebate. A few countries, Argentina for example, even impose a separate tax on foreign interest payments. These taxes increase the cost of borrowing in U.S. dollars or other foreign currency.[6] Such policies encourage MNCs to prefer the use of host-country financing. As a matter of fact, many firms require that all foreign projects be financed in the currency of the host country.

The use of host-country currency for financing limits the foreign exchange exposure and, hence, the risk.[7] Experience in India is relevant here.[8] Traditionally, foreign investors did not think that India provided an opportunity for raising capital locally. Back in 1985, however, Honda Motor Company's issue was oversubscribed 165 times within a span of 72 hours. Similarly, Burroughs Corporation's stock and debenture issue was oversubscribed 30 times. In brief, even in many developing countries there is no shortage of local capital.

Translation risk still arises from foreign financing decisions. On the whole, however, such translation risk is less severe because, while exchange risk leads to a realizable gain or loss, translation risk is a paper gain or loss. Besides, the former is taxable, while the effects of translation risk are rarely taxable.[9] Thus, an effective argument can be made for host-country financing. The argument, however, is based on a variety of assumptions, both economic and noneconomic. In many LDCs, for example, the government may make it virtually impossible to raise money locally. In other situations, the local currency may be unusable. Thus, despite all the arguments advanced in favor of host-country financing, a company may be forced to seek funds in other markets.[10]

Although money management involves many facets, our discussion has been limited mainly to the question of host-country financing. For our purposes, however, such limited treatment of the subject is sufficient as all that is intended is to provide a bird's-eye view of money management.

Repatriation of Funds

In domestic business, an important financial decision made by a corporation is the establishment of dividend policy; that is, the amount of earnings to be distributed to the owners, the stockholders. Likewise, a multinational firm needs to formulate a strategy on remission of dividends from overseas affiliates to headquarters. According to Eiteman, Stonehill, and Moffett, the international dividend policy is determined by the following six factors:

1. Tax implications
2. Political risk
3. Foreign exchange risk
4. Age and size of affiliate
5. Availability of funds
6. Presence of joint venture partners[11]

Many countries—Germany, for example—tax retained earnings, which would yield higher dividend payouts. Countries that levy withholding taxes on dividends paid to a foreign parent, on the other hand, discourage distribution of earnings in the form of dividends. Taxes aside, in the case of countries exhibiting higher political risk, the parent might require the remission of all earnings minus funds needed for working capital and approved capital projects planned for the next few months. Such a perspective would more often apply to developing countries. Where political risk may not be an important factor to reckon with, the dividend policy will be based on availability and use of funds. For example, if funds are needed in the U.K., headquarters might decide to transfer its retained earnings from a German subsidiary to the U.K. rather than transferring funds from the U.S. An alternative to this would be the investment of funds in German marks.

Another factor that affects international dividend payment is foreign exchange risk. If the value of the host-country currency is expected to decline substantially, other things being equal, common business wisdom will direct conversion of funds into a strong currency. Age and size of affiliates also influence the dividend policy. Research on the subject showed that older affiliates provide a larger proportion of their earnings to the parent since their reinvestment needs decline with time. By the same token, recently established affiliates provide only marginal dividends. As far as size is concerned, larger firms usually have a formal policy for dividend payout, but small firms depend on ad hoc decisions. Finally, if a foreign affiliate is formed as a joint venture, the interests of local stockholders force the company to follow a more stable dividend policy because the worldwide corporate perspective cannot be pursued at the cost of valid claims by local investors who do not necessarily benefit from the global dividend strategy of the parent.

On the basis of the six factors listed and discussed, a multinational firm may follow either a *pooled strategy* or a *flexible strategy* for distribution of earnings generated by foreign affiliates.[12] The pooled strategy refers to a stated policy of remittance of profits to the parent on a regular basis. The flexible strategy, on the other hand, leaves the decision on dividends to factors operating at the time. The flexible strategy permits the parent to make the most viable use of funds vis-à-vis its long-term corporate objectives. Overall, the flexible approach in foreign earnings permits a better utilization of the total financial resources available and eventually leads to a higher level of inflow of funds to the parent company in all forms—dividends, royalties, and various fees.

Making International Investments

Successful international companies continue to be interested in growth prospects. They receive a variety of proposals from different sources that potentially could lead to investments abroad. These sources include company employees, unknown host-country firms, licensees, distributors, and joint-venture partners. Essentially, two processes of an investment proposal determine its fate: the selling of the proposal and its review. Proposal selling and reviewing go through a variety of formal and informal human interactions. The processes are significantly affected by the firm's internal politics—that is, factors such as who is backing the proposal, what the company's organization is, how company personalities interact—and by factors outside the firm. Ultimately, the winning strength of a proposal depends on the diligent work of those who prepare it (see Exhibit 4.1).

Selling an Investment Proposal

Depending on the organizational arrangements of the company, the selling job begins at the middle-management level in the international division or department. When an opportunity arises that seems worthwhile, the manager involved, usually the manager of international development, begins checking with colleagues in manufacturing, marketing, and legal departments in a very informal fashion on such matters as sales projections, manufacturing estimates, patents, and taxes. The manager would also apprise superiors of the forthcoming proposal.

Throughout the early investigatory period that leads up to a formal presentation of the proposal to an international executive, it is important to concentrate on the really critical matters involved. Although these vary somewhat from industry to industry, the overriding emphasis should be put on marketing, because it is in this area that major problems occur. Once the investigation has been completed, a formal proposal is developed and submitted to the head of the international section.

The international head will make a more detailed study of the proposed project with the objective of strengthening the proposal. The location of the investment, market estimates and sales forecasts, equipment costs, total capital required, sources of funding, raw materials availability, and human resources will be examined.[13] On the basis of this examination, the proposal is completed for submission to the corporate headquarters. Accompanied by a letter, the final proposal will include an appropriation request, an engineering report, the project proposal, and financial analysis. The letter activates the formal review procedure, first through the finance committee, and then through the board of directors.

Reviewing the Investment Proposal.

The nature of the review process is intimately related to the perspectives of a company's top management. Often the process and philosophy behind the review of investment opportunities change dramatically with a new person at the helm.[14] In any event, most companies have a comprehensive system for reviewing investment proposals.

While the review procedure may vary, all corporations strive to determine whether the investment will be sound and provide a long-term, lasting benefit for the owners. It is important that the chief executive or another top officer participate actively in the review process of individual major investment decisions from the viewpoint of the long-term strategic posture of the company.

EXHIBIT 4.1 Checklist for Getting an International Investment Proposal Approved

1. Check with all the people whose approval is needed.

2. Check with all the people *they* will call on for advice.

3. If possible, determine who is most important for which aspects of the proposal (but be careful not to categorize people too narrowly).

4. Sell at the highest possible level—there's nothing like having the president's office behind you from the opening whistle.

5. Establish "people priorities"—who, in descending order, is most important for passing on the project. (This will by no means necessarily be in order of rank.)

6. Set up a flexible "people timetable"—who should be won over in what order.

7. Think ahead as to what each person is going to want to know about the project, and program that into the project analysis. (As one executive put it, you should "do *their* homework" for *them*.)

8. Measure your proposal against *all* stated corporate policy objectives; although sales and profit objectives are the easy ones, don't forget others.

9. Identify any potential enemies to your project and any points of potential resistance, and then establish strategies, or at least mental contingency plans, for dealing with them.

10. Make sure that the investment proposal format corresponds exactly to that used for domestic proposals so as to avoid having it appear to be exotic and thereby attract special detailed scrutiny regarding risk.

11. Give careful thought to any objections that may be raised against your proposal.

12. Be sure you know where your allies stand at all times.

13. In terms of the proposal itself, check carefully that you have not overlooked any obviously important details. Then check for more subtle omissions, and be particularly aware of problem areas and weak points. Have a good idea of the margin of error in the estimates.

14. Anticipate as many objections as possible, but don't be defensive and show your refutations of the objections too hastily.

15. At all times, carefully monitor the pulse of the project's momentum. Momentum can change abruptly. Be ready to facilitate steady progress and to forestall hitches.

16. Be particularly wary of dangerous "parabusiness" environmental criticism of overseas projects, that is, qualitative or essentially subjective, negative social and political judgments. (A domestic officer wishing to shoot down an international proposal may revert to the very thing that is seldom, or rarely, considered for domestic investment proposals, namely, a careful analysis of the political and social climate.)

17. Try to keep the project moving forward at a deliberate speed. Don't let it get stalled in excessive reviewing.

The checklist in Exhibit 4.2 indicates the type of information needed for review in order to approve an international investment project. With this information, a framework for evaluating foreign investment projects can be laid out. In the final analysis, the evaluation should provide the cost-benefit effects of the project for the host country, parent corporation, and foreign subsidiary.

EXHIBIT 4.2 Checklist for Reviewing an International Investment Proposal

1. Carefully examine the record and predilections of the individual most directly responsible for the proposal. Is he or she chronically optimistic? Does he or she usually underestimate costs or overestimate future sales?

2. Who has been won over to her or his side? Why do certain managers support the proposal? Why do others oppose it?

3. Determine as best you can the politics of the situation and try to discount each aspect in your analysis.

4. Systematically review all the estimates and projections of the proposal.

5. Look at the details, but also sit back and broadly scrutinize the project. Does it hang together, not only in its details but also as a whole? Does it fit in with the company's long-term objectives?

6. Give particularly close attention to the most crucial elements in your industry—marketing, manufacturing, technical know-how, or financing.

7. Look for holes. Errors of omission are sometimes harder to spot than outright mistakes.

8. Probe the weak or questionable assumptions that lie behind the figures.

9. Make sure you don't overlook anybody on the corporate staff, or elsewhere in the company, whose advice would be useful and who should see the proposal.

10. Don't let the proposal get rapidly "railroaded" through the process without sufficiently careful analysis.

11. Make sure that the difficulties—present and future—of doing business in the country and region in question are not minimized. What about the future effects of nascent regional trade groups? Any serious chance of low-price competition from new sources, for example, in the Pacific Rim or Eastern Europe?

12. Take a hard look at the broad political, social, and financial prospects of the country involved. Can you foresee the possibility of anything like an Iraqi attack on Kuwait or European currency turmoil in 1992?

13. Look at the overall conditions of doing business in the country involved. What are the chances of price controls, nationalization of retail outlets (such as pharmacies are in Sweden), greater mandatory fringe benefits, new labor legislation, work permit problems (as exist in Switzerland)?

14. Test the key assumptions of the proposal by subjecting them to a test of their elasticity, and test the overall flexibility of the project by projecting the effects of changes on the project. Suppose, for example, that the sales forecast is off by 10 percent. What will that do to profitability?

International Accounting

Global economic interdependence and the existence of large, multinational enterprises create needs for measurement, information transfer, and evaluation of microinformation and macroinformation on an unprecedented scale. International accounting addresses these issues. Traditionally, the flow of information between the parent and its subsidiaries was limited. In the last 20 years or so, however, the communication of accounting data across national boundaries has increased enormously. The rapid development of computer capability, as well as achievements in the field of air travel and telecommunications, has made it possible for an MNC to assemble detailed data from its worldwide operations on short notice. But this raises the question of what information a parent corporation should request to serve both internal and external needs.

An international accounting system serves the same two basic purposes as domestic accounting. It provides information on the business conducted during a certain period and the results obtained. The first purpose is achieved through the income statement. The second purpose is accomplished through the balance sheet, which shows the position of a business, its assets, and its liabilities at a particular time. Accounting information is needed for the internal workings of the organization and to satisfy the requirements and expectations of the external community. But the internal contexts of an international corporation are obviously more complex and larger in scope. For internal purposes, accounting information must adhere to the needs of *both* the parent company and its foreign subsidiary. The internal use of information is related to decision making and control. This raises the question of how much of what information a corporation should compile in its internal accounting system. The external interest of corporate public (e.g., stockholders, governments, financial communities, labor, customers, creditors, and employees) in *both* the parent and host country should also be served adequately through accounting information. The external use of information creates the company image of an economic institution of significance for current and potential investors.

International Accounting Reports

The income statement and the balance sheet mainly constitute accounting reports all over the world. The emphasis placed on these statements, however, varies from country to country. In the U.S., for example, the income statement is of primary interest. This is so because most large U.S. corporations are publicly owned and stockholders' wealth depends primarily on stock market prices, which, in turn, are greatly affected by earnings per share. In Europe, however, as well as in Latin America and Asia, the major concerns are the ownership of wealth (rather than the generation of income) and the position of the firm vis-à-vis its assets and the claims against them. This view makes the balance sheet of primary importance among Europeans, Latin Americans, and Asians.

The format of an income statement and a balance sheet also varies among countries.[15] In the U.S. balance sheet liabilities appear on the right and assets on the left. But in most European countries, the order is reversed, liabilities appearing on the left and assets on the right. Along the same lines, non-U.S. balance sheets usually show fixed assets and stockholders' equity sections at the top, and current assets and current liabilities near the bottom. Such variations in format do not make a substantial difference in the information but simply indicate the styles and traditions adhered to in different parts of the world.

Another interesting facet of international accounting reports pertains to the information disclosed in them. By and large, in the U.S. much more information is disclosed than in accounting statements elsewhere. This is largely due to the requirements of the U.S. Securities and Exchange Commission, as well as the stock exchanges' listing requirements, particularly those of the New York Stock Exchange (see International Marketing Highlight 4.3). Among non-U.S. corporations, practices vary from country to country. Overall, European firms tend to maintain secrecy and disclose less than U.S. firms.[16]

International Marketing Highlight 4.3

Let the Investor Beware

So you want to invest overseas? That makes sense. After all, foreign stock markets often outperform the U.S. market. Now all you have to do is figure out what you're investing in.

It won't be easy. Disclosure and accounting rules overseas differ sharply from those in the U.S.—and also differ significantly among the foreign countries.

Only companies in the U.S. and Canada, for example, issue reports quarterly on profits and other key financial data. Most companies in Japan and Germany don't consolidate the financial data of majority-owned subsidiaries.

In some nations, the lack of a strong enforcement body like the Securities and Exchange Commission permits overseas companies to be more footloose and fancy-free with disclosures. Insider trading is often greeted with a wink by government regulators. In Holland, Spain, and France, where stock exchanges are relatively small, government regulation and oversight of company disclosures are very relaxed.

Source, The Wall Street Journal, September 22, 1989, p. R30.

Harmonization of International Accounting

In recent years there has been growing interest in making it more feasible to compare accounting information provided by multinational firms. Authorities on the subject, while discounting complete standardization and rejecting uniform accounting, recommend harmonization, which implies a reconciliation of different points of view. It is argued that harmonization of accounting would permit better communication of information in a form that could be interpreted and understood internationally.[17]

Multinational firms raise capital in different countries. It is desirable, therefore, that investors and creditors be provided common information in order to shape their investment decisions. Thus, a set of international accounting standards would facilitate the generation of common information. The principal force behind the accounting profession's attempt at harmonization has been the International Congress of Accountants (ICA). ICA, in its tenth meeting in Sidney in 1972, established the International Coordination Committee for the Accounting Profession (ICCAP) to provide leadership in the harmonization effort. One of the outcomes of ICCAP's efforts was the 1973 formation of the International Accounting Standards Committee (IASC), which was formed to (1) develop basic standards to be observed in presenting audited financial statements and (2) promote worldwide acceptance and observance of these standards.[18]

Very much in the manner of the Financial Accounting Standards Board (FASB) in the U.S., the IASC issues international accounting standards. By 1992, IASC had issued 44 standards.

The IASC has had only an indirect effect on the external financial reporting practices of U.S. multinational enterprises. The American Institute of CPAs (AICPA), for example, has pledged its best efforts to gain acceptance of IASC standards. Yet the FASB, not the AICPA, presently sets U.S. accounting standards and has done little to harmonize their standards with those of the IASC, nor has the IASC attempted to harmonize its pronouncements with those of the FASB. Thus, U.S. firms are bound by FASB, not IASC, standards and are not presently required to disclose whatever differences exist between these two sets of standards.

The IASC appears to have more influence with financial institutions in other countries. For example, the World Federation of Stock Exchanges has asked member exchanges to require compliance with IASC standards. In addition, the London Stock Exchange requires that listed companies conform with IASC standards.

The ultimate success of the IASC and its eventual effect on multinational enterprises depend primarily on the kinds of standards it issues. To be successful, the IASC must issue statements that either develop broad accounting principles acceptable to most countries or require disclosures that would enable users to compare more easily multinational enterprises.

Consolidation of Accounts

Most MNCs consolidate the accounting information from their different entities to present a single income statement and balance sheet for both parent and affiliates. The consolidation process is based on legal requirements of the parent company, information available from subsidiaries, and the practice established over time within the corporation. In the U.S., MNCs are generally required by law to consolidate the accounts of a subsidiary if the parent owns 50 percent or more of the affiliate. In order to publish consolidated financial statements within a reasonable time after the end of the parent corporation's financial year, the U.S. multinationals usually require the affiliates to prepare their accounts earlier. For example, if the parent's financial year ends on December 31, the subsidiaries may end their financial year on October 31. This way subsidiaries' financial accounts will be available to the parent by December 31 for consolidation with its own.

Most corporations have standard procedures for the subsidiaries to report their accounting information. Thus, the management of subsidiaries not only have to satisfy the legal accounting requirements of their host countries, but also make the information available in the required format demanded by their corporate headquarter.[19] Usually U.S. multinationals require their subsidiaries to submit quarterly accounts, comparing actual results against the standards. But some corporations request monthly accounts. Review meetings are held to examine the future outlook of the business, on the basis of such periodic information. The recent trend has been to seek as much detailed information on the subsidiaries' activities as feasible including, in addition to accounting information, data on markets, industry, climate, and economic environment.

National differences and delayed international standardization make it necessary for each multinational enterprise to deal individually with the issue of adequate

Summary

reporting (see International Marketing Highlight 4.4). Unfortunately, varying national approaches to inflation accounting, new regional requirements for consolidation, demands for social accounting data, and uncoordinated actions by international "standardizing" organizations create additional problems. Consequently, there is a great need for new developments in accounting theory and practice to provide adequate multinational information.

International Marketing Highlight 4.4

A Computer Comparison

To illustrate how tough it is to compare profit performance in different nations, three accounting professors at Rider College in Lawrenceville, New Jersey, set up a computer model of an imaginary company's financial reports in four countries. Starting with the same gross operating profit of $1.5 million, the company had net profit of $34,600 in the U.S., $260,600 in the U.K., $240,600 in Australia, and $10,402 in Germany—all because of varying accounting rules in each country.

Although many companies have worldwide operations, their financial results in different countries aren't comparable. This is a serious problem for accountants who may be called upon to analyze a foreign company's financial statements.

The results of companies in Japan, Germany, Switzerland, and Spain are among the most difficult to compare with those of their U.S. counterparts. In Japan and Germany, many corporations don't consolidate results of their majority-owned subsidiaries; in Switzerland and Spain, some concerns set up hidden reserves, which result in lower reported profits.

Investing in Korean companies can also be tricky. Some Korean companies create "special gains and losses" that sometimes don't relate to company successes or failures.

Source: *The Wall Street Journal*, September 22, 1989, p. R30.

Summary

International marketing decisions are deeply affected by the finance and accounting function; therefore, a brief review of their conduct in the international business field is in order. Essentially, international finance deals with the management of financial resources such as the sources and uses of funds and the remission of profits from subsidiaries. The underlying force behind finance decisions is a corporation's financial objectives. These objectives usually are defined in terms such as desired return on investment or assets, desired profit growth, hurdle rate (for accepting new projects), proportion of earnings desired to be paid in the form of dividends, and others.

With certain objectives given, a corporation can then decide how to raise funds—whether to borrow money or to make a stock offering; where to raise money—in the U.S. or in another capital market; and who should trigger certain actions—the parent or a subsidiary. Among other things, two important factors influence international finance decisions: (1) the varying and fluctuating exchange rates of different currencies and (2) the restrictions imposed by host countries on the transfer of funds. Thus, before the source of funds can be settled, the exchange rates of the countries where the funds are to be raised must be predicted. Then funds can be raised to avoid exchange losses on the one hand and to minimize the cost of capital on the other. Another factor that must be dealt with in money management is the political climate of the host country involved. If problems that may jeopardize the ownership of corporate funds can be foreseen, it might be desirable to transfer funds out of the country while there is still time, even at the cost of substantial exchange loss.

Remission of profits from one country to another is determined by such factors as tax implications, political risk, foreign exchange risk, age and size of affiliate, availability of funds, and presence of joint-venture partners. MNCs pursue either a pooled or flexible strategy in the matter of profit transfer from a subsidiary to the parent and/or to another subsidiary. The pooled strategy spells out profit to the parent by each subsidiary on a predetermined basis. The flexible strategy leaves the decision on remission of profits to the circumstances of the critical moment.

Marketing is affected by financial decisions in many ways. Among these, two deserve mention. One is the area of transfer pricing—the price that a subsidiary charges to another subsidiary belonging to the same parent for its goods, services, and technology. The second is that the approval of projects that seem crucial from a marketing standpoint may be denied because overall corporate financial objectives do not support the project.

The chapter described the process that companies follow in making international investment decisions. Most multinationals have a systematic procedure to receive, evaluate, and approve projects requiring capital expenditures. The presentation for approval of such projects is approached in two ways: the selling of an investment project and the review of an investment proposal.

The section on international accounting described the varying importance placed on the income statement and the balance sheet in different countries. For example, in the U.S. the income statement is considered of prime importance. In Europe, Asia, and Latin America, the balance sheet has a greater significance.

Accounting systems and procedures, although essentially following the double entry system, differ worldwide. Therefore, it is difficult to draw comparisons from the information provided in accounting reports. Efforts at harmonization of international accounting are being spearheaded by the International Accounting Standards Committee (IASC).

Review Questions

1. Describe the meaning of money management in the international context.
2. What risks does a multinational enterprise sometimes face in international money management?
3. What are the arguments for and against raising capital in host-country currency?
4. What factors determine international dividend policy?
5. Explain the meaning of transfer pricing. What factors affect transfer pricing?
6. What sorts of reports usually are included with a project proposal?
7. Explain why the income statement is considered important in the U.S. while the balance sheet is more crucial in Europe.
8. Why is more information usually disclosed by U.S. firms in their financial accounts than by their counterparts in Europe?

Creative Questions

1. The format of an income statement and a balance sheet in the U.S. varies from the conventions followed elsewhere in the world. What difference will it make if U.S. companies follow the practices pursued in other nations? Will it not make it easier for U.S. MNCs to consolidate their subsidiaries' accounts and interpret their performance?
2. What is ECU? Can a company raise money in ECUs? What are the pros and cons of such a decision?

Endnotes

1. *See* Steven J. Cochran and Igbal Mansur, "The Interrelationships Between U.S. and Foreign Equity Market Yields: Tests of Granger Causality," *Journal of International Business Studies*, Fourth Quarter 1991, pp. 723–36.

2. Helmut Hagemann, "Anticipate Your Long-Term Foreign Exchange Risks," *Harvard Business Review*, March–April 1977, p. 82.

3. Kwang Chul Lee and Cluik C. Y. Kwok, "Multinational Corporations vs. Domestic Corporations: International Environmental Factors and Determinants of Capital Structure," *Journal of International Business Studies*, Summer 1988, pp. 195–218.

4. *Investment, Licensing and Trading Conditions Abroad* (New York: Business International Corporation, 1989).

5. *See* Alan C. Shapiro, *Multinational Financial Management*, 3rd ed. (Boston: Allyn & Bacon, 1988), Chapter 13.

6. Lee H. Radebaugh and Sidney J. Gray, *International Accounting and Multinational Enterprises* (New York: John Wiley, 1993), Chapter 2.

7. Jongmoo Jay Choi, "Diversification, Exchange Risk, and Corporate International Investment," *Journal of International Business Studies*, Spring 1989, pp. 145–56.

8. Matt Miller, "India's Stock Market Is Soaring as Investors Snap up Spate of Issues by Foreign Firms," *The Asian Wall Street Journal Weekly*, September 9, 1985, p. 1. Also see "Indian Shares—Over Sensitive," *The Economist*, February 9, 1994, p. 80.

9. *See* William S. Sekely and J. Markham Collins, "Cultural Influences on International Capital Structure," *Journal of International Business Studies*, Spring 1988, pp. 87–100.

10. John D. Daniels and Lee H. Radebaugh, *International Business Environments and Operations*, 6th ed. (Reading, MA: Addison-Wesley, 1992), Chapters 3–6.

11. David Eitemann, Arthur I. Stonehill, and Michael M. Moffett, *Multinational Business Finance*, 6th ed. (New York: Addison Wesley, 1992), Chapter 19.

12. Alan C. Shapiro, *Multinational Financial Management*, 4th ed. (Boston: Allyn & Bacon, 1992), pp. 369–78.

13. Joshua Mendes, "Go Abroad for Bigger Returns," *Fortune*, 1993 Investor's Guide, p. 88.

14. *Evaluating New Projects Abroad*, Management Monographs No. 45 (New York: Business International Corporation, undated), pp. 14–15.

15. Timothy S. Doupink and Stephen B. Salter, "An Empirical Test of a Judgemental International Classification of Financial Reporting Practices," *Journal of International Business Studies*, Vol. 24, No. 1, 1993, pp. 41–60.

16. Frederick D. S. Choi and Vinod B. Bavishi, "A Crossnational Assessment of Management's Geographic Disclosures," *Working Paper* (Storrs, CT: Center for Transnational Accounting and Financial Research, University of Connecticut, 1983).

17. "MNCs Home Competitive Edge With Activity-Based Costing," *Business International*, January 29, 1991, p. 37.

18. Lee H. Radebaugh and Sidney J. Gray, *Op. cit.*, pp. 166–73.

19. Michael J. Kane and David A. Ricks, "The Impact of Transborder Data Flow Regulation on Large United States Based Corporations," *Columbia Journal of World Business*, Summer 1989, pp. 23–30.

CHAPTER 5

Regional Market Agreements

CHAPTER FOCUS

After studying this chapter, you should be able to:

- Describe the rationale behind regional market agreements

- Discuss how market agreements affect international marketing

- Examine the historical perspectives of market agreements

- Discuss the European Community and its various aspects such as the Europe 1992 program and the Monetary Union

- Describe other agreements, especially the North American Free Trade Agreement

A previous chapter discussed the worldwide postwar efforts to restore free trade. These efforts included the elimination of tariff barriers through the General Agreement on Tariffs and Trade (GATT) and stabilization of currencies through the International Monetary Fund (IMF). At the same time these efforts went forward on the international level, an interest in economic cooperation at the regional level also developed, resulting in different forms of market agreements. Regional economic cooperation is based on the premise that, while responding to global agreements to promote trade, nations in a region connected by historical, geographic, cultural, economic, and political affinities may be able to strike more intensive cooperative agreements for mutually beneficial economic advantages.

An outstanding example of regional economic cooperation is today's **European Union (EU)**, often called "the (European) Common Market."* At the time of development of the Marshall Plan, the U.S. strongly felt that European nations should seek an adequate economic integration to cope with the problems of reconstruction. Such economic integration, it was argued, would permit Western Europe to emerge both in a market the size of the U.S. and in the viable competitive position necessary for achieving economies of scale via mass production. Simultaneously, however, the self-interest of the U.S. was also a force in the initial stimulus for the European economic integration. The creation of a large, and at least homogeneous, market was certainly beneficial to U.S. corporations.

Economic cooperation has an effect on international marketing, and different forms of market agreements among nations have different effects. The international marketer should be aware of early attempts at regional cooperation and economic integration like the European Community and the cultivation of existing market agreements in different parts of the world.

Effects of Market Agreements on Marketing

Market agreements affect international marketing in a variety of ways. *First, the scope of the market is broadened.* For example, after the formation of the Common Market, the French market ceased to be just a French market; it became a part of the larger Common Market. Such an expanded market provides a *flexibility* that would not be feasible dealing with individual countries. For example, under one type of market agreement called a *free trade area agreement*, internal trade barriers among member countries are abolished and a company may move products from one country to another freely. This permits a company to achieve economies of scale not only in production but also in product promotion, distribution, and other aspects of business. For example, the establishment of the Common Market made it feasible for the Ford Motor Company to integrate its operations in Germany and Britain.

> A new management organization was created to make all the critical decisions for both the British and German companies. There were obvious operating economies in the

---

*Originally called the European Economic Community (EEC) in 1958, the name was changed in 1980 to European Community (EC), and in 1992 to European Union.

arrangement—the duplicate dealer organizations in third markets could be eliminated and responsibility went where the skill was: body development work was concentrated in Germany, power train development concentrated in Britain. The pooling cut the engineering bill in half for each company, provided economies of scale with double the volume in terms of purchase—commonization of purchase, common components—and provided the financial resources for a good product program at a really good price.[1]

Since the formation of the EU, U.S. business activity in the region has grown significantly. U.S. investment in the EU increased fourfold during the 1970s. In 1972, for example, 30 percent of U.S. investment in Canada had increased almost four times, while investment in the EU had gone up almost seven times to $212 billion. In 1992, EU investments in the U.S. amounted to nearly two-thirds of all foreign investments in the U.S., about $272 billion.

Second, market agreements change the nature of competition. For example, before the formation of the Common Market, many American MNCs found little local competition in Western Europe, but afterward local companies were encouraged to expand quickly. They became factors in the market, through mergers and such, with the encouragement of member governments. In the computer area, Siemens A.G. (German), Compagnie International pour L'Informatique (French), and Philips N.V. (Dutch) entered into a joint venture to compete effectively against IBM.

Despite IBM's best efforts, in 1985 the EU denied IBM the opportunity to join European firms for basic research to close Europe's technology gap with the U.S. and Japan. This research was sponsored to use Esprit, a $1 billion program focusing on basic information technology, and encourage Britain's ICL, France's Bull, Italy's Olivetti, former West Germany's Nixdorf, and the Netherlands Philips to cooperate with each other to compete against giants such as IBM.[2] Such cooperation among businesses need not necessarily be between companies of different nations. In Italy, for example, Montecatini and Edison companies merged to form Montedison.

Third, market-agreement firms expand through mergers and acquisitions and thereby become highly competitive outside their market area as well. For example, after the formulation of the Common Market, French and German companies were able to compete aggressively against U.S. and Japanese multinationals worldwide. Consider Airbus Industrié, a consortium of French, German, English, and Spanish companies formed in 1970. This company grabbed 30 percent of newcraft orders in 1991 in a short span at the cost of American airframe manufacturers.[3]

Finally, market-agreement countries are able to make decisions favorable to all member-country companies. It would not be feasible for an individual country to enforce such measures.[4] For example, Common Market antitrust policies could adversely affect an American company and its subsidiaries or licensees that previously had been given exclusive rights in, say, Italy and the Netherlands.

It is important to mention also that economic integration, while leading to a variety of benefits, can create some problems. Consider, for example, the potential for trouble with the freedom of labor movement within the European Union. With relatively poor countries like Spain and Portugal having joined the group, controversy over guest workers from these countries, in Germany in particular, is likely. In the long run, the freedom of labor movement may become illusory. Further, free entry for Spanish and Portuguese agricultural products has worsened the EU's agricultural problems, boosting output of such products as olive and citrus fruit and thus depressing prices. This is likely to put further pressure on the EU's budget, two-thirds of which is already spent on supporting farm subsidies.[5]

Another problem is the jeopardy into which existing agreements of a nation are thrown when it joins a market group.[6] Entry into the EU caused Great Britain's commitments to the Commonwealth to diminish. Agricultural overproduction and inefficiencies are always potentially controversial among member countries since no nation wants its output outpriced by cheap imports. As a matter of fact, agricultural exports have been a chief issue of conflict between the U.S. and the EU, and to a large extent have been responsible for the delay in concluding the Uruguay Round deadlock, as was discussed in Chapter 2.

A market agreement does not create a homogeneous market; it simply broadens the market base. Within the enlarged, heterogeneous market, segments ought to be identified for the development of effective marketing strategy—each segment served by a unique marketing mix. Such an approach might not be possible for each individual country, however, Many marketers erroneously thought that with the establishment of the Common Market, Western Europe would present a single homogeneous market.[7] While there apparently is not a homogeneous market of consumers, there are homogeneous segments within the Common Market that must be recognized and served through unique marketing programs.

Early Attempts at Regional Economic Integration

Current efforts toward regional economic integration among nations of the world began with the creation of the European Economic Community (EEC) in 1958, born through a long history of trial and deliberation. In 1948, the Organization for European Economic Cooperation (OEEC) was established to administer the Marshall Aid program. Very soon it became obvious to all concerned that European nations would have to seek some form of economic cooperation in order to emerge as a large autonomous market.

The drive toward European economic unity continued to gain momentum in the early 1950s, although many leaders doubted that perpetual cooperation, other than on an ad hoc basis, would ever be feasible. The proponents of the movement met with their first success with the establishment of the European Coal and Steel Community (ECSC) in 1952. The ECSC was created to develop a common market in coal, steel, and iron ore. The 6 countries participating in this effort were France, Germany, Italy, Belgium, the Netherlands, and Luxembourg. The success of the ECSC led these 6 nations to venture further into the 1958 establishment of the EEC and its long-term plans. Initially, it was established as a customs union that was gradually to include both industrial and agricultural goods and to lead to the abolition of restrictions on trade among member nations and the creation of common external tariffs. The EEC's organizers looked to eventual economic union among the member countries to enable free movement of people, services, and capital, and gradual development of common social, fiscal, and monetary policies.

Simultaneously with the formation of the EEC, another seven-nation regional group was established. Unable to come to agreement within the OEEC, U.K., Denmark,

Sweden, Norway, Switzerland, Austria, and Poland formed the European Free Trade Association (EFTA) in 1960.

With Europe as an example, regional agreements have come into existence all over the world—in Africa, in the Arab world, in Latin America, and in Asia. Communist countries also made their own regional cooperative arrangements.

The Bases of Cooperation

Economic cooperation among nations is mainly dictated by economic, political, geographic, and social factors. Nations may be willing to cooperate with each other simply as a matter of economic necessity.[8] For example, 77 countries located distantly around the world have joined together to form a group called the New International Economic Order (NIEO), which negotiates concessions from richer countries for the purpose of enhancing NIEO member trade.

Nations also may cooperate for political reasons. The Commonwealth is an interesting example of a political union of nations. Commonwealth countries are economically far apart from each other. For example, Australia is among the developed nations while Pakistan is a developing country. Geographically, the Commonwealth countries are spread over different continents. Canada is in North America, Great Britain in Europe, Nigeria in Africa, and India in Asia. Even some political similarities of the past are different today as nations pursue different political modes—Burma is a military dictatorship; New Zealand a democracy. The commonality of these nations is their historical partnership in the British Empire.

Geographic proximity is another factor that facilitates economic cooperation and integration among nations. Presumably countries in the same geographic region have a better appreciation of each other's strengths and weaknesses, and together they may come to realize synergies that would make them economically stronger. For example, a mass market is necessary for mass production. Nations located near each other would be better able to develop a mass market and could recognize this potential and join together. A notable example of such cooperation among nations in geographic proximity to one another was the formation of the European Union, or Common Market.

Finally, countries also may associate with each other on the basis of social customs, traditions, taboos, and culture. Arab countries, for example, share a long Islamic heritage. Such bonds favor economic union.

The Success of Cooperation

A question may be raised as to what factors account for the success of economic integration. Briefly, economic cooperation is likely to flourish when member countries have diverse products and raw materials. The most successful case of economic integration has been the European Union. Nations belonging the EU have more or less complementary economies, diverse industries, different natural resources, and varying agricultural bases. Further, it is desirable that member nations be of compatible economic status in terms of balance-of-payments position and level of development.

Types of Market Agreements

There are five principal forms of market agreements among nations: free trade area, customs union, common market, economic union, and political union. Such agreements are differentiated on several bases.

Types of Market Agreements

Free Trade Area (FTA)

The free trade area (FTA) type of agreement requires nations to remove all tariffs among the members. Let us assume there are three nations—A, B, and C—that agree to an FTA agreement and abolish all tariffs among themselves to permit free trade. Beyond the FTA, nations A, B, and C may impose tariffs as they choose. For example, if nation X trades extensively with nation B, nation B may have very low tariffs for goods imported from nation X while nations A and C impose high tariffs on goods from nation X. Under an FTA agreement, nation B is free to continue its *preferred* relationship with nation X while nations A and C are at liberty to decide their own external tariff policies. The European Free Trade Area (EFTA) and the Latin American Free Trade Area (LAFTA) illustrate the free trade area type of agreement.

Customs Union

A customs union, in addition to requiring abolition of internal tariffs among members, further obligates the members to establish common external tariffs.[9] To continue with example nations A, B, and C, under a customs union agreement (instead of an FTA), B would not be permitted to have a special relationship with nation X. Nations A, B, and C would have to have a common tariff policy toward X. A customs union agreement exists among Caribbean countries. Their cooperative effort started as a free trade area and later developed into a customs union. As mentioned earlier, the EU began as a customs union.

Common Market

In a common market type of agreement, members not only abolish internal tariffs among themselves and levy common external tariffs, but they also permit the free flow of all factors of production (capital, labor, technology) among themselves.[10] Our illustration nations A, B, and C, under a common market agreement, not only would remove all tariffs and quotas among themselves and impose common tariffs against other countries such as nation X, but also would allow capital and labor to move freely within their boundaries as if they were one nation. This means, for example, a resident of nation A is free to accept a position in nation C without a work permit. Likewise, an investor in nation B is at liberty to invest money in nations A, B, or C without restriction from either home or host government when transferring funds for investment.

Economic Union

Under the economic union arrangement, common market characteristics are combined with harmonization of economic policy. Member countries are expected to pursue common monetary and fiscal policies. Ordinarily this means synchronizing taxes, money supply, interest rates, and regulation of capital market, among other things. In effect, the economic union calls for a supranational authority to design an economic policy for an entire group of nations. The EU, to a great extent, can be called an economic union. This designation is justified by the fact that the union has a common agricultural policy and shares the European monetary system.

Political Union

A political union is the ultimate market agreement among nations. It includes the characteristics of economic union and requires, in addition, political harmony among the members. Essentially, it means nations merging with each other to form a new nation.

In its pure form, an example of the political union does not exist. In the 1950s, however, Egypt, Syria, and Yemen formed a short-lived political union. To an extent, the Commonwealth of Nations and perhaps the newly formed Commonwealth of Independent States can be characterized as politically based agreements. In the future, in a very limited sense, the EU with the European Parliament in place could be considered a political union.

Market Agreements in Force

Most current market agreements are organized by geography. Some agreements are not formed according to region, however, but extend over different geographic areas of the world.

Europe

European nations have been by far the most aggressive in seeking economic integration. They have formed the European Union, the European Free Trade Association, and the now-defunct Council for Mutual Economic Assistance.

European Union (EU) Often called the European Common Market, the agreement came into existence in January 1958. Its purpose was to abolish over a 12-year period all customs tariffs and other economic barriers among the 6 member countries: Germany, France, Italy, the Netherlands, Belgium and Luxembourg. In 1973, the U.K., Denmark, and Ireland joined the EU. Greece became a full member in 1982. Spain and Portugal joined the EU as full members on January 1, 1986. As it stands today, the EU is the world's largest exporter, producing over one-fourth of world exports.

The EU today represents a true customs union, having abolished all customs duties and restrictions on trade in industrial goods within the community while imposing common external tariffs and supporting free internal movement of labor and capital. In the area of agriculture, the EU has developed a protective common agricultural policy that consists of a support system designed to promote domestic agricultural production and guaranteed farm incomes.

The European Community's 1957 Rome Treaty called for the eventual formation of an economic union. While some progress has been made toward this end in the form of a common antitrust policy, complete economic and monetary union, not to mention political union, has a long way to go. However, the name change from European Economic Community to European Community in 1980 and to European Union in 1992 indicated the broadened political role this group was likely to play in the later years.

A number of other countries are linked with the Common Market as associate members. Turkey is one. The EU also has preferential trade agreements with a number of Mediterranean countries and with the countries in the European Free Trade Association (EFTA).

Following the Lomé (capital of Togo) Convention in 1975 and its latest extension in 1990 (the fourth Lomé Convention) the EU agreed to a trading program with 66 African, Caribbean, and Pacific (ACP) countries that is valid for 5 years (i.e., 1990–1995). The fourth Lomé agreement consolidated and built on the earlier Lomé agreements, and provided, in particular, trade opportunities and development aid to selected Third World countries from EU members.[11] It established a vast, privileged domain of cooperation among multiform (economic, commercial, and even cultural) northern (the members of the EU) and southern (the associated states of Africa, the Caribbean, and the Pacific) countries.

Today, the EU is a viable world economic force with as large a market as the U.S. If the present trend continues, the EU will grow in coming years as other countries join the group. Austria, Sweden, and Finland, for example, are likely to become full members in 1995. Similarly, some Eastern European countries are likely to seek entry into the EU.

Due to the EU program, Western European nations are doing more together than ever. The Common Market is expanding, both in members and in terms of trade, after settling a protracted dispute over budgetary share. New cooperation agreements on matters important in future European development—space, broadcasting, and computer research—were negotiated in 1985 among countries and companies.

In 1992, exports by Common Market countries to other Common Market countries grew by 24 percent in local currency terms to the equivalent of 4 billion. In the U.S. view, Western Europe's appreciation of the economic importance of trade has been traditionally poor. But to Western Europe, expanding trade has been, and continues to be, the greatest achievement of the Common Market.

The rate of expansion in European trade during the 1990s was seven times the rate of economic growth. This means several things. First, trade is acting as a propellant to Europe's overall economy—exactly what the continent's leaders had in mind when they launched the Common Market over 35 years ago. The key provision of the treaty, the elimination of tariffs among member states, touched off a trade boom that continues to this day, despite the severe recession in the 1990s.

Despite the tremendous achievements of the EU, in the mid-1980s, the organization faced a variety of problems (see International Marketing Highlight 5.1). A critical examination of the EU showed that it never really became a common market. After the first heady years, various kinds of nontariff barriers once again began to choke off trade between member nations. A common currency, even a single free capital market, remained little more than a goal for the distant future. Less soaring aims, like harmonizing economic policies and standardizing member countries' value-added taxes, also appeared remote. Freedom of trade in services hardly existed at all, and there was little consensus on how to bring it about. The EU's common agricultural policy (CAP), which guarantees farmers high prices without limiting production, had produced huge surpluses that disrupted international markets and strained the EU budget. Yet farmers were not happy; their gripes about prices and market share erupted in violence.

The most disappointing failure, however, was a lack of progress in creating a true common market in manufactured goods, the EU's original reason for existence. Before the EU's birth, Europe was a maze of protectionism. Tariffs and quotas were the most visible and significant barriers, but they were backed by a host of regulations and other protectionist devices, some more than 100 years old. After the tariffs and quotas were eliminated, much of their protectionist function was gradually taken over by the nontariff barriers, many of which have proliferated over the years (see International Marketing Highlight 5.2).

International Marketing Highlight 5.1

Crazy Quilt of Regulations

If a commercial truck driver who left New York and drove the 5,000 or so kilometers to Los Angeles respected all the applicable work and rest rules, he could drive that entire distance at an average speed of 60 kilometers per hour. If that same rule-obeying driver in the same heavy lorry were to leave the Midlands in the U.K., pass by London, and drive down to Athens, also a distance of some 5,000 kilometers, he would be able to average only 12 kilometers per hour. It is worth noting that 12 kilometers per hour happens to be the speed of a horse and cart.

International Marketing Highlight 5.2

How Nontariff Barriers Hindered European Growth

A recent study by the EC Commission listed no fewer than fifty-six different categories of nontariff barriers, ranging from discrimination in government procurement contracts through national health and technical regulations to sheer customs chicanery at national borders. Many customs restrictions, such as taking currency in or out of France and Italy, are more stringent now than they were in the past. The time wasted getting goods through borders adds significantly to European industry's costs—as much as $1 billion a year. The total cost to industry of complying with all of the customs formalities is estimated at more than $10 billion, or between 5 percent and 10 percent of the value of the goods traded. This amounts to a substantial hidden tariff. In 1983, several truckloads of West German freezers were turned back at the French border for failing to have new certification documents in French, a requirement that had been introduced almost overnight. At the Italian border, customs officials often are simply unavailable, which halts truck traffic. Moreover, Italy still requires, as it did before 1958, that any pasta sold there must be made of durum wheat, not the soft wheat normally used for pasta-type products elsewhere. In Germany, a law whose origins go back several centuries specifies that beer sold there may be made only of barley malt, hops, and water. Since brewers in France, Belgium, and the Netherlands, like those in the United States, now use other grains or additives, this means that not a single bottle of Kronenbourg, Stella Artois, or Heineken can be sent across the Rhine.

Governments take action under many guises that discriminate against foreign products. France and Italy, for instance, impose disproportionately heavy taxes on big, powerful cars, which suits their automobile manufacturers whose output is concentrated in the small-car end of the line. As buyers of goods and services—telecommunications equipment, for example, or pharmaceuticals for national health services—governments can be decidedly protectionist.

Source: European Community Press and Information Service, New York, March 1985.

The EU members realized that as markets and industries globalize, those constraints—physical, technical, and fiscal—are no longer endurable. Further, as the forces of globalization have increased, the influence of European countries, both political and economic, has weakened. During the first half of the 1980s, Europe lost jobs at 0.5

percent per year, while its economy, roughly the same size as that of the U.S., grew at 1.5 percent per year. At the same time, the unemployment rate in Europe climbed from 4 percent to around 6 percent. These numbers pointed to a troubling decline in the international competitiveness of European companies.

Thus, to create jobs, restore international competitiveness, and boost the value to European customers of the goods and services available to them, the EU members were led to adopt a new course, that is, the Europe 1992 program.

The 12 member countries of the EU committed to integrating into a single internal market by the end of 1992. The result was to be a $4 trillion market of 340 million people. This Internal Market Program has made sweeping changes in virtually every aspect of business life, and has greatly altered the way U.S. firms do business in Europe.

Initially described in a 1985 EU Commission White Paper, the Internal Market Program consisted of 285 legislative directives intended to eliminate present barriers to the free movement of goods, people, and capital among the 12 EU member states. Internal Market Directives reached into every aspect of commercial activity, from eliminating border controls and duplicative customs documents, to setting uniform product standards, to establishing guidelines for company mergers. By 1992, 80 percent of all regulations affecting business in the EU were EU regulations and directives instead of national laws.

European officials believe that the integration of the EU market has increased economic growth and employment, and led to greater consumption and imports. A study by the EU Commission predicted that the removal of existing barriers would result in a 5 percent increase in EU gross domestic product, more than $260 billion, through more economies of scale and greater economic efficiency.[12]

European industry should receive the most direct benefits from the program. The ability to compete in a continental scale market and to avoid duplication of administrative procedures, production, marketing, and distribution systems should offer great advantages.

A unified EU market offers tremendous opportunities to U.S. companies, both those located in Europe and those exporting. At the same time, however, U.S. companies face tougher competition from their European counterparts (see International Marketing Highlight 5.3).

U.S. company sales in the 12-nation European Union are over $650 billion, almost 4 times greater than sales to Japan. Achieving a single EU internal market should mean greater economic growth for Europe, which, in turn, should bring increased demand for American products. In addition, the uniformity of trade and financial regulations have allowed U.S. companies easier access to all the EU countries by eliminating the need to meet national registration requirements in each country. This means that a product or service that meets the EU requirements in one member state can then be freely marketed throughout the EU. U.S. industries are thus able to reach a greater number of European consumers at a lower cost.[13]

The 1992 program dealt with three general objectives: the removal of physical barriers, the removal of technical barriers, and the removal of fiscal barriers through standardization of value added tax (VAT) rates and excise taxes.

The removal of physical barriers eliminated the regulations and procedures that gave rise to such border controls as vehicle safety checks or animal and plant inspec-

---

International Marketing Highlight 5.3

Europe 1992: Industries Most Affected

1. Industries that are losing protection and becoming more susceptible to competition:
   - financial services (banking and insurance)
   - pharmaceuticals
   - telecommunications services

2. Industries shifting from fragmented local to integrated community-wide markets:
   - distribution
   - food processing
   - transport (trucking)

3. Industries gaining technical economies of scale through sale of homogeneous goods and services:
   - electronics
   - packaging
   - white goods and other consumer products

4. Industries dependent on public procurement:
   - computer equipment and services
   - defense contractors
   - telecommunications equipment

5. Industries where the single market leads to import substitution, i.e., EU goods instead of imports:
   - chemicals
   - electrical components and products
   - office equipment

6. Industries where price disparity exists between countries with different indirect taxation (VAT) levels:
   - consumer goods and services

Source: Business International, November 27, 1989, p. 365

---

tions. One important aspect of the program, and one with an immediate impact, was the adoption as of January 1, 1988, of a Single Administrative Document, which eliminated the need for duplicative customs documents for goods shipped to and within the EU.

Perhaps the most significant aspect of the program from the point of view of U.S. industry is the directives related to the removal of technical barriers. EU directives mandate the creation of uniform EU industrial standards, the opening of public procurement procedures, the removal of restrictions on trade in services and capital movements, and stricter guidelines against barriers to competition.

The Europe 1992 program concluded on time, although there have been a variety of hindrances relative to the national interests of member nations. For example, a

German law discourages the import of parallel pharmaceuticals (drugs bought cheaply in one market and exported to where they are expensive) by requiring them to bear a certificate proving they meet German standards.

The EU Commission, however, is getting tougher as it seeks to ensure that national governments effectively administer EU rules. To resolve this problem, the Commission persuaded Germany to tell its customs offices to ignore the law.[14]

As a matter of fact, the 1991 historic accord (the Maastricht Treaty) on monetary and political union is a milestone that will transform the way Europe does business. The EU's 12 government leaders launched a monetary union that will give Europe its own currency and central bank by the end of the century. Exhibit 5.1 summarizes the main points of the Maastricht Treaty. Like its precursor, the 1986 Single Europe Act, which paved the way for free trade within the EU after 1992, the accord promises to become a powerful force for even closer economic and political integration. The new European Currency Unit, or ECU, has the potential to become a strong rival to the dollar in international finance and trade.[15]

EXHIBIT 5.1 Major Points of the Maastricht Treaty

Monetary Union: The EU would form a central bank by 1999 that would issue a single EU currency. Britain could opt out of monetary union.

Political Union: The EU states would forge common foreign and security policies, generally by consensus. In 1996, the EU would review political cooperation and could form a defense arm with a common defense policy.

New Policies: By replacing unanimity with majority voting at EU meetings, the EU *would get more say in education, public health, culture, consumer protection*, industry, research and development, environment, and development cooperation. Britain would have the right to opt out of decisions on social affairs.

European Parliament: The EU's 518-member assembly, primarily a consultative body, *would get some legislative say*, notably in internal trade, environment, education, health, and consumer protection.

Immigration: The EU would set goal of *common rules on immigration from outside* the EU, movement of immigrants within the community, and increased immigration-law enforcement. Decisions would require unanimity.

Citizenship: The EU would introduce *"Citizen of the Union"* guaranteeing free movement within the community, *granting after 1994 the right to vote and run in municipal elections in any EU nation.*

The peaceful revolution that swept Eastern Europe in 1989 is one of the most significant global events of the past 45 years. The EU and its member states are uniquely placed to help their Eastern neighbors on their way to becoming capitalist economies. The EU, with more than 30 years of experience in bringing small and medium-sized nations together in an economic unit, also serves as a model for bringing market-driven economic policies to the eastern part of the continent.[16]

From the modest business that EU countries conducted with Eastern European nations, the contacts grew rapidly between 1988 and 1990 with the conclusion by the EU of trade and cooperation agreements with Hungary, Czech Republic, Poland, Bulgaria, and Romania.

But the rapid pace of events in Eastern Europe has also forced the EU to develop additional new responses. These first-generation agreements are modest instruments with which to meet the challenge of helping g the emergence of democracy and market economies in Poland and Hungary and the rest of Eastern Europe.[17] The Eastern European nations, of course, aspire to eventual membership in the EU. But this may work out until their economies are strong enough to compete with more-developed nations.

European Free Trade Association (EFTA) The European Free Trade Association was formed in Stockholm in 1959 after a series of negotiations among those Western European countries that for one reason or another did not join the European Economic Community. (Great Britain, for example, had certain arrangements with Commonwealth countries that hindered their joining the EEC.) Austria, Denmark, Norway, Portugal, Sweden, Switzerland, and the U.K. were the original seven members of the EFTA. Finland (as an associate) and Iceland joined later. Denmark and the U.K. ceased to be members in 1973 after joining the EU. Currently, EFTA has seven members: Austria, Finland, Iceland, Norway, Sweden, Switzerland, and tiny Liechtenstein

The 12-nation European Community, the world's largest trading bloc, and the 7-member European Free Trade Association agreed in October 1991 to form a new common market, to be known as the European Economic Area (EEA). The agreement (after it is approved by each of the 19 national parliaments) would allow for the free flow of most goods, services, capital, and people among its 19 member nations. It went into effect just as a single regional market was formed by the EU on January 1, 1993.[18] The EEA consists of 18 countries except Switzerland, whose voters narrowly rejected membership of the giant free-trade area.[19] The agreement also paved the way for several new countries to seek full membership in the EU, which is rapidly moving toward social and political, as well as economic, integration.

Of the 7 members of EFTA, the three Nordic countries (Sweden, Norway, and Finland) and Austria have joined the EU as full members in 1995. Switzerland by referendum on EU membership has decided to stay out. Iceland and Liechtenstein are still undecided.[20]

Council for Mutual Economic Assistance (CMEA) In 1949, communist countries, led by the Soviet Union, formed the Council for Mutual Economic Assistance (sometimes called the Council of Mutual Economic Cooperation or COMECON) to coordinate trade and promote economic cooperation. Before it was disbanded on January 1, 1991, CMEA's membership included Bulgaria, Czechoslovakia, East Germany, Hungary, Mongolia, Poland, Romania, the Soviet Union, Cuba, and Vietnam.

The CMEA was formed more as a political group than as an economic association. It was organized and tightly controlled by the Soviet Union.

Although some trade gains were recorded among its member nations, CMEA did not promote economic integration through product specialization in any significant way. This may be partly attributed to the fact that foreign trade among the centrally planned economies had been looked upon as a means of balancing shortages and surpluses generated by the domestic sector.[21]

Africa   Influenced by the EU, a number of African countries have attempted to draw up market agreements in order to benefit from economic integration and cooperation. There are several major African market groups. The Afro-Malagasy Economic Union was formed in 1974 with Cameroon, Central African Republic, Chad, Congo-Brazzaville, Dahomey, Ivory Coast, Mali, Mauritania, Niger, Senegal, Togo, and Burkina as members. The East Africa Customs Union was formed in 1967 with Ethiopia, Kenya, Sudan, Tanzania, Uganda, and Zambia as members. The West African Economic Community (WAEC) was established in 1972 with Ivory Coast, Mali, Mauritania, Niger, Senegal, and Burkina as its member countries. The Maghreb Economic Community consisting of Algeria, Libya, Tunisia, and Morocco was formed. The Economic Community of West African States (ECOWAS) also was created with Benin, Cape Verde, Gambia, Ghana, Guinea, Guinea-Bissau, Ivory Coast, Liberia, Mali, Mauritania, Niger, Nigeria, Senegal, Sierra Leone, Togo, and Burkina as members.

Despite the fact that there are many market agreements in force in Africa, they have had no significant effect in promoting trade or economic progress because most African nations are small and have no economic infrastructure to produce goods to be traded among themselves.

The Economic Community of West African States (ECOWAS) is a recent attempt by 16 African countries to seek economic cooperation for their mutual advantage. The agreement called for complete economic integration by 1992. However, Nigeria accounts for almost two-thirds of the community's exports, and its latest economic woes, created by a decline in oil prices, have hindered smooth achievement of the goal of full integration.

On the other hand, considering the unique set of difficulties that the member countries have been going through, it is incredible that ECOWAS has survived. In 1994, the ECOWAS nations have been relaunching their efforts at economic reforms and trade liberalization. Although these are problems, the regional economy it covers offers significant opportunities for international marketers.

Latin America   Of all the developing areas of the world, Latin America has struggled the longest for the benefits of economic integration and cooperation. Market agreement attempts have been made to have certain countries specialize in certain industries, such as textiles, metal working, or shoe manufacturing, in order to derive benefits of scale and experience. The U.S. has played a major role in helping Latin American countries with market agreements. Yet, overall, the low level of economic activity and the political instability in the region have repeatedly been stumbling blocks.

There are five major market agreements in operation in Latin America: (1) the Latin American Integration Association (formerly called the Latin American Free Trade Association or LAFTA), (2) the Central American Common Market, (3) the

Andean Common Market, (4) the Caribbean Community Common Market, and (5) Mercado Comun del Sur (Mercosur).

The Latin American Free Trade Association (LAFTA), originally formed in 1960, was renamed the Latin American Integration Association (LAIA)[23] via the Treaty of Montevideo in August 1980. Its members are Argentina, Brazil, Chile, Mexico, Paraguay, Peru, Uruguay, Colombia, Ecuador, Venezuela, and Bolivia. LAFTA was the first attempt at economic cooperation among Latin American counties, but its large membership has hampered its effectiveness. The fact that some member countries (Argentina, Brazil, Chile, Mexico, and Venezuela) are economically more advanced than others, like Uruguay and Bolivia, has made it difficult to make agreements for free trade among themselves.

The Central American Common Market, comprised of Costa Rica, El Salvador, Guatemala, Honduras, and Nicaragua, was established in 1960. Its scope was more limited, and the countries, which are essentially on the same level of economic development, have found it mutually beneficial to implement the agreement.

However, it collapsed in 1969, when war broke out between Honduras and El Salvador after a riot at a soccer match involving the two countries. The members decided in 1992 to re-establish the Common Market by 1995.[24]

The Andean Common Market was created in 1969 by Bolivia, Chile, Colombia, Ecuador, Peru, and Venezuela as a subgroup of LAFTA.[25] Chile is no longer a member, while Panama holds associate status in the group.

The Caribbean Community and Common Market (CARICOM) was formed in 1968. Its original members were Barbados, Guyana, Jamaica, Trinidad and Tobago, Antigua, Dominica, Grenada, Montserrat, St. Kitts-Nevis-Anguilla, St. Lucia, St. Vincent, and Belize.

Mercosur originated in 1988 as a free-trade pact between Brazil and Argentina and was expanded to embrace Uruguay and Paraguay. By the end of 1994, it is supposed to enshrine a completely free market in goods, services, and labor for Argentina and Brazil, with Uruguay and Paraguay following a year later. Chile may move toward closer integration with Mercosur countries in the future. Mercosur is likely to emerge into a full-fledged customs union.[26]

Of the aforementioned agreements, LAIA is almost defunct, while Mercosur offers that most hope for integration in the area. The ultimate dream of most Latin American countries is to join, together or alone, with the North American Free Trade Area of Mexico, Canada, and the U.S.

Asia

Asia is a vast continent with a large population. In the past, meager industrial development combined with the diversity and size of the region gave little reason for market arrangements. Nonetheless, Japan and the Pacific countries, Australia and New Zealand, along with the U.S. and Canada, may enter into some sort of market arrangement. In fact, these countries created the Pacific Basin Economic Council to encourage intraregional trade, but it failed to develop into a market agreement.

In Southeast Asia, however, the emerging countries of Indonesia, Malaysia, the Philippines, Singapore, and Thailand have made a first attempt at establishing a market agreement. With these countries as members, the Association of South East Asian Nations (ASEAN) became operational in 1978. Brunei became a member later. Vietnam and Laos have become associate members and participate in such functional programs of the group as science and technology, tourism, and human resources development. Cambodia may also become an associate member in the near future.[27]

The association seeks closer economic integration and cooperation through the establishment of complementary industries and investment incentives to nonmember countries.[28] Although the group initially had setbacks in meeting its goals, it now shows slow progress.[29]

An interesting development in Asia is the emergence of a new group called Asia-Pacific Economic Cooperation (APEC) among 14 Pacific Rim economies, who had their first meeting in 1993. APEC, whose membership includes China, Japan, the Four Tigers, Australia, New Zealand, and ASEAN members, had a combined GDP of $14 trillion in 1992, nearly equal to the $15.7 trillion GPD of the Group of Seven (U.S., U.K., Germany, France, Italy, Canada, and Japan). By the year 2000, APEC will be larger than the G-7 and will dominate U.S. trade; 40 percent of U.S. foreign commerce will by then be with APEC nations, twice that with Europe.[30]

The Indian subcontinent region, with a population of over one billion people, provides another possibility for a regional market group. In December 1985, seven nations of the region (India, Pakistan, Bangladesh, Sri Lanka, Nepal, Bhutan, and Maldives) put aside their differences and launched the South Asian Association for Regional Cooperation (SAARC). SAARC's initial purpose has been limited to cooperation in noncontroversial areas such as agriculture, rural development, telecommunications, postal services, transport, science and technology, meteorology, tourism, and sports. Important elements like the formation of a common market or a free trade zone have been omitted. However, even a small beginning in this region augurs well for the future, since there is a vast potential for mutually beneficial economic cooperation and growth.

Countries in the Arab region have already made some progress in making market agreements. Several market groups are operating there. One of these is the Arab Common Market (ACM) formed in 1964 with Egypt, Iraq, Kuwait, Jordan, and Syria as members. This group planned to achieve free internal trade within 10 years, but it has not yet achieved this goal. External tariffs are likely to be regulated sometime in the 1990s.

The Regional Cooperation for Development (RCD) represented a new kind of regional agreement. It was created in 1964 among Iran, Pakistan, and Turkey for the purpose of undertaking such projects as the building of a hydroelectric dam to serve the entire region. Unlike other market agreements, this agreement did not provide for free trade between member nations or for the setting of common external tariffs, yet it did have a regional economic base and its aims were to benefit regional market potential. With the fall of the Shah of Iran, however, RCD virtually ceased to exist.

U.S.–Canada Free Trade Agreement

On January 2, 1988, President Reagan and Prime Minister Mulroney of Canada signed the U.S.–Canada Free Trade Agreement (FTA). This historic agreement represents the culmination of efforts stretching back more than 100 years. FTA was designed to strengthen an already extensive trading relationship and enhance economic opportunity on both sides of the common border.

Each year the U.S. and Canada exchange more goods and services than any other two countries in the world. Bilateral trade in goods and services exceeded $200 billion in 1993. The elimination of tariffs and most other barriers to trade between the two countries under the FTA has increased economic growth, lowered prices, expanded employment, and has enhanced the competitiveness of both countries in the world marketplace (see International Marketing Highlight 5.4).

International Marketing Highlight 5.4

Success in Open Markets

The U.S.–Canada Free Trade Agreement has already achieved a number of notable successes in facilitating trade in investment:

Accelerated Tariff Removal. U.S. and Canadian companies are anxious to move to free trade, as has been demonstrated by the number of industry petitions to remove bilateral tariffs faster than specified in the agreement. Based on industry requests, the tariffs on some 400 products, accounting for almost $6 billion in bilateral trade, were removed in April 1990. Additional petitions are being considered for the second round of accelerated tariff elimination.

Standard Simplification. Under the agreement umbrella and through the efforts of the private sector, progress has been achieved in harmonizing standards. For example, 121 Canadian and U.S. standards have been combined to form one single binational heating and air conditioning standard. Now the manufacturers can produce only one standard; in addition, consumers have wider product selection at lower cost.

New Government Procurement Opportunities. Since implementing the agreement, more than 200 additional Canadian government contracts, totaling nearly $13 million, have been awarded to U.S. companies of all sizes. Without the agreement, these contracts would not have been open to U.S. exporters.

Because of the agreement, Americans and Canadians are discovering new ways to work together in business, tourism, education, and the environment. For example, a New Brunswick manufacturer of file folders recently began buying paper stock from a U.S. company in Raleigh, North Carolina. Canadian tariffs on paper, previously as high as 25 percent, have been reduced by 60 percent, making American products more price competitive.

Source: Business America, April 8, 1991, p. 4.

While the FTA does not eliminate all trade problems between the U.S. and Canada, it does provide a consultative framework within which these problems can be managed before they create serious economic and political friction. Predictably, industries in both the U.S. and Canada can expect to undergo some structural readjustment in the years ahead to adapt to changing market conditions. However, the less-restricted trade permitted by the FTA will spur both the American and Canadian economies to higher growth rates, increased efficiency, and improved competitiveness with other trading partners.[31]

The agreement came into force on January 1, 1989. The two governments have established a joint Canada–U.S. Trade Commission to oversee its implementation. A

North American Free Trade Agreement

On January 1, 1994, the U.S.–Canada–Mexico free trade agreement emerged as the North American Free-Trade Agreement (NAFTA). NAFTA creates the largest market in the world of 370 million consumers and $6.5 trillion in output. NAFTA bodes well for U.S. and Canadian marketers who stand to gain much in meeting the long pent-up demands of newly affluent Mexicans (see International Marketing Highlight 5.5). The Mexicans will be able to attract a variety of manufacturing to their country. The following are NAFTA's key provisions.[32]

- America and Canada to phase out tariffs on *textiles and apparel* over 10 years. Mexico to eliminate many tariffs in this sector immediately.
- All tariffs on *cars and car parts* to be eliminated over 10 years.
- In *agriculture*, Mexico and America to phase out 57 percent of trade barriers immediately, 94 percent after 10 years, and 100 percent after 15 years. Mexico and Canada also to phase out tariffs. U.S.-Canada Free Trade Agreement unchanged.
- Pemex, Mexico's state oil company, to keep its constitutional monopoly over most of the country's *oil industry*. However, foreigners could invest in petrochemicals, electricity generation, and coal mines. Procurement contracts for Pemex and Mexico's state electricity commission would be opened for foreigners.
- Foreign *banks and securities brokers* to have unrestricted access to Mexico by the year 2000. Some restrictions would remain on sales of policies in Mexico by American and Canadian *insurers*, but with gradual freeing of direct investment.
- *Lorry-drivers* to cross the Mexican border freely by 1999.
- Most of Mexico's trade barriers on *tele-communications equipment* eliminated. Basic voice services would remain protected, but with foreigners authorized to provide value-added telephone services.
- Modest agreement to open *central-government procurement* to competition. However, this provision need not bind lower layers of government.
- *Intellectual property* to be protected to industrial-country standards.
- NAFTA *investors* generally to receive national treatment, with freedom to seek binding arbitration from an international forum. However, special protection would be given to Mexican energy and railway industries, American airline and radio communications industries, and Canadian culture.
- Each country to apply its own *environmental standards*, provided such standards have a scientific basis. Lowering of standards as a lure to investment would be "inappropriate."
- Two *commissions* to be established with power to impose fines and remove trade privileges (as a last resort) when environmental standards or legislation involving health and safety, minimum wages, or child labor ignored. However, governments would pay the fines, and only after a long bureaucratic process.

International Marketing Highlight 5.5

NAFTA: Mutually Beneficial Business Opportunities

Farming: As NAFTA is phased in, Mexico will supply more citrus, vegetables, and fruits. The U.S. will ship south more meat and grains, including corn and soybeans. Canadian wood exports will grow.

Autos: The Big Three automakers expect to boost exports to Mexico to 60,000 vehicles yearly from 7,700 currently. Over time, Mexico will win some manufacturing jobs such as assembling small cars and light trucks for the region.

Consumer Goods: Wal-Mart, J.C. Penney, and Radio Shack are part of a U.S. retail move into Mexico. Add fast-food franchisers and powerhouses such as Procter & Gamble, and it's an invasion.

Telecom: Massive integration is under way. Canada's Northern Telecom builds switches in North Carolina and installs them in Mexico City. Southwestern Bell owns a piece of Telefonos de Mexico. AT&T, MCI, and Sprint will try to move into long distance in Mexico, as they did in Canada.

Financial Services: Newly deregulated Mexican financial markets will grow by 15 percent annually in the next 5 years. Credit cards, mortgages, and life and property insurance are all virgin markets in Mexico.

Textiles: Strong local-content rules will help revive U.S. textiles, which will supply apparel manufacturing returning from Asia to Mexico.

Energy: Mexico's oil patch remains off-limits, but NAFTA would spark a boom for U.S. oil field services and power generation. The U.S. would still be dependent on Mexican oil imports.

Source: "Overview on NAFTA," (Washington, D.C.: U.S. Trade Representative's Office, 1993).

The way the three economies (U.S., Canadian, and Mexican) complement each other allows for greater room for growth and efficiency gains from free trade. Increasing economic ties through NAFTA would result in net growth for the three partners.

Free trade agreements have promoted growth for the European Union, Australia, and New Zealand, among others. Even when trade agreements occur between economies with different levels of development, the net result has been positive. The accession of Greece, Spain, and Portugal to the EU did not depress real wages within the EU. In fact, during the 1980s, real manufacturing wages rose in the Federal Republic of Germany, France, and the U.K. by at least 20 percent. EU programs have resulted in the continued lowering of barriers to trade and investment and prompted a renewal of economic and job growth.

NAFTA, which is expected to be concluded by 1996, will power the region's economic growth, productivity, and global competitiveness into the twenty-first century.

Other Forms of Agreements

We have discussed the important types of market agreements extant among nations in different regions of the world. In addition to these, various nations have made a variety of other arrangements for their economic benefit. For instance, four different forms of agreement are the Commonwealth of Nations, the Commonwealth of Independent States, commodity agreements, and producer cartels. Although the Commonwealth of Nations was mentioned in relation to political unions, it is not strictly speaking a political union. The only political bond among the Commonwealth nations existed in the past when they constituted part of the British Empire. On the economic front, the member nations accord one another preferential treatment by agreeing to import from each other on a selective basis. Still, this situation has changed greatly since its beginnings in the post-World War II period, partially on political grounds and partially in response to individual economic interest.

The Commonwealth of Independent States (CIS) is a confederation of 11 countries that were previously part of the Soviet Union.[33] The shape that this agreement will ultimately take is difficult to say since its scope is not clear, but there is little doubt that it would be dominated by Russian, which has half of the former superpower's people and most of its resources and industrial base. Some people are skeptical that the CIS will survive long. Most of the member republics, especially Ukraine, are deeply suspicious of Russian intentions.

Another significant type of market agreement is the *commodity agreement*. Some have been entered into under the auspices of GATT to stabilize the price of commodities such as textiles, coffee, olive oil, sugar, tin, cocoa, and wheat. The underlying purpose of commodity agreements, which are made between producing and consuming countries, has been to prevent excessive price fluctuations that would be detrimental to the developing countries.[34]

The term *producer cartel* refers to a unilateral agreement among producers of a commodity, or suppliers of a natural resource, to deal collectively as a group with the buyers for purposes of trading the commodity. The producer cartel became a popular mode of economic cooperation among producers of strategic commodities after the success of the OPEC petroleum cartel. Since 1975, a number of producer cartels have been organized by countries exporting bauxite, phosphate, chromium, rubber, and copper. However, it is unrealistic to expect other cartels to duplicate OPEC's record.

Summary

In the post-World War II period, nations came to realize that the task of economic reconstruction and expansion could be achieved more smoothly through cooperation among governments. The cooperation took two forms: global and regional. Global cooperation was reflected in steps such as the establishment of the World Bank, the International Monetary Fund (IMF) and the General Agreement on Tariffs and Trade (GATT). Chapters 2 and 3 examined these efforts.

Regional cooperation took the form of economic integration through market agreements among nations in geographical proximity to each other. Five types of market agreements are free trade area, customs union, common market, economic union, and political union. Market agreements are based on commonality of interest among nations. For example, developing countries share the common objective of economic development. Likewise, political systems and culture may influence nations to enter into economic cooperation. However, geographic proximity turns out to be the basis for market agreements more often than any other reason for cooperation. It is natural because, other things being equal, nations located in the same region are usually influenced by common social and economic environments.

Historically, the economic cooperation among nations that influences governments today first emerged in Europe. Six European countries—former West Germany, France, Italy, the Netherlands, Belgum, and Luxembourg—agreed to form what is popularly called the European Common Market or the European Union. Its example was followed by the establishment of market agreements in other parts of Europe and elsewhere throughout the world.

From the marketing viewpoint, the importance of market agreements lies in the potential generation of markets. Inasmuch as mass production can be justified only by mass markets, market agreements boost industrial development and economic activity. For example, the European Union is about equal in size to the U.S. market. Thus, certain economies of scale, which previously could not be achieved in Western Europe, are now feasible as a result of the formation of the Union.

Review Questions

1. What factors lead nations to work toward economic integration?
2. What role did the U.S. play in the establishment of the European Economic Community (EEC)?
3. Why did Great Britain not join the EEC at the time of its creation, but do so later?
4. List the differences between the arrangements of a free trade area and a customs union.
5. Is economic integration workable among Third World nations?
6. Examine why Japan might be hindered in establishing a market agreement in the Pacific region on the basis of your general knowledge of the factors that promote such arrangements.
7. In what way is the unification of the European market in 1992 likely to benefit U.S. businesses?

Creative Questions

1. Do regional market agreements contradict multilateral agreements? Why do we need the regional agreements if we have the latter? Are there any major provisions in NAFTA that have not been covered by the Uruguay Round Agreement?
2. Is a market agreement among the Indian Ocean countries (i.e., India, Pakistan, Iran, South Africa, and others) feasible? What problems discourage such an agreement? How can these problems be resolved?

Endnotes

1. "Common Marketing for the Common Market," *Forbes*, July 1, 1972, p. 23. *Also see* John Drew, "European Markets: A Business Overview," *Europe*, July–August 1984, pp. 18–19.

2. "IBM Finds a Club that Doesn't Want it as a Member," *Business Week*, February 11, 1985, p. 42.

3. "Collision Course in Commercial Aircraft: Boeing-Airbus-McDonnell Douglas-1991 (A)," A Case #9-391-106 available from the Publishing Division, Harvard Business School.

4. Stefan H. Robock and Kenneth Simmonds, *International Business and Multinational Enterprises*, 2nd ed. (Homewood, IL: Irwin, 1983), p. 149. *Also see* "EC Backs French Ban on Japanese TV Sets," *The Asian Wall Street Journal Weekly*, March 9, 1981, p. 2.

5. Lawrence Ingrassia, "As Spain Joins the EC, Its Shielded Industries Get Ready for a Shock," *The Wall Street Journal*, October 14, 1985, p. 1; "The Haggling that May Stall Spain and Portugal's Entry into the EC," *Business Week*, May 28, 1984, p. 54.

6. *See* "What Bilateral Deals Mean for Trade," *The Economist*, February 6, 1988, p. 63.

7. Etienne Cracco and Guy Robert, "The Uncommon Common Market," in Ronald C. Curham, *1974 Combined Proceedings* (Chicago: American Marketing Association, 1975), p. 601.

8. *See* Bela Balassa, *The Theory of Economic Integration* (Homewood, IL: Irwin, 1961), pp. 1–21.

9. R. Lipsey, "The Theory of Customs Unions: A General Survey," *Economic Journal*, Vol. 70 (1960), pp. 496–513.

10. D. Swann, *The Economics of the Common Market* (Harmondsworth, England: Penguin Books, 1970).

11. Lomé IV Convention," *Development Forum*, May–June 1989, p. 20.

12. Francine Lamoriello, "Completing the Internal Market by 1992: The EC's Legislative Program for Business," *Business America*, August 1, 1988, pp. 4–7.

13. *See* Andrew I. Millington and Brian T. Bayliss, "Non-Tariff Barriers and U.K. Investment in the European Community," *Journal of International Business Studies*, Vol. 22, No. 4, pp. 695–710. *Also see* Patrick W. Cooke and Donald R. Mackay, "The New EC Approach to Harmonization of Standards and Certification," *Business America*, August 1, 1988, pp. 8–9.

14. *The Economist*, April 10, 1993, p. 74. *Also see Crossborder Monitor*, August 17, 1994, p. 3.

15. "One Big Currency—And One Big Job Ahead," *Business Week*, December 23, 1991, p. 40.

16. Charles Goldsmith, "EU Will Broaden Foreign-Policy Ties With Six Nations in Eastern Europe," *The Wall Street Journal*, March 9, 1994, p. A12.

17. "A New Economic Miracle," *Business Week*, November 27, 1989, p. 59.

18. Alan Riding, "Europeans in Accord to Create Vastly Expanded Trading Bloc," *The New York Times*, October 23, 1991, p. A1. *Also see* "Tearing Down Even More Fences in Europe," *Business Week*, November 4, 1991, p. 50.

19. *The Economist*, September 4, 1993, p. 68.

20. "EU Enlargement: Opportunities Open As Frontiers Go East," *Crossborder Monitor*, May 11, 1994, p. 1.

21. "COMECON's Crumbling Credit-Worthiness," *The Wall Street Journal*, September 18, 1985, p. 31.

22. Thomas V. Greer, "The Economic Community of West African States," *International Marketing Review*, Vol. 9. No. 3, 1992, pp. 25–39.

23. *See* "New Latin American Association Carries on Traditions of LAFTA," *Business America*, April 6, 1981, p. 15.

24. "Free-Trade-Free-for-All," *The Economist*, January 4, 1992, p. 63.

25. " A Common Market of Sorts," *The Economist*, February 19, 1983, p. 25.

26. "Growing Markets Lure Companies to Mercosur Region," *Crossborder Monitor*, June 8, 1994, p. 1.

27. Barry Wain, "ASEAN Faces New Threats to Prosperity," *The Asian Wall Street Journal Weekly*, March 14, 1994, p. 12.

28. "ASEAN: Whatever For," *The Economist*, October 7, 1989, p. 40.

29. George Paine, Linda Droker, and John Sitnik, "ASEAN Economic Dialogue Returns to Washington," *Business America*, February 1, 1988, p. 2.

30. "This Isn't Your Usual Clinton Grabfest," *Business Week*, November 15, 1993, p. 52.

31. Alan Freeman, "Free-Trade Pact Creates Winners, Losers," *The Wall Street Journal*, February 7, 1989, p. A20.

32. *See* "Border Crossings," *Business Week*, November 22, 1993, p. 40; "Overview, The North American Free Trade Agreement," a paper issued by the office of the U.S. Trade Representative, 1993; Gary A. Knight, "NAFTA Holds Promise for Stronger, Prosperous North America," *Marketing News*, October 25, 1993, p. 14; and Lew S. Richman, "How NAFTA Will Help Americans," *Fortune*, April 18, 1993, p. 95.

33. "How Long Can Yeltsin Hold It All Together?" *Business Week*, January 13, 1992, p. 49.

34. Steve Mufson, "Third World Pleas on Commodity Prices Get No Sympathy in Developed Nations," *The Wall Street Journal*, October 2, 1985, p. 34.

PART · 2

Cases

Case 7: Shanghai Volkswagen Corp.

"When you see a Santana car running behind you, you had better make way for it, for it is certain to outrun you," the government news agency quoted an unidentified Shanghai driver's views in early 1985 on the "Shanghai Santana," which was the admirable product made by the Shanghai Volkswagen Corp. This driver's words did not only point to the car itself, but also predicted that the Shanghai Volkswagen Corp. was going to have great success in the potentially huge Chinese car market.

Recently, there are almost no carmakers who don't turn their eyes to the Chinese car market. Despite difficulties all major auto companies are seeking entry into the Chinese market. Volkswagen AG, Germany's biggest carmaker, has finally pulled off the China deal every big motor manufacturer has lusted for. It was the winner among all foreign competitors. In 1990 and 1991, the Shanghai VW Corp., the joint venture between Volkswagen and China, stood No. 1 on the list of Top Ten Joint Ventures in China. The rankings were jointly sponsored by the *Economic Daily* of China and *China Industrial and Commercial Times*, and included the following indexes: ratio between investment and profit; per-capita profit; labor productivity; accumulative rate of depreciation; per-capita investment; balance of foreign currency; ratio between cost and output value; export rate; and ratio between R&D input and total sales income (*Li Rongxia*, 1992, pp.14–16). The Shanghai Volkswagen success story has inspired people's interests: Why did this company have such significant success? How is it possible?

Company Background

The Shanghai Volkswagen Corp. agreement was signed on October 10, 1984, by Volkswagen AG and the People's Republic of China. The signing took place in the Great Hall of the People, which is the most noble place in the hearts of the Chinese people, in Beijing. West German Chancellor Helmut Kohl was present for the signing and, a short time later, for the laying of a cornerstone on the 50-acre site in the suburb of Shanghai. The former vice premier Li Peng, who is the present Premier Minister of China, also appeared at the cornerstone ceremony. It is the first passenger-car manufacturing agreement of its kind with mainland China for foreign carmakers. One Chinese official told the XinHua News Agency that

---

This case was prepared by Hang Li, D.B.A. Candidate, under the supervison of Professors Theodore F. Smith and C.P. Rao of Old Dominion University, College of Business and Public Administration, Dominion University, Norfolk, VA 23529. It is intended as a basis for class discussion and student analysis. Printed by permission.

the VW deal represented a "40-year leap forward" for China.

Under the deal, an initial investment of $165 million was made to cover the first stages of the ambitious undertaking. The joint company, to be known as Shanghai Volkswagen Automobile Co., Ltd., was established in March 1985, and was initially set to run for 25 years. Volkswagen AG holds a 50 percent share in the venture. Shanghai Tractor & Automobile Co. has 25 percent; Shanghai Trust and Consultancy, a subsidiary of the Bank of China, 15 percent; and China National Automobile Industry Corp., the remaining 10 percent. The company's capital stock was about $67 million.

While the original production target was 20,000 VW Santanas (US Quantum), the agreed-upon plant's nominal capacity was 30,000 units annually. Actually, it produced 10,000 cars in 1987 and reached 35,000 units in 1991. The original purchasers were Chinese authorities and taxi companies. With increased income for Chinese people, private individuals emerged as new buyers. Domestic consumption had first priority, but the company actually exported some products recently. The daily production of the company increased from 17 cars in 1985 to 100 in 1991. Only 13 percent of the value of the cars was made in China in 1987. This rose to 60 percent local content in 1991 (*The Economist*, 1988, pp. 81–82; *Beijing Review*, 1991, pp. 14–16).

There is equal Chinese and German representation on the 10-member board of directors, with a Chinese representative as chairman. A four-person management committee runs the business activities. They report to the board of directors. China nominates the managing director and head of personnel, and VW supplies the commercial and financial directors for the committee (*Automotive News*, 1984, p. 8). In 1988, there were 2,300 employees in this company. The German technicians are running training schools for the Chinese workers in all aspects of assembly work. The overall cost of labor for Shanghai VW is far below that paid in Germany or other Volkswagen locations.

The company was established on the site of the former Shanghai Car Factory, which stood in rice fields 20 miles southwest of Shanghai, China's leading industrial city. The hallways in the office building are clean and bright, in sharp contrast to the ill-lighted interiors and clutter of many other Chinese factories. Neat signs are tacked on every office door, identifying the German and Chinese who work inside. There is an air of efficiency and a bustle not usually found in other factories of this country.

For a long time, China depended heavily on imports from Japan. The Chinese government even signed a contract in 1983 with the Japanese to import 250,000 Japanese vehicles. In reality, Japan's exports to China soared from 10,800 in 1983 to nearly 85,000 in 1984. In January and February of 1985, Japanese shipments increased by 58 percent. Since Shanghai Volkswagen was founded, its managers have been enthusiastic about the eventual goal to cut China's dependence on Japan, and about Volkswagen's new Asian base, from which it can challenge Japanese auto makers in Asia in the coming decade. For Volkswagen, this company is a symbol of its foothold in three important and—for outsiders—difficult markets. The other two are: Nissan, which puts together up to 60,000 Santanas a year in Japan, and Seat in Spain, which assembles four Volkswagen models, reaching 120,000 units a year in 1985.

The company is equipped with internationally advanced technology and facilities. Its engine factory, painting workshop, and assembly workshop are equal to the advanced international standards of the 1980s. Four production lines concentrate on the assembly of Santana CKD parts shipped from Germany.

The Germans offered much technical and financial help for this project, which could cost as much as $1 billion over the 1990s. They dispatched many experts to Shanghai to help the Chinese people modernize and expand the antiquated, existing plant. Cheap labor was readily available. The profits of the company are equally shared. Li Jian, the manager of the government-owned Shanghai Automotive Industry Corp., one of Volkswagen's three Chinese partners, was quoted in the Chinese press as predicting a profit of US$154 million in 1991.

Environmental Review

Business people around the world have been well aware of the huge potential market for consumer goods and the 1.2 billion newly materialistic citizens in China. But only recently have the world's carmakers begun to pay attention to China's appetite for automobiles. There were too many car plants making too few cars. Although China's own vehicle output doubled to 300,000 units since 1980, even such a rapid growth could not keep up with the surge in demand. The demand in 1985 jumped by nearly 50 percent, to 500,000 units. Even in 1987, seventy-three vehicle-making plants produced only 440,000 cars and trucks (*The Economist*, 1988, pp. 81–82), far from meeting the strong demand for cars in China. With one car for every 2000 citizens in China (compared with one car for every two citizens in the U.S. and West Germany, and for every 24 in Hong Kong), and with the country's fast-growing standard of living, the opportunities were obviously there.

Before the 1980s, owning a car was a symbol of power and high social class in China. Only the government, state-owned enterprises, and companies could buy cars. Also, only officials who were at the level of a county magistrate and above had the right to use a car. Car prices were astronomically high for average people. After Deng's open and reform policy was adopted by the Chinese government in 1978, some regions along the sea became prosperous, and some people in lines such as entertainment and private business became wealthy. They were eager to buy a car in order to show their superiority to the average people. Some film stars and private entrepreneurs constituted the first part of the populace who could afford a car by themselves. With the general expansion of economic activities, the demand for cars from state-owned companies and enterprises and the government also increased a great deal. A company wishing to buy a car must first obtain a quota from the government.

China's domestic industry was unable to serve this market, resulting in the creation of black markets for all cars, whether imported outright, made in China, or joint-venture factories. Lured by enormous profits, some people in Shandong province and the southern island of Hainan smuggled a large quantity of foreign cars for resale to the mainland. Back door deals abounded. Many people had to register on a two-year waiting list (*Abrahamson*, 1989, p. 30–21).

However, importation was not the most feasible solution, as China was short of hard currency. "Money should be spent on the edge of the knife," as people say in China. China needed to buy high-production technology and equipment from abroad to replace its present, obsolete machines, some of which were imported from the former Soviet Union 30 years ago. Importing consumer goods was of second-order importance to the Chinese leaders. The principle political decision to bolster China's auto industry was confirmed at the highest level. It would be accomplished through more joint manufacturing ventures and a further cutback in direct imports. Contracts to bring in more Japanese vehicles were phased out after 1985, with corresponding savings of hard currencies. Through joint ventures, the Chinese car industry planned to learn advanced technology and make use of foreign currencies from foreign partners. Also, the quality of the Chinese labor force would be improved. So the government offered many favorable terms to attract foreign investment. Priority of land, labor, taxation, transportation, utilities, and raw materials were given to joint ventures. To some extent, this hurt some state-owned enterprises. Although the government encouraged the joint ventures to export their products, the major portion of the outputs were sold in China, due to heavy demand.

Auto Industry in China

There was no auto industry when the People's Republic of China was founded in 1949. With the Soviet's help in supplying equipment and expertise, China's first truck rolled off the assembly line in 1956. Since then, China has built about 2,400 auto and auto-parts factories, including 119 auto and truck assembly plants up to 1985. The industry employed 1.3 million people and produced about 600,000 vehicles, light trucks for rural use, dump trucks for mining, transport vehicles, limousines, cars, and tourist buses.

China is self-sufficient in production of raw materials and components used in making its old models. It can produce more than 95 percent of the sheet steel, gear steel, spring steel, and alloy steel plates needed to make frames, and also has capabilities in producing rubber and plastic fittings, meters and instruments.

But the models produced in these factories were too old and out-of-date. They were generally technically backward products based on models from the 1950s, or even the 1940s. The cars produced were available in only a few models, were inefficient in fuel consumption, and offered poor performance. The manufacturing plants needed urgently to be improved in management, equipment, technology, and research. Also, the industry was too decentralized and fragmented, especially in making components. It was obvious that some inefficient factories should be closed and the scattered components makers grouped.

Beginning in 1985, advanced production technology and equipment were introduced to upgrade China's outdated models to meet international standards. To rationalize operations, the Chinese government set up six large motor-vehicle companies. According to Mr. Liu Xianzeng, a 64-year-old mechanical engineer from the National Automotive Trading Corp. of China, China's "Big Three" plants include the Shanghai Volkswagen Auto Co., producer of the Santana car; the Changchun Volkswagen Auto Co., producer of Jettas and Golfs; and the Dragon Auto Co., a joint venture between China's Second Auto Works and Citroen, the French manufacturer. The so-called "Little Three" are Chrysler's joint venture, Beijing Jeep; Guangzhou Peugeot Automotive Co., maker of Peugeot 505 cars and station wagons and 504 pickup trucks; and a Daihatsu plant in Tianjin, maker of the Charade car. Trucks and buses are made at the First Auto Works in Changchun and the Second Auto Works in Shi Yan (*Bradford, 1992, p. 9*).

In fact, the Changchun Volkswagen Auto Co. has not yet achieved mass production capabilities of making cars, and the Dragon Auto Co. is still under negotiation between China and France. But this is the future skeleton of China's auto industry.

Beijing Jeep Corp. started in 1983 as a joint venture between American Motors (purchased by Chrysler in 1987) and Beijing Automotive Works. The Americans have a 38 percent stake in its partnership with the Chinese. Although this venture had some problems at the beginning, it built on strong returns and in 1990 ranked no. 2 among all foreign joint ventures in terms of revenue. In 1991, Beijing Jeep raised the output of its U.S.-designed Cherokee by 73 percent from 1990 to 13,000 units and built 35,000 Chinese four-wheel drive vehicles known as Beijing 212. An official from the company, who was unwilling to be identified, acknowledged that it had 1991 net income of about US$40 million on revenue of US$400 million. It plans to invest RMB1.2 billion (US$225 million) through 1995 to upgrade its plant, bolster annual output of its Cherokee vehicle to 80,000 units, and introduce an all-new model based on the Jeep Wrangler to replace the existing BJ2020.

Guangzhou Peugeot is a joint venture between China and France. Peugeot owns a 22 percent stake in the company, with Guangzhou Automobile Manufacturing holding 46 percent, Chinese International Trust & Investment Corp., 20 percent, Banque Nationale de Paris, 4 percent, and the World Bank's International Finance Corp. 8 percent. After three years of manufacturing about 6,000 cars, Guangzhou Peugeot doubled its output in 1991, having RMB233 million in profit with RMB1.5 billion in revenue (*Karp, 1992, pp. 49–50*).

The Chinese government has set goals for dramatically increasing production in its two 5-year plans (1991–2000). The industry produced 78,000 passenger cars in 1991; the government hopes to increase that to 700,000 by the end of the century (*Bradford, 1992, pp. 66–68*).

Marketing Mix Strategies

Volkswagen of AG's decision to pursue a joint venture with China was made after carefully analyzing the particular environment of China, and was based on a number of fundamental operational strategies.

Product

In twenty-seven years, the forerunner of Shanghai VW Corp.—Shanghai Car Work—made 50,000 Shanghai sedans at a rate of 6,000 a year. The Shanghai sedan was based on Mercedes 170 model, a big, four-door car that reminds people, who see it staggering along the streets in Beijing and many big cities (usually carrying government officials) of an American Dodge, vintage 1950s. This car dated from the early 1950s and is definitely out of fashion nowadays.

Following formation of the joint venture, the company decided to make the VW Santana model. It was the first model especially designed for the local market by foreign manufacturers. They gave it a sound name, "Shanghai Santana," which proved successful in building a strong brand identification. The Santana was painted white, red, and grey, which are popular colors in China. They planned no two-door models, because in China, a car often must take as many passengers as possible. Four-door cars were thought to be more convenient and were already accepted by Chinese people. So the plant made all cars with four doors. To meet the technical manufacturing ability of the Chinese industry and in keeping with a prevailing view that driving is a special technical skill that cannot be easily learned, the factory manufactured only manual transmissions for the car. Drivers in China are a in special social class, which is higher than average. Partially because they drive for officials, they have more chances to be with officials, the symbol of power in China. Sometimes the drivers can even influence the official decisions.

Quality control is based on the standard of Volkswagen in Germany, which is 2.3 (on a five-point scale, with 1 being highest quality). The company periodically has an international quality audit where the car is checked from the customer's point of view. This audit reached the figure 2.3 in 1988, which is a higher quality standard than that achieved in Brazil and Mexico. The Shanghai VW started at 3.5.

The company has consistently placed emphasis on increasing the use of Chinese-made parts and components in the manufacture of its cars. In 1991, 83 percent of domestically made models with 60 percent of parts made in China reached approved quality levels (*Li Rongxia*, 1992, p. 36). Body frames, engines, and gear-boxes are all produced in China.

Designing a new model is in process. According to plan, beginning in 1995, a new car will be produced at the company's expanded facilities in Shanghai. It is being designed with VW's Brazilian subsidiary and will be based on the current-generation Passat, which is not built in China. The wheelbase will be extended 3.5 inches, and the car will get an all-new body with a larger space inside. "This is the first step toward developing a car by ourselves," said Stefan Messman, the Shanghai Volkswagen's deputy managing director in 1992.

Price, Promotion, and Distribution

The company knows that millions of eager buyers are waiting for their cars. Each car is driven away by its buyer immediately after it rolls off the assembly line. There is no real need for promotion at the present stage of the Chinese economy. Once in a while the company advertises on TV or newspapers to increase awareness of "Shanghai Santana" and upgrade its position in people's eyes. Because of China's history as a central-planned economy country, there are no private car dealers. All cars are distributed by state-owned companies, and Shanghai Volkswagen is no exception. All Santana cars are distributed by a state-owned company in Shanghai. But because of the strong demand and the high profit potential, many people bypass that company and directly buy the cars from the factory through personal relationships. In the market, no other cars of the nature of the Santana are made in the domestic industry. Although Beijing Jeep makes Jeep Cherokee and the Soviet-designed 2020N series, Guangzhou Peugeot makes Peugeot cars, and the Charade cars are made in Tianjin, their production level is too low to fill this market. The imported Japanese cars are sold for over RMB250,000 (US$53,000 at the 1990 official exchange rate), and the quantity is decreasing.

Concerned with this situation, the Shanghai VW Corp. sells their cars, after tax, at RMB178,000 (US$37,800 at the 1990 rate)—roughly six times the price the joint venture could charge if it ever exports its cars (*The Economist*, 1990, pp. 66–68). The profit margin is so high that the company's books in the 1988 tax year, showed profits handsomely above Volkswagen's worldwide targets. Although the Shanghai Santana factory price is unbelievably high compared with that of other countries, the price offered by a few automobile trade corporations in some cities is well above RMB210,000, an even more unbelievable price. And personal relationships to buy a car are still relied on. This supports the conclusion that China is a huge market, whose potential has come.

However, to a great extent, China is still a centrally planned economy. Sometimes when problems happen to the economy, the government has to make some temporary policies to remedy the economy. This would definitely influence all industries. When the government adopted an austerity program in 1989 to curb the inflated economy, the economy went into recession and the market shrank. At this time, in order not to hurt foreign investors' zeal and show the government's confidence for the open policy, the government bought 1,500 Santanas produced in Shanghai, according to an official in charge of auto venture in the State Planning Commission as quoted in the official *China Daily* on November 19, 1989. On the other hand, the company made their efforts, too. As they are very familiar with the importance of the personal relationship in doing business in China, they used it. They even persuaded President Jiang Zeming, who is also China's Communist Party general secretary and a former mayor of Shanghai, to order state authorities to buy the factory's unsold backlog of 3,000 cars (*The Economist*, 1990, pp. 66–68). This problem occurred just once following establishment of the joint venture.

Present and Future

With seven years' great effort, the Shanghai Volkswagen has formed a manufacturing capacity for 60,000 cars and 100,000 engines a year, positioning itself as the sole car producer with mass production facilities in China.

In order to upgrade features, the company has always adhered to the technical standards of Santanas of the Volkswagen Corp. of Germany. The Shanghai Santana has been rated the best vehicle of its kind in an appraisal of manufacture of similar models produced by the Volkswagen Corp. subsidiaries in four countries.

By the end of 1991, the company had total production of 106,725 cars and 110,000 engines. Labor productivity reached 9.5 cars per worker, the highest in China and on a close par with the German parent corporation. And in 1992, Volkswagen had sales of 90,000 vehicles with 7.11 billion yuan in the Chinese market. It has become the largest car maker in China.

At present the company is entering the second phase of technological renovation. A new model will be introduced in 1995 and the joint venture plans to produce 90,000 the first year and 150,000 per year thereafter.

As time goes by, the Chinese car industry will develop very fast. Other car makers will raise their output greatly and grow up as competitors against Shanghai Volkswagen. Although it has a long way to go to meet the demand of this market which has 1.28 billion people, the Shanghai VW should make a long-term strategic plan to position itself against the future competition. The first impending change will be the distribution channel. After the reform reaches a new stage, the company cannot expect the government to distribute all cars and cannot rely on personal relationships to sell a large quantity of cars. The company needs to consider building its own distribution channels. Perhaps local automobile trade companies that now exist all over the country can be part of the solution. They can possibly change into tomorrow's car dealers in China. Another question is, as Volkswagen hopes to use its China operations as a bridgehead for exports to the Asian market, How can it make exports profitable under the present condition that the domestic price is several times higher than that for export?

In conclusion, both the Chinese and Germans are very optimistic about Shanghai Volkswagen's future.

Case 8: Hillebrand Estates Winery Limited: Competing Against the World on the Basis of Unique Quality

The New Challenges of the Global Economy

Prior to recent decisions by the General Agreement on Tariffs and Trade (GATT) and prior to the Canada-U.S. Free Trade Agreement (FTA), Canada's wine industry existed behind a set of protective barriers. Not surprisingly, the discussions leading up to the FTA included considerable concern about the potential damage that the FTA could cause to an industry that had experienced this protection. Would Canada's wineries be able to adjust to the global market? Hillebrand, an Ontario company, took a strong public position that it could, in fact, successfully compete under the new international trade arrangements, with the lowering of Canadian protective measures. In fact, the former president of Hillebrand, John Swan, wrote a letter to the Toronto Star in November 1987, in which he discussed the FTA in a positive light. Swan also advocated the elimination of interprovincial barriers to trade as another important stimulus to competitive efficiency.

> Yes, some wineries will close down, but those committed to producing world-class wines will challenge the competition. Canadian wineries are now producing international award-winning wines from the grapes grown in Niagara, where climatic conditions are ideal for growing world-class premium grapes.
>
> The 'big boys' in Canada have been forced to open up secondary divisions in other provinces to avoid paying the high tariffs being placed on wines traded between the provinces. If inter-provincial tariffs are dropped as part of the free trade deal or to conform with this week's ruling of the General Agreement on Tariffs and Trade, you will see these secondary plants phased out. But you'll also see expansion at the home base and much more efficiency in the long run. Operating costs will be drastically reduced and prices will reflect that, which will make them more competitive with California's so-called 'big boys'. It will take a strong political will from Federal and Provincial governments to remove the inter-provincial liquor board tariffs. We must receive national treatment East to West as well as North and South.[1]

Faced with the prospect of the FTA, Hillebrand initiated a thorough corporate restructuring that impacted most aspects of its operations. As indicated in its President's 1987 public statement, Hillebrand had a clear vision of its potential international competitiveness. This case study discusses various elements of Hillebrand's corporate restructuring, and it raises questions as to whether or not businesses in other sectors may also compete successfully, internationally, through the pursuit of such a vision.

Background

Hillebrand was founded in 1979 by Joseph Pohorly as a family business; then it was called Neward Wines Inc. Pohorly was for many years a grape grower. However, within a few years, shares in the winery were sold to Underberg, a European firm involved in the wine business. This decision by Pohorly to give up sole ownership—and, in particular, to involve a European investor—was an important element in the success of Hillebrand Estates Winery Ltd. Corporate restructuring depended upon large capital investments in order to obtain state-of-the-art equipment, and it involved dramatic changes in production and distribution processes. The experience of the European owner, and its ability to raise the requisite capital, was the foundation for this restructuring.

At the outset, we should note that Hillebrand's sales success, particularly in the past few years, was outstanding. In 1989, Hillebrand ranked as the fifth fastest growing company in Canada.[2] Between 1988 and 1990, its revenues rose from $5.2 million to more than $8.2 million.

This case was prepared by David W. Conklin of the Western Business School. Copyright © 1994 by The University of Western Ontario.

This material is not covered under authorization from CanCopy or any reproduction rights organization. Any form of reproduction, storage or transmittal of this material is prohibited without written permission from Western Business School, The University of Western Ontario, London, Canada N6A 3K7. Reprinted with permission, Western Business School.

[1] *Toronto Star*, 13 November 1987, A25.

State of the Art

When George Sorensen became president of Hillebrand near the beginning of 1990, only 14% of Hillebrand's wines were in the premium end of the market. By the end of 1992, Hillebrand predicts that 40% of its wines will have achieved similar status. However, it is true that Hillebrand had a strong emphasis on quality in previous years as well. For example, Hillebrand carefully chose exceptional winemakers in the past. Winemakers must not only be masters of the process of making the wines and creating blends of them, but they must also be masters of the technical side of the processing equipment as well. Hillebrand always brought winemakers from Europe to work at Hillebrand, winemakers who were accustomed to producing top-quality wines. The prospect of world competition led Hillebrand to further intensify its quality objectives by undertaking several more initiatives.

Hillebrand undertook substantial capital investments, choosing state-of-the-art equipment. In this, the company was helped significantly by the fact that the controlling shareholder, Emil Underberg, is a European with considerable experience in European wineries. Consequently, in the late 1980s, Underberg invested $9 million to update Hillebrand's equipment and wine stores. This relationship brought not only necessary capital but also an expertise that has been important to Hillebrand's overall objectives. On a continuing basis, Hillebrand employees discuss technical matters with their European counterparts. As George Sorensen has explained:

> Hillebrand has invested in state-of-the-art winemaking equipment, state-of-the-art wine processing equipment, and state-of-the-art production equipment. We have the very best equipment you can buy in the wine industry. And, this investment was made very specifically to assure that we could make the best wine that could be made.

New Brands

Hillebrand worked closely with the farmers who grow its grapes as well, seeking to improve the quality of the grapes that Hillebrand uses. Hillebrand negotiated long-term contracts with growers in order to ensure a secure supply of top-quality grapes. In order to assist Canadian growers, Hillebrand, once again, sought help from its European associates, sometimes sending Canadian growers to Europe to learn from the best practices there. A special goal in the pursuit of quality was the development of varietal brands that could be priced considerably higher than many other Canadian wines. These came from grapes grown in particular vineyards—grapes that have an unique capability to produce a distinctive flavour.

Premium Wines

Hillebrand created many new brands in the premium wine category. Sales of these new brands increased as a percentage of total sales. Hillebrand, for example, is the only winery in Canada to have method champenoise cellars. Its production process for champagne follows the traditional European method, and Hillebrand developed this process with a sister winery, Mounier, of Austria, which is a member of the Underberg Family Group. Hillebrand placed a gradually increasing emphasis on the creation of new brands of red wines as well, where it expects a growth in consumer interest in the coming years. It has also been the first to develop the now famous "Icewine." In order to strengthen its market image, it has designed new labels and special bottles that make these and other products distinctively different on the shelves in a wine store.

Hillebrand has been able to achieve some of these quality objectives because it is vertically integrated. Each division has its own director. Vertical integration includes the growing and the purchase of grapes, the production of wine, warehousing, distribution, retailing, and exports.

Systems: Physical/Automated

In developing its unique quality, Hilebrand has been extremely concerned about efficiency in cost. It is not enough to focus solely on quality improvements and a distinctive product. For Hillebrand, the pursuit of cost efficiency has meant a restructuring of its internal

[2] "Fine Foods Goes to Zand," *Small Business* (June 1990):50

systems, both the physical procedures of production, warehousing, and selling, and also the information and control systems that utilize modern computer equipment and software. As George Sorensen has explained:

> We're now placing greater emphasis, internally, from the point of view of systems. We're looking at the efficiency of our systems—that is both in physical systems terms and in automated systems terms. We've just completed a review of our operations systems. We've put in some improvements that will increase the efficiency of processing, and the efficiency of distribution. We have almost completed an integrated computer system—a system that links our wine making with our production planning, our distribution, and our retail.
>
> Of course, the fermentation process itself has always involved a separate system of information and supervision. It is necessary to manage the bulk inventory. After the wine is made, then the management of that bulk inventory involves information and control systems all the way through the process to the customer—right to the point of sale. And, we have pretty well 'nailed that down'. It's a very clean system. What we've done, in the first instance, is to develop a PC-based networking system. We're looking over the next 2 to 3 years at having a fully integrated system. And, we're talking to some people about fully integrated software packages with various modules. We'll have a module, if you will, for the winemaking side, a module on the production side, the distribution side, and the retail side. Each software package will be linked. Our goal is to have an interface among the packages, but each package could be independent of the others. Each of the operating entities will have its own subsystem to help it to guide and to measure its own performance.

COSTS

> Cost control is absolutely the golden priority every day. We have had a lot of success, but it all comes down to efficiency. We have a very, very good system for monitoring and measuring our costs: a highly disciplined system of accountability and responsibility for each of the operating entities. Each individual division is financially accountable. We have a budgetary system which essentially breaks out each of the elements, and also includes the capital investments. Consequently, we deal with both the capital investment side and the operating expense side. It's a very clear definition of accountability; our controller monitors operations very effectively.

INVENTORY

The amount of money that we have tied up in inventory is very significant. There are many aspects to production planning: the cost of labour, processing, and warehousing, the efficiency of the materials handling processes, and the cost of the system which distributes to 42 stores. It is important that the most economical shipment of quantities is made to each store. Exporting presents a further set of inventory issues.

The retail stores phone in their orders; they have an order entry system. The efficiency of the processing on that side, is the efficiency of organizing the orders and deliveries, the efficiency of laying out the warehouse to minimize the amount of time and motion, the elements of the order picking, and the truck loading and distribution. All of those elements have to be monitored and measured very carefully and quantified as best we can to be sure that we are maximizing the efficiency of these elements. There is a tremendous amount of money involved if it is done efficiently compared to doing it 'sort of ad hoc' or letting one activity be isolated from the other. I'm very strong on integration.

New Marketing Strategies: Linking a Quality Product with Customer Perceptions

Retail Stores

For many years, Hillebrand, like some other Ontario wineries, operated retail stores that sold its product lines. As part of its corporate restructuring, Hillebrand examined these existing stores, carefully, especially from the perspective of their locations. Realizing that the FTA would likely limit the creation of future stores, it decided to extend this aspect of its business just prior to the FTA decision. The existing Ontario licenses were "grandfathered" under the FTA, with their continued operation being permitted. However, no more private retail licenses would be granted. Thus, as part of its retail emphasis, over the 1990–92 period, Hillebrand closed 14 stores and opened 16 new ones.

New Locations/New Training

George Sorensen explains that the choice of location has recently been based upon a greater in-depth analysis of a professional nature. This has included the analysis of a wider variety of types of stores. For example, Hillebrand has been experimenting with the concept of operating its own retail boutiques within larger stores and supermarkets. These have included several within Loblaws supermarkets, as well as a couple within gourmet specialty stores. Hillebrand has undertaken a number of new approaches that have strengthened the competitive position of its stores in attracting consumers, and in encouraging them to be repeat customers. For example, store staff are well trained to assist the public. Assistance includes technical advice that customers find essential in this kind of product. It also includes encouraging the customer to taste the wines that Hillebrand offers. Each store has an extensive range of tastings, particularly for its newer brands. This tasting process is especially important for customers who are considering premium wines. Staff are also trained in the skills of salesmanship, including the process of encouraging the customer to choose better quality and higher-priced brands. Not only direct but indirect salesmanship is an important marketing tool. Hillebrand places a heavy emphasis on training staff in the technicalities of in-store merchandising and "shelf management," including special display racks.

Hillebrand uses its stores to deal effectively with the greater interest of Canadian consumers in the alternative qualities of wines that are now available to them. Increasingly, prospective purchasers express an interest in trying new kinds of foods. As Sorensen explains, "So, we find people much more curious and they want to experiment more, and the more curious they are and the more they want to experiment, the more we have an ability to influence the decision."

Pricing/Packaging

A related area of corporate restructuring has been Hillebrand's new approach to the pricing and packaging of its products. George Sorensen feels that this is another essential element in strengthening international competitiveness:

The other thing is in packaging—new package design, new product packaging concepts, price positioning—giving much more attention to the demand elasticity, if you will, as it relates to our price position. Today, we don't necessarily price position against the competition. We price position on the basis of what we think the consumer perceives as a rational relationship between price and quality. We don't just look at what the competition is doing in its pricing. We watch it continually, we analyze it, we study it. But, we don't follow the competition on the pricing side of it.

We try to get as close to the customer as we can, and we try to get a feel for what the customer is prepared to pay. And, again, given the size of our operation, given the emphasis we put on quality and the money we spend on the quality side of the business and the relatively high quality level of our wines, there's a cost to our pursuit of quality. The best way to recover it, of course, is to have the right retail price. We found that given the captive retail environment in which we operate, which is highly convenience oriented, the consumers are prepared to pay. And, they are prepared to come back and buy again if the quality is there. If, their perception of value is enhanced, then they will be back. I was always satisfied that we could price position to the point whereby we wouldn't have to be looking over our shoulders at the competition. We should be looking more directly in the eyes of the consumer, and asking the consumer, "What are you prepared to pay for the wine you are buying?"

The Impact of the FTA

Many commentators believed that the FTA would severely hurt Canada's wineries. Writing in the *Financial Post* in 1988, for example, the columnist John Schreiner stated that:

No industry faces a more rapid adjustment under the terms of the free trade pact: the bulk of the protective measures will be gone in two years. The Canadian negotiators threw in the towel for two reasons. First, Canada was losing before the General Agreement on Tariffs & Trade tribunal a challenge to the two-tier provincial markups which have given domestic wines a price advantage compared with imports. Secondly, there were bigger trade issues to argue. Former Trade minister Pat Carney said there was no point to arguing "about plonk."[3]

Prior to the FTA, the wine industry was closely regulated both at the Federal and Provincial levels. These regulations influenced the structure of the industry, the cost of production, and the product pricing and marketing. There has been a wine industry presence in seven out of the ten provinces.

Ontario/British Columbia

The wine industry in Ontario and British Columbia has been closely linked to the grape-growing sector and, as such, has been heavily influenced by agricultural policies. Provincial agricultural regulations influenced the ability of wineries in these provinces to source competitively priced inputs and and to select desirable grape varieties. In these two provinces, for example, there were—prior to the FTA—blending restrictions which tied the use of imported grapes, grape equivalent, or wine to a proportion of domestically grown grapes purchased. In addition, there were limits to the proportion of imported material in any one product. In Ontario, wineries utilized between 50% and 70% of the annual domestic grape crop with the remainder being used for non-wine purposes such as juice and fresh fruit markets or for purchase as surplus. In British Columbia, wineries were required to purchase all the grape crop, except some 5% which found its way into the market for juice or fresh fruit consumption. In contrast, the other eight provinces used primarily imported juice, grapes or concentrates to make wine, which could be blended with wine imported in bulk and then bottled for the domestic market, or imported and bottled without blending.

Tariffs

Prior to the FTA, tariffs on wine products were low and had little influence on trade in wine. Canadian tariff rates were C$0.20 per gallon for still-grape wines, while U.S. tariffs were higher at US$0.375 to US$0.625 per gallon (C$0.454 to C$09.756, based on an exchange rate of C$1.21 = US$1.00). In the case of sparkling wine, the Canadian tariff was C$4.00 per dozen bottles (approximately C$2.00 per gallon) whereas U.S. tariffs were US$1.17 (C$1.42) per gallon.

Pricing Practices

Of greater importance than tariffs in influencing trade were provincial listing and distribution and pricing practices. These became major irritants to Canada's trading partners. In the late 1980s, there was also a formal complaint by the EC upheld by a GATT Panel Report (October 1987) that these practices were inconsistent with international trading rules. In the FTA, several important changes were made to ease access of U.S. wines to the Canadian market.

U.S. Wines

Under the FTA, national treatment is granted to U.S. wines for listings and distribution. U.S. wines are to be treated no less favorably than Canadian products, and an administrative appeal process will review disputed listing decisions. Differences in price mark-ups in excess of those justified for cost-of-service considerations were reduced by 25% on the effective date of the agreement, with a further 25% reduction one year later. The remaining difference was to be eliminated in equal steps over the remaining five years.

Other FTA Effects

Other effects of the FTA are that: Quebec may continue its requirement that wine sold in grocery stores be bottled in Quebec, provided there are alternative outlets, such as the liquor stores, available for U.S. wines. Private wine stores in British Columbia and Ontario are permitted to continue operating, but new licenses will not be granted. Current listings of estate wineries in British Columbia will be retained. U.S. state-controlled liquor agencies, which are the equivalent of Canada's liquor control boards, will be required to accord Canadian wines national treatment. Both U.S. and Canadian tariffs will be reduced to zero in equal steps over a 10-year period. It should be noted that the FTA does not require changes to either Canada's internal interprovincial barriers to trade in wine or to domestic wine content regulations.

---

[3] *Financial Post Daily*, 4 August 1988, v. 1 (108), 5.

Foreign Wines

An essential aspect of Canadian protectionism has been the practice of provincial stores that sell alcoholic beverages, and the regulatory bodies that supervise them, to purchase only a limited number of foreign wines that could compete effectively against Canadian wines. Wineries in other countries have argued before GATT that their wineries have been excluded from Canadian provincial listings as a result. In addition, Canadian provincial regulatory bodies and provincial retail outlets have added extra markups to foreign wines, making them relatively more expensive than Canadian products. To some degree, these higher markups are justified, Canadian supporters claim, because of the higher handling costs for foreign lines. Such actions have also been criticized by foreign wineries.

This subject raises the interesting question of the degree to which a federal international commitment can bind provincial jurisdictions. The Ontario government, in particular, took the position that its practices could not be controlled by these trade agreements, since its practices were within provincial jurisdiction under the Canadian constitution. Apart from the interjurisdictional question, this subject also raises the point that various interpretations can be given to the ruling concerning equal treatment. To what degree do the higher costs involved with importing foreign wines really justify higher retail prices? In choosing among a huge number of potential wines to list, it may be a matter of subjective judgement as to the number that should be from Canada as opposed to the number that should be from other countries.

Hillebrand's response to the FTA has been to undertake the corporate restructuring discussed above. An unique aspect, of course, was the decision by Hillebrand to participate actively in the retail store business. Under the FTA, U.S. wineries are not permitted to own and operate stores in Canada. This gives Hillebrand and other wineries a marketing advantage vis-à-vis foreign wineries. Hillebrand also sells through the provincially owned and operated retail outlets, in which it competes directly with all the other brands that the government stores sell. Hillebrand's decision to focus on the creation of its unique quality has been the basis for its competitive position. As discussed above, it has been essential that Hillebrand accompany this quality emphasis with new approaches to cost control, packaging, and pricing.

Clustering: The Porter Thesis

No doubt Hillebrand has also been helped by the recent success of other Niagara area wineries. Hillebrand is not alone in the restructuring processes that it has put in place, nor is it alone in the public recognition of its success. Among our group of case studies, Ontario's wineries and grape growers come closest to illustrating Michael Porter's "cluster" theories.

Awards

The magazine *The Ontario Grape Grower* serves this burgeoning sector. It relates many success stories of Ontario wineries. Throughout the world, and particularly in various European countries, there are frequent competitions in which recognized authorities from many vineyards taste the wines and award medals. Ontario's wineries have, indeed, been able to win gold, silver, and bronze medals in competition with leading European wineries. Hillebrand is Canada's most award winning winery and has won gold medals for its Chardonnay and Icewine in International Competitions. The most prestigious award was the Decanter Trophy for its Riesling at the International Wine & Spirits Competition in London, England in 1990. The Hillebrand Riesling ranked above 28 entries from wineries around the world. The summer 1991 issue of the *Ontario Grape Grower* featured a victory of Inniskillin wine and emphasized the favourable impact of this even on the reputation of other Ontario wineries.

> The bi-annual global wine competition held in Bordeaux attracted 4,100 wine entries from 38 wine producing nations in June. Inniskillin Wines, of Niagara-on-the-Lake, walked off with one of the nine gold medals awarded—the Grand Prix d'Honneur, and instantly elevated the wines of Ontario into international fame and acclaim. Inniskillin's 1989 Vidal Ice

Wine brought back to Canada the greatest honor ever awarded to a Canadian wine.[4]

The winter 1991-92 edition of this magazine reports as follows:

> Brights Wines showed its class and versatility in Barcelona, Spain, taking gold and silver medals at the 1991 International Mode Selection Competition. Capturing the gold was Brights 1989 Vidal. The silver was awarded to its late harvest 1989 Baco Noir. And Niagara wines continue to prove their excellence. The Cellars of the World competition was a Canadian triumph, with wines winning 18 of 60 awards.[5]

It is important to emphasize that many of Ontario's vineyards have been able to restructure successfully. It is also interesting to ask the question whether this successful restructuring would have occurred without the new competitive pressures of the GATT ruling and the FTA. John Godfrey discussed this subject in a *Financial Post* article entitled "From Plonk to Vintage." He quoted Hillebrand's John Swan, "Without GATT and the FTA, the industry would have died a lingering death. This has been a useful jolt. We can produce world-class grapes here."[6]

Ontario Grape Growers

It is also important to understand the radical transformation within Ontario's grape-growing industry, and to see how the success of wineries depended upon the success of Ontario's grape growers. As indicated above, Hillebrand worked very closely with grape growers in their efforts to improve the quality of their crop. Other vineyards have also assisted the growers. The result was that the growers themselves became internationally competitive. An article on this subject in *The Ontario Grape Grower* entitled "1991 Harvest Outstanding," presented the following summary:

> Ontario's grape industry is one of the few real bright spots in Canada's beleaguered agricultural sector these days. We can boast of an outstanding 1991 harvest of the best quality grapes ever produced in Ontario. This vintage comes on the heels of three successive vintages which have won recognition here at home and around the world. And for the first time in 12 years, there was no surplus of Ontario grapes. We sold all grapes we produced. Prices, at least for wine grapes, are also up moderately.
>
> After four successive years of consistent high quality vintages, we can say with a great degree of confidence that Ontario grape growers have mastered the art of growing vinifera varieties in Ontario.
>
> New plantings since 1988 assure an excellent and steadily increasing supply of high quality grapes, at least through the next three years. These new plantings represent an investment by Ontario grape growers exceeding $10 million.
>
> Also looking to the future, we continue to expand existing markets and to diversify into new markets. This year growers will complete the planting of 500 acres of currently underused agricultural land to supply 2,500 additional tonnes of Ontario Niagara grapes to the U.S. juice market.[7]

Advertising

In order to convince consumers to pay higher prices for the better quality wines now being produced by many of Ontario's wineries, multi-million dollar advertising campaigns were developed. The various wineries contributed to the cost of these advertising campaigns. It is important to note that the Ontario government also contributed financially to these advertising programs. Various reports, as well as substantial sales increases, suggest that these promotional activities have, in fact, changed the Canadian consumers' perception of Ontario wines.

VQA

Another contribution to this change in public perception was made by the decision to offer wineries a classification system in which those brands that meet certain quality-oriented criteria can be labeled as VQA (Vintage Quality Alliance). From the perspective of our case study, it is interesting to note that Hillebrand claims to produce over 50% of all the

---

[4] "Ontario Wine takes Gold in Bordeaux," *The Ontario Grape Grower* 23/2 Summer 1991, 1.
[5] "Medals and More Medals," *Ontario Grape Grower* Winter 1991-92, 6.
[6] *The Financial Post*, find date.
[7] Art Smith, "1991 harvest outstanding," *The Ontario Grape Grower*

VQA wines in Ontario, and that Hillebrand uses the VQA designation as a marketing tool.

Experimenting in the World Market

Hillebrand's first general response to being exposed to world competitive pressures was to defend its own territory. The various activities discussed above were aimed primarily at the Canadian market, and particularly, the market within Ontario. This creation of a strong home base, and the later exploration of foreign markets is another theme that is central to Porter's competitiveness literature.

An important element of Hillebrand's decision making was the strategic alliance with European wineries also owned by Emil Underberg. Hillebrand's stationery proudly states, "A member of the Underberg family." Geroge Sorensen described the process as one of continually exchanging information. While this information is often related to production technology, it also deals with new marketing concepts.

Exports

In recent years, Hillebrand gradually established relationships with certain distributors and sales agents in other countries. For example, Hillebrand now exports to Japan. In order to be accepted in the Japanese market, Hillebrand met extremely strict Japanese beverage standards. This it did successfully. The United States, however, poses different difficulties, since like Canada, each state has jurisdiction over alcohol sales, and the practices and procedures vary from one state to another. In some situations, a wholesale distributor buys the product from Hillebrand. In other states, government liquor boards purchase Hillebrand's exports under a system similar to that of Ontario's. Overall, 5% of Hillebrand's production is currently exported to a variety of countries.

The emphasis on quality, discussed above, was an essential foundation for this export success. The ability to win medals in international wine competitions was an important aspect of export promotion, since it assured the foreign consumer that Hillebrand's wines were indeed "world-class."

As part of this venture into world competitiveness, Hillebrand diversified. It produces a wide variety of brands; it sells in many different markets. Consequently, it positioned itself well in order to respond to any future changes in the world wine market, even though it may not be possible at this time to predict what changes may occur.

Issues and Implications

The FTA brought radical change to Canada's wine industry. The strong protection provided, in the past, by the listing and markup practices of provincial authorities shielded this sector from foreign competition. Faced with the clear threat of new competitive pressures, many firms within this sector have quickly adjusted through a series of measures illustrated in the Hillebrand case. What has made this sector so successful in understanding and adopting these measures? Is this sector unique, or does it provide a helpful example for others?

To what degree is the remarkable success due to its close relationships with its suppliers—the grape growers—and the close geographical proximity within which both the wineries and the grape growers find themselves? Does the success of this "cluster" of activities illustrate and support Porter's competitiveness theories? The Ontario government has encouraged cooperation among these firms, particularly in marketing, and it has contributed financial assistance for these cooperative efforts. Does this illustrate and support Porter's views concerning the appropriate role for Canada's governments today?

In Hillebrand's case, it is clear that foreign ownership has been a valuable element underlying success. Is this an exception, or can foreign owners assist other Canadian companies in a similar way, when major corporate restructuring is necessary in order to become competitive in the world market? Is this a new role for foreign ownership, and should Canadians be more receptive to this role, perhaps instituting public policies that encourage it?

Case 9: EQ Bank

On October 20, 1988, Michael Banks, political risk manager of EQ Bank in New York, was approached by Daniel Whitman, president of Enviro-systems, to arrange financing for the construction of a refuse recycling facility to be built in Senegal, Africa. This project called for shipping human refuse from the eastern seaboard of the United States to the West African country where the labor-intensive job of sorting would take advantage of the lower wage rate. The bulk of the refuse was to be sorted into recyclable components such as metals, glass, and plastic; the remainder was to be shredded, sterilized, and then seeded with a bacteria to ferment into a clean compost that would be superior to the local African soil. The human waste and some of the refuse was to be combined to produce methane. Both end products would be sold locally.

Banks was now preparing for a meeting, on November 15, 1988, with Joseph Gergacz, vice president of EQ's venture capital fund management division to discuss procedures for the project.

EQ Bank

EQ Bank, established in 1975, deals primarily in Africa. EQ Bank is a private non-deposit bank whose personnel see themselves as deal makers. They buy and sell a wide variety of African products, for both import and export. They also find buyers and suppliers for African manufactures and provide financial services and capital. Their variety of clients include private businesses, state-owned firms, governments, and international agencies that deal with Africa.

The company is divided into EQ Trade, EQ Aviation, EQ Capital Markets, and EQ Bank. These four units can operate separately or in concert depending on the needs of the client.

The import-export trade division is based on the belief that Africa's future depends on advanced technology and improving methods of production. To this end EQ Trade helps by providing a conduit for knowledge as well as products. It also encourages worldwide purchases of African products. They are manufacturers' agents for mining equipment (drills, bores, dump trucks, heavy earth moving machinery), surface transportation (fishing vessels, oil-field service vessels, railway locomotives and rolling stock, buses, commercial lorries, tractor-trailers), and commercial and general aviation (new and used aircraft, aircraft parts, ground service). They offer financial support in the form of supplier credit lines, short-term bridge financing, and currency hedging. They also act as consultants giving advice on markets, product information, and economic development assistance agency packages. The latter involves products that qualify for special treatment under bilateral or multi-lateral institutions providing grant or concession financing for development projects.

EQ Aviation is a worldwide network of airplanes, parts, and aviation services. Its personnel can provide the equipment to operate an airport and the expertise to form an airline.

EQ Capital Markets provides general managerial, financial, and technical skills in support of a wide variety of economic and business activities in Africa. Personnel in this division advise on mergers, acquisitions, divestitures, and joint ventures. They often counsel senior executives of African government ministries, financial institutions, state-owned enterprises, and private firms. They help corporations expand capital, structure debt and equity, and, in general, work to present the enterprise to the financial markets effectively and efficiently.

Through its affiliation with the Hong Kong Bank Group and other contacts in financial centers, EQ Capital Markets works to match capital with worthwhile projects in need of funds. It is also working to establish financial institutions in Africa.

Through its close relationship with African finance ministers and commercial banks, EQ Capital Markets is in an ideal situation to participate in debt-for-equity and debt-for-debt swaps—a practice personnel like to call debt arbitrage.

EQ Bank is the original EQ company. This merchant banking division concentrates most of its activities in trade and capital equipment financing. It is a registered Bahamian bank, and its personnel pride themselves on being able to create a variety of specialized financing structures tailored to specific client needs. They offer a variety of offshore banking services, including foreign currency exchange, hedging, interest rate futures, and interest rate swaps, all performed under the Bank Secrecy Act of the Bahamas.

The projects at EQ Bank were given to teams that had specific knowledge on the business aspects as well as a strong background in the region of Africa involved. With respect to the refuse conversion project, Banks worked with a Senegal and an Ivory Coast national. They were required to report their progress to their superior; however, when questioned on reporting procedures, Banks stated that he "reports occasionally, and sometimes not at all."

Banks had spent two years in the Peace Corps after graduating from Stanton College with a degree in philosophy. He then earned a master's degree in international affairs from Columbia University. After working for Chase Manhattan Bank for sixteen months, he returned to his undergraduate university and taught for one year. He then came to EQ Bank, and has been there for almost two years. He is a humanitarian and always stresses how he and his company are in business to help Africa, not just to make money.

The Rubbish

Currently the United States is producing 200 million tons of rubbish per year and it is disposed of by either landfall, incineration, or recycling. Burying is the cheapest and accounts for 90 percent of American disposal; however, this is likely to decrease in the future. Americans are voting to keep the smelly dump sites away from their homes and environmentalists are constantly campaigning to eliminate them altogether. Environmentalists are armed with many cases of poisoned land—completed dump sites where the rubbish is producing methane, thus making the land unusable.

Landfill sites are also being exhausted. One-third have closed since 1980, and more than half the cities on the East Coast will exhaust their sites by 2000. In New York fourteen sites have closed in the past ten years and now most of the city's 24,000 tons of trash per day is put into the Fresh Kills landfill on Staten Island. This site produces 5 million cubic feet of methane per year, enough to heat 50,000 homes. As landfill sites fill up, municipalities have looked to other locations. The notorious garbage barge, the Mobro, publicized this crisis when it spent two months in the summer of 1987 meandering around the Caribbean looking for a dump site for its 3,100 tons of New York's trash before returning home with it.

Incineration has the advantage of reducing the rubbish to ash, greatly decreasing the volume, and generating energy that by law, the local utility must buy. At this time there are several domestic American companies operating profitable incineration plants.

The major drawback to incineration is pollution. The smoke plume can contain hydrogen chloride and dioxin if the smokestack is not equipped with expensive scrubbing equipment. This added cost increases the incinerator's burning charge by almost 50 percent. However, not all states require such equipment and many believe that in the long run this will give incinerators a black eye. Also, the ash, which still must be disposed of, often contains dioxin and heavy metals. The introduction of these contaminants can be reduced with an extensive sorting of the input but this, too, is very expensive.

In other parts of the world recycling is a major solution to the problem of rubbish disposal. In Japan, for example, more than half of the waste paper is recycled and in Germany nearly 40 percent of the glass is recycled. Yet Americans only recycle 28 percent of their aluminum, 27 percent of their paper, and 10 percent of their glass. This seems to be a product of capitalism, as the sale of recycled material will not pay for the cost of collecting and reprocessing it in a free market.

The cost of landfills is estimated to be from $40 to $60 per ton and incineration is between $70 and $120 per ton. This implies that a net gain to society would occur if a subsidy of up to $40 per ton were made—potentially a politically dangerous move. But even if such a subsidy were granted, recycling only affects specific components and is only as effective as the consumers make it.

The newest approach to disposal problems comes from companies like Enviro-systems. Their system of converting rubbish into fertilizer by shredding, sterilizing, and seeding the waste with bacteria is already in use in France, producing 800,000 tons a year, and another plant in Pompano Beach, Florida, will open soon.

The Project

The people at Enviro-systems estimate that with the cheaper labor in Africa they will be able to collect, transport, and process rubbish for $70 per ton. This low cost is due mainly to the wage rate in Senegal, which is approximately $10 per day.

Senegal was selected not only for its low wage rate but also because it had a relatively stable dictatorship government that had been in power for the past twenty years. Furthermore, the country was in an economic decline, so the prospect of employing 700 to 800 people should outweigh the undesirable aspects of foreign rubbish processing.

The beauty of recycling is that the accepting country is paid to receive rubbish from municipalities and private collection agencies as well as being paid for the recycled product.

Enviro-systems estimates that it will require $25 million to build the collection site in the United States and the facility in Africa, which will have a 4000 ton per day capacity. They would also like to purchase a 10,000 ton vessel for transporting the rubbish. They believe the project will be very profitable; in fact, they predict making $378 million over the first six years.

The demand for fertilizer and methane in Africa is quite strong, and even though other disposal techniques are being explored, their impact on the demand for disposal is expected to be minimal. If the system is operational soon and the company lands some long-term contracts, the profit predictions may be fulfilled.

EQ Bank's Problem

To obtain financing EQ Bank must first convince the host country, Senegal, that the project will be beneficial to its society and not harmful to its environment. To help in this, Banks was trying to get endorsements from environmental organizations such as Greenpeace and the EPA. As a backup and bartering chip, he was also looking at nearby countries that would be acceptable.

EQ Bank then had to convince lenders of the viability of the project. Banks was planning to solicit funds from the World Bank, a very conservative donor group. In order to get funds from the World Bank, Banks knew that he would need to prove the soundness of the project both financially and environmentally, especially the latter. This aspect worried Banks, who did not have a technical background and was not quite sure what to look for or how to prove the system's safety. This is where the competition comes into play.

The Competition

Many of the large investment banking houses on Wall Street saw refuse recycling projects as a means to accomplish two goals. First, as the statistics presented above illustrate, there is a growing demand for this kind of facility, and investment bankers saw this project as a new niche in the market. They were working to develop a small staff of experts who understood the problems associated with installing such a facility and with environmental legislation, lobbying, and environmental engineering.

Secondly, this was an ideal opportunity to improve their public image. With all the negative publicity coming out of the insider trading scandals, firms like the former Drexel Burnham were eager to be involved in projects that were considered to be in the best interest of the country.

The Meeting

It is now the beginning of November, and Banks and his cohorts have approximately two weeks to formulate a strategy and gather the appropriate data to support it.

Case 10: International Machine Corporation

International Machine Corporation (IMC) manufactures food-processing and packaging equipment. IMC's revenues in 1983 amounted to $12 billion, of which 45 percent was generated outside the United States. IMC has subsidiaries in twenty-three countries and licensing arrangements in eight others.

IMC management was contemplating the establishment of a subsidiary in Mexico where it was thought that demand was sufficient for their product and that the local market and economy were expanding and would be receptive to such an investment. IMC had exported products to Mexico for several years. Before proceeding to invest money in the Mexican project, IMC wanted to determine the financial reliability of the project. IMC's president, Charles Futell, asked Lewis Harvey, vice president of the International Division of the company, to work out a detailed financial analysis of the project. At his request, IMC's controller's office had supplied Harvey with considerable information.

Annual inflation was projected at 5 percent in Mexico and 2.5 percent in the United States. The current exchange rate, $1 for 22 pesos, was expected to remain fixed over the life of the investment.

Initial Investment

It was estimated that it would take one year to purchase and install plant and equipment.

Imported machinery and equipment would cost $9 million. No import duties would be levied by the Mexican government. With a small allowance for banking fees, the bill would come to 200 million Mexican pesos.

The plant would be set up on government-owned land, which would be sold to IMC for 20 million pesos.

IMC planned to maintain effective control of the subsidiary with ownership of 60 percent of equity. The remaining 40 percent was to be distributed widely among Mexico's financial institutions and private investors. Accordingly, IMC needed to invest $6 million U.S. in the project.

Working Capital

The company planned to maintain 5 percent of each year's sales as a minimum cash balance.

Accounts receivable were estimated to be seventy-three days of annual sales.

Inventory was estimated to be 20 percent of the following year's sales.

Accounts payable were estimated to be 5 percent of the year-end inventory.

Other payables were estimated to be 5 percent of sales for the current year.

Licensing and overhead allocation fees were to be paid annually at the end of the year.

Sales Volume

Sales volume for the first year was estimated to be 200 units.

Selling price in the first year was estimated to be 1,400,000 pesos per unit.

Sales growth of 10 percent was expected during the project life.

An annual price increase of 20 percent was contemplated.

Cost of Goods Sold

The U.S. parent company was expected to provide parts and components adding up to 180,000 pesos per unit in the first year of operation. These costs (in U.S. dollars) were expected to rise on an average of 10 percent annually, in line with the projected U.S. inflation rate.

Local material and labor costs were expected to be 420,000 pesos per unit, with an annual rate of increase of 20 percent.

This case is printed here with the permission of the authors, Vinod Bavishi of the University of Connecticut, and Hany A. Shawky of the State University of New York at Albany.

Manufacturing overhead (without depreciation) was expected to be 28 million pesos the first year of operation. An average annual rate increase of 15 percent was expected.

Depreciation of manufacturing equipment was to be computed on a straight-line basis, with a project life of ten years and zero salvage value to be assumed.

Selling and Administrative Costs

Variable selling and administrative costs were expected to equal 10 percent of annual sales. These costs were likely to be incurred within Mexico and were expected to rise at 20 percent annually.

Semi-fixed selling costs were expected to equal 5 percent of annual sales. These costs were estimated to rise at 15 percent annually.

Licensing and Overhead Allocation Fees

The parent company would levy 70,000 pesos per unit as licensing and overhead allocation fees, payable at year-end in U.S. dollars.

This fee would increase 20 percent per year to compensate for Mexican inflation.

Interest Expense

Local borrowing could be obtained for working capital purposes at 15 percent. Borrowing would occur at the end of the year with the full year's interest budgeted in the following year.

Any excess funds could be invested in Mexican marketable securities with an annual rate of return of 15 percent. Investment was likely to be made at the end of the year, with the full year's interest to be received the following year.

Income Taxes

Corporate income taxes in Mexico were 42 percent of taxable income. Withholding taxes on licensing and overhead allocation fees were 20 percent.

The parent company's effective U.S. tax rate was 44 percent, which was the rate used in analyzing investment projects. It could be assumed that the parent company could take appropriate credits for taxes paid to, or withheld by, the Mexican government.

Dividend and Terminal Payments

No dividend was planned to be paid for the first three years.

Dividends equal to 70 percent of earnings would be paid to the shareholders, beginning in the fourth year.

It was assumed that, at the end of the tenth year of operation, IMC's share of net worth in the Mexican subsidiary would be remitted in the form of a terminal payment.

Loss of Export Sales

At present, IMC was exporting about twenty-five units per year to Mexico. If IMC decided to establish the Mexican subsidiary, it was expected that the after-tax effects on income due to the lost exports sales would be $648,000, $742,000, and $930,000 in the first three years of operation, respectively.

IMC assumed it could not count on export sales for more than three future years, as the Mexican government was determined to see that such machinery was manufactured locally in the near future.

Case 11: Sperry/MacLennan

In August of 1988 Mitch Brooks, a junior partner and director of Sperry/MacLennan (S/M), a Dartmouth, Nova Scotia, architectural practice specializing in recreational facilities, is in the process of developing a plan to export his company's services. He intends to present the plan to the other directors at their meeting the first week of October. The regional market for architectural services is showing some signs of slowing and S/M realizes that it must seek new markets. As Sheila Sperry, the office manager and one of the directors, said at their last meeting: "You have to go wider than your own backyard. After all, you can only build so many pools in your own backyard."

About the Company

Drew Sperry, one of the two senior partners in Sperry/MacLennan, founded the company in 1982 as a one-man architectural practice. After graduating from the Nova Scotia Technical College (now the Technical University of Nova Scotia) in 1966, Sperry worked for six years for Robert J. Flinn before deciding that it was time to start his own company. By then he had cultivated a loyal clientele and a reputation as a good design architect and planner. In the first year, the business was supported part-time by a contract with the Province of Prince Edward Island Department of Tourism to undertake parks planning and the design of parks facilities from park furniture to interpretive centers. At the end of its first year, the company was incorporated as H. Drew Sperry and Associates; by then Sperry had added three junior architects, a draftsman, and a secretary. One of those architects was John MacLennan, who would later become a senior partner in Sperry/MacLennan.

Throughout the 1970s, the practice grew rapidly as the local economy expanded, even though the market for architectural services was competitive. The architectural program at the Nova Scotia Technical College (TUNS) was graduating more architects wishing to stay in the Maritimes than could be readily absorbed. But that was not the only reason why competition was stiff; there was a perception among businesspeople and local government personnel that, if you wanted the best, you had to get it from Toronto or New York. The company's greatest challenge throughout this period was persuading the local authorities that they did not have to go to Central Canada for first-class architectural expertise.

With the baby boom generation entering the housing market, more than enough business came their way to enable Sperry's to develop a thriving architectural practice, and by 1979 the company had grown to fifteen employees and had established branch offices in Charlottetown and Fredericton. These branch offices had been established to provide a local market presence and meet licensing requirements during their aggressive growth period. The one in Charlottetown operated under the name of Allison & Sperry Associates, with Jim Allison as the partner, while in Fredericton, partner Peter Fellows was in charge.

But the growth could not last. The early 1980s was not an easy time for the industry and many architectural firms found themselves unable to stay in business through a very slow period in 1981–82. For Sperry/MacLennan, it meant a severe reduction in staff and it also marked the end of the branch offices. Financially stretched and with work winding down on a multipurpose civic sports facility, the Dartmouth Sportspex, the company was asked to enter a design competition for an aquatics center in Saint John, New Brunswick. It was a situation where they had to win or close their doors. The company laid off all but the three remaining partners, Drew, Sheila Sperry, and John MacLennan. However, one draftsman and the secretary refused to leave, working without pay for several months in the belief that the company would win; their faith in the firm is still appreciated today.

Their persistence and faith were rewarded. In 1983 Sperry won the competition for the aquatics

---

This case has been prepared by Mary R. Brooks of Dalhousie University as a basis for classroom discussion rather than to illustrate effective or ineffective handling of an administrative situation, and is printed here with her permission. The author gratefully acknowledges the support of the Secretary of State, Canadian Studies Program, in developing the case.

facility for the Canada Games to be held in Saint John. The clients in Saint John wanted to build a new aquatic center that would house the Canada Games competition *and* provide a community facility that was self-supporting after the games were over. The facility needed to project a forward-thinking image to the world and act as a linchpin in the downtown revitalization plan. Therefore, it was paramount that the facility adhere to all technical competition requirements and that the design include renovation details for its conversion to a community facility sporting a new Sperry design element, the "indoor beach." The Saint John Canada Games Society decided to use Sperry for the contract and were very pleased with the building, the more so since the building won two design awards in 1985, the Facility of Merit Award for its "outstanding design" from *Athletics Business* and the Canadian Parks and Recreation Facility of Excellence Award. Sperry had gained national recognition for its sports facility expertise and its reputation as a good design firm specializing in sports facilities was secured.

From the beginning, the company found recreational facilities work to be fun and exciting. To quote Sheila Sperry, the type of client "wants you to be innovative and new. It's a dream for an architect because it gives him an opportunity to use all the shapes and colors and natural light. It's a very exciting medium to work in." So they decided to focus their promotional efforts to get more of this type of work and consolidate their "pool designer" image by associating with Creative Aquatics on an exclusive basis in 1984. Creative Aquatics provided aquatics programming and technical operations expertise (materials, systems, water treatment, safety, and so on) to complement the design and planning skills at Sperry.

The construction industry rebounded in 1984; declining interest rates ushered in a mini building boom that kept everyone busy for the 1984–1987 period. Jim Reardon joined the company in 1983 and quickly acquired the experience and knowledge that would ease the company through its inevitable expansion. John MacLennan, by then a senior shareholder in the firm, wanted to develop a base in the large Ontario market and establish an office in Toronto. Jim Reardon was able to take over John's activities with very little difficulty as he had been working very closely with John in the recreational facilities aspect of the business. Reardon became a junior partner in 1986.

With John MacLennan's move to Toronto in 1985, the company changed its name to Sperry/MacLennan in hopes that the name could be used for both offices. But the Ontario Association of Architects ruled that the name could not include "Sperry" because Drew Sperry was not an Ontario resident, and the Toronto office was required to operate under the name of MacLennan Architects. The Ontario office gradually became self-supporting and the company successfully entered a new growth phase.

Mitch Brooks joined the practice in 1987. He had graduated from TUNS in 1975 and had been one of the small number in his class to try and make a go of it in Halifax. The decision to add Brooks as a partner, albeit a junior one, stemmed from their compatibility. Brooks was a good production architect and work under his supervision came in on budget and on time, a factor compatible with the Sperry/MacLennan emphasis on customer service. The company's fee revenue amounted to approximately $1.2 million in the 1987 fiscal year; however, salaries are a major business expense and profits after taxes (but before employee bonuses) accounted for only 4.5 percent of revenue.

Now it is late August, and with the weather cooling Mitch Brooks reflects on his newest task, planning for the coming winter's activities. The company's reputation in the Canadian sports facility market is secure. The company has completed or has in construction five sports complexes in the Maritimes and five in Ontario, and three more facilities are in design. The awards have followed and, just this morning, Drew was notified of their latest achievement—the company has won the $10,000 *Canadian Architect* Grand Award for the Grand River Aquatics and Community Center near Kitchener, Ontario. This award is a particularly prestigious one as it is given by fellow architects in recognition of design excellence. Last week Sheila Sperry received word that the Amherst, Nova Scotia, YM-YWCA won the American National Swimming Pool and Spa Gold Medal for pool design against French and Mexican finalists, giving them international recognition. Mitch Brooks is looking forward to the task ahead. The partners anticipate a slight slowdown in late 1988 and economists are predicting a recession for 1989. With nineteen employees to keep busy and a competitor on the west coast, they decided this morning that it is time to consider exporting their hard-won expertise.

The Architecture Industry

In order to practice architecture in Canada, an architect must graduate from an accredited school and serve a period of apprenticeship with a licensed architect, during which time he or she must experience all facets of the practice. At the end of this period, the would-be architect must pass an examination similar to that required of U.S. architects.

Architects are licensed provincially and these licenses are not readily transferable from province to province. Various levels of reciprocity are in existence. For this reason, joint ventures are not that uncommon in the business. In order to "cross" provincial boundaries, architecture firms in one province often enter into a joint venture arrangement with a local company. For example, the well-known design firm of Arthur Erickson of Vancouver/Toronto often engages in joint ventures with local production architects, as was the case for their design of the new Sir James Dunn Law Library on the campus of Dalhousie University in Halifax.

In the U.S., Canadian architects are well-respected. The primary difficulty in working in the U.S. has been founded in immigration policies, which limit the movement of staff and provide difficulties in securing contracts. These policies will be eliminated with the Free Trade Agreement and the reciprocity accord signed between the American Institute of Architects and the Royal Architectural Institute of Canada, a voluntary group representing the provincial associations.

As architects in Nova Scotia are ethically prohibited from advertising their services, an architect's best advertisement is a good project, well done and well received. The provincial association (Nova Scotia Association of Architects [NSAA]) will supply potential clients with basic information about licensed firms, their area of specialization, and so on. NSAA guidelines limit marketing to announcements of new partners, presentations to targeted potential clients, advertisements of a business card size with "business card" information, and participation in media events.

The provincial association also provides a minimum schedule of fees, although many clients view this as the maximum they should pay. Although architects would like to think that the client chooses to do business with them because they like their past work, the price of the service is often the decision point. Some developers prefer to buy services on a basis other than the published fee schedule, such as a lump-sum amount or a per square foot price. Although fee cutting is not encouraged by the professional organization, it is a factor in winning business, particularly when interest rates are high and construction slow.

As the "product" of an architecture firm is the service of designing a building, the marketing of the "product" centers on the architect's experience with a particular building type. Therefore, it is imperative that the architect convince the client that he has the necessary experience and capability to undertake the project and complete it satisfactorily. S/M has found with its large projects that the amount of time spent meeting with the client requires some local presence, although the design need not be done locally.

The process of marketing architectural services is one of marketing ideas. Therefore, it is imperative that the architect and the client have the same objectives and ultimately the same vision. Although that vision may be constrained by the client's budget, part of the marketing process is one of communicating with the client to ensure these common objectives exist.

Architects get business in a number of ways. "Walk-in" business is negligible and most of S/M's contracts are a result of one of the following five processes:

1. By referral from a satisfied client.
2. A juried design competition will be announced. (S/M has found that these prestigious jobs, even though they offer "runners-up" partial compensation, are not worth entering except to *win* as costs are too high and the compensation offered

other entrants too low. Second place is the same as last place. The Dartmouth Sportsplex and the Saint John Aquatic Center were both design competition wins.)
3. A client will publish a "Call for Proposals" or a "Call for Expressions of Interest" as the start of a formal selection process. (S/M rates these opportunities; unless they have a 75 percent chance of winning the contract, they view the effort as not worth the risk.)
4. A potential client invites a limited number of architectural firms to submit their qualifications as the start of a formal selection process. (S/M has a prepared qualification package that it can customize for a particular client.)
5. S/M hears of a potential building and contacts the client, presenting its qualifications.

The fourth and fifth processes are most common in buildings done for institutions and large corporations. As the primary buyers of sports facilities tend to be municipalities or educational institutions, this is the way S/M acquires a substantial share of its work. While juried competitions are not that common, the publicity possible from success in landing this work is important to S/M. The company has found that its success in securing a contract is often dependent on the client's criteria and the current state of the local market, with no particular pattern evident for a specific building type.

After the architect signs the contract, there will be a number of meetings with the client as the concept evolves and the drawings and specifications develop. On a large sports facility project, the hours of contact can run into the hundreds. Depending on the type of project, client meetings may be held weekly or every two weeks; during the development of working drawings and specifications for a complex building, meetings may be as often as once a day. Therefore, continuing client contact is as much a part of the service sold as the drawings, specifications, and site supervision and, in fact, may be the key factor in repeat business.

Developers in Nova Scotia are often not loyal buyers, changing architects with every major project or two. Despite this, architects are inclined to think the buyer's loyalty is greater than it really is. Therefore, S/M scrutinizes buyers carefully, interested in those that can pay for a premium product. S/M's philosophy is to provide "quality products with quality service for quality clients," and thus produce facilities that will reflect well on the company.

The Opportunity

In 1987 the Department of External Affairs and the Royal Architectural Institute of Canada commissioned a study of exporting opportunities for architects on the assumption that free trade in architectural services would be possible under the Free Trade Agreement. The report, entitled *Precision, Planning, and Perseverance: Exporting Architectural Services to the United States*, identified eight market niches for Canadian architects in the U.S., one of which was educational facilities, in particular post-secondary institutions.

This niche, identified by Brooks as most likely to match S/M's capabilities, is controlled by state governments and private organizations. Universities are known not to be particularly loyal to local firms and so present a potential market to be developed. The study reported that "post-secondary institutions require design and management competence, whatever the source." Athletic facilities were identified as a possible niche for architects with mixed-use facility experience. Finally, the study concluded that "there is an enormous backlog of capital maintenance and new building requirements facing most higher education institutions."

In addition to the above factors, the study indicated others Brooks felt were of importance:

1. The U.S. has 30 percent fewer architectural firms per capita than Canada.
2. The market shares many Canadian values and work practices.
3. The population shift away from the Northeast to the Sunbelt is beginning to reverse.
4. Americans are demanding better buildings.

Although Brooks knows that Canadian firms have always had a good reputation internationally for the quality of their buildings, he is concerned that American firms are well ahead of Canadian ones in their use of

CADD (computer-assisted design and drafting) for everything from conceptual design to facility management. S/M, despite best intentions, has been unable to get CADD off the ground but is in the process of applying to the Atlantic Canada Opportunities Agency for financial assistance in switching over to CADD.

Finally, the study cautions that "joint ventures with a U.S. architectural firm may be required but the facility managers network of the APPA [Association of Physical Plant Administrators of Universities and Colleges] should also be actively pursued."

Under free trade, architects will be able to freely engage in trade in services. Architects will be able to travel to the U.S. and set up an architectural practice without having to become qualified under the American Institute of Architects; as long as they are members of their respective provincial associations and have passed provincial licensing exams and apprenticeship requirements, they will be able to travel and work in the U.S., and import staff as required.

Where to Start?

In a meeting in Halifax in January 1988, the Department of External Affairs had indicated that trade to the U.S. in architectural services was going to be one positive benefit of the Free Trade Agreement to come into force in January 1989. As a response, S/M has targeted New England for their expansion, because of its geographical proximity to S/M's home base in the Halifax/Dartmouth area, and also because of its population density and similar climatic conditions. However, with all the hype about free trade and the current focus on the U.S., Brooks is quite concerned that the company might be overlooking some other very lucrative markets for his company's expertise. As part of his October presentation to the board, he wants to identify and evaluate other possible markets for S/M's services. Other parts of the U.S., or the affluent countries of Europe where recreational facilities are regularly patronized and design is taken seriously, might provide a better export market, given their string of design successes at home and the international recognition afforded by the Amherst facility design award. Brooks feels that designing two sports facilities a year in a new market would be an acceptable goal.

As part of searching for leads, Brooks notes that the APPA charges $575 for a membership, which provides access to their membership list once a year. But this is only one source of leads. And of course there is the U.S. Department of Commerce Bureau of the Census as another source of information for him to tap. He wonders what other sources are possible.

S/M looks to have a very good opportunity in the New England market with all of its small universities and colleges. After a decade of cutbacks on spending, corporate donations and alumni support for U.S. universities has never been so strong, and many campuses have sports facilities that are outdated and have been poorly maintained. But Mitch Brooks is not sure that the New England market is the best. After all, a seminar on exporting that he attended last week indicated that the most geographically close market, or even the most psychically close one, may not be the best choice for long-run profit maximization and/or market share.

PART · 3

Environmental Factors Affecting International Marketing

CHAPTER 6

Economic Environment

CHAPTER FOCUS

After studying this chapter, you should be able to:

■ Describe the macroeconomic and microeconomic environment

■ Examine the effect of the economic environment on marketing strategy

■ Analyze the economic environment of a country

■ Appreciate the emerging opportunities in developing countries

This chapter deals with the phenomenon of economic environment. In most cases, economic environment can be viewed from two different angles: the macro view or the micro view. From a macro view, people's wants and needs and the economic policy of a country establish market scope and economic outlook. A microenvironmental view focuses on a firm's ability to compete within a market.

Different countries provide varying market potential with respect to population. However, potential per se does not mean that there is a realizable opportunity for any given firm. For example, a low level of economic activity in a country may force most people there to live modestly. In such a country, many foods and services taken for granted in the U.S. are truly luxuries. In addition, even if there is a market, the competition from both existing and other potential businesses may make it difficult for a new firm to establish itself. In brief, the economic environment of a country, both from the macro and micro viewpoints, largely defines the marketing opportunity for international business. The economic environment of the home country, to an extent, also influences marketing overseas. For example, the economic perspectives of the U.S. at a given time will have an effect on the international activity of U.S. firms during that time.

This chapter begins with an examination of the factors that compose macro and microeconomic environments. This explanation is followed by an illustration of the economic environment's impact on international marketing strategy. Finally, a framework for measuring economic potential and conducting opportunity analyses is furnished.

Macroeconomic Environment

A country's economy includes sources of domestic livelihood and the allocation of resources. Because not all of the world's economies operate at the same level of efficiency, it is necessary to form a clear idea of the economic situation of a particular host country in order to make adequate marketing decisions.

Population and Income

The most basic information to be considered is about the nature of the population, because the people, of course, constitute the market. Table 6.1 shows the population of different countries of the world, but population figures alone provide little information, since people must have the means in terms of income to become viable customers. Thus, Table 6.1 also shows population combined with per capita GNP, providing an estimate of consuming capacity. An index of consuming capacity depicts the absolute or aggregate consumption, both in the entire world and in individual economies. The consumption rate can be satisfied either domestically or through imports.

The information in Table 6.1 should be interpreted cautiously because it makes no allowances for the diffcrences in the purchasing power of different countries. The point may be illustrated with reference to Thailand. Although its per capita GNP is lower than that of the U.S., the Thai bhat goes much further than the dollar. For example, one dozen eggs cost only $.79 in Bangkok, while in New York they cost $1.15; an apartment rents for $950 in Bangkok, while the rent for an equivalent apartment in New York is $1,680; the taxi fare for a five-mile ride in New York and Bangkok comes to $8.12 and $1.83, respectively.[1]

TABLE 6.1
Consuming Capacities of Selected Countries

Country	Population*	Per Capita GNP†	Index of Consuming Capacity‡
United States	255.4	23,240	5935.5
Japan	124.5	28,190	3509.7
Germany	80.6	23,030	1856.2
France	57.4	22,260	1277.7
Italy	57.8	20,460	1182.6
United Kingdom	57.8	17,790	1028.3
Canada	27.4	20,710	567.5
Brazil	153.9	2,770	426.3
Netherlands	15.2	20,480	311.3
Australia	17.5	17,260	302.1
Mexico	85.0	3,470	295.0
India	883.6	310	273.9
Switzerland	6.9	36,080	249.0
Belgium	10.0	20,880	208.8
Argentina	33.1	6,050	200.3
Denmark	5.2	26,000	135.2
Turkey	58.5	1,980	115.8
South Africa	39.8	2,670	106.3
Thailand	55.8	1,260	70.3
Israel	5.1	13,220	67.4
Philippines	64.3	770	49.5
New Zealand	3.4	12,300	41.8
Peru	22.4	950	21.3
Ecuador	11.0	1,070	11.8
Paraguay	4.5	1,380	6.2
Uganda	17.5	170	3.0

World Bank Report, 1994. Figures in millions.
†*Statistical Abstract of the United States:* 1994 (Washington, D.C.: U.S. Department of Commerce). Figures in U.S. dollars.
‡Per capita GNP (gross national product) multiplied by total population in billions.

Two conclusions are obvious, however: (1) aggregate consuming capacity depends on total population as well as per capita income, and (2) advanced countries dominate as potential customers. In Chapter 1, it was noted that the U.S. MNCs are mainly active in Western Europe, Japan, and Canada. The reason for this is not difficult to find. In contrast, despite a large population, Bangladesh does not offer a realizable market potential. This is true also of other poor countries. It must be noted, however, that many countries belonging to the Third World are slowly emerging from their traditional poverty. Thus, it would be shortsighted to write them off. As a matter of fact, there is an interesting development taking place in the economic arena as far as the U.S. is concerned: Western Europe and Japan are becoming more competitive with the U.S., while developing countries are becoming potential markets. Indeed, U.S. exports to developing countries as a group already substantially exceed exports to its traditional trading partners.

Concept of Economic Advancement

Developing countries are becoming important markets as their economies advance. According to the concept of international product life cycle examined in Chapter 2, more and more developing countries may become significant markets. It would be desirable for a marketer, therefore, to keep abreast of countries slowly reaching that point where market potential becomes worthwhile. GNP per capita may be relied on as a measure of the economic viability of a market. It provides a reasonable estimate of the market in cases where detailed analysis is not feasible.

Economic advancement is characterized by such factors as comparatively small allocation of labor force to agriculture; energy available in large amounts at low cost per unit; high level of GNP and income; high levels of per capita consumption; relatively low rates of population growth; complex modern facilities for transportation, communication, and exchange; a substantial amount of capital for investment; urbanization based on production as well as exchange; diversified manufacturing that accounts for an important share of the labor force; numerous tertiary occupations; specialization of both physical and mental labor; surpluses of both goods and services; and a highly developed technology that includes ample media and methods for experiment. These factors can be utilized to examine economic standing. Needless to say, a large variety of information is needed to categorize countries on an economic development scale. For many characteristics, hard data may not be available and judgment becomes the determining factor.

As a generalization, the conditions in underdeveloped economies would be the mirror image, or reverse, of those that characterize economic advancement. This raises an interesting question. Can poor countries be converted into advanced countries through reversing the conditions that hamper economic progress? The answer to such a question is far from simple because economic development is not a simple, discrete process. Many historical, geographic, political, and cultural factors are intimately related to the economic well-being of a nation. For example, no wars have been fought on U.S. soil in the last 100 years, which to an extent helped the U.S. achieve its present economic greatness. The impact of this factor has been thoroughly covered elsewhere.[2]

Structure of Consumption

Nations' overall patterns of consumption can be viewed not only on the basis of potential but also on the basis of structure. While it is important to measure the volume of consumption among various cultures, nations, and societies, the characteristics of that consumption reveal its structure. Particularly conspicuous in this respect are differences in emphasis. Depending on economic factors, a country may have to emphasize producer goods over consumer goods. Also, what are considered necessities in one economy may be luxuries in another. In addition, consumption in most advanced countries is characterized by a higher proportion of expenditures devoted to capital goods than consumption in poor countries, where substantially more is spent on consumer goods.

However, proportionate expenditures for producer goods within a given economy are only moderately high if that economy enjoys the benefits of past (preferably long-term) capital accumulation. When a less-developed economy decides to become technically and economically more advanced, an extraordinary percentage of national income must be diverted to producer goods, especially if that economy is unable to attract substantial amounts of foreign currency in the form of direct investment, loans, or other aid. This is one important reason why less-developed economies find the transition period to technical advancement so difficult.

The structural differences with regard to expenditures among nations can be explained by a theory propounded by the German statistician Engel. The *law of consumption* (Engel's law) states that poorer families and societies spend a greater proportion of their incomes on food than well-to-do people.[3] Table 6.2 substantiates Engel's law on a global scale. Shown is the percentage of per capita income spent for food, housing, clothing, and other purposes in selected countries. Third World countries like the Philippines and Sri Lanka are shown to spend a larger percentage on food than countries like the U.S. Further, in any country, rural people spend a larger percentage on food than urban dwellers (not shown in the table). Housing, in particular, receives a much smaller share of income in underdeveloped countries than in the advanced nations (see International Marketing Highlight 6.1).

TABLE 6.2 Consumption Expenditures of Selected Countries

Country (Base Year)	Food & Beverage	Clothing & Footwear	Housing & Operations	Household Furnishings	Medical Care & Health	Transportation	Recreation	Other*
Industrial Market Economies								
Belgium (1985)	19.7	6.8	17.7	10.7	10.6	13.1	6.6	14.8
Canada (1986)	16.2	5.7	22.4	9.7	4.2	15.8	11.3	14.7
France (1980)	19.4	6.2	17.8	8.2	10.5	6.8	8.1	13.0
Japan (1985)	20.8	6.1	18.6	6.3	10.4	10.7	10.6	16.5
Sweden (1980)	22.3	8.4	23.5	6.8	2.7	17.9	10.5	8.0
United Kingdom (1985)	21.1	6.7	18.4	7.2	1.3	18.3	10.1	17.0
United States (1980)	13.3	7.7	17.4	6.3	12.4	16.4	11.7	14.8
[Former] West Germany (1980)	23.6	8.6	19.8	9.7	3.1	16.4	10.7	8.2
Middle-Income Countries								
Mexico (1980)	37.4	8.2	12.6	12.4	4.0	9.1	5.6	10.8
Philippines (1972)	60.0	5.3	3.1	13.5	n.a.	2.3	n.a.	15.8
Republic of Korea (1985)	36.8	4.7	9.9	6.1	7.2	11.2	11.9	12.3
Low-Income Countries								
India (1980)	53.5	13.1	11.1	4.9	2.4	7.5	3.2	4.3
Sri Lanka (1975)	52.7	10.1	4.2	5.5	1.3	18.3	4.1	3.9

Other includes expenditures for personal care, restaurants, and hotels.
n.a.: data not available.
Note: The expenditures are expressed as percentages of total consumption in constant prices.

International Marketing Highlight 6.1

Acquiring a Vacation Spot

One CEO visited North Africa and fell in love with Morocco. Imagining frequent trips to this desert kingdom, he established a Marrakesh subsidiary for his firm, which manufactures kitchen cabinets. Unfortunately, he neglected to notice that most Moroccans don't have indoor kitchens, much less kitchen cabinets. The branch operation was a total failure. The lure of exotic climes had distorted this executive's previously sound business judgement.

Source: Charles F. Valentine, *The Arthur Young International Business Guide* (New York; John Wiley & Sons, 1988), p. 22.

The structure of consumption varies among developed countries, too. While the average American home covers 1583 square feet and the typical European dwelling is more than 1050 square feet, Japanese families manage with 925 square feet. The U.S. nuclear family boasts 2.2 cars on average; comparable households in the European community average 1.3 cars. In Japan, the average is 0.88. And while food costs absorb 26 percent of the typical Japanese household's income, the amount is less than 15 percent for the average American family, and about 20 percent for the Europeans.[4] As shown in Table 6.3, while the average person in England eats 13 pounds of cereal a year, per capita consumption in France is just 1 pound, and in Japan less than one-fourth of a pound. Americans eat about 10 pounds of cereal each per year.

TABLE 6.3
Food Consumption Differences Among Nations

Country	Food Market And Habits		
	Per Capita Cereal Consumption (in pounds)	Per Capita Frozen-Food Consumption (in pounds)	Percent of Homes with Microwave Ovens
United States	9.8	92.4	80
Britain	12.8	48.2	43
[former] West Germany	2.0	33.4	21
Denmark	4.6	53.9	—
Sweden	—	51.7	—
France	1.1	40.5	16
Norway	—	38.3	—
Netherlands	—	34.8	8
Switzerland	—	33.2	—
Spain	0.4	—	13
Ireland	15.4	—	—
Australia	12.3	—	—
Canada	8.7	—	—
Belgium	—	—	10
Italy	—	—	3
Japan	0.2	18.6	—

Source: Kellogg Co. for cereal consumption; Birds Eye Wall Ltd. for frozen-food consumption, and GE Mintel Ltd. for homes with microwave ovens.

Other Economic Indicators

Population, income, and expenditure data provide basic insights into the economies of different nations. For a certain point in time, however, a variety of other aspects of economic environment may be pertinent in a given case. This economic information may be found in categories such as:

- Production indicators (such as the production of raw steel, automobiles, trucks, and electric power; crude-oil refinery runs, coal production, paperboard production, lumber production, and rail freight traffic)
- Prices (such as the price of gold, finished steel, aluminum, wheat, cotton, industrial raw materials, and foodstuffs)
- Finance (such as corporate bond yield, prime commercial paper, Eurodollar rate, money supply)
- Other indicators (such as index of industrial production, retail sales, installment credit debt, and wholesale and retail inventories)

It is not necessary for a marketer to gather information about and review all these indicators. As a matter of fact, complete information would be difficult to obtain from each country.[5] Thus, at any given time, the choice of economic indicators to be examined is determined by the purpose of the project at hand. For example, a company contemplating manufacturing tires abroad needs to look into the foreign country's automobile and truck production data for a number of previous years as well as the data for those countries that are likely to import tires from the foreign country. A processed food manufacturer, on the other hand, would be interested in such information as inflation rate, foodstuff prices, and retail sales data. In brief, marketers should examine only those economic indicators that are relevant to their marketing decisions. Relevancy can be determined in part by the marketer's domestic operations but should also reflect the new situation in the foreign country.

Economic Systems

The economic system of a country is another important factor that a marketer must understand. Traditionally, there are two types of economic systems: capitalist systems and state-owned systems. The U.S. comes close to being a pure capitalist system. The state-owned, or Marxist, system is pursued in communist countries where all activities related to production and distribution are controlled by the state. Between the two extremes are many countries that follow mixed economic systems where certain industries are allowed to run freely while others are strictly or partially controlled.

The nature of economic systems affects the political/regulatory control of the economy. Today, the pure capitalistic system propounded by Adam Smith is a thing of the past. Even in the U.S., there are some laws and conditions imposed on various businesses. The nature of these laws and other government regulations and controls will be examined in Chapter 9.

An interesting development of the recent past appears to have given rise to an economic system that is new to the modern world and links economic life with religion.[6] Some Muslim countries have adopted a national economic perspective based on Islam. While the trend, led by Iran, is still emerging, it is difficult to say how far it will go or what impact it will have on marketers interested in doing business with Muslim countries.[7]

Mutual Economic Dependence

The U.S. economy is profoundly related to the economies of other nations, particularly those of the advanced countries. The U.S. market is so large that despite its ability to supply most of its needs from domestic output, it is also a dominant factor in international trade. For example, what happens in Western Europe cannot be ignored by the U.S. While there may be a time lag, happenings there are bound to ultimately affect the U.S. economy. It has been estimated that a recession in Western Europe affects the U.S. after a lag of about six months. Thus, when performing an economic analysis, an international marketer needs to consider the economic perspectives of the overall world economy, particularly those of its major trading partners and the host country.

The depth of economic analysis varies from case to case. For example, if the enterprise concerns Saudi Arabia, economic development in the Pacific region can be discounted. On the other hand, if a project is related to Japanese industries, the economic environment in emerging countries of Southeast Asia must be reviewed.

Microeconomic Environment

Microeconomic environment refers to the environment surrounding a product and/or market of interest to a company. An examination of microenvironment indicates whether the company can successfully enter the market. Essentially, the microeconomic environment concerns competition.

Sources of Competition

A U.S. company may face competition in an international market from three different sources: local business, other U.S. corporations, and foreign companies. For example, if Chrysler Corporation were to consider entering the German market, it would compete against General Motors, Volkswagen, and Honda Motors of Japan. Different competitors, however, may satisfy different types of demand: existing demand, latent demand, or incipient demand.[8] *Existing demand* refers to a product bought to satisfy a recognized need. *Latent demand* applies in a situation where a particular need has been recognized, but no products have been offered. *Incipient demand* describes a projected need that will emerge when customers become aware of it sometime in the future. To illustrate the point, consider demand in the computer industry. Overall, IBM may be strong in, let us say, Spain. But a firm like Dell Computers may choose to enter the Spanish market to serve *latent demand* there. This way Dell avoids direct confrontation with IBM and Apple, at least in the short run. Competition can also be analyzed by the characteristics of products. Three product categories are considered here: breakthrough products, competitive products, and improved products.[9] A *breakthrough product* is a unique innovation that is mainly technical in nature, such as a digital watch, a VCR, or a jet plane. A *competitive product* is one of many brands currently available in the market and has no special advantage over the competing products. An *improved product* is not unique but is generally superior to many existing brands.

The nature of the competition that a company faces in entering an overseas market can be determined by relating the three types of products to the three types of demand. Upon examining the competition, a company should be able to ascertain which product/market it is most capable of pursuing. For example, let us assume Procter & Gamble is interested in manufacturing hair shampoo in Egypt and seeks entry into the emerging Arab market. The company finds that in addition to a number of local brands, Johnson & Johnson's baby shampoo and Helene Curtis Industries' Suave Shampoo are the *competitive* products in the market. Gillette has recently entered the market with its Silkience brand, which is considered an *improved* product. Most of the competition appears to be addressing the *existing* demand. No attempts have been made to satisfy *latent* demand or *incipient* demand. After reviewing various considerations, Procter & Gamble may decide to fulfill latent demand with an improved offering through its Head & Shoulders brand. Based on market information, the company reasons that a hair problem most consumers face in that part of the world is dandruff. No brand has addressed itself to that problem. Even Gillette's new entry mainly emphasizes silkiness of hair. Thus, analysis of the competition with reference to product offerings and demand enables Procter & Gamble to determine its entry point into the Arab market.

Competitive Advantage

The above analysis indicates an open space in the market for entry. But this in itself is not enough. Competitors may follow right on the heels of Procter & Gamble's entry steps. Thus, further analysis is needed to figure out the competitive advantage the company has over rivals, existing and potential. The following questions could be raised to analyze the competition:

- Who are the competition now, and who will they be in the future?
- What are the key competitors' strategies, objectives, and goals?
- How important is a specific market to the competitors, and are they committed enough to continue to invest?
- What unique strengths do the competitors have?
- Do they have any weaknesses that make them vulnerable?
- What changes are likely in the competitors' future strategies?
- What are the implications of competitors' strategies on the market, the industry, and one's own company?

The best way to examine competition is to draw up a demographic profile of the industry. Markets dominated by small single-industry business or small national competitors differ significantly from those dominated by multi-industry companies, and those in turn are different from those controlled by multinational or foreign companies.

A simple listing of major competitors is not enough. It is also important to learn about their goals and aspirations. In fact, an attempt should be made to know competitors' total financial situations, including their serious problems as well as their advantages and opportunities.

Further, the competitors' relative strengths and weaknesses should be examined. Exhibit 6.1 lists areas to be considered in order to assess competitive strengths and weaknesses. Note that most areas of strength either are related to the excellence of personnel or are resource-based. Not all factors have the same significance for every product/market. Therefore, it is desirable first to recognize the critical factors that could directly or indirectly bear on a product's performance in a given market. For example, adequate distribution may be critical in a developing country with inadequate means of transportation and communication, while development of new products through research and development might be strategic to gain the competitive edge in Western Europe.

EXHIBIT 6.1 Assessing Competitor's Areas of Strength

1. Excellence in product design and/or performance (engineering ingenuity)
2. Low-cost, high-efficiency operating skill in manufacturing and/or in distribution
3. Leadership in product innovation
4. Efficiency in customer service
5. Personal relationships with customers
6. Efficiency in transportation and logistics
7. Effectiveness in sales promotion
8. Merchandising efficiency—high turnover of inventories and/or of capital
9. Skillful trading in volatile price movement commodities
10. Ability to influence legislation
11. Highly efficient, low-cost facilities
12. Ownership or control of low-cost or scarce raw materials
13. Control of intermediate distribution or processing units
14. Massive availability of capital
15. Widespread customer acceptance of company brand name (reputation)
16. Product availability, convenience
17. Customer loyalty
18. Dominant market share position
19. Effectiveness of advertising
20. Quality salesforce

An example of strength is provided by BMW car company. It is commonly known that selling foreign cars in Japan is not easy. Yet BMW sold almost 50,000 cars annually in the 1980s to the Japanese, and the number was expected to be four times as high by the end of the 1990s. With Japanese consumers' increasing interest in luxury cars, a new market segment had been emerging that was not being tapped by the Japanese companies. BMW took advantage of the situation. Avoiding the pitfalls that make doing business in Japan difficult, it established a comfortable niche for itself. After buying its own dealer network and expanding it, the company advertised heavily, set up a service-and-parts system, and lowered interest rates to single digits (5 percent), when consumer interest rates were 15 percent. In brief, despite the fact that Japan is a difficult market to enter, analysis of the microeconomic environment showed that BMW could successfully seek entry into the Japanese market.[10]

Japanese auto companies, in turn, have captured a major share (in 1991, approximately 28 percent) of the U.S. auto market. Let us assume Ford Motor Company decides to retaliate by exploring the possibility of entering the Japanese market. Despite all its strengths and experience in international business, however, Ford may find itself greatly constrained in its endeavors. In the past, cost was a major factor. Because of U.S. wage-price and managerial efficiency differentials, the Japanese companies were able to build a car and ship it to the U.S. for $2,000 to $2,300 less than it costs Detroit to produce an equivalent vehicle. Now, due to the appreciation in the value of yen against the dollar and U.S. companies' attempts to overhaul their operations, cost differential is not significant anymore. Yet U.S. companies may find it difficult to match Japanese selling methods—one-half the cars sold are peddled by door-to-door salesmen. Such sales tactics, coupled with high-quality vehicles, stack the odds against Ford Motor Company.[11] Thus, even if Ford were to assemble cars in Japan, other things being equal, it would still be severely handicapped due to lack of selling experience in Japan. In this instance, analysis of the microeconomic environment paints a discouraging picture for Ford's entry into the Japanese market.

Economic Environment and Marketing Strategy

The overall macroeconomic climate of the host country as well as the microeconomic environment surrounding the product/market has a significant effect on marketing strategy. The macroeconomic environment sets the limit of activity in different sectors of the economy. Thus, when the economy is booming, there will be plenty of jobs, consumers will be optimistic, and cash registers will ring often. In a booming economy situation, the international marketer will have more opportunity in the marketplace, although marketplace opportunities may attract new competition. However, when an economy is down, unemployment may rise, interest rates may go up, sales could be more difficult to generate, and the international marketer's decisions will take a different shape.

Impact of Macroeconomic Environment

Brazil, one of a few countries fast emerging into developed economies, provides a case where there would be ample opportunities for U.S. international marketers. Yet, in the early 1990s, the Brazilian economy was beset by a variety of problems that restricted the realization of opportunities there. By the end of 1991, the country had accumulated a huge external debt, over $100 billion attributed to oil imports, so that despite severe import restrictions, a record soybean crop, and excellent performance by manufactured exports, until 1991 inflation ran about 250 percent. Although the economy maintained its approximate 4.8 percent annual growth rate, Brazil had severe problems. In addition, strict import restrictions limited the opportunity for exports to Brazil, and soaring inflation and falling consumer demand, attributed to Brazil's recession and delayed implementation of liberalization measures, required caution in establishing manufacturing there, since new plant construction would be costly. Further, Brazilian exports to the U.S. and other markets were less competitive in price.

But then the monetary reforms that the country introduced in 1993 began to show results. For example, the launching of a new currency, the Real, helped slash inflation from 50 percent a month in June 1994 to just under 2 percent in August 1994. The revival of consumer credit triggered a spending surge, giving new strength to many industrial sectors.[12]

Betting on continuing recovery, billions of dollars of foreign investment have been flowing into Brazil's stock market. At the end of 1993, Brazil was the biggest receiver of U.S. direct investment, amounting to $16.9 billion against Mexico's $15.4 billion. Thus, the economic outlook for Brazil in 1994 appeared very promising.

The health of an economy affects consumer confidence, which is then reflected in consumer buying plans. A favorable economic climate generates a spirit of optimism that makes consumers more willing to spend money. The reverse occurs when economic conditions are unfavorable. In Brazil's case, 1993–94 were exciting years from the viewpoint of consumers. With inflation under control, Brazil's consumers felt optimistic and were ready to spend.

Consider the impact on Brazil's car industry. For the first time since the 1970s, it may be about to live up to its ambitions. In 1993, the vehicle output rose 29.5 percent to 1.39 million units; thus, Brazil became the world's tenth largest producer, overtaking Italy and Mexico. Sales of passenger cars almost doubled during 1992–94, while exports in 1993 amounted to $2.7 billion. By the end of the decade, Brazil's car industry could be the world's fifth largest, producing more than 2 million units a year.[13]

While economic climate affects all businesses, some businesses are affected more deeply than others. International marketers should calculate the extent to which their business is susceptible to economic conditions. For example, in a booming economy, consumers tend to buy durable goods. Thus, the economic environment in Brazil during 1994 seemed attractive for consumer goods manufacturers interested in entering the market. It should be noted, however, that current economic environment is just one variable. Despite the fact that the short-run economic environment is conducive to profits, a company should enter an overseas market based on good long-term economic prospects in that economy and such other favorable factors as growing political stability or existence of low wage scales. The long-run perspective is the most important one if a firm has sufficient resources to endure waiting for the future favorable environment.

Impact of Microeconomic Environment

The following example shows how the microeconomic environment of a product/market would affect marketing strategy:

> A very successful U.S. company, for many years a leader in its field, launched a cheaper version of its traditional product almost simultaneously in the United States and in Europe. The product design, pricing, and advertising copy—in fact, the whole marketing approach—were quite similar in both areas. The strategy was very successful at home, but in Europe sales fell far below expectations.
> What was the cause of the trouble? The company had neglected several significant differences between the two market areas:
>
> 1. In the United States it had a major share of the market, while in Europe it was an insignificant factor.
> 2. At home, the company's product concept was in the mature phase of its life cycle, while in Europe it was at its beginning.
> 3. In the United States roughly 85 percent of all households knew the company and its products, whereas in Europe the awareness level was barely 5 percent and few customers understood the nature of this innovative product.
> 4. As a result, the advertising copy that featured a low price without explaining the product concept was meaningful to most U.S. consumers but unsuitable for most of the European market.

It is evident from this illustration that the U.S. company got into problems in Europe because its competitive strength there was meager (small market share), the product, relatively speaking, was new to the market (starting life cycle position), and the product presented an unfamiliar concept. In other words, the company did not orient its marketing program with the product/market environment existing in Europe.

Impact of the Domestic Economic Environment

While international marketers should be concerned with economic environment overseas, they should also be sensitive to economic perspectives in the U.S., just as the reverse is true for domestic marketers. Thus, in appraising domestic economic development, short-run, foreign trade and international economic movements can no longer be ignored even when we are looking at the world's largest and most self-sufficient economy. Indeed, firms react to changing domestic and international economic environments and can be expected to shift their relative emphasis in promoting domestic versus foreign trade. During 1990, as the recession deepened in the U.S., U.S. companies appeared to put greater stress on foreign markets than on U.S. markets. Similarly, in 1993, as the dollar fell, companies became more anxious to tap export markets.[14] Briefly, during slack conditions in the U.S., overseas markets provide a realistic alternative for maintaining business tempo.[15] However, to develop perpetual foreign markets, firms cannot simply shift gears in favor of overseas markets when something goes wrong in the domestic market, and then abandon foreign markets once the domestic economy picks up again. Such tactics are harmful to long-term market development abroad, and they damage the reputation of the business.[16]

Analysis of Economic Environments

Given the perspectives of macro- and microeconomic environment, an opportunity analysis may be performed to determine if it is worthwhile to seek entry into a foreign country's market. A conceptual scheme is helpful for analyzing economic environment in practice in order to assess marketing opportunities. The conceptual scheme requires consideration of such variables as those shown in Exhibit 6.2. With the use of these variables, analysis of marketing opportunity centers on two sets of criteria: cost-benefit criteria and risk/reward criteria.*

Cost-Benefit Criteria Analysis

Cost-benefit criteria answer a series of questions that stress markets, competition, and the financial implications of doing business in a foreign country.

Markets Will people want our products? More importantly, will they want them enough to pay a price that will yield us a profit? Is the market large enough for the firm to venture in?

Competition What kind of competition will we have to face, and will the rules apply equally to all? Concern about equal treatment within a market comes from situations of altered marketplace. In many countries, *altered marketplace competition* comes from host governments, through direct ownership of competitors, subsidization, or participation. In such cases, the foreign business usually is at a disadvantage, even though it is pitted against inefficient local business, and therefore cannot compete on an equal footing.

---

*Inasmuch as this chapter deals with economic environment only, the risk/reward criteria will be examined here solely with reference to economic situation. The risk/reward analysis should be extended by relating it to cultural environment (Chapter 7) and the political environment (Chapter 8).

EXHIBIT 6.2 Considerations in the Evaluation of Economic Environment

Financial Considerations
1. Capital acquisition plan
2. Length of payback period
3. Projected cash inflows (years one, two, and so forth)
4. Projected cash outflows (years one, two, and so forth)
5. Return on investment
6. Monetary exchange considerations

Technical and Engineering Feasibility Considerations
7. Raw materials availability (construction/support/supplies)
8. Raw materials availability (products)
9. Geography/climate
10. Site locations and access
11. Availability of local labor
12. Availability of local management
13. Economic infrastructure (roads, water, electricity, and so forth)
14. Facilities planning (preliminary or detailed)

Marketing Considerations
15. Market size
16. Market potential
17. Distribution costs
18. Competition
19. Time necessary to establish distribution/sales channels
20. Promotion costs
21. Social/cultural factors affecting products

Economic and Legal Considerations
22. Legal systems
23. Host government attitudes toward foreign investment
24. Host attitude toward this particular investment
25. Restrictions on ownership
26. Tax laws
27. Import/export restrictions
28. Capital flow restrictions
29. Land-title acquisitions
30. Inflation

Political and Social Considerations
31. Internal political stability
32. Relations with neighboring countries
33. Political/social traditions
34. Communist influence
35. Religious/racial/language homogeneity
36. Labor organizations and attitudes
37. Skill/technical level of the labor force
38. Socioeconomic infrastructure to support families

Financial Examination How many resources (and how much of each) must be committed, and what will they cost? What return may be expected, and how long might it take to recover the investment?

Of course, there are other cost-benefit criteria. The level of training and skills of a national workforce are important considerations, as well as the availability of educated, experienced local managers. Most MNCs have learned the value of having local or regional executives in host countries. For example, Sperry Rand Corporation in Japan shares a joint venture that is manned entirely by Japanese workers and executives.[17] In addition, transportation, the communications system, and the availability of local resources (especially energy) should be considered. This list could go on, but enough has been said to illustrate some of the assessable conceptual factors influencing market entry decisions.

Risk/Reward Criteria Analysis

The *risk/reward criteria* emphasize the overall constantly changing mix of situations in the social, political, and economic climates of a host country. In terms of economics, the macroeconomic characteristics of a nation will almost always affect the specific economics of business. The national economic objectives of the country, therefore, also figure in a firm's decision to explore entry there. For example, the firm needs to know how fiscal policy (the control of the nation's economy through taxes) translates into business taxation, or how income policy (wage/price guideposts) may affect wage and price controls. The firm also needs to know about a country's monetary policy (the control of the nation's economy through increasing or decreasing interest rates by the central bank; The Federal Reserve does it in the U.S. by establishing the rate at which commercial banks borrow from it). Does the country's policy place restrictions on international cash transactions, such as the repatriation of profits? What is the outlook, for example, for the cost and availability of credits? Is the currency strong, and, more important, what is the inflation situation?

Social/Cultural and Political Factors

Although it is convenient to categorize a country's environment into social/cultural, political, and economic aspects, they each overlap, and they all influence the intelligent analysis of any one aspect. Thus, in economic analysis, the social/cultural and political environments should be duly considered.

In the social area, the demographic characteristics of the population should be taken into account. The general level of education is an important indicator of the society's development, the likelihood of its accepting new ideas, and possibly, its attitude toward a foreign investor. The standard of living and the general expectations of the country tell a great deal. Is it a progressive society or a static one? Does it aspire to development, or is it frozen into old social patterns and mores? Are its expectations pragmatic or unrealistic? Class structure, where it exists, also yields useful information.

The political area reflects both the social and economic situations and vice versa. However, some political aspects are particularly relevant to economic analysis:

- What kind of political system does the country have? Is it a democratic/parliamentary society? Or is it authoritarian and possibly repressive?

- Is the national leadership popular or unpopular? The answer might indicate the probability of radical change.

- By our standards, are the national policies successful or unsuccessful?

- What is the level of insurgency, if any? This might range all the way from random terror or occasional violence to guerrilla warfare or foreign-supported insurgency. One of the most graphic signs of change in international business is that business must be prepared to defend itself not only economically, but also physically and ideologically in foreign countries.

If there is a common denominator of both the cost-benefit and risk/reward equations, it is stability. That is not to suggest that business should want some imposed stability at the price of reduced performance. Rather, what is desired is a reasonable level of stability in all of the areas just discussed. The aim should be to ensure that capital investment is recovered over a reasonable period, generates a satisfactory profit, and provides a base for the further expansion of international business.

An Illustration

Decisions related to foreign market entry, expansion, and conversion, as well as phasing out from foreign markets, call for systematic frameworks for analysis, as discussed previously. Illustrated here is one method of putting a framework into practical use; other approaches are available to assess international marketing opportunities.[18] The suggested framework consists of three phases:

1. Appropriate national markets are selected by quickly screening the full range of options without regard to any preconceived notions.
2. Specific strategic approaches are devised for each country or group of countries, based on the company's specific product technologies.
3. Marketing plans for each country or group of countries are developed, reviewed, revised, and incorporated into the overall corporate concept without regard to conventional wisdom or stereotypes.

Phase One: Selecting National Markets There are over 150 countries in the world; of these the majority may appear to offer entry markets. Many countries go out of their way to attract foreign investment by offering lures ranging from tax exemptions to low-paid, amply skilled labor. These inducements, valid as they may be in certain individual cases, have repeatedly led to hasty foreign market entry.

A good basis for decision is arrived at through a comparative analysis of different countries, with long-term economic environment having the greatest weight. First, certain countries, on account of their political situations (for example, Libya under Qadhafi) would be considered unsuitable for market entry. It might help to consult an index that rates different countries for business attractiveness. The final choice should be based on the company's own assessment and risk preference. Further, markets that are either too small in terms of population and per capita income or economically too weak should be eliminated.

For example, a number of countries with populations of less than 20 million and annual per capita incomes below $2,000 are of little interest to many companies because of limited demand potential.

The markets surviving this screening are then assessed for strategic attractiveness. A battery of criteria should be developed to fit the specific requirements of the corporation. Basically, the criteria should focus on the following five factors (industry/product characteristics may require slight modifications):

1. Future demand and economic potential of the country in question
2. Distribution of purchasing power by population groups or market segments
3. Country-specific technical product standards
4. "Spillover" from the national market (via standards, regulations, norms, or economic ties) to other markets (for example, the Andes Pact provides for low-duty exports from Colombia to Peru)
5. Access to vital resources (qualified labor force, raw materials sources, suppliers)

There is no reason to expand the list since additional criteria are rarely significant enough to result in useful new insights. Rather, management should concentrate on developing truly meaningful and practical parameters for each of the five criteria listed above, so that the selection process does not become unnecessarily costly and the results are fully relevant to the company concerned. For example, a German flooring manufacturer, selling principally to the building industry, selected the following yardsticks:

1. *Economic potential:* new housing needs, GNP growth
2. *Wealth:* per capita income, per capita market size for institutional building or private dwellings (the higher the per capita income, market volume, and share of institutional buildings, the more attractive the market)
3. *Technical product standards:* price level of similar products, for example, price per square meter for floor coverings (the higher the price level, the more attractive the market tends to be for a technically advanced producer)
4. *"Spillover":* area in which the same building standards (especially fire safety standards) apply (for example, the U.S. National Electrical Manufacturers' Association standards are widely applicable in Latin America, and British standards apply in most of the Commonwealth countries)
5. *Resource availability:* annual production volume of PVC (an important raw material for the company)

Through these criteria, the analysis of economic potential was based on two factors: housing needs and economic base (see Figure 6.1). In specifying these criteria, the company deliberately confined itself to measures that (1) could readily be developed from existing sources of macroeconomic data, (2) would show trends as well as current positions, and (3) match the company's particular characteristics as closely as possible.

Since German producers of floor covering employ a highly sophisticated technology, it would have been senseless to give a high ranking to a country with only rudimentary production technology in this particular facet. Companies in other industries, of course, would have to consider other factors—auto registrations per thousand population, percentage of households with telephones, density of household appliance installations, and the like.

The resulting values are rated, for each criterion, on a scale of one to five, so that by weighing the criteria on a percentage basis, each country can be assigned an index number indicating its overall attractiveness. In this particular case, the result was that, out of the 49 countries surviving the initial screening, 16 were ultimately judged attractive enough—on the basis of market potential, per capita market size, level of technical sophistication, prevailing regulations, and resource availability—to warrant serious attention.

Interestingly, the traditionally German-favored markets of Austria and Belgium emerged with low rankings from this strategically based assessment because the level of potential demand was judged to be insufficient. Some new markets such as Egypt and Pakistan were also downgraded as offering an inadequate economic base. Likewise, even such high-potential markets as Italy and Indonesia were eliminated for objective reasons (in the latter case, the low technical standard of most products).

Phase Two: Determining Marketing Strategy After a short list of attractive foreign markets has been compiled, the next step is to group these countries according to their respective stages of economic development. Here, the criterion of classification is not per capita income, but the degree of market penetration by the generic product in question. For example, the floor covering manufacturer already mentioned grouped the

Analysis of Economic Environments

FIGURE 6.1 Assessing Country Economic Potential: The Case of a Building Industry Flooring Supplier

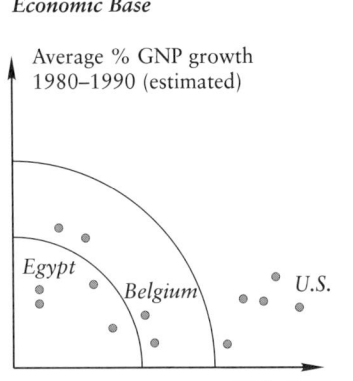

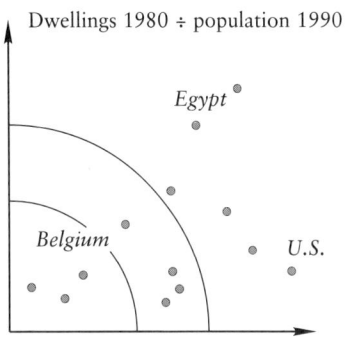

*Assumes 1990 target = 2.5 persons per dwelling (catch-up and new demand).

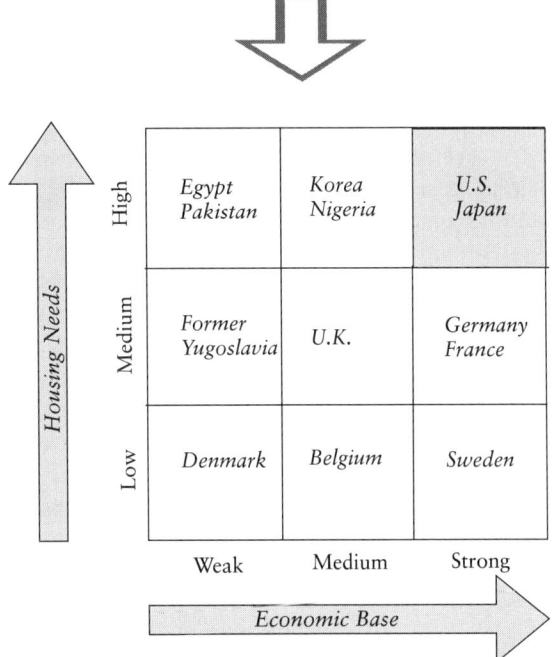

Examples: Sweden—needs only in replacement sector, Pakistan—economically too weak to meet needs.

countries into three categories—developing, take-off and mature—as defined by these factors (see Figure 6.2):

1. *Accessibility of markets*: crucial for the choice between export and import production
2. *Local competitive situation*: crucial for the choice between independent construction, joint venture, and acquisition
3. *Customer structure*: crucial for sales and distribution strategy
4. *Re-import potential*: crucial for international product/market strategy

FIGURE 6.2   Grouping Countries by Phase of Development

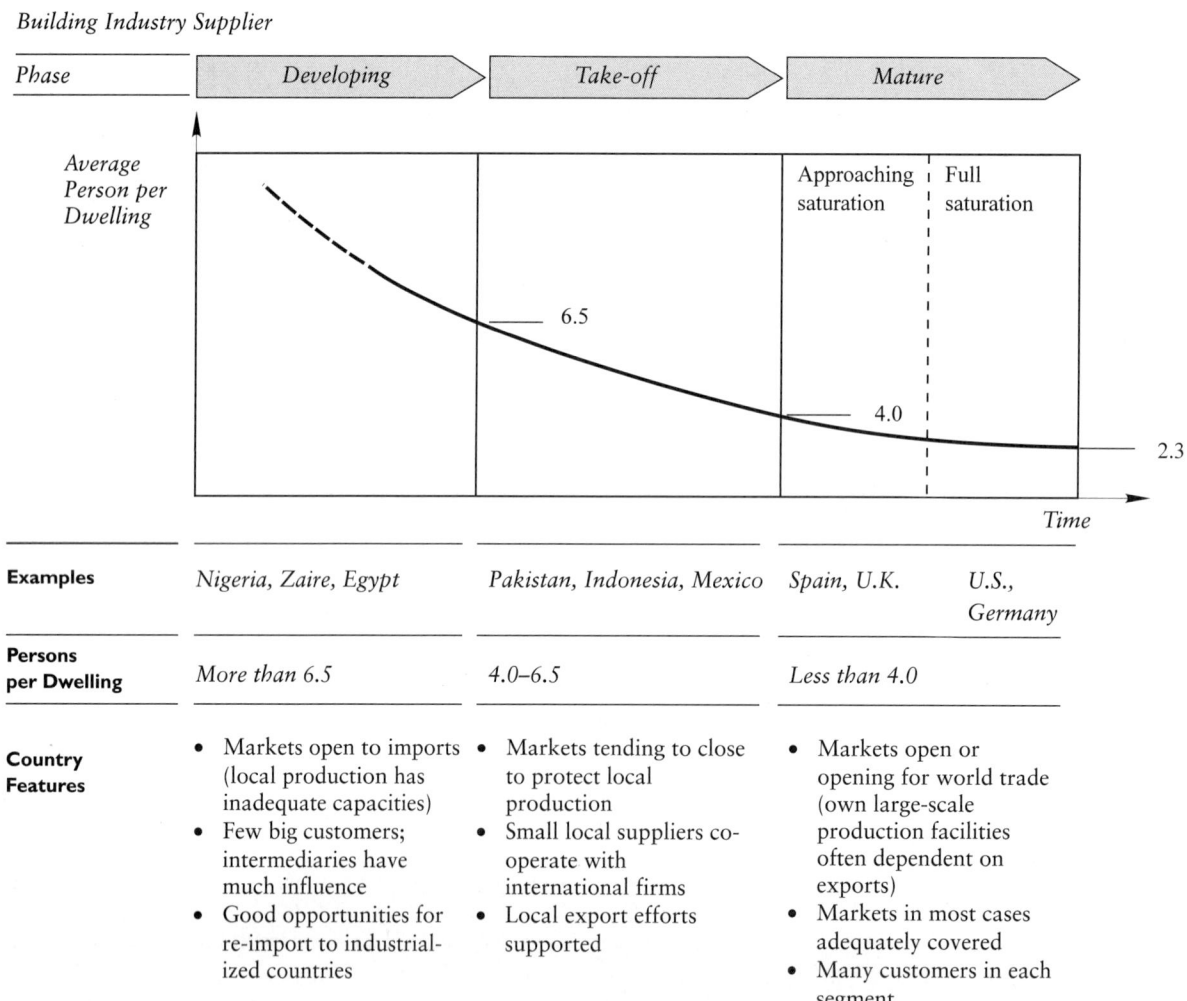

The established development phases and their defining criteria must be very closely geared to the company situation, since it is these factors—not the apparent attractiveness of markets—that will make or break the company's strategic thrust into a given country.

This being the case, for each country or group of countries on the short list, management should formulate a generic marketing strategy with respect to investment, risk, product, and pricing policies, that is, a unified strategic framework applicable to all the countries in each stage of development. This step should yield a clear understanding of what the respective stages of economic development of each country entail for the company's marketing strategies (see Table 6.4).

Companies are too often inclined to regard "overseas" as a single market, or at least to differentiate very little among individual overseas markets. Another common error is the assumption that product or service concepts suited to a highly developed consumer economy will work as well in any foreign market. This is rarely true—different markets demand different approaches.

Across-the-board strategic approaches typically result in ill-advised and inappropriate allocation of resources. In less-developed markets that could be perfectly well served by a few distributors, companies have in some cases established production facilities that are doomed to permanent unprofitability. In markets already at the take-off point, companies have failed to build the necessary local plants, and instead have complained about declining exports only to finally abandon the field to competitors. And in markets already approaching saturation, companies have often sought to impose domestic technical standards where adequate standards and knowledge already exist or tried to operate like minireplicas of parent corporations, marketing too many product lines with too few salespeople. Again and again, product line offerings are weighted toward either cheaper or higher-quality products than the local market will accept. Clearly, the best insurance against such errors is to select strategies appropriate to the country.

Phase Three: Developing Marketing Plans In developing detailed marketing plans, it is first necessary to determine which product lines fit local markets, as well as the appropriate allocation of resources. A rough analysis of potential international business, global sales, and profit targets based on the estimates worked out in Phase One will help in assigning product lines. A framework for resource allocation can then be mapped out according to rough comparative figures for investment quotas, management needs, and skilled-labor requirements. This framework should be supplemented by company-specific examples of standard marketing strategies for each group of countries.

Table 6.5 illustrates the resource allocation process. Different product lines are assigned to different country groups, and for each country category different strategic approaches are specified, for example, support on large-scale products, establishment of local production facilities, cooperation with local manufacturers.

The level of detail in this resource allocation decision framework will depend on a number of factors: company history and philosophy, business policy objectives, scope and variety of product lines, and the number of countries to be served. Working within this decision framework, each product division should analyze its own market in terms

TABLE 6.4 Developing Standard Strategies

Phase	Developing	Take-off	Mature
Basic Strategy	Test Market Pursue profitable individual projects and/or export activities	Build Base Allocate substantial resources to establish leading position in market	Expand/Round Off Operations Allocate resources selectively to develop market niches
Elements of Strategy			
Investment	Minimize (distribution and services)	Invest to expand capacity (relatively long payback)	Expand selectively in R&D, production, and distribution (relatively short payback)
Risk Know-how transfer (R&D)	Avoid Document know-how on reference projects	Accept Use local know-how in • Product technology • Production engineering	Limit Transfer know-how in special product lines; acquire local know-how to round off own base
Market share objective	Concentrate on key projects; possibly build position in profitable businesses with local support	Extend base with • New products • New outlets • New applications	Expand/defend
Cost leadership objective	Minimum acceptable (especially reduction of guarantee risks)	Economies of scale, reduction of fixed costs	Rationalize; optimize resources
Product	Standard technology, simple products	Aim for wide range, "innovator" role	Full product line in selected areas, products of high technical quality
Price	Price high	Aim for price leadership (at both ends)	Back stable market price level
Distribution	Use select local distributors (exclusive distribution)	Use a large number of small distributors (intensive distribution)	Use company sales force (selective distribution)
Promotion	Selective advertising • With typical high-prestige products • Aim at decision makers	Active utilization of selective marketing resources	Selected product advertising

TABLE 6.5 A Specimen Framework for Resource Allocation

Phase	Specimen Countries	Resource Allocation By Product Division*					
		PVC Floor Coverings	Carpeting	Suspended Ceilings	Wall Paneling	PVC Tubes	Plastic-Coated Roof Insulation
Developing "Test Market"	Nigeria	Intensive	None	Moderate	None	Intensive	Intensive
(Share of total resources: 20 percent)		Specific Plans • Develop own plastics-processing facilities • Acquire plastics processors					
Take-off "Build base"	Indonesia	Moderate	None	None	None	Moderate	Moderate
(Share of total resources: 50 percent)		Specific Plans • Give support in key projects • Cooperate with state-owned construction organization					
Mature "Expand/round off operations"	Spain	Moderate	Moderate	Intensive	Intensive	None	None
(Share of total resources: 30 percent)		Specific Plans • Develop local facilities for tufting and paneling • Acquire/cooperate with suppliers using unique product and production technology • Develop own distribution channel • Extend range to provide complete interior equipment program (system concept)					

of size, growth, and competitive situations; assess its profitability prospects, opportunities, and risks; and identify its own current strategic position on the basis of market share, profit situation, and vulnerability to local risks. Each product division will then be in a position to develop country-specific marketing alternatives for servicing each national market. Top management's role throughout is to coordinate the marketing strategy development efforts of the various divisions and constantly monitor the strategic decision framework.

This three-phase approach exhibits a number of advantages.

- It allows management to set up, with a minimum of planning effort, a strategic framework that gives clear priority to market selection decisions, thus making it much easier for the divisions to work out effective product line strategies, unhampered by the usual "chicken or egg" problem.

- Division managers can foresee, at a fairly early stage, what reallocations of management, labor, and capital resources are needed and what adjustments may have to be imposed from the top due to inadequate resources.

- The company's future risk profile can be worked out in terms of resource commitment by country group and type of investment.

- The usual plethora of "exceptional" (and mostly opportunistic) product/market situations is sharply reduced. Only the really unique opportunities pass through the filter; exceptions are no longer the rule.

- The dazzling-in-theory but unrealistic-in-practice concept of establishing production bases in low-wage countries, buying from the world's lowest-cost sources, and selling products wherever the best prices can be had is replaced by a realistic country-by-country market evaluation.

- Issues of organization, personnel assignment, and integration of overseas operations into corporate planning and control systems reach management's attention only after the fundamental strategic aspects of the company's overseas involvement have been thoroughly prepared.

In brief, the three-phase approach enables management to profitably concentrate resources and attention on a handful of really attractive countries instead of dissipating its efforts in vain attempts to serve the entire world.

Opportunities in the Developing World

The framework just discussed is applicable for analyzing the economic environment in both developed and developing countries. However, further examination of opportunities in developing countries is appropriate for two reasons. First, more and more developing countries are pursuing the growth path. South Korea, Taiwan, Singapore, and Hong Kong were first, while Brazil and China followed. Now India and Eastern European countries have been opening up. As a matter of fact, several other nations are following suit. The developing world is beginning to rely on the market mechanism to attract investment and technology and become industrialized. Second, government plays a significant role in business decisions. The bureaucrats approach foreign investment with much less sophistication and confidence than do private sector executives.

These characteristics suggest that in analyzing opportunities in the developing countries, a company should be willing to lay more emphasis on long-term potential than on short-term gains (see International Marketing Highlight 6.2). In addition, adequate treatment should be given to political and social variables. Further, business conditions vary so much from one country to the other that a comparative (i.e., multicountry) analysis may be difficult. Availability of reliable and timely information makes the opportunity analysis more difficult in developing countries, Thus, there is no way to systematically evaluate such factors as sociopolitical conditions. Instead, broad guidelines and a general feel for the situation are necessary, for which a trusted native could be of immense help.

For example, it has been estimated that basic packaged foods sales take off when GDP per head increases $5,000.[19] Based on this guideline, only a few Asian countries qualify for packaged foods. However, many of these nations are already more affluent than the aggregate figures imply. In countries such as Indonesia and Thailand, a rising middle class can afford to indulge itself. Besides, Asia has a higher percentage of younger people, a trend likely to continue for the next 30 years or so. That is important because young people are more willing to change their living habits than older ones.

In general, many U.S. firms' overall approach to developing-country foreign investment decision making is much less sophisticated than their developed-country approach. The former is often characterized by a lack of breadth in consideration of important variables, a biased perspective, and a lack of adequate preparation.[20] The key to future improvement of opportunity analysis in developing countries may lie in the motivation generated by the inevitable increase in competition. In the past, the sheer power, dynamism, and momentum of U.S. business virtually ensured its success in almost any developing nation. As competition, particularly from Japan, becomes more significant, the recognition of shades of difference and finer distinctions with regard to opportunities becomes more important as well.[21]

International Marketing Highlight 6.2

Procter & Gamble's Foreign Formula

The day after a 34-year-old Peruvian became manager of Procter & Gamble Co.'s Peru subsidiary in September 1988, the economy hit the skids. By the end of the year, inflation had soared to 2,000 percent. Key managers fled. Leftist terrorists kidnapped or murdered business leaders. The P&G subsidiary's sales plunged more than 30 percent, and the unit posted a loss. Money became tight.

But while many MNCs pulled out of Peru. P&G remained. Now, the consumer-products company is expanding there.

Throughout Latin America, P&G is shaking the stranglehold of government controls and its own strict U.S. culture. The Latin American division began as a fledgling detergent company but now is a $1 billion business that contributes 15 percent of P&G's international sales. The company expects the division, which has subsidiaries in 9 countries and sells in 10 others through distributors, to double its revenue again in 5 years. The division's profit margins exceed its international average.

P&G's success is attributed to an important lesson: U.S. management and marketing plans often don't work outside the U.S. For example, Ace detergent, launched in Mexico in the early 1950s, was clobbered by local competitors. Developed for U.S. washing machines, the product had a low-suds formula. But at that time, many Mexicans washed their clothes in the river or in a basin of water, and they judged detergent by its suds.

Eventually, the formula was changed. Similarly, P&G switched from cardboard boxes to plastic bags, which kept the detergent drier and were cheaper. Besides, many consumers shop every day and can afford only small amounts of detergent each time. Now, one top seller throughout Latin America is the 100-gram bag, enough to wash just one basket of clothes.

Source: *The Wall Street Journal*, June 5, 1990, p.1.

Summary

The economic environment of a foreign country is an important factor that should be examined before an international marketer decides to enter its market. A country burdened with economic problems may lack stability and become vulnerable to political radicalism. On the other hand, a growing and burgeoning economy usually stimulates business activity and offers new opportunities. Thus, a careful review of economic conditions, both short-and long-term, is a prerequisite for a decision about entering an overseas market.

Economic environment can be divided into macro- and microeconomic environments. Macroenvironment describes the overall economic situation in a country and is analyzed using economic indicators such as GNP per capita, index of industrial production, rate of economic growth, inflation rate, balance-of-trade surplus (deficit), interest rates, unemployment data, and the like. The economic system of a country is also part of the macroenvironment. Two extreme types of economic systems are the capitalist system and state control. The latter is mainly found in socialist countries; most Western countries pursue a mixed form of capitalism.

Microenvironment refers to economic conditions relevant to a particular product/market. Analysis of microeconomic environment is largely performed with reference to competition. A firm should properly identify different sources of competition and examine its own strengths and weaknesses relative to major competitors. Equipped with a competitive advantage over its rivals, a firm will be able to develop a workable marketing mix.

Economic environment does affect international marketing decisions, whether changes occur in the macro- or microeconomic environments. The impact of the U.S. economic environment on international business activity should not be ignored. For example, many U.S. firms enter the international market during a recession to sustain their business, only to withdraw as the domestic scene improves.

Conceptual schemes or frameworks are helpful for analyzing economic environment. Analysis can be performed with reference to cost-benefit criteria and risk/reward criteria. Cost-benefit criteria includes markets, competition, and financial implications of doing business in a country. The risk/reward criteria include the broad social, economic, and political climates of a nation. The successful application of a conceptual scheme yields a marketing strategy that will foster the development of market plans appropriate to a particular foreign market at a particular time. The conceptual scheme can be used to analyze opportunities in developed and developing economies. In many cases, however, lack of adequate information on developing countries may mean depending more on the feel of the situation than on actual data.

Review Questions

1. Should different types of economic indicators be used to examine the macroeconomic environments of different countries? Discuss.
2. Discuss the following statements: "While advanced countries offer an immediate market opportunity, the competitive activity is excessively keen there. It may, therefore, be more advantageous for a firm to gain a permanent foothold in one or more developing countries, since often there is no competition to reckon with."
3. What are the distinguishing characteristics of Muslim economic ideas?
4. Present a scheme for analyzing the economic environment of Mexico from the viewpoint of an appliance manufacturer.
5. What relevance does Engel's law have in the analysis of economic environment for overseas business?
6. How can a firm examine its competitive advantage overseas?
7. Illustrate how the economic perspectives of different countries are related.

Creative Questions

1. A company is interested in selling telecommunications equipment (telephone exchanges, etc.) to India—a country with 900 million people, a billion by decade's end—and only 7 million phone lines. What kind of economic analysis would you conduct to determine the viability of opportunity in India?
2. The product life cycle theory alleges that the nature and number of competitors vary at different stages. During the early (introduction, growth) stages of the product life cycle the product has little or no competition, and at later stages (maturity, decline), the competition becomes tougher. Does that mean if a company enters a growth market overseas, it need not worry about competition? Does it not have to undertake competitive analysis?

Endnotes

1. "A Snapshot of Living Standards," *Fortune*, July 31, 1989, p. 92.
2. Gunnar Myrdal, *The Asian Drama: An Inquiry into the Poverty of Nations* (New York: Pantheon, 1968).
3. Bill Saporito, "Where the Global Action is," *Fortune*, Autumn/Winter 1993, p. 63.
4. *The Economist*, April 2, 1994, p. 100. *Also see* "The Myth of the Japanese Middle Class," *Business America*, September 12, 1988, p. 49.
5. The most up-to-date statistics on a world-wide basis are available from the World Bank. *See World Development Report—1988* (New York: Oxford University Press, 1988).
6. Benjamin R. Barber, "Jihad vs McWorld," *The Atlantic*, March 1992, pp. 53–56, 58–63.
7. Art Pine, "Pakistan Bends Economy to the Koran," *The Wall Street Journal*, September 9, 1981, p. 33.
8. Subhash C. Jain, *Marketing Planning and Strategy*, 3rd ed. (Cincinnati, OH: South-Western Publishing Co., 1992), pp. 77–78.
9. Ibid.
10. "How German Auto Makers Penetrated Japan's Market," *The Wall Street Journal*, May 17, 1988, p. 34. Information updated from BMW Marketing Division in Germany.
11. Valerie Reitman, "In Japan's Car Market, Big Three Face Rivals Who Go Door-to-Door," *The Wall Street Journal*, September 28, 1994, p.1.
12. "Brazil: Is the Recovery for Real?" *Business Week*, October 3, 1994, p. 60.
13. "Brazil's Car Industry: Party Time, *The Economist,* September 17, 1994, p. 76.
14. "U.S.-Based MNCs say Weak Dollar is Nothing to Cry About," *Crossborder Monitor*, July 20, 1994, p. 1.
15. C.P. Rao, M. Krishna Erramilli, and Gopala K. Ganesh, "Impact of Domestic Recession on Export Marketing Behavior," *International Marketing Review*, Vol. 7, No. 2 (1990), pp. 54–65.
16. John Jelacic, "U.S. Trade Facts," *Business America*, April, 1994, p. 40.
17. *See* Jeremy Main, "How to Go Global and Why," *Fortune*, August 28, 1989, p. 70.
18. V. Kumar, Antonie Stam, and Erich A. Joachimsthaler, "An Interactive Multi-Criteria Approach to Identifying Potential Foreign Markets," *Journal of International Marketing*, Vol. 2, No. 1, 1994, pp. 29–52. *Also see*: Marie E. Wicks Kelly and George C. Philippatos, "Comparative Analysis of the Foreign Investment Evaluation Practices by U.S.-Based Manufacturing Multinational Companies," *Business Studies*, Winter 1982, pp. 19–42; Robert Weigand, "International Investments; Weighing the Incentives," *Harvard Business Review*, July–August 1983, pp. 146–53; and Philip Kotler and Liam Fahey, "The World's Champion Marketers: The Japanese," *Journal of Business Strategy,* Summer 1982, pp. 3–13.
19. "Adam Smith and the Wok," *The Economist*, December 4, 1993, p. 15.
20. *See* H.J. Heinz Company's annual report for 1993.
21. Anthony J.F. O'Reilly, "Establishing Successful Joint Ventures in Developing Nations: A CEO's Perspective," *Columbia Journal of World Business*, Spring 1955, pp. 3–9. Information updated based on interviews with company executives.

CHAPTER 7

Cultural Environment

CHAPTER FOCUS

After studying this chapter, you should be able to:

■ Explain the meaning of culture and its various aspects

■ Describe the impact of culture on product, price, promotion, and distribution decisions

■ Analyze cultural implications for a product/market

■ Discuss cultural adaptation

■ Examine the process of cultural change

Doing business across national boundaries requires interaction with people and their institutions and organizations nurtured in different cultural environments. Values that are important to one group of people may mean little to another. For example, typical U.S. attitudes and perceptions of various things may be at variance with other people's ideas and views of the same things. In brief, there exist among nations striking and significant differences of attitude, belief, ritual, motivation, perception, morality, truth, superstition, and an almost endless list of other cultural characteristics.

Cultural differences deeply affect market behavior. International marketers, therefore, need to be as familiar as possible with the cultural traits of any country they want to do business with. International business literature is full of instances where stereotyped notions of countries' cultures have led to insurmountable problems. More than any other function of a business, marketing perhaps is most susceptible to cultural error, since marketing by definition requires contact with the people of the country concerned. Practically all marketing decisions are culture-bound.

The effect of culture on international marketing ventures is multifaceted. The factoring of cultural differences into marketing mix decisions to enhance the likelihood of success has long been a critical issue in overseas operations. With the increasing criticism leveled at multinational enterprises, cultural forces have taken on additional importance. Naiveté and blundering about culture can also be expensive.

This chapter begins by examining the meaning of culture and goes on to explore the profound effect of culture on marketing outside the U.S. Various elements of culture are discussed. A framework for analyzing culture is introduced. The impact of the sociocultural fabric of the host nation on different marketing decisions is analyzed. Following this, a procedure for cultural adaptation overseas is recommended. Finally, the impact of foreign business on local culture as an agent of cultural change in the host country is examined.

The Concept of Culture

It was the middle of October and a marketing executive from the U.S. was flying to Saudi Arabia to finalize a contract with a local company to supply hospital furnishings. The next day, he met the Saudi contacts and wondered if they would sign the deal within two or three days, since he had to report the matter to his board the following Monday. The Saudi executive made a simple response: "Insha Allah," which means "if God is willing." The American felt completely lost. He found the carefree response of the Saudi insulting and unbusinesslike. He felt he had made an effort by going all the way to Saudi Arabia in order for them to question any matter requiring clarification before signing the contract. He thought that the Saudi executive was treating a deal worth over $100 million as if it meant nothing.

During the next meeting the American was determined to put the matter in stronger terms, emphasizing the importance of his board's meeting. But the Arabs again ignored the issue of signing the contract. "They were friendly, appeared happy and calm, but wouldn't sign on the dotted lines," the American later explained. Finally on orders from the president of his company, he returned home without the contract.

Why did the Saudi executives not sign the sales contract? After all, they had agreed to all the terms and conditions during their meeting in New York. But in Riyadh they did not even care to review it, let alone sign it.

Unfortunately, the U.S. executive had arrived at the wrong time. It was the time of Ramadan, holy month, and most Muslims fast. During this time, everything slows down, particularly business.[1] In Western societies, while religion is important, it is for most people only one aspect of life and business goes on as usual most of the time. In the Islamic countries, religion is a total way of life for the majority of people. It affects every facet of living. Thus, no matter how important a business deal may be, it would be undesirable to conduct a deal during the holy month. Such is the Arab value system. The executive from the U.S., however, was not aware of Muslim culture.

Culture has been defined in different ways. Essentially, it includes all learned behavior and values that are transmitted to an individual living within the society through shared experience. A classic definition of culture is provided by Sir Edward Tylor:

> Culture is that complex whole which includes knowledge, belief, art, morals, law, custom, and any other capabilities and habits acquired by [individuals as members] of society.[2]

Culture develops through recurrent social relationships that form patterns that are eventually internalized by members of the entire group.

It is commonly agreed that a culture must have these three characteristics:

1. It is *learned*, that is, acquired by people over time through their membership in a group that transmits culture from generation to generation.
2. It is *interrelated*, that is, one part of the culture is deeply connected with another part such as religion and marriage, business and social status.
3. It is *shared*, that is, tenets of a culture extend to other members of the group.[3]

The concept of culture is broad and extremely complex. It encompasses virtually every part of a person's life. This suggests that culture serves virtually all human needs, both physical and psychological. Further, culture continues to evolve through constant embellishment and adaptation, partly in response to environmental needs and partly through the influence of outside forces. In other words, a culture does not stand still, but slowly, over time it may change. Finally, cultural differences are not necessarily visible but can be quite subtle and can surface in situations where one would never notice them.

A nation may embody more than one culture. Canada has a dual culture: English-speaking and French-speaking. The two cultures may exhibit fundamental cultural differences. Two distinctive cultures also exist in Israel, a so-called Western group consisting of European and U.S. immigrants whose culture corresponds to their backgrounds, and a so-called Oriental group consisting of immigrants from Asian and African countries, most Arab-speaking Muslim societies. The contrasts between the two groups have been described this way:

> The oriental set of values corresponds to the values generally attributed to traditional societies described as: compulsory in their force, sacred in their tone and stable in their timelessness. They call for fatalistic acceptance of the world as is, respect for those in authority, and submergence of the individual in collectivity.

In contrast to this, the norms and values of Israelis of western ancestry can described as stressing acquisitive activities, an aggressive attitude toward economic and social change, and a clear trend toward a higher degree of industrialization. The oriental Israeli immigrants, having arrived later than the western immigrants, were expected to be absorbed in a western society, having a strong emphasis on specificity, universalism and achievement.[4]

Cultural Field

Knowledge of a culture can be gained by probing its various aspects—but which aspects? Since culture is such a vast concept, it is desirable to develop a field for cultural understanding. From the viewpoint of an marketer one way of gaining cultural understanding is to examine the following cultural elements within a country: material life, social interactions, language, aesthetics, religion and faith, pride and prejudice, and ethics and mores.[5]

Material Life

Material life refers to economics, that is, what people do to derive their livelihood. The tools, knowledge, techniques, methods, and processes that a culture utilizes to produce goods and services, as well as their distribution and consumption, are all part of material life. Thus, two essential parts of material life are knowledge and economics.

Material life reflects standard of living and degree of technological advancement. In a hypothetical country, for example, a large proportion of the population is engaged in agriculture. Agricultural operations are mainly performed by manual labor; mechanization of agriculture is unknown. Modern techniques of farming such as use of fertilizers, pesticides, and quality seeds are unfamiliar. The medium of exchange is a barter system, markets are local, and living is entirely rural. Such a composite description suggests that the society is primitive. Opportunities for multinational business in a primitive environment will be limited.

By contrast, consider a different society where manufacturing industry serves as the major source of employment, and agriculture supports about one-tenth of the population. People live in urban centers and have such modern amenities as TVs, cars, VCRs, newspapers, and so on. Money is the medium of exchange. In such a culture, business across national boundaries would make sense.

The material life of a society cannot be described simply, but falls on a continuum of material life whose two poles are traditional and industrialized. A position on the material-life continuum indicates a society's way of life. Each position would then become the basis of analyzing opportunities for an international marketer. For example, Brazil and Pakistan are both developing countries, but the study of material life in the two countries would show that Brazil is ahead of Pakistan, offering market opportunities for such projects as electrical appliances, stereos, and TVs. Pakistan, however, is still emerging from total dependence on farming, suggesting the importance of agricultural tools and inputs in that culture.

Social Interactions

Social interactions establish the roles that people play in a society and their authority/responsibility patterns. These roles and patterns are supported by society's institutional framework, which includes, for example, education and marriage.

Consider the traditional marriage of a Saudi woman. The woman's father chooses the husband-to-be. After agreeing on a small payment for the bride, the two men hold hands in front of a judge to finalize the marriage. The woman sees her husband for the first time when he comes to consummate the marriage. The social role assigned to women in the strict Islamic world is one of complete dependency on men; their authority and their command cannot be questioned. A woman's place is always in the home. Outside the home, if women are seen at all, they are veiled. As has been said:

> Moslems [sic] believe in the segregation of men and women, with the exception of husbands and wives and close family members. Men who are strangers to the family are not even supposed to see a man's female relatives. Moslems are not receptive to the western concept of liberation of women. Males are more privileged. It is not uncommon, as an example, to witness some Moslem males traveling by air in the first-class section of an airliner and their wives in the back, flying economy.[6]

Social roles are also established by culture. For example, a woman can be a wife, a mother, a community leader, and/or an employee. What role is preferred in different situations is culture-bound. Most Swiss women consider household work (e.g., washing dishes, cleaning floors) as their primary role. For this reason, they resent modern gadgets and machines. Behavior also emerges from culture in the form of conventions, rituals, and practices on different occasions such as during festivals, marriages, get-togethers, and times of grief or religious celebration.

Likewise, the authority of the aged, the teacher, and the religious in many societies is held high. The educational system, the social settings (celebrations and festivities), and customs and traditions reassert the prescribed roles and patterns of individuals and groups.[7] A good example is the caste system in India. A person's social and occupational status is determined by birth in a certain family/community. Such is the strength of social heritage that, despite discrimination on the basis of caste being unconstitutional and legally punishable, the system still prevails today, especially in the rural areas.

With reference to marketing, the social interactions influence family decision making and buying behavior and define the scope of personal influence and opinion. In Latin America, as is true of Asian societies as well, the extended family is considered the most basic and stable unit of social organization. The extended family is the center for all economic, political, social, and religious life. It provides companionship, protection, and a common set of values with specifically prescribed means for fulfilling them. By contrast, in the U.S., the nuclear family (husband, wife, and children) is the focus of social organization.

An empirical study by Tan and McCullough showed how cultural differences affect the husband-wife influence in buying decisions. A Singapore husband played a more dominant role than his U.S. counterpart in family decision making.[8] Similar results were obtained in a study of Dutch and U.S. housewives. The U.S. wife played a more autonomous role than the Dutch wife in family decision making. Thus, social roles vary from culture to culture and likely to affect marketing behavior.[9]

Language

Language as part of culture is considered not only in the literal sense as the spoken word, but also as symbolic communication of time, space, things, friendship, and agreements.[10] Communication occurs through speech, gestures, expressions, and other body movements.

The many different languages of the world do not literally translate from one to another, and the understanding of the symbolic and physical aspects of different cultures' communication is even more difficult to achieve. For example, a phrase such as "body by Fisher" translated literally into Flemish means "corpse by Fisher." Similarly, "Let Hertz put you in the driver's seat" translated literally into Spanish means "Let Hertz make you a chauffeur."[11] Nova translates into Spanish as "it doesn't go." A shipment of Chinese shoes destined for Egypt created a problem because the design on the soles of the shoes spelled "God" in Arabic. Olympia's Roto photocopier did not sell well because "roto" refers to the lowest class in Chile, and "roto" in Spanish means "broken."[12]

In addition, meanings differ within the same language used in different places. For example, English language meaning differs from one English-speaking country to another. A store sign in Hong Kong read, "Teeth extracted by the latest methodists," while the sign in a tailor's window in Jordan advised, "Order your summer suits. Because in big rush we will execute customers in strict rotation."[13] In England the words for "truck," "gasoline," and cookies" are "lorry," "petrol," and "biscuits."[14]

Sometimes the same word may mean an entirely different thing in different cultures. "Table the report" in the U.S. means postponement; in England it means "bring the matter to the forefront." Therefore, an international marketer must be careful in handling the matter of language in business dealings, contracts, negotiations, advertising, and so on. Coca-Cola Co., for example, did not use the diet name in France since the word "diet" suggests poor health. Instead, the company called it Coca-Cola Light.

Symbolic communication is equally important. To be on time for an appointment is an accepted norm of behavior in the U.S. A person is looked down upon if he or she fails to be on time. But in many other cultures, people are not particular about time and an appointment at 11 a.m. may not mean 11 a.m. sharp, but only mean at *about* that time (see International Marketing Highlight 7.1). Something as simple as a greeting can be misunderstood. The form of greeting differs from culture to culture. Traditional greetings may be a handshake, hug, nose rub, kiss, placing the hands in praying position, or various other gestures.

For example, in Chile, women typically greet everyone, even strangers, with a kiss on one cheek. In Brazil, it is kisses on both cheeks. But in Spain, in business circles, it may be better to wait until becoming friends to kiss or pat someone on the shoulder.[15] Lack of awareness concerning the country's accepted form of greeting can lead to awkward encounters.[16]

International Marketing Highlight 7.1

Being on Time

Attitudes toward punctuality vary greatly from one culture to another and unless understood can cause confusion and misunderstanding. Romanians, Japanese, and Germans are very punctual, while many of the Latin countries have a more relaxed attitude toward time. The Japanese consider it rude to be late for a business meeting, but it is acceptable, even fashionable, to be late for a social occasion. In Guatemala, on the other hand, a luncheon at a specified time means that some guests might guests might be 10 minutes early while others may be 45 minutes late.

Aesthetics

Aesthetics include the art, the drama, the music, the folkways, and the architecture endemic to a society. These aspects of a society convey the concept of beauty and expression revered in a culture. For example, different colors have different meanings worldwide. In Western societies, wedding gowns are usually white, but in Asia, white symbolizes sorrow.[17]

The aesthetic values of a society show in the design, styles, colors, expressions, symbols, movements, emotions, and postures valued and preferred in a particular culture. These attributes have an impact on the design and promotion of different products.

Likewise, space and the way that a person occupies it communicates something about position in the terms of each culture. For example, a large office on the top floor of a building in the U.S. may mean that the person is important in an organizational hierarchy. Such a conclusion elsewhere would not always be right. Japanese executives usually share an office. Likewise, in the U.S., worldly possessions and material things are often used as symbols of success. A Lincoln Continental or a Mercedes automobile would signify achievement. However, in many countries, such automobiles would not signal respect. Particularly in the Islamic countries, such emphasis on material possessions is frowned upon.

In many situations the symbolic language of communication is more important than the actual words, and people respond accordingly. Therefore, an international businessperson must understand cultural differences and behave accordingly to avoid inadvertently communicating the wrong message.

Religion and Faith

Religion influences a culture's outlook on life, its meaning and concept. Islam considers emphasis on material wealth ignoble. In Christianity, particularly in Western cultures, the ideal of people taking dominion of the earthly environment has combined with the Calvinist ethic of hard work and success to promote the idea of the acquisition of wealth as a measure of achievement. Hinduism, while it places no sanction on the acquisition of wealth, is fatalistic about the acquisition of riches. In general, the religion practiced in a society influences the emphasis placed on material life, which in turn affects the attitudes toward owning and using goods and services. Religious traditions may prohibit the use of certain goods and services altogether. For example, Hinduism prescribes vegetarianism, with special stress on abstinence from beef. Islam, on the other hand, forbids the eating of pork.

A fatalistic belief leads Asians to choose an auspicious time to buy a car or to plan a wedding. Car salespeople in Japan, for example, deliver a car to a consumer on a lucky day, while contractors check for an auspicious day before breaking ground, and insurance salespeople are careful to pick a good day before going for a customer's signature on a life insurance policy.[18]

Religion also influences male-female roles, as well as societal institutions and customs such as marriage and funeral rites. Islam restricts the role of the female to the household. She is also confined to an inferior role. In addition, a Muslim man may have more than one wife, but a woman must practice monogamy.

Religion affects patterns of living in various other ways. It establishes authority relationships, an individual's duties and responsibilities both in childhood and as an adult, and the sanctity of different acts such as hygiene.[19] In the name of religion,

Iranians in 1979 disrupted their whole country.[20] The Catholic church officially continues to prohibit the use of birth control devices. Animism, religion emphasizing magic practiced in many parts of Africa, demands human sacrifices. In general organized religion and faith inevitably motivate people and their customs in numerous ways.[21] The impact of religion is continuous and profound (see International Marketing Highlight 7.2).

International Marketing Highlight 7.2

Cultural Diversity

When a manager from the dominant U.S. culture saw two Arab-American employees arguing, he figured he had better stay out of it. But the employees *expected* a third-party intermediary, or *wasta* in Arabic, and without one the incident blew up.

The expectation goes back to the Koran and Bedouin tradition. While the dominant American culture is likely to take an individualistic, win-lose approach and emphasize privacy, Arab-Americans tend to value a win-win result that preserves group harmony but often requires mediation.

A Latino manager starts a budget-planning meeting by chatting casually and checking with his new staff on whether everyone can get together after work. His non-Latino boss frets over the delay and wonders why he doesn't get straight to the numbers. Latino culture teaches that building relationships is often critical to working together, while the dominant American culture encourages "getting down to business."

Source: *The Wall Street Journal*, September 12, 1990, p. B1

Because religious traits and tenets may profoundly affect marketing, international marketers must be sensitive to the religious principles of the host country.

Pride and Prejudice

Every culture fosters a certain pride and prejudice in its inhabitants. Thus, even the culture most backward in the eyes of a Westerner will have a certain inherent pride in its traits and ways.[22] The Chinese are jealous of their cultural heritage, and they speak of it with great emotion. So do the Egyptians of their heritage. As a matter of fact, despite economic achievements, Americans feel deprived of cultural history in a country so young and diverse by nature (see International Marketing Highlight 7.3).

International Marketing Highlight 7.3

Cultural Islands

Japan: The strongest work ethic, the greatest concern about the work ethic of the rest of the workforce, and strongly in favor of free trade.

South Korea: Strongly favors protectionism, puts country ahead of company, a strong sense of corporate responsibility toward employees, and more optimistic about the future.

India: More optimistic about the future and strongly favors protectionism.

Hungary: Organizationally different from companies in other countries and very focused on economic regeneration.

Source: Rosabeth Moss Kanter, "Transcending Business Boundaries: 12,000 World Managers View Change," *Harvard Business Review*, May–June 1991, p. 153.

Cultural pride and prejudice make many nations reject foreign ideas and imported products. But the reverse may also be true, and a perception of greatness attributed to another culture may lead to the eager acceptance of things reflecting that culture. For example, the Japanese are proud of their culture and economic achievement and prefer to buy Japanese manufactures. On the other hand, the words *Made In U.S.A.* marked on a product communicate quality and sophistication to people in many developing countries.[23] The Japanese respond to names. They like dealing with people of standing. It is for this reason that Mead Corporation, which has successfully operated in Japan for 35 years, had Nelson Mead, the son of the founder, handle that business.

Ethics and Mores

The concept of what is right and wrong is based on culture. To be straightforward and openly honest are considered morally right in the U.S., even if feelings are hurt. In Latin cultures, however, people avoid direct statements that would embarrass or make another uncomfortable. Thus, even if a Latin businessman does not mean to do business, he would appear to participate, only later to excuse himself from the transaction process.

In an empirical study of U.S., French, and German managers, for example, substantial differences were noted on ethical issues. On an issue that may benefit the firm at the expense of the environment, the French and German managers were more likely to side with their employers and participate in what they perceived as a relatively minor infraction of environmental law. The American managers were less likely to approve a production run that would result in illegal air pollution.[25]

The differences in mannerisms between the Japanese and the Koreans also illustrate the point. The Japanese are formal and reserved; the Koreans informal and outgoing. A Korean saleswoman puts her hand on a customer's shoulder as she walks him to the door; a Korean executive invites a business acquaintance home to meet the family. Such acts of familiarity would be very unusual in Japan.[26] Graham noted that culture has significant influence on the process of business negotiations conducted by the executives in the U.S., Japan, and Brazil. For example, substantial differences in bargaining style existed across the three cultures. Brazilians made fewer commitments and more demands. Their first offers were more greedy. Americans were more apt to offer a fair price, one that was closer to the eventual solution. Japanese consistently asked for higher profit solutions when making the initial offer in a negotiation.[27] (see International Marketing Highlight 7.4).

Culture and Marketing

Culture influences every aspect of marketing. Figure 7.1 describes the linkage between culture and marketing action. A marketing-oriented firm should make decisions based on customer perspectives. Customers' actions are shaped by their lifestyles and behavior patterns as they stem from their society's culture. Thus, the products that people buy, the attributes that they value, and the principals whose opinions they accept, are all culture-based choices. As a matter of fact, it is not an overstatement to say that a person's perspectives or resources, problems, and opportunities to a considerable extent are generated and conditioned by culture. The influence of culture on marketing perspectives is cited in Exhibit 7.1, showing how Brazilians have reacted negatively to products that were successful in the U.S. (see International Marketing Highlight 7.5).

International Marketing Highlight 7.4

Why Can't People Do Things the American Way?

Bill Hastings, the assistant director of marketing for a small American manufacturing company, visited Bangkok to investigate the possibility of distributing the company's products in Southeast Asia. Bill traveled with Cheryl Acosta, field director for the company's international operations. Neither of them had any prior experience in Asia. Bill, in fact, had never traveled outside the U.S. Both executives felt mildly apprehensive about being neophytes in the field, but they felt great excitement, too, as if they were the first explorers in an uncharted area. (Neither acknowledged that their counterparts in other companies probably had had years of international experience and had developed a mastery of Southeast Asian business practices.)

Bill and Cheryl attempted to complete a 12-country marketing study in 6 weeks. Bill figured that once he obtained the facts and made a quick decision on how to proceed, sales would start rolling in. But they found the environment baffling and made little headway. Frustrated, they impulsively recommended a plan to headquarters that ended in a fiasco one year later.

"I can't understand what happened," Bill reflected in the aftermath. "The same method worked just fine when we started operations in Los Angeles."

Figure 7.1 Impact of Culture on Marketing Decisions

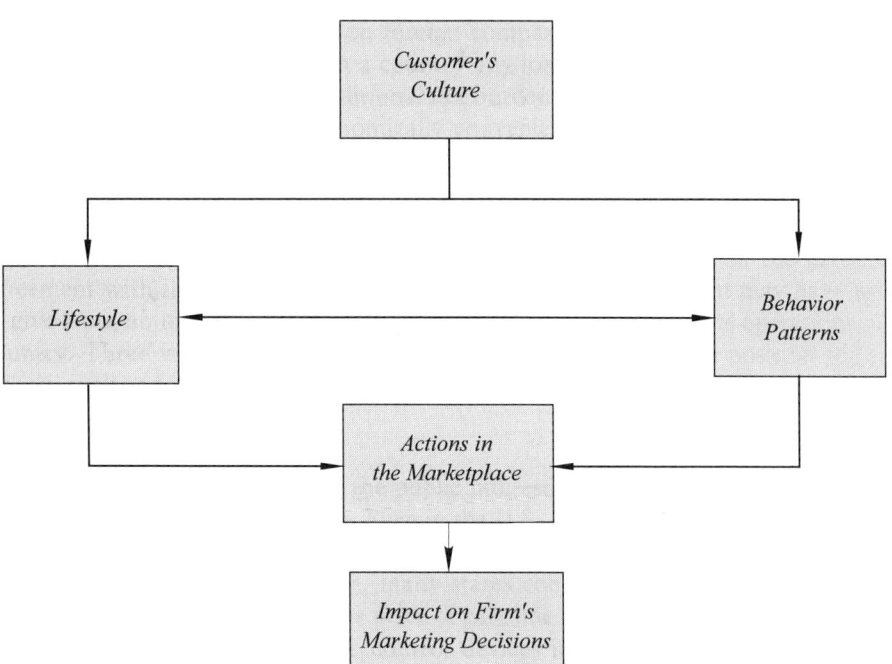

A practical example of cultural impact is illustrated by the foods that people prefer. Of all the universals that constitute "culture," few, if any, are so ingrained and consistently reinforced as are food habits. The daily physiological requirement of nutrition in some form exists for every human inhabitant in any society or culture—there is no escape from eating for an extended period. Food consumption, acquisition, and preparation also are interrelated with many of the other universals of the culture, including religious observances and ceremonies, feasting, folklore, and the division of labor.[28]

EXHIBIT 7.1   How Cultural Backgrounds Vary: An Example

Imaginative Brazilians do not always use products in the same way as Americans. "Marketers assume they can segment markets and position products, but Brazilian housewives find multiple uses for things," says Ian Gardner, a former Reckitt & Colman product manager. "If you try to sell a product specifically for cleaning floor surfaces, Brazilians will use it for disinfecting the toilet bowl, cleaning the cat, and washing the kids' hair."

Recently, sales of a certain brand of floor wax dropped mysteriously, says an American adman. The perplexed manufacturer soon discovered many Brazilians had been using the floor wax as lighter fluid to ignite their Sunday barbecues. When the company added more water to the solvent base, the floor wax became less flammable and Brazilians stopped buying it.

Products must be tailored to local tastes and customs. In Rio de Janeiro, consumers are used to butter that is usually slightly rancid from the tropical heat.

Unilever and Anderson-Clayton learned that to sell margarine successfully in Rio, it should taste slightly rancid.

Advertising as well as the product itself should be directed at the way Brazilians do things like washing dishes. Brazilians squirt liquid detergent on a sponge rather than filling the kitchen sink with soapy water and submerging plates and silverware.

A recent commercial for a successful liquid dishwashing detergent featured a row of nuns, plates in hand, correctly doing the dishes by passing a soapy sponge down the line.

Why should [Brazilian] Portuguese speakers try to pronounce Kentucky Fried Chicken? "Some names are ridiculous, like [Pepsi's] Mountain Dew and [R.J. Reynolds'] Chesterfield," says Mr. Gardner. "Brazilians can't pronounce them."

Since its introduction in southern Brazil at the end of 1981, Mountain Dew has been working on the pronunciation problem with a mnemonic device. Ads read: "*Peca* [ask for] Mao-Tem-Du," a close approximation of Mountain Dew in a Brazilian accent.

"If you have to spend lots of money just to teach people to pronounce your product's name, there are much better ways to spend money," Mr. Gardner said.

Few Brazilians seem to be asking for Mountain Dew. A Pepsi marketing exec said the soft drink started very strong but sales have flattened. "But Brazilians can pronounce the name" he said. "They just need a little help."

Brazilians may have a similar problem when local beverage manufacturer Antarctica launches the national fruit flavored soft drink—called Guarana and pronounced "Gaw-ra-nuh"—in the U.S. later this year.

Source: Laurel Wenz, *Advertising Age*, July 5, 1982, p. m–25. Copyright © 1982 by Crain Communications, Inc. All rights reserved. Reprinted by permission.

International Marketing Highlight 7.5

Embarrassment in the Air

United Airlines' experiences in the Pacific market show how cultural mistakes could be embarrassing. As one of their officials reported:

> The map we inserted into our sales promotion brochure left out one of Japan's main islands.
>
> Our magazine ad campaign, "We Know the Orient," listed the names of Far Eastern countries below pictures of local coins. Unfortunately, the coins didn't match up with the countries.
>
> I leave to your imagination how Chinese businessmen felt taking off from Hong Kong during the inauguration of our concierge services for first-class passengers. To mark the occasion, each concierge was proudly wearing a white carnation . . . a well-known Oriental symbol of death.
>
> Perhaps the most embarrassing mistake was our inflight magazine cover that showed Australian actor Paul Horgan wandering through the Outback. The caption read, "Paul Hogan Camps It Up." Hogan's lawyer was kind enough to phone us long distance from Sydney to let us know that "camps it up" is Australian slang for "flaunts his homosexuality." The Paul Hogan story is particularly instructive. Americans often assume that the folks Down Under are just like Americans because we all speak English. This does not make for happy customers. Australians expect real cream in their coffee—not artificial whitener. And the American hand gesture for "thumbs up" has quite a different meaning Down Under. It does *not* mean "OK."

Source: John R. Zeeman, "Service—The Cutting Edge of Global Competition: What United Is Learning in the Pacific," a presentation before the Academy of International Business, Chicago, Illinois, November 14, 1987.

The human perception of edibility has little to do with logical nutritional fulfillments. Culture creates the system of communication among humans about edibility, toxicity, and repleteness. Cultural pressures easily overrule physiological necessities; therefore, it becomes even more difficult for an individual alien to a culture to predict that culture's preference for or rejection of certain food habits. Similarly, gift giving varies from country to country as has been said:

> Customs concerning gift giving are extremely important to understand. In some cultures, gifts are expected, and failure to present them is considered an insult, whereas in other countries, offering a gift is considered offensive. Business executives also need to know when to present gifts—on the initial visit or afterward; where to present gifts—in public or in private; what type of gift to present; what color it should be; and how many to present.
>
> Gift giving is an important part of doing business in Japan. Exchanging gifts symbolizes the depth and strength of a business relationship to the Japanese. Gifts are usually exchanged at the first meeting. When presented with a gift, companies are expected to respond by giving a gift.
>
> In sharp contrast, gifts are rarely exchanged in Germany and are usually not appropriate. Small gifts are fine, but expensive items are not a general practice.

Gift giving is not a normal custom in Belgium or the U.K. either, although in both countries flowers are a suitable gift if invited to someone's home. Even that is not as easy as it sounds. International executives must use caution to choose appropriate flowers. For example, avoid sending chrysanthemums (especially white) in Belgium and elsewhere in Europe since they are mainly used for funerals. In Europe, it is also considered bad luck to present an even number of flowers. Beware of white flowers in Japan where they are associated with death, and purple flowers in Mexico and Brazil.[29]

These descriptions are merely summaries; they do not encompass all trends, etiquettes, and traditions observed in the respective cultures, and each country deserves an in-depth report to provide meaningful data for planning a thorough marketing strategy.

Empirical evidence on lifestyle and behavior differences is provided by a number of authors. Although some of the studies examined here are old, they nevertheless underline the importance of cultural differences from the viewpoint of marketers.

Basing his findings on a number of cross-cultural consumer studies, Plummer demonstrates significant differences among people belonging to different countries on a variety of dimensions.[30] On the topic of housecleaning, for example, the normal attitude toward this chore appears much more casual in Australia, Germany, and the U.S. than in Italy and the U.K. Likewise, people in the U.K., Italy, France, and the U.S. hold a more traditional and conservative perspective of moral principle statements than those in Germany and Australia.

On the topic of personal hygiene, Plummer found that "Americans would be lost without their deodorant." The French and Australians, on the other hand, "appear less concerned about the use of a deodorant."[31] These differences vividly point out the importance of assessing cultural differences among nations before developing marketing strategy.

Similar differences in cross-national comparisons were discovered by Douglas. In her study of wives working at home and outside the home in the U.S. and France, she found that even after accounting for structural differences between the two countries, the U.S. wives tended to shop more in large supermarkets and less in neighborhood supermarkets and corner stores than French housewives. Further, the U.S. husbands seemed more likely to assist in grocery shopping, though infrequently, than French husbands.[32]

Muller and Bolger discovered major differences in the pattern of prepurchase information search for a new automobile between the two major cultural groups in Canada. First, French Canadians considered fewer cars during the search process than did English Canadians. Second, the French Canadian car buyers devoted less time to search than their English Canadian counterparts. Third, French Canadians conducted a generally less thorough and less extensive search for a new car than did English Canadians. Fourth, on the average, before choosing a new car, English Canadians made three times as many test drives as French Canadians. To sum up, the French Canadian buyers of new autos search less than English Canadians, not only because of their traditional reliance on the family and on word-of-mouth communications, but for other reasons which were not made clear from this study.[33] Similarly, Schaninger, Bourgeois, and Buss found significant consumption, shopping, and media usage differences between the French-speaking, bilingual, and English-speaking Canadian families.[34] A recent study indicated, although the trend is slowly shifting, that Germans still consume six times as much beer per capita as the Italians, and the French six time times as much wine per capita as the British.[35] Despite their geographic closeness, Japan and Korea couldn't have more different coffee markets. The average Japanese drinks 800 cups of coffee a year, a Korean about a quarter of that.[36]

Nonetheless, no matter who shops, or where, cultural differences always affect decision making when it comes to the product and its price, as well as to the way it is distributed and promoted. Briefly, understanding and heeding cultural variables is critical to success in international marketing. Lack of familiarity with the business practices, social customs, and etiquette of a country can weaken a company's position in the market, prevent it from accomplishing its objectives, and ultimately lead to failure.

The Product

Two similar products are introduced into a country. One does extremely well; the other flops. Why? Although the performance of a product/market depends on a variety of factors, in many cases *failure is directly traceable to cultural blunders*. For example, Kentucky Fried Chicken was received well in France (as in Germany and the U.K.), but McDonald's stumbled.[37] Similarly, the British prefer a wood handle on their umbrella while we in the U.S. find the plastic handle satisfactory. Apparently, what is a "right" product for one culture may be unsuitable for another culture.

A product that has been highly profitable in the U.S. may not achieve the same success elsewhere because the product attributes desired in the U.S. may not necessarily be desired in another part of the world. The Campbell Soup Company found out the hard way that the condensed soups so popular and acceptable in the U.S. were not liked in England. Accustomed to ready-to-eat soups, the English consumer found it hard to believe that water or milk could be added to soup without spoiling the taste.[38] Similarly, Phillip Morris ran into difficulties because of taste differences among nations. One of its popular brands was a dismal flop in Canada despite adequate promotion. Canadians have a preference for Virginia-type tobacco blends, which are different from what the popular brand had to offer.[39]

Sometimes a product that is unacceptable in its U.S. form may succeed if it is adapted to the culture of the new market. Mister Donut's success in Japan is the result of a series of minute but sensible modifications. Their coffee cup is smaller and lighter to fit the finger size of the average Japanese consumer. Even their donuts are a little smaller there than those in the U.S. Similarly, Japanese mothers found the Beechnut babyfood jar too big. After the jar was made smaller, the sales increased. After years of painstaking market research, P&G finally realized that Japanese parents are very concerned with keeping their babies clean, and they change their children's diapers far more often than Americans do. In response, P&G devised Ultra Pampers, a more-absorbent diaper that keeps the child drier and makes frequent changing a less-messy task. P&G also discovered that in land-starved Japan, shelf and closet space is almost as precious to housewives as their children, so it made the diapers thinner so the same number fit in a much smaller box. The popularity of the new diapers spread rapidly, and today Ultra Pampers is the market leader in Japan.[40]

Another good example is the Barbie doll. This all-American best-seller did not do very well in Japan for a long time. Finally, Mattel Toys, its creator, gave the manufacturing license to Takara, a Japanese company. Takara's own survey revealed that most Japanese girls—and their parents—thought the doll's breasts were too big and the legs unrealistically long. After correcting these minor defects, and converting the Barbie doll's blue eyes to dark brown, Takara started selling the same doll under the same brand name and concept, and found that its production could not keep up with the demand. Takara sold some two million Barbie dolls in just two years. According to a Takara executive, dolls in Japan are a reflection of what girls want to be. With the target customer group in Japan being eighth-graders, the doll had to look more Japanese than the original version.[41]

In India, the Barbie doll had a slightly different problem. In a conservative country like India, the concept of a boyfriend was unacceptable, so Ken did not accompany her. However, since brothers and sisters in India are much closer than in Western societies, Mattel created Mark as Barbie's brother for the Indian market.

The positioning of the product in different countries should be in line with the cultural traits of each society. Renault's strategy in different countries illustrates the point. In France, the Renault car was introduced as a little "supercar," which was fun to drive both on highways and within the city. In Germany, where auto buying is viewed as a serious matter, the emphasis was put on safety, modern engineering, and interior comfort. In Italy, road performance—road handling capacity and acceleration—was stressed. In Finland, the focus was on solid construction and reliability. For Holland, the Renault car had to be redesigned because the Dutch consider a small car cheap and mechanically inferior.[42] The same principle applies to the personal computer. American computer companies learned early on that they could not simply target Europe as one market, but must court each country market separately, acknowledging cultural differences. The French, for example, are very nationalistic, looking for more French-made parts in the product. The German market, on the other hand, has a very high perception of quality.[43]

In general, product positioning in a foreign market should match the country's unique cultural environment (see International Marketing Highlight 7.6).

The importance of perceived risk is subject to cultural influences as well. Thus, risk is a more important determinant of purchase behavior in the U.S. than in Mexico, where consumers are influenced by fatalism, the belief that humans have no control or recourse on the shape of things in the future. Therefore, for cultural reasons, the use of product warranties to reduce the risk of negative outcomes associated with purchases may not be as effective in Mexico as in the U.S.

Distribution

The cultural dimensions of a nation make certain distribution arrangements more viable. For example, in the U.S., Sears, Roebuck merchandises a big percentage of products under its own brand name. In Mexico, however, Sears has done two things differently in order to respond to pride aspects in the local culture. First, it buys over 90 percent of its items from national manufacturers. Second, it carries U.S. national brands made in Mexico to cater to well-to-do customers who like to distinguish themselves by using U.S. brands.

International Marketing Highlight 7.6

The Marlboro Man

What do college students in different countries think when considering Marlboro cigarettes? A researcher at Northwestern University posed this question and put it to the test by researching college students in five countries: Brazil, Japan, Norway, Thailand, and the U.S. Small samples of students in each country participated in a word-association test by responding to the statement: "Smoking a Marlboro cigarette . . ."

Responses were sharply mixed. Thai students considered smoking a Marlboro cigarette to be relaxing. Norwegian students most closely linked smoking Marlboros to disease, and Brazilians associated the brand with pollution. U.S. students responded to "Smoking a Marlboro cigarette . . ." with words like "cowboy," "horse," and "macho"—all relating directly to Marlboro's longstanding advertising campaign. The Japanese associated smoking Marlboros with social occasions.

These different images point out that products and brands mean different things around the world because the cultural contexts in which they are interpreted vary greatly. This means that creative advertising needs to be adjusted to accommodate the specific cultural context in which it is placed. For example, because Japanese consumers associate Marlboro cigarettes with being sociable, Marlboro advertisements in Japan could show the cowboy with other cowboys rather than by himself. In Thailand, where consumers perceive cigarettes to be suggestive of relaxation, it may be most effective to show the cowboy in a subdued context rather than chasing wild horses.

Source: Lenore Skenazy, "How Does Slogan Translate," *Advertising Age*, October 12, 1987, p. 84.

Channels of distribution may need to be modified to suit local conditions. Avon uses door-to-door and other direct selling in the U.S. This provides men and women with the opportunity to make buying decisions in the privacy of their homes or workplaces. Such arrangements, however, did not work abroad. European women considered calls by Avon representatives as intrusions on their privacy, and the representatives felt uncomfortable selling to friends in their homes for a profit.[45]

Cultural boundaries affect the mapping of sales territories. For example, a French company decided to divide sales territories in Africa based on market potential (respecting local administrative boundaries), something it had done successfully in the Wester European market. This type of territory structure, however, did not allow for the fact that the countries contained a number of tribes, each with a particular person authorized to buy in the community. The territory arrangements overlapped with these tribal areas and created a great deal of confusion in the assignment of sales responsibilities.[46]

Promotion

Promotion practices, particularly advertising, are perhaps most susceptible to cultural error. Examples abound where advertising copy and design were culturally repugnant, and, therefore, totally ineffective. For example, in Thailand the Warner-Lambert Company used its U.S. ad for Listerine showing a boy and a girl being affectionate with each other. This type of appeal was ineffective since the boy-girl relationship shown was ultra-modern and hence against the cultural norms of Thailand's conservative society. A slight modification—two girls talking about Listerine—had a positive effect on sales.[47] Similarly, Colgate Palmolive Company introduced its Cue toothpaste in France only to find out later that *cue* in French is a pornographic word.[48] Pepsi ran into difficulties in Germany for using its U.S. ad, "Come alive, you're in the Pepsi generation," which in German meant "Come alive out of the grave."[49] Pepsodent's promise of white teeth backfired in Southeast Asia where betel nut chewing was an acceptable norm, and therefore, yellow teeth were taken for granted.[50] A P&G soap commercial showed a Japanese husband in the room as his wife was bathing. The Japanese considered it an invasion of privacy and distasteful.[51] An airline ad campaign urged Hispanics to fly *en cuero*. It is hard to figure out what the airline had in mind given that the phrase means stark naked.[52]

Ajax's white tornado was not perceived as a symbol of power in many countries, Ultra Brite's sexy girl throwing kisses was ineffective in Belgium and the company was forced to drop the theme "Give your mouth sex appeal."[53] Carlsberg had to add a third elephant to its label of Elephant beer for an ad in Africa since two elephants are a symbol of bad luck there.[54] Usage of color in ads must be attuned to cultural norms as well. In Japan, as in many Asian countries, the color white is for mourning; purple is associated with death in many Latin American countries; and brown and gray are disliked in Nicaragua[55] (see International Marketing Highlight 7.7).

■ International Marketing Highlight 7.7 ■

Taboos Around the World

Never touch the head of a Thai or pass an object over it, as the head is considered sacred in Thailand. Likewise, never point the bottoms of the feet in the direction of another person in Thailand or cross your legs while sitting, especially in the presence of an older person.

Avoid using triangular shapes in Hong Kong, Korea, or Taiwan, as the triangle is considered a negative shape in those countries.

Remember that the number seven is considered bad luck in Kenya, good luck in Czechoslovakia, and has magical connotations in Benin.

Red is a positive color in Denmark, but represents witchcraft and death in many African countries.

A nod means "no" in Bulgaria, and shaking the head side-to-side means "yes."

Source: Business America, Vol. 112, No. 2 (Special Edition 1991), pp. 26–27.

Pricing

The price that a customer may be willing to pay for a product depends on both its perceived and actual values.[56] The value of goods imported from a Western country, for example, is perceived as much higher in developing countries. As an example, Indians perceive imported products as superior to those manufactured locally. For this reason, U.S./English brands sell at an inflated price. A story is told of an Indian who on a trip to England bought an expensive sweater for his wife from a London department store. He was disenchanted on returning home to find that the sweater had been manufactured in India.

An empirical investigation by Cattin and his colleagues showed that U.S. and French purchasing managers attached varying degrees of importance to products manufactured in different countries. For example, *Made in England* appeared to be more favorably perceived by the French, as promising more luxurious and more inventive products than *Made in U.S.A*. On the other hand, *Made In Germany* products were more highly regarded by American than French consumers. It would appear in countries where one's image is high, a premium price may be charged. However, where a national image is weak, an international business could do well to deemphasize "made in" information and perhaps seek entry in the market through a joint venture or some other form of close association with a domestic firm.[57]

Cultural Analysis—The Primacy of Host Country Viewpoint

The analysis of cultural differences is necessary for the formulation of international marketing strategy. Conceptually, cultural analysis may be based on any of the following three approaches: ethnocentrism, assimilation, and primacy of host country viewpoint.[58]

The *ethnocentrism approach* assumes "We are the best." Many U.S. companies are guilty of assuming that what is good at home should work in foreign markets as well.[59] The examples discussed in the previous section illustrate how ethnocentrism can lead to costly mistakes. The *assimilation approach* assumes that since the U.S. is a cultural melting pot, the cultural traits demonstrated in U.S. society are relevant anywhere. The third viewpoint, the *primacy of host country approach*, concerns market composition and emphasizes basing decisions on host country cultural traits. This approach considers domestic information as inappropriate to successful operation in markets outside the U.S. The discussion that follows assumes the primacy of host country viewpoint.

Assessment of Culture

An assessment of a country's culture for marketing's sake involves analyzing the people's attitudes, motivations, perceptions, and learning processes. Exhibit 7.2 summarizes more specifically the cultural determinants. The information contained in this exhibit attempts to relate cultural traits to marketing decisions. For example, simply knowing about the religion or morality of a culture is not enough. What must be analyzed is whether or not the product slated to be introduced into the country has any direct or indirect connotations that conflict with the cultural patterns of the society. Similarly, an examination of advertising themes, phrases, words, or expressions should confirm viability of promotional decisions.

The cultural values of a nation may be studied through either observation or fieldwork. *Observation* requires living in a culture over a long period in order to become deeply involved in its pattern of living. *Fieldwork*, on the other hand, involves gathering information on a set of variables relative to the culture. While the observation method may be more desirable for a fuller understanding of the culture, from the standpoint of business it is impractical. Thus, the study of culture in the realm of international marketing must be based on fieldwork. One fieldwork approach for assessing culture has been worked out by Rokeach. He has developed a list of 18 terminal and 18 instrumental values (see Exhibit 7.3). Rokeach's framework can be employed productively to discriminate people of culturally diverse backgrounds.[60]

Thus, one way to approach the cultural analysis of a country for the purpose of making marketing decisions might consist of two steps. First, a general notion of the culture is gained by using Rokeach's 36 values. This general information may be further interpreted by answering the specific marketing-related questions raised by Engel and his colleagues in Exhibit 7.2.

EXHIBIT 7.2 Outline of Cross-Cultural Analysis of Consumer Behavior

1. **Determine Relevant Motivations in the Culture**

    What needs are fulfilled with this product in the minds of members of the culture? How are these needs presently fulfilled? Do members of this culture readily recognize these needs?

2. **Determine Characteristic Behavior Patterns**

    What patterns are characteristic of purchasing behavior? What forms of division of labor exist within the family structure? How frequently are products of this type purchased? What size packages are normally purchased? Do any of these characteristic behaviors conflict with behavior expected for this product? How strongly ingrained are the behavior patterns that conflict with those needed for distribution of this product?

3. **Determine What Broad Cultural Values are Relevant to This Product**

    Are there strong values about work, morality, religion, family relations, and so on, that relate to this product? Does this product connote attributes that are in conflict with these cultural values? Can conflicts with values be avoided by changing the product? Are there positive values in this culture with which the product might be identified?

4. **Determine Characteristic Forms of Decision Making**

    Do members of the culture display a studied approach to decisions concerning innovations or an impulsive approach? What is the form of the decision process? Upon what information sources do members of the culture rely? Do members of the culture tend to be rigid or flexible in the acceptance of new ideas? What criteria do they use in evaluating alternatives?

5. **Evaluate Promotion Methods Appropriate to the Culture**

    What role does advertising occupy in the culture? What themes, words, or illustrations are taboo? What language problems exist in present markets that cannot be translated into this culture? What types of salespeople are accepted by members of the culture? Are such salespeople available?

6. **Determine Appropriate Institutions for This Product in the Minds of Consumers**

    What types of retailers and intermediary institutions are available? What services do these institutions offer that are expected by the consumer? What alternatives are available for obtaining services needed for the product but not offered by existing institutions? How are various types of retailers regarded by consumers? What alternatives are available for obtaining services needed for the product but not offered by existing institutions? How are various types of retailers regarded by consumers? Will changes in the distribution structure be readily accepted?

Source: James F. Engel, Roger D. Blackwell, and David T. Kollat, *Consumer Behavior*, 3rd ed. (Hinsdale, IL: Dryden Press, 1978), p. 90.

EXHIBIT 7.3 Terminal and Instrumental Values

TERMINAL VALUE	INSTRUMENTAL VALUE
A comfortable life (a prosperous life)	
An exciting life (a stimulating, active life)	Ambitious (hardworking, aspiring)
A sense of accomplishment (lasting contribution)	Broadminded (open-minded)
A world at peace (free of war and conflict)	Capable (competent, effective)
A world of beauty (beauty of nature and the arts)	Cheerful (lighthearted, joyful)
Equality (brotherhood, equal opportunity for all)	Clean (neat, tidy)
Family security (taking care of loved ones)	Courageous (standing up for your beliefs)
Freedom (independence, free choice)	Forgiving (willing to pardon others)
Happiness (contentedness)	Helpful (working for the welfare of others)
Inner harmony (freedom from inner conflict)	Honest (sincere, truthful)
Mature love (sexual and spiritual intimacy)	Imaginative (daring, creative)
National security (protection from attack)	Independent (self-reliant, self-sufficient)
Pleasure (an enjoyable, leisurely life)	Intellectual (intelligent, reflective)
Salvation (saved, eternal life)	Logical (consistent, rational)
Self-respect (self-esteem)	Loving (affectionate, tender)
Social recognition (respect, admiration)	Obedient (dutiful, respectful)
True friendship (close companionship)	Polite (courteous, well-mannered)
Wisdom (a mature understanding of life)	Responsible (dependent, reliable)
	Self-controlled (restrained, self-disciplined)

Source: M. Rokeach, *The Nature of Human Values* (New York: Free Press, 1973), p. 28

Hall's Map of Culture

A different way of understanding foreign cultures is recommended by Edward T. Hall. His framework, which he calls a map of culture, consists of a two-dimensional matrix containing different human activities, which he calls primary message systems. These activities are interaction, association, subsistence, bisexuality, territoriality, temporality, learning, play, defense, and exploitation.[61] Exhibit 7.4 explains briefly the 10 primary message systems.

A person interested in learning about a culture need not study all 10 aspects but can examine any one of them fully and gain an adequate understanding of the culture. Hall remarked: "Since each [aspect] is enmeshed in the other, one can start the study of culture with any of the ten and eventually come out with a complete picture.[62] For example, to understand buyer behavior, a marketer could analyze the culture by examining the association aspect; association intersects with all other nine aspects just as they intersect with association. With each intersection, a variety of questions can be raised to gain cultural understanding. To illustrate the point, the intersection of association with learning may be examined by seeking answers to such questions as: How do different groups of the society learn about new things? Whose opinions are respected in each group? Similarly, the intersection of learning with association would be revealed in connection with such problems as how learning takes place through different sources in different groups.

EXHIBIT 7.4   The Primary Message System of Edward Hall's Map of Culture

1. *Interaction.*   The interaction with the environment through different modes such as speech and writing.
2. *Association.*   The structure and organization of society and its various components.
3. *Subsistence.*   The perspective of activities of individuals and groups that deal with livelihood and living.
4. *Bisexuality.*   The differentiation of roles and functions along sex lines.
5. *Territoriality.*   The possession, use, and defense of land and territory.
6. *Temporality.*   The division and allocation of time and its use for various activities.
7. *Learning.*   The patterns of transmitting knowledge.
8. *Play.*   The process of enjoyment through relaxation and recreation.
9. *Defense.*   The protection against natural and human forces in the environment.
10. *Exploitation.*   The application of skills and technology to turn natural resources to people's needs.

Source: Excerpt from *The Silent Language* by Edward T. Hall, © 1959 by Edward T. Hall. Used by permission of Doubleday, a division of Bantam, Doubleday, Dell Publishing Group, Inc.

The use of Hall's framework for international marketers is exemplified by Robock and Simmonds in an analysis of the play activity for a toy and games company.[63] Presumably, perspectives of play vary from one culture to another. To suit the marketing program to the cultural traits of the local market, Hall's framework would create 18 categories of questions (see Exhibit 7.5). For example, categories 13 and 14 deal with learning as it emerges in play and play as it leads to learning.

Hall's approach provides an overall perspective on the culture through analysis of one or two primary message systems. In relation to the needs of business, this system works well because the time and expense for a comprehensive cultural perspective are not required. Only the particular element of the culture directly related to a particular international marketing decision needs to be analyzed.

Cultural Adaptation

Cultural adaptation refers to the making of business decisions appropriate to the cultural traits of the society. In other words, adaptation requires that the decisions should be sensitive to the local culture to ensure that the native customs, traditions, and taboos offer no constraint to their implementation.

The previous sections underscored the importance of culture as a factor in conducting business outside the U.S. The impact of culture is ubiquitous in all marketing decisions. Obviously, international marketers must seek cultural adaptation overseas. All their decisions and actions should be fully congruent with local culture.

While the necessity for cultural adaptation is widely recognized, its realization can be difficult in practice. The major reason for this difficulty is what one author calls

EXHIBIT 7.5 A Business Application of Edward Hall's Map of Culture

	Intersections of Play and Other Primary Message Systems	Sample Questions Concerning Cultural Patterns Significant for Marketing Toys and Games
1.	Interaction/play	How do people interact during play as regards competitiveness, instigation, or leadership?
2.	Play/interaction	What games are played involving acting, role-playing, or other aspects of real-world interaction?
3.	Association/play	Who organizes play, and how do the organization patterns differ?
4.	Play/association	What games are played about organization; for example, team competitions and games involving kings, judges, or leader-developed rules and penalties?
5.	Subsistence/play	What are the significant factors regarding people such as distributors, teachers, coaches, or publishers who make their livelihood from games?
6.	Play/subsistence	What games are played about work roles in society such as doctors, nurses, firemen?
7.	Bisexuality/play	What are the significant differences between the sexes in the sports, games, and toys enjoyed?
8.	Play/bisexuality	What games and toys involve bisexuality; for example, dolls, dressing up, dancing?
9.	Territoriality/play	Where are games played and what are the limits observed in houses, parks, streets, schools, and so forth?
10.	Play/territoriality	What games are played about space and ownership; for example, Monopoly?
11.	Temporality/play	At what ages and what times of the day and year are different games played?
12.	Play/temporality	What games are played about and involving time; for example, clocks, speed tests?
13.	Learning/play	What patterns of coaching, tuition, and training exist for learning games?
14.	Play/learning	What games are played about and involving learning and knowledge; for example, quizzes?
15.	Defense/play	What are the safety rules for games, equipment, and toys?
16.	Play/defense	What war and defense games and toys are utilized?
17.	Exploitation/play	What resources and technology are permitted or utilized for games and sport; for example, hunting and fishing rules, use of parks, cameras, vehicles, and so forth?
18.	Play/exploitation	What games and toys about technology or exploitation are used; for example, scouting, chemical sets, microscopes?

Source: Stefan H. Robock and Kenneth Simmonds, *International Business and Multinational Enterprises*, 4th ed. (Homewood, IL: Irwin, 1989), p. 426.

SRC, that is, the tendency to use a ***self-reference criterion***, which can be explained this way: Whenever people are faced with unique situations, their own values are the measure for their understanding and response to the circumstances. Dependence on SRC comes naturally. For example, if someone in the U.S. is late for an appointment, that person will most likely feel guilty about it and apologize for being late—the value of punctuality and the importance of time have been instilled. The same person visiting an Arab country and scheduled for a business meeting would respond to the time of appointment with SRC and arrive on time for the meeting. If the other party fails to be on time, the visiting representative may be unhappy and angry and expect the latecomer to have the courtesy to apologize. Unfortunately, punctuality is not given the same priority the world over. To the Arab, the time of meeting would not mean that it has to be at the exact hour, but only means at about that time. For example, a 9 a.m. meeting does not communicate an exact time to the Arab but would be understood as some time in the morning. The tendency toward SRC is a stumbling block in cultural adaptation.

Framework for Adaptation

Lee proposes a four-step procedure for checking the influence of SRC in business adaptation:

- *Step 1*. Define the business problem or goal in terms of the cultural traits, habits, or norms of the U.S.
- *Step 2*. Define the business problem or goal in terms of the foreign cultural traits, habits, or norms. Make no value judgments.
- *Step 3*. Isolate the SRC influence in the problem and examine it carefully to see how it complicates the problem.
- *Step 4*. Redefine the problem without the SRC influence and solve for the optimum business goal situation.[64]

To illustrate the implementation of this four-step procedure, consider the question: What automobile would be appropriate for the Pakistani market?

Step 1. In the U.S., the automobile is a necessity for most people. Two cars per family is an accepted concept. Highway systems are designed for speeds of up to 70 miles per hour, but the legal limit for many highways is 55 miles per hour. Gasoline of high octane without lead is conveniently available. Consumers look for comforts in the automobile such as air conditioning, AM/FM radio, cruise control, and leg room. Manufacturing techniques are sophisticated, and foreign exchange problems are unknown. Purchasers have a choice of buying either domestic or foreign-made automobiles. Introduction of yearly models of different cars is an accepted practice. Imports have achieved a significant share of the U.S. market and continue to challenge the viability of the domestic industry.

Step 2. Pakistan is a poor country. Over 60 percent of the people are illiterate and live in villages with muddy roads. Even in urban areas, lack of modern roads restricts speed to 35–40 miles per hour. Gasoline is very expensive—the equivalent of almost $3 for a U.S. gallon—and it is only 60 octane. The country is committed to a thoroughly Islamic way of life. Islamic thinking is finding its way into economic, political, educational, and family life. The Western attitude toward acquisition of goods and toward materialistic life is frowned upon. The rich have to live inconspicuously. The bicycle is the major mode of individual transportation and may be compared to having a good used car in the U.S. Some people, a little more well-to-do, drive scooters, smaller versions of the motorcycle. Automobile ownership is a symbol of status and achievement. Ownership of an imported car is the equivalent of owning a Mercedes in the U.S. With per capita GNP of $420 (1992 estimate), discretionary income is minimal.

Step 3. Review of steps 1 and 2 brings out the significant differences between the two countries. Even the cheapest American car, say a Geo, would not match Pakistan's needs. In brief, an automobile manufacturer interested in entering Pakistan may not be able to successfully penetrate the market simply by modifying a U.S. model. Pakistan's needs call for a new product concept.

Step 4. The company seeking to enter the Pakistan market will be obliged to design an entirely new car. Such a car should be simple in all aspects: lightweight, few, if any, castings, and no compound body design; capable of giving very high mileage, say 80–100 miles per gallon, with cruising speeds up to 40 miles per hour. The car could simply be made of scrap iron with a low-powered engine and no frills. Such a car should be manufactured using local materials with minimum dependence on imported technology and/or parts. In other words, foreign exchange requirements of the project should be minimal. Overall, the feasible price for the car would have to be around $3,000.

Pakistan is not the only country that needs such a car. A large majority of Third World countries offer potential opportunities for a product of this type. Unfortunately SRC criteria, so deeply ingrained among Western auto manufacturers, have interfered with the development of an automobile for poorer nations. However, the experience of a nonprofit British-Dutch consortium, the Foundation for Transportation Development (FTD) in Lancaster, England, with their Africar is interesting. As has been said:

> Developed at a cost of $6.7 million, the vehicle has a body made of plywood—impregnated with epoxy to withstand the elements. Its angular contours are designed for easy production, but the shape also has low air drag to boost fuel economy. To smooth the ride, all four wheels have independent suspensions with hydraulic springs slung high off the ground for better clearance. With an air-cooled Citroën engine that needs minimum maintenance, the novel car has already proved its mettle in a rally from the Arctic Circle to the equator.
>
> Africar can turn a profit for licensed Third World producers on volumes of as few as 5,000 units per year.[65]

Areas of Adaptation

Essentially, there are three areas of foreign business adaptation: product, institutional, and individual. The *product* may be marketed abroad as is, or it may be modified to fit the foreign country's climate, electrical specifications, color preferences, and the like, or it may be completely redesigned to match local requirements—a $3,000 automobile for the Third World. *Institutional* behavior includes adaptation of the organization and business interactions to match the host's perspective. For example, the U.S. firm in Spain may allow the workers time for a siesta during the day.

Most important, the adaptation of *individuals'* responses to foreign situations should strive to be free of SRC. Such adaptation may be required in all regards—the meaning of time, social behavior, play behavior, family interactions, and more. For example, adaptation may require that the female spouse of a U.S. executive not accompany him to a dinner party in an Islamic country. Unfortunately, in international situations, each culture is so deeply imbued with its own values that only what is normally seen and done appears appropriate and right.

Appropriate adaptive behavior is necessary to the successful conduct of foreign business. Adaptation should not be misinterpreted to mean that one should adapt the foreign country's attitudes and traits. Rather, one should, while inhibiting SRC, gain understanding and develop a spirit of tolerance and appreciation of different cultures.

Neglect of cultural factors limits marketing success, and can even lead to failure. Thus, marketing strategy should be duly attuned to local cultural traits.

Cultural Change

While international marketers must be aware that culture influences all aspects of a country's environment and that they therefore must be familiar with culture and then orient the marketing mix accordingly, they must also know that over time *cultures do change*.

This characteristic of culture brings up interesting possibilities. Products and services, which at one time may not be introduced into a particular culture, may become acceptable at a later time because of cultural change. In other words, cultural change affects acceptance of innovations. For example, back in the 1950s the filter cigarette was rejected in many Southeast Asian countries, because its basic for-health's-sake promotion over regular cigarettes made no sense in countries where the average life span was 30 years. After 10 years, the filter cigarette slowly began to gain more acceptance. To an extent, the shift in attitude toward this product may be attributed to cultural change.

Basis of Cultural Change

The matter of cultural change is a controversial one and different anthropologists would specify different reasons for it. Although it may be disputed, one way of looking at cultural change is through economic development and Maslow's hierarchy-of-needs theory. Maslow ranked five human needs in lowest to highest order with lowest needs coming first: *physiological needs* (food, water, shelter, sex); *safety needs* (protection, security, stability); *social needs* (affection, friendship, acceptance); *ego needs* (prestige, success, self-esteem); and *the need for self-actualization* (self-fulfillment).[66] As a country begins to move from a subsistence economy, where fulfillment of physiological needs has been the major goal, to a situation where basic needs are easily achievable, new needs take precedence. This change forces cultural adjustments. In other words, as the economic well-being of a society satisfies one level of needs, it gives rise to new needs whose satisfaction requires cultural change.

Consider the role of an Asian homemaker. In a village economy, she would be fully confined to her home. However, a job for her husband in a factory in a nearby city enables the family to move to town. This move assures the family of basic needs fulfillment. There will be no more dependence on the farm for survival, but instead a weekly check. At this time, safety needs become important. Safety requires buying groceries at the factory store as soon as they are available. In many developing countries items such as cooking oil, sugar, and bar soap are often in short supply. Thus, while the husband is at work, the wife must shop. This imposes a new role on the wife, a cultural change that results from economic prosperity. No longer are her activities confined within the home; now she can go out alone to shop, something that would have been culturally prohibited in the village.

Whether all aspects of a culture change when a single aspect changes is a question that may be answered by referring to Hall's classification of cultural aspects into formal, informal, and technical. *Formal* aspects constitute the core of a culture. They are most deeply rooted and are extremely difficult to change. Formal aspects are taught as absolute rights and wrongs. Nonobservance of formal aspects cannot be forgiven. *Informal* aspects are traits that one learns by being a member of the society. Everyone is supposed to be aware of these aspects. If an informal aspect is not adhered to, an expression of disapproval or concern would be shown. In other words, accommodation is feasible in relation to informal aspects. *Technical* aspects are transmitted in the form of instruction and have reasons behind them. Change can be most easily accomplished in technical cultural aspects. So long as change can be reasoned in a logical fashion, no emotions stand in the way.[67]

The definition of formal, informal, and technical cultural aspects will vary from country to country. For example, take the case of cigarette smoking among middle-class teenage girls. In India, this matter would be concerned with a formal aspect of the culture and completely rejected. In Latin America, it would be in conflict with an informal aspect of the culture. While parents might not like their daughters smoking, they might accept it after registering their disapproval. In Germany and Sweden, a young girl's smoking could be categorized as a technical aspect. Parents might not mind if the cigarettes are low-tar and, therefore, on technical grounds will resist smoking for health reasons. Once it is agreed that the cigarettes will be low-tar, there would be no objection to the girl's smoking.

MNCS as Agents of Change

A family's move from village to town, from farm work to factory work, describes how industrialization forces cultural change. A country may industrialize by exploiting its indigenous resources. But in the modern era, an important source of industrialization is the multinational corporation (MNC). An MNC rapidly and effectively transfers features of one cultural society to certain sectors of another perhaps very different society. In this process, it is uniquely capable of forcing cultural change.

> In fact, given the magnitude of international business, the prevailing pattern of close headquarters control over foreign affiliates, and the various linkages between foreign and host countries, the introduction of novel business value and behavioral patterns can be expected to have a profound impact on the cultural and social fabric of the societies in which international business is entrenched.[68]

MNCs transmit home country values in two ways: (1) through the vast network of affiliates, which introduce, demonstrate, and disseminate new behaviors while increasing and shaping the manufacturing sector of host countries, and (2) through the business service structure including advertising and business education.

Millions of people in host countries work for foreign affiliates of MNCs. While the latest data are not available, in the early 1990s 33 million people were directly employed by MNC affiliates in other countries. These people, while living in their own culture, spend their working lives in a foreign environment. Foreign affiliates are in most cases highly integrated with the parent corporation. They are subject to close headquarters control through a variety of mechanisms, notably majority equity ownership, managerial control in key decision areas, and the presence of expatriate managers among the senior employees of the affiliate. Thus, the working life of the affiliate to a large extent reflects the values common in the corridors of the parent corporation. The affiliate employees may initiate, learn, and internalize new values and become channels to further diffuse these values in the host country culture at large.

The advertising media of MNCs is another avenue that transmits cultural values in host countries. The move of manufacturing companies to foreign countries has frequently been accompanied by a simultaneous move by advertising agencies. Of the top six advertising agencies of the world, five stem from the U.S. Therefore, MNC affiliates in their marketing efforts abroad have easy access to the agencies handling parent company business. These foreign agencies transmit and reinforce attitudes that fit nicely with the requirements of the MNCS. Change in the acceptance of advertising was influenced by American practices. Today most European countries permit commercials on their broadcasting networks.

The role of advertising in the context of international marketing is summarized well in the following words:

> It should be noted that advertising does more than merely sell products and form consumption patterns; it informs, educates, changes attitudes, and builds images. For purposes of illustration, we may quote the statement of a marketing manager who answered the basic marketing question, "What do we sell?" in the following way: "Never a product, always an idea." In other words, the function of advertising agencies is to seek "to influence human behavior in ways favorable to the interests of their clients," to "indoctrinate" them.[69]

Another interesting development is the spread worldwide of U.S. business education. Business schools, especially the Harvard Graduate School of Business Administration, have trained thousands of foreign students through professional education in business. Additionally, many U.S. business schools have aided in the establishment of similar institutions in host countries. The Harvard Business School alone has helped Switzerland, Japan, France, Turkey, India, the U.K., and a number of other countries in creating institutions for offering advanced education in business. In all these schools, staff and alumni from Harvard are an influential, if not dominant, group within the faculty, and in most cases, teaching and reading reflect a decidedly U.S. business philosophy. The coming generation of top managers in Europe, all more or less similarly trained to put the commercial interests of their enterprises above other considerations, are increasingly divorced from their particular national framework and reflect to various degrees the business philosophy of the top U.S. schools.[70]

The U.S.-educated students, whether actually instructed in the U.S. or their homeland, generate and support ideas, values, and viewpoints that refer to the cultural traits revered in U.S. business circles. At the product/market level, they demand products and services in market categories where international marketers have traditionally had more experience. Included is a range of products from nutritious and more hygienically packaged goods to various kinds of household furnishings, appliances, and entertainment-oriented products. Also, new products are more easily accepted.

Summary

The cultural traits of a country have a profound effect on people's lifestyle and behavior patterns, and these are reflected in the marketplace. *Culture* is a complex term, and its precise definition is difficult. Broadly defined, however, it refers to all learned behavior of all facets of life and living transmitted from generation to generation. Cultural differences among countries can be subtle and zealously followed.

The study of culture includes material life (the means and artifacts people use for livelihood); social interactions between individuals and groups in formal and informal situations; language (spoken/written words, symbols, and physical expressions that people use to communicate); aesthetics (art, drama, music); religion and faith; pride and prejudices; and ethics and mores. Cultural traits account for such differences among nations as color preferences, concept of time, and authority patterns. For example, in Western countries a bride's gown is usually white. In the far East, however, women wear white during mourning.

Cultural differences have impact on marketing decisions affecting product, price, distribution, and promotion. Two frameworks for analyzing culture are Rokeach's 36 values used to seek information on the cultural differences of national societies, and Hall's cultural map, with its two-dimensional matrix using 10 human activities to generate a cultural analysis by focusing on the intersections of 1 with the 9 others.

To conduct business successfully across national boundaries, marketers must adapt themselves to local cultures. A four-step framework for cultural adaptation, which encourages the avoidance of dependence on self-reference criteria (SRC), is important for developing an understanding of foreign situations. The tendency toward SRC reinforces the idea that what is good at home is good—and relevant—anywhere else as well.

A discussion of culture must also deal with cultural change. Cultures do change, but change is usually slow in coming. Industrialization is an important factor behind cultural change. MNCs, through involvement in the industrialization process, serve as change agents in foreign cultures. Their worldwide networks of affiliates transmit the values of the parent corporation's culture. Cultural change also takes place through advertising media and through the internationalization of business education.

Review Questions

1. What elements of culture may be most relevant to marketing? Why?
2. How might a marketer of cosmetics assess significant cultural traits for his or her business in the Muslim world?
3. Americans share a variety of common traits with the English. Based on this assumption, will it be safe to conclude that the two societies have a more or less common culture?
4. Illustrate how an international marketer can use Hall's map of culture.
5. How has the spread of professional education in business affected local culture?
6. Describe how MNCs influence host country culture through their network of affiliates.
7. How could aesthetics, as an element of culture, affect marketing decisions in the international context?
8. Should an international marketer deliberately attempt to seek cultural change in a society?

9. "It is economic not cultural differences that count. Given the economic environment and income levels of the U.S., people in any country, Muslim or Christian, would follow the U.S. lifestyle and materialistic living." Discuss this statement.

Creative Questions

1. China has a large population and its economy is booming. However, in 1994, cola consumption in the country was only 10 servings (8 oz. per serving) per capita. For a comparison, the consumption in the U.S. in the same year was 149.8 servings per capita. Apparently, there is a huge potential for soft drinks in China. Are there any cultural barriers that may become hurdles in realizing this potential? Discuss the nature of these barriers and examine how they may affect cola consumption.
2. What cultural adaptations are required to make U.S. cars more acceptable in Japan?

Endnotes

1. "Making Do During Ramadan," *Business Week*, April 8, 1991, p. 18A.
2. Edward B. Tylor, *Primitive Culture* (London: John Murray, 1871), p. 1.
3. Edward T. Hall, *Beyond Culture* (Garden City, NY: Anchor Books, 1977), p. 16. *Also see* Edward T. Hall, "Learning the Arabs' Silent Language," *Psychology Today*, August 1979, p. 54.
4. Abraham Pizam and Arie Reichel, "Cultural Determinants of Managerial Behavior," *Management International Review*, No. 2 (1977), p. 66.
5. Martin J. Gannon, *Understanding Global Cultures* (Thousand Oaks, CA, 1994), pp. 3–18.
6. Karen Elliott House, "Saudi Marriage Mores Are Shaken as Women Seek a Stronger Voice," *The Wall Street Journal*, June 8, 1981, p. 1. *Also see* "Marriage-Minded Japanese Turn to Mama," *The Asian Wall Street Journal Weekly*, August 24, 1981, p. 13.
7. Martin J. Gannon, *Understanding Global Cultures*, op. cit., p. xi.
8. Chin Tiong Tan and James McCullough, "Ethnicity and Family Buying Behavior." Paper presented at the Annual Meeting of the Academy of International Business, Cleveland, Ohio, October 1984.
9. Robert T. Green, Bronislaw J. Verhage, and Isabell C. M. Cunningham, "Household Purchasing Decisions," *Working Paper* (Austin, TX: University of Texas, 1983). *Also see* John I. Reynolds, "Developing Policy Responses to Cultural Differences," *Business Horizons*, August 1978, pp. 30–31.
10. Edward T. Hall, "The Silent Language in Overseas Business," *Harvard Business Review*, May–June 1960, pp. 88–96. Also *see* Sir Horace Phillips, "Language, the Passport to Global Business," *The Asian Wall Street Journal Weekly*, March 23, 1981, p. 11.
11. David A. Ricks, "How to Avoid Business Blunders Abroad," *Business*, April–June 1984, pp. 3–11.
12. David A. Ricks, "International Business Blunders: An Update," *B&E Review*, January–March 1988, p. 11.
13. Ibid., p. 12.
14. Vern Terpstra, *International Marketing* (Hinsdale, IL: Dryden Press, 1983). *Also see* Robert Howells, "Culture Clash: An American's Guide to English," *The Wall Street Journal*, October 30, 1984, p. 34.
15. Susan Barciela, "Know the Customs of the Country," *The Hartford Courant*, March 14, 1994, p. 7.
16. *See* Jeffrey A. Rosenweig and Wayne D. Gantt, "Doing Business in Japan," *Emory Business Magazine*, Spring 1990, pp. 34–36.
17. *See* Lawrence Jacobs, Charles Keown, Reginald Worthley, and Kyung-Il Gihymn, "Cross-Cultural Colour Comparisons: Global Marketers Beware," *International Marketing Review*, Vol. 8, No. 3, 1991, pp. 21–30.
18. "Before Buying Insurance, Consult This Calendar," *The Asian Wall Street Journal Weekly*, October 10, 1988, p. 8.
19. Geraldine Brooks, "Riddle of Riyadh: Islamic Law Thrives Amid Modernity," *The Wall Street Journal*, November 9, 1989, p. 1.
20. *See* Youssef M. Ibrahim, "Revolutionary Islam of Iran Is Neutralized by Policies of Bahrain." *The Wall Street Journal*, August 11, 1987, p. 1; and Karen Elliott House, "Rising

Islamic Fervor Challenges the West, Every Moslem Ruler," *The Wall Street Journal*, August 7, 1987, p. 1.

21. P. Wright, "Organizational Behavior in Islamic Firms," *Management International Review*, No. 2 (1981), p. 87. *Also see* Ernest Dichter, "The World Customer," *Harvard Business Review*, July–August 1962, p. 116; S. G. Redding, "Cultural Effects on the Marketing Process in Southeast Asia," *Journal of Market Research Society*, April 1982, pp. 86–98.

22. Tim Carrington, "Chief of European Reconstruction Bank Faces Challenges on Financial and Cultural Fronts," *The Wall Street Journal*, November 26, 1990, p. A5.

23. *See* Robert A. Jackson, "Are American Buyers the Prisoners of Politicians?" *San Francisco State University School of Business Journal*, Summer 1984, pp. 33–40.

24. George Mellon, "Trade Curbs Would Threaten Many Companies," *The Wall Street Journal*, April 28, 1987, p. 35.

25. Helmut Becker and David J. Fritzsche, "A Comparison of the Ethical Behavior of American, French and German Managers," *Columbia Journal of World Business*, Winter 1987, pp. 87–96.

26. Lee Smith, "Korea's Challenge to Japan," *Fortune*, February 6, 1984, p. 94.

27. John L. Graham, "The Influence of Culture on Business Negotiations," *Journal of International Business Studies*, Spring 1985, pp. 81–96.

28. *See* Tara Parker-Pope, "Will the British Warm Up To Iced Tea?," *The Wall Street Journal*, August 22, 1994, p. B1.

29. *See* Kathleen Reardon, *International Business Gift-Giving Customs* (Jamesville, WI: The Parker Pen Company, 1981). *Also see* Michael Lynn, George M. Zinkham, and Judy Harris, "Consumers Tipping: A Cross-Country Study," *Journal of Consumer Research*, Vol. 20, December 1993, pp. 478–88.

30. Joseph T. Plummer, "Consumer Focus in Cross-National Research," *Journal of Advertising*, Summer 1977, pp. 5–15. *Also see* Vern Terpstra and Kenneth David, *The Cultural Environment of International Business*, 2nd ed. (Cincinnati, OH: South-Western Publishing Co., 1985).

31. Ibid., p. 11. *Also see* I. G. M. Cunningham and Robert T. Green, "Working Wives in the United States and Venezuela: A Cross-National Study of Family Decision Making," *Journal of Comparative Family Studies*, Spring 1979, pp. 67–80.

32. Susan P. Douglas, "Cross-National Comparisons and Consumer Stereotypes: A Case Study of Working and Nonworking Wives in the U.S. and France," *The Journal of Consumer Research*, June 1976, pp. 12–20.

33. Thomas E. Muller and Christopher Bolger, "Search Behavior of French and English Canadians in Automobile Purchase," *International Marketing Review*, Winter 1985, pp. 21–30.

34. Charles M. Schaninger, Jacques C. Bourgeois, and W. Christian Buss, "French-English Canadian Subcultural Consumption Differences," *Journal of Marketing*, Spring 1985, pp. 82–92.

35. *The McKinsey Quarterly*, No. 4, 1991, p. 6. *Also see* Philip R. Harris and Robert T. Moran, *Managing Cultural Differences*, 2nd ed. (Houston, TX: Gulf Publishing Co., 1987).

36. Damon Darlin, "Coke, Nestlé Launch First Coffee Drink," *The Wall Street Journal*, October 25, 1994, p.42.

37. Susan Douglas and Bernard Dubois, "Looking at the Cultural Environment for International Marketing Opportunities," *Columbia Journal of World Business*, Winter 1977, p. 102. *Also see* Ian R. Wilson, "American Success Story—Coca-Cola in Japan." in Mark B. Winchester, ed., *The International Essays for Business Decision Makers* (Dallas: The Center for International Business, 1980), pp. 119–27.

38. "The $30 Million Lesson," *Sales Management*, March 1967, pp. 31–38. *Also see* Henry Lane, "Systems, Values, and Action: An Analytic Framework for Intercultural Management Research," *Management International Review*, No. 3 (1980), pp. 61–70.

39. Robert D. Buzzell, "Can You Standardize Multinational Marketing?" *Harvard Business Review*, November–December 1968, pp. 102–13.

40. *Fortune*, November 6, 1989, p. 86. *Also see* Patriya Tansuhaj, et al., "Across National Examination of Innovation Resistance," *International Marketing Review*, Vol. 8, No. 3, 1991, pp. 7–20.

41. Kenichi Ohmae, *Triad Power* (New York: The Free Press, 1985), pp. 102–04.

42. Susan Douglas and Bernard Dubois, "Looking at the Cultural Environment for International Marketing Opportunities," *Columbia Journal of World Business*, Winter 1977, pp. 106–07.

43. L. Erik Calonius, "As a Market for PCs, Europe Seems as Hot as the U.S. Is Not," *The Wall Street Journal*, August 19, 1985, p. 1.

44. Robert J. Hoover, Robert T. Green, and Joel Saegart, "A Cross-National Study of Perceived Risk," *Journal of Marketing*, July 1978, pp. 102–08. *Also see* Chin Tiong Tan and Christina Chua, "Effects of Attitudes and Social Influence in Bank Selection: A Study in an Oriental Culture," a paper presented at the Annual Meeting of the Academy of International Business, Washington, D.C., October 1982.

45. Susan Douglas and Bernard Dubois, "Looking at the Cultural Environment for International Marketing Opportunities," *Columbia Journal of World Business*, Winter 1977, p. 107. *Also see* Erdener Kaynak and Lionel A. Mitchell, "Cultural Barriers to the Full-Scale Acceptance of Supermarkets in Less-Developed Countries," a paper presented at the Annual Meeting of the Academy of International Business, new Orleans, October 1980.

46. Ibid.

47. R. S. Diamon, "Managers Away From Home," *Fortune*, August 15, 1969, p. 50.

48. Howe Martyn, *International Business—Principles and Problems* (New York: Collier-Macmillan, 1964), p. 78.

49. *Advertising Age*, May 9, 1960, p. 75.

50. Matt Miller and Sundeep Chakravarti, "For Indians, a 2,000 Year-Old Habit of Chewing Red Goo Is Hard to Break," *The Wall Street Journal*, May 12, 1987, p. 28.

51. *Fortune*, November 6, 1989, p. 86.

52. "Catch As Catch Can," *World*, No. 2, 1992, p. 2.

53. S. Watson Dunn, "Effect of National Identity on Multinational Promotional Strategy in Europe," *Journal of Marketing*, October 1976, pp. 54–55.

54. J. Douglas McConnell, "The Economics of Behavioral Factors on the Multinational Corporation," in Fred C. Allvine, ed., *Combined Proceedings* (Chicago: American Marketing Association, 1971), p. 264. *Also see* Arndt Sorge and Malcom Warner, "Culture, Management and Manufacturing Organization: A Study of British and German Firms," *Management International Review*, No. 1 (1981), pp. 35–48.

55. Charles Winick, "Anthropology's Contribution to Marketing," *Journal of Marketing*, July 1961, p. 59. *Also see* D. E. Allen, "Anthropological Insights into Customer Behavior," *European Journal of Marketing*, No. 5 (1971), pp. 45–47.

56. Saled Samiee, "Customer Evaluation of Products in a Global Market," *Journal of International Business Studies*, Vol. 25, No. 3, 1994, pp. 579–604.

57. Philippe Cattin, Alain Jolibert, and Colleen Lohnes, "A Cross-Cultural Study of 'Made-in' Concepts," *The Journal of International Business Studies*, Winter 1982, pp. 131–42. *Also see* Victor V. Cordell, "Competitive Context and Price as Moderators of Country of Origin Preferences," *Journal of the Academy of Marketing Science*, Spring 1991, pp. 123–28.

58. Nancy J. Adler, "Cultural Synergy: The Management of Cross-Cultural Organizations," in W. Warner Burke and Leonard D. Goodstein, eds. *Trends and Issues in OD: Current Theory and Practice* (San Diego, CA: University Associates, 1980), pp. 163–84.

59. "Hidden Agenda," *Marketing Insights*, Summer Issue 1990, pp. 40–45.

60. J. Michael Munson and Shelby H. McIntyre, "Personal Values: A Cross-Cultural Assessment of Self Values and Values Attributed to a Distant Cultural Stereotype," in H. Keith Hunt, ed., *Advances in Consumer Research*, Vol. 5 (Ann Arbor, MI: Association for Consumer Research, 1978), pp. 103–04. *Also see* Van R. Wood and Roy Howell, "A Note on Hispanic Values and Subculture Research: An Alternative View," *Journal of the Academy of Marketing Science*, Vol. 19, No. 1, pp. 61–7.

61. Edward T. Hall, *The Silent Language* (Garden City, NY: Doubleday, 1959), pp. 61–81.

62. Ibid., p. 61.

63. Stefan H. Robock and Kenneth Simmons, *International Business and Multinational Enterprises*, 4th ed. (Homewood, IL: Irwin, 1989), pp. 424–28.

64. James A. Lee, "Cultural Analysis in Overseas Operations," *Harvard Business Review*, March–April 1966, p. 110. *Also see* James R. Schiffman, "Korea Promises to Build a People's Car Affordable to Burgeoning Middle Class," *The Asian Wall Street Journal Weekly*, February 7, 1983, p. 11.

65. "A 'Jeep' that May Tame the Third World's Road," *Business Week*, February 13, 1989, p. 100.

66. *See* Abraham H. Maslow, *Motivation and Personality* (New York: Harper & Row, 1954).

67. Edward T. Hall, *The Silent Language* (Garden City, NY: Doubleday, 1959), pp. 110–13.

68. Karl P. Sauvant, "Multinational Enterprises and the Transmission of Culture: The International Supply of Advertising Services and Business Education." *Journal of Peace Research*, No. 1 (1976), p. 49.

69. Paul C. Harper, Jr., "The Agency Business in 1980," *Advertising Age*, November 29, 1978, p. 35.

70. *See* Shawn Tully, "Europe's Best Business Schools," *Fortune*, May 23, 1988, p. 106.

CHAPTER · 8

Political Environment

CHAPTER FOCUS

After studying this chapter you should be able to:

- Describe how political situations affect marketing decisions

- Discuss sources of political problems

- Examine different ways that governments may intervene in the affairs of foreign firms

- Explain how the political perspectives of a country can be examined

- Compare alternative strategies a company may pursue in the event of political intervention

The political environment of each country is unique. An apparently rich foreign market may not warrant entry if the political environment is characterized by instability and uncertainty. In brief, a thorough review of the political environment must precede commitment to a new market in a foreign country.

Furthermore, the political environments of countries do not remain static. Political changes and upheavals may occur after an international marketer has made a commitment and has an established business. The revolution in Iran exposed U.S. companies to potential losses of $1 billion and drove home the lesson that the political situation in a country must be reviewed on a continuing basis. Political environment connotes diverse happenings such as civil difficulties (for example, the conflict between the rival tribes in the African country of Somalia); acts of terrorism against businesses (for example, kidnappings, arson); and conflicts between countries in a particular region, which may be one-time occurrences like the war between India and China or perennial problems like the enmity between the People's Republic of China and Taiwan.

Political stability has been found to be one of the crucial variables that companies weigh when considering going overseas. Unstable political environment subjects foreign business to risks such as violence, expropriation, restriction of operations, and restrictions on repatriation of capital and remittances of profits. If the risk is high in a particular politically unstable country, it is necessary to know how to monitor that country's ongoing political situation. This chapter examines the occurrence of political conflicts and difficulties in foreign countries and their effects on overseas business, and discusses ways to analyze politics and measure risk. Strategic responses to political change available to multinational marketers also are covered.

Politics and Marketing

A few years ago, the French president François Mitterrand invited Apple Computer executives to lunch at his residence, Élysée Palace. The Apple executives jumped at the invitation since for months they had been trying to sell their personal computers to the French government. The French government had authorized a $156 million purchase of teaching computers for the French school system, but Apple's foreign citizenship had hindered its efforts to get a piece of the order.

During the private, two-hour lunch, with a translator present, the Apple executives praised the government's computer program and offered to help in any way they could. But President Mitterand rebuffed them. Later one aide said that the president had invited the Apple executives to discuss technological cooperation with French companies, not the educational computer purchase program.[1]

How Apple tried, and failed, to get a significant share of the computer order is a revealing tale of international marketing and politics. The total order, for 120,000 microcomputers, was the biggest single purchase of educational computers in Europe and part of an ambitious campaign to teach almost everybody in France how to use computers. Although Apple is the largest vendor of professional microcomputers in France, when the list of suppliers for the new program was announced, Apple received no order.

The head of Apple's subsidiary near Paris, a Frenchman, blamed the company's exclusion on lobbying by competitors and Apple's U.S. nationality: "The color of our passport is wrong."

On hearing about Apple's difficulties, the U.S. government complained to France about what it considered the unfair handling of the microcomputer order, raising the possibility of retaliatory moves in U.S. government contracting procedures. Other than registering its annoyance on the matter, the U.S. government did not pursue it, perhaps for political reasons.

Whether such nationalistic buying will get French students the best equipment is a matter of debate. Yet this clearly brings out the political underpinnings involved in conducting international marketing.

Marketing decisions in the international context are deeply affected by the political perspectives of both home and host countries.[2] For example, government decisions have significantly affected the U.S. automotive industry. Stringent requirements such as the fuel efficiency standards have burdened the industry in several ways.

Governments around the world help their domestic industries to strengthen their competitiveness through various fiscal and monetary measures. Such political support can play a key role in an industry's search for markets abroad. Without such assistance, an industry may face a difficult situation. The U.S. auto industry would benefit from U.S. government concessions favoring U.S. automotive exports. European countries, for example, rely on value-added taxes to help their industries. These are applied to all levels of manufacturing transactions up to and including the final sale to the user. However, if the final sale is for export, the value-added tax is rebated, thus effectively reducing the price in international commerce. Japan imposes a commodity tax on selected lines of products, including automobiles. In the event of export, the commodity tax is waived. The U.S. has no corresponding arrangement. Thus, when a new automobile is shipped from the U.S. to Japan, it receives no rebate or relief of its U.S. taxes upon export and also must bear the cost of the Japanese commodity tax (15 or 20 percent depending on the size of the vehicle) when it is sold in Japan[3] (see International Marketing Highlight 8.1).

The competition facing U.S. manufacturers, therefore, both at home and in international markets, is potent and resourceful. Moreover, a number of these overseas competitors are wholly or partly state-owned and respond to the direction of their governments, which depend heavily on their export business for the maintenance of employment and the earning of foreign exchange. This makes politics important, deeply influencing the perspectives of international marketing.

Politics may affect international marketing in various ways. In January 1985, Ford Motor Company divested itself of its auto operations in South Africa to take a 40 percent minority position.[4] At about the same time, Japan liberalized tobacco imports by lifting restrictions on price, distribution, and the number of retail outlets that can handle their products, thus encouraging foreign suppliers to intensify their marketing efforts.[5] In July 1985, Mexico approved the long-delayed, once-rejected 100 percent IBM-owned microcomputer plant to encourage more foreign investment.[6] After waiting for several years, toward the end of 1988, PepsiCo got the Indian government's approval for a joint venture there.[7] In 1991, after much politicking, the French government permitted IBM to link up with France's state-owned computer maker, Groupe Bull, to develop high-speed RISC computer technology.[8]

International Marketing Highlight 8.1

Politics of Smoking

The federal government officially discourages cigarette smoking in the U.S. But if people in other countries are going to smoke anyway, why shouldn't they puff away on American tobacco?

Armed with this logic, the Reagan administration strong-armed Japan, South Korea, and Taiwan to dismantle their government-sanctioned tobacco monopolies. This opened lucrative markets and created such growth for U.S. cigarette makers that skyrocketing Asian sales did much to offset the decline at home.

However, Thailand, with a government tobacco monopoly of its own, has been fighting U.S. pressure to open up, and U.S. tobacco companies approached the Bush administration to take up trade sanctions against the Thais. That raises many questions about U.S. trade policy, including: Should Washington use its muscle to promote a product overseas that it acknowledges is deadly? Are trade disputes to be decided by lawyers and bureaucrats on the basis of commercial regulations, or should health and safety experts get into the act? Should the U.S. use trade policy to make the world healthier, just as it does to save whales, punish South Africa, or promote human rights?

Source: *Business Week*, October 9, 1989, p. 61.

Conceptually, multinational enterprises are affected by politics in three areas: (1) the pattern of ownership in the parent company or the affiliate, (2) the direction and nature of growth of the affiliate, and (3) the flow of product, technology, and managerial skills within the companies of the group. Take, for example, the case of Vietnam. The impact of politics on the strategies adopted by MNCs there leads to one important conclusion: The strategic choices made by MNC affiliates are a response more to political environment than to the interaction of market forces or to technological innovation. In other words, the government can substantially influence the strategy of MNC affiliates in ways that were thought impossible even a few years ago. In India, many MNC affiliates had to diversify into areas where neither the parent company nor the affiliate had the core capabilities. Competence ceased to be an important factor in strategy formulation compared to the need to comply with political directives and regulations. In general, the transfer of product and technology from the parent company in order to exploit new markets in the host country meets with obstruction from the government unless the technology is in the areas specified by regulation.

Sources of Political Problems

Figure 8.1 illustrates sources of political problems from firms doing business in foreign countries. Political impact on business comes mainly from political sovereignty and political conflict.

FIGURE 8.1 Politics and Foreign Business

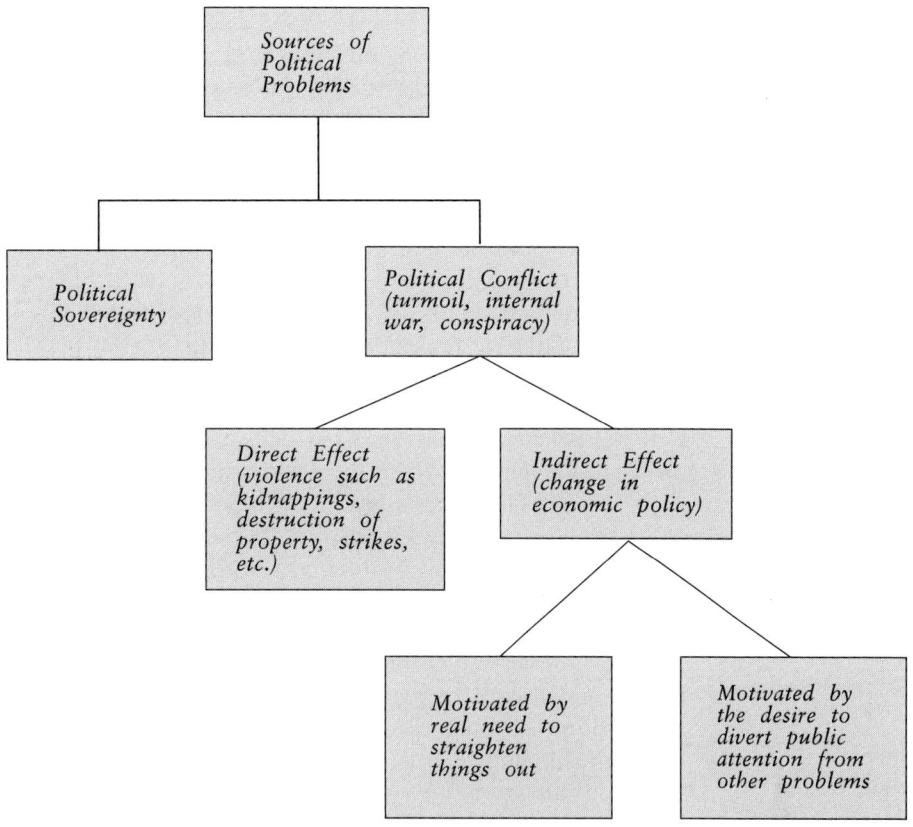

Political Sovereignty

Political sovereignty refers to a country's desire to assert its authority over foreign business through various sanctions. Such sanctions are regular and evolutionary, and, therefore, are predictable. An example is increases in taxes over foreign operations. Many of the less-developed countries impose restrictions on foreign business to protect their independence (economic domination is often perceived as leading to political subservience). These countries are jealous of their political freedom and want to protect it at all costs, even if it means going at a slow economic pace and without the help of MNCs. Thus, the political sovereignty problem mainly concerns developing countries.[9]

The industrialized nations, whose political sovereignty has been secure for a long time, require a more open policy for the economic realities of today's world. Today, governments are expected simultaneously to curb unemployment, limit inflation, redistribute income, build up backward regions, deliver health services, and not abuse the environment. These wide-ranging objectives make developed countries seek foreign technology, use foreign capital and foreign raw materials, and sell their specialties in foreign markets. The net result is that these countries have found themselves exchanging guarantees for mutual access to one another's economies. In brief, among the developed countries, multinationalism of business is politically acceptable and economically desirable.

Political Conflict

Many countries in different parts of the world undergo political conflict of various sorts. *Political conflict* can be irregular, revolutionary, and/or discontinuous, and basically may be categorized as turmoil, internal war, and conspiracy. *Turmoil* refers to instant upheaval on a massive scale against an established regime (for example, the Islamic fundamentalists' mass protest against the Shah of Iran). *Internal war* means large-scale, organized violence against a government such as guerrilla warfare (for example, Vietnam's actions in Cambodia). *Conspiracy* represents an instant, planned act of violence against those in power (for example, the assassination of Egyptian President Anwar Sadat). Political conflict may or may not have an impact on business. For example, while the ouster of the Shah of Iran incurred heavy losses for U.S. business there, the murder of Anwar Sadat made no difference to international business in Egypt at that time.

As a matter of fact, political change sometimes may lead to a more favorable business climate. For example, after the Peronist regime was overthrown in Argentina, the new government's policy was so favorable toward multinationals that the previously nationalized firms were returned to their owners. Similarly, Sukarno's departure from the Indonesian scene improved the business climate there, as did Nkrumah's absence from Ghana. After the assassination of Prime Minister Rajiv Gandhi in 1991, India's policy became highly favorable for international business. Suddenly, U.S. multinationals found India an attractive place to do business.[10]

It is important to make a distinction between political risk and political conflict. Political conflict in a country may lead to unstable conditions, but those conditions may or may not affect business. Therefore, political risk may or may not result from political unrest. Businesses must analyze each occurrence of political conflict and assess the likelihood of its impact on business. Consider the case of the Philippines. During 1988, communist threats posed insurmountable problems for foreign companies although the economy had been doing well. For example, Dole Philippines' banana plantation was attacked and two warehouses were destroyed. Yet, in the interest of long-term opportunity, Dole officials refused to take any drastic steps.[11]

Sometimes the conflict is in response to a particular political event that subsides with time. For example, disgruntled French farmers ransacked a Coca-Cola plant in a series of demonstrations brought on in part by U.S. pressure on Europe to reduce agricultural subsidies.[12]

The effect of political conflict on business may be direct or indirect. *Direct effects* would be violence against the firms in such forms as the kidnapping of an executive, damage to company property, a labor strike, and the like. Overall, direct effects are usually temporary and do not result in huge losses.[13] (see International Marketing Highlight 8.2). *Indirect effects* occur because of changes in government policy. In other words, political conflict leads to some change in a government's economic perspective. Such change may come from a new attitude on the part of an existing government or through a new government. Further, the changes may be motivated by a sincere desire to straighten things out or simply to divert public attention from other domestic problems plaguing the country.

International Marketing Highlight 8.2

Executives in Peru Don't Leave Home Without It

Herbert Dunn, a former police officer and SWAT-team member in the U.S., came to Peru in 1984 as a security consultant. He now teaches local executives how to defend themselves in a terrorist attack—a common occurrence in Peru.

With two major terrorist groups and a variety of smaller ones carrying out bombings, killings, and kidnappings, security is an obsession here. In 1990 alone, political violence claimed 3,384 lives—more than were lost in Lebanon's civil war in 1990—and caused material damage estimated by one research firm at $3 billion. That's about 15 percent of Peru's gross domestic product.

Many top businesspeople, some journalists, and even usually sedate political scientists don't leave home without a revolver. Visitors to corporate headquarters routinely check their guns, along with IDs, upon entering. Factories are fortified bunkers, surrounded by high walls and barbed wire, with armed guards looking out from watchtowers.

Even some of Lima's Kentucky Fried Chicken outlets have three armed guards at the entrance—not, as one resident jokes, to guard the quality of the product, but to keep the stores standing after two bomb attacks this year. Terrorists "seem to have an obsession about fried chicken," says Bustavo Gorriti, a journalist. "They must think it's the food of choice of the American plutocracy."

Source: The Wall Street Journal, April 10, 1991, p. 1.

From the viewpoint of foreign businesses, it is important to understand the nature of political conflict and the motivation behind government action. If a change in government policy is merely for symbolic purposes, it represents less risk to foreign businesses. Also, when new policy is expressed through the imposition of certain constraints, requirements, and/or controls on foreign businesses, it is important to assess the host government's administrative ability. The government must have the capacity to promulgate and enforce the new policy. If such capabilities are lacking, the new policy will remain a well-intentioned effort without any actual effects on foreign businesses.

Political Intervention

Carefully chosen overseas markets provide substantial opportunity. The opportunity, however, is coupled with risks of intervention by host governments seeking to further their own interests. Nations are not monolithic, or even bipartisan. Rather they are composed of different groups, each of which is intent on maximizing its individual interests. In countries where foreign investment plays a significant role in the economy, the goals of special interests frequently necessitate interference in the operations of foreign firms.[14] For example, if a foreign company is prominent in the economy of such countries as Zambia, Guinea, Chile, and Tanzania, the possibilities of government intervention are relatively great. While certainly not limited to developing countries, intervention in the affairs of foreign enterprise is more frequent in these countries. Developed countries respond to foreign enterprise by establishing their own multinationals to challenge foreign firms both on the home front and abroad. Developing countries may have to intervene directly in the operations of MNCs operating in their lands in order to pursue their own special interests.

Political intervention can be defined as a decision on the part of the host country government that may force a change in the operations, policies, and strategies of a foreign firm. The intervention may range from some sort of control to complete takeover or annexation of the foreign enterprise. The magnitude of intervention would vary according to the company's business in the country and the nature of the intervention. There are different forms of intervention: expropriation, domestication, exchange control, import restrictions, market control, tax control, price control, and labor problems. Figure 8.2 shows different ways that governments may intervene in the affairs of foreign firms. Also specified are the likely effects of political intervention on marketing mix variables.

FIGURE 8.2 Classification of Governmental Intervention in the Operations of Foreign Firms

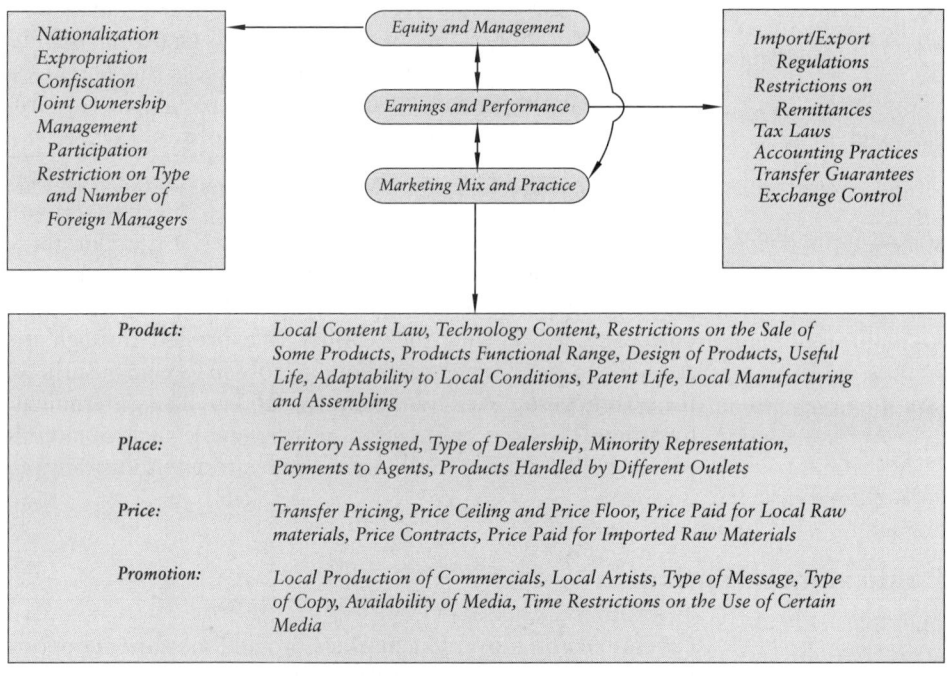

Source: Humayun Akhter and Robert F. Lusch, "Political Risk and the Evolution of the Control of Foreign Business: Equity, Earnings and the Marketing Mix," *Journal of Global Marketing*, Spring 1988, p. 117.

Expropriation

Of all the forms of political intervention, *expropriation* is most pervasive. As defined by Eitemen and Stonehill, it is:

Official seizure of foreign property by a host country whose intention is to use the seized property in the public interest. Expropriation is recognized by international law as the right of sovereign states, provided the expropriated firms are given prompt compensation, at fair market value, in convertible currencies.[15]

The second part of this definition points out the source of much of the controversy associated with expropriation. Other terms used interchangeably with expropriation are nationalization and socialization. *Nationalization* refers to a transfer of the entire industry within that country from private to public ownership with no discrimination as to foreign ownership or local ownership. *Socialization*, also referred to as communization, differs from nationalization in that it is a transfer of all the industries within the country. *Confiscation* means expropriation without compensation.

Traditionally, patterns of expropriation have been differentiated according to industry, geographic region, type of ownership, technology, degree of vertical integration, asset size, and politicoeconomic situation.[16] Based on an older study, Latin America accounted for 49 percent of all expropriations between 1960 and 1976, followed by the Arab countries with 27 percent, black Africa with 13 percent, and Asian nations with 11 percent.[17] A study by the United Nations of foreign firm takeovers between 1960 and 1974 showed that two-thirds of all takeovers were accounted for by just 10 nations, including Argentina, Chile, Cuba, Peru, Algeria, Libya, and Iraq.[18]

For a long time it was believed that ownership shared with host nations through joint ventures was advantageous. This has been proven false. For example, Bradley has found that joint ventures with host country governments, as opposed to wholly-owned foreign subsidiaries, have a greater rate of expropriation.[19] Technology can serve as the defense against expropriation, if the technology of the enterprise cannot be duplicated by the host country or cannot be made operable by the expropriators. Further, if a firm is vertically integrated with the parent firm so that the parent controls either the supplies for production or the market for the product, the firm is then an unlikely target for expropriation. Asset size also makes a difference here. A firm with total assets in excess of $100 million has a 50 times greater chance of being expropriated than a firm with assets of less than $1 million.[20]

Finally, the politicoeconomic backdrops against which expropriations have taken place have been associated with sweeping and violent upheavals, which transformed the basic governmental structure and politicoeconomic ideologies of the nations involved.

Recent trends show that expropriation activity has decreased over time. Many developing countries now protect foreign direct investors from expropriation. This change reflects a shift away from ideologies and politics to a more functional need for economic development desired by the less developed countries. In light of this trend, expropriations have become more selective, directed toward those foreign-owned enterprises whose policies or aspirations have collided with the economic plans and priorities of the developing nation. A recent study on the subject supports this conclusion.[21] It indicates that expropriation is unlikely to resurface in the near future as a source of MNC-developing country contention. The broad-scale movement in developing countries to privatize state-owned enterprises also indicates that governments will not be eager to replace private-sector activity with state ownership. In sum, for the foreseeable future, significant expropriation activity is unlikely.

Domestication

Domestication, which can be thought of as *creeping expropriation*, is a process by which controls and restrictions placed on the foreign firm gradually reduce the control of the owners. Although domestication may lead ultimately to expropriation, in a way it offers a compromise to both parties. The MNC continues to operate in the country while the host government is able to maintain leverage on the foreign firm through imposing different controls. Domestication involves several measures, including:

- Gradual transfer of ownership to nationals
- Promotion of a large number of nationals to higher levels of management
- Greater decision-making powers accorded to nationals
- More products produced locally rather than imported for assembly
- Specific export regulations designed to dictate participation in world markets

From the viewpoint of the host country, domestication is preferable to expropriation. It provides the host country enough control to carefully scrutinize and regulate activities of the foreign firm. In this way, any truly negative effects of the MNC's operations in the country are discovered and prompt corrective action taken, either through negotiations or through legislation and decree for further control.

Other Forms of Intervention

In addition to expropriation and domestication, there are various means of government intervention in foreign enterprise. The intervention usually takes the form of legislative action and/or a decree enacted in the best national interest. Further, intervention appears to apply to both domestic and foreign businesses. But a deeper probe often reveals that certain aspects of the law/decree are irrelevant for domestic business and are meant specifically to control foreign business. For example, a clause in a decree restricting repatriation of profits to stockholders outside the country would be meaningless for native companies.

The following means of intervention are discussed below: exchange control, import restrictions, market control, tax control, price control, and labor restrictions.

Exchange Control Countries having difficulties with the balance of trade often impose restrictions on the free use of foreign exchange. For example, import of luxuries from outside the country is restricted. Similarly, restrictions are placed on the remittances from the country involving hard currency. The exchange control may also be an effort to encourage domestic industry.

Exchange control measures affect foreign business in two ways. First, profits and capital cannot be returned to the parent company at will. Second, raw material, machinery, spare parts, and the like cannot be liberally imported for operating purposes.

Many developing countries utilize exchange control to regulate their hard currency balances. The need for such regulations is one important reason for restrictions on imports of consumer goods (for example, cars, appliances, clothing, perfumes) in most emerging countries. Sometimes even developed countries may resort to exchange control. One example is France in 1981 after the socialist government took over.[22]

Import Restrictions Import restrictions are primarily for the support of native industries. Consider a foreign pharmaceutical company traditionally importing certain compounds and chemicals from the parent company. If the host country places restrictions on imports, the company may be forced to depend on local sources of supply for these new materials. This can create two types of problems for the foreign firm. First, the local product may be of inferior quality, which would affect the quality of the finished product. Second, locally the product may be in such short supply that the pharmaceutical manufacturer cannot acquire it in adequate quantity.

Presumably, governments legislate import restrictions with the total industry, and not a particular company, in mind. Thus, the difficulties likely to be faced by a foreign company do not figure in the discussion. Further, when a country wants to encourage domestic industry as a matter of industrial policy, import restrictions are adopted with the realization that the local product will be inferior, at least initially. Strictly from the point of view of the government, import restrictions seem reasonable, but they ordinarily jeopardize the functions of foreign business.

Market Control The government of a country sometimes imposes control to prevent foreign companies from competing in certain markets. For example, until recently Japan had prohibited foreign companies from selling sophisticated communications equipment to the Japanese government. Thus, AT&T, GTE-Sylvania, and ITT could do little business with Japan.

The Arab boycott, until recently, of companies doing business with Israel is an interesting example of market control. Since the Arab states had not recognized Israel's right to exist, the Arabs hoped that the boycott eventually would bring about the collapse of the state of Israel. Although many companies had given in to Arab demands, the U.S. government had adopted strict laws to prevent companies from becoming susceptible to the Arab blackmail.

Tax Control Governments may also impose excessive and unconventional taxes on foreign business. For example, a new form of excise tax for which there is no precedent may be placed on the output of a foreign firm. Such taxes are imposed for three reasons. First, an out-of-the-way burden on foreign companies is an indirect way of warning them that they are not wanted in a country any longer. Second, when a country is in dire need of new revenues, an additional tax burden on foreign companies appears not only politically prudent but economically convenient. And third, taxes can be retaliatory if a government, for example, learns that foreign corporations have abused differences in international taxation and have deprived the country of due revenue.

Taxes per se do not hinder foreign enterprise. However, problems do arise over excessively discriminatory taxes or taxes imposed at variance with the company's agreement with the government. For example, the host government may have agreed to give a tax holiday to a company, say for five years, to establish its operations in the country. Three years later, the government chooses to reverse its position for some reason, such as a new government's refusing to live with the agreement entered into by its predecessor.

Price Control For the sake of the public interest in difficult economic times, countries often resort to price controls. Even in the U.S., the price control weapon has been used many times. For example, President Nixon imposed price controls in the early 1970s to fight inflation. Likewise, many states control the price that a vendor may charge for milk. Until recently, the price of gasoline was regulated.

Similarly, countries use price control devices in various ways to improve their economies. For example, a country may set an official price on essential products such as drugs, heating oil, sugar, and cereals. Price control becomes a special problem if it is imposed randomly; for example, a price limit is placed on a company's finished product, but the prices of the raw materials used in the production of that product are left to market forces. Further, if the product of a particular foreign country has been singled out for price control without any economic rationale, such a measure amounts to undesirable intervention in the working of a foreign firm.

Labor Restrictions   In many nations, labor unions are very strong and have great political clout. Using its strength, labor may be able to talk the government into passing very restrictive laws that support labor at heavy cost to business. Traditionally, labor unions in Latin America have been able to prevent layoffs, plant shutdowns, and the like, even when business could not afford to meet such demands. Labor unions are gradually becoming strong in Western Europe as well. For example, Germany and a number of other European nations require labor representation on boards of directors.

Foreign firms may find it difficult to accommodate labor demands transformed into laws. Even where there are no labor laws to comply with, there may be labor problems. Problems can reach such a level that the foreign enterprise is left with no other choice but to leave.[23]

Political Perspectives

Given today's climate of global economic and political change and the experience of widespread nationalizations and expropriations in the 1960s and 1970s, there is a growing recognition in the business world of the need for a company to "look before it leaps" when considering entry into a foreign country. Any multinational marketer would be well-advised to compile a thorough analysis of the political risks peculiar to a foreign country's political system as well as risks peculiar to the company's industry in foreign settings.

History shows that far and away the riskiest ventures are those in countries of the Third World where appeals to nationalism are most damaging to multinationals.

On the other hand, these countries cannot simply be ignored. For the U.S., the developing countries are increasingly important both economically and politically. They are major suppliers of raw materials including, of course, oil; moreover, they constitute the most rapidly growing U.S. export markets. For example, from 1988 to 1993 U.S. exports of capital goods to developing countries almost doubled from under $59 billion to over $114 billion. In fact, taken as a group, developing countries (excluding OPEC countries) now account for more U.S. exports than the Western European countries. During the recessionary period of the early 1990s, while U.S. exports to industrial countries stagnated or declined, exports to developing (including oil-exporting) countries continued to expand. Without that demand for U.S. goods, unemployment and production would have been far worse. In 1992, about 25 percent of $775 billion in direct overseas U.S. investments was in developing countries. The Third World also accounted for around 40 percent of the $535 billion in U.S. bank claims on foreigners. Profits and interest from these investments and loans play an important role in offsetting U.S. trade deficits.

The political perspectives of a nation can be studied using factors such as those in the following list:
- Type of government
- Stability of government
- Quality of host government's economic management
- Change in government policy
- Host country's attitude toward foreign investment
- Host country's relationship with the rest of the world
- Host country's relationship with parent company's home government
- Attitude toward assignment of foreign personnel
- Extent of anti-private-sector influence or influence of state-controlled industries
- Fairness and honesty of administrative procedures
- Closeness between government and people

The importance of these factors varies from country to country. Nevertheless, it is desirable to consider them all to ensure a complete knowledge of the political outlook for doing business in a particular country.

Type of Government

World governments can be realistically grouped in four categories: democratic republics, communist dictatorships, dictatorships, and monarchies. In each category there is a spectrum of variation. Democratic governments are formed through regular elections and have different party systems. In the U.S. and England, two major political parties are active. Italy and France have several political parties. In India and Mexico, one dominant party controls. Although economic policies are an important issue in democracies, different parties hold different views on how the country's economy can be strengthened. In England, the two major parties, Labour and Conservative (or Tory), have different economic approaches. A Labour government usually seeks greater government control, while a Tory government stands for programs similar to those of the Republican party of the U.S.

Communist governments are rigidly regulated by complete government control of all business activity. Such governments exist in Cuba, the People's Republic of China, Vietnam, North Korea, and Burma. Communist countries maintain various types of ties with foreign business. Because China desires to achieve economic progress through using Western technology and skills, the business climate there has been favorable. On the other hand, Burma has totally isolated itself from the rest of the world. The attitude of the Chinese government swings with changing events. It is convinced that the best way for the country to survive is to keep the screws on political dissent but also energize the economy with free-market reforms.

Dictatorships are authoritarian regimes. These governments are run either by military dictators such as in Nigeria, or by civilian dictators such as in South Korea. Military dictators often eventually adopt a civilian posture, usually by holding an election that gives the appearance of a government elected by popular vote.

Authoritarian governments can be further categorized according to economic philosophy. They may be left wing or Marxist oriented, or right wing and directed toward free enterprise. Angola and Nicaragua reflect, for instance, left-wing characteristics, while both Indonesia and Nigeria follow right-wing policies.

Finally, monarchy refers to a government whose ruler derives power through inheritance. A country may have a monarchy and yet be democratic such as Great Britain, whose Queen Elizabeth II is titular head of the country but not head of the British government. But in many countries, the government is actually run with the monarch as the head. Saudi Arabia and Jordan have monarchies. The Shah of Iran was a reigning monarch. A monarch may have inclinations to either the left or the right.

Any review of a country's political system and its impact on foreign business must remain free of stereotyped notions. Political philosophies change over time. Thus, what a government or a party stood for in the 1960s may not hold true in the 1990s. Obviously, current and emerging perspectives should be analyzed and understood.

Government Stability

In many countries, there are frequent changes of government. In such a climate, a foreign business finds that the government has changed by the time it is ready to implement an agreement. In other words, the government with whom the initial agreement was arranged was different from the one currently in office. Such changes may create difficulties in implementing the agreement because the new government may or may not subscribe to the commitments made by its predecessor.

Thus, it is important for international marketers to examine, before making agreements, whether the current government will continue to be in office to implement agreements made with it (see International Marketing Highlight 8.3). In a democratic situation, the incumbent party's strength and/or the alternative outcomes of the next election can be weighed to assess the likelihood of a change in government. In other situations, a variety of symptoms could point toward the instability of a government:

- Public unrest (demonstrations, riots, or other demonstrations of social tension)
- Government crises (opposition forces trying to topple the government)
- Armed attacks by one group of people on another, or by groups from a neighboring country
- Guerrilla warfare
- Politically motivated assassinations
- Coup d'état
- Irregular change in top government leaders

A report covering these points would provide good evidence of a government's stability or instability.

Government Economic Management

Another factor to examine is the quality of the host government's economic management. A country that manages its economic affairs according to sound economic principles, whether through free economics or socialist policies, will, all things being equal, provide a more favorable environment than a country governed by political emotions and abrupt practices. The economic environment of a country should be studied in the political context with reference to:

- The ability of the government to sustain its internal and external debt
- The country's pursuit of stable and diversified economic growth
- The country's ability to generate an adequate amount of foreign exchange

Political Perspectives

International Marketing Highlight 8.3

Change in Command

Sam Parry was the assistant director of a corporate team investigating the prospects of a manufacturing venture in a small Caribbean country. After six weeks in the field, the team received a request from the government to address the head of state and his cabinet about their proposal. The team spent several days preparing a presentation. At the last minute, however, the project director was called away; she assigned Sam to address the assembled leaders in her place.

Sam had spent enough time helping to prepare the presentation that he felt comfortable with it. He even practiced his introduction to the prime minister—the honorable Mr. Tollis—and to the prime minister's cabinet. Finally, the day arrived for the address. Sam and the team were received at the governmental palace.

Once settled into the prime minister's meeting room, Sam opened the presentation. "Honorable Mr. Tollis," he began, "and esteemed members of the cabinet. . . ."

Abruptly, the prime minister interrupted Sam. "Won't you please start over?" he asked with a peeved smile.

Sam was taken aback. He hadn't expected his hosts to be so formal. They always seemed so casual in their open-necked short-sleeved shirts while Sam and his team sweated away in their suits. But Sam soon regained his composure. "Most honorable Mr. Tollis and highly esteemed members of the cabinet. . . ."

"Be so kind as to begin again," said the prime minister, now visibly annoyed.

"Most esteemed and honorable Mr. Tollis—"

"Perhaps you should start yet again."

Shaken, Sam glanced desperately at his team, then at the government officials surrounding him. The ceiling fans rattled lightly overhead.

One of the cabinet ministers sitting nearby took pity on Sam. Leaning over, the elderly gentleman whispered, "Excuse me, but Mr. Tollis was deposed six months ago. You are now addressing the honorable Mr. Herbert."

Source: Charles F. Valentine, *The Arthur Young International Business Guide* (New York: John Wiley & Sons, 1988), p. 400.

- The nature of the various fiscal and monetary means used to steer the economy
- The quality of the long-term planning of economic policy and its implementation

As an example, a country that continues to live on borrowed funds, either from private sources or international agencies like the IMF, and frequently defaults on payments demonstrates poor economic management.

Change in Government Policy

More than anything else, MNCs dislike frequent policy changes by host countries. Policy changes may occur even without a change in government. When this type of environment exists, it makes things so uncertain that foreign business cannot know what it is getting into. It is important, therefore, for the foreign business to analyze the mechanism of governmental policy changes. Information on the autonomy of legislatures and study of the procedures followed for seeking constitutional changes can be crucial.

Attitude Toward Foreign Investment

Many nations look upon foreign investment with suspicion. This is true of both developed and developing countries. Take, for example, Japan, where it would be extremely difficult for a foreign business to establish itself without first generating a trusting relationship in order to gain entry through a joint-venture opportunity. Developing countries, on the other hand, are usually afraid of domination and exploitation by foreign business. In response to national attitudes, nations legislate a variety of laws and regulations to prescribe the role of foreign investment in their economies. It is appropriate, therefore, to review the host country's regulations and identify underlying attitudes and motivations. Indirectly, the success of other multinational businesses in a country indicates a favorable attitude.[24]

The International Stance of Government

Countries that maintain amicable political relationships with the rest of the world and have respect for international law and order show political maturity. These countries can be expected to behave in a responsible fashion. Iran, for example, in the post-Shah period behaved erratically without regard for international treaties and obligations. Uganda during Dada's regime fell in the same category. Usually, extreme cases can be easily identified. For less spectacular situations, membership in regional and international organizations as well as adherence to bilateral and multilateral principles and agreements provides evidence of a country's relationship with other nations.

Relationship with Parent Company's Home Government

In theory, MNCs have no political alignment. Yet a company originating in the U.S. will continue to be known as a U.S. company even though it may derive a major portion of its revenues and profits from operations outside the U.S. Nestlé, for example, generates close to 50 percent of its revenues in the U.S. and only 4 percent in its home country, Switzerland. Nevertheless, it is identified as a Swiss company. Thus, the relationship between the host country government and the parent company government also will affect, either directly or indirectly, the MNC. Thus, a U.S. international marketer should trace the history of the relationship between the host country's government and the U.S. government. Do the two governments agree on issues debated in international agencies? Are there any points of discord between the two countries? Are there reasons to believe that relations between them will improve or deteriorate in the future? (see International Marketing Highlight 8.4).

Attitude Toward Foreign Managers

A company making an investment in a foreign country needs to make sure that its business there is managed effectively. Among other factors, a crucial determinant of success in overseas operations is the assignment of experienced persons to key positions. But in a country where appointment of local nationals to key positions is a requirement and where qualified nationals are in short supply, there are bound to be difficulties.

Anti-Private-Sector Influence

An interesting development of the post-World War II period has been the increased presence of government in a wide spectrum of social and economic affairs that were previously ignored. As an example in the U.S., concern for the poor, the aged, minorities, consumers' rights, and the environment has spurred government response and the adoption of a variety of legislative measures. In a great many foreign countries, such concerns have led governments to take over businesses to be run as public enterprises. Sympathies for public-sector enterprises, successful or not as businesses, have rendered private corporations suspect and undesirable in many countries. Also, it should not be mistakenly thought that public-sector enterprises are limited to developing countries. Great Britain and France have many government corporations, from airlines to broadcasting companies to banks and steel mills. An example is Airbus Industrié, a civilian aircraft manufacturer owned by the British, French, German, and Spanish governments.

Obviously, in nations where there is an ongoing bias against home-grown private businesses, a MNC cannot expect a cordial welcome. In such a situation, a MNC would have to contend with being a private business and being foreign. Sound business intelligence and familiarity with the industrial policy of the government and related legislative acts and decrees should provide clarification of the role of the private sector in any given economy.

International Marketing Highlight 8.4

Copyright Struggle in New York

A copyright squabble in 1988 between two small companies in New York's Chinatown over videotapes of Taiwanese soap operas illustrates how a relationship between governments could erupt into a political problem. U.E. Enterprises Inc., accused of pirating the Taiwanese television programs, claims that Taiwanese nationals no longer are entitled to copyright protection, as a result of the decision by the U.S. to recognize the People's Republic of China as the "sole legal government" of China in 1979. That decision, the defendants claim, negated the U.S.–Taiwan Friendship, Commerce and Navigation Treaty of 1948, which is the legal framework for trade as well as copyright agreements between the U.S. and Taiwan. The defendant's case relies on a complex argument that a law passed by Congress in 1979, purporting to maintain normal trade relations with Taiwan after recognition of the People's Republic, is constitutionally invalid because it effectively amended the treaty by changing the parties from the Republic of China to the "governing authorities of Taiwan." Only the president, with the consent of the Senate, has the power to make or amend treaties, U.E. Enterprises' attorneys say. On the other hand, legal experts feel that the very existence of the act refutes U.E.'s defense. The Justice Department, which filed a brief in the case, agreed.

On the surface, the case concerns only the unauthorized use of Taiwanese products in the U.S. However, the disputed treaty also protects U.S. companies such as International Business Machines Corp., E-II Holdings Inc.'s Samsonite Unit, Walt Disney Co., and many others from the pirating of their products in Taiwan. Because of this the case received wide publicity.

While the judgement was against U.E. Enterprises, the case highlights the significance of political relations between countries.

Source: *The Wall Street Journal*, October 25, 1988, p. B8.

Administrative Procedures

Every country has its own unique administrative scheme. The scheme emerges from such factors as experience, culture, the system of reward and punishment, availability of qualified administrators, and style of leadership. Additionally, the availability of modern means of transportation and communication helps to streamline governmental administration. Businesses often complain about the U.S. federal bureaucracy and its states' agencies, but if they were to compare U.S. administration with other nations', they would be pleasantly surprised to learn that government in the U.S. is far more efficient than elsewhere. It is not extraordinary in many African countries for administrators to be altogether unavailable, the telephones not to work, or files to be lost. Similar difficulties would not be unusual in either Asia or Latin America. Such hindrances, in addition to the usual red tape, make business dealings uncomfortable and unpleasant. While a company may not bypass an overseas opportunity solely because of this factor, knowledge about the inefficiency of administrative machinery might lengthen schedules and force patience through understanding. The wisdom of engaging the services of a local broker or an agent could also be considered.

Closeness of Government to People

Iran's 1979 crisis suggests that economic development cannot be imposed on a nation; rather, it must evolve over time. The breakneck speed with which the Shah of Iran invested billions of dollars in development in the late 1960s and early 1970s created a fragile society. The Shah imposed a modern infrastructure, an industry dependent on foreign technology, and a Western lifestyle on a Muslim society that was opposed to change. This swift modernization, with GNP per capita increasing from $200 to over $2,000 in a decade's time, triggered a reaction that led to the Shah's fall. The people, in other words, could not absorb modernization quickly enough to adapt their lives accordingly, and they revolted. Religious priests became the leaders of a people disillusioned by Western living and material progress.

The Islamic revolution in Iran provides a classic case of how the distance between government and people can lead to the total disruption of a country. Many political scientists have noted the similarities between Saudi Arabia's modernization and Iran's. There also, a tribal nomadic society is being transformed seemingly overnight into an industrial society with modern amenities and facilities.[25] To an extent, South Vietnam presented a similar problem. The government kept developing programs, with U.S. aid, that widened the distance between the government and the people.

It is sometimes difficult to ascertain whether the people and the government of a country are in accord. The U.S. government, despite all its resources, failed to foresee that the Shah would fall. However, contact with journalists, religious leaders, and the intelligentsia of a country can provide some insights into the feelings of ordinary citizens toward their government and its programs.[26] In traditional societies, where a windfall such as oil revenues suddenly offers an opportunity for multinational business, it would be prudent to investigate the sentiments of the people before making major commitments.

Political Models

On the basis of the factors discussed so far, a country can be categorized as having one of the following political slants: state-centric international politics, pluralistic national politics, bureaucratic organizational politics, or transnational politics. Each of these political model systems presents different kinds of risk for doing business.

The *state-centric model* of international politics assumes that national governments seek power and status in relation to one another, that they do so in the context of a competitive, decentralized international political system, and that they utilize whatever internal political resources are available in pursuit of their international objectives. National governments' actions are thus assumed to be functions of the officials' desire for international power and status and of their reactions to political pressures exerted by other national governments.

The *pluralistic model* of national politics assumes that national governments are responsive to the diverse and conflicting interests and pressures of multiple interest groups within a political system. Group interests and pressures are expressed through electoral processes but are especially important in legislative and administrative processes, where they take the form of lobbying activities. National governments' actions are thus assumed to be functions of the officials' desire to remain in office and/or of their reaction to internal political pressures.

The *bureaucratic organizational politics behavior model* assumes that national governments' actions are the result of organizational processes within government bureaucracies. Intragovernmental conflicts are generated, for instance, by the differing policy preferences of individual officials and agencies. These variances arise from conflicting organizational interests, differences in career experiences, differences in ties to domestic clientele groups, and other factors. This model also suggests that government policies are slow to change because of bureaucratic inertia.

The *transnational politics model* emphasizes the increasingly important role played in world politics by organizations other than those of national governments. Thus, not only MNCs but also international organizations and nongovernmental association such as transnational interest groups are all assuming greater influence, often at the expense of national governments.

Each model contains numerous variables and propositions about relationships among the variables. Each one is also evident in an abundance of impressionistic case studies, systematic quantitative studies, and historical narratives. However, even this abbreviated discussion suggests the utility of these models in political risk assessment, for they can be used to develop a lengthy and systematic list of potential sources of political risk.[27]

Political Risk Assessment

Political risk assessment (PRA) is useful for three reasons:

1. To identify countries that may turn out to be the Irans of tomorrow. (PRA should sound a warning signal of mounting political risks so that a firm can protect itself by minimizing its exposure.)
2. To identify countries unnecessarily discounted as politically unsound, for example, Cambodia, and to identify countries where political conditions have changed for the better, for example, Vietnam and Haiti.
3. To provide a framework to identify countries that are politically risky, but not so risky as to be automatically ruled out. (Most developing countries fall into this category.)

Methods of Political Risk Assessment

Corporations utilize any number of methods to analyze political risk. The currently favored approaches are the so-called qualitative grand tour and old hand approaches, the delphi technique, and the use of quantitative methods.

Grand Tour This approach involves an executive or a team of executives visiting the country in which investment is being considered. Usually, prior to the visit, there has been some preliminary market research. Upon arrival, there are usually meetings with government officials and local businesspersons. The results of this type of visit can be very superficial, representing only selected pieces of information and therefore possibly camouflaging undesirable aspects of the market.

Old Hand This approach relies on the advice of an outside consultant or a person deemed to be an expert. Usually such persons are seasoned educators, diplomats, local politicians, or businesspersons. The capability and experience of the advisor is the factor determining the quality of this report.

Delphi Technique This technique involves asking a group of experts to share their opinions independently on a given problem, in a form that can be scored in order to produce a statistical distribution of opinion. The experts are shown the resulting distribution and given the chance to alter their original views. The process is repeated several times. For some problems, it has been found that the average opinion of the group at the last round is usually more nearly correct than any of the individual views in the beginning.

To use this method, a group of experts would be asked to rate different political factors, for example, the stability of government, the role of its armed forces, and its political conflicts. Based on the final expert opinion, a go or no-go decision can be made.

Quantitative Methods In addition to qualitative methods, many businesses have tried quantitative methods to judge political risk.[28] Among the quantitative methods, discriminant analysis is the most rigorous. This technique involves developing a mathematical relationship among a series of quantifiable factors in order to predict (within specified probability ranges) the likelihood of certain events. Banks have utilized this technique before granting loans to foreign countries. This technique requires collection of different forms of quantitative data, complex analysis of data using an appropriate computer program, and expert interpretation of the results.

Political Risk Assessment Models

Political risk assessment (PRA) has become a fact of U.S. corporate life. The surge of interest in PRA began with the unexpected fall of the Shah's regime in Iran and was reinforced by the overthrow of apparently secure governments in Nicaragua and South Korea. Several independent political risk consultants are available to help corporate clients develop general political risk summaries or provide studies of specific countries. The best known-risk raters are the Economist Intelligence Unit (EIU), a New York-based subsidiary of The Economist Group, London; the *International Country Risk Guide (ICRG)*; and BERI S.A.[29] According to the Economist Intelligence Unit, a rating of A, or 0–20 points, is the least risky; followed by B, 25–40 points; C, 45–55 points;

D, 60–75 points, and E, 80–100 points. The ratings break down into three categories: medium-term lending risk, covering such factors as external debt and trends in the current account, with a maximum score of 45 points; political and policy risk, including factors such as the consistency of government policy and the quality of economic management, with a maximum score of 40 points; and short-term trade risk, including foreign-exchange reserves, with a cap of 15 points.

The International Country Risk Guide is put out by a U.S. division of International Business Communications Ltd., London. *ICRG* offers a composite risk rating, as well as individual ratings for political, financial, and economic risk. The political variable, which makes up 50 percent of the composite figure, includes factors such as government corruption and how economic expectations diverge from reality. The financial rating looks at such things as the likelihood of losses from exchange controls and loan defaults. Economic ratings take into account such factors as inflation and debt service costs. The maximum, or least-risky, score is 100 for the political category and 50 each for financial and economic risk. For the composite score, 85–100 is considered very low risk; 70–84.5, low risk; 60–69.5, moderate risk; 50–59.5, moderately high risk; and 0–49.5, very high risk.

BERI S.A.'s political risk index (PRI) reviews 54 countries 3 times a year.

Consider Brazil's ratings in 1993. EIU puts Brazil in category C, giving it a total score of 54 (which is a slight improvement over the 1991 score of 50). The reason behind this improved showing is easy to see. The inflation is down and the country has liberalized the economic to become attractive to foreign investors. *ICRG* gives Brazil an overall score of 72, ranking it 48th out of 127 countries.

Comparatively, Mexico's prospects are more bullish, and the investment climate has rarely been better. President Carlos Salinas de Gortari during his tenure made solid progress to open the country to foreign competition. In addition, the NAFTA agreement is a positive factor in favor of Mexico.

In its 1993 report, EIU gave Mexico a risk rating of 50, adding 5 points to the previous rating because of a high current-account deficit. Mexico still stays in EIU's C category.[30]

In *ICRG*'s ratings, Mexico gets a score of 70.5 and a rank of 32. For political risk, it gets 71; for financial risk, 41; and for economic risk, 28.5.

Among Southeast Asian countries, Thailand is perceived as one of Asia's most attractive investments. Economic growth is strong, wages are relatively low, and the government is hospitable to foreign investment. The country is once again under military rule after a brief period of democracy. EIU gives Thailand a score 25, putting it in the B category. Political risk drags down the score. *ICRG* gives Thailand a score of 68, ranking it 40th. Political risk is scored at 57, financial risk at 42, and economic risk at 37.

Indonesia is rated a medium-risk country. Though the government of President Suharto is authoritarian, it follows conservative fiscal and monetary policies and has steadily slashed restrictions on domestic and foreign investment in recent years. EIU gives Indonesia an overall rating of B. It has raised Indonesia's medium-term lending-risk rating to B from C, reflecting an expected improvement in the debt service as a percentage of gross domestic product. *ICRG* gives Indonesia a score of 68.5, putting it in the moderate-risk category. However, the country gets a relatively weak 57 for political risk, reflecting rising discontent with authoritarian rule and corruption. Indonesia chalks up a strong 44 for financial risk and 35.5 for economic risk.

In Eastern Europe, EIU rates Hungary 55, which puts it in the C category. *ICRG* ranks it 54th, with a composite score of 62, made up of 68 for political risk, 32 for financial risk, and 24 for economic risk. EIU gives Poland a score of 45, putting it in the D category. Poland gets a composite score of 61 from *ICRG*, putting it in 56th place (62 for political risk, 29 for financial risk, and 31 for economic risk). Finally, EIU gives Czech Republic a rating of 45, putting it in the C band. *ICRG* gives the country a composite risk rating of 69.5, ranking it 36th. Political risk comes in at 73, financial risk at 36, and economic risk at 30.

The general perspective provided by these studies does not help in monitoring political developments in a practical fashion. Too often, consultants' reports are of dubious usefulness to subsidiary managers, since they are mainly oriented to corporate headquarters. The objectives of a good political risk analysis system should not be to collect and evaluate information, but rather to include the best political intelligence in decision making.[31] Toward this end, a specific study tailored to a particular purpose is more useful. Although there is some debate about the usefulness of the indexing services, the client lists of the three organizations include a number of Fortune 500 companies.[32]

Strategic Response

When a company has become susceptible to political risk or has been politically victimized, it must make an effort to salvage its position. While there is little a company can do to ward off internal violence or political instability in the host country, it can employ a number of responses to discourage expropriation or to generally strengthen its position. As one author has stated:

> In sum, host governments should not be seen by MNC top managers exclusively as an impediment to global strategic freedom, to be avoided at all cost. Occasionally they may provide enough of a helping hand—through privileged market access, export credits, and subsidies—for smaller MNCs to face global competition, to make it worthwhile for those smaller, often weaker, MNCs to relinquish wholeheartedly some strategic freedom to gain competitive strength through government support. Host governments can thus either hamper or help global strategies, depending on their policies and on the strategic options of the affected firms. It is important, therefore, to make an analysis of host government goals, policies, and actions an integral part of the strategy formulation process in a global business.[33]

Strategic Choices

Essentially a company has three strategic options to choose from in response to political difficulties in a host country. These responses are to adapt, to withdraw, and to take counteractive measures.[34] For example, in the 1970s, IBM completely withdrew from India because the company could not live with the restrictions imposed by the government on freedom of strategy in product development, pricing, and other areas. Nestlé, on the other hand, accepted India's infringements in return for continued presence in the market. CPC International, du Pont, and Brown Boveri (a European company) likewise seek market presence rather than complete withdrawal. The third choice, counteractive response, amounts to making a new move to gain a competitive advantage based on company strengths and the needs of the host government. For example, Honeywell merged its French subsidiary, Honeywell Bull, with the French government company, Compagnie Internationl pour L'Informatique, which was losing money. This arrangement gave Honeywell access to the French market and qualified it to receive French government grants for R & D (see International marketing Highlight 8.5).

International Marketing Highlight 8.5

Managing Government Intervention

Bristol-Myers pursued the counteractive strategy in Indonesia. It had successfully marketed one of its nutritional products in Indonesia, which was centrally obtained from its Nijmegen facility in Holland. This worked well for Bristol-Myers since the Indonesian market wasn't developed enough to justify the cost of building a plant there to service this market. The problem started when the Indonesian government decided to close its borders to the "finished product" that Bristol-Myers had introduced so successfully into the market. Bristol-Myers had to decide whether to find an alternative that could circumvent the new regulation or withdraw from the Indonesian market. Bristol-Myers decided to follow the former route. The concerned product was composed of a highly sophisticated powder that was blended with a heat-sensitive key raw material and canned. Bristol-Myers solved the problem by ascertaining what the Indonesian government really meant by "finished product." It worked closely with the ministry of health and the ministry of economics in Indonesia to come up with a mutually acceptable solution: Bristol-Myers was permitted to import a "base" powder that it would blend with an indigenous raw material. Bristol-Myers successfully subcontracted with an Indonesian company to produce and blend the raw material with the base. The "finished product" was subsequently canned, carried the Bristol-Myers label, and continued to be sold in Indonesia.

Keep in mind, however, that no single strategy works best in a single country or even in a single industry. If the MNC's managers are flexible and imaginative in responding to government demands, the consequences could be surprisingly favorable. Encarnation and Vachani found that new product lines and markets, risk diversifications, and higher earnings are among the benefits MNCs operating in India enjoyed in the wake of that country's "hostile" equity laws. Some, for example, negotiated for manufacturing licenses and other concessions in exchange for "Indianization." Others successfully sought entry to new markets, hitherto forbidden.[35] The choice, of course, among the three options depends on the bargaining power of the company in respect to the bargaining power of the host government.

MNCs' Bargaining Power

The bargaining power of MNCs stems from such factors as technology, economies of scale, and product differentiation. Companies with technology badly needed by the host country and unobtainable on comparative terms elsewhere bargain from a leverage position. For example, in the late 1970s Indonesia desperately sought to boost its oil exploration activity. This goal required sophisticated technology, and Indonesia was willing to go to any length to get it. In other words, oil companies negotiated with the Indonesian government on very favorable terms since they had the necessary technology.[36] Mexico willingly permitted IBM to establish a wholly owned microcomputer plant. The Mexican government was concerned that without a major microcomputer plant the local market would consists of outmoded and overpriced products. If a company like IBM entered the market, it could pull other companies in the production chain along with it.[37]

Economies of scale, which a foreign firm might realize through its worldwide production and distribution arrangements, also yield a unique bargaining strength. If the low cost of the local multinational firm's output is directly related to the MNC's worldwide network or vertical integration (via the establishment of specialized plants in various countries and the transfer of components or end products among them), the host country will hesitate to intervene out of fear that any intervention would cancel out the benefits that the firm derives from being a part of the network. In the case of Marcona Mining's iron milling operation in Peru, for example, the firm signed long-term supply agreements with its customers that stipulated that, in the event of nationalization, the contracts with its Peruvian subsidiary would be considered void and that Marcona Mining would supply its customers from its other milling operations. When the firm was expropriated, the Peruvian government found it had no outlet for iron ore concentrate. Since the trade in this commodity is based almost entirely on long-term controls, there was no well-developed spot market to which the Peruvian government could turn.[38]

Product differentiation (i.e., differentiation based on the nature of the product and product quality/performance attributes, and not on consumer perceptions) can serve as another area of strength in foreign firms' bargaining with the host governments. For example, a firm producing quality agricultural machinery will have greater leverage in dealing with a host government than will a cosmetics manufacturer.

To sum up, firms with technical, operational, and managerial requirements that are within the reach of the abilities of the host nation will have little bargaining power. Such firms are more likely to experience intervention than those in complex fields. For example, there is considerable local pressure on governments in Kenya, Indonesia, Brazil, and India to restrict such areas as consumer goods manufacturing, retailing, importing and exporting, and distribution to nationals only.

Bargaining Power of the Host Country

The bargaining power of the host country mainly depends on two factors: control of market access and inducements. The host country controls access to the market in many ways. It may restrict entry for other competitors, or it may open up rights to restricted markets. For example, Spain attracted Ford Motor Company by making it feasible for the company to sell enough cars there. Similarly, Japan has permitted foreign companies to sell communications-related products to its government, which may serve as an incentive for such firms as Western Electric to become more active in that market.

In addition, host countries may offer such inducements as R&D funds, tax holidays, market information, land subsidies, and financial concessions (repatriation arrangements) to attract the businesses sought. For example, ITT's European units have received large government grants to develop communication equipment tailored to local conditions.

Making a Response

The strategic response a company makes to intervention by the host country should depend on the bargaining power on each side. Bradley recommends the following strategies for improving the odds in international investing:

- Seek joint ventures with local private parties.
- Concentrate proprietary research, product development, and process technology in the U.S.
- Ensure that each new investment is economically dependent on the parent corporation in the U.S. (For example, establish the parent as the sole supplier of essential materials.)
- Avoid local branding or establish a single global trademark.
- Adopt a low-profile, multiplant strategy, with a number of investments in different countries.[39]

To conclude, the major benefits to a host country from a foreign investment usually appear at the beginning. Over time, the incremental benefits become smaller and the costs more apparent. Unless the firm continually renews these benefits, by introducing more products, say, or by expanding output and developing export markets, it is likely to be subject to increasing political risks.[40] The common government attitude is to ignore the past and instead ask what will be done for them in the future. In a situation where the firm's future contributions are unlikely to evoke a favorable government reaction, the firm had best concentrate on protecting its foreign investments by striking a balance between the company's goals and those of its host. For example, a company may introduce higher technology products and thereby foster the government's economic plans.[41]

Summary

An international marketer needs to examine carefully the political environment of a country before making major commitments in that country. The political situation of a country may or may not be conducive to profitable business there.

Political problems related to foreign business occur mainly because of political sovereignty, a country's desire to assert its authority, and political conflict—either internal ones such as civil war or external troubles with another country. Such troubles may lead a country to intervene politically in the affairs of private business, particularly those of foreign firms. Intervention may range from some form of control to complete takeover, or expropriation, which is the official seizure of foreign property by a host country. Other forms of intervention include exchange control, import restrictions, market control, tax control, price control, and labor restrictions. At one time, political intervention mainly occurred in developing countries. Now, even industrially developed countries seek to control foreign enterprises in various ways.

The possibility of political intervention makes it necessary for a foreign marketer to carefully analyze the political situation of a country before investment there. This analysis can be made through study of the country's type of government (such as republic, dictatorship, and so forth); the stability of the government; the government's economic management; the frequency of changes in government policy; the attitudes that the country maintains toward foreign investment, other governments, the parent company's home government, foreign managers, and private business; the viability of the government's administrative procedures; and the closeness between the government and its people. On the basis of the preceding factors, the foreign firm can determine the political risk of doing business with a given country. Various methods or models can be employed for political risk assessment.

In theory, a company should not enter a politically unsafe country. However, things sometimes change within a country after entry has been made. For example, traditionally Iran provided a workable environment. However, beginning in 1978, it became an extremely high-risk country. What can a company do if problems arise afterward? There are three strategic responses for a company to make in response to political intervention: adapt and accept infringements and mold the business operations to suit the foreign government's requirements; withdraw and call it quits even if it means taking a loss of property; and attempt counteractive measures by making counterproposals that would provide the government with what it wants and at the same time allow the company a few concessions. In the final analysis, the host government's willingness to grant concessions to the foreign enterprise would depend on the MNC's own bargaining leverage. For example, a host government would be willing to concede to the terms of a multinational enterprise involved in business that is of strategic national importance and that cannot be replaced. On the other hand, a company manufacturing consumer goods such as bar soaps and shampoo may not have much bargaining power with the host government.

Review Questions

1. Why is it necessary for international marketers to study political environment? How can foreign politics affect marketing decisions?
2. What are the underlying causes of political unrest? Discuss.
3. Discuss different ways in which a host government may intervene in the affairs of a multinational firm.
4. Define the term *expropriation*. What can a company do to counteract expropriation?
5. What factors should a company study to gain insight into a country's politics?
6. Why is it desirable to undertake political risk assessment?
7. Examine the alternative responses a company can use to strengthen its position with the host government.

Creative Questions

1. In 1994, the Clinton Administration extended the Most Favorite Nation trading status to China, despite that country's poor record in respecting human rights. What political factors influenced this decision? Should America have compromised its policy on human rights for economic gains? What influence is this decision likely to have on other nations with questionable records on maintaining human rights?
2. Have causes of war disappeared from the face of the earth? According to *Economist*, they have not. There might be a general war between Islam and the West. Such a war has three sorts of potential ignites: ideology, skin color, and conflict of interest. Examine this proposition, suggesting ways it can be averted.

Endnotes

1. Richard L. Hudson, "Apple Computer vs. French Chauvinism: Politics, Not Free Trade, Wins in the End," *The Wall Street Journal*, February 22, 1985, p. 34.

2. See Roberto Friedmann, "Political Risk and International Marketing," *Columbia Journal of World Business*, Winter 1988.

3. "Toyota's Fast Lane," *Business Week*, November 4, 1985, p. 42. Also see "Asian Auto Makers Find a Back Door to the U.S. Market," *Business Week*, December 9, 1985, p. 52; "Import or Die," *The Economist*, February 19, 1983, pp. 11–12.

4. "The Screws Are Tightening on U.S. Companies," *Business Week*, February 11, 1985, p. 38.

5. "Foreign Cigarette Makers Aim for Bigger Share of Japan Market," *The Asian Wall Street Journal Weekly*, October 28, 1985, p. 23.

6. Steve Frazier, "Mexico Hopes Its Approval of IBM Plant Encourages More Foreign Investment," *The Wall Street Journal*, July 25, 1985, p. 25.

7. Anthony Spaeth and Amal Kumar Naj, "PepsiCo Accepts Tough Conditions for the Right to Sell Cola in India," *The Wall Street Journal*, September 20, 1988, p. 44.

8. *Business Week*, February 10, 1992, p. 43.

9. Raymond Vernon, "Multinational Enterprises and National Governments: Exploration of an Uneasy Relationship," *Columbia Journal of World Business*, Summer 1976, p. 11.

10. See Subhash C. Jain, *Market Evolution in Developing Countries: The Unfolding of the Indian Market* (New York: The Haworth Press, Inc. 1993).

11. Lynne Reaves, "U.S. Marketers Fend Off Turmoil in Philippines," *Advertising Age*, May 16, 1988, p. 10.

12. *Fortune*, November 2, 1993, p. 18.

13. See Adi Ignatius, "Crimes Against Foreigners Are Adding to Burden of Doing Business in Russia," *The Wall Street Journal*, September 10, 1993, p. A6.

14. See Xiao-Hong Sun and Peter D. Bennett, "The Effect of Political Events on Foreign Direct Investment in Marketing," *Journal of Global Marketing*, Spring 1988, pp. 7–28.

15. David K. Eiteman and Arthur I. Stonehill, *Multinational Business Finance* (Reading MA: Addison-Wesley, 1979), p. 186.

16. David G. Bradley, "Managing Against Expropriation," *Harvard Business Review*, July–August 1977, pp. 75–84.

17. Ibid.

18. *Transnational Corporations in World Development: Third Survey* (New York: United Nations, 1983).

19. David G. Bradley, op. cit.

20. Ibid.

21. Michael S. Minor, "The Demise of Expropriation as an Instrument of Old LDC Policy, 1980–1992," *Journal of International Business Studies*, Vol. 25, No. 1, 1994, pp. 177–88.

22. "Europe's Economic Malaise," *Business Week*, December 7, 1981, p. 74.

23. Richard F. Janssen, "Hitachi Bid to Build Television Plant in Britain, Creating Jobs, Provokes a Storm of Opposition," *The Wall Street Journal*, November 1, 1977, p. 46.

24. See Gerald Pollio and Charles H. Riemenschneider, "The Coming Third World Investment Revival," *Harvard Business Review*, March–April 1988, pp. 114–27. Also see *Business America*, March 13, 1989, pp. 16–17.

25. See "Saudi Arabia's Dilemma: Too Much, Too Fast," *Business Week*, December 8, 1980, p. 53.

26. "The Fundamental Fear," *The Economist*, August 6, 1994, p. 15.

27. Thomas L. Brewer, *American Foreign Policy: Contemporary Introduction* (Englewood Cliffs, NJ: Prentice-Hall, 1980), Chapter 2.

28. See P. Nagy, "Quantifying Country Risk: A System Developed by Economists at the Bank of Montreal," *Columbia Journal of World Business*, Fall 1978, pp. 135–47; Elizabeth Goldstein and Jan Vanous, "Country Risk Analysis: Pitfalls of Comparing Eastern Bloc Countries with the Rest of the World," *Columbia Journal of World Business*, Winter 1983, pp. 10–16.

29. Monua Janah, "Rating Risk in the Hot Countries," *The Wall Street Journal*, September 20, 1991, p. R4. Also see William D. Coplin and Michael K. O'Leary, "World Political/Business Risk Analysis for 1987," *Planning Review*, January/February 1987, pp. 34–40. Also see Jean-Claude Cosset and Jean Ray, "The Determinants of Country Risk Ratings." *Journal of International Business Studies*, Vol. 22, No. 1 (First Quarter 1991), pp. 135–42.

30. "World Risk Ratings Review," *Crossborder Monitor*, May 25, 1994, p. 12.

31. See Thomas W. Shreeve, "Be Prepared for Political Changes Abroad," *Harvard Business Review*, July–August 1984, pp. 111–18.

32. William D. Coplin and Michael K. O'Leary, "1991 World Political Risk Forecast," *Planning Review*, January/February 1991, pp. 16–23.

33. C. K. Prahalad and Yves L. Doz, *The Multinational Mission* (New York: The Free Press, 1987), p. 68.

34. Yves L. Doz and C. K. Prahalad, "How MNCs Cope with Host Government Intervention," *Harvard Business Review*, March–April 1980, pp. 149–57.

35. D. J. Encarnation and Sushil Vachini, "Foreign Ownership: When Hosts Change the Rules," *Harvard Business Review*, September–October 1985, pp. 152–60.

36. "Foreign Countries Offer Wide Range of Incentives to Invest," *The Asian Wall Street Journal Weekly*, August 24, 1981, pp. 12–14.

37. Steve Frazier, "Mexico Hopes Its Approval of IBM Plant Encourages More Foreign Investment," *The Wall Street Journal*, July 25, 1985, p. 25.

38. Brad Bueermann, "Marcona Mining: A Study in Risk Avoidance," unpublished paper, Stanford University, Graduate School of Business, June 1979.

39. David G. Bradley, "Managing Against Expropriation," *Harvard Business Review*, July–August 1977, pp. 75–83. *Also see* Stephen Weiss-Wik, "Enhancing Negotiators' Successfulness," *Journal of Conflict Resolution*, December 1983, pp. 706–39.

40. Alan C. Shapiro, "Managing Political Risk: A Policy Approach," *Columbia Journal of World Business*, Fall 1981, pp. 63–69.

41. James E. Austin and John C. Ickis, "Managing After the Revolutionaries Have Won," *Harvard Business Review*, May–June 1988, pp. 103–09.

CHAPTER 9

Legal Environment

Chapter Focus

After studying this chapter, you should be able to:

- Describe two types of legal systems

- Discuss jurisdiction of laws

- Examine relevant host country laws, U.S. laws, and international laws and conventions

- Explain arbitration and how companies may resort to it to resolve conflict in a foreign environment

Multinational enterprise in its global exercise must cope with widely differing laws. A U.S. corporation not only has to consider U.S. laws wherever it does business, but also must be responsive to the host country's laws as well. For example, without requiring proof that certain market practices have adversely affected competition, U.S. law makes them violations. These include horizontal price fixing between competitors, market division by agreement between competitors, and price discrimination. These laws must be respected by a U.S. corporation regardless of its place of business. Simultaneously, local laws must be adhered to. For example, in Europe a clear-cut distinction is made between agencies and distributorships. Agents are deemed auxiliaries of their principal; distributorships are independent enterprises. Exclusive distributorships are considered restrictive in European Union (EU) countries. The foreign marketer must be careful in making distribution arrangements in, say France, so as not to violate the regulation concerning distributorship contracts.

Worldwide, different countries pursue legal systems of varied complexity and dimension. In some countries, laws only provide a broad guide, and the interpretation is left to the courts. In other countries, laws spell out virtually every detail. A foreign enterprise, therefore, has to be scrupulously careful to ensure that it fully abides by local laws and regulations. From the marketing standpoint, a U.S. company doing business in other countries should be primarily concerned with laws pertaining to competition, price setting (for example, price discrimination, resale price maintenance), distribution arrangements (for example, exclusive dealership), product (for example, wholesomeness, packaging, warranty and service, patents and trademarks), personal selling (for example, white-collar employment/labor laws), and advertising (for example, media usage, information provision).

In addition, there are both host country and U.S. laws concerned with taxes, tariffs, licensing, and other areas related to business that should be understood and complied with, along with certain international laws and conventions that affect marketing decision making in the global context. The international marketer should also understand the use of arbitration as an alternative to legal recourse.

The impact of legal aspects on marketing is illustrated by an Italian law allowing wine coolers to be sold there. Although Italy had been producing wine coolers for export for years, existing law had prohibited wine from being mixed with other ingredients, basically to protect consumers from tampered wine. The new law prevents the beverage from being called a wine cooler. Instead, it's to be described as a wine-based "fantasy" beverage with a minimum of 75 percent wine and grape juice. The Italian word *fantasia* also means multicolored. No artificial flavors, sugar, or water are allowed.

Both Riunite and Cantina Sociale di Foggia launched their wine beverages in Italy within days of official publication of the laws.[1]

International Legal Perspectives

Two important aspects of international legal systems are pertinent to marketing: the philosophical bases of the laws and the jurisdiction of these laws.

Common Law Versus Code Law

Philosophically, two types of legal systems may be distinguished: common law and code law. ***Common law*** is based on precedents and practices established in the past and interpreted over time. Common law was first developed in England, and most of the countries that at one time or another formed a part of the British Empire follow this system. ***Code law*** is based on detailed rules for all eventualities. Code law was developed by the Romans and is popularly practiced by a number of free world countries. Most countries of the free world may be divided into those that follow common law, as do Great Britain, U.S., Australia, India, and Kenya, and those that have code law, as do Italy, France, Germany, Mexico, and Switzerland.

It is important for an international marketer to be familiar with the genesis of a country's law, for it frequently has far-reaching effects on all kinds of decisions. For example, right to a property (which would cover such things as trademark) in a common-law country would depend on the history of use of the property, that is, in a dispute which party actually used the trademark on its package and in its advertising campaign. According to code law, however, the right of property would be established based on which party actually registered the trademark. Assume two companies, say Alpha and Beta, are claiming rights to a trademark. Alpha registered the trademark but never used it. On the other hand, Beta has been using it all along in various commercial ways without ever bothering to register it. Legally, in a common-law country, the trademark would belong to Beta Company. In the code-law country, however, it would be the property of the Alpha Company.

Similarly, so-called acts of God in contractual obligations are interpreted differently in the two legal systems. Consider a Japanese company that entered into contracts with firms in England and Italy to deliver certain electronic equipment on a specified date. When a hurricane on the high seas destroyed the Japanese shipment, the company could not fulfill the contract. In both England and Italy, this is considered an act of God, and the Japanese company would not be held liable for not meeting the contractual terms. However, assume the shipment was destroyed not by a hurricane but by a breakdown in the air conditioning of the building where the goods were stored. In this case, the common law might not release the Japanese exporters from noncompliance because air conditioning failure during summer heat can be expected and therefore is not an act of God. Under code law, both circumstances would most likely be considered acts of God.

The division between code-law and common-law countries, broad in nature, narrows in actual practice. Some common-law countries also have specific codes, particularly in the area of commerce, that must be followed. Furthermore, although two countries follow the same system, the interpretation in a particular case may differ, based on the experiences and precedents in the two environments. For example, air conditioning failure might be considered an act of God in Egypt, even though it is a common-law country, because air conditioning is limited there and the climate is sultry most of the year.

An emerging development is the difference between the legal system of free countries and communist rules. This difference becomes significant as former communist countries liberalize their economies and come in contact with people/companies from the capitalist world (see International Marketing Highlight 9.1).

Jurisdiction of Laws

Remarkably enough, while business across national boundaries is an accomplished fact, there is no international body to make rules and oversee their fulfillment by different parties. Thus, a business incorporated in a particular country carries the burden of complying with the laws of both the incorporating nation and the host country. For example, a large U.S. manufacturer may have subsidiaries incorporated/registered in different parts of the world. Such expansion makes the parent company liable to the laws of all the nations where it does business.

Major problems occur when laws of more than one country must be respected and these laws have different values. In other words, if a conflict occurs between two contracting parties, the question arises as to which nation's laws should be used to resolve the problem. If the contract contains a jurisdiction clause stipulating which country's legal system should be used to settle disputes, the matter can be settled accordingly. However, if the parties have failed to include a jurisdiction clause in the contract, two alternatives exist: (1) settle the dispute by following the laws of the country where the agreement was made, or (2) resolve the dispute by applying the laws of the country where the contract has to be fulfilled. If the two alternatives are likely to lead to different conclusions, each party naturally would like to settle the issue according to the legal system that favors its position. Obviously, this may lead to legal and counterlegal actions, presumably in different courts, perhaps in different countries. An alternative to legal action is arbitration, which will be discussed in a later section.

Consider the Bhopal tragedy in which over 2,000 people died from a gas leakage accident in a Union Carbide plant in India in 1984. The Indian government would have liked the question of compensation to survivors settled in the U.S. courts, because the U.S. courts have been more liberal than the Indian courts in granting compensation to victims in such cases. Despite India's viewpoint, Union Carbide would have preferred that the case be settled in the Indian courts, in the hope that their liability would be reduced substantially. In the end, the case was settled in India (for readers' interest, it was an out-of-court settlement).

Host Country Laws

Countries enact laws to control foreign businesses in their economies. Some of the laws are discriminatory against foreign goods and businesses. Laws are sometimes designed to allow reciprocity with nations on good trading terms with the country. In some instances, extremely favorable laws may be passed to attract foreign investment. In general, the legal environment of a country for foreign commerce depends on that country's economic objectives and its obligations and position in relating to worldwide commerce. In some situations, however, the laws may have political aims as well. For example, a government may decide to restrict all imports in order to promote a national feeling among the people and their political supporters. On the other hand, political considerations may require a country to liberalize its laws pertaining to foreign business. For example, in 1988 in the wake of a high U.S. trade deficit and under pressure from Washington, Taiwan reduced tariffs on some 3,500 items by an average of 50 percent, including telecommunications, medical equipment, pharmaceuticals, sophisticated electronic equipment, forest products, agricultural goods, and cigarettes.[2] South Korea and

Japan, other trading partners of the U.S. with whom it had a substantial negative trade balance, have been similarly tilting their trade policy toward the U.S.

Laws that bear on entry into foreign markets take several forms, including tariffs, antidumping laws, export/import licensing, investment regulations, legal incentives, and restrictive trading laws. Japan has finally scrapped its Staple Food Control Act that restricted free trade in rice. With this, U.S. rice should be easy to sell in Japan. Also, the freer competition should bring down the price for the Japanese consumers, which has been roughly nine times the world market price.[3]

■■■■■■■■■■ **International Marketing Highlight 9.1** ■■■■■■■■■■

Trial of a Salesman

Kwok Siu-wah, a Hong Kong salesman, was alleged to have defrauded three Shenzhen (China) companies of $12,800 by altering shipping invoices between May 1984 and July 1985. He was detained in July of 1985. In December, the Shenzhen Public Security Bureau turned the case over to the prosecutor's office, which demanded that Mr. Kwok repay the money. Because he was not able to do so, court proceedings were instituted against him. Simultaneously, the court temporarily confiscated the travel documents of Mr. Kwok's son, Kwok Wai-hung, who was not charged. The January 1986 verdict sentenced the elder Kwok to seven years in prison.

Since Hong Kong will come under Chinese rule in 1997, a comparison of the proceedings of the Shenzhen court with the proceedings of a Hong Kong court today is interesting.

In a Hong Kong court, the identity and authority of all the participants are made clear at the outset. In Shenzhen, however, the accused was isolated and opposed by all other participants in the case, who were themselves united under party leadership. None of the identities of the court personnel—police, lawyers, court staff, the plaintiff, or the accused themselves—were made public.

Moreover, the Public Security Bureau, the prosecutor's office, the court, and the plaintiff were united in a pursuit of the defendant and his family in an attempt to persuade them to turn over $12,800.

In Hong Kong, even though a defendant has confessed, a court must still render its verdict according to the evidence and to statements made in court. In the Shenzhen case, it was pointed out that the documents allegedly altered by the defendant also bore the signatures of every responsible official of the company he allegedly defrauded. Yet none of these officials was called to present evidence before the court. Instead, the court delivered its verdict based solely on the confession of the defendant—a man who had been isolated for six months prior to the trial.

Under these circumstances, the defendant's confession could have been influenced by threats, coercion, and possibly even mistreatment. The fact that Mr. Kwok's accusers never appeared in court to give evidence and that Mr. Kwok was not allowed to cross-examine them also leads one to raise the possibility that the charges in the case resulted not from Mr. Kwok's actions alone, but from actions involving him with Chinese officials in the alleged fraud. Was the money taken by Mr. Kwok alone, or was it split with the others? The joint pursuit of this money by Shenzhen's police, prosecutor, and plaintiff makes one wonder about motives that have not been revealed. The fact that Mr. Kwok's accusers were not brought before the court for cross-examination raises the question of whether there was an attempt at some sort of cover-up.

In the courtroom—a temporary location rather than a formal, permanent site—the defendant was seated on a low stool, giving onlookers an impression of guilt before he had even been sentenced. The plaintiffs did not appear in court. The Defense attorney told the defendant's wife, "You should not entertain any suspicions, nor should you make complaints to any one."

At the beginning of the trial, the travel documents of the defendant's son, Kwok Wai-hung, were confiscated. He was not allowed to return to Hong Kong until his mother disclosed his plight at a news conference in Hong Kong. His release was apparently the result of the publicity that attended the incident in Hong Kong and China's fear of Hong Kong public opinion.

When the case concluded, the court stated that "During the period when the case was under investigation, this court had, according to the law, educated the defendant's wife Tin Yun-kiu, daughter Kwok Sui-ling, and son Kwok Wai-hung, that they should pay back the sum embezzled by the defendant. This was totally legitimate."

Source: *The Wall Street Journal*, March 10, 1986, p. 7.

Tariffs

A *tariff* is a tax that a government levies on exports and imports. If the tax is charged on exports it is called *export duty*. The tax associated with imports is referred to as *import duty* or *customs duty*. The purpose of export duty is to discourage selling overseas to maintain adequate supply at home.

The import duty is levied for different reasons: to protect home industry from being outpriced by cheap imports, to gain a source of revenue for the government, and to prevent the dilution of foreign exchange balances through consumer goods purchased by a few privileged people. In developing countries, where new industries cannot compete with imports from the Western world and their resources are limited, the import duty serves as an important measure to promote economic development. While most of the reasons for levying import duties make little sense in the U.S. and other industrialized countries, the influx of Japanese imports, particularly automobiles, has led many concerned groups in the U.S. to recommend heavy import duty on Nissans and Toyotas.

An import duty may be assessed either according to the value of the product (called ad valorem), or on a unit basis (called specific duty), or both. Computation of a specific duty is easier because the price factor does not come into the picture as it does in ad valorem duty.

A related term, called subsidy, is relevant here also. A *subsidy* is a reverse tariff. Many countries provide a subsidy for local manufactures for export abroad. For example, South Korea provides a subsidy to its steel manufacturers to compete effectively in the world market. A subsidy may also be provided to local products to make them competitive against imports. For example, the U.S. government subsidized certain types of steel to protect the U.S. industry against Japan's.

Antidumping Laws

Dumping is a type of pricing strategy for selling products in foreign markets below cost, or below the price charged to domestic customers. Dumping is practiced to capture a foreign market and to damage rival foreign national enterprises. For example, in the

1980s, foreign car manufacturers were charged with dumping cars in the U.S. Japanese television manufacturers and steel companies also have been similarly charged. In 1993, the U.S. government accused India, France, and Brazil of dumping stainless steel wire rods and forged stainless steel flanges.[4]

Host governments often pass laws against dumping with a view to protecting local industries. Dumping can be a problem for developed and developing countries alike. Thus, the U.S. Treasury Department found that 23 of 28 foreign automakers had been dumping cars in the U.S. It demanded that the foreign manufacturers increase their car prices. Subsequently, Volkswagen, for instance, raised its car price an average of 2.5 percent. In the same way, on the recommendation of the International Trade Commission, under the provisions of the 1974 Trade Act, the Treasury Department set minimum steel import price levels to enable U.S. manufacturers to compete against Japanese steelmakers.[5] Among the developing countries, Brazil has passed antidumping legislation against imports from the U.S. and Japan. Similar laws exist in South Korea, Taiwan, India, and Nigeria.

In theory, the practice of dumping cannot be criticized. A business should be free to set any price it finds would be beneficial in the long run. Thus, different prices may be set in different markets, based on the demand and the competition. The counterargument, however, is that price differentials are intended strictly to weaken competition and over the long run will hurt everyone. Particularly in international business, dumping does inhibit the orderly development of national industry. From this viewpoint, attacks on rival markets by dumping amount to destructive as well as unscrupulous means of securing market position. It is for this reason that countries pass antidumping laws.

Export/Import Licensing

Many countries have laws on the books that require exporters and importers to obtain licenses before engaging in trade across national boundaries. For example, Singapore requires importers of video games to obtain an import permit from the Board of Film Censors to distribute their product in Singapore.[6] The purpose of an export license may be simply to allow for the statistical tracking of export activities. Licensing may also help to ensure that certain goods are not exported at all, or at least not to certain countries. Chapter 17 discusses U.S. government prohibition of exportation of certain high-tech defense-related goods to certain countries and government requirements for permission to sell bombers and fighter planes to any country. Readers may recall the debate in the Congress in 1993 about the sale of Cray Super Computers and Nuclear Power plants to China, which finally was approved.[7]

Import licensing is enforced to control the unnecessary purchase of goods from other countries. Such restraints save foreign exchange balances for other important purposes like the import of pharmaceuticals, chemicals, and machinery. India, for example, has strict licensing requirements for the import of cars and other luxury goods.

Foreign Investment Regulations

One of the primary aims of laws and regulations on foreign investment is to limit the influence of MNCs and to achieve a pattern of foreign investment that contributes most effectively to the realization of the host country's economic objectives. There are several broad areas of legislation concerned with foreign investment such as administration of the investment process, screening criteria, ownership, finance, employment and training, technology transfer, investment incentives, and dispute settlement.

General Motors Corporation's problems in Germany show how varying investment laws could pose difficulty. The affair stems from GM's sale of its unprofitable Terex subsidiary, which made earthmoving equipment, to IBH Holding AG of Mainz in 1980. Over the next two years, before IBH declared bankruptcy in 1983, GM made four equity investments in the increasingly troubled German holding company. In return, the automaker received immediate repayments of millions owed to it by IBH.

Such a maneuver, called "round-tripping," is generally considered illegal, unless properly disclosed, in Germany—though not in the U.S. The Germans contend that it could hide a company's true financial condition and thus mislead investors and creditors.

Criminal investigation was launched against GM and its chairman Roger Smith. It took two years for the problem to be settled and GM to be exonerated of any wrongdoing. Meanwhile, however, before making a routine visit to Germany in 1986, Mr. Smith directed GM attorneys to seek assurances from a German prosecutor's office that he would not be arrested. He further requested the audit committee of the GM board to conduct its own review to satisfy itself that he had acted properly.[8]

Legal Incentives

Investment incentives enacted to attract foreign investment are an important part of government policy in most developing countries. In a few cases, the regulation of investment through incentive schemes is still the only significant regulation of foreign investment. Although incentive benefits are rarely exclusively reserved for foreign enterprises, in certain countries foreign private investment is in fact the main or sole beneficiary of incentives, because local capital and entrepreneurship cannot undertake the kind of investment encouraged by the incentives. On the other hand, there are some instances where incentives are restricted to local enterprises, joint ventures, or enterprises with a minority foreign participation.

Depending on the basic approach to investment regulation, incentives may be awarded automatically to all enterprises meeting the conditions specified in the relevant legislation, or incentives may be granted for a specific performance or contribution to the host country's economy such as export promotion and diversification, the development of a backward area, the transfer of modern technology, the encouragement of applied research in the host country, and so forth. Incentives also are often awarded on the basis of case-by-case negotiation in accordance with ad hoc criteria.

The main incentive to the establishment of an enterprise is ordinarily an income-tax holiday of several years' duration. Some governments are inclined to reduce the length of such tax holidays when they involve important tax revenue losses. Tax measures such as accelerated depreciation (which are often used in developed countries as stimulants to investment) have proven less effective for various reasons as incentives in the economic environment of developing countries where the main interest is in new investment rather than the encouragement of expenditure on plant replacement. Other fiscal incentives obtainable in developing countries include the waiver of import duties on equipment and materials essential for production, exemptions from property taxes, and numerous minor tax concessions granted by the provinces or localities where the enterprise is located.

Restrictive Trading Laws

In addition to the tax incentive laws, many governments adopt measures that restrict imports or artificially stimulate exports. Usually such laws are referred to as nontariff barriers to international trade. There are several major types of nontariff barriers.

- *Government participation in trade*: subsidies, countervailing duties, government procurement, and state trading

- *Customs and entry procedures*: valuation, classification, documentation, and health and safety regulations

- *Standards*: product standards, packaging, and labeling and marking

- *Specific limitations*: quotas, exchange controls, import restraints, and licensing

- *Import charges*: prior import credit restrictions for imports, special duties, and variable levies

    For example, suppose Germany imposes an 11 percent value-added tax on a domestic product and a 13 percent tax adjustment at the border on a product of identical price and quality imported from the U.S. This would induce German buyers to choose the German product over the U.S. import because the tax is 2 percent lower. On the contrary, if a German exporter were given a rebate of 13 percent, he would be able to sell at 2 percent below U.S. price levels and would benefit from an equivalent export subsidy.[9]

- *Other measures*: voluntary export restraints whereby agreement is made between two trading countries to limit the exports of a specific product to a particular level, such as the agreement between Japan and the U.S. in the 1980s to limit Japanese car exports to the U.S.; and orderly marketing agreements, which are specific agreements between trading partners whereby they agree to negotiate trade restrictions (see International Marketing Highlight 9.2).

International Marketing Highlight 9.2

Tough Move on Gum Control

Like spitting, public chewing may wind up on the wrong side of the law in the sternly ruled island republic of Singapore. The government has banned the manufacture, sale, and importation of chewing gum. Mere possession of the stuff is not illegal yet, but offending sellers face fines of up to $1,200 and importers could get a year in jail. Gum, explains a government spokesman, "causes filthiness to our public facilities."

Singapore's subway trains have been halted several times recently when wads of chewing gum jammed their doors. The gum lobby argues that gum does not clog doors, people do. The government is unmoved.

Gum fanciers arriving from abroad must declare any gum they have with them on their customs forms. They will be allowed to bring in small amounts for their personal use, but the government reserves the right to define how much that may be.

Source: Time, January 13, 1992, p. 31.

U.S. Laws

Both U.S. corporations and their U.S. officers working abroad remain liable to the laws of the U.S. For instance, individuals must comply with U.S. Internal Revenue Service (IRS) laws and corporations are bound by U.S. antitrust laws. One application of the U.S. antitrust laws to an American company overseas is the Gillette Company case. In a February 1968 suit, the Justice Department sought an injunction against Gillette for its acquisition of shares in Braun AG of Germany. The Justice Department held that Gillette's acquisition of Braun would restrict competition in shaving devices in the U.S., given the fact that Braun makes electric razors and that Braun had previously relinquished to a third company its rights to sell in the U.S. market until 1976.[10]

There are some laws, however, that have been specially enacted to direct multinational marketing activities such as the Foreign Corrupt Practices Act of 1977. Basically, the intention of these laws is to protect American economic interests, ensure national security, maintain recognized standards of ethics, and promote fair competition. There are particular U.S. laws that a marketer should pay heed to when engaged in international activities.

Laws Affecting Foreign Trade

The U.S., relative to other nations, has a liberal attitude toward exports and imports. However, there are many regulations that an exporter must be aware of in the conduct of business. The government prohibits trading with some nations, for example, Iran and Cuba, and, until recently, Vietnam. Likewise, exportation of several products, among them defense-related equipment, must be cleared with the U.S. Department of Commerce by obtaining a license permitting shipment (licensing requirements will be discussed in Chapter 17). The Omnibus Trade and Competitiveness Act of 1988 affects U.S. exporters in many ways (principal features of this act are discussed in Chapter 2).

The government of the U.S. also imposes restrictions, via the IRS, on pricing for intracompany foreign transactions. The IRS ensures that prices are not underestimated to save U.S. taxes. For example, a U.S. corporation may export certain goods to its subsidiary, say, in Germany, at a very low price. This would reduce the corporation's U.S. taxes. It is for this reason that the IRS is authorized to review pricing and demand change, if necessary, in such company-to-company overseas transfers.

In regard to imports, the U.S. markets traditionally were open to all nations with few restrictions. However, for health and safety reasons, food products from many developing countries are prohibited. For example, in 1985 the Food and Drug Administration detained Sri Lankan tea imports for special testing following terrorist threats to contaminate that nation's black tea with cyanide. Sri Lanka provides about 11 percent of U.S. tea imports, or about 21 million pounds of black tea annually. Another example occurred in 1989. For several weeks, Chilean grapes and other fruits were prohibited from entering the U.S., since some of these products had been poisoned.

While the federal government basically subscribes to free trade and has supported through GATT the worldwide effort toward this goal, various legislative and nonlegislative measures have been adopted to protect domestic U.S. industry. However, things changed in the 1970s when more and more U.S. companies showed signs of crumbling, often from an inability to compete in the world market. The textile, tire, and auto industries cut production or closed down entire factories, largely because U.S. consum-

Antitrust Laws

ers purchased imports. Consequently, workers and industries applied continuing pressure for tougher tariffs and trade quotas. Thus, for some products, like automobiles, import duties were increased. For other products, like textiles, quotas were imposed on imports from various countries. For steel, the government set minimum prices on imports to make domestic steel competitive.

As noted earlier, the U.S. antitrust laws apply to U.S. corporations in their international dealings as well as in their domestic transactions. More specifically, U.S. businesses must carefully ascertain if antitrust laws would be violated in any way in the following situations:

- When a U.S. firm *acquires* a foreign firm

- When a U.S. firm *engages in a joint venture* abroad with another American company or a foreign firm

- When a U.S. firm *enters into a marketing agreement* with a foreign-based firm[11]

The Justice Department has become very strict in the application of U.S. antitrust laws on foreign operations of U.S. corporations. Justice Department enforcement takes several forms.

- In 1980 the Justice Department initiated criminal grand jury probes into allegations that U.S. and foreign competitors illegally set the prices of uranium, phosphate, and ocean shipping rates.

- In 1985 it reviewed the overseas licensing agreements of some two dozen multinationals to see whether their prices or territorial arrangements unreasonably prevented overseas producers from selling in the U.S.

- In 1987 it investigated oil company reactions to the new two-tier pricing system for foreign crude along with other aspects of their relations with oil-producing countries.

Foreign Corrupt Practices Act (FCPA)

The Foreign Corrupt Practices Act, passed by Congress in 1977, makes stringent antibribery provisions prohibiting all U.S. companies on file with the Securities and Exchange Commission from making any unauthorized payments. These payments include those made to foreign officials, political parties, and/or candidates.[12] The law prescribes a one million dollar penalty to a corporation for violation of the law. Corporate officers connected with illegal payments may be fined $10,000 or be subjected to a 5-year imprisonment, or both.

How FCPA may create hindrances is illustrated with reference to the Coca-Cola Company's deal with the former Soviet Union. In 1986, Coca-Cola signed a $30 million 6-year agreement to expand its business in the U.S.S.R. Until then, Coke was sold only in Moscow shops for tourists, and the company's Fanta orange soda was available in a few other cities. Published reports indicated that the Coca-Cola Company paid bribes to people in the Soviet Union to crack the Soviet market. Subsequently, a federal grand jury initiated an investigation to determine if the allegations of wrongdoing were correct. Although the company was finally proven innocent, it had to endure subpoenas of its documents and other inconveniences to prove its innocence[13] (see International Marketing Highlight 9.3).

In part, the FCPA is an effort to extend American moral standards to other countries. The act also seeks to enlist U.S. MNCs as instruments of U.S. foreign policy. The FCPA, therefore, marks a major attempt by the U.S. government to enforce a series of noneconomic foreign policy objectives through private enterprise, whose principal purpose and rationale has traditionally been considered to be economic. The act places American corporations doing business abroad in an awkward position. On the one hand, they must comply with U.S. law, and on the other, they have to compete with other foreign countries whose governments do not prohibit such payments. In some nations where American business is conducted, bribery is commonplace; the FCPA could weaken the competitive position of U.S. corporations in such countries.[14]

International Marketing Highlight 9.3

Making Payments to Seek Business

In October 1989, a federal grand jury indicted Young & Rubicam on charges it paid kickbacks to Jamaican businessman Arnold Foote, Jr., to help the agency win the tourist account in 1981. According to the indictment, Mr. Foote, in turn bribed Eric Anthony Abrahams, at the time Jamaica's minister of tourism, to award the account to Y&R. The agency subsequently created the award-winning "Come Back to Jamaica" campaign for the tourist board.

As part of the settlement, the Justice Department agreed to drop charges that Y&R violated federal racketeering prohibitions. However, the agency pleaded guilty to conspiring to violate the Foreign Corrupt Practices Act, and to making $132,000 in payments.

In making the plea, Young & Rubicam acknowledged that it had "reason to know" that when it paid Mr. Foote, he would in turn make payments to the tourism minister, Mr. Abrahams. The ad agency paid a $500,000 fine to end the case.

Source: The Wall Street Journal, February 12, 1990, p. B4.

Although macroeconomic research on the subject shows that the FCPA did not adversely affect U.S. trade,[15] the U.S. cannot force its moral principles and concepts of right and wrong on the whole world. Questionable payments will continue whether U.S. corporations participate or not. International bribery might be controlled through an international agreement effected through WTO or the IMF.

The Omnibus Trade and Competitiveness Act of 1988 amended the FCPA in many respects to lessen concern among U.S. companies about the scope of the statute. The primary change concerns payments to third parties by a U.S. firm "knowing or having reason to know" that the third party would use the payment for prohibited purposes. Under the new law, the U.S. firm must have actual knowledge of or willful blindness to the prohibited use of the payment. The act also clarifies the types of payments that are permissible and do not run afoul of the prohibition against bribery.[16] For example, under the FCPA as originally enacted, payments to low-level officials who exercise only "ministerial" or "clerical" functions were exempt. Unfortunately, this provision provided little guidance to companies in determining whether a given foreign official exercised discretionary authority: special problems arose in countries in the Middle East and Africa where foreign officials can be employed part-time. The trade act provides a U.S. business with better guidance by specifying the types of payments that are permissible rather than which individuals can receive them. The act specifies that a payment for a routine governmental action such as processing papers, stamping visas, and scheduling inspections, may be made without subjecting the businessperson to the worry of whether this type of payment may lead to criminal liability. The changes in the law make it easier for U.S. exporters to do business in foreign countries by removing concerns about inadvertent violations.

Antiboycott Laws

From time to time nations attempt to put pressure on each other through programs of economic boycott. The early 1980s Arab boycott of companies doing business with Israel is an example of such a tactic. Most Arab states did not recognize Israel and hoped that an economic boycott would contribute to Israel's collapse.

The oil fortunes of the Arab countries gave them significant economic clout to implement the boycott. The Arab boycott blacklisted companies that dealt with Israel with the intention of squeezing Israel from all directions and forcing the country into economic isolation.

The U.S. government adopted various measures to prevent U.S. companies from complying with the Arab boycott. For example, the Tax Reform Act of 1976 included a measure that denied foreign income tax benefits to companies that subscribed to the boycott. The law preempts any state or local regulations dealing with boycotts fostered or imposed by foreign countries.[17]

The Arab boycott crumbled toward the end of the 1980s, making it easier for U.S. companies to continue their operations in Israel, and at the same time seek out business in Arab states. For example, Coca-Cola began making inroads into the Gulf, Lebanon, Jordan, and Saudi Arabia as the boycott became ineffective.[18]

Laws to Protect Domestic Industry

The U.S. government has legislated many laws to protect domestic industry. From time to time, the government sets quotas on imports. For a number of years the sugar import quotas were set so as to preserve about half the market for U.S. producers. Often, quotas are split among several countries interested in exporting to the U.S. Such allocation is partly influenced by political considerations. For example, a certain proportion of a quota may be assigned to a developing country even though its price is higher than that of other exporters. For a few years early in the 1980s, the U.S. government had imposed quotas on Japanese car imports. Recently, a debate has been going on in the federal government about limiting Japanese textile exports to the U.S. by establishing quotas for different categories of textiles.

Quotas, while providing relief to domestic industry, turn out to be only temporarily effective. In the long run, a domestic industry must stand on its own. If a domestic industry is inherently inefficient, quotas amount to a support of inefficiency, which is counterproductive. However, if quotas are used to buy time so an infant industry can mature and compete effectively, that may be appropriate and productive.[19]

Laws to Eliminate Tax Loopholes

There are many federal laws meant to eliminate tax loopholes. A prominent example is legislation against tax havens. *Tax havens* are countries that provide out-of-the-ordinary privileges to multinationals in order to attract them to their lands. Tax havens make it more profitable for companies to locate there than in the U.S. Doucet and Good categorize four types of tax havens:

1. Countries with no taxes at all such as the Bahamas, Bermuda, and the Cayman Islands.
2. Countries with taxes at low rates such as the British Virgin Islands.
3. Havens that tax income from domestic sources but exempt income from foreign sources, such as Hong Kong, Liberia, and Panama.
4. Countries that allow special privileges, which generally are suitable as tax havens only for limited purposes.[20]

Corporations find tax havens a legal way to save on taxes. Their response, however, to a country's offer is not motivated simply by tax benefits alone. Political stability in the country, availability of adequate means of communication and transportation, economic freedom for currency conversion, and availability of professional services serve as important criteria when a company locates itself in a tax haven.[21]

Tax Treaties

Tax treaties are arrangements between nations that prevent corporate and individual income from being double-taxed. The U.S. has tax treaties with over 42 nations. Thus, foreigners who own securities in U.S. corporations and who are from countries with which there is a tax treaty pay a withholding tax of about 15 percent, while those from non-tax treaty countries pay a 30 percent tax.

The tax treaties are meant to provide a fair deal to individuals and corporations from friendly countries, which encourages mutually beneficial economic activity. Usually, under a tax treaty, the country where the primary business activity takes place is provided the right to be the principal receiver of tax revenue. A small proportion of the tax, however, may accrue to the other nation. Take, for example, the case of a Pakistani exporter with a business in the U.S. Since there is a tax treaty between the U.S. and Pakistan, the income of the Pakistani businessman, as far as his U.S. operations are concerned, would be taxable under the U.S. IRS rules. However, he would pay only a negligible tax in Pakistan.

Businesses, particularly the MNCs, use tax treaties in various ways to seek maximum benefits. Consider the following situations:[22]

- A tax treaty between the U.S. and England requires a 15 percent withholding tax on dividends.
- A tax treaty between the U.S. and the Netherlands specifies a 5 percent withholding tax.
- A tax treaty between the Netherlands and Great Britain calls for a 5 percent withholding tax. Additionally, dividends from foreign sources are not taxed in the Netherlands.

According to these arrangements, a U.S. company may establish a holding company in the Netherlands, which might receive dividend income from a British subsidiary.

U.S. Government Support

Finally, the dividends may be remitted to the parent company in the U.S. The combined tax in the whole process will amount to 10 percent rather than 15 percent.

Tax treaties between the U.S. and different countries are reviewed from time to time. This permits periodic changes in treaty agreements to accommodate changes in the country's domestic monetary and fiscal policies. Usually, a treaty spells out the procedure for consultation and negotiation between officials of the two countries, should disagreements occur.

Nations provide many kinds of support to their companies to enable them to compete successfully for foreign business. For example, companies belonging to EU countries are often eligible for such government support as low-cost or no-cost bank guarantees, low-cost or no-cost working capital loans, and protection from price escalation.

Traditionally, this type of support has not been available from the U.S. government. In the fall of 1985, however, the U.S. government established a program of bank guarantees, similar to those of EU countries.[23] Congress approved the creation of a "war chest" of $300 million to allow the Export-Import Bank to match or beat competitors' subsidies for the benefit of U.S. exporters (see International Marketing Highlight 9.4). In 1992, under pressure from the U.S. during President Bush's trip to Japan, the Japanese automakers promised to increase their purchases of U.S. parts from $9 billion annually to $19 billion in 4 years and import an estimated 20,000 more U.S. cars a year.[24] However, this program did not go far.

International Marketing Highlight 9.4

U.S. Subsidizes Big Food Companies in Their Search for Foreign Markets

McDonald's got $465,000 from the U.S. Agriculture Department in 1991 for ads, paper tray liners, and counter displays promoting Chicken McNuggets to customers around the world.

Campbell Soup Co. spent part of the $450,000 it got from the government to remind the people of Japan, Korea, Argentina, and Taiwan to have a V8 juice. Joseph E. Seagram and Sons touted its Four Roses whiskey in Europe and the Far East with $146,000 from the department.

The three companies are among dozens of well-known corporate giants that have collected money under a U.S.D.A. program to find new overseas market for U.S. food, candy, bourbon, wine, ginseng, cotton, mink pelts, and bovine semen.

The $200-million-a-year Market Promotion Program is supposed to help U.S. farmers by promoting exports of products that contain at least 50 percent U.S. agricultural commodities.

Two-thirds of the grants in 1991 went to industry associations that conduct promotions for products such as strawberries, kiwis, or cling peaches.

The remainder went to a long list of companies to advertise their brand-name products. Those brands include Burger King, M&M-Mars, Hershey Foods, Del Monte, Welch's, Ocean Spray Cranberries, Nabisco, and Quaker Oats.

Source: Marketing News, March 2, 1992, p. 7.

In October 1994, however, America and Japan made four new trade deals.[25] Two of these deals made it easier for Americans (and other foreigners) to sell telecom equipment to the Japanese government and to NTT, Japan's biggest telephone firm, which is 65 percent state-owned. The third deal helped foreign firms to seek government's contracts to supply medical equipment. The fourth deal clarified regulations in the Japanese insurance market, permitting companies to change premium and introduce new products without permission from regulators.

International Laws

A variety of international laws regulate business across national borders. International law is an area of study in and of itself. It would be impossible to discuss here, even perfunctorily, all the different types of international laws related to business. The General Agreement on Tariff and Trade (GATT), the International Monetary Fund (IMF), and the World Bank were discussed in Chapter 3. Agreements under these institutions compose international laws of sorts that influence business in different ways. The GATT (now WTO) regulations are particularly relevant for marketers since they deal with trade restrictions and barriers that affect market potential.

To give the reader an idea of other areas covered by international law and the agencies that administer these laws, a brief discussion of particular international laws follows.

Protection of Property

Property here refers to patents, trademarks, and the like. In the U.S., businesses seek protection of their property under U.S. laws. For example, a trademark can be registered. In an overseas situation, a multinational enterprise runs the risk of piracy. Stories are told that jeans manufactured in Hong Kong are given the Calvin Klein brand name and sold in Europe at half the usual price. Computer pirates in Taiwan incur the wrath of IBM Corporation. IBM-compatible computers are sold widely in Taiwan by scores of small companies, who manufacture counterfeit machines in violation of IBM's copyrights.[26] The U.S. Patent Trademark Office estimates that intellectual property losses for U.S. industry, measured in terms of lost licensing opportunities and cost of enforcement, totaled at least $30 billion in 1998 alone[27] (see International Marketing Highlight 9.5).

Companies spend millions of dollars to build up and establish trademarks and brand names. Consider, for example, Coca-Cola, Tide, and Corningware's cornflower pattern. If a foreign firm steals a company's established brand name and uses it on a locally conceived and manufactured product, the interests of the established company could be hurt. It would mean not only losing potential markets, but also perhaps gaining a bad name for poor performance if a disappointed customer did not know that a product was an imitation.

U.S. companies are particularly susceptible to piracy because of their lead in many technologies and number of household brand names.

In 1992, a federal jury ordered Minolta Camera Co. to pay Honeywell Inc. $96 million for infringing two Honeywell patents in its autofocus cameras.[28] The intellectual property protection problem, however, is not limited to U.S. companies. Multinationals from other parts of the world face similar problems. For example, Hitachi Ltd. has accused Korea's Samsung Electronics Co. of using its technology to make dynamic random access memory chips. Hitachi also has a problem with the U.S.'s Motorola, Inc. It has sued the latter, charging that its MC88200 chip infringes on a Hitachi patent.[29]

The traditional way of protecting property outside the home country is by obtaining parallel protection in each host country. This process, however, is cumbersome and expensive. For example, it cost one large company almost $2 million to obtain foreign patents. This process is diverse, expensive, and is replete with risks that the patent will not be granted because the standards for patentability in some countries are not compatible with accepted practices in other countries. Fortunately, there are international conventions and agreements that can make it easier to secure property rights.

International Marketing Highlight 9.5

Rounding Up Counterfeiters

Levi Strauss & Co. touts its trousers as "America's original jeans." But these days, so do a lot of others. The famous apparel maker is fighting an unprecedented explosion of counterfeit pants. In 1991, Levi seized 1.3 million pairs of knockoffs, more than 5 times as many as it usually confiscates in a year. But the new knockoffs, most of which are made in China, differ from the crude copies the company has seen in the past.

Counterfeiters have crossed the threshold. The typical consumer would not be able to detect that they are buying counterfeits. The fakes bear labels saying that they're made in the U.S. and proclaiming that their colored tab and stitched pocket design are registered trademarks to help you identify garments made only by Levi Strauss & Co.

Only someone well-versed in the "construction and engineering" of Levis could tell the difference. There are a few identifying marks on the real McCoys, but Levi doesn't want to tell consumers what they are for fear of tipping its hand to counterfeiters. (One difference is that real Levi labels note that they are "made from recycled paper.")

Though the fake Levis look nearly identical, the company contends they may fall apart at the seams. After a few washes, belt loops fall off, rivets rust, and shrinkage control is not what it should be. Levi contends that poor-quality jeans will hurt its reputation.

Counterfeiters are trying to cash in on the huge demand for Levi jeans overseas. Though fakes have been seized in 31 countries, most are destined for the booming European market, where Levis are a status symbol, commanding up to $100 a pair. In 1990 alone, the company's sales in Europe, where Levi sells mostly jeans, rose 55 percent. But Levi can't meet worldwide demand for its best-selling button-fly "501" jeans, most of which are manufactured in the U.S.

Counterfeiters are eager to take up the slack. To combat them, Levi has spent about $2 million on more than 600 investigations, relying on a network of informants in Asia and Europe and trying to build paper trails on the middlemen who drive the market.

Source: *The Wall Street Journal*, February 19, 1992, p. B1.

Before describing these conventions, however, it should be noted that overall international arrangements for property protection are insufficient and inadequate, and brand name/trademark piracy is not actually alleviated. The real problem arises when the question of copyright infringement is not clear cut. Consider the fight between Lego System (a Danish company), the world's leading maker of children's building blocks, and a U.S. company, Tyco, popularly known for its model trains. Tyco spotted Lego's lack of competition and launched its own high-quality Lego copies called Super Blocks at retail prices 25 percent below Lego's. Thanks in part to its hard-hitting advertising campaign ("If you can't tell the difference, why pay the difference?"), in 1986 Tyco captured more than one-fifth of the $100 million U.S. market for blocks. Lego sued Tyco for copyright infringement in Hong Kong, where Tyco's blocks were made before production was shifted to Taiwan. Following a trial in 1986 that cost each company $2 million, the Hong Kong lower court decided in favor of Lego. However, the appeals court reversed parts of the decision, and both toy makers have appealed to the London Court of Arbitration. In early 1987, the London court upheld the decision of the appeals court.[30]

Interestingly, owing to philosophical differences between code and common law, sometimes injured parties lose in legal dispute. For example, under common law, the right to property is established by actual use, while under code law the right emerges from legal registration. Thus, if a pirate registered a well-known brand (say, Colgate) in a code-law country (say, Italy), in a legal dispute the actual owner (the Colgate Palmolive Company) may lose to the pirate, at least in Italy. Of course, if the country in question happens to be a friendly country, the U.S. government may be willing to help.

There are several important international conventions for property protection:

International Bureau for the Protection of Industrial Property. This bureau was established by the Paris Convention, to which over 50 nations including the U.S. subscribed. Currently the membership includes some 94 countries. Under this convention, once a company has filed for a patent in one country, it has priority for 12 months in seeking the patent in all other member countries. Further, the convention requires each member country to extend to the nationals of other member countries the same rights it provides to its own nationals.

The Inter-American Convention. Most Latin American countries and the U.S. are parties to this convention. This convention provides its members protection similar to that of the Paris Convention for inventions, patents, designs, and models.

Madrid Arrangement for International Registration of Trademarks. This forum has 26 members in Europe. The U.S. is not a member of the Madrid Convention. Under the Madrid arrangement, the member countries grant automatic registration in all countries through registration in one of the countries upon payment of the required fee. For example, if a company registers a trademark in Spain, a member country, registration is simultaneously ensured in the other 25 member countries after the appropriate payments are made.

The Trademark Registration Treaty. In the early 1970s, 16 European nations signed a convention to establish a European patent office. Under this convention, the patent office makes one grant for all the member countries under a single European patent law. The European patent office became operational in 1978 in Munich, Germany.

Intellectual property protection has improved in several problem countries in recent years (particularly Taiwan, Indonesia, and China). This has largely been the result of political pressure from the U.S. (see International Marketing Highlight 9.6). The following is a checklist for guarding intellectual property protection:[31]

- Find out how the country protects intellectual property, if at all.

- Register your copyrights and trademarks in countries in which you do business.

- Clearly spell out dispute resolution procedures in contracts.

- Explore entering into licensing contracts with likely problem competitors, especially in countries without strong intellectual property laws.

- Consider distributing only older material overseas, especially in countries where the state of technology is somewhat less advanced.

- Establish relations and cooperate with local customs officials and police.

- Hire a private investigator to gather evidence of piracy and work with local officials.

International Marketing Highlight 9.6

Saudi Copyright Law

Saudi Arabia passed a copyright law to curb widespread piracy of such material as videotapes and computer software. The law, approved by King Fahd in December 1989, was in response to pressure from the U.S., where the Motion Picture Association of America has claimed industry losses of about $200 million a year due to piracy of videotapes in Saudi Arabia alone. The new law strictly forbids piracy, but diplomatic sources said much will depend on how the Saudis enforce the law.

Source: The Wall Street Journal, January 18, 1990, p. A16.

UN Treaties and Conventions

The United Nations has established a number of autonomous bodies and agencies to encourage worldwide economic cooperation and prosperity.

World Health Organization. WHO's work concerns the improvement of health conditions. It deals with such matters as drug standardization, epidemic control, health delivery systems, and related programs.

International Civil Aviation Organization. ICAO promotes safe and efficient air travel through regulating flow of air traffic, air-worthiness standards, airport operations, and related communications.

International Telecommunications Union. ITU regulates international communications via radio, telephone, and telegraph. For example, ITU controls and allocates radio frequencies and facilitates intercountry telegraph and telephone communications.

Universal Postal Union. UPU facilitates postal communication. For example, it conducts settlements among nations related to revenue sharing.

International Labor Organization. ILO protects workers' rights, promotes worker welfare, and enhances the effectiveness of their organizations.

International Telecommunications Satellite Consortium. INTELSAT deals with matters of telecommunication. Its work mainly concerns new satellite communications technology.

International Standards Organization. ISO is another specialized UN agency. It is particularly important because its administration bears directly on marketing. ISO promotes standardization of different products and processes. The ultimate purpose is to encourage world trade and business without hindrance from design/style/feature variations among nations. As an example, the ISO has over 100 committees that are actively engaged in developing uniform international standards in various fields.

The impact of these agencies on international business varies. (For example, an airframe industry is affected by the ICAO regulations; a WHO agreement might apply to a pharmaceutical company.) But the importance of the need for standardization does not vary. For example, a grinding machine still usable in the U.S. might be unsuitable in England for such reasons as differences in electric current and weight measures (in England, power is normally supplied at 220 volts and the metric system is used). Thus, in order to sell a U.S.-made grinding machine, the tolerance measurement may have to be varied to conform to measurements commonly used in Great Britain. Similarly, the electrical wiring may require change for the machine to operate with a different supply power.

Consider the European telecommunications industry:

In Spain, the busy signal is three pips a second; in Denmark it's two. Telephone numbers within French cities are seven digits long; in Italy they're almost any length. German phones run on 60 volts of electricity; elsewhere, it's 49. Only about 30 percent of the technical specifications involved in phone systems are common from one country to the next.[32]

Needless to say, standardization in the European telecommunications industry is overdue.

Metric Transition

The differences in standards are among the major hindrances to world trade and business development. These differences have led to market opportunity losses for U.S. companies in many nations. This is another area where international cooperation is overdue. Traditionally, U.S. industry and government have played almost no role in seeking common standards worldwide. This may be attributed to the fact that the overseas business of U.S. firms is proportionately small. In the future, however, U.S. businesses are more likely to participate actively in the standardization effort. The U.S. Department of Commerce's National Institute of Standards and Technology (NIST), which previously was known as the National Bureau of Standards (NBS), has been given several new assignments to boost U.S. industry in the world marketplace by seeking standardization. The assignments result from the 1988 Omnibus Trade and Competitiveness Act, which addresses the problem by moving the U.S. closer to the metric system, now used by most of the world's population. The "inch-pound" system of measurement used in the U.S., known as the "Customary" or "English" system, was abandoned even by the English when the U.K. switched to the metric system in the early 1970s.

The 1988 act states that the metric system is "the preferred system of weights and measures for U.S. trade and commerce." It directs the federal government to provide leadership in metric conversion and calls for a preference in government purchasing for metric products. The act requires federal agencies to use the metric system wherever it is practical to do so in procurements, grants, and other business-related activities, by October 1, 1992. The agencies have notified grantees, contractors, and suppliers of the new requirements and of time schedules for meeting the government's deadline.

The act specifies that the federal government has a responsibility to develop procedures and techniques to assist industry, especially small business, as it voluntarily converts to the metric system. Individual groups and industries are still free to decide whether to convert and to determine conversion timetables according to their own needs.

The trade act requires government and industry to use metric units in documentation of exports and imports as prescribed by the International Convention on the Harmonized Commodity Description and Coding System. The Harmonized System is an international goods classification system designed to standardize commodity classification for all major trading nations. The international metric system (SI) is the official measurement system of the Harmonized System.

Congress spelled out in the act the reasons it believes the U.S. would benefit from converting to the metric system:

World trade is increasingly geared toward the metric system of measurement.

Industry in the U.S. is often at a competitive disadvantage when dealing in international markets because of its nonstandard measurement system, and is sometimes excluded when it is unable to deliver goods that are measured in metric system.

The inherent simplicity of the metric system of measurement and standardization of weights and measures has led to major cost savings in certain industries that have converted to that system.

The metric system of measurement can provide substantial advantages to the Federal Government in its own operations.[33]

The EU is proceeding aggressively with plans to standardize differing national specifications and testing and certification procedures into a single EU-wide body of uniform standards and regulations. This can offer real advantages to U.S. businesspeople interested in a large market for their goods. A U.S. product that meets the EU requirements in one member state can then be freely marketed throughout the European Union.

UN Guidelines on Consumer Protection

After more than six years of work, in April 1985 the United Nations General Assembly adopted by consensus a set of guidelines on consumer protection. The guidelines cover the following basic consumer principles:[34]

- Insurance of the physical safety of consumers and their protection from potential dangers caused by consumer products
- Protection of consumers' economic interests

- Consumers' access to the necessary information to make informed choices according to their individual wishes and needs
- Availability of effective consumer redress
- Freedom to form consumer groups or organizations and the opportunity of such organizations to be consulted and to have their views represented

These guidelines are important because without acceptance of such principles and strong information links on products that have been banned or severely restricted in various countries, sales could continue unabated. In other words, profit motive may override consideration for the harm many products may induce.

Implementation of these guidelines by countries currently lacking adequate consumer protection will enable them to cope with these and similar consumer problems.

Regional Laws

Regional laws pertain to specific areas involving a group of countries tied together through some kind of regional economic cooperation. (Chapter 5 examined different forms of regional groupings.)

Market groups may legislate laws applicable to MNCs conducting business within the member countries. The most progressive market agreement is represented by the European Union. The EU has debated a variety of legislative measures that would deeply affect multinational enterprises. For example, there was consideration of a proposal that would not only force the head offices of MNCs with European-based subsidiaries to make disclosures of their global operations to local labor unions twice a year, but also would oblige them to inform and consult with the labor unions on any major decision affecting workers. Another proposal would require MNCs to consolidate the accounts of European subsidiaries. A third proposal, related to product-liability standards, would effectively eliminate the need for plaintiffs to show negligence to justify injury claims. Under a fourth proposal, workers would sit on the boards of all public companies. The most radical of all is a proposal to make corporate directors *personally* liable for damages should minority stockholders or creditors or even employees of a subsidiary suffer as a result of a corporate headquarters' decision favoring the interests of the parent company and its stockholders.[35]

These kinds of proposals are not accepted quickly; the EU lawmaking process in unparalleled for ponderousness. Proposals to harmonize the national laws of the 12 members of the EU must first be endorsed by a majority of the 16 European commissioners (2 each from Britain, France, Germany, and Italy, 1 each from the rest, and all appointed for 4-year terms by their governments). Draft-stage directives then go to the 460-member European Parliament in Strasbourg, whose main role is to propose amendments for the commissioners' consideration. After receiving the parliament's views, the commission prepares a final draft of the directive and submits it to the Council of Ministers, composed of the appropriate cabinet-level officers from each national government. With the council's consent, a proposal becomes a legally binding EU directive, but even then it does not become law automatically. Enacting legislation to fulfill the intent of EU directives remains a prerogative of national parliaments. For example, in 1985 a European Union product liability directive was adopted by the Council of Ministers after more than eight years of talks. The directive allows consumers to collect damages for injuries from defective products without showing that the manufacturer was at fault. Member nations should pass laws that comply with the directive within three years, which they did.

Arbitration

Despite their best efforts, U.S. business people working at the international level may run into difficulties from time to time with people, companies, and/or organizations in foreign countries. The conflict may be with the host country government; a native firm, either in the public or private sector; or a multinational firm belonging to a third country. The difficulty may arise because of differing interpretations of the contractual terms or because of opposing positions on an ad hoc issue that was not anticipated at the time the contract was made. There are three ways for an international firm to resolve conflicts. First, the two parties mutually agree to settle the differences. Second, the firm decides to sue the other party. Third, the conflicting parties agree to arbitration. Of the three alternatives, the first one is the best, if at all possible. Usually, however, the conflicting parties cannot realistically be expected to resolve their differences between themselves. As far as legal action is concerned, for a variety of reasons, it may not be in the best long-term interest of the international marketer. Legal action against a native firm would surely affect the reputation of the foreign enterprise, no matter how strong the case of the latter might be. Further, there is no guarantee that the court would make a fair, unbiased decision on behalf of the domestic party. Finally, the legal route can be messy, time consuming, and expensive.

For example, taking legal action in a trade case can range from an average $54,700 for a Section 301 violation (an unfair foreign trade practice) to $715,000 or more for a Section 337 case (an infringement or theft of intellectual property rights such as patents, trademarks, and copyrights.) Similarly, legal costs in a dumping case may range from $151,000 to $553,000, while an import threat to national security may cost $181,300 to $537,500.[36]

Therefore, arbitration is usually the best recourse of a multinational firm to resolve conflict in a foreign environment. *Arbitration* can be defined as a process of settling disputes by referring the matter to a disinterested party for a review of the merits of the case and for a judgment, which may or may not be binding on the conflicting parties. Traditionally, the disputing parties resorted to ad hoc arrangements for arbitration because prior to 1966 there was no international authority to serve as arbitrator between an international marketer and a host country party. Currently, there are a number of arrangements available for arbitration.

1. *The International Center for Settlement of Investment Disputes (ICSID)* was established in 1966 by the World Bank convention to enable private investors to obtain redress against a foreign state for grievances arising out of an investment dispute. The convention established strict rules for arbitration that may explain in part why it is seldom used:

   The Convention provides that, where both parties have consented to arbitration under the auspices of the Center, neither may withdraw its consent unilaterally; and should either party refuse to submit to the jurisdiction of the Center thereafter, an award can nevertheless be entered which will be final, binding, and enforceable without relitigation, in all nations that are members of the Convention. To facilitate the enforcement of awards, each member nation is obliged to designate a domestic court or other authority responsible for enforcement of awards made.[37]

ICSID has not been able to play the role expected by the signatories who created the convention. The problem is that large developing countries, important prospects for direct foreign investment, are not ICSID members. Most of Latin American countries are among the nonsignatories; they subscribe to the Calvo doctrine for representation of their position. *The Calvo doctrine*, named after an Argentine jurist, provides that a foreign investor by virtue of making an investment implicitly agrees to be treated by the host government as a national and gives up the right to involve any outside agency or home government in the resolution of a dispute.

In brief, ICSID has received lukewarm support from host countries as an arbitrator of disputes.

2. *The Inter-American Commercial Arbitration Commission* serves to arbitrate disputes between businesses of 21 Western hemisphere countries including the U.S.
3. *The International Chamber of Commerce (ICC)* is an association of chambers of commerce worldwide. It has established a court of arbitration that has set rules used in conducting arbitration proceedings.

   Perhaps of all the arrangements for arbitration, ICC is the most successful. Of the over 200 decisions that the ICC Court of Arbitration made in recent years, only about 24 were questioned by the disputants. Of these 24, 21 decisions were upheld in the courts when further legal action was pursued.

   The ICC arbitration procedure is rather simple. In the first instance, it tries to settle the dispute through mutual conciliation. If that fails, each party is allowed to choose one member of the Court of Arbitration from its current list of distinguished lawyers/jurists/judges. The third member is appointed by ICC. The Court of Arbitration schedules hearings and, after reviewing the facts presented by the plaintiff and the defendant, makes a decision.
4. *The American Arbitration Association (AAA)* is basically a U.S. tribunal originally established to conduct arbitration among businesses in the U.S. More recently, the AAA extended the scope of its activities outside the U.S.
5. *The Canadian-American Commercial Arbitration Commission (CACAC)* serves as arbitrator between U.S. and Canadian businesses.
6. *The London Court of Arbitration* has jurisdiction that is restricted to cases that should legally be arbitrated in the U.K. The decisions of this court are legally binding on the parties in dispute under the English law.

A number of other agencies and organizations arbitrate in disputes about foreign direct investment. One of these is the *International Court of Justice (ICJ)*. ICJ, also sometimes referred to as the World Court, is a special judicial UN agency. ICJ can be approached for the arbitration of disputes between sovereign nations. Thus, if the U.S. government decides to take up a matter on behalf of a U.S. company that is in a conflict with a government overseas, the dispute can be referred to ICJ for decision. Needless to say, the federal government would pursue the matter only if it involved a national issue. Since ICJ only deals with disputes between nations, and not those between individuals or their companies, and since the government would involve itself only if the matter is of national importance, ICJ has not been extensively used for the settlement of investment disputes.

Another agency is the *Permanent Court of Arbitration (PCA)*. The PCA was established by the Hague Conventions of 1899 and 1907. It consists of a small bureau at the Hague and a panel of arbitrators, four from each member country. The arbitrators are chosen from the panel members whenever a case must be examined. PCA has played an insignificant role in connection with international investment disputes. Like the ICJ, use of PCA for arbitration in international investment disputes comes only through the U.S. federal government.

Finally, arbitration may also be conducted by the various *International Claims Commission (ICC)*. The ICC is an ad hoc arbitration arrangement. When a substantial number of claims between two countries accumulate, an ICC arbitration tribunal may be established by agreement between the interested nations. ICC's use requires that the U.S. government espouse and raise the MNC's claim against the other nation. To invoke the jurisdiction of any of the last three bodies, the foreign nation in question must consent to arbitration.

Summary

A U.S. corporation involved in international marketing should comply not only with U.S. laws but also with host country laws. Worldwide, different countries follow different sets of laws. An international marketer should be particularly familiar with host country laws pertaining to competition, price setting, distribution arrangements, product liability, patents and trademarks, and advertising.

To fully grasp a country's laws, it is essential to understand the legal philosophy of the country. Countries may follow common law or code law. Common law is based on precedents and practices; England, for example, is a common-law country. Code law is based on detailed rules; Mexico, for example, is a code-law country. The legal basis of a country can affect marketing decisions in multifaceted ways.

Another important legal environment aspect is the jurisdiction of laws. The question of which laws will apply in which particular matters must be known. In some instances, those of the country where the agreement was made apply; in others, those of the country where the business was conducted apply. It is desirable to have a jurisdictional clause in agreements. If there is none, when a conflict of interest occurs, it may either be settled through litigation or be referred for arbitration.

In addition to heeding both U.S. and host country laws, international marketers must be aware of treaties and international conventions. By and large, the relevant laws of the host country would be those concerning tariffs, dumping, export/import licensing, foreign investment, foreign investment incentives (provided by the government to attract foreign business), and restrictions on trading activities. The relevant U.S. laws would be those affecting foreign trade, antitrust laws, antiboycott laws, laws to protect domestic industry, laws to prevent loopholes in the existing tax laws (tax haven laws), tax treaties, and laws that pertain to U.S. government support of U.S. business abroad.

Some international treaties and conventions are concerned with the protection of property such as patents, trademarks, models, and the like, in foreign countries. Some international laws have provisions for the encouragement of both worldwide economic cooperation and prosperity and the realization of international products and processes standardization.

If a legal conflict occurs between parties from different countries, one way of resolving it is through arbitration. There are a number of organizations available for arbitration of disputes: the International Center for Settlement of Investment Disputes, the Inter-American Commercial Arbitration Commission, the International Chamber of Commerce, the American Arbitration Association, the Canadian-American Commercial Arbitration Commission, and the London Court of Arbitration.

Review Questions

1. Distinguish between code law and common law. Illustrate how the differences between the two may affect marketing decisions.
2. Explain how one might determine which country's laws would be applicable in the event of a dispute.
3. Define the term *dumping*. Why do countries pass antidumping laws?
4. Do U.S. antitrust laws apply to U.S. corporations in their international dealings? If so, how does this affect the competitive position of U.S. corporations?
5. What sort of support could the U.S. government provide to help U.S. corporations compete effectively against non-U.S. multinationals?
6. What is arbitration? Discuss the role of the International Chamber of Commerce as an arbitration agency.

Creative Questions

1. Internationally adequate protection of intellectual property rights is important for the U.S. since we as a nation have a higher stake than others in the matter. The recently concluded GATT agreement provides 20 years protection of patents, trademarks, and copyrights for book, software, film. and pharmaceutical industries. Developing countries were given 10 years to phase in patent protection for pharmaceuticals. Is this enough to protect U.S. interests? If not, what additional measures should be adopted?
2. In developing countries, governments have large procurement programs. Often multinational corporations outside the U.S. have high-level government support to successfully compete for these programs. Should the U.S. provide such help to its companies? What if such help leads to government interference in other business matters?

Endnotes

1. *Advertising Age*, April 2, 1988, p. 34.
2. Ford S. Worthy, "Tightwad Taiwan Starts to Spend," *Fortune*, December 5, 1988, p. 177.
3. "Japanese Rice: The End of An Era," *The Economist*, August 20, 1994, p. 52.
4. Aziz Haniffa, "India Accused of Dumping Steel," *India Abroad*, August 6, 1993, p. 24.

5. Warren J. Keegan, *Multinational Marketing Management*, 3rd ed. (Englewood Cliffs, NJ: Prentice-Hall, 1984), p. 346. *Also see* "Antidumping Levies Assessed on Imports from Three Nations," *The Wall Street Journal*, March 7, 1980, p. 14. *Also see* Eduardo Lachica, "Anti-Dumping Suits in the U.S. Get No Relief for Unit of Hanson," *The Wall Street Journal*, June 24, 1992, p. 1.

6. *Asia Wall Street Journal Weekly*, February 21, 1994, p. 8.

7. "President Pitchman," *Business Week*, December 6, 1993, p. 42.

8. Doron P. Levin and Thomas F. O'Boyle, "GM's Chairman Runs into Bizarre Problem Under German Law," *The Wall Street Journal*, June 10, 1987, p. 1.

9. A. O. Cao, "Nontariff Barriers to U.S. Manufactured Exports," *Columbia Journal of World Business*, Summer 1980, p. 95.

10. Raymond Vernon, "Antitrust and International Business," *Harvard Business Review*, September–October 1968, p. 86. *Also see* Robert H. Brumley, "How Antitrust Law Affects International Joint Ventures," *Business America*, November 21, 1988, pp. 2–4.

11. Vern Terpstra, *International Market* (Hinsdale, IL: Dryden Press, 1983). *Also see* "Antitrust Guide in International Operation," United States Department of Justice, Antitrust Division, January 26, 1977, p. 63.

12. *See* "The Destructive Costs of Greasing Palms," *Business Week*, December 6, 1993, p. 133.

13. "Coke Said to Face Inquiry Over Sales in Soviet Union," *The Wall Street Journal*, June 12, 1988, p. 22.

14. Jack G. Kaikati and Wayne A. Label, "American Bribery Legislation: An Obstacle to International Marketing," *Journal of Marketing*, Fall 1980, pp. 38–43. *Also see* Brooks Jackson, "Overseas Bribery Gets a Lot Less Attention After Cutbacks by the Justice Department," *The Wall Street Journal*, February 22, 1983, p. 33.

15. *See* John L. Graham, "Foreign Corrupt Practices: A Manager's Guide" *Columbia Journal of World Business,* Fall 1983. pp. 89–94. *Also see* John L. Graham, "The Foreign Corrupt Practices Act: A New Perspective," *Journal of International Business Studies*, Winter 1984, pp. 107–22.

16. "Doing Business Abroad with Few Restraints," *The Wall Street Journal*, June 5, 1990, p. B1.

17. Sandra MacRae Huszagh, "Exporter Perceptions of the U.S. Regulatory Environment," *Columbia Journal of World Business*, Fall 1981, pp. 22–31; Samuel Rabino, "An Examination of Barriers to Exporting Encountered by Small Manufacturing Companies," *Management International Review*, No. 1 (1980), pp. 67–74.

18. "A Red Line in the Sand," *The Economist*, October 1, 1994, p. 86.

19. John F. Stacks, "The Administration's Split on Auto Imports," *Fortune*, May 4, 1981, p. 158.

20. Jean Doucet and Kenneth J. Good, "What Makes a Good Tax Haven?" *Banker*, May 1973, p. 493. *Also see* "The U.S. Targets a Tax Haven," *Business Week*, April 19, 1982, p. 106.

21. Caroline Doggart, *Tax Havens and Their Uses* 1987 (London: Economist Intelligence Unit, 1987).

22. John D. Daniels, Ernest W. Ogram, Jr., and Lee H. Radebaugh, *International Business: Environments and Operations*, 2nd ed. (Reading, MA: Addison-Wesley, 1979), p. 480.

23. "The New Trade Strategy," *Business Week*, October 7, 1985, p. 90.

24. Allan T. Demaree, "What Now for the U.S. and Japan," *Fortune*, February 10, 1992, p. 80.

25. "U.S. – Japan Trade: Big Deal," *The Economist*, October 8, 1994, p. 76.

26. "IBM Hints for Taiwanese Pirates," *The Wall Street Journal*, October 16, 1984, p. 32. *Also see* Gunter Hauptamn, "Intellectual Property Rights," *International Marketing Review*, Spring 1987, pp. 61–64.

27. Business International, May 29, 1989, p. 166.

28. "From the Mind of Minolta — Oops, Make that 'Honeywell'," *Business Week*, February 24, 1992, p. 34.

29. "Japanese Reverse Tack on Patent Protection," *The Wall Street Journal*, October 24, 1989, p. B1. *Also see* Thomas J. Maronick, "European Patent Laws and Decisions: Implications for Multinational Marketing Strategy," *International Marketing Review*, Summer 1988, pp. 31–40.

30. Erik Bjerager, "Denmark's Lego Challenges Imitators of its Famous Toy Blocks Across Globe," *The Wall Street Journal*, August 5, 1987, p. 18.

31. *Business International*, May 29, 1989, p. 166.

32. Richard L. Hudson, "European Officials Push Idea of Standardizing Telecommunications—But Some Makers Resist," *The Wall Street Journal*, April 10, 1985, p. 32.

33. *Business America*, August 1, 1988, p. 9.

34. "U.N. Rallies to Consumers," *Development Forum*, July–August 1985, p. 14.

35. *See Opening Up the Internal Market* (Brussels: EC, 1991).

36. Virginia M. Citrano, "So, Sue Me," *Northeast International Business*, May 1989, p. 38.

37. William R. Hopkins, "How to Counter Expropriation," *Harvard Business Review*, September–October 1970, p. 109.

PART 3

Cases

Case 12: Collision Course in Commercial Aircraft: Boeing-Airbus-McDonnell Douglas—1991 (A)

You don't succeed in this business by being cautious. If you don't want to play the game, maybe you ought to do something else.... The willingness to gamble, whether in product innovation or product introduction, is very important. The worst thing for us is to overreact and get so conservative that we try to live off our past accomplishments...[1]

At various points in the previous two decades, accusations of unfair trade practices had led the United States and the European Community to the brink of trade war in commercial aircraft. Booming demand at the end of the 1980s seemed to signal a respite in the fight between companies and countries on both sides of the Atlantic. The three major manufacturers—Boeing, Airbus Industrie, and McDonnell Douglas—were struggling to produce enough aircraft to satisfy a seemingly unquenchable need for passenger and freight transport around the world.

But the political and competitive battle showed signs of heating up again in mid-1991. Airbus, a consortium of European aircraft manufacturers formed in 1970 and backed by their various national governments, grabbed 30% of new aircraft orders in 1991, largely from McDonnell Douglas (MD). With MD holding only 14% of industry backlog, it was questionable whether MD's commercial operations could stay out of the red. Moreover, Airbus Managing Partner, Jean Pierson, confidently predicted at the Harvard Business School in 1991 that there would "only be two manufacturers in the year 2000," implying that MD was unlikely to be around.

Having proclaimed victory in one competitive arena, Airbus publicly committed to the biggest pie in the industry: intercontinental jumbo jets. This was Boeing's territory, the lucrative Boeing 747 market. When it first introduced them in 1966, Boeing sold 747s for about $18 million each. In 1991, the same airframe (albeit with some improvements and renovations) cost about $150 million apiece. One industry analyst estimated that Boeing's 1991 profit on each 747 sold was about $45 million. (See **Exhibit 1**.) Yet if Airbus wanted to develop a long-range jumbo jet, it would have to invest billions of dollars in research

---

Copyright © 1991 by the President and Fellows of Harvard College. Harvard Business School Case 391-106.
Research Associate Eric J. Vayle prepared this case under the supervision of Professor David B. Yoffie as the basis for class discussion rather than to illustrate either effective or ineffective handling of an administrative situation.
Reprinted by permission of the Harvard Business School.

1. Boeing Chairman and CEO Frank Shrontz, interviewed in *Fortune*, October 17, 1989.

301

Exhibit 1 Manufacturer's Operating and Financial Statistics

	1990	1989	1988	1990	1989	1988
	TRANSPORT AIRCRAFT[1]			TOTAL OPERATIONS[2]		
McDonnell Douglas						
Revenues	$5,812	$4,511	$4,637	$16,246	$14,581	$14,435
R & D				620	617	562
Oper Income	(177)	(167)	110	185	250	737
Depreciation	140	116	96	581	542	538
Net Income				275	(37)	372
Cash & Equivalents				226	119	107
Assets	5,432	4,030	2,949	14,965	13,397	11,783
LT Debt				5,584	4,935	3,626
Equity				3,514	3,287	3,186
Cap'l Exp	146	213	219	406	582	619
Rtn on Sales				1.7%	−0.3%	2.6%
Rtn on Avg. Equity				8.1%	−1.1%	12.1%
Boeing						
Revenues	$21,230	$14,305	$11,369	$28,043	$20,623	$17,340
R & D				827	754	751
Oper Income	2,189	1,165	585	1,972	922	820
Depreciation	349	280	264	672	622	563
Net Income				1,385	973	614
Cash & Equivalents				3,326	1,863	3,963
Assets	6,267	6,675	4,558	14,591	13,278	12,608
LT Debt				311	275	251
Equity				6,973	6,131	5,404
Cap'l Exp	1,001	612	326	1,586	1,362	690
Rtn on Sales				5.0%	3.3%	3.6%
Rtn on Avg. Equity				19.9%	11.0%	11.4%

Source: Boeing and McDonnell Douglas Annual Reports

1. Transport Aircraft operations at McDonnell Douglas include production of the C-17, a military transport aircraft. Transport aircraft operations are exclusively commercial.
2. Non-transport aircraft operations for these two companies include the manufacture of military aircraft and other aerospace products.

and fixed assets over the next few years. Furthermore, it would not earn any revenues in this segment before the year 2000, and cash flow from continuing operations were grossly insufficient to cover development costs.

The early 1990s would be a watershed for the commercial aircraft industry. McDonnell Douglas had to fend off Airbus to survive; Airbus had to finance its ongoing assault against its American competitors; and Boeing faced the prospect of its first direct threat to its cash cow. At stake for the companies *and* their respective countries was over $600 billion in orders over the coming decade.

The Business of Making and Marketing Airframes

Industry-Government Interaction

In 1917, just 14 years after the Wright brothers took the first manned flight, the U.S. government built a major aeronautics research center in Langley, Virginia. Since that time, the industry had been characterized by close collaboration between the private and public sectors. In the United States, government investment in civil aircraft manufacture was substantial before and during World War II, as the industry mobilized to meet the country's military needs. As a consequence, U.S. manufacturers emerged from the war with a distinct technological and economic advantage over competitors in Europe. The industry continued to be a high government priority after World War II. Governments around the world recognized that nations could benefit from investment in aircraft. When a country had a viable aerospace industry, the economic and technological spillovers created dozens of new industries and thousands of new jobs.

While federal funding in the U.S. was targeted for military aviation, European government support was directly aimed at the commercial sector. Government subsidies were instrumental in creating and sustaining Airbus. Government funds were the sole source of capital for the development of the A300, Airbus's first aircraft, and European subsidies continued to underwrite substantial portions of the R&D for new models. This ongoing government role produced intense pressure on both sides of the Atlantic for government officials to tip the balance of industry economics in the favor of their country's home producers.

Economic Factors

Launch costs Commercial airframe manufacturers tended to be in the business for the long haul. Years of investment were needed before production began and revenues appeared. Launch investment costs typically fell into three categories: 40% for development, 20% for tooling, and 40% for work-in-process and overhead costs. The total amount, spent over an average five years of development, was necessary to develop and certify the aircraft and set up a production line, all before any assessment of success in the market. Manufacturers tried to book as many launch orders as possible, but in the history of the industry there had never been enough to ensure breakeven profitability before the launch date. As a measure of investment risk, Boeing's combined investment in the 1970s for its new 757 and 767 aircraft totaled more than the company's net worth.

The development period began with an aircraft design known as the "paper airplane," a three-way-view model with estimates of performance and operating costs. The manufacturer used these models to demonstrate new technology and, most important, to assess the response of potential buyers. Typically, manufacturers held discussions with key airlines about adaptations and options to incorporate into the prototype. Often these airlines became launch customers, making initial orders that guaranteed a minimum volume, while sending a signal to the marketplace that the aircraft would likely succeed. A launch customer's reputation was important for subsequent sales.

Once minimum backing was achieved—either through orders received from a group of airlines or financial commitments from government agencies—the program could proceed and full-scale development begin. The design and development phase faced built-in costs, such as regulatory approval and costly and time-consuming flight tests, in addition to prototype construction and assembly.

The majority of the tooling costs were associated with the construction jigs, which were expensive to build and required precise specifications. Work-in-process and general administration costs were large because the manufacturer was required to start production of a new model long before it was government certified; otherwise, there would be a delay of 12 to 24 months (the length of the manufacturing cycle) before any aircraft were delivered. The initial inventory was equivalent to about 40 aircraft, although the costs of the inventory buildup could be offset partly by customer progress payments and subcontractor credits. All in all, launch costs could total up to $20 million per seat, as inferred from estimates of the launch investment of $2.5 billion for Airbus's A-320. In the 1990s, a new development project from scratch was more likely to cost between $4 billion and $5 billion, adding to the sales volume necessary to break even. In addition, any upgrades or derivatives, a normal part of the development phase for long production runs, could add 30% to 40% to the overall investment.

An aircraft's sale price typically included purchased parts, direct expenses (labor and supplies), and the launch investment. With normal 25% gross margins, manufacturers typically reached breakeven (recovered launch costs) at 400 units, 12-14 years after the decision to launch the program. Realizing profits in this industry followed a traditional learning curve. As more were produced, the marginal cost to produce each unit decreased. Yet not every manufacturer faced exactly the same curve. When Airbus decided to produce the A-320, it was more likely that 600 sales were needed to break even. However, only one of the 14 European jetliners that had entered service since 1952 ever reached 300 sales (the A300 in 1991), and only 6 out of 12 American models—the Boeing 707, 727, 737, and 747 and the McDonnell Douglas DC-9 and MD-80 had ever generated over 600 shipments each.

Civil aircraft selling was also a long-term relationship business. A manufacturer's sales force and designers worked closed with engineers at the airlines during the development phase. Customers demanded that manufacturers provide service worldwide, with minimum delay. To obtain operational and maintenance efficiency, airlines did not usually mix directly competitive types of aircraft or engines in their fleets. Neighboring airlines also found it advantageous to have access to one another's spare parts and maintenance services. Thus, an initial order tended to have substantial ripple effects. It established an airline's fleet composition by aircraft or engine type for a decade or more. With an aircraft's normal service life of 22 years, a lost sale could easily have a ripple effect of 15 to 20 years. In addition to the hurdle of launching costs, suppliers faced the challenge of selling several jetliners to a few large customers at the outset, rather than marketing initial units to a large cluster of small airlines, which was far more costly. All of the major competitors in the industry strived to make large sales at the launch, and to maintain their fleets at important airlines. Harry Colwell, an analyst at Chase Manhattan Bank, commented that "the manufacturer feels that he has to win each competition. It becomes so important as to be obsessive—a kind of phobia."[2]

Future demand Demand for new aircraft was driven by traffic growth and fleet replacement. At the end of 1990, there were over 7,800 aircraft in service. The industry expected air travel at the end of the century to be nearly double its 1990 level (**Exhibits 2 and 3**). In 1991 dollars, this represented about $600 billion in new orders; of this, about $200 billion was replacement demand, and the rest was new growth. These figures also did not take into account the Soviet Union and Eastern Bloc countries. Hungary, Romania, and Poland had entered into negotiations with Boeing, and Airbus Industrie was completing an application to sell two widebodied planes to East Germany. The Soviet Union's state-run airline, Aeroflot, was the world's largest, and was also considering its fleet in 1991, possibly to include Western aircraft for the first time.

Historically, most non-U.S. carriers had been small, government-owned airlines, which tended to place small orders. However, some European and

---

2. John Newhouse, *The Sporty Game* (New York: Alfred A. Knopf, 1982), p. 21.

EXHIBIT 2 World Aircraft Demand

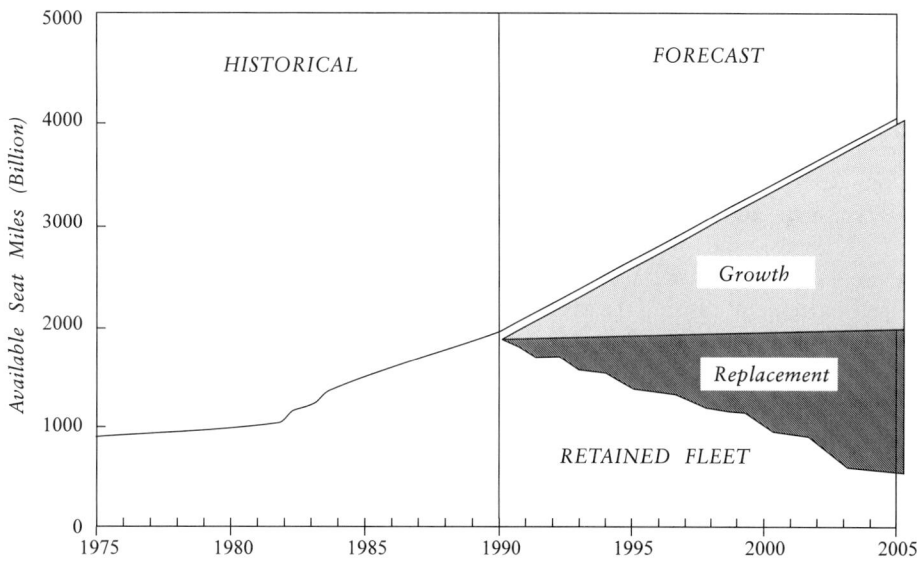

EXHIBIT 3 Aircraft Delivery Forecast

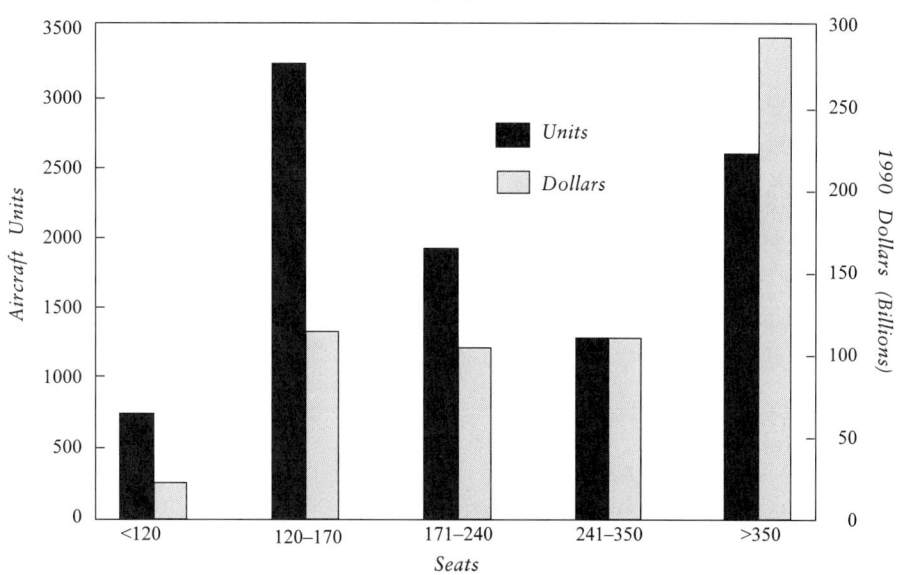

Source: *1991 Current Market Outlook*, The Boeing Company, 1991

Asian carriers were approaching the size and scope of U.S. mega-carriers and were placing huge orders. Also, some international carriers had formed purchasing alliances that allowed them to order greater quantities of aircraft.

The rate of aircraft replacement was determined by the airlines' ability to pay for new equipment and the cost of keeping old equipment in service. Other factors that affected the replacement life were the resale value of old aircraft and routes to be served. As of 1984, the average for retiring an aircraft had been 18.5 years. But many airlines continued to postpone aircraft retirement, causing the average aircraft age to climb. By 1990, it had reached 22 years. Postponing aircraft replacement allowed carriers lower depreciation charges and delayed major capital outlays. However, replacement of older jetliners lowered airlines' charges for fuel and maintenance (between them, the lion's share of operating expenses). Newer technology allowed savings on skilled labor (two instead of three in the cockpit), which also represented a substantial portion of operating cost. According to an estimate by Boeing, about 300 planes per year were expected to be retired between 1991 and 2005.

Engine noise restriction was the one aircraft replacement factor that airlines did not control. By 1985, the industry's oldest jetliners (e.g., Boeing's 707) were no longer able to serve U.S. markets due to noise regulations. In 1990, Congress set a timetable for airlines to have Stage 2 aircraft (aircraft built with some noise control, after initial noise restrictions were put into effect) like 727s, 737s, and some 747s from Boeing, and McDonnell-Douglas DC-9s and DC-10s, either retired or modified to further reduce engine noise by the year 2000. These regulations were only for U.S. airports, but similar restrictions existed in Europe and elsewhere.

Although demand for new planes seemed high and steady in 1991, the major players understood that demand in this industry was cyclical and that the risk of an eventual slowdown in orders existed. Industry players faced the challenge of positioning themselves so that they were able to keep up with demand during booming periods, but were not caught with overcapacity during the busts.

The Boeing Company

The Boeing Company, founded in July 1916 in Seattle, Washington, was the world's largest private commercial aircraft manufacturer and America's largest exporter. In 1990, Boeing delivered 385 airplanes while taking new orders for 543 aircraft. Boeing also produced military aircraft and products for NASA and other aerospace organizations.

During the 1970s and 1980s, Boeing's stated goal was to be the dominant competitor in every segment of the commercial transport market. To accomplish its goal, Boeing identified several strategies. First, it had to be a technological leader, spending between 4% and 9% on research and development programs for commercial aircraft. Boeing was nearly pushed into bankruptcy in 1971, for example, because of the large expense of developing the 747. It had been forced to take measures as drastic as cutting its work force by over 60% at that time, but Boeing had expanded tremendously since 1981. By 1990 its manufacturing capacity was over 430 planes per year—about 70% of worldwide demand.

The military aircraft and space product programs at Boeing and McDonnell Douglas also helped promote the development of new technology and commercial products. By absorbing the heavy research and development costs for jet engines, jumbo airframes and wings, and advanced avionics, federal military grants enabled Boeing to move down the learning curve on commercial planes with far smaller investments of their own capital. In the 1960s, for example, the U.S. military ordered 600 KC-135 military transports from Boeing. Because the 707 was such a close derivative of the KC-135, its initial profitability was ensured before production commenced. Similarly, development work on airframes and engines for the Air Force's giant C-5 transport led to commercial jumbo jets like the Boeing 747 and McDonnell Douglas's DC-10.

Boeing also developed a family of base models for a wide variety of flight ranges and passenger capacities. From these, derivatives could be developed to expand markets and to extend product life cycles (see **Exhibit 4**). In 1991, Boeing's airframe families included the 727 and 737, both short-range aircraft; the 757 and 767, both larger, medium-range craft; and

747, a massive widebody airplane that held 400 passengers and could fly further than any other commercial airliner. Until 1987, Boeing had planned to offer a short-range, 150-seat plane called the 7J7 starting in 1992. It had so much difficulty finding launch customers for the plane, given competitive products by Airbus already available to airlines, that it repeatedly postponed and eventually canceled the project. It transferred some of the 7J7's technical innovations to development of the 777, a medium-to-long-range widebody aircraft that Boeing expected to deliver in 1995.

Cancellation of the 7J7 development program strengthened Boeing's cash position and helped its strong, well-coordinated marketing team to sell planes more aggressively on a global scale. Salespeople endeavored to identify potential sales earlier than competitors when possible. Without the costs of 7J7 development, Boeing had better financial wherewithal to compete on the basis of price as well. While the team attempted to sell to all airlines and aircraft-leasing companies worldwide, it targeted certain carriers that it refused to relinquish as customers at any price. These tended to be the world's largest, best-capitalized carriers, such as United Airlines, Lufthansa, British Airways, Air France, and Japan Airlines. United, for example, placed a $22 billion order for new aircraft in 1990, calling for 128 planes to be delivered between 1991 and 2004. The entire order was for Boeing aircraft; not only was this the largest order in aviation history but it would also make United an all-Boeing carrier. According to James Bryan, president of Airbus North America, "There was no way that Boeing was going to let Airbus into United. They would have given away the airplanes if it had come to that."

Boeing also developed a reputation for providing rapid, worldwide service and parts replacement for its customers. By 1991, Boeing boasted an enormous customer base: nearly 6,300 commercial aircraft had been delivered to more than 450 owners and operators. Boeing's range of products made it the only civil aircraft producer that met the demands of most large continental and intercontinental carriers.

Airbus Industrie

Airbus Industrie was formed in 1980 as a GIE (Groupement d'Intérêt Economique), an entity of French origin under which separate companies pooled their interests and activities for mutual gain. The GIE itself, however, did not exist to make a profit. All of the financial accounts associated with the Airbus programs were incorporated into the partners' own accounts, and the GIE did not report its financial results. Each participant's profit depended upon its own costs, and the costs of one participant were not borne by the others. In effect, profits (and losses) were not shared.

A major reason for Airbus's existence was the desire of several European governments to have a viable aerospace industry. Although European competitors had existed in the industry from its outset, they had historically comprised a minute portion of high-capacity aircraft sales. In 1970, the consortium was formed. Its initial two members were France's Aérospatiale and West Germany's Deutsche Airbus. Later, British Aerospace and Spain's CASA would join as well. Discussions on cooperation stemmed from perceived opportunities in the short- to medium-range market. At that time, over 60% of the world's airline traffic flew routes less than 2,500 nautical miles and the short- to medium-range airliner market was virtually untapped.

The partners focused their discussions around the development of the A-300, the world's first twin-engine widebodied aircraft, seating 240 to 345 passengers with a range of 2,000 to 4,000 nautical miles. Airbus Industrie was responsible for managing the development, production, marketing, and after-sales service of the aircraft. Functions specifically associated with the engineering, production, and program finance, while coordinated by Airbus Industrie, were primarily executed by the partner companies.

In 1974, the first A-300s were delivered. The consortium's second effort was the A-310, a smaller and longer-ranging widebody, which began delivery in 1983. Recognizing the importance of having a range of aircraft "families" available to fill various niches for customers in the 1980s, Airbus followed these with the A-320, a small-capacity, short-range craft in 1988. This craft was built to accommodate

EXHIBIT 4A Existing Airframe Models of Boeing, Airbus, and MD in 1975

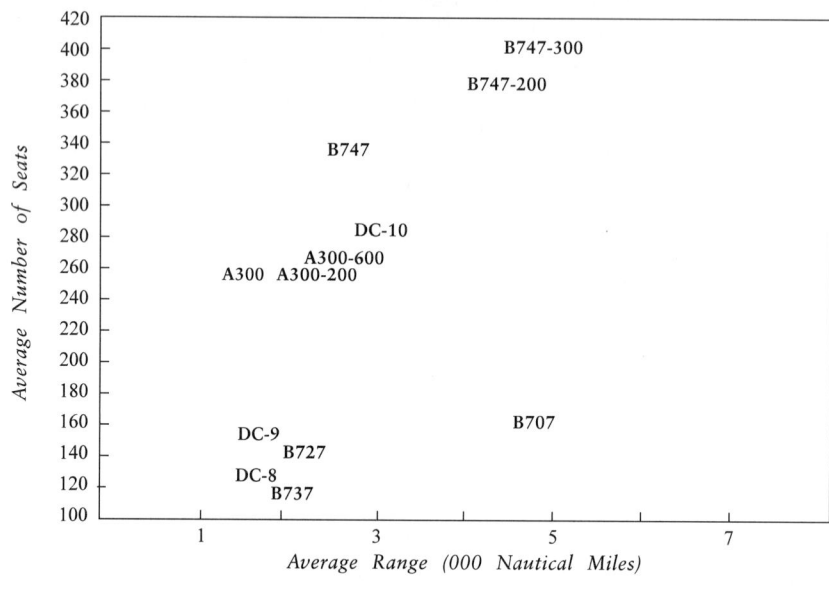

Source: R. Moriarty "The Airframe Industry (M)," Harvard Business School Case no. 582-013, 1982.

EXHIBIT 4B Existing and Proposed Airframe Models of Boeing, Airbus, and MD in 1991

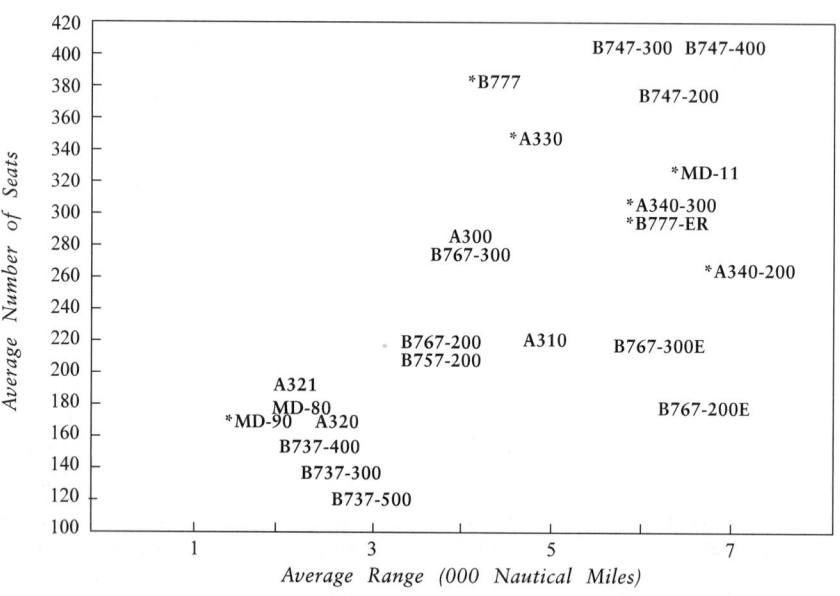

*Proposed models are preceded by an asterisk.

Source: Boeing *1991 Current Market Outlook*, Airbus and MD documents.

two new trends in the industry. First, many new airlines had appeared since deregulation in the United States and Europe in the 1980s. These new carriers operated at lower cost, offered discounted fares, and required smaller seating capacity. Second, flight scheduling focused around the hub-and-spoke pattern, under which short-haul routes fed into major airports for connection with longer-haul segments of the trip. During the late 1980s, the company began taking orders for two new airframes, the A330 and A340, to compete with the MD-11 and 747 on medium- to long-range routes. They were built to access the expected increase in intercontinental (especially trans-Pacific) travel and were expected to be ready for delivery in 1993.

Airbus aircraft boasted technological advances over U.S. planes. Technological firsts for Airbus on the A-320 and the A-330 and A-340 included, among other features, active controls, variable camber wing, fly-by-wire, digital auto-flight system, side-stick controllers, and advanced composite materials in the aircraft's structure. Several of these technologies would be incorporated into new Boeing and MD designs like the 777 and MD-11.

Between 70%-90% of R&D costs for Airbus's technological development were financed by money from the participant nation governments. According to a 1990 consultant's report commissioned by the U.S. Department of Commerce, over $13 billion in government subsidies for development and production had been granted to Airbus partners since its inception. If that money had been borrowed at commercial rates, Airbus would owe more than $25 billion. The report continued that further aid would be available to Airbus, as needed for future development projects. Airbus claimed that government "launch aid" consisted only of loans, which were repaid by an agreed-upon share of the proceeds of each aircraft sale, transferred by Airbus Industrie to the partners. Evidence suggested that interest rates on these loans were below market rates, and that interest was sometimes forgiven altogether. Some government assistance was also provided to offset currency difficulties faced by subsidiaries: Airbus was paid in U.S. dollars for its deliveries, and in turn paid its member companies in dollars. The subsidiaries paid their expenses in local currencies. In 1989, the German government sold Deutsche Airbus to MBB, a German heavy manufacturing conglomerate. The sale was accomplished only with the stipulation that the German government would reimburse MBB for profit shortfalls caused by any exchange rate losses.

McDonnell Douglas Corporation

The industry's third major manufacturer was McDonnell Douglas (MD). MD had been making commercial airliners since 1920, and MD's Douglas Commercial (or DC) line of planes had been in service for over half a century. The majority of McDonnell Douglas's revenues came from U.S. government orders in 1991. MD was the largest defense contractor in the United States, producing about $10 billion worth of combat aircraft, helicopters, missiles, and defense electronic systems for the U.S. Armed Forces in 1990. During the 1960s and 1970s, the Commercial Aircraft Group at MD developed two major airframe designs that would become the backbones of its modern fleet. They were the DC-9, a narrow-body, short-range craft seating about 150 passengers, and the DC-10, a widebody, medium-range jet seating 250-350.

McDonnell Douglas was in financial disarray in 1990. Both its government sector business and its commercial business were faced with strong competitors and rapidly dropping demand for its products. Despite combat in the Persian Gulf, the defense sector underwent a major downturn in research and procurement during the late 1980s and early 1990s. Amidst the general slowdown, McDonnell Douglas's military group faced particularly serious setbacks due to the cancellation of the $4.8 billion A-12 Stealth attack plane in early 1990.

The company's transport aircraft sector had faced financial difficulties since the early 1980s. Competition between MD's DC-10 and Lockheed Corporation's L-1011 had cost the commercial division precious profitability in the late 1970s, and the strong emergence of Airbus squeezed MD's market share (see **Exhibits 5** and **6**). In 1985, MD's fleet comprised 28% of aircraft in service. By 1989, MD had only 26% of the worldwide fleet. In an attempt to revive lagging profits, MD undertook a massive restructuring in 1989. Personnel in production and other departments were cut by 8,400 jobs. Managers were required to interview for their own jobs. The restructuring, while having little effect on the division's profitability, was a devastating blow to employee and management morale. In 1990, the division lost over $177 million despite the restructuring and an Air Force procurement program for the C-17 transport.

In the late 1970s, McDonnell Douglas had needed to develop a new set of aircraft to replace aging DC-9s and DC-10s. Given its financial difficul-

EXHIBIT 5 Market Share of Orders, 1974–1990

	1974	1975	1976	1977	1978	1979	1980	1981	1982	1983	1984	1985	1986	1987	1988	1989	1990
Boeing	70%	69%	72%	67%	68%	68%	81%	57%	62%	56%	50%	61%	47%	53%	57%	53%	45%
Airbus	1%	4%	5%	5%	14%	15%	6%	29%	13%	0%	22%	9%	25%	28%	15%	24%	34%
MD & Others	29%	27%	28%	28%	18%	17%	13%	14%	25%	44%	28%	30%	28%	19%	28%	23%	21%

EXHIBIT 6 Forecast of Aircraft Deliveries

	91	92	93	94	95	96	97	98	99	2000	Total
Boeing											
B737	210	210	210	142	104	106	81	78	46	38	1,225
B747	67	72	72	73	60	60	50	51	40	38	583
B757	96	96	94	96	86	74	74	80	78	84	858
B767	60	60	60	55	54	27	27	18	20	8	389
B777	0	0	0	1	16	46	50	67	57	60	297
Airbus											
A300	37	39	18	15	8	0	0	0	0	0	117
A310	25	24	15	13	8	0	0	0	0	0	85
A320	110	100	88	65	40	30	20	20	14	20	507
A321	0	0	2	15	36	50	60	60	48	50	321
A330	0	2	13	35	66	52	37	43	59	64	371
A340	2	11	22	25	33	22	22	22	22	17	198
McDonnell Douglas											
MD-80	140	119	101	71	30	5	12	0	0	0	478
MD-90	0	1	14	38	39	48	58	80	80	84	442
MD-11	44	63	68	44	35	30	23	22	14	10	353
MD-12	0	0	0	2	2	20	20	20	23	37	122

Source: Forecast International/DMS Market Intelligence Report, May 1991.

ties, MD chose to use the basic airframe and wing technologies of the DC-9 to develop the MD-80 series of twinjets, rather than invest in a completely new start-up development program. The MD-80 series, put into service in 1980, was available to carriers in a wide variety of passenger configurations and was MD's biggest seller. By 1990 over 1,600 MD-80s were in service. The MD-90 series, a derivative of the MD-80, was expected to enter service in 1994.

A similar development decision was made with the MD-11 in the late 1980s; instead of being developed from scratch, this tri-engine widebody craft was derived from DC-10 technology, and was put into service in 1990. By March 1991, 377 MD-11s had been ordered, selling out MD's production capabilities through 1995. MD hoped that the launch of the MD-11 would mark the company's turnaround. Instead, the MD-11 was filled with technical and manufacturing difficulties. The first planes off the assembly lines were delivered several months behind schedule and with several engineering deficiencies. As a result, the airplane was incapable of reaching its advertised maximum range when filled to its maximum capacity. Major launch customer American Airlines had inaugurated service from Boston to San Jose to Tokyo with this new craft, and the airplane was unable to make the full journey. American Airlines CEO Robert Crandall was infuriated, claiming he was "unhappy with the single MD-11 [American] has received, and very disappointed with McDonnell Douglas"[3] in January 1991. By May 1991, the craft was still not being used for the trans-Pacific portion of the trip. With over 200 MD-80s in its fleet, and with 19 firm orders and 31 options for MD-11s, American was McDonnell Douglas's largest single customer.

While in the midst of MD-11 development in 1988, McDonnell Douglas approached Airbus about potential joint ventures. An alliance between the two would have made them equal to, if not larger than, Boeing in terms of market share. According to a news report, McDonnell Douglas [was] willing to use spare production capabilities in southern California to help Airbus produce its A-320, and there were "possibilities for joint production of a 100- to 120-seat aircraft [to rival the Boeing 737] and an aircraft in the 400-seat range to compete with the Boeing 747."[4] The two discovered that neither could abandon its current plans for a medium- to long-range craft. "Airbus was proceeding with plans for [its] two new widebody jets, the A-330 and the A-340, to be introduced in 1992,"[5] while McDonnell Douglas adhered to plans to deliver the competing MD-11 by 1990. However, they considered a stretched version of the MD-11, fitted with an Airbus A-330 wing. This "McAirbus" would have had two engines under the wing and a third (McDonell Douglas style) in the tail. The plane could carry more than 500 passengers and would be the first direct competitor to Boeing's 747. Moreover, with one less engine, the McAirbus would be able to do what a 747 did more cheaply. Negotiations broke down when the companies hit an impasse over which should build the cockpit, the critical portion of the craft. The two broke off all discussions and continued on their separate projects. Talks had not resumed by 1991.

International Collaboration

Despite the lack of an agreement between Airbus and MD, success in the commercial aircraft industry had become dependent upon multinational joint ventures by the mid-1980s, and the industry was expected to become even further globalized as the century ended. Sharing the risks and rewards of development programs reduced market, financial, and technological uncertainties for manufacturers undertaking new projects.

Airbus, in addition to being an international consortium, depended on non-EC suppliers for a substantial portion of each aircraft. The largest of these foreign contributors were General Electric (GE) and CFM, an engine manufacturer that was a joint venture of GE and SNECMA, a French manufacturer. Both of these American manufacturers fitted Airbus planes with engines. In 1987, Airbus ordered $2 billion worth of engines from these companies. (See **Exhibit 7**.)

In the late 1980s, McDonnell Douglas joined forces with Aeritalia to produce over 10% of the

---

3. *Aviation Week and Space Technology*, February 25, 1991, p. 29.

4. *Financial Times*, March 4, 1988, p. 5.

5. *Business Week*, March 21, 1988, p. 51.

MD-11 airframe; other international partners produced substantial amounts as well. In April 1985, McDonnell Douglas also signed an agreement with Shanghai Aviation Industry Corporation (SAIC) to co-produce 25 MD-80 twin-jet transports, with an option for 15 more. McDonnell Douglas was forging a long-term relationship in China with an eye toward further collaboration with SAIC.

Boeing contracted with three Japanese heavy manufacturers to build 20% of the airframe of its new 777 twin-engine widebody. In return, the Japanese Aircraft Development Corporation (a subsidiary of MITI, Japan's Ministry of International Trade and Industry) agreed to fund a substantial percentage of the development costs of the project. When asked whether or not Airbus would become similarly involved with Japanese manufacturers, Airbus Managing Partner Jean Pierson replied that Airbus was "considering the opportunity of taking, perhaps, a 15% risk partner. We're examining a new widebody project for 1997 or 1998, and we might bring them in on that." Manufacturers feared cooperating with Japan because MITI had publicly announced its intention to develop the aerospace industry in Japan as it had electronics and automobiles. In 1991, Japanese manufacturers did not have enough expertise to develop whole aircraft, but they had made great strides in that direction.

Pricing Competition

Since Airbus's entry into the world market with the A-300 and A-310, selling competition had increased steadily and substantially among the manufacturers. In a 1978 sale to Eastern Airlines, Airbus offered a financial arrangement known as a "Deferred Seat Plan." Under the plan, 12 of 23 planes were sold as if they had only 170 seats rather than 240. After four years or if Eastern's load factors exceeded a certain level, Eastern would be required to repay the "deferral." By offering to finance about 85% of a 1985 sale to Indian Airlines, Airbus clinched a sale even after the airline had signed a letter of intent with Boeing. To get the sale, Airbus offered to deduct from the sale price the costs of several aircraft that the airline leased while the ordered planes were being built. According to one published report, the French government also intervened in the sale on Airbus's behalf. French officials allegedly proposed offers of assistance to the Indian government, ranging from help in securing loans at the World Bank to accelerating deliveries of French military aircraft to India, to technical assistance in cleaning up the polluted Ganges River.[6]

Another financing package offered by manufacturers was the "walk-away lease." In 1988, American Airlines became the first carrier to utilize such a package when it split an order between the Boeing 767 and the Airbus A-300. Both manufacturers agreed to buy back the jets with as little as 30 days' notice. Another was the "trade-in" of competitor aircraft. All of the competitors had organizations to refurbish and sell used aircraft from competitors, which they purchased in exchange deals for new planes. In one deal, Boeing repurchased three *brand new* A-310s from Kuwait Airways in order to sell 767s to the airline. Tightening profits among the world's airlines made competitive financing increasingly risky for manufacturers in 1991. Eastern went bankrupt in 1991, leaving creditors including Airbus with billions of dollars' worth of uncollectible debt. If losses continued to plague airlines, manufacturers would continue to be stuck with bad debt and airplanes to resell.

Some of the fiercest competition came in the form of underbidding. Prior to 1988, Airbus often forced Boeing and MD to choose between losing a sale or cutting the prices below operating expenses. "We were pricing for market share," admitted Airbus Chairman Alan Boyd, "we had to do it in order to get our feet in the door." The further that Airbus was willing to price its aircraft below what U.S. manufacturers believed its operating costs to be, the more U.S. manufacturers believed Airbus was competing unfairly. U.S. trade officials stepped in to examine whether Airbus was in violation of international trade agreements.

Government Intervention

In the late 1970s, representatives of the United States, EC, and other governments drew up major fair trade

---

6. *International Herald Tribune*, October 31, 1985.

Case 12: Collision Course in Commercial Aircraft 313

Exhibit 7 Examples of International Cooperation

A Typical "European" Aircraft Program

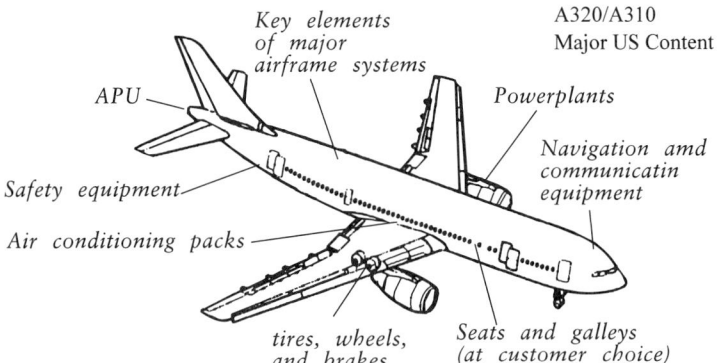

A320/A310 Major US Content

Over 500 U.S. companies participate in the Airbus Industrie industrial programs. In terms of initial investment, every Airbus aircraft sold generates approximately the same amount of business for the U.S. manufacturing industry as an MD-80.

Over a 15 year cycle each Airbus widebody generates more business for the United States that a 727.

88% of all maintenance items are U.S. manufactured.

Since 1979, Airbus Industrie contracts with the U.S. aerospace industry have exceeded $3.5 billion—an average of $1.2 million per day for 8 years.

A Typical "American" Aircraft Program

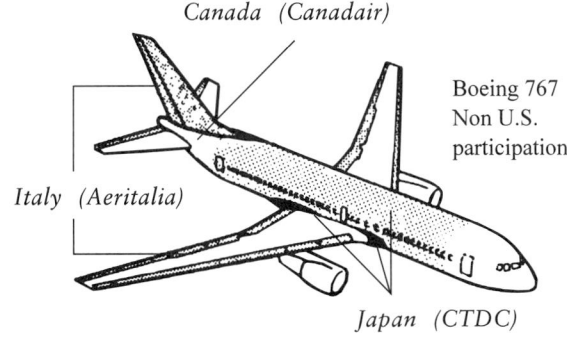

Boeing 767 Non U.S. participation

—Well over 30% of the 767 is manufactured outside the U.S.

—Because of the scale of resources required the same situation will apply for any new front-line airplane, from whatever primary source.

MD-80 AIRFRAME TEAM

McDonnell Douglas — 51.9%
Douglas Aircraft — 34.5%
Other locations — 17.4%

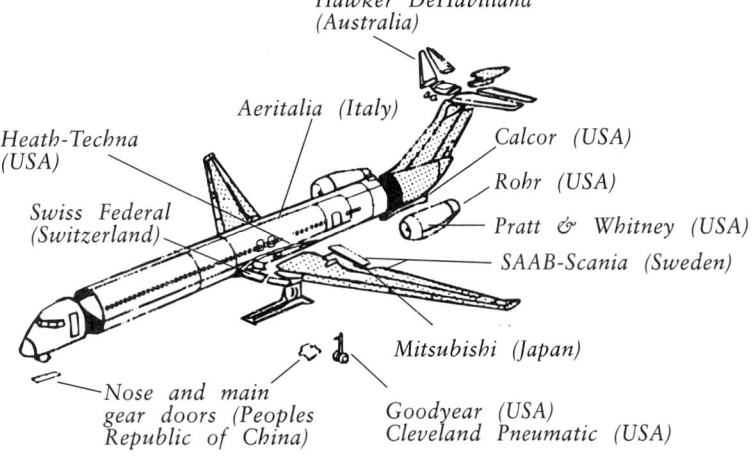

Source: Airbus Industrie company document

agreements for aircraft sales as part of the General Agreement on Trade and Tariffs (GATT). The 1979 GATT Agreement on Trade in Civil Aircraft set forth an international legal framework governing the conduct of trade in civil aircraft. The framework included the elimination of duties and technical barriers for civil aircraft, the avoidance of disruptions in trade (including fair pricing), and a ban on governmental interference on sales or purchases. (**Exhibit 8** highlights the salient points of the GATT Aircraft Agreement.) The Large Aircraft Sector Understanding, signed in July 1985, updated the GATT agreement and sought to remove government financial assistance from the selling process by using interest rates to equilibrate customer financing opportunities among manufacturers.

Through the early 1980s, Airbus's sales were relatively few and American manufacturers were not concerned about competitive pressure from Europe. As Airbus's sales expanded in the mid-1980s and as the consortium developed products to compete in a wide range of market segments, industry officials began to pressure the U.S. Department of Commerce and the Office of the United States Trade Representative to help counter the trend. Government officials lodged protests over actions by European governments that seemed to violate the intent of the trade agreements to which they were signatories. European governments rejected American claims and put forth counter claims about U.S. government involvement in the industry. The diplomatic debate over active and financial involvement raged between them for the rest of the 1980s and into the 1990s.

Embassy Assistance

The United States and European Community governments accused one another of intervening to provide "embassy assistance" to their manufacturers in situations where airlines were state-run agencies. In addition to reported French government activities in India, Airbus aircraft sales were also linked to French investments in a Kuwait petrochemical plant and to landing rights in Paris allowed to Korean Airlines. Along the same lines, however, Boeing's Vice President Boris Mishel admitted in 1988 that "U.S. embassy personnel have been extremely helpful in promoting the export of aircraft as well as all other U.S. manufactured goods."

Airbus's three largest partners also offered export credits, loans, and guarantees for the purchase of aircraft outside the consortium countries through institutions owned by their governments. France's Compagnie Française d'Assurance du Commerce Extérieur (COFACE) along with the Banque Française du Commerce Extérieur (BFCE) provided insurance and financing for up to 85% of the total purchase at the interest rates set out by the Large Aircraft Sector Understanding. Great Britain's Export Credit Guaranty Department (ECGD) performed both roles, insurance and banking, under the international guidelines. West Germany's Hermes, a private insurance agency owned by a consortium of large commercial banks but acting on behalf of the government, provided export credit guarantees for Deutsche Airbus. The conditions that were offered were reportedly in accordance with the Understanding.

Government Subsidies

Even more than political interference and export financing, U.S. industry and government officials were concerned about what they considered unfair subsidies provided to Airbus by European governments. McDonnell Douglas Vice President James Worsham encapsulated the U.S. position in the trade dispute: "No private U.S. company in our capital-intensive industry can compete indefinitely with the national treasuries of the most powerful European governments." Bruce Smart, undersecretary for international trade in the Department of Commerce, estimated that "about $12 billion of U.S. value-added [in 1984 dollars] would have resulted from shipments of U.S. rather than Airbus aircraft from 1974 to 1986, [and furthermore, that] translated to about 8,000 U.S. jobs in the aerospace industry and another 24,000 jobs in related industries." U.S. officials reacted skeptically when told that over a billion dollars' worth of commercial loans for the A300 and A310 were forgiven

---

7. Section 301 refers to the sections of the U.S. Trade Act of 1974, in which the president was empowered to take action to enforce the rights of the United States under any trade agreement and to eliminate unfair trade practices by a trading partner.

EXHIBIT 8 Highlights of the GATT Agreement on Trade in Civil Aircraft

Signatories:

Austria, Belgium, Canada, Denmark, EEC, West Germany, France, Ireland, Italy, Japan, Luxembourg, Netherlands, Norway, Romania, Sweden, United Kingdom, United States

Purpose:

1. Achieve expansion and ever-greater liberalization of world trade through the progressive dismantling of obstacles to trade;
2. Maximize freedom of world trade;
3. Promote technological development;
4. Ensure fair and equal competitive opportunities;
5. Affirm importance in civil aircraft sector
6. Recognize aircraft sector as a particularly important component of economic and industrial policy;
7. Eliminate adverse effects on trade in civil aircraft resulting from governmental support in civil aircraft development, production, and marketing, while recognizing that such government support, of itself, would not be deemed a distortion of trade;
8. Accept that civil aircraft activities operate on commercially competitive bases, and government-industry relationships differ widely among them;
9. Provide for international notification, consultation, surveillance, and dispute settlement procedures;
10. Establish an international framework governing conduct of trade.

Highlights of Articles Agreed to by Signatories

1. Ensure airlines' freedom from governmental pressures to select suppliers on basis of commercial and technological factors; purchase of products covered by this Agreement should be made only on a competitive basis; avoid attaching inducements of any kind to the sale or purchase of civil aircraft from any particular source which would create discrimination against suppliers from any signatory.
2. No application of trade restrictions such as import quotas, import licensing requirements, or export licensing to restrict imports or exports.
3. Avoid adverse effects on trade in civil aircraft and take into account the special factors which apply in the aircraft sector, in particular the widespread governmental support in this area, their international economic interests, and the desire of producers of all signatories to participate in the expansion of the world civil aircraft market; pricing should be based on a reasonable expectation of recoupment of all costs, including nonrecurring program costs, identifiable and prorated costs of military research and development on aircraft, components, and systems subsequently applied to the production of such civil aircraft.

The agreement was signed April 12, 1979, in Geneva and went into effect January 1, 1980.

Source: GATT Agreement on Trade in Civil Aircraft

Deutsche Airbus by the German government in 1988. "This confirms," claimed Orvil Roetman, Boeing VP of international Business and Government Affairs, "the commercial insolvency of Airbus."

Airbus countered the charges of subsidization by stating that government assistance was necessary to overcome American monopoly status in the industry. It further claimed that the U.S. government was equally guilty of providing indirect subsidies to manufacturers through development and production contracts for military products with commercial applications. According to one Airbus claim, U.S. aircraft manufacturers (military as well as commercial) received a total of $23 billion in indirect government support between 1960 and 1988.

Conflict and Negotiations

In a 1985 press conference, President Ronald Reagan announced several alleged violations of trade agreements by U.S. trading partners, one of which was Airbus. The press conference resulted in speculation that the U.S. would file a Section 301 case against Airbus.[7] It did not. On June 23, 1987, however, the dispute escalated when the House Subcommittee on Commerce, Consumer Protection, and Competitiveness held its first hearing on competition between Airbus and the U.S. industry. Committee Chairperson James Florio (D-NJ) advocated the use of Section 301 of the U.S. trade law if the continuing negotiations failed to produce a resolution. He declared that "our trade partners should understand. . . that the Congress cannot, and will not, ignore the failure of negotiations to produce an acceptable agreement. The aerospace industry is too important to our nation's trade, economic, and defense interests to allow this situation to continue."

With such high stakes for trade balances and employment on the one hand, and the threat of lost aircraft sales on the other, GATT negotiators were pressed to provide a solution to the lingering civil aircraft trade dispute. On October 27, 1987, U.S. and E.C. negotiators agreed upon a framework of principles to resolve the dispute. Future meetings would aim at resolving embassy involvement and government financial support. Negotiations continued after that meeting, as negotiators attempted to find a diplomatic solution. However, exchanges were frank and often heated. Each side accused the other of violations, and each defended its actions on the basis of economic necessity. Little progress was made before a March 18, 1988, ministerial meeting. Convened in Konstanz, West Germany, U.S. Trade Representative Clayton Yeutter debated the remaining differences in the civil aircraft trade dispute with his counterparts from Britain, France, Germany, and the EC. They sought to resolve misunderstandings about direct government procurement, mandatory subcontracts and inducements, and issues concerning government support, both direct and indirect. The meeting, like its predecessors, yielded little progress. The parties agreed to eliminate state funding of *production*, as opposed to *research* and *development*, and agreed that both direct and indirect production funding would be covered by the agreement. However, as the meeting drew to a close, it was apparent that principles, and not details, were agreed upon. Progress had not led to resolution.

Between 1988 and 1991, U.S. Trade Representatives threatened four times to take trade action against the EC and Airbus. American government officials were concerned about maintaining the U.S. position in aerospace because it was one of the few shining stars in the U.S. trade balance: in 1989, for example, American aerospace companies exports totaled more than $23 billion (about 6.5% of total U.S. exports), and the sector's trade surplus stood at nearly $18 billion. In contrast, the United States's overall trade deficit was $104.2 billion in 1989. Yet retaliation never materialized since "satisfactory progress" was made at preliminary meetings. By 1991, trade negotiators had agreed to limit Airbus government subsidies to 45% of total costs, down from 75% in the past. American negotiators still hoped to lower the amount to 25%. Beyond that issue, negotiations were at an impasse. Requests for financial transparency, an opening of the accounting books on both sides, were denied. European negotiators refused to disclose the true amount of subsidization until American negotiators disclosed the amount of indirect support available to American producers through military and NASA contracts. In 1991, the political situation appeared to be intensifying again. Aerospatiale's president, Henri Martre, urged the EC to harden its stance in subsidy negotiations, calling for "a strong, comprehensive case to defend European interests." This closely followed a claim by Airbus Managing Partner Jean Pierson that the U.S. was "deliberately manipulating [instruments like] the exchange rate to hurt European companies like Airbus Industrie." Alan Boyd of Airbus North America warned that "neither the EC nor Airbus will roll over and play dead" in the face of U.S. pressure.

Funding a New Jumbo

Managing Partner Pierson proudly exclaimed that, counter to the claims of American industry and government officials, "Airbus reached [operating] profitability in 1991, four years ahead of original expectations." Yet it would not be enough to cover development costs of the new craft; government subsidies would be required for the development of any new airframe. Yet in 1991, the government subsidies that had proven necessary in the past were being negotiated away. For Airbus, the key questions were, How do we continue financing our R&D and launch costs? What are our options and how do we frame the arguments?

The 747 was Boeing's last bastion of monopoly, and an Airbus competitor to the 747 could cement the European consortium's position squarely in the thick of the industry as the twenty-first century approached. Creative selling by Airbus had revolutionized the industry already, and American producers were faced with another possible assault. As they watched Airbus gather its political and economic weapons to prepare for the development of a new Airbus jumbo jet, U.S. manufacturers and government officials were faced with a number of questions. Would government-subsidized development of an Airbus competitor to the 747 be unfair or in violation of the GATT agreement? If Airbus could sell airlines directly competitive to the 747, what would that do to the industry structure? How should Boeing and MD respond to Airbus's relentless drive for market share?

Case 13: El Norte Chemicals, Ltd.

Juan Cavasantes, assistant to the director of countertrade and Latin American specialist for El Norte Chemicals, collected his notes and headed for the boardroom. The El Norte board of directors was waiting to evaluate his proposal that El Norte Chemicals should swap various chemical products for wine from the country of Bocotania. Cavasantes believed that the board should approve his proposal and hoped that the directors would agree to the proposed transaction quickly, so that he could import at least a few containers of Bocotanian wine in time for the upcoming Christmas and New Year's holidays.

This case is printed here with the permission of the author, David K. Smith, Jr., of Michigan State University.

The Company

El Norte Chemicals, Ltd. (hence, ENC), is a Delaware corporation formed in 1902. The company manufactures plastics, organic and inorganic chemicals, pharmaceuticals, and other specialty products including polymeric materials and fabricated products of various sorts. A substantial portion of ENC's business consists of high volume/low markup (and low value added) chemical products. Raw materials used by ENC to produce its products are as indicated in Table 1. In general, availabiity of these raw materials (feedstocks) has not been a problem.

TABLE 1 Major Feedstocks Utilized by ENC Chemicals, Inc.

Liquified petroleum gas
Naphtha
Natural gas
Benzene
Crude oil
Ammonia
Coal
Limestone
Salt
Styrene
Ethylene
Acrylonitrile
Octane
Propylene oxide
Cellulose
Butadiene
Aniline
Toluene diamine

Up until the Second World War, ENC was a relatively small firm doing business primarily in the United States. After the war, however, the company expanded vigorously into petrochemicals. As indicated in Table 2, the average growth in ENC revenues associated with the move into petrochemicals was substantial.

In the 1970s, the growth rate realized over the previous two decades was no longer sustainable on petrochemicals alone. Consequently, ENC spent considerable time and effort working to identify new growth opportunities. Ultimately, a decision was made to shift from a primarily domestic focus to the solicitation of business on a global basis.

ENC's decision to adopt a global focus was accompanied by considerable soul-searching as to the corporate structure that would best support the new global focus. Ultimately, the centralized decision-making structure and culture that had evolved over the first seventy years of ENC's existence was scrapped. In its place, a decentralized structure based on relatively autonomous geographic regions was adopted. Figure 1 gives an overview of the structure in existence at the time the decision to "go global" was made as well as the new decentralized structure.

Results associated with the decision to become a global supplier of chemical products were impressive. As Table 2 indicates, the growth in revenues during the 1970s not only matched but, in fact, exceeded the results produced during the years when growth had been petrochemical-induced.

While the growth in revenues during the decade of the 1970s was acceptable to management, ENC's profitability over this period was very erratic. Consequently, ENC's management began looking for ways to reduce the large oscillations in corporate profits and return on investment (ROI). Ultimately, management decided that ENC's heavy dependence on the sale of commodity and basic chemicals would be reduced by focusing corporate attention and resources on the development of specialty chemicals

TABLE 2 Growth in ENC Revenues over the Period 1950–1981

YEAR	REVENUES (MILLION $U.S.)	YEAR	REVENUES (MILLION $U.S.)
1950	102	1966	425
1951	120	1967	450
1952	130	1968	455
1953	145	1969	460
1954	160	1970	465
1955	180	1971	475
1956	200	1972	495
1957	220	1973	554
1958	230	1974	620
1959	260	1975	690
1960	280	1976	770
1961	305	1977	860
1962	330	1978	970
1963	370	1979	1064
1964	395	1980	1225
1965	410	1981	1395

businesses.[1] Since the early 1980s, nearly all ENC's capital expenditures have been dedicated to the strengthening of ENC's specialty chemical businesses.

Bocotania

Bocotania, located in South America, is approximately 1.2 million square kilometers—about one-sixth the size of the United States. Part of the country is very desolate, part is very mountainous, and part is covered by jungle vegetation. Total population is about 19 million people, many of whom are descendants of the Spaniards who conquered Bocotania in the 16th century. In addition, however, a large percentage of the population is composed of descendants of the Indians who controlled the area before the arrival of the Spaniards.

Bocotania has been richly endowed with a number of natural resources including silver, gold, and a variety of other nonferrous metals. Thus, a substantial portion of the Bocotanian economy is devoted to the mining, refining, and fabricating of nonferrous metal products of various sorts. Bocotania has a number of other natural resources as well, including timber and petroleum. In addition, the climate and soil conditions are conducive to the production of agricultural products such as sugar, cotton, coffee, fruits (including plums, apricots, peaches, grapes, and mangoes), vegetables (asparagus, broccoli, bell peppers), and spices (oregano).

---

[1] The definitions ENC uses for commodity, basic, and specialty chemicals are as follows: commodity chemicals: chemicals that are not differentiable from those of competitors; basic chemicals: chemicals that can be differentiated from those of competitors because of the addition of services and/or technical capabilities; specialty chemicals: chemicals that offer characteristics that differentiate them from competing products.

FIGURE 1 Evolution of ENC Chemicals, Inc., Organizational Structure

(a) Pre-1970s Organizational Structure of ENC Chemicals, Inc

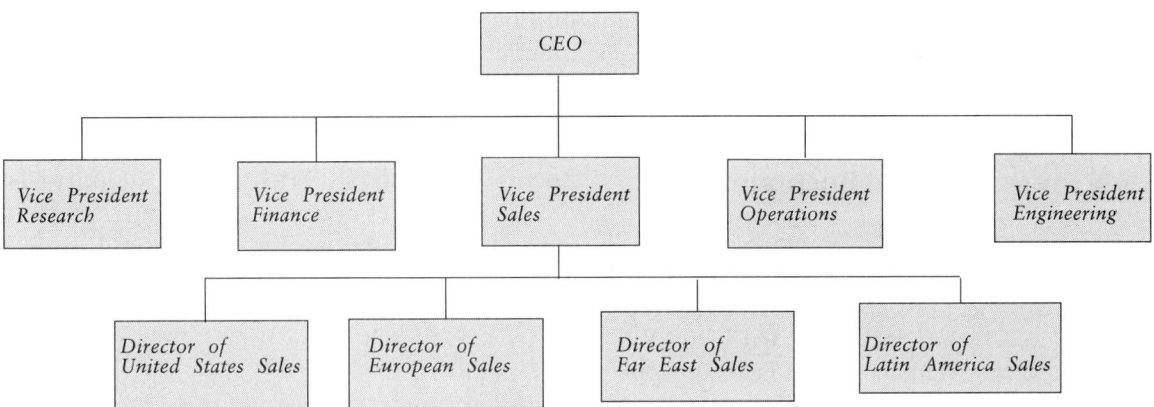

(b) Post-1970s Organizational Structure of ENC Chemicals, Inc.

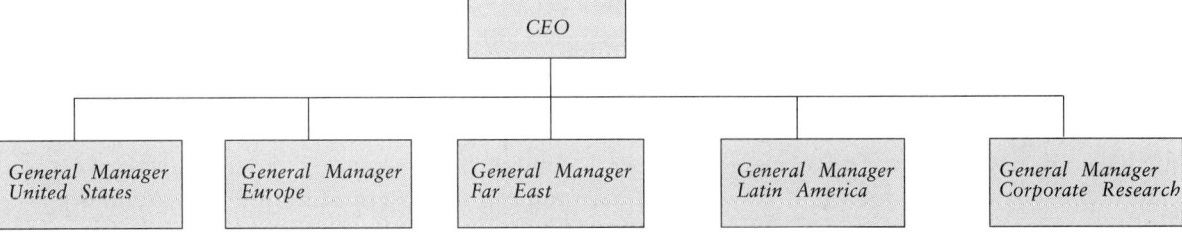

Much of the political and economic life (as much as 90 percent of Bocotanian business ventures) has been and continues to be controlled by a small number of very powerful families of European heritage. Unfortunately, the Indians, with their very different languages and culture, have not been well integrated into the Bocotanian economy. Levels of literacy and education for Indians are substantially lower than for Bocotanians of European descent. Furthermore, it is very uncommon for Bocotanians of Indian descent to be promoted to positions of power and influence. As a consequence, the history of working conditions in factories and mines is very bad, and the dominant theme of union/management relationships for many years has been conflict rather than cooperation. More recently, the tensions and bitterness generated by the disenfranchisement of the large Indian population by the oligopolistic ruling families has manifested itself in the emergence of a violent guerrilla movement against the government and the status quo. Over the last five years, numerous mayors and other government officials living in rural areas have been murdered. To date, however, terrorism against business managers has not been a major problem.

ENC'S Involvement in Bocotania

ENC had entered the Bocotanian market in the late 1960s, during the waning days of the petrochemical boom. At that time, ENC had discovered that relatively small and remote locations far from the intensely competitive triad markets of Europe, Japan, and the United States represented attractive pockets of business at above-average margins. Over the ensuing years, the company's involvement in Bocotania grew steadily, until at one point ENC's fully staffed office (that is, managers for most functions including traffic, credit, treasury, marketing and sales, etc.) was generating about $16 million of sales per year, all to local companies manufacturing for local consumption, and all at margins 10 percent higher than the 20 percent ENC was able to achieve at that time in the triad markets of Europe, Japan, and the United States. Products supplied by ENC to these local producers included low- and high-density polyethylene (for plastic bags), polystyrene (for disposable cups), ABS (for the plastic housing on electrical appliances), industrial chemicals such as caustic soda (used by paper and soap manufacturers), and agricultural chemicals (fungicides, insecticides).

While the decade of the 1970s had been good for Bocotania and for ENC's operations there, the decade of the 1980s was a disaster. With expectations buoyed by high prices for a number of their mineral products, Bocotanian managers borrowed heavily during the 1970s to expand and/or upgrade their mining and processing operations. Unfortunately, other producers worldwide reacted the same way, so when new facilities started operations early in the 1980s, world prices for nearly all of Bocotania's raw material-related products fell dramatically.

The initial effect of the decline in global resource prices was limited to the natural resource sector of the Bocotanian economy. Sales by ENC of floculants and other chemicals used in the mining industry decreased considerably during the early to mid-1980s. Over time, however, as resource-related companies declared bankruptcy and workers lost their jobs, the effect on the Bocotanian economy broadened. Manufacturers of a wide range of consumer and industrial goods began to suffer, too, as it became more and more difficult for Bocotanian buyers (individual and industrial) to acquire the funds necessary to purchase anything but the most basic necessities. Ultimately even companies manufacturing basic consumer goods began to suffer sales declines. Thus, ENC's sales of the plastics used for bags, cups, and a variety of other consumer products began to evaporate. For many people, purchases in 1988 were limited to bread, milk, and other essentials of existence. Demand for nonessential consumer goods had virtually disappeared, and the economy was shrinking. Of those ENC customers, both consumer and industrial goods companies, that were still in business, many were laying off staff or in the process of shutting down completely.

Enter ENC's Countertrade Unit

Early in 1989, with ENC revenues in Bocotania plunging, ENC's managing director in Bocotania asked Mike Jones, director of ENC Global Trading, to review this situation. Specifically, the managing director asked Jones to analyze the situation in Bocotania and to make recommendations as to how the Global Countertrade unit could help Bocotanian customers continue purchasing ENC chemicals, given the deteriorating economic environment in Bocotania.

In February of 1989, Jones and Cavasantes flew to Bocotania to review the situation. While their trip confirmed the dismal situation faced by most Bocotanian companies manufacturing for local consumption, it also uncovered a few bright sports in the economic picture. For example, some Bocotanian companies manufacturing primarily for export were actually doing quite well. This was especially true for producers and fabricators of copper. As indicated in Table 3, prices of copper have recovered from their mid-1980s low and are currently at historic highs. Jones and Cavasantes also found that export-oriented companies taking advantage of Bocotania's relatively low labor costs to export labor-intensive manufactured goods using locally available inputs could compete quite effectively in world markets. However, their review of ENC's customers confirmed the fact that few of these customers had any experience marketing in the international marketplace.

During their stay in Bocotania, Jones and Cavasantes spent a considerable amount of time talking with ENC customers. One evening, a manufacturer of plastic bags and disposable cups for local consumption who had until recently been one of ENC's largest customers commented that his family also ran a winery. This customer went on to say that he would be eager to buy considerable quantities of polyethylene and polystyrene for his plastics factory operations if ENC would accept wine as payment for these chemicals. When asked about the quality of the family wine, their customer smiled and asked if they had enjoyed the red and white wine that had been served earlier in the evening. As it happened, both Jones and Cavasantes had remarked earlier (and positively) on the quality of the wine they had been served, particularly the red.

TABLE 3 Nine-Year Trend in Copper Prices (price per pound)

1989	1.38
1988	1.01
1987	0.84
1986	0.63
1985	0.62
1984	0.65
1983	0.78
1982	0.67
1981	0.78

The last night of their trip, Jones and Cavasantes reviewed the alternative business opportunities they had uncovered for ENC Global Countertrade during their trip. To qualify as an "opportunity," proposals had to involve products that met two criteria: (1) substantial quantities of consistent-quality products appeared to be available in Bocotania; and (2) informal discussions with bankers and/or government officials suggested that the Bocotanian government would be willing to allow an item to be countertraded. Products meeting these two criteria included nonferrous metallic compounds of various sorts, rare earths used by paint manufacturers to control the drying times for various sorts of paints, suits and/or other textile products sewn in Bocotania for export markets, and a couple of different vegetable products including asparagus and broccoli. Of these, Jones and Cavasantes knew that while ENC itself used moderate amounts of nonferrous metallic compounds, ENC had experienced problems with various nondomestic sources of these products and that, subsequently, ENC purchasing agents preferred to work with domestic sources. They also knew that paint dryers would require extensive testing and certification procedures to assure buyers that the properties of paints incorporating these rare earths would be those desired, that development of large, assured sources of supply of vegetables would be a multiyear challenge, and that development of substantial suppliers of high and consistent quality suits would take considerable time. Thus, their initial predisposition as they examined the proposals brought to them was to focus their attention and energies on wine. Jones urged Cavasantes to place the wine opportunity at the top of their priority list, and to follow up on it as soon as they returned to the States.

Because of the importance of the quality issue, Cavasantes' first step following their return to the U.S. was to deliver several bottles of their customer's wine to a testing agency. As indicated in Table 4 the tests confirmed the initial reactions of Jones and Cavasantes, which had been that both red and white were quite acceptable but that the red was more impressive.

TABLE 4 Evaluation of 1987 Vintage White and Red Wines from Bocotania

EVALUATIVE DIMENSION	SCORES	
	Red	White
Empirical Evaluations		
color	+	=
sugar content	+	+
viscosity	+	−
Subjective Assessments		
aroma (nose)	+	+
body	+	=
mouth persistence	+	+
overall taste assessment	+	=
Other Issues		
bottle	+	=
label	+	+
residue	+	+
Summary Assessment Score	+	=

Note: Tests were conducted using as benchmarks a Yugoslavian red wine and a Czechoslovakian white wine that are well established and accepted in the United States. + indicates that the tested wine was evaluated more favorably than the benchmark wine, = indicates that the tested wine was evaluated as equal to the benchmark wine, and − indicates that the tested wine was evaluated as inferior to benchmark wine. Both benchmarks are priced at $2.99 retail.

Given an assurance of acceptable quality, Cavasantes turned next to consider the issue of distribution. His first move was to call a broker of brandy he knew in Houston, to learn a bit about the distribution of alcoholic beverages. Next, he went to his local liquor store to discover the names of the importers of the wines that were for sale there. He discovered that while many of the wines available in his store were imported by nationwide distributors such as "Monsieur Henri," a few brands were imported by a small Chicago wholesaler named N. J. Phillips, Inc. Because Cavasantes suspected that "Monsieur Henri" had little need for one more brand, he called N. J. Phillips, Inc. He found that Nancy Phillips carried several smaller brands, that she had been importing wines for approximately five years, and that she was willing to consider adding Bocotanian wines to her product portfolio.

Based on the strength of her interest, Cavasantes flew to Chicago to provide Ms. Phillips with samples of both the Bocotanian red and white wines. While she preferred the red, she found both wines quite acceptable. By the end of Cavasantes' trip, Ms. Phillips had, on the basis of commitments from several Latin American specialty restaurants in the Chicago metropolitan area, agreed to accept half a container (400 cases of twelve bottles each) of Bocotanian wines as soon as they were available, assuming the retail price could be kept under $3.00 per bottle. In addition, using relationships with her suppliers, Ms. Phillips had initiated a search for importers like herself in the Detroit, New York, and West Coast markets who would be interested in sampling the Bocotanian wines and were big enough to be able to commit to the purchase of at least half a container per order.

On his flight back to ENC headquarters, Cavasantes reviewed the status of his efforts on the wine project. He was pleased with the results of the quality tests and with the progress he had made toward solving the distribution issue. His primary concern at the moment, he decided, related to the fact that the Bocotanian wine should carry a retail price not higher than $3.00 per bottle. As Cavasantes had discovered, both wholesalers and retailers of wine expected a 50 percent markup. While he felt certain that his source of Bocotanian wines would be open to negotiation on price, Cavasantes was not sure how far below the quoted price of slightly more than one U.S. dollar his source would be willing to go.

Presentation Day Minus One

This day, Cavasantes had expected to be able to devote himself to resolving the price issue. However, on his initial attempt to call Bocotania, he discovered that phone, fax, and telex connections to Bocotania were out of order. Later in the morning, before Cavasantes could try again to place his Bocotanian call, he received a call from Houston asking whether he could sell sixty metric tons of copper sulfate for a European seller. Because ENC people in Europe indicated that speedy attention to this opportunity could open important doors for them, Cavasantes felt obliged to respond immediately. As it happens, his secretary had just run a PIERS report on copper sulfate, showing the major importers of this material to the United States over the previous twelve months. Consequently, before lunch Cavasantes was able to place the copper sulfate for the European seller with a major user in Florida, at a price of $2.00 per pound. For acting as intermediary on this transaction, ENC Global Trading earned a commission of 10 percent.

After lunch Cavasantes again tried to place phone, fax, and telex messages to Bocotania. Again, he was unsuccessful. Cavasantes decided to draft his proposal regarding Bocotania wines to show the directors. With luck, he reasoned, he would get through to Bocotania early the next morning, and be able to fill in blanks in his proposal to the directors. As always, his guide for drafting this proposal was the set of framing guidelines that Jones had developed when ENC first began doing countertrade transactions (see **Exhibit 1**).

Presentation Day

Once again, phone and fax communications were out of order. However, Cavasantes was able to get a telex through to ENC's Bocotanian office. Thus, while Cavasantes knew he would not be able to get answers to his questions on price, he would at least be able to indicate to the directors that the question had been raised and that answers should be forthcoming shortly.

EXHIBIT 1 Items to Be Addressed in ENC Purchase-Side Countertrade Contracts

1) Identity of parties to the contract
2) Products to be purchased by ENC, and the quantities involved for some period of time (often a year)
3) Specifications (country and standard) that product specifications must match
4) Packaging and shipment methods to be used by seller
5) Assignment of responsibility for freight expenses (place to which products will be delivered F.O.B.)
6) Price ENC will pay for the product
7) Payment arrangements (how and when ENC will remit funds to the seller)
8) Documentation seller shall present to ENC to claim payments due them under this contract (often, one commercial invoice together with several copies, a clean-on-board bill of lading, an original certificate of origin together with a couple of copies, and an original packing list together with several copies)
9) Any ancillary materials to be included with each product (for example, a users manual, a warranty card, etc.)
10) Agreement by seller that ENC or any other buyer is entitled to resell these products using their own trademarks
11) A force majeure clause (means that in event of certain specified events such as floods, strikes, major mechanical problems, war, and acts of God the parties shall notify each other promptly of the condition and at that point the contract shall be suspended until the problem can be resolved)
12) Legal system that shall be used in event of litigation
13) Right of ENC and/or other involved parties including certification-to-standards inspectors to inspect the factory
14) Seller agreement to maintain an adequate inventory of spare parts and components for a period (say, five years) after the last shipment made under this agreement
15) Agreement that seller will ship spare parts quickly (say, within fifteen days) after receipt of telex or fax requesting such shipment
16) Controlling definitions for commercial terms used in this agreement (often, International Rules for the Interpretation of Trade Terms [INCOTERMS], published by the International Chamber of Commerce, Paris, France
17) Starting date and period for which this contract shall be valid (often, one year)

Case 14: Kellogg In Europe

Arnold G. Langbo, President and Chief Operating Officer of Kellogg, Inc. and President of Kellogg International, was uneasy as he read the 1990 annual market analysis coming out of Europe. Since late 1989, for the first time in their sixty-plus-year presence in Europe, Kellogg of Battle Creek, Michigan, had a formidable opponent in the ready-to-eat cereal market there. Nestlé, S.A. of Switzerland had formed a joint venture with Kellogg's biggest competitor, General Mills. Cereal Partners Worldwide (CPW, as the new enterprise was called, was out to cut into Kellogg's 51 percent share of cereal sales outside the United States.

The U.S. market for cereals was mature. There was little growth, high competition, with more than 200 brands to choose from, under heavy attack from the private label brands and their lower prices. These private labels targeted many of Kellogg's core products such as Corn Flakes and Frosted Flakes. When Kellogg raised its U.S. prices 3 percent in 1990, Corn Flakes was not involved.

General Mills had already chipped away at Kellogg's market share in the U.S. From 1987–1990, Kellogg saw its share in the market fall from 41.2 percent to 37.5 percent, while General Mills' share of the $6.9 billion dollar industry had risen from 21.2 percent to 23.8 percent (**Exhibit 1**). The only other share growth was seen in the private label segment of the industry. And now it appeared that the Big G of General Mills was aiming for Kellogg International.

Langbo knew that beyond Europe were the markets of Latin America and the East. While Kellogg already had a more than 90 percent share in Brazil, the Japanese marketplace was going to be much more difficult to master. In Japan they were accustomed to eating something warm and soft for breakfast, and to change that into a taste for a cold, crisp cereal was going to take tremendous marketing skills. The society was deeply entrenched in tradition, but was not impenetrable, as the presence of McDonald's and Kentucky Fried Chicken attested to.

Kellogg could not afford to tackle those obstacles while still worrying about losing market share in Europe. No, Cereal Partners Worldwide would have to be put in its place and fast.

Langbo called in Holger U. Birkigt, Vice President and Director, Continental European Operations, and Thomas A. Knowlton, Vice President and Managing Director of Kellogg Company of Great Britain, to discuss the situation.

Kellogg of Battle Creek

Kellogg was founded in 1906, focusing on the manufacture of nutritious, ready-to-eat breakfast cereal made from corn. Nutrition and good taste had always

Exhibit 1 Percent of U.S. Market in Pounds

Company	1987	1988	1989	1990	1991
Kellogg	41.2	41.4	39.7	37.5	38.8
General Mills	21.2	21.1	23.4	24.3	23.8
Post/General Foods	13.2	12.2	10.9	11.3	11.2
Quaker Oats	7.5	8.1	7.9	7.4	7.4
Ralston Purina	5.6	5.2	5.6	6.1	4.7
Nabisco	5.4	5.2	4.8	4.4	3.4
Private Labels	3.6	4.3	5.2	6.5	7.4
Others	2.3	2.5	2.5	2.5	3.3

been their trademark, and at the height of their kingdom, in the 1950s, they had attained a 45 percent market share in the U.S.

Through the 1970s, the market grew rapidly and became increasingly competitive. Women were joining the work force in record numbers, and the lure of a quick, healthy breakfast for the family caused cereal sales to soar.

Kellogg had not been prepared for what came in the 1980s. Health experts everywhere were touting the benefits of oat bran as a preventative against heart disease and certain cancers. With 80 percent of their products made from corn, Kellogg saw their market share slip away. They were slow to respond to this phenomenon, and competitors such as General Mills, with 40 percent of their cereals oat-based, grew.

The oat-based cereals that Kellogg did develop came too late and at a great cost to the company. From 1985 to 1990 the number of cereals on the American shelves increased by 52 percent. Customers had over 200 names to choose from and the new ones from Kellogg were lost in the avalanche.

In 1990, the U.S. market was growing at a relatively slow 0.2 percent annually. Market share could only be gotten at a competitor's loss, which could be quite expensive in an industry where the cost of introducing a new product had risen from $5 million in the 1970s to $30–$40 million in the 1990s. Langbo knew the answer lay in the underdeveloped markets overseas, where current growth rates were 8–9 percent annually and were expected to continue for some time to come. After all, he thought, ready-to-eat breakfast cereals were currently marketed to less than half of the world's population.

Kellogg International

Kellogg had been a player in the European breakfast market since 1922, when Kellogg's Corn Flakes were introduced in London. A production facility was built in 1938, and the cereal giant from Battle Creek, Michigan, set down its roots and began to expand, crossing over to the Continent in the 1950s.

Kellogg had to create their market in most of Europe. The consumption of cereal for breakfast was traditional only in Britain and Ireland, where a big, American-style breakfast was the norm. In France, for instance, croissants and sweet rolls were more common, and in some countries, meat and cheese were the first meal of the day. Kellogg had always felt that being first in markets like these would help secure a first place position in the market.

Kellogg had been somewhat successful in developing the cereal market throughout most of Europe. The market was expanding, but there were still drastic differences in consumption among consumers in different European countries. In Great Britain, for instance, the average consumer ate 13 pounds of cereal a year, which even exceeded U.S. consumption of 10 pounds annually. In France and Germany, however, consumption levels in 1989 were 2 pounds per person. **Exhibits 2 and 3** show the growth in sales in Germany and Great Britain. The significantly higher growth rate in Germany can be attributed to this lower consumption per capita. It was clear to Langbo that there was still plenty of room for growth in this market.

Kellogg had production facilities in several locations throughout Europe poised to accept increased production as sales increased. Their distribution channels were also up to the task. All that was needed was the demand.

In 1990, Kellogg products were distributed in 130 countries worldwide, a distribution exceeded only by

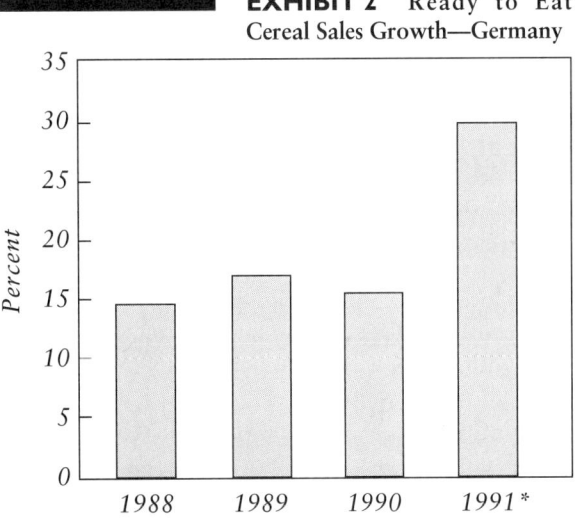

EXHIBIT 2 Ready to Eat Cereal Sales Growth—Germany

* 1991 Sales are based on First Quarter

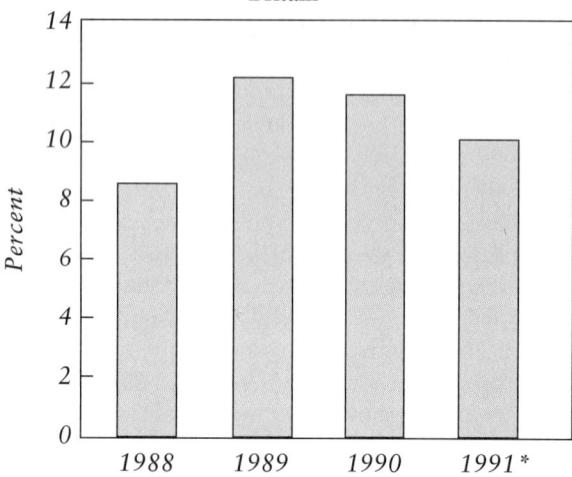

EXHIBIT 3 Ready To Eat Cereal Sales Growth—Great Britain

* 1991 Sales are based on First Quarter

Coca-Cola. If this trend continued, international sales were expected to top domestic sales by 1992.

Kellogg International was organized as a subsidiary of Kellogg, with Langbo as its President reporting to C.E.O William E. LaMothe. Each International Operating Manager in turn reported to Langbo. With the pending retirement of LaMothe, Langbo was considering an organizational change, giving each manager more responsibility and authority in their respective areas of control, since they each had unique characteristics.

Cereal Partners Worldwide

In 1989, Nestlé approached General Mills with an offer that they found impossible to turn down: Create a joint venture combining their individual strengths to tap into the rapidly expanding ready-to-eat cereal market in Europe. They had first approached Quaker Oats with their offer of a joint venture, but had been rejected.

The products would be the same that General Mills sold elsewhere, but would carry the Nestlé name, which was well known in Europe. Initially they would be manufactured in Nestlé production facilities, using General Mills' knowledge and technology. Nestlé would also provide the distribution channels and access to the local markets. This mix of General Mills' collection of products, technology, and knowledge of the cereal business along with Nestlé's distribution network, name recognition, and knowledge of the European market was creating quite a wave in the European marketplace.

CPW entered the European market with much fanfare and its requisite advertising. All this hoopla had caused an increase in overall cereal consumption and as such, was helpful to Kellogg's bottom line. In 1990, although Kellogg's market share had remained steady at 51.2 percent, total sales in Europe had increased by 6.5 percent and were expected to continue their upward climb.

To counter CPW's emergence as a competitor, Kellogg had thus far introduced products that were nearly identical to those launched by Cereal Partners. Cereals such as Golden Crackles competed with General Mills' Golden Grahams. Honey Nut Loops, made by Kellogg, was launched to compete with Big G's biggest seller, Cheerios. Kellogg even went so far as to introduce a cereal called Golden Oatmeal Crisp, akin to General Mills' Oatmeal Crisp, which they marketed in the U.S. Although it helped soften the blow, this strategy gave Kellogg the appearance of being a follower, not the leader that they were accustomed to being. While this strategy might prove beneficial in the short term, the Battle Creek giant needed a defence that would protect its market position against all competitors.

Kellogg's Name Recognition

The Kellogg name had always been associated with quality and nutrition. In order to project this image worldwide, the company had been a leader in product labeling, had sponsored nutrition workshops with health professionals, been a corporate sponsor of the Olympics, and had even entered into a co-marketing arrangement with the French government to preach the benefits of a good breakfast.

The Kellogg name was well known throughout Europe and was perceived by many people in England to be an English corporation. This would give them the "home court" advantage on the battlefield.

Market

In 1990, Kellogg was the number one seller of cereal in much of Europe (**Exhibit 4**). Sales were growing at an alarming rate and showed no signs of ebbing. Even countries in Eastern Europe were discovering ready-to-eat cereals, and Kellogg was planning to open production facilities in Latvia in late 1991. There were still areas where consumption was low enough to warrant a special effort by the company, and Birkigt thought they should concentrate their efforts there. Some of these markets, such as Spain and France, were virtually untouched. Birkigt pointed to Kellogg's popularity in these countries (**Exhibit 5**), saying that Kellogg had the market share, what they needed to do was develop the market.

EXHIBIT 4 Top Sellers in Europe, December 1990

Company	U.K.	France	W. Germany	Italy
Kellogg	42%	54%	42%	42%
Quaker	7%	16%	—	18%
Nabisco	8%	–	—	4%
Nestlé	—	12%	—	—
Wheetabix	14%	—	—	6%
Banania	—	9%	—	—
CPC	—	—	8%	—

EXHIBIT 5 Top Ten Brands in Selected Markets, As of March 1991 (* Denotes a Kellogg cereal)

Great Britain	France	Spain
1. Corn Flakes*	1. Corn Flakes*	1. Smacks*
2. Wheetabix	2. CPW Chocapic	2. Coco Pops*
3. Frosted Flakes*	3. Coco Pops*	3. Corn Flakes*
4. Rice Krispies*	4. Smacks*	4. All Bran*
5. All Bran*	5. Frosted Flakes*	5. Frosted Flakes*
6. Bran Flakes*	6. Corn Pops*	6. Corn Pops*
7. Crunchy Nut*	7. Quaker Cruesli	7. CPW Chocapic
8. CPW Shredded Wheat	8. Extra*	8. Krispies*
9. Sugar Puffs	9. Country Store*	9. Rice Krispies*
10. Fruit n' Fibre*	10. Rice Krispies*	10. Chocos*

This growth could be attributed to several things: the ever-increasing number of women in the workforce who are attracted to the convenience of the product; Europeans traveling to the U.S. and bringing their newly developed tastes for cereal back home (in fact, for many years some of Kellogg's products were sold in Europe in specialty import stores); and the development of commercial television, making advertising more profitable.

Kellogg had answered the growing demand by continually introducing new products in the different countries. Each product was slightly different in each country, making it impossible for Kellogg to take advantage of the economies of scale, or to market a truly global product. Changes had been made recently to eliminate the differences, with Kellogg's Corn Flakes consistent across borders, and Frosted Flakes and Rice Krispies almost there.

Marketing efforts were also becoming global. Tony the Tiger now hawks Frosted Flakes all over the world, and Toucan Sam of Fruit Loops fame is fast becoming a household character.

All this gave Kellogg a solid base from which to defend their cereal kingdom on the Continent. But CPW is a worthy opponent and Langbo felt that further steps in streamlining production, distribution, and marketing were warranted.

Entrenchment

Knowlton questioned whether the constant introduction of new products in a developing market such as Europe was prudent. He was already hearing rumblings from distributors that the store managers did not want to devote any more shelf space to cereal. If a new product went up, an old one came down. Kellogg had also suffered severe financial setbacks from recent flops such as Big Mixx and SW Graham in the U.S. and Raisin Splitz and Toppas abroad. Maybe concentrating on a few core products, creating consistency in manufacture and marketing, would give them the solid growth everyone wanted.

Case 15: The Clondike Works

In March 1989, Robert Lenore, an executive in the International Division of the Clondike Works, was faced with deciding what tactics the company could employ against a Taiwanese manufacturing company that was exporting counterfeit products labeled with the "Clondike" name. Among many products, the company was most concerned about power-lock tape rules, of which it had lost 50 percent of its sales to the Taiwanese competitor.

The Taiwanese firm had duplicated the tape lock and sold it with either the "Clondike" name or a close facsimile for $2.00 to $2.50 below the Clondike price. Clondike's biggest customers for the power tape lock were in the Middle East, and during the previous two years the sales there had dropped over 50 percent. Mr. Lenore expressed deep concern over what could be done to rectify this situation.

The Clondike Works

In 1840, James and Patrick Clondike earned a reputation for manufacturing quality hardware products with Yankee craftsmanship. This reputation for quality continued to grow over the years, and Clondike always stood behind the quality of its work. For example, Clondike "Life Span" hinges were guaranteed for the life of the building in which they were installed. Over 10,000 of these hinges were used in the twin towers of the World Trade Center in New York City.

As the company's product lines grew, so did its quality control capability. New techniques and procedures, and new instruments and controls had been added to ensure that Clondike's reputation for quality could keep pace with the nation's growing technological sophistication. Because of its high standards, "Clondike" was the preferred name in tools, as well as builder's hardware. During the 1970s, the company registered tremendous growth. Its sales increased from $1 billion in 1981 to $1.8 billion in 1988. Earnings in 1988 amounted to about 6 percent of sales. The company was headquartered in Newton, Massachusetts.

Product Lines

Clondike manufactured and sold over 20,000 products. These products were divided into three product lines: consumer products ("do-it-yourselfers"), industrial products, and construction and maintenance products. The "do-it-yourselfer" (DIY) industry was seen as a major strategic thrust for Clondike works. Products in this category were introduced to enable the consumers to do everyday repair work, simple construction, and other types of improvements. The products in the DIY line were grouped into five categories: hand tools, hardware, drapery hardware, garden tools, and automatic garage door openers. DIY products accounted for about 42 percent of Clondike's sales. Industrial products were categorized into five groups: air tools, electrical tools, hand tools, hydraulic tools, and systems. Clondike's industrial products, sold worldwide, contributed about 35 percent toward the company's sales. Construction and maintenance products were divided into five categories: hand tools, electrical tools, hardware, doors, and hydraulic tools, and provided 23 percent of Clondike's sales.

Clondike International

International sales accounted for more than 42 percent of Clondike's total business. Besides the United States, Clondike had manufacturing operations in nine countries—England, France, Germany, Italy, Australia, Colombia, Brazil, Guatemala, and Mexico. The company had sales offices in thirty-three countries around the globe. International sales of the company's products began through overseas representation fifty years ago. The steady sales growth of Clondike's products in overseas markets was based largely upon the customer's approval of Clondike quality

Internationally, the company was extremely diversified, which added to its strengths and protected it against currency fluctuations. For example, during the 1970s when the U.S. dollar was very strong, U.S.

products were more expensive compared with products of countries whose currencies were weak against the dollar. Thus, the distributors in Europe found it to their advantage to source out of England, France, or Germany. During the 1980s, the U.S. dollar was weak and U.S. products were in great demand on the export market because they were cheaper. Many Middle Eastern orders, which formerly had gone to England or Europe, began coming to the United States because of the difference in currency values, and Clondike was able to make the best of the situation.

Competition from Taiwan

Clondike's 3-meter, 1½-inch-wide 10-foot power lock was sold all over the world. "Power lock" is a Clondike trademark registered in the United States. Its reproduction and sale throughout the Middle East, Africa, and Asia by the Taiwanese manufacturers were illegal. Originally the quality of the Taiwanese product had been inferior to the Clondike product, but in recent years the reproduction had been improved to a level comparable to the Clondike product.

The Taiwanese manufacturers capitalized on Clondike packaging and its logo and name to sell their product by outright use of the word *Clondike* on a label and package that duplicated Clondike's. In some instances, the Clondike logo was utilized by simply rearranging the design, colors, and background. In other cases, the imitation product was stamped with a look-alike "Clondike" name—minus the "e." In most ways, it was difficult to distinguish between the reproduction and Clondike's product. The only discernible difference was the stamped USA logo on the original products. Most dealers overseas exhibited the forged product side-by-side with the original product, and customers could not distinguish between the two, except by the prices.

Customer Loyalty

Clondike experienced customer losses based solely on price criteria. Sales had dropped over 50 percent in the previous two years in the firm's primary market—the Middle East, Far East, and Nigeria. In addition, costly labor and high overhead costs placed constraints on Clondike's ability to compete with the Taiwanese producer. Clondike's experience was comparable to the U.S. automotive industry's competition from the Japanese in the 1980s, whose labor costs were $10 to $12 per hour compared with U.S. costs of $14 to $16 per hour. Because of a similar discrepancy, the Taiwanese were able to offer quality goods, manufactured with cheap labor at prices well below their U.S. competition.

In an effort to compete with the Taiwanese on a price basis, Clondike attempted to supply the Middle East with tape locks produced in England, France, and Mexico. However, customer loyalty to the U.S.-made product discouraged the purchase of products manufactured elsewhere. Foreign customers were intrigued with the prestige of buying a product manufactured in the United States. Clondike's attempt to sell a less-expensive product proved unsuccessful, and it returned to supplying foreign dealers from the United States.

The Effects of International Politics, Economics, and Legislation

In early 1988, Clondike tried to take legal action against the Taiwanese firm. It proved to be a difficult task. There are no international courts and no enforceable laws. Legal action, therefore, had to be pursued through either the U.S. or the Taiwanese courts. Of basic importance to international legal action are (1) the cooperation given by the foreign government and (2) the strength of the company's representation in the foreign country.

Cooperation from the Taiwanese government was negligible for economic reasons. At the time, Taiwan was experiencing a difficult period of economic growth and development. The increase in its exports had a positive influence on its balance of payments. Therefore, the manufacturing and exporting of Taiwanese tape locks were good for the economy, even if they were illegally manufactured. Also, export was the only market for counterfeit products since selling them within Taiwan would result in court action for patent infringement.

Politically, Taiwan and United States were no longer staunch allies. The United States had withdrawn its ambassador to Taiwan, and the UN had expelled the Taiwanese representative. Such political actions precluded any cooperation from the Taiwanese government. As Mr. Lenore pondered the facts, he realized a decision had to be made regarding what action Clondike would take against Taiwanese counterfeiting. Part of the answer, he realized, was to stay in the market rather than pull out altogether. Also, there was reassurance in the idea that 50 percent of something was better than 50 percent of nothing.

Case 16: All Shave in Saudi Arabia

On a hot summer day in 1990, Mike Lacey lay on his bed and watched as the fan went around. He felt whipped and didn't really know what to do next. All week he had been trying to influence Mustafa Almin, and he had no more effect than the fan was having on the heat of Riyadh.

Three years ago the All Shave Company, of which Mike was Middle Eastern manager, had been very successful exporting razors and blades to Saudi Arabia. Then, in the face of possible import restrictions, the company had turned over its business to a new company financed by the Almin family. The family members were leading Saudi industrialists who had built a fortune on the production of steel products, like picks and shovels, and were then interested in expanding to new fields. All Shave received a minority interest in the new business in return for its trade name and technical aid.

The contract with the Almin family had also specified that they would "actively promote All Shave products." Mike thought that it was clearly understood that this meant continuing the aggressive promotion that had been used in Saudi Arabia to build the company's sales in the 1970s from nothing to a high level. Under Almin management, however, All Shave sales had dropped steadily. It was soon evident that the Almins were not pushing sales, and in visits and correspondence, the company applied increasing pressure for more activity.

When nothing happened, Mike finally decided he would go to Saudi Arabia and stay until he could find a way to get the Almins moving. That was over six weeks ago. After spending the first month in the field, Mike had worked up a detailed program designed to reestablish All Shave's market position. He had found All Shave products were being sold from Almin warehouses with virtually no sales effort and that promotion was limited to a few newspaper advertisements and a scattering of posters distributed by the Almin family's industrial sales reps. No additional salespeople had been added for All Shave accounts. The selling activity fell far short of All Shave's former program and that of its leading competitor.

For the past week, Mike had been trying to convince Mustafa Almin, the sixty-year-old head of the family, to adopt a better program. But he had argued in vain. Mike had pointed to the low sales volume and the Almins' limited program, which he pointed out did not meet their agreement. He had supported his proposals in the greatest detail, arguing particularly that All Shave's previous success and the present results achieved by their competition proved that strong promotion was worthwhile.

Mustafa Almin expressed appreciation for Mike's interest and efforts but had agreed to nothing. He explained that a sales drop was inevitable with the change to the Saudi manufacturer. Although sales were lower, the company was making a reasonable profit. He said that to fulfill the contract terms he had undertaken newspaper advertising even though he did not believe in it. He felt its blatant character reflected on the prestige of the Almin family name.

This case is printed here with the permission of the authors Ellen Cook, Philip Hunsaker, and Mohammed Ali Alireza of the University of San Diego.

Mustafa Almin believed that a good product was its own best advertisement and on that basis the Almin family had built a great business. He also observed that the closest competitor sold a higher-quality blade than All Shave and it was quite probable that this, rather than promotion, accounted for their success. In any case, several British concerns in related fields did very little advertising, and since they had been in India for many years, Mr. Almin felt their approach to the market was probably sounder.

Mike found it hard to counter these arguments. He was sure he was right, and equally sure that Mr. Almin was a very competent businessman who should be able to see the logic of Mike's proposals. He had great respect and liking for Mr. Almin, and he believed that once Almin grasped the value of promotion, he would do great things for All Shave in Saudi Arabia.

But how could he convince him?

Mustafa Almin settled himself to relax before the evening meal and reflected for a moment on the events of the past week. He had spent a great deal of time with the boy from the United States. He was a good boy, full of energy and ideas. He wished he could do something to help him. He drove so hard, and for what? This whole arrangement with the All Shave Company had turned out rather differently from what the Almins had expected. The product was good, and left to themselves, his family could develop it into a good business, as they had with the rest of their operations.

But they were not left to themselves. Instead, there had been constant pushing and arguing. These people from the United States never seemed to be satisfied with anything. Now they sent this young man who scarcely knew Saudi Arabia to tell the Almins how to run their business. It was not pleasant at all. He hoped the young man would give up soon.

PART 4

Perspectives of International Markets

CHAPTER 10

International Marketing Research

CHAPTER FOCUS

After studying this chapter, you should be able to:

- Explain the importance of marketing research in the context of international business

- Discuss the procedure for undertaking marketing research across national boundaries

- Identify sources of secondary data both in the U.S. and abroad

- Describe the problems of conducting primary research overseas

- Examine the perspectives of an international marketing information system

The prime function of marketing is to make and sell what buyers *want*, rather than simply selling whatever can be most easily made. Therefore, what consumers require must be assessed through marketing research so that a firm can direct its activities toward optimal marketing through the satisfaction of those requirements.

The role of marketing research is equally important in domestic and international marketing. The worldwide marketing research industry had a value of about $3.8 billion in 1985. Of this, the largest single market was the U.S., accounting for some $1.8 billion or about 47 percent of the total. Europe accounted for $1.4 billion, 35 percent of the total global marketing research expenditures. Japan, Australia, and New Zealand added another 9 percent. Canada accounted for 4 percent. The remaining $156 million, about 4 percent of the world total, came from the Third World. Half of the amount was spent in Latin and South America, mainly Mexico, Brazil, Argentina, and Venezuela. The Far East, excluding Japan, accounted for $38 million. The African total would have been very small if not for the $15 million of the $17 million total spent by South Africa. The Middle East, with Saudi Arabia the main market, contributed about $10 million and is a growth area, but one that has shown some slowing in recent years. India, Pakistan, and Sri Lanka added a further $9 million.[1]

The differences in international environments make conducting marketing research more difficult.[2] Consider the research information needed by these potential international marketers in order for them to make decisions on how to proceed:

> A manufacturer of a specialized industrial product, iron fitting, believes that there is potentially a good market for export and wants to begin to develop it. Neither the company's management nor any of its sales force, however, has knowledge of possible markets or of the nature of the competition.
>
> A large U.S. corporation is contemplating building a factory in Western Europe. Management wonders if its product should be changed to suit the new market.
>
> A pharmaceutical company has to decide how to price a prescription drug item manufactured in its factory in Brazil for the Latin American market. Should the same pricing schedule used in the U.S. be followed? If not, what criteria should be used to set the price?
>
> A soft drink company must determine how effective its U.S. advertising strategy will be in promoting its product in Southeast Asia.

Such situations are examples of international marketing problems that require marketing research. In each case, the firm's past experience cannot provide an adequate basis for decision. In fact, the information necessary to support management action is more likely to be found outside the organization. Specialized trade journals or government studies or discussions with professional-level personnel who have special industry expertise are likely to be helpful. Or, if all these fail, it may finally become necessary to conduct a customer survey.

This chapter examines the meaning of marketing research and provides a framework for conducting such research. The two types of research, primary and secondary, are differentiated and their procedures discussed. Alternative ways of organizing international marketing research and the need for establishing an international marketing information system are included.

Meaning of Marketing Research

The term *marketing research* refers to gathering, analyzing, and presenting information related to a well-defined problem. The focus of marketing research is a specific problem or project with a beginning and an end. Marketing research differs from *marketing intelligence*, which is information gathered and analyzed on a continual basis. Further, intelligence is evaluated information whose credibility, meaning, and importance have been established.

Often in practice, marketing research is used interchangeably with the term *market research*, which is conceptually narrower in scope because it deals with information concerned with current and potential customers—who they are; why they buy a product or service; and where they buy it, when they buy it, what they buy, and how they buy it. Marketing research, in addition to market research information, also deals with information relative to *marketing mix variables*: product, price, distribution, and promotion; marketing organizational matters; and the marketing environment. A *marketing information system* is the organization of market research, marketing research, and marketing intelligence into a workable system.

The procedures and methods of conducting marketing research are conceptually the same for both domestic marketing and international marketing. For example, before collecting data the researcher must have a clear idea of the research problem. Likewise, only an appropriate sample will yield valuable results. Procedural similarities aside, international marketing research differs from domestic marketing in three major ways:

1. The effects of the international environment on the whole company as a profit-oriented unit are considered. For example, the marketing research project concerned with the ramifications of a substantial price hike in a particular foreign country must consider questions that do not apply to the domestic market; for example, will the company's subsidiary be nationalized if prices are increased beyond a certain level? (See International Marketing Highlight 10.1.)
2. Many concepts and frameworks (i.e., market segmentation), which constitute the core of marketing decision making in the domestic arena, may be unusable in international marketing, not because the concept cannot be transferred, but because the information necessary to make such a transfer is not available. For example, if there is a lack of current income distribution data on a country, any analysis of the demand for a product will assume incorrect income categories and, therefore, cannot mean much for practical purposes.
3. Finally, the ethnocentric nature of marketing makes cultural differences among nations a significant factor. Thus, culture in a domestic market can be considered to be naturally understood, but in international marketing the culture must be fully investigated.

To illustrate the point, consider a recent study that explored the effect of a monetary incentive on the questionnaire response rate. Receipt of one U.S. dollar increased the response rate from Japanese businesspeople but decreased the response from Hong Kong business people. The author noted:

In this study, Japanese business executives were more compliant than Hong Kongese in general, and the monitary incentive was successful in more than doubling the response from Japan but decreased the response from Hong Kong. These findings may be biased because of the small sample, the sampling frame, or the questionnaire content. However, the results may imply a cultural difference either toward responding to questionnaires, or toward monetary incentives. The cross-cultural researcher should be aware of such problems, and explore the effect of monetary incentives prior to the mass mailing or surveys. Theoretically, monetary incentives may increase response rates in any culture or country; however, the type (local or foreign currency) and amount may be important factors.[3]

Such factors raise a variety of conceptual, methodological, and organizational issues in international marketing research relating to:

1. The complexity of research design, caused by operation in a multicountry, multicultural, and multilinguistic environment
2. The lack of secondary data available for many countries and product markets
3. The high costs of collecting primary data, particularly in developing countries
4. The problems associated with coordinating research and data collection in different countries
5. The difficulties of establishing the comparability and equivalence of data and research conducted in different contexts
6. The intrafunctional character of many international marketing decisions
7. The economics of many international investment and marketing decisions.[4]

International Marketing Highlight 10.1

Local Culture and Market Potential

The chairman of a large American soft drink company decided that the firm should target Indonesia for sales of its most popular beverage. With a population of nearly 180 million people, Indonesia is the fifth most populous country in the world. Management considered this huge potential market irresistible and worked out a bottling and distribution arrangement to serve the country. The company sold the soft drink syrup to a bottler, who then bottled the drink and distributed it.

Unfortunately, sales were terrible. The drink simply didn't sell. The marketing campaign flopped despite predominantly good initial research, including research into the local competition and government attitudes, because the chairman and his project directors forgot to consider two major factors. First, Indonesia does have 180 million inhabitants, but most of them live in rural areas still functioning within a preindustrial economy. Most Indonesians simply don't have much money. Second, many of them prefer sweet, coconut-based drinks; they are unaccustomed to American-style carbonated beverages. A market for American drinks does exist, but almost exclusively in the major cities. That market—consumers with Western tastes and sufficient disposable income to purchase foreign-style beverages—totals only about 8 million people.

Framework for International Marketing Research

Most marketing research studies proceed through a common series of major tasks:

- Define the problem and the information needed for support of management's decision-making process.
- Identify alternative sources of information.
- Plan and execute data collection.
- Analyze the data and prepare a report.

Defining the Problem

This first task, which sounds deceptively simple, may be the pivotal task in the entire study. In defining the problem, two important considerations are market structure and product concept. *Market structure* refers to the size of the market, its stage of development, the number of competitors and their market shares, and the channels through which the market is approached. The importance of market structure in a problem definition is shown by a 1963 *Reader's Digest* study, which reported that French and German consumers ate significantly more spaghetti than Italians.[5] This finding was wrong. The study had concerned itself with only packaged, branded spaghetti, and not *total* spaghetti consumption. Because much of the spaghetti sold in Italy has been unpackaged and unbranded, the results of the study were totally invalid. The *Reader's Digest* researchers should have clearly defined the kind of spaghetti consumption to be studied in each of the different countries (see International Marketing Highlight 10.2).

■ International Marketing Highlight 10.2 ■

Health Clubs in Singapore

A widely franchised health club opened a facility in Singapore. With its young, urban population and a widespread appreciation of Western culture, Singapore seemed a site destined for success. Moreover, the club's physical appearance and stock of equipment equaled or surpassed that of comparable facilities in the U.S.

Yet the club couldn't sign up enough members. Despite the Singaporeans' interest in sports, the club attracted few of them and ended up catering to the relatively small expatriate community instead. Citizens of Singapore felt little enthusiasm for the American-style health club; they were more attracted either to Western competitive sports or to Chinese calisthenics and other traditional Asian forms of exercise.

Source: Charles F. Valentine, *The Arthur Young International Business Guide* (New York: John Wiley & Sons, 1988), p. 74.

In addition, a product may be viewed differently in different cultures. Thus, even before attempting to define the marketing research problem for study, exploratory research may be necessary to understand the *product concept*, that is, the meaning of the product in a particular environment. In this way, problem definition will be appropriate to the concept of the product held in the particular country of interest.

Berent points out that milk-based products are viewed very differently in the U.K. and Thailand.[6] In England, they are usually consumed at meals and bedtime for their sleep-inducing, soothing, relaxing properties. In Thailand, the same products are consumed on the way to work and often away from home, for they are considered invigorating, energizing, and stimulating.

Let us assume a multinational marketer is interested in finding out the potential market for a brand of yogurt in England and Thailand. The problem definition in the two countries will have to be stated differently. In the U.K., the yogurt might be primarily perceived by the consumers as a healthful and relaxing product to be used prior to retiring. In Thailand, the research problem would determine if yogurt would be considered mainly an energy food used to start the day.

Identifying Alternative Information Sources

After the problem has been defined, where the necessary information may be found and how to obtain it must be determined. In some cases, the study may be confined to *secondary data*, that is, published information that has been collected elsewhere. It may be available free (for example, government statistics), for a price (for example, syndicated research supplies), or through restricted distribution sources (for example, trade association statistics).

Let us assume that Ford Motor Company is interested in assembling its new world car in India in collaboration with an Indian company. Before committing itself to the joint venture, Ford would like to study the car's market potential in India over a 10-year period. Fortunately, the Indian government collects a variety of socioeconomic-demographic information on a regular basis. This information is conveniently available. Ford, therefore, can use with confidence such secondary information as population projections, income data, consumer expenditure patterns, and rural-urban population shifts to assess the market potential.

Sometimes internal data are also useful. Existing files, in fact, can often provide important insights into the question at hand. In the above example, Ford might have found that it already had sufficient information on population trends in India gathered when the company had earlier negotiated for the assembly of tractors there. Thus, there would be no need for another source of information.

In cases where no amount of investigation of secondary sources or of internal data provides the required information, *primary data* will have to be compiled from scratch through interviews and other direct collection of information. Primary data may be gathered in various ways (to be discussed later) from trade association representatives, governmental experts, managerial personnel, and/or the buying public.

For example, a company may be interested in introducing its prefabricated houses in Latin America. The company would have to study house-buying behavior in the target countries. Since this type of information may not be conveniently available from secondary sources, primary data gathering may be necessary. The importance of such information for decision making is revealed in a study on the subject done in the U.K.

> Home ownership in different countries could also have completely different implications. The proverb that "a man's home is his castle" is far more applicable in the U.K. (where castles can in fact be found) than in the U.S., where the geographic and social mobility of the population means that the regular exchange of homes is a commonplace experience during the life cycle of most families. Therefore, the decision-making patterns of husband and wife, and the amount of effort spent in making a home-buying decision, should be quite different between these two countries.[7]

Thus, before entering the market with prefabricated houses in Latin America, the company has to learn through primary research in which ways houses might mean home in various locales.

Data Collection

The actual collection of data must be planned and executed carefully. While data collection will be discussed at length in later sections of this chapter, it should be noted here that tracking down reliable, usable data sources can be time consuming. This is particularly so when a variety of sources are pursued concurrently. In fact, the search can go on with decreasing returns unless personnel with knowledge of the country appraise what progress is being made.

Interview questions must be tested for their appropriateness so that they produce the desired results. A sound approach is to conduct professional-level interviews in two phases: (1) collect basic data and (2) explore interview questions not anticipated at the start of the project.

Once basic data have been collected, the process of cross-checking can begin. This step requires that all information be examined critically for its relevance. Cross-checking establishes the reliability of data by comparing one source with another. It is important to document the criteria used by the project team to determine the reliability of collected data.

Analysis, Interpretation, and Report Preparation

For the final step, the preparation of the report, the data must be analyzed and interpreted.[8] Here also, attention should be paid to a country's cultural traits. For example, in an examination of the beer market, it was found that beer was perceived as an alcoholic drink in Northern European countries, but it was considered a soft drink in Mediterranean countries. Thus, other products listed with beer as alternative drinks would influence the research findings. Similarly, in Japan noncarbonated fruit juices are often substituted for bottled soft drinks. This seldom occurs in the U.S.[9] In brief, *the significance of different concepts of the product in various countries must be taken into account.*

Reports must be complete, factual, and objective. It is particularly important to communicate the reliability as well as the limitations of the facts presented. Particular attention should be given to the following aspects of a report:

1. Data sources must be identified. Different sources of data warrant varying degrees of confidence. For example, information on a Third World country obtained from the United States Agency for International Development is probably more reliable than the information available from the government of that country.
2. Data projection must be explained. As a matter of fact, the statistical computations should be simplified as much as possible.
3. The identity of all those interviewed should be included as well as their titles or qualifications. (This rule does not apply to consumer research.) This requirement may have to be relaxed when anonymity has been guaranteed.
4. The alternative courses of action developed from analysis and interpretation of the data must be labeled as such, clearly reserving to management the responsibility for selecting the appropriate course of action.

Information Requirements of International Marketers

The nature of marketing decisions does not vary from country to country, but the environment differs from country to country. For this reason, the sort of information required to complete a marketing study may vary from one country to another. For example, in a situation where a marketer is free to set prices based on competition, a detailed analysis of competition should be made. However, in a country where the price is set by government, information on governmental cost analysis would be of greater importance. The fact that environment determines what kind of information is needed makes international marketing research efforts quite different from domestic marketing research work.[10]

Figure 10.1 shows the types of marketing studies a company may want to conduct in different areas such as promotion, distribution, price, product, or market. Each of these area studies takes a different form of information, as the following discussion makes clear.

FIGURE 10.1 Types of Marketing Studies Required for Doing Business Abroad

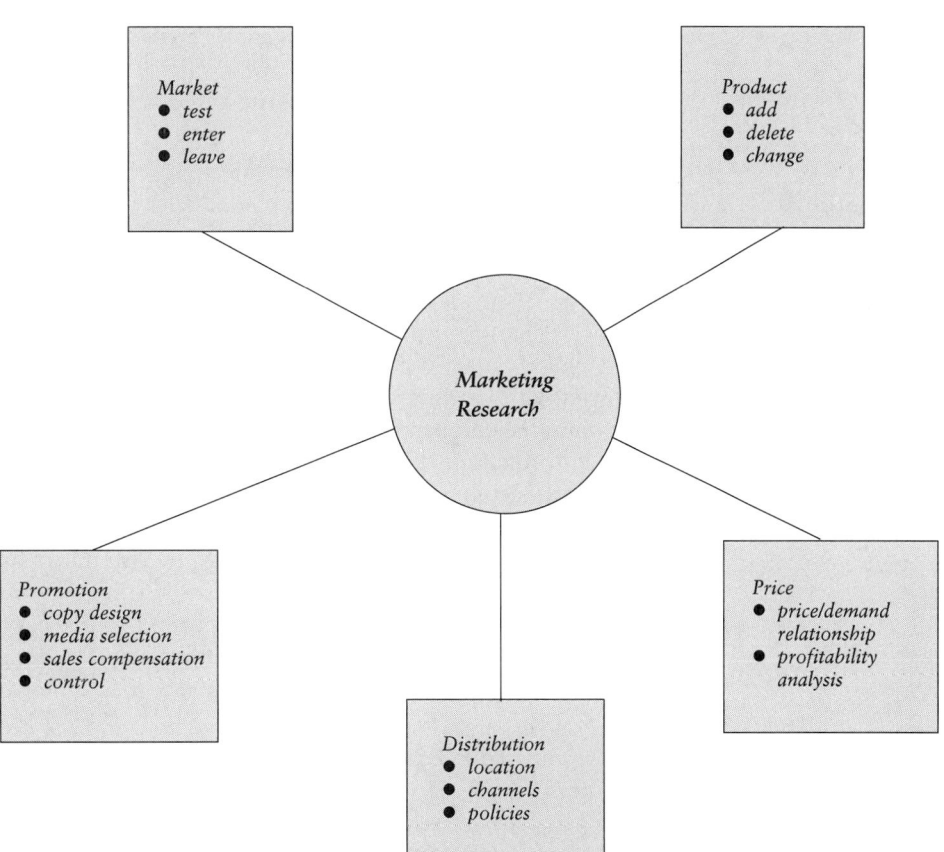

Market Information

Market research is required for testing, entering, or leaving a market and deals with market performance, market shares, and sales analysis and forecasting. *Marketing performance research* involves market measurements, either to compare a company's performance against specified standards or to project a possible future outcome. *Market potential* refers to the total market demand under optimal conditions; *market forecast* shows the expected level of market demand under the given conditions. To illustrate, when PepsiCo decided to expand its Pizza Hut business into certain Middle Eastern countries like Saudi Arabia, it conducted beforehand market potential research for five years in each country.

Market share refers to a company's proportion of total sales in an industry during a set time, usually a year. The market shares held by competitors shape marketing strategy for a company. The competitor with a respectable market share will have a cost advantage over its rivals. This cost advantage can be passed on to the customers through lower prices, which in turn strengthens the company's hold on the market. Because of the strategic importance of market share, business corporations keep constant watch on its fluctuations. Data supplied by industry associations, if properly analyzed, usually show respective market shares.

Past *sales information* can be analyzed in different ways: by amount of profit from different products, by productivity of sales territory (for example, Latin America or Western Europe), or by customer type. Sales analysis can pinpoint problems.

Sales forecasts refer to estimates of future sales of a product during a specific period. The sales forecast is the single most important basis for preparing budgets.

Product Information

Product research means both product line research and individual product research. This kind of research bears on when to add, delete, or change the product.

A company operating overseas must often decide which product line it should add, which it should drop, and which needs rejuvenation. These decisions require a variety of information. Consider this example. A large paper products company manufactured an expensive line of writing paper, as well as other kinds of paper products. The company had about a 30 percent market share in Latin America, but the demand had been constant for a number of years. As part of a program for simplification of product lines, the company wondered if there had been changes in the office environment in Latin countries that made the use of expensive paper obsolete. In other words, should the product line be abandoned? The company undertook marketing research to find an answer to this question.

A manager may also require marketing research information on each individual product. As a product passes through its life cycle, different marketing programs must be developed for every stage. Thus, it is important to place a product on its life cycle curve in order to choose the appropriate marketing program, and marketing research can be of real value in plotting a product's life cycle in different countries.

Promotion Information

Promotion research indicates research for advertising and personal selling. Companies consult the findings of objective research before spending money on advertising campaigns in order to select appropriate copy and appeals and make the best media selection. A trading stamp company operating in Europe, for example, redeemed stamps saved by consumers in two ways, either in merchandise or in travel. Over the years, it was found that more and more customers preferred overseas travel to merchandise. For the company, however, merchandise was more profitable; so the company considered starting an ad campaign to entice consumers into redeeming their stamps in merchandise. The company wondered if a merchandise catalog, which emphasized the virtue of material acquisitions as status symbols, would be persuasive in Europe. The production of the catalog would cost about two million dollars, and the catalog's market effectiveness had to be tested beforehand.

Personal selling, just as advertising, must produce profits. Consider the complaint of the sales manager of a U.S. pharmaceutical company: "My salespeople in Italy are not productive enough even though we pay them a lot more than the industry average there." Marketing research can provide insights into problems related to *personal selling*, which involves questions about how many salespeople to hire and how much to pay them, how to form sales territories, and how much time to spend on retaining old customers and how much on developing new accounts.

Distribution Information

Distribution research consists of channel research and location research. *Channel research* can help a company decide which channels to use for distribution of its products. Marketing research can provide information on the availability of channels and their relative desirability.

A water systems manufacturer, for instance, traditionally used manufacturer's representatives for the distribution of its water pumps in the Canadian market. The company, however, was becoming dissatisfied with manufacturer's representatives and wanted to use its own sales force. A marketing research firm was asked for a study of the effect on sales of making such a change.

Location research concerns decisions about warehousing, inventory, and transportation. For example, the decision to own a warehouse in Germany or to use a public warehouse there requires marketing research.

Price Information

A company sets the prices of its products to meet both short-term and long-term objectives. To set prices, information about the ability of consumers to pay, about dealer reaction, and about the effect of price on demand is necessary. Studies that measure the public perception of a product's quality in relation to price also help in making pricing decisions.

Environment Information

No matter which sort of international marketing study is planned, the researchers must take into account the foreign country's environment in all its aspects: legal, political, social, cultural, and attitudinal, as shown by both the buying habits of its consumers and the business practices of its enterprises. Naturally, familiarity with the environment is equally important in domestic marketing, but knowledge of domestic environment can come more easily from personal experience. For example, if a U.S. company is interested in doing business in China, it must learn about a political system that is different from what is taken for granted in the U.S. political structure.

General Research Information

All marketing research requires four general groups of overall information in addition to the more specific categories already discussed:

1. General information about:
   a. Community-type conditions (for example, political happenings such as campaigns and elections; cultural events such as county fairs and special annual ethnic or religious celebrations; and national events such as sports, championships, and holidays)
   b. Business conditions (for example, business ethics and traditional associations)
   c. Lifestyles and living conditions, that is, social and cultural customs and taboos (for example, marriageable age for men and women and the role of women in society).[11] (See International Marketing Highlight 10.3.)
   d. General economic conditions (for example, the standards of living of various groups of people and the economic infrastructure—transportation, power supply, and communication)
2. Industry information about governmental decisions affecting the industry; resource availability (for example, labor and land); current or potential competitors (that is, general information about their markets and their problems); competition from U.S. companies, local companies, and/or third country companies; industry policy, concerted actions in the industry, and so forth.

International Marketing Highlight 10.3

Hands-On Market Research

When Sony researched the market for a lightweight portable cassette player, results showed that consumers wouldn't buy a tape player that didn't record. Company chairman Akio Morita decided to introduce the Walkman anyway, and the rest is history. Today it is one of Sony's most successful products.

Morita's disdain for large-scale consumer surveys and other scientific research tools isn't unique in Japan. Matsushita, Toyota, and other well-known Japanese consumer goods companies are just as skeptical about the Western style of market research. Occasionally, the Japanese do conduct consumer attitude surveys, but most executives don't base their marketing decisions on them or on other popular techniques.

Of course, Japanese corporations want accurate and useful information about their markets as much as U.S. and European companies do. They just go about it differently. Japanese executives put much more faith in information they get directly from wholesalers and retailers in the distribution channels. Moreover, they track what's happening among channel members on a monthly, weekly, and sometimes even daily basis.

Japanese-style market research relies heavily on two kinds of information: "soft data" obtained from visits to dealers and other channel members, and "hard data" about shipments, inventory levels, and retail sales. Japanese managers believe that these data better reflect the behavior and intentions of flesh-and-blood consumers.

Source: Reprinted by permission of *Harvard Business Review*. An excerpt from "Market Research the Japanese Way" by Johny K. Johansson and Ikujiro Nonaka, May–June 1987, p. 16. Copyright © 1987 by the President and Fellows of Harvard College; all rights reserved.

3. Study-related information: collateral data generated to complete a specific market research study. For example, a study concerned with market potential needs information on supply and demand in market areas of current and potential interest (for example, capacity, consumption, imports, exports). On the other hand, a study concerned with the introduction of a new product requires information about existing products, the technical know-how available in the country, sources of raw material, and leads for joint ventures.

The amount of information to be gathered in a given case depends on the cost-benefit relationship of such information. For example, let us assume a company has an opportunity to export machinery to Kenya. Although normally the company checks on the credit rating of an importer before making a shipment, such a delay might ruin a particular transaction. The company figures out that, if the importer does not make the payment as stipulated, it stands to lose $2,000 after accounting for the advance from the importer. On the other hand, the company could have a market research firm do a study on the credit worthiness of the importer for $3,000 in a very short time. In other words, the cost exceeds the benefit and the study is not worth it. This example, while oversimplified, illustrates the importance of relating the cost to benefit in terms of time and money before deciding to undertake marketing research.

Finally, the nature of information required will vary based on the objective of research.[12] To illustrate the point, Exhibit 10.1 lists the type of information a firm needs to determine the export potential. The firm must examine different types of environments as well as undertake market and product research.

Gathering Secondary Data at Home

There are two kinds of data—primary and secondary. Primary data are gathered by the researcher. Secondary data, on the other hand, refer to information collected by someone else, either an individual or an organization. Exhibit 10.2 characterizes the two kinds of data. Research based on secondary data may be conducted either at home or abroad. This section discusses secondary research in the U.S.

U.S. Sources of Data

There are five sources of information in the U.S.: international agencies, the U.S. government, consulting firms, foreign government offices, and banks.

International Agencies The United Nations (UN), the World Bank, and the International Monetary Fund (IMF) gather a variety of economic and social information on different countries of the world. This information is available to the public. For example, the UN yearbook provides information on worldwide demographics.[13] Also, the World Bank's *The World Development Report* summarizes information on living patterns via such indicators as daily calorie supply, life expectancy at birth, and school enrollment.[14] The IMF provides historical information on national economic indicators (GNP, industrial production, inflation rate, money supply) of its member countries. This information is available on computer tapes.[15]

Exhibit 10.1 Information Needs for Determining Export Potential

STAGE ONE: PRELIMINARY SCREENING

Preliminary screening involves defining the physical, political, economic, and cultural environment.

Demographic/Physical Environment

- Population size, growth, density
- Urban and rural distribution
- Climate and weather variations
- Shipping distance
- Product-significant demographics
- Physical distribution and communications network
- Natural resources

Political Environment

- System of government
- Political stability and continuity
- Ideological orientation
- Government involvement in business
- Government involvement in communications
- Attitudes toward foreign business (trade restrictions, tariffs, nontariff barriers, bilateral trade agreement)
- National economic and developmental priorities

Economic Environment

- Overall level of development
- Economic growth: GNP, industrial sector
- Role of foreign trade in the economy
- Currency, inflation rate, availability, controls, stability of exchange rate
- Balance of payments
- Per capita income and distribution
- Disposable income and expenditure patterns

Social/Cultural Environment

- Literacy rate, educational level
- Existence of middle class
- Similarities and differences in relation to home market
- Language and other cultural considerations

The export marketer will eliminate some foreign markets from further consideration on the basis of this preliminary screening. An example would be the absence of comparable or linking products and services, a deficiency that would hinder the potential for marketing products.

STAGE TWO: ANALYSIS OF INDUSTRY MARKET POTENTIAL

Market Access

- Limitations on trade: tariff levels, quotas
- Documentation and import regulations
- Local standards, practices, and other nontariff barriers
- Patents and trademarks
- Preferential treaties
- Legal considerations; investment, taxation, repatriation, employment, code of laws

Product Potential

- Customer needs and desires
- Local production, imports, consumption
- Exposure to and acceptance of products
- Availability of linking products
- Industry-specific key indicators of demand
- Attitudes toward products of foreign origin
- Competitive offerings
- Availability of intermediaries
- Regional and local transportation facilities
- Availability of manpower
- Conditions for local manufacture

STAGE THREE: ANALYSIS OF COMPANY SALES POTENTIAL

The third stage of the screening process involves assessing company sales potential in those countries that prove promising based upon the earlier analyses.

Sales Volume Forecasting

- Size and concentration of customer segments
- Projected consumption statistics
- Competitive pressures
- Expectations of local distributors/agents

Landed Cost

- Costing method for exports
- Domestic distribution costs
- International freight and insurance
- Cost of product modification

Cost of Internal Distribution

- Tariffs and duties
- Value-added tax
- Local packaging and assembly
- Margins/commission allowed for the trade
- Local distribution and inventory costs
- Promotional expenditures

Other Determinants of Profitability

- Going price levels
- Competitive strengths and weaknesses
- Credit practices
- Current and projected exchange rates

Source: S. Tamer Cavusgil, "Guidelines for Export Market Research," *Business Horizons*, November–December 1985, pp. 30–31.

Exhibit 10.2 Characteristics of Primary and Secondary Data

PRIMARY DATA	SECONDARY DATA
• From knowledgeable individuals at the professional level	• From published sources or collected by others
• May be costly in time and travel	• Usually free or low cost
• May tend to be subjective	• Can be collected quickly
• Must be pilot-tested	• May be biased or incomplete
• Can be very specific to problems at hand	• May be out of date
• Cannot require disclosure of proprietary information	• Requires careful analysis of limitations

The information available from these international organizations, however, has two drawbacks. First, the information is based on data supplied by each member country. It is difficult to determine what criteria and means have been used. In some cases, the reliability of the data should be questioned because the information compiled has been passed along by various bureaucrats who may have slanted the data for their own purposes. Second, the information is dated. It takes time for an international organization to gather information from all over the world, analyze it, and make it available to the public in summary form.

Most university libraries and public libraries in major cities carry the UN and the World Bank publications. The IMF information may be available only in more specialized libraries.

U.S. Government The U.S. Department of Commerce is the single most important source of secondary information. Forty-eight international trade administration district offices and 19 branch offices of the U.S. Department of Commerce in cities throughout the U.S. and in Puerto Rico provide information and professional export counseling to businespeople. Each office is headed by a director, supported by trade specialists and other staff. These professionals can help a company's decision makers gain a basic understanding of profitable opportunities in exporting and assist them in evaluating the company's market potential overseas.

Each district office can give information about:

- Trade and investment opportunities abroad
- Foreign markets for U.S. products and services
- Services to locate and evaluate overseas buyers and representatives
- Financing aid for exporters
- International trade exhibitions
- Export documentation requirements
- Foreign economic statistics
- U.S. export licensing and foreign national import requirements
- Export seminars and conferences

Most district offices maintain an extensive business library containing the department's latest reports.

The U.S. Department of Commerce information is obtained in two ways: on a regular basis from periodicals such as *Business America*,[16] and on an ad hoc basis from special reports prepared on opportunities for American companies, for example, in Saudi Arabia.

The U.S. Department of Commerce informs businesses not only about international business conditions abroad, but also about events and happenings in Washington and their impact on international business. Information is available on all phases of marketing.

Useful information may also be available from other departments/agencies of the federal government such as the U.S. State Department's Agency for International

Development (USAID) or the U.S. Department of Agriculture. Most of these organizations issue newsletters and other publications. An international marketer could subscribe to those pertinent to particular products or markets. Currently, all U.S. government information is available on CD Rom, updated every three months.

U.S. Consulting Firms Many management consulting firms (including accounting firms) specialize in services for U.S. business abroad. Some of these firms conduct original research. Their findings are available to the international marketer. One such firm is Business International Corporation, a division of *The Economist*. It puts out a number of publications (newsletters issued periodically, studies issued on a regular basis, and ad hoc studies). Another firm that specializes in providing secondary data is Predicasts of Cleveland, Ohio. Similarly, major accounting firms and major banks issue a variety of finance- and accounting-related information on different countries of the world. For example, Price Waterhouse regularly publishes booklets on select countries, providing perspectives on doing business there. Bank of America offers a service entitled World Information Services, which tracks, analyzes, and forecasts economic and business conditions in 80 countries.

U.S. Foreign Government Offices Almost all countries maintain embassies in Washington, D.C. In addition, these countries have consulates and UN mission offices in New York City. A country may have more than one consulate office in the U.S. For example, the government of Brazil maintains consulate offices in New York, Chicago, Dallas, and Los Angeles, in addition to their embassy in Washington, D.C. Usually, an embassy has a commercial attaché who may be a good source of secondary information on the country. The consulate and the UN mission usually have basic information on their country to offer the researcher. For example, let us assume research is being done to prepare a market-potential study in order to decide whether a company should assemble TVs in Nigeria. Import data on TV sets in Nigeria for the past five years are needed. The Nigerian consulate in New York might have a government publication that quickly and easily provides such information.

Other units of a foreign government in the U.S. can serve as important sources of data. For example, a hotel chain interested in constructing a hotel in the Caribbean island of St. Lucia may find the St. Lucian government tourist office in New York City an important source of information on tourist trade there.

Many governments maintain special offices in the U.S. for the purpose of promoting trade and business with U.S. companies. For example, the Indian government's Indian Investment Center in New York City offers all sorts of business-related information. If the center does not have the information, it can guide the researcher to the proper source.

U.S. Multinational Banks Both U.S. banks active worldwide (e.g., Citicorp, BankAmerica Corp., Chase Manhattan Bank), and branches of foreign banks in the U.S. are additional sources of secondary information. Many of these banks maintain libraries. They usually offer free access to customers, present and prospective. In some instances, however, a bank may have information a researcher seeks in one of its reports, but the data may not be made available. It is worthwhile, nevertheless, to contact a multinational bank for secondary data.

Advantages of Secondary Research at Home

Secondary research conducted in the U.S. is less expensive and less time-consuming than research abroad.[17] The research at home keeps commitment to future projects at a low level: no contacts have to be made overseas, and no high-level decisions have to be made on exploring markets outside the U.S. Research in the home environment affords easy communication with sources of information. In addition, requests for certain kinds of information are often more favorably received by foreign sources located in the U.S. where political pressure and business customers do not inhibit response. Research undertaken in the U.S. about a foreign environment also gains objectivity. The researcher is not constrained by overseas customs or mores and can apply the same standards of quality and analysis as would be used for a project related to domestic business.

Disadvantages of Secondary Research at Home

Secondary research undertaken in the U.S. has various limitations. First, current information may be scarce in the U.S. After all, there is a time lag between data gathering in a foreign country and its transmission to the U.s. Further, certain things may be uncovered in the foreign environment that ultimately will bear on the project. For example, a company may be exploring the feasibility of establishing a plant in Saudi Arabia to manufacture air conditioners. Research done in the U.S. is likely to reveal good potential there for air conditioners based on secondary data such as high per capita income, hot climate, low rate of air conditioners per hundred households, and encouragement by the Saudi government. However, these data omit an important fact about Saudi living: a large proportion of the people live in mud houses. Additionally, there are regions without electricity. Such facts would become immediately obvious to a researcher on the spot.

Secondary Research Abroad

An alternative to doing secondary research in the U.S. is undertaking secondary research abroad. It should be recognized that the abundance of information available in the U.S. from both government and private sources is not found in most countries of the world, including the developed ones. Since World War II, however, interest in collecting socioeconomic information has greatly increased. As countries progressed economically, it became important to collect and publish statistical information on commercial matters on a regular basis. As a matter of fact, it may be claimed that availability of reliable secondary data is directly related to the level of economic development of a country. Even among Third World countries, data-gathering activity has greatly improved since the 1970s. This may be attributed partly to the UN's efforts to impress upon countries the desirability of keeping national statistical information accurate and current.

Foreign Sources of Information

The following are the major sources of secondary information for an international marketer:

Government Sources The single most important source of secondary information in a country is the national government. The quality and quantity of information will vary from country to country, but in most cases information on population statistics, consumption standards, industrial production, imports and exports, price levels, employment, and more is conveniently available. On the other hand, data on retail and wholesale trade may be found only in certain countries. The government data are usually available through a government agency or major publishers in the country. In many countries, marketing-related information gathered by the government is not separated from other sorts of information. Thus, the researcher must go through a plethora of information to choose what is relevant.

Private Sources In many countries there are private consulting firms (like Gallup Research, Business International Corporation, New York City; and Predicasts, Cleveland, Ohio) that gather and sell commercial information (see International Marketing Highlight 10.4). Information from private sources may, in fact, have been collected by the government originally. However, consulting firms analyze and organize it in such a manner that business executives can more easily make sense of it. The commercial attaché at the U.S. Embassy should be able to provide the names and addresses of local consulting firms. For example, International Information Services Ltd. (IIS), a global product pick-up service located in Sussex, United Kingdom, provides answers to such specific issues as the most popular pizza flavors in France and retail pricing structure for shampoos in Venezuela compared with that of its neighbors in Colombia and Brazil. Each day over 400 IIS shoppers visit supermarkets in 120 countries searching for information requested by clients such as Coca-Cola, General Foods, Procter & Gamble, Nestlé, and Unilever. The information gathered by IIS shoppers is stored, along with data from the company's comprehensive library of foreign trade publications, in a computerized database, enabling IIS to offer clients continuous updates on new food, household, and pharmaceutical products introduced worldwide. IIS uses these data to compile bimonthly indexes of the new products.[18]

Research Institutes, Trade Associations, Universities, and Similar Sources
Although not every country in the world has trade associations or research institutes, in both developed and developing countries (like India, Brazil, South Korea, Egypt), such sources could be important sources of secondary data. In some countries, they are set up with the help of international agencies and/or the government. Information on these sources should be sought from the appropriate U.S. embassy.

Local Businesses A U.S. company may be in contact with one or more businesses in a foreign country. These contacts can serve as important sources of secondary data. Even if these businesses have collected no data on their own, they could gather and communicate data available through other local sources such as those mentioned earlier.

International Marketing Highlight 10.4

Direct Mail Responders Love to Shop

The 1990 Target Group Index (TGI) survey by the British Market Research Bureau found that people who respond to direct-response advertising are less brand-loyal and more likely to experiment in their purchasing behavior.

The TGI is a national product and media survey. It measures the use of over 3,000 brands in more than 200 product areas and the use of 450 other services. The survey can be used to link responsiveness data with geographic and demographic information to more accurately target cold mailings.

Although the traditional image of the direct mail respondent is someone who doesn't like to shop, the response to the TGI survey contradicts this notion.

People who respond to direct mail enjoy their shopping more than anyone else, even though they are also the busiest people. They also hunt for bargains more enthusiastically, and are more likely to try new brands.

The TGI also found that in the past 12 months, at least 62 percent of the adult population (over age 15) in the U.K. purchased goods through a mail order catalog or responded to a direct-response advertisement, or did both.

Seventeen million adults (39 percent) responded to direct-response ads, and 19.5 million (43 percent) made purchases through mail order companies.

Source: Direct Mail Information Service, 14 Floral Street, Covent Garden, London WC2E 9RR, United Kingdom.

U.S. Embassies The U.S. embassy (including the resources of other U.S. government agencies abroad such as the Agency for International Development) may also provide secondary data on the country. Embassy personnel may have gathered information on a particular industry in a country in order to understand its impact on U.S. business at home (for example, the impact of the Japanese auto industry on U.S. automobile companies might be better understood with information from the U.S. embassy in Japan). Embassy appointees may be requested to be mindful of U.S. trade prospects for particular raw materials (for example, the U.S. embassy in Colombia would be aware of Colombian coffee bean trade). In addition, the embassy could lead the marketing researcher to other sources of secondary data in the country such as trade associations or research institutes.

Problems with Foreign Secondary Data

Secondary data available in a foreign country suffer in comparison with similar information available from U.S. sources at home. The researcher must be aware of problems and deficiencies when interpreting information. The following brief summaries deal with some of the difficulties with the reliability of foreign secondary data.

The Underlying Purpose of Data Collection As mentioned earlier, the single most important source of marketing-related secondary data in a country is the government. The government as a political institution may not approach data collection with the same objectivity as a business researcher. This problem is particularly severe in developing countries where governments may enhance the information content in order to paint a rosy picture of economic life in the country. In this way, political considerations overshadow the reliability of the data.

It is worth noting that the U.S. as a society is more open than other countries. No matter how embarrassing data may appear to be for the government or the nation, the free flow of information is considered desirable. This, however, is not true elsewhere. It is not surprising, therefore, that the plight of the poor in the U.S. seems exaggerated when measured by standards of poverty in developing countries. The researcher must ascertain that the data available are accurate within the limits of its source and that there are no hidden assumptions that might distort the information from the researcher's point of view.

Currency of Information Information gathering is an expensive activity. When the government has limited resources, data gathering becomes a lower priority. Thus, information may not be gathered as frequently as desirable. The researcher needs to be very careful that the information available overseas has not become outdated. For an example close to home, in the U.S. a sensible decision about a housing project could not be made on the basis of 1960s' house prices.

Reliability of Data It was mentioned that political considerations may affect the reliability of data. In addition, the reliability of data may be affected by data collection procedures. For example, the sample may not be random, so that the results cannot be assumed to reflect the behavior of the total population. Even when a good sampling plan has been laid out, it may not be properly adhered to (i.e., the interviewers might substitute subjects when those required by the sampling plan cannot be reached). In brief, numerous factors may affect the reliability of data.[19]

It may be difficult for the researchers to judge the reliability of secondary data available in a country, and it would be dysfunctional to try to test that reliability. If the researchers are indeed concerned with reliability, they would be better off undertaking primary data gathering. Researchers should judge for themselves how far to accept the data on the basis of inputs from different contacts in the country about their own experiences with secondary data there.

Data Classification Another problem has to do with the classification scheme of the available data. In many countries, data reported are too broadly classified for use at the micro level. For example, in Malaysia the category "construction equipment, machinery, and tools" includes large bulldozers as well as hand-operated drills. Thus, a company interested in manufacturing heavy construction machinery in Malaysia cannot get a clear idea about the current availability of such equipment in the country from the information given under such a category.

However, the problem of data classification is being solved. The international trading community has for years had to confront the lack of a standardized goods classification system for products being traded in the international marketplace. The use of diverse systems has complicated the preparation of documents, hampered the analysis of trade data, created uncertainty in the negotiation and interpretation of trade agreements, and slowed the movement of traded goods. However, as countries adopt the Harmonized Commodity Description and Coding System, information across countries will be similarly classified, eliminating many of the problems that arise from the use of a nonstandardized system. In the U.S., the Harmonized System (HS) was adopted on January 1, 1988, requiring all U.S. exporters and importers to conform to the revised classification.

The Harmonized Commodity Description and Coding System is an international goods classification system designed to standardize commodity classification for all major trading nations. The system assigns all products a six-digit code, which would be used by all countries for both imported and exported goods. The HS was developed under the auspices of the Customs Cooperation Council (CCC) in Brussels, Belgium, and is based on the Customs Cooperation Council Nomenclature (CCCN), formerly known as the Brussels Tariff Nomenclature (BTN). It is more detailed and contains many new subdivisions to reflect changes in technology, trade patterns, and user requirements.

The Harmonized System replaces the Tariff Schedules of the United States Annotated (TSUSA) and Schedule B. The U.S. import and export schedules under the HS will be nearly identical and completely compatible. The only differences will occur with regard to level of detail; in some areas such as textiles, the import schedule will need to be subdivided in much finer detail than is necessary for exports. In addition, both the U.S. import and export schedules will be identical through the first six digits with those of trading partners adopting the Harmonized System. Under the current system, a product may be given one code when it is imported, a separate code when it is exported, and various other codes in foreign countries. If the Harmonized System were applied on a worldwide basis, any single product would share a common six-digit base code. National subdivisions beyond the six-digit level are possible for tariff and statistical purposes.

The system will also provide U.S. exporters with information concerning the tariff classification of their goods in other countries as well as a procedure for bringing goods classification disputes before an international customs council.

Use of a common system would accelerate the movement of goods and their associated paperwork. International traders would no longer have to redescribe and recode goods as they move through the international marketplace. All this elimination of the above-mentioned obstacles would save time and money.

The Harmonized System consists of 5,019 4-digit headings and subheadings. Developing countries will be able, under certain circumstances, to adopt the system at the four-digit level; developed countries, however, must use all six digits. The first two digits represent the chapter in which the goods are found, the next two digits represent the place within the chapter where the goods are described, and the next two digits represent the international subdivisions within the heading. The U.S will further subdivide the 5,019 6-digit international headings and subheadings into approximately 8,800 8-digit rate lines, or classification lines, and into approximately 12,000 10-digit statistical reporting numbers. This represents an increase in rate lines of about 1,500 and a decrease of about 2,000 in the statistical reporting numbers from the present system.

Another noteworthy development in making international economic information more useful is a new framework for national-income accounting, the new System of National Accounts (SNA).[20] The new SNA takes into account changes in both the world's economy and in accounting practices in the past 25 years. Its guidelines on accounting for inflation have been beefed up, and the way it measures trade flows has been improved. The new SNA will account for trade in the same way as the IMF's balance-of-payments statistics. Imports of goods will now be valued "free-on-board," that is, at the point of export (the old system incorrectly lumped in cost, insurance, and freight). The system will also adopt the IMF's approach to the return on foreign direct investment, treating retained profits of foreign-owned businesses as though they had been repatriated. The new SNA is a joint effort by the UN, the IMF, the World Bank, the OECD, and Eurostat, the Statistical Office of the European Union.

Comparability of Data   Multinational corporate executives often like to compare information on their host countries about such matters as review of market performance, strategy effectiveness in different environments, and so on. Unfortunately, the secondary data obtainable from different countries are not readily comparable. Keegan reports, for example, that in Germany purchases of TVs are considered expenditures for recreation and entertainment, while in the U.S., TV purchases are in the category of furniture, furnishing, and household equipment.[21] These discrepancies make brand share comparison nearly impossible.

Availability of Data   Finally, in many developing nations, secondary data are very scarce. Information on retail and wholesale trade is especially difficult to obtain. In such cases, primary data collection becomes vital.

Primary Data Collection

An alternative to secondary data is primary data collection. Primary data presumably provide more relevant information because they are collected specifically for the purpose in mind. However, the collection of primary data is an expensive proposition in terms of both money and time. Thus, the underlying purpose must justify the effort. For example, when a company has to make a decision about appointing a dealer for the occasional sale of its product in a developing country, it is not necessary to have primary data on the long-term market potential. On the other hand, if the company is considering the establishment of a manufacturing plant in the country, it may be important to undertake a market potential study.

Problems of Primary Data Collection

Primary data collection in a foreign environment poses a variety of problems not encountered in the U.S.[22] These problems are related to social and cultural factors and the level of economic development, and can be grouped under three headings: (1) sampling problems, (2) questionnaire problems, and (3) the problem of nonresponse.

Sampling Problems   A good piece of research should reflect the perspectives of the entire population. This is feasible, however, only when the sample is randomly drawn (see International Marketing Highlight 10.5). Unfortunately, in many countries it is difficult to get completely representative information on the socioeconomic characteristics of the population because such information is lacking or, at best, is inadequate. Most samples in the end are biased. Cateora adds:

In many countries, telephone directories, cross-index street directories, census tract and block data, and detailed social and economic characteristics of the universe are not available on a current basis, if at all. The researcher then has to estimate characteristics and population parameters, sometimes with little basic data on which to build an accurate estimate. To add to the confusion, in some cities in South America, Mexico, and Asia, street maps are unavailable; and in some large metropolitan areas of the Near East and Asia, streets are not identified nor houses numbered.[23]

International Marketing Highlight 10.5

Who Drinks More Wine?

According to a recent study, the Italians drink the most wine of any country—about 116 liters per capita a year, compared with 77 for the French and just over 9 for the British. But another study disagrees. It gives the French first place in the wine-drinking competition, finding that annual per capita intake in France is 70 liters and that the Italians drink only 62 liters a year. (The difference may well be in the way the population is defined or the way the questions were asked.)

No matter what the reason, the study by the French Inter-Professional Office of Wine (ONIVINS) says that the French have cut their wine consumption. More than half of the 12,400 people interviewed in this study said they abstain from drinking wine.

In 1980, according to ONIVINS, nearly one-third of the French drank wine daily, compared with only 18 percent this year. Families spend less time together and eat together less often, forcing wine to take a back seat to other options such as mineral water and soft drinks. The ONIVINS study also found that the French are choosing to drink higher-quality wine, when they choose to drink wine.

Source: The European, August 10-12, 1990.

Limitations aside, directories are available to help the international marketing researcher draw an adequate sample, especially in the industrial marketing area. *Boltin International,* for example, provides names and addresses of more than 300,000 firms in 100 countries, under 1,000 product classifications, by trade and by country.[24] Another source is *Kelly's Manufacturers and Merchants Directory,* which lists firms in the U.S. and other major trading countries in the world.[25]

Even if a workable random sample is drawn, inadequate means of transportation may prevent interviewing people as planned. For example, in developing countries, many areas, especially rural ones, are quite inaccessible. Thus, data gathering may have to be confined to urban areas. Further, only a small percentage of the population may have telephones. The World Bank statistics indicate, for example, that there are only 4 telephones per 1,000 population in Egypt, 6 in Turkey, and 32 in Argentina. In many countries, the postal system is so inefficient that letters may not be delivered at all or may reach the addressee only after a long delay. In Brazil, for example, an estimated 30 percent of the domestic mail is never delivered.[26] In brief, it may be extremely difficult to obtain a proper random sample, especially in developing countries.

Questionnaire Problems In many countries, different languages are spoken in different areas. Thus, the questionnaire has to be in different languages for use within the same country. In India, for example, 14 official languages are spoken in different parts of the country, while most government and business affairs are conducted in English. Similarly, in Switzerland, German is used in some areas and French in others. In the Republic of Congo, the official language is French, but only a small part of the population is fluent in French. Unfortunately, translating a questionnaire from one language to another is far from easy. In the translating process many points are entirely eclipsed, because many idioms, phrases, and statements mean different things in different cultures. For example, in Spanish there is no word that means "value" as we define it in English. Therefore, a U.S. restaurant chain conducting marketing research in Spain had to ask guests such questions as "Do you think the quality of the food was equal to the price you paid?"[27] A Danish executive observed:

> Check this out by having a different translator put back into English what you've translated from the English. You'll get the shock of your life. I remember "out of sight, out of mind" had become "invisible things are insane."[28]

This translation problem may be partially averted with the help of computers; however, experience with computers shows that they cannot fathom the subtleties of language.[29]

Problem of Nonresponse Even if the interviewee is successfully reached, there is no guarantee that he or she will cooperate and furnish the desired information. There are many reasons for nonresponse. First, cultural habits in many countries virtually prohibit communication with a stranger, particularly for women. For example, a researcher simply may not be able to speak on the phone with a housewife in an Islamic country to find out what she thinks of a particular brand. Second, in many societies such matters as preferences for hygienic products and food products are too personal to be shared with an outsider. In many Latin American countries, a woman may feel ashamed to talk with a researcher about her choice of a brand of sanitary pad, hair shampoo, or perfume. Third, respondents in many cases may be unwilling to share their true feelings with interviewers because they suspect the interviewers may be agents of the government, for example, seeking information for imposition of additional taxes. Fourth, middle-class people, in developing countries in particular, are reluctant to accept their status and may take false claims in order to reflect the lifestyle of wealthier people. For example, in a study on the consumption of tea in India, over 70 percent of the respondents from middle-income families claimed they used one of the several national brands of tea. This finding could not be substantiated since over 60 percent of the tea sold nationally in India is unbranded, generic tea sold unpackaged. Fifth, many respondents, willing to cooperate, may be illiterate, so that even oral communication may be difficult. In other words, their exposure to the modern world may be so limited and their outlook so narrow that the researchers would find it extremely difficult to elicit adequate responses from them. Sixth, in many countries, privacy is becoming a big issue. In Japan, for example, the middle class is showing increasing concern about the protection of personal information. Information that people are most anxious to protect includes income, assets, tax payments, family life, and political and religious affiliation.[30] Finally, the lack of established marketing research firms in many countries may force the researcher to count on ad hoc help for gathering data. How far such temporary help may be counted on to complete a job systematically can only be guessed.

Resolving the Problems

There are no foolproof methods to take care of all the problems discussed above. The following suggestions, however, may help to eliminate some of the problems.

The international marketing research effort should be undertaken in conjunction with a reputable local firm. Such a firm may be a foreign office of a U.S. advertising firm like J. Walter Thompson, a U.S. accounting firm like Price Waterhouse, or a locally owned firm belonging to a third country like a Japanese advertising agency in Italy. The resources of the cooperating firm will be invaluable; for example, its knowledge of local customs, including things like the feasibility of interviewing housewives while husbands are at work; its familiarity with the local environment, including modes of transportation available for personal interviews in smaller towns; and its contact in different parts of the country as sources for drawing a sample.

From the beginning, a person fully conversant with both sound marketing research procedures and the local culture should be involved in all phases of the research design. Such a person can recommend the number of languages the questionnaire should be printed in and what sort of cultural traits, habits, customs, and rituals to keep in mind in different phases of the research. Such a person may be a U.S.-educated marketer or a person with good business education or experience, preferably in marketing.

The questionnaire may first be written in English, and then a native fluent in English can translate it into the local language(s). A third person should retranslate it into English. This retranslated version can then be compared with the original English version. The three people involved should work together to eliminate differences in the three versions of the questionnaire by changing phrases, idioms, and words. Ultimately, the questionnaire in the local language should accurately reflect the questions in the original English questionnaire.

If feasible, the persons hired to conduct the interviews should have prior experience. The local cooperating firm discussed earlier may be helpful here. In any event, complete instructions and training should be given before work starts. As a matter of fact, the conducting of interviews should be practiced. Ways to ensure that the interviewers follow the instructions must be found for proper sampling control. For example, the researcher might accompany the interviewer sporadically.

Finally, the researcher should draw the best possible sample. If the sample is not random, the researcher should employ appropriate statistical techniques in analyzing the collected information so that the results reflect the reality of the situation.

Organization for International Marketing Research

International marketing research can be carried out both at the headquarters in the U.S. and in the host country. Marketing research at the headquarters is useful in two areas: short-term planning and budgeting, and strategy formulation. For example, yearly forecasts of sales for different products in different countries will be a part of the annual budget. But a study undertaken to determine if a new product successfully sold in the U.S. should be introduced in international markets would have a strategy focus.

Marketing research studies in host countries are concerned mainly with day-to-day operations, tactics to achieve designated goals, and short-term marketing planning. For example, a study may examine the factors responsible for poor sales performance in the previous quarter. Similarly, marketing research may be undertaken to decide if a concentrated 6- or 10-week advertising campaign is preferable to spreading advertising over the whole year. Naturally, sales forecasting will be done to develop budgets. As mentioned earlier, the headquarters may also make sales forecasts. Thus, for discussion of annual plans and budgets, the host country manager would use his or her forecasts as the basis for resource allocation, while the headquarters' people use their forecasts to negotiate and approve the country budgets.

Marketing research is unquestionably an important function that must be conducted both at the headquarters and in the host countries. The persons to take charge at the two different locations would vary from company to company. For example, at NCR a staff assistant reporting to the vice president of international marketing is responsible for marketing research at the corporate headquarters. The marketing research function for NCR in host countries is performed at different levels according to the importance of each country to the parent company. In Japan, in the U.K., and in Germany, NCR has large marketing research departments simply because the company is extremely active in these markets. On the other hand, in a country like Pakistan where NCR commitment is meager, marketing research study might be assigned to an outside consultant.

In addition to undertaking marketing research at the corporate level and in the host countries, in many companies marketing research may also be conducted at the regional level. A company may divide its international operations into regions; for example, Western Europe, Far East, Latin America, Middle East, Africa, and Southeast Asia. Each country manager in a region would report to the regional executive. Under such arrangements, the regional executive may seek marketing research information to formulate regional marketing strategy or to develop the marketing perspective of a country within the region. There may be a specific person responsible for marketing research in the region, or one of the staff persons may carry this responsibility.

What is important to recognize is that marketing information is important at all levels. However, the process of gathering, analyzing, and reporting market-related information may not necessarily be called marketing research. Further, marketing research responsibility may not necessarily be assigned to a marketing person. Of course, the extent of marketing research that a company undertakes would vary according to the style of management and the importance of a particular foreign country for a given product.

International Marketing Information System

Earlier in this chapter, three terms were introduced: *market research, marketing research,* and *marketing intelligence.* An international marketing information system is a formal way of structuring the information flow through these three modes. Large, complex organizations may do business in a great number of countries with any number of products and services. This complexity combined with today's difficult and demanding business environment makes it particularly important for international marketers to have adequate and timely information available in order to make the right moves.

The following mishap illustrates the critical need for information:

"I never dreamed this would happen to us," exclaimed the chairman of the American drug firm G.D. Searle & Co. (sales over $600 million) in an interview published in *Business Week*. The company was apparently unaware that it would be investigated by a Senate subcommittee on health involving charges that the company mishandled research data on two of its best selling products. It is obvious that this company—like many others—did not have an adequate "early warning" capability or intelligence system which could have enabled management to anticipate the crisis. One result of the threat: a corporate committee of social scientists was established to study economic and political trends and their potential effect on the company.

Another recent example of an intelligence mishap involved Westinghouse Corporation's agreement to sell utility companies 80 million pounds of uranium at an average contracted price of $10 a pound over a period of twenty years. At the time the agreement was signed, Westinghouse owned only about 20 percent of the contracted amount of uranium. Since then, its price rose to $40 and if the company would have fulfilled the terms of the agreement it could have lost about $2 billion. Obviously top management were unaware that such an agreement was being negotiated, an intelligence failure concerning internal operations.[31]

Steps for Establishing an Information System

Figure 10.2 shows the essential steps for developing and maintaining an international marketing information system. As indicated in Figure 10.2, five essential components must be considered: determining information needs, identifying information sources, gathering information, analyzing information, and disseminating information. Information will be needed at corporate headquarters, regional offices, and country locations. Another way of looking at information needs is to differentiate between strategic and operational information. Still another way of grouping information is to form the following categories: market information, competitive information, foreign-exchange related data, resource information, prescriptive information (e.g., foreign taxes), and general conditions.

It is difficult to suggest a general framework for classifying the information needs of all companies or any particular company. Every company should work out its own information categories, which may be based on one scheme or another. Which kind a company will establish is influenced by the marketing information needs of the company and the attitude of top management toward systematic information management. Whatever the ultimate system is—highly structured and/or computerized or primitive, unstructured, and manual—it must meet in sophistication and range the anticipated information needs it will be called upon to supply.

Aspects of System Use

The information sources may be internal and external. Both internal and external sources may be further divided between international and domestic sources. Another way of classifying sources of information is to distinguish between secondary and primary sources. The information may be gathered in various ways—by mail, by

FIGURE 10.2 Components of an International Marketing Information System

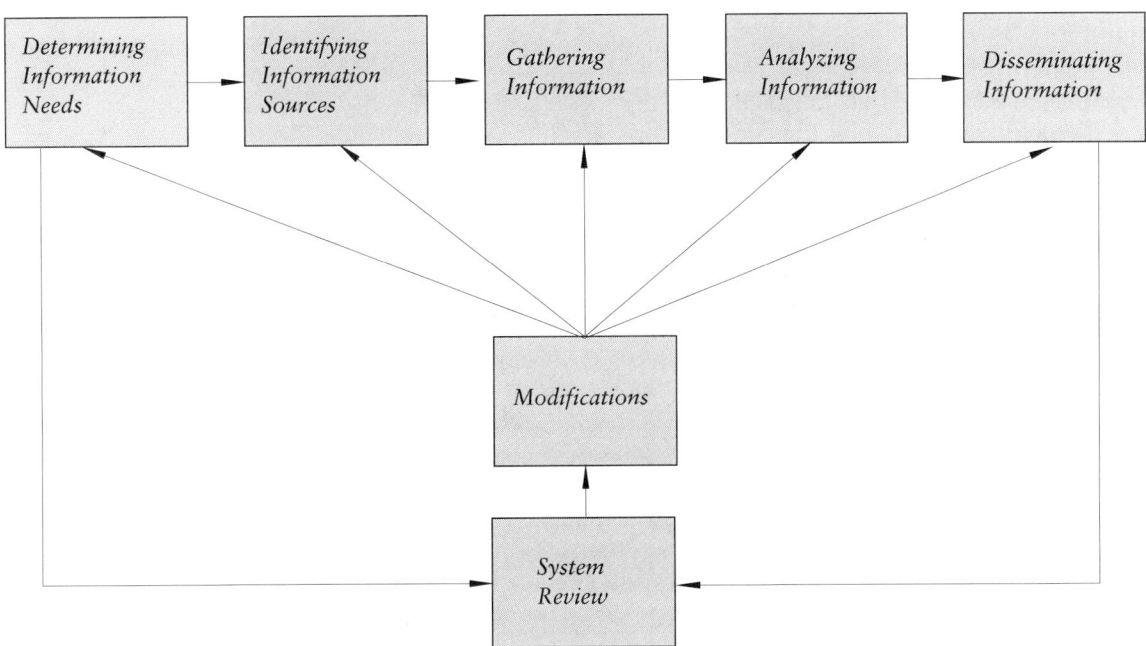

telephone, or via computer terminal through remote entry. Some information may be gathered regularly, and some may be collected on an ad hoc basis. Also, information may be gathered in a structured fashion or simply in an open-ended fashion. In gathering information, duplication should be avoided, as it is wasteful in most cases to gather the same information from different sources. In certain cases, though, duplication can be used as a control device. Next, the gathered information must be analyzed for use in the most convenient form. Finally, the information needs to be disseminated to all designated users. Some information may be made widely available to all managers and those above them. Other information may be restricted for senior people in the organization. Information may be disseminated on a regular basis or irregularly. Still other information may be available only on request.

The system design should be reviewed from time to time to ensure it still meets the demands placed on it. The review should also evaluate the cost–benefit relationship of the entire system. The review may recommend modifications in any one or more of the system components.[32]

Most large multimarket, multiproduct companies have some sort of multinational marketing information system in operation. It is difficult to say, however, how many of these systems can be labeled "sophisticated" or "advanced." Nonetheless, the increasing popularity of the international data networks made available by such companies as Data Research Inc., and Predicasts indicates that companies are moving toward the establishment of computerized information systems. These systems may serve information needs of marketing and of other functional areas of the business as well in the following manner:[33]

1. To aid in decisions relating to international market expansion, for example, whether new countries are potential candidates for market entry or existing products might be carried into new markets
2. To monitor performance in different countries and product markets based on criteria such as return on investment and market share, so as to diagnose where existing or potential future problems appear to be emerging and, hence, where there is a need to adapt current marketing tactics or strategies
3. To scan the international environment in order to assess future world and country scenarios and to monitor emerging and changing environmental trends
4. To assess strategies with regard to the allocation of corporate resources and effort across different countries, product markets, target segments, and modes of entry to determine whether changes in this allocation would maximize long-run profitability.

Summary

The techniques and tools of international marketing research do not vary according to whether research is done in the U.S. or abroad. An international marketing research project essentially follows domestic procedures: problem definition, research design, data collection, analysis, and report preparation. However, several factors make international marketing research more challenging and more difficult.

The two sources of data are secondary data and primary data. There are a variety of sources of information from which secondary information may be gathered at home; foremost among them is the U.S. Department of Commerce. Secondary information available in host countries may be plagued by problems of timeliness, reliability, and comparability. The collection of primary data abroad also poses difficulties such as the inability to draw a random sample, unwillingness of the sample population to cooperate, and the inability to develop an adequate questionnaire.

Despite the inherent problems, a researcher can adopt measures to solve some, if not all, of the difficulties involved. Two helpful measures are the involvement of talented individuals in data collection and cooperation with respectable foreign marketing information sources.

The international research activity may be formally organized at home or in the host country, or at both locations. Further, the marketing research organization may be just a one-person department or a large entity in accordance with the scope of marketing activity in a country. A company deeply involved in business around the globe should establish an international marketing information system with formal structuring to determine information needs, to identify information sources, and to gather, analyze, and disseminate information.

Review Questions

1. What factors make conducting international marketing research more difficult than domestic marketing research?
2. What are the principal sources of secondary data in the U.S.?

3. What difficulties are associated with secondary data on marketing in host countries?
4. Discuss the problems a researcher may face in primary data collection overseas.
5. What factors account for the unreliability of secondary data in foreign countries?
6. What steps may be taken to resolve the problems of primary data collection in the developing countries?
7. What kind of companies should consider developing an international marketing information system?
8. What help can be expected from international agencies in the search for secondary data?

Creative Questions

1. Pizza Hut, a division of PepsiCo, is interested in surveying consumers in France, Singapore, and Mexico. A consultant suggests conducting a telephone survey using the same questionnaire (initially written in English but duly translated into local languages). Evaluate the consultant's recommendation. Do you have any alternative recommendation for conducting the survey?
2. The U.S. government collects and disseminates an abundance of foreign trade data. Yet the marketing-related data is commonly not available. If you were to make a case to the U.S. government to provide data readily usable by marketers, indicate what type of data, in what format, and how current the government should make data available.

Endnotes

1. "Third World Research Is Difficult, But It Is Possible," *Marketing News*, August 29, 1987, p. 50.
2. *See* Kjell Gronhaug and John Graham, "International Marketing Research Revisited," in S. Tamer Cavusgil, ed., *Advances in International Marketing* (Greenwich, CT: Jai Press, Inc., 1987), pp. 121–38.
3. Charles F. Keown, "Foreign Mail Surveys: Response Rates Using Monetary Incentives," *Journal of International Business Studies*, Fall 1985, p. 153. *Also see* Robert J. Hoover, Robert T. Green, and Joel Saergert, "A Cross-National Study of Perceived Risk," *Journal of Marketing*, July 1978, pp. 107–08.
4. Susan P. Douglas and C. Samuel Craig, *International Marketing Research* (Englewood Cliffs, NJ: Prentice-Hall, Inc., 1983), p. 16.
5. *European Market Survey* (Pleasantville, NY: Reader's Digest Association, 1963).
6. Paul H. Berent, "International Research Is Different: The Case for Centralized Control," in *International Marketing Research: Does It Provide What the User Needs?* (Amsterdam: European Society for Opinion and Marketing Research, 1986), pp. 110–11.
7. Charles S. Mayer, "The Lessons of Multinational Marketing Research," *Business Horizons*, December 1978, p. 9.
8. Essam Mahmoud and Gillian Rice, "Use of Analytical Techniques in International Marketing," *International Marketing Review*, Autumn 1988, pp. 7–14. *Also see* David R. Wheeler, "Content Analysis: An Analytical Technique for International Marketing Research," *International Marketing Review*, Winter 1988, pp. 34–40.
9. Charles S. Mayer, Op. cit., p. 10.
10. *See* S. Tamer Cavusgil, "Qualitative Insights into Company Experiences in International Marketing Research," in V. H. Kirpalani, ed., *Changing Currents in International Marketing* (Chicago: American Marketing Association, 1984).
11. Tatsuo Ohbora, Andrew Parsons, and Hajo Riesenbeck, "Alternate Routes to Global Marketing," *The Marketing Quarterly*, 1992, No. 3, pp. 52–74.

12. *See* Van R. Wood and Jerry R. Goolsby, "Foreign Market Information Preferences of Established U.S. Exporters," *International Marketing Review*, Winter 1987, pp. 43–52.

13. *See Statistical Yearbook of the United Nations* (New York: United Nations, an annual publication).

14. *See World Development Report* (Washington, D.C.: World Bank, an annual publication).

15. *See International Financial Statistics* (Washington, D.C.: International Monetary Fund, an annual publication).

16. *See Business America* (Washington, D.C.: U.S. Government Printing Office, a bi-weekly publication).

17. *See* Leonard M. Field, "How to Gather Foreign Intelligence Without Leaving Home," *Marketing News*, January 4, 1988, p. 24.

18. "Product Pick-UP Firm Samples International Supermarkets," *Marketing News*, March 1, 1985, p. 10.

19. *See* Ravi Parameswaran and Attila Yaprak, "A Cross-National Comparison of Consumer Research Measures," *Journal of International Business Studies*, Spring 1987, pp. 35–50.

20. "Grossly Distorted Picture," *The Economist*, February 5, 1994, p. 71.

21. Warren J. Keegan, *Multinational Marketing Management*, 3rd ed. (Englewood Cliffs, NJ: Prentice-Hall, 1984), p. 224.

22. *See* Erdener Kaynak, "Difficulties of Undertaking Marketing Research in the Developing Countries," *European Research*, November 1978, pp. 251–59. *Also see* Mary Goodyear, "Qualitative Research in Developing Countries," *Journal of the Marketing Research Society*, Vol. 24, No. 2 (1982), pp. 80–96.

23. Philip R. Cateora, *International Marketing*, 5th ed. (Homewood, IL: Irwin, 1983), pp. 267–68.

24. *Boltin International* (Los Angeles, CA: Boltin International, an annual publication).

25. *Kelly's Manufacturers and Merchants Directory* (New York: Kelly's Directories Ltd., an annual publication).

26. Susan P. Douglas and C. Samuel Craig, *International Marketing Research* (Englewood Cliffs, NJ: Prentice-Hall, Inc., 1983), p. 224. *Also see* David Jobber and John Saunders, "An Experimental Investigation into Cross-National Mail Survey Response Rates," *Journal of International Business Studies*, Fall 1988, pp. 483–90.

27. Wallace Doolin, "Taking Your Business on the Road Abroad," *The Wall Street Journal*, July 25, 1994, p. A14.

28. Ferdinand F. Mauser, "Losing Something in Translation," *Harvard Business Review*, July–August 1977, p. 14.

29. J. Terence Gallagher, "A Problem of Translation," *The Asian Wall Street Journal Weekly*, September 30, 1985, p. 11c.

30. "Japanese Grow Anxious to Protect Their Privacy," *The Asian Wall Street Journal Weekly*, November 11, 1985, p. 23. *Also see* Naresh K. Malhotra, "Administration of Questionnaires in International Marketing Research," *Journal of Global Marketing*, Vol. 4, No. 2 (1991), pp. 63–92.

31. E.D. Jaffee, "Multinational Marketing Intelligence: An Information Requirements Model," *Management International Review*, Vol. 19, No. 2 (1979), pp. 53–60.

32. Benjamin Gilad, "The Role of Organized Competitive Intelligence in Corporate Strategy," *Columbia Journal of World Business*, Winter 1989, pp. 29–36.

33. Susan P. Douglas and C. Samuel Craig, *International Marketing Research* (Englewood Cliffs, NJ: Prentice-Hall, Inc., 1983), pp. 278–79.

Global Marketplace

CHAPTER FOCUS

After studying this chapter, you should be able to:

- Compare market opportunities in different parts of the world
- Discuss the dimensions of global markets
- Describe the forces behind market globalization
- Explain the rationale for segmenting the international market
- Evaluate different criteria for grouping countries

The World Bank lists 132 countries. It is difficult to imagine that a marketer would be interested in serving the entire global market. Granted, some companies such as Kodak and Coca-Cola are active in over 100 countries. However, such a vast coverage of market develops gradually. Initially, a company may enter just one country or a few countries. From there, the scope may broaden as the company brings other countries within its fold.

Obviously, the company must choose among the countries of the world in order to identify its target markets. Worldwide there is great contrast economically, culturally, and politically among nations. These contrasts mean that an overseas marketer cannot select target countries randomly, but must employ workable criteria to analyze the world market and choose those countries where the company's product/service has the best opportunity for success. While individual countries have peculiarities, they also have similarities that they share with other countries, and such bases render some grouping device feasible.

What are the characteristics of that global marketplace, the international market? What is the rationale for grouping countries into segments? What procedure would a company employ to segment the international market? How can in-country segmentation be achieved?

Global Market

The most basic information needed to appraise global markets concerns population, because the people, of course, constitute the market. The population of the world reached an estimated 5.5 billion in 1992. According to the latest estimates from the Population Division of the United Nations, this total is expected to increase to 6.2 billion by 2000 and to almost 8.5 billion by 2025. Current world population is growing at about 1.7 percent per year. This is a slight decline from the peak rate of 1.9 percent, but the absolute number of people being added to the world's population each year is still increasing. This figure is expected to peak in the late 1990s at about 90 million additional people per year (see International Marketing Highlight 11.1).

Population growth rates vary significantly by region. Europe has the lowest rate of population growth at only about 0.3 percent per year. Several European countries are experiencing declining populations, including Austria, Denmark, Germany, Luxembourg, and Sweden. Growth rates are also below 1 percent per year in North America.

The regions with the highest population growth rates are Africa (3 percent per year), Latin America (2 percent per year), and South Asia (1.9 percent per year). China, the world's most populous country, is growing at only about 1.2 percent per year. Even so, that rate means that China's population increases by over 12 million each year. The world's second-largest country, India, is growing at over 1.7 percent per year. It is expected to grow from 850 million today to the 1 billion mark by about 2003.

One striking aspect of population growth in the developing countries is the rapid rate of urbanization. The urban population is growing at less than 1 percent in Europe and North America, but it is growing at almost 3.5 percent in the developing world. Today, 13 of the 20 largest urban agglomerations are in the developing world. By the year 2000, 17 of the 20 largest cities will be in the developing world. The only developed-country cities in the top 20 will be Tokyo, New York, and Los Angeles. The world's largest cities will be Mexico City (26 million), Sao Paulo (24 million), and Calcutta and Bombay (both over 16 million).[1] This information shows that the total markets in Europe and North America will not be increasing; population will not add much to total market size. Of course, these populations are growing older, so that certain segments will have increasing numbers. For example, the total population of Europe will increase only 1.6 percent from 1995 to 2000, but the over-65 population will increase by 12 percent during the same period.

International Marketing Highlight 11.1

Babies Are Our Only Customers Worldwide

Gerber Products Co. is going global with a host of child-care products in an effort to break out of its mild-mannered, domestic baby-food niche.

The company has been fine-tuning its "superbranding" campaign for years. It feels it has developed a real following among mothers, and it is going to utilize its brand name to market products in three different categories: food and formula, baby-care products, and clothing.

Market research shows that moms around the globe recognize and trust the Gerber logo. The company's baby food already is sold in Mexico, Puerto Rico, Europe, and the Far East. Sales have expanded into Poland, Egypt, Russia, and Eastern Europe.

However, internationally, the company is an infant. About 95 percent of the babies born in the world are born outside the U.S. Yet right now, international sales account for only about 5 percent of the company's total sales.

Gerber will introduce the baby-food lines in new international markets first, then follow with baby-care products and apparel.

Source: Marketing News, September 26, 1991, p. 22.

While the population variable provides a snapshot of market opportunity in a country, a variety of other factors must be considered to identify viable markets. For example, in the developing world, the increase in numbers does not necessarily mean increased market opportunity. The fastest growing region, Africa, is also experiencing low or negative rates of economic growth per capita. Much of Latin America is hampered by huge external debts that force those countries to try to limit imports while using their resources to generate foreign exchange for debt service. In most of these cases, the problem of foreign debt will have to be solved before the growing populations will translate into large markets.

Taking into account factors such as urbanization, consumption patterns, infrastructure, and overall industrialization, different parts of the global market are examined below.

Triad Market

The *triad market* refers to the U.S. and Canada, Japan, and Western European countries. They account for approximately 14 percent of the world's population, but they represent over 70 percent of world gross product. As such, these countries absorb the major proportion of capital and consumer products, and, thus, are the most advanced consuming societies in the world. Not only do most of the product innovations take place in these countries, but they also serve as the opinion leaders and mold the purchasing and consumption behavior of the remaining 86 percent of the world's population.

For example, over 90 percent of the computers worldwide are used by triad countries. In the case of numerically controlled machine tools, almost 100 percent are distributed in the triad market. The same pattern follows in consumer products. Triad accounts for 90 percent of the demand for electronic consumer goods. What these statistics point to is that a company that ignores the market potential of the triad does so at its own peril.[2]

An interesting characteristic of the triad market is the universalization of needs. For example, not too long ago manufacturers of capital equipment produced machinery that reflected strong cultural distinctions. West German machines reflected that nation's penchant for craftsmanship while American equipment was often extravagant in its use of raw materials. But these distinctions have disappeared. The best-selling factory machines have lost the "art" element that distinguished them and have become much more similar, both in appearance and in the level of skills they require. The current revolution in production engineering has brought ever-increasing global standards of performance. In an era when productivity improvements can quickly determine their life or death on a global scale, companies cannot afford to indulge themselves in a metallic piece of art that will last 30 years (see International Marketing Highlight 11.2).

At the same time, consumer markets have become fairly homogeneous. Ohmae notes:

> The Triad consumption pattern, which is both a cause and an effect of cultural patterns, has its roots to a large extent in the educational system. As educational systems enable more people to use technology, they tend to become more similar to each other. It follows, therefore, that education leading to higher levels of technological achievement also tends to eradicate differences in lifestyles. Penetration of television, which enables everyone possessing a television set to share sophisticated behavioral information instantaneously throughout the world, has also accelerated this trend. There are, for example, 750 million consumers in all three parts of the Triad (Japan, the United States and Canada, the nations of Western Europe), with strikingly similar needs and preferences. . . . A new generation worships the universal "now" gods—ABBA, Levi's and Arpege. . . .Youngsters in Denmark, West Germany, Japan, and California are all growing up with ketchup, jeans, guitars. Their lifestyles, aspirations, and desires are so similar that you might call them "OECDites" or Triadians, rather than by names denoting their national identity.[3]

There are many reasons for the similarities and commonalities in the triad's consumer demand and lifestyle patterns. First, the purchasing power of triad residents, as expressed in discretionary income per individual, is more than 10 times greater than that of residents of developing countries. For example, TV penetration in triad countries is greater than 94 percent, whereas in newly industrialized countries it is 25 percent, and for the developing countries less than 10 percent. Second, their technological infrastructure is more advanced. For example, over 70 percent of triadian households have a telephone. This makes it feasible to use such products as facsimile, telex, and digital data transmission/processing equipment. Third, the educational level is much higher in triad nations than in other parts of the world. Fourth, the number of physicians per 10,000 in triad countries exceeds 30, which creates demand for pharmaceuticals and medical electronics. Fifth, better infrastructure in the triad leads to opportunities not feasible in less-developed markets. For example, paved roads make rapid adoption of radial tires and sports cars possible.

International Marketing Highlight 11.2

Who Sells What, Where?

There may be "global markets" out there, but "global brands" have not captured them yet. This was the finding of a survey of U.S.-based manufacturers of consumer nondurable goods. Of the 85 brands included in the survey, 29, or 34 percent, were not marketed outside the U.S. at all. Others were only marketed marginally abroad.

Companies surveyed showed a clear preference for selling their goods in markets culturally similar to the U.S.: Canada and the U.K. While one might argue that Canada was targeted so frequently because of its geographical proximity to the U.S., the choice of the U.K. cannot be so easily explained. It is as far away as many other foreign countries, and its population and economy are smaller than several other foreign markets.

Among the survey's other key findings:

- *Canada is the star.* Canada was the largest foreign market by far for U.S. brands (33 of the 56 sold abroad). In fact, for 13 brands, Canada is the only foreign market. The U.K. was a distant second, being the largest foreign market for five brands. Mexico was next, with four brands, followed by [the former] West Germany with three.

- *Few mega-brands.* There were only 14 "mega-brands," ones that could be termed truly global in that they were marketed in more than 50 countries. Those most internationalized were mainly soft drinks, cleaning products, and over-the-counter drugs. Food products rely less on standard branding worldwide.

- *Older products are more international.* An interesting finding was that a majority (57 percent) of the brands sold abroad were launched before 1960. This challenges the notion that new brands are more likely than older brands to be designed for global markets.

- *No name changes.* One might expect the limited distribution of U.S. brands overseas to be offset somewhat by foreign production of exports under different brand names, but this is not the case. Few survey respondents indicated that they sell similar items abroad under different brand names.

Source: International Marketing Review, Vol. 6 (1989), pp. 7–19; and *Journal of Advertising*, No. 17 (1988), pp. 14–22.

Pacific Rim

The Pacific Rim's growing power is the corporate challenge of the 1990s. The long-anticipated emergence of the countries in the region (South Korea, Singapore, Taiwan, Hong Kong, Malaysia, Thailand, Indonesia, and the Philippines) as economic powerhouses is shaping up. Steel consumption in the region (including Japan) is higher than in the U.S. and in Europe. Similarly, demand in the Pacific Rim (again, including Japan) for semiconductors exceeds that of the EU.

Some view Pacific Rim nations as a better business bet than Eastern Europe. According to them, Eastern Europe's embrace of free enterprise is just the first step. The hard part will be catching up with the work habits and entrepreneurship of a capitalistic system. These countries will find it difficult to shed the effects of 40 years of Marxism-Leninism to become "gung-ho" like the Japanese and citizens of the newly industrializing economies.

The Pacific Rim offers a variety of opportunities for American companies, from cars to telecommunications equipment, airline seats and banking services, and a host of other products. However, it is a very competitive market. Not only are potent Japanese companies active in this market, but so are aggressive, growing conglomerates from other countries in the region. Asian producers outside Japan have already gained 25 percent of the global market for personal computers.

Without the fanfare of a common market, the Pacific Rim is becoming an economically cohesive region. A new division of labor on manufacturing is taking place. Japan and the "four dragons"—Singapore, Hong Kong, Taiwan, and South Korea—provide most of the capital and expertise for the region's other nations, which have an abundance of natural resources and labor.

Unlike Japan, other countries in the region are more amenable to buying Western products and forming manufacturing alliances with Western companies.

The point may be illustrated with reference to General Motors Corporation. The company owns 30 percent stake in a $100 million plant in China that will produce up to 60,000 light trucks annually by 1998. It has boosted distribution and marketing of Opels in Hong Kong and Singapore. In addition, it exports 14,000 U.S.-made cars to Taiwan annually and plans to assemble 20,000 Opels a year there. Further, it has set up auto assembly operations in Indonesia, Malaysia, and Thailand.[4]

Singapore in particular is promoting what it calls a "growth triangle," in which multinational companies can offset the high wages of Singapore's skilled workers by also using lower-paid, less-skilled workers in nearby Indonesia and Malaysia.

American investments in the region generally pay off handsomely. A U.S Department of Commerce study showed average annual returns of 31.2 percent in Singapore, 28.8 percent in Malaysia, 17.9 percent in South Korea, 23.6 percent in Hong Kong, 22.2 percent in Taiwan, and 14.1 percent in Japan versus 15.2 percent for U.S. investments in all foreign countries.[5] For all its burgeoning strength, however, the Pacific Rim faces risks. The region's political stability in the long run could be shaken here and there as strong leaders hand over power.

With the lifting of the 19-year-old trade embargo on Vietnam, another potentially lucrative market is opened in Southeast Asia.[5] The risks of not tapping the region's potential are global. If U.S. companies do not establish a firm position in the region, competitors from Japan, Taiwan, and Korea will gain more strength at home for even bigger assaults on markets in America and Europe.

Postcommunist Countries

The pace of the political transformations that have swept through Eastern Europe and the former Soviet Union is unprecedented. With irresistible force, the people of these communist countries have toppled their governments. With this, a new market is taking shape in the region. The tattered nations are lurching toward a Western economic orbit, and when they reach it, Western Europe's focus will shift eastward. Europe's accent will become more Germanic and Slavic, and its potential economic might will grow to a staggering size—nearly as large as the U.S. and Japan combined. The West stands to gain new markets as well as a labor supply that is well-trained and socially stable. It is a tantalizing prospect that Europe may produce the world's next economic miracle, harnessing the rich dynamism of the West to the untapped talent and energy of the East.[7]

Yet the immediate task of rescuing the backward economies of Eastern Europe is an enormous challenge. Unwinding the command economies without heaping too much pain on the populace is a Herculean job. Privatizing industrial units, keeping inflation down, and coping with massive layoffs are difficult tasks. So far, the biggest economies—Czechoslovakia, Hungary, and Poland—are making the most progress. Yugoslavia, racked by ethnic conflict, split into different nations, which are at war with each other. Less-developed Romania and Bulgaria are barely out from under their former rulers.

The difficulties ahead are large, but if the East can forge new links with the West without inflaming the continent's old nationalistic passions, the world may well be headed for a "Pax Europa," with prosperity helping to ensure the peace.

At this time, Eastern Europe is more of a market for foreign investment and aid than manufactured goods. Since communism crumbled in 1989, foreign investors have been looking hard at Eastern European countries. By the end of 1990, almost 10,000 foreign joint ventures had been established in Poland, Hungary, and former Czechoslovakia.[8] Once the changeover to the market economy is complete, these countries should become attractive markets to serve. How long this may take is difficult to predict.

Experts claim that Eastern Europe's progress depends on two factors: its ability to attract adequate capital and the ability of the people to tolerate hardships during the changeover. According to one estimate, the cost of modernizing industry and infrastructure in Eastern Europe would be $500 billion over the next 10 to 15 years.[9] Considering the enormity of the task, it may be safe to say that Eastern Europe markets may not evolve into mass markets on Western lines for another 20 years. In the interim, this will be an ad hoc opportunity for capital equipment, telecommunications, and, from time to time, limited amounts of consumer goods.[10]

The Commonwealth of Independent States poses similar problems. Russia is taking drastic steps to liberalize its economy quickly. The country is adopting a high-risk austerity program to stabilize its collapsed economy and integrate it with the rest of the world's.[11]

Russian leaders are convinced that only a radical reform program can save the country from return to dangerous central control. However, many wonder if too much is being done too soon. Although prices have begun to increase at a slower pace and more food is available in stores, enterprises around the country are hurting badly, and unemployment is increasing sharply.

Time is clearly of the essence. With economic pain stirring, Russia could become explosive. On the other hand, Russia could emerge as a healthy economy in the late 1990s.

To Westerners, Russia offers both a challenge and an opportunity. By and large, companies are optimistic about the country, and they are carefully watching its progress. If the economic measures succeed, Russia will offer all sorts of attractive opportunities.

Among other members of the commonwealth, the Baltics (Estonia, Latvia, and Lithuania) are expected to switch to market economies sooner than others. With a total population of less than eight million, these countries are mere blips on the map of Europe, but they have a highly motivated, well-trained, and low-paid work force.[12] Baltic workers are more productive than Russian workers and the Baltic countries could emerge as a viable market if their goods could be sold for hard currency in Western Europe. That is highly uncertain, however. Isolated from the West for more than 50 years, much of what they make is not competitive in today's European market—even at lower prices. Even so, there are plenty of companies willing to wait for several years. The Baltics provide a viable place to establish a manufacturing or service operation for serving the emerging Russian market.

Opportunities in other former Soviet republics are hard to pinpoint at this time. Five of them (Azerbaijan, Uzbekistan, Turkmenistan, Kyrgyzstan, and Tajikistan) have joined Iran, Turkey, and Pakistan to become part of an Islamic common market.[13] Presumably, their economic perspectives would be determined by the policies pursued by their Muslim brethren. Largely Christian Georgia and Armenia will stay closer to Russia in their endeavor to revamp their economies. The direction that Moldavia, Ukraine, and Belorussia may adopt is uncertain. For example, Moldavia might link up with Romania, while Ukraine and Belorussia may follow an independent course.[14] In any event, considering their smaller populations, they are unlikely to offer any substantial market opportunity.

Latin America

As governments cut tariffs, welcome foreign companies, and unshackle their economies, market opportunities in Latin America abound. The severe miseries of the 1980s shocked the Latin countries into abandoning the statism, populism, and protectionism that have crippled their economies since colonial times. One after another in the late 1980s, governments in Latin America have thrust their businesspeople into the free market, cutting tariffs, welcoming foreign investment, and unloading hopelessly unprofitable state enterprises. Debt is becoming manageable, and incomes are growing.

The U.S. has a better opportunity in the region since it has the inside track. Western European nations are largely occupied with Eastern Europe, and the Japanese remain focused mainly on developed countries.

Latin America offers a better opportunity, especially for U.S. firms, than Eastern Europe. It can feed itself and has a business infrastructure, albeit rickety. U.S. trade with the region is already 15 times greater than with Eastern Europe. Indeed, Latin America holds the key to the U.S. trade deficit.[15]

Although opportunities beckon, Latin America still suffers from acute economic problems. For example, inflation continues to be high and the debt problem still looms large. Slow or disappointing progress could turn the poor against free markets and back to a populist, anti-Yankee leader. Nonetheless, the rewards often outweigh the risks. Latin American consumers prefer U.S. products. Capital goods companies (e.g., telecommunications, transportation systems, mining and manufacturing equipment) have a special opportunity as these countries make investments to globalize their businesses.

China and India

China and India are by far the two most populous developing countries on earth. Notwithstanding the large differences in history, politics, and culture that separate them, the size of their populations and the vastness of their lands have stimulated similar responses to the changing global business environment. Both countries seek self-sufficiency, and at the same time are liberalizing their economies to link themselves to the global network.[16]

Since the Tiananmen Square killings in 1989, China has become suspect in Western capitals. Yet business opportunities in the country continue to grow. For example, Procter & Gamble launched its China efforts in the Guangzhou region in 1988, focusing on two products, Head & Shoulders shampoo and Oil of Olay skin cream. Both were quick hits. Avon started in 1990 and sold 6 months' worth of inventory in the first 30 days. Capital goods companies—for instance, Lockheed and Westinghouse—had similar experiences.[17]

Despite communism, capitalistic values are slowly permeating select parts of the country, particularly the delta area closer to Hong Kong. As Hong Kong accedes to China, the level of business activity in the country, and hence the market opportunity, should accelerate. If a firm has the patience to endure endless negotiations and maddening bureaucratic tangles, China is a potentially growing market (see International Marketing Highlight 11.3).

India's economic growth has occurred in a political culture that places a high value on national self-reliance and social equity. Thus, despite the fact that India is the world's largest democracy, in the realm of business it has pursued socialist policies. In recent years, however, dismayed by discouraging economic performance, India has started liberalizing the economy. The current government has taken drastic measures to encourage foreign investment and promote capital markets and exports. The government wants to establish a worldwide economy through a large-scale liberalization by freeing foreign investment conditions, cutting down protection for Indian industry, and streamlining bureaucratic procedures.

At the same time, India is in the throes of a middle class revolution that could transform its attitude toward business. The middle class accounts for some 200 million people and is growing rapidly. The rise of the middle class has sparked a boom in a variety of consumer products, durable and nondurables, a market once confined to a wealthy few.

More and more foreign companies are taking advantage of the changing business conditions in India. Recently, such well-known corporations as Timex, Kellogg, and McDonald's have entered the Indian market, something that would have been impossible in the mid-1980s.

Markets in Developing Countries

A basic management reality in today's economic world is that businesses operate in a highly interdependent global economy, and the 100-plus developing countries are very significant factors in the international business arena. They are the buyers, suppliers, competitors, and capital users. In order to determine market opportunity in developing countries, it is important to recognize the magnitude and significance of these roles.

Traditionally, Third World countries (including India and China, some Pacific Rim nations, and most Latin American countries) have provided a market for about one-third of all U.S. exports. The largest U.S. exports to developing countries are machinery and transport equipment, agricultural products, and chemicals, but all major product categories share in these markets.

International Marketing Highlight 11.3

"Hmmm. Could Use A Little More Snake"

On any weekday morning, a dozen or so consumers take the elevator to the 19th floor of Cornwall House, a nondescript office building that's home to Campbell Soup Co.'s Hong Kong taste kitchen. There, they split off into carrels and take their seats before bowls of soup and eager food scientists. Chosen carefully to get the right demographic mix, such groups are assembled to taste the offerings that Campbell hopes will ignite consumer interest in China and other parts of Asia.

The menu might include cabbage soup, scallop broth, or a local delicacy, such as pork, fig, and date soup. After up to an hour of tasting and observing, the technicians get their answers. Too much pork? Enough scallops?

Such insights are crucial to Campbell as it tries to create new products to whet regional appetites. Diet is a function of local culture, and Asia in particular puts huge demands on a Western food company seeking to crack its exotic markets. Campbell opened the Hong Kong kitchen in 1991 to reach two billion Asian consumers.

Cooking up regional specialties isn't easy. Fewer than 1 in 20 varieties tested may hit the stores. Nonetheless, Campbell can score big if it gets the formula right. At an average of one bowl a day, the Chinese are among the highest per capita soup eaters in the world.

Campbell enters new markets gingerly. It typically launches a basic meat or chicken broth, which consumers can doctor with meats, vegetables, and spices. Then it brings out more sophisticated soups. The Hong Kong kitchen already has a couple of hits to its credit—new scallop and ham soups came out of the lab. Campbell has also discovered a few surprises. Among the company's biggest sellers across Asia are such U.S. standbys as cream of mushroom and cream of chicken, which researchers believe attract westernized Chinese. One Campbell breakthrough in China, watercress and duck-gizzard soup, was developed in the U.S.

Local ingredients may count, but Campbell draws the line on some Asian favorites. Dog soup is out, as is shark's fin, since most species are endangered. However, the kitchen staff keeps an open mind when it comes to other fare.

Source: Business Week, March 15, 1993. p. 53.

U.S. business with the Third World follows closely the economic growth trends recorded in those countries. For example, U.S. exports declined sharply in the early and mid-1980s as purchasing power in those countries was reduced by debt-service problems, declining commodity prices, and the global recession. By 1987, however, the Third World market recovered more rapidly. U.S. exports to those countries showed a 16 percent gain over the preceding year, compared with increases of only 9 percent in sales to developed countries.[18]

As we move toward and into the 21st century, developing countries will become even more important in the global economy. Market opportunity in these countries rests on their ability to develop economically. That development will depend on two factors:[19] (1) their governments' willingness to encourage growth through liberal monetary and fiscal policies, and (2) the capacity of their managers to operate the productive apparatus in an efficient, effective, and equitable manner.

Traditionally, our trade focus has been on Europe and Japan. While the industrial nations will continue to be our largest markets for decades to come, another category of country holds far more promise for large incremental gains in exports. These nations, the "Big Emerging Markets" (BEMs), comprise the Chinese Economic Area (China, Hong Kong, Taiwan), Indonesia, South Korea, India, Turkey, South Africa, Poland, Argentina, Brazil, and Mexico.

The U.S. Department of Commerce estimates that nearly three-fourths of the growth in world trade in the next two decades is likely to take place in the developing countries. Most of this expansion will occur in the BEMs. The BEMs are likely to double their share of world GDP in that time to 20 percent from today's 10 percent. By the year 2010, their share of world imports is likely to exceed Japan and the European Union combined.

The BEMs will also be the competitive battleground of the future. Japan, Europe, and several developing countries can be expected to be fierce rivals in these markets.

Pursuing U.S. interests in these countries will require DEFT balancing of commercial and foreign policy considerations. It is in the BEMs that commercial opportunities co-exist so closely with complications of human rights, worker rights, nuclear non-proliferation, and violations of intellectual property right laws. The BEMs, moreover, have enough political influence and aspiration to often effectively challenge U.S. policies in multilateral organizations such as the IMF, the GATT, and the UN.

Dimensions of the Global Market

A statistical perspective of the world market is helpful to international marketers to equip them with basic information on socioeconomic life in the world via macro data. Presumably, such information should assist in segmenting the international market and in formulating marketing strategy. The macro information is conveniently available from such international organizations as the United Nations, the World Bank, and the International Monetary Fund.

The information relates to such economic aspects as population, income, trade, private consumption expenditures, total stock of durable goods (e.g., passenger cars, trucks, and buses), service facilities (e.g., telephone access lines), consumption of basic materials (e.g., cement, steel), average hourly wage rates, and other.

Analysis of macro information leads to useful conclusions. For example, per capita GDP of most Western European countries is over $15,000, while those of most Asian countries (except Japan, Hong Kong, South Korea, Taiwan, and Singapore) is less than $1,000. The per capita GDP of the two largest countries (China and India) is $367 and $274, respectively.

In most developed countries, the average hourly wage is over $5, while in most developing countries it is less than $1. In some countries (Sri Lanka, for example), it is as low as $0.19 an hour.

As can be expected, total private consumption expenditures are much higher in industrialized countries than those in the middle-and low-income brackets. By the same token, ownership of passenger cars and other durable goods, as well as consumption of energy and basic materials, is skewed in favor of advanced countries. As a matter of fact, it is the low level of energy consumption and meager use of such materials as steel and cement that characterize less-developed countries.

Based on the kind of information mentioned above, *Crossborder Monitor* has identified the 12 largest markets in the world (see Table 11.1). Interestingly, of these 12 markets, as many as 5 are the developing countries of Russia, Mexico China, Brazil, and India. Based on this information, it will be foolhardy for a company to treat all developing countries alike. Apparently, there are countries that offer a better market opportunity than the industrialized countries.

TABLE 11.1 Size, Growth, and Intensity of World's Twelve Largest Markets

Major Markets	Market Size (% of World Market)			Market Intensity (World = 1.00)			Cumulative Five-Year Market Growth (%)
	1982	1987	1992	1982	1987	1992	1992
United States	21.39	19.41	20.27	4.56	4.21	5.41	5.47
Japan	9.42	8.07	10.04	3.56	3.17	5.30	21.02
China	4.70	12.24	9.98	0.19	0.48	0.26	22.73
Russia	13.62	12.86	5.71	2.11	1.99	1.72	−9.29
India	1.49	2.31	4.91	0.09	0.13	0.13	29.83
Germany	4.79	4.21	4.86	3.81	3.56	5.04	9.43
Italy	4.04	3.58	3.69	3.36	3.22	4.46	9.05
France	3.81	3.34	3.62	3.44	3.15	4.30	15.16
United Kingdom	3.23	2.81	3.15	2.78	2.67	3.75	2.47
Brazil	2.46	3.00	2.56	0.88	1.01	0.85	−4.65
Mexico	1.28	1.49	2.47	0.85	0.80	1.44	94.71
Canada	2.07	1.99	1.96	3.98	3.89	4.66	1.66

Notes:

Market Size shows the relative dimensions of each national or regional market as a percentage of the total world market. The percentages for each market are derived by averaging the corresponding data on total population (double weighted), urban population, private consumption expenditure, steel consumption, electricity production and ownership of telephones, passenger automobiles and televisions.

Market Intensity measures the richness of the market, or the degree of concentrated purchasing power it represents. Taking the world's market intensity as 1, the EIU has calculated the intensity of each country or region as it relates to this base. The intensity figure is derived from an average of per-capita ownership, production, and consumption indicators. Specifically, it is calculated by averaging per-capita figures for automobiles in use (double weighted), telephones in use, TVs in use, steel consumption, electricity production, private consumption expenditure (double weighted) and the percentage of population that is urban (double weighted).

Market Growth is an average of cumulative growth in several key economic market indicators: population; steel consumption; electricity production; and ownership of passenger automobiles, lorries, buses, and TVs.

Source: Crossborder Monitor, August 31, 1994, p.4.

An interesting characteristic of global markets is their emerging universality. In other words, a one-world market exists for products ranging from cars to consumer electronics to carbonated drinks. Firms today are engaged in world competition to serve consumers globally (see International Marketing Highlight 11.4). It must be cautioned, however, that each nation still has its own cultural peculiarities. Thus, a firm cannot assume that in each case what is good for the home country is good for the world.

A number of broad forces have led to growing globalization of markets.[20] These include:

- *Growing similarity of countries.* Because of growing commonality of infrastructure, distribution channels, and marketing approaches, more and more products and brands are available everywhere. This manifests similar buyer needs in different countries. Large retail chains, TV advertising, and credit cards are just a few examples of once-isolated phenomena that are rapidly becoming universal.

- *Falling tariff barriers.* Successive rounds of bilateral and multilateral agreements have lowered tariffs markedly since World War II. At the same time, regional economic agreements such as the European Union have facilitated trade relations among member countries.

- *Strategic role of technology:* Technology is not only reshaping industries, but contributing to market homogenization. For example, electronic innovations permit the development of more compact, lighter products that are less costly to ship. Transportation costs themselves have fallen with the use of containerization and larger-capacity ships. Increasing ease of communication and data transfer make it feasible to link operations in different countries. At the same time, technology leads to an easy flow of information among buyers, making them aware of new and quality products and thus creating demand.

Global markets offer unlimited opportunities. However, competition in these markets is intense. To be globally successful, companies must learn to operate and compete as if the world were one large market, ignoring superficial regional and national differences. Corporations geared to this new reality can benefit from enormous economies of scale in production, distribution, marketing, and management. By translating these benefits into reduced world prices, they can dislodge competitors who still operate with the perspectives of the 1970s and 1980s. Companies willing to change their perspectives and become global can attain sustainable competitive advantage (see International Marketing Highlight 11.5).

Segmenting the Global Market

A *market segment* refers to a group of countries that are alike in respect to their responsiveness to some aspect of marketing strategy. *Market segmentation* may be defined as a technique of dividing different countries into homogeneous groups. The concept of segmentation is based on the fact that a business cannot serve the entire world with a single set of policies because there are disparities among countries—both economic and cultural. An international marketer, therefore, should pick out one or more countries as target markets. A company may not find it feasible to do business immediately with the entire spectrum of countries forming a segment. In that case, the firm may design its marketing programs and strategies for those countries it does enter and draw upon its experience with these countries in dealing with new markets.

International Marketing Highlight 11.4

Global Disorientation

She arrives on her British Airways flight, rents a Toyota at the Hertz desk in the terminal, and drives to the downtown Hilton hotel. She drops into a chair, flips on the Sony TV, and gazes glassily at this week's scandal on "Dallas." Room service delivers dinner along with the bottle of Perrier and the pack of Marlboro cigarettes she ordered. While eating dinner she catches herself nodding off, but is brought back to consciousness by a sudden feeling of disorientation. Is she in Sydney, Singapore, Stockholm, or Seattle? Her surroundings and points of reference over the past few hours have provided few clues.

With the expansion of the international economy and the growth of international business in the post-World War II era, the marketplace has taken on a recognizably similar face in countries around the globe. No longer is the overseas traveler surprised to see a familiar logo flashing from a neon sign or to find a favorite brand from home on sale in a foreign location. The most interesting phenomenon is not just that MNCs have entered the foreign markets. Increasingly, it has become evident that the same few companies compete against each other for leadership positions in numerous national markets worldwide. In automobiles, construction equipment, consumer electronics, cameras, office copiers, airframes, computers, and a variety of other industries, not more than half a dozen MNCs dominate the major markets worldwide.

Source: From a note entitled "Global Competition and MNC Managers," by Christopher A. Bartlett, Harvard Business School, 1985.

International Marketing Highlight 11.5

Why Go Global?

The rules for survival have changed since the beginning of the 1980s. Domestic markets have become too small. Even the biggest companies in the biggest countries cannot survive on their domestic markets if they are in global industries. They have to be in all major markets. That means North America, Western Europe, and the Pacific Rim countries.

Take, for example, the pharmaceuticals business. In the 1970s, developing a new drug cost about $16 million and took 4 to 5 years. The drug could be produced in Britain or the U.S. and eventually exported. Now, developing a drug costs about $250 million and takes as long as 12 years. Only a global product for a global market can support that much risk. No major pharmaceuticals company is in the game for anything other than global products. That helps explain a series of mergers of major drug companies, most recently the marriage of Bristol-Myers and Squibb.

Source: Fortune, August 1989, p. 70.

The importance of segmentation can be illustrated by a reference to Massy-Ferguson Ltd., a Toronto-based farm equipment producer. As far back as 1959, this company decided to concentrate on sales outside of North America and thus avoid competing head-on with Ford Motor Company, Deere & Company, and International Harvester Company. It took the company years to implement successfully its segmentation strategy before reaching a point where it derives almost 70 percent of its sales outside of North America. As a matter of fact, as the market matured in North America, Massey continued to grow and earn substantial income, since demand overseas accelerated in the 1980s. While Ford, Deere, and International Harvester struggled hard to maintain profitability, Massey-Ferguson, because of its decision to avoid the North American segment, showed a fine performance.

To survive and prosper in the increasingly competitive global marketplace many companies are learning to find and dominate "niche markets." For companies of all kinds and sizes, nichemanship is rapidly becoming the new business imperative.

Simply defined, a niche is a relatively small segment of a market that the major competitors or producers may overlook, ignore, or have difficulty serving. The niche may be a narrowly defined geographical area. It may relate to the unique needs of a small and specific group of customers, or it may be some narrow, highly specialized aspect of a very broad group of customers. In some cases, the niche market may actually be very large—particularly if the company operates globally.

The possibilities are virtually endless. So too are the opportunities, as effective niche strategies can be extremely profitable.

By focusing on a niche market, companies often develop an excellent understanding of their customers' operations—and how those customers make money. This understanding in turn provides an edge when it comes to identifying opportunities for new products and marketing programs. This emphasis on a niche provides a very clear focus for the development of business strategies and action plans.

The importance of niche strategy may be illustrated by the experience of Linear Technology, a Canadian firm.[21] It successfully carved out a niche in the world integrated circuit ("chip") business. Although this market as a whole is dominated by major Japanese and American firms, Linear Technology dominates the global market for one narrow segment—audio amplifier chips for hearing aids. Even in Japan, it has achieved more than a 50 percent market share in competition with companies like NEC. By having a broad product line within its specialized area and by focusing on the needs of one set of customers, it has managed to beat all competitors.

A basic problem in market segmentation is how it should be accomplished. Virtually all international marketers segment the world market, but typically their criteria do not provide categories that are truly significant. Traditionally, geography has been employed to divide the world. However, segmentation based on geography overlooks the possibility of economic and cultural differences among countries.

For example, the countries of the Middle East in no way constitute a homogeneous market. Iran, Iraq, Kuwait, the United Arab Emirates (UAE), Saudi Arabia, Egypt, and Lebanon are all very different. Lebanon has had special problems, while all the others have different legal and political systems. The Emirates have no formal business laws at all, Saudi Arabia has a fairly new and sophisticated statute, while Egyptian law has a long history and is based on French law. Lately, the Middle Eastern countries have made attempts to present a common economic posture through regulation tariffs, duties, and the like. Despite that, a U.S. business cannot take full advantage of the fragmentation of bureaucracies and laws because the natural fragmentation of Middle Eastern markets is reinforced by nationalist tendencies. Therefore, it is not possible for a company simply to go into the cheapest or most liberal country and expect to maximize its profit by trading into the whole area from that base.

The Middle East description illustrates the point that world markets need to be grouped judiciously. It requires carefully finding and verifying the dimension(s) to be employed in classifying the countries.

Segmentation Process

Five procedural steps should be followed to gain information and insights into the segmentation criteria suitable for classifying world markets:

1. Develop a market taxonomy for classifying the world markets.
2. Segment all countries into homogeneous groups having common characteristics with reference to the dimensions of the market taxonomy.
3. Determine theoretically the most efficient method of serving each group.
4. Choose the group in which the marketer's own perspective (its product/service, and strengths) is in line with the requirements of the group.
5. Adjust this ideal classification to the constraints of the real world (existing commitments, legal and political restrictions, practicality, and so forth).

A company interested in expanding business overseas can utilize this procedure by first deciding on a criterion for classifying the countries for its product. Not all countries should be analyzed, but only those that appear to offer a viable potential. For example, a machine-tool manufacturer may segment countries based on need: those requiring simple machines (first-generation machine-tools); those requiring medium-size machine-tools (say, second-generation machines); and those requiring large, sophisticated machines. The company may find it is well placed to serve the second segment, those countries that require medium-size machine-tools. Let us assume the following countries fall into this segment: Malaysia, Brazil, Thailand, Indonesia, Philippines, Mexico, and Nigeria. To serve this targeted segment of countries, the company may establish three assembly plants, one in Nigeria, one in Brazil, and one in Malaysia (assuming other countries in the geographic area would be served through exports from these three countries). However, because the machine tool industry often encounters a lack of scientific personnel in such foreign countries, the company may consider establishing an assembly plant in India (instead of Malaysia), which has a large pool of scientific talent, to serve the Asian part of its segment. It may do so even though the Indian market is highly competitive. This is what is meant by adjustment of the ideal system to the real world.

Criteria for Grouping Countries

As is true in domestic market segmentation, countries of the world can be grouped using a variety of criteria. For example, a company may group world markets (countries) based on a single variable such as per capita GNP or geography. Similarly, religion or political system may serve as a criterion for grouping countries. Alternatively, the classification of countries may be based on the combination of a few selected variables. One may use just a few variables such as political system, geography, and economic status (GNP per capita), or use a large number of variables, similar to what is done in establishing lifestyle or psychographic segments in domestic marketing.

Our discussion is developed based on economic status grouping, geographic grouping, political system grouping, grouping by religion, cultural grouping, multiple-variable grouping, intermarket grouping, and quality of life grouping. The discussion ends with a recommended scheme for country classification.

Of the different ways for grouping countries together, the choice of an appropriate method will depend on the reasons for segmenting the world market. The main purpose of grouping is usually related to the nature of the product. For example, a defense equipment manufacturer may classify countries based on their political systems. But for an appliance company, economic status may be a more appropriate choice.

> The manner in which countries are to be grouped will depend, to a large extent, on the nature of a company's product or product lines. Companies marketing capital goods may find that Rostow's classification of countries into five economic states is the most effective way to view operations. On the other hand, companies in the consumer durable-goods field may find that grouping countries by personal consumption expenditures is a more meaningful way to study world-wide activities. A series of composite indicators developed for each group may prove to be of substantial help in evaluating overseas division and area performance, and in applying the lessons learned in one market to the formulation of plans and strategies for the other areas.[22]

Economic Status Grouping

The simplest way to form economic groups is to classify countries on the basis on GNP per person. For example, countries may be grouped as high-income countries with GNP per capita over $12,000; middle-income countries (GNP per capita between $1,000 and $7,500); and low-income countries with GNP below $1,000. If we follow this scheme, about 55 countries will fall in the low-income category, 50 in the middle-income category, and 23 will be considered high-income.[23] (Economic status groupings should be differentiated from regional market agreements, discussed in Chapter 5, which are formed using more than strictly economic considerations.)

There is no empirical study showing that the economic status classification of countries by GNP per capita is a viable system. Based on domestic marketing experience, however, it is questionable if a single variable should be used to group countries into homogeneous categories. For example, GNP per capita of Kuwait, Libya, and Saudi Arabia would put them in the category of industrialized countries, but these countries by no means constitute the same market as industrial countries such as the U.S., Germany, Italy, and so on. Additionally, emphasis on economic status alone in classifying countries misses the crucial impact of cultural differences among nations.

The grouping of countries based on GNP per capita assumes, like other economic criteria for segmentation, that market behavior is directly related to income. In domestic marketing, a number of studies have questioned the relevance of income as a discerning variable. In the international arena as well, sole reliance on GNP per capita for international comparisons is considered inadequate. For example, in 1992 Ghana had a per capita GNP of $450, compared with India's $310. However, if the purchasing power of a dollar in the 2 countries is considered, the per capita GNP for Ghana comes out to be US$540, while that for India is $850.

Based on the current international situation, a slightly different way of forming segments is to group countries in the following five categories: First World, Second World, Third World, Fourth World, and Fifth World. These categories may be defined in the following terms.[24]

First World This includes the advanced industrialized nations of Europe, North America, and Asia that accept a more-or-less capitalistic, market-oriented economy. The core of the First World consists of members of the OECD (Organization for Economic Cooperation and Development); that is, the industrialized West and Japan. New Zealand and Australia also qualify, and Greece and Spain are borderline cases.

Second World This group includes high-income oil exporters and newly industrialized countries. These countries have in the past 20 years achieved significant economic progress, either through investing their oil revenues (for example, Saudi Arabia) or by competing aggressively in the international market such as South Korea.

Third World This group is made up of countries that need time and technology, rather than massive foreign aid, to build modern developed economies. These include nations whose development may be guaranteed by other key resources and nations that are developed enough to attract foreign investment and borrow on commercial terms. Examples of the former group are Zambia (copper) and Morocco (phosphate). Mexico, Brazil, and India fall into the latter group.

Fourth World This group includes the 1.5 billion people of the world's hitherto centrally planned communist-run nations, with the exception of former Yugoslavia, which has a mixed economy, and the People's Republic of China.

Fifth World The 200 million inhabitants of the Fifth World live in hard-core poverty. Many Fifth World countries have few presently known resources. Usually a large part of the population is engaged in subsistence farming or nomadic herding, and some are isolated from the outside world. Life expectancy is below 50 years, and nutritional intake is significantly less than the minimum considered necessary for health. Notable exceptions are Mali, Chad, Ethiopia, Somalia, Rwanda, and Bangladesh.

The aforementioned groupings, while interesting and seemingly relevant, do not appear to lend themselves to practical use. Assignment of different countries to these categories is arbitrary. Besides, no evidence exists to support the viability of these categories from the standpoint of marketing.

Geographic Grouping

One popular way of grouping nations is to classify them along regional lines. Many MNCs organize their worldwide operations into such regions as Western Europe, Latin

America, Far East (including Australia and New Zealand), Middle East, and Africa. A variety of reasons makes geographic grouping of countries an acceptable criterion for overseas marketers. First, geographic proximity makes it easier to manage countries blocked together. For example, all countries in Latin America can be managed, say, from a regional headquarters in Brazil. Both transportation and communication are easier to handle on a regional basis. Consider, if Argentina is grouped with Italy, Spain, and New Zealand, while Brazil is grouped with South Korea, Taiwan, and India (assuming some viable basis), how difficult it would be for an executive to manage these far-flung countries theoretically grouped together.

As a matter of fact, one might even argue that nations in the same geographic regions should share common cultural traits with each other. This added facet gives credence to geographic grouping. One more factor that supports regional classification of countries is the post-World War II organization of countries into trading groups, such as the European Economic Community (EEC), now the EU, the Latin American Free Trade Association, and the European Free Trade Area. These organizations are regional in character; that is, countries in the same geographic region decided to join with each other to become large economic entities. Typically, members of a group agree to trade freely with each other without any barriers, as do the Common Market countries. In fact the EU countries go even further and levy common external tariffs. From the point of view of an international marketer, the existence of common economic arrangements among nations by means of groups will mean that entry into one country will automatically smooth entry into another country belonging to the same group; the same marketing strategy perspective can be applied to one or all. Thus, geographic division of countries appears sound.

Despite these reasons, geographic lumping of countries to form market segments is not always sound. Geographic proximity of countries does not automatically guarantee they will present the same market opportunity for international business. For example, the Philippines and Thailand do not provide as viable markets as Singapore, Malaysia, South Korea, Taiwan, and Hong Kong, even though all these countries are in the same geographic region. Similarly, Mexico is geographically part of the same continent as the U.S. and Canada, but Mexico obviously differs culturally and economically from the other two.

What Rossman says about Latin America applies to other parts of the world as well:

> Many U.S. marketers think everything between the Rio Grande River and Tierra del Fuego at the southern tip of South America is the same, including the 400 million inhabitants. In fact, the Dominican Republic is no more like Argentina than Sicily is like Sweden.
>
> Many Latin Americans don't speak Spanish, including 140 million Portuguese-speaking Brazilians and the millions in other countries who speak a variety of Indian dialects.[25]

In general, geographic classification of countries for the purposes of international marketing may not be the most desirable alternative to use.

Political Grouping

Another way of grouping countries is to classify them by their political perspective. For example, countries may be categorized politically in the following types: democratic republics, dictatorships, communist dictatorships, and monarchies. These categories are used simply to facilitate discussion. As appropriate to a marketer's purposes, these categories may be refined further. Political segments may be established with reference to party systems. For example, the two-party system of the U.S., the multiparty systems of Italy, Israel, and Germany, or the single-party systems of Mexico and India could be used. Dictatorships may be military or civilian.

Once a suitable set of political categories has been worked out, countries in each category or group may then be considered as homogeneous for purposes of developing marketing strategy. In other words, a different marketing strategy may be developed for each political group that would be relevant for the firm's international business with all the countries in that group.

If politics is used as the segmentation criterion for grouping countries, Nigeria, Bangladesh, and Argentina would have belonged in the same category in 1988. For example, all then had military dictators, with inclinations toward holding free elections to establish democratic governments. However, from the vantage point of the multinational marketer, their political closeness did not render them potentially similar customers. Argentina was economically much closer to the Western European countries. Nigeria's economic potential is linked with oil prices. Highly populated Bangladesh, on the other hand, ranked among the low-income countries of the world. The differing economic perspectives of the three countries seem to negate their grouping according to political environment in order to develop a common marketing strategy. One strategy would not be adequate to serve these markets.

The concept of political grouping appears most relevant to categorizing communist countries. Because of common marketing approaches like centralized buying, barter, and countertrade that were practiced in Eastern Europe, these countries, in the past, could be served with a common marketing strategy.

Grouping in Religion

Religion constitutes an important element of society in most cultures. It thus greatly influences lifestyle, which in turn affects marketing. Following this logic, religion could work out to be a viable criterion for grouping countries. What has been said of Latin America applies to many other parts of the world with different religions.

> The life of the family and of the individual is greatly and continuously involved with the Church. One must not exaggerate the implications of this relationship of the individual, the family, and the community to the Church. But one should also be careful not to underestimate it. It gives the life a certain quality and adds something to the meaning of daily activities which is lacking in the United States.[26]

Religion can be defined as the quest for the values of the ideal life and as involving three phases: the ideal, the practices for attaining the value of the ideal, and the theology or world-view relating the quest to the surrounding universe. This definition covers virtually all aspects of a country's life—its aesthetics, its material culture, its social organization, its language, even its politics and economics.

Animism, Hinduism, Buddhism, Judaism, Islam, and Christianity are the major religions of the world. Religion as an aspect of cultural environment is discussed in Chapter 7. Briefly, however, animism is a prehistoric form of religion—ancient religion without religious texts and specific words but with some magic. Animism today is found all over the world but is practiced most obviously in African countries. Some Latin American countries have animistic tendencies as well.[27]

Hinduism, defined more as a way of life than a religion, is practiced mostly in India. Considered to be 4,000 years old, it reflects a complex set of tenets and beliefs but lacks a common creed or dogma.

> Hinduism has no dogma; it is not even a religion when you come to think of it; it is a way of life. This in itself makes the task of change harder. You are not up against dogma, you are just up against a total way of life, which is much more difficult to change than dogma.[28]

Buddhism sprang from Hinduism in India in the sixth century B.C. Buddhists are found mainly in Southeast Asia and Japan. In Burma, Sri Lanka, Thailand, Laos, and Kampuchea it is the dominant religion. There are some Buddhists in Western countries, and, presumably, in the People's Republic of China as well.

Judaism is the monotheistic religion of the Jewish people, tracing its origin to Abraham, having its spiritual and ethical principles embodied chiefly in the Bible and the Talmud. Jews do not belong to one race of people. The term *Jew* applies correctly to anyone who is a member of the Jewish faith. Nationally speaking, Jews are Germans, Arabian, American, and almost everything else.

Islam is practiced by over 500 million people living in about 30 countries. The Islamic countries are located mainly in the Middle East, Northern Africa, and South Asia. Islam tends to define a total way of life that its adherents should follow. It includes legislation that organizes all human relationships.

Christianity, sometimes referred to as the religion of the Western world, is found all over the globe. With the Protestant Reformation, Christianity began to emphasize individuality more than other religions. Although marked differences exist between the two major divisions of Christianity, Roman Catholicism and Protestantism, basically it stresses similar values such as achievement and thrift. Interestingly, the Protestant countries in particular rank economically among the highest in the world in terms of GNP per capita.

The effect of religion on lifestyle makes it a relevant criterion for grouping countries. Exhibit 7.2 shows, for example, how Islam affects business. Yet the formulation of a common marketing strategy for a group of countries following Islam, or any one religion, may not suffice. Both Pakistan and Saudi Arabia are strong adherents to Islam. However, the economic differences between the two countries would invalidate lumping them together for marketing decision making. Saudi Arabia, with a per capita GNP of $7,510 (1992 estimate), is a customer for a variety of consumer and industrial products. On the other hand, Pakistan, with its per capita GNP of $420 (1992 estimate), offers a very low potential for international marketers. Similarly, France and the Philippines, both primarily Catholic countries, cannot be served by following the same marketing perspective. In brief, while religion via culture plays an important role in determining lifestyle, by itself it may not serve as a viable criterion for grouping countries.

Cultural Classification

It is conceivable that countries can be classified in stereotyped cultural groupings. Presumably, countries in a cultural group should be amenable to the same marketing strategy. To an extent, cultural groupings make sense since lifestyle is affected intimately by culture, and hence this form of classification for marketing decision making should be adequate. The problem here, however, is what constitutes a cultural category. Unless we use a variable like religion to serve as a surrogate for culture, it will not be easy to establish cultural categories.

The Human Relations Area Files Inc., associated with Yale University, has identified about 700 major cultural groups in the world, further collapsing of which resulted in over 60 blue-ribbon culture types.[29] Even if only 60 categories are used, it will be an enormous task for an international marketer to relate all the different countries of the world to each of these categories and formulate an individualized strategy for each of the 60 cultural groups.

Multiple-Variable Grouping

A number of studies have been reported in marketing literature that used a large number of variables to form country clusters.[30] The argument behind the use of multiple variables has been that countries relate to each other in accordance with their cultural, religious, socioeconomic, and political characteristics. Therefore, it is desirable to form international segments using variables in all these areas rather than simply grouping countries on the basis of geographic proximity or economic status.

An important grouping study using cluster analysis was done by Sethi. He used 29 variables to cluster 91 countries.[31] The method adopted by Sethi requires two procedural steps. First, a large number of variables are collapsed into smaller, more meaningful groups of clusters. These groups are called *variable clusters* or *V-clusters,* and are discriminatory variables pertaining to countries such as GNP per capita, cars per capita, and single-family homes per capita. Second, objects (for example, countries) are scored on the basis of each V-cluster. With the use of O-analysis (one method for accomplishing the second step), a large number of countries are classified into subgroups called O-clusters (or O-types). Each country is scored for each of the V-cluster dimensions mentioned in the first step. These scores are used to identify O-types or countries with similar characteristics. The multiple-variable approach assumes that countries with similar social-economic-political perspectives should be combined into segments. The approach falsely assumes that countries are indivisible, heterogeneous units.

Intermarket Segmentation

In recent years, a refined approach has been advanced: the formation of intercountry segments.[32] Groups of customers who are alike in different countries form segments. In other words, each country's market consists of different segments. A particular segment in a country may be very much like a similar segment in one or more other countries.[33] These similar segments belonging to different countries may be combined to form a viable intermarket segment (see International Marketing Highlight 11.6).

Assume a U.S. chemical manufacturing company is interested in foreign expansion. The company manufactures different types of chemicals such as pharmaceuticals, fine chemicals, and fertilizers. In its attempts to segment the world market, the company may find small farmers in developing countries a segment worth serving. These customers, whether from Pakistan or Indonesia or Kenya or Mexico, appear to represent common needs and behavior patterns. Most of them till the land using bullock carts and have very little cash to buy agricultural inputs. They lack the education and exposure to appreciate fully the value of using fertilizer and depend on government help for such things as seeds, pesticides, and fertilizer. They acquire their farming needs from local suppliers and count on word-of-mouth to learn and accept new things and ideas. Thus, even though these farmers are in different countries continents apart, and even though they speak different languages and have different cultural backgrounds, they may represent a homogeneous market segment.

Take the case of the Mercedes-Benz. Considered a luxury car, it has a world-wide market niche among the well-to-do. Even in Japan, Mercedes is considered the most popular foreign luxury car.[34] Similarly, a designer of men's clothing may find that elites of different countries compose a market of segment themselves. Likewise, the teenagers of different countries may work out to be a viable segment. (see International Marketing Highlight 11.7). Table 11.2 illustrates the perspectives of these intermarket segments.

International Marketing Highlight 11.6

Segmenting the Global Market

A critical element in fending off the competition is being aware of who one's consumer is and what that consumer wants. Global Scan, an annual survey developed by the advertising agency, Network Backer Spielvogel Bates Worldwide Inc., that measures style of life and consumer attitudes and purchasing pattern of over 15,000 customers in 14 countries (Australia, Canada, Colombia, Finland, France, Germany, Hong Kong, Indonesia, Japan, Mexico, Spain, the U.K., the U.S., and Venezuela), has classified global consumers into 5 distinct categories: strivers, achievers, pressured, traditionals, and adapters. Although all five consumer classes were found to exist in almost all of the Global Scan countries, segment sizes vary widely—sometimes dramatically—from one country to the next. The same five consumer groups can be found in the U.S. and in Japan—countries with totally different histories and cultures. The Japanese strivers and achievers, for instance, have more in common with their U.S. counterparts than they do with their own parents.

Global Scan has determined that, throughout the world, more strivers (26 percent) set highest priority on good service than all other groups, followed closely by achievers (22 percent). In fact, service will become increasingly important as these two segments age—or grow wealthier.

- *Strivers.* These are defined as young people on the run. Their median age is 31, and their average day is nonstop. They push hard to achieve success, but they are also hard-pressed to meet all their goals. They are materialistic, look for pleasure, and insist on instant gratification. Short of time, energy, and money, they seek out convenience in every corner of their lives. Strivers think that others are getting more out of life—and most are envious.

- *Achievers.* Those who fall into this category are slightly older and several giant steps ahead of the strivers. They are affluent, assertive, and on the way up. Opinion leaders and style-setters, they shape the world's mainstream values. Achievers are hooked on status and high on quality; together with the strivers, they create the youth-oriented values that drive society today.

Source: *Business International,* July 23, 1990, p. 237.

While the concept of intermarket segmenting is relevant on a worldwide basis, it is especially workable within a region. For example, women all over the world could be considered mistakenly to have similar cosmetic-usage behavior patterns. It is widely recognized that lifestyle behavior is deeply affected by culture. Muslim women are supposed to veil in public; some Latin women consider excessive cosmetic usage as self-indulgence. Thus, from the viewpoint of a cosmetic company, stereotyping people globally may prove to be unproductive. Instead, grouping people in a region where culture and economic conditions do not vary substantially from country to country may represent a viable segment.

Applying the concept of intermarket segmentation in Europe, many companies are pursuing the idea of a *Eurobrand,* that is, a product/brand destined for a market consisting of niches in different Western European countries. The development of satellite communication makes it feasible to simultaneously reach customers in different countries, which would not have been possible through the traditional TV channel.[35]

Estee Lauder, Inc. recently made its first foray into intermarket marketing with a strategy to sell products designed specifically for the West Coast of the U.S. and Japan. The cosmetics company's Aramis division launched a line of men's fragrances, called NewWest, in the fall of 1988 in California and Japan. At least initially, the company did not plan to sell the products elsewhere in the U.S. Such intermarket strategies have also been pursued by Campbell Soup Company and Chrysler Corp.[36]

International Marketing Highlight 11.7

The Global Teen Segment

In the world divided by trade wars and tribalism, teenagers, of all people, are the new unifying force. From the steamy playgrounds of Los Angeles to the stately boulevards of Singapore, kids show amazing similarities in taste, language, and attitude. African Americans, Asians, Latinos, and Europeans are zipping up Levi's, dancing to the Red Hot Chili Peppers, and punching the keyboards of their Macintosh PCs. Propelled by mighty couriers like MTV, trends spread with sorcerous speed. Kids hear drumbeats a continent away, absorb the rhythm, and add their own licks. For the Coca-Colas and the Nikes, no marketing challenge is more basic than capturing that beat. There are billions to be earned.

Teens almost everywhere buy a common gallery of products: Reebok sports shoes, Procter & Gamble Cover Girl makeup, Sega and Nintendo videogames, PepsiCo's new Pepsi Max. They're also helping pick the hits in electronics, from Kodak cameras to Motorola beepers. Teen choices are big business. Last year America's 28 million teenagers spent $57 billion of their own money. In Europe, Latin America, and the Pacific Rim, a swath of over 200 million teens are converging with their American soul mates in a vast, free-spending market that circles the globe.

Source: Shawn Tully, "Teens–The Most Global Market of All," *Fortune,* May 16, 1994, p. 9. ©1994 Time Inc. All rights reserved.

Portfolio Approach

A new approach based on strategic planning frameworks for classifying countries has been recommended by Rizkallah.[37] This *portfolio approach,* as shown in Figure 11.1, proposes dividing countries on a three-dimensional basis: country potential, competitive strength, and risk. Following this method, 18 country segments are obtained.

Country potential in the portfolio approach refers to the market potential for a firm's product/service in a given country and is based on such factors as population size, rate of economic growth, real gross national product, per capita national income, distribution of population, industrial production/consumption patterns, and the like. Both internal and external factors determine *competitive strength.* In a given country,

TABLE 11.2
Behavioral Aspects Related to the Identification of Global Consumer Segments

	GLOBAL ELITES	GLOBAL TEENAGERS
Shared Values	Wealth, success, status	Growth, change, future, learning, play
Key Product Benefits Sought	Universally recognizable products with prestige image High-quality products	Novelty, trendy image, fashion statement Name brands/novelty
Demographics	Very high income, social status and class/ well-traveled /well-educated	Age 12–19, well-traveled, high media exposure
Media/Communication	Upscale magazines, social-selective channels (i.e., cliques), direct marketing, global telemarketing	Teen magazines, MTV, radio, video, peers, role models
Distribution Channels	Selective (i.e., upscale, retailers)	General retailers with name brands
Price Range	Premium	Affordable
Targeted by Global Firms Such as	Mercedes Benz, Perrier, American Express, Ralph Lauren's Polo	Coca-Cola Co., Benetton, Swatch International, Sony, PepsiCo, Inc.
Related Microsegments/Clusters	Affluent women, top executives, highly educated professionals, professional athletes	Preadolescents, female teens, male teens
Factors Influencing the Emergence of the Segment	Increased wealth, widespread travel	Television media, international education

Source: Salah S. Hassan and Lea Prevel Katsanis, "Identification of Global Consumer Segments," *Journal of International Consumer Marketing,* Vol. 3 (2), p. 24. Copyright 1991 by the Haworth Press, Inc. (Binghamton, NY).

the *internal factors* include the firm's market share; its resources; and facilities, including knowledge of the unique features of that country and the skills and facilities it owns to match these features. *External factors* include strength of competitors in the same industry, competition from industries of substitute products, and the structure of the industry locally and internationally. *Risk*—that is, political risk, financial risk, and business risk (like change in consumer preferences)—is any factor that causes variation in profit, cash flow, or other outcomes generated by involvement in a country.

The author of this approach claims the following advantages for the portfolio approach:[38]

- It is three-dimensional, which implies greater representativeness of the multinational environment.

- Its dimensions are relevant to marketing.

- It treats risk as a separate dimension, which makes it closed to the real world situation, since many countries of the world could have high potential and be attractive but have different degrees of risk.

FIGURE 11.1 An International Market Taxonomy Matrix for Classifying Countries

		Competitive Strength			
		Strong	Average	Weak	
Risk	High			High	Country Potential
				Medium	
				Low	
	Low			High	
				Medium	
				Low	

Source: Elias G. Rizkallah, "Multiple Product: Multiple Market Allocations—A Portfolio Approach," a paper presented at the Academy of International Business Annual Meeting in New Orleans, October 24, 1980, p. 10.

- Each of the preceding dimensions is a composite measure of a variety of subfactors. For example, neither GNP nor income level, each by itself, is adequate as a descriptor of overall country potential.

- It uses an 18-cell matrix with 3 levels each of the country potential and competitive strength dimensions, and 2 levels of risk. This is important because the world contains not only highs and lows, but middle positions as well.

This approach presents an interesting method for achieving country segments. It requires, however, an abundance of information, both internal and external to the firm, which may not be easy to collect and analyze. Additionally, this approach is more relevant for use at a product/market level than at a headquarters level. Thus, a company involved in marketing a number of products/services abroad will have to work out a number of segmentation schemes. The scheme, however, makes strategic sense and provides an important framework for analyzing opportunities for chosen products in select markets that appear to be potentially viable.

In-Country Segmentation

So far the discussion has dealt with grouping the countries of the world from the point of view of the MNC. However, the concept of segmentation also is relevant within a particular country. Just as marketers segment their markets in the U.S., in each country there may be a variety of submarkets or segments that vary substantially from one another. The marketing strategist should identify these segments and choose those that are to be served.

One may use simple demographic and socioeconomic variables, personality and lifestyle variables, or situation-specific events (such as use intensity, brand loyalty, attitudes) as the bases for segmentation. For example, a U.S. food company segmented the French market into modern and traditional segments, defining the modern French consumer as liking processed foods while the traditional type looks upon them as a threat. A leading industrial manufacturer discovered that the critical variable for segmenting the Japanese market was the amount of annual usage per item, not per order or per any other variable. A toiletries manufacturer used geographic criteria—urban versus rural markets in West Africa. Exhibit 11.1 provides an inventory of different bases for market segmentation. Most of these bases are usually covered in a principles of marketing text.

Besides products and customers, a market can also be segmented by level of customer service, stage of production, price-performance characteristics, credit arrangements with customers, location of plants, characteristics of manufacturing equipment, channels of distribution, and financial policies.

The key is to choose a variable or variables that so divide the market that customers in a segment have similar responsiveness to some aspect of the marketer's strategy. The variable should be measurable; it should represent an objective value such as income, rate of consumption, or frequency of buying, not simply a qualitative viewpoint such as the degree of customer happiness.[39] Also, the variable should create segments that may be responsive to promotion. Even if it were feasible to measure happiness, segments based on the happiness variable cannot be reached by a specific medium. Thus, happiness cannot serve as an appropriate criterion because it is not easily manipulated.

Once segments have been formed, the next strategic issue is deciding which segment should be selected. The segment chosen should fulfill the following conditions:

1. It should be one in which the maximum differential in competitive strategy can be developed.
2. It must be capable of being isolated so that the competitive advantage can be preserved.
3. It must be valid, even though imitated.

EXHIBIT 11.1 Bases for Segmentation

1. Demographic factors (age, income, sex, etc.)
2. Socioeconomic factors (social class, stages in the family life cycle)
3. Geographic factors
4. Psychological factors (lifestyle, personality traits)
5. Consumption patterns (heavy, moderate, and light users)
6. Perceptual factors (benefit segmentation, perceptual mapping)
7. Brand and loyalty patterns
8. Product attributes

The success of Volkswagen in the U.S. can be attributed to its fit into a market segment that had two unique characteristics. First, the segment served by VW could not be adequately served by conventional U.S. cars or modifications of them. Second, the manufacturing economies of scale could not be brought to bear by U.S. manufacturers as a whole to the disadvantage of VW. However, American Motors, like Volkswagen, was successful in identifying a special segment to serve with its compact car, the Rambler. In the long run, the critical difference between Volkswagen and American Motors was that American Motors could not protect its segment from the superior scale of manufacturing volume of the other three U.S. automobile manufacturers.

Summary

Worldwide there are about 5.5 billion consumers belonging to over 132 countries. Not all people, however, are viable consumers. The global market may be split into different regions such as the triad market, Pacific Rim market, postcommunist countries, Latin America, China and India, and developing countries. Different regions offer different market opportunities. The richest and most advanced among these is the triad market.

An interesting aspect of today's international business is the globalization of markets. World markets are slowly becoming homogeneous, requiring companies to develop marketing programs to serve consumers across national boundaries. A company interested in marketing abroad needs to decide which countries to enter and how those countries may be grouped together in homogeneous categories. The use of categories limits the need for developing marketing programs for each country separately and permits countries in each group to be served through a common marketing perspective.

Countries may be classified by such criteria as their economic status, geographic location, cultural traits, religious perspective, political system, socioeconomic-political characteristics, or common intermarket characteristics. In addition, a new approach for grouping countries, the portfolio method, recommends grouping countries based on three factors: competitive strength, risk, and country potential.

The concept of segmentation in the context of international marketing ought to be examined at another level, that is, segmenting the in-country market. Just as the U.S. market is segmented by marketers in different ways, it may be desirable to segment the market within each country and choose one or more segments to be served. The process of accomplishing in-country segmentation is essentially the same in international marketing as in domestic marketing.

Review Questions

1. What factors make the triad market most attractive?
2. What forces account for the growing globalization of markets?
3. Between the Pacific Rim market (excluding Japan) and the Eastern European market, which one appears to offer better market opportunities?
4. What is the rationale behind grouping countries together?

5. Even countries that appear to be the same in so many ways, Great Britain and Canada, for example, are nevertheless very different. Thus, does grouping of countries really help in making sound marketing decisions?
6. Discuss the following: "Philosophical imposition of political boundaries as the starting point in the matter of segmenting the world market is superfluous and dysfunctional. Why should we segment countries? We should rather segment the customers of the world. After all, it may be hypothesized that high-income people, whether living in the U.S., France, Brazil, India, Nigeria, Egypt, Sweden, or Mexico, provide a similar potential for a product. If this is true, then it is the customer segmentation on a worldwide basis that should be sought and not country classification. Like income, education, geography, political views, age, and a host of other demographic and socioeconomic criteria may be used to segment the world market."
7. What are the variables used in the portfolio approach to classify countries? What problems do you anticipate in adapting the portfolio approach in practice?

Creative Questions

1. According to the U.S. government, the most growth in the next century will be in 10 nations called the Big Emerging Markets (comprising China, Indonesia, South Korea, India, Turkey, South Africa, Poland, Argentina, Brazil, and Mexico). Debate this list indicating if it should be refined. What countries might warrant inclusion in this list? Why? What countries should be dropped?
2. Often a case is made for making investments in developing countries since their long-run business potential is high. However, the term "long-run" usually is not defined. Should the MNCs invest money in LDCs under the illusion of long-run benefits? If not, should these countries be ignored until they present sustainable business opportunity?

Endnotes

1. *The Futures Group Reports,* March 1989.
2. Kenichi Ohmae, *Triad Power* (New York: The Free Press, 1985).
3. Ibid., p. 23.
4. "GM Finally Discovers Asia," *Business Week,* August 24, 1992, p. 42.
5. Louis Kraar, "The Rising Power of the Pacific," *Fortune,* Pacific Rim Issue, 1990, p. 80.
6. Robert S. Greenberger, "Clinton Lifts Ban on Trade With Vietnam," *The Wall Street Journal,* February 4, 1994, p. A12. Also see: "Destination, Vietnam: *Business Week,* February 14, 1994, p. 26.
7. "Rising from the Ashes," *Business Week,* May 23, 1994, p. 44.
8. Paul Hofheinz, "Yes, You Can Win in Eastern Europe," *Fortune,* May 16, 1994, p. 110.
9. Shawn Tully, "What Eastern Europe Offers," *Fortune,* March 2, 1990, p. 51. Also see W.W. Rostow, *The States of Economic Growth* (New York: Cambridge University Press. 1960).
10. "Reawakening: A Market Economy Takes Root in Eastern Europe," *Business Week,* April 15, 1991, p. 46. Also see Janusz Bugajski, "Eastern Europe in the Post-Communist Era," *Columbia Journal of World Business,* Spring 1991, pp. 5–9.
11. "Yeltsin's Economic Shock Trooper," *Business Week,* February 24, 1992, p. 67.
12. Paul Hofheinz, "Opportunity in the Baltics," *Fortune,* October 21, 1991, p. 68.

13. *The Wall Street Journal,* February 18, 1992, p. 1.
14. "As the Empire Shrinks, Russian Nationalists Vie for Power," *Business Week,* February 5, 1990, p. 40.
15. Jeremy Main, "How Latin America is Opening Up," *Fortune,* April 8, 1991, p. 84.
16. "GE's Brave New World," *Business Week,* November 8, 1993, p. 74. *Also see* Rahul Jacob, "The Big Rise," *Fortune,* May 30, 1994, p. 74.
17. Ford S. Worthy, "Where Capitalism Thrives in China," *Fortune,* March 9, 1992, p. 71.
18. *The Global Century: A Source Book on U.S. Business and the Third World* (Washington, D.C.: National Cooperative Business Association, 1989).
19. "Africa: A Flicker of Light," *The Economist,* March 5, 1994, p. 21.
20. George S. Yip, "Global Strategy in a World of Nations," *Sloan Management Review,* Fall 1991, pp. 29–39.
21. Federal Industries (a Canadian firm) Annual Report, 1986.
22. "Value Segments Help Define International Market," *Marketing News,* November 21, 1988, p. 17.
23. *World Development Report,* 1994 (New York: Oxford University Press, 1994), pp. 162–63.
24. *See* Richard D. Steade, "Multinational Corporations and the Changing World Economic Order," *California Management Review,* Winter 1978, p. 87.
25. Marlene L. Rossman, "Understanding Five Nations of Latin America," *Marketing News,* October 11, 1985, p. 10.
26. Frank Tannenbaum, *Ten Keys to Latin America* (New York: Knopf, 1962) p. 65. *Also see* Lane Kelley and Reginald Worthley, "The Role of Culture in Comparative Management: A Cross-Cultural Perspective," *Academy of Management Journal,* No. 1 (1981), pp. 164–73.
27. *See* Vern Terpstra and Kenneth David, *The Cultural Environment of International Business,* 2nd ed. (Cincinnati, OH: South-Western Publishing Co., 1985) pp. 77–116.
28. Prakash Tandon, "Maturing of Business in India," *California Management Review,* Spring, 1972, p. 80.
29. *See Nature and Use of the HRAF Files* (New Haven: Human Relations Area Files, Inc., 1974).
30. *See* Ellen Day, Richard J. Fox, and Sandra M. Huszagh, "Segmenting the Global Market for Industrial Goods: Issues and Implications," *International Marketing Review,* Autumn, 1988, pp. 14–27.
31. S. Prakash Sethi, "Comparative Cluster Analysis for World Markets," *Journal of Marketing Research,* August 1971, pp. 348–54. *Also see* Kenneth Matsuura, *A Classification of Countries for International Marketing,* Master's thesis, University of California, Berkeley, 1968.
32. *See* Sudhir H. Kale and D. Sudharshan, "A Strategic Approach to International Segmentation," *International Marketing Review,* Summer, 1987, pp. 60–70.
33. "Citibank in Indonesia: Targeting the Affluent," *Crossborder Monitor,* July 13, 1994, p. 8.
34. "How Germany Sells Cars Where Detroit Can't," *Business Week,* September 9, 1985, p. 45.
35. John K. Ryans, Jr., "Have Communications Technological Developments Made Current European Marketing Practices/Strategies Obsolete? a presentation made at the Netherlands School of Business, July 5, 1982. *Also see* Gerald D. Sentell, "Modern, Traditional, and Transnational Consumer Groups in a Developing Dual Economy: An Empirical Investigation of Thai Consumers," a paper presented at the Academy of International Business Meeting, Washington, D.C., 1982.
36. "Estee Lauder Hoping to Sell Men's Perfume to Affluent Japanese," *The Asian Wall Street Journal Weekly,* September 26, 1988, p. 8.
37. Elias G. Rizkallah, "Multiple Product: Multiple Market Allocations—A Portfolio Approach," a paper presented at the Academy of International Business Annual Meeting in New Orleans, October 24, 1980.
38. Ibid.
39. Robert A. Garda, "A Strategic Approach to Market Segmentation," *The McKinsey Quarterly,* Autumn 1981, pp. 16–29. *Also see* Ivor Mitchell and Tom O. Amioku, "Brand Preference Factors in Patronage and Consumption of Nigerian Beer," *Columbia Journal of World Business,* Spring 1985, pp. 55–68.

PART 4

Cases

Case 17: McIlhenny Company: Japan

In January 1988, Carlos Malespin, vice-president, International, of the McIlhenny Company, was reviewing all the market and product studies for a new line of Tabasco brand spaghetti sauces to be introduced in Japan later that year. While reassured by the findings, Mr. Malespin realized that this product was an important "first" for this old-line company, and he was anxious that each detail should withstand careful analysis and scrutiny. He was also a firm believer in action, however; as he said, "Any idea can be killed by hypothesizing it to death." Therefore, he was prepared to proceed with the next step, which was to introduce the product at FoodEx (Harumi), a major trade show, in March. Now he needed the go-ahead from his boss, Ned Simmons, a fourth-generation McIlhenny and president of the company.

Company Background

McIlhenny Company was a closely held family business located on Avery Island, Louisiana. Although the company name was relatively unknown, its major product, Tabasco pepper sauce, was marketed in at least 103 countries, with labels in 20 different languages. The brand was over 120 years old, but its recipe had changed little since Edmund McIlhenny first invented and refined it at the close of the Civil War. He had been given the seeds of a pepper (*Capsicum frutescens*) by a friend who had brought them from Mexico; he experimented extensively with both the plants and the sauce he made from the peppers. Finally, because of the product's distinctive flavor and uncompromising quality, his friends and family had recommended that he bottle it for the retail market.

In 1907 McIlhenny Company was formally incorporated with the ownership and rights to all the titles, copyrights, formulas, and trademarks for Tabasco sauce. In 1949 Walter S. McIlhenny was elected president, and under his leadership, McIlhenny Company was launched on an impressive period of growth; in addition, the company introduced the Tabasco brand Bloody Mary mix and Tabasco brand picante sauce. As the demand for Tabasco sauce increased, its quality was never compromised, and continual improvements were made to the growing, bottling, and other aspects of its manufacture.

This case is intended as the basis for classroom use only. Some figures have been disguised. "Tabasco®" is a registered trademark of the McIlhenny Company. Copyright © 1989 by the Darden Graduate Business School Foundation, Charlottesville, VA. Printed with permission.

In 1982 Ned Simmons, great grandson of the founder, assumed the presidency. Mr. Simmons began an aggressive marketing and sales program, and he was also extremely concerned with improving productivity, streamlining operations, and reducing overhead to improve bottom-line profit. As a closely controlled organization, McIlhenny's financial data were not available, but industry experts estimated that 1988 sales would be $50 million, up over 1987. The company's excellent trade relations indicated that the company was well managed and had the resources necessary to finance new-product introductions. U.S. sales of 40 million 2-ounce bottles were growing about 5 percent a year (representing about one-third of the pepper-sauce market), but overseas growth was about 8 percent annually. Mr. Simmons said that the U.S. business, divided about equally between home use and use in restaurants, had the highest market saturation, but that

> the potential even here for added penetration is tremendous. Our penetration is far less in foreign markets, but growth in those areas will require a slow build. We can take advantage of the interest in "international cuisine"—such as, for example, the popularity of western food in Japan—to increase usage.

His goal was to double corporate sales over the next five years.

Tabasco Sauce in Japan

Tabasco was introduced in Japan at the end of World War II by the U.S. occupation forces. By 1988 Japan was McIlhenny's largest international market, followed by West Germany, Canada, and Mexico. The product was handled in Japan by the company's sales agent, PBI Japan, which received a 5 percent sales commission; in return, the agent recommended and worked with the five exclusive importers, formulated an annual sales and marketing plan, searched out new markets, commissioned market research, supervised the work of the advertising agency (Dentsu), kept alert for new opportunities, and in every other respect acted as Mr. Malespin's alter ego in Japan. Recent annual sales growth in Japan was about 8 percent.

Five exclusive importers carried the line; they included some of the largest trading companies in Japan (Sumitomo, Marubeni, Meidi-ya, Toyota, and Nippon coffee). These importers distributed to "primary wholesalers," who in turn sold to "secondary wholesalers," who then sold to tertiary wholesalers or small neighborhood grocery shops and restaurants. About 80 percent of Tabasco sales were to restaurants and coffee shops, and the little red bottle was a familiar sight to all Japanese. The product was not used on traditional Japanese foods, which were typically mild dishes, but on "western food," particularly pizza and spaghetti.[1]

Surveys indicated that Tabasco enjoyed 95 percent unaided awareness, that it could be found in about 60 percent of all homes, and that it was on the tables of practically all restaurants serving western food. Consumer research indicated that it enjoyed a reputation as "a U.S. product of very high quality." The company had worked with local chefs and cooking schools to develop new recipes using Tabasco sauce that would appeal to the new "hot taste"; these recipes were promulgated via package inserts, quarterly news letters distributed through the Cajun Cooking Club, and at the company's booth at FoodEx, which annually attracted over 100,000 distributors, retailers, and sales agents. There was no direct competitor to Tabasco.

Japan: The Spaghetti-Sauce Opportunity

Mr. Malespin was the company's first manager for international marketing. Prior to his arrival, the company used a New York-based export-management company for sales overseas and had licensing agreements with a few foreign firms for manufacturing and/or marketing Tabasco. Mr. Malespin had obtained an MA in economics and an MA in international trade from the Catholic University of Louvain in Belgium. After graduation, he spent eight years in various international assignments, including working on tariff and trade matters in the Nicaraguan Central Bank and as an export sales manager for a trading company in New Orleans.

---

[1] More information on Japan and its people is given in Appendix A.

Upon joining McIlhenny in 1985, Mr. Malespin spent a great deal of time studying the company's various international markets and preparing a handbook on "how to do business abroad." He took a long tour of the company's major international markets to meet licensees, importers, and major retail accounts.[2] From these studies, he concluded that the Tabasco name had built up as much equity abroad as it had in the United States and that attractive opportunities existed to offer other products under this ample umbrella.

He decided to make his first move in Japan, where the size of the market, the trend toward western foods, and the rapid growth of U.S. fast-food chains (especially Kentucky Fried Chicken and McDonald's) seemed to offer McIlhenny a platform for new growth. For example, a growing interest in Cajun food was a felicitous opportunity to popularize jambalaya and gumbo (Cajun specialties based on rice, vegetables, and seafood), because these dishes used basic Japanese culinary ingredients and cooking systems. Through the services of Paul Prudhomme (a gifted U.S. chef specializing in Cajun delights), these recipes were introduced at the 1986 Matsuo Food Fair; they received national attention, and over time, jambalaya became part of the repertoire of modern Japanese cooks and housewives.

By 1987, however, Mr. Malespin could not envision any further accelerated growth for Tabasco through recipe programs. He therefore explored other avenues by asking such questions as, "What is Tabasco Sauce? What does it mean to Japanese consumers? How do they use it?" In the process of answering these questions, he and the managers of PBI Japan concluded that the spaghetti-sauce market offered a promising opportunity. PBI agreed to undertake research on this market and on consumer attitudes toward and use of spaghetti sauce.

Market Research

PBI's research indicated that wholesale **canned** spaghetti sauce accounted for $86 million of the total estimated market of $110 million (the balance of sales was in retort pouches). The meat-sauce portion had sales of $73 million.[3] Of the approximately 35 brands of canned sauce currently on the market, none was dominant. The top four brands controlled 62 percent of market share; they were Kewpi ($15 million), Mama ($13.5 million), Kagome ($12.5 million), and Oh-My ($11.8). Five other brands had sales of $30 million altogether, and the remaining brands controlled $2.5 million. All were Japanese companies with the exception of a Heinz joint venture ($6.8 million).

The industry spent $4.2 million annually in 1986 for advertising (based on data for five of the top seven brands). Mr. Malespin observed that 10 feet of gondola space was devoted to this product in grocery stores ("a tremendous amount of shelf space!") and that spaghetti was perceived in Japan to be a western dish.

Mr. Malespin believed that the market was ready for a new entry that (1) built on the excellent reputation and distribution of the Tabasco name, especially given its powerful association in Japan with spaghetti and pizza products and (2) offered a better product but priced the same as competition. The new product was to offer more beef, yet be formulated to appeal to Japanese tastes.

For the past 20 years, the company had retained a food consultant, Ms. Ichikawa, to create recipes using Tabasco sauce. Now she was asked to develop a new spaghetti-sauce recipe using not only Tabasco sauce but other ingredients that she believed would improve on the major brands and still appeal to Japanese palates. At this point, the decision on sourcing the product was deliberately held open.

In her lab, Ms. Ichikawa analyzed the current brands with respect to flavors, size of cans, texture, appearance, etc., based on both taste tests and ingredient analysis. From this analysis, she elicited complaints ranging from "thin, color drab" and "smells too spicy, bad can smell" to "good but doesn't go with spaghetti well," and so on.

---

[2] "Too long!" he said. "I spent 5 weeks on that trip, and increasingly found that my clients were far more refreshed than I was! Most practitioners would say that 15-18 days abroad is max, before lose your acuity in cutting deals."

[3] At this time, the exchange rate was $1.00 = ¥128.

Ms. Ichikawa then experimented with different ingredients, including red wines, beef, pork and mutton, cheeses, olive and sunflower oils, and such different vegetables as carrots, onions, potatoes, celery, and many more. These recipes were tested among small consumer groups and, once refined, were subjected to production in larger quantities in order to see if the "homemade" characteristics were preserved.

By December 1987, the product formulation was complete: compared with U.S. brands, the product was darker (a "meaty-brown"), thicker, and sweeter. Containing 12 percent meat solids, it could be imported into Japan under current beef tariff restrictions (20 percent maximum) yet still be called "meat sauce" under U.S. standards. (By now the company had determined that the high price of beef in Japan made production in the United States more profitable than in Japan.) Ms. Ichikawa reported that, based on the taste tests, "Texture, aroma, freshness, and can smell all got highest marks."

Based on an assumed first-year sales level of 1 percent of the market, Mr. Malespin estimated the production and marketing costs (see Exhibit 1). The proposed retail price of ¥300 for a 300-gram can would yield a factory price of $1.09 and a unit profit of $0.24.

For the typical three layers of distribution between the retailer and the factory, the margins (over the buyer's cost) were as follows: importer, 12 percent; primary wholesaler, 6 percent; secondary wholesaler, 6 percent; and the retailer, 38 percent. For companies importing into Japan, the sales agent received a fixed commission, usually 5 percent. In addition, promotional allowances were frequently given to the importer, which were in turn passed down the chain in the form of price discounts; these allowances could include "1 free case in 10" or discounts off invoice. Thus a 300-gram can of spaghetti sauce with a list price of ¥300 normally sold for ¥220 to ¥240. (See Exhibit 2 for a projection of distribution costs and trade pricing.)

EXHIBIT I McIlhenny Company: Japan
Spaghetti-Sauce Estimated Product and Selling Costs, 1988
(300-gram can)

	$	¥	%
Gross Sales[a]	$1.09	¥139.5	100.0%
Cost of Goods Sold	.64	81.9	58.7
Gross Profit	.45	57.6	41.3%
Selling Expenses			
Advertising and Promotion	.07	9.0	7.8
Returns and Allowances	.025	3.2	3.3
Interest	.005	0.6	0.5
Containerization[b]	.02	2.5	1.8
Freight to Japan	.024	3.1	2.2
Commission	.06	7.7	5.5
Miscellaneous	.01	1.3	0.9
Total Selling Expenses	.21	26.9	19.3
Net Profit	$0.24	¥30.7	22.0%

[a] C&F Japan. That is, all McIlhenny prices were quoted in U.S. dollars.
[b] Including inland cartage (U.S.).

Consumer Surveys

In July 1987, the sales agent, PBI, had conducted had conducted an initial written survey involving 110 respondents (basic conclusions are in Exhibit 3). In October PBI commissioned two focus groups (selected results from this research are in Appendix B). Two more focus-group sessions were conducted in December to test the actual Tabasco formulation, packages, and "catch phrases"; selected results from these sessions are found in Appendix C.

The Proposal

In its review of the situation, PBI stated,

There is currently no clear, overall leader in the canned meat sauce market. Tabasco brand spaghetti sauces will interface well with the Tabasco pepper sauce principal market position as the pasta/pizza condiment. Tabasco spaghetti sauce offers an opportunity to capitalize on consumer brand awareness. The sauce will expand McIlhenny's product base and its distribution channels can carry the product along with the pepper sauce. Tabasco brand spaghetti sauce products would increase tabasco pepper sauce sales by 1) creating more Tabasco brand merchandising space at the retail level, 2) standardizing Tabasco brand merchandising space at the retail level, 3) creating Tabasco pepper sauce impulse-buy opportunities, and 4) broadening the entire Tabasco brand base of consumers in Japan.

Mr. Malespin proposed offering the spaghetti sauce in Japan in three 300-gram versions: a mild

EXHIBIT 2 McIlhenny Company: Japan
Distribution Costs and Trade Pricing
(300-gram can)

A. Importer's Cost

McIlhenny Price	¥139.5*
Insurance	0.5
Duty Charges	13.5
Landed Cost	¥153.5
Customs	2.5
Warehouse (90 days)	5.0
Delivery	5.0
Interest (150 days)	5.4
Total Cost	¥171.4

B. Typical Trade Selling Prices

	¥	Percentage of Retail Price	Profit Margin[b]
Retail Price	300	100.0	38%
Secondary Wholesaler Price	216	72.0	6%
Primary Wholesaler Price	204	68.0	6%
Importer Selling Price	192	64.0	12%

[a]Based on $1.00 = ¥128.

[b]The gross margin is based on the buyer's cost.

Source: Company records.

EXHIBIT 3 McIlhenny Company: Japan Findings from Initial Written Questionnaire, July 1989 (N = 110 respondents)

- 4% were between 25–40 years old; 40% had children, mostly ages 1–17; dinner meals were probably eaten at home.
- 72% prepared spaghetti at least every 2 weeks; 65% prepared it for family consumption, 22% for themselves; 74% prepared 2–4 servings.
- 66% bought spaghetti in a supermarket; the frequency of purchase was at least every 2 months.
- 62% prepared meat sauce or Japanese-style sauce—could be soy-based, sukiyaki type, fermented soy bean sauce, fish egg, ground white radish and barbecue meat slices, Japanese mushrooms, or even seaweed.
- Spice was the most popular additive (38%), then meat (30%), mushrooms (14%), tomato or onion (11%), and Tabasco (7–11%).
- 65% had no regular brand; those who were loyal cited "taste" and "price" as the reason for their loyalty.
- 76% would try new brands.

version (suitable for children), a regular, and a "spicy" version. Because even the spicy version was relatively mild by American standards, there was still opportunity for consumers to use Tabasco on the product. In order to offer a fuller product line, McIlhenny would also produce a chile con carne sauce (in mild and regular flavors), which was similar to spaghetti sauce but had pinto beans. This product had been as thoroughly tested by Ms. Ichikawa as had the spaghetti sauce.

By this time, about ¥6.5 million had been spent on the consumer research, product development, and product/consumer tests. The next step was to introduce the product to the trade in the company's booth at the March FoodEx show. In addition to this chance for the 100,000 distributor/retailer representatives to taste the product, Mr. Malespin planned a private showing to the five trading companies that imported Tabasco pepper sauce into Japan.

Mr. Malespin believed there was no point in conducting a regional test market, because Japan was so concentrated: a regional test would be tantamount to a national introduction. As he pointed out, 45 percent of the country's population lived within 100 miles of Tokyo.

Thus, given no surprises at the show, Mr. Malespin anticipated a national introduction in November 1988. He would give one of the usual trade allowances to spur trial, which in this case would be "one case free with ten." Advertising for the product would be piggybacked by taking the top third of the one-page newspaper and magazine ads normally used for advertising Tabasco sauce; two ads were scheduled for November and two for December in the three major national Japanese newspapers. The copy points were:

> Tabasco made it—it must be delicious! There are a number of sauces with meat, but Tabasco has made a real meat sauce as it should be: 1) High volume of meat; 2) only high quality, 100% beef; 3) best-quality ingredients carefully selected to complement nutrition and taste.
>
> These production criteria have guided Tabasco's recipe development. We hope that you and your family will enjoy this sauce soon.

Mr. Malespin's target was to get the product on the shelves by November 20 and to attain a 1 percent share by the end of the first year. While he believed that the Tabasco brand could be the market leader in five years, he knew the project had some risks. The greatest was the possible loss of good will among the many levels of distribution should the product fail. Mr. Malespin was aware that few of the 80,000 new products introduced into the market each year survived. A major contributor to this worry was the fact that the Japanese government could ban the product if it did not live up to the inspectors' very high quality standards, including the prohibition of food additives. So far, only samples of the imported Tabasco sauce had been submitted for government inspection, and any question about the company's standards could lead to more rigorous inspection of that product as well. Not only would such an eventuality cloud the company's name, it could substantially increase the difficulty and costs of working in this most important market.

Appendix A— McIlhenny Company: Japan, Selected Facts on Japan and the Japanese[1]

Part I. Selected Data From Student Report, December 1987

Population Japan was one of the most densely populated nations in the world. The total Japanese population approximated 120 million densely settled, highly literate, and homogeneous inhabitants. The total population was estimated to peak at 130 million soon after the coming century, at that time reaching a zero population growth rate. The land area of Japan was about 146,000 square miles (378,000 square kilometers), approximately the size of the state of Montana. Over half the population was concentrated within the Tokyo/Osaka urban belt. The population continued to grow at a .6 percent rate annually, but the average age was increasing. It was estimated that, by the year 2000, the elderly (those over age 65) would account for over 15 percent of the total population. Japan currently had the highest life expectancy in the world for both males and females, at 72.2 and 77.4 years, respectively. The total labor force was over 60 million. Japanese women were becoming increasingly significant in Japanese industry. Currently, women were over one third of the total work force.

Language and education Japanese was the language of Japan and was understood throughout the land. There were regional dialects, but on the whole the language was the same. The writing system consisted of the three alphabets of Hiragana, Katakana, and Kanji (Chinese characters). There was compulsory and free education up to the age of 15. English was a required subject from junior high through college. About 41 percent of men and 33 percent of women went on to higher education.

Religion The basic religions of Japan were Buddhism and the Japanese religion of Shinto. However, some Japanese (0.8 percent) practiced Christianity and other religions. Most Japanese actively practiced Buddhism only when honoring the dead. Shintoism, on the other hand, was associated with happy occasions such as weddings, purification of buildings, ground-breaking ceremonies, etc. Many national holidays were closely related to significant religious events.

Psychographics Traditionally, housewives held the purse strings in the Japanese family. Except for very large purchases, the housewife made most shopping decisions. Typically, the Japanese housewife made several trips a week to the neighborhood grocery store.

The Japanese consumer was one of the most demanding in the world. She was brand conscious and expected high quality regardless of price. Because of the immeasurable number of consumer goods available (both foreign and domestic), the Japanese consumer placed great emphasis on the reputation of the producer. When it came to consumer goods, the Japanese were obsessed not only with product quality, but also with the way the product was packaged. The market almost seemed to require "over-packaging."

The *Shinjinrui* (new humankind) was a new breed of image-conscious Japanese consumer who was the driving force behind the current restructuring of the Japanese retail industry. The young adults' affluence and changing personal value system had forced mom-and-pop corner store retailers to specialize or be left behind. Specialty stores carrying a single line of merchandise continued to gain share in the Japanese market. In many cases, their success was a result of their ability to market a slice of American life. The young Japanese generation was very attuned to American culture.

Fish, vegetables, rice, or noodles were the main fare of most Japanese, but such food as pizza, hamburgers, steak, etc., had been receiving attention among younger Japanese consumers. The Japanese tended to distinguish types of food depending on the occasion and location. For example, pizza, hamburgers, or fried chicken could replace Chinese or Japanese

---

[1] Part I if the material in this appendix was taken from parts of "Tabasco in Japan," a study performed by students at the American Graduate School of International Management in the fall of 1987. Part II is taken from a presentation made by PBI in its yearly presentation to McIlhenny executives at Avery Island.

food for lunch. These types of food were usually consumed for lunch or a snack rather than as a main dish at dinner. Traditional Japanese cooking was often time consuming and required the preparation of many kinds of food; as many as 30 dishes might be served at one meal.

The Japanese did not invite guests into their homes as frequently as Americans did. This was partially because Japanese homes were not large enough to accommodate guests. Seventy-six percent of the population were urban dwellers, and Japanese urbanites often lived in very small apartments, or "rabbit hutches," as some foreigners called them.

Legal environment By far the most common problem experienced by exporters of food to Japan was the prohibition of food additives. There were several hundred inadvertent violations per year. Consumer co-ops existed that viewed additives as one of the key trade issues, ranking them more important than market access or pricing and distribution of goods. Japan allowed 347 synthetic chemical compounds to be used as food additives, fewer than in many western countries.

Japan's customs tariff was administered by the Ministry of Finance through its Customs Bureau. All imported food products had to be labeled in Japanese. Any artificial coloring or preservatives, the name and address of the importer, and the date of manufacture had to be stated on the outside label.

There were few legal restrictions on advertising in Japan. Commercials for liquor and cigarettes flourished, and sexy images were not uncommon. One of the few restraints placed on advertising concerned the amount of time allotted to commercials during each broadcast hour: the limit was set at six minutes. However, networks had colluded with advertisers in finding a loophole: by rearranging program scheduling, they stretched hourly advertising to eight minutes.

Income distribution and expenditure Japan's gross national product was the second largest in the Free World, amounting to approximately half of U.S. GNP. The average family income was between ¥4 and ¥6 million, which at an exchange rate of ¥142.41 to the dollar (as of September 11, 1987) equaled $28,000 to $42,000. Japan had one of the highest savings rates in the world, at slightly under 20 percent of total net income. Real disposable income had stagnated since 1978, resulting in more women entering or remaining in the work force. Because of the contribution of working women to the family budget, two-income families were able to save and consume more.

Communication Japan was ideally suited for much mass-media advertising because of its literate, highly concentrated, and homogeneous population. There were over 4,000 advertising agencies servicing the country through newspapers, television, magazines, radio, and outdoor advertising. Traditionally, Japanese advertising agencies had assumed the role of "space broker," buying media space or time and reselling it to clients. The top 5 advertising agencies in Japan did over 50 percent of the total business, with the largest, Dentsu, accounting for 26.5 percent of the total. There were 102 commercial television broadcasters across Japan, 5 in the Greater Tokyo area alone. The largest national daily newspapers were the *Yomiuri* and the *Asahi*. Each printed roughly 13 million copies (morning and evening editions) and carried 37 percent of all newspaper advertising.

Distribution For a foreign company looking to establish a presence in Japan, the most common approach to market entry was the use of the existing distribution channels of the large trading companies (*sogo shosha*). They could handle up to 25,000 different products and provide a range of services that included financing, warehousing, transporting, wholesaling, and servicing. However, many foreign companies believed that the *sogo shoshas* were too large and would not aggressively market their products. Of the 2,300 U.S. companies operating in Japan, the majority chose subsidiaries or joint ventures.

The traditional distribution system was changing, albeit gradually, to the advantage of the foreign manufacturer. This was partially a result of the formation and growth of specialty, chain, and convenience stores. Recently, supermarkets and department stores had been moving toward selling their own brands.

Part II. Excerpts From a PBI Presentation to McIlhenny, 1988

A. Macroenvironment Overview

1. Japan's population is about 122 million. Its GNP is the second largest in the free world at $2.5 trillion. In consumer spending and capital investment, Japan's domestic market is the world's second largest.

2. The typical Japanese household consists of 4 persons living on an average monthly income of about $3,600, nearly 85 percent of which is disposable. Purchasing power in dollars has doubled since 1981.

3. Japanese consumers can afford to be selective and choose products that meet strict standards of quality. Ownership of consumer durables is high, with over 98 percent of households owning refrigerators, washing machines, and color televisions. Central heating is uncommon, and space heaters remain the most prevalent to heat residences.

4. Standards of education are high—compulsory through 9th grade, but 95 percent of all students go on to senior high school and 35 percent on to higher education. The five leading newspapers have a combined morning circulation of more than 25 million.

5. Medical and health facilities are good, with life expectancy among the highest in the world, and nearly the entire population is covered by national or company health insurance provided at a cost that varies according to income.

6. Crime-related injury is low. In 1985 there were 15 murders per million population in Japan (compared with 79 in the U.S. and 37 in the U.K.). Property crime is low, while arrest and conviction rates are very high.

7. Housing standards are lower than western industrialized countries, since both land and construction are expensive in Japan. About 60 percent of Japanese households own their homes.

8. Japanese consumers spend less time at home than people in other industrialized countries. The number of workers having only a five-day workweek is increasing but is still far lower than in the U.S. The number of national holidays is greater than in the U.S. or Germany, but companies give fewer individual paid holidays to employees. The working year in Japan in recent years has been 253 days (compared with 233 in the U.S. and 230 in the U.K.). The Japanese take 10 days paid vacation yearly (compared with 19 in the U.S. and 31 in Germany).

B. Japanese Consumers

1. Consumer spending in Japan is highly influenced by the compensation used by most companies. Although changing, the features of the current system show that wages are tied to seniority and that lifetime employment provides security for significant portions of the population and their families. Also, the practice of paying semiannual bonuses coincides with the two gift-giving seasons. The bonuses are paid in mid-summer and in December, the best times for purchases of high-quality foods, accessories, and other gifts as well as for major consumer durables such as color televisions, VCRs, etc. These bonus seasons are prime marketing targets for both domestic producers and imported goods manufacturers.

2. The largest expenditures in the typical family's budget are for food, transportation, communication, reading and recreation, and apparel. The Japanese have a reputation for demanding quality at reasonable cost and place emphasis on product appearance and packaging as well as superior functions.

3. The Japanese sense of taste for color is affected by a long heritage and differs from that of most other nations. For consumer items other than clothing, there has been a trend toward individuality, leading to a wider variety of colors in appliances and interior furnishings.

4. The Japanese diet has become greatly influenced by other cuisines, and families eat a wide range of foods.

5. The Japanese market is highly segmentable by income, region, age, sex, and lifestyle. Mass media and compulsory education have had substantial influence on growing homogeneity, but climate, food, and consumer preferences nevertheless vary from region to region.

6. Different age groups in Japan have very different tastes and lifestyles. While a majority of men go on to university, more women attend shorter programs at junior colleges. Single working women have high discretionary incomes. After marriage, women leave their jobs to take care of the household and budget, while men concentrate on career advancement within the company.

C. Dietary Habits and Trends

1. The Japanese diet has been strongly influenced by other countries' cuisines over the past 15 years and has become more westernized and diversified. It is characterized by a high consumption of cereals and fish, and by a low consumption of dairy products.

2. As a proportion of food expenditures, rice has declined since 1970, and bread has taken up the slack. Fish and meat expenditures have increased, while spending on dairy products has declined slightly.

3. The proportion of frozen foods consumed has risen with the increase in ownership of home freezers, and a rise in the ownership of microwave ovens has laid the groundwork for an increasing use of prepared frozen foods and oven-cooked foods.

4. The predominant flavors in Japan tend to remain the traditional ones, such as soy sauce and miso, but the Japanese diet has diversified to a great extent. Many products in the growing category of prepared foods are sauces and bases for Chinese and other types of cuisine.

5. Although the Japanese welcome an increasing variety of foods, they still generally tend to prefer the milder flavors. In addition, foods are presented in a pleasing manner—attractive to the eye with subtle combinations of color and design.

6. Salt intake, most of which comes from the traditional flavorings, has been high in the past but has dropped as consumers have become more concerned with salt-related health problems. Growing concern with health has also created a growing demand for low-calorie foods.

D. Summaries of Market Research Surveys

1. Sumitomo Bank: Eating Habits in the Gourmet Age. 800 wives of salaried workers in Tokyo and Osaka (multiple answers).
   - 73% often watch TV programs featuring eating and cooking.
   - 64% try to choose foods without additives.

Annual Household Expenditures—Major Food Items

Year	Rice	Bread	Fish	Meat	Vegetables	Dairy	Prepared Foods
1970	¥41,890 (20.2)	5,814 (2.8)	44,670 (21.6)	33,189 (16.0)	44,830 (21.6)	24,791 (12.0)	12,044 (5.8)
1986	¥74,397 (13.7)	24,059 (4.4)	130,191 (24.0)	96,567 (17.8)	112,663 (20.8)	42,657 (7.9)	61,972 (11.4)

*Figures in parentheses indicate percentage of food expenditures.

- 59% like to read books and articles on dining out.
- 22% think they are "gourmet"; 44% definitely not.
- 55% of families dine out once a month or more.

2. Ministry of Health and Welfare: National Nutrition Survey. 7,000 households throughout the country.
   - Intake of animal fat continues to decrease.
   - Intake of salt continues to decrease.
   - Levels of calcium considered inadequate by Ministry of Health.
   - Intake of green vegetables continues to increase.
3. Ajinomoto: Food Preferences. 5,000 men and women aged 12 and up in 16 cities around the country.
   - Those below the age of 30 prefer a variety of western foods.
   - Those aged 50 and up prefer traditional Japanese foods.
   - Those in the 30s and 40s have no strong likes or dislikes.
   - Women seem to prefer carbohydrates.

Source: Company records.

Appendix B—McIlhenny Company: Japan, Selected Findings from Focus-Group Study (conducted October 12, 1987)

I. OBJECTIVE:

To evaluate the concept of a Tabasco brand canned spaghetti meat sauce and to estimate future potential for this product in Japan.

II. RESEARCH SCHEME:

1. Focus Group Participants—Users of canned spaghetti meat sauce. Half of the participants use it 2–3 times per month, and the rest use it less often (no habitual usage).
2. Region—Tokyo and suburban areas.
3. Sampling—Two groups of eight participants.

Group No. 1   Housewives from 23–24 years old with annual income of ¥4 million or more.

Group No. 2   Singles women 21–30 years old with annual income of ¥2.5 million or more.

III. FINDINGS:

Conditions of Usage and Purchase

Housewives' group Demographics of participants' family members are widely dispersed. The largest family is seven members of three generations. Children vary from kindergarten to adult ages. Eating habits include Japanese, western, and Chinese dishes, but there is an inclination toward western-style foods. Spaghetti is one dish favored by children and appears on the family's dinner menu frequently.

Although participants make small efforts at consuming lots of vegetables and maintaining a low-sodium diet, they are not very strict about it, and the desire for tasty food seems to be somewhat stronger.

Dining-out frequency is two-to-three times per month, and spaghetti is one of the meals ordered most often. On these occasions, they tend to order Tarako (cod eggs), Natto (soy beans), Wafu (soy sauce), and other flavors that they don't usually prepare at home.

Single women's group All but one live with their parents and all but one bring their lunch to work. All claim that their cooking repertoire is very limited. They eat out two or three times a week and often frequent spagetti resturants, where they order sauces not usually home prepared such as Tarako (cod eggs), white sauce, etc.

Household usage About 70 percent of the participants use canned spaghetti meat sauce 1-3 times per month, and the other 30 percent, most of whom are housewives, use it once per week. Usage by housewives varies from normal meals to lunch with children, late-night snacks, sudden visitors, and Sunday lunch. When they have time, they add meat or vegetables that are on hand such as green peppers, carrots, onions, tomatoes, and mushrooms. Spices added are usually oregano, cinnamon, black pepper, Tabasco, basil, or flavorings such as broth, Worcestershire sauce, and wine according to taste. If time does not allow for additional ingredients, they use it as is.

Compared with the housewives, single women tend to use canned spaghetti meat sauce for breakfast or lunch on days when the mothers are away, or when supper has not been made for them. Most of them simply heat the sauce and put Tabasco on it.

In most cases, usage of the sauce is for two or more people—especially housewives who eat with their children.

Utilization of canned meat sauce varies from such dishes as gratin and lasagna to potato casseroles and stews for housewives. Single women say they use it for cheese casseroles with noodles or broccoli and often simply use it as stuffing for hot-dog buns.

The majority of housewives use 2.3 300-gram cans at once, whereas single women use only 1 can.

Reasons for usage The major attraction for canned spaghetti meat sauce is that it is "very handy and easy to use," and some participants think the flavor is close to sauce in restaurants. Also, it's difficult to make from scratch.

The reasons housewives add things to canned meat sauce are to: (1) eliminate the can smell, (2) increase the meat content, and (3) insure enough flavoring to suit everyone's taste. A psychological element is that they don't want to appear lazy by using sauce "as is." Historically, most housewives started using canned sauce when they got married, while single women began usage five to six years ago in high school home economics classes.

The most common reason for use is "Mother used it." Other reasons given include TV commercials, noted products on store shelves, and heard about it from others.

Although retort pouch and packaged sauces from hotels or restaurants are sometimes used by participants, canned meat sauce is by far the main vehicle. Single women think the retort pouch is convenient because of its one-serving size, but housewives say the pouch is uneconomical and show little intent to purchase.

Canned-sauce and retort-pouch comparisons
Advantages of the can include long storage time, easy to store, restaurant flavor, and easy to prepare. Advantages of the retort pouch are convenient for one, easy to prepare, no can smell; disadvantages are insufficient amount and hands get dirty.

Purchasing conditions Within the single-women's group, two claim they buy the product themselves, while others eat the brand their mother buys. Hardly any participants recognize any taste difference between one brand and another.

Housewives claim they buy canned meat sauce when supermarkets are having a sale or when they don't have much other shopping to do. They buy from two to four cans at each purchase.

Most participants show no brand loyalty and are only concerned that the brand name is a well-known one or that they have seen the product advertised on TV. Taste is thought to be standard among most brands.

Brands Purchased

Kewpi	9
Heinz	5
Kagome	5
Mama	3
Oh-My	2
Meidi-Ya	1

- Kewpi is purchased by both groups, but housewives buy mostly Heinz.
- Reasons for purchasing Kewpi are: commercials, packaging (red and white), used to taste, and usage of other Kewpi products.
- Reasons for purchasing Heinz are: used to taste, safe product, and children seem to like it. No real brand loyalty noted among participants.

Other brand images and reasons are: Mama: often discounted and same brand as spaghetti noodles. Meidi-Ya: high quality, reliable, can be used as a gift. Kagome: same brand as famous ketchup.

Housewives said that average prices for the 300-gram can were ¥250, but they said it could be bought for ¥200 on sale. Single women had very little idea on prices but thought that ¥300 sounded reasonable.

Flavor Evaluations

Canned meat sauce General complaints about flavor and contents of canned meat sauce are made concerning its sweetness and lack of spice, but are for the most part focused on the scarcity of meat. Both housewives and single women, however, think that's all they can expect from canned sauces and seem to value convenience above any other factors.

Housewives Flavor suits everyone, but too sweet/not enough spice; to thin/watery; insufficient amount; tomato too strong; flavor unsatisfying; strong can smell; gets lumpy. Therefore: add Tabasco and more spices, more base ingredients, and more parmesan cheese.

Single women School lunch flavor, children like it, but not enough meat; too sour or too sweet; too much for single serving; too rich, can't finish. Therefore: add sugar, put Tabasco for more flavor, add spices for distinct taste.

Evaluation of Overall Concept

Brand not shown to participants Housewives' group said the concept photo had "lots of ingredients and seems thick enough not to soak through the noodles... actually looks very tasty." On the other hand, single women showed very little interest in the photo, saying "all products look alike."

Both groups, nevertheless, felt a difference between the concept brand and the ordinary types. Housewives felt the concept brand is one that can be served to family or visitors without having to add anything. All of them wanted to try it and thought it was a "real meat sauce." The single women split into two factions: One saying they had no interest in it, since "all canned meat sauces taste the same," and if they want a special dish, they could go to a restaurant. The other half of single women wanted to try the concept brand because they could make it and "it really looks think and complete."

Standard and mild types Single women thought the brand was aimed at those who were unsatisfied with conventional products and those who like spicy and hot tastes. The housewives think the concept is attractive because it seems to have an adult taste and uses many spices. Both groups felt the concept sauce would be difficult to make at home by themselves with any success.

Pricing of ¥500. Housewives accept this price if the product is tasty, since it would still be cheaper than going out to eat. Also, most said the price should be in accord with the taste.

Some of the single women felt it would be acceptable if tasty and if ¥500 is for two servings, but others said it was expensive for a canned meat sauce and showed surprise and hesitation. Most said they would go to a special restaurant if the price difference was trivial.

100% lean beef Participants felt that the secret in making an ideal sauce is to use 100% beef. Many do not know what kind of meat is in the canned sauces they currently use, a fact especially true with the single women's group. It was pointed out that it would be better to use ground beef than shredded beef or chunks of beef.

Some felt that the phrase "Beef—40 percent of the contents" was somewhat ambiguous and desired a clearer, easily understood explanation of all ingredients in the product.

Tabasco brand shown to participants The initial response from both groups upon hearing the brand "Tabasco" was similar: "It sounds hot and spicy." The housewives said they welcomed the concept of a Tabasco brand as a flavor for adults, while the single women showed surprise, having a strong image of "Tabasco" as a spice manufacturer.

Although all the participants thought about a spicy type for adults and a mild type, it was a common opinion that the "Tabasco" name gives a direct impression that it is too hot and spicy for children, regardless of the two different types. Therefore, it was felt that a phrase which emphasizes its mild flavor be used to convey the idea that it would suit anyone's taste.

Some housewives thought Tabasco originated from the U.S.A. or Mexico. Most, however, thought it came from Italy, where pasta has its origins, since Tabasco is used on pizza and spaghetti in Japan. Single women had an impression that Tabasco came from some area in Latin America.

Even after the brand name "Tabasco" was opened to the participants, there was no change in response to the ¥500 price inquiry put to them earlier regarding the 300-gram can. The housewives were still positive, and the single women were split into two groups.

Evaluation of Current Packaging

Both groups showed amazingly similar tastes in packaging. Favorable responses came forth on all the existing brands except for extremely negative comments on Mama and Showa.

Type of packaging About half the participants prefer litho cans, claiming paper labels (1) are easily torn, (2) fade quickly, and (3) get dirty if stored a long time. Some showed a strong rejection of paper labels and said they project an "image of pineapple cans." The other half say they receive a high-class image form paper labeling.

Colors Both groups shared the common opinion that a combination of red, white, and green colors give an Italian image. However, nearly every manufacturer uses them in some way, and group participants suggested a unique design and color pattern to create a high-class image.

Tabasco logo Housewives think the Tabasco logo is quite fashionable and feel it should be on the label, using its quality image to assist in advertising and promotions. The single women split again; half saying the logo should be used, and half insisting it will confuse the consumer by implying the product is a type of spicy flavoring and not a meat sauce.

Source: Company records.

Appendix C
McIlhenny Company: Japan
Second Focus Group, Conducted with Actual Product

PARTICIPANT PROFILES

Housewives

Twelve housewives aged between 25 and 45 who reside in the suburbs of Tokyo. Four participants have no children. The others all have two children each from kindergarten to high-school ages. In terms of eating habits, most of them make home meals where children's tastes get first consideration since husbands arrive home late. The trend, therefore, is to light and sweet flavors. Those with no children cook easy-to-prepare foods when husbands come home late and tend to favor hot and spicy tastes.

Single Working Women

Four single working women participated. Two of them work full time, and the two others work part time. One lives with her parents, two live by themselves, and one lives with a grandfather. All but the one who lives with her parents prepare meals regularly. Most of them claim they dine out almost half of the time. The three who cook regularly make simple meals at home.

EATING AND PURCHASING HABITS

Almost half the participants claim they eat spaghetti two or three times a month, and the other half claim they eat it at least once a week. Housewives with children use it largely for lunch or snacks on holidays, when schools do not serve lunches, or when the husband comes home late. Housewives with no children and single women don't specify times of use.

Housewives with children normally add some ingredients like onions, carrots, mushrooms, and meat for nutritional purposes, and tend to adjust flavors by adding spices and some condiments such as ketchup or tomato puree. Housewives with no children and single women use salt, pepper, Tabasco, and often spices and Worcestershire sauce or soy sauce. They take more advantage of convenience factors.

Housewives with children also tend to make other dishes—such as eggplant gratin, omelets, and lasagna—with canned spaghetti meat sauce.

TASTE TESTING

Mild Meat Sauce

Close to conventional meat sauce; weak tomato taste, seems thin, lacks spices, lacks richness.

Regular Meat Sauce

Plus points: conventional flavor, flexible usage; minus points: instant taste, ordinary. Because of its light flavor and admitted flexibility, nearly half felt that it would be suitable for children. [Note: The focus group moderator cautions that panel members feel a psychological need to be critical of the product.]

Spicy Meat Sauce

Nearly all of the participants in this, the second, focus group felt that the spicy variation of sauce offers a unique alternative to what is currently on the market in Japan. The level of spiciness is judged to be stimulating and with a flavor that differs from other products.

Those who prefer a spicy product (about one-third of the group participants) are usually in their 20s and feel the spicy product has both flavor and character. The rest of the participants feel it is too spicy and kills the flavor of the meat sauce itself, leaving a lingering taste which is unsuitable to them.

Most housewives feel it is too strong and spicy for children to eat, and the overall impression is that the product is one for young adults and grown men.

The smell of red peppers in the sauce is believed to be attractive to men, and its was felt that the sauce would go well with beer in the evening.

Plus points: elaborate taste, good overall aroma; minus points: too spicy for children.

RELATIVE EVALUATION

Almost 40 percent of the participants picked the mild meat sauce as the best among the flavors, and if we consider the number of second-place votes mild meat sauce received, that flavor gets a 60 percent vote of confidence.

Family considerations: Housewives with younger children chose the mild meat sauce and the regular meat sauce because of their relatively sweeter flavors. The choices by single women were spread across the mild, regular, and spicy meat sauces in near-equal sectors. The spicy meat sauce was least popular due to its high spice level.

CATCH-PHRASE EVALUATION

[Ten "catch phrases" were shown to respondents: (1) Beefy sauce made by Tabasco, the spaghetti specialist; (2) A supreme sauce with supreme beef—dedicated to spaghetti lovers; (3) Pasta luxury—supreme beef and secret flavors; (4) Ungrudging amount of supreme beef—ungrudgingly real; (5) Thick and profound—finished with supreme beef and ripe spices; (6) Starting today, learn the taste of a real sauce full of selected beef; (7) Real sauce with simmered beef—the epitome of a luxurious pasta; (8) Supreme beef meets supreme spices; (9) Full of the tasty flavor of excellent beef. The true sauce of luxury; (10) Finally—a sauce that's too tasty for words.]

General comments: Participants in this focus group chose each of the ten proposed catch phrases except "Starting today, learn the taste of a real sauce full of selected beef."

Fully 40 percent of the participants liked the last copy best of all. Reasons for this particular selection were: simple and unpretentious; concise and clear; sounds nice; easy to imagine.

The phrase that was thought to be second by the groups was: "Supreme beef meets supreme spices." Reasons given were" easy to understand; simple and clean.

The third-place phrase was: "A supreme sauce with supreme beef—dedicated to spaghetti lovers." This phrase was chosen based on the idea that it sounds as though people would like to hear it in commercials on TV or read it in magazine and newspaper advertisements.

PURCHASING INTENTIONS

(Prior to being told the price): Judging from the average existing price of canned sauces, which is felt to be between ¥250-¥260 at most supermarkets, housewives showed an intent to purchase if it is below ¥350. They claim they would definitely buy if it were ¥300 or less.

On the other hand, single women showed intent to purchase if the price is ¥340-¥350 or up to ¥400 at most; reflecting a wider range than housewives.

(After being shown the price): When a target price of ¥350 was shown, most participants showed intent to purchase once on a trial basis, and if it doesn't taste any different from the others, they will go back to their old brands.

The image of canned meat sauce is that they all taste about the same, and the focus-group participants felt that the ¥300 will be lowered to the mid-¥200 range on sale eventually.

A couple of participants admit that their decision on purchasing is affected greatly by the image they get form packaging.

Source: Company records.

Case 18: Currency Concepts International

Dr. Karen Anderson, Manager of Planning for Century Bank of Los Angeles, settled down for an unexpected evening of work in her small beach apartment. It seemed that every research project Century had commissioned in the last year had been completed during her ten-day trip to Taiwan. She had brought three research reports home that evening to try to catch up before meeting with the banks' Executive Planning Committee the next day.

Possibly because the currency-exchange facilities had been closed at the Taiwan Airport when she first arrived, Dr. Anderson's attention turned first to a report on a project currently under consideration by one of Century Bank's wholly owned subsidiaries, Currency Concepts International (CCI). The project concerned the manufacture and installation of currency-exchange automatic teller machines (ATMs) in major foreign airports.

CCI had been responsible for the development of Century Bank's very popular ATM ("money machine"), now installed in numerous branches of the bank, as well as in its main location in downtown Los Angeles. The current project was a small part of CCI and Century Bank's plan to expand electronic banking services worldwide.

As she started to review the marketing research effort of Information Resources, Inc., she wondered what she would be able to recommend to the Executive Planning Committee the next day regarding the currency-exchange project. She liked her recommendations to be backed by solid evidence, and she looked forward to reviewing results of the research performed to date.

Activities of Information Resources, Inc.

Personnel of Information Resources, Inc., had decided to follow three different approaches in investigating the problem presented to them: (1) review secondary statistical data; (2) interview companies that currently engage in currency exchange; and (3) conduct an exploratory consumer survey of a convenience sample.

Secondary Data

The review of secondary data had three objectives:

1. To determine whether the number of persons flying abroad constitutes a market potentially large enough to merit automated currency exchange

---

This case is printed with the permission of the author, Grady D. Bruce of the California State University, Fullerton.

2. To isolate any trends in the numbers of people flying abroad
3. To determine whether the amount of money that these travelers spend abroad is sizeable enough to provide a potential market for automated currency exchange.

The United States Department of Transportation monitors the number of people traveling from United States airports to foreign airports. These statistics are maintained and categorized as follows: citizen and noncitizen passengers, and civilian and military passengers. Since this study was concerned only with Americans who travel abroad, only citizen categories were considered. Furthermore, since American military flights do not utilize the same foreign airport facilities as civilian passenger flights, the military category was also excluded. The prospect that non-Americans might also use these facilities causes the statistics to be somewhat conservative. The figures, for 1978, were summed for each foreign airport; the results by geographical area are shown in Exhibit 1. The top ten gateway cities from all American ports are shown in Exhibit 2.

The second objective, to determine any growth trends in air travel, was addressed by studying the number of Americans flying abroad in the last five years. Exhibit 3 shows the number of American travelers flying to various geographic areas and the associated growth rates in each of those areas. Europe, clearly, has the greatest number of travelers; and, although it did not show the greatest percentage growth in 1978, it does have the largest growth in absolute numbers. Generally, growth rates in overseas air travel have been good for the last four years; at this time, these trends appear to be positive from the standpoint of a potential market. However, there are also some potential problems on the horizon. As the world's energy situation increasingly worsens, there is the possibility of significant decreases in international travel.

In order to address the third objective, whether the amount of money spent by American travelers abroad constitutes a potential market, per capita spending was examined. Exhibit 4 shows per capita spending, by geographic area, for the last five years as well as yearly percentages of growth. The category that includes the Far East, "other areas," shows the highest per capita spending. This may be the result of the relatively low prices found in the Far East.

Europe shows the second-highest figures for per capita spending; this area also exhibited strong growth in the last year. These figures indicate that Americans are spending increasing amounts of money abroad; even when inflation is taken consideration, these figures are positive.

EXHIBIT 1 American Citizens Flying Abroad in 1978 to Foreign Ports of Entry with Over 25,000 Arrivals

Europe	3,725,952
Caribbean	1,930,756
Central America	1,356,496
South America	301,347
Far East	516,861
Oceania	133,584

Note: Included in these area totals are all ports of entry that receive more than 25,000 passengers annually (68 per day). Ports of entry with lower through-put rate were excluded.

Source: Based on data provided in United States Department of Transportation, *United States International Air Travel Statistics*, 1978, Washington, D.C.

EXHIBIT 2 Most Frequented Foreign Ports of Entry from All American Ports

	PORT	PASSENGERS
1.	London, England	1,420,285
2.	Mexico City, Mexico	641,054
3.	Frankfurt, Germany	446,166
4.	Hamilton, Bermuda	378,897
5.	Nassau, Bahamas	361,791
6.	Tokyo, Japan	320,827
7.	Freeport, Bahamas	309,288
8.	Paris, France	295,823
9.	Rome, Italy	272,186
10.	Acapulco, Mexico	226,120

Source: Based on data provided in United States Department of Transportation, *United States International Air Travel Statistics*, 1978, Washington, D.C.

EXHIBIT 3 Growth in Number of Americans Flying Abroad 1974–1978 (Thousands)

	1974	% Change	1975	% Change	1976	% Change	1977	% Change	1978
European and Mediterranean	3,325	(4.2)	3,185	10.6	3,523	11.3	3,920	5.2	4,105
Western Europe	3,118	(4.1)	2,990	10.0	3,245	11.2	3,663	6.9	3,914
Caribbean and Central America	2,147	(3.8)	2,065	6.6	2,201	—	2,203	7.4	2,365
South America	423	5.7	447	(2.5)	436	10.8	483	6.6	515
Other Areas	572	14.9	657	12.2	737	6.4	784	2.7	805
Total	9,585	8.5	9,344	36.9	10,142	39.7	11,053	28.8	11,704

Source: United States Department of Commerce, *Survey of Current Business*, June 1979, Washington, D.C.

EXHIBIT 4 Per Capita Spending by Americans Traveling Abroad 1974–1978

	1974	% Change	1975	% Change	1976	% Change	1977	% Change	1978
Europe	542	11.1	602	1.3	610	—	612	17.2	717
Caribbean and Central America	319	19.4	381	(6.6)	356	—	359	4.5	375
South America	494	9.5	541	(1.7)	532	(1.1)	526	12.9	594
Other Areas	786	1.9	802	0.9	809	3.7	839	20.0	1,007
All Areas	489	12.6	547	—	545	1.8	555	14.6	635

Source: United States Department of Commerce, *Survey of Current Business*, June 1979, Washington, D.C.

Information Resources, Inc., concluded, therefore, that Europe holds the greatest market potential for introduction of the new system. As Dick Knowlton, coordinator of the research team, said, "Not only are all of the statistics for Europe high, but the short geographic distances between countries can be expected to provide a good deal of intra-area travel."

Company Interviews

In an attempt to better understand the current operations of currency exchange in airports, four major firms engaged in these activities were contacted. While some firms were naturally reluctant to provide information on some areas of their operations, several were quite cooperative. These firms, and a number of knowledgeable individuals whose names surfaced in initial interviews, provided the information that follows.

In both New York and Los Angeles, there is only one bank engaged in airport currency exchange: Deak-Perera. American Express, Bank of America, and Citibank, as well as Deak-Perera, are engaged in airport currency exchange in a variety of foreign locations. Approval of permits to engage in airport currency exchange activity rests with the municipal body that governs the airport and is highly controlled. It appears that foreign currency exchange is a highly profitable venture. Banks make most of their profits on the spread in exchange rates, which are posted daily.

Both Citibank and Bank of America indicated that they attempt to ensure their facilities' availability to all flights. The more profitable flights were found to be those that were regularly scheduled, rather than chartered. The person most likely to use the facilities was the vacationer rather than the businessperson.

Neither bank could give an exact figure for the average transaction size; estimates ranged from $85 to $100.

It was the opinion of bank/Deak employees, who dealt with travelers on a daily basis, that the average traveler was somewhat uncomfortable changing money in a foreign country. They also believed it to be particularly helpful if clerks at the exchange counter converse with travelers in their own language. A number of years ago Deak attempted to use a type of vending machine to dispense money at Kennedy Airport. This venture failed; industry observers felt that absence of human conversation and assurance contributed to its lack of success.

Most of the exchange perform the same types of services, including the sale of foreign currency and the sale of travelers checks. The actual brand of travelers checks sold varies with the vendors.

American Express has recently placed automated unmanned travelers check dispensers in various American airports. This service is available to American Express card holders and the only charge is 1 percent of the face value of the purchased checks; the purchase is charged directly to the customer's checking account. As yet, the machines have not enjoyed a great deal of use, although American Express has been successful in enrolling its customers as potential users.

Methods of payment for currency purchases are similar at all exchanges. Accepted forms of payment include: actual cash, travelers checks, cashier checks drawn on local banks, and Master Charge or Visa cards. When using a credit card to pay for currency purchase, there is a service charge added to the customer's bill, as with any cash advance.

Traveler Interviews

To supplement and complement the statistical foundation gained by reviewing secondary data sources, the consumer interview portion of the study was purposefully designed to elicit qualitative information about travelers' feelings toward current and future forms of exchanging currency. Approximately sixty American travelers were interviewed at both the San Francisco and Los Angeles International Airports, due to the accessibility of these locations to Information Resources' sole location. An unstructured, undisguised questionnaire was developed to assist in channeling the interview toward specific topics (see Appendix A). Questions were not fixed and the question order was dependent on the respondent's answers. Basically, the guide served to force the interview conversation around the central foreign currency exchange theme. The interviews were conducted primarily in the arrival/departure lobbies of international carriers and spanned over four weeks, beginning in mid-December 1979. A deliberate attempt was made to include as many arriving as departing passengers to neutralize the effect of increasing holiday traffic. Additionally, to reduce interviewer bias, three different interviewers were used. Interviews were intentionally kept informal. And Dick Knowlton cautioned the interviewers to remain objective and "not let your excitement over the product concept spill over into the interview and bias the responses."

The interviews were divided almost evenly between those who favored the concept and those who did not. Those who did perceive value in the concept tended also to support other innovations such as the automated teller machine and charging foreign currency on credit cards. Those who would not use the currency exchange terminals wanted more human interaction and generally did not favor automation in any form; a fair proportion also had previous problems exchanging foreign currency. However, even those who did not favor the currency exchange idea did seem to prefer the system of having twenty-four-hour availability of the machines, and of using credit cards to get cash under emergency situations.

The respondents represent a diverse group of individuals ranging in age from eighteen to eighty years, holding such different positions as oil executive, photographer, housewife, and customs officer. Primarily bound for Europe, Canada, and Mexico, the interviewees were mainly split between pleasure-seekers and those on business. Only three individuals interviewed were part of tour groups, and of these three, only one had previously traveled abroad. The majority of the others had been out of the United States before and had exchanged currency in at least one other country. Many had exchanged currency in remote parts of the world, including Morocco, Brazil,

Australia, Japan, Tanzania, and Russia. Only five individuals had not exchanged money in airports at one time or another. The majority had obtained foreign currency in airports and exchanged money in airports primarily in small denominations for use in taxi cab fares, bus fares, phones, and airport gift shops, as well as for food, tips, and drinks. Most respondents agreed a prime motive for exchanging money in airports was the security of having local currency.

Exchanging currency can become a trying ordeal for some individuals. They fear being cheated on the exchange rate; they cannot convert the foreign currency into tangible concepts (for example, "how many yen should a loaf of bread cost?"); they dislike lines and associated red tape; and many cannot understand the rates as posted in percentages. Most individuals exchange money in airports, hotels, or banks, but sometimes there are no convenient facilities at all for exchanging currency.

People like to deal with well-known bank branches, especially in airports, because they feel more confident about the rate they are receiving. However, major fears of individuals are that many exchange personnel will not understand English and that they will be cheated in the transaction. Furthermore, a few people mentioned poor documentation when they exchange currency in foreign airports.

The travelers were divided as to whether they exchange currency before or after they arrive in the foreign country, but a few said that the decision depended on what country they were entering. If a currency, such as English pounds, could easily be obtained from a local bank before leaving the United States, they were more likely to exchange before leaving. However, in no case would the traveler arrange for currency beyond a week in advance. Most preferred to obtain the foreign currency on relatively short notice—less than three days before the trip. Of the individuals on tours, none planned to obtain currency in the foreign airport. Apparently, the tour guide had previously arranged for the necessary transportation from the airport to the hotels, and there would be only enough time to gather one's luggage and find the bus before it would depart, leaving no time to enjoy the facilities of the airport which required foreign currency. All three tour individuals did mention that they planned to obtain foreign currency once they arrived at the hotel. All individuals mentioned that they had secured their own foreign currency, but a few of the wives who were traveling with their husbands conceded that their spouses usually converted the currency in the foreign airport.

Very few of the interviewees had actually used an automated teller machine, but the majority had heard of or seen the teller machines on television. Those who had used the automated machines preferred their convenience and were generally satisfied with the terminal's performance. Many of those who had not used the automated teller machines mistrusted the machine and possible loss of control over their finances. Concerns about security and problems with the machines breaking down were also expressed. One woman described the teller machines as being "convenient, but cold." Apparently, many people prefer having human interaction when their money is concerned.

As noted earlier, approximately thirty of the respondents would favor the exchange terminals over their normal airport currency exchange routine, while the same number would have nothing to do with the machines. However, the majority of potential users qualified their use by such features as competitive rates, knowing the precise charges, or knowing they could get help if something went wrong. Individuals who indicated no preference were included in the favorable category, simply because they would not refuse to try the machine. Most of the indifferent people seemed to indicate they would try such a machine if some type of introductory promotional offer was included, such as travel information, currency tips, or a better rate.

With virtual unanimity, the respondents felt that twenty-four-hour availability made the currency exchange machines more attractive, yet that alone would not persuade the dissenters to use the terminals. Some individuals felt that a machine simply could not give the travel advice that could be obtained at the currency exchange booths.

The opportunity to charge foreign currency against a major credit card, such as Master Charge or Visa, was a definite plus in the minds of most respondents. One individual clearly resented the idea, however, feeling that he would "overspend" if given such a convenient way to obtain cash. Respondents offered a number of suggestions concerning implementations of the product concept and a number of specific product features:

1. Add information about the country.
2. Provide small denominations, and include coins.
3. Have it communicate in English.
4. Put in travelers checks to get cash.
5. Put in cash to get foreign currency.
6. Post rates daily.
7. Keep rates competitive and post charges.
8. Have television screen with person to describe procedure.
9. Place the machines in hotels and banks.
10. Have a change machine nearby that can convert paper money.
11. Place machine near existing currency exchange facilities for convenience when normal lines become long.
12. Demonstrate how to use the machine.
13. Use all bank credit cards.

Appendix A: Interview Guide for International Travelers (U.S. Citizens)

These interviews should remain as informal as possible. The object is not to obtain statistically reliable results, but to get ideas that will help to stimulate research. These questions are not fixed; the order, however, is sometimes dependent on answers the respondents give.

Introduce Yourself

1. Are you going to be traveling to a foreign country? Arriving from a foreign country? A United States resident?
2. Where is/was your final destination?
3. Why are you traveling (business, pleasure, a tour)?
4. How often do you travel outside of the United States?
5. Have you ever exchanged currency in a foreign country. (If no, go to #6.) Where? Does anything in particular stand out in your mind when you exchanged currency?
6. Have you ever changed money in an airport? (If no, go to #7.)
7. Where do you plan to exchange currency on this trip?
8. Where do you change money normally?
9. Have you ever had any problems changing currencies? Explain circumstances.
10. Normally, would you change money before entering a country or after you arrive? If before, how long in advance? Where? (Probe.)
11. Are you familiar with automated teller machines that banks are using? (If not, explain.) Have you used one of these machines?
12. What are your feelings toward these machines?
13. If a currency exchange terminal, similar to an automated teller machine, was placed in your destination airport, would you use the machine or follow your normal routine?
14. Would 24-hour availability make the currency exchange machines more attractive? Would you use the terminals at night?
15. None of the currency exchange machines currently exists. What features or services could be provided so that you might choose to use a terminal rather than other currency exchange facilities?
16. If you could charge the foreign currency received to a major credit card, such as Master Charge or Visa, would you be more likely to use the machine?
17. Demographics—Age range (visual)
    Occupation?
    Sex?
    Traveling alone?

Case 19: Mondetta Everywear

In June 1992, the office of Mondetta Clothing Company in Winnipeg, Manitoba, was alive with activity as Mondetta's four owners and their support staff were busy at work. In the company's meeting room, samples were being examined for the upcoming fall fashion line, while in the back warehouse, new clothing shipments were being sorted. After several years of rapid growth in the Canadian casual wear industry, Mondetta's managers were committed to making their company a success through further market penetration. They wondered whether they should continue to solidify clothing sales in Canada or proceed with their desire to expand into the American, and eventually, the European markets. In order to make a reasonable decision, each expansion alternative would require careful examination of market and industry data as well as the company's ability to handle another phase of increased growth.

Company Background

Mondetta Clothing Company was founded as a partnership in Winnipeg, Manitoba by brothers Ash and Prashant Modha, and Raj and Amit Bahl. The brothers were close friends who started by operating a small business selling cards and stationery while studying at University. In 1987, they decided to offer local casual wear buyers unique fashions by designing and manufacturing a line of beachwear and casual pants. Working out of their families' basement, they managed product designs, production, marketing and distribution and were rewarded with $10,000 in sales in that year.

During the following two summers, the company's casual cotton pants, shorts and tops were sold outside the city from a booth at Winnipeg's popular Grand Beach. In 1988, their sales grew to $25,000 and reached $125,000 by 1989. As the Mondetta name proceeded to gain exposure in the Winnipeg market, the brothers were awarded the Small Business Achiever Award by Winnipeg's Uptown Magazine as well as other distinguished industry and media honours. In May 1990, after most of them had completed their undergraduate studies, they incorporated the business and started full time company operations. Soon Mondetta expanded from a few Winnipeg retail stores to more than 350 outlets across Canada, with sales beyond $2.4 million. The company's financial statements are presented in Exhibits 1, 2, and 3.

Mondetta Everywear

Mondetta's most popular items were their "flagshirts", sweatshirts adorned with the flags of world countries. The name Mondetta was based on a play of French words for "small world" and the focus of the collection was the high quality applique and embroidery on cotton clothing. The company's styles were targeted to the socially or politically concerned man, woman or young adult who enjoyed superior quality casual or street wear.

The Casual Wear And Street Wear Market

Mondetta catered to a market that bordered between casual and street wear, and which could be classified as trendy wear. There were numerous types of casual wear in the rapidly changing Canadian apparel market. Regular or mainstream casual wear consisted of similar clothing styles that could easily be found in any department or chain store. Street wear included casual clothing that appealed to more unique and diverse tastes. Trendy wear shoppers generally desired clothing that offered them something different from what was available in most regular stores. They specifically searched for eye catching products and often purchased from companies with an established brand name reputation.

This case was prepared by Leena Malik, Instructor, under the supervision of Professor John F. Graham, for the sole purpose of providing material for class discussion at the Western Business School. Certain names and other identifying information may have disguised to protect confidentiality. It is not intended to illustrate either effective or ineffective handling of a managerial situation. Copyright © 1993 The University of Western Ontario. This material is not covered under authorization from CanCopy or any reproduction rights organization. Any form of reproduction, storage or transmittal of this material is prohibited without written permission from Western Business School, The University of Western Ontario, London, Canada N6A 3K7. Reprinted with permission, Western Business School.

EXHIBIT 1 Statement of Operations (For the Year Ended April 30)

	1990[1]	1991	1992
Total Revenue	$ 104,896	$ 247,970	$2,436,644
Cost of Goods Sold	75,506	178,543	1,863,427
Gross Profit	29,390	69,427	573,217
Operating Expenses:			
Accounting and Legal	2,649	2,699	7,732
Advertising and Promo	1,224	8,964	29,135
Bank Charges and Interest	3,198	8,762	14,726
Bad Debts	3,702	4,031	21,735
Deprec. & Amortiz.	0	2,504	9,038
Factoring Commissions	0	920	52,006
Insurance	0	593	810
Leases and Equipment	265	1,398	8,498
Management Bonus	0	0	110,400
Miscellaneous	307	1,521	1,328
Printing and Stationery	695	1,167	9,055
Parking	0	207	46
Property and Business Tax	0	822	1,276
Rent	1,288	9,246	12,696
Repairs and Maintenance	0	182	528
Salaries and Benefits	1,437	29,005	75,339
Telephone	1,136	6,516	12,091
Travel and Entertainment	1,693	7,974	14,731
Utilities	0	477	970
Total Operating Expenses	17,594	86,998	382,140
Earning (Loss) Before Tax	11,796	(17,571)	191,077
Income Taxes	0	0	43,517
Income Tax Reduction Resulting from Loss Carry Forward	0	0	3,864
Net Earnings (Loss)	$ 11,796	$ (17,571)	$ 151,424

[1] For the period covered by this date the organization was a partnership. The firm was incorporated May 1, 1990.

EXHIBIT 2 Balance Sheet (As of April 30)

	1990*	1991	1992
ASSETS			
Current Assets:			
Accounts Receivable	$ 76,473	$ 72,789	$ 875,641
Inventories	38,780	54,961	433,653
Prepaid Expenses	1,472	1,794	3,752
Total Current Assets	116,725	129,544	1,313,046
Fixed Assets:			
Equipment and Leasehold improvements	0	13,583	53,895
Accumulated Deprec.	0	2,306	10,982
Fixed Assets (Net)	0	11,277	42,913
Other Assets	0	3,588	6,593
TOTAL ASSETS	$ 116,725	$ 144,409	$1,362,552
LIABILITIES:			
Current Liabiities:			
Bank Overdraft	$ 1,539	$ 14,041	$ 57,936
Bank Loan	41,400	58,880	185,840
Accounts Payable	27,585	62,676	790,847
Bonus Payable	0	0	110,400
Income Taxes Payable	0	0	39,653
Total Current Liabilities	79,524	135,597	1,184,676
Long-Term Liabilities:			
Note Payable	34,049	7,820	0
Payable to Shareholders	0	18,379	22,218
Total Long-Term Liabilities	34,049	26,199	22,218
SHAREHOLDER'S EQUITY:			
Share Capital	N/A	184	21,804
Retained Earnings	12,152	(17,571)	133,854
Total Equity	12,152	(17,387)	155,658
TOTAL LIABILITIES AND SHAREHOLDER'S EQUITY	$ 116,725	$ 144,409	$1,362,552

* 4 month period

EXHIBIT 3 Ratio Sheet

	1990	1991	1992
PROFITABLITY			
Total Revenue	100.0%	100.0%	100.0%
Cost of Sales	72.0%	72.0%	76.5%
Gross Margin	28.0%	28.0%	23.5%
Operating Expenses:			
Accounting and Legal	2.5%	1.1%	0.3%
Advertising and Promotion	1.2%	3.6%	1.2%
Bank Charges and Interest	3.0%	3.5%	0.6%
Bad Debts	3.5%	1.6%	0.9%
Deprec. & Amortiz.	0.0%	1.0%	0.4%
Factoring Commissions	0.0%	0.4%	2.1%
Insurance	0.0%	0.2%	0.0%
Leases and Equipment	0.3%	0.6%	0.3%
Management Bonus	0.0%	0.0%	4.5%
Miscellaneous	0.3%	0.6%	0.1%
Printing and Stationery	0.7%	0.5%	0.4%
Parking	0.0%	0.1%	0.0%
Property and Business Tax	0.0%	0.3%	0.1%
Rent	1.2%	3.7%	0.5%
Repairs and Maintenance	0.0%	0.1%	0.0%
Salaries and Benefits	1.4%	11.7%	3.1%
Telephone	1.1%	2.6%	0.5%
Travel and Entertainment	1.6%	3.2%	0.6%
Utilities	0.0%	0.2%	0.0%
Total Operating Expenses	16.8%	35.1%	15.7%
Earning (Loss) Before Tax	11.2%	(7.1%)	7.8%
Income Taxes	0.0%	0.0%	1.6%
Net Earnings (Loss)	11.2%	(7.1%)	6.2%
LIQUIDITY			
Current Ratio	1.66	0.96	1.11
Acid Test	1.11	0.55	0.74
Working Capital	46,201	(6,053)	128,370
EFFICIENCY			
Age of Accounts Receivable	266	107	131
Age of Inventory	187	0	0
Age of Payables	133	117	129
STABILITY			
Net Worth/Total Assets	10%	(12%)	11%
Interest Coverage	4.7	(1.0)	14.5
GROWTH		1990–1991	1991–1992
Sales		136.4%	882.6%
Net Income		(249.0%)	—
Assets		23.7%	843.5%

The casual and street wear market was more easily divided into two age groups: older and younger buyers. The older casual wear consumer was about 30 years old and wanted a product made of high quality materials with superior graphics designs. Younger customers aged 13 to 30 looked mainly for quality through an established brand name. Although younger consumers were highly influenced by fashion trends, the price of the apparel nonetheless remained an important consideration in their buying process. Word of mouth and the visual appearance of the clothing also influenced both consumer groups, who approached trendy wear stores to find the hottest new clothing available. Consequently, innovative clothing companies often started their businesses by selling clothing to trend setting stores in hopes that their products would create a new fashion craze. Once a trend had been created, product visibility and sales were increased through movement into the mainstream clothing stores.

The Canadian Trade Environment

In the casual and street wear market, the graphics design either led to rapid product acceptance or rejection. Thus, retailers were hesitant to take on new products since rejection forced them to mark down prices in order to dispose of unwanted inventories. To protect themselves, retailers looked for product quality and fit within their stores, as well as for the visual graphics appeal of the clothing. In addition, they usually made a small trial order to test the product's saleability before ordering in larger quantities.

Since the Canadian apparel market was dominated by a limited number of large department and chain stores, clothing companies tried to sell their products through their own sales representatives or independent agents at the most advantageous prices available. Some casual and street wear firms also sold to local independent or specialty stores.

Department stores such as Eaton's, the Bay and Sears were generally less flexible and entrepreneurial than other retail outlets and relied on more tightly controlled planning of operations. Department stores purchased clothing (based on product type) from central or regional buying offices through designated buyers. Some department stores also specifically allocated budgets for the exploration of goods from local companies to match merchandise with local demand. In order to get placement in a department store, clothing company representatives had to approach the appropriate buying officer. For casual and street wear, this officer was more likely to be the men's or ladies' wear buyer.

Department store demands were usually very high. Most expected signed contracts specifying desired prices, mark-ups, volume discounts and early payment discounts. Mark-ups on cost for casual wear were close to 50%, while volume and early payment discounts ranged between 3–5% each. Although product distribution was usually allocated per store location by the clothing firm, products had to be sent to the department store's central warehouse before being shipped to designated store outlets. This system resulted in an additional 2% warehousing discount. Some department stores also demanded a 1–2% advertising discount. The resulting 9–14% worth of discounts allowed Canadian department stores to sell products at a lower price than other retailers, thereby creating the perception that department stores sold discount low quality clothing.

The chain store network was divided into regional chains which serviced either western or eastern Canada and national chains. Chain stores were more stable and credit worthy than independent stores and had more purchasing power than the department stores. Chain stores expected a 55% product mark-up as well as a 2% warehousing discount. Early payment terms were 3% in 10 days net 60 days. Most chain stores offered relatively little product advertising and relied on in-store displays and word of mouth to attract customers. The need to approach only one or two buying offices for each chain offered the provision of wide geographic distribution with less selling effort than required for the independent stores.

Independent store owners usually managed one or at most two local stores in a city or town. Some independents were considered to be local trend setters, while others were followers who copied the trend makers after product exposure had been created. Purchases were performed from one location, usually the store itself, using fashion trend information.

Many independents were considered to be poor credit risks due to their limited financial resources, unstable management and variable clientele. Even though placement in an independent store appeared risky, it was an important channel for brand name and trend creation. The most successful independents distinguished themselves through their management style and the establishment of their own reputation, visibility and local market niche. Since independent stores generally did not have the ability to purchase in large quantities, volume and early payment discounts were not granted. Payment terms to producers were 30 to 60 days with 50% mark-up to retail customers.

The American Trade Environment

American trade dynamics differed from Canadian dynamics in several ways. First, the discount image of Canadian department stores made independent and chain stores hesitant to take on products originally featured in a department store. In the United States, department stores such as Bloomingdales, Macy's and Nordstroms were perceived as leaders in the fashion industry. Therefore, initial placement in these stores created a fashion trend that the independent and chain stores were willing to endorse. Second, the American market was dominated by numerous strong retail stores and apparel companies that were more aggressive and demanding than their conservative Canadian counterparts. Third, highly diverse consumer tastes and the desire for more bold and flashy items resulted in an intensely competitive retail environment. These factors and the specific demands of American retailers are outlined in Exhibit 4.

The American apparel industry was also undergoing a period of change and restructuring. By 1989, discount stores and mail order firms had gained market share at the expense of specialty department and chain stores. In fact, discounters replaced department stores as the largest retail segment. Another trend in the American apparel industry was the formation of close, interdependent relationships between retailer and supplier based upon a joint commitment to mutual profitability through in-store boutiques. In addition, in order to improve efficiency and lower costs, retailers were making efforts to narrow their supplier structure with larger commitments and bigger orders.

The Competition

Competitors in the casual wear industry sold similar products (jeans, sweatshirts and t-shirts) adorned with their brand names in retail chain, department and independent stores throughout Canada and the United States. Because competing products were normally placed side-by-side in the store, sales depended more on brand name and reputation rather than product differentiation. Top industry names were Guess Jeans, Buffalo Jeans and B.U.M. Equipment and were all associated with large American and European firms. The success of these companies was due to the creation of a highly visible media hype focused on brand name and product promotion. Brand names were also heavily promoted in well known fashion and trend setting magazines such as Vogue, Rolling Stone, and GQ. Guess, and B.U.M. were also beginning to license themselves in the European market. Buffalo Jeans was a European label licensed in Canada. Through licensing, a European manufacturer had the right to produce and sell approved designs using a clothing's brand name and logo.

The management style among smaller Canadian apparel firms could be characterized as entrepreneurial. Owners, supported by informally organized executive staffs, performed all the functions required in the day-to-day operations of the business. Some of the medium and larger sized firms had started to rely on the specialized skills of their management teams to bring a more corporate approach to executive decision making. Nevertheless, many apparel firms were averse to the long-term strategic reinvestment of profits and tended to concentrate on short-term operation decisions rather than the development of long-term business planning and market positioning.

The fragmentation and volatility of market conditions as well as the entrepreneurial management nature made financial institutions hesitant to extend long-term financing to apparel firms. A number of companies had tried to reorganize their financial positions by becoming public companies. However, this

EXHIBIT 4 American Retail Channel Profiles By Store Type[1]

	Department Stores	Chain Stores	Specialty Stores	Independent Stores
Market Flows	• have their own private label programs • want unique & exciting fashions to service customer needs • medium quality/medium price • high volume	• wide geographic distribution • medium volume • diversity and uniqueness • fit in the store • right goods at right price • look for brand names • country of origin less important	• highly prestigious names (Neiman Marcus, Sak's, Tiffany's) • considered to be in world of fashion and luxury • great variety • variable volume • unique designs • very high quality / high price	• small (1–2 stores) • competitive pressure • in-depth customer knowledge • unique styles • high quality/high price • low volume
Sales Force & Relationships	• can suddenly drop suppliers • not loyal, will depend on sales performance and profitability	• prefer long-term cooperative relationships	• want exclusivity • less loyal to suppliers • less loyal to suppliers • will drop suppliers which fail to meet performance goals • market trade shows are key for establishing contacts & selecting products	• personal/flexible service • value long-term relationship • trust
Merchandising & Packaging	want: • attractive return policies • shared mark-downs • 48–52% mark-up • early payment discounts 8% • volume discounts 4–5% • co-op advertising 2–3%	want: • 45–50% mark-up • early payment disc. up to 8% • volume discounts 1–2% • co-op advertising 2–3% • 90-day terms	want: • liberal return policies • no risk product testing • shared mark-downs • 50–60% mark-up • early payment disc. 6–8% • volume discounts 2–5% • co-op advertising 2–3%	• limited financial resources to finance inventory • rapid refills • 50–60% mark-up
Distribution Concerns	• centralized distrib. centres • may request customized store orders • want on-time delivery • value exclusivity		• centralized distr. centers • customized store orders may be requested • value exclusivity	• value on-time delivery
Electronic Linkage	• behind, but starting to get more sophisticated	• sophisticated response and inventory systems	• few linkages in place	• no sophisticated procedures in place • electronic cash registers for inventory management

[1] Preparing for Free Trade: Apparel Retailing in the United States

Reproduced with permission from Industry, Science and Technology Canada

strategy appeared unsuccessful due to the poor performance of share offerings in public exchanges.

Exhibit 5 presents an overview of major international apparel markets and producers as well as their main strengths and weaknesses. The United Kingdom, Germany, France and Italy were perceived as leaders in the European and international fashion industries. Countries such as China, Hong Kong, Singapore and the Philippines were well known for their ability to provide high quality products using cheaper labour. The Canadian apparel market, once a stable market, faced increased competitive pressure from these low-cost imports and, by 1989, imports had increased at rates in excess of Canadian market growth despite protective import restraints. As a result, apparel firms faced greater pressure to rationalize and restructure their operations.

Exports were not a major influence in the apparel industry's overall sales performance. In 1989, sales to the United States accounted for approximately 85%

EXHIBIT 5 The International Apparel Market[2]

Country	Characteristics
CANADA:	• Relatively unknown • Lacks reputation • The future?
CARIBBEAN:	• Political tensions dissipating • Developing strong ties with the U.S. • Item 807
CHINA:	• Well known for silk • Plentiful cheap labor • Large internal textile industry • Destined to be a vast resource as apparel sophistication improves
EASTERN EUROPE:	• Low wages • Entering a phase of rapid industrialization • Outlook for apparel is good
FRANCE:	• Fashion leadership • Reputation for quality and taste
GERMANY:	• Reputation for quality and taste • Consistent styling
HONG KONG:	• Historical reputation for superior handwork and "one-stop shopping" • Critical labor shortage • Questionable future - Beijing's intentions are unclear
ITALY	• Fashion leadership • High quality • Renowned flexibility
PHILIPPINES	• Low wages • Reputation for excellent handwork • Destination resource for gloves, undergarments, and children's apparel products
SINGAPORE	• Emerging apparel "Hub" for Pacific rim • Large port city • Strong infrastructure • Migration of Hong Kong, Taiwanese, and Japanese interests
UNITED KINGDOM	• Established fashion signature • High taste level • Quality tailored clothing & knitwear

[2] *Apparel Retailing in the United States*

of Canada's apparel export shipments. Canada's competition in foreign markets was primarily from European producers. Among the products exhibiting the best performance record were ladies' designer fashions, winter outerwear, some types of men's fine clothing, children's wear and occupational apparel. In the European and American high fashion markets, country of origin was less important than factors such as quality, style and price, particularly in the medium to higher price ranges.

The Environment

The casual and street wear market was highly volatile and vulnerable to changing fashion trends, lifestyles and leisure activities. Sometimes, a popular trend enticed companies to saturate the market, a move which eventually led to the deterioration of the trend. During recessionary periods, apparel companies generally experienced reduced demand for their products. However, since trendy wear sales were highly dependent on the intensity of the latest trend, it was difficult to relate sales to poor business conditions.

Increased opportunities for Canadian apparel firms to enter the large American market were becoming available due to the gradual reduction of trade tariffs under the recent Canada-U.S. Free Trade Agreement. However, Canadian companies wishing to export to the United States faced many established competitors. In addition, their flexibility was reduced due to a requirement to place 50% Canadian content in their goods. As a general rule, apparel made from third country fabrics was not eligible for duty-free treatment under the agreement. Freer trade with the United States also prompted several large American retailers to expand into Canada, thereby increasing competition for the Canadian consumer. By June 1992, North American Free Trade talks with Mexico were well underway and an agreement was expected to be reached before the end of 1992.

Currency fluctuations appeared to have little impact on export competitiveness with the United States. On the other hand, the devaluation of the Canadian dollar relative to European currencies over the past two years had sparked renewed interest by Canadian manufacturers in the European market. However, in Europe the duty-free movement of goods among European community countries, strong competition from European designer labels, and the aggressive marketing of private-label manufacturers, hindered Canada's apparel trade in this market.

Technological systems were becoming more advanced and useful to both producers and retailers. The computerization of sales and inventory data allowed companies to keep informed of rapidly changing market conditions in order to improve their market position and service to customers. Some retailers made arrangements with suppliers to transmit orders by computer when a minimum inventory level was reached. These "quick response" systems created better relationships between retailer and supplier and provided apparel firms with the flexibility to switch from one style or product to another as profitable market opportunities were discovered. In Canada, sophisticated response systems were still relatively unknown to retailers while in the United States, large chains stores were more experienced in the use of quick response systems. Although American department stores had no sophisticated systems in place, they were starting to plan for the future installation of new technology.

Mondetta's Current Strategy

Mondetta's strategy focused around product exclusivity rather than market saturation. This was achieved through careful selection of industry sales agents and retailers for clothing promotion. In 1989 and early 1990, Mondetta clothing was sold throughout western Canada in high quality regional and national chain stores and local independent stores. Since heavy price discounting by department stores compromised Mondetta's high quality exclusive image, department store sales were restricted to Eaton's in Winnipeg. In late 1991, after the establishment of western Canadian sales, Mondetta expanded into Ontario, Quebec and the Maritimes. Management's sales goal for the 1992 fiscal year was $5–6 million which they hoped to achieve through increased national and international market penetration.

Finance

Although monthly cash flow forecasts based on pre-booked orders were prepared, the frequent opening of new accounts resulted in completely different cash requirements than those projected. This situation was beginning to strain Mondetta's $250,000 line of credit for inventory financing. While government incentives to support small business were available to companies that promoted local employment, poor economic conditions in 1992 and the company's young age made government agencies hesitant to provide funds. Banks were also afraid to lend funds to what they labelled as "here today, gone tomorrow" businesses. This feeling was created by the recent bankruptcy of several highly successful Winnipeg clothing companies which were owned and operated by young managers.

In order to deal with a difficult cash situation, Mondetta operated by customer order. This system enabled the company to match receivables with payables while carefully managing supply relationships to ensure timely payments. Management hoped that a new computerized system for accounting, purchase orders, production, marketing, and receivables would assist with the development of strict cash management plans.

Marketing

Mondetta's most popular logos, "Mondetta Everywear" and "The Spirit of Unification", were company trademarks. Traditionally, the two fashion lines (spring and fall) focused on the theme of international awareness and globalization. Exhibit 6 outlines Mondetta's production timeline for 1992. In 1993, the company hoped to sell four fashion lines (one per season) which placed more emphasis on the Mondetta name instead of flags.

Mondetta's managers tried to foster a mystique cult following and to avoid market saturation by restricting their products to a limited number of superior quality stores. To create visibility for its flag-shirts, the company employed industry agents who targeted trendy name-setting stores in each location before distributing to the high quality chain stores. Agents received a 10% commission on the Mondetta selling price (industry commissions ranged from 8–12%). Marketing communications consisted mainly of press exposure, word of mouth and the graphics appeal of the clothing. In Winnipeg, Mondetta clothing was also displayed on transit shelters.

The brothers participated in two semi-annual trade shows hosted by Salon International. Trade shows created product visibility and were attended by numerous retail sales agents and buyers. The Spring/Summer show was held during February in Montreal while the Fall/Winter show was held during August in Toronto. A trade show booth cost approximately $20,000, with a space cost of $5,000. Travelling and on-site expenses resulted in a total cost of $30,000 per show.

EXHIBIT 6 Production And Operations Time Line For 1992

Jan.	Feb.	Mar.	Apr.	May	June	July	Aug.	Sept.	Oct.	Nov.	Dec.
• finalize and complete fall 1992 designs and product line	deliver orders taken in Oct/Nov 1991	continue spring shipments	finish spring shipments	finalize and complete spring 1993 designs and product line		begin shipment of fall orders	attend trade show in Toronto for spring line	process orders for spring 1993	continue order processing for spring 1993	continue spring line production	
	attend trade show in Montreal for fall line	take and process orders for the fall fashion line	cut-off for fall orders in the third week	ship, repeat orders for spring 1991			continue shipment of fall fashion line	continue shipment of fall fashion line	spring line production begins	finish fall shipments	ship repeat orders to fall 1992
	begin shipment of spring fashion line		fall line production begins in fourth week	continue production of fall 1992 line					design and complete Summer 1993 fashion line		

*By 1993 fiscal year, the company will move from the design and manufacture of Spring and Fall fashion lines to spring, summer, fall and winter lines.

Mondetta's major customers were: Bootlegger (nation-wide), Below the Belt, and Off the Wall (western regional chains), and Eaton's in Winnipeg. Approximately 40% of the company's sales volume resulted from these accounts. Exhibit 7 compares Mondetta's Canadian sales with those of the Canadian apparel industry. Western Canadian sales comprised 80% of the company's business with 18% in Ontario and only 2% in Quebec and the Maritimes. Canadian retail apparel sales in 1991 were around 37% in Ontario, 34% in Quebec and the Maritimes, and 29% in western Canada.

Competition

Nationally, Mondetta clothing was placed side by side with other established brand name products such as the Guess Jeans, Request and Pepe Jeans. However, the companies selling these labels had wider retail distribution networks in both Canada and the United States.

In Winnipeg, an independent company called "Passport International" had recently opened a retail outlet next to Eaton's downtown store. Passport's designs were identical to Mondetta's with the exception of the logo, and the clothing was also sold at a lower price. For example, Mondetta's highly successful flagshirt which retailed for $79.95 was sold for $64.99 in Passport. Passport also offered customized flags of any country compared to Mondetta's 45 flags. Although Passport was made of lower quality materials, customers wanting a Mondetta but not being able to afford one generally turned to Passport for their designs. Passport International was rumoured to be opening a new location in Toronto's Fairview Mall by fall 1992.

Operations

The apparel design either led to rapid product acceptance or rejection thus making it the first and most crucial step in the production process. Other major steps in apparel manufacture were material sourcing, pattern making, fabric cutting, sewing, and finishing. When Mondetta first began operations, the brothers sourced their own materials and transported them to the manufacturer to cut, make, trim and finish the product. This method created numerous problems and often resulted in inconsistent quality, as they continuously researched, purchased and stored inventories of shirt materials, embroidery thread and coloured flag patches. This purchase process not only consumed a considerable amount of management time, but it also required elaborate inventory controls

EXHIBIT 7 Percentage of Retail Apparel Sales in Canada[3]

Region	Canada*	Mondetta
Quebec and Maritimes	33.9	2.0
Ontario	37.3	18.0
Manitoba/Saskatchewan	6.5	20.0
Alberta/British Columbia	22.2	60.0
Yukon/Northwest Territories	0.1	0.0

* Canadian sales data do not include department stores.

[3] Source: Statistics Canada: Catalogue 63-005, December 1991

EXHIBIT 8 Production Costs of Selected Products

World Flag Shirts	
Manufacturing Cost	$19.50
Applique	$7.50–$10.40
Labels, Tags	.26
Total Cost	$27.56–$30.16
World Flag T-Shirts	
Manufacturing Cost	$4.88
Embroidery	6.83
Bag, Tag, Labels	.78
Total Cost	$12.49
Call Letter Sweatshirt	
Manufacturing Cost	$20.93
Embroidery	10.73
Labels	.26
Total Costs	$31.92

* Canadian sales data do not include department stores.

[3] Source: Statistics Canada: Catalogue 63-005, December 1991

EXHIBIT 9 Comparison Of Local Versus Overseas Costs Of World Baseball Jersey

	Overseas	Local
Manufacturing Costs	$19.83	$31.85
Customs Duties (25% of cost)	4.96	0
Shipping Costs to Winnipeg	.39	0
	$25.18	$31.85
Commissions (10% of Mondetta selling price)	4.00	4.00
Total Cost	$29.73	$37.05
Mondetta Selling Price	$40.00	$40.00

and vast amounts of storage space. To alleviate the situation, management started to rely on their producers to source and produce clothing materials based on their specified quality standards. As a result, the brothers had more time to concentrate on company operations and design.

During the first two years of operations, Mondetta clothing was produced in Winnipeg by eight to ten medium sized clothing manufacturers. However, when the product's quick success raised producer demands, unit labour and material costs escalated, forcing management to search for offshore manufacturers in order to reduce production costs and increase production capacity. An agent was subsequently secured for Hong Kong through some well established industry contacts. Although offshore production created periodic quality control problems, the cost of wasted production was much less than the cost of local production. Exhibit 8 outlines Canadian production costs of the company's t-shirt and sweatshirts. Exhibit 9 presents a cost comparison of local versus offshore production of the company's t-shirts and indicates a 20% savings on every t-shirt produced abroad.

By 1992, approximately 40% of Mondetta's product line was produced in Hong Kong. While both local and offshore manufacturers had the capacity to produce approximately 10,000 t-shirts per month, shipment time for overseas production took an additional month. To avoid sales forecast misjudgments, Mondetta relied on pre-booked orders to trigger production with an additional 20–25% buffer inventory built into each order.

Imports from Hong Kong were highly dependent on a quota system whereby the Canadian government allowed a maximum number of goods to be imported annually from Hong Kong based on product type and category. After the appropriate quota had been determined, the Hong Kong government divided it among manufacturers who produced goods for Canadian companies. This system placed the burden on the manufacturer to find adequate quota to supply the desired amount requested by the Canadian importer. If quota was unavailable, the manufacturer had to purchase the desired amount from a quota market before beginning production.

Human Resources

Mondetta Clothing Company was managed by Ash, Prashant, Raj and Amit. The company also employed a customer service representative and a support staff of four people. Ash, Modha, Mondetta's President and Chief Executive Officer, was 23 years old and had just completed a Bachelor of Arts in Economics from the University of Manitoba. His brother, Prashant, aged 25, had completed a Bachelor of Science in 1988 and received a Master of Business Administration degree from the University of Manitoba in June 1991, Raj Bahl, also 25 years of age, had a Bachelor of Arts degree in Applied Economics from the University of Manitoba. His brother, Amit, attended the University of Winnipeg but chose to work instead.

The company had no structured hierarchy and the brothers operated in an informal team-oriented atmosphere. Internal communications and reporting structures were also not formally specified. Traditionally, day-to-day operations were completed by the most experienced and available person. Major operating decisions were given deliberate individual consideration before a consensus was reached. During crisis situations, decisions were made quickly after careful consideration of available alternatives.

Although responsibilities were not formally segmented, increased growth had started to create a more divisionalized approach to management. Ash and Raj were primarily responsible for the company's fashion designs. Ash also managed the company's production requirements while Raj was responsible for marketing and salesforce management. Prashant monitored the company's financial operations and Amit organized distribution, shipping and receiving.

Future Strategy

The four brothers were committed to the company's growth and were considering several growth opportunities such as expansion into the United States, further penetration into Eastern Canada, and licensing in western Europe.

Expand to the United States

The nature of the apparel industry demanded that management approach their American entry with caution in order to avoid unmanageable rapid acceptance or damaging product rejection. First, management had to consider which areas of the country to target. Exhibit 10 outlines American apparel consumption by region. Largely populated areas with the highest apparel consumption were the eastern states, while the northwestern states more closely resembled the Canadian market. In addition, the appropriate distribution channels and distribution strategy for market penetration and trend creation had to be determined. A geographic segmentation map of the United States and a breakdown of American department stores per region is presented in Exhibit 11.

The brothers also needed to determine suitable product selection and market penetration strategies. Since production in Manitoba would be insufficient for demand, apparel would have to be shipped directly from Hong Kong to the United States, requiring quota negotiations similar to those for Canada. The company's popular flagshirts and flag t-shirts could be made available for sale as well as its new product line which focused on the Mondetta name. Sales agent commissions would be approximately 10% of Mondetta's selling price and American retailers would

EXHIBIT 10 American Apparel Consumption by Region[4]

U.S./Canadian Region	Consumption
Northwest	4%
Southwest	12%
North Central (Midwest)	16%
South Central	14%
Northeast	39%
Southeast	15%

[4] *Source:* U.S. & Canadian Governments

EXHIBIT 11 — American Department Stores Segmented by Geographic Location[5]

Region	Western	Southcentral	Northcentral	Southeast	Northeast	Total
Bloomingdales	0	0	1	4	10	15
Bullocks	22	2	0	0	0	24
Macy's East	0	4	0	21	46	71
Macy's West	26	0	0	0	0	26
Macy's South	0	10	0	15	0	25
Lord & Taylor					majority	49
Nordstroms	27	0	3	0	25	55
Hechts	0	0	0	0	43	43
Marshall Field	0	2	22	0	0	24

[5] *Sheldon's Retail Directory by the United States and Canada, 1991.* Reproduced with permission from Phelon, Sheldon & Marsar, Inc.

likely demand a 50 to 60% product mark-up on cost. Some chains would also try to negotiate buy back options or replacement of non-selling styles and volume discounts. Annual travelling and other expenses were estimated around $5,000 to $10,000 (Canadian), while annual trade show expenses would be $25,000 for the summer Magic Show in Las Vegas. The Magic Show was one of the largest trade shows in America, attracting 52,000 agents, buyers and retailers.

American sales growth could not expand beyond $500,000 (Cdn) in the first year due to Mondetta's limited ability to handle rapid international growth. Profit margins would be similar to those earned in Canada since losses on export duties would likely be recovered with the currency exchange.

Continue Penetration into Eastern Canada

Consumer acceptance of Mondetta clothing in eastern Canada, particularly in Quebec, appeared slower than in western Canada. Mondetta's managers believed that slow sales in Quebec were due to poor product visibility created by inexperienced sales agents. In addition, retail sales in Quebec were controlled by large powerful buying groups. Established relationships with the buyers of these groups would be essential to product acceptance.

Although the company was experiencing healthy growth in Ontario, the Mondetta name was still relatively unknown in a large potential market. Management's biggest concern was Passport International's expansion to Toronto's Fairview mall where Mondetta was also sold. If necessary, mall advertising and billboards would cost approximately $6800 for six months.

Other marketing communications could also be used to speed up product exposure in both Ontario and Quebec. Economical advertisements such as point of purchase ads would cost approximately $25,000 per year. A Mondetta fashion catalogue could also be printed and distributed at an annual cost of $10–15,000. Advertising in the French version of Elle fashion magazine in Quebec would cost $7,000 per issue. Management wondered which forms of advertising should be purchased in eastern Canada, and what sales level would be required to break-even.

Pursue Licensing in Europe

Successful name licensing could create new product demand and expand brand name exposure in both the

United States and western Europe. Many well known names such as Guess Jeans and Buffalo Jeans were already licensed. Guess Jeans already had 22 licenses across the world while Buffalo was licensed in major European centres.

Through licensing, another company would be granted exclusive rights to manufacture, promote, distribute, and sell products using the Mondetta name with Mondetta designs or approved designs. The major advantage of licensing was widespread market penetration with minimal capital and financing requirements. There were also several risks. First, finding appropriate licensees could be difficult due to the required product specifications, quality and commitment. Second, licensees could demand that Mondetta handle the majority of product advertising. Third, a licensee could copy Mondetta's sample designs and sell clothing under a new brand name. The brothers hoped that careful selection of licensees would reduce the risks and were planning to attract licensees for kidswear, shoes and women's wear while continuing their main fashion designs and product lines.

The average license agreement was usually three years. During the three year term, the licensee would be required to pay a non-refundable initial license fee as well as an annual license fee. Initial and annual fees could range from $10,000 to $1,000,000 depending on the size and reputation of the licensee. Management hoped major licensees would generate $2 to 3 million in sales during their first year of operations. In each and every calendar year throughout the term, licensees would have to spend an average of 6% of sales to advertise and promote the apparel. In addition, a royalty of 8–10% of sales would be owed to Mondetta. Mondetta would also incur lawyers' fees and trademark costs for different geographic areas. For example, Canadian trademarks for "Mondetta Everywear" and "The Spirit of Unification" each cost approximately $1,500.

Decisions

Clearly, the task of determining where to take Mondetta Clothing Company was not an easy one. While the company's rapid market acceptance appeared to promise greater success in the future, further market penetration demanded careful consideration of alternatives before making the appropriate strategic decisions.

Case 20: Idéale Imprimerie

Well established as the leading printer in Morocco, Idéale Imprimerie is located in Casablanca, the country's commercial capital. In the spring of 1991, the management of Idéale identified an attractive opportunity for market expansion, namely, local production of wallpaper. Production of wallpaper would be within their field of expertise, and some evidence existed to suggest that this would be an important growth market in the future. The only problem appeared to be the lack of published data on consumer demand and purchasing patterns. This information would be necessary for decisions concerning production plant capacity, production scheduling, product lines, and distribution. Curious to know more about the feasibility of such a venture, the managing director of Idéale Imprimerie contacted the national business school, the Institut Supérieur de Commerce et d'Administration des Entreprises (ISCAE), for help in evaluating this new market.

The Company

Idéale Imprimerie is recognized as the leader in its sector for printing on both paper and cartons. With

---

This case is printed here with the permission of the author, Lyn S. Amine of St. Louis University.

its group of 175 employees, it dominates the sector not only by its size, but also by its reputation. Any reference in the business community to "Idéale" is immediately understood. Idéale's premises cover three times the surface area of its closest competitor, Belles Impressions. About fifteen other small printers compete in specific segments of the market, specializing in certain production processes, types of materials (e.g., billboards, handouts, letterhead stationery), or regions of the country.

Idéale was set up in 1975. The managing director, Maurice Pichot, is actively assisted by two working directors, Luigi Ghislanzoni and Mohamed Boukhari. This small team has the advantage of familiarity with the French market (Maurice), the Italian market (Luigi), and the local market (Mohamed). They are constantly on the lookout for new ideas that will give their company a competitive edge, in order to maintain their leadership position.

The Market Environment

Morocco is a Muslim Arab kingdom situated at the western end of the Mediterranean. Because Morocco was formerly a French protectorate (until 1956), the French influence still persists through use of the French language in business. Elsewhere, Moroccan Arabic is the everyday language. Topographically and politically Morocco is part of North Africa and a member of the "Maghreb" trading group composed of Morocco, Algeria, and Tunisia. Recent involvement in the war with Algeria over possession of the western Sahara has had serious repercussions on the Moroccan economy. Current national problems focus on management of the heavy burden of foreign debt. Long-term development objectives include maintenance of a free market economy directed by five-year plans; rapid modernization of the way of life (compatible with Islamic traditions); and the general emancipation of the people through education, health services, and equal employment opportunities. However, unemployment, under-employment, and illiteracy are major problems among a population of approximately 20 million, 50 percent of whom are under age 20.

The concept of marketing is steadily growing in significance in the business community. Instrumental factors include the presence of numerous multinational marketing companies (Nestlé, Unilever, Procter & Gamble, Ford, International Harvester—some of which are "Moroccanized" in name, ownership, and management); the existence of a university-level business school in Casablanca (ISCAE); and the activities of five major advertising agencies (Shem's, Univas, TOP, KLEM, Cinémapress) and one international marketing research agency (Middle East Marketing Research Bureau).

Notable characteristics of Moroccan business customs are:
- A relentless drive to preserve business and administrative secrecy at all levels
- A general fascination with novelty and innovation in all its forms
- Widespread and rapid imitation of successful new ideas

Marketing research activities of any type meet with much resistance, being considered an invasion of privacy by businesspeople and consumer alike. However, once successful inroads are made, then "me-too" activities will soon follow.

The Product Market

Traditionally homes in Morocco were built to the classic Arab model: single-family homes with two floors built around an open courtyard. Floors and walls are decorated by ceramic tiles, and ceilings are covered with wood carvings or stucco reliefs. Modern homes consist of villas with two floors or two-to three-bedroom condominium apartments for sale or rent. These modern homes represent the target market for wallpaper. From 1973 until the present time, nine importers were the sole source of wallpaper supply for the local market. Therefore, an opportunity for import substitution existed that would benefit from government support grants accorded to "infant" industries.

Idéale's initial research requirements specified items such as historical import data by value and volume, domestic sales records, discretionary income

Case 20: Idéale Imprimerie

TABLE 1 Summary of Calculation of Consumption of Wallpaper (by number of rolls; Years 1–11)

	Year 1	2	3	4	5	6	7	8	9	10	11
A	14,174	14,529	14,893	15,267	15,692	16,124	16,570	17,025	17,450	17,887	18,334
B = 20%A	2,834.8	2,905.8	2,978.6	3,053.4	3,138.4	3,224.8	3,314	3,405	3,490	3,577.4	3,666.8
$C = \frac{B}{A}$	566.96	581.16	595.72	610.68	627.68	644.96	662.80	681.0	698.0	715.48	733.3
D = 10%C	56.69	58.11	59.57	61.06	62.76	64.49	66.28	68.1	69.8	71.54	73.3
E = 25%D	14.17	14.52	14.89	15.26	15.69	16.12	16.57	17.02	17.45	17.88	18.3
F = E × 30	425.1	435.6	446.7	457.8	470.7	483.6	497.1	510.6	523.5	536.4	549.9
G	425,100	435,600	446,700	457,800	470,700	483,600	497,100	510,600	523,500	536,400	569,900

A = Population of Morocco in thousands.
B = Estimated one-fifth of the population with substantial purchasing power: *Libération.*
C = Estimate of five persons per household.
D = One-tenth of the population estimated responsible for the largest part of consumer expenditures: *Libération.*
E = Estimate of potential proportion of wallpaper purchasers (10 percent).
F = Estimated consumption of 30 rolls per household (in thousands): survey data.
G = Total estimated consumption by number of rolls.

by type of household (traditional or modern), home construction data, and general lifestyle data.

Marketing Research Efforts

Intensive searching by Ghislanzoni revealed four potentially useful sources of secondary data. However, all suffered from various deficiencies.

Import Statistics

Although recorded for ten years prior to the date of Idéale research, imports of wallpaper were recorded by weight (kgs) and value (thousands of dirhams). Wallpaper is sold by the roll, and different qualities and designs have different weights. Since the number of rolls was not specified, Idéale management could not even speculate on the number of "modern" households buying wallpaper over the past ten years.

Domestic Water-Heater Industry Study

This study was completed by the national economic development bank (BNDE) and offered two types of indirectly useful data, population growth statistics and annual home construction figures. The BNDE's objective was to determine the market for large, electric, domestic water heaters. Pichot and his colleagues considered it reasonable to assume that if a home featured this important "modern" convenience, then in all probability family lifestyle (along with home decorations) would also be more modern than for families in traditional homes. Consequently they thought these modern homes could be considered legitimate members, actual or potential, of the target market for wallpaper sales.

Boukhari had heard importers claim that the expected life of the product was five years. The "ballpark" figure for number of modern households (equal to the proxy market for water heaters) was therefore divided by five to establish a base number of assumed customer households per year. Population growth statistics of 5 percent per annum gave some indication of expected expansion rates of the total consumer market, but not specifically of the identified "modern" segment.

Study of the Potential Market for Locally Produced Wallpaper

Although of great apparent relevance, this research by the Office for the Development of Industry (ODI) proved virtually useless. As imports were recorded by weight, ODI researchers had calculated future de-

TABLE 2
Calculation of Consumption of Wallpaper Using Proxy Data (by number of rolls; Years 6–11)

	Year 6	7	8	9	10	11
A	6,444	7,546	9,986	11,612	12,462	14,297
B	35,051	35,051	35,051	35,051	35,051	41,495*
C = (A + B)	41,495	42,597	45,037	46,663	47,513	55,792
D = (C × 30)	1,244,850	1,277,910	1,351,110	1,399,890	1,425,390	1,673,760

A = Number of new homes equipped with a water heater: BNDE.
B = Number of existing homes equipped with a water heater, less an estimated 15 percent of traditional homes, spread equally over the five-year period to reflect assumed demand among established households.
C = Total number of estimated customer households.
D = Total estimated consumption by number of rolls, assuming thirty per household: survey data.
*Year 11 would be the first year of expected replacement purchases, assuming a product life of five years.

TABLE 3
Calculation of Imports of Wallpaper (by number of rolls; Years 1–11)

Year	Kilograms*	Dirhams (in Thousands)*	Rolls†
1	14,465	182	20,090
2	19,348	283	26,872
3	43,449	463	60,346
4	78,439	707	108,943
5	81,624	670	113,367
6	81,510	680	113,208
7	109,468	1,351	152,039
8	207,579	1,804	288,304
9	265,625	2,176	368,924
10	472,917	3,356	656,829
11	511,255	3,211	710,076

*Annuaires Statistiques des Importations, Dept. of Commerce, Morocco

†Weight per roll varies from 500 gm to 1300 gm, standard quality weight being 500 to 600 gm and deluxe quality 1200 to 1300 gm. A guesstimated average weight per roll of 720 gm was used to convert weight of imports into number of rolls.

mand per inhabitant also by weight. The study assumed that all consumers, traditional or modern, urban or rural, were potential customers with the result that the final weight per inhabitant was infinitesimal.

Income Distribution Study

Again, although of great apparent use, the propagandist nature of this study, entitled "Inequality for How Long?" and published by the local periodical *Libération*, made Pichot cautious in using these statistics. The study asserted that 6.54 percent of national income was owned by 20 percent of the population making up the "class A." Moreover, a mere 10 percent of class A was responsible for 37 percent of total consumer expenditure. Many members of class A would clearly be customers for wallpaper along with other luxury and status items. Pichot, Ghislanzoni, and Boukhari therefore assumed that the maximum size of the target market (in terms of individuals) would include this 20 percent of the national population. Making the further assumption of five persons per household, they were then able to estimate the

TABLE 4 Comparison of Estimated Values Calculated Using Proxy Data and Improvisation (Year 6–11)

	Year 6	7	8	9	10	11
Table 1	483,600	497,100	510,600	523,500	536,400	549,900
Table 2	1,244,850	1,277,910	1,351,110	1,399,890	1,425,390	1,673,760
Table 3	113,208	152,039	288,304	368,924	656,829	710,076
Average value	613,886	642,350	716,671	764,105	872,873	977,912
Percentage change	—	+4.6%	+11.6%	+6.6%	+14.2%	+12.0%

number of households in the target market.

Some informal visits to the showrooms of the nine importers by specially briefed staff members yielded the following lifestyle information:

- Consumers shop for wallpaper as a complementary decoration to fitted carpets (in place of traditional rugs) and modern living room and bedroom sets.
- Generally, the wife makes all decisions regarding quality and style.
- Customers are members of the upper class consisting of professional, technical, and commercial leaders and high-ranking administrators.
- Homes are modern and situated in the new and/or prestigious residential areas in Casablanca (whose estimated population is about 3 million).
- Average annual household consumption of wallpaper is about thirty rolls.

The Decision

Idéale's management turned over all these data to the marketing department at ISCAE. Recognizing that use of "guesstimates" and proxy data would not produce statistically reliable results, Pichot requested only a go/no go decision regarding the advisability of entering the wallpaper market as a local producer. What would you recommend as members of the marketing department at ISCAE?

Case 21: California Foods Corporation

In early 1990, the international marketing manager at California Foods Corporation (CFC), Lois Verbrugge, was considering how to react to the continuing decline of CFC grape juice sales in the Puerto Rican market. In 1989, the marketing staff in the international division estimated that sales of CFC grape juice had fallen off by approximately 30 percent from the previous year. To determine why this loss of volume had taken place, extensive consumer research was utilized. But, as of February, Ms. Verbrugge and her staff had not come up with any clear-cut remedies for CFC's problems in the Puerto Rican market.

Company Background

CFC was a wholly owned subsidiary of the Federation of Grape Growers' Associations. The federation purchased the California Foods Corporation in 1956 as part of a strategy to integrate its business forward into the processing and distribution of grape products. CFC continued in 1990 to operate as an agribusiness largely as it had in 1956. The federation supplied the grapes, and CFC handled all processing and marketing of the products. CFC's sales had increased every year since the takeover by the federation. CFC was generally considered the foremost leader in the juice industry. It set the standards for progressive marketing techniques and new product development for the industry. With sales reaching a quarter billion dollars in 1989, the growers and CFC were the largest grape growing, processing, and marketing enterprise in the world.

Originally, CFC had produced only grape-related products: grape jams, grape jelly, frozen grape concentrate, grape drink, and grape preserves. In recent years, however, CFC had expanded to include non-grape products, too. Between 1970 and 1982, CFC introduced thirty-six new products. In 1990, CFC incorporated a complete line of fruit juices with a selection of fruit drinks and a line of fruit-flavored preserves.

CFC's International Division

CFC distributed an assortment of products to foreign markets with the majority of sales derived from juices and fruit drinks. It marketed its products to over forty countries. Major markets included Puerto Rico, Mexico, and Japan. CFC products were distributed by food brokers and distributors to retail stores and food service institutions. In 1988, the International Division experienced record sales and greater than expected profitability. Sales slipped slightly during 1989, largely the result of sales erosion in the Puerto Rican market.

The Juice and Drinks Market in Puerto Rico

Most of the juice consumption in Puerto Rico was composed of imported products. Some of the more popular brands competing for market share were CFC, Seneca, Pueblo, and Grand Union. There was only one domestic grape juice producer, selling under the name Richy. Richy had been in business for a few years, but its impact on the market had been minimal. Table 1 outlines the imported volumes of juices and drinks into Puerto Rico over the last three years. As the table reveals, grape juice imports (California Foods' and others) were declining rather sharply. Still, the grape juice market was by far the largest juice market in Puerto Rico.

The "fruit drink" category was quite large too and was growing, especially the miscellaneous/all-others subgroup, which included Tang's imported powdered grape and orange drinks. Because many Puerto Ricans equated powdered grape with grape juice, it was possible that at least some of CFC grape juice's volume loss could be traceable to these imports, although no hard evidence existed.

Frozen concentrates represented another competing group that was large and had shown strong growth in the preceding three years. Again, the miscellaneous/all-others subgroup had shown steady growth. Perhaps some of CFC grape juice's loss could be attributable to a shift of sales across generic categories.

CFC's Entry into Puerto Rico

CFC's first experience in Puerto Rico came in the 1950s when it introduced CFC grape juice. At that point, grape juice was practically unheard of by the majority of Puerto Ricans. Despite this, the introduction was a resounding success and CFC grape juice became the best-selling juice in Puerto Rico.

Rumour had it that CFC grape juice's success was traceable to the Puerto Rican belief that grape juice was good for men's virility and for women's hemoglobin during their menstrual cycles. Pseudomedicinal drinks were concocted by mixing egg with grape juice. The resulting mixture was referred to as an "egg punch." To take advantage of this seemingly unique consumer behavior, CFC launched an "egg punch" campaign in 1985. One television spot showed a young Puerto Rican man at a disco drinking an egg punch and subsequently departing with an attractive young woman. Print advertising featured a mother nursing her newborn and copy expounding the nutritional value of grape juice.

Grape juice was indeed CFC's biggest seller in Puerto Rico. Sales for 1989 were 412,000 cases. Frozen concentrated grape juice accounted for sales of 32,000 cases during 1989. Other CFC products were Calfood fruit drink, California instant powdered grape drink, CFC grape soda, and CFC strawberry soda.

TABLE 1
Juices and Drinks Imported into Puerto Rico

	Thousands Of Cases (not Equivalents)			Percent Of Change
	1987	1988	1989	1988–1989
Fruit juices				
Vegetable juice	20.6	23.4	23.9	+2.1
Tomato juice	45.5	21.2	26.3	+24.6
Apple juice	84.5	109.0	105.6	–3.1
Citrus juice	203.5	198.7	183.4	–7.7
Nectars	—	5.0	1.8	–64.0
Pineapple juice	22.5	22.9	29.1	+27.1
Prune juice	25.8	23.3	29.5	+26.6
Grape juice-CFC	569.1	586.5	412.1	–29.7
Grape juice-other	40.6	37.1	26.6	–28.3
Fruit drinks				
RJR	114.1	161.0	116.3	–27.8
Borden*	92.9	124.4	132.6	+6.6
Miscellaneous/all others†	260.5	296.4	356.0	+20.4
Fruit juice—frozen and concentrated				
Citrus Central	184.8	236.6	219.5	–7.2
CFC	34.4	23.4	32.5	+33.2
Miscellaneous/all others	378.1	431.5	499.8	+15.8

*Includes Orange Burst instant breakfast drink, Wyler's ades.

†Includes Tang powdered grape and orange drinks.

Source: Maritime Reports (Washington, D.C.: U.S. Government Printing Office, 1990).

Consumer Research

In order to ascertain the causes for CFC's rapid decline in grape juice sales, an "Awareness, Usage, and Attitude Study" was compiled in February 1990 to update the marketing department's understanding of Puerto Rican grape juice consumers. Two hundred personal interviews were done with people who had used grape juice during the previous two years. The study was administered by a Puerto Rican consulting group. Results are listed in Table 2.

The results of the study showed that the demand for orange juice had increased tremendously since 1988. Both current and previous study users of CFC grape juice were drinking much more orange juice by 1990. In addition, the percentage of respondents who did not use orange juice was practically nil.

Current users of CFC juice continued to drink large quantities of grape juice, as the figures reveal. In fact, 86 percent of all CFC users said that they drank as much, or more, grape juice in 1989 as they had previously. However, among the previous CFC users, there were many more who had decreased their consumption of grape juice than had increased it. Therefore, it was implied that they were not switching from one grape juice brand to another, but drinking more orange juice instead. Over 57 percent of previous CFC users drank more orange juice by 1990 than they had in early 1988.

The main motive for the purchase of grape juice by mothers in the sample was because their children had asked for and/or liked it. The study also revealed

TABLE 2 Consumption Results of Sample of Puerto Rican Grape Juice Users During 1988 and 1989

Juices	Previous Users (n = 45)				Current CFC Users (n = 155)			
	More	The Same	Less	Don't Use	More	The Same	Less	Don't Use
Orange	57.7%	28.9%	11.1%	2.3%	43.5%	42.2%	11.7%	2.6%
Grape	13.3	37.8	24.5	24.5	38.9	47.4	13.0	0.7
Pineapple	22.2	26.7	33.3	17.8	23.3	29.9	31.1	15.7
Grapefruit	15.6	11.1	51.2	22.1	5.2	16.9	45.4	32.5
Fruit drinks	17.7	20.0	33.5	26.8	13.6	29.2	23.3	33.9
Fruit nectar	20.0	35.6	26.7	17.7	13.6	30.5	30.5	25.4
Powdered drinks	31.1	17.8	24.4	26.7	9.1	32.5	34.4	24.0

that Puerto Ricans perceived grape juice to be both tasty and nutritious. On the negative side, respondents who were buying less grape juice had a variety of reasons for not buying it; most notably, very high price and preference for other juices were mentioned.

It was discovered that previous CFC users replaced grape juice with three other types of beverages: other canned juices (pineapple, orange, grapefruit), natural juices (orange, grapefruit, tamarind, lemon), and carbonated drinks (Pepsi, Coca-Cola, and the like).

Researchers had asked the question "Why aren't you using more CFC grape juice?" The most frequent response indicated that CFC's price was too high and that the respondents tried to buy products that were more economical. Secondary reasons suggested that they did not like the taste and preferred other flavors to grape. Table 3 summarizes consumers' reasons for buying either less or no grape juice in general and of CFC's in particular.

CFC had performed a similar consumer study in 1985 to determine grape juice drinkers' attitudes toward CFC grape juice. One section of the 1985 questionnaire involved consumers' opinions of the characteristics of CFC grape juice. Likewise, part of

TABLE 3 Respondents' Reasons for Not Buying Grape Juice

	Reasons for No Longer Serving Grape Juice	Reasons for No Longer Serving CPC Grape Juice
High price	22.6%	23.2%
Only use it occasionally	9.7	4.4
Prefer other flavors	29.0	22.2
Harmful to stomach/diet	12.9	10.3
Prefer natural juices	16.1	6.7
Not accustomed to using it	n.a.	8.9
Prefer powdered drinks	n.a.	8.7
Other	9.7	15.6
Total	100.0%	100.0%

the 1990 survey was devoted to similar questioning. In both studies, respondents rated CFC grape juice on the basis of eight criteria, on a scale from 1 to 6. The figures in Table 4 represent average ratings for each of the product characteristics.

Both studies seemed to suggest that CFC grape juice had been, and still was, well regarded in the Puerto Rican market. There had not been too much change in the general opinion that CFC grape juice was a good-tasting, nutritious, high-quality product. In consumers' minds even the price had become more reasonable in relation to the generally stormy economic conditions. So, what seems to be the problem with CFC grape juice in the Puerto Rican market?

The study data appear to support the notion that CFC grape juice is held in high esteem in Puerto Rico, yet a solution to CFC's sales problem is needed. With this in mind, Ms. Verbrugge arranged a meeting with Jeff Hartman, Market Research Manager, to discuss and review the situation. Ms. Verbrugge wanted to examine the problem in more detail and was prepared to commit additional funds for marketing research. Before making any decision, however, she wanted Mr. Hartman's assessment of the situation.

TABLE 4 Averaged Ratings of CFC Grape Juice (Scale of 1 to 6)

	1990 Study (n = 200)	1985 Study (n = 200)
Sweetness	4.95	3.96
Taste	4.96	4.73
Economy	3.86	3.47
Nutrition	5.06	5.24
Naturalness	4.91	5.05
Best for children	4.97	4.92
Best for adults	4.88	4.74
Quality	5.13	5.17

Case 22: Chivaly International

In early 1991, Martin Creich, product manager for Chivaly International's urethane foam product division, was considering a recommendation that the firm establish a regional sales office in Singapore. Since marketing its products in Indonesian markets in 1984, Chivaly had captured 10 percent of the urethane foam market. By establishing a sales office in Singapore, Creich could foresee increasing the Indonesian market share for Chivaly's urethane foam to 25 percent and expanding into Malaysian and Thai markets. In addition, a regional sales office would strengthen Chivaly's competitive posture, allowing the firm to conduct sales directly to distributors and commission agents.

Before presenting his recommendations to top management, Creich wanted to compile necessary information to support his decision.

Chivaly Corporation

Chivaly was a major manufacturer of chemicals, metals, flax-based papers, cellophane, sports equipment, and home building products. Incorporated in South Dakota in 1892, the firm had since established its executive offices in Oklahoma City.

Urethane foam, a part of the chemical division, had been marketed since 1949 and was one of the world's most adaptable products. It was used primarily as cushioning material in chairs, beds, spring mattresses, auto upholstery, and other products that needed foam cushioning. As a result of the product's adaptability, its major chemical component, tuluene duso cyanate (TDI), had become one of the world's largest chemical commodities. Chivaly was also a large producer of TDI, supplying the chemical division with adequate proportions of the commodity for urethane foam production.

Urethane foam was produced for the firm's worldwide markets in two plants located in Lake Charles, Louisiana, and in Mansville, West Virginia. Each plant separately produced more than 50,000 tons of urethane foam per year. Production inefficiencies resulted if either plant fell below the standard 50,000-ton level.

From a process standpoint, urethane foam was a difficult chemical to produce. The product's toxic and lethal components made production and process controls vital steps in manufacturing. Orders were shipped directly from each plant to Chivaly's distributors throughout the world.

International Markets

In 1990, approximately 16 percent of Chivaly's $2 billion in sales were derived from international markets. By 2000, the company planned to obtain a significant portion of its sales and profits from its overseas businesses. Management believed that investing substantial sums of capital to establish sales offices around the world would help the firm strengthen its international presence. Chivaly already had established offices in Mexico City, Caracas, Dublin, London, Paris, Frankfurt, Johannesburg, Madrid, Cape Town, and Sydney.

Chivaly's entry into specific foreign markets was a result of thorough market analyses. Specifically, the firm performed market profiles and market attractiveness analyses that considered pertinent factors such as target markets, resource requirements, cultural factors, and personnel requirements. After such basic information had been gathered, corporate representatives then traveled to the targeted countries to meet with regional sales representatives, who helped gather further information based on questionnaires distributed to local contacts. The corporate representatives then used this information to formulate a final area profile with analyses and recommendations, eventually determining which markets were most attractive. This process determined which consumers, commission agents, and distributors were to be used if the market proved profitable.

Indonesian Operations

Chivaly entered the Indonesian market in 1984, selling urethane foam on a freight alongside basis through a Japanese trading company. The trading company, in turn, sold the urethane to local companies in Indonesia. Chivaly's entry into the Indonesian market was haphazard. Initially, the firm knew nothing about the market or how their product was sold. As Chivaly's Indonesian operation grew, the firm established sales representatives in the region, providing a direct link to the market.

The Indonesian market was heavily influenced by corruption. Indonesians expected "royalty payments" in exchange for special treatment and favors. Chivaly representatives, however, had been instructed to refrain from participating in these payments. To avoid this situation, Chivaly sought clients whose executives were American-educated and familiar with Western business procedures.

Indonesia's cultural environment also restricted the way foreign firms could do business. For example, Indonesians preferred to do business with local people; therefore, Chivaly hired a large number of local people as sales representatives.

Chivaly also sold its urethane foam through local distributors. Sales were volume oriented, and long-term business relationships were valued more than short-term profits. Because American companies concentrated on profits, firms would often lose their distributors and commission agents. Asians also refused to wage price wars and, more often than not, refused to sell any product at a price higher than that of their competitors.

Indonesia had few political constraints; however, Chivaly was prohibited from opening regional offices in the country unless a majority of the subsidiary was owned by nationals. Chivaly also was prevented from purchasing and stockpiling urethane foam in local warehouses, which was a major factor in establishing an office in Singapore. As a free-trade zone, Singapore adopted a laissez-faire attitude toward free enterprise.

Chivaly's major Indonesian competitor was the German firm Bayer. Chivaly also competed on a smaller scale with Dow Chemical and BASF. There was little product differentiation among these suppliers. Factors that provided the competitive edge included service, local relationships, and the strength of letters of credit.

Bayer was the largest producer of urethane in the world, while Chivaly ranked second. As the first company to enter the Indonesian urethane foam market, Bayer had captured roughly 45 percent of the Indonesian market, with sales of over 7,500 tons of urethane.

Bayer's German production facilities provided the firm with huge production capacity and economies of scale. The firm used its extensive distribution network to distribute its full line of urethane foam chemical components to Indonesian markets. However, Bayer did not adapt to cultural factors. Sales representatives maintained a strict European attitude in business affairs, which proved a handicap in Indonesia.

There was little advertising in the urethane foam business. Sales were made strictly through sales contacts. Prices were based on open market demand. In 1990, the price for urethane foam components was $1,550 a ton.

Competitors often mislabeled chemicals for shipment to get cheaper freight rates. Because TDI was a Poison B chemical that caused several health hazards, the word *Tylene* was often painted over the TDI label in Indonesia. Tylene was a comparatively harmless chemical and could be shipped at lower freight rates. Chivaly made sure its products were always represented in the correct manner.

By 1990, Chivaly had captured 10 percent of the Indonesian market, but management believed they were underpricing their product. To combat its price problem, Chivaly wanted to achieve two objectives: (1) to sell 4,000 tons of TDI and (2) to increase its urethane foam market share to 25 percent. Management felt that the Singapore office would fulfill these objectives.

PART · 5

International Marketing Decisions

CHAPTER · 12

Product Policy and Planning

CHAPTER FOCUS

After studying this chapter, you should be able to:

■ Discuss the perspectives of international product planning

■ Debate the pros and cons of following standardization versus customization of product in overseas markets

■ Describe various aspects of new product introduction in international markets

■ Explain the factors that affect global adoption and diffusion of new products

■ Compare various branding alternatives for international markets

■ Examine the role of international product warranties and services

The product decision is among the first decisions that a marketing manager makes in order to develop a marketing mix. Traditionally, product decision in international marketing simply has meant exporting products already produced and marketed in the U.S. In the future, and even now, such a simple perspective on product policy will not work. Today, U.S. companies face strong competition from European and Japanese companies, as well as from newly industrialized countries and Third World nations. At the same time, foreign markets have become more sophisticated and an American product may not be acceptable any longer simply because it is an American product.

Thus, the product decision must be made on the basis of careful analysis and review. The nature, depth, and breadth of the product line; the possibilities of new product development and product innovation; the importance attached to product design (the adaptation and customization of products to suit local conditions vis-à-vis standardization); the decision on foreign R&D; and a planned screening and elimination of unsuccessful products bear heavily on success in foreign markets.

This chapter examines these product-related issues and suggests conceptual approaches for handling them. Also discussed are international packaging and labeling matters, international brand strategy, and warranty and service policies.

Meaning of Product

Products are all around us, and yet it is not easy to define precisely what a product is. The difficulty is that the same product may have a different significance for people in different countries. A refrigerator is a necessity in the U.S. because people tend to depend on a variety of frozen foods and weekly shopping. In Mexico, however, as in other developing countries, food shopping most commonly occurs on a daily basis. A refrigerator there is a luxury for the rich to store either leftovers or perishable foods for a short time.

A definition of *product*, thus, must be comprehensive in order to serve an operational purpose. A product can be defined as a bundle of attributes that satisfies a customer demand. It may be offered in the form of a tangible item, a service, or an idea. For example, the attributes of a wine are flavor, taste, consistency, and its quality as a thirst quencher or cool refreshment. Different wines have different attributes, and each brand is intended to meet the demands of a particular set of target customers. Likewise, the attributes of a corporate jet plane are width of cabin, fuel economy, flight range, speed, and noise level. Businesspersons around the world would prefer different sets of attributes in choosing a plane for their use.

Putting it differently, customers do not simply buy products in the physical sense, they buy *satisfaction*, which is derived from the product's attributes, various features, and characteristics. This fact has important ramifications in defining product objectives.

A company can offer different versions of the same product and thus broaden its product line by catering to the needs of heterogeneous segments of the market. In the U.S., the Coca-Cola Company is a *full-line* soft drink manufacturer producing Classic Coke, New Coke, Diet Coke, Sprite, Minute Maid, and other soft drinks to cater to the needs of different target groups. Outside the U.S., the company offers just Coca-Cola in most countries. Thus, the Coca-Cola Company is considered a full-line manufacturer at home, but a limited-line manufacturer internationally.

International Product Planning

International product planning involves determining which products to introduce into which countries; what modifications to make in the products; what new products to add; what brand names to use; what package designs to use; what guarantees and warranties to give; what after-sales services to offer; and finally, when to enter the market. All these are crucial decisions requiring a variety of informational inputs. Chapter 10 on marketing research specifies different ways and sources for gathering appropriate information. Basic to these decisions are three other considerations (1) product objectives, (2) coordination of product planning activities between headquarters and subsidiary, and (3) foreign collaboration.

The process of product planning in the international context is diagrammed in Figure 12.1. A company interested in an international market should first define its business intent based on the objectives of both the corporation and the host country. The product objectives of a company would flow from the definition of its business.

FIGURE 12.1 Perspectives of International Product Planning

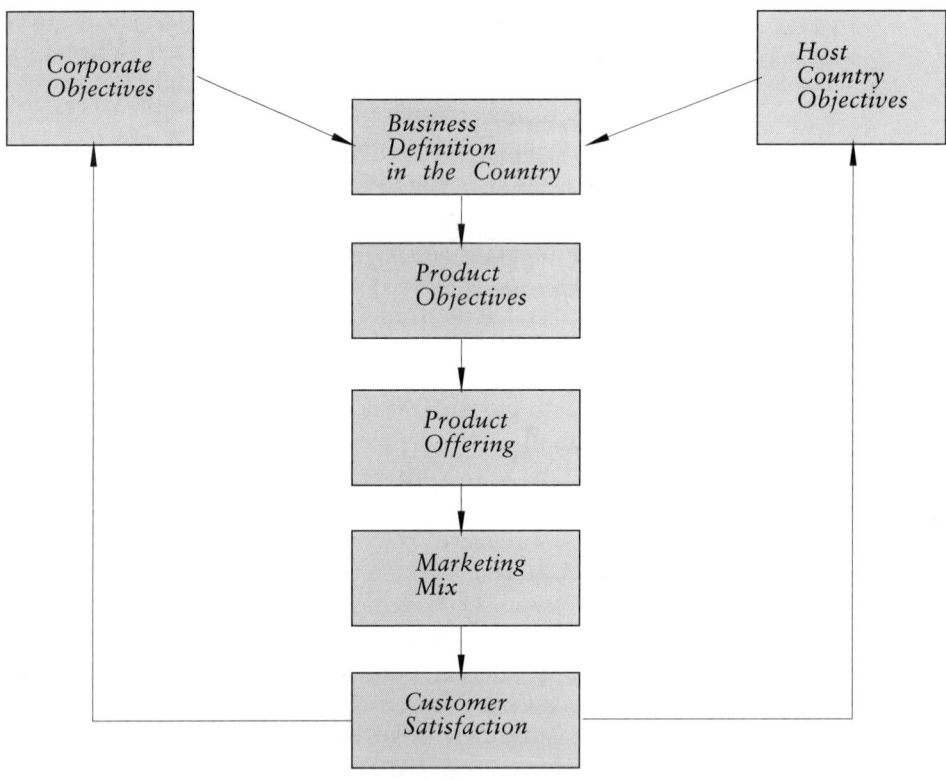

Product Objectives   Product objectives emerge from host country and corporate objectives combined via the business definition. The company's goals usually are *stability*, *growth*, *profits*, and *return on investment*. Stated differently, the corporate objectives may be defined in terms of *activities* (the manufacture of a specific product, or export to a particular market), *financial indicators* (to achieve a targeted return on investment), *desired position* (its market share and relative market leadership), and all these in combination with each other. The parent company usually also has a series of objectives on behalf of the various *stakeholders' interests* for which it is accountable. Host country objectives vary depending on the country's economic, political, and cultural environment. For example, the typical goals of a less-developed country would be to seek faster economic growth, to build a balanced industrial sector, to create employment opportunities, and to earn foreign exchange. On the other hand, the objectives of an oil-rich country might be to provide a modern living standard to its masses in a short time without disrupting the cultural structure of its society and/or to diversify its economy to reduce its dependence on oil over the long term.

Obviously, the objectives of the host country and the company are poles apart. In any emerging market worldwide, however, no company can hope to succeed without aligning itself with the national concerns of the host country. There are no models to use in seeking a description of such an alignment. Conceptually, however, a macroanalysis of a country's socioeconomic perspectives should provide insights into its different concerns and problems. The company can then figure out if its business would help the country in any way, directly or indirectly. The business definition should then be developed accordingly. For example, the shortage of foreign exchange might be a big problem for a country. A multinational marketer's willingness to pursue a major effort of export promotion in the country would amount to an objective in line with the country's need. On the other hand, a company simply interested in manufacturing and selling such consumer goods as toiletries and canned foods, in a nation that is interested in establishing a basic infrastructure for industrial development in the country, may not be serving the national interest.

The definition of product objectives should emerge from the business definition. Product objectives can be defined in physical or marketing terms. "We sell instant coffee" is an example of defining objectives in physical terms. In marketing terms, the objective statement would emphasize the satisfaction of a customer need. The latter method is preferred because it reinforces the marketing concept.

To illustrate the point, assume that Maytag is interested in establishing a plant for manufacturing washing machines and dryers in Egypt. The product objectives may be defined in the following manner:

- *Maytag corporate objective.* Earn a minimum of 25 percent return on investment in any developing country.

- *Egypt's national concerns.* Create employment opportunities and build up faltering foreign exchange balances.

- *Business definition.* Establish a large appliance plant in Egypt to compete effectively in the Middle East.
- *Product definition.* Meet the laundry needs of the masses.

Product Planning

The perspectives of international product planning can be categorized between issues of day-to-day concern on the one hand and strategic issues on the other. The day-to-day issues arise in implementing decisions already made. For example, following up on the Maytag example, an issue may arise concerning the need for extra precautions to be taken to protect working washers and dryers from dust. This issue applies only to the Middle East market where the climate requires that windows be open all the time, and where the winds carry a lot of dust into the houses. The issue would be handled appropriately by local managers. If any specific technological help is needed, it would be sought from the parent corporation on an ad hoc basis.

Strategic issues require major commitments, which must be taken up with the parent corporation. For example, using the Maytag illustration, the question might be raised whether motors for the appliances should be imported from Maytag in the U.S. or from a relatively new Japanese subsidiary located in Egypt. Another strategic question could arise with reference to trading with a country that is not on friendly terms with the U.S. Let us assume Egypt does a lot of trade with Libya. Assume further that the U.S. has a trade embargo against Libya. Will it be all right for the Maytag subsidiary in Egypt to export the appliances to Libya in view of the U.S. government's trade embargo? Strategic questions cannot be handled by subsidiary management alone and must be referred to the parent organization.

It is difficult to accumulate an inventory of decisions to label as day-to-day or strategic. It all depends on the individual situation. The subsidiary management must decide if the matter involved is strategic enough to require input from or a decision by the parent. At the risk of overgeneralization, an issue/matter/decision can be considered strategic:

- If the U.S. government comes into the picture
- If substantial investment needs to be made
- If previously agreed-upon arrangements would be overturned by a decision
- If long-term financial interests of the parent are affected
- If the host government appears to be imposing regulations that might affect the long-term survival of the company
- If technical problems have arisen that cannot be handled locally
- If certain accusations have been made against the subsidiary that could flare up in labor trouble or have other ramifications

In addition to ad hoc problems which may be day-to-day or strategic, the parent should require inputs in the form of the subsidiary's plans. Product planning for established product lines and plans for the development and marketing of new product lines would then be prepared by each host country/geographic area and separately submitted to corporate management for approval.

Foreign Collaboration/ Investment

Often international businesses seek foreign collaboration in order to enter world markets. Such collaboration may take shape in a licensing agreement or in a joint venture with a business in the host country. Traditionally, the concept of foreign collaboration has been explained with reference to the international product life cycle. As discussed in Chapter 2, essentially this has meant that U.S. exports dominate the world market, and then the producers from other developed countries become increasingly competitive, first in their markets and then in third-country markets, and finally in the U.S. market. The cycle may be repeated with successive challenges from producers in less-developed countries.

In theory, a U.S. corporation should seek foreign collaboration in the third and fourth stages of the international product life cycle; that is, when it is competitively more desirable to produce abroad and compete effectively in foreign markets, as well as in the U.S., through importing from the foreign source. The theory would work if worldwide markets were perfect. This, of course, is not so. Host governments insist on establishing plants even when the plants are not economic propositions in the international context. For example, a country may opt for a steel mill although it can import steel from a neighboring country much more economically. In brief, market imperfections brought about by tariff and nontariff barriers intrude upon the practical application of theory. As a matter of fact, in some industries, such as the automobile industry, the theory may fail because investment requirements at the third and fourth stages are tremendous. Thus, we should not expect auto industries to move from Japan and Europe to emerging developing countries.

An international marketer can still seek foreign collaboration by producing a specialized product in another country in order to take advantage of the peculiar strengths of that country. For example, labor in some nations is cheap, particularly in most developing countries. Some other countries have a big pool of scientific talent—India, for example. By collaborating with a foreign company to produce and/or distribute a product, a multinational marketer can gain competitive leverage.

Coca-Cola Company's recent collaboration with Nestlé S.A. of Switzerland illustrates the point. The two companies have undertaken a multimillion dollar effort to market canned coffee, either warm or cold, to Koreans. If the effort succeeds, the Coca-Cola Nestlé Refreshments Co. would roll out Nescafé canned coffee through Asia, Europe, and the U.S.[1]

Product Design Strategy

An important question that multinational marketers need to answer is whether the same product approach will be adequate in foreign markets. In other words, a decision must be made about which is the more appropriate of two product design strategies—standardization or customization. *Standardization* means offering a common product on a national, regional, or worldwide basis. *Customization* means adaptation, that is, making appropriate changes in a product to match local perspectives. On the one hand, the environmental differences between nations abroad are great. The degree of difference recommends product customization or adaptation over standardization in order to cater to the unique situation in each country. On the other hand, there are potential gains to consider in product standardization.[2] International marketers must examine all the criteria in order to decide the extent to which products should vary from country to country.

Decision Criteria

Whether to standardize or to customize is a vexing question with which international marketers have long wrestled. It is simple enough to figure out the rationale for standardization. Nothing new needs to be done to make the offering ready for any market. The literature, however, is full of illustrations showing how standardization has led to complete market failure. General Electric Company's debacle in the small appliance field in Germany and Polaroid's difficulties with the Swinger camera in France are classic examples. At the same time, Volkswagen's success worldwide with the Beetle supports standardization. Excessive concern with local customization can be troublesome, too. Holland's Philips Company learned the hard lesson that it cannot afford to customize TVs for each European market separately. Standardization became necessary to obtain R&D and manufacturing efficiencies.[3] Because neither strategy alternative is superior on its merits, certain criteria can be used instead to determine if adaptation would be desirable and, if so, to what extent.[4]

Nature of Product Research on the subject shows that foreign product design strategy varies with the nature of the product. More standardization is feasible in the case of industrial goods than for consumer goods. Among consumer goods, nondurables require greater customization than durables, because nondurable consumer goods appeal to tastes, habits, and customs. These traits are unique to each country; therefore, adaptation becomes significant. An alternative to customization, however, is to limit the target market to a small identifiable segment.

Market Development Different national markets for a given product are in different stages of development. A convenient way of explaining this phenomenon is through the product life cycle concept. Products go through several life cycle stages over a period of time, and in each stage different marketing strategies are appropriate. The four stages usually identified in the life cycle of a product are introduction, growth, maturity, and decline.

If a product's foreign market is in a different stage of market development than its U.S. market, appropriate changes in the product design become desirable in order to make an adequate product/market match. The claim is that Polaroid's Swinger camera failed in France because the company pursued the same strategy there as in the U.S., when the two markets were in different stages of development. The U.S. market was in the mature stage, while the French market was in the introductory stage.[5]

Even within a country one segment may be ready for a standardized product, while the product must be appropriately adapted for other segments. For example, Hill and Still found that products targeted to urban markets in less-developed countries need only minimal changes from those marketed in developed countries. On the other hand, the rural markets in LDCs require greater adaptation.[6]

Cost-Benefit Relationship Product adaptation to match local conditions involves costs. These costs may relate to R&D, physical alteration of the product's design, style, features, changes in packaging, brand name, performance guarantee, and the like. As far as standardization is concerned, no R&D is required since manufacturing technology and quality control procedures have been established. Performance has been tested and improved. In brief, standardization brings certain cost savings. One important cost, however, that standardization may involve and that is difficult to quantify is opportunity cost. If the product is customized, presumably it would have a greater appeal to the mass market in the host country. Thus, to determine whether adaptation would be in order, a cost–benefit analysis in terms of what it would cost to customize and what benefits may be expected in the form of market growth must be undertaken. The cost–benefit analysis should then be compared with the growth and profitability that would result from standardization. The net difference should indicate the relative desirability of seeking product adaptation.

Legal Requirements Different countries have different laws about product standards, patent laws, and tariffs and taxes. These laws may require product adaptation. For example, in Europe the 220-volt electrical system is used. This has led European governments to set stringent safety standards for such products as irons—cord connections must be stronger, radio interference must be shielded, and so on.[7] Likewise, foreign auto manufacturers must adapt their cars for export to the U.S. because of the U.S. government safety standards and emission control requirements (see International Marketing Highlight 12.1).

International Marketing Highlight 12.1

Oh, How Life Would Be Easier if We Only Had a Europlug

Those of you who have traveled Europe know of the frustration of electrical plugs, different electrical voltages, and other annoyances of international travel. But consider the cost to consumers and the inefficiency of production for a company that wishes to sell electrical appliances in the European "common" market.

Philips, the electrical appliance manufacturer, has to produce twelve kinds of irons to serve just its European market. The problem is that Europe does not have a universal standard. The ends of irons bristle with different plugs for different countries. Some have three prongs, others two; prongs protrude straight or angled, round or rectangular, fat, thin, and sometimes sheathed. There are circular plug faces, squares, pentagons, and hexagons. Some are perforated and some are notched. One French plug has a niche like a keyhole; British plugs carry fuses.

Europe's plugs and sockets are balkanized partly because different countries have different voltages and cycles. But the variety of standards also has other causes, such as protecting local manufacturers. The estimated cost of the lack of universal standards is between $60 billion and $80 billion a year, or nearly 3 percent of the EC's total output of goods and services.

Source: *The Wall Street Journal*, August 7, 1985, p. 1.

Competition In the absence of current and potential competition, a company may continue to do well in a market overseas with a standard product. However, the presence of competition may require customization to gain an advantage over the rivals by providing a product that ultimately matches local conditions. For example, the firms from the newly industrializing countries of Asia successfully compete by rapidly adapting their products to changing markets and adopting more innovative product strategies. In this way the MNCs from these countries are able to gain leverage against the MNCs from the industrialized countries. Thus, the latter must anticipate and understand market requirements better than ever and appropriately adapt their products to be competitive.

Traditionally, Kodak could get away by selling a standard film globally because it was so rich, efficient, and powerful. However, with changing competitive conditions, Kodak cannot succeed with parochial attitudes. It is not the only company in the market anymore. Now, for instance, Kodak sells film in Japan with the ruddier flesh tones preferred by the Japanese.[8]

Support System The support system refers to institutions and functions that are necessary to create, develop, and service demand. These include retailers, wholesalers, sales agents, warehousing, transportation, creditors and media. The availability, performance, and cost of the support system profoundly affect the product design strategy. For example, frozen foods cannot be marketed in countries where retailers do not have facilities with freezers. The point can be illustrated by a reference to Lever Brothers' attempts to introduce packaged foods in developing countries. In the absence of refrigeration facilities at the retail level (as well as in homes), the frozen vegetables could not be introduced. The company, therefore, developed and sold a line of dehydrated vegetables such as peas, carrots, and beans in countries like India, Pakistan, Thailand, and the Philippines.

Physical Environment The physical conditions of a country (i.e., climate, topography, and resources) may also require product adaptation. For example, such products as air conditioners in a hot climate, as in the middle East, require additional features for satisfactory performance. Differences in the size and configuration of homes affect product design for appliances and home furnishings. European kitchens are usually smaller than U.S. kitchens. Further, European homes generally do not have basements. Thus, compactness of design in such appliances as washers and dryers is a necessity since they must be accommodated within a crowded area.

Market Conditions Cultural differences, economic prosperity, and customer perceptions in the foreign country would also influence the decision to adapt a product. The British prefer a slightly more bitter taste in soup than Americans do. This required the Campbell Soup Company to modify soup ingredients in Britain to cater to the local taste. To cater to local taste in Japan, Domino's offers pizza with such toppings as chicken teriyaki, apple, rice, and corn.[9] The masses in many countries cannot afford the variety of products that U.S. consumers consider essential. To bring such products as automobiles and appliances within the reach of the middle class in developing countries, for example, the products must be appropriately modified to cut costs without reducing functional quality. Finally, foreign products in many cultures are perceived as high-quality products. In such cases, standardization would be desirable. On the other hand, if the image of a country's products is weak, it would be strategically desirable to adapt a product so that it could be promoted as a different, rather than typical, product of the country. For example, U.S. automobiles are considered substandard. Thus, entry by American auto manufacturers into Japan would require changes in the product design to gain acceptance in Japan.[10]

Standardization: A Common Practice

Other things being equal, companies usually opt for standardization. A recent study on the subject lends support to the high propensity to standardize all or parts of marketing strategy in foreign markets. For example, an extremely high degree of standardization appears to exist in brand names, physical characteristics of products, and packaging.

> More than half the products that MNCs sell in less developed countries originate in the parent companies' home markets. Of the 2,200 products sold by the 61 subsidiaries in the sample, 1,200 had originated in the United States or the United Kingdom.[11]

The arguments in favor of standardization are realization of cost savings, development of worldwide products, and achievement of better marketing performance. Standardization of products across national borders eliminates duplication of such costs as research and development, product design, and packaging. Further, standardization permits realization of economies of scale. Also, standardization makes it feasible to achieve consistency in dealing with customers and in product design. The consistency in product style—features, design, brand name, packaging—should establish a common image of the product worldwide to help increase overall sales. For example, a person accustomed to a particular brand is likely to buy the same brand overseas if it is available. The global exposure that brands receive these days as a result of extensive world travel and mass media requires the consistency feasible through standardization. Finally, standardization may be urged on the grounds that a product that has proven to be successful in one country should do equally well in other countries that present more or less similar markets and similar competitive conditions. For example, Gillette's Sensor razor, launched in 1989 at a cost of $200 million, is the same razor throughout the world, sold with the same advertising[12] (see International Marketing Highlight 12.2).

Rewards of Adaptation

Although standardization offers benefits, too much attachment to standardization can be counterproductive. Marketing environment varies from country to country, and thus a standard product originally conceived and developed in the U.S. may not really match the conditions in each and every market (see International Marketing Highlight 12.3). In other words, standardization can lead to substantial opportunity loss.

> Pond's cold cream, Coca-Cola, and Colgate toothpaste have been cited as evidence that a universal product and marketing strategy for consumer goods can win worldwide success. However, the applicability of a universal approach for consumer goods appears to be limited to products that have certain characteristics, such as universal brand-name recognition (generally earned by huge financial outlays), minimal product knowledge requirements for consumer use, and product advertisements that demand low information content. Clearly, Coca-Cola, Colgate toothpaste, McDonald's, Levi jeans, and Pond's cold cream display these traits. Thus, whereas a universal strategy can be effective for some consumer products, it is clearly an exception rather than the general rule. Those who argue that consumer products no longer require market tailoring due to the globalization of markets brought about by today's advanced technology are not always correct.

An MNC that intends to launch a new product into a foreign market should consider the nature of its product, its organizational capabilities, and the level of adaptation required to accommodate cultural differences between the home and host country. An MNC should also analyze factors such as market structures, competitors' strategic orientations, and host government demands.[13]

International Marketing Highlight 12.2

Gillette Tries to Nick Schick in Japan

For Gillette Co., the leading razor maker in most parts of the world, Japan has always been a sore spot. The company, which averages a 65 percent market share in 70 percent of its markets, hobbles along with a 10 percent share of the razor and blade market in Japan.

What has barred the giant Gillette from growing in Japan isn't a closed market, unfair Japanese customs, or anything else Japan is accused of. It is rival American Warner-Lambert Co., owner of the Schick brand name. Although Schick trails Gillette in the U.S., it has gained 62 percent of Japan's "wet-shaving" razor and blade market by using the Japanese style of marketing.

Now, the battle is heating up as both sides promote new products worldwide. Armed with its popular Sensor brand, Gillette is launching a new strategy. While Schick stresses its Japanese way of marketing, Gillette is emphasizing its "Americanness." It is airing the same ads it runs in the U.S. and selling Sensor in the same packages, with the brand name in bold English letters and a Japanese version of it only in tiny letters in a corner. The company vows to double market share in Japan in the next three to five years. Previously, Gillette had TV ads made just for the Japanese market, although it did use foreign models and sports personalities.

Source: *The Wall Street Journal,* February 4, 1991, p. B1

International Marketing Highlight 12.3

Taking on Japanese Flavor

Fast-food outlets in Japan are trying to become more Japanese, offering burgers dipped in teriyaki sauce and making buns out of rice.

McDonald's Japanese subsidiary, the country's biggest fast-food chain, has added a sandwich of fried chicken soaked in soy sauce to its menu. The company tested the 320-yen ($2.25) item, called Chicken Tatsuta, and found that it sold nearly as well as the Big Mac.

Japanese-style burgers appeal to consumers because they seem more healthful. Moreover, tastes are changing. When U.S. chains first entered Japan two decades ago, what Japanese consumers were looking for in a hamburger was America. But now, consumers say they've gotten the American taste down, and they're asking if we have something else. Wendy's restaurants in Japan offer sandwiches with deep-fried pork cutlets—usually served with a bowl of rice—as well as a version of the teriyaki burger.

Source: *The Wall Street Journal,* June 19, 1991, p. B1.

The international marketplace is far more competitive today than in the 1960s, and most likely will remain so. Thus, some sort of adaptation might provide a better match of the product with local conditions for competitive advantage.[14] Vachani and Wells, for example, argue that based on a study of the product decisions of Indian subsidiaries of five multinationals, there remain important consumer segments that have special needs that are not met by global products.[15] Ohmae's charges against American companies for not adapting their products to Japanese needs are also revealing.

> Yet, American merchandisers push such products as oversize cars with left-wheel drive, devices measuring in inches, appliances not adapted to lower voltage and frequencies, office equipment without *kanji* capabilities and clothes not cut to smaller dimensions. Most Japanese like sweet oranges and sour cherries, not vice versa. That is because they compare imported oranges with domestic *mikans* (very sweet tangerines) and cherries with plums (somewhat tangy and sour).[16]

There are several patterns and various degrees of differentiation that firms can adopt to do business on an international scale.[17] The most common of these are obligatory and discretionary product adaptation. An *obligatory*, or minimal, product adaptation implies minor changes or modifications in the product design that a manufacturer is forced to introduce for either of two reasons. First, it is mandatory in order to seek entry into particular foreign markets. Second, it is imposed on a firm by external environmental factors, including the special needs of the foreign market. In brief, obligatory adaptation is related to safety regulations, trademark registration, quality standards, and media standards. An obligatory adaptation requires mostly physical changes in the product. *Discretionary* or voluntary product adaptation reflects a sort of self-imposed discipline and a deliberate move on the part of an exporter to build stable foreign markets through a better alignment of product with market needs and/or a cultural alignment of the product. An empirical study on the subject showed that product adaptation is most directly influenced by two factors: cultural aspects and legal requirements, one of which is discretionary, and the other is obligatory.[18]

Swiss-based pharmaceutical maker Ciba-Geigy's efforts in adapting its products to local conditions are noteworthy. Basic to the company's adaptation program are the quality circles. These circles include local executives with line responsibilities in packaging, labeling, advertising, and manufacturing. They are responsible for determining if (1) Ciba-Geigy's products are appropriate for the cultures in which they are sold and meet the users' needs, (2) products are promoted in such a way that they can be used correctly for the purposes intended, and (3) when used properly, products present no unreasonable hazards to human health and safety.[19]

Developing an International Product Line

Continued success in overseas markets requires the individual designing of a viable product line for each country. To achieve this viability, the composition of the product line may need to be periodically reviewed and changed. Such environmental changes as customer preferences, competitors' tactics, host country legal requirements, and a firm's own perspectives (including its objectives, cost structure, and spillover of demand from one product to another) can all render the current product line inadequate. Thus, it may become necessary to add new products and/or eliminate existing products. Additions to the product line may take different forms. A firm may simply extend additional domestic products abroad. Alternatively, certain specific products may be sought for a particular foreign country, either locally abroad or in the home country. Finally, new products may be developed for international markets. Also, product(s) may be either eliminated or selectively cut from a line in some countries. There are various ways of obtaining an optimum product line for different international markets.

Extension of Domestic Line

The extension of domestic products to foreign markets follows the logic of the concept of international product life cycle. Companies develop products for the home market that prove successful and lead to some export orders. As the exports grow, the firm considers setting up a warehouse, a sales branch, or a service center in the foreign locale. Later, the firm finds it more economical to assemble or manufacture the product in the host country.

Relating this process to product line extension, a firm may initially market a few products overseas. As those markets grow or change, an opportunity may emerge to extend the line by selecting additional products from the domestic line for overseas distribution. A TRW subsidiary in the 1960s, for example, exported fractional horsepower motors to Egypt, Nigeria, India, and a number of other developing countries. In the 1970s, many of these countries started manufacturing sophisticated equipment that required large horsepower motors. This change at the customer level made the company's international division choose additional motors for export to these countries. The Coca-Cola Company began marketing Coca-Cola in Japan in 1958. As the market developed, it appeared viable to introduce additional beverages. Thus, Fanta was added in 1968, and Sprite in 1970. By 1983, these other flavors were outselling Coke.[20]

Introducing Additional Products to the International Line

Products may be added to the line for two reasons: (1) to serve an unfulfilled customer need in a particular market overseas or (2) to optimize the existing marketing capacity. For example, a chemical company selling fertilizer and pesticides overseas in developing countries may discover a dire need for quality seeds and thus may add seeds to its line. Alternatively, the same company may feel it has established a good distribution network to serve rural customers and that it is not being fully utilized. The company may, therefore, consider products that could be successfully distributed to their rural customers. Such products may or may not be related to the company's business. For example, in Japan Coca-Cola markets two fruit drink products, a canned coffee-flavored noncarbonated drink, and a carbonated orange fruit drink (both under the "Hi-C" name) that it does not sell in the U.S. Similarly, Coca-Cola markets potato chips in Japan, a business unknown to the company at home.[21] Campbell Soup Company sells gourmet cookies in Europe and Japan and not in the U.S.[22]

Implementation of this strategy alternative can be illustrated with reference to Colgate-Palmolive Company's experience. Colgate distributes internationally a variety of products that belong to other companies. For example, Colgate sold Wilkinson razor blades for their British manufacturer. Colgate did the same for Henkel's (a German company) Pritt Glue Stick.[23]

MNCs often add products differently to their parent country market than to the international market, where product line strategy alternatives are pursued in response to the needs and opportunities of world markets. The products for addition to the line are determined according to inputs or product specifications received from different markets abroad. Insofar as possible, attempts are made to develop one standardized product to serve customers worldwide.

The decision to add a product to the line is influenced by such considerations as marketing compatibility, finances, organization, and environment. Marketing compatibility involves the match between the new addition and the current and potential marketing compatibilities of the parent company and its foreign subsidiary in matters such as product, price, promotion, and distribution. The closer the proposed product is to current marketing perspectives, the easier it would be to market the product successfully. A low compatibility, however, may affect profitable marketing. Thus, in the earlier example, the chemical company may find adding seeds to its line more compatible than offering leased agricultural machinery.

Sound business judgment requires a full examination of the financial risks and opportunities relative to the product addition under consideration. The common criteria for use in determining the financial compatibility of the proposed addition are profitability and cash flow implications.

The environmental compatibility includes concern for the customer, competitive action, and legal/political problems. The inclusion of a product in the line should not pose any problem for either existing or potential customers. At the same time, the competitive reactions to the company's product addition should be projected and evaluated. If the political/legal problems are likely to become a big stumbling block, it might be best to cancel plans to add the product.

Introducing a New Product to a Host Country

For the purposes of this discussion, a new product is defined as one that is new to the host country, but not new to the international market. For example, when Kodak started distributing its pocket camera in Southeast Asia in 1982, it was a new product to Sri Lanka, Pakistan, Thailand, and other countries in the region. However, in the other markets, like the U.S., Western Europe, and Japan, it was not a new product. Many decisions are required for the introduction of new products in foreign markets. These include decisions about which products to introduce in different foreign markets; decisions about timing and the sequence of introduction; and whether to introduce the product as it is marketed in the U.S., that is, in the standardized form, or to adapt it to the peculiar requirements of the host country.

An empirical study on new product introductions overseas showed that U.S. corporations frequently introduced new products first to countries culturally similar to the U.S.[24] Thus, Great Britain, Canada, and Australia were the leading recipients of new U.S. international offerings, accounting for almost half of the new product introductions, and other developed countries accounted for more than one-third. Only one-sixth of new product introductions were made in developing countries. New product introductions to foreign markets also varied by industry. New products in the category of office machines, computers, and instruments were introduced across national boundaries in less than half the cases. On the other hand, textiles, paper, and fabricated metal innovations were entered in foreign markets in 85 percent of the cases. As far as timing is concerned, the U.S. corporations have been introducing new products to overseas markets faster than before. For example, the percentage of foreign introductions within one year of domestic introduction went up from 5.6 percent of all innovations in the period from 1945 to 1950 to 38.7 percent between 1971 and 1975.

This testifies to the growing importance of new products for successful competition in international markets. Although no empirical evidence is available, presumably, in the wake of increasing competition, this percentage should prove to have been still higher in the 1980s, and should go up further in the 1990s.

Alternative Ways of Seeking New Products for Foreign Markets A company can develop a new product for a foreign market either internally or by acquisition of another company. Internally, new products are developed through R&D. R&D may be conducted in either the home or the host country. For example, Colgate-Palmolive developed in the U.S. a manual washing device—an all-plastic, hand-powered washer for developing countries. IBM developed IBM 2750 and 3750 electronic private business telephone exchanges within the U.K.[25] For most companies, however, R&D is centralized at home. (A later section will examine the role of foreign R&D in international product policy in detail.)

Many companies add new products through acquisitions. For example, Gillette acquired Braun AG of Germany in order to add electric shavers to its line. Similarly, Gulf Oil acquired Shawinigan Chemical of Canada to enter the field of carbon black. International Telephone and Telegraph (ITT) acquired Rimmel Ltd. of England to enter the cosmetics field.[26]

Rationale Behind New Products A firm may introduce new products in foreign markets as either a defensive or an offensive measure. Defensively, the new product is expected to help the company compete effectively. For example, a well-established company may be challenged by competition. In response to this, the introduction of a new product may appear to be the most desirable course against the competition. For example, with coffee drinking gaining in popularity over tea, the Brooke Bond Tea Company, a British company, decided to introduce its own brand of coffee in a number of Southeast Asian countries. Alternatively, a new product may be introduced to satisfy host government requirements for business related to national development. For example, Union Carbide, a chemical company, seriously considered adding men's shirts to its portfolio of businesses in India.

New products may also be added because the corporation had earlier licensed its company/brand name to someone else. For example, Union Carbide had to develop a new product/brand for Europe because a German firm had the license for Eveready.

New products may also be introduced as an offensive weapon for growth. For example, Polaroid Corporation sought growth by developing a conventional film since the instant photography market had matured and showed no signs of survival. Branded as Polaroid Super Color, the film was introduced in Spain and Portugal in 1986. In 1988, the company entered it in several other markets.[27] Coca-Cola company introduces dozens of new products every year to keep up with local competition. In Japan, for example, the company's product line includes Ginseng-based still drink (Real Gold) and a milk-based drink (Ambassa) as well as a honey-and-lemon flavored juice (Mone).[28]

The rationale for new product introduction can take three shapes: (1) to serve a segment hitherto ignored, (2) to satisfy an unfulfilled need, and (3) to adapt a domestic product for better product/market match. Often there is no single reason, but rather a number of considerations figuring into a new product decision.

Overall, new products are appearing more frequently because so-called product life cycles (from drawing board until the last is sold) are getting shorter as companies cut their development times and reorganize their factories to build new things more quickly (see International Marketing Highlight 12.4). Products survive for a shorter time in the market because they are rapidly outdated by products from rivals who are speeding up their operations, too. The incentive for successful innovation is great. Premium prices can be charged for novel things, particularly if they create new markets. IBM did this with its personal computers. America's Compaq then stole some of IBM's market by developing the next generation of IBM-compatible computers before IBM.[29]

International Marketing Highlight 12.4

Japanese Passion for New Products

The Japanese system rests, in large part, on the dynamic that drives its consumer products companies perpetually to create and introduce new products. This "product churning" reflects, of course, the Japanese consumer's well known passion for new products. It also reflects, among manufacturers, the speed-to-market in new product development, in which the Japanese completely outclass their American or German rivals.

In the soft drinks industry, for example, more than 700 new products and brands are marketed each year, but about 90 percent of them disappear after only one year in the market. This is a common pattern. Ajinomoto, the largest packaged foods company in Japan, launched between 20 and 35 new frozen food brands each year between 1986 and 1989. Only about half survived for one year, and most have gone entirely from today's market. Such product churning activity is not limited only to packaged goods, but applies as well to consumer electronics. Sony launched 182 new products in 1990, almost 1 new product per business day.

Source: Tatsuo Ohbora, Andrew Parsons, and Hajo Riesenbeck, "Global Marketing," *The McKinsey Quarterly*, No. 3, 1992, p. 59.

The following example of the lives of devout Muslims illustrates the way in which new product opportunities can develop in overseas markets. Muslims must face Mecca and pray five times each day. Because the proper time for each prayer is measured from either sunrise or sunset, it changes from day to day and greatly from place to place. In addition, the Koran specifies that the body face Mecca within 2½ degrees. The Muslim faithful can obtain charts of every part of the globe that show the direction to Mecca, but attaining the proper accuracy can be tough, even with a compass. Therefore, Sensortron Technology Ltd. brought high technology to bear on the problem. The company, which was founded in Monaco by an American, Romm Doulton, developed two pocket-sized aids. One points to Mecca, the other emits an electronic Hadan, or call to prayer. Both have microprocessors that calculate the direction of Mecca based on a person's proximity to one of 11,000 programmed locations. Sensortron figured its potential market is 10 percent of the one-half billion Muslims.[30]

New Product Development Process Usually, six steps are involved in new product development: *idea, screening, evaluation, prototype product, market testing,* and *entry*. Organizations spend varying amounts of time on each step. At each step, management must make a go or no-go decision. As a product progresses from one step to the next, it requires a greater commitment of resources.

Idea derives from different sources, the principal ones being host government, customers, subsidiary employees, and international agencies such as the World Health Organization. The ideas received go through the *screening* process to choose the promising ideas for detailed consideration. Screening begins by matching the product idea with the overall objectives of the subsidiary in the host country. Next comes a determination of product feasibility vis-à-vis the resources of both the subsidiary and the parent company, including finances, raw materials, energy, past experience, management skills, patents (for example, the ownership of a technical design/process), and the like.

Product ideas that seem feasible are carried on through the *evaluation* step. Evaluation mainly concerns total market potential and demand analysis. At this time, accounting information such as fixed costs, unit variable cost, and likely price is used to conduct the break-even analysis to figure out the point at which the company would be at a no-profit/loss situation in terms of either volume or dollar sales.

Once the evaluation step has been completed, the management must make the go or no-go decision. If it is *go*, the idea is next given physical shape in the form of a *prototype product*. Engineering and production groups work jointly in this task. Marketing astuteness demands *market testing* before final commitment to full-scale commercialization. Testing the market helps in two ways: (1) it furnishes information on the chances of product acceptance and (2) it indicates an appropriate strategy. If the market tests are encouraging, the company should go ahead with *entry* of the product into the market.

Conceptually, the whole process appears to be logical and sequentially possible. However, a variety of difficulties can arise that might require accepting shortcuts or even omissions of certain things. For example, the test marketing may be rendered difficult for lack of a marketing research firm specializing in market testing in the host country. Similarly, if the product development effort is located outside the host country, the coordination between engineering/production and the host country marketing group would prove difficult. Further, the host government requirements can pose problems in systematically following the product development procedure. For example, the target date for full-scale introduction may have to be altered. Finally, internal organization and management style may hinder smooth and timely development of new products.[31]

Difficulties aside, new products provide a viable route for growth as much in foreign markets as at home (see International Marketing Highlight 12.5).

Management of Product Line

Based on the experiences of successful companies, a few generalizations can be made about profitably managing an international product line. These suggestions relate to market segmentation, product design, product quality, product innovation, and economies of scale. First, any product added to the line, whether entirely new or extended overseas from the home country, must be directed toward a well-defined target group.

International Marketing Highlight 12.5

Better than the Best

Getting the Lexus out of Toyota, whose forte is rolling out wheels for the world's millionaires, is like producing beef Wellington at McDonald's. Toyota had to target its customer precisely, create all-new management organizations, rethink components down to the tiniest screw, and invest more time and money—six years and over $500 million—than anyone had originally imagined.

Toyota set out to do what nobody else had done: design a sedan that would travel 150 mph while carrying four passengers in relative quiet, comfort, and safety—and without incurring the American gas-guzzler tax. Even though 65 mph is the legal limit in the U.S., Toyota figured Lexus owners would want to brag about outrunning radar.

Those specifications dictated breakthroughs in aerodynamics, noise dampening, suspension, and, most of all, the engine. The company devised a nine-stage process to reach each design target. It included: discussing how goals would be met, making continual follow-ups, and trying wherever possible to have it both ways. For example, the company wanted the optimum solution—the biggest engine with the least noise—even though the two objectives are difficult to reconcile. Compromise was unacceptable. "We had to push the engineers to achieve the vision we wanted to create," said the chief engineer. Despite obstacles aplenty, the product looks like a stunning success.

Source, *Fortune*, August 14, 1989, p. 63.

For example, Riunite became the largest-selling imported wine in the U.S. through advertising itself as a beverage drink for young consumers: "More than a wine, it's a beverage. It can be drunk by anybody who is legal, anywhere, at any time of day. Its real competitors are soft drinks, beer, vodka and tonic, and iced tea."[32]

Further, it is helpful to distinguish products according to aesthetic appeal and functional design. This holds true for both consumer and industrial goods. Additionally, well-made, long-lasting products obtain a permanent place in the market that competitors find difficult to challenge. Inasmuch as foreign markets vary, a novel product created to match the characteristics of a particular market can be an extremely useful step to gain an advantage over competition selling "me-too" products extended from the parent company. Product innovation is especially helpful for mature industries with static demand. Finally, a cost advantage over the competition provides a strong, enviable position. Thus, realization of economies of scale in managing the product line is a desirable objective. For example, before the value of the yen hit the ceiling, the Japanese automakers occupied an unbeatable position in the U.S. market, based largely on a cost advantage of almost $2,000 over an equivalent U.S.-built car.

Overseas R&D

Research and development is essential to originating new products. U.S. corporations spend billions of dollars annually on R&D. For example, in 1993, American industry spent over $200 billion on R&D over and above the R&D supported by the federal government. Although U.S. companies make significant investments in R&D, their performance is lagging behind the Japanese. For example, of the top ten patent winners in the U.S. in 1980, seven were U.S. companies (G.E., RCA, U.S. Navy, AT&T, IBM,

Westinghouse, and General Motors), two were European, and one was Japanese. In 1990, however, five were Japanese companies, three were U.S. (G.E., Kodak, and IBM), and two were European.[33]

Most of the R&D activity of MNCs is centralized in the U.S. A Conference Board study on the subject, conducted in the early 1970s, indicated that U.S. R&D expenditures overseas came to about 10 percent of the total.[34] The overseas R&D is concentrated mainly among the large multinationals, just as domestic R&D is highly concentrated among the large industrial corporations.

Terpstra lists several reasons that lead companies to centralize R&D in the home country:[35]

- Critical mass and economies of scale (By expanding R&D in the home country, a company can realize economies of scale rather than incur initial costs.)
- Easier communication (Social and cultural barriers such as language differences are avoided.)
- Better protection of know-how (A company finds it easier to protect its research output and patents at home than abroad.)
- More leverage with host government (Host country's interest in seeking R&D would make the overseas company more vulnerable to foreign government action.)
- Ease of control of coordination (R&D activity can be controlled better by centralization of the entire program in one country; centralization permits better coordination with marketing and production.)

Although U.S. multinationals and those of other nations centralize the major portion of R&D in their home countries, companies do undertake some R&D abroad as well. Foreign R&D is explained by factors such as adaptation of home products abroad; response to subsidiary pressures; response to host government incentives for local R&D; public relations tool; local professional talent; cost savings; broader base for seeking new product ideas; proximity to markets; and continuation of R&D activities of a firm acquired abroad.

Obviously, there are many reasons that justify undertaking overseas R&D. In the future, it would be reasonable to expect more and more companies to initiate or enlarge their R&D activity abroad. This can be predicted from the known facts that the foreign marketplace is becoming highly competitive and that host countries are becoming very aggressive in seeking technology. Today, U.S. MNCs have to compete against non-U.S. MNCs, not only from Europe but also from the developing countries. The sharing/transferring of technology serves as an effective tool for entry into many countries. An obvious form of technology transfer takes place when the parent company engages in research and development activities abroad.[36]

Procter & Gamble's experience illustrates how research and development is becoming an international process for more and more companies. P&G recently introduced Liquid Tide, which, by drawing on ideas and technology from around the world, has a distinctly international R&D connection. A new ingredient that helps suspend dirt in wash water came from the company's research center near P&G's Cincinnati headquarters; the formula for Liquid Tide's surfactants, or cleaning agents, was developed by

P&G technicians in Japan; and the ingredients that fight the mineral salts present in hard water came from P&G's scientists in Brussels.[37] Thus, by pooling its research and development strength worldwide, P&G was able to develop a successful product that would not have been feasible if it had relied only on its R&D in the U.S., since certain technologies are more advanced in particular countries because of endemic needs and conditions.[38]

Unilever, a company whose core products include soaps and detergents, as well as margarine and other inexpensive edible oils, provides another example of an MNC that has globalized its R&D. The company has four major laboratories that conduct basic research: one in the Netherlands, one in India, and two in the U.K. It also has some 40 applied research centers in foreign subsidiaries, 24 of which are in LDCs. Unilever makes a practical organizational distinction between basic research and applied research, granting subsidiaries responsibility for the latter.[39]

Product Elimination

In international marketing, primary attention is frequently given to the problem of developing, adding, and modifying new products. Less emphasis is placed on product deletion decisions. This section discusses the importance of international product deletion and its strategic implications.

In recent years, global competitive pressures have caused many MNCs to reappraise their product mixes. The worsening scarcities of raw materials, price controls in some countries, increasing entry difficulties, tariffs, and the fear of a global energy crunch have forced multinational companies of every size, shape, and kind to reexamine their overseas product mix and make appropriate changes in it. Very often a small proportion of a company's products, say 20 to 30 percent, accounts for a large percentage, say between 60 and 80 percent, of its profits. The majority of the products, accounting for most of the losses or a smaller proportion of profits, should be examined very carefully. In many cases, the breadth and depth of the worldwide product line is greater than that of the domestic line. Weak products, on the basis of estimated future contribution to the product line, must be phased out to prevent dispersion and fragmentation of effort.

There are many reasons for failure of overseas products. Honeywell, Inc., decided to sell a substantial part of its 47 percent interest in its French subsidiary, Honeywell Bull, because of continuing losses. J.C. Penney decided to pull out of Belgium since economic and political conditions made it impossible to operate profitably there. For example, Belgium's strict price controls made it difficult for the company to pass along cost increases to customers.[40] Volkswagen AG closed its U.S. manufacturing operations under pressure from Japanese competitors and poor U.S. sales, which had been linked to an image problem that hurt the company's U.S.-produced cars.[41] ITT Corporation closed most of its telecommunications in Argentina primarily because of unstable economic conditions—delays in payments from the government-owned telephone company and a lack of new orders.[42]

Another important reason for product deletion overseas is customer rejection of the product. For example, after three years and an advertising campaign of $2 million, the Campbell Soup Company decided to close its Brazilian canned soup operation. Campbell failed to interest Brazilian cooks who felt they could serve only soup that they could call their own.[43] Campbell's offerings—mostly vegetable and beef combinations packed in extra large cans bearing a variant of the familiar red and white label—failed to catch on. Instead, Brazilian cooks seemed to prefer the dehydrated products of competitors such as Knorr and Maggi, which they could use as soup starters and add ingredients of their own. Campbell's soup was considered an emergency solution when cooking time was short.

Like the Campbell Soup Company, Gerber Products Company also decided to leave the Brazilian market. The company failed to convince mothers to use baby food as an everyday feeding item despite an award-winning advertising campaign telling mothers they would have more time to show affection to their infants if they were not bent over a sink preparing food. The company underestimated a cultural factor. Brazilian mothers are not willing to accept that prepared baby food is a good substitute for food freshly made by themselves—or, more likely, by their live-in maids, since most women in Brazil who can afford to buy prepared baby food can afford to have a maid.[44] In general, Brazilian women like to use prepackaged baby food only for convenience, when visiting friends and relatives or going to the beach.

All in all, appropriate organizational procedures for systematic review of products must be established. Specific criteria to evaluate product performance such as minimum level of sales, market share, profitability, and condition of the product line should be set. The criteria can be established by local organizational units relative to specific market conditions, by headquarters' management, or by both, depending on the organizational structure. Some coordination of these criteria is ordinarily desirable. The review of products based on these criteria can be carried out on a market-by-market and/or on a regional or global basis depending on the uniformity of the product mix in different markets. Typically, however, some informational input from local organizational units is necessary.

Adoption and Diffusion of New Products

A paramount concern in the introduction of new products is acceptance by the public. One way of determining whether a new product would be accepted by a sufficient number of potential customers is through an analysis of expected product adoption and diffusion in the foreign market.

Customers do not instantly buy new products. They go through a step-by-step mental process of acceptance or rejection of a new product. Typically, this process occurs in sequential stages:

- Awareness (Being exposed to a new product, consumers become aware of it.)
- Knowledge (Consumers develop enough interest in the product to seek additional information.)
- Evaluation (An attitude forms, negative or positive, about the product.)
- Trial (Consumers buy the product to see if it indeed meets their needs.)
- Adoption (The product is accepted for continuing use after satisfactory experience during trial.)

Adoption and Diffusion of New Products

Not all customers pass through all these stages in their adoption of new products. For example, a customer may move straight from awareness to evaluation to adoption. Similarly, different customers take varying amounts of time to move from stage to stage. Further, the time lapse between stages also varies with the nature of the product. For an inexpensive product, the whole process may involve only a few minutes. But the adoption process for an expensive product may require months.

A classic study on the subject showed how a new product is accepted by people over time. Initially, only a small percentage of people accept it. A little larger percentage follows. Eventually the product is accepted by the masses. The adoption over time can be represented by a bell-shaped curve. Based on this conceptualization, five categories of customers can be identified: innovators, early adopters, early majority, late majority, and laggards. Innovators constitute a small proportion. The real market develops when early and late majority consumers enter the market.

While the actual adoption might not pattern itself so neatly, it is reasonable to expect a tendency toward such a distribution. Assuming this, the adoption framework can be utilized to forecast the initial demand for a new product in a foreign country and how the demand would mature with time. Thus, even where economies of scale are important for a product to achieve satisfactory performance, a company may not establish production facilities if customers cannot be expected to enter the market for several years.[45]

In international marketing, the concept of the diffusion of new products is essential. *Diffusion* refers to how a new product captures a target market. The adoption process is concerned with acceptance by individuals, while the diffusion process emphasizes the aggregate of individual decisions to adopt a new product. Thus, an analysis of the diffusion process in a country/culture indicates if the new product would be acceptable.

Research on the subject shows that diffusion is influenced by a number of organizational factors such as effectiveness of communication between the parent and the subsidiary.[46] In addition, a variety of product-related and market-related characteristics facilitate diffusion. The product-related characteristics are relative advantage, compatibility, complexity, divisibility, and communicability. The market-related characteristics include innovativeness of target customers and their clearer perception of need and economic ability.

Product-Related Characteristics

Relative Advantage Relative advantage refers to the degree of superiority of the new product compared with current offerings. If the new product is perceived as more beneficial, that is, it appears to make a stronger promise of need fulfillment, it is likely to diffuse more quickly. One of the major causes of faster diffusion of superior products is word-of-mouth from the innovator, or initial adopter, to other customers.

Compatibility The higher the compatibility of the new product to the current ones, the more rapidly it will diffuse. Compatibility refers to social/cultural perspectives and the consistency of the product with existing tastes, values, and behaviors. Socially, a product requiring little change will be more readily accepted. Change is painful because it necessitates adjustments, both physical and mental, in established patterns. New products, or innovations, can be classified into three categories in order to judge compatibility. They may be labeled *continuous* innovations, *dynamically continuous* innovations, or *discontinuous* innovations.

> A continuous innovation has the least disrupting influence on established patterns. Alteration of a product is involved, rather than the establishment of a new product. Examples: fluoride toothpaste; new-model automobile changeovers; menthol cigarettes.
>
> A dynamically continuous innovation has more disrupting effects than a continuous innovation, although it still does not generally alter established patterns. It may involve the creation of a new product or the alteration of an existing product. Examples: electric toothbrushes; the Mustang automobile; Touch-Tone telephones.
>
> A discontinuous innovation involves the establishment of a new product and the establishment of new behavior patterns. Examples: television; computers.[47]

A product representing continuous innovation would diffuse more rapidly than those in the other two categories. The diffusion of products in the last category, discontinuous innovation, would require the longest time.

Complexity A product that is easy to comprehend and use would be diffused relatively quickly. A complex product requires detailed instructions for customer use. A customer must not only be made aware of the new product but also be educated in its use; the more complex the product, the slower the learning process. Nestlé baby formula ran into difficulties in many African countries because mothers in rural sections of Africa did not understand the quantities of baby formula they needed to buy in order to feed their babies adequately and they watered the formula down.

Divisibility If a product is available for trial on a limited basis, it diffuses far more rapidly. Customers can try it without making major commitments. In other words, divisibility reduces the risk to the customer, because a product can be sampled or can be had on a returnable basis—for example, 10 days' free trial.

Communicability A product with attributes that can be conveniently communicated to the target customers and so distinguish it from other products can be more readily diffused. In other words, the degree to which the benefits/qualities of a product are obvious to potential customers dictates the pace of diffusion. By the same token, if a product is visible in a culture, it tends toward fast diffusion.

Market-Related Characteristics

Customer Innovativeness Wherever customers by virtue of their social/cultural traits are open and prone to accept new things, diffusion becomes easier. Thus, diffusion occurs more rapidly in Western societies than in Eastern cultures. Within the same country, different cultural groups show different tendencies toward acceptance of a new product. For example, in Israel most Arab Jews would be less inclined to accept new innovations than would most European Jews.

Need Perception In situations where customers have a clear perception of their needs, new products are more likely to be diffused rapidly, because it is easier to determine if the product matches the need. Where customers do not know whether they need the product or not, diffusion would be rather slow, even if the product is desirable.

For example, in many developing countries birth-control-related products are not diffused since customers are not convinced of the need, or aware of the option, to limit family size. In such situations, even when birth-control devices are offered free, they are not accepted.

Economic Ability   Despite the presence of all the characteristics favorable to rapid diffusion, a new product may fail if the customers are unable to afford it. Thus, the economic ability of the customers would be another determining factor in the rate of diffusion. Many poor countries failed in their family planning campaigns because couples could not afford birth-control pills.

Impact of Diffusion Process on New Products

The characteristics that affect the diffusion process can be added up for an estimate of the length of diffusion time. While the exact time of product spread cannot be predicted, the approximate length of time can be identified. If the diffusion time is longer than anticipated or desirable, it may become necessary to make some changes in the new product to achieve more rapid diffusion. For example, the product design may have to be simplified to make it convenient for the customers to understand and use the product. Likewise, new features added to the product could provide an additional advantage to the users vis-à-vis the competing products.

As a matter of fact, adjustments may have to be made in the entire marketing mix to increase the pace of diffusion. However, the variable most related to diffusion, other than the product variable, is promotion. For example, promotional perspectives could be reoriented to provide customers an opportunity to try the product before making a commitment.

Foreign Product Diversification

Diversification refers to seeking unfamiliar products or unfamiliar markets, or both, for the purpose of expansion. Every company is at its best offering certain familiar products; diversification requires substantially different and unfamiliar knowledge, thinking, skills, and processes. Thus, diversification is at best a risky strategy, and a company should choose this path only when current product/market orientation seems to provide no further opportunities for growth.

Most large multinationals are diversified and have no need to undertake product diversification solely for international business. In other words, their diversification is usually planned in the home market, say, the U.S., and once the diversified product succeeds in the U.S., it can be introduced in foreign markets as well.

For a variety of reasons, however, a company may decide to diversify in a particular market overseas. First, in a particular country, government pressure may force a foreign company into unrelated areas. As mentioned earlier, Union Carbide considered entering the field of men's dress shirts in India to fulfill a government regulation.[48] Second, a special opportunity in a field may lead a company to diversify in that country. For example, a U.S. hotel chain might enter the car rental business in Latin America but not in the U.S., where there is fierce competition in the car rental business. Third, a strictly one-product international company may diversify overseas if its main business has reached maturity. Take the case of the Hoover Company, for example. In the U.S., it is basically a vacuum cleaner company, In Europe, the company has long been active in washing machines as well. The European business accounted for more than 50 percent of Hoover's sales. In the late 1970s and early 1980s, the European business slowed down because of recession and aggressive, low-priced continental competitors, causing chronically depressed earnings. The company, therefore, decided to adopt a new strategy that included diversifying into a new line of cleaners and washing machines just for the European market, particularly Britain.[49]

Similarly, Unilever has diversified into different fields to strengthen its position in the U.S. market. In 1987, the company paid $3.1 billion to acquire Chesebrough-Pond's, which sells personal-care items and cosmetics including Pepsodent, Vaseline, Pond's, Q-tips, and Fabergé. In August 1989, for a total of $1.5 billion, Unilever acquired Elizabeth Arden, whose products include Visible Difference cosmetics, Elizabeth Taylor's Passion perfume, Erno Laszlo skin-care products, and Red Door salons. Subsequently, the company acquired Calvin Klein Cosmetics, which sells Eternity and Obsession fragrances.[50]

Brand Strategy

Corporate identification is a valuable asset in marketing, in both domestic and international markets. Firms face the choice of linking the company closely with its products and brands or of establishing market strength for each individual product line or brand. In the context of international business, the factors that usually determine policy on identification are further complicated by problems of nationalism, language and cultural differences, and customer preferences that vary with the distinctive characteristics in each market. Despite these difficulties, a company must make decisions on multinational identification about the use of brand names, use of trademarks, and names of subsidiaries.

Brand Alternatives

An overseas marketer has several alternative ways to decide on the brand name:

- Use one name with no adaptation to local markets.
- Use one name but adapt and modify it for each local market.
- Use different names in different markets for the same products.
- Use the company name as a brand name under one house style or the corporate umbrella approach.

One Brand Name Worldwide This strategy is useful when the company primarily markets one product that is widely distributed, and the brand name does not seem to conflict with local cultures of different societies. Coca-Cola, for example, is marketed around the globe under the brand name Coke without any adaptation to local markets.

The worldwide use of one brand name provides a greater identification of the product with the company on an international basis. It helps to achieve greater consistency and coordination of advertising and promotion on a worldwide basis. It permits clear identification of a brand with a company noted for quality or technical superiority. It eliminates confusion with products of other companies. Finally, a great sense of consumer familiarity through customer identification of trademarks is realized.⁵¹ (see International Marketing Highlight 12.6).

International Marketing Highlight 12.6

Power Brands

What would happen if you tried to compare the world's best-known brand with those held in the highest esteem? To find out, Landor Associates, a San Francisco design consulting firm, assembled a list of what it calls "brands with global image power."

Landor surveyed 10,000 consumers in the U.S., Western Europe, and Japan, asking them to judge 6,000 brands by both measures. The top 10: Coca-Cola (a U.S. brand); Sony (Japanese); Mercedes-Benz (German); Kodak (U.S.); Disney (U.S.); Nestlé (Swiss); Toyota (Japanese); and McDonald's, IBM, and Pepsi Cola (all U.S.).

Source: Landor Associates, San Francisco, 1991.

Modifying Brand Name in Each Market Some factors overseas may lead a company to adapt a brand name to suit local conditions. Nestlé, for example, introduced several new products in Europe in the 1960s by modifying the brand name for each country. Its soluble coffee was introduced in Germany under the name "Nescafé Gold" and in Britain under "Nescafé Gold Blend."

Very often when a company leaves its home market, it tries to shake its so-called foreignness. Back in 1950 when the Campbell Soup Company entered the British market on a national scale, it attempted to take advantage of its Scottish-origin name. Each of its brands of soups was introduced at a tasting party for the press with a number of Campbell families living in Britain. These ranged from the Duke of Argyll, head of the Campbell clan, right down to Donald Campbell, the racing motorist. To add further to the name, some 5,000 Campbells in the London telephone directory were sent a sample can of Campbell's soup. Today, Campbell Soup is thought to be a British company by a large portion of its consuming public in Britain.⁵²

The adaptation of the parent brand name to local conditions would also be affected by media considerations. For example, Unilever sold one of its detergents in Germany under the brand name Radion, but for special reasons it was sold under another name in Austria. For a few years this worked out well. Then a great majority of Austrians began to watch German TV programs and read German magazines. Thus, German advertisements gained importance among Austrians. In the case of Radion detergent, however, this was a problem since it was sold under a different brand name in Austria. The company finally decided to substitute Radion for the Austrian brand name.

Different Brand Names in Different Markets Local brands are often used when the brand name cannot be translated into the local language; when a product is manufactured, sold, and consumed locally; when it is a leading selling brand and part of a new local acquisition; and when the company wants to play down its foreignness and be thought of as a local company.

A local brand name is necessary for products for which there has been no local manufacturer and the imported international brand is too expensive for the typical local consumer. The British American Tobacco Company has a number of markets where it caters to the full range of purchasing power. It provides cigarettes at the lowest possible prices for the mass consumer (through purely local brands, unheard of elsewhere), as well as international brands for the relatively wealthy minority who can afford them.

Individual brand names permit greater identification of the product by consumers with a name more suited to the local language or jargon. For example, in the U.S. Frigidaire was synonymous with the word "refrigerator," but this could not be the case in a non-English-speaking market. The local brand name, however, may have a strong market following; in the case of acquisition, it would be preferable to retain the local name, perhaps linking it with the corporate name of the acquiring company. For example, the local name on the package could be underscored with the caption "A Product of the XYZ Company." A local brand name or trademark can support a general campaign by the company to "go local" in its total approach to the market. A local trademark or brand name lessens the impact on other company products and the total corporate image if the new product proves to be a failure.

Company Name as Brand Name Many companies use standard trademarks for all their products, but are flexible in the case of brand names, taking into consideration local consumer motivation, language and translation problems, and other market factors. Some use both worldwide brands and local brands according to each market situation, and thus avoid the major disadvantage of a worldwide brand policy—inflexibility.

Trademarks in the form of symbols, logos, letters, and initials have all become forms of corporate identification. Just as the brand name is identified with the product, the trademark goes further and identifies both the product and the company. The double task carries a much stronger corporate message back to the consumer. Whereas the brand name may contend with the company name for first place, the trademark usually complements and reinforces it.

Some companies can benefit from the double impact of a trademark that is the same as or similar to the company name. Levi Strauss & Company has profited from Levi's jeans identity. However, success in the foreign markets has brought with it the problem of keeping others from using the same name, because as international sales have increased, so have the infringements upon Levi trademarks. (The problem of infringements will be discussed in a later section.)

The dilemma of brand name versus company name is a contested issue. Even the largest international companies, such as Unilever, Shell, and Imperial Chemicals Industries (ICI), differ on this point. Shell and ICI promote products under the company name and are heavy corporate advertisers. Unilever promotes brands and products and does not emphasize its corporate name, especially in areas outside its home territory.

The 3M Company (Minnesota Mining and Manufacturing) is an example of a firm that has successfully taken the umbrella approach and has created a family look around its products. Faced with an ever-growing number of new products and a constant need for new brand names, 3M decided on a corporate packaging theme for all its products. Previously, names and packaging had not conveyed the impression of one versatile company offering products to industry, to commercial business, and to the home consumer. The new corporate design system consists of three rectangular elements. One rectangle always carries the 3M logo, another the product identification, and the third the divisional identification, such as the Scotch™ plaid of the retail tape and gift wrap division. 3M considers the one look worldwide more important internationally than in the U.S., since identity and packaging problems had become quite difficult internationally with multiple sources of supply, different languages, and various modes of distribution.

Three trends are pushing companies into increasingly making their corporate names more noticeable on their products. First, product proliferation; second, product commoditization; and third, eternal values. With regard to the first two, the proliferation of brands and the fact that product differences are usually copied within six months mean that consumers will look to the company behind a brand to simplify the buying decision. As for the third, consumers are redefining brand loyalty as a two-way street: If a firm wants them to be loyal to its brands, then it must show them a commitment as well. Trust, integrity, reputation—such values will provide the emotional connection consumers seek and the necessary reassurance that they are making the right product choices.[53]

Brand Piracy

One persistent problem that well-known brands face in foreign markets is counterfeiting. Consider, for example, the irritation it would cause Procter & Gamble to find out that its Crest brand name is being used falsely on a toothpaste sold for one-fifth the Procter & Gamble price in various markets abroad. Unfortunately, the laws pertaining to brand piracy in many countries are loose, with little punishment for shady practices.

Of the many factors that encourage brand piracy, two stand out. First, a variety of U.S. goods are held in high esteem, particularly those of long standing, such as Singer sewing machines. In the developing countries, goods from advanced countries, especially the luxury goods, serve as status symbols and most of the time are in short supply. Thus, a ready-made market exists for imported brands that the counterfeiter likes to exploit. Second, the technological knowledge required to produce a counterfeit product is readily available. For example, a person in Taiwan interested in counterfeiting a Seiko watch will encounter little difficulty in acquiring the know-how and parts required.

As U.S. companies do more manufacturing offshore, developing countries acquire the technology to product bogus goods. But not all offenders are foreign. According to a *Business Week* report, 20 percent of the world's fakes are made in the U.S., mostly by marginal producers who cannot make a profit legally. No one knows the exact number of shoddy goods being traded, but experts estimate that up to $60 billion in annual world trade is in fakes.[54]

Three forms of piracy can be labeled: imitation, faking, and preemption.[55] *Imitation* amounts simply to copying an established brand. For example, a manufacturer in Italy may produce cheap jeans and put on the Calvin Klein label for sale as a genuine Klein product. *Faking* refers to identifying the fraudulent product with a symbol, logo, or brand name that is very similar to the famous brand. For example, in Europe several companies have sold jeans under the brand names of "Lewis" (in France) and "Levy's" (in Germany), which are pronounced very similarly to Levi's. A Hong Kong firm advertises its blue jeans under its own brand name, but displays the figure of the Levi Strauss trademark, "The Levi's Saddleman," with the only difference being that the branding iron in the hand of saddleman is replaced by a horsewhip.[56] Here is another example:

Recently, McDonald's filed a request for a temporary injunction against McDavid's, a Tel Aviv hamburger outlet. The restaurant looks distinctly American—from the plastic counters and beeping digital cash registers to the Uncle Sam hat atop the McDavid's symbol. The owner of McDavid's was quoted as saying that he had McDonald's 120-page manual for its franchise owners translated into Hebrew.[57]

Piracy through *preemption* of brand names is feasible in those countries where the law permits wholesale registration of brand names. In such countries, a person may register in his or her name a large number of well-known brand names, and then either sell these names to those interested in counterfeiting or better still to the multinational when it is ready to move into the country. In Monaco, for example, a person registered 300 famous brand names such as Chase Manhattan, Bankers Trust, du Pont, Sears, Texaco, NBC, and CBS.

Needless to say, brand piracy can cause unfair competition to multinational enterprises in many markets. Worse still is the export of the counterfeit product to the home market. For example, while the loss of a particular country as a market may not cause much worry to Proctor & Gamble, a fake product in the U.S. sold at a meager price would create a real problem.

Unfortunately, MNCs have little protection in the form of international laws to protect their brands overseas. There are some conventions, such as the Paris Convention and the Madrid Convention, discussed in Chapter 9, that make it convenient to obtain registration of the brand simultaneously in member countries. Other than that, the international marketer is left with few alternatives. Legal recourse overseas can be ill-advised since it would be difficult to ensure an unbiased decision. Besides, legal action is expensive and can result in adverse publicity in the foreign market. Thus, the only option of the international firm to protect its brand is either to withdraw from the market where it must compete against imitations and fakes or to promote its product in such a way as to make the customer aware of false brands. The best defense for business victimized by brand piracy is to strike back rather than to rely on government agencies. In this regard, the experience of Paris-based Cartier is illuminating. Despite Cartier's best efforts, Mexican officials were uncooperative about pursuing a Mexico City retail store owner who was selling fake Cartier products, even with 49 legal decisions against him. So Cartier opened its own store directly across the street and forced the retailer to strike a deal: in return for not selling forgeries, he would become Cartier's sole local distributor.[58]

A few years ago, a coalition of 25 U.S. and European businesses helped to mitigate the problem of invasion of the U.S. home market. Through their efforts, an amendment in U.S. customs laws now requires officials to confiscate counterfeit goods at the port of entry.

Identifying Country of Origin

A related question here is the identification of country of origin on a product. For example, should a U.S. company use the "Made in the USA" label on its product? The answer to this question depends on the market for which the product is destined. There was a time when U.S. products were held in high esteem worldwide. Traditionally, therefore, as far as U.S. companies were concerned, identifying the country of origin was considered very desirable. However, more recent events suggest that the country of origin not be identified indiscriminately.[59]

A recent study showed that consumer perceptions of product quality vary across product perspectives, i.e., U.S.-branded/U.S.-made, U.S.-branded/foreign-made, foreign-branded/U.S.-made, and foreign-branded/foreign-made. However, the sourcing country stimuli came out stronger than brand name when the consumers evaluated bi-national products.[60]

Thus, the made-in-the-USA label is not the sole mark of prestige, technical advancement, and innovativeness. Lately, however, the names that connote "America" or, more specifically, the American West, are hot, particularly in Asia.[61] From Beijing to Bombay, American brands are commanding big premiums over inferior hometown competitors.[62] In many developing countries, nationalist sentiments favor locally produced products. In the light of these developments, an international marketer may choose not to use the "made in" attribute as a regular practice. Where laws require such identification, the company has no choice. For example, goods entering the U.S. must be identified by their origin. However, in countries where there are no such legal requirements, the "made in" identification should be used if research findings and business acumen indicate that the identification would benefit the business (see International Marketing Highlight 12.7).

International Marketing Highlight 12.7

What America Makes Best

A deep concern for product quality is turning many U.S. manufacturers into the world's top competitors. Among the many products that restore the definition of quality to the words "Made in America" are:

- F-16 aircraft (General Dynamics)
- Computer workstations (Sun Microsystems)
- Biotechnological drugs (Genentech)
- Pacemakers (Medtronic)
- Satellites (Hughes Aircraft)
- Stereo speakers (Advent, Allison, Infinity)
- Towels and bed sheets (many companies)

Source: *Fortune*, March 28, 1988, p. 40

Private Branding for Foreign Markets

Private branding refers to identifying a product with the brand name of another business. For example, a food processor may can soups and put the A&P label on them. Private branding is a common practice in many countries whereby large retailers sell a variety of products under their house brand. For example, products sold under stores' labels (private brands) comprise 30 percent of supermarket sales in Britain and are rising in France, Switzerland, and Italy.[63] The question is to what extent this practice is relevant in international marketing.

An essential requirement for private branding is the existence of a developed distribution system in the market, particularly at the retail level. Thus, only industrialized societies qualify for successful private branding outside the U.S. In other words,

U.S. businesspersons may find it advantageous to enter a country, say, England, by producing private brands for a large retailer there. The danger with such a decision is that the U.S. exporter is entirely at the mercy of the English retailer: the manufacturer's name is not known. As the product becomes popular, the retailer might want to strike such a hard bargain that the U.S. producer is caught in an unfavorable cost/profit situation, and ends the association. This is likely to happen because the retailer can easily find alternative sources of supply for the product both in the U.S. and elsewhere. It is for such reasons that H.J. Heinz Co. is opposed to the retailers' big push into private labels in Britain. While Heinz's major competitors, Campbell Soup and Nestlé, have succumbed to pressure from the food chains, Heinz decided against private branding. To compete with private-label brands, which retail up to 15 percent less than its own products, Heinz feels confident that consumers will continue to consider its products superior and demand them despite higher prices. Thus, the retailers eventually will lose their leverage.[64]

Even in nonfood areas, private branding at the international level is slowly becoming popular. For example, Polaroid agreed to let Minolta Camera Co. of Japan sell the Spectra Pro, its most expensive consumer instant camera, in the U.S. as the Minolta Instant Pro. Polaroid considers the agreement to be a logical move to find new ways to grow through private branding.[65] Private branding for U.S. retailers by foreign companies, however, is quite prevalent. For example, J.C. Penney has an array of its electronic products and appliances (radios, toasters) manufactured in Southeast Asia under the J.C. Penney brand.

International Packaging

Good marketing practice requires that products be offered to customers in serviceable shape and pleasing form. Thus, the product must be moved in a proper fashion from the production point to the retail shop. Therefore, packaging plays an important role that can be described basically in two ways—physical and psychological. Physically, the packaging should be sturdy enough to undergo all the strain involved in shipment. The psychological aspect involves the package as a promotional tool. In general, international packaging decisions ought to take into account the requirements of four groups of people: customers, shippers, distributors, and host governments.

Customer Requirements

Packaging requirements for the customer will vary from country to country, based on socioeconomic-cultural factors. Customer characteristics should be examined in order to make sound packaging decisions. The aesthetics of the package is the first important consideration. The shape of the package and the logo, symbols, and figures used on it; the words and phrases describing the product; and the color scheme must all be appropriately attuned to the cultural traits of the host country. While in developed countries the major emphasis in packaging is on visual aesthetics, in developing countries the overall physical quality of the package is important because the package will most likely be kept and used as a container. Thus, the package itself may become a selling point. The higher the quality of the package, however, the higher the cost. If package costs substantially increase the product price, demand will be adversely affected. Another aesthetic factor to reckon with is size. An eight-ounce jar of coffee may be all right in the U.S., but thoroughly inappropriate in a tea-drinking nation where coffee is used infrequently.

Climate is another consideration in foreign packaging decision. The package chosen should be sturdy enough to withstand extreme climatic conditions. For example, food product packaging may have to be redesigned for shipping to zones of high temperature, such as Saudi Arabia. Package failure would mean that customers would be buying a stale product and the brand name would earn a bad image.

Finally, packaging should be safe in every way, both when it is used to house the product and during after-use. It is particularly important that after-use should not lead to any bad side effects, including ecological concerns. The disposal of the package should not be hazardous to humans or pets and should not lead to pollution of the environment.

Shipper Requirements

Regardless of the mode of transportation, the main concern of shippers involved in international marketing is getting goods to their destination without damage, theft, or loss, and doing that with the least possible cost. The key to accomplishing this is in efficient packing and packaging methods. The major questions to answer in order to design proper packaging for international shipment are : Where is the shipment going? Will it be stacked? For how long and where (in a warehouse or in an open space)? What are the handling requirements (net weight and type of load)? Are there any unusual or additional requirements? Sometimes these questions are difficult to answer in advance. In such cases, a consulting firm with expertise in packaging for international shipments can be helpful.

Distributor Requirements

The distribution channels for dispersion and conversion of products for worldwide markets require that theft, pilferage, and damage of shipped goods be avoided through proper packaging. For example, advertising the company or product on the shipping case is inadvisable. Not only does it involve unnecessary printing cost, but it is also an invitation to pilferage. Most of the requirements of channels of distribution in international marketing are similar to domestic marketing channels. For example, the package should not waste shelf space, should handle easily, and should permit easy and efficient price marketing/labeling. Foremost, the package should protect the contents and be aesthetically attractive to promote the product at the point of purchase.

Government Requirements

Government requirements in the area of packaging are mainly related to labeling and marking. Labeling applies to retail packages and is intended to provide consumers with essential information about the contents of the package in order to assure them that both the package and its contents conform to the regulations in force within the market. Marking regulations concern only the transport container and normally do not affect the labeling on the retail package inside.

To illustrate government labeling requirements, many countries with two common languages require bilingual labeling. Likewise, nations on the metric system require provision of information on weight and measure in metric designation. Canada's law pertaining to labeling illustrates the point. It requires:

1. That the identity of the product by its common or generic name or its function be shown on the principal display panel in English and French

2. That the net quantity of the product be declared in metric units and in the French and English languages
3. That the person by or for whom the product was manufactured be identified sufficiently for postal purposes

Special "other information" requirements are set forth for food products related to the use of artificial flavorings.[66]

International Warranties and Services

Customers buy not only the physical product but also the benefits that the product provides. To assure the customer that the product will do what it is meant to do, it is usual in U.S. domestic business to provide a warranty. The question arises whether such a warranty should be extended internationally. Similarly, certain products, particularly consumer durables and industrial products, require servicing throughout their useful life. International marketers have to decide on servicing arrangements for products sold overseas.

Warranties

A *warranty* is a guarantee from the manufacturer that the product will perform as stipulated. There are various reasons for companies to give warranties. First, a warranty serves as a competitive tool. A good warranty policy tends to differentiate the product in the marketplace. It enhances the customer's confidence in the product. Second, a warranty sometimes helps in gaining additional business. For example, the warranty may hold good only if the product is regularly serviced. Thus, to keep the warranty viable, the customer might contract with the company for servicing. (To illustrate the point, in 1990, Boeing sold six jet airliners to Moroccan Airways for $300 million. Along with the sale went a service contract for $20 million for training personnel and servicing the airliners. Third, an explicit warranty limits the liability of the company should the product fail to meet the expectations of the buyer.

The design of a warranty policy raises an important managerial question: Should a standard warranty be provided worldwide, or should the warranty be customized for each country or region? For example, on most electronic toys, manufacturers provide one-year guarantees in the U.S. Whether this one-year warranty should be extended to toys sold outside the U.S. is a question that must be investigated.

The answer to this question would involve a variety of considerations. First among these considerations is the nature of the market. If the international market is represented as one market, such as the Common Market where goods move freely within the market, it is desirable to offer a standard warranty. *Competition* within international markets would be another consideration. For example, the company may not have an elaborate warranty policy at home, but in an international market it might be forced into matching the warranty offered by competitors. For example, in 1986, Ford did not offer extensive warranties on most of its cars in the U.S. However, outside the U.S., Ford continued its two-year or 60,000-kilometer warranty. The warranty may have to be different if the conditions of the use of the product vary in different markets. A warranty may have to be made much more restrictive if wear and tear on the product because of, say, climatic conditions is likely to be excessive. For example, in the dusty conditions and hot climate of Saudi Arabia, equipment such as air conditioners would wear out in a shorter period than in Switzerland. A company, therefore, may offer a more liberal warranty in Switzerland than in Saudi Arabia. Another consideration is the nature of the product. Conventionally, a warranty on certain products is limited to basic performance. In such cases, a standard warranty could be offered worldwide. For example, Allis Chalmers, Bell & Howell, Brunswick (bowling equipment), Caterpillar, AB Dick, Parker Pen, Sunbeam, and Volkswagen offer a basic performance warranty common to all markets. A final consideration in deciding between a standard and localized warranty is the ability of the company to service the product under warranty. Servicing requires servicing facilities. If it is not feasible to have facilities in all the markets and countries the company sells in, it may offer different warranties to fit the situation.

Service

Service constitutes an offer to maintain the original product through overhauling, replacement of parts, adjustments, and the like. Most industrial products and many consumer durables require servicing on a regular basis. Provision of service on an international basis is important on two accounts. First, service must be provided to comply with the warranty policy. For example, if a piece of equipment carries a year's warranty on certain parts and functions, the manufacturer should make arrangements to ensure that the terms of the warranty are adequately fulfilled by providing appropriate service facilities. Second, service ranks as a promotional tool. When a product by its very nature periodically requires after-sale service, the company that provides such a service has an edge over a competitor who does not offer service.

International customer service has not received the same degree of attention from U.S. firms as has domestic customer service. Typically, U.S. exporters delegate the responsibility for service to third parties such as importers. Consequently, the service needs of foreign customers often are handled ineffectively.[67]

The formulation of a service policy requires an objective assessment of needs. The need may vary by country, depending on such factors as intensity of use, climatic conditions, and the technical skills of the people using the product. For example, in the U.S. higher labor costs mean that various industrial machine tools are used much more intensively than in Japan. In an extreme climate, a product is very likely to require greater care. Also, when the people using the product have marginal skills, the need for service escalates.

A prerequisite to an offer of service is an adequate supply of spare parts. Companies often fail in this regard and thereby earn a bad reputation among their customers. The problem in supplying parts is that many products come in different models and parts frequently vary from model to model. Furthermore, a product may have a large number of parts, some of which are exorbitantly expensive, and a service facility has to carry all of them. There is no easy solution to this problem. Usually, companies consult their own past experience to work out a list of parts that often need replacing and then carry these parts in the inventory.

Providing service also necessitates trained personnel to perform the servicing. Most companies handle the training process in one of two ways: Either the native service personnel are trained in their own country by one or more technicians from the U.S., or they are brought to the U.S. for training. Usually training involves on-the-job experience as well as classroom instruction. Training of high-technology products is rendered on an ongoing basis. Many companies have teams of trainers who visit country after country to update local personnel on new materials/processes/parts related to the product.

In conclusion, a good service program is helpful, directly and indirectly, in getting feedback from customers on various aspects of the marketing mix. The service organization, based on customer inputs, can serve as a catalyst to generate ideas on product improvement. Similarly, this information can shed light on other aspects of the marketing mix.

Summary

Decisions about products involve such issues as what products and product lines to introduce in various countries; to what extent a product should be adapted or modified to match local customs and characteristics; whether new products should be introduced; where the R&D effort should be concentrated; whether the firm should diversify into unrelated areas; which products should be eliminated; how products should be packaged; what brand policy to pursue; what after-sale services to offer; and what guarantees the company should provide on various products.

Product means a bundle of attributes put together to satisfy a customer need. The product objectives for each country or market should be defined separately and be based on overall corporate objectives on the one hand, and on the concerns of the individual national governments on the other. Product planning decisions, both immediate and strategic, are based on product objectives.

Product design is a major strategic issue. A company can either offer a standard product worldwide or adapt it to local requirements. Adaptation can be physical (for example, changes made in the electrical wiring system of a machine to match voltage requirements of a country) or cultural (for example, a color change in response to a cultural preference). The decision to standardize or adapt is dictated by the nature of the product, market development, cost-benefit considerations, legal requirements, competition, support system, physical environment, and market conditions. Generally, companies try to market a standardized product internationally. Although this helps in cost savings, standardization can also lead to missed opportunities.

To operate overseas successfully, periodic review of the product line is necessary. Product line development essentially involves three alternatives: (1) extension of the domestic line, which refers to the introduction of domestic products to overseas markets; (2) adding additional products to the overseas line even if the company does not carry those products domestically; and (3) adding new products. New products for international markets can be either developed internally or acquired. The rationale behind the addition of new products and the procedure for undertaking new-product development are complex marketing issues. Product review may also result in product elimination. There are several reasons for product elimination and different ways of implementing elimination decisions.

Another issue examined is the R&D activity. Some companies undertake R&D across national boundaries, but companies largely centralize R&D activity at home for a variety of reasons. More recently, however, R&D effort in host countries has been initiated by some companies. There are relative pros and cons of centralization versus decentralization of R&D.

The diffusion of innovations in overseas markets involves adoption and diffusion processes that are affected by a series of factors. In fact, the diffusion process itself may have an impact on new products.

There are four alternatives for formulating an international brand strategy: using one name worldwide, using one name with adaptations for each market, using different names in different markets, and using the company name as a family name for all brands. An important problem that companies face in brand management is that of brand piracy, the illegal use of famous brand names in various ways. In the absence of any international law to protect the brands, each company must independently guard its brand from invaders. The identification of country of origin on the product as well as private branding for international markets are decisions that must be made in relation to specific situation.

International packaging is influenced by such considerations as customers, distribution channels, shippers, and host governments. The service/warranty component provides a company with an important opportunity to differentiate its product from the competition.

Review Questions

1. What are the advantages of product standardization worldwide?
2. Under what circumstances should the product be adapted to local conditions?
3. Distinguish between obligatory and discretionary adaptation. Give examples.
4. Illustrate the logic behind the extension of the domestic product line to overseas markets.
5. What factors influence a decision to add products to the overseas product line?
6. Discuss the rationale behind the introduction of new products across national boundaries.
7. What factors help in the successful management of the international product line?
8. Why do MNCs mainly centralize R&D at home?
9. What alternative strategies can a company adopt to brand its international products?
10. What factors enhance the diffusion of innovations overseas?

Creative Questions

1. Academic research confirms that the country-of-origin of a product affects its perception and evaluation by the consumers. Thus, consumers in developed countries attach lower value to products from developing countries. What strategies might be adopted to successfully sell products with developing country origins in industrialized nations?
2. The powerful force of technology is driving the world toward a converging commonality: the emergence of a global market. To serve the global market, one school of thought recommends adopting a common marketing mix worldwide.

This way, companies can benefit from enormous economies of scale. By transferring these benefits into reduced world prices, they can gain competitive leverage. On the other hand, experience shows that socioeconomic, legal/political, and cultural differences among nations do not permit complete marketing standardization. Accepting the latter viewpoint, divide products into these categories: where more or less complete standardization is desirable, where complete customization is necessary, and where at least one aspect of the marketing mix must be adapted to local conditions.

Endnotes

1. Samon Darlin, "Coke, Nestlé Launch First Coffee Drink," *The Wall Street Journal*, October 25, 1991, p. B1

2. Subhash C. Jain, "Standardization of International Marketing Strategy: Some Hypotheses," *Journal of Marketing*, January 1989, pp. 70–79.

3. Donald S. Henley, "Evaluating International Product Line Performance: A Conceptual Approach," in *Multinational Product Management* (Cambridge, MA: Marketing Science Institute, 1976), pp. II-1–II-19.

4. *See* Saeed Samiee and Kendall Roth, "The Influence of Global Marketing Standardization of Performance," *Journal of Marketing*, April 1992, pp. 1–17; David M. Szymanski, Sundar G. Bharadwaj, and P. Rajan Varadarajan, "Standardization Versus Adaptation of International Marketing Strategy: An Empirical Investigation," *Journal of Marketing*, October 1993, pp. 1–17; and Martin S. Roth, "Customizing Brand Image Strategies Across International Markets: Effects on Financial Performance," A paper presented at the 1993 Summer Educators' Conference of the American Marketing Association.

5. Jose De La Torre, "Product Life Cycle as a Determinant of Global Marketing Strategies," *Atlantic Economic Review*, September–October 1975, pp. 9–14.

6. John S. Hill and Richard R. Still, "Effects of Urbanization on Multinational Product Planning: Markets in Lesser-Developed Countries," *Columbia Journal of World Business*, Summer 1984, pp. 62–67.

7. Robert D. Buzzell, "Can You Standardize Multinational Marketing?" *Harvard Business Review*, November–December 1968, pp. 1, 2, and 113.

8. Seth Luboro, "Aim, Focus, and Shoot," *Forbes*, November 26, 1990, p. 67.

9. Yumiko Ono, "Pizza in Japan Is Adapted to Local Tastes," *The Wall Street Journal*, June 4, 1993, p. B1.

10. Allan T. Demaree, "What Now for the U.S. and Japan," *Fortune*, February 10, 1992, p. 90

11. John S. Hill and Richard R. Still, "Adapting Products to LDC Tastes," *Harvard Business Review*, March–April, 1984, pp. 93–4. *Also see* John S. Hill and William L. James, "Product and Promotion Transfers in Consumer Goods Multinationals," *International Marketing Review*, Vol. 8, No. 2 (1991), pp. 6–17.

12. "Blade-Runner," *The Economist*, April 10, 1993, p. 68.

13. W. Chan Kim and R. A. Manborgue, "Cross-Cultural Strategies," *Journal of Business Strategies*, Spring 1987, p. 31. *Also see* M. P. Kacker, "Export-Oriented Product Adaptation—Its Patterns and Problems," *Management International Review*, No. 6 (1976), pp. 61–70.

14. Warren J. Keegan, Richard R. Still, and John S. Hill, "Transferability and Adaptability of Products and Promotion Themes in Multinational Marketing—MNCs in LDCs," *Journal of Global Marketing*, Fall/Winter 1987, pp. 85–101. *Also see* Kamran Kashani, "Beware the Pitfalls of Global Marketing," *Harvard Business Review*, September–October 1989, pp. 91–8.

15. Sushil Vachani and Louis T. Wells, Jr., "How Far Should Global Products Go?" *Vikalpa*, April–June 1989, pp. 3–10.

16. Kenichi Ohmae, *Triad Power* (New York: The Free Press, 1985), pp. 101–02.

17. Based on a case study titled "Sodima-Yoplait" completed by a French student, Marie Colongo, under the supervision of Subhash C. Jain, University of Connecticut, 1990. Subsequently updated in 1994.

18. S. Tamer Cavusgil, Shaoming Zou, and G. M. Mehta, "Product and Promotion Adaptation in Export Ventures: An Empirical Investigation," *Journal of International Business Studies*, Third Quarter, 1993, pp. 479–506.

19. W. Chan Kim and R. A. Manborgue, "Cross-Cultural Strategies," *Journal of Business Strategies*, Spring 1987, p. 30.

20. Ian R. Wilson, "American Success Story—Coca-Cola in Japan," in Mark B. Winchester, ed., *The International Essays for Business Decision Makers*, Vol. 5 (Dallas: The Center for Business, 1980), p. 121.

21. Ibid.

22. "Campbell Soup Unit's Cookies Will Be Sold in Japan by Meiji Seika," *The Asian Wall Street Journal Weekly*, September 30, 1985, p. 22.

23. Vern Terpstra, "International Product Policy: The Role of Foreign R&D," *Columbia Journal of World Business*, Winter 1977, p. 25.

24. William H. Davidson and Richard Harrigan, "Key Decisions in International Marketing: Introducing New Products Abroad," *Columbia Journal of World Business*, Winter 1977, pp. 15–23.

25. *See* Georges Leroy, *Multinational Product Strategy* (New York: Praeger, 1976).

26. *Ibid. Also see* Richard Klavans, Mark Shauley, and William E. Evan, "The Management of International Corporate Venture: Entrepreneurship and Innovation," *Columbia Journal of World Business*, Summer 1985, pp. 21–8.

27. "A New Focus for Polaroid: Conventional Film," *Business Week*, July 25, 1988, p. 36.

28. "Fizzing," *The Economist*, September 4, 1993, p. 63.

29. "Another Day, Another Bright Idea," *The Economist*, April 16, 1988, p. 82.

30. "Computers That Point Moslems Toward Mecca," *Business Week*, March 25, 1985, p. 46.

31. "Taking on the World," *Time*, October 19, 1987, p. 47.

32. Charles G. Burck, "The Toyota of the Wine Trade," *Fortune*, November 30, 1981, p. 155.

33. Thomas A. Stewart, "The New American Century," *Fortune*, The New American Century Issue, 1991, p. 12.

34. *See* Daniel Creamer, *Overseas Research and Development by United States Multinationals, 1960–1975* (New York: The Conference Board, 1976).

35. Vern Terpstra, "International Product Policy: The Role of Foreign R&D," *Columbia Journal of World Business*, Winter 1977, pp. 24–32. *Also see* Tamara J. Erickson, "Worldwide R&D Management: Concepts and Applications," *Columbia Journal of World Business*, Winter 1990, pp. 8–13.

36. *See* Susan Moffat, "Picking Japan's Research Brains," *Fortune*, March 25, 1991, p. 84.

37. Paul Ingrassia, "Industry Is Shopping Abroad for Good Ideas to Apply to Products," *The Wall Street Journal*, April 29, 1985, p. 1.

38. Alphonso O. Ogbuehi and Ralph A. Bellas, Jr., "Decentralized R&D for Global Product Development: Strategic Implications for the Multinational Corporation," *International Marketing Review*, Vol. 9, No. 5, 1992, pp. 60–70.

39. W. Chan Kim and R. A. Manborgue, "Cross-Cultural Strategies," *Journal of Business Strategy*, Spring 1987, pp. 28–35.

40. "The Frustrations Behind Penney's Cutback," *Business Week*, November 16, 1981, p. 60.

41. Joseph B. White and Thomas F. O'Boyle, "Volkswagen AG to Close or Sell Its U.S. Plant," *The Wall Street Journal*, November 23, 1987, p. 2.

42. "ITT Corp. May Close Unit in Argentina," *The Wall Street Journal*, February 22, 1985, p. 34.

43. "Campbell Soup Fails to Make It to the Table," *Business Week*, October 12, 1981, p. 66.

44. "Gerber Abandons a Baby-Food Market," *Business Week*, February 9, 1982, p. 45.

45. Zoher E. Shipchandler, "Change in Demand for Consumer Goods in International Markets," in Subhash C. Jain and Lewis R. Tucker, Jr., eds., *International Marketing Managerial Perspectives*, 2nd ed. (Boston: Kent Publishing Co., 1986).

46. Sumantra Ghoshal and Christopher A. Bartlett, "Creation, Adoption, and Diffusion of Innovations by Subsidiaries of MNCs," *Journal of International Business Studies*, Fall 1988, pp. 365–88.

47. Thomas S. Robertson, "The Process of Innovation and the Diffusion of Innovation," *Journal of Marketing*, January 1964, pp. 15–16.

48. Yves L. Doz and C. K. Prahalad, "How MNCs Cope with Host Government Intervention," *Harvard Business Review*, March–April 1980, p. 149.

49. "Hoover: Revamping in Europe to Stem an Earnings Drain at Home," *Business Week*, February 15, 1982, p. 144. *Also see* Sushil Vachini, "Distinguishing Between Related and Unrelated International Geographic Diversification: A Comprehensive Measure of Global Diversification," *Journal of International Business Studies*, Vol. 22, No. 2 (Second Quarter 1991), pp. 307–22.

50. "The New, Improved Unilever Aims to Clean Up in the U.S.," *Business Week*, November 27, 1989, p. 102.

51. *See* Sak Onkvisit and John J. Shaw, "The International Dimension of Branding: Strategic Considerations and Decisions," *International Marketing Review*, Vol. 6, No. 3 (1989), pp. 22–34. *Also see* Robert Johnson, "Naming a New Product Is Tough When the Best Names Are Taken," *The Wall Street Journal*, January 19, 1988, p. 31.

52. This and other examples in this section are taken from *Choosing Corporate, Product, and Brand Names for Worldwide Marketing* (New York: Business International Corporation, 1966), pp. 24–32.

53. "Branding Strategies: Should Products Carry the Corporate Name?" *Business International*, March 19, 1991, p. 91.

54. "The Counterfeit Trade," *Business Week*, December 16, 1985, p. 64.

55. *See* Jack G. Kaikati and Raymond LaGrace, "Beware of International Brand Piracy," *Harvard Business Review*,

March–April 1980, p. 46. *Also see* "The Pirates of Taiwan," *Dun's Business Month*, February 1983, p. 13.

56. *Choosing Corporate, Product, and Brand Names for Worldwide Marketing* (New York: Business International Corporation, pp. 24–32.

57. Jack A. Kaikati and Raymond LaGrace, "Beware of International Brand Piracy," *Harvard Business Review*, March–April 1980, p. 54.

58. "The Counterfeit Trade," *Business Week*, December 16, 1985, p. 64.

59. Paul Chao, "Partitioning Country of Origin Effects: Consumer Evaluations of a Hybrid Product," *Journal of International Business Studies*, Second Quarter 1993, pp. 291–306.

60. C. Min Han and Vern Terpstra, "Country-of-Origin Effects for Uni-National and Bi-National Products," *Journal of International Business Studies*, Summer 1988, pp. 235–56. *Also see* Graham J. Hooley and David Shipley, "A Method for Modelling Consumer Perceptions of Country of Origin," *International Marketing Review*, Autumn 1988, pp. 67–76.

61. "U.S. Locations Make Hot Brand Names Abroad," *Business International*, April 6, 1992, p. 101.

62. Patricia Sellers, "Brands: It's Thrive or Die," *Fortune*, August 23, 1993, p. 52.

63. "The Eurosion of Brand Loyalty," *Business Week*, July 19, 1993, p. 22.

64. "Heinz Struggles to Stay at the Top of the Stack," *Business Week*, March 11, 1985, p. 49.

65. "Polaroid and Minolta: More Developments Ahead," *Business Week*, July 16, 1990, p. 32. *Also see* Ron Suskind, "Minolta Puts Name on Polaroid," *The Wall Street Journal*, August 29, 1990, p. B1.

66. "Law and Rulings," *Modern Packaging*, July 1975, p. 55. *Also see* Hans B. Thorelli, "Consumer Information Policy in Sweden—What Can Be Learned?" *Journal of Marketing*, January 1971, pp. 50–55.

67. Martin Christopher, Richard Lancioni, and John Gattorna, "Managing International Customer Service," *International Marketing Review*, Spring 1985, pp. 65–70.

CHAPTER · 13

International Pricing Strategy

CHAPTER FOCUS

After studying this chapter, you should be able to:

- Describe the importance of the pricing decision in the international context
- Explain the parent company's role in pricing
- Discuss factors that must be considered in setting prices
- Compare the cost approach versus the market approach for price setting
- Examine factors that affect transfer pricing
- Discuss issues of dumping and leasing

Pricing is a particularly critical and complex variable in overseas marketing strategies. The pricing decision ultimately affects an organization's ability to stay in the market. At the same time, the uncertainties of entirely unpredictable forces such as costs, competition, and demand, threaten with numerous pitfalls for international pricing. This chapter develops a framework for understanding the international pricing process with a description of the problems and tactics of international marketers.

International pricing has several processes and ramifications. Corporate headquarters has a role in making pricing decisions. Different price-setting approaches are available, and a variety of concerns influence pricing decisions including intrafirm pricing, dumping, and leasing. An international marketer must work with facility through all these complex variables.

Importance of Pricing

Pricing, an important decision in any business, be it domestic or international, directly affects revenue and thus profitability. Further, appropriate pricing aids proper growth, as development of a mass market depends to a large extent on price. For businesses dependent on acquiring business contracts through competitive bidding, such as the construction and mining industries and drilling companies, a poor pricing decision threatens survival. Too high a price may mean no business, while a lower price may lead to an unprofitable operation. In many cases, the price indicates a product's quality.[1] If the Mercedes car, for example, were priced in the same range as the Oldsmobile, the Mercedes would lose some of its quality image. Finally, price affects the extent of promotional support to be allocated to a product.

Parent Company's Role in Pricing

One question in overseas pricing pertains to the role of the parent corporation. The parent company must decide how much say it wants to reserve for itself in international pricing, including whether the pricing decision will be made centrally or delegated to foreign subsidiaries. To an extent, the pricing role of the parent company is determined by the emphasis put on price competition in the total marketing mix.

Strategic Significance of Pricing

The role assigned to the pricing variable in developing the marketing mix depends on its strategic significance. Traditionally, U.S. companies have relied more on nonprice competition than on pricing. For example, Terpstra found that U.S. companies generally avoided price competition in the Common Market and more often went after competitive leverage through advertising, selling, and product differentiation.[2] This sort of behavior can be attributed to the fact that U.S. manufacturing costs were usually high, which made it difficult to compete pricewise. Further, the quality of U.S. goods had been considered high, which permitted targeting the product for a segment in which price did not matter.

In the last few years, however, price competition has been stressed more than before. Sales promotion, presale and postsale service, advertising and product differentiation, and product quality are no longer depended upon exclusively.[3] This change has been necessitated partly by the importance of focusing on mass markets overseas, particularly in Western Europe. A small decrease in price can be an effective way of increasing penetration in many foreign markets, especially wherever there is considerable price consciousness and where products are not highly differentiated. For example, the Italian appliance industry made significant inroads in the Western European markets through price competition. Furthermore, costs in many countries, Germany for example, have been rising faster than in the U.S. Thus, price competition is feasible in some cases.

Leff makes an interesting case for penetrating Third World markets through judicious use of pricing. The high elasticity of demand for consumer products and the highly skewed income distribution in developing countries lead him to recommend making changes in the pricing/output strategy. In this way, mass markets can be developed, enabling the MNC to achieve higher profits and larger growth, and enabling the host country to enhance the rate of economic development.[4]

Uniform Versus Differentiated Pricing

To what extent the setting of uniform prices is desirable in worldwide markets is a question that MNCs perpetually face. Some international marketers argue for uniform prices. Others, however, observe that the obvious differences in the markets of various countries favor the use of an internationally differentiated pricing policy. In brief, pricing in overseas markets is a controversial issue involving legal, economic, governmental, and marketing aspects, both in the practice of differentiated pricing and in price uniformity.

In theory, it is desirable on economic grounds to set different prices in different markets, because demand and supply differ from country to country. This occurs under any form of imperfect competition such as pure monopoly, oligarchy, and monopolistic competition.

> In evaluating each foreign market, the firm may find that there exist different demand elasticities than those encountered in the home market. Hence it behooves the firm to take advantage of these different demand elasticities by charging the appropriate price in each market.[5]

Thus, it makes economic sense for the multinational firm to vary prices from market to market. Such a strategy, however, may cause the firm to be charged with dumping in the host country. So from a legal standpoint, it may be desirable to set a uniform price globally. The host country may frown upon differentiated pricing since it may expose the domestic firm to foreign competition. Such an argument would even be economically justified in the case of an infant industry.

Empirical research on the subject corroborates the conceptual framework. Boddewyn found that over two-thirds of consumer-nondurable marketers and almost 50 percent of industrial-good manufacturers among U.S. MNCs adapted pricing to local conditions. This adaptation is justified on the grounds that manufacturing costs, competitor's prices, and taxes all vary from country to country, making local market considerations a critical factor in pricing.[6]

Despite the importance of differentiated pricing, some firms try to standardize at least the relative price level. As a matter of fact, some sort of uniformity in international pricing ensures adequate product positioning and control.

All in all, the decision between uniform and differentiated pricing would be dictated by such factors as competitive conditions, life cycle position of the product, product diffusion process, regulatory considerations, channel structure, company objectives, and consumer price perceptions. If the competitive position of the firm does not vary from market to market, it may be worthwhile to pursue a uniform pricing strategy. A firm essentially in a monopoly or differentiated oligopolistic situation may price its product uniformly on a global scale. For example, Boeing sells a highly differentiated jetliner. To all intents and purposes, therefore, it charges the same price for its planes everywhere, whether they are sold in the U.S. or Europe. Even the Third World countries pay the same price. In the introductory product stage when the product is not highly diffused, markets are limited to a few daring or innovative customers. These customers constitute homogeneous segments even though they may be geographically apart. Thus, a new product may initially be priced uniformly throughout the world. Further, if the diffusion process of an innovation has a similar pattern worldwide, standardized pricing will make sense. The perspectives of pricing—uniform versus differentiated—are also affected by local laws. Even when other conditions favor a standard price worldwide, local taxes, for example, may oblige a company to price the product higher in a particular country than elsewhere.

The wholesale and retail distribution structure of a country also influences the price decision. A *Business International* study, although dated, found, for example, that radios and TVs were priced lowest in Germany; prepared foods were more expensive in Italy and least expensive in the Netherlands. Such differences were attributed to retail structure.[7] Thus, where the channel structure is inefficient, additional distribution costs will be incurred, which must be absorbed through accelerating prices, resulting in nonuniformity of price worldwide.

The corporate objectives in a country may vary. Such differences in objectives would make standardized pricing ineffective. For example, a company may enter one market to develop a mass market through penetration and plan to be there for a long time. On the other hand, its entry in another country may be considered an ad hoc opportunity, expected to last a few years until the domestic industry, currently in its infancy, matures. Such a difference in objectives would suggest the development of different pricing strategies in the two countries. In the latter case, skimming the cream off the top of the demand curve will make sense. In the first case, however, a penetration pricing strategy would be in order.

Finally, the price perceptions of customers may vary from country to country, requiring differentiated pricing. For example, in the competitive environment of Western Europe, an American product may be perceived as the equivalent of local products and hence must be competitively priced. However, the same product in a developing country might be perceived as superior in quality, and a low standard price would disturb the customer.

Responsibility for Price Setting

The corporate headquarters should spell out who is responsible for price setting. Three ways to allocate price-setting responsibility are (1) headquarters only decides, (2) each overseas subsidiary decides independently, and (3) decisions are jointly made between the parent and the subsidiary. Because of differences in local manufacturing and market situations, it would appear impractical for the parent organization to set the price for foreign markets. Many companies assign pricing responsibility exclusively to country managers.

Most frequently, however, companies follow some sort of joint decision-making procedure. The parent company specifies a basic framework for pricing, leaving considerable leverage for overseas affiliates to set actual prices. The framework may consist of a formula to be adopted for figuring out base price or simply a few guidelines. The following is an example of a price guideline issued by one headquarters to each of its foreign affiliates.

> Our products should command a premium price, although not necessarily the top price in the market, and therefore should appeal to the consumer to whom superiority. . . is important.

Pricing Factors

The factors to consider in international pricing exceed those in strictly domestic marketing not only in number, but also in ambiguity and risk. Domestic price is affected by such considerations as pricing objectives, cost, competition, customer, and regulations. Internationally, these considerations apply at home and in the host country. Each of these considerations composes a number of components that vary in importance and interaction in different nations. This section reviews pricing factors and looks at their influence on pricing in international business operations.

Pricing Objectives

Pricing objectives should be closely aligned to marketing objectives, which should in turn be derived from overall corporate objectives. Essentially, objectives can be defined in terms of profit or volume. The profit objective may take the shape of either a percentage markup on cost or price or a target return on investment. The volume objective is usually specified as a desired percentage of growth in sales or as a percentage of the market share to be achieved. Sometimes businesses define their pricing objectives in such general terms as *image building* (that is, pricing should project a certain image of the product/company), *stability*, (that is, pricing should realize a stable level of sales and profits), and *ethics* (that is, the setting of a price should meet the ethical standards of good and fair business.

Two questions must be answered in setting price objectives: (1) Who should set the pricing objectives in different countries (the parent organization or the host country subsidiary)? (2) Should there be common objectives worldwide, or should objectives vary by country? (These questions will be examined in later sections.) Suffice it to say here that, inasmuch as market conditions differ in each country, it would be dysfunctional to set common pricing objectives globally. Further, no matter who sets the final price, both parent/regional and subsidiary inputs should be properly reviewed before making the decision. For example, what price the market will bear should be properly related to the parent corporation's profit goal.

Cost Analysis

Cost is one important factor in price determination. Of all the many cost concepts, fixed and variable costs are the most relevant to our discussion. *Fixed costs* are those that do not vary with the scale of operations, such as number of units manufactured. Salaries of the managerial staff, office rent, and other office and factory overhead expenses are examples of fixed costs. On the other hand, *variable costs* such as costs of material and labor used in the manufacture of a product bear a direct relationship to the level of operations.

It is important to measure costs accurately in order to develop a cost-volume relationship and to allocate various costs as fixed or variable. Measurement of costs is far from easy. Some fixed, short-run costs are not necessarily fixed in the long run; therefore, the distinction between variable and fixed costs matters only in the short run. For example, in the short run, the salaries of the marketing staff in the home office would be considered fixed. However, in the long run, the sales staff could be either increased or cut, no longer making sales salaries a fixed expense.

Further, some costs that initially appear fixed can be considered variable costs when properly traced. A company manufacturing different products can keep a complete record of the sales manager's time spent on each product and thus may treat this salary as variable, However, the cost of that record keeping will far exceed the benefits to be derived from making the salary a variable cost. Also, no matter how well a company maintains its records, some variable costs cannot be allocated to a particular product or line of business. In the final analysis, allocation of costs must be examined on the merit of each particular case.

The impact of costs on pricing strategy can be studied by considering the following three relationships: (1) the ratio of fixed costs to variable costs; (2) the economies of scale available to a firm; and (3) the cost structure of a firm vis-à-vis competitors. If the fixed costs of a company in comparison with variable costs form the higher proportion of its total costs, adding sales volume will be a great help in increasing earnings. Consider, for example, the case of an airline whose fixed costs are as high as 60 percent to 70 percent of total costs. Once fixed costs are recovered, the additional tickets sold add greatly to earnings. Such an industry would be termed *volume sensitive*. There are some industries, such as the paper industry, where variable costs constitute the higher proportion of total costs. Such industries are *price sensitive* because even a small increase in price adds much to earnings (see International Marketing Highlight 13.1).

International Marketing Highlight 13.1

Pricing at Replacement Cost

Why did gas prices go up so fast? It's hard to blame consumers for wondering why gas should increase by 10 to 20 cents a gallon just 5 days after Iraqi tanks rolled into Kuwait City—the oil companies were selling gasoline from old, cheap crude, weren't they?

The real answer is a combination of accounting and price-setting practices for crude oil. The last-in first-out method of accounting for inventory that most U.S. oil companies use causes them to price products according to the cost of replacing them, not according to historical cost. Reason: When it's time to figure profits for a given quarter, the cost of the most recently purchased oil is what gets subtracted from revenues. Since that cost went up quickly, oil companies must increase revenues quickly as well to maintain profit margins.

Source: Joel Drefuss, "Gas Pump Economics 101," *Fortune*, September 10, 1990, p. 42.

If substantial economies of scale are obtainable through a company's operations, market share should be expanded. In considering prices, the expected decline in costs should be duly taken into account—that is, prices may be lowered to gain higher market share in the long run. The concept of obtaining lower costs through economies of scale has often been referred to in the literature as *experience effect*, which means that all costs go down as accumulated experience increases. Thus, if a company acquires a higher market share, its costs would decline, enabling it to reduce prices. If a manufacturer is a low-cost producer, maintaining prices at competitive levels will earn additional profits. The additional profits can be used to promote the product aggressively and increase the overall scope of the business. If, however, the costs of a manufacturer are high compared with other competitors, prices cannot be lowered in order to increase market share. In a price-war situation, the high-cost producer is bound to lose.

Competition

The nature of competition in each country is another factor to consider in setting prices. The competition in an industry can be analyzed with reference to such factors as the number of firms in the industry, product differentiation, and ease of entry. In addition, competitive environment can be categorized as privileged position, leadership, chaotic, or stabilized competition, as shown in Table 13.1. The privileged position amounts to a monopoly situation. The supply of spare parts is one example in this category, particularly in industrial markets. The leadership position refers to oligopolistic competition in which the leader reaps high margins while the followers receive only adequate margins. The chaotic situation also operates in oligopoly. Only long-run programs can rescue a company from chaos. Finally, the stabilized competition applies to a monopolistic situation where a high degree of product differentiation prevails.

The impact of market structure on pricing is illustrated in the following quotation with references to the Japanese market:

> The oligopolistic structure of Japanese industry in the main reason for widespread price coordination. In most branches of industry, many company or industrial groups exist, each of which has strong connections in the financial sector, in the Diet and in the bureaucracy. Any attempt by one of these companies to engage in heavy price competition could provoke such a powerful negative reaction from the others that it would probably produce more harm than benefit. Furthermore, price coordination and resale price maintenance (RPM) have various advantages for manufacturers. In the Japanese market, with its overwhelming number of small retail outlets, RPM also serves to protect the small retailers. When prices are uniform, consumers do not have much incentive to prefer large outlets (which can cut prices as a result of economies of scale) over small, more expensive shops. Thus, price coordination and RPM are strongly supported by small retailers, who in sheer numbers are a politically visible segment of the population.
>
> Examples of price coordination and industrial cooperation are clearly evident. In the summer, electric fans that are identical in color, shape, quality, and price are on the market—but are produced by several different companies. Even discount prices tend to be coordinated. In Akihabara, Tokyo's largest consumer electrical goods shopping area, numerous outlets will offer identical models of vacuum cleaners at discount prices. Although each shop sells the products of different manufacturers, the discount prices are all at the same level.[8]

Customer Perspective

Customer demand for a product is another key factor in price determination. Demand is based on a variety of considerations among which price is just one. These considerations include the ability of customers to buy, their willingness to buy, the place of the product in the customer's lifestyle (whether a status symbol or a daily-use product); prices of substitute products; the potential market for the product (whether there is an unfulfilled demand in the market or if the market is saturated); the nature of nonprice competition; consumer behavior in general; and segments in the market. All these factors are interdependent, and it may not be easy to estimate their relationships accurately.

TABLE 13.1 Competitive Environment

POINTS OF DIFFERENTIATION	COMPETITIVE ENVIRONMENT			
	Privileged Position	**Leadership**	**Chaotic**	**Stabilized Competition**
Definition	Lack of significant direct competition	Leader has ability to set price level Leader affects degree of variation from basic level	Price level and variation are unpredictable and frequently changing	Firms have pricing latitude Price levels and variations adjust smoothly to each firm's strategy
Characteristics	High degree of technical/service differentiation High cost of entry Good customer, competitor intelligence Considerable latitude in pricing	Few competitors, high cost of entry Leader has high market share Leader has recognized technical and marketing leadership, and generally is low-cost producer Leader has reputation for good pricing decisions Leader is able to communicate its policies Leader's actions are predictable	Price is the major competitive tool "Commodity" products—everybody viewed the same Customers are price sensitive, or made to be price sensitive Tendency to excess capacity No recognized leader and no restraint	No recognized industry price leader No firm has dominant market share Firms employ product differentiation and market segment Competition based on technology, service, delivery; not based on price Infrequent price changes
Implications	High margins and profits Responsibility for market development	Good margins and profits for leader Acceptable margins and profits for followers Customers are satisfied	Nobody making even acceptable profits Customer probably dissatisfied	Good or acceptable margins for all Customers are satisfied

Source: Donald S. Henley, "Evaluating International Product Line Performance: A Conceptual Approach," in *Multinational Product Management* (Cambridge, MA: Marketing Science Institute, 1976), pp. II–13–II–16.

Demand analysis involves predicting the relationship between price level and demand, simultaneously considering the effects of other variables on demand. The relationship between price and demand is called *elasticity of demand,* or sensitivity of price, and it refers to the number of units of a product that would be demanded at different prices. Price sensitivity should be considered at two different levels: total industry price sensitivity and price sensitivity of a firm.

Industry demand for a product is elastic if demand can be substantially increased by lowering prices. If lowering price has little effect on demand, it would be considered inelastic. Environmental factors, which vary from country to country, have a direct influence on demand elasticity. For example, when gasoline prices are high, the average U.S. consumer seeks to conserve gasoline. If gasoline prices should go down, people would be willing to use gas more freely, Thus, in the U.S., the demand for gasoline can be considered somewhat elastic. On the other hand, in a Third World country like Egypt, where only a few rich people own cars, no matter how much gasoline prices change, the total demand would not be greatly affected, making it inelastic.

When the total demand of an industry is highly elastic, the industry leader may take the initiative to lower prices. The loss in revenues due to increased prices will presumably be more than compensated for by the additional demand generated, thus enlarging the total dollar market. Such a strategy will be highly attractive in an industry where economies of scale are possible. Where demand is inelastic and there are no conceivable substitutes, prices may be increased, at least in the short run. In the long run, however, the government may impose controls, or substitutes may be developed.

An individual firm's demand is derived from the total industry demand. An individual firm seeks to find out how much market share it can command in the market by changing its own prices. In the case of undifferentiated, standardized products, lower prices should help a firm in increasing its market share, as long as competitors do not retaliate by matching the firm's prices. Similarly, when business is sought through bidding, lower prices should help. In the case of differentiated products, however, market share can even be improved by maintaining higher prices (within a certain range). The products may be differentiated in various real and imagined ways.

For example, a manufacturer in a foreign market who provides adequate warranties and after-sale service might maintain higher prices and still increase market share. Brand name, an image of sophistication, and the impression of high quality are other factors that can help in differentiating a product and hence afford an opportunity to increase prices and not lose market share. Of course, other elements of the marketing mix should reinforce the image suggested by the price. In brief, a firm's best opportunity lies in differentiating the product. A differentiated product offers more opportunity for increasing earnings through higher prices.

Government and Pricing

Government rules and regulations pertaining to pricing should be taken into account in setting prices. Legal requirements of both the host government and the U.S. government must be satisfied.

Chapter 9 discusses legal aspects that affect marketing decisions. In brief, the provisions of U.S. antitrust laws (for example, the Robinson-Patman Act related to price discrimination) would apply to any foreign pricing decision that would adversely affect competition on the U.S. For example, suppose an electronics company exports integrated circuits (ICs) to South Korea at a price lower than the one it charges U.S. customers. Suppose further that the Korean importer uses these ICs to assemble computer terminals that are exported to the U.S. to compete against U.S-made terminals. If the Korean company gets an advantage over the U.S. terminal manufacturers because of the lower price it pays for the ICs bought form the U.S., the IC manufacturer could be charged with price discrimination.

A host country may have different laws concerning price setting. These may range from guidelines for the setting of prices to complete procedures for arriving at prices, amounting to virtual control over prices.

Government regulations evolve over time. For example, relatively new antitrust laws have been enacted in the European Union (EU). These laws may be even more stringent than those of the U.S. The first company cited for violations in the EU was United Brands for selling bananas at lower prices in the Netherlands than in other countries.

Briefly, the international pricing decision depends on such factors as pricing objective, cost, competition, customer, and government requirements. An empirical study on the subject, however, has shown total costs to be the most important factor in setting international price. The competitors' pricing policies rank as the next important factor, followed by the company's out-of-pocket costs, return on investment policy, and the customer's ability to pay.[9]

International Price Setting

International pricing is affected by such factors as differences in costs, demand conditions, competition, and government laws. The impact of these factors on pricing is figured in by following a particular pricing orientation. This section examines different pricing orientations and discusses export price setting. Perspectives of price setting in foreign markets are also considered.

Pricing Orientation

Companies mainly follow two different types of pricing orientation: the cost approach and the market approach. The *cost approach* involves first computing all relevant costs and then adding a desired profit markup to arrive at the price. The cost approach is popular because it is simple to comprehend and use and leads to fairly stable prices. This approach, however, has two drawbacks. First, definition and computation of costs can become troublesome. Second, this approach brings an element of inflexibility into the pricing decision.

This approach arrives at a tentative price based strictly on costs. The final price emerges after making adjustments, dictated by considerations of government, demand, competition, company objectives, and others. The principal emphasis, however, continues to be on costs, which forces inflexibility. More than that, a problem arises in defining the meaning of cost. Should all (both fixed and variable) costs be included or only variable costs? What proportion of fixed costs should be included, if any? Particularly, should costs related to R&D and parent corporation administrative overhead costs be included? The answers to these questions are far from easy.

A conservative attitude would favor using full costs as the basis of pricing. On the other hand, an incremental cost pricing could allow for seeking business otherwise lost.

International Price Setting

Exhibit 13.1 illustrates this point. The Natural Company would not be able to conduct its foreign business if it insisted on recovering the full unit cost of $11.67. If the full costing method were the decision criterion, the company would actually pass up the opportunity to add $3,000 to profit.

The profit markup applied to the cost to compute final price may simply be a markup percentage arbitrarily decided upon. Alternatively, the profit markup may represent a desired percentage return on investment.

For example, if the total investment in a business is $16,000,000 and the total cost of annual output (averaged over the years) is $25,000,000, the capital turnover ratio would be $16,000,000/$25,000,000, or 0.8. Multiplying the capital turnover ratio, 0.8, by the desired return on investment, say, 20 percent, would give a markup of 16 percent (0.8 X 0.20) on standard cost. It can be shown as:

$$\text{Percentage markup on cost} = \frac{\text{Total invested capital}}{\text{Standard cost of annual normal production}} \times \text{Percentage desired return on investment}$$

This method is an improvement over the pure cost-plus method since markup is derived more scientifically. Nonetheless, the determination of rate of return poses a problem. Academically, the rate of return should be based on the minimum fair return on investment. In other words, rate of return has to be equal to, or more than, the current cost of capital. In actual practice, a certain amount usually comes to be accepted as a fair return. Thus, 15 percent is considered a normal return in manufacturing industries, while 8 percent to 10 percent suffices in services industries. In this method, markup is linked to the total investment and, therefore, does not consider changes in price of cost components.

Under the *market approach* pricing starts in a reverse fashion. First, an estimate is made of the acceptable price in the target segment. An analysis is performed to determine if this price would meet the company's profit objective. If not, then the alternatives are either to give up the business or to increase the price. Additional adjustments in price may be required to cope with competitors, host country government, expected cost increase, and other eventualities. The final price is based on the market rather than estimated production costs.

EXHIBIT 13.1 Full Costing Versus Incremental Costing

The following is an illustration of the full costing and incremental costing methods. The Natural Company has a production capacity of 20,000 units per year. Presently the company is producing and selling 15,000 units per year. The regular market price is $15.00 per unit. The variable costs are listed below.

Material	$5/unit
Labor	$4/unit
Total Variable Cost	$9/unit

The fixed cost is $40,000 per year

EXHIBIT 13.1 (Continued)

The income statement reflecting the situation above would appear as follows:

Income Statement

Sales (15,000 @ $15.00)		$225,000
Cost: Variable Cost (15,000 @ $9.00)	$135,000	
Fixed Cost	40,000	175,000
Profit		$ 50,000

Now suppose the company has the opportunity to sell an additional 3,000 units at $10.00 per unit to a foreign firm. This is a special situation and would not have an adverse effect on the price of the product in the regular market.

If Natural Company uses the full costing method to make its decision, the offer would be rejected. The reasoning behind this is that the price of $10.00/unit does not cover the full cost of $11.67/unit ($175,000 15,000 = $11.67). By using the full costing method as a decision criterion, the company would actually be giving up $3,000 in additional profits.

If the incremental costing method is used, the offer would be accepted, and thus, a gain of $3,000 in profits would be realized. The incremental costing method compares additional costs to be incurred with the additional revenues that will be received if the offer is accepted.

Additional Revenue (3,000 @ $10.00)	$30,000
Additional Costs (3,000 @ $9.00)	27,000
Additional Income	$ 3,000

The difference between the two decision methods results from the treatment of fixed costs. The full costing method includes the fixed cost per unit calculation. The incremental cost method recognizes that no additional fixed costs will be incurred if additional units are produced. Therefore, fixed costs are not considered in the decision process.

The following is an income statement comparing the results of the company with and without the acceptance of the foreign offer:

Income Statement

	Rejecting the offer	Accepting the offer
Sales (15,000 units @ $15.00)	$225,000	$225,000
(3,000 units @ $10.00)	—	30,000
Total Sales	$225,000	$225,000
Costs: Variable (@ $9.00/unit)	$135,000	$162,000
Fixed	40,000	40,000
Total Cost	$175,000	$202,000
Net Income	$ 50,000	$ 53,000

NOTE: An important factor in such a decision is considering what the effects of accepting the offer will be on regular market price. If the additional sales were made in the regular market at the $10.00 price, it could depress the regular market price below $15.00. This would severely hamper operations in the future.

Market approach is widely used in Japan. For example, one Japanese firm first examines likely competitors and their products, then estimates the unit cost necessary for viable entry into the market. The engineers then try to design and make a product to meet the target cost. When Canon set out to challenge Xerox in the personal copier business, it set a target price of $1,000 for a home copier. At that time, Canon's least expensive copier sold for several thousand dollars. Trying to reduce the cost of existing models would not have given Canon the radical price improvement it needed. Instead, Canon engineers were challenged to reinvent a cheaper copier, without compromising quality standards. The challenge was met by substituting a disposable cartridge for the complex image transfer mechanism used in other copiers.[10]

Both the cost and market approaches essentially consider common factors in determining the final price. The difference between the two approaches involves the core concern in setting prices. The market approach focuses on pricing from the viewpoint of the customer. Unfortunately, in many countries it may not be easy to develop an adequate price-demand relationship, and therefore implementation of the market approach may occur in a vacuum. It is this kind of uncertainty that forces marketers to opt for the cost approach (see International Marketing Highlight 13.2).

In theory, pricing is based on either of the two pricing approaches. In most cases, however, the cost approach turns out to be a more viable approach. The difficulty of gaining adequate knowledge of the foreign market and the desire to ensure satisfactory profit on export transactions leads companies to choose the cost approach.

Export Pricing

Export pricing is affected by three factors:

1. The price destination (that is, who it is that will pay the price—the final consumer, independent distributors, a wholly owned subsidiary, a joint venture organization, or someone else)
2. The nature of the product (that is, whether it is raw or semiprocessed material, components, finished or largely finished products: or services or intangible property—patents, trademarks, formulas, and the like)
3. The currency used for billing (that is, the currency of the purchaser's country, the seller's home country currency, or a leading international currency)

The *price destination* is an important consideration since different destinations present different opportunities and problems. For example, pricing to sell to a government may require special procedures and concessions not necessary in pricing to other customers. A little extra margin might be called for. On the other hand, independent distributors with whom the company has a contractual marketing arrangement deserve a price break. Wholesalers and jobbers that shop around have an entirely different relationship with the supplier than the independent distributors.

As products, raw materials and commodities give a company very little leeway for maneuvering; there is usually a prevalent world price that must be charged, particularly when the supply is plentiful. However, if the supply is short, the seller may be able to demand a higher price. Similarly, when it is a sellers' market, the seller can make the buyer pay for adverse exchange fluctuations, and vice versa.[11]

International Marketing Highlight 13.2

Approach to Price Setting

Seiko Epson, the Japanese computer peripherals manufacturer, sets floor prices at headquarters after considering costs, recommendations from executives in the company's various manufacturing divisions and country markets, and a corporate profit markup target for the particular product. Starting from this figure, product division presidents at headquarters establish flexibility parameters. The low-end products, such as Epson's LQ-500 series printer, are usually restricted to a variability range of less than 5 percent, while the prices charged for high-end products like computers and laser-jet printers can range from 10 percent to 25 percent above or below the base price. Salespeople in headquarters are allowed to negotiate prices within these parameters with country-level sales affiliates. In view of the rapid technological change and rapid entry of new products in that industry, this sort of price flexibility is considered essential by marketing staff.

Source: *Marketing Strategies for Global Growth and Competitiveness* (New York: Business International, no date), p. 64.

A pricing choice in export pricing that a company must consider is whether to set a common price or different prices for domestic and international markets. Although some companies have common prices, more often, for reasons discussed in the previous section, a firm develops two price lists, one for the domestic and one for the foreign market. The salesperson or distributor for a particular foreign market receives the foreign price list, which would be used in discussing price with customers. Usually, a company would charge the same price to a given customer even if a product is supplied from various plants. For example, a Brazilian order might be filled from either a U.S. plant or a plant in Italy. Normally, the Brazilian market would be served from the U.S. and the U.S. price list would be used. In an emergency, if the order must be filled from Italy, the parent company would absorb the extra cost of shipping the product from Italy in order to maintain stable prices.

Often, a margin is built into the price list so that, if necessary, it is feasible to adjust prices in response to local market conditions. Such conditions would include overall competitiveness based on production and related costs, the export incentives other governments give their manufacturers, and the actual margin another product has in a given country.

Price lists are periodically reviewed for adjustments. In the economic environment of the 1990s, such reviews are becoming more frequent. For example, a chemical MNC reviewed prices every three months instead of semiannually, mostly because of world supply/demand conditions. Usually, exporting firms give anywhere between 30 to 90 days' notice of an impending price increase, depending on the nature of the product.

As far as currency conditions are concerned, the appropriate strategy would depend on the currency used and its relative strength. For example, if domestic currency is used, Cavusgil recommends alternative strategies depending on whether it is weak or strong (see Table 13.2).

A company may make sales on a spot basis or for future delivery. For sales on a spot basis, prices are determined according to the daily exchange rate at the time of the order. On orders for future delivery, a company may either quote at the current rate or

International Price Setting

Price Escalation

use a forward rate. The final decision on the use of the exchange rate will depend on the company's overall export exposure and its past experience with exchange losses.

The retail price of exports is usually much higher than the domestic retail price for the same product. This escalation in foreign price can be explained by such costs as transportation, customs duty, and distributor margins, all associated with exports. The geographic distance that goods must travel results in additional transportation cost. The imported goods must also bear the import taxes in the form of customs duty imposed by the host government. Further, the completion of the export transaction may require the passage of the goods through many more channels than in a domestic sale. Each channel member must be paid a margin for services it provides, which naturally increases cost. Also, a variety of government requirements, domestic and foreign, must be fulfilled, incurring further costs.

The process of price escalation is illustrated in Exhibit 13.2. It is evident that the retail price for exported goods is about 60 percent more than the domestic retail price. For example, about $80 more is spent on transportation alone. An additional $90 is accounted for by the import tariff. Finally, the agent costs for the exported goods amount to about $371, compared with $194 for domestic distribution.

TABLE 13.2 International Pricing Strategies Under Varying Currency Conditions

WHEN THE DOMESTIC CURRENCY IS WEAK	WHEN THE DOMESTIC CURRENCY IS STRONG
Stress price benefits.	Engage in nonprice competition by improving quality, delivery, and after-sale service.
Expand product line and add more costly features.	Improve productivity and engage in vigorous cost reduction.
Shift sourcing manufacturing to domestic market.	Shift sourcing and manufacturing overseas.
Exploit export opportunities in all markets.	Give priority to exports to countries with relatively strong currencies.
Use a full-costing approach, but employ marginal-cost pricing to penetrate new or competitive markets.	Trim profit margins and use marginal-cost pricing.
Speed repatriation of foreign-earned income and collections.	Keep the foreign-earned income in host country; slow down collections.
Minimize expenditures in local or host country currency.	Maximize expenditures in local or host country currency.
Buy needed services (advertising, insurance, transportation, etc.) in domestic market.	Buy needed services abroad and pay for them in local currencies.
Bill foreign customers in their own currency.	Bill foreign customers in the domestic currency.

Source: S. Tamer Cavusgil, "Pricing for Global Markets," in *Marketing Strategies for Global Growth and Competitiveness* (New York: Business International, no date), p. 61.

13 International Pricing Strategy

The price escalation could raise the final price to the foreign customer so much that demand drops. An exporter has various means to counteract such a problem:

1. Ship modified or unassembled products, which might lower transportation costs and duties.
2. Lower the export price at the factory, thus reducing the multiplier effect of all the markups
3. Get its freight and/or duty classifications changed for a possible lowering of these costs.
4. Produce within the export market to eliminate the extra steps.[12]

EXHIBIT 13.2 An Example of Price Escalation (Export from the U.S. to the Middle East)

	DOMESTIC TRANSACTIONS	MIDDLE EAST TRANSACTIONS
Manufacturing price in the U.S.	$362.00	$362.00
Transportation to wholesaler/point of shipment	18.00	23.00
	$380.00	$385.00
Export documentation (i.e., bill of lading, counselor's invoice)		4.00
Handling for overseas shipping		2.50
Overseas freight and insurance		58.50
		$450.00
Import tariff: 20 percent of landed cost		90.00
		$540.00
Handling at foreign port of entry		3.00
		$543.00
Transportation from port of entry to importer		17.00
		$560.00
Importer margin (on sale to wholesaler): 10 percent		56.00
		$616.00
Wholesale margin: 8 percent	30.40	49.28
	$410.40	$665.28
Real margin: 40 percent	164.16	266.12
Final retail price	$574.56	$931.40

Export Price Quotation

An export price may be quoted to the overseas buyer in any one of several ways. Every alternative implies mutual commitment by exporter and importer and specifies the terms of trade. The price alters according to the degree of responsibility that the exporter undertakes, which varies with each alternative.

There are five principal ways of quoting export prices: ex-factory; free-along-side-ship (F.A.S.); free-on-board (F.O.B.); cost, insurance, and freight (CIF); and delivered duty-paid. The ex-factory price represents the simplest arrangement. The importer is presumed to have bought the goods right at the exporter's factory. All costs and risks from thereon become the buyer's problem. The ex-factory arrangement limits the exporter's risk. However, an importer may find an ex-factory deal highly demanding. From another country, it could prove difficult to arrange for transportation and to take care of the various formalities associated with foreign trade. Only large companies such as Japanese trading companies can handle ex-factory purchases in another country smoothly.

The F.A.S. contract requires the exporter to be responsible for the goods until they are placed alongside the ship. All charges incurred up to that point must be borne by the seller. The exporter's side of the contract is completed on receiving a clean wharfage receipt indicating safe delivery of goods for foreign embarkation. The F.A.S. price is slightly higher than the ex-factory price since the exporter undertakes to transport the goods to the point of shipment and becomes liable for the risk associated with the goods for a longer period.

The F.O.B. price includes actual placement of goods aboard the ship. The F.O.B. price may be the F.O.B. inland carrier or F.O.B. foreign carrier. If it is the former, then the F.O.B. price will be slightly less than the F.A.S. price. However, if it is an F.O.B. foreign carrier, then the price will include the F.A.S. price plus cost of transportation to the importer's country.

Generally, U.S. companies prefer quoting export prices as F.O.B. This limits their responsibility to activities in the U.S. In fact, companies usually favor F.O.B. inland carrier over F.O.B. foreign carrier.[13]

Under the CIF price quotation, the ownership of the goods passes to the importer as soon as they are loaded aboard the ship, but the exporter is liable for payment of freight and insurance charges up to the port of destination. Finally, the delivered duty-paid alternative imposes on the exporter the complete responsibility for delivering the goods at a particular place in the importer's country. Thus, the exporter makes arrangements for the receipt of the goods at the foreign port, pays necessary taxes/duties and handling, and provides for further inland transportation in the importer's country. Needless to say, the price of delivered duty-paid goods is much higher than the goods exported under the CIF contract.

Price Setting in Foreign Markets

The pricing decision of an MNC for a foreign market is essentially based on the same considerations as those affecting pricing in the domestic market. As discussed earlier in this chapter, these considerations include overall parent company objectives, the competition, the customer costs, and government regulations. In the international field, however, there is a range of additional factors to be examined before finalizing the price. First, the price in various regions of the world should be kept fairly uniform. Such parity prevents unrelated dealers in home markets from competing with the overseas company units. For example, if a firm in Europe makes and sells products identical to those it makes and sells in the U.S., a customer in Europe would not have any reason to prefer one source over another except for a significant price differential. If the price for a given product sold in Europe goes up substantially above the selling price in the

U.S., the European customer will very likely import the U.S.-made product and undercut the U.S. firm's European manufacturing subsidiaries.

Second, ethical considerations in the foreign market differ from those in the domestic market. For example, a pharmaceutical company may find it ethically desirable to sell drugs in developing countries at a lower margin despite the feasibility of realizing a higher profit. Third, price segmentation becomes more significant in the foreign market. The nomads of the Sahara, although they are extremely poor, need expensive clothes because of harsh conditions and extreme temperatures. As a matter of fact, a small market for expensive products always exists anywhere in the world.

Fourth, U.S. businesspersons characteristically like to maximize short-term performance. In foreign markets, however, it may be preferable to seek long-term gains, even if less-than-optimum profits are earned in the initial years. Thus, pricing to realize a designated rate of return may have to be staggered over several years. In this way, the return in the first few years would be lower, but much higher in the later years, averaging our overall to a figure considered satisfactory by the parent corporation (see International Marketing Highlight 13.3).

Finally, government plays a much more prominent role in pricing in almost all countries outside the U.S. In many countries, prices are strictly controlled and all price changes have to be cleared with the government before taking effect.[14] Price control is not limited to developing countries. In recent years, for example, a number of European countries (Belgium, France, Ireland, the Netherlands, Spain, Sweden, and the U.K.) instituted price controls.

Ordinarily, price control means that an application to increase price must be filed with the government, together with supporting data of cast increases. Government approval may take several months, and often the price increase only takes effect after an additional several months.[15] In other words, a future price increase is publicly announced several months ahead of time. This leads to obsessive buying to beat the price increase. The price control problem can eventually force a company to leave a country. The following case is an illustration:

> Gerber Products Co. had been operating in Venezuela since 1960. Unprofitable operations forced the firm to sell out in 1979. The company blamed price controls as a major factor in losses. Some of Gerber's products were still being sold at prices set in 1968. The government had refused repeated requests for price increases. The price squeeze forced Gerber to cut output from 88 varieties to as low as 12. The company reportedly lost $500,000 in the first 6 months of 1979.[16]

Transfer Pricing

Transfer pricing refers to the pricing of goods/services among units within the corporation. It serves as a measure of the economic performance of profit centers within the enterprise. It differs from market price, which measures exchanges between a company and the outside world, for the net effect of transfer pricing is borne by the same organization. The determination of transfer prices in MNCs is an important issue because a substantial proportion of international exchanges consists of transactions between a parent corporation and its affiliates. For example, in the case of the U.S., 58 percent of 1993 exports and 45 percent of 1993 imports were within related firms.

Similarly, in the case of OECD countries, about one-third of merchandise imports and exports represented transfers among affiliated enterprises.

International Marketing Highlight 13.3

Giveaway Pricing

Japanese companies definitely conduct business differently. Consider Japan's number one computer maker, Fujitsu Ltd., which won a contract to design a computer system for the city of Hiroshima by bidding 1 yen, or 0.7 cents. Fujitsu's strategy is simple: give away the design job, which hopefully should lead to the city's equipment orders. Japanese companies hope that once they get the inside track, they will enjoy a lifetime of orders. Such lowball pricing is a common practice in Japan. In the past, Fujitsu and NEC Corp. had both submitted a 1 yen bid to design a library computer system. They drew straws and Fujitsu won. Earlier, Fujitsu had won a contract to design a telecommunications system in Wakayama Prefecture by bidding 1 yen.

The lowball pricing highlights Japanese companies' managerial philosophy: Shoot for the long-term. They don't mind giving away business in the short run and dividing up the bidding with their Japanese competitors to ultimately hype the market share, the end-game of Japanese business strategy.

Giveaway pricing shows how difficult it is to break into the Japanese market. Even if other structural barriers to trade, i.e., distribution system, exclusionary business practices, and land-use policies, are eliminated, the rigged bids would be an insurmountable hurdle for U.S. companies to cross.

Another kind of price distortion practiced in Japan is the government's price floor enforcement, applicable in such industries as airlines, insurance, agriculture, and fertilizer, whereby the business is divided up in cartels. This way competitors are prevented from entering the market.

Source: Business Week, November 20, 1989, p. 50.

Factors Affecting Transfer Pricing

Economic theory holds that price reflects demand and supply. For intracompany transactions, however, the parent corporation can control transfer pricing because the exchange is little more than an accounting entry between units of the same corporation. The principal objective of the parent corporation in setting intrafirm prices is to maximize the long-term economic interests of the total corporation. In this endeavor, one or more affiliates of the company may often end up losing, which leads to conflicts that must be resolved. Essentially, transfer pricing decisions are affected by the following factors:

1. Income tax liability within the host country
2. Income tax liability within the U.S.
3. Tariffs and/or customs duties within the host country
4. Exchange controls within the host country
5. Profit repatriation restrictions within the host country
6. Quota restrictions within the U.S.
7. Credit status of the U.S. parent firm

8. Credit status of the foreign subsidiary or affiliate
9. Joint-venture constraints within the host country

The importance of these factors varies from company to company and according to the location of affiliates. An older study, however, indicated that income tax liability was the most important variable influencing transfer pricing.[18] This conclusion was based mainly on research conducted to investigate MNCs' experiences vis-à-vis industrialized countries. In the case of developing countries, however, Kim and Miller ranked profit repatriation restrictions, exchange control constraints, and joint-venture constraints within the host country as the three most important factors affecting the pricing decision.[19] Despite the importance of different factors in different parts of the world, the motivation behind transfer pricing is the same—maximize overall corporate performance.[20]

Transfer Pricing Methods

For setting transfer prices, companies usually set guidelines like the following:

- All domestic and foreign units are profit centers, and transfers must be set at levels that yield a reasonable profit to both the selling and buying units.
- Profit is divided according to functions performed in producing and marketing goods to unrelated buyers.
- Gross margins (the spread between production and distribution costs and the sale to an unrelated buyer) are divided more or less evenly between domestic producing and foreign marketing units.
- Overall impact on consolidated profit is the paramount consideration, and profit is taken where it is best for the total corporation.

Such guidelines are meant to provide a broad perspective for arriving at prices. The actual price is left to the discretion of the manager concerned, since differences in corporate objectives and environmental conditions may not permit a uniform method. For instance, in order to cover certain costs, transfer prices may be raised in countries that limit or refuse to allow royalties as a deductible business expense for a local subsidiary or in countries with exchange controls on dividends that delay remittances. Prices to high-tariff countries may be kept as low as legal requirements permit. A company that is attempting to enter a foreign market, or to expand its share of a market, frequently suppresses initial administrative, research, or other expenses when establishing costs in its transfer price.

Since the transfer price has a variety of repercussions both at home and in host countries, many governments have developed rules for setting transfer prices following the "arm's length" principle, which is more or less arriving at the price based on competitive conditions. In practice, the arm's length approach yields decisions by national tax authorities. Companies that strictly follow the arm's length principle, which is more or less arriving at the price based on competitive conditions.

Government involvement in the setting of transfer prices is understandable. In addition to profit shifting and tax avoidance in safe havens, transfer pricing can also affect the international price structure in critical areas, thereby possibly fueling the inflationary process or creating a balance-of-payments problem (see International Marketing Highlight 13.4).

In many industries, the products planned for transfer from the parent or another affiliate are commonly available from sources outside the corporate family. In such cases, many companies let their contracting units negotiate the transfer price. The negotiated price may be based on market price or landed cost plus an agreed-upon profit markup.

Handling Interdivisional Conflicts

Decentralized units of a corporation usually are profit centers. Each profit center's rewards and benefits are dependent on its bottom-line performance. Thus, if the transfer pricing system affects the profits of a unit, it is likely to lead to a conflict between the units involved. Interdivisional conflict because of transfer pricing is unhealthy and should be avoided or minimized by setting the transfer price in such a way that a balance exists between each division's perception of the other's advantage in the transfer situation. If one of the divisions enjoys an advantage, the performance of the other division is adversely affected.

An empirical study on the subject showed that where either the supplier or the customer division is seen as making excessive profits from transfer pricing transactions, interdivisional conflict is increased; that is, conflict results not only from the real impact of a transfer price on a unit's performance, but also from the perception about the impact on the divisions involved. It is necessary, therefore, to provide adequate information to both the affiliates to prevent misconceptions about impact. Further, arrangements should be made through some sort of organizational set-up at headquarters to handle any conflict. The thrust of the conflict-handling effort should be to remove the imbalance that may favor one unit over the other.

Dumping

Dumping refers to the practice of pricing exports at levels lower than the domestic price. Strictly as a business strategy, dumping is a way of setting differential prices to achieve certain objectives. Thus, if a product is sold in the U.S. in two different markets at different prices (assuming this is feasible within the Robinson-Patman Act), there is nothing wrong with that practice. However, in the context of the international market, if this strategy is used intentionally to destroy a domestic industry, it becomes a matter of concern for the host country government on behalf of the greater interest of its nation. It is for this reason that many nations have antidumping laws on the books.

An international marketer must make sure that pricing decisions are free from liability for dumping in the host country. Countries usually levy a heavy penalty against dumping, which may cause the imported goods to be much higher than the market price.

━━━━━━━━━━━━━━━━ **International Marketing Highlight 13.4** ━━━━━━━━━━━━━━━━

Two Ways to Skin the Cat

To reduce the MNC's exposure to significant tax and penalty costs in the area of transfer pricing, a company has only two choices: rely on self-compliance or obtain an advance pricing agreement (APA). Self-compliance involves a consistent, documented effort to report arm's length results from intercompany transactions. An APA is an agreement between the MNC and the IRS in advance covering the transfer-pricing methods that will apply in the future—a period of three to five years—to the MNC's transactions with its affiliates.

MNCs should consider the following factors in choosing among transfer-pricing alternatives:

- **Protection against IRS adjustments and penalties.** With self-compliance, there is a risk of IRS-imposed adjustments and penalties because the area is so fact-specific and complex. An APA offers more reliable protection against an unforeseen tax bite.

- **Protection against double taxation.** With self-compliance, there is the risk that the foreign country will not agree to an MNC's method and will tax the same income that the IRS taxes. With a binational APA, as an extension of the one in the USA, this risk is eliminated.

- **Practical pricing policies.** An APA allows for negotiation of a pricing method that best suits the company. Under self-compliance, the MNC must fit into the IRS cookbook of rules.

- **Up-front costs.** The initial costs incurred in satisfying self-compliance procedures may be less than those involved in obtaining an APA.

- **Ongoing costs.** There may be significant costs under self-compliance in trying to comply with all the rules. With an APA, yearly costs would only entail the time and effort needed to comply with the agreement.

- **Best earnings results for MNCs.** IRS agents' responsibility is to make adjustments favorable to the government whereas the APA division's job is to reach reasonable agreements with tax-payers. Thus, savings are more likely to result from an APA than from an audit of self-compliance methods.

Source: *Crossborder Monitor*, July 20, 1994, p. 12.

Actually, the problem of dumping is more prevalent in developed markets. It is in these markets that exporters find the best opportunity for growth. Dumping is one way to render the domestic industry noncompetitive. If carried to its extreme, dumping can force the domestic manufacturers out of business. Once that happens, the price of imported goods can be increased. In brief, an exporter may practice dumping with lower profits in the short run, but with extremely high profits in the long run. As an example, the U.S. is a large market. Overall, U.S. tariff barriers are very low. Exporters from Japan, South Korea, Brazil, and even from Europe find it a lucrative market to expand in. Dumping provides an opportunity to exporters to undercut the price of U.S.-manufactured goods. Thus, in the past, many exporters have been charged with dumping, particularly the Japanese (for example, TV manufacturers and steelmakers). Responding to the steel industry's pleas, the Treasury Department established minimum prices for different types of imported steel. Prices below the minimum prices would automatically initiate an investigation of possible dumping.

Meeting the Import Challenge

Many business face competition from imports. Foreign goods are often sold at prices that seem so ridiculously low that they can only be explained as dumping. A company can consider several strategic options to protect its markets from imports and possibly develop new opportunities for its products. A company facing competition from imported goods should:

- Evaluate its underlying competitive position and that of foreign competitors.

- Assess whether it is feasible to drive the domestic value-added component down to the same level as that of the import.

- Look at import competition in the context of changes in world production and trade factors. Adopting this approach will help differentiate between the short-and long-run impact of imports.

- Clearly understand the impact of changes in either its own or the foreign competitor's value-added and raw-material components.

- Be aware that the basis for import competition will vary with the country of origin. European imports require a different response than Japanese imports, and these, in turn, will require still a different response than that for, say, Korean or Taiwanese imports.

- When there are fundamental differences in cost that cannot be eliminated, attempt to change the product. The domestic producer should ensure, however, that value-added additions to its products result in differences in real value in the marketplace and that the foreign producer cannot emulate them. If the foreign competitor can follow with relative ease, the foreign competitor's leverage is actually increased.

- Segment the market so that efforts are concentrated where competitive leverage is greatest. Attempting to match imports across a wide spectrum of products can often be disastrous. The domestic producer should be both thoughtful and explicit in the method of segmentation.

- Fully assess the impact of volume on value-added. If this is significant, and if reasonable changes in volume can be made, then this, combined with the ability to purchase raw material at internationally competitive prices, can bring about significant changes in total cost. As a result, the domestic producer could possibly become competitive with imports. The remaining domestic producers may then face an abrupt change in their respective strategies for competing with domestic competitors as well as a need to change the strategy for competing with imports.

Leasing

In domestic marketing, leasing serves as an important alternative to outright buying, especially in the area of industrial marketing. In recent years, however, leasing has emerged in international marketing as well. For example, several years ago TAW Company founded TAW International Leasing Inc., to rent different types of heavy equipment, especially in Africa. Similarly, Clark Equipment Company leases equipment overseas through its Clark Rental Corporation subsidiary.[21] As a matter of fact, leasing strategy is employed by essentially all capital goods and equipment manufacturers active in foreign markets.

A variety of conditions operating in foreign markets make leasing a viable pricing strategy to pursue. These conditions are capital shortage, availability of maintenance and servicing personnel, intermittent need, customer's unwillingness to make a long-term commitment, and the tax advantages of leasing. Capital shortage may make it difficult for customers to buy certain equipment. This is particularly true in the case of developing countries. Leasing, however, provides a way to procure use of the equipment. By the same token, leasing permits the international marketer an entry into the market, which otherwise might be closed because of capital shortage.

Further, many kinds of equipment require regular maintenance and servicing. Customers may shy away from buying equipment because they fear a lack of adequate servicing. Leasing, however, transfers the burden of servicing and maintenance onto the lessor and relieves the customer of the worry about servicing. In many situations, a customer may be unwilling to buy a product outright either out of concern about possible technological obsolescence or because its relevance for the business is unclear. In such cases, leasing provides a viable compromise. The customer can use the equipment without being stuck with it. As a matter of fact, in many leasing arrangements, the customer is given an option to buy the product at a specified price after having the opportunity to use it for some time. Finally, many countries offer investment incentives that are available for both outright purchase and leased equipment/plant. Where capital shortage becomes a hindrance to an outright purchaser, the incentive still can be sought through leasing. To the U.S. marketer, leasing offers an additional advantage: the entire lease price or rental may be written off as an expense for income tax purposes. The marketer may even be willing to pass on a portion of this tax benefit to the overseas customer.

Advantages aside, leasing poses two problems. First, how should the leasing price be set? Second, what may a lessor do if the customer overseas abruptly calls the deal off? For example, in the U.S., an attempt is usually made to recover the total cost of the leased equipment in about half its useful life. Thus, the leasing charge/rental during the second half of life would be strictly profit. However, the life of the equipment may be longer or shorter in a foreign setting depending on the intensity of use and the conditions under which the use takes place. Thus, the establishment of the useful life of the product might not be easy. Further, it would be difficult to compute the monetary value of risks involved in a long-term foreign transaction. Finally, the inclusion of foreign inflation factors in setting the lease price would pose problems too because computation of inflation rates and related forecasts are not reliable.

A still greater problem occurs when a foreign party backs out of a deal. For example, in 1984, the Zambian government canceled its contract with TAW to rent 330 tractors and 400 trailers. TAW had gone out of its way to manufacture the equipment custom-designed for heavy-duty usage on inferior roads at a time when U.S. business was good and parts were short. The Zambian government's decision created a big problem for TAW. How was it to dispose of the equipment?[22]

Despite the problems that leasing may pose, in the years to come leasing is likely to become more popular. In recent years, many governments have facilitated marketing overseas through leasing plans. For example, the French government tried to establish a market for its Concorde, the supersonic jetliner, through backing a leasing program.[23] Similarly, the U.S. Export-Import Bank provides guarantees on foreign leasing by U.S. companies. Such support helps companies venturing into new foreign markets through leasing.

Summary

Prices determine the total revenue and to a large extent the profitability of any business. Because of the crucial importance of pricing, top management often plays a significant role in making pricing decisions. Top management must decide the strategic significance of pricing in the marketing mix. For example, U.S. companies traditionally have competed overseas based on nonprice factors. Lately, however, more and more companies emphasize price competition. Further, top management's goals must determine the extent to which uniform versus differentiated prices are set worldwide. It is argued usually that dissimilar conditions in overseas markets favor differentiated prices. However, it is felt that standardized pricing increases overall corporate effectiveness. Finally, top management assigns the pricing responsibility either to headquarters or to subsidiaries, or jointly between them.

In making any pricing decision, the following factors deserve consideration: pricing objectives, cost, competition, the customer, and government regulations. In international marketing, these factors must be examined both at home and in the host country. Each factor, composed of a number of components, varies in each nation both in importance and in interaction.

Prices in overseas business are set by following either a cost approach or a market approach. The cost approach involves computing all relevant costs and adding a profit markup to determine the price. The market approach examines price setting from the customer's viewpoint. If the price that appears satisfactory to the potential customer does not meet the company's profit goal, either the business is given up or the price is increased. Thus, either approach brings a viable decision on price.

Export pricing is affected by three additional considerations: the price destination, the nature of the product, and the currency used in completing the transaction. Usually companies prepare separate price lists for different overseas markets. The price list contains a profit margin that makes it feasible to adjust the price following local market conditions, including competitive price, the government's export incentives in some countries, and the flexibility for competitive reduction of the price.

Price escalation is an important consideration in export retail pricing. The retail price of exports usually is much higher than the domestic retail price for the same good.

This difference can be explained by the added costs associated with exports such as transportation, customs duty, and distributor margin. To counteract the excessive escalation of export prices, a variety of strategic alternatives is available to management.

Price setting by multinational marketers in foreign markets essentially follows the procedure practiced in domestic markets. Internationally, however, a few additional factors become important. The price in various regions of the world should be kept relatively uniform to avoid competition for company units from unrelated dealers in the home market. Especially in developing countries, the ethics of pricing requires careful examination. Also price segmentation acquires more significance in foreign markets. Further, it may not always be desirable to pursue short-term pricing goals in foreign markets. Finally, governments outside the U.S. play a significant role in pricing.

An important topic in international marketing concerns pricing intracompany transfer of goods and services, that is, prices for goods and services exchanged within the corporate family. When transactions between units of the same enterprise take place across national frontiers and the units are subject to different environmental factors such as customs duties, tax rates, and currency risks, adjustments in transfer prices can be used to advance various corporate goals and increase overall corporate profits. Since the transfer price has repercussions for both the home and host countries, many governments have designed rules to monitor such prices. In the U.S., for example, the IRS requires setting transfer prices according to the arm's length principle, which more or less means arriving at the price based on competitive conditions.

The chapter ends with a discussion on dumping and leasing. Dumping refers to the practice of pricing exports at lower levels than the domestic price for the same goods. As dumping may adversely affect domestic industry, many nations have legislated antidumping laws. As an alternative to outright purchase, leasing is slowly emerging in importance in international marketing. While setting leasing prices presents difficulties for various reasons, it nevertheless provides a good entry into markets otherwise inaccessible because of capital shortage.

Review Questions

1. What role does corporate management play in price setting for international markets?
2. What arguments favor a strategy of differentiated pricing in international markets?
3. Under what circumstances may uniform prices make sense?
4. Briefly discuss various factors that affect the pricing decision internationally.
5. Differentiate between the cost and market approaches to pricing.
6. What is meant by price escalation? What strategic options are available to international marketers to counteract escalation in export prices?
7. Under what circumstances might dumping be useful to the people of the importing country? Explain.
8. What advantage does leasing offer in international markets?

Creative Questions

1. U.S. steel manufacturers feel that Korean steel companies are dumping their products into the U.S. steel market. What recourse do the U.S. companies have to redress their concern? Does the U.S. government have any rules to punish foreign countries dumping goods in the U.S. market? How do the U.S. companies go about establishing their claim against the Koreans?
2. Since demand and supply conditions vary from market to market, setting of uniform prices on a global basis is unrealistic. Do you agree? Are there conditions under which uniform pricing would make sense? What kinds of products are more amenable to uniform pricing?

Endnotes

1. Bill Saporito, "Why the Price Wars Never End," *Fortune*, March 23, 1992, p. 68. *Also see* Johny K. Johansson and Gary Erickson, "The Price-Quality Relationship and Trade Barriers," *International Marketing Review*, Autumn 1985, pp. 52–63.
2. Vern Terpstra, *American Marketing in the Common Market* (New York: Praeger, 1967), pp.109–10.
3. J.J. Boddewyn, "American Marketing in the European Common Market, 1963–1973," in *Multinational Product Management* (Cambridge, MA: Marketing Science Institute, 1976), pp. VII–1–VII–25.
4. Nathaniel H. Leff, "Multinational Corporate Pricing Strategy in the Developing Countries," *Journal of International Business Studies*, Fall 1975, p. 55.
5. Peter R. Kressler, "Is Uniform Pricing Desirable in Multinational Markets?" in Subhash C. Jain and Lewis R. Tucker, Jr., eds., *International Marketing Managerial Perspectives* (Boston: CBI Publishing Company, Inc. 1979), p. 389.
6. J. J. Boddewyn, "American Marketing in the European Common Market, 1963–1973," in *Multinational Product Management* (Cambridge, MA: Marketing Science Institute, 1976), pp. VII–1–I–25.
7. "Why Common Market Does Not Mean Common Prices," *Business International*, February 2, 1973, p. 47.
8. Raphael Elimelech, "Pricing for the Japanese Market," in Subhash C. Jain and Lewis R. Tucker, Jr., eds., *International Marketing: Managerial Perspectives*, 2nd ed. (Boston: Kent Publishing Co., 1986), pp. 285–97.
9. "Factors that Influence Pricing Decisions, *International Management*, June 1981, p. 3.
10. "MNCs Home Competitive Edge With Activity-Based Costing," *Business International*, January 28, 1991, p. 37.
11. Sharon V. Thach and Catherine N. Axinn, "Pricing and Financing Practices of Industrial Exporting Firms," *International Marketing Review*, Vol. 8, No. 1 (1991), pp. 32–46.
12. Vern Terpstra, *International Dimensions of Marketing* (Boston: Kent Publishing Company, 1982), p. 141. *Also see* Pamela Sherrid, "Learning the Tricks of the Japanese Trade," *Fortune*, November 20, 1978, p. 63.
13. Warren J. Keegan, *Multinational Marketing Management* 3rd ed. (Englewood Cliffs, NJ: Prentice-Hall, 1984), p. 511.
14. *See* Amanda Bennett, "Peking Is Finding It Difficult to Let Prices Float," *The Wall Street Journal*, February 22, 1985, p. 34.
15. Venkatakrishna V. Bellur, Radharao Chagauti, Rajeswarnrao Chagauti, and Saraswati P. Singh, "Strategic Adaptions to Price Controls: The Case of the Indian Drug Industry," *Journal of the Academy of Marketing Science*, Winter–Spring 1985, pp. 143–59.
16. Vern Terpstra, *International Dimensions of Marketing* (Boston: Kent Publishing Company, 1982), p. 151.
17. U.S. Department of Commerce (Based on an ad hoc inquiry.)
18. Jeffrey S. Arpan, "Multinational Firm Pricing in International Markets," *Sloan Management Review*, Winter 1973, pp. 1–9.
19. Seung H. Kim and Stephen W. Miller, "Constituents of the International Transfer Pricing Decisions," *Columbia Journal of World Business*, Spring 1979, pp. 69–77.
20. Mohammad F. Al-Eryani, Pervaiz Alam, and Syed H. Akhter, "Transfer Pricing Determinants of U.S. Multinationals," *Journal of International Business Studies*, Vol. 21, No. 3 (Third Quarter 1990). pp. 409–26.
21. *Business Abroad*, May 13, 1986, p. 15.
22. "Zambia: The TAW Truck Deal Runs Out of Gas," *Business Week*, April 27, 1984, p. 56.
23. *See:* "Collision Course in Commercial Aircraft: Boeing-Airbus-McDonnell Douglas-1991 (A)," A Case Study, Harvard Business School, 1989.

CHAPTER 14

International Channels of Distribution

Chapter Focus

After studying this chapter, you should be able to:

- Compare alternative international channels of distribution
- Describe the international channel selection process
- Discuss wholesaling and retailing in foreign environments
- Examine international franchising and physical distribution

As for domestic marketing, the distribution process for international programs involves all those activities related to time, place, and ownership utilities for industrial and ultimate consumers. The selection, operation, and motivation of effective channels of distribution are often crucial factors in a firm's differential advantage in international markets. The diverse activities and culturally differentiated roles of channel intermediaries make the formulation of distribution strategies a challenge for any firm entering foreign markets.

The channels of distribution available in a country are the result of culture and tradition. For example, in Japan there are usually too many channels involved in the distribution of a product. In the developing countries, channels of distribution are scattered, small in scope, inefficient, and insufficient. An international distribution system must be adapted to the country's established practices. Channel innovations ought to emerge from customer need rather than through an arbitrary attempt to streamline the distribution system.

This chapter describes the alternative channels of distribution for an international marketer to consider. There are examples of different types of intermediaries, both domestic and foreign, for distribution across national boundaries. Guidelines are provided for selecting, motivating, and controlling the channels most appropriate for a firm's distribution mix. In addition, wholesale and retail patterns in overseas markets are examined. Also explored is the rationale of overseas franchising relationships along with their patterns of development. Finally, the perspectives of international physical distribution are discussed. International distribution, which requires special knowledge of complex rate structures and tariffs, presents many unique problems. These call for an adequate management information system. Throughout the chapter, examples are given to illustrate how to achieve an effective distribution system in international markets.

Alternative Distribution Channels

Distribution channels are the link between producers and customers. As Figure 14.1 shows, there are various ways of creating this link. Basically, an international marketer distributes either directly or indirectly. Direct distribution amounts to dealing with a foreign firm. The indirect method means dealing through another U.S. firm that serves as an intermediary. The choice of a particular channel link will be founded on considerations to be discussed in a later section of this chapter.

Channel Theory

It has long been held that the channels of distribution available in a country depend on its stage of economic development, which is reflected in the per capita real income and the sociopsychological, cultural, or anthropological environment. From this premise, it can be concluded that:

- The more-developed countries have more levels of distribution, more specialty stores and supermarkets, more department stores, and more stores in the rural areas.

- The influence of the foreign import agent declines with economic development.

- Manufacturer-wholesaler-retailer functions become separated with economic development.

- Wholesaler functions approximate those in North America with increasing economic development.

FIGURE 14.1 Selected Channels of Distribution in International Marketing

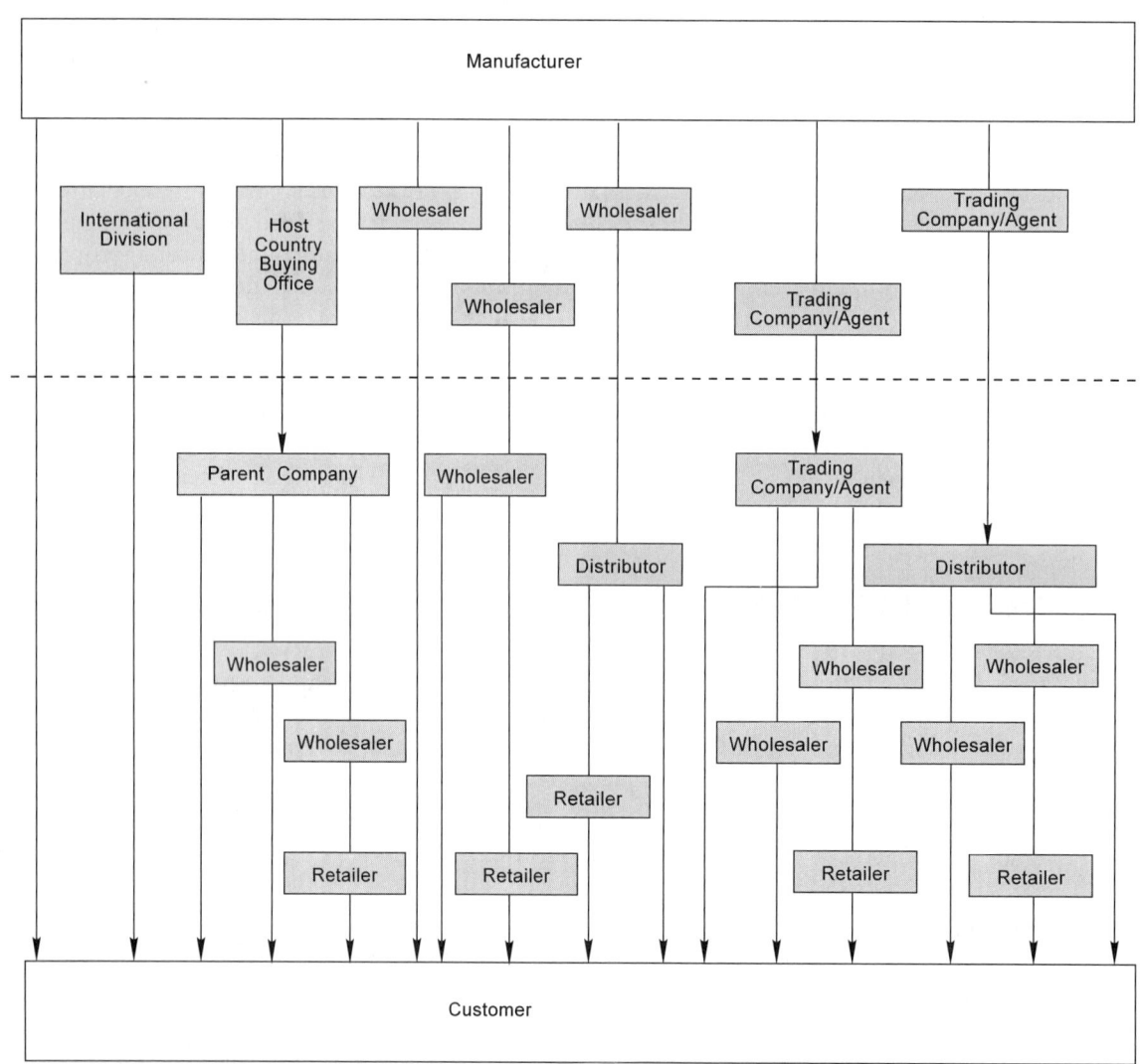

Note: Middle agents above the dotted line are U.S.-based. Those below the dotted line are foreign channels.

- The financing function of wholesalers declines and wholesale markups increase with increasing development.

- The number of small stores declines and the size of the average store increases with increasing development.

- The role of the peddler and itinerant trader and the importance of the open-garden-fair decline with increasing development.

- Retail margins improve with increasing economic development.[1]

According to this theory, changes in the channel structure of a country can be introduced only in response to changes in its economic and other environments. Channel changes cannot be enforced from without. At the cost of oversimplification, for example, supermarket distribution would not work in poor countries such as Egypt, Kenya, Sudan, and Pakistan because the economy and other environments operating in those countries are not conducive to such a form of distribution.

An empirical study on the subject, however, casts doubts on the viability of this theory. The results of the study showed little evidence to support the idea that the development of a distribution system in a country is determined by the limits of its social, economic, technological, and cultural environments. For example, it was found that channel structure and relationships mainly depend on the relative size of the firms at different channel stages, rather than on the country's level of development.

Apparently, the relationship between a country's channel structure and its environment remains undefined. How else to explain the channels of distribution in a country is a matter of speculation. All that can be said, given the current state-of-the-art, is that distribution channels, like any other socioeconomic phenomenon, evolve slowly from a multitude of factors, some direct and some indirect. We do not quite know what these factors are, let alone their relationships.

Distribution Channels in Japan: An Example

Each country, rich or poor, has its own unique distribution system, evolved over time. International marketers must carefully examine the various aspects of a country's established distribution system to determine how to obtain distribution for their goods.

Despite the fact that Japan is the second economic power in the world today, its distribution system has been labeled outmoded, complex, cumbersome, and inefficient. The purpose of focusing this discussion on Japan is to emphasize that distribution structure is country-specific, and it would be naive for international marketers to enforce their own new distribution system on a country. Thus, distribution channels must be used as they are, and efforts should be made to fit into the country through the established patterns.

In general, the Japanese system encompasses a wide range of wholesalers and other agents, brokers, and retailers, differing more in number than in function from their American counterparts. There are myriad tiny retail shops. An even greater number of wholesalers supplies goods to them, layered tier upon tier, many more than most U.S. executives would think necessary. For example, soap may move through three wholesalers plus a sales company after it leaves the manufacturer before it even reaches the retail outlet. A steak goes from rancher to consumer in a process that often involves a dozen middle agents. Furthermore, Japan's distribution channels have traditionally been segregated by product type, with the consequent development of many specialized marketing routes.[2]

The Japanese distribution system is built into the fabric of its society. It is a sort of welfare system that provides a living for so many people that the government does not have to pay welfare. In this way, the seemingly inefficient distribution system serves an important social function: It has been a flexible make-work device, acting as a buffer to absorb excess workers, particularly those on the verge of retirement. Many observers expect this social role to increase as the current slowdown in Japan's economic growth shrinks employment in manufacturing.[3]

Another reason for the longevity of Japan's distribution system is that it serves most companies well. Some suppliers, for instance, keep their inventories at or near their customers' headquarters to ensure rapid deliveries. Foreign companies, of course, can't compete with such service unless they maintain substantial stockpiles and facilities in Japan.

Consumers are also served well. Lacking much storage space in their small homes, most Japanese homemakers shop several times a week and prefer convenient neighborhood shops. The little shops often strengthen their position by doing more for customers than just selling goods. In brief, Japanese distribution channels are more complex than comparable channels in the U.S. However, the dominant view in Japan is that the system suits the needs of Japanese consumers. For example, while furniture stores in the U.S. may take up to 10 weeks for delivery, Japanese consumers usually receive delivery within a week.

Moreover, statistics indicate that the distribution system is not likely to change soon. According to government figures, the number of mom-and-pop retailers employing 4 or fewer workers increased almost 60 percent between 1975 and 1990 to 2 million outlets. During the same period, the number of similar-size wholesalers rose to more than 413,000 from about 250,000.[4] The papa-mama stores control 56 percent of Japan's retail sales (versus 3 percent for U.S. mom-and-pops and 5 percent in Europe).[5]

Japan has 1 retailer for every 74 people, compared with 1 for every 144 Americans. The U.S. has 145,000 food stores to serve a nation of 250 million; Japan has more than 620,000 to serve a population one-half the size.[6]

Similarly, Japan has one million bars and restaurants, more than three times as many per person as in the U.S. More than one-half of these establishments are independent operators, so they need frequent deliveries in small quantities. Wholesalers of perishable foods make as many as three drop-offs a day. Campbell Japan Inc.'s typical delivery of soup to a retailer is minuscule by U.S. standards: six cans. Campbell's average shipment to wholesalers is 3 to 5 24-can cases. That and a 19 percent duty increase the price of a can of tomato soup in Tokyo to $1.45, compared with $.39 in New York.[7]

It costs U.S. and German retailers about $25 to deliver a market basket of groceries to a customer, but in Japan the cost to retailers is about $35. This means the average Japanese must work 40 percent longer than his or her German or American counterpart to buy a weekly supply of groceries.[8]

In conclusion, the way the Japanese distribution channels are structured and managed presents one of the major reasons for the failure of foreign firms to establish major market position in Japan. Further, despite the fact that the Japanese channels have been held inefficient and cumbersome, they seem to serve the customer well (see International Marketing Highlight 14.1).

International Marketing Highlight 14.1

Customer Service—The Japanese Way

My husband and I bought one souvenir the last time we were in Tokyo—a Sony compact disk player. The transaction took seven minutes at the Odakyu Department Store, including time to find the right department and to wait while the salesman filled out a second charge slip after misspelling my husband's name on the first.

My in-laws, who were our hosts in the outlying city of Sagamihara, were eager to see their son's purchase, so he opened the box for them the next morning. But when he tried to demonstrate the player, it wouldn't work. We peered inside. It had no innards! My husband used the time until the Odakyu would open at 10:00 to practice for the rare opportunity in that country to wax indignant. But at a minute to 10:00 he was preempted by the store ringing us.

My mother-in-law took the call and had to hold the receiver away from her ear against the barrage of Japanese honorifics. Odakyu's vice president was on his way over with a new disk player.

A taxi pulled up fifty minutes later and spilled out the vice president and a junior employee who was laden with packages and a clipboard. In the entrance hall the two men bowed vigorously.

The younger man was still bobbing as he read from a log that recorded the progress of their efforts to rectify their mistake, beginning at 4:32 p.m. the day before, when the salesclerk alerted the store's security guards to stop my husband at the door. When that didn't work, the clerk turned to his supervisor, who turned to his supervisor, until a SWAT team leading all the way to the vice president was in place to work on the only clues, a name and an American Express card number. Remembering that the customer had asked him about using the disk player in the U.S., the clerk called thirty-two hotels in and around Tokyo to ask if a Mr. Kitasei was registered. When that turned up nothing, the Odakyu commandeered a staff member to stay until 9 p.m. to call American Express headquarters in New York. American Express gave him our New York telephone number. It was after 11 p.m. when he reached my parents, who were staying at our apartment. My mother gave him my in-law's telephone number.

The younger man looked up from his clipboard and gave us, in addition to the new $280 disk player, a set of towels, a box of cakes, and a Chopin disk. Three minutes after this exhausted pair had arrived they were climbing back into the waiting cab. The vice president suddenly dashed back. He had forgotten to apologize for my husband having to wait while the salesman had rewritten the charge slip, but he hoped we understood that it had been the young man's first day.

My Tokyo experience contrasts sharply with treatment I've received at home. In late July, without explanation or apology from Bloomingdale's, a credit of $546.66 appeared on my American Express statement for china ordered January 12, paid for April 17, and never received.

Source: Hilary Hinds Kitasei, "Japan's Got Us Beat in the Service Department Too," *The Wall Street Journal*, July 30, 1985, p. 30.

International Channel Members

The previous section mentioned two forms of distribution: direct and indirect. While a direct distribution channel may appear more effective, in practice it is better only if the customers are geographically homogeneous, have similar buying habits, and are limited in number. Indirect channel is preferable when customers and buying habits are heterogeneous.[9]

Either way, a company may go through one or more agents or merchant intermediaries. The essential difference between them concerns the legal ownership of goods. An agent, without taking title to the goods, distributes them on behalf of the principal, the manufacturer. Merchant intermediaries do business in their own names and hold title to the goods they deal in. Figure 14.2 identifies important types of intermediaries. The type of intermediaries and their names vary from country to country and from industry to industry in the same country. For this reason, the discussion here is limited to certain intermediaries popularly used worldwide for distribution across industries.

Indirect Distribution Through Agents

Important among these types of agents are export management companies, manufacturers' export agents, cooperative exporters, Webb-Pomerene associations, foreign freight forwarders, commission agents, and country-controlled buying agents and trading companies. While these agents do not take title, they do take possession of goods. However, they have different duties in respect to continuation of relationship with the principal (long-term versus ad hoc); degree of control maintained by the principal (complete versus slight versus none); pricing authority accorded to the agent (full versus partial versus advisory); affiliation with buyer or seller; number of principals served at a time (few versus many); involvement or noninvolvement with shipping or handling of competitive lines; provision of promotional support (continuous versus one-time versus none); extension of credit to principal (regularly versus occasionally versus rarely versus never); and provision of market information (good versus fair versus poor).

Export Management Company (EMC) An export management company is an independent export organization that serves different companies in their export endeavors. The EMC regards the exporter as a client, not as an employer. The EMC deals in a number of allied but noncompetitive lines. Usually, the EMC handles the entire export function for a manufacturer. In all contacts and communications overseas, the EMC operates under the client's name, using client stationery and promotional materials such as catalogs. EMCs differ in the scale of their operations. Some handle export sales for as few as four or five manufacturers; others serve as many as fifty companies. A typical firm represents ten manufacturers. EMCs are especially helpful to small companies that are unable to afford experienced and skilled export managers. EMCs understand foreign cultures. They are up-to-date on international politics, logistics, taxation, and legal problems. They provide a viable alternative for small firms to launch themselves in the export business.

An EMC may be just a 1-person operation, or it may employ as many as a 100 people. Some firms are relatively new, while others have decades of experience. Large export management firms often maintain overseas offices in strategic locations. Senior

International Channel Members

FIGURE 14.2 Intermediaries in International Distribution

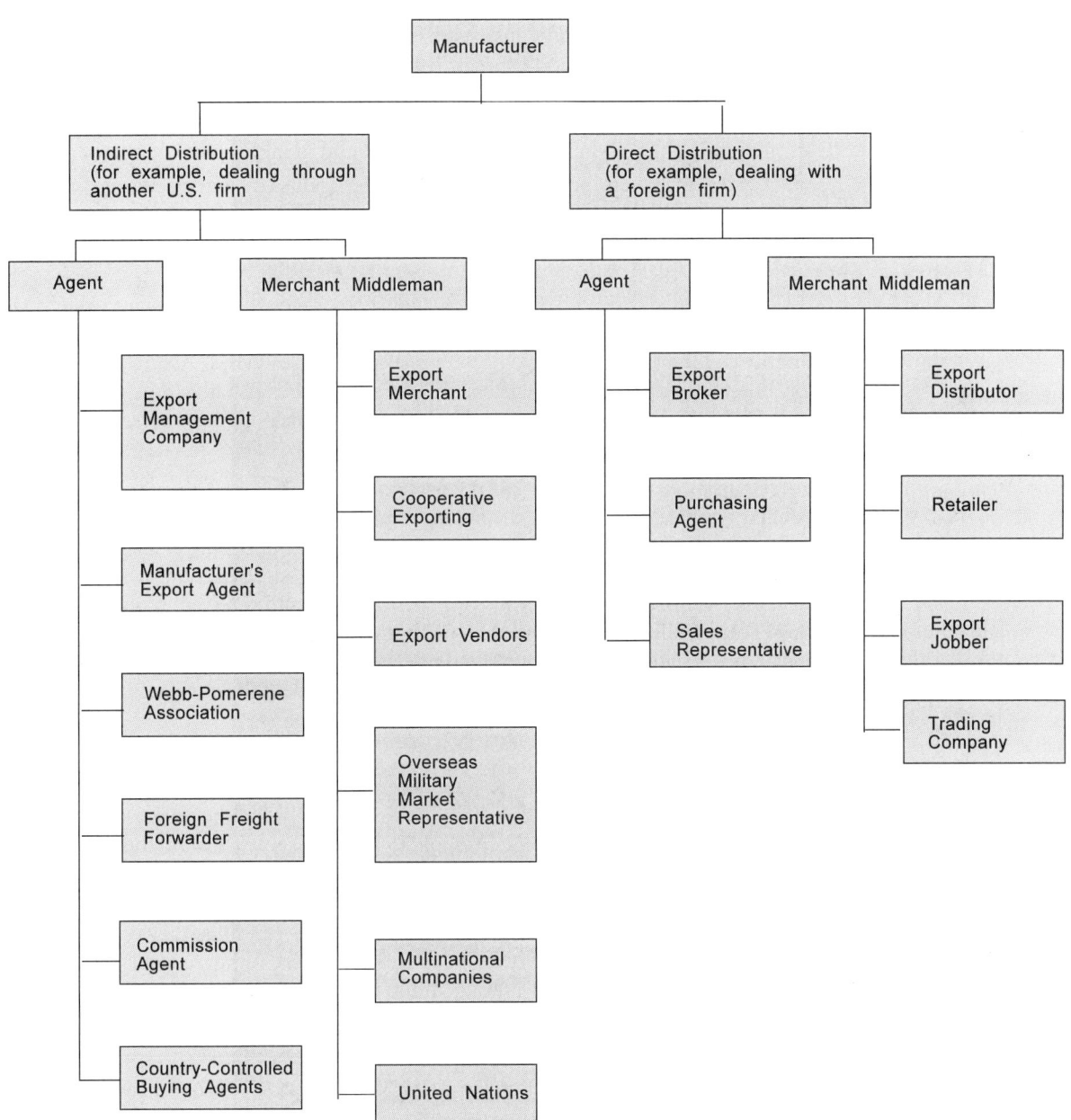

executives of these firms frequently travel overseas to seek orders and develop relationships with the customers.

There are about 1,200 EMCs in the U.S. Most are located in the larger seaport cities. The important sources for locating an EMC are the U.S. Department of Commerce, port authorities, and banks handling foreign trade. The National Federation of Export Management Companies, based in Washington, D.C., and local chambers of commerce are also good sources. An exporter should attempt to find an EMC that specializes in its product type, has in place a well-organized and controlled worldwide distribution system, is well-financed and managed, and is willing and eager to devote significant amounts of managerial effort and money to launching its product.

EMCs generate their income either from commissions or from discounts on goods they buy for resale overseas. The commission/discount varies from 10 percent or less to 30 percent or more, based on the services provided and the difficulty of the marketing task.

EMCs are used by both large and small companies, simply because they can undertake exporting more effectively and generally at a lower cost than other channels. Further, it is quite common for exporters to use multiple EMCs. A single EMC may not be able to reach all world markets. In addition, EMCs usually come to specialize by product. Thus, a company that deals in diverse products may use several EMCs.

Manufacturer's Export Agent (MEA) Manufacturer's export agents provide services similar to those provided by the export management company with the exception that they cover limited markets. Further, the contractual relationship is short-term only, from a few months, to a year or two. Sometimes the contract applies only to a particular transaction. The MEA acts under his or her own name and receives a commission for services. Thus, while an international marketer might deal with one export management company, he or she would be represented by several MEAs. Because the MEA does not serve the export department of the principal as an EMC does, he or she cannot be relied upon to perpetuate business for an export-minded company.

Webb-Pomerene Association A Webb-Pomerene association is formed among competing U.S. manufacturers, especially and exclusively for the purpose of exports according to the Webb-Pomerene Act of 1918. An agreement in the form of a Webb-Pomerene association is exempt from antitrust laws.

The members of a Webb-Pomerene association can engage in different international marketing activities to their mutual advantage. For example, they can set prices, combine shipments, jointly undertake marketing research, or share information with each other, and allocate orders among different members of the association. It is estimated that there are currently over 30 active Webb-Pomerene associations.

Foreign Freight Forwarder Foreign freight forwarders specialize in handling overseas shipping arrangements. Their services can be utilized for handling goods from a U.S. port to the foreign port of entry. Occasionally, they may handle inland shipments also. A foreign freight forwarder receives a discount or fees from the shipping company. For extra services such as packing, they would be paid by the export manufacturer.

Commission Agent   Commission agents represent foreign customers interested in buying U.S. products. They serve as so-called finders for their principals and locate the appropriate goods at the lowest price. The commission agents receive a commission for their services from their foreign clients.

Country-Controlled Buying Agent   This type of agent is an official buyer of a foreign government, seeking to buy designated goods for his or her country. Many developing countries, for example, maintain supply missions in the U.S. with a number of officers who are entrusted with the task of procuring different goods for their countries.

American Trading Company (ATC)   The ATC is a relatively new form of indirect channel that can be formed under the Export Trading Company Act of 1982 (also see Chapter 17). The goal of this act is to increase U.S. exports by encouraging more efficient provision of export trade services to producers and suppliers alike, by improving the availability of trade finance, and by removing the anti-trust disincentive to export activities.[10] Before the Export Trading Company Act, U.S. firms were handicapped in forming trading companies because of the fear of antitrust prosecution and inadequate capitalization. Since the passage of this legislation, however, there has been an increasing interest among businesses of all sizes to form trading companies.

Although the act provides a legal basis for the development of ATCs, the shape of their operating characteristics (i.e., type of product exported, the export role adopted—agent or merchant—services provided, etc.) is left in the hands of private business. Because the whole concept of trading companies is new to the U.S., it is too early to say what products they normally will handle, how they will be managed, and what services they will concentrate on. Thus far, agribusiness firms are taking more interest in trading companies than are any other types of business.[11]

Empirical research on the subject indicates that ATCs are likely to be more diversified both in handling products and in geographic coverage. In addition, unlike the EMCs, the ATCs have the potential to be much larger in size and operations. By the same token, decision making in ATCs should be diversified, since the membership would be shared by firms (e.g., banks, manufacturers, EMCs) with different backgrounds and cultures.[12]

Indirect Distribution Through Merchant Intermediaries

Merchant intermediaries located in the U.S. serve as middle agents for manufacturers in their export endeavors. Export merchants, other manufactures, export vendors, overseas military market representatives, MNCs, and the U.N. principally fill this role.

The merchant intermediaries invariably take title to the goods and deal in their own names. They may or may not undertake delivery of the goods, and the services they provide vary. Likewise, the authority exercised by these intermediaries differs. For example, the export merchant usually has pricing authority, but a cooperative exporter does not.

Export Merchant Export merchants buy directly from manufacturers according to their specifications, taking title to the goods. They have overseas contacts through which the goods are sold either to wholesalers or retailers. They assume all the risks and sell in their own names. Their compensation consists of a markup percentage that is based on market conditions. In general, an export merchant resembles a domestic wholesaler.

Cooperative Exporter Cooperative exporter is the name given to any company that has an established system of handling exports for its own goods and distributes products overseas for other manufacturers on a contractual basis. For example, several years ago Colgate-Palmolive Company distributed Wilkinson blades in many international markets. Recently, Colgate and Kao Corporation of Japan formed a joint venture to manufacture toiletry products in the U.S. The products of this venture would be distributed worldwide through the former's distribution network.[13] Similarly, Sony Corporation serves as a distributor in Japan for different U.S. and European companies. Kao Corporation of Japan, a diversified chemical and detergent company, markets Dow Chemical Co.'s corrosion-resistant vinyl ester resin, a type of fiberglass-reinforced plastic used in industry.[14] Whirlpool used Sony in Japan, Perrier marketed the Swiss chocolate Lindt in the U.S., Breck Shampoo used Schick in Germany, and Champion Spark Plug used a Nanjing spark plug manufacturer to distribute its products in China.[15]

These cooperative arrangements are also called *piggybacking*. The cooperative exporter may assume the role of an EMC or may just serve as a commission agent for a short period in select markets. The principal asset of cooperative exporters is their experience in dealing overseas as manufacturers themselves. Therefore, they are more aware of and sympathetic toward the problems of the manufacturer interested in developing export markets.

Export Vendor Export vendors are companies that specialize in buying poor-quality and overproduced goods for distribution overseas. The companies buy goods outright, taking title to them. They ship the goods to one or more countries and sell them through their established contacts. Such intermediaries are useful in times of depressed business conditions in the U.S. and/or when company for some reason gets stuck with certain unwanted products. For example, many small U.S. manufacturers used such intermediaries to get rid of goods they produced for the 1980 Olympic Games in Moscow. Since the U.S. did not participate in the games, these goods could not be sold in a normal way.

Overseas Military Market Representatives These are representatives who specialize in selling to US. military post exchanges (PXs) and commissaries. More than $3 billion annually in consumer goods, not all of them made in the U.S., are sold by U.S. military PXs and commissaries overseas. The bulk of this market is made up of the joint Army-Air Force PX system. PX managers abroad decide what to buy. Commissary managers are restricted by a "brand name contracts" list, but still have considerable discretion. All PX and commissary orders are placed through central headquarters in the U.S.

The PX and commissary system primarily serves young consumers, among whom ethnic products are popular. Usually, these products are purchased in bulk at top discounts. These representatives generally work for a commission, but on occasion will buy on their own for resale. Some representatives handle all types of consumer products; others are specialized.

Multinational Companies Some 5,000 U.S. companies, through overseas subsidiaries, have overseas operations including factories, branch and regional offices, and in some countries elaborate residential compounds for American personnel. (American compounds with more than 1,000 residents are not unusual in the Middle East.)

Not all of these companies are committed to buy products from the U.S. Usually they do, however, for three important reasons: (1) their staff is familiar with products from the U.S.; (2) purchasing of major items can be done in the home office; (3) it is cheaper to consolidate purchasing and buy the same brand for all subsidiaries.

The MNC market generates massive demand for plant machinery, supplies, testing equipment, vehicles, spare parts, process control systems, training equipment, computer systems, appliances, office machines, furniture, and other goods. Residents of the compounds require all types of household appliances, fixtures, foods and other consumables, educational equipment and materials, and entertainment and leisure products.

United Nations The UN's purchasing is spread out among a number of agencies. Some have headquarters in the U.S., others in Europe. Any member nation can compete for this business. Each agency is specialized.

The UN agencies themselves do not purchase goods in the same quantities as do projects financed by organizations such as the World Bank. The UN agencies often act as advisors rather than actual buyers.

A good example is UNESCO (the United Nations Educational, Scientific, and Cultural Organization). A $50 million educational development project in Zaire, for instance, may be jointly financed by the government of Zaire, the African Development Bank, and the World Bank, but designed (including product specifications) by UNESCO advisors. Purchasing and contracting will be done by the Ministry of Education of Zaire, probably with advice from the same UNESCO team who helped write the specifications.

Other UN agencies operate in much the same manner. A notable exception is UNICEF (the United Nations Children's Fund). UNICEF maintains in Copenhagen a large warehouse with substantial stocks of basic equipment and teaching aids for primary schools in developing countries. UNICEF ships from Copenhagen and issues replacement orders as stocks are depleted.

In the U.S. all UNICEF buying is done through the UN's New York headquarters. To qualify as a vendor, one must submit catalogs and specifications, and sometimes samples for evaluation. UNICEF has very strict requirements governing the types of products included on its basic list and carried in its regular inventory.

Direct Distribution Through Agents

A company may deal with different types of agent intermediaries overseas. These agents do not take title to the goods and usually work for a commission. The product involved, and the way it is marketed in the U.S., will provide a clue as to who might be employed to undertake overseas distribution—sales representatives, purchasing agents, or export brokers.

Sales Representative These agents resemble a manufacturer's representative in the U.S. A manufacturer supplies the sales representatives with literature and samples to conduct sales in a predesignated territory. These representatives usually work on a commission basis, assume no risk or responsibility, and are under contract for a definite period. They may operate on either an exclusive or nonexclusive basis, and they do not handle competing lines. They serve as a good source of market information.

Purchasing Agent These agents are also referred to as buyers for export, export commission houses, or export confirming houses. They are active in U.S. markets, seeking goods of interest to their foreign principals. Their product quality and price demands stem from the requirements of the principals.

Usually, foreign purchasing agents represent governments or big contractors, either for a specified time or for a particular task. In any event, they do not provide continual service and stable volume to vendors. For example, a foreign government might authorize a purchasing agent to buy designated goods in the U.S. for the completion of a large mill or plant. Once the mill or plant is constructed, the purchasing agent ceases to be active.

Purchasing agents receive commissions from their principals. A transaction with a purchasing agent is completed, as in domestic marketing, with the agent handling all packing and shipping details. A purchasing agent may represent several principals requiring the same goods and may deal with different competing vendors.

Export Broker An export broker brings the foreign buyer and U.S. seller together. Usually, export brokers receive a commission or fee from the seller for their services. They take neither title nor possession of goods and assume no financial responsibility relative to the export transaction. Export brokers generally are used in the export of commodities such as grain and cotton. Only rarely is the export broker involved in the export of manufactured goods.

Direct Distribution Through Merchant Intermediaries

The foreign merchant intermediaries take title to the goods and sell them under their own names. They may or may not take possession of the goods. They render services similar to a domestic wholesaler. Major types of foreign merchant intermediaries are export distributors, foreign retailers, export jobbers, and trading companies.

Export Distributor The export distributors purchase goods from a U.S. manufacturer at the greatest possible discount and resell them for a profit. They are especially active in distributing products that require periodic servicing. They commit themselves to provide adequate service to the customers through carrying a sufficient quantity of spares and parts, maintaining facilities, and providing technicians to perform all normal servicing operations.

Export distributors buy in their own names and usually maintain an ongoing relationship with the exporter. Export distributors have exclusive sales rights in a country or region and receive easy payment terms from exporters.

Foreign Retailer   In some cases, U.S. manufacturers deal directly with foreign retailers, particularly in the case of consumer goods. For example, Campbell Soup Co. sells its Pepperidge Farm Cookies in Japan by directly dealing with a 3,300-store 7-Eleven chain throughout Japan.[16] The contact may be made either through a traveling salesperson or by mail using catalogs or brochures. In many countries, large retailers perform dual roles. While they sell directly to consumers through their own outlets, they also distribute imported goods to smaller retailers. Thus, exports handled by the retailer may receive wide coverage.

Export Jobber   Export jobbers determine customer needs overseas and fill them by making purchases in the U.S. Some jobbers reverse the process, filling needs of U.S. customers by supplying imported products. The jobbers mainly deal in staples, openly traded products for which brand names have little importance.

Trading Company   In modern times, the so-called trading companies usually are associated with Japan. Actually, the concept of the trading company is much older. During colonial times many European countries, particularly Britain and France, used trading companies to develop trade with other nations. For example, the East India Company was England's major means to enter India. Similarly, the French trading companies Cie Française de l'Afrique Occidentale and Ste Commerciale de l'Ouest Africain were active in Africa.

In Japan, the trading company originated as a commodity dealer that outgrew its wholesale functions. When the country was opened to the West, the trading company primarily served as a buffer between Japanese merchants and foreign businesses. Then Japan began to industrialize. Having neither raw materials at home nor an empire to exploit, the new industry needed imports. Rather than depend on foreigners, they adapted their trading companies to the task of acquiring the raw materials in addition to moving Japanese goods overseas.

Japanese trading companies have been very successful in promoting Japan's exports. They offer a broad range of services, from marketing research to financing, and present a relatively inexpensive way for the small or medium-size firm to do international marketing.

Some major functions of trading companies include trading and distributing, risk-hedging in exchange rates and commodity price fluctuation, domestic and overseas marketing of exported and imported technology, management consulting, participation in manufacturing, joint ventures abroad in resource developments and urban and rural development, and organizing new industries. The only functions that trading companies do not perform are production and retailing, but they may become involved even in these activities through joint ventures.

There are approximately 7,000 trading companies in Japan today, but only about 300 of them are engaged in foreign trade. The six largest trading companies in Japan, referred to as the Big Six, are Mitsubishi Corporation, C. Itoh & Company, Nissho-Iwai Company, Sumitomo Shoji, Marubeni Corporation, and Mitsui & Company. They had combined sales of over $375 billion in 1986.[17] They are responsible for bringing in about 68 percent of Japan's imports and shipping out about 44 percent of its exports. These 6 companies have over 500 offices outside Japan, employing over 15,000 people.[18]

The big trading companies control 56 percent of Japan's foreign trade. Together, they are the main exporters of almost every product (except cars and electrical appliances) exported directly by manufacturers. Japanese trading companies have expert knowledge about the lures most attractive to distributors of Japanese exports in all major foreign countries. By contrast, foreign exporters cannot compete so easily in Japan, because they will usually have to sell through a trading company that is part of a Japanese group probably making a competing product.[19]

In addition to privately controlled trading companies such as those in Japan, many countries have state-controlled trading companies. Such companies are active in countries like those in Eastern Europe where business is conducted by a few government-sanctioned and -controlled trading outfits. (Currently, attempts are in progress, especially in Poland and the Czech Republic, to privatize their trading companies.) In many countries, the state-controlled trading companies may be the only means of doing business. In many other nations, however, trading companies bridge the gap between Western business style and local cultural practices for conducting business.

Dealing with Intermediaries

After an exporter successfully locates prospective intermediaries, terms of agreement must be defined between them. A written agreement often avoids later disputes and misunderstandings. However, some companies have a simple agreement, leaving details to be settled when and as questions arise. As long as the intent of both parties is good, it is feasible to work without spelling out every detail in a written document. Yet, it is still considered a better alternative to prepare a written contract after the manufacturer has investigated the channel member's overall integrity, financial soundness, community standing, share of the market, and other product lines carried. Exhibit 14-1 shows the items included in a typical agreement.

In addition to the items shown in the sample agreement, it is desirable to specify that the intermediary will not deal in competing lines, disclose confidential information, or make agreements that bind the exporting firm in any way. Further, the place and time for the title to the merchandise to pass from the seller to the buyer should be clearly stated because of tax implications in the countries of both the exporter and the intermediary. Finally, the contract should avoid articles that directly or indirectly conflict with U.S. antitrust laws.

Company-Owned Distribution

An alternative way for a company to arrange for distribution in other countries is to establish its own distribution instead of going through intermediaries. An exporter may choose this alternative for three reasons: to enhance coverage with the objective of increasing sales, to maintain complete control over foreign distribution, and to seek distribution when channels are unavailable.

Foreign company-owned channels not only take a long time to establish, but also may not always provide the desired sales results. Difficulties are likely to occur, especially when a change is made in channel arrangements. For example, if an exporter drops existing channels in favor of company-owned distribution, it will face tough competition from them. Further, in many countries it may not be easy to find qualified individuals to serve as salespersons. As a matter of fact in many nations, Japan for example, a company may face insurmountable problems in seeking distribution of its own. Occasionally, a joint venture with a host country business is preferable to a strictly company-owned distribution. The host country business may already have a distribution set-up. The joint venture route provides the exporter an opportunity to enhance control and market coverage without the problems of building channels from scratch.

EXHIBIT 14.1 Items to Include in an Agreement with Foreign Intermediaries

- Names and addresses of both parties
- Date when the agreement goes into effect
- Duration of the agreement
- Provisions for extending or terminating the agreement
- Description of product lines included
- Definition of sales territory
- Establishment of discount and/or commission schedules and determination of when and how paid
- Provisions for revising the commission or discount schedules
- Establishment of a policy governing resale prices
- Maintenance of appropriate service facilities
- Restrictions to prohibit the manufacture and sale of similar and competitive products
- Designation of responsibility for patent and trademark negotiations and/or pricing
- The assignability or nonassignability of the agreement and any limiting factors
- Designation of the country (not necessarily the U.S.) and state (if applicable) of contract jurisdiction in the case of dispute

Gray Market

The Gray Market refers to distribution through unauthorized channels. The term is derived from "black market," the infamous underground economy for goods and services. However, where a black market typically deals with illegal goods and services (or the illegal trading of otherwise legal goods), the line between proper and improper is not as clear in a gray market. The pipeline in a gray market is legal, but somewhat controversial. Many consider it unethical. Others argue that it is economically unsound because it often involves purchasing goods and selling them at a profit without adding any value.

Typically, a gray market transaction would work as follows: A broker buys goods from a distributor overseas, where wholesale prices are low, then diverts them to the U.S., where he/she undersells domestic distributors who have paid a higher wholesale price. The usual scenario involves four steps:

1. *Authorized Sale* — This is usually direct from a manufacturer or exporter to a distributor.
2. *Diversion* — This is the critical step in a gray market transaction. The distributor diverts the shipment to another storage site, where it is either held or transported to a free-trade port (such as Panama).
3. *Import* — Discounters learn of the stored products through brokers and purchase huge quantities at the lower overseas wholesale prices.
4. *Retail Sale* — The discounter sells the product in the U.S. at below-market prices, but still makes a profit.

Gray markets are especially prevalent in the trading of luxury goods (such as autos, furs, jewels, and upscale clothing and perfumes) and high-tech goods (disc drives, computers, and computer chips). A specific example helps to illustrate the problems facing a company caught in gray market trading. A customer of a certain computer company buys components (such as disc drives) at a volume discount. The contract calls for "adding value," but instead, the customer resells the "raw" drives to major dealers, systems houses, and original-equipment manufacturers (OEMs). In doing so, the customer can undercut the prices set by the manufacturer's authorized distributors. These distributors become angry and, more important, they are now unmotivated to highlight and sell the manufacturer's product. The company is caught in a real trap — it risks losing the loyalty of a valuable distributor base, but satisfying this base hurts the company's sales force, which may depend on gray market sales for a good portion of their quotas.

High-tech industries become particularly entrenched in gray markets because their products usually involve short life cycles, which translates into a short shelf-life. Salespeople are willing to sell to anybody, before their product becomes outdated or obsolete. A vicious circle is created: the sales force is pressured to move product, which forces sales to the gray market, which erodes prices, which causes further pressures to move products.

It is the manufacturers who are on the defensive. Some are simply absorbing profit losses to the gray market as an acknowledged cost of doing business. Others are taking a more aggressive stand, through privately funded fraud investigations, litigation, and even corporate guerrilla tactics.

One key step for companies determined to fight the gray market is self-examination. The perfume industry is a classic example. Wholesale prices charged to U.S. retailers can be 25 percent higher than the currency-adjusted wholesale prices charged in Europe. Such price discrepancies are meant to guarantee that U.S. perfume distributors limit their distribution network to select dealers and upscale stores. Yet, it is exactly this type of discrepancy among markets that allows the gray market to flourish through "underground distribution systems."

One would think that perfume manufacturers would be somewhat hesitant to ship huge quantities of their priciest potions to such questionable havens of the rich such as

Poland, Egypt, and Panama. In 1986 alone, for example, French perfume exports directly to Panama totaled $40 million—theoretically making that country's per capita consumption of perfume 35 times that of the U.S.[20] Critics argue that the perfume companies know full well that such shipments are heading directly for major gray-market trans-shipment points, but a companys' financial results and product positioning simply take priority. Stated another way, the companies attempting to fight the gray market system become their own worst enemies. They regularly sell to known gray market diverters to meet sales targets, and they have allowed their own distribution systems to spin out of control.

Channel Management

Channel management covers selecting appropriate channels of distribution and making them work. The selection process requires decisions on distribution structure and choice of specific channel members. Once the selection is made, the goal is to make the channel arrangements work adequately. This requires maintaining cordial relationships and minimizing conflicts.

Channel Selection

The channel selection process in international marketing is similar to the one for a domestic situation. Usually, the selection process involves establishing channel objectives and feasible channel alternatives, evaluation of alternatives, and the choice of appropriate channels.

Establishing Objectives The objectives of an international channel of distribution derive from total marketing objectives in the foreign market. Channel objectives are concerned with a clear-cut definition of the target customers. Implicit in the definition of target customers is the decision about whether the company wants intensive, selective, or exclusive distribution. Intensive distribution is an attempt to reach the mass market, and it requires a broad-based channel structure. Selective distribution is letting a designated channel undertake distribution on a monopoly basis.

Objectives should not only designate the target customers, but also specify the type of service to be rendered to each group of customers. For example, the acceptable time lag between the receipt of an order and delivery of goods should be clearly defined. Similarly, an original equipment manufacturer should state not only the types of services the company intends to make available but also with what frequency.

Establishing Feasible Channel Alternatives The characteristics of customers, product, intermediaries, competitors, marketing environment, and company's strengths and weaknesses determine the various possible alternatives for the distribution of a line of products.[21] If the number of customers is large and/or geographically widespread rather than concentrated, and if they make their purchases in smaller quantities at frequent intervals, the company will have to opt for intensive distribution, that is, a large number of channel outlets. Another factor to be considered here is the desire of the customer to deal with a particular type of channel. For example, the customer in a country may dislike the idea of buying groceries from large supermarkets. In other words, a customer's susceptibility to different selling methods is an important factor to be considered.

A variety of product characteristics have an effect on the selection of channels of distribution. Perishable goods require direct channels. Bulky but inexpensive products can use long channels. Shorter channels are employed when the unit value of a product is high, as in the case of computers, and/or when the product has to be custom-made, like air-conditioning equipment for a large building. Proximity to the customer helps in cutting down costs as well as in rendering good service. Also, products requiring installation and regular maintenance would call for shorter channels of distribution. Most capital equipment falls into this category.

The kinds of channels available constrain channel selection. The company should consider the terms demanded by different channel constituents and evaluate them in comparison with services and benefits provided including factors such as channel location, credit granted, quality of the sales force, warehousing facilities, reputation in the market, outlay on advertising, and overall experience. Consideration must also be given to the demands of the intermediaries from the company (i.e., what the channels expect from suppliers in such matters as decision-making authority, services, and financial assistance). Depending on other factors such as customer and product characteristics, the company will choose those channels that make the maximum impact in the market at minimum cost.

Host country trade practices concerning the distribution of a particular product is another influential variable. For example, innovations may not be easily accepted in all countries. Even today, many Swiss homemakers prefer buying groceries from mom-and-pop-type outlets.

The environment of the host country constitutes another variable to weigh in making a channel selection decision. For example, the economic structure affects the suitability of a particular channel. In free economies, it is common practice to use private agents/distributors who buy and resell at a markup. Most agents/distributors function as parts of local companies that deal in a large number of product lines ranging from candy to sophisticated machine tools. In state-controlled markets, like those of Jordan and Syria, international marketers must do business with state-owned trading companies operating on very low margins that cover physical distribution costs but usually no other necessary marketing activities. In such countries, international marketers often retain the services of private agencies to promote their products to the final consumers. Poor economic conditions may not justify committing the company to excessive fixed costs, and thus distribution through wholesalers may be deemed the best alternative. A depressed economy may also demand cutting down on nonessential services.

The final factor in evaluating channel alternatives is the company's own strengths and weaknesses in the overseas market. A well-known company of long standing in the market will tap channels more easily than the new entrant. A financially strong company need not necessarily opt for channels that absorb a part of the distribution costs of inventory, transportation, advertising, and/or training. Similarly, a company with a large number of products for the same market could deal directly with the customers.

All these factors serve as a basis for determining the feasible alternative channels of distribution. Generally, the company would have three channel alternatives: selling direct to the customers, selling through intermediaries based in the U.S., and selling through foreign distributors. In practice, however, channels in international marketing can be a labyrinth of complicated relationships. For example, the company might sell directly in some countries while employing U.S.-based distributors in another country and utilizing overseas distributors in still other cases.

Evaluation of Alternative Channels Each channel alternative should be evaluated on the basis of three factors: coverage, control, and cost. Coverage refers to both qualitative and quantitative coverage of customers and is determined by an analysis of customers, including such factors as their geographic locations, sales potential, and service requirements. Usually, customers are grouped into homogeneous categories. Each channel alternative can then be evaluated for different customer segments according to geographic coverage, coverage of big accounts, meeting the needs of different segments, and the like. If deemed necessary, different weights can be assigned to these factors. Often, it will be found that no one channel provides optimum coverage for each segment. Thus, to cater to different segments, the company may be obliged to choose more than one channel.[22]

Control refers to the discretion that the company has, or wants to have, in seeing the goods through to the customers. Dealing with some intermediate agents leaves the company in better control of various activities such as establishing prices, recommending cooperative advertising, and suggesting inventory level. On the other hand, some intermediaries will demand flexibility in pricing, the right to refuse to enter into cooperative advertising, freedom in deciding how much inventory they would like to carry, and so forth. In brief, going through the agent/distributor necessitates sharing control. If a company wants complete control, it must develop company-owned distribution. Direct distribution, however, requires patience and ingenuity (see International Marketing Highlight 14.2).

A third factor in evaluating channel alternatives is cost. Direct distribution by the company is usually more costly if the sales base is small, but it gives the company full control over distribution. In the final analysis, a balance has to be struck between cost, coverage, and control. No one factor can be considered in isolation. Probably a composite index should be utilized to measure each channel. The channel with optimum coverage and control at minimum cost would be the obvious choice.

Choosing the Channels After alternative channels have been evaluated, the one most appropriate to the stated objective should be chosen. In practice, however, it may be difficult to state the objective in concrete terms for clear matching with each alternative. Thus, subjective judgment becomes important in the final decision. Management should not only consider the implications of the short run, but also allow sufficient flexibility to meet changing requirements. Sometimes a channel is chosen as a stopgap arrangement that will allow for a new alternative in the future.

International Marketing Highlight 14.2

"Boutique" Marketing System

Fieldcrest Mills' bed and bath division decided in 1976 to export its "boutique" marketing system to Western Europe and Japan. "It seemed an obvious thing to do," the president explains. "Department stores in those countries were decades behind the United States. They still looked on towels and sheets as mundane products with no fashion pizzazz whatever. And just like our stores decades ago, they were selling unattractive products at virtually no profit, sort of like a public service to customers."

The firm embarked on a campaign to convince department stores in Europe and Japan that they could, like their U.S. counterparts, make money by selling high-fashion (that is, high markup) towels and sheets. At first there was considerable resistance to Fieldcrest's selling efforts. The owner of a Stuttgart department store flatly rejected the offer of a written guarantee that installation of a Fieldcrest boutique would double the profits generated on that floor space within two years.

But Fieldcrest eventually succeeded in convincing a number of overseas department stores to take a fling. Stores in Hamburg, Munich, London, and Tokyo agreed to install boutiques in especially favorable locations—usually on the main floor near the cosmetics counters, where customer traffic is heavy. Fieldcrest provided the design and even the lighting systems at its own cost. Foreign consumers are now developing a taste for those fashionable U.S. bed and bath products. At London's famed Harrods, the Fieldcrest boutique has become one of the most successful profit centers. As a result of its boutique concept, Fieldcrest's exports jumped in 1980 by a most respectable 58 percent.

Source: Herbert E. Meyer, "How U.S. Textiles Got to Be Winners in the Export Game," *Fortune*, May 5, 1980, p. 261.

Pros and Cons of the Use of Intermediaries

Independent intermediaries play a significant role in the total global marketing effort of many companies. Although even some large companies use intermediaries for seeking distribution in smaller foreign markets or for distribution of certain product lines in larger markets, the distribution through intermediaries is especially important for smaller companies, which generally do not have the scale of operations, financial resources, or experience to operate more directly in foreign markets.

The popularity of this mode of distribution has been attributed to the many advantages that intermediaries provide in foreign markets. A distributor brings immediate new assets to the multinational marketer by providing local market know-how, knowledge, and contacts with little expenditure on the part of the exporter. In the case of selling computers in the Middle East, a computer executive noted:

> Although you know more about the product, inevitably the local guy will know more about the market. And make no mistake—market knowledge is more important than product knowledge in getting sales in the Middle East.

Further, the overseas distributor adds to the effective capital available for a company's worldwide marketing efforts, because distributors have funds of their own, as well as local borrowing power that a firm located in another country may not have. Further, intermediaries afford an opportunity for the stocking and sale of a company's product in a new market at negligible cost. The cost of a company-owned local operation, involving support staff, office space and equipment, overhead, and the like is worthwhile only when a certain volume of business and a certain operating margin are achieved. A distributor may be able to do a good job with a smaller volume by spreading his costs among many lines of products.

The point can be illustrated with this example. A chemical company charges its distributors of textile fibers F.A.S. price less 3 percent. That 3 percent would never cover the costs of maintaining a sales force, local travel expenses, or overhead. But the distributor handles other noncompetitive products—such as textiles machinery—with larger margins. The irregularity of this machinery business is balanced by the steadiness of the fiber sales. Spreading the costs makes it possible for the distributor to carry economically and profitably both lines of goods where neither might be viable separately (see International Marketing Highlight 14.3).

On the other hand, there are some serious disadvantages to using independent distributors. First, the manufacturer has less direct control over an independent distributor than over his or her own employees. Second, there is a risk of violation of U.S. or European Union antitrust laws when a distributor is being directed, particularly in the area of pricing. Third, the manufacturer may have little contact with, or knowledge of, the retail outlets used by the distributor. Fourth, the manufacturer has little or no control over the marketing, sales techniques, and credit policies of the distributor. Finally, in some cases, it may be very difficult and costly for the manufacturer to cancel an agreement.

Briefly, then, a company should use distributors in markets where sales volume would not justify its own distribution or when it does not have the staff and know-how to set up its own operations. A firm may or may not change a satisfactory distributor arrangement when local volume could pay the costs of a company's own operation. In some markets, such a volume may never be reached, but in others when it is reached, the distributor relationship is retained for any of a host of reasons. Alternatively, the company may acquire or just continue to use the distributor as an adjunct to its own operations in the market.

International Marketing Highlight 14.3

Schick Versus Gillette in Japan

In Japan, a product's success often depends on how widespread the distribution network is. And that is a classic strength of Schick. After entering the market along with Gillette and other foreign makers in 1962, when Japan liberalized the razor market, Schick decided to leave distribution to Seiko Corp. Seiko imports Schick razors from the U.S. and now sells them to 150,000 wholesalers nationwide.

Gillette, meanwhile, flopped when it tried to crack the market on its own and never caught up with Schick. Instead of going through a sole Japanese agent like Seiko, Gillette mainly tried to sell razors through its own salespeople, a strategy that failed because Gillette didn't have the distribution network available to Japanese companies—which was crucial. Now Gillette is making another try on its own. It has doubled salespeople in Japan to forty, and for the first time held lavish parties last year for wholesalers.

Source: The Wall Street Journal, February 4, 1991, p. B1.

Selection of Intermediaries

Finding reliable distributors is a major challenge for firms entering markets in other countries. There are a number of potential sources of overseas distributors ranging from local trade and banking houses to chambers of commerce, officials of foreign embassies in the U.S., and various state and the U.S. departments of commerce. Of all of these, the U.S. Department of Commerce provides the most thorough information. It offers several aids to assist U.S. exporters, which are described in Chapter 17. There is, however, one important service, titled Agent/Distributor Service (A/DS), that is designed exclusively to help U.S. firms identify suitable representatives abroad for a fee. The exporters may seek the names of agents and/or distributors abroad who have indicated an interest in handling specific products from the U.S.

The following four criteria could be employed to identify suitable intermediaries: financial strength, good connections, the number and kinds of other companies represented, and the quality of local personnel, facilities, and equipment.

Financial Strength Sales in foreign markets take time to mature. Yet, the distributor must invest in personnel and equipment ahead of the actual business activity if the organization is to have an effective beginning. Thus, the prospective distributor must be financially sound and should have the strength and will to take the risks involved. Financial strength involves both credit standing and cash flow position.

Good Connections In a large number of countries, business is conducted on a personal basis. In many cases, the government is deeply involved in business. Thus, for agents and distributors to be effective, they should be well connected both in private and in government circles. They should be regarded as respectable businesspersons by all concerned and follow established traditions and practices.

Other Business Commitments Information should be gathered on other commitments that the potential intermediary is involved in. For example, someone currently dealing in noncompeting goods and enjoying a good reputation for providing service, handling complaints and problems, and carrying inventory might be a viable candidate. Information on performance can be sought from the companies he or she has been representing. In addition to an encouraging reputation, any experience gained through handling complementary goods would be advantageous in representing the firm's products. However, sound business practice prohibits distributors from handling competing lines.

Personnel, Facilities, and Equipment The number and quality of the representatives's employees, equipment, and facilities should be examined. After all, the reputation of the foreign firm in the host country depends on the activities and behavior of the people representing it. The people should not only be skilled and qualified in their trade, but also have good public relations. Further, the distributor's facilities and equipment should be adequate, as well as properly located. If certain equipment is lacking, the distributor should be willing to make additions. Often potential representatives are willing to hire more people and purchase additional facilities and equipment, if selected. To ensure that the distributor lives up to such promises, these provisions should be specified in the agreement.

The following are additional considerations in the selection of intermediaries:

- Capability to provide adequate sales coverage
- Overall positive reputation and image as a company
- Product compatibility (synergy or conflict?)
- Pertinent technical know-how at staff level
- Adequate infrastructure in staff and facilities
- Proven performance record with client companies
- Positive attitude toward the company's products
- Mature outlook regarding the company's inevitable progression in market management

Channel Control and Performance

Distribution in foreign locales through intermediaries always entails compromise. The compromise involves the loss of control over the MNC's foreign marketing operations in exchange for relatively low-cost representation. Although some control must be relinquished to intermediaries even in domestic markets, in foreign markets it is more significant because the firm has no permanent presence abroad. A distributor, the only means of accomplishing all the related tasks—selling, servicing, providing market information—often falls short of the manufacturer's expectations. The independent distributor represents an entity separate from the exporter, and their goals may not match exactly. Despite the fact that the exporter/manufacturer lacks full control of foreign distribution, he or she still wants adequate information. This raises the dilemma of how to encourage high performance by channels that are not a part of the firm's own network.

No matter how one looks at it, companies using independent distributors will have great difficulty in controlling them. It is difficult for the exporter to make sales forecasts, set sales targets, and develop customer-contact plans when there is no access to the distributor's books, sales reports, or other records. Thus, the manufacturer should not depend on controls to optimize distributor performance, but instead use motivational methods.

> A distributor wants to do the best possible job for each of his manufacturers, but he really cannot. So he concentrates on (1) where he makes the most money and (2) where he has the least aggravation or the greatest personal pull. The following are some thoughts on how the company may build loyalty:
>
> 1. Build the distributor with the company; bring him into your picture; discuss future plans as they affect his area with him; seek his advice.
> 2. Give the distributor an attractive profit margin; try to keep in mind that the company wants to be in business with him for several years; make him want to continue the relationship.
> 3. Be sure he has credit terms which make him competitive, or more so, in amount and length of payment.
> 4. Maintain regular correspondence, and make sure he can clearly understand the company's viewpoint.

5. Make a point of commenting on successful distributors in whatever communication the company uses in his area (advertising, publicity, house organs, sales bulletins, and so on).
6. Keep the obvious control to a minimum; as his performance improves, the supervision can be reduced.
7. If financing is needed locally and the company has the ability to help, do so if his situation justifies this.
8. Bring the distributor to the U.S. on occasion and let him see what goes on.
9. Offer a scholarship to the children of a successful distributor.
10. Establish a recognition system: recognition certificates, cash prizes, trips, and so on.
11. Make available remembrance items: giveaways with the company name—perhaps, if warranted, with his name too.

An empirical study on the subject notes that the performance of an overseas distributor is affected by such relational factors as formalization, standardization, reciprocity, intensity, and conflict.[23] *Formalization* refers to the extent to which the relationship is agreed upon and made explicit. *Standardization* indicates the extent to which the established roles and trading routines are followed. *Reciprocity* means the extent to which the manufacturer and distributor are *both* involved in decision making, despite the traditional domains of each part. *Intensity* is the level of contact and resource exchange between the parties. Finally, conflict refers to the level of tension and disagreement between the two parties. The findings of this study strongly recommend that high performance is associated with certain relational characteristics. High performance requires that the two parties:

- Adapt their roles and routines (or make them less standardized)
- Display a commitment to developing business in the market in question (or focus on contact and resource intensity)
- Exhibit lower levels of intercompany tension and disagreement (or conflict)

In addition, the manufacturer should demonstrate (1) a genuine interest in the foreign market and in the overseas distributor, (2) a willingness to adapt his or her ways of doing business to be an effective competitor abroad, and (3) an ability to minimize disagreements with the overseas distributor.[24]

Modification of Channel

Environmental forces, internal or external, may force a company to modify existing channel agreements. A shift in the trade policy/practice of a country, for instance, may render distribution through a state trading organization obsolete. The experience of companies in Europe is relevant here. MNCs in the EU area, in response to the 1992 single internal market program, have been changing their distribution channels from covering only one national market to covering two or more national markets and serving areas reflecting natural rather than national boundaries. Similarly, technological changes in product design may require service calls to customers more frequently than the current channels can manage, and thus require the company to opt for direct distribution.

Ordinarily, a company new to the international market starts distribution through intermediaries. The company has little, if any, knowledge of the conditions overseas and has neither the insight nor capabilities necessary to deal successfully with the vagaries of the market. For good reasons, therefore, intermediaries are patronized. With their knowledge of the market, they play an important role in establishing demand for a company's products. However, once the company attains a foothold in the market, it may discover that it does not have enough control of distribution to make further headway. At this time, modification becomes essential.[25]

Managerial astuteness requires that the company do a thorough study before deciding to change existing channel arrangements. No matter how long a U.S. company has been engaged in business with other countries, there are customs and conditions that may constrain a non-native firm in establishing its own distribution system. In other words, hurried measures could create insurmountable problems, resulting in loose control and poor communications. Further, the affected intermediary agents should be taken into the company's confidence about future plans and compensated for any breach in terms. Any modification of channels should tally with the total marketing system. This requires consideration of the effect of a modified plan on various ingredients in the marketing mix such as pricing, promotion, and so on. The managers in different departments (as well as the customers) should be informed so that the change does not come as a surprise. In other words, care must be taken to ensure that a modification in channel arrangements causes no distortion in the overall distribution system.

Wholesaling in Foreign Environments

An international marketer interested in overseas distribution must acquire complete knowledge of the existing wholesale and retail patterns of the host country. Such knowledge reveals what sort of distribution is feasible; what economic, social, and cultural factors influence the distribution structure of the country; and what legal and political requirements must be followed. The following two sections examine different aspects of wholesaling and retailing in foreign markets.

Overall, wholesalers worldwide perform such functions as purchasing, selling, transportation, storage, financing, information gathering, production planning, risk management, and even management consulting. However, in some countries, some of the functions are reserved for manufacturers or retailers or both. Briefly, functions performed by wholesalers vary from country to country. Table 14.1 provides statistical information on wholesaling in foreign markets.

Status and Role of Wholesalers

The status and role of wholesalers vary from country to country. In developing countries, they play a crucial role by handling imports as well as products of small, domestic manufacturers and by financing the flow of goods between the producers and retailers. Despite their importance in many developing countries, wholesalers are held in low esteem for two reasons. First, the major economic emphasis in developing countries is on production since goods are scarce in virtually all sectors. Second, wholesale trade, like retail, in many countries is dominated by foreigners. The local population, therefore, looks down upon wholesalers as they consider them to be getting rich by exploiting them. For example, in many African countries like Kenya and Sierra Leone, people of the Indian subcontinent control the trading sector of the economy. About 75 percent of Kenya's retail and wholesale business even today is controlled by

Asians. Similarly, the Chinese have been dominant in the Philippines and Indonesia. European companies control a large proportion of Hong Kong's and Singapore's trade.

Further, the size of wholesaling operations differs significantly from country to country. In Finland, four wholesaling houses handle the major portions of all trade. One of these 4 houses, Kesko, controls over 20 percent of the market.[26] On the other hand, Japan is known for its myriad wholesalers linked to each other in a multilevel arrangement.

TABLE 14.1 Wholesaling in Selected Countries

Country	Number of Wholesalers	Number of Wholesale Employees	Employees per Wholesaler	Retailers per Wholesaler	Population per Wholesaler
United States	416,000	5,355,000	13	5	564
Ireland	3,073	42,100	14	11	1,139
Austria	12,890	148,900	12	3	582
Sweden	27,913	193,200	7	3	145
(The former) Soviet Union	1,000	120,000	120	481	174,922
Belgium	57,079	177,400	3	2	174
United Kingdom	80,104	1,087,000	14	3	698
Israel	4,862	36,900	8	8	782
Japan	429,000	4,091,000	10	4	278
India	116,000	—	—	32	5,612
Turkey	24,592	87,200	4	20	1,923
Chile	561	15,900	28	42	20,856
Brazil	46,000	442,000	10	61	2,820
South Korea	45,568	173,200	4	21	878
Italy	120,366	547,000	5	8	473
Egypt	1,766	42,300	24	1	25,595
Yugoslavia	1,110	138,100	124	70	20,000

Sources: *United Nations Statistical Yearbook*, 1983–1984, pp. 866–89, and 1979–1980, pp. 404–19, and *Statistical Abstract of the United States*, 1986, p. 774.

Services Offered by Wholesalers

Services provided by wholesalers are related to competition. In a country like India, where there are virtually hundreds of wholesalers, the margins are low and the competition is fierce. In such an environment, wholesalers provide a variety of services from financing to inventory maintenance. On the other hand, the large trading companies usually provide a good service mix, but at a substantial cost to the manufacturer/retailer. In most industrialized countries, the merging trend toward vertical integration has squeezed the wholesaler from both sides. The wholesalers, therefore, have tried to streamline by carefully limiting the areas of operation and strictly controlling them. For example, wholesalers continue to be a major factor in Western Europe in food products. Thus, even though Kraft distributes in Germany through company-owned channels, it must provide the wholesalers their commission without receiving any services.[27]

Merchandising Policies

Smaller wholesalers usually limit their business to handling a particular family of goods. Whenever they expand, they venture only into related goods. Large wholesalers, however, deal in different products without any underlying relationship among them. For example, Hamashbir Hamerkazi, a large wholesale group in Israel, handles different kinds of products and has interests in 12 large manufacturing firms.[28]

Margins and Efficiency

The margins and efficiency of wholesalers depend on the services they provide and the competition they face. Where competition is lacking, wholesalers run an inefficient operation. The wholesaling function simply amounts to an intermediate function for the flow of goods. The inefficiency of operations has no relationship to margins. When the business develops into a monopoly and the goods are in short supply, margins are rather high, despite the low level of services (related to credit, storage, shipping, and market research information). Keen competition, however, raises the level of services that wholesalers provide without simultaneous improvement in either the margins or efficiency. In brief, wholesaling worldwide is not marked by efficiency; with poor efficiency and keen competition, the margins are meager.

Retailing in Overseas Markets

Diverse retailing patterns can be observed from country to country, even more than in wholesaling. Retailing in many respects is a localized activity, deeply influenced by prevailing social and cultural norms and government controls. An international marketer should gain as much insight into the retailing practices of the host country as necessary for his or her marketing endeavors.

Worldwide Retailing Patterns

Retailing operations vary widely in size. Some countries have large stores comparable to those in the U.S. In other nations, retailing is a small family business. Harrods of England, Mitsukoshi of Japan, and Au Printemps of France are well known names in retailing. These stores have a large clientele and carry an extensive line of merchandise along the lines of a typical department store in the U.S. For example, Mitsukoshi serves over 100,000 customers every day. Contrast this with retailing in Pakistan and Nigeria, where retailers in a large city number in the thousands and carry one or two lines of goods, serving a very few customers. The relative size of retail patterns is illustrated in Table 14.2. Relatively speaking, not only is the number of retail stores in the developing countries much greater than in the industrialized nations, but also by contrast the number of customers served is low. As a matter of fact, even among developed countries, retailing patterns vary significantly. For example, in 1991 the average sales volume per store was $695,000 in the U.S., $532,000 in Great Britain, and $182,500 in Japan.[29]

The level of services that retailers provide to manufacturers varies according to their size. Thus, large retail houses generally carry inventory, render financial help, display and promote merchandise, and furnish market information. On the other hand, smaller retailers would depend entirely on the manufacturer or wholesaler. On their own, they would carry a limited quantity of products (which might lead to out-of-stock items) and would expect the vendor to provide credit. Promotion and merchandise display material would have to be handled by the manufacturer or the wholesaler.

The smaller retailers carry limited lines of goods in limited variety. Usually, their operations are run inefficiently and their margins are low. On the other hand, large-scale

TABLE 14.2 Retailing in Selected Countries

Country	Year	Retail outlets (000s)	Pop. per outlet	Retail staff (000s)
Algeria	1971	3.6	5,146	18
Argentina	1974	445.8	40	1,868
Australia	1986	160.2	100	929
Brazil	1980	885.6	143	2,817
Egypt	1981	2.1	20,000	48
Ghana	1983	1.5	8,693	16
Guatemala	1982	88.2	84	n/a
India	1978	450	1,450	n/a
Iran	1971	214	175	328
Israel	1982	30	144	83
Japan	1985	1,628.6	74	633
Kenya	1987	4.3	4,930	250
Malaysia	1980	96	142	247
Mexico	1975	463.6	122	985
Morocco	1972	4	3,900	20
New Zealand	1983	30	107	129
Nigeria	1982	22.2	4,045	266
Pakistan	1976	276	325	502
Saudi Arabia	1981	80.3	130	174
Singapore	1986	15.5	166	63
South Africa	1983	58.1	408	373
South Korea	1986	637.7	63	1,221
Tanzania	1983	1.6	12,963	17
Thailand	1988	6.7	7,910	42
United States	1984	1,035	228	9,834
Zimbabwe	1982	1.2	5,843	13

Source: Adapted from *International Marketing Data and Statistics*, London: Euromonitor Publications Limited, 1990

operations are able to achieve economies of scale and infuse professionalism into the operations. Their margins are relatively high, but at the same time so are their services.

An international marketer would have difficulty dealing directly with smaller retailers. Thus, in nations where retailing is a mom-and-pop business, the wholesaler becomes important. By the same token, new ideas and innovations overseas at the retail level can be successfully introduced only in countries that have large retail houses.

Theory of International Retailing

Any institutional framework in a country is a function of its environment. Available evidence suggests that efficiency in distribution channels, and consequently in retailing, depends largely on a country's infrastructure and the level of economic development.[30] In the area of international retailing, this thesis is supported by empirical work on the subject. For example, supermarkets were found to be more common and retail outlets much larger in countries with relatively higher GNPs per capita. As a matter of fact, time lags in the development of retailing innovations and improvements appeared similar in length to lags in environmental development.[31] In brief, it can be theorized that the retailing structure (that is, the number of inhabitants per retail establishment and sales per retail establishment) emerges from the environmental characteristics of the country. The environmental determinants of retail structure are personal consumption expenditures per capita, passenger car ownership, and geographical concentration of population. The theory of retailing propounded here has a variety of implications for multinational marketers. For example, Western capital-intensive mass-market technology clearly is ill-suited to serve low- and middle-income consumers in the Third World. Instead, the traditional labor-intensive food retailer is more suitable for marketing staples to the bulk of the world's population—that is, neither so primitive as to offer no escape from low production and low income, nor so highly sophisticated as to be out of the reach of poor people.

Until recently, the transfer of capital-intensive marketing technology was recommended as a solution to Third World problems. The horizontally and vertically integrated systems surrounding institutions known as supermarkets were considered generators of substantial benefits as a result of economies of scale, self-service, and a shortened distribution channel. Supermarkets supposedly help to by-pass the public wholesale markets; replace the crowded, old-fashioned, noisy, disorderly, dirty but picturesque food stands in municipal retail bazaars; and do away with street vendors who cause health and safety hazards in busy downtown areas. In short, the small, limited-line retailers of consumer staples—plus the long, labor-intensive, and haphazardly coordinated distribution chain—were being arrogantly brushed aside as inadequate, inefficient, and irrelevant.

The experience of the past 25 years, however, shows that Western marketing technology is too big and too expensive. It does not create the jobs needed to absorb the rapidly expanding labor force in the Third World, and it is not appropriate for the small firms and businesses that make up the bulk of the economic activity in developing countries.

Global Retailing Trends

Worldwide, various changes are emerging on the retail scene.[32] Although most changes are limited to advanced nations, different sorts of retailing trends are evident even among developing countries.

Adoption of U.S. Retailing Innovations Such U.S. retailing innovations as self-service supermarkets, discount houses, and suburban shopping centers gradually are finding their way everywhere (see International Marketing Highlight 14.4). The growth of discounting in Germany illustrates the point. Starting with the first discount store in 1953, the number of discounters exceeded 1,000 by 1991. The new discount houses, called *verbraucher markte* (consumer markets), are in some cases larger than a typical discount store in the U.S. Similarly, discounting has taken off in France, where 1960s supermarkets have evolved into hypermarkets, selling not just food but furniture, clothing, and hardware. To illustrate the point, cat food costs 2.80 francs at a hypermarket compared with 5.30 francs at a neighborhood shop.

Incidentally, hypermarkets did not succeed in the U.S. For example, Wal-Mart Stores Inc. established four hypermarkets in different cities to penetrate suburban markets. But the company had trouble in running them profitably. Similarly, K-Mart Corporation's hypermarket failed to meet expectations.[33]

Discounting is becoming popular in Japan as well. Daiei Inc. has 204 stores that conduct American-style discounting business. Its cut-rate stores are shaking up Japan's protective distribution system, where manufacturers tend to dictate prices to retailers.[34] For example, in a Tokyo department store, a pair of designer jeans costs $63, while in a suburban discount store the same product costs $39. A can of Coors costs 240 yen in a neighborhood liquor store, 178 yen in a supermarket, and 139 yen in a discount store.[35]

American retailing innovations are also finding their way to developing countries. Foe example, McDonald's, Kentucky Fried Chicken, Pizza Hut, Burger King, Ponderosa, and Wendy's are thriving in many Southeast Asian areas including China.[36]

Even mail-order business is catching up.[37] For example, mail-order business traditionally had a shoddy image in Japan. Only such products as contraceptive devices and aphrodisiacs, which reputable stores refused to sell, were convenient to channel through mail. With more Japanese women working and with mail-order houses trying hard to improve their image, the mail-order business has begun to boom. Well-known companies have begun selling jewelry, kitchen utensils, fur coats, baby clothes, and even automobiles by mail. This trend is visible in other countries as well.[38]

Further, the share of business for the large retailers has been increasing as retailing becomes concentrated in fewer hands. This trend is noticeable throughout Western Europe with the exception of Italy.[39] In Japan, large department stores have captured about 10 percent of domestic retail sales. However, their strong market position has been overtaken by so-called supers or general merchandise stores, which handle about 15 percent of retail sales. Self-service and convenience chain stores have also grown rapidly and together hold another 15 percent of the market.[40]

Internationalization of Retailing The growing interest among the large retailers of industrialized countries in expansion overseas is another noticeable change. Sears, Roebuck & Company has ventured into Mexico, South America, and Spain; J.C. Penney Company moved into Mexico and Italy; Safeway entered Great Britain, Germany, and Australia; and Federated Department Stores found its way into Madrid. Likewise, Avon representatives and Tupperware parties have become common in a number of countries. Since 1984, Toys 'R' Us Company has opened megastores in Canada, Britain, Singapore, Germany, France, Italy, and Japan.[41]

Wal-Mart has made a major commitment to the Canadian market. It acquired 120 Woolco discount department stores from Woolworth and plans to build additional outlets of its own.[42] Wal-Mart has also expanded into Argentina and Brazil.[43]

The internationalization of retailing, however, is not limited to U.S. business. Harrods, Britain's best-known department store, has branched out into Japan. France's Au Printemps department store opened stores in Japan, Singapore, Saudi Arabia, South Korea, and Turkey. In 1987, it opened its first U.S. store in Denver and plans to open many more in the 1990s.[44]

International Marketing Highlight 14.4

The Mall, The Merrier

On August 21st, the largest shopping mall in Asia threw open its glass and chrome doors to Bankok's overeager shoppers. Set by a dusty suburban highway, Seacon Square incorporates all the latest tricks of the mega-mall trade: a vast fountain-filled atrium, a 14-screen cinema complex, an amusement park complete with roller coasters—and miles and miles of shops.

The arrival of Seacon Square is the latest symptom of Asia's retailing revolution. The mall craze is driven by demographics. Residents of Bankok now earn on average around $4,000 a year. The number of households is growing by a steady 2 – 3% a year. The expanding middle class has more than enough disposable income to make a trip to the mall a feasible alternative to a visit to a pollution-choked park.

As Thais find new ways to spend their money, the landscape of Bangkok is rapidly changing. The dowdy shophouses that have lined the city's commercial districts for a century are giving way to mega-malls, out-of-town hypermarkets and 24-hour convenience stores.

Source: *The Economist,* August 27, 1994, p. 59.

Social Marketing An interesting trend in the developing countries has been the retailers' entry into social marketing. For example, retailers in Kenya, Jamaica, and India willingly display and sell contraceptives to support their governments' efforts to popularize family planning. This shows the awareness of even small businesses/retailers in developing countries toward the need for social programs and their willingness to participate. It seems that the primitive distribution networks in developing counties can be counted on for delivery of medically and socially oriented products, ideas, and services. In other words, psychologically, physically, and economically, the retailers are accessible for distribution of such products as health-related foods, over-the-counter medicines, and nutrition and hygiene information, even though each of them may run a small, inefficient operation.

Cooperative Retailing The emergence of consumer retail cooperatives is another trend that deserves mention. Traditionally, consumer cooperatives have been popular in Europe. for example, consumer cooperatives control almost one-fourth of food sales in Switzerland. Presumably, the two largest Swiss cooperatives have over one-third of

Swiss households as members. In Japan, consumers' cooperative union stores, which are nonprofit institutions, are fast emerging as a viable force in food retailing.[45]

The cooperative movement at the retail level, however, is spreading much faster in the developing countries of Asia and Africa. In many countries (for example, Mexico and India), government-sponsored cooperative societies have been formed to undertake distribution of essential products. The presence of the cooperatives reduces the volume of trade handled by private retailers and increases the government's control over trade. Interestingly, however, cooperatives do not succeed in many nations because in an economy of scarcity, cooperatives are often out of stock of the most-needed goods and products. This forces consumers to depend on private sources for their crucial purchases, even though it means paying a higher price.

International Franchising

Expansion into international markets represents a major growth opportunity for domestic franchise operations. This section focuses on the entry motivations, ownership practices, marketing strategies, and problems associated with U.S. franchise operations abroad.

The term *franchising* has many connotations; therefore, its meaning must be delineated in the context of private enterprise, where it refers to a form of marketing or distribution in which a parent company customarily grants an individual or relatively small company the right or privilege to do business (for a consideration from the franchisee) in a prescribed manner over a certain period of time in a specified place. An important aspect of a franchise arrangement is the continuing relationship between the parties. The current growth of the franchise industry is of recent origin and is strictly an American phenomenon.

Perspectives of International Franchising

Companies are primarily motivated by three factors in the expansion of their franchising operations internationally: market-growth opportunities, profit potential, and the desire to be known as an international firm. Companies usually initiate franchising in other countries on a limited scale—one or two countries with a few outlets in key locations. Initial success, however, leads to further expansion. Like the international expansion of U.S. business in general, foreign franchising operations usually start with Canada, Western Europe, and Japan. For example, Canada has the largest number of U.S. franchise operations, followed by England and Japan.[46] In Australia, U.S. fast-food chains—McDonald's, KFC, and Pizza Hut—and the convenience store chain 7-Eleven are included within the top 25 retailers.[47] Fast foods and business services account for over 50 percent of international franchising operations of U.S. firms. In 1987, 354 U.S. franchisers operated 32,000 outlets in foreign countries, and their gross sales amounted to almost $6 billion.[48]

Marketing Strategy

Firms entering overseas markets by establishing franchising operations must determine if they will follow a standardized or differentiated strategy with reference to product, price, and promotion. Most firms follow a standardized approach, particularly the soft drink and business services organizations. However, some fast-food companies have made adaptations in their overseas operations in response to particular cultural habits and customs of different nations. For example, in Japan Denny's serves ginger pork, curried rice, and dishes flavored with soy sauce. McDonald's offers tomato and beet-root in Austria; in France it serves wine with meals. Dairy Queen is attempting to penetrate the Middle East market by adding *roti*, a type of bread, and a fried vegetable and meat dish to the fare.

Similarly, price is duly adjusted to local competition. Promotion also varies, depending on media availability. For example, the use of television in foreign markets is much less popular. The dominant means of promotion are radio and different forms of sales promotions.

Future Trends

For numerous reasons, the international franchising operations of U.S. corporations should grow at a fast pace in the 1990s.[49] First, as the people in Western Europe and Japan move away from downtown areas into suburbs and as more and more women start working, the fast food industry should prosper. Second, there has been a gradual break in the tradition of going home for lunch, particularly in France, Germay, England, and Scandinavian countries. This is attributed to tightening of working hours, forced by the need to increase productivity. Third, the rise in discretionary income in Europe and Japan has enhanced the need for convenience foods. For example, companies like McDonald's and Kentucky Fried Chicken are showing annual sales increases of 50 percent a year. Fourth, franchising permits a substantial involvement of the local entrepreneur (for example, in the franchisee-owned ownership arrangement) right from the beginning. This makes entry into the country easier. Fifth, even among the emerging developing countries or otherwise large Third World countries, franchising has a great potential because it permits mass distribution, involves native businesspersons, and offers a standard product/service at a price trimmed by economies of scale. In conclusion, the future of franchising operations in the international markets appears promising, and more and more companies may seek foreign market entry through franchising.

International Physical Distribution

International physical distribution (PD) encompasses the logistics or movements of goods across countries from the sources of supply to the centers of demand. In other words, it is concerned with getting the right product to the right place at the right time, in good condition and at reasonable cost. Warehousing, transportation, and inventory are the major components of physical distribution. The final purpose of physical distribution activity is to provide adequate service to the customer. For satisfactory performance of this function, the various components of PD should be properly integrated for worldwide distribution.

Importance of International Physical Distribution

The importance of international physical distribution is illustrated by Japan. Two large metropolitan areas in Japan—Tokyo and Osaka—consume approximately 85 percent of all gasoline sold in Japan. The physical distribution system for a particular oil company serving Japan is made up of four different levels of intermediary agents—a national wholesaler, a regional wholesaler, a local wholesaler, and a retailer. The gasoline is physically delivered to the national wholesaler, who then has it delivered to the regional one, then on to the local one, and finally the retailer. There is nothing odd about this distribution system until one stops to consider that all channel members are located within the same metropolitan area. It would be considerably more convenient and far cheaper to ship the gasoline directly from the oil company's tanks to the retailer. However, because of the cultural environment in Japan, it may not be entirely feasible to streamline this distribution system. Nevertheless, the example serves to indicate that, by evaluating and implementing an alternative system, the delivery cost of the gasoline could be lowered. For example, an American manufacturer trying to penetrate the Japanese consumer goods market satisfied the cultural requirements by routing the paperwork through various levels of appropriately compensated intermediaries while distributing the product itself directly. Distribution is a marketing area that management might have a tendency to view as a so-called cost sink without realizing that considerable savings can be achieved by proper analysis and revision of distribution systems.

Management of International Physical Distribution

The three important aspects of physical distribution are warehousing, transportation, and inventory management. The basic decisions to be made concerning warehousing are how many warehouses of what size a company needs (if any at all), and in which country they should be located. The decision on warehousing requires information such as where the firm's customers, both current and potential, are geographically located around the world; what is the pattern of their current demand, and what demand pattern is likely to emerge in the future; and what level of customer service should be followed. The last item refers to the number of days within which the customer order would be filled. Often customers are categorized based on their importance for the company. The service level is varied in different categories. All this information is analyzed before making the warehousing decision.

The transportation decision mainly involves the choice of a mode of transportation for shipping the goods both internationally and locally within a foreign nation. This decision is affected by such factors as the availability of transportation, nature of product, size of shipment, distance to be traveled, type of demand (routine versus urgent demand), and cost of different shipping alternatives.

Inventory management deals with stocking inventory to fill customer orders. It involves two decisions—how often to order in a given period and how much to order. The costs involved with these decisions are inversely related. For example, if too many orders are placed in a year, the ordering costs go up. On the other hand, if large quantities are bought at a time, the total number of orders is reduced and hence the total ordering cost, but the costs of carrying large purchases goes up. Thus, an optimum point must be found for the number of orders and the size of each order. This can be figured by using different forms of informational inputs and an appropriate mathematical formula. (Such details, however, are beyond the scope of this book.)

So far, the three aspects of physical distribution have been discussed separately. For an integrated decision on international physical distribution, however, these three aspects should be considered simultaneously. This amounts to considering physical distribution as a system with three components—warehousing, transportation, and inventory management.

The logic of applying a systems approach to physical distribution is simple. Because the costs involved in administering warehousing, transportation, and inventory functions are interrelated, they must be considered simultaneously for effective decision making. For example, if the number of warehouses is increased, transportation costs will decrease, but inventory costs will increase—inventory will have to be duplicated at more places. Similarly, if an attempt is made to decrease inventory costs by cutting down inventory levels, transportation costs will go up. Obviously, an optimum decision mandates that all relevant costs be considered in an integrated fashion and in relation to the desired service level.

International Physical Distribution: An Example

Illustrated here are the highlights of Eastman Kodak Company's international physical distribution arrangements as an example of how a large MNC moves goods internationally.[50] For Kodak, proper distribution means getting the right product to the right place at the right time, in good condition, and at a reasonable cost. To achieve this, Kodak has developed a highly integrated worldwide distribution system.

International Organization Sophistication, coordination, and cooperation are required in order for Kodak to provide a wide range of products manufactured in both the U.S. and foreign factories to all of its corporate installations around the world. The center of Kodak's organization in this important area is the International Distribution Operations Committee. The committee provides a focal point for the Distribution Division's interface with the International Photographic Division and also develops and evaluates new ideas in the export area.

Inventory Management Kodak's inventory management system consists of two subsystems. The automatic replenishment subsystem determines the timing and amount of an order to be placed with one of the manufacturing companies. If stock is below a predetermined reorder point, the system prepares a replenishment order that is reviewed by the local planning department, thereby eliminating the time the stock planner usually spends in clerical review of the product line and leaving more time for true planning. In addition, the system automatically establishes control points used in the reorder cycle, which is the second part of the inventory management process. This system provides each of Kodak's computerized foreign facilities with an effective and efficient means of maintaining properly balanced inventories.

The results of the dual process are replenishment orders sent to Kodak manufacturing plants from one location to another. Transmission of computerized information is relayed over telephone lines in Northern Europe among six non-manufacturing companies. One large computer in Sweden services smaller computer systems in Denmark, Norway, Finland, Belgium, the Netherlands, Mexico, Singapore, Brazil, Japan, and Spain. Each night, replenishment orders from these 10 Kodak companies are transmitted from Sweden to New York and then to Rochester. By reducing lead time, inventories at the ordering locations can also be reduced. In attempting to maintain a proper worldwide balance of inventories, the main considerations are efficiency, accuracy, and timing.

Shipping Kodak's General Transportation group coordinates product movement from Rochester to foreign markets. Kodak's goods are shipped to New York City by truck and then by either ocean or air freight. In-transit time accounts for the majority of time between the issuance and receipt of an order by a foreign company. Therefore, the General Transportation group must try to make this time as short as practical, and the product as safe as possible, during the in-transit time interval. Also, they must schedule the timing and method of shipment so that Kodak gets the best possible rates for the service it uses.

Warehousing Kodak's international distribution system is based on the assumption that the supplying factory has sufficient inventory in its distribution center to fill the order. This is the most important link in the entire chain of events. Along with its marketing and manufacturing divisions, Kodak's Distribution Division is responsible for ensuring that the factory distribution centers will have the product when it is needed. This means that Rochester must maintain close contact with the international marketplace to see that sales requirements for the foreign market are properly incorporated into the marketing, distributing, and manufacturing chain of events.

This function is performed by International Estimating, and an international information system has been developed to aid them in the task. This information system consists of three parts. Weekly information is provided to International Estimating for a select number of key items. The second part generates monthly stock and product sales data in card format from each of the international companies to the supplying factory. The final portion of the system operates on a quarterly basis and is involved with medium-term forecasting. The last step helps International Estimating in establishing sales estimates to present to marketing as the first step in the production scheduling process.

Summary

Once opportunities in other countries have been determined, arrangements must be made to get the product to the market. Essentially, a company has two options concerning foreign distribution: establish company-owned channels or deal with different types of intermediaries. Initially, most companies use an existing system of distribution rather than attempting to build their own channels.

An important consideration in channel selection for overseas distribution is the availability of appropriate channels. Theory has it that the channel structures of a country reflect the stage of its economic development. According to this concept, channels of distribution in developed countries would be similar to those in the U.S., while in developing countries channels would be fragmented, smaller in operation, and inefficient. Unfortunately, limited research on the subject fails to support this theory. Presumably, the contradiction occurs because the channel structure of a country is more complex than has previously been suggested. For example, Japan is an advanced country, yet the Japanese channels of distribution are labeled by some as outmoded, complex, cumbersome, and inefficient.

Different types of intermediaries are active in the field of international distribution. Essentially, they can be categorized either as domestic agents and merchant intermediaries who provide channels of indirect distribution, or as foreign agents and merchant intermediaries who make it feasible to distribute directly. An essential difference between agents and merchant intermediaries is that the agents do not take title to the goods and operate only on behalf of their principals. The merchant intermediaries take title to the goods and conduct business on their own.

An international marketer should select appropriate channels and make them work. The selection process includes the establishment of channel objectives, feasible alternatives, and the choice of appropriate channels.

Once the distribution channel is determined, reliable foreign distributors must be found. The U.S. Department of Commerce provides different forms of services in this area. The actual selection of an intermediary is based on criteria such as the candidates' financial strength, their connections, the number and kind of other companies they represent, and the quality of their local personnel, facilities, and equipment.

Overall, independent intermediaries play a crucial role in international marketing. Their knowledge of the market and of the relevant business customs and practices adds to the strength of the manufacturer/exporter. They are especially important for smaller companies. Even some large companies with particular products prefer distributors over company-owned channels.

Use of intermediaries necessitates that manufacturers relinquish part of the control of the channel. It is important, therefore, for the manufacturer to design and implement an appropriate program to motivate channel members for effective performance.

An international marketer should gain knowledge of the host country's wholesale and retail patterns. Such knowledge will provide insights into the social, economic, political, and cultural factors that will affect distribution. Wide variations exist in the wholesaling and retailing characteristics of developed and developing countries. As a matter of fact, even among the advanced countries, channels differ significantly.

A discussion on physical distribution concludes the chapter. Physical distribution concerns the flow of goods from the manufacturer to the customer. Essentially, there are three aspects of physical distribution—warehousing, transportation, and inventory management—and they are related to each other. For an optimum physical distribution decision, they should be considered as a system. Physical distribution is one area where cost savings through efficiency are feasible provided the decision is systematically made.

Review Questions

1. What accounts for the differences in available channels in developed and developing countries?
2. Examine the distinguishing characteristics of Japanese distribution channels.
3. Discuss the role played by an export management company in international distribution.
4. Why do MNCs undertake distribution for other multinationals? What are the pros and cons of such piggybacking?
5. Discuss the importance of trading companies in foreign trade. Why are there no U.S. trading companies comparable in size and scope to the Japanese trading companies?
6. What criteria should an international marketer adopt in channel selection?
7. What factors weigh heavily with international firms in the selection of particular distributors/dealers?

8. What steps can a firm take to motivate the channel members to perform effectively?

Creative Questions

1. Gradually, U.S. retailing innovations are being adopted in other nations. Even some U.S. retailers like J.C. Penney, Toys 'R' Us, and Sears have selectively gone overseas. Yet, we don't find U.S. department stores venturing into foreign markets. What rationale do they have in not seeking overseas expansion? What conditions might attract them to operate stores outside the U.S.?
2. Trading companies have played a key role in helping small Japanese companies to export. In the U.S., while small companies are being encouraged to export, the trading company distribution route has been neglected. Why have trading companies not been considered important in the U.S.? Are there any cultural reasons that prevent us from preferring trading companies for distribution in export markets?

Endnotes

1. George Wadinambiaratchi, "Channels of Distribution in Developing Economies," *The Business Quarterly*, Winter 1965. *Also see* Leon V. Hirsch, *Marketing in an Underdeveloped Economy: The North Indian Sugar Industry* (Englewood Cliffs, NJ: Prentice-Hall, 1962); and George Wadinambiaratchi, "Theories of Retail Development," *Social and Economic Studies* (a publication of the University of West Indies), December 1972, pp. 391–403.
2. *See* Michael R. Czinkota, "Distribution of Consumer Products in Japan," *Industrial Marketing Review*, Vol. 2, No. 3 (1985), pp. 39–51. *Also see* L. Joseph Rosenberg, "Cultural Background: Implication and Effects on Japanese Distribution Channels," in Michael G. Harvey and Robert F. Lusch, eds., *Marketing Channels: Domestic and International Perspectives* (Norman, OK: Center for Economic and Management Research, School of Business Administration, The University of Oklahoma, 1982), pp. 52–58
3. *See* Robert E. Weigand, "Japan's Changing Marketing Channels," *Working Paper*, The University of Illinois at Chicago, 1988. *Also see* Jean L. Johnson, Tomuaki Sakano, and Naoto Onzo, "Behavioral Relations in Cross-Culture Distribution Systems: Influence, Control and Conflict in U.S.-Japanese Marketing Channels," *Journal of International Business Studies*, Vol. 21, No. 4 (1990), pp. 639–56.
4. "Selling in Japan Gets Less Befuddling," *Business Week*, February 20, 1989, p. 122D. *See Statistics of Commerce* (1985) (Tokyo: Japanese Ministry of International Trade and Industry).
5. Damon Darlin, "Papa-Mama Stores in Japan Wield Power to Hold Back Imports," *The Wall Street Journal*, November 14, 1988, p. 1.
6. *The McKinsey Quarterly*, No. 3, 1992, pp. 52–62
7. "Selling in Japan Gets Less Befuddling," *Business Week*, February 20, 1989, p. 122D.
8. Yumiko Ono, "As Discounting Rises in Japan, People Learn to Hunt for Bargains," *The Wall Street Journal*, December 31, 1992, p. A1.
9. *See* Bruce Seifert, "Export Distribution Channels," *Columbia Journal of World Business*, Summer 1989, pp. 15–22.
10. Donald G. Howard and James M. Maskulka, "Will American Export Trading Companies Replace Traditional Export Management Companies?" *International Marketing Review*, Winter 1988, pp. 41–50.
11. Don Stow, "Export Trading Companies: An Update," *Business America*, January 20, 1994, p. 9.
12. Daniel C. Bello and Nicholas C. Williamson, "The American Export Trading Company: Designing a New International Marketing Institution," *Journal of Marketing*, Fall 1985, pp. 60–69.
13. "Colgate-Palmolive, Kao Join to Create Hair Products Line," *The Asian Wall Street Journal Weekly*, January 24, 1983, p. 22.
14. "Kao Takes Over Sales of Dow Chemical Vinyl Ester in Japan," *The Asian Wall Street Journal Weekly*, October 7, 1985, p. 21.
15. Vern Terpstra and Chow-Ming J. Yu, "Piggybacking a Quick Road to Internationalization," *International Marketing Review*, Vol. 7, No. 4 (1990), pp. 52–63.
16. "Campbell's Taste of the Japanese Market is MM-MM Good," *Business Week*, March 28, 1988, p. 42.

17. "Corporate Scoreboard," *Business Week*, July 20, 1987, p. 162.

18. Bradley K. Martin, "Japan's Trading Giants Look to Year 2000," *The Wall Street Journal*, March 31, 1986, p. 23.

19. *See* Lyn S. Amine and S. Tamer Cavusgil, "Japanese Sogo Shosha and the U.S. Export Trading Companies," a paper presented at the Academy of International Business Annual Conference, Cleveland, Ohio, 1984.

20. Dale F. Duhan and , Mary Jane Sheffet, "Gray Markets and the Legal Status of Parallel Importation," *Journal of Marketing*, July 1988, p. 75.

21. *See* Bert Rosenbloom and Trina L. Larsen, "International Channels of Distribution and the Role of Comparative Marketing Analysis," *Journal of Global Marketing*, Vol. 4, No. 4 (1991), pp. 39–54.

22. *See* Saul Klein, "Selection of International Marketing Channels," *Journal of Global Marketing*, Vol. 4, No. 4 (1991), pp. 21–37.

23. Philip J. Rosson and I. David Ford, "Manufacturer-Overseas Distributor Relations and Export Performance," *Journal of International Business Studies*, Fall 1982, pp. 57l–72. *Also see* Gary L. Frazier, James D. Gill, and Sudhir H. Kale, "Dealer Dependence Levels and Reciprocal Actions in a Channel of Distribution in a Developing country," *Journal of Marketing*, January 1989, pp. 50–69.

24. Philip J. Rosson, "Success Factors in Manufacturer-Overseas Distributor Relationships in International Marketing," in Erdener Kaynak, ed., *International Marketing Management* (New York: Praeger Publishers, 1984), pp. 91–107.

25. Kenichi Ohmae, "Myths and Realities of Japanese Corporations," *The McKinsey Quarterly*, Summer 1982, p. 17.

26. Vern Terpstra, *International Marketing*, 4th ed. (Hinsdale, IL: Dryden Press, 1987), p. 388.

27. Ibid., p. 390.

28. Philip R. Cateora, *International Marketing*, 7th ed. (Homewood, IL: Irwin, 1990), p. 589.

29. *United Nations Statistical Yearbook*, 1993–94.

30. *See* Saeed Samiee, "Retailing and Channel Considerations in Developing Countries: A Review and Research Propositions," *Working Paper*, College of Business Administration, University of South Carolina, 1992.

31. Erdener Kaynak, *Transnational Retailing* (Hawthorne, NY: Walter de Gruyter, Inc., 1988).

32. *See* Madhav Kacker, "Coming to Terms with Global Retailing," *International Marketing Review*, Spring 1986, pp. 7–20.

33. "Wal-Mart Gets Lost in the Vegetable Aisle," *Business Week*, May 28, 1990, p. 48.

34. "A Retail Rebel Has the Establishment Quaking," *Business Week*, April 1, 1991, p. 39.

35. Yumiko Ono, "As Discounting Rises in Japan, People Learn to Hunt for Bargains," *The Wall Street Journal*, December 31, 1993, p. 1.

36. "Kentucky Fried Chicken Finds Favor in Bejing," *Asian Wall Street Journal Weekly*, September 26, 1988, p. 25.

37. "Otto the Great Rules in Germany," *Business Week*, January 31, 1994, p. 70.

38. "The Japanese Go on a Mail-Order Shopping Spree," *Business Week*, September 7, 1987, p. 44; and "Next, a Mail-Model," *The Economist*, January 16, 1988, p. 65.

39. Vern Terpstra, *International Marketing*, 4th ed. (Homewood, IL: Irwin, 1987), p. 391.

40. Kaoru Kobayashi, "Marketing in Japan," *Tradepia International*, Winter 1980, pp. 22–23.

41. "Guess Who's Selling Barbies in Japan Now," *Business Week*, December 9, 1991, p. 72; and "Toy Joy," *The Economist*, January 4, 1992, p. 62.

42. *Business Week*, January 31, 1994, p. 38.

43. Bob Ortega, "Wal-Mart Looks Beyond North America, Plans to Expand in Argentina, Brazil," *The Wall Street Journal*, June 6, 1994, p. A8.2.

44. "Printemps Finds Tough Climbing in the Rockies," *Business Week*, November 28, 1988, p. 101.

45. Bradley K. Martin, "Japan's Mom-and-Pop Stores Cooped Up," *The Wall Street Journal*, September 18, 1985, p. 23.

46. *Business America*, May 9, 1988, p. 27.

47. Madhav Kacker, "Australia Retailing Offers Growth for U.S. Marketers," *Marketing News*, April 12, 1993, p. 22.

48. *Business America*, May 9, 1988, p. 27. *Also see* "Franchising Is Still Proving Its Validity as a Marketing Method," *Business America*, March 16, 1987, p. 18.

49. *See* Niazamettin Aydin and Madhav Kacker, "International Outlook of U.S.-Based Franchisers," *International Marketing Review*, Vol. 7, No. 2 (1990), pp. 43–53.

50. Based on author's interview with Kodak managers, 1993.

CHAPTER • 15

International Advertising

CHAPTER FOCUS

After studying this chapter, you should be able to:

- Compare the pros and cons of using standardized versus localized advertising
- Examine the development and availability of international media
- Describe the steps in an international advertising program
- Discuss global advertising regulations
- Explain the role of advertising agencies internationally

Promotion is the fourth and final decision about marketing mix. Promotion means communication with the customer. The creation of awareness, interest, desire, and action is the universal aim of the promotion mix. Coordinating and integrating promotion with other aspects of a marketing strategy are often quite difficult to achieve in overseas markets. The quality, availability, and scheduling of promotional tools all influence the degree of success realized by a product or service.

Promotion includes advertising, personal selling, sales promotion, and publicity. Advertising refers to the corporate-sponsored messages transmitted through the mass media. Personal selling involves person-to-person contact with the customer. Sales promotion consists of different techniques (for example, samples, trading stamps, point-of-purchase promotion, coupons, contests, gifts, allowances, and displays) that support and complement advertising and personal selling. Publicity includes seeking favorable comments on the product/service and/or the firm itself through a write-up or presentation in mass media for which the sponsor is not charged. The focus of this chapter is on advertising. (Personal selling and other forms of promotion will be examined in Chapter 16.)

There are several important considerations in the design of international advertising and what it communicates. One important strategic consideration is whether to standardize advertising worldwide or to adapt it to match the environment of each country. Another consideration is the availability of media, which varies around the world. The development of advertising programs for foreign markets should take these differences, as well as advertising regulations in international markets, into account. The expertise of international advertising agencies can be valuable.

Perspectives of International Advertising

Worldwide, advertising plays a crucial role. In the case of many products/markets, a successful advertising campaign is the critical factor in achieving sales goals. As a matter of fact, more and more companies consider successful advertising to be requisite to profitable international operations.[1]

Global advertising expenditures were estimated to be $223.4 billion in 1988, and projected to increase to $650 billion by the year 2000. Outside the U.S., advertising expenditures could rise from $180 billion in 1990 to $300 billion by 2000.[2] These are impressive projections. Marketers abroad more and more are emulating U.S. advertising practices. The broad dimensions of the U.S. advertising industry changed significantly between 1960 and 1990. The total amount of money spent for advertising rose from a little less than $12 billion to more than $88 billion, more than a sevenfold increase. During the same period, the economy of the U.S. also increased approximately six times. Advertising as a percentage of GNP should rise in many countries as their media and marketing practices move increasingly in directions pursued in the U.S. For example, with the advent of current development in China, the advertising industry has been growing at a rate of 50 percent a year.[3] (see International Marketing Highlight 15.1).

Table 15.1 summarizes advertising expenditures during 1990 in selected countries. As might be expected, advanced countries account for a greater proportion of the expenditures than do developing nations. As a matter of fact, it may be postulated that advertising expenditures are significantly related to economic development.

International Marketing Highlight 15.1

Television Advertising in Asia

Commercial TV in Asia has emerged and expanded, stimulating fresh marketing efforts. Japan, the most mature television advertising market in Asia, has seen its market more than double since 1982 to $8.2 billion. Additionally, two of the largest potential consumer markets on the continent—China and India—have opened their doors to commercial television by expanding Western programming. General evening viewing in India is expected to climb to 400 million people by 1995.

TV ad expenditures in Asia do not come close to matching those of Western Europe, but the pace of growth has been more dramatic. In fact, between 1980 and 1986, Asian ad expenditures (excluding Japan) climbed 58.5 percent, versus 27.5 percent in Europe.

The signs of change can be discerned in TV advertising data for selected Asian nations. For its survey, *World Advertising Expenditures* (1982–1987), Starch, INRA, Hooper, Inc. recorded these gains:

- India, up from $16.2 million to $108 million;
- Japan, up from $3.6 billion to $8.2 billion;
- South Korea, up from $194 million to $430 million;
- Malaysia, up from $21 million to $66 million;
- Taiwan, up from $95 million to $266 million;

Source: *Business International,* February 20, 1989, p. 54.

Advertising is a key tool in international marketing. While the rationale for advertising may vary from country to country and among industries within a country, its overall relevance remains beyond question.[4] Like any other tool, of course, advertising can be misused and misapplied. Nonetheless, as long as the ethics of advertising are maintained, it serves a useful purpose. More specifically, advertising is important for the following reasons. First, advertising involves a significant commitment of funds—the cost of effective and ineffective advertising varies little. Further, an effective advertising campaign represents a tangible resource, transferable from one market to another. Obviously, every effort must be made to achieve effective advertising performance and so create a durable asset. Second, for many companies, advertising is their sole representative internationally. The image and impression created by advertising reflect on the entire corporation. If advertising succeeds in establishing and maintaining desired market images, it can pave the way for expansion. Third, advertising should establish the desired position for a product in a market. Once this position has been achieved, any local disturbances and changes, such as price-related effects, are less significant. Fourth, global advertising requires a certain degree of centralization, which in itself becomes a measure of control over global activities. Finally, advertising provides the most cost-effective method for communicating with potential buyers and creating markets in other countries (see International Marketing Highlight 15.2).

TABLE 15.1 Distribution of Advertising Expenditure in 1990 by Media and Select Countries (millions of U.S. dollars)

Country	Total	Print	TV	Radio	Cinema	Outdoor Transit	Direct Advertising	Miscellaneous
Argentina	829.1	262.3	250.9	72.4	27.7	79.6	58.4	78.8
Australia	3,548.0	1,869.7	1,057.9	335.2	63.3	221.9	—	—
Austria	1,012.0	566.0	264.7	119.3	—	62.0	—	—
Bahrain	11.0	6.1	4.9	—	—	—	—	—
Belgium	1,223.5	527.4	321.4	21.5	13.8	134.5	204.9	—
Bolivia	64.6	14.0	46.8	2.7	0.5	0.6	—	—
Brazil	3,186.5	1,121.8	1,825.9	153.0	—	63.6	—	22.2
China, People's Republic	523.1	159.7	117.4	19.1	0.5	—	126.0	100.4
Colombia	476.4	103.3	283.4	89.7	—	—	—	—
Costa Rica	67.9	26.1	32.7	—	9.1	—	—	—
Cyprus	4.8	1.6	2.2	0.9	—	—	—	0.1
Denmark	1,377.2	897.1	129.3	22.6	12.1	19.6	—	296.5
Dominican Republic	58.5	11.3	37.6	7.4	0.2	1.9	—	0.1
Ecuador	45.8	9.4	27.4	3.9	0.1	0.7	0.4	3.9
Finland	1,800.2	1,167.3	210.3	62.5	1.3	40.8	318.0	—
France	12,891.9	3,627.0	2,523.3	619.8	84.5	1,138.6	—	4,898.7
Germany, Federal Republic	13,944.4	8,429.8	1,708.2	550.8	136.2	420.9	2,698.5	—
Greece	526.2	232.8	221.1	35.6	1.3	35.4	—	—
Guatemala	16.3	4.8	10.5	1.0	—	—	—	—
Hong Kong	861.3	363.0	421.9	37.9	11.2	27.3	—	—
India	895.8	599.9	177.1	22.9	4.6	91.4	—	—
Indonesia	286.9	172.2	26.1	53.5	4.1	31.0	—	—
Ireland	321.1	168.8	84.9	35.2	—	22.1	—	10.1
Israel	587.9	415.3	20.0	30.1	4.5	42.0	20.6	55.4
Italy	5,709.7	2,466.9	2,908.1	91.7	—	243.0	—	—
Japan	38,433.6	11,971.1	11,164.4	1,612.7	—	4,347.7	3,628.7	5,709.0

(continued)

Country	Total	Print	TV	Radio	Cinema	Outdoor Transit	Direct Advertising	Miscellaneous
Kenya	20.5	9.6	3.0	4.0	0.6	1.2	0.2	1.9
Korea, South	2,826.2	1,370.0	845.2	134.7	—	476.3	—	—
Malaysia	321.6	153.5	130.7	5.5	1.1	26.2	—	4.6
Malta	14.6	9.5	4.0	0.2	—	0.6	0.3	—
Mexico	2,199.3	314.4	1,649.1	235.8	—	—	—	—
Netherlands	4,334.6	2,232.4	331.7	59.9	7.1	80.7	1,277.9	344.9
New Zealand	624.5	281.2	210.1	83.6	—	—	—	49.6
Norway	1,233.4	730.9	20.0	8.0	9.6	17.6	447.3	—
Oman	11.9	6.9	5.0	—	—	—	—	—
Pakistan	89.6	39.9	39.2	2.5	0.2	4.6	—	3.2
Panama	54.0	16.0	32.0	3.5	0.5	2.0	—	—
Portugal	415.6	154.9	181.7	32.6	—	46.4	—	—
Qatar	10.7	7.3	3.4	—	—	—	—	—
Saudi Arabia	139.7	89.4	50.3	—	—	—	—	—
Singapore	314.7	200.3	95.4	6.6	1.9	8.3	—	2.2
Spain	10,348.3	4,051.8	2,393.8	784.9	58.9	363.0	1,299.9	1,396.0
Sri Lanka	21.0	12.7	3.8	2.5	0.1	1.9	—	—
Sweden	2,729.3	1,706.8	39.9	—	11.8	78.9	891.9	—
Switzerland	4,098.0	1,895.3	162.7	41.0	22.3	299.5	1,677.2	—
Taiwan	1,569.2	710.4	458.1	84.7	5.5	35.3	44.5	230.7
Trinidad and Tobago	23.4	7.4	0.4	5.2	0.2	0.8	0.4	—
United Arab Emirates	69.4	47.9	21.5	—	—	—	—	—
United Kingdom	15,726.0	9,055.6	4,149.4	200.9	69.6	503.3	1,747.2	—
United States	128,640.0	42,174.0	28,405.0	8,726.0	—	1,084.0	23,370.0	24,881.0
Venezuela	439.2	136.5	285.7	8.5	—	8.5	—	—
Zambia	4.1	3.3	0.4	0.2	—	—	—	0.2
Zimbabwe	26.3	17.9	4.6	3.0	0.5	0.3	—	—

Source: World Advertising Expenditures (New York: Starch, INRA, Hooper and International Advertising Association, 1992). pp. 36–37.

Determining Advertising Strategy: Standardization Versus Localization

An important strategic decision for international marketers to make is whether the basics of an advertising campaign developed at home can be transferred to other nations with changes like translation into local languages. Many marketers strongly believe that a successful advertising concept will do well anywhere. Critics, however, are quick to reject standardization on the ground that cultural differences between nations require advertising to be tailored to each country. This section examines the arguments for and against global transferability of advertising and proposes an analytical approach the formulation of advertising strategy.

International Marketing Highlight 15.2

International Coffee War

When you think of coffee, what country do you think of? When researchers asked that question in 1959, most U.S. consumers replied, "Brazil." The National Federation of Coffee Growers of Colombia found to their dismay that the country of Colombia received almost no mentions.

Obviously, the Colombia coffee growers felt a major awareness campaign was needed. They also wanted U.S. consumers to identify brands with 100 percent Colombian coffee as quality or premium. This might sound like an impossible mission. Who, after all, cares which country grows the coffee beans?

The Colombian coffee growers federation accepted the challenge. It developed the slogan, "The Richest Coffee in the World," and the character of Juan Valdez as a spokesperson who taught consumers how to identify brands that contain 100 percent Colombian coffee. The Valdez character also explained the unique properties of Colombia that enabled it to grow the best coffee in the world.

DDB Needham ads established the premium image by featuring upscale settings with discriminating consumers enjoying 100 percent Colombian coffee. For example, one ad featured a businessman sitting in a lush grand parlor in front of a fireplace reading *The Wall Street Journal* and drinking a cup of Colombian coffee. The copy featured only the headline: "50% Tax Bracket, 100% Colombian coffee," the Juan Valdez logo, and the campaign slogan.

By the mid-1980s, unaided awareness of Colombia as a coffee-producing country reached an all-time high of 96 percent. Additionally, 62 percent of consumers believed that Colombia grows the best coffee. In the great coffee war, Colombia took the offensive away from Brazil. In 1983, only 35 coffee brands featured the Colombia logo. Today, 640 brands are in the program. People are willing to pay 15 percent more for the Colombian coffee compared with the blends.

Source: "The Richest Coffee in the World," DDB Needham Case Study, unpublished document.

Standardized Approach

Many practitioners and scholars believe that universal advertising can work advantageously. A Swedish executive, for example, found that savings bank promotions were successfully transferable all over Scandinavia.[5] Similarly, Fatt supports a standardized approach, believing that "the desire to be beautiful is universal. Such appeals as 'mother and child,' 'freedom from pain,' and 'glow of health,' know no boundaries."[6]

Empirical research on the subject and the experiences of many marketers confirm that such sentiments abound among advertisers. In their study sample of Fortune 500 firms, Donnelly and Ryans discovered that 90 percent of the firms to at least some degree extend their U.S. advertising approach to nondomestic situations.

International Playtex, Inc.'s efforts in developing a standardized campaign for its Wow bra are all the more revealing. The company traditionally ran 43 versions of its ads worldwide, employing different ad agencies in various countries. For Wow, the company assigned the entire global business to Grey Advertising, Inc. The ad theme was based on a single feature: Wow provides the extra support features of underwire bras without using uncomfortable wires. The company uses a plastic that took three years to develop. Beyond the basic theme, however, the commercial for each market had to be fine-tuned to meet local requirements. For example, the most noticeable change in the commercial had to be made for South Africa, where TV standards don't allow women to be shown modeling bras. In this market, fully clothed models hold up the bra on a hanger, while in other countries the models wear the bras. Further, some commercials had to be 29 seconds long, while others had to be 30 seconds long, because some countries want one second of silence at the beginning of the ad, while others do not. Certain national preferences also had to be observed: the French like lacy bras, while Americans prefer plainer, opaque styles.

Creating a global commercial that met government regulations and industry standards in different countries required good logistics. Grey Advertising, for example, showed Playtex foreign managers videotapes of potential models for ads. Three models were selected by consensus from over 50 prospects. Overall, the standardized approach did pay off. The Wow campaign allowed Playtex to present one unified message and save money. Grey was able to produce the Wow ad for a dozen countries for $250,000; the average cost of producing a single U.S. ad is $100,000.[8]

Similarly, Unilever, a British-Dutch consumer-goods maker's cross-border advertising campaign for the Impulse line of fragrances is a good example of standardized approach. Impulse was developed as a spray-on perfumed deodorant by Unilever's South African subsidiary. The parent company decided that the line had pan-European potential.

Subsequently, a cross-border campaign was devised, based on a simple but powerful advertising idea: When a woman wears Impulse, men cannot help but give her flowers. It did what every campaign, whether national, regional, or global, should do, i.e., tapped into a really provocative consumer insight. It brought together the impulsiveness of the male/female interaction and created an embodiment of that. The earliest campaigns varied because of the way relationships are conducted from country to country. For example, in Italy the boy plucked flowers from a garden, while in France he bought flowers.[9]

There is an apparent trend toward standardization. A number of companies, including A.T. Cross Pencil company, Deere & Co., and Nike, have been reported as favoring standardization.[10] Proponents of the standardized approach advance various reasons to support their viewpoint. First, there is the cost savings. Once an advertising concept is developed, it can be transferred to other nations with minor additional cost. Second is the realization of economies of scale made possible by the centralization of worldwide advertising authority to the home office. Third, standardization permits full utilization of home office advertising expertise hard won on the field. Fourth, it prevents the generation of disparate messages in different nations, which eventually may blur the established image of the product. Fifth, the common approach to advertising ensures proper concern for corporatewide objectives in promoting the product. Finally, similarities in the usage of media among specific segments across nations justify the standardized approach. For example, Urban's study on the subject showed that French and American women belonging to the same socioeconomic groups revealed similar media usage behavior.[11] Culture aside, this means that a particular type of segment in one country exhibits behavior comparable to that of a similar segment in another country. Thus, businesspeople in France may not differ from those in the U.S., Egypt, or Singapore. Presumably, then, a standard advertising strategy can be employed to reach businesspeople in many countries (see International Marketing Highlight 15.3).

International Marketing Highlight 15.3

Gillette's Panregional Approach

Gillette has organized its advertising plans according to regional and cultural clusters: pan-Latin America, pan-Middle East, pan-Africa, and pan-Atlantic. This is the result of what Gillette calls convergence, which is based on the belief that the company can identify the same purchase incentives and needs among consumers in regions or in countries that are linked by culture, consumers' habits, and development of the company's market for products.

For example, Gillette may use the same European-style advertising for Australia, New Zealand, and South Africa. In Asia, the company will link the less economically developed countries of Malaysia, Thailand, the Philippines, and Indonesia. It will market Singapore, Hong Kong, and Taiwan together, but handle Japan, China, and India separately.

The overall objective of Gillette's panregional strategy, which sells some 800 products in 200 countries, is to approximate a global marketing strategy while remaining sensitive to regional and national differences. Every two years, Gillette conducts research on brand usage of its products and those of competitors in most major markets.

Source: Business International, February 20, 1989, p. 51.

Localized Advertising

Customization of advertising for each nation is justified on the grounds of cultural differences among countries.[12] The international marketing literature is full of examples illustrating how efforts at standardization have backfired. Consider the following example:

> A worldwide leader in the toilet goods field built up one of its toothpaste brands to a leadership position in its home market with a promise of decay prevention. Given this success, the same promise was used to introduce the product in Latin American markets. The company was well-established in that part of the world, and together with its advertising agency developed on-site a new advertising campaign to carry the decay-prevention message—an execution tailored to those markets in every detail. At the end of one year of broad-scale advertising and selling effort, the product was withdrawn. It had achieved only a 3 percent share of market instead of the 15 percent achieved in the U.S.

A leading producer of farm equipment was particularly pleased with the success of a North America advertising campaign which was built around the testimonials of small farmers. The manufacturer felt that this campaign combined the traditional virtues of an endorsement by actual users with the added element of those customers to whom economy of use was a vital factor in their purchase decision. For these reasons, the testimonial campaign was introduced into Europe. The advertising vice president was dismayed to receive an urgent Telex from the largest distributor organization demanding that the campaign be withdrawn after only two weeks. The distributor had been flooded with telegrams from his dealers. They all found the campaign to be insulting and described it like this: "Most of our farms in Europe are small to begin with. When you stress 'smallness' so much, our customers think you are talking about peanuts. And who likes advice from them?"[13]

Briefly, product-related attributes influence buyer behavior differently around the globe. Thus, a standard approach to advertising may not be practical. For example, General Motors' Nova car did not do well in Latin America since *no va* translated into Spanish means "doesn't go." Emphasis on "whiteness" from a laundry detergent will not work in Brazil because Brazilians do not wear white clothes. Chileans buy their coffee strictly on the basis of price, but for Germans good coffee is a must for which they would pay any price.[14] Kentucky Fried Chicken is viewed as an ordinary meal in the U.S., while the Japanese consider it to be a treat.[15] A TV candy commercial for South Africa with a circus elephant had to be changed since the animal is sacred to the Venda people, the segment to which the ad was directed. Besides, the royal title of the wife of the king of neighboring Swaziland is "she-elephant," and it was feared the ad might offend that country.[16] Students of West African culture recommend against printing an advertisement on white paper there. In West Africa, white is associated with death and it might be perceived as a death notice. Grammatical errors in copy annoy the French. The macho image of a model wearing a hard hat does not excite Latin Americans. They prefer their macho men in suits suitable for executives. Testimonial advertising is considered "pushy" and "phony" among the Japanese.[17] Gillette, in its efforts to introduce its Trac II razor to Europe in 1972, found that products in the toiletries category are geared to cultural traits and life-styles and thus the U.S. advertising approach would fail abroad. In its attempt to develop localized advertising, the company changed the Trac II name to G II in some nations, since marketing research showed that *trac* in some of the Romance languages meant "fragile." Similarly, the copy design was adapted to match the local perspective. The U.S. copy showed builders constructing a new and unique razor. In Europe a sports analogy made sense, emphasizing synchronization of two moves to score a goal, or the closest shave through G II.[18]

Although product attributes and functions are generally similar in different countries, the perception of these attributes varies from nation to nation. Thus, the common needs of people belonging to different nations do not mean necessarily that the same products will be appreciated in the same ways. This suggests that standardized advertising will not work globally.

> Product [need] universality cannot imply global message appeal. . . . [Israeli and American women] might manifest the same need for cosmetics (i.e., preservation of beauty), but this certainly does not mean that an Israeli woman perceives the American cosmetic ad the same way it is perceived by the American. Therefore, understanding consumer wants, needs,

motives, and behavior is a necessary condition to the development of an effective promotional program.[19]

A standardized advertising approach seems particularly unsuited in developing countries because an international advertiser is likely to encounter marked differences in lifestyle, level of wealth, market structure, and various other aspects of the environment in the countries. Amine and Cavusgil, for example, found localized advertising more appropriate in Morocco, since knowledge of local environment and campaign targeting are essential for effective advertising.[20]

Strategy Selection

The determination of international advertising strategy is not a simple matter of choosing between standardization and localization. Conditions differ from nation to nation. Further, while one campaign may have been successfully transferred, another campaign might flop in the same country.[21] Besides, even where localization appears satisfactory, companies naturally do not want to give up the benefits of standardization. To resolve the problem, strategy should be formulated after careful analysis and consideration. The recommended procedure consists of three steps: apply choice criteria, analyze advertising transferability, and make organizational arrangements.

Choice Criteria The extension of the home country advertising program to a host country is affected by the following factors: host country environment, advertising objectives relative to the host country, target market, product characteristics, media availability, and cost-benefit relationship. Although it may not be feasible to combine all these influencing factors into a quantitative model, and international advertiser should find even a qualitative, sequential examination of these criteria helpful.

Environmental Factors A variety of environmental factors affect advertising transferability across national boundaries:

Rate of economic growth of country
Per capita income and distribution of income
Average size of household
Level of literacy
Level of education
Vocational training
Social class structure
Attitudes toward authority
Attitudes toward the U.S.
Degree of nationalism in country
Attitudes toward achievement and work
Attitude toward risk taking
Attitudes toward wealth and monetary gain
Similarity of ethical and moral standards to U.S. standards
Availability of time on commercial broadcast media
Adequate coverage of market by broadcast media
Availability of satisfactory outdoor media
Availability of satisfactory print media

Independence of media from government control
Political organization and stability
Import/export rate of country
Legal restraints on advertising within the country
Availability of prototype campaigns
Relative importance of visual versus verbal in ad message
Experience and competence of personnel in foreign subsidiary and distributor
Experience and competence of personnel in foreign agency or branch of U.S. agency
Eating patterns and customs
Importance of self-service retailing
Import duties and quotas in country
Development and acceptance of international trademark or trade name
Applicability of product's theme or slogan to other markets

Not all these factors would be relevant in every case. It would be desirable, therefore, to diagnose and identify the most salient environmental concerns for a product/market.

For example, factors considered important from the viewpoint of consumer goods companies in developed countries might comprise level of education; level of literacy; attitudes toward risk taking, achievement, work, wealth, and monetary gain; experience and competence of personnel in foreign agency or branch of U.S. agency, foreign subsidiary, or distributor; degree of nationalism in the country and attitudes toward the U.S.; rate of economic growth of country; per capita income and distribution of income; import duties and quotas in the country; development and acceptance of international trademark and trade name; eating patterns and customs; importance of self-service retailing; attitudes toward authority; social structure; applicability of product or slogan to other markets; independence of media from government control; and availability of satisfactory media. Clearly, a different set of factors would be applicable to developing countries. Similarly, relevance of environmental factors would vary based on the type of goods. However, if the overall perspectives of the environmental factors vis-à-vis the host country are similar to those of the U.S., standardization might be feasible. A significant difference in the environment, however, would suggest localized advertising (see International Marketing Highlight 15.4).

Advertising objectives. Advertising objectives vary from market to market. Advertising does not lead directly to sales. A sale is a multiphased phenomenon, and advertising can be used for transferring the customer from one phase to the next. Advertising attempts to move consumers from unawareness of a product or service—to awareness—to comprehension—to conviction—to action. Presumably, customers in the host country may not be at the same point in the product adoption cycle as those in the home country. If this is so, the advertising objectives of the two markets would differ and thus the home-country advertising concept might not work in the host country. For example, a television manufacturer's advertising objectives for Mexico would have to be different from those for the U.S. because in the U.S., TV is in the maturity stage of the product life cycle, while in Mexico it is in the growth stage. In Mexico, the major focus of advertising may be to move the customer from awareness to comprehension, while in the U.S. from conviction to action. Thus, the U.S. advertising concept for marketing TVs would not be effective in Mexico.

Target market. If the proposed ad campaign for another country is aimed toward a segment that is more or less similar in characteristics to the segment served in the U.S., standardized advertising would appear satisfactory. However, if the target segments differ, a localized campaign would be desirable. For advertising purposes, dividing the market is to split it into three consumer categories:

1. International sophisticates: a select group of well-to-do and successful people who are mainly in the developed countries and who have international exposure because of travel, education, responsibility and the like.
2. Semisophisticates: a large group of middle-and high-income individuals who are largely in developed countries and who have substantial discretionary income.
3. Provincials: people who have a narrow outlook and ethnocentric orientation.

Of the three groups, the first one would be most receptive to standardized advertising. The provincial group can effectively be reached through localized advertising. The semisophisticates may or may not be convinced by the standardized approach, depending on the nature of the product.

International Marketing Highlight 15.4

The Euroteens (and How To Sell To Them)

For years, marketers have been heralding the arrival of the Global Teen, a new breed of youth who share universal tastes in food, fashion, and attitude. However, despite the rise of global media, differences still abound, making life complicated for marketers.

Take Levi Strauss & Co. It sells a key part of the international teen uniform, but found that European teens reacted negatively to the gritty urban realism of its U.S. ads, which evoked a side of America that makes them uncomfortable. So Levi's European ads draw on a mythical America. One example: a mini-Western of two girls traveling by covered wagon who stop to watch a young man bathe in a creek wearing nothing but his Levi's.

Marketers say European kids are also starting to look toward Central and Eastern Europe for music and fashion clues. The hottest cities on teens' travel itineraries are not Los Angeles and New York but Berlin, Prague, and Budapest. It's cool to look to America, but there's a deep-seated need and pride for one's own roots and heritage.

Research underscores the difference among kids. Compared with Yanks, European teens enjoy closer relationships with their parents, and—except for Britons—don't watch as much TV, according to a 1993 study by Yankelovich Partners Inc. A study by Paris-based Martine Thiesse of Research International found that teens in such recession-wracked countries as Germany, Denmark, and Belgium worry that they'll never match the living standards of their parents. Europe's teens also prefer a more irreverent style of ad. A British spot aimed at 15-year-old boys, for example, urges them to buy the snack food Nik Naks, not because they taste good but because they're revolting. Two cartoon characters in the macabre ads torture one another into misshapen forms.

Source: Business Week, April 11, 1994, p. 84.

Product characteristics. The characteristics of the product involved also determine the usage of standardized advertising.[22] These characteristics would include product attributes, both purchase and usage patterns; psychological attributes associated with the product (e.g. attitude); and cultural factors. The following questions should be raised for each characteristic to determine the appropriate advertising approach.

   a. **Product Patterns:** Is the product or service purchased by relatively the same consumer income group from one country to another? Do the same family members motivate the purchase in all target countries? Do the same family memebers dictate brand choices in all target countries? Do most consumers expect a product to have the same appearance? Is the purchase rate the same regardless of the country? Are most purchases made at the same kind of retail outlet? Do most consumers spend the same amount of time making the purchase? Do most consumers use the product for the same purpose or purposes? Is the product or service used in different amounts from one target area or country to another? Is the method of preparation the same in all target countries? Is the product or service used along with other products or services?

   b. **Psychological Attributes:** Is brand loyalty the same throughout target countries for the product or service under consideration? Will past advertising strategies conflict with the projected standardized approach? Are the media of the target countries suitable for a common advertising strategy? Are the basic psychological, social, and economic factors motivating the purchase and use of the product or service the same for all target countries? Are the advantages and disadvantages of the product or service in the minds of consumers basically the same from one country to another? Does the symbolic content of the product or service differ from one country to another? Is the cost of purchasing or using the product or service the same, whatever the country? Does the appeal of the product or service for a cosmopolitan market differ, thus crossing national boundaries? Is the brand name equally known and accepted in all target countries? Are customer attitudes toward pricing basically the same?

   c. **Cultural Factors:** Does society restrict the purchase and/or use of the product or service to a particular sex, age group, religious group, or education level? Is there a stigma attached to the product or service—the brand name, advertising content, or type of artwork in one or more of the target countries? Does usage of the product or service as suggested by advertising interfere with tradition in one country and not the others?

Consider product patterns. One of the questions is "Do the same family members motivate the purchase in all target countries?" If the answer to this question is positive, standardized advertising would be attractive. Although it may not be feasible to specify a definite "yes" or "no" answer to all the aforementioned questions, a sense of direction can be gained by considering the questions. If the consideration of a product yields an affirmative sense of direction, then the use of standardized advertising would be recommended. Localized advertising would be preferable in cases where a negative sense dominates.

Media availability. Media availability is another consideration that determines the feasibility of using standardized advertising. For example, a U.S. TV ad would not be suitable in India since commercial advertising on TV is limited there. Because of legal restrictions in France, the International Playtex Company could not use coupons and door-to-door samples as it could in the U.S. for a promotion campaign for its Jhirmack line of hair-care products. The company was, therefore, obliged to launch instore demonstrations.[23]

Cost-benefit relationship. In the final analysis, the choice between the standardized approach and localization should be based on a careful consideration of cost-benefit. If the cost of local adaptation exceeds the benefit that an adaptation might provide, it is desirable to opt for standardized advertising. On the other hand, it would be reasonable to incur costs, as a form of investment, if the localized advertising could open up new opportunities that might be lost by sticking to the standardized advertising concept.

Transferability Analysis   There are two aspects to consider in advertising propositions for international transfer: the buying proposal and the creative presentation. The *buying proposal* refers to the content, not the form, of the advertisement. Its focus is on the most persuasive and most relevant elements of the advertisement. The *creative presentation* assists in transferring the buying proposal into an advertising message, which consists of the headline idea and all the visual and verbal elements of the advertisement. The difference between the two aspects can be illustrated with reference to toothpaste: (a) buying proposal–cosmetic benefits; (b) creative presentation–cavity prevention. A buying proposal is far easier to transfer across national boundaries than are creative presentations because certain needs are basic worldwide and customer motivations for such products do not vary much. For example, expectations for a laundry detergent may not differ from nation to nation. Similarly, emphasis on punctuality by an airline would catch the fancy of businesspersons who fly frequently, regardless of their nationality.

The creative presentation, on the other hand, is difficult to transfer in its original form. The following barriers limit an intact transfer of creative presentation:

- Cultural barriers (In most Anglo-Saxon countries, women are accepted without question as family spokespersons, but much less so in Latin America and seldom in Muslim countries.)

- Communication barriers (Something accepted as funny in one country might be considered silly in another. Exxon's tiger ad, putting a cartoon character in the gas tank, did not make sense to the Swedes.)

- Legislative barriers (Laws and regulations imposed on the advertising industry differ among nations.)

- Competitive barriers (Competition for a product varies from one national market to another and sometimes necessitate changes in advertising viewpoint for proper positioning.

- Implementation barriers (such barriers might include poor printing and reproduction because of the level of facilities available, and the necessity of using local landscapes and models to avoid negative connotations.)

It would be naive to expect that a standardized creative presentation would succeed globally. Therefore, appropriate marketing research must be conducted to determine what elements of the creative presentation can be retained, what must be eliminated or replaced, and what should be added. As a matter of fact, once the creative presentation has been reworked, the advertisement should be tested in the prospective market before becoming final.

Organizational Support Whatever strategy is selected, its successful implementation requires appropriate organizational arrangements. If the standardized approach is adopted, the company should establish and adequately staff the international advertising office. For example, Deere & Company has organized its international advertising at a central office at its headquarters that develops yearly several hundred pieces of advertising in as many as 12 languages with the assistance of one advertising agency.

Similarly, if a localized strategy is decided upon, then communication links must be established to coordinate the advertising efforts of far-flung subsidiaries. Such a coordination not only would serve as a control device, but also should be shared with subsidiary advertising people to avoid the necessity of reinventing the wheel, so to speak, for each operation.

In conclusion, it should be noted that no particular strategy is appropriate for all companies at all times. In fact, two companies in the same industry may well pursue different strategies (see International Marketing Highlight 15.5). Some companies adhere to a policy of standardization. This group includes such multinationals as International Playtex Company, British Airways, and Philip Morris, Inc. For example, Philip Morris has used the Marlboro-country concept and has kept the basic Marlboro look in all its ads worldwide. Traditionally, British Airways had decentralized advertising arrangements and its local managers enjoyed a great deal of autonomy. However, the decentralized arrangement led country managers to position British Airways in different markets differently. Therefore, British Airways introduced a widely publicized global advertising campaign to present a common image worldwide. The campaign included the well-known 90-second Manhattan Landing television commercial created by the Saatchi & Saatchi advertising agency, one of the leading proponents of global advertising.[24]

At the other end of the spectrum are those companies that have delegated almost the entire advertising responsibility to locals. Nestlé S.A., for example, utilizes 130 different ad agencies in over 40 countries and has given near autonomy to country managers. There are companies in between the British Airways and Nestlé styles that pursue a patterned approach, establishing basic guidelines for global advertising centrally and leaving development of individual campaigns to locals. In the final analysis, whatever the advertising strategy, a company must consider local factors. Even products that had been considered sure winners have been hurt by a failure to reckon with local realities. General Food's Maxwell House was dismayed to find that the great American coffee had little respect among the Germans. Similarly, Procter & Gamble's Crest fluoride appeal did not mean much to English customers.[25] The theory that people are alike and that they have the same generic needs and preferences does not always hold true in international advertising. A recent study of Japanese advertisements, featuring products and services in a home setting, showed significant differences between the two countries. The Japanese advertising emphasized status to a much greater degree than did U.S. ads. The reverse was true with personal efficacy, which was more prominent in U.S. ads.[26] (see International Marketing Highlight 15.6).

International Marketing Highlight 15.5

Nike vs. Reebok: Marching to Different Drummers

Nike, the worldwide sports and fitness company, has created a global advertising program and tailored it regionally to local markets. The basic vehicle is the popular "Bo Knows" commercial that was used in the company's U.S. campaign. In that ad, Bo Jackson, an American professional football and baseball star, was seen taking part in a wide variety of other professional sports, such as tennis and basketball while wearing Nike shoes and apparel. Well-known professional athletes from other sports exclaimed that "Bo knows" their sports as well.

For international use, Nike used Jackson in a similar ad while including athletes whose names were well known in the target countries such as cricket star Ian Botham for ads that ran in the U.K. and soccer star Ian Rush for ads that ran in France, Sweden, Denmark, and Norway. The ads ran in the local European language without subtitles.

In contrast, another leading U.S. athletic shoe producer, Reebok, bases its international ad strategy on addressing the individual needs and national brand identities of each country while remaining under a global umbrella theme. Individual strategies may differ from country to country and are designed to capitalize on international talents and unique country differences, but the common thread of a global brand identity remains consistent.

For the most part, Reebok's foreign advertisements feature actors and athletes famous in each country, who promote the company's shoes in campaigns devised locally. However, U.S. commercials and print ads are often adapted for foreign use. For example, Reebok's new brand image campaign, "It's Time to Play," is in use in France, but with a revised edit that is more in tune with the demographics of that market.

Source: Marketing News, December 4, 1989, p. 10.

Media

The global growth of the advertising industry is directly related to the development and availability of mass media. Mass media are most highly developed in the U.S., followed by Britain, Germany, France, Japan, and Italy. In the less-developed countries, where a majority of the world population lives, the mass media are far behind. This is evident in the information contained in Table 15.2 and Table 15.3.

Table 15.2 shows the number of newspapers (local and regional/national) and magazines (consumer/trade and technical) for selected countries. Although the number of newspapers is one indicator of the media resources of a country, the extent of their circulation also matters. For example, in 1990, Pakistan had as many as 168 local and regional newspapers, but their total circulation was rather small, limited to about 5.3 million (figure not given in the table). On the other hand, that same year, Japan achieved a circulation of over 16.5 million (figure not given in the table) with 79 local and regional newspapers. Thus, in many countries, the lag is not in overall numbers of newspapers published, but in the extent of the circulation. In some countries, however, poor media development is a factor, as typified by such a large country as South Korea with only 68 newspapers in 1990. On the other hand, Mexico typifies media inefficiency. In 1990, 317 magazines achieved a circulation of 6 million there. By comparison, Sweden with 239 magazines had a circulation of 7 million in 1990 (see International Marketing Highlight 15.7).

Table 15.3 examines the broadcasting media of radio and TV. In the U.S. and many other industrialized countries, TV constitutes the most important medium for advertising, accounting for anywhere from 15 percent to 27 percent of advertising expenditures.[27] In the developing countries, TV is still in its primitive stages. As a matter of fact, in many poor countries, TV cannot be considered a mass medium; even if TV is available, TV commercials are more or less prohibited. Thanks to the development of transistor technology, radio is becoming a popular mass medium worldwide

■ International Marketing Highlight 15.6 ■

Is Global Branding More Myth Than Reality?

Despite the prominence of some well-known global brands, a recent study indicated that most U.S.-based MNCs do not seriously pursue the ideas of global branding. According to the survey, which examined U.S.-based manufacturers of consumer nondurable goods, "global markets" may be out there, but global brands have not yet captured them. Of 85 brands included in the survey, 29 (or 34 percent) were not marketed outside the U.S. at all, and many of the remaining brands were only minimally marketed abroad (see table below).

Largest Foreign Markets for U.S. Brands

	Number Of Brands For Which Listed Country Is Largest Foreign Market	Number Of Brands For Which Listed Country Is Second-largest Foreign Market
Canada	33	2
United Kingdom	5	9
Mexico	4	0
Germany	3	5
Japan	2	4
Australia	2	4
France	1	1
Italy	1	2
Nigeria	1	1
Norway	1	0
Missing	3	14
Total	56	42

Companies surveyed showed a clear preference for selling their goods in markets culturally similar to the U.S. market, i.e., Canada and the U.K. (see table). While one might argue that Canada was targeted so frequently because of its geographical proximity to the U.S., the choice of the U.K. cannot be so easily explained. It is as far away as many other foreign countries, and its population and economy are smaller than those of several other foreign markets.

Source: Marketing Strategies for Global Growth and Competitiveness (New York: Business International Corp., October 1990), p. 36.

TABLE 15.2
1990 Media Information: Newspapers and Magazines for Selected Countries

Country	NEWSPAPERS			MAGAZINES		
	Total	Local & Regional	National	Total	Consumer	Trade & Technical
Argentina	255	—	255	850	450	400
Austria	197	164	33	129	59	70
Belgium	17	—	17	64	64	—
Brazil	1,939	1,939	—	745	195	550
China, People's Republic	773	—	773	5,751	?	?
Colombia	32	30	2	110	52	58
Costa Rica	4	—	4	31	6	25
Cyprus	13	—	13	21	7	14
Dominican Republic	10	1	9	36	34	2
Ecuador	41	37	4	26	20	6
Greece	225	195	30	540	30	510
Guatemala	6	2	4	25	15	10
Hong Kong	43	43	—	613	—	613
Indonesia	109	107	2	109	104	5
Ireland	73	60	13	90	30	60
Israel	147	135	12	—	—	—
Japan	84	79	5	3,889	—	—
Kenya	8	3	5	70	45	45
Korea, South	68	35	33	145	97	48
Malaysia	41	21	20	165	115	50
Malta	8	—	8	26	16	10
Mexico	332	332	10	317	120	197
Netherlands	78	70	8	1,200	—	1,200
New Zealand	133	127	6	500	—	—
Pakistan	180	168	12	1,640	1,630	10
Panama	7	2	5	4	3	1
Portugal	51	15	36	88	54	34
Singapore	14	—	14	3,700	3,700	—
Spain	120	110	10	3,200	200	3,000
Sri Lanka	86	—	86	—	—	—
Sweden	157	152	5	239	30	209
Switzerland	220	220	—	2,050	50	2,000
Taiwan	226	—	226	193	193	—
Trinidad & Tobago	6	—	6	—	—	—

(Continued)

	NEWSPAPERS			MAGAZINES		
Country	Total	Local & Regional	National	Total	Consumer	Trade & Technical
United Kingdom	1,680	1,660	20	6,667	2,373	4,304
United States	1,622	1,620	2	15,350	11,050	4,300
Zambia	9	3	6	3	2	1
Zimbabwe	16	14	2	38	18	20

Source: *World Advertising Expenditures* (New York: Starch, INRA, Hooper and International Advertising Association, 1992) pp. 48–49.

Advertising and Mass Media

Advertising is the principal source of revenue for most commercial mass media throughout the world. Although the dependence of media on advertising revenues is generally considerable, cross-national comparisons show some variations. In the case of most developed countries including the U.S., TV relies heavily on advertising revenues. In those countries where TV is subsidized or owned by the government, as in Western European countries, the high costs of transmission require considerable support from commercial advertising. However, in those countries where the TV owner pays an annual fee to the government for television viewing, as in Italy, Finland, and Sweden, advertising revenues are not so significant. Newspapers and magazines are not dependent on advertising revenues alike. In some countries, the reader pays most of the cost, while in others the advertiser does. The dependence of radio on advertising revenues also varies by country and is lowest in Western Europe.[28]

Throughout the world, a trend toward commercialization of mass media is apparent. In the printed media, this trend is reflected in the substantial increase in the commercial content of newspapers and magazines. In the case of TV, the amount of time devoted to advertising is not very significant compared with the proportional amount of space in newspapers and magazines. This is partly because the amount of advertising time allowed on TV is regulated in most countries. In Mexico, for example, a maximum of 15 percent of total broadcasting time may be used for advertising, and individual advertisements may not exceed two and one-half minutes in length. However, worldwide there has been a tendency toward the commercialization of TV. In Colombia, where the control of television was originally in the hands of the state, the system was modified to allow for the sale of time to commercial interests. Israel commercialized its system in 1976. Even in Europe, the traditionally strong state-owned systems have shifted one by one to allow some commercial support. Italy has become one of the world's most commercial and competitive television markets. The U.K. opened a commercial channel in 1955, which claims to have taken away more than half of the BBC's viewers. Switzerland, which long held out against TV advertising, has yielded to commercial support. In France and the Netherlands, TV became commercial in 1968. Although in many countries including Belgium, Denmark, Sweden, and Norway, government broadcasts still carry no TV advertising, deregulation is sweeping the TV industry in Europe. Guided by free market policies, governments are selling their own stations or letting entrepreneurs into the game.[29] Cable networks covering as many as 18 countries have started broadcasting programs from different countries.

The demand for time to broadcast commercials and increased programming costs have led to a dramatic rise in the cost of TV advertising. To begin with, compared to the U.S., media costs are much higher in foreign markets and, as a recent study of 9 major global markets shows, the costs are increasing at a rate of 10 percent to 15 percent annually. In part, the increase can be explained by shortages of advertising time. In the U.K, for example, instead of paying fixed rates, companies bid for TV time, which escalates the prices. Moreover, stations follow a preempt system. Even though a company has booked a spot at $57,000, another company that is willing to pay more will get it.[30]

Table 15.3 1987 Media Information: TV Sets and Radio Receivers for Selected Countries

Country	TV SETS Total (millions)	TV SETS Per 1,000 Population	CABLE Subscribers (thousands)	RADIO RECEIVERS Total (millions)	RADIO RECEIVERS Per 1,000 Population	Cinemas
Argentina	9.8	310.7	600	10.4	329.5	511
Australia	7.0	429.8	—	26.2	1,619.3	514
Austria	1.9	252.7	447	—	—	470
Bahrain	—	—	—	—	—	—
Belgium	3.5	355.0	2,950	—	—	371
Bolivia	0.3	36.8	—	0.6	87.6	45
Brazil	27.8	196.8	—	59.5	421.3	1,423
Canada	9.1	351.9	—	—	—	—
Chile	3.2	253.6	80	5.6	446.7	180
China, People's Republic	90.0	84.2	—	300.0	280.7	—
Colombia	5.0	169.5	200	9.0	305.1	—
Costa Rica	0.3	92.3	90	0.4	147.6	35
Cyprus	0.2	243.0	—	0.2	316.6	20
Denmark	2.1	411.4	—	3.8	744.4	315
Dominican Republic	4.9	732.6	100	6.0	893.4	79
Ecuador	—	—	—	—	—	350
El Salvador	0.4	76.4	20	1.2	241.3	30
Finland	2.6	525.6	345	—	—	328
France	—	—	—	—	—	2
Germany, Federal Republic	23.4	384.7	3,800	—	—	3,281
Greece	3.5	349.9	—	—	—	220
Guatemala	0.9	110.8	80	2.5	291.5	50
Hong Kong	1.6	295.9	—	4.8	873.9	110
India	16.0	20.1	10	50.0	62.7	12,400
Indonesia	9.0	53.0	—	—	—	2,115
Ireland	1.0	276.9	320	1.8	498.5	101
Israel	1.0	228.6	—	1.1	251.5	250
Italy	19.0	331.3	—	14.3	248.6	5,500

	TV SETS		CABLE	RADIO RECEIVERS		
Country	Total (millions)	Per 1,000 Population	Subscribers (thousands)	Total (millions)	Per 1,000 Population	Cinemas
						(continued
Jamaica	0.4	170.1	—	1.4	582.7	33
Japan	83.0	679.6	4,935	153.0	1,252.8	2,109
Jordan	—	—	—	—	—	—
Kenya	1.0	45.3	—	4.2	190.1	67
Korea, South	9.3	221.2	—	9.8	233.5	676
Kuwait	—	—	—	—	—	—
Lebanon	0.5	181.2	—	0.6	235.5	50
Malaysia	2.0	120.8	—	2.2	132.9	205
Malta	1.2	3,333.3	—	0.2	611.1	14
Mexico	11.9	144.7	152	12.9	157.4	1,000
Morocco	3.0	130.6	—	—	—	250
Netherlands	—	—	—	—	—	—
New Zealand	0.9	282.3	—	3.5	1,046.1	154
Nigeria	5.3	49.2	—	84.0	787.0	147
Norway	—	—	—	—	—	—
Oman	—	—	—	—	—	—
Pakistan	1.5	14.6	—	12.5	122.0	—
Panama	0.2	105.6	3	0.4	155.8	22
Peru	3.1	148.1	—	—	—	—
Philippines	4.1	70.4	25	8.0	137.3	940
Portugal	2.4	237.4	—	—	—	324
Puerto rico	1.5	448.3	225	1.7	508.1	115
Qatar	—	—	—	—	—	—
Saudi Arabia	—	—	—	—	—	—
Singapore	0.5	206.5	—	0.6	247.1	42
South Africa	—	—	—	—	—	400
Spain	13.0	334.5	—	—	—	2,083
Sri Lanka	0.6	39.7	—	3.0	183.4	200
Sweden	3.3	388.9	—	—	—	1,236
Switzerland	2.3	353.8	1,100	—	—	431
Taiwan	4.3	219.1	—	2.8	145.8	600
Thailand	6.3	117.1	—	8.2	153.2	262
Trinidad & Tobago	0.3	265.8	—	0.4	344.2	20
Turkey	8.5	160.8	—	7.0	132.5	88
United Arab Emirates	—	—	—	—	—	—
United Kingdom	33.0	580.5	—	—	—	1,252
United States	87.4	359.1	39,700	482.3	1,981.7	8,600
Venezuela	3.1	169.7	500	3.2	176.6	436

Source: World Advertising Expenditures (New York: Starch, INRA, Hooper and International Advertising Association, 1988), pp. 52–53.

Relative Importance of Different Media for Advertising

A comparison of advertising expenditures by media category around the world reveals that print is still the most important: 40 percent of the reported expenditures by 53 countries in 1990 were made in newspapers and magazines. TV is second with 24 percent, and radio is third with 7 percent. The remaining expenditures go to media such as outdoor posters and transit advertising, cinema, direct mail, exhibits, sales promotion, and reference publications.[31]

International Marketing Highlight 15.7

24,629 Journals—In 92 Languages

Despite the low literacy rate of around 40 percent, perhaps no country matches India in the number of newspapers published in an incredible variety of languages, shapes, sizes, and opinions.

Newspapers and periodicals are published in 92 languages—the 16 main languages recognized by the constitution, 76 others, and a few foreign languages.

At the end of 1987, the total of newspapers and magazines was 24,629 of which 2,151 were dailies, 7,501 weeklies, 3,366 biweeklies, 8,123 monthlies, and the rest quarterlies and annuals. In contrast, the U.S. has 1,642 dailies and about 8,000 weeklies.

Although English is the mother tongue of fewer than 250,000 people in India, the overall circulation of the English-language press is second only to that of Hindi. While the Hindi press had a total readership of 14 million, English was next with 10 million, followed by Malayalam with 6 million.

Hardly any major urban center is without at least two English papers. New Delhi alone has six English dailies, compared to two in Washington and five in London.

About 30 percent of newspapers published in the country are concentrated in the four metropolises of Delhi, Bombay, Calcutta, and Madras. Among multiple-edition dailies, *The Indian Express*, published in 11 centers in English, leads with a circulation of 632,199, followed by another English daily, *The Times of India*, with a circulation of 573,552 in 6 editions.

Source: *India Abroad,* August 25, 1989, p. 12.

Of course, patterns and levels of expenditures vary from country to country, and from region to region (see Table 15.1). Differences in media expenditures do not always reflect the preferences of advertisers, since in several countries, particularly in Europe, there are restrictions on TV and radio advertising. Thus, print advertising is relatively high in Western Europe and Australia and relatively low in Latin America. On the other hand, TV advertising is well above average in Latin America and Asia and below average in Western Europe and the Middle East/Africa. The use of TV as an advertising medium continues to expand proportionately faster than the use of other media, with the most pronounced increases occurring among the LDCs. Radio advertising is very popular in Latin America but is less so in Western Europe, where commercial radio is even more limited than commercial television.[32] Despite variations among regions and countries, a trend has emerged: advertising expenditures on TV are increasing, while expenditures on print and radio advertising are decreasing in relative terms. The growing importance of TV advertising is due largely to the continuing increase in the number of TVs throughout the world. For example, China now has about 150 million homes with TV. Seven years ago, it had 30 million TV homes.[33]

Mention must be made of two emerging media, cable TV and satellite TV, which are expected to have significant effects on advertising in the 1990s and beyond. Consider Germany. Back in 1990 there were only three TV channels—all state owned. In 1994, there were more than 20 channels on cable, 15 of which were privately owned. Cable is available in more than three-quarters of all households in Germany.[34] In other European countries, the situation is similar.

It is predicted, for example, that by the year 2000, 125 million European families will watch the same cable programs, despite the cultural impediments.[35] The European communications satellite (ECS-1), used by major pan-European TV stations in the U.K., Germany, France, Italy, the Netherlands, and the U.S., has a range of coverage beyond the EU, including some parts of Eastern Europe and the former Soviet republics.

With the market for satellite TV growing, Europe's broadcasting regulators have accepted that national monopolies on TV transmissions are no longer defensible. For example, the arrival of pan-European satellite broadcasting has breached the long-standing barrier to TV advertising in Sweden. It is expected that Swedish TV will go commercial within a few years.

Satellite TV is not limited to Europe alone. Developing countries are experimenting with satellite broadcasts to reach the masses. India, for example, has launched a satellite to reach people in remote villages, making broadcasts of the same program in different languages. Currently such broadcasts are limited to social programs such as family planning, but may eventually be opened for commercial advertising.

International Advertising Program

The development of an international advertising program depends on the advertising strategy that an MNC pursues. For the sake of discussion, let us assume that a company has decided to decentralize its advertising and let its overseas subsidiaries play a major role in determining their advertising program. The parent corporation maintains sufficient control through periodic review and approval authority over the final budget. The advertising program essentially includes nine steps:

1. Provision of guidelines by headquarters
2. Definition of advertising goals
3. Preparation of a campaign plan
4. Review and approval of plan
5. Copy development and testing
6. Media planning
7. Budget approval
8. Campaign implementation
9. Measurement of advertising effectiveness

Basically, an advertising program, in both domestic and international advertising, involves decisions concerning the media, the message, and the budget allocation. However, differences in number and types of media in conjunction with cultural and other environmental aspects necessitate tailoring themes, messages, presentations, and illustrations to the target market. As an advertising executive remarked:

> It is the advertising environment embracing language, culture, and socio-economic conditions that change from one country to another, not the approach taken to plan and to prepare effective advertising campaigns.

Head Office Guidelines

The head office guidelines should include procedural, discretionary, and format guidelines.

Procedural Guidelines These should include what should be done, and when. For example, the guidelines may specify that no commitments be made to the media except with budget approval. Likewise, subsidiaries may be required to prepare a minimum of four different ads and market test them to single out the final copy. Procedural guidelines are requirements that must be followed. Their purpose is to bring about global consistency in advertising. These guidelines essentially draw upon the parent corporation's past experience.

Discretionary Guidelines These are bits of advice that a subsidiary may or may not choose to accept. The following is an example of such a guideline: "Experience in the U.S. and elsewhere supports the usage of testimonial advertising. You may, therefore, consider using a local model to promote the product."

Format Guidelines These define any form, design, or procedure that should be followed in planning the campaign. These guidelines also include dates that must be adhered to. The major purpose of format guidelines is to make it easy for the corporation to impose and maintain control over the advertising activities of the subsidiaries.

Advertising Goals

Advertising goals should be appropriately related to product/market objectives. Thus, a subsidiary serving two markets (business customers and household consumers) may have different advertising goals in the two markets. Because advertising produces changes in attitudes, advertising goals should be defined in order to influence attitudinal structures. Accordingly, advertising may be undertaken to: (1) affect those forces that strongly influence the choice criteria used for evaluating brands belonging to the product class; (2) add characteristic(s) to those considered salient for the product class; (3) increase/decrease the rating for a salient product class characteristic; (4) change perception of the company's brand with regard to some particular salient product characteristic; and (5) change perception of competitive brands with regard to some particular salient product characteristic. Based on these additional perspectives, advertising objectives may be defined as:

- Increasing consumers' or buyers' *awareness* of the product . . . either generally or comparatively

- Improving the product's *image* among consumers or buyers . . . either generally or comparatively

- Increasing a target group of opinion leaders' or consumers'/buyers' *awareness* of the company . . . either generally or comparatively

- Increasing the company's *image* among a target group of opinion leaders or consumers/buyers . . . either generally or comparatively

- Increasing the product's *sales* or market share among consumers or buyers . . . either generally or comparatively (These objectives are more appropriate for retail or direct-response advertising.)[36]

A good definition of objectives aids in writing appropriate copy and in selecting the media. The firm's headquarters should make sure that the objectives have been defined by the proper managerial person.

Campaign Plan

The campaign plan outlines what sort of advertising campaign the subsidiary has in mind. It spells out the dimensions of strategy and media and indicates the preliminary budget estimates. For example, a subsidiary may plan along the following lines:

- Develop ad copy using a female model to promote the product, and run it simultaneously in six different magazines every other month for one year.

- Estimate the impact of the campaign by twice exposing 60 percent of the target customers to the new version of the product.

- Remember that the rationale behind this campaign is to reinforce the product's image among customers and counteract the competitor's recent entry into the market with a product similar to ours.

- Measure the effectiveness of the campaign by having an ad agency do a recognition test with a sample of women in the third, sixth, and ninth months of the campaign.

- Continue to position the product among women between 20 and 40 years of age from middle-income families.

- Estimate that the costs of this campaign during the first year will be $2 million.

- Decide that, for implementation of this plan, approval is needed by December 15.

Review and Approval of Plan

Headquarters should review each subsidiary's advertising schemes to ensure that they will contribute to the realization of the subsidiary's marketing goals and to assess that the planned campaign is realistic and entails a proper use of resources. In the review process, it is important to judge matters from the viewpoint of the individual subsidiary's business and related environments. In other words, headquarter's managers should avoid using self-reference criteria. Where insufficient information has been provided by the subsidiary, further information should be requested. Finally, reviewers at corporate headquarters should remember that events do not move at the same pace in every country. Thus, every effort should be made to meet the deadline set by the subsidiary.

Copy Development and Testing

Copy refers to the content of an advertisement. In advertising, the term copy is used in a broad sense to include words, pictures, symbols, colors, layout, and any other ingredients of an ad. Copywriting is a creative job, and its quality depends to a large extent on the creative genius of persons in the advertising agency or the company. However, creativity alone may not produce good ad copy. The marketing managers should provide their conception of the copy and furnish adequate information on the product, objectives, target customers, competitive activity, and legal aspects. The copywriter uses these facts as well as talent and imagination to develop ad copy. Before finalizing copy, it should be screened and revised as necessary. Sometimes several versions of the copy are developed and tested simultaneously, and the final version is chosen on the basis of test results.

Often subsidiaries have available various ads used in the U.S. and elsewhere in the world. If the copy of one of the available ads appears basically appropriate, it may well be worthwhile to use it. But such "foreign" copy should be adapted for local conditions. This point is especially noteworthy when expatriate managers have to make ad copy decisions.

To avoid snarls, it is best for subsidiary management to work closely with their advertising agency. The task of adaptation becomes easier if the agency that initially worked on the campaign has an office in the subsidiary's country. Multinational ad agencies have global experience and contacts that facilitate locating and using the best talent for adapting the ad to local conditions. Interestingly, often local native-born managers are as bad as expatriate managers in the localization of ad copy. Long accustomed to the outside world, they may be quite divorced from the realities of life in their home countries and may approach the task with imported ideas.

The final test of the appropriateness of copy is the marketplace. Three or four different versions should be sample-tested, using appropriate statistical procedures. Unless a subsidiary is very well equipped, the copy-testing task should be assigned to the agency. The final copy should be selected based on test results. In some cases, it may become necessary to develop yet another entirely new copy if none of the original ones appears sufficiently effective.

Media Planning

The decision on media is made simultaneously with the copy decision. It is influenced by media availability, media coverage, and media cost.

Media availability elsewhere in the world is more restricted than in the U.S. Even in developed countries like Switzerland, commercial advertising is permitted only during certain hours. In Germany, Europe's richest and largest national market, TV spots are kept to barely 40 minutes a day and none on Sunday.[37] Many countries ban the advertising of certain products. For example, Venezuela bans foreign cigarette and liquor advertising. In England, the government once questioned the high expenditures budgeted by Unilever and Procter & Gamble for advertising detergents. In brief, in media planning, careful analysis is necessary to figure out first what media are practical before making the actual selection.

Media coverage varies from country to country. The average is affected by the range of exposure and ownership of receivers. Ownership is a problem in the developing countries, where only a small percentage of the population owns radios and/or TVs. Printed media present similar problems. The masses may be illiterate, may not afford to subscribe to newspapers and magazines, or may live beyond circulation centers. In addition, the heterogeneity of a country with different languages or cultural and religious groups may make it difficult to reach enough people through a single campaign. A related problem here is the availability of coverage statistics. In many countries, the sole source of such information is the government, whose figures may be overstated for political reasons, besides being haphazardly gathered and/or outdated. In other countries, absolutely no information may be available on the coverage of different media, except the best guesses of bureaucrats. In other words, Starch's coverage data and Nielson's ratings are not widely known outside the U.S. In any event, subsidiary management should gather as much information on media coverage as possible in order to select the media focus.

The final consideration is cost. In many countries, media prices are subject to negotiation. Thus, the cost could be affected by the bargaining abilities of the subsidiary management. On the other hand, in some countries, media rates are arbitrarily set and increased without any market justification. This often happens where media are government-controlled and do not depend solely on advertising revenues to operate. Further, in LDCs, media costs are relatively high compared with those in the advanced nations. In newspaper advertising, the most popular medium worldwide, the rates are much higher in the developing countries in proportion to circulation. Besides, the real cost of reaching potential buyers with advertising messages may also be high because the media are not readily available and a large proportion of the population is scattered in rural areas. After considering all the problems, the subsidiary management must judiciously choose the best media available for its purposes.

Budget Approval

Budget approval is generally granted during the review process, but some companies keep budget approval pending until the copy has been developed and tested and the media planning completed. Although it may seem odd that subsidiaries proceed to develop and test copy as well as undertake media selection without budget approval, changing business environments, which are subject to political situations like threatened nationalization and/or business conditions that are declining because of competition, may make it essential to postpone commitments.

Campaign Implementation

Once budget approval has been received, the campaign should be undertaken as planned. Contingency plans are also necessary in case of unexpected difficulties. For example, one company in Pakistan had planned an ad using a female model to promote a brand of bar soap. Everything seemed fine during the planning stages. As release time approached, the Pakistani government banned all use of female models in ads. In such eventualities, contingency plans can save the day.

The thrust of the program may also require change if initial feedback on the campaign is discouraging. In any event, a certain amount of flexibility can accommodate changes for an effective campaign.

Measuring Effectiveness

There are various means to measure advertising effectiveness. Such research can be undertaken both before and after an ad is run. Pretesting measures include:

- Opinion and attitude ratings, gathered by questioning a sample of the prospective audience

- Projective techniques, which are indirectly elicited responses from the audience using motivation research techniques

- Laboratory testing, gathered by exposing a sample of customers to the ad and asking their reactions

- Post-testing measures include:

- Recognition and recall

- Changes in attitude ascribable to the ad

- Inquiries and sales measures; for example, the return of a card included with the ad

The methods discussed thus far are the same as those utilized in domestic marketing. However, their utilization may not be feasible in every nation. The facilities, talent, and resources needed for advertising effectiveness studies may be lacking.

Problems

Many problems can arise overseas to hinder the smooth development of an advertising program. Some countries lack facilities for fine printing. In other nations, government restrictions on advertising cause difficulties. In still other cases, illiteracy and language differences within the same country have an adverse effect. Mostly these problems arise in developing countries.

There are no easy answers for these problems. In some cases, advance planning and patience may help. For example, if an ad must be approved by the country government beforehand, enough time should be allotted so that, if a delay occurs in the process, the prompt release of the ad is assured. Similarly, if some printing/recording must be done in the home country for lack of facilities in the host country, advance planning is vital. Beyond that, an advertiser must accept the problems as an environmental constraint in doing business internationally.

Global Advertising Regulations

Most countries impose some regulations on advertising. The purpose behind these regulations is twofold: (1) to protect the consumers against misleading advertising and their own gulliblitiy and (2) to protect smaller businesses from the competitive threats of large corporations. It is interesting to note that advertising regulation is more common in developed societies than in developing countries. This may be explained by the fact that the advertising industry is still in its infancy in most developing countries, and therefore ignored as yet. Besides, not all developing countries have the administrative machinery to enforce regulations.

Exhibit 15.1 illustrates the types of issues that lead to regulation in different parts of the world. For example, while France and Mexico resist the use of foreign language, the Muslim countries regulate the use of foreign material themes and illustrations. Essentially, advertising regulation is focused on specific areas (see International Marketing Highlight 15.8):

- Certain classes of product/service, such as alcoholic beverages, tobacco, non-prescription pharmaceuticals, and financial and real estate deals
- Mail-order distribution
- Ads targeted toward children
- Foreign ownership of advertising agencies
- Comparative advertising
- "Puffery" or superlative claim—for example, "this brand is *the* best"
- Use of foreign language/words, models, backgrounds, and illustrations
- Media—for example, time limits for advertising
- Sexism in advertising

EXHIBIT 15.1 Taboo on TV

Egypt	Sex; anything more than a little kiss
Poland	References to the Church or sex
Hong Kong	Indecent matter; obscene or vulgar language
Iran	Women whose heads, arms, and legs are not covered; drinking
Most Arab Countries	Nudity, sex, enthusiastic necking; criticism of the head of state; criticism of any religion
Brazil	Explicit sex and violence during prime time; references to government repression
Mexico	Criticism of the government
Thailand	Anything remotely critical of the royal family
Japan	Criticism of the imperial family or religious sects
Israel	Any shot of a political candidate; terrorists' opinions
Turkey	Ethnic problems
Indonesia	Anything offending religion
South Africa	Any reference to Jesus Christ; all expletives containing the word God, including "Oh, God"

Source: John Lippman, "Television Is Fast Changing the Way the World Works, the Way It Plays, the Way It Goes to War and Makes Peace," *The Milwaukee Journal,* December 20, 1992, J1, J3.

International Marketing Highlight 15.8

War on Smoking

While cigarette smoking in the U.S. is declining, in many countries overseas it is a growth industry. Nonetheless, these are protective markets not open to outsiders. Consider Thailand's $744 million cigarette market, which was finally open to imports under heavy pressure from U.S. trade negotiators only after Thailand imposed high import duties, a cumbersome customs-clearance procedure, and stiff restrictions on cigarette advertising.

What is interesting about Thailand's efforts to curb American tobacco imports is that it relied heavily for help on an alliance of local and international antismoking activists. As a spokesperson from the American Cancer Society, an alliance member, notes, "The Thais complained to us that your government is trying to force U.S. cigarettes down our throats." Now these antismoking groups are actively campaigning against smoking throughout Asia, and have seriously hurt the U.S. tobacco industry.

As U.S. companies stepped up their efforts to develop the Asian markets, the antismoking activists intensified their efforts to keep them away. For example, a 14-nation group called the Asian Consultancy on Tobacco Control met in Hong Kong to formulate a 4-year strategy to prevent smoking in the area. The group's aim is to persuade Asian countries to adopt uniform tobacco-control regulations and thus prevent U.S. companies from making inroads in the region.

Source: "Asia: A New Front in the War on Smoking," *Business Week,* February 25, 1991, p. 66.

Regulations affecting advertising in various regions of the world have grown both in number and stringency over the years.

Some examples of advertising regulations include:

- China, the world's largest and potentially most lucrative cigarette market (with nearly 1.2 billion people and one out of every three smokers) has banned tobacco advertising.

- India announced an upper limit of $10,000 for advertising expenses for all companies doing business in India; expenditures over that limit were to be taxed at the rate of 50 percent. Widespread cancellation of advertising in reaction to this law, however, caused the withdrawal of this tax, as the government was concerned with effects that the cancellation of advertising might have on the level employment.

- In Costa Rica, a law provides for the national majority ownership of the media and the agencies.

- In Germany, TV advertising on the commercial stations is restricted to 20 minutes per day in blocks of 5 to 7 minutes between 5:00 p.m. and 8:00 p.m. with no advertising on Sundays and holidays. In the Netherlands, TV commercials must be confined to five-minute blocks in the evenings.

- In Turkey, the state-owned commercial TV carries 12 minutes of non-commissionable advertising each evening in 3-minute blocks.

- In Denmark, Germany, and Italy, medical product advertising must be supervised as to content.
- In Germany, France, Belgium, Austria, Italy, and the Netherlands, restrictions on comparative advertising are enforced.
- A French law forbids the use of foreign words and expressions when French equivalents can be found in the official dictionary.[38]

Industry Self-Regulation

The growing trend toward governmental action has led the advertising industry to attempt self-regulation in order to prevent undesirable governmental regulations. Self-regulation also shields the industry from unfair internal competition. Standards are set, and objective arbitration settles complaints and disputes outside the framework of government. The degree of self-regulation throughout the world varies from country to country according to each country's cultural and social values and level of development.

Most self-regulation measures are spearheaded by advertising industry associations. In many countries, Belgium for one, specialized self-regulatory bodies have been formed to deal with the problems related to advertising. Large advertising agencies and even the media in some countries have set their own standards or codes of conduct.

Advertising Agencies

Advertising agencies serve advertisers. As MNCs have circled the globe, their advertising agencies as well as involved banks and accounting firms have followed suit. The principal reason that advertising agencies go international has been to continue to serve their clients both at home and abroad. Chapter 1 examined the domination of the multinational scene by U.S. corporations. This domination is even more apparent in the case of advertising agencies. Of the 10 largest advertising agencies in the world, all but 2 are U.S.-based.

Globally, the major thrust of the advertising agencies' business is in the developed countries. Their principal clients focus most of their activities in these countries. It has been estimated that over 85 percent of their income is derived from activities in developed countries. The major portion of their income from developing countries originates in the Pacific rim, followed by Latin America.

Advertising agencies use various modes of foreign entry. One form of foreign entry is the opening of a local office. Such an arrangement permits complete control over the nature and size of the foreign office. However, it is a costly alternative, as it takes 8 to 10 years for a new office to generate enough clients to become financially self-sufficient. Another alternative is to acquire full or partial interest in existing agencies. This offers an ongoing business with a trained staff and a roster of clients. However, in practice, it is difficult to impose control over an acquired business that has established procedures of its own. A third alternative is to form a joint venture that may later develop into full ownership. Finally, a holding company can be formed. The choice of mode of entry would depend on the captive business, availability of a viable firm for acquisition, future prospects, financial resources of the agency, and national regulations.

A multinational firm uses a home-based advertising agency in order to achieve and maintain control. Even when strategy decisions are delegated to nationals, if a subsidiary works with the same agency that the MNC uses in the U.S., then there is sufficient assurance that the overall advertising function should be performed satisfactorily.

Often multinational enterprises retain the same agency for U.S. and international advertising. One problem with the use of a foreign agency is a lack of cultural insight into the market. Frequently, however, the foreign agency will have local employees. In nations where the dearth of local talent may force an agency to depend entirely on expatriate managers, chances are there is no local agency, leaving the MNC no choice but to use the foreign agency. Overall, the trend among MNCs is toward employing one individual advertising agency worldwide rather that a separate agency in each country. For example, IBM has put its worldwide advertising business including the U.S. into a single agency, Ogilvy & Mather.[39] This practice is reinforced by the desire to avoid diverse advertising approaches and the consequent loss of overall advertising effectiveness.[40]

As in the U.S., a foreign advertising agency (unless prohibited by the national law) receives a 15 percent discount from the media on the business it places. This constitutes the main source of revenue for ad agencies. In some countries, however, there is a movement away from the 15 percent compensation plan to a schedule of fees. Further, in many countries, local agencies aggressively compete against the multinational agencies by passing along a portion of their discount to their clients. Fifteen percent is a standard charge for a routine advertising job. In cases where a client requires help beyond the simple work of creating copy and scheduling the media, the agency normally charges more.

Summary

The promotion of goods and services is an important part of the marketing mix. The purpose of promotion is to inform, persuade, and remind the customer that certain goods and services are available. The four ingredients of promotion are advertising, personal selling, sales promotion, and publicity.

Advertising is an American institution born of U.S. economic progress. However, the rest of the world is catching up fast. World advertising expenditures, other than those of the U.S., are likely to rise from $130 billion in 1988 to $300 billion in 2000.

An important decision for international advertisers to make is whether the advertising campaign should be standardized worldwide or localized. Standard advertising has advantages in that a successful campaign in one country is likely to be effective in another nation as well. Further, standard advertising is economical. On the other hand, localized advertising recognizes cultural differences among nations. An effective advertising campaign in the U.S. will not necessarily be well received in, say, Saudi Arabia because of differences in cultural traits, language, economic life, and the like. For example, a female ad model is not likely to be acceptable in a Muslim country. In the final analysis, the choice between standard and local advertising should be based on such environmental considerations as levels of education; experience and competence of personnel in the foreign agency; degree of nationalism and rate of economic growth in the country; eating patterns and customs of the country; attitudes toward authority; and independence of media from governmental control. If overall environmental differences are significant, then advertising should be localized. Besides the environment, other criteria to be weighed before using a standardized campaign overseas are advertising objectives relative the host country, target market, product characteristics, media availability, and cost–benefit relationship.

The growth of global advertising is directly related to media development. However, in many countries, media have not yet developed adequately. Besides, many nations strictly regulate media availability. Statistical information reflects worldwide media differences. Unlike those in the U.S., overseas media do not derive revenues solely from advertising.

The steps to follow to build an international advertising program are provision of headquarters guidelines, definition of advertising goals, preparation of a campaign plan, review and approval of plan, copy development and testing, media planning, budget approval, campaign implementation, and measurement of advertising effectiveness.

Overseas countries impose different regulations on advertising. While the thrust of the regulations varies from nation to nation, the essential focus is on certain classes of products/services; mail-order distribution; ads targeted toward children; foreign ownership of advertising agencies; comparative advertising; superlative claims in ads; use of foreign language/words; and media. Many U.S. advertising agencies have expanded outside the U.S.

Review Questions

1. What factors argue for an internationally standardized approach to advertising?
2. Is the fact of cultural differences among nations strong enough to justify localized advertising?
3. Define the terms *buying proposal* and *creative presentation*. How do they affect standardized or localized advertising?
4. In the U.S., advertising is the principal source of revenue for the media. Is this true in other countries? If not, how do media derive their incomes?
5. List the various steps for developing an international advertising program.
6. Illustrate with examples the types of regulations that countries overseas impose on media.
7. Why is it desirable for a U.S. company to use a U.S.-based advertising agency in other countries?

Creative Questions

1. An MNC is interested in standardizing its advertising worldwide. However, advertising rules and regulations vary from country to country, which means in each nation, some form of adaptation will be necessary. In view of this, the company faces the dilemma if it should hire a large ad agency with contacts in most major

markets, or let each subsidiary hire a local ad agency. What are the pros and cons of hiring a global agency versus local agencies? Should the company make separate arrangements for concept and tactical advertising?

2. Critically examine the impact of technological changes on global advertising through electronics media.

Endnotes

1. *See* Tom Griffin, *International Marketing Communications* (Oxford, U.K.: Buttersworth-Heinemann Ltd., 1993).

2. "U.S. Outspends the World in Ads," *Marketing News*, February 2, 1988, p. 15. *Also see* "Hubris and Humble Pie," *The Economist*, August 27, 1994, p. 55.

3. "China Is Planning to Hold Its First Advertising Parley," *The Asian Wall Street Journal Weekly*, December 2, 1985, p. 11.

4. Peter S.H. Leeflang and Jan C. Reuiji, "Advertising and Industry Sales: An Empirical Study of the West German Cigarette Market," *Journal of Marketing*, Fall, 1985, pp. 92–98.

5. Erik Elinder, "How International Can Advertising Be?" in S. Watson Dunn, ed., *International Handbook of Advertising* (New York: McGraw-Hill, 1964), pp. 59–71.

6. Arthur C. Fatt, "The Danger of 'Local' International Advertising," *Journal of Marketing*, January, 1976, p. 61. *Also see* Gordon E. Miracle, "Internationalizing Advertising Principles and Strategies," *MSU Business Topics*, Autumn, 1968, pp. 29–36.

7. James H. Donnelly, Jr., and John K. Ryans, Jr., "Standardized Global Advertising: A Call as Yet Unanswered," *Journal of Marketing*, April, 1969, pp. 57–60. *Also see* George Fields, "How to Scale the Cultural Fence," *Advertising Age*, December 13, 1982, pp. 4–11.

8. "Playtex Kicks Off a One-Ad-Fits-All Campaign," *Business Week*, December 16, 1985, p. 48.

9. *Crossborder Monitor*, August 17, 1994, p.7.

10. Dean M. Peebes and John K. Ryans, Jr., *Management of International Advertising: A Marketing Approach* (Rockleigh, NJ: Allyn & Bacon, 1984), p. 73. *Also see* Ken Wells, "Global Ad Campaigns, After Many Missteps Finally Pay Dividends," *The Wall Street Journal*, August 27, 1992, p. 1.

11. Christine D. Urban, "A Cross-National Comparison of Consumers' Media Use Patterns," *Columbia Journal of World Business*, Winter, 1977, pp. 53–64.

12. Edward T. Hall, *The Silent Language* (New York: Doubleday, 1959). For discussion on cultural influences see Chapter 8.

13. James Killough, "Improved Payoffs from Transnational Advertising," *Harvard Business Review*, July–August, 1978, p. 103.

14. B.G. Youovich, "Maintain a Balance of Planning," *Advertising Age*, May 17, 1982, p. M-7.

15. Based on an interview with a Kentucky Fried Chicken executive.

16. *Washington Post*, January 11, 1982, p. 38.

17. Ann Helming, "Pitfalls Lie Waiting for Unwary Marketers," *Advertising Age*, May 17, 1982, p. M-8.

18. Jamie Talan, "Gillette Company on Track with Sharp Marketing for GII," *Advertising Age*, May 17, 1982, p. M-14.

19. Jacob Hornik, "Comparative Evaluation of International vs. National Advertising Strategies," *Columbia Journal of World Business*, Spring, 1980, p. 43.

20. Lyn S. Amine and S. Tamer Cavusgil, "Mass Media Advertising in a Developing Country," *International Journal of Advertising*, Vol. 2(1983), pp. 317–30.

21. Roger Blackwell, Riad Ajami, and Kristina Stephan, "Winning the Global Advertising Race: Planning Globally, Acting Locally," *Journal of International Consumer Marketing*, Vol. 3, No. 2 (1991), pp. 97–120.

22. John S. Hill and William L. James, "Consumer Nondurable Products: Prospects for Global Advertising," *Journal of International Consumer Marketing*, Vol. 3, No. 2 (1991), pp. 79–96.

23. "Playtex Conditions Its Strategies," *Advertising Age*, May 17, 1982, p. M-16.

24. John A. Quelch, "British Airways," a Harvard Business School case.

25. S. Watson Dunn, "Effect of National Identity on Multinational Promotion Strategy in Europe," *Journal of Marketing*, October 1976, pp. 50–57.

26. Russell W. Belk and Richard W. Pollay, "Materialism and Status Appeals in Japanese and U.S. Print Advertising," *International Marketing Review*, Winter 1985, pp. 38–47.

27. *See World Advertising Expenditures* (Mamaroneck, NY: Starch INRA Hooper, Inc., 1989) pp. 32–33.

28. F. Callahan, "Does Advertising Subsidize Information?" *Journal of Advertising Research*, No. 18 (1978), pp. 19 and 20.

29. "The Media Barons Battle to Dominate Europe," *Business Week,* May 25, 1987, p. 158; and Shawn Tully, "U.S.-Style TV Turns on Europe," *Fortune,* April 13, 1987, p. 5.

30. Tim Harper, "U.K. Eyes New Channel to Ease Demand Prices," *Advertising Age,* May 16, 1988, p. 68.

31. *World Advertising Expenditures* (New York: Starch, INRA, Hooper and International Advertising Association, 1992), pp. 36–37.

32. *See* Cynthia Webster, "The Effect of Nationality on Media Usage Patterns: A Study of Consumers From Countries of Various Levels of Development," in James E. Littlefield and Magdolna Csath, eds., *Marketing and Economic Development* (Budapest, Hungary: Karl Marx University of Economic Sciences, 1988), pp. 238–41.

33. Lynn Elber, "U.S. TV Networks Expand Interests Overseas," *Marketing News,* November 7, 1994, p. 7.

34. Tutsuo Ohbora, Andrew Parsons and Hajo Risenbeck, "Alternate Routes to Global Marketing," *The McKinsey Quarterly,* No. 3, 1992, pp. 52–74.

35. S. Tamer Cavusgil and Karl Hutchinson, "Pan-Europe TV Opens up New Multinational Markets," *Marketing News,* March 27, 1987, p. 8.

36. Dean M. Peebes and John K. Ryans, Jr., *Management of International Advertising* (Rockleigh, NJ: Allyn & Bacon, 1984), p. 25.

37. "The Media Barons Battle to Dominate Europe," *Business Week,* May 25, 1987, p. 158.

38. Based on information reported in various issues of *Advertising Age* during 1992–94.

39. *Crossborder Monitor,* August 10, 1994, p. 3.

40. Jon Lafayette, "Picking the Right Ad Agency," *International Business,* December 1992, pp. 106–08.

CHAPTER 16

Multinational Sales Management and Foreign Sales Promotion

CHAPTER FOCUS

After studying this chapter, you should be able to:

- Discuss the role of personal selling in international business

- Examine the problems of expatriates and third country nationals

- Describe the formulation and implementation of policy guidelines regarding the transfer of people from nation to nation

- Define the steps in building foreign sales promotion and public relations programs

Personal selling, sales promotion, and public relations are all devices of a company's total promotional scheme, but each one has certain characteristics that assign it a unique role. When a company begins selling in export markets, or switches from export selling to international marketing, or launches a new product line or service in a new foreign market, or takes an established line of products into a new country or region, it invariably has more promotion tasks to undertake than funds available. In other words, marketers' aspirations with respect to foreign marketing almost always exceed their ability or willingness to allocate funds. This chapter highlights the significance of different types of promotion and examines their relevance in different foreign situations. Unfortunately, no ready-made formulas are available to give priority to different forms of promotion. However, the discussion here identifies considerations that may help in determining where and how to begin.

Sales Personnel and Personal Selling Abroad

Sales personnel in international business can be classified in two ways, either by the task they perform or by their nationality. Principally, there are three categories of selling tasks: sales generation, sales support, and missionary work. *Sales generation* is the creative task of helping the customer to make a purchase decision. *Sales support* is concerned with after-sale service. *Missionary work* is undertaken by a manufacturer's salespersons to stimulate demand to help the distributors. When classifying sales personnel by nationality, there are also three categories: expatriates, natives, and third country nationals. *Expatriates* are home-country employees on deputation in the host country. For example, a G.E. sales manager from the U.S. assigned to launch the G.E. sales effort in Spain would be considered an expatriate. *Natives* are employees belonging to the host country. A Spanish national working for G.E. as a salesperson in Spain is a native. *Third country nationals* are employees transferred from one host country to another. For example, a French national transferred to Spain would be defined as a third country national.

For the most part, U.S. companies do not transfer selling personnel abroad. There are two reasons for this. First, selling requires deep familiarity with the local culture, which an expatriate cannot be expected to have, and second, it is extremely expensive to assign expatriates to selling positions. Such reasons lead companies—IBM as an example—to depend mainly on nationals for selling jobs. Similarly, Unilever only employs nationals of a country for marketing jobs in that country.[1] There are occasions, however, when companies may assign expatriates to work, usually for short periods, in the selling area. Such a practice is more commonly followed in the marketing of big-ticket items. The expatriate who has a proven track record at home can be quite helpful in resolving difficult foreign situations, and/or in serving as a catalyst for the natives. For example, Otis Elevator had to assign a sales engineer from the home office to provide after-sale service for its elevators in a large office complex in Singapore for a year. This became necessary because the native salesforce had failed to ensure smooth functioning of its elevators. Likewise, NCR Corporation uses expatriates to provide on-the-job training to natives. As a matter of fact, the company has a cadre of seasoned salespeople who travel from country to country assisting native salesforces in selling the company's products. Many big-ticket items require selling directly from the home office, which usually involves expatriates. For example, Boeing bids for selling airliners to foreign airlines from its headquarters in Seattle. Its salespeople, mainly expatriates, travel extensively worldwide to call on its customers. In 1983, Greece decided to rejuvenate its air force by buying 100 new fighter bombers. This amounted to over $3 billion worth of business, Greece's biggest-ever defense contract. A number of U.S. aircraft companies and European companies sent sales personnel to Athens to make sales presentations and contacts.[2]

The management of a native salesforce is a local matter to be handled according to business practices in the host country. From the viewpoint of parent corporations, therefore, the major concern is with expatriates and third country nationals. Foreign sales positions are demanding assignments that require long hours of hard work, perseverance, and self-sacrifice. Developing the long-term relationships necessary for successful selling in a foreign environment takes tremendous effort.

Expatriates

The recruitment, transport, and risks connected with sending expatriate salespeople overseas are time consuming an expensive, ranging from two-and-a-half to three times the costs involved with an equivalent domestic salesperson. In addition, an MNC risks a loss of time and money if the salesperson fails to stay the length of the assignment. Productivity may suffer too if the person becomes a so-called brownout—someone who stays on the foreign assignment but becomes inefficient because either he or she or the family is unhappy. Also, an expatriate's lack of knowledge or disregard for the host country's cultural practices may damage a company's reputation or cause the loss of a critical contact. Finally, the MNC should be concerned with the repatriation of expatriates in order to reassimilate them into the stream of domestic corporate activity without the loss of efficiency. (see International Marketing Highlight 16.1).

In addition to using expatriates for sales positions overseas for limited periods, many companies place expatriates in foreign subsidiaries for reasons that may be hard to accept. A study by Galbraith and Edstrom offers four reasons for using expatriates. While the study deals with foreign placement in general, it has equal application for the assignment of salespeople overseas. The reasons were (1) to fill a position, (2) to utilize managerial talent, (3) to give an executive international experience, and (4) to facilitate coordination and control with the parent company.[3]

The first reason usually results from a technical position becoming vacant in a subsidiary located in a developing country, where the lack of technically qualified personnel motivates the move. One example is the recruitment of engineers for high-paying positions in the Middle East. According to the study, this reason accounted for 60 percent to 70 percent of all transfers.

The second reason, to use managerial talent, is explained by the authors as follows: "a job opportunity and a promotable individual do not always occur in the same subsidiary." This situation complements the first. An absence of opportunity at home and a need overseas would encourage the transfer of a talented individual to a subsidiary outside the U.S.

The third reason, to provide international experience for executives, was cited by U.S. firms in the study as the second most important criterion for foreign assignment. This consideration, however, is not independent of the need to fill a position. If there are qualified local managers and the transfer occurs, then the probable reason is valuable international experience and exposure. Knowledge gained during the assignment would increase the firm's global perspective in relation to existing markets. Firsthand information is always preferable. This leads to the fourth reason, coordination and control, which is particularly crucial in situations where the firm is initiating large efforts to crack a local market, where the organization is implementing policy changes, or where the firm lacks confidence in developing countries.

International Marketing Highlight 16.1

Indifference at Home

In a survey of personnel managers at 56 MNCs based in the U.S.:

56 percent say a foreign assignment is either detrimental to or immaterial in one's career.

47 percent say their returning expatriates aren't guaranteed jobs with the company upon completion of their foreign assignments.

65 percent say their expatriates' foreign assignments are not integrated into their overall career planning.

45 percent view returning expatriates as a problem because they are so hard to fit back into the company.

20 percent consider their company's repatriation policies adequate to meet the needs of their returning expatriates.

Source: Moran, Stahl & Boyer, New York.

It is quite logical to bring in expatriates for specific so-called fire-fighting assignments (for example, to supervise and/or train locals) or for a developmental assignment, that is, to expose a promising executive to multinational experience. The problems occur when people are sent overseas for historical, egocentric, or nationalistic reasons like: "But we've always had an expatriate do that job. No one can manage that operation except an American." Political maneuvering within a company can also cause problems, like sending an employee overseas to clear the way for another person to take up an emerging position. Retreading the path of least resistance—that is, the best solution is always to bring in an American whenever there is any problem—can be counterproductive.

Third Country Nationals

In recent years, a new trend has been to assign employees at all levels from one host country to another. This trend has arisen for two reasons. One, in many countries of the world there is a surplus of workers, while other countries lack adequate workforces. For example, Saudi Arabia's population is about 9 million people. If a company is developing fast there, it may need a large salesforce, but finds it difficult to find suitable Saudis to fill sales positions. Saudi Arabia is, therefore, forced into accepting salespeople from other developing countries, like Pakistan, India, or South Korea. Too, a company often needs a salesperson with certain requisite experience for a subsidiary. Looking around, the company discovers the most appropriate person for the job is a third country national (see International Marketing Highlight 16.2).

International Marketing Highlight 16.2

Wooing Third Country Nationals

Multinational firms are tapping more third country nationals for overseas posts. Nationality matters less as businesses race to enlarge their ranks of global managers. So-called TCNs—neither Americans nor local nationals—often win jobs because they speak several languages and know an industry or foreign country well. The average number of TCNs per U.S. company rose to 46 in 1989 from 33 in 1988.

Pioneer Hi-Bred International employs 29 TCNs in key jobs abroad, triple the number 5 years ago, partly because they accept difficult living conditions in Africa and the Middle East. Raychem has a dozen such foreigners in top European posts, up from eight in 1986. The numbers are going to increase as Europe's falling trade barriers ease relocation. A French citizen runs the company's Italian subsidiary, a Belgian is a sales manager in France, while a Cuban heads the unit in Spain.

Scott Paper, whose TCN managers have increased to 13 from 2 in 1987, will step up recruitment of young foreigners willing to move around Europe or around the Pacific.

Source: The Wall Street Journal, September 16, 1990, p. B1.

Third country individuals face unique organizational problems (see Exhibit 16.1). For example, third country employees naturally want to know to which organization, the parent corporation of the host country company, they belong in regard to promotion and benefits and their feeling of identity. To manage third country employees effectively, both headquarters and host country management should study their special problems. An appreciation of their needs enhances performance for the benefits of the corporation. Although the episode in International Marketing Highlight 16.3 concerns an executive, it is equally relevant for salespersons. The story illustrates the type of management thinking and planning that ought to precede actual transfer of people across national boundaries. Cultural biases, financial interests, and individual preferences all play a role in a person's life. A person's success in one environment doesn't guarantee success elsewhere. A company needs a sound policy for moving people from country to country.

International Marketing Highlight 16.3

Managing Third Country Nationals

The scene is the West Coast headquarters of a worldwide high-technology company. It is late in the afternoon and an all-day conference involving the personnel director and the vice president of international operations is in progress.

What is the problem? The problem is Pierre. Who is Pierre? He is not just another militant employee off the assembly line. Pierre is a key executive, two levels from the top of the organization, and, heretofore, regarded as a comer headed for a key top-management position in the U.S. upon conclusion of his current assignment.

How did Pierre get in this fix? He was hired in Paris and managed the French subsidiary until it achieved significant market penetration in France. One day Pierre woke up and found that the job had lost challenge. There was nowhere for him to go. He was a big fish in a small pond. About the same time, the company was beginning operations in Australia. What was better logic than to send Pierre from France to Australia to utilize his flair for building up the business? After he had opened up operations in Australia, there were vague plans to move him back to headquarters.

Pierre was a task-oriented man. For six months, he left his family in Paris, took a flat in Sydney, and worked day and night, making only two brief return trips to France. Then he moved his family to Australia and the trouble began.

The problems started simply enough. How did he get paid? The French subsidiary wanted him off their books. "No problem," said the personnel director, "we will pay you like an American. After all, you work for an American company, so we will pay you in U.S. dollars."

Pierre received his first paycheck and could not believe it. When transferred to the U.S. scale, he made less money than in France. (Top management salaries in parts of Western Europe have reached parity and in many cases have surpassed their U.S. counterparts—this is not even considering benefits, which have historically been much better in Europe than in the U.S.)

Pierre took the salary reduction in stride, primarily because he was too involved in building up the market and did not have time to worry about it then. After his family had been there one month, the U.S. dollar was devalued and the Australian dollar revalued. Since Pierre used U.S. dollars to buy Australian dollars, his purchasing power was cut.

The problems then increased in intensity. There was the matter of taxes. He was in Australia and legally responsible for Australian taxes. But Pierre's Australian taxes were more than he would have paid had he stayed in Paris. The first of many cables was sent to corporate headquarters.

"What about my salary and taxes?"

"Pay him like an American, tax him like an American," said the personnel director.

The next round of cables soon followed. "But I am not an American; I am a Frenchman. I want a French salary and French tax levels, and while I'm at it, what about my French profit sharing? Do I lose this while in Australia?" (In France, many companies set aside, at least by U.S. standards, a rather liberal amount of money for profit sharing.) "What about my company car?" (Having a company car is another European custom for top management.) "How about vacation?" (Holidays in France are longer.) "How about home leave? When can I go back to France?"

As if this were not enough, further cables kept rolling in "What about housing? I pay more housing in Sydney than I did in Paris."

Then there was education. Who would pay the fee for correspondence courses to keep Pierre's children involved in the French education system?

The crowning blow was when Pierre asked for a cost-of-living allowance. "It couldn't cost him more to live in Sydney than in Paris!" shouted the vice president of international operations. "What's happened to Pierre? He has turned into a greedy, me-first employee. Is this the kind of manager we want representing us overseas? Get him back here; let's talk this out now!"

Pierre gladly caught the next plane. How did all this happen? What caused Pierre's metamorphosis? It was another common fault of multinational companies engaging in the movement of people across borders. In the heat of battle, decisions are made to move people without being thoroughly thought out. Moreover, these decisions are made without an underlying philosophy and plan.

Source: David M. Neor, *Multinational People Management* (Washington, D.C.: Bureau of National Affairs, 1975), pp. 9–11.

EXHIBIT 16.1 Problems Faced by Third Country Nationals

- *Blocked promotions.* The tendency of MNCs to reserve top positions at headquarters for parent country managers.

- *Transfer anxieties.* The third country managers' anxieties caused by uncertainty about the timing of their next transfers, the countries to which they will be transferred, the positions to which they will be assigned, and the extent of managerial autonomy involved in their next assignments.

- *Income gaps.* The tendency of third country managers to feel deprived in terms of income in comparison to parent country managers, and the tendency of host country managers to feel deprived in comparison to third country managers.

- *Unfamiliarity and adaptability difficulties.* The natural tendency of newly arrived third country managers to make mistakes and their compulsion to cover them up.

- *Avoidance of long-range projects.* The tendency of third country managers to concentrate on short-range, nonrisk, and demonstration-type projects.

- *Inappropriate leadership style.* The tendency of third country managers to imitate the managerial style prevalent at headquarters.

- *Nonparticipative decision making and screening of information.* The tendency of third country managers to adopt a detached leadership style because of their perception of headquarters as their positive reference group.

- *Insufficient authority in industrial relations.* The tendency of MNCs to delegate insufficient authority to third country managers in top positions for dealing with critical industrial relations issues in their subsidiaries.

- *Lack of commitment of top-ranking third country managers to the perpetuation of the host country organizations.* The conviction of host country managers that third country managers are less committed to the perpetuation of the host country organization and to the welfare of their host country subordinates.

Source: Yoram Zeira and Ehud Harari, "Managing Third Country Nationals in Multinational Corporations," *Business Horizons,* October 1977, p. 84.

Formulating Policy Guidelines

The high rate of expatriate failure among U.S. multinationals is a matter of great concern. It stems from several factors: the family situation, lack of cross-cultural relational abilities, the short duration of overseas assignments, problems of repatriation, overemphasis on the technical competence criterion to the disregard of other important attributes such as relational abilities, and inadequate training for cross-cultural encounters.

Companies can no longer afford to transfer people from nation to nation without having an appropriate policy for a guide. Too many people and too much money are involved. While the common practice is to hire natives for sales positions, the number of short-term specific assignments for solving ad hoc problems is on the increase, which requires bringing in expatriates or third country nationals.

The policy should cover determination of the most appropriate nationality, the selection of the nonnative salesperson, plans for repatriation and reassignment, work assignments, and the development of native salespersons by the nonnative selected. In actuality, companies may not have a thoroughly articulated policy for expatriates and third country nationals that covers all these points. Nonetheless, increasingly companies attach importance to the problems that occur when people work in different cultures. As an example, Westinghouse Corporation has defined the following corporate procedure for assignment, repatriation, and reassignment of international employees:

Background

The long-term interest of the Corporation is best served by limiting international assignments to those management and professional employees who have an established record of competence. International assignments can be a valuable supplement to the normal training and development programs for the high-potential employee.

Management and professional people with international experience are an invaluable corporate asset, and every effort should be made to assure that experience gained by employees through such assignments is retained and properly utilized.

Consequently, all organization units assigning personnel internationally should develop specific plans for the selection, assignment, and repatriation of management and professional employees. Consistent with the needs for international staffing, organization units should identify competent employees who have the desire and potential to successfully undertake an assignment abroad.

Guidelines

1. Pre-assignment—a pre-assignment orientation program should be planned and implemented on a timely basis to assure that candidates and their dependents are fully prepared to undertake international assignments. Organization units assigning personnel internationally will define in writing all known conditions of assignment, including but not limited to the employee's salary, allowances, duration of assignment, etc. The employee should be provided copies of all applicable policies and procedures. 2. Repatriation and reassignment—Organization units should periodically review the status of their international assignees and develop specific repatriation plans for each employee. Where performance continues to be satisfactory, it is the responsibility of these units to assure that personnel

selected for international assignments will have upon return a position at least equivalent to the level held by the employee prior to accepting the international assignment. For coordination reasons, it is also the responsibility of these units to keep Key Personnel Services advised of their repatriation plans or problems. 3. Application—This procedure applies to all organization units assigning personnel internationally, as well as to all management and professional personnel who accept an international assignment, with the exception of those engaged in service and other activities which normally require international travel or who are assigned for a limited time to specific international customer contracts abroad.[4]

Abroad as at home, poor supervision and inappropriate policies produce negative results. Deficiencies in management away from home can be costly. More and more attention, therefore, is likely to be given to recruiting, selecting, developing, and motivating managers for overseas assignments, however brief the assignment.

Tung suggests that to enhance expatriate success and minimize failure, U.S. multinationals (1) adopt a longer-term orientation with regard to expatriate assignments and provide support mechanisms at corporate headquarters to allay concerns about repatriation, (2) develop a more international orientation, and (3) provide more rigorous training programs to prepare expatriates for cross-cultural encounters.[5]

Implementing Policy Guidelines

The first step after formulating a policy for the management of both expatriates and third country nationals is the pursuit of this policy to administer adequately the selection, orientation and training, compensation, and placement procedures inaugurated for salespeople for positions away from home.

Selection

Selection is crucial to the success for an overseas appointment. It is desirable to establish adequate selection criteria and to adapt the criteria carefully to ensure that the right person is chosen. Selection criteria include motivation, health, language ability, family considerations, resourcefulness and initiative, adaptability, career and financial planning. Potential candidates could be rated as either satisfactory or unsatisfactory on each of the criteria listed. Then the person showing the highest satisfactory ratings overall could be the final choice. In addition to the factors included in the sample list, the candidate's spouse should be involved in the selection process right from the start. Many failures stem from the spouse's reluctance to transfer in the first place and an inability to adapt to host country conditions. An expatriate rated as having a marginal chance of success might do very well because of a supportive spouse. It is, therefore, crucial to consider spouse evaluation in an expatriate selection system. Further, before accepting the assignment, the candidate and his or her spouse should be given an opportunity to see the country. An advance trip of a week or two cannot give anyone a thorough understanding of a country's culture, but if properly done, it enables the prospective expatriate to make a more intelligent decision (see International Marketing Highlight 16.4).

International Marketing Highlight 16.4

Spouses Must Pass Test Before Global Transfers

Employees' families are playing a bigger role in international transfers. The inability of spouses or children to adapt to their new surroundings is the number one cause of failure in overseas transfers, including premature returns, job-performance slumps, and other problems. With overseas postings costing an average of $225,000 to $250,000 a year, companies are trying to smooth the way.

Many companies include spouses in the screening process for overseas assignments, including a formal assessment of such qualities as flexibility, patience, and adaptability. Ford Motor interviews spouses before the move. Exxon also meets with the spouses or children. Minnesota Mining & Manufacturing offers spouses educational benefits and uses electronic mail to introduce employees' children to peers in the target country. 3M recently found new housing for one Japanese executive in the U.S. so his 65 pound dog could rejoin the family.

The programs are largely a response to pressure from employees. As many as 75 percent of international transfers end in such family problems as marital discord or adjustment problems in children. Companies are finding that it's difficult to get someone to go unless they address those issues.

Source: *The Wall Street Journal,* September 6, 1991, p. B1.

Orientation and Training

Sales personnel slated for foreign assignment should be oriented to the new job and provided relevant training. Essentially, orientation and training should cover the terms and conditions of the assignment, language training, and cultural training.[6] (see International Marketing Highlight 16.5).

Terms and Conditions of the Assignment The employee should be provided with a clear and concise overview of the company's expatriate policies, procedures, and compensation system; information on housing, transportation, and schools in the host country; and information on moving arrangements.

Language Training Language training is perhaps the most basic type of knowledge that a foreigner needs for a productive life in a host country. Language is the key to a country's culture. It permits understanding of the subtleties of the country and the reasons why certain things are done differently. A language can be learned in different ways: in a language school with a regular program lasting several months; through a short, intensive program offered either by a commercial school or a local university, or at home through a self-study program. Do-it-yourself kits are available for home study programs in the form of records, cassette recordings, books, telephone conversations with instructors, and different combinations of these alternatives. Regardless of the method, the one central ingredient in learning a language is proper motivation on the part of the employee and family. It is incumbent upon the multinational employer to emphasize the need for language training.

International Marketing Highlight 16.5

The Colgate-Palmolive Global Marketing Training Program

Few companies pour as much money and management expertise into training marketing managers as New York-based Colgate-Palmolive. Although much smaller than Lever Brothers and Procter & Gamble, Colgate derives 60 percent of its revenue from abroad. The company prides itself in its ability to penetrate new markets (sometimes before its giant competitors arrive) and maintain good profitability. To retain its position as one of the world's preeminent consumer products companies, Colgate decided years ago to develop a program to ensure itself of a steady supply of superior marketers with the skills to operate almost anywhere.

The "Global Marketing Training Program" Colgate created, which gives its participants a two-year immersion in global marketing, has acquired considerable prestige since its establishment. Admission is highly competitive and is sought by some of the brightest B.A.'s and M.B.A.'s from the world's best colleges and business schools. Successful applicants must have not only excellent academic credentials but also leadership skills, fluency in at least one other language in addition to English, and some international-living experience, for example, a year of study in a country other than the applicant's own.

The program itself consists of assignments in various departments at Colgate, with a strong emphasis on marketing functions. A typical rotation includes some time in finance and manufacturing and larger blocks of time at Colgate's ad agency, in market research, and in product management. The trainees serve for seven months as field salespeople in the U.S., and they actually perform the job rather than merely accompanying regular salespeople on their rounds.

The program gives trainees the basic skills global marketing managers need. The participants learn to use computers, devise budgets, formulate sales promotion strategies, manage work groups, and so on. They also begin to develop relationships that will help them when they start to operate in the international environment.

Most of Colgate's new marketing "graduates" are sent to markets in developing countries. Some are initially assigned to work in the U.S., but they, too, are soon posted overseas. Because non-U.S. markets are so important to Colgate, it does not automatically bring its international marketers back to the U.S. after a foreign assignment, as do many other MNCs. Often, the marketers go directly from one overseas post to another, in essence, career internationalism.

Source: *Business International,* September 10, 1990, p. 306.

Cultural Training Both academic and interpersonal cultural training should be given. Academic training includes the provision of things like books, maps, brochures, films, and slides. The interpersonal training consists of making arrangements for candidate and family to make a trip to the host country, in addition to meeting with host country natives living in the U.S. and people who have lived previously in the host country.[7]

Compensation Salespeople away from their home base cost more because they must be paid extra compensation. The extra compensation covers three factors. First, it is a premium for climatic conditions in the host country, separation from friends and relative, cultural shock, and subjection to situations of political instability and economic risk in conditions of unstable currencies. Second, it is an allowance for housing, children's schooling, return trips home on a periodic basis, income tax, and overall cost-of-living expenses. Third, there are certain perquisites common in host countries for particular positions, like car and driver, servants, and club memberships.[8]

The elements of compensation and the amount paid under each heading differ from country to country depending on the living costs. According to Union Bank of Switzerland, for example, giving New York an index of 100, the cost-of-living index in Tokyo would be 199, Stockholm 131, Geneva 127, London 101, Frankfurt and Paris 95, Milan 94, Toronto 88, Sydney 84, Los Angeles 76, Hong Kong 72, Cairo 62, Mexico City 55, and Bombay 54 (based on a basket of 108 goods and services excluding rent for a typical European family of three).[9]

Exhibit 16.2 illustrates a typical expatriate compensation package. Note that the total additional compensation is over three times more in the U.K. than in the U.S. Even in a developing country, an expatriate may cost more depending on demand and supply conditions relative to different elements of compensation. In a city like Tokyo, housing would be very expensive since suitable apartments are very scarce. In many developing countries, housing is expensive because Western-style accommodations are difficult to locate, and a high premium must be paid for the few that are available. Similarly, if taxes are very high in a country and if the foreigner is taxed like a native, the company must bear the tax burden over and above what the employee would have paid in the U.S. or other home country.

Placement

Once a salesperson accepts an overseas position, the company should provide adequate information to prepare for the departure to the host country. This information includes advice on such matters as how to apply for a passport; how to obtain necessary visas and immunizations; how expenses should be handled for reimbursement; how to obtain transportation and arrange accompanied baggage and unaccompanied baggage shipment; tax matters; and current status under the various company benefit, pension, stock, and insurance plans. Information is also needed on obtaining an international driver's license, making financial arrangements, deciding what clothing to take, and even reminding the salesperson to notify correspondents of a change of address. Some of these arrangements and details are quite complicated, and generous advice and counsel for each individual can smooth the passage of personnel and their families to transfer assignments.

Repatriation and Reassignment

Traditionally, salespeople have welcomed overseas assignments. It has meant taking extra compensation and seeing the world at company expense; besides, going abroad was considered to be a route to the executive suite. More recently, however, fewer jobs are opening up in Euro-capitals. The Middle East and the developing countries are the new foreign-assignment destinations, where hardship pay lives up to its name and the experience offers little beyond just that—experience. A returning salesperson faces a severe penalty for being out of the home office working environment and a severe shock when confronted with the domestic real estate market.

EXHIBIT 16.2 The Price of an Expatriate

An employer's typical first-year expenses of sending a U.S. executive to Britain, assuming a $100,000 salary and a family of four.

Direct compensation costs
Base salary	$100,000
Foreign-service premium	15,000
Goods and services differential	21,000
Housing costs in London	39,000*

Transfer costs
Relocation allowance	$5,000
Air fare to London	2,000
Moving household goods	25,000

Other costs
Company car	$15,000
Schooling (two children)	20,000
Annual home leave (four people)	4,000
U.K. personal income tax	56,000*

Total — $302,000

Note: Additional costs often incurred aren't listed above, including language and cross-cultural training for employee and family, and costs of selling home and cars in the U.S. before moving.
* Figures take into account payments by employee to company based on hypothetical U.S. income tax and housing costs.
Source: Organizational Resource Counselors Inc., New York.

Fewer salespeople are willing to accept overseas positions, particularly those personnel who perceive the risk of an inferior position upon return. On a number of occasions, there has been no job for a returning expatriate, who has then spent months in a holding pattern. Many companies lose good marketing people for lack of job vacancies in the U.S. when their time comes to return.

Returning home amounts to facing previously familiar surroundings. Yet, as the following quotes show, expatriates have found the reentry into the home environment more of a problem than going abroad.[10]

> Repatriating executives from overseas assignments is a top management challenge that goes far beyond the superficial problems and costs of physical relocation... the crux of the matter is the assumption that since these individuals are returning home—that is, to a familiar way of life—they should have no trouble adapting to either the corporate or the home environment. However, experience has shown that repatriation is anything but simple.

> Managers know that there is always a risk of being stuck, at least temporarily, in a mediocre job when they return.

> Few, if any, executives ever come out ahead financially in a transfer back to the U.S. . . . An even more serious shock [than the financial shock], because it can have a long-range impact on the executive's career, is the re-adaptation to corporate life. . . a foreign assignment [tends to]. . . keep the executive out of the mainstream of advancement. . . . In some respects the more outstanding a performer the executive was overseas, the more uncomfortable his return will be.[11]

The returning executives themselves have made these comments:

> Going home is a harder move. The foreign move has the excitement of being new. . .more confusing, but exciting. Reentry is frightening. . . . I'll be happy to be home . . . I wonder if I can adjust back.
>
> There's some kind of traumatic reaction to it. It evidenced itself in my insomnia. There was something there . . . waking me up at 4 a.m.
>
> Career . . . it didn't help. I got personal learning. I lost time. My career stopped when I left and started again when I returned.
>
> Colleagues view me as doing a job I did in the past. I had the experience before going . . . they don't view me as gaining while overseas.
>
> The organization has changed . . . work habits and norms and procedures have changed and I have lost touch with all that. . . I am a beginner again.
>
> Colleagues are indifferent to my international assignment.
>
> Before going overseas I thought that it might help my career. Within the home organization, international is more remote from domestic. You are visible only within international.
>
> I have no specific reentry job to return to . . . I want to leave international and return to domestic . . . Working abroad magnifies problems while isolating effects . . . i.e., you deal with more problems, but. . . [the home office] does not know the details of the good or bad effects . . . managerially, I'm out of touch with financial policies. . . I'll be less confident in managing . . . If this job had been in North America, . . . my old management style would have worked.[12]

The repatriation problem is not limited to U.S. expatriates. Even Japanese returnees find it hard to assimilate their own culture after having spent a few years in the U.S. Because most Japanese white-collar workers generally have a negative attitude toward overseas assignments, many returnees end up taking jobs with the U.S. subsidiaries in Japan.[13]

To alleviate the reluctance of personnel to be recruited for foreign assignments, companies are providing prospective expatriates with written guarantees on company foreign personnel policy. These repatriation agreements are really no more than general promises in writing that include a limit of a two-to five-year maximum on time spent abroad and assurances of return to a mutually acceptable job. Union Carbide assigns senior executives to act as sponsors for overseas managers, including salespeople. Sponsors scout six months prior to the expatriates' return to locate a suitable position. The Dow Chemical Company has 10 full-time counselors who visit with each of the company's expatriate employees, including those in sales, once a year. The counselors let the expatriates know that they have not been forgotten and act as advocates for possible promotion considerations. Also, repatriation supervisors are assigned to expatriates to monitor compensation, performance, and potential career paths.[14]

Sales people with international experience are an invaluable corporate asset. Repatriation agreements should ensure that the experience gained by personnel through such assignments is retained and properly utilized.

International Sales Negotiations

Face-to-face negotiations with the customer is the heart of the sales job. Negotiations are necessary to reach an agreement on the total exchange transaction, comprising such aspects as the product to be delivered, the price to be paid, the service agreement, the payment schedule, and other issues. Briefly, negotiations are the means of deciding the terms of sales.

International sales negotiations have many characteristics that distinguish them from negotiations in the domestic setting. First and foremost, the cultural background of the negotiating parties is different, which may inhibit understanding of each other's viewpoint.[15] Second, political factors often complicate and delay international business negotiations. Third, in many cases, the host government must be involved in bringing the negotiations to a conclusion.

Sales negotiations may involve such issues as product features, service, price, delivery date, mode of payment, training of buyer personnel, and financing. While these issues are usually negotiated between buyer and seller in domestic situations as well, they assume greater importance in international marketing for a variety of reasons. Consider service. In the U.S. a company selling a product that requires periodic servicing will presumably have adequate service facilities and parts inventory. However, if the product sale is negotiated in, say, Thailand, and the company's closest service facilities in the area are located in Japan, the customer would want certain assurances about timely servicing at a reasonable cost. The customer may demand that the company establish facilities in Thailand itself. On the other hand, the company may not find it financially feasible to do so. In such a situation, negotiations become essential. As a matter of fact, the Thai government may step in and refuse to grant foreign exchange until the company agrees to make local service arrangements.

Negotiating Process

The objective of a negotiating process is to reach an agreement of mutual benefit.[16] The process begins from a situation of *contention,* meaning each party has its own agenda to strike the deal. It ends with *conclusion,* whereby a mutually satisfying agreement has been reached. The distance from contention to conclusion is covered through the stages of clarification, comprehension, confidence, credibility, convergence, conciliation, and concession. The first stage, *clarification* and *comprehension,* involves seeking information to form a better idea of each other's position on significant issues. The second stage includes *confidence* and *credibility,* which refer to the formation of attitudes among the parties based on an appreciation of each other's requirements and the reasons behind them. At the conclusion of this stage, the two parties would reach a *convergence* of views on many aspects of the deal. The third stage, *concession* and *conciliation,* requires the parties to reach a compromise on the remaining unsettled issues through give and take. The final stage is the conclusion of negotiations. The shape of the negotiated agreement depends on the bargaining power of the two parties, which in turn is determined by the importance of the deal for each of them. For example, if the product involves substantial business for the seller now and potential additional sales later, the buyer would be in a relatively strong bargaining position. On the other hand, if the product is not readily available from another source, the seller will approach negotiations from a point of leverage.

In addition to the bargaining power of the two parties, negotiations are considerably affected by the negotiating skills of the people involved in the process. Issues such as how people perceive each other, how they interact, how the ambience of negotiations can be altered, how confidence and trust can be established, and how they threaten and intimidate each other will significantly influence the outcome.[17] These issues, along with the fact that the negotiating parties come from different economic, political, and cultural backgrounds and may speak different languages, make international negotiating a complex exercise. It is for this reason that many scholars consider international negotiating an art.

Negotiating Strategies

Basic to negotiating well is the ability to put yourself in the other person's shoes, understand his or her way of thinking, recognize his or her perspective, and allocate sufficient time for the task. Even when you start from a point of weakness, there are strategies that a salesperson can pursue to negotiate to his or her advantage. For example:

1. Increase your variables and know your alternatives. Price is not the only flexible factor. Consider every aspect of the deal—R&D, specifications, delivery, and payment arrangements. The more options you have, the greater your chances of success.
2. When attacked, listen. Keep the customer talking and you will learn valuable things about his or her business and needs.
3. To reduce frustration and assure the customer that you're hearing what he or she is saying, pause often to summarize your progress.
4. Assert your own company's needs. Too much empathy for the customer can reduce the emphasis on problem solving and lead to concessions.
5. Try to make your customer commit to the outcome of the whole negotiation. Make sure the full solution works for both parties.
6. Save the hardest issues for last.
7. Start high, concede slowly, keep your expectations high, and remember that every concession has a different value for buyer and seller.
8. Never give in to emotional blackmail. If the customer loses his temper, don't lose yours. Withdraw, postpone, dodge, sidestep, listen. As a last resort, declare the attack unacceptable, but always refuse to fight.[18]

Negotiating style varies from culture to culture, and often involves language differences, cultural conditioning, approaches to problem solving, implicit assumptions, gestures and facial expressions, and the role of ceremony and formality. In preparing for and analyzing a negotiation, it is useful to review these dimensions fully. As has been said: "The negotiator must enter into the private world or cultural space of the other, while at the same time, sharing his or her own perceptual field."[19]

Foreign Sales Promotion

Sales promotion devices tend to stimulate new attitudes toward the promoted product through the lure of getting something for nothing. The very feeling that something can be had for free creates a strong desire for the product among buyers no matter which country/region they belong to. Historically, sales promotion is a uniquely American phenomenon. Nonetheless, today sales promotion techniques are popularly used to supplement advertising and personal selling throughout the world (see International Marketing Highlight 16.6).

International Marketing Highlight 16.6

Globalization of Coupons

International coupon use is on the rise, a trend that will continue through the 1990s, according to a recent study.

"Coupon Distribution and Redemption Patterns Report," released by NCH Promotional Services, Chicago, examines the couponing and promotion trends in major world markets including the U.S., Canada, the U.K., Spain, Italy, and Belgium.

Although the U.S. remains the world's leading coupon market, with over 279.4 billion coupons issued in 1990, several other markets around the world are beginning to experience the same couponing growth that occurred in the U.S. during the early 1980s.

The European Community's recent gains in political and economic freedoms have given marketers the opportunity to use more creative promotional techniques. The European market has enormous, untapped promotional possibilities.

As distribution methods standardize and multinational firms introduce tried-and-true coupon promotion practices on a large-scale, the barriers to couponing will begin to dissolve.

The study said consumers in the U.K. and Belgium are the EU's most active coupon users. In 1990, an average of 17 coupons per household were redeemed in the U.K., and 18 coupons per household were redeemed in Belgium. The U.K., Europe's largest coupon market, has had redemption growth of 21 percent since 1989, the largest increase in the world.

The study also reported that the U.K.'s coupon industry outlook is bright, since 7 out of 10 consumers already use coupons regularly. Newspapers and magazines are the most popular means of distribution in the U.K. Spain and Italy rely heavily on in- or on-pack promotions for their coupon distribution. In several European markets, door-to-door coupon distribution is common, although this technique is virtually unheard of in the U.S.

In other parts of Europe, couponing has had relatively stagnant growth. In Spain, distribution has declined over the past few years, and Italy's couponing has shown only modest increases. In both countries, an average of 3 coupons were redeemed per household, compared with 77 in the U.S. and 26 in Canada.

Although couponing has just become legal in Denmark, other European countries have limited access to coupons. In Holland and Switzerland, major retailers refuse to accept coupons.

Source: "Global Coupon Use Up; U.K., Belgium Tops in Europe," *Marketing News,* August 5, 1991, p. 6. Copyright 1991 by the American Marketing Association.

Besides increasing sales at the retail level, sales promotion helps in building the morale of the sales force. Some companies use sales promotion simultaneously with sales incentive schemes to make them complement each other. For example, Hoover Company promoted its vacuum cleaners in England through providing a packet of one dozen throw-away vacuum bags as a lure. At the same time, the company organized a sales contest for its dealers and salesforce for a vacation in the U.S. Sales promotion also acts as a push-through device by making customers want the product. Once the image of a product is established among customers, dealers and retailers will be compelled to stock it. For example, Coca-cola Company introduced its orange soda, Fanta, in many developing countries through free gifts of ballpoint pens and pencils and the like. Through consumer demand, even the very small retailers were forced into carrying Fanta.

Devices of sales promotion can be classified on the basis of the function to be performed and the target to be reached. Three main types of sales promotion functions can be distinguished: sales promotion for introducing a new product, sales promotion for increasing the use of a product, and sales promotion for the direct enticement of customers at the retail level. Free samples, price-off coupons, and refund offers are the devices used for introducing new products. Price-off deals, premiums, contests, and sweepstakes constitute the methods for securing greater use of a product. Trading stamps, retailer coupons, and point-of-purchase demonstrations are resorted to for action at the retail level. Sales promotion techniques can be consumer-oriented, and dealer-and distributor-oriented. Sampling, demonstrations, or instructions; premium offers or temporary price reductions; and contests and sweepstakes are consumer-oriented promotion devices. Intermediary or agent-oriented techniques include assistance in store layout, assistance in planning and developing strategy such as accounting and inventory instructions, cooperative advertising, dealers' sales training, provision of point-of-purchase materials, and money and merchandise allowances.

The above categorization is based on U.S. practices. The marketing environment in a foreign market, however, may require making appropriate adaptations in sales promotion offerings. As a matter of fact, in some nations, a marketer may be forced into coming out with an entirely new sales promotion idea that is in line with the country's environment. Poor economic conditions in developing countries may suggest putting greater emphasis on the economic value of the offering, assuming the product is directed at the mass market. Legal restrictions in many countries call for adaptation. In Germany, giveaways (other than items of insignificant value such as calendars and diaries) are legally prohibited. Further, the sales promotion campaign should not create conflict in the marketplace so as to raise eyebrows in political circles. Inasmuch as some sales promotion campaigns must be implemented through wholesalers and retailers, their structure and practices would also be a consideration in planning a sales promotion campaign. For example, retailers in most developing countries are small, scattered, and disorganized. They may not be able to handle the equivalent of a cents-off type of sales promotion. Above all, the sales promotion offering should be culturally acceptable. The customization of sales promotion to match the perspectives of a country is well illustrated by Ford Motor company's efforts in Brazil.[20] In the midst of high inflation, banks in Brazil were not willing to finance purchases of big-price items by low-income families. Ford Motor Company, therefore, established car-buying clubs of

60 members in each. Each member made 60 monthly payments toward a car. A drawing was held each month and the member whose name appeared on the drawing received the car that month. This way the low-income Brazilian families continued to buy the cars without being burdened with high interest costs. The company, on the other hand, generated a guaranteed number of customers each month.

Management of sales promotion requires (1) a clear definition of *objectives* (for example, introducing a new product, increasing sales of an existing product, reducing seasonal declines in sales, countering competitor's gains, and registering new customers); (2) making *budget* allocations (which must be done in the context of a total promotional budget including advertising and personal selling); (3) drawing a *plan of action* covering such points as length of the campaign, details of sales promotion offerings, instructions required for the salesforce and middle agents, coordination needed with other departments of the company, media announcements, and cost estimates; and (4) an *evaluation* of the campaign to determine its viability for future use in the same country, and in other nations.

Public Relations Overseas

Public relations serves as a useful device for establishing a foothold and/or strengthening existing position in an overseas market. The public relations activity is directed toward an influential, though relatively small, target audience of editors and journalists who work for publications or in broadcasting aimed at a firm's customers and prospects. Since the target audience is small, it is relatively inexpensive to reach.

To do an effective public relations job overseas, an international marketer needs to hire an established public relations firm. It is desirable to look for a firm that has relevant experience and adequate resources. If the U.S. public relations firm of the company has an office in the host country, it may be retained there too. Alternatively, one may have to choose from among the local firms. After the public relations firm is recruited, the company should develop a dossier, that is, a package of information that editors may file for future reference. A typical dossier runs to 10 pages and includes information on the company's capabilities, its technologies, its preeminence, and why it operates in the host country. The dossier may be supplemented with a corporate brochure, preferably in the host country language, identifying worldwide manufacturing, research and development, and sales/service locations. Usually, the dossier is accompanied by a letter inviting editors to contact a designated person for further information. The letter may also state that articles and releases will be regularly issued by the company in the future.

The company should decide, in consultation with the public relations firm, how an initial contact should be made with the target audience, editors and journalists. At this stage, the public relations firm is better known to the audience than is its client. As a matter of fact, some public relations firms are so well accepted in a country that a release on the company's behalf signals editors that the story is newsworthy, factual, and worth publishing. Thus, the public relations firm should play a lead role in establishing initial contact for the firm.

Future announcements and releases may either be custom-developed for the host country or extracted from among those prepared for the domestic market. In other words, a firm entering an overseas market may reuse some of its U.S. news releases, application case histories, technical and feature articles, trends articles, and the like. The appropriateness of domestic material in an overseas market may be judged by the host country marketing management and the public relations firm. Wherever necessary, however, original releases must be produced and issued as desired.

Once a story or article on the firm appears in print, it will be read by only a small fraction of customers. Nonetheless, it is important to get all the promotional value one can from a good placement. One way of doing this is to send story/article reprints in quantity to the firm's salespeople and distributor salespeople for use in their sales calls and mailings. The reprints support sales training programs, too. New salespeople can learn much about the company's products and applications from a file of articles.

International Marketing Highlight 16.7

Global Philanthropy

American Express—Developed an academic course to educate secondary school students on travel and tourism issues. Cost: $500,000.

DuPont—Sent 1.4 million water-jug filters to 8 nations in Africa. Their synthetic fabric removes debilitating parasitic worms from drinking water. Cost: $400,000.

Alcoa—Teamed up with local authorities in southern Brazil to build a sewage plant serving 15,000 rural residents. Cost: $112,000.

H.J. Heinz—Funded infant nutrition studies in China and Thailand through Heinz's Institute of Nutritional Sciences in Chengdu, China. Cost: $94,000.

IBM—Donated computer equipment and expertise to Costa Rica's National Parks foundation to develop strategies for preserving rain forests. Cost: $60,000.

Hewlett-Packard Co.—Donated computers to the University of Prague.

Source: *Business Week*, February 25, 1991, p. 91.

These activities help in establishing a good name for the company and its product during the start-up period. To continue to generate news and be visible in the long run, a variety of techniques can be used. These include interviews and the publicizing of talks by area executives, publicity for new product designs or services developed in or for the overseas area, case histories from customers' experiences in the area, special activities for key media, invitations to the press to cover company-sponsored seminars, meetings, and workshops, and photographs to meet an editor's express needs. These techniques assist in *localizing* the company. Beyond that, as the company becomes fully established, the public relations activities may include sponsored speeches and seminars, and management leadership in professional associations (see International Marketing Highlight 16.7).

The role of public relations abroad does not differ greatly from what it is in the U.S., but somehow U.S. companies do not emphasize it overseas as thoroughly as at home. The public relations activity internationally should not be directly limited to market a product/service. Public relations programs should serve as a company's antenna, gathering and analyzing information on events, trends, and legislation, and as a contact point with the firm's various audiences.

Summary

Personal selling is an important ingredient of any marketing program. Three sources of sales personnel are identified: expatriates (U.S. nationals working in a host country, say, England), natives (an English national working in England), and third-country nationals (a French citizen transferred by a U.S. company to work in England). In the realm of international business, most personal selling jobs are handled by the local management. The head office, however, can provide useful support to local management on such aspects as selection, training, supervision, compensation, and evaluation.

The chapter concentrates on the problems involved in managing expatriates and third country nationals. MNCs should have a well-defined policy for expatriates and third country nationals that deals with such matters as determining the most appropriate nonnative nationality selection in host country personnel situations, employment upon repatriation, and plans for natives' development. Also covered are various aspects of managing expatriates and third country salespeople: selection, orientation, training (including terms and conditions of the assignment, cultural training, and language training), compensation, and placement, Finally, the process of international sales negotiations and strategies for successful negotiations are discussed.

In ways similar to domestic marketing, sales promotion and public relations are also relevant to international marketing. The role of sales promotion in other countries does not vary from what it is in the U.S. However, an appropriate sales promotion program for an overseas market should be geared to the local environment. For example, in a country where retailing organizations are small and scattered, it may be difficult to use the equivalent of cents-off coupons. Public relations provide a justification and an identity for the foreign enterprise in the economic sphere of the host country. It is desirable to hire the services of a public relations firm with relevant experience in order to get started on a solid program. Publicity programs, which give the firm and its products broad exposure to customers and prospects as well as third-party endorsement by the media, provide a cost-efficient use of a limited promotional budget.

Review Questions

1. Define the term *expatriate*. What problems are expatriates likely to face overseas?
2. Discuss the problems that pertain to the employment of third country nationals as salespeople.
3. What are the elements of policy guidelines for sales management overseas?
4. What precautions should be taken in selecting salespeople for overseas positions?
5. What type of training should be provided to expatriates?
6. Why do expatriate salespeople cost more? Illustrate with examples.
7. What steps may be adopted to adequately repatriate and reassign salespeople located abroad?
8. What role does a public relations firm play for an international marketer?

Creative Questions

1. Many developing countries have a surplus of skilled people who are willing to work at substantially lower wages than their counterparts in the industrialized countries. Despite this problem, should an MNC prefer nationals over third-country workers to be a good corporate citizen?
2. Often it is said that marketing students interested in international business should be fluent in at least one foreign language. On the other hand, English is the commercial language of the world. Is the emphasis on learning a foreign language unnecessary? Even if one were to learn a foreign language, which language should be chosen? (Keep in mind that at this stage, the student cannot be sure in which part of the world he/she will be involved.)

Endnotes

1. W. Chan Kim and R. A. Manborgue, "Cross-Cultural Strategies," *Journal of Business Strategy*, Spring, 1987, p. 29.
2. "The Sale of the Decade?" *The Economist*, February 19, 1983, p. 43.
3. O. Jay Galbraith and Anders Edstrom, "International Transfer of Managers: Some Important Policy Considerations," *Columbia Journal of World Business*, Summer, 1976, pp. 100–26.
4. *Corporate Procedure* (Pittsburgh: Westinghouse Electric corporation, 1992), pp. 2–5.
5. Rosalie L. Tung, "Expatriate Assignments: Enhancing Success and Minimalizing Failure," *Executive*, No. 2 (1987), pp. 117–26.
6. See Joann S. Lublin, "Younger Managers Learn Global Skills," *The Wall Street Journal*, March 31, 1991, p. B1.
7. See: Cyndee Miller, "Growing Overseas Requires Marketers to Learn More Than a New Language," *Marketing News*, March 28, 1994, p.8. *Also see* Bob Hagerty, "Trainers Help Expatriate Employees Build Bridges to Different Cultures," *The Wall Street Journal*, June 14, 1993, p. B1.
8. See "The Fast Track Leads Overseas," *Business Week*, November 1, 1993, p. 64.
9. *Business Week*, November 7, 1988. *Also see* Shawn Tully, "Where People Live Best," *Fortune*, March 11, 1991, p. 44.
10. Susan Carey, "Expatriates Find Long Stints Abroad Can Close Doors to Credit At Home," *The Wall Street Journal*, May 17, 1993, p. B1. *Also see* Joan M. Inzinga, "The Perceived Learning Needs and Intercultural Experiences of Corporate Expatriates: American and Asian Pacifics," Ph.D. dissertation, The University of Connecticut, 1988.
11. "Successful Repatriation Demands Attention, Care and Dash of Ingenuity," *Business International*, March 3, 1978, p. 65.
12. Nancy J. Adler, "Re-Entry: Managing Cross-Cultural Transitions," a paper presented at the Academy of International Business Meetings in New Orleans, October 1980.
13. Nan M. Sussman, "A Hard Homecoming for Japan's Expats," *The Asian Wall Street Journal Weekly*, January 13, 1986, p. 15.
14. See "How MNCs Ease Expatriates' Return to Home Countries," *Business International*, February 25, 1991, p. 65. *Also see* "Bringing Our Expatriates Home: A Fresh Look at Reentry," *Business International*, February 11, 1991, p. 49.
15. John L. Graham, Dong Ki Kim, Chi-Yuan Lin, and Michael Robinson, "Buyer-Seller Negotiations Around the Pacific Rim: Differences in Fundamental Exchange Processes," *Journal of Consumer Research*, June 1988, pp. 48–54.
16. Discussion in this section draws heavily on Claude Cellich, "Skills for Business Negotiations," *International Trade Forum*, October/November 1990, p. 8.
17. Nigel C. G. Campbell, John L. Graham, Alain Jolibert, and Hans Gunther Meissner, "Marketing Negotiations in France, Germany, the United Kingdom and the United States," *Journal of Marketing*, April 1988, pp. 49–62.
18. Thomas C. Keise, "Negotiating With a Customer You Can't Afford to Lose," *Harvard Business Review*, November–December 1988, pp. 30–37.
19. Philip R. Harris and Robert T. Moran, *Managing Cultural Differences*, 2nd ed. (Houston: Gulf Publishing Co., 1987), p. 57.
20. "How Brazilians Beat the Credit Squeeze," *Business Week*, November 1, 1976, p. 50.

CHAPTER 17

Export Marketing

CHAPTER FOCUS

After studying this chapter, you should be able to:

- Describe perspectives of U.S. export trade

- Discuss how the U.S. government encourages and hinders exports

- Define the steps in conducting export business

- Examine duty free zones and barter trade

The United States is the world's largest exporter. Yet, its exports are a meager percentage of the U.S. gross national product (GNP). The balance has shifted, however, to an extraordinary extent in the last decade. In 1970, the ratio of US. exports to GDP was 4.3 percent. Exports almost doubled to 7.5 percent of GDP in 1986, and fell to 7.3 percent of GDP in 1993. However, in comparison with the exports of European nations and Japan, U.S. exports (as a percentage of GNP) are still small. For Germany and the U.K., exports amount to roughly 20 percent of GDP.[1]

The international trade environment provides U.S. business with a variety of opportunities for export growth. The U.S. government is moving toward policies and procedures that encourage exports. The world economy began to recover in early 1993 from a long recession. Economic liberalization in developing countries provided an additional boost to world economies, and narrowing inflation differentials among nations have always favored export growth.

Nonetheless, trends alone cannot prompt higher exports. U.S. businesses must make conscious efforts to boost exports. About 37,000 U.S. manufacturing companies, slightly more than one-third of all U.S. companies, export. However, only 1 percent of U.S. companies accounted for about 74 percent of all 1993 U.S. exports. Big MNCs account for the vast share of exports. However, there is continued potential opportunity for other U.S companies to conduct export business successfully.

Some marketing managers do not fully explore potential sales abroad because of an uneasiness or lack of understanding about foreign credits and collections. Others shy away because of a fear that selling abroad involves too much red tape. Of course, selling abroad differs from selling in the domestic market, yet export sales can be handled without much difficulty if management has the vision and energy to make the attempt.

This chapter begins with an analysis of certain U.S. exports. Then, the procedural details for conducting an export business are outlined. Significant export management issues are discussed, and the emerging area of barter trading is examined.

U.S. Export Trade

The U.S. imports more merchandise than it exports, resulting in the problem of a negative balance of trade. To an extent, the negative trade balance is caused by excessive oil imports. During the 1950s, U.S. exports amounted to 18 percent of world trade. This declined to about 13.5 percent in 1970 during a period of indifference toward export trade. For example, either U.S. exports then were unique products that sold themselves—without significant competition from other countries—or export markets were used as last resorts to absorb periodic excess domestic inventories. Only a few companies were really committed to exporting. In the recent past, the U.S. government had no clear-cut policy for the encouragement of exports. Not until the mid-1960s did the U.S. government become particularly concerned about the U.S. balance of payments. During the 1970s, two compelling reasons to expand exports emerged. First, U.S. economic growth had slipped to less than 2 percent annually from about 4 percent over the preceding 20 years. U.S. companies began to consider export markets as a way of sustaining their own growth rates. Second, the dramatic increase in the price and consumption of imported oil made it essential to boost exports to help offset the huge outflow of U.S. dollars paid for oil. The U.S. share of world exports climbed as high as

20.6 percent in the early 1980s. It declined to 13 percent in 1990 and stood at 12.3 percent in 1993.[2]

The U.S. potential for export growth is enormous There is a $2.5 trillion market abroad, and with its capture come millions of jobs and income security for average Americans. So far, only a fraction of U.S. export potential has been tapped. Eight out of 10 new manufacturing jobs created between 1987 and 1992 were in export-related industries. A $10 billion increase in exports generates about 193,000 American jobs both directly and indirectly. A similar increase in imports eliminates about 179,000 jobs. Thus, the export job-generation effect is about 7.8 percent larger than the import job-loss effect.[3]

Thousands of U.S. companies offer products and services that could be competitive abroad. Entry into export markets should help domestic business as well because, as the market expands via exports, economies of scale should be realized in lower costs of products both for overseas shipment and for those to be sold in the U.S. Also, exports provide a cushion against slumps in the domestic market.

The Level and Direction of U.S. Export Activity

In the last few years, thousands of American companies have taken a fresh, aggressive approach to selling in the international markets. They are venturing into new markets, exporting goods and services that had never gone abroad before, using novel approaches to marketing products, and thinking up new ways to apply their technological know-how. This export vigor can be attributed to many factors. The fall of the dollar makes U.S. products cheaper for foreign buyers. Further, U.S. productivity has been rising since the late 1980s. Finally, U.S. labor costs have fallen since the 1990s.[4]

In 1993, U.S. industries exported $465 billion worth of goods to foreign customers; during the same year the U.S. imports amounted to $581 billion. (see Table 17.1) This resulted in a trade deficit of $116 billion. For 17 years, the U.S. continued to incur trade deficits; from $9.3 billion in 1976 to $148.5 billion in 1985—the largest deficit on record. Since then, the picture has been a little more encouraging. Between 1985 and 1991, exports rose at a faster pace than imports. In 1991, while exports increased over 7 percent, imports registered a decline of 1.4 percent. The trend reversed in 1992 and again in 1993. A major reason for the decline in export growth has been the European and Japanese recession leading to cutbacks in purchases of U.S. products. The net result was a substantial trade deficit in 1993.

This deficit refers to U.S. balance of trade and *not* to balance of payment. The *balance of trade* is the difference between merchandise exports and imports. The *balance of payment*, on the other hand, includes all international transactions such as merchandise exports and imports; transfers under U.S. military agency sales contracts; travel and transportation by U.S. citizens abroad and by foreigners in the U.S.; and direct investments, foreign aid, and other payments. Such international transactions (excluding merchandise exports and imports) usually are called "invisibles" in international commerce. Their significant role for the U.S. is borne out by the fact that at times our deficits in merchandise trade have been largely balanced or exceeded by growing positive "invisible" balances.

American exports consist primarily of agricultural products and ready-for-sale manufactured goods, as well as component parts and intermediate products used in manufacturing—in other words, from soybeans to computers and aircraft, and from blue jeans to machine tools. The U.S. import list includes oil, autos, TVs, and other consumer and industrial goods. Among the 10 key industries in U.S. foreign trade, aerospace, computer equipment, oil field machinery, medical equipment, and chemicals enjoy export surpluses, while cars and trucks, textiles and apparel, electronics, steel, and machine tools remain huge losers.

During the last 10 years, U.S. trade has undergone interesting changes. First, trade with Pacific Basin countries has registered a significant increase, while trade with Western Europe has relatively declined. The Geneva-based General Agreement on Tariffs and Trade (GATT) says transpacific trade overtook transatlantic trade in value for the first time in 1984. Second, trade with developing countries has been increasing faster than with developed countries. Third, the role of manufactured products has increased in importance over basic products. The above shifts reflect the changes in the world economy. More nations today participate in trade than ever before. U.S. trade is shifting away from its traditional markets of Canada and Western Europe to a broader base of nations, indicating that U.S. business is truly becoming international in character (see International Marketing Highlight 17.1).

International Marketing Highlight 17.1

America's Hottest Export: Pop Culture

There is good news for the U.S. these days on the export front: Around the globe, folks just can't get enough of America. They may not want our hardware anymore—our cars, steel, or television sets. But when they want a jolt of popular culture—and they want more all the time—they increasingly turn to American software: our movies, music, TV programming, and home video, which together now account for an annual trade surplus of some $8 billion. Only aerospace—aircraft and related equipment—outranks pop culture as an export.

Like it or not, Mickey Mouse, Michael Jackson, and Madonna—her overseas sales are two and a half times her domestic number—prop up what's left of our balance of trade.

Broaden the definition of pop culture to include licensed consumer products—say, Teenage Mutant Ninja Turtle bubble bath—throw in such culture-driven products as McDonald's burgers, Levi's jeans, and Coca-Cola's soft drinks, and you're looking at America's top seller abroad. Last year Walt Disney Co. sold $1.5 billion worth of consumer products—hats, watches, comic books—in Japan, where Coca-Cola earns more money than it does in the U.S.

In the past five years the overseas revenues of Hollywood studios doubled, and in a couple of years they should surpass domestic. The $20-billion-a-year American music business—basically rock & roll—collects 70 percent of its revenue outside the U.S. Sales of U.S. television programming to Europe are estimated at about $600 million a year. Almost everybody in the world watches Cosby, and everybody in the world watched Dallas. The most popular film of all time in Israel and Sweden is "Pretty Woman," which already has garnered more than $360 million worldwide at the box office and hasn't yet opened in the two biggest markets outside the U.S.—Japan and France.

Source: Fortune, December 31, 1990, p. 50 © 1990 Time Inc. All rights reserved.

TABLE 17.1 Merchandise Exports and Imports*

Type of Transaction	1960	1965	1970	1975	1985	1986
Exports of goods and services	$19,650	$26,461	$42,469	$107,088	$213,100	$217,300
Imports of goods and services	$14,758	$21,510	$39,866	$98,041	$361,600	$387,100

Type of Transaction	1987	1988	1989	1990	1991	1092	1993
Exports of goods and services	$254,100	$322,200	$363,800	$394,000	$421,600	$448,000	$465,000
Imports of goods and services	$406,200	$459,500	$473,200	$495,000	$488,100	$532,000	$581,000

*In millions of dollars.
Source: U.S. Department of Commerce, *Statistical Abstract of the United States: 1994* (Washington, D.C.: U.S. Government Printing Office, 1994), p. 727; *Business America*, April,1994, p. 40; and *Business America*, April 22, 1991, pp. 2-7.

Approximately two-thirds of U.S. goods exports are by U.S. owned MNCs, with over one-third of these exports by U.S. parent corporations, shipped to foreign affiliates. These affiliates usually include both local manufacturers and companies that market products from the U.S. parent. For example, General Motors, Ford, and IBM exported and sold over $1 billion of goods almost exclusively through foreign affiliates.

The direction of U.S. trade is indicated in Table 17.2. The EU countries account for about 20 percent of U.S. exports. As a single country, Canada is the most important U.S. customer, followed by Japan. Moreover, almost one-third of U.S. exports are to developing countries. As far as U.S. imports are concerned, Canada was the U.S. leading import supplier, followed by Japan, and then by Mexico, China, Germany, Taiwan, and the U.K.

U.S. Export Problems

The U.S. export situation is adversely affected by various factors. Chief among these are that (1) many corporate managers consider exports to be only marginal business and (2) while the U.S. government pays lip service to the promotion of exports, it actually inhibits them through laws and regulations. Notably, the traditional business factors (the high costs of labor and capital, or low productivity) that at one time were considered responsible for limiting U.S. exports are no longer influential; U.S. companies are now competitive. Instead, exports are hurt by an overall negative attitude. Sometimes agricultural exports are discouraged because of domestic price pressures; other times military exports are blocked for political reasons.

There are historical reasons for the U.S. indifference toward international trade. In the 1950s and 1960s, the U.S. had little need of export markets because the home market was large enough to absorb mass production. However, today, to balance the cost of oil imports, the U.S. needs to generate additional exports in the tens of billions of dollars. The disinterest in the export sector also costs jobs, corporate profits, and business growth. Consequently, it is likely to lead to slower economic growth and, ultimately, to a slower rise in living standards.[5]

For nearly 20 years, the economies of overseas production, compared with high costs at home, compelled U.S. companies to continue building plants abroad rather than exporting goods to serve foreign markets. Nonetheless, factors that made that practice desirable no longer apply. For example, the percentage increase in unit labor costs in the U.S. since the early 1980s has been the lowest among the major industrial

TABLE 17.2 U.S. Trade : 1993

Top 25 US. Markets U.S. Domestic and Foreign Goods Exports, 1993 (F.a.s. Value)		$billions
1.	Canada	100.2
2.	Japan	48.0
3.	Mexico	41.6
4.	United Kingdom	26.4
5.	Germany	19.0
6.	Taiwan	16.3
7.	South Korea	14.8
8.	France	13.3
9.	Netherlands	12.8
10.	Singapore	11.7
11.	Hong Kong	9.9
12.	Belgium-Luxembourg	9.4
13.	China	8.8
14.	Australia	8.3
15.	Switzerland	6.8
16.	Saudi Arabia	6.7
17.	Italy	6.5
18.	Malaysia	6.1
19.	Brazil	6.0
20.	Venezuela	4.6
21.	Israel	4.4
22.	Spain	4.2
23.	Argentina	3.8
24.	Thailand	3.8
25.	Philippines	3.5

Leading U.S. Suppliers U.S. General Goods Imports, 1993 (Customs Value)		$billions
1.	Canada	110.9
2.	Japan	107.3
3.	Mexico	39.9
4.	China	31.5
5.	Germany	28.6
6.	Taiwan	25.1
7.	United Kingdom	21.7
8.	South Korea	17.1
9.	France	15.2
10.	Italy	13.2
11.	Singapore	12.8
12.	Malaysia	10.6
13.	Hong Kong	9.6
14.	Thailand	8.5
15.	Venezuela	8.1
16.	Saudi Arabia	7.7
17.	Italy	7.5
18.	Switzerland	6.0
19.	Netherlands	5.5
20.	Indonesia	5.4
21.	Belgium-Luxembourg	5.4
22.	Nigeria	5.3
23.	Philippines	4.9
24.	India	4.6
25.	Sweden	4.5

U.S. Trade Balances, 1993 — Listing of U.S. Goods Trade Balances
Domestic and Foreign Exports, F.a.s. Value, General Imports, Customs Value

U.S. Surplus Positions		$billions
1.	Netherlands	+7.4
2.	Australia	+5.0
3.	United Kingdom	+4.6
4.	Belgium-Luxembourg	+4.0
5.	Argentina	+2.6
6.	Turkey	+2.2
7.	Egypt	+2.2
8.	Mexico	+1.7
9.	Russia	+1.2
10.	Spain	+1.2
11.	Chile	+1.1
12.	United Arab Emirates	+1.1
13.	.Panama	+0.9
14.	Switzerland	+0.8
15.	Iran	+0.6
16.	Bahrain	+0.6
17.	Greece	+0.5
18.	Paraguay	+0.5
19.	Poland	+0.5
20.	Brunei	+0.4
21.	Morocco	+0.4
22.	Jamacia	+0.4
23.	El Salvador	+0.4
24.	Bahamas	+0.4
25.	South Africa	+0.4

U.S. Deficit Positions		$billions
1.	Japan	−59.3
2.	China	−22.8
3.	Canada	−10.8
4.	Germany	−9.6
5.	Taiwan	−8.9
6.	Italy	−6.8
7.	Thailand	−4.8
8.	Malaysia	−4.5
9.	Nigeria	−4.4
10.	Venezuela	−3.5
11.	Indonesia	−2.7
12.	South Korea	−2.3
13.	Sweden	−2.2
14.	France	−2.0
15.	Angola	−1.9
16.	India	−1.8
17.	Brazil	−1.4
18.	Phiolippines	−1.4
19.	Singapore	−1.1
20.	Saudi Arabia	−1.0
21.	Gabon	−0.9
22.	Kuwait	−0.8
23.	Sri Lanka	−0.8
24.	Finland	−0.8
25.	Norway	−0.7

Source: Business America, April 1994, p. 10

countries.[6] All that is needed is determination among U.S. managers to export, and more help and less hindrance from the government.

It is estimated that although 37,500 U.S. companies export, another 20,000 that could successfully sell in foreign markets are not doing so. The resulting asymmetry in U.S. trade relations with the rest of the world is typified by the auto industry. Very few of the big cars that Detroit designs for the U.S. market are exported, while Europeans and the Japanese build smaller cars for world markets.[7] In 1991, combined they shipped 2.6 million cars to the U.S.. With the entry of the Japanese luxury cars into the U.S. auto market, the domestic industry is going to be further squeezed.[8]

At the same time, a number of countries impose barriers against U.S. exports (see International Marketing Highlight 17.2). These barriers comprise government laws, regulations, policies, or practices that either protect domestic producers from foreign competition or artificially stimulate exports of particular domestic products.[9]

International Marketing Highlight 17.2

Prince for Sale or Rent

The biggest rip-off in the music industry—the widespread transfer to cassettes of compact discs (CDs) that people rent in Japan—looks like it is being outlawed. The Japanese authorities, who have hitherto turned a blind eye to the practice, had until the end of December 1991 to put a stop to piracy that cost foreign record companies upwards of $1 billion a year in lost sales. Record producers in America and Europe wanted the Japanese to ban the rental of new CDs for one year following their release.

At present, the Japanese CD rental stores are supposed to hold back new record releases for one to three weeks. Few bother. However, if Japan fails to come up with an answer soon, America will push ahead with the (rather fanciful) 50-year renting moratorium it has proposed at the GATT trade talks.

Under Japan's present copyright laws, record companies can ban the renting of CDs and records for up to a year after release, and demand a royalty fee from rental stores for 29 years thereafter. However, the agreement applies only to Japanese CDs and records, not foreign ones. The stores pay a one-time fee of 400 yen ($3) for the right to rent each new Japanese release. With foreign CDs and records accounting for a third of the rental market in Japan, Western record companies understandably feel cheated.

Source: The Economist, December 21, 1991-January 3, 1992, p. 80.

Thus, the structure of international trade is moving further and further from the classical model of unimpeded commerce based strictly on comparative advantages. Eventually, the large reverse flow of foreign multinational investment now coming into the U.S. should help narrow the U.S. trade gap by substituting U.S.-made products for imports.

Table 17.3 shows how the U.S. is losing its markets to imports in industry after industry. This situation cannot be allowed to continue; U.S. businesspeople must learn to export aggressively.

Despite the gloomy picture that Table 17.3 depicts, there are products such as pulp and wastepaper, electronic components and parts, and timber in which American

TABLE 17.3
Share of U.S. Market Occupied by Imports

PRODUCT	1972	1992
Blowers and fans	3.6%	37.6%
Converted paper products	10.4	22.2
Costume jewelry	10.4	59.6
Dolls	21.8	61.9
Electronic computing equipment	0.0	12.8
Lighting fixtures	4.2	27.5
Precious metal jewelry	4.9	34.4
Primary zinc	28.4	58.5
Printing trade machinery	8.5	21.8
Radios and TVs	34.9	69.7
Semiconductors	12.3	43.8
Shoes	17.1	62.3
Luggage and personal goods	20.7	52.9
Men's and boys' outerwear	8.7	41.3
Men's and boys' shirts and nightwear	17.8	58.5
Musical instruments	14.9	26.2
Nitrogenous fertilizers	4.3	21.4
Power-driven hand tools	7.5	27.2
Sporting and athletic goods	13.0	33.8
Telephone and telegraph equipment	2.1	27.5
Tires and inner tubes	7.2	24.5
Women's blouses	14.9	47.8
Women's suits and coats	7.3	38.2
Wool yarn mills	6.1	22.4

Source: Different publications of the U.S. Department of Commerce.

companies maintain leads. If adequate encouragement is provided, these products offer an opportunity to offset the U.S. trade balance.

U.S. Government Encouragement of Exports

Worldwide, governments play a vital role in encouraging exports. Traditionally, in the U.S. the issue of exports has not been given the status that issues such as tax reform, armaments, corporate corruption, the Arab boycott of Israel, and antitrust enforcement received. Nonetheless, the importance of balancing the trade deficit has led the government in the past few years to adopt programs to boost exports.

The U.S. government aids exports through the Export-Import Bank, foreign sales corporations, Commerce Department programs, the Overseas Private Investment Corporation, and pressure on major trading partners to spur their economies. The Omnibus Trade and Competitiveness Act of 1988 has been hailed as landmark legislation intended to spur U.S. exports. The National Export Strategy formulated in 1994 enhances the inherent strengths of the U.S. economy and helps our firms compete globally into the next century.

Export-Import Bank

The Export-Import Bank was created by the U.S. government in 1934 to provide low-cost financing to encourage exports of aircraft, nuclear plants, and other "big-ticket" items. The bank's lending capacity is based on appropriations approved by Congress. The bank's subsidy supposedly helps U.S. businesses to meet European and Japanese competition vis-à-vis their export-subsidy programs. For example, the bank might lend money equal to 45 percent of the price of the American goods to prospective buyers at low rates of interest. In some cases, the bank has financed up to 85 percent of the price. As a matter of fact, in at least one case—a proposed $16 million sale of gas turbines to Malaysia by United Technologies Corporation—the bank agreed to provide 100 percent financing. Despite the bank's program, it is not easy to match Japanese and European competition. For example, in the Malaysian deal, a Japanese company won the sale with a government-backed 4 percent 20-year loan. General Electric Co. lost the contract for Thailand's new power plant generators to Japan's Fuji Electric Co., since Japan's export-finance agency offered a highly subsidized, last-minute loan.[10]

In the 1980s, the bank's lending authority was vastly enhanced. For example, export credit programs were strengthened by increasing the level of the Export-Import Bank ceiling on export guarantees. Further, in accordance with the provisions of the Export Trading Company Act (ETC) of 1982, the bank's new ETC Loan Guarantee Program was developed in a way that should be especially helpful to small and medium-size minority and agricultural exporters and producers. For example, exporters can obtain short-term, preexport loans to be used to finance export-related activities when arrangements cannot be made in the private credit market.

In the 1990s, the Export-Import Bank redesigned and streamlined its loan, guarantee, and insurance programs to make them more accessible, especially to the small and medium-sized businesses with the greatest potential for increasing U.S. exports and improving the balance of trade. The bank also works with cities and states on a program to educate local officials about trade assistance available from the U.S. government.[11]

Foreign Sales Corporations (FSCs)

Before the creation of FSCs, U.S. companies could establish domestic international sales corporations (DISCs) under the Revenue Act of 1971. The purpose behind the DISC legislation was to encourage businesses, especially small ones, to engage in export activity through the tax sheltering of income. A DISC could be established in any state with nominal capital of $2,500. To tax shelter the income, a minimum of 95 percent of the DISC sale had to be export-related and, whether the goods were grown, extracted, or manufactured in the U.S., they must have come from an organization other than the DISC. In other words, the DISC acted as a parent company and served as an export channel. DISCs ran into conflict with some of the fair-trade rules of GATT. After years of complaints from U.S. trading partners, GATT ruled in 1982 that DISCs are an illegal export subsidy. This ruling forced the U.S. government to abolish DISC legislation.

Thus, DISCs ceased after December 31, 1984. However, to continue to encourage U.S. businesses to export, the Deficit Reduction Act of 1984 replaced DISCs with FSCs. An FSC is a foreign corporation not located in the U.S. Customs Zone that is allowed to earn some exempt and nontaxable income on its exports from the U.S. In most cases, this partial exemption can result in U.S. tax savings of up to 7.4 percent of the profit on the export transaction for a manufacturer/exporter and 14.7 percent for a trading company/exporter. The FSC is required to pay U.S. tax on the balance of its nonexempt income. The FSC's trade income dividends to its U.S. corporate shareholders are not taxable to them.[12]

The FSC legislation has an advantage over the DISC legislation: it allows a permanent tax exemption to the U.S. corporate shareholders on dividend distributions that may be as frequent as the FSC desires and that may be invested anywhere. However, the DISC legislation required investing the proceeds in qualified foreign assets. Thus, U.S. farmers and agricultural cooperatives can benefit from the FSC but not from the DISC. These benefits aside, overall FSCs provide for limited tax exemption and are more costly to operate.[13]

Commerce Department Programs

The U.S. Department of Commerce offers a variety of services through the International Trade Administration (ITA) to help businesses in their export activities. Forty-eight ITA district offices and 19 branch offices in cities throughout the U.S. and in Puerto Rico provide information and professional export counseling to businesspeople. Each office is headed by a director and supported by trade specialists and other staff. These professionals can help a company's decision makers gain a basic understanding of profitable opportunities in exporting and assist them in evaluating the company's market potential overseas (see International Marketing Highlight 17.3).

Each district office can give information about:

- Trade and investment opportunities abroad
- Foreign markets for U.S. products and services
- Services to locate and evaluate overseas buyers and representatives
- Export seminars and conferences

Most district offices maintain an extensive business library containing the department's latest reports.

The major elements of ITA programs are summarized below.

U.S. and Foreign Commercial Services The U.S. and Foreign Commercial Services (US/FCS) were combined a few years ago to offer the American exporter coordinated trade assistance both at home and abroad. Overseas, the US/FCS maintains 136 offices in 69 countries that are considered to be the principal U.S. trading partners. More than 175 commercial officers direct export promotion activities at these sites and manage promotional programs developed by ITA.

Commercial officers gather data on specific export opportunities, country trends affecting trade and investment, prospects for specific industries, and other commercial intelligence. They also identify and evaluate importers, buyers, agents, distributors, and joint-venture partners linked with U.S. firms; and they monitor and analyze local laws and practices that affect business conditions.

The domestic side of the US/FCS operates, as mentioned above, 48 district offices in industrial and commercial centers throughout the nation. These offer a broad range of trade-related information, as well as one-on-one counseling by experienced trade specialists.

The district offices can tell exporters or prospective exporters about trade and investment opportunities abroad, foreign markets for U.S. products and services, financing aid, insurance from the Foreign Credit Insurance Association (FCIA), tax advantages of exporting, international trade exhibitions, export documentation requirements, economic facts on foreign countries, and export licensing and import requirements.

International Marketing Highlight 17.3

Obstacles Small Exporters Face

Small firms starting to export say the single largest source of information—the Department of Commerce—is also one of the biggest sources of frustration. They condemn trade-promotion programs throughout the federal government as unfocused, overlapping, and inefficient. Worse, U.S. commercial banks, citing too little profit and too much risk, routinely refuse to lend to small exporters. Talk of recession has amplified their concerns.

As more small companies search out business abroad, many say their two greatest needs, reliable trade information and trade financing, are in short supply.

When N&N Contact Lens International Inc. of Lywood, Washington, began looking for information on overseas markets two years ago, the local Department of Commerce office was stumped by simple, specific questions. When asked who sells contact lenses in Caracas, Venezuela, it gave the company lists, many of which were outdated, of distributors of such broad categories as "medical devices."

Among major industrialized nations, the U.S. spends the least per capita to promote exports. Number 1, Canada, shelled out 18 times more in 1987, the latest year for which figures are available: $21.44 for each inhabitant versus $1.20 in the U.S. The U.S. government itself brands the services of the U.S. and Foreign Commercial Service, a unit of the Commerce Department's International Trade Administration, as unfocused and inefficient.

Source: Mark Robichaux, "Exporters Face Big Roadblocks at Home," *The Wall Street Journal*, November 7, 1990, p. B1.

Besides the district offices, an export counseling unit in Washington, D.C., helps U.S. firms develop or expand markets abroad. Counselors advise exporters on the choice of support services and guide them in the use of export practices and procedures.

The counseling unit also maintains an export information reference room in Washington, D.C., where interested persons may examine a wide range of information on major foreign projects under consideration by international financial institutions.

Publications That Assist Exporters   A variety of publications are available to help exporters reach and expand foreign markets. The foremost of these publications are

Business America, Commercial News USA, A Basic Guide to Exporting, Market Share Reports, Global Market Surveys, and *Overseas Business Reports.* (See International Marketing Highlight 17.4.)

Commerce Export Assistance Programs ITA maintains a wide range of programs to help U.S. companies begin exporting and to locate or expand foreign markets. Major programs include:

Automated Information Transfer System (AITS). AITS, a linked system of small computers, has been installed in most ITA district offices and nearly 50 overseas posts to make market-related information accessible worldwide on a timely, efficient, and inexpensive basis. The AITS system can match U.S. producers with overseas buyers interested in their products; retrieve trade leads, company contacts, and other information; and send messages from one ITA location to another.

Trade Opportunities Program (TOP). Export opportunities, originating from either private or government sources overseas, are transmitted daily to TOP in Washington, D.C., by U.S. and Foreign Commercial Service posts around the world. As subscribers to TOP, U.S. business firms indicate the products or services they wish to export, the countries they are interested in, and the type of opportunities desired, whether direct sales, overseas representation, or foreign government tenders. The TOP system matches the product interests of foreign buyers with those indicated by U.S. subscribers, mailing the leads to subscribers on a daily basis.

■■■■■■■■■■ **International Marketing Highlight 17.4** ■■■■■■■■■■

The Export Yellow Pages

Reaching out to the global marketplace became much easier in 1992 with the inaugural publication of *The Export Yellow Pages.* Produced as part of a public/private initiative with the U.S. Department of Commerce—which spearheads distribution of 50,000 copies worldwide—*The Export Yellow Pages* is uniquely designed to help:

- Foreign firms buy U.S. products and services
- U.S. executives locate export service providers

Source: *Business America,* January 13, 1992, p. 34.

New Product Information Service (NPIS). This program provides worldwide publicity for new U.S. products available for immediate export. Promotional descriptions are published in *Commercial News USA* magazine for dissemination to business and government leaders around the globe. Information on selected NPIS products is also broadcast overseas by the U.S. Information Agency's "Voice of America" radio shows.

Export Contact List Services. ITA collects and stores data on foreign firms in a master computer file called the Foreign Trade Index (FTI). Covering 143 countries, this file contains information on more than 140,000 importing firms, agents, distributors, service organizations, manufacturers, retailers, and potential end-users of U.S. products and services. The information is made available in various forms such as mailing labels and computer printouts, to meet company requirements.

World Traders Data Reports (WTDRs). Prepared by U.S. commercial officers abroad, WTDRs are business reports providing background information on potential foreign trade contacts. Each report also contains a general narrative prepared by the U.S. commercial officer conducting the investigation as to the reliability of the foreign firm.

Agent/Distributor Service (A/DS). The A/DS provides U.S. firms with the names of agents and/or distributors abroad who have indicated an interest in handling specific products from the U.S. ITA's commercial officers conduct "customized" on-site searches to identify representatives who are both interested and qualified to handle specific products.

Overseas Trade Fairs. ITA sponsors participation by U.S. firms in worldwide international trade fairs, assisting with many preshow promotional services such as marketing, provision of exhibit space, and design and construction of exhibits. The cost to the U.S. participant varies by country and event.

Commerce Assistance on Specific Markets. Commercial and economic information on most trading partners of the U.S. are available through ITA's international economic policy unit.

Assistance on Foreign Industry Sectors. Trade information on most industry sectors is available through the trade development unit in ITA.

Comparison Shopping. This is a custom-tailored service that provides firms with key marketing and foreign representation information about their specific products. Commerce Department staff conduct on-the-spot interviews to determine nine key marketing facts about the product such as sales potential in market, comparable products, distribution channels, going price, competitive factors, and qualified purchasers.

Foreign Buyer Program. Exporters can meet qualified foreign purchasers for their products or services at trade shows in the U.S. The Commerce Department promotes the shows worldwide to attract foreign buyer delegations, manages an international business center, counsels participating firms, and brings together buyer and seller.

Overseas Catalog and Video-Catalog Shows. Companies can gain market exposure for their product or service without the cost of traveling overseas by participating in a catalog or video catalog show sponsored by the Commerce Department. Provided with the firm's product literature or promotional video, the Department's U.S. and Foreign Commercial Service will send an industry expert to display the material to select foreign audiences in several countries.

Overseas Trade Missions. Officials of U.S. firms can participate in a trade mission, which will give them an opportunity to confer with influential foreign business and government representatives. Commerce Department staff will identify and arrange a full schedule of appointments in each country.

Matchmaker Events. Matchmaker Trade Delegations offer introductions to new markets through short, inexpensive overseas visits with a limited objective: to match the U.S. firm with a representative or prospective joint venture/licensee partner who shares a common product or service interest. Firms learn key aspects of doing business in the new country and meet, in one-to-one interviews, the local people who can help them be successful.

Exporters Licensing Services This ITA activity assists U.S. firms in fulfilling their obligations under the Export Administration Act. The act helps to ensure U.S. national security and to further U.S. national foreign policies by controlling exports to certain destinations of certain kinds of sensitive, high-technology equipment and data.

Exporters Licensing group gives speedy advice to business executives who need to determine whether their exports require advance, validated licenses or who need help in filing the requisite application.

Service Industries Development Program The Trade and Tariff Act of 1984 mandates that the Commerce Department establish a service industries development program. An essential element of this program is an updated survey of the services sector, which includes statistics on exports and imports of services, receipts, employment, and wages paid by service firms.

Improved data on service industries help analysis of this sector's contribution to the U.S. economy and advance the marketing of U.S. services abroad.

Foreign Requirements for U.S. Products and Services U.S. companies wishing to sell abroad must know how to deal with foreign national requirements, standards, testing, and certification requirements. The National Center for Standards and Certification Information (NCSCI), a branch of the Commerce Department's National Bureau of Standards, is the government's central repository for standards-related information about foreign countries.

Foreign Metric Regulations The Office of Metric Programs provides exporters with information about foreign metric import regulations. It also provides guidance and assistance on matters relating to U.S. transition to the metric system.

Overseas Private Investment Corporation (OPIC)

Established as a federal agency in 1969, OPIC provides insurance coverage for U.S. companies in countries where annual per capita income does not exceed $1,000. Recently, this limit was raised to include countries with per capita income up to $2,200. Boosting this limit permitted OPIC to operate in such emerging developing countries as Brazil, where U.S. companies are offered the promise of quick growth

OPIC offers 20-year coverage to U.S. companies abroad, compared with the 3-year policies typically available from private insurers.

OPIC has been designed to be self-sufficient. It operates on its own profit without congressional funds. In 1992, OPIC wrote $7.6 billion worth of insurance covering 100 countries. It is authorized to write up to $7.5 billion.

In addition to these services, OPIC has special programs to meet specific needs of the investor involved in contracting and exporting, energy exploration, and development and leasing arrangements.

Many developing countries require foreign firms to post performance or advance payment guarantees in the form of standby letters of credit. OPIC's political risk insurance for contractors and exporters protects against arbitrary or unfair drawing of these letters of credit. It also protects against confiscation of tangible assets or bank accounts and losses due to a government owner failing to live up to contract provisions.

Energy programs are special insurance and finance programs geared toward U.S. investors involved in oil, gas, oil shale, geothermal, mineral, solar, and other energy projects. OPIC can provide a loan guaranty of up to $50 million to finance as much as 50 percent of a new project deemed commercially feasible.

Leasing programs provide specialized insurance and finance services for U.S. investors involved in international leasing. Political risk insurance is available for cross-border operating and capital leases running for at least 36 months. Loan guaranties to leasing companies can range from $500,000 to $30 million, with the fees paralleling OPIC's general finance programs. Direct loans are available to foreign leasing projects in which small U.S. businesses have significant interests.

Pressure on Trading Partners

For many years, the U.S. government has tried to increase demand for U.S. products abroad by prodding the governments of Germany and Japan in particular to stimulate their economies and thus draw in more U.S. goods. This idea is based on the assumption that recovery abroad would stimulate U.S. exports.

In addition, the U.S. government has been pressuring the Japanese to reduce barriers that restrict the sales of U.S. goods in Japan. For example, traditionally, the Japanese government required purchase of telecommunications equipment from native sources only. Recent pressure, however, has led Japan to eliminate this restriction and thus has opened the door for U.S. firms such as Western Electric, a subsidiary of American Telephone and Telegraph, to explore export opportunities in Japan.[14] Similarly, pressure is being put on South Korea, Taiwan, and other trading partners to open their markets to American goods.

Export Trading Company Act, 1982

This act was the first major export expansion legislation in more than a decade. It encourages businesses to join together and form export trading companies. It provides antitrust protection for joint exporting, and permits banking institutions to own interests in these exporting ventures. This act makes exporting practical for small- and medium-size firms by permitting them to join forces and hire specialists to handle all the complicated details of exporting without fear of antitrust prosecution and inadequate capitalization.[15] The following are the highlights of the provisions of the Export Trading Company Act.

Banking Provisions Bank holding companies and bankers' banks may invest up to 5 percent and loan up to 10 percent of their capital and surplus to an export trading company.

Bank holding companies and bankers' banks may own up to 100 percent of the stock of an export trading company.

The Federal Reserve Board (FRB) must approve any proposed investment. Under this process, a bank need only notify the FRB of the intended investment. If no objection is made within 60 days thereafter, the bank may proceed with the intended investment.

A bank is exempted from the collateral requirements contained in the Federal Reserve Act for loans to its export trading company.

Antitrust Certification Provisions The antitrust certification is provided by the Commerce Department. A certificate holder has complete immunity from U.S. antitrust laws, except for private party lawsuits for actual damages.

By the end of 1990, the Commerce Department issued 132 certificates providing antitrust protection to 46 firms and individuals. Small and medium-sized firms constituted a majority of the holders of these certificates. Interestingly, the agribusiness community is taking more interest in the ETC program than other industries. Further, by the end of 1990, a total of 73 bank ETCs had been formed with the approval of the Federal Reserve Board, and had invested $148 million in them. Despite these achievements, the ETC program has received lukewarm support in the business community. Critics consider these achievements insignificant. Empirical research shows that such large companies as Sears, General Electric, Rockwell International, and General Motors would have formed export trading companies with or without the ETC legislation. Banks and small- and medium-sized manufacturers, which were supposed to benefit most from the legislation, have not responded well.[16]

One reason for this lackluster support may be the ignorance of smaller companies about the act's relevance and usefulness to their business. The U.S. Department of Commerce's educational programs (e.g., conferences and publications) may encourage these firms to take advantage of the export opportunities furnished under the ETC Act.

Omnibus Trade and Competitiveness Act of 1988

On August 23, President Reagan signed the Omnibus Trade and Competitiveness Act of 1988. The major provisions of the act are discussed in Chapter 2. The act maintains U.S. commitment to free trade and provides better trade remedy tools to open foreign markets. It strengthens the ability of U.S. firms to protect their patented, copyrighted, and trademarked goods and ideas from international thievery.[17]

Further, the act supports the Uruguay Round trade talks to adapt or expand GATT by improving existing rules with respect to agriculture and to dispute settlement, and by extending GATT discipline to new areas such as services, investment, and intellectual property.

The act also provides for the establishment of an interagency committee to assure the timely collection of accurate trade and economic data and to provide the private sector and government officials with efficient access to this data for policy-making and export promotion (see International Marketing Highlight 17.5).

As discussed in Chapter 2, in 1994, Congress approved a new trade strategy to boost U.S. exports. The strategy is founded on the conviction that exports play a vital and ever-increasing role in creating new jobs driving the nation's economic growth. It is expected that exports of U.S. goods and services will reach $1 trillion by the beginning of the next decade, resulting in over 6 million new jobs. According to the

Clinton Administration, the National Export Strategy makes government more responsive to its "customers"—businesses and individuals who export goods and services throughout the world and ensure the creation of dynamic new export-oriented strategic alliances among business, labor, and government.

International Marketing Highlight 17.5

Trade vs. Environment

In the past few years, a new problem has arisen concerning trade barriers and environmental laws. In these trade versus environment conflicts, developing nations with an abundance of natural resources are pitted against industrialized nations. For example, fishermen in Mexico were harvesting yellowfin tuna by using nets that trap scores of dolphins in the process. As a result, tens of thousands of dolphins drowned. In 1988, the U.S. banned all imports of tuna caught using this technique. However, in response to a Mexican complaint, a GATT panel ruled that such a ban was an unfair trade barrier. The GATT panel ruled against a member country restricting imports of a product merely because it came from a country with different environmental policies than its own.

The Mexican government did not push the matter further despite the GATT ruling in its favor. However, if other countries transhipping Mexican tuna are banned from exporting, they may protest under the GATT ruling.

Concern for the environment is laudable. Nonetheless, the problem is that countries pursue trade protectionism in the name of a "safe" environment. For example, Canadians protect their prized Pacific salmon against overfishing by virtually counting the catch. Atlantic lobsters are safeguarded by New England states by banning sales of adolescent crustaceans. Europeans demand that imported beef must be untainted by artificial growth hormones. As world trade grows, such conflicts are likely and there is no easy way to resolve them. Resource-rich developing nations see imperialism in the efforts of industrialized nations to force environmental reforms on them. Rich nations, on the other hand, fear deterioration of the environment as a genuine concern.

Source: "Save the Dolphins—or Free Trade," *Business Week*, February 17, 1992, p. 130D.

U.S. Government Hindrance of Exports

Although the government encourages exports in various ways, several U.S. rules and regulations have acted as obstacles (although many of them are not as significant anymore as they used to be) to increasing exports:[18]

- The Foreign Corrupt Practices Act of 1977, which imposes jail terms and fines for overseas payoffs by U.S. companies

- Limits on the sale and financing of nuclear plants (these restrictions have been designed to halt the spread of nuclear weapons)

- Human rights legislation, which denies credits to rights violators

- U.S. trade embargoes, which ban exports to Cuba, Iran, Zimbabwe, and many other countries

- Strategic controls restrictions, which stop exports with potential military uses to many countries
- Antitrust laws, which prevent U.S. companies from bidding jointly on major foreign projects
- Super 301 trade law, which has been used against barriers in such countries as Japan, Brazil, and India.
- Imposition of U.S. environmental protection standards on trading partners.
- Restrictions on hi-tech exports to protect national security

The U.S. policy in foreign trade matters continues to be based on *helping and reforming* other nations. Such a policy reinforces the view that major trading partners of the U.S. are so weak that they require very substantial U.S. concessions in trade and other economic matters, and that the U.S. is so strong that it is immune from economic injury no matter what concessions are made by its government. The validity of such an appraisal is questionable, as is the expectation that other nations will accept U.S. values and ethics as a basis for their exports.

Export Management

U.S. companies face a challenge to succeed in a time of growing protectionism and keen competition. While U.S. government programs are some help, the proper management of export activity at the company level is equally important. This section discusses select strategies to improve export performance.

Export markets offer a variety of opportunities. However, to capitalize on these opportunities, companies should develop an export focus and do a thorough job in identifying products/markets. Consider Japan. Often companies grumble about its closed markets, but they fail to realize that the new generation of Japanese crave U.S. goods and have plenty of purchasing power. Foreign products selling well in Japan are those not requiring much after-sale service, which foreign producers are relatively poor at providing, and those in which foreign producers maintain a competitive edge vis-à-vis their Japanese competitors in terms of either price or performance. These products are primarily nondurable consumer and specialty goods that satisfy individual tastes. Examples include black tea (market share of imports to the overall market equals 60 percent), canned soup (40 percent), neckties (25 percent), climbing ropes (90 percent), paper diapers (50 percent), skiing goods (30 percent), and fountain pens (35 percent).

Choosing Attractive Markets

A framework for selecting potential growth markets for exports is diagrammatically depicted in Figure 17.1. Market attractiveness may be based on company competencies, industry practices, and competitive conditions. A sustainable competitive position in selected foreign markets can be built if a company is able to reach a minimum level of

FIGURE 17.1 Setting Development Priorities in Overseas Markets

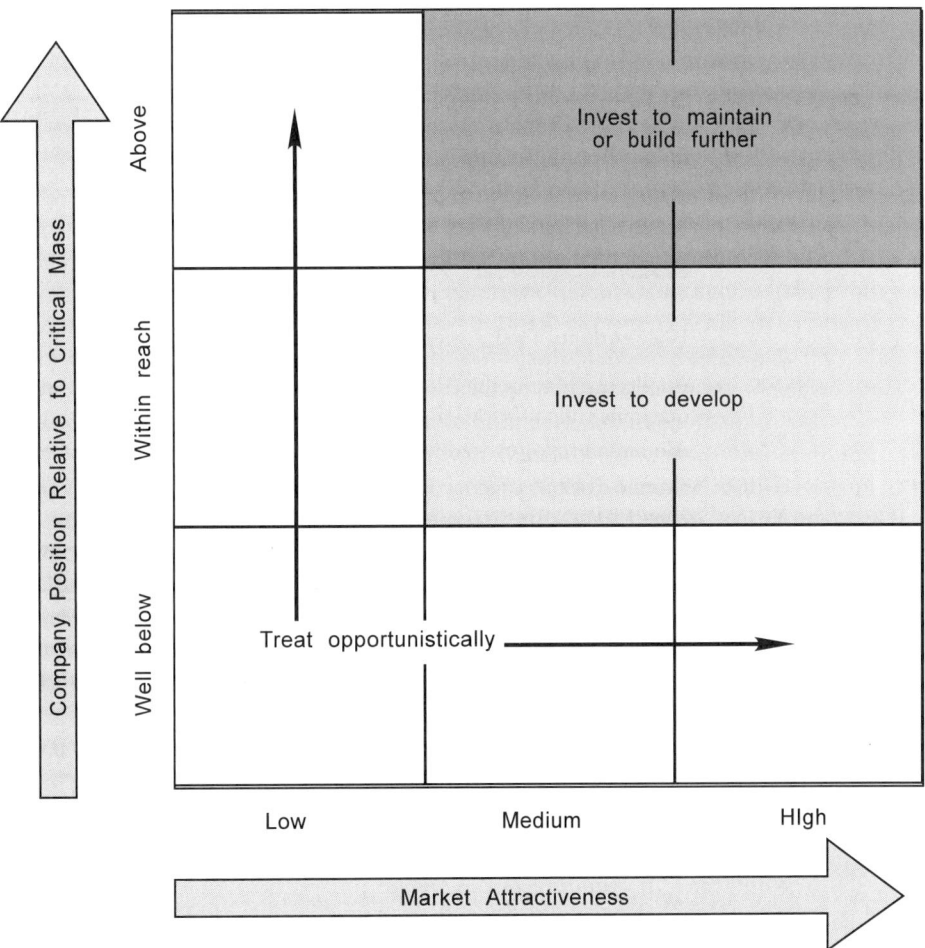

size and effectiveness; that is, critical mass. *Critical mass* is determined by the ability of the company to match the product, price, distribution, and promotion requirements of the market vis-à-vis competition. Once different markets are located on the grid, the approximate allocation of resources for foreign market development may be made as follows: In the dark-shaded areas, at the upper right-hand corner of the grid, are found attractive markets where the company already has a strong position. In these markets, the appropriate strategy is usually to maintain that position or build it further. The light-shaded areas indicate attractive markets where the company is within reach of critical mass. Here, the company can improve results by investing the necessary time and resources to gain the step-function benefits of crossing the threshold. The white areas of the grid are those markets with low attractiveness, or markets where it is unlikely that the company can reach critical mass. Here, a strategy of careful opportunistic response and limited or reduced investment is probably called for.

17 Export Marketing

Product Specialization

There was a time when U.S. products everywhere were considered superior across the board. In the past 20 years, however, other countries have achieved similar distinction in a variety of products. No longer are U.S. electronic goods considered the best. German machinery is often held superior to that of the U.S. Moreover, many Third World countries are able to produce high-quality, low-technology products at significantly lower costs. In brief, U.S. corporations cannot expect to do well overseas with all products. A careful choice of both products and market is essential. For example, high-technology products have provided a unique opportunity for U.S. business to

International Marketing Highlight 17.6

100 Products That America Makes Best

All-electric plastics injection-molding machine, Cincinnati Milacron
Aluminum foil, Reynold Metals
Atomic clock, Frequency Electronics, Hewlett-Packard
Ball point pens, A.T. Cross
Balloon and laser angioplasty catheters, C.R. Bard, Eli Lilly, Trimedyne
Bamboo fly-fish rods, Walt Carpenter
Bed sheets and towels, Burlington Industries, Dan River, Dundee Mills, Fieldcrest, Cannon, J.P. Stevens, Springs Industries, West Point-Pepperell
Biotech drugs: t-PA, Genentech
Bobcat skid-steer loaders, Melroe
Boots and hunting shoes, Timberland, L.L. Bean
Brain electrical activity mapping system, Nicolet Instrument
Camera film (color), Eastman Kodak
Central office switching equipment, AT&T
Charcoal briquettes, Kingsford Products
Charge couple device image sensor, Eastman Kodak
Clothes dryers, Whirlpool
Combines, Case IH, Deere
Computer operating systems software: MS-DOS, Unix, VM, VMS, Microsoft, AT&T, IBM, Digital Equipment
Copiers, Eastman Kodak, Xerox
Cotton denim, Cone Mills

Cruising sailboats, 37 feet and under, Pacific Seacraft
Crystal, Steuben Glass
Data parallel supercomputers, Thinking Machines
Digital plotters, Hewlett-Packard
Dishwashers, General Electric
Distributed database management technology, Tandem Computers
Ditch Witch trenchers, Charles Machine Works
Drugs: Capoten and Vasotec, Squibb, Merck
Dustbuster Plus hand-held cordless vacuum cleaners, Black & Decker
Electrodeposition primers, PPG Industries
Electrohydraulic servo valves, Moog
F-16 jet fighters, General Dynamics
Fast food: hamburgers, McDonald's
Financial, engineering, and scientific hand-held calculators, Hewlett-Packard
501 jeans, Levi Strauss
Flashlights, Mag Instrument
Flutes, Wm. S. Haynes
FM two-way radios, Motorola
Frequency and time interval analyzers, Hewlett-Packard
Fur coats, Peter Dion, Goldin-Feldman Ben Kahn, Maximilian, Louis Milona
Glass fiber for communications, Corning Glass Works
Gore-Tex waterproof breathable fabric, W.L. Gore

Handbags, Coach Leatherware

Hay and forage equipment, Ford New Holland

Heating controls, Honeywell

Heavy earthmoving equipment, Caterpillar

Ice cream and sorbet, New York Fruit Ice

Industrial and commercial floor sweepers and scrubbers, Tennant

Instant camera films, Polaroid

Integrated voice and data communications systems (T-1 multiplexers), Network Equipment Technologies

Intelsat VI satellite, Hughes Aircraft

Ion chromatographs, Dionex

Jazz music

Jet aircraft: 747 family of planes, Boeing

Jet engines, General Electric

Kevlar fiber, Du Pont

Load/backhoe, Case IH

Locomotives, General Electric

Longwall mining systems, Joy Technologies

Lycra spandex fiber, Du Pont

Magnetic resonance imaging scanners, General Electric

Marlboro cigarettes, Philip Morris

Mass spectrometers, Finnigan

Men's ready-to-wear suits, Oxford Clothes

Micro-precision machine and measuring tools, Moore Special Tool

Microprocessors: Motorola 68000 family, Intel 80X86 family, Motorola, Intel

Microwavable food in shelf-stable packaging: Impromptu, Top Shelf, General Foods, Geo. A. Hormel & Continental Can

Microwave ovens, Litton Industries

Minicomputers, Digital Equipment, Hewlett-Packard, IBM

Minisupercomputers, Alliant Computer Systems, Convex Computer

Multimeters, Hewlett-Packard, John Fluke Mfg.

Offshore drilling equipment, Cameron Iron Works

Oscilloscopes, Tektronix

Pacemakers, Medtronic

Paper towels, Procter & Gamble, Scott Paper

Personal computer applications software, Lotus Development, Microsoft, Word-Perfect

Personal computers, Apple Computer

Pianos, Steinway & Sons

Post-it-note pads, 3M

Powerboats, Cigarette Racing Team, Donzi Marine

Pressure transmitters for industrial process plants, Rosemount

Row-crop planters, Case IH

Scotch S-VHS videotape, 3M

Scotchcal drag reduction tape, 3M

Sheet and strip stainless steel, Allegheny Ludlum

Soft drinks, Coca-Cola

Stationery, Crane

Stereo loudspeakers, International Jensen, Allison Acoustics, Infinity Systems

Sunglass lenses, Corning Glass Works

Supercomputers, Cray Research

Symbion J-7 and Thoratec artificial hearts, Symbion, Thoratec Medical

Tampax, Tambrands

Technical workstations, Apollo, Silicon Graphics, Sun

Teflon, Du Pont

Telephone sets, AT&T

Thermos vacuum containers, Halsey Taylor/Thermos

Thin film hard disks, Komag, Seagate Technology

Tillage equipment, Krause Plow

Tractors, 100 hp and over, Deere

Washing machines, Maytag, Whirlpool

Source: Richard L. Kirkland, Jr., "Entering a New Age of Global Business," *Fortune*, March 14, 1988, p. 40 © 1988 Time Inc. All rights reserved.

acquire leverage in entering export markets. However, other industrialized nations are slowly challenging the U.S. position even in this area.[19] U.S. companies need to be active in protecting their advantage in the export of high-technology products (see International Marketing Highlight 17.6).

Appropriate Management Orientation

To compete effectively abroad and develop and expand foreign markets, U.S. business persons need to develop a particular management orientation. Different firms, depending on their experience, face different problems in the export arena. The management focus of each firm, therefore, should be directly related to its actual experience. For example, exporters may be divided into three categories: (1) exporters with only a partial interest in exporting, (2) exporters who export on an experimental basis, and (3) experienced exporters. The perspective of each type of export operation is significantly different from the others. Obviously, management style and strategy should vary accordingly. To illustrate this point, experienced firms need to devote more attention to financial aspects and funds transfer, while new entrants should tackle packaging, funds transfer, document handling, and the mechanics of exporting. By the same token, as the dynamics of a firm's business change from the experimental to the experienced level, the nature of the problems changes, and then a different managerial emphasis is required.[20]

Appropriate Export Strategy

Finally, for a longer-term effective export performance, a company must develop an appropriate marketing strategy. For the foreseeable future, the global environment dictates that U.S. export sales cannot be generated simply by repeating what a company does in the U.S. Overseas markets should be properly analyzed to search out and identify product/market niches where a certain company might have a particular opportunity. Next, adequate product, price, distribution, and promotion strategies need to be formulated to serve those target markets.

The textile industry's export performance during the late 1980s illustrates how a well-planned strategy can pay off.[21] For example, U.S. textile exports (yarn, fabric, and carpeting) increased 50 percent, from $3.2 billion in 1980 to $4.8 billion in 1985. To accomplish this, the textile companies took three strategic measures.

First, they identified market segments that currently were not adequately served. For example, British carpetmakers mainly produced two types of carpets—woven wool carpet and synthetic carpet. The middle class could not afford the wool carpet because it was expensive; and the synthetic carpet looked cheap. To cater to the middle class, American mills introduced mid-priced carpeting in different shades, colors, and textures.

Second, riding on the tidal wave of enthusiasm for such U.S. fashions as blue jeans, U.S textile producers started exporting denim and corduroy to European apparel makers. These foreign companies compete head-on with U.S. apparel makers such as Levi Strauss. Thus, the move to supply denim to a customer's competitors was risky. However, in the long run, the textile mills found it to be a sound strategy.

Third, the textile producers introduced new product concepts overseas. For example, towels and sheets in Europe and Japan had been stable, commodity-type products in standard shapes and designs, without fashion appeal. U.S. companies decided to introduce a "boutique" marketing system to develop an export market for bed and bath textile products. One company that stands out in the successful pursuit of this strategy is Fieldcrest Mills.

Export Procedure

Many marketing managers fail to explore fully potential business abroad because of their uncertainty about, or simply lack of understanding of, export mechanics. While exporting is certainly more demanding than a strictly domestic business, by using the information provided by the U.S. Department of Commerce and employing agents and other professionals familiar with the formalities, export sales can be handled almost as easily as domestic sales. One need not travel abroad and meet with customers in person to be successful in exports. As with most any undertaking, there are basic procedural tasks involved in exporting.

Locating Customers

Overseas customers can be located in many ways. Large corporations have their established contacts. Firms new to exports can identify likely prospects overseas through the information available from the U.S. Department of Commerce. For example, as discussed earlier in this chapter, the *World Traders Data Reports* (WTDRs), a service of the Commerce Department, provide detailed commercial information on foreign firms—background information on the organization, year established, number of employees, sales area, type of operation, products handled, name of contact officer, general reputation in trade and finance circles, names of other foreign firms the company represents, and even a U.S. foreign service officer's comment on the firm's suitability as a trade contact.

Before proceeding with a prospect, it is advisable to examine the socioeconomic-political-regulatory environment of the importing country. Such an examination would indicate if an export can be successfully transacted. For example, many countries prohibit the importation of certain products. Some require that an import license be obtained from the government. Other countries impose restrictions on the quantity imported. Thus, if an import license is required, the exporting firm should insist that the importer obtain it first. Similarly, if a government levies a heavy import duty, the exporter should remind the interested overseas party of the impact of such a barrier on the final cost of the product.

Obtaining Export Licenses

Exporters should be aware of U.S government regulations affecting the export of certain strategic commodities to certain destinations. Essentially, all items intended for export require an export license. This rule is mandated by the need for national security, and by the foreign policy and economic interests of the U.S. The rule, however, applies neither to U.S. territories and possessions nor, in most cases, to Canada. There are two types of licenses: general and validated. A general license permits exportation within certain limits without requiring that an application be filed or that a license document be issued. A validated license authorizes exportation within specific limitations; it is issued only on formal application. Most goods can move from the U.S. to free-world countries under a general license. A validated license is required to export certain kinds of strategic goods regardless of the destination.

An exporter needs to know whether a general or validated license is necessary and which office to contact to obtain the license. For most commodities, the license is granted by the Commerce Department's Office of Export Administration (OEA). For certain specific products and commodities, however, export licenses are provided by other U.S. government departments and agencies (see Table 17.4). For example, in the case of arms, ammunition, and other war-related items, the license is given by the Department of State.

TABLE 17.4
U.S. Export Licensing Authorities for Specific Commodities

COMMODITY	LICENSING AUTHORITY
Arms, ammunition, and other war related products	Department of State
Atomic energy material (including fissionable materials and facilities for their manufacture)	Atomic Energy Commission
Gold and silver	Department of Treasury
Narcotic drugs	Department of Justice
Natural gas and electric energy	Federal Power Commission
Tobacco plants and seeds	Department of Agriculture
Vessels	Maritime Commission
Endangered wildlife	Department of the Interior

Source: U.S. Department of Commerce. *The Export Administration Regulations* (Washington, D.C.: U.S. Government Printing Office, 1993).

The type of license—general or validated—required for exporting is based on two considerations: country of destination and commodity to be exported. For export purposes, the U.S. government has classified countries (except Canada) into seven categories:[22] Q—Romania; S—Libya; T—all countries of the Western Hemisphere except Canada and Cuba; W—Poland and Hungary; Y—Albania, Bulgaria, Czech Republic, the Commonwealth of Independent States, and several communist countries; Z—North Korea and Cuba; and V—all other countries except Canada. Exports to countries in the Z category are almost completely banned. There is a selective embargo, based on the type of commodity, on exports to countries in the Y group. In brief, different licensing requirements apply to countries in each category. Thus, exports to countries in the Y category would require a validated license, while those in the T category, a general license.

Items requiring a validated license include, but are not limited to, certain chemicals, special types of plastics, sophisticated electronic and communication equipment, scarce materials, and related technical data. By referring to the commodity control list of the Export Administration regulations available from the U.S. Department of Commerce, one can determine whether a validated export license is needed for a particular commodity to a particular country.

To obtain a validated export license, an application must be prepared following the procedures described in the Export Administration regulations. Where the value of the shipment is $5,000 or more and a validated license is needed, special forms generally must be completed by importers or their government to support the request for license.

A general license is a published authorization for the exporting of commodities that do not require a validated license. The majority of U.S. products exported require a general, not a validated, license. An exporter need not obtain formal authorization to ship products requiring a general license. Those products can be shipped by merely inserting the correct general license symbol or code on the export control document, that is, the shipper's export declaration. In other words, no formal application has to be made to export products for which a general license is needed.

Collecting Export Documents

A variety of documents is needed to complete an export transaction. The documents help to clear exported goods at shipping points and through customs, and to receive payment. Documentation requirements vary from country to country. The following documents are required most commonly.

Commercial Invoice A commercial invoice summarizes details of the sales contract and lists the names and addresses of the exporter, shipper, and consignee; date of order; shipping data; mode of shipment; delivery and payment terms; description of product; and prices, discounts, and quantities.

Some countries require additional information in the commercial invoice; for example, the invoice must be signed and notarized or countersigned by the exporter's chamber of commerce. Similarly, some countries require the invoice to be visaed by the resident consul of the importer's country. Details for the inclusion or attachment of additional information in the commercial invoice can be obtained from any of the 48 U.S. Department of Commerce district offices located in major cities across the nation.

Consular Invoice This term refers to a certificate pertaining to exports that should be obtained from the consulate office of the importer's country. A consular invoice is prepared on forms available from the consulate and often is in the language of the importing country. It is visaed by the resident consul, certifying the authenticity and correctness of the proposed shipment.

Certificate of Origin Many countries require a certificate, either on a prescribed form or on the exporter's letterhead, that specifies the origin of the merchandise. Usually such a statement is made on the commercial invoice, but some countries require an additional separate certificate. The certificate of origin makes it easier to establish possible preferential rates for import duties under a most-favored-nation arrangement.

Inspection Certificate An inspection certificate is an affidavit, either by the shipper or by an independent inspection firm, certifying the quality, quantity, and conformity of goods in relation to the order. Importers often request such a certificate to ensure the correctness of the shipment.

Shipper's Export Declaration This document summarizes shipping information and contains a description of the merchandise in a special nomenclature, both in words and by commodity identifying number per Export Administration regulations. The reference to a specific validated or general export license also appears on this document.

Export Packing List The export packing list summarizes information about the merchandise and facilitates shipping. The list is also used by customs officials to check the cargo at both the point of shipment and the port of entry. The list helps the importer to inventory the merchandise received. The list itemizes the material in each package; specifies the type of package (box, crate, drum); shows the package dimensions and weight; and provides the shipper's and buyer's references. The packing list is attached to the outside of one of the packages in a waterproof envelope marked "packing list enclosed."

Dock, or Warehouse, Receipt This document stipulates the receipt of goods at the pier or warehouse for further shipment abroad. This receipt is usually needed when the exporter has to deliver goods only to the U.S. port of export.

Insurance Certificate This certificate specifies the type and amount of insurance coverage. Virtually all shipments overseas are insured to protect the goods against political risks and damage by natural causes. An exporter can obtain an open cargo policy to cover all foreign shipments or insure individual shipments.

Bill of Lading This is the single most important export document. A *bill of lading* establishes the ownership of goods, testifies to the carrier's obligation to ship the goods, and serves as a receipt of goods from the carrier. A bill of lading may be negotiable or nonnegotiable. The nonnegotiable bill of lading is usually used for air shipments; the goods are addressed to the named consignee. However, most shipments are made via negotiable bills of lading. The goods may be consigned to the consignee or to a third party but are delivered to the bearer of the bill of lading, that is, the party presenting the properly endorsed bill of lading. Following commercial practice, a bill of lading, to be valid and acceptable, must be marked "Clean on Board." This amounts to a certificate by the carrier that the goods were received on board in good and satisfactory condition. Conversely, a bill of lading marked "Foul" by the carrier would mean that the goods were received on board either damaged or spoiled.

A bill of lading includes the name and address of the exporter, the forwarding agent, and the overseas consignee (both intermediate and ultimate); it identifies the carrier, the U.S. port of export, and the foreign port of unloading; and it includes the name of the party to be notified on arrival of the goods. It also contains details pertaining to the merchandise; nature of goods (e.g., "four boxes: textiles"), weight, value, and other pertinent information.

Packing and Marking

The importance of adequate packing for overseas shipment is discussed in Chapter 12 on product policy. Briefly, packing should be designed to prevent breakage and to protect against pilferage and exposure to moisture. Further, every effort should be made to keep package weight down to save on shipping costs, while ensuring that the package is sufficiently sturdy to withstand the violent handling, stocking, loading, and unloading so common to ocean shipping.

The package should be properly marked for easy identification. Legible and clear marking will ensure its shipment to the correct destination. Besides, it will help the consignee to identify the package without difficulty. Usually, overseas buyers specify special identification marks to be imprinted on the package. Frequently, exporters

Shipping Abroad

avoid showing trademarks or other clues that might reveal the contents of the shipment. Such precautions help to avoid pilferage.

Shipping of merchandise to overseas destinations involves observing different formalities that not every exporter is able to handle independently. It is desirable, therefore, to enlist the services of a *foreign freight forwarder*, an agent who specializes in moving the cargo to overseas destinations. After the goods have been delivered to the port of export, the freight forwarder takes over to clear the goods through U.S. customs and delivers the cargo to the pier in time for loading aboard the selected vessel. In addition, a freight forwarder furnishes useful advice to the exporter relative to freight costs, port changes, consular fees, export documentation, and customs rules, both in the U.S. and the importer's country.

Shipment may be made from the U.S. by either air or ocean carrier; in the case of countries accessible by land, such as Mexico and Canada, trucks can also be used. Carrier companies provide various types of contracts for overseas shipments. For example, three types of ocean service are available: conference lines, independent lines, and tramp vessels. The conference and independent lines operate on a predetermined schedule, while tramp vessels sail on ad hoc arrangements and usually carry bulk cargo. Conference lines are carriers who have formed an association to establish common freight rates and shipping conditions. Exporters who contract to deal exclusively with conference lines ship at lower rates than noncontract shippers. Independent lines price their services individually and aggressively compete for noncontract exporters, vying with the conference lines.

The shipping arrangement is finalized after a *booking contract* is obtained, reserving space for the cargo on a specified vessel.

Receiving Payment

There are various methods of receiving payment for export such as cash in advance, open account, consignment sales, dollar draft, and letter of credit. The method of payment used and the terms and conditions agreed upon would depend on the credit standing of the importer, the exchange restrictions operating in the importer's country, and the competition the exporter faces. Usually, the international services of a commercial bank are used to receive payment.

Cash in Advance As far as the seller is concerned, cash in advance is the safest method. Payment received before shipping the goods relieves the seller of worry about collection. Besides, the money is available for use right away. From the buyer's viewpoint, this is not a preferred method for two main reasons. First, certain foreign exchange restrictions prohibit paying cash in advance. Second, there is no guarantee of shipment of the merchandise as specified.

Overall, this method of payment is not used frequently; trade conducted via cash in advance constitutes a small portion of the total trade.

Open Account In an open-account arrangement, goods are shipped without any prior financial deal. This is a risky method of receiving payments unless the seller is dealing with a known party whose financial integrity is held in high esteem. Even where there is no danger of not receiving payment under this mode of payment, the trade practice in the buyer's country may be to pay only when the goods have actually been received. In developing countries, exchange problems may create an additional difficulty if the buyer fails to receive foreign exchange.

This method is most often used between organizations under the same corporate umbrella, for example one subsidiary of a company ships goods to another subsidiary in another country. Open-account shipments are also feasible between large organizations in industrialized countries; for example, General Motors may ship parts to Volvo in Sweden.

Consignment Sales   Consignment sales refer to an arrangement whereby goods are shipped to the overseas party while the seller retains title to the goods. The consignee makes payment to the seller after the goods have been sold. The consignment arrangement, like the open account, is feasible if the consignee's country provides a stable economic and political environment, and the consignee has a good reputation and offers a deal that is a sound business risk. Consignment sales are made mostly to exporters' overseas branches or affiliates.

Export Drafts   An export draft is an unconditional order drawn by the exporter asking the importer to pay the designated amount either on presentation (sight draft) or at a future date mutually agreed upon (time draft). Usually the future date specified in the draft is 30, 60, 90, 120, or 180 days after presentation. The draft may name either the seller as the party to receive payment or a bank to handle collection.

If a bank is to handle payment, the exporter delivers the draft and shipping documents to the named bank. The bank then forwards them to its branch, affiliate, or correspondent bank in the importer's country. The branch contacts the buyer or the buyer's bank and demands immediate payment if it is a sight draft, or acceptance on the time draft. Once payment or acceptance is received, the shipping documents are delivered to the buyer.

An export draft can be drawn in U.S. dollars or in a foreign currency. A payment-on-draft agreement is usually used when the protection provided by a letter of credit (discussed next) is not necessary. This mode of receiving payment is less expensive, and, therefore, enhances the exporter's competitive position in seeking export business.

Letter of Credit   A frequently used method of receiving payment for exports is through the letter of credit. It is a document issued by a bank at the buyer's request in favor of the exporter. The document promises to pay the specified sum of money in the designated currency within a specified time upon receipt by the bank of shipping documents (bill of lading).

Essentially, there are two types of letters of credit: revocable and irrevocable. An irrevocable letter of credit, once given to and accepted by the seller, cannot be altered in any way without permission of the seller. On the other hand, a revocable letter of credit may be declared invalid by the buyer, either personally or through a bank, for any discretionary reason. Except for cash in advance, the irrevocable letter of credit offers the exporter the highest degree of protection. Inexperienced exporters, particularly when dealing with unknown parties, and especially in developing countries, should find the letter of credit a safe way to secure themselves financially.

Duty-Free Zones

In order to encourage international trade despite import barriers, many countries have resorted to the opening of foreign-trade enclaves. There are different types of such enclaves. Among these, however, *duty-free zones* (also called free-trade zones or foreign-trade zones) are the most popular. The duty-free zones are unique because they let businesses store, process, assemble, and display goods from abroad without paying a tariff first. Once these products leave a zone and are delivered within the U.S., a tariff must be paid—but not on the cost of assembly, or on profits.[23] For example, a furnituremaker will have to pay a duty only on the imported raw wood used, not on the cost of assembling the item or on the profits. Consider Timex Co.'s example. It used the Little Rock, Arkansas, free-trade zone to store machinery it had bought overseas. By storing the equipment in the duty-free zone, the company deferred import duties until it had decided in which U.S. plant to use the foreign machinery. Finished goods can be stored in free-trade zones for reasons other than deferring customs duties. One firm ages wine in the New Orleans duty-free zone and thus defers import duties for years.[24]

If a product is re-exported, a company never has to pay a tariff. That means a U.S. cameramaker can assemble foreign parts in a Florida free-trade zone and ship the finished cameras to Latin America without paying U.S. duty.

Even if half the plants in these zones are foreign owned, it benefits the U.S. to have them because of the jobs created. Common for years in other countries, duty-free zones are becoming popular in the U.S. as the cost of doing business abroad rises.

Currently, there are 195 foreign-trade zones in the U.S., in such large cities as New York, Boston, San Francisco, and Chicago; and in such remote places as Duluth, Minnesota; Little Rock, Arkansas; Bangor, Maine; and Burlington, Vermont. More than $60 billion worth of merchandise was processed in these zones in 1992, over one-third more than in 1982. About 2,000 business firms used foreign-trade zones during 1992. About 700 firms occupied zone facilities on a permanent basis.[25]

The cost advantages of foreign-trade zones are exemplified by Berg Steel Pipe Co., a German-French joint venture in Panama City's zone.[26] Berg produces large-diameter pipe for, among others, the oil industry, importing some of the needed steel plate from Germany and Italy for about $450 to $500 a ton. Imported as materials, the plate normally would be taxed on 6 percent. However, with trade-zone status, Berg can convert the plate into pipe and move it into the U.S. market at the rate for finished products—1.9 percent—or export it free of tariff.

With such savings, companies of all kinds are setting up in foreign-trade zones. The variety of goods processed runs from Ambrosia Chocolate Co.'s bulk chocolate in Milwaukee to Xerox Corp.'s copiers near Rochester, New York. General Motors Corp. has 11 plants in foreign-trade zones, Ford Motor Co., 12, and Chrysler Corp. 9. Other trade zones include Bethlehem Steel Corp.'s shipbuilding yard in Sparrows Point, Maryland, a Caterpillar Inc. engine plant near Peoria, Illinois, and three Eli Lilly & Co. plants in Indiana. Many foreign firms such as Porsche, Nissan, and Mazda are active, too. Although both the tonnage and dollar value are dominated by giant corporations, more small than big companies are involved in foreign-trade zones.

Barter

An interesting development in recent years has been the emergence of barter, whereby goods/services are exchanged for goods/services without resorting to money-swapping. In other words, barter replaces money and credit as the medium of international exchange. Several types of barter deals are popular in the international market: counterpurchases, switch trading, clearing agreements, and buyback barter.

Counterpurchase (or Pure Barter)

Counterpurchase refers to a set of parallel cash agreements in which the supplier sells a service or product and orders unrelated products to offset the costs to the buyer.[27] For example, a few years ago, Caterpillar Tractor sold tractors to a Latin American logger and sawmill operator and took coffins in exchange.[28]

In the past, countertrade was used primarily by the [former] Soviet Union and by Eastern European and foreign-exchange-poor developing economies. However, recently these practices have spread as countries such as Canada, Switzerland, Sweden, and even the U.S. have joined this trend. One example of a countertrade deal is the New Zealand Meat Board's agreement to sell $200 million worth of frozen lamb to the Iranian government in exchange for crude oil. Another example is General Electric's agreement to sell Swedish products in overseas markets in exchange for a contract to build engines for Sweden's JAS fighters.[29]

Switch Trading

In a *switch-trading* arrangement, additional parties are brought into the picture whereby part of the exchanged goods is shifted to the new party, often for cash. When one party has an unwanted balance of goods to be received from a second party, a third party in need of the goods offered by the first party is found to purchase the available goods, with the proceeds going to the second party. In one transaction, Mitsui, a Japanese company, bought tanning material in the [former] Soviet Union and delivered it to Argentina in return for plastic products. These Mitsui materials sold in the U.S. for cash.[30]

Clearing Agreement

The objective of the *clearing agreement* is to balance the exchange of products over time between two governments without having to transfer funds by using an agreed-on value of trade, tabulated in nonconvertible "clearing account units." The contracting parties establish an exchange ratio of their respective currencies to determine the amount of goods to be traded. Usually, the exchange value is figured in U.S. dollars. An advantage of the clearing agreement is that flexibility is normally provided so that either side may accumulate a limited import/export surplus for the short term. The following example illustrates clearing agreements:

> Morocco and the [former] Soviet Union agree to exchange capital equipment and fresh oranges for a new phosphate plant. Morocco might prefer to buy the equipment elsewhere, but it has little foreign exchange, so it buys from the country that will take oranges in payment rather than hard currency. But Morocco needs the equipment more than the Soviets need the oranges. At settlement date, Morocco corrects the deficit by either paying the difference in hard currency or hoping the Soviets will enter a new agreement and permit the deficit to be carried over to the next contract.[31]

Buyback Barter

Under *buyback barter*, one party's purchase of capital equipment (e.g., plant, process) is paid for through the output made feasible by the capital equipment. For example, a U.S. tire company may sell equipment to establish an auto-tire plant in Egypt and get paid for it through tires manufactured by the Egyptian plant.

The barter agreements are really a form of protectionism because making any seller trade goods he or she would not otherwise buy eliminates part of free trade. Countries in the former Soviet bloc have been the chief practitioners of barter. In recent years, they have been joined by OPEC and other developing countries. As a matter of fact, more and more industrialized countries are following the same route to sell such big-ticket items as aircraft.

While Japanese and European companies have adapted themselves to barter, U.S. companies find it hard to absorb such practices. Long accustomed to straight cash deals, they are being dragged very reluctantly into barter agreements. Nonetheless, because rival companies outside the U.S. are so accustomed to writing barter contracts, more and more U.S. companies are likely to be forced into barter. How barter-type deals can hurt business is illustrated by General Electric's efforts to sell computerized axial tomographic (CAT) scanners for Austria. G.E. lost the deal for CAT scanners for Austrian hospitals after the German competitor, Siemens, agreed to step up production of unrelated electronic goods from an Austrian plant it operates, preserving 4,000 jobs.[32]

Barter trade is a wave of the future. While it tends to complicate overseas sales agreements, U.S. companies may have no choice. Stiff competition from European and Japanese companies, particularly in the case of high-value products, may force U.S. firms into barter deals.[33] More and more, U.S. companies are finding out that having a good product isn't enough. Countries with low hard-cash reserves now look as closely at an exporter's countertrade and financing terms as they do at its product. If competitors from Europe and Japan are willing to offer countertrade, the American companies must be, too. After all, barter accounts for over one-third of the world trade and appears to be increasing at a fast pace.[34]

Summary

The U.S. is the largest exporter in the world. Compared with other nations, however, U.S. exports constitute a small percentage of the GNP. Because the U.S. alone provided a large and growing market for labor-expensive American manufactured goods, export markets had not held much attraction for U.S. businesses. The situation changed in the 1970s. In particular, the high cost of oil imports made it necessary for the U.S. to put greater emphasis on exports and to seek a positive trade balance. Moreover, the devaluation of the U.S. dollar and wage increases overseas made U.S. goods competitive worldwide.

The U.S. government has a variety of programs to encourage exports. Through the Export-Import Bank, the government provides low-cost financing for overseas customers to buy American goods. An exporter can establish a foreign sales corporation to save taxes on his or her export earnings. The U.S. Department of Commerce's 48 district offices provide export-related information and counseling. The Overseas Private Investment Corporation, a federal government agency, insures U.S. business activity abroad in developing countries. Exporters are permitted to join together, without fear of antitrust prosecution, to form export trading companies under the 1982 Export Trading Company Act. Stronger tools to open foreign markets and help U.S. exporters are provided by the Omnibus Trade and Competitiveness Act of 1988. The 1994 National Export Strategy should significantly boost U.S. exports.

Although the government supports export growth in principle, many of its programs hinder export growth. For example, antitrust laws prevent U.S. companies from bidding jointly on major foreign projects.

Export markets provide a unique growth opportunity, but competition in these markets is fierce. Businesspersons, therefore, should adopt appropriate marketing strategies to conduct export trade profitably. They should be aware of attractive markets; specialize in the export of products, where American business has a lead; adopt private measures (in addition to those available from the U.S. government) to strengthen their competitive position in relation to foreign competitors; and develop an appropriate orientation for managing export business.

Procedurally, exporting requires locating customers, obtaining an export license from the federal government (a validated or a general license); collecting export documents (such as bill of lading, commercial invoice, export packing list, insurance certificate); packing and marketing; shipping abroad; and receiving payment. Various methods of receiving payment include cash in advance, open account, consignment sale, dollar draft, and letter of credit. Of these the latter two are most popular.

The provision of customs-privileged facilities, via the establishment of free-trade zones, is a recent trend that many countries have adopted to encourage and facilitate international trade. The U.S. government has approved 195 foreign-trade zones in different communities.

The age-old practice of barter is recurring as a new force in international trade, whereby goods are exchanged for goods without money swapping. Initiated by the former Soviet bloc, barter has spread to both the developing and industrialized nations. Currently, it accounts for 25–30 percent of world trade. Unaccustomed to noncash dealings, American companies have not been very enthusiastic about barter. Since it is likely to become more important, more and more U.S. corporations could be forced into barter agreements in the future.

Review Questions

1. Traditionally, what reasons explain America's meager interest in the export business?
2. Currently, why is it important for the U.S. to emphasize exports?
3. How does the Export-Import Bank help in enhancing U.S. exports?
4. Briefly, list the services of the U.S. Department of Commerce that assist exporters.
5. What is a foreign sales corporation? What role does it play in the context of U.S. exports?
6. What is a bill of lading? What functions does it serve?
7. Illustrate how a letter of credit helps in receiving payment for exports.
8. What is a free-trade zone? How does it help in increasing international trade?

9. Why is barter becoming important? What reasons account for U.S. companies' lack of interest in this activity?

Creative Questions

1. Currently Canada accounts for over one-fourth of U.S. exports. Potentially, in view of NAFTA, the importance of Canada should grow. Yet, Canada does not figure much in government export programs. By the same token, U.S. companies take the Canadian market for granted. To ensure that our largest export market is not jeopardized, what programs may the U.S. government develop to strengthen U.S. exports to Canada?
2. A mail-order sportswear company is interested in globalizing its business. It is planning to mail its monthly catalog to 18 to 30 year olds in select countries all over the world. What preparation does the company need to successfully take its business outside the U.S.?

Endnotes

1. Rob Norton, "Strategies for the New Export Boom," *Fortune*, August 22, 1994, p. 129.
2. "U.S. Trade Facts," *Business America*, April 1994, p. 40.
3. Richard S. Belous and Andrew W. Wyckoff, "Trade Has Job Winners Too," *Across the Board*, September 1987, pp. 53–55.
4. "Export Policy," *The Economist*, September 25, 1993, p. 34.
5. *See* Subhash C. Jain, *Export Strategy* (Westport, CT: Greenwood Press, Inc., 1989).
6. "Exports: This Show Has Legs," *Business Week*, September 19, 1994, p. 34.
7. *The Economist*, January 11, 1992, p. 60.
8. According to the Japanese Desk at the U.S. Department of Commerce, Japan has extended the laws applicable to Japanese CDs and records to those of foreign origin as well beginning 1993. However, it is uncertain if the rental stores comply with the new regulations.
9. "Report Cites Significant Foreign Barriers to U.S. Exports," *Business America*, April 9, 1990, p. 9.
10. Michael R. Sesit, "Foreign Nations Offer Cheap Export Loans, Rile American Firms," *The Wall Street Journal*, September 19, 1985, p. 1.
11. Kenneth D. Brody, "Ex-Im Bank Marks World Trade Week With Reorganization," *Business America*, April 1994, p. 7.
12. "Forming an FSC in the U.S. Virgin Islands," *Business America*, September 17, 1984, p. 3.
13. B. E. Lee and Donald R. Bloom, "Deficit Reduction Act of 1984: Change in Export Incentives," *Columbia Journal of World Business*, Summer 1985, pp. 63–67.
14. Rob Norton, "Clinton's High-Risk Trade Tactics," *Fortune*, May 16, 1994, p. 73. *Also see*: "Talking to Japan," *The Economist*, February 12, 1994, p. 16.
15. *See* Joanne Hvala, Anne C. Perry, and Jean J. Boddewyn, "General Electric Trading Company: The Sogoshosha That Wasn't," *Journal of Global Marketing*, Vol. 3, No. 4 (1990), pp. 7–32.
16. Michael R. Czinkota, "The Business Response to the Export Trading Company Act of 1982," *Columbia Journal of World Business*, Fall 1984, pp. 105–11. *Also see* Steve Weiner and Robert Johnson, "Export Trading Firms in U.S. are Failing to Fulfill Promise," *The Wall Street Journal*, May 24, 1984, p. 1.
17. "America's Frugal New Year," *The Economist*, December 19, 1987, pp. 13–14. *Also see* "The New Trade Act," *Business America*, October 24, 1988, pp. 2–6.
18. *See*: J. David Richardson, *Sizing Up U.S. Export Disincentives*. (Washington, D.C.: Institute for International Economics, 1993).
19. Patricia Gray, "Asian Computer Firms Invade the U.S. Market," *The Wall Street Journal*, January 10, 986, p. 1.
20. "Ready to Take on the World," *The Economist*, January 15, 1994, p. 65.
21. *See* David A Ricks, Jeffrey S. Arpan, Andy H. Barnett, and Brian Toyne, "Global Changes and Strategies for Increasing the International Competitiveness of the U.S. Man-Made

Fibers Industry," *Columbia Journal of World Business*, Summer 1986, pp. 75–84.

22. U.S. Department of Commerce, *Export Control Regulations* (Washington, D.C.: U.S. Government Printing Office, 1993).

23. T. Bettina Cornwell, "Foreign-Trade Zones in the United States: A Longitudinal Management Perspective," *International Marketing Review*, Vol. 6, No. 6 (1989), pp. 42–52.

24. Peter Wright, "International Partnerships and Foreign Trade Zones: Strategies for Small Firms," *The Collegiate Forum*, Spring 1984, p. 4.

25. Information for this section was obtained from Foreign Trade Zones Board, International Trade Administration, U.S. Department of Commerce, Washington, D.C. *Also see Business America*, January 27, 1992.

26. Ken Slocum, "Foreign-Trade Zones Aid Many Companies, But Stir Up Criticism," *The Wall Street Journal*, September 30, 1987, p. 1.

27. *See* Jean-Francois Hennart, "Some Empirical Dimensions of Countertrade," *Journal of International Business Studies*, Second Quarter 1990, pp. 243–70.

28. "Better Barter?" *Fortune*, February 18, 1985, p. 105.

29. Anant R. Negandi and Peter A. Donhowe, "It Is Time to Explore New Global Trade Options," *Journal of Business Strategy*, January–February, 1989, pp. 27–31.

30. Everett A. Martin and Thomas E. Ricks, "Countertrading Grows as Cash-Short Nations Seek Marketing Help," *The Wall Street Journal*, March 13, 1985, p 29.

31. Robert E. Weigand, "International Trade Without Money," *Harvard Business Review*, November–December 1977, p. 28.

32. "New Restrictions on World Trade," *Business Week*, July 19, 1982, p. 118.

33. Cyndee Miller, "Worldwide Money Crunch Fuels More International Barter," *Marketing News*, March 2, 1992, p. 5.

34. "Countertrade Increases Worldwide," *Development Forum*, March 1986, p. 16.

PART 5

Cases

Case 23: Schweppes Drinks — Export Light

Daryl MacGraw chuckled as he folded up the beverage-industry trade magazine he'd been reading and laid it to the side of the papers on his desk. He'd been amused to read, in one of the magazine articles, a reference to "the interesting battle now shaping up in Australia's market for low-alcohol beers." As New South Wales[1] (NSW) Sales Manager for Schweppes Drinks, and the person responsible for the marketing strategy for all Schweppes brands in Australia, MacGraw knew just how "interesting" the battle was. In fact, at this moment, in late November 1984, MacGraw needed to begin formulating a major decision for the continued marketing of Schweppes' low-alcohol beer, Export Light.

MacGraw's decision involved the possible repositioning of a relatively new product, Export Light, in a market—low-alcohol beers—that was also new and whose characteristics were not yet clear. Export Light had gained the major share of that market, but the product had been out such a short time that it was still difficult to say precisely whether its sales were improving or declining, in year-to-year or season-to-season terms. Although the seasonal nature of beer sales might be masking the overall trend, MacGraw thought his figures showed a softening in the NSW market for low-alcohol beer. At the same time, a new competing low-alcohol brand, produced by a prestigious Australian brewery and already popular in Western Australia, was entering the NSW market. This new entry, along with changing NSW state government regulations concerning the labelling and selling of low-alcohol beer, had prompted Schweppes to reconsider its entire direction for Export Light.

Cadbury-Schweppes Pty. Ltd. and Schweppes Drinks

Cadbury Schweppes Pty. Ltd. was a major force in the Australian soft drink industry, via its division Schweppes Drinks, which had several leading brands. Schweppes was the oldest soft drink company in the world, having been established for more than 200 years. Some of its major brands were Schweppes Mixers, Schweppes Lemonade, Schweppes Mineral Water, Solo (a lemon-flavored drink), and Tarino. Newer brands were Zapple (an apple juice drink with

---

[1] New South Wales, one of eight Australian states and territories, had an estimated population in 1981 of 5 million, out of a total Australian population of 15 million.

This case was written by William Van Doren under the supervision of Professor Paul W. Farris. This study was prepared as a basis for class discussion rather than to illustrate either an effective or ineffective handling of an administrative situation. Copyright © 1985 by the Darden Graduate Business School Foundation, Charlottesville, VA. Reprinted with permission.

a nutritional appeal) and Orchy fruit juice drinks. Also important to the business of Schweppes in Australia was its role as distributor of Pepsi-Cola and Diet Pepsi.

The Market for Low-Alcohol Beer

Low-alcohol beers—known in some forms as "near beer" and often, recently, as "non-alcoholic" beer—had been introduced commercially in Europe and North America at various times since as early as the 1890s. Essentially regular beer from which much of the alcohol was removed, the low-alcohol brews had been largely unsuccessful until methods were devised to remove the alcohol without destroying the beer's taste. Improved brewing and distilling processes for these beers, pioneered by Swiss breweries such as Hurlimann (brewer of the brand Birrell) in the mid 1960s, coincided with new stirrings of consumer interest in such a beverage in European and other markets.

In Australia, as elsewhere, interest in low-alcohol beers had been building since the late 1970s. On the consumer side, personal concerns about health and dietary effects of alcoholic-beverage consumption[2] and concerns about the dangers of drunk driving, along with a fashion for "lighter" drinks as part of an active lifestyle, had combined to create a potentially significant, although still largely undefined, demand for a beer beverage without the effects of alcohol. Of these factors, it appeared that the social pressures and law-enforcement crackdowns against drunk driving were probably the most compelling in changing beer-consumption habits. Drivers were being subjected to stricter enforcement of drunk-driving laws; stricter laws were being passed; movements were afoot to raise legal drinking ages; and law-enforcement officers in Australian states and localities were being authorized to stop drivers virtually at random and, if need be, conduct tests for the level of alcohol in the driver's blood. The government of New South Wales had spent millions of dollars in a publicity campaign against drunk driving.

In most areas of Australia the legal threshold of "driving under intoxication" was a blood alcohol level of .05 percent (.08 percent in Western Australia)—and a frequently cited selling point of low-alcohol beers was that one would have to drink an extremely large quantity, such as 10 to 20 bottles in an hour, to risk reaching this level.

To offer this as well as other perceived "low-alcohol" advantages, the beers so designated in various world markets were almost always under one percent alcohol, compared to the four percent of most regular lagers. Many low-alcohol beers were under .5 percent alcohol, the legal limit in several countries, such as West Germany and the United States, for beverages to be described as "non-alcoholic." The lower limit for an Australian "beer" was a source of current controversy. Export Light, the Schweppes entry, was .9 percent alcohol, as was its emerging chief competitor, Swan Special Light.

In addition to the concerns of consumers, the worries of brewers had also helped to spur development and marketing of the new low-alcohol products. Brewers in both the United States and Australia had been encountering slack demand for their major brands, as people turned to alternatives such as wine, soft drinks, bottled waters, and juices.[3,4] Referring to the U.S. market, one observer noted that other industries might have responded to the crisis by "pulling in their marketing horns" and concentrating on proven flagship brands, but the brewing industry's response had been to expand into new categories as well as new brands, including various "light" and "low-alcohol," as well as "superpremium," beers.

> ... One brewing executive calls it a "panic".... But analysts and brewing executives say the brewing industry may have no choice ... that it reflects the new rules under which the beer marketing game is being played. A shrinking market means brewers now must steal shares from competitors in each of the increasingly segmented price and product categories. As a result, product lines have been extended and marketing budgets have exploded.[5]

---

[2] Low-alcohol beers tended to range between 50 and 90 calories; many purchasers were thought to be women who were watching their weight or who were pregnant and concerned about effects of alcohol on the unborn.

[3] Scott Hume, "Brewers Enlist New Brands to Battle Problems," *Advertising Age* (January 31, 1985): 16.

[4] *National Times* (Perth?)¶, October 28, 1983.

[5] Hume, *Advertising Age*, p. 16.

In Australia, Swan Brewery, the second largest brewery in the country, acknowledged falling beer sales as one of its motivations for moving into the low-alcohol market.[6] And in both the U.S. and Australia, another reason cited for the low-alcohol strategy was to avoid alcoholic-beverage excise taxes and their squeeze on narrowing profit margins.

The consumer interest and the expanded brewery activity did not necessarily transplant, however, into bankable markets for low-alcohol beer. Widely considered to be unproved, "tiny," and "embryonic," at least in the U.S.,[7] the low-alcohol segment included a sizable and growing graveyard for brands that had ventured into the market—often without market research or a clear strategy—and then faded away.

Schweppes executives in Australia were mindful of the experience of Anheuser-Busch in the U.S. with its first low-alcohol entry, called Chelsea. The .5 percent alcohol product had sparked a furor when it was introduced, in 1978, with a pronounced "soft drink" image. The company withdrew its advertising campaign for Chelsea largely in response to complaints that the ads' appeal encouraged youngsters to start consuming an alcoholic drink.[8] Anheuser-Busch quickly came out with a new campaign touting Chelsea as "natural" and "not-so-sweet," in ads that the company said were "frankly, more adult."[9] But these actions were apparently not sufficient to dispel confusion about the product, or to locate its niche, and chelsea was abandoned after only a year. Many other low-alcohol entries had failed in various world markets. In New South Wales, of the eight low-alcohol beers being charted by Nielsen in May 1983, three had disappeared by August 1984. A more recent entry by Anheuser-Busch, L.A., was clearly positioned in the "beer" market.

---

[6] *National Times,* October 28, 1983.

[7] Carol Cain, "No-Alcohol entries Add Marketing Punch," *Advertising Age* (January 31, 1985): 28, 30.

[8] *Advertising Age,* October 30, 1978, p. 2.

[9] *Advertising Age,* December 18, 1978, p. 3.

The Development of Export Light

Shortly before Christmas of 1982, Daryl MacGraw and others in the management of Schweppes Drinks were discussing the effects of the government campaign against drunk driving. The idea of marketing a product which would permit one to drink without risk of intoxication led to the concept of Export Light. After approaching a local brewery and determining that a beverage could be produced which tasted like beer, but had less than 1 percent alcohol, the decision to launch Export Light was made. Less than three months later, Export Light was on the market. The only commitment to the producing brewery was to order at least one production run of 40,000 cans. Other than this, no projected sales or budget was undertaken. The packaging and advertising campaigns were accelerated to make the full introduction in time for summer. After looking at the margins available, Daryl decided that the product should be sold at prices which would yield margins much closer to those in the soft drink industry than the beer industry profit rates. This meant lower prices than existing premium beers. Subsequent market research tended to confirm the wisdom of this tactic.

Introduction of Export Light

Schweppes introduced its Export Light in outlets throughout New South Wales and Victoria by March 1983. Available in 375 ml cans and nonreturnable bottles—familiar types of containers in Australia for either soft drinks or beers—Export Light was presented not as a low-alcohol beer but as a "brewed soft drink" and, elsewhere on its label, a "traditional brewed malt beverage." NSW trade regulations prohibited use of the word "beer" if the product was less than 1.15 percent alcohol. The label might have been considered a hybrid of beer and soft drink motifs, with its grain logo, foaming glass, and unusual (for beer) large italic lettering. Any alcohol content was not at all prominent on the containers, although the relative lack of alcohol was very prominent in advertisements: "IT'S .05 FREE." This phrase did not mean, of course, an ".05" alcohol content—which in fact was .09 percent—but freedom from concern about reaching the .05 blood alcohol level. One advertisement managed to convey this connection to driving without words, simply by portraying a can, bottle, and foaming glass of Export Light next to a judge's gavel.

Along with samples of Export Light, Schweppes sent NSW retailers promotional material that stressed the new campaigns against drunk driving. For the customer, these would mean "1) He *must* watch what he drinks. 2) He can *no longer* enjoy a few beers with the boys. 3) He definitely *can't* drink and drive. 4) He *must* have an alternative." For the retailer licensed to sell alcoholic beverages, this would mean a drop in sales, increased emphasis on take-home trade (an important point for outlets which served drinks), loss of profits, and thus the need to "find an alternative." The alternative was Export Light—"brewed light, tastes right." Schweppes emphasized Export Light's "continuity of supply," and repeated near the end of the promotion: "very importantly, no supply problems." This was a reference to Export Light's local NSW origins and the well-established Schweppes distribution system, and was an implicit comparison to such competitors as Swans, which were located in Western Australia, and to low-alcohol beers with small and inconsistent volumes of sales, little or no advertising, and relatively inefficient distribution system.[10] The first attribute of Export Light featured in the material, however, was taste, followed by "the pack,"[11] "the price," and the "advertising/media" (the promotional packet emphasized "national advertising as well as local TV, radio and press").

Advertisements for Export Light in retailing trade publications strongly linked driving laws and the need to capture the sales volume of any alternative beverages; they portrayed a policeman and a Schweppes route driver, each with a glass of Export Light, over the motto, "The .05 drink that will keep your customers on the road—Make sure the traffic is through your door!" This advertisement emphasized Export Light's taste, but did not mention the word "beer." However, it did say, "Now you can enjoy a drink with a friend—anytime!"

The 1983–84 advertising strategy for Export Light was to "gain consumer interest and trial" by emphasizing the product's "great beer taste." To reach the actual target audience—"male beer drinkers who drive"—advertising would portray "male beer drinkers 25–35 years old." Positioning would be as "the great-tasting beer you drink when you're driving," with the message that "Export Light . . . has a full-brewed beer taste that is satisfying and thirst-quenching and won't put you over .05." The drink's image was to be "male, Australian, confident, brash."

Pricing and Distribution

Wholesale prices for a case of Export Light differed according to type of retail outlet and/or wholesale dealer. Retail outlets could be divided into two categories: grocery stores, including supermarkets, which could not legally sell regular beer, and licensed outlets, including pubs and liquor stores (bottle shops). Schweppes recorded sales of Export Light in the greater Sydney area in these two categories—Grocery and Licensed or Route Trade—and recorded all sales outside the Sydney area in a third category, "Franchise," since these were franchised to dealers and involved a different wholesale price. Roughly the same ratio of Grocery to Licensed (Route) Trade sales held true in the Franchise area as within the Sydney region.

Export Light was priced at approximately $1 less than regular beer per case of twenty-four 375 ml bottles or cans, as follows: to groceries/supermarkets, $11 wholesale ($13.99 retail); to route/licensed outlets,[12] $12 wholesale ($15.99 retail); to franchise wholesalers, $8 wholesale ($13.99 retail); a single can or bottle sold at retail for approximately 58¢ to 67¢.

Market Results

When introduced in early 1983, Export Light quickly captured 35 percent of the low-alcohol beer market, measured by sales, in the Sydney area, outselling

---

[10] * However, Swan did experience lower freight rates available from trucks returning (usually empty) from Western Australia to New South Wales. Daryl estimated that normal rates would be $.50 a case, but that Swan was paying only $.30–$.35 a case.

[11] Beer-like label and can.

[12] Both pubs and bottle shops (stores selling packaged whiskey, wine, and beer).

EXPORT LIGHT DISTRIBUTION OUTLET/CHANNELS

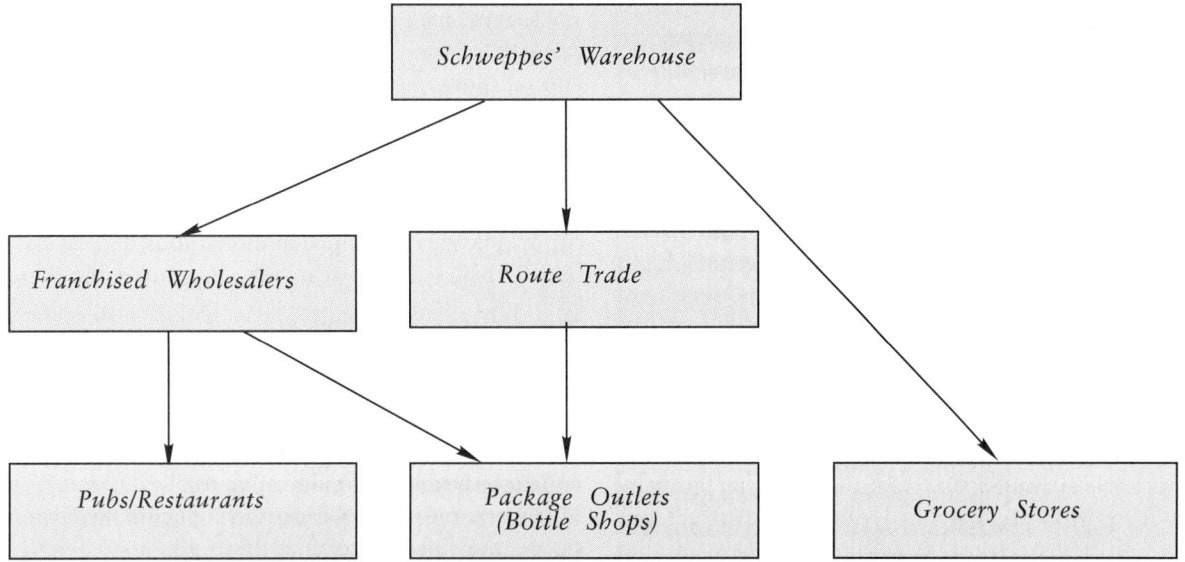

Note: Grocery outlets were supplied directly from Schweppes Drinks' own delivery vehicles, as was the Route Trade. Generally, franchised wholesalers *supplied* the smaller establishments and Schweppes Route trade served the larger licensed outlets directly. Schweppes' Route trade was also concentrated in the Sydney area.

already-established competitors Northern Light, A.S.A., and Birrell, among others. By year's end, Export Light had taken 60 percent of this market, and by mid-1984, 75 percent.

In November 1984, with eight weeks of sales still to be made and compiled to complete the year, Export Light had achieved sales for the year of 34,000 cases in grocery outlets, 85,000 cases in route trade, and 136,000 cases in the franchise category.

The total market for beer in Australia had been estimated at 645 million liters or 71 million cases. The dollar value of this market was $1.24 billion. Total beer advertising in Australia was estimated at 5 percent of the sales value. Twenty-two percent of the beer sold in bottles, 43 percent in cans, and the remaining 45 percent in bulk containers. The New South Wales market was approximately 33 percent of the total Australian beer market.

Advertising for Export Light

Advertising for Export Light during the year had involved 303 thirty-second television airings at an average cost (for broadcast time only, not including production) of $1,320, 218 thirty-second radio spots at $110, and a print media budget of $26,000. Figures for one month, August 1983, not long after the product introduction showed that Export Light's TV advertising was presenting three different thirty-second commercials a total of 89 times in NSW, during popular prime-time series and special sports events, as well as during movies and specials. There was also a full schedule of thirty-second radio spots, and print advertising. In that month, Export Light was selling approximately 3,900 cases through franchise dealers, 1,800 through grocery outlets, and 9,100 cases to route/licensed outlets.

Entry of Swan Special Light Lager

Swan Brewery, located in Perth on Australia's west coast, was a long-established brewer well known around the world for its lagers and beers. It was particularly dominant in the state of Western Australia, of which Perth was the capital and major city, and had recently gained additional fame as sponsor of the yacht that had finally wrested the America's Cup away from the United States. In July 1983, Swan launched its low-alcohol beer, Swan Special Light Lager, in Western Australia, with an alcohol content of .9 percent. The label design featured the Swan logo so widely associated with Swan's other beers and identified the product as a "lager" and "reduced alcohol beer." Suggested retail price was 53¢ for a 375 ml can. Soon after launch, in October–November of 1983, Swan Special Light was gaining publicity as being "too popular" in Western Australia; Swan executives were cheerfully admitting to the press that they were having to ration the new product among their outlets.

As Swan geared up in 1984 for entry into the far more populous NSW market, it again demonstrated a flair, whether intentional or not, for notoriety. The Labor-Party government of New South Wales had established the regulation requiring a beverage to be at least 1.15 percent alcohol before it could be called a "beer" or "lager." The regulation, if kept in place, would have forced Swan to change the name, labelling, and image—or the formula—of Special Light in order to compete in New South Wales.

However, readers of the July 8, 1984 Sydney *Sunday Telegraph* were treated to a full-page advertisement by a major wine and spirits merchant identifying this regulation with NSW's Labor Party leader, Wran, and proclaiming in boldface banner headlines: "WRAN'S BAN HYPOCRITICAL." Around the picture of a can of Swan Special Light Lager, the merchant declared that "You could drink 8 of these in an hour and stay out of gaol, BUT BY SELLING JUST ONE CAN—WE COULD GO TO GAOL!" The advertisement attacked the paradox of a state government working to cut down on drunk driving and yet keeping a low-alcohol product out of liquor stores, then boldly asserted: "We will break the law and sell this Beer at $12.99 for 2 doz. 375 ml Cans." The advertisement not only captured attention in itself but was the subject of news stories.

Daryl MacGraw and other Schweppes executives knew that Swan's image as a brewery was very strong and considered the impending Swan entry a serious threat to Export Light. At the end of July 1984, knowing that NSW regulations were about to be changed to allow the words "beer" and "lager" on low-alcohol brews, Schweppes marketing researchers conducted four focus-group discussions with Sydney beer drinkers. The researchers structured the focus group as follows:

1. Current Export Light drinkers (mainly drank Export Light but also consumed other light or regular beers); males 25 to 40 years old.
2. Current Light Beer drinkers (excluding Export Light Drinkers); males 25 to 40.
3. Current Light Beer drinkers (including Export Light drinkers); females 25 to 40.
4. Current Regular Beer drinkers (non-users of Light Beer); males 25 to 40.

The study included open and blind taste tests of Export Light and Swan Special Light, discussions, and several "semi-projective" exercises in which participants individually completed sentences and cartoon captions, filling in what they projected would be said about Export Light and Special Light, and who they projected would be saying it.

The Schweppes study found that awareness of both brands and of their advertising appeared to be high. "Both products," the researchers concluded, "have clearly established a presence in the marketplace."

Details of the Export Light TV commercial are well recalled:

Brewed soft drink

Drink 12 in an hour

Avoidance of D.U.I., the car keys

A very masculine pub setting

"It's that ad in the pub with all the blokes singing and you see the car keys."

"You can drink it all night is a line, I think."

"It's all to do with drink[13] driving."

"But why does it say soft drink? It does have some alcohol, doesn't it?"

The heart of the study concerned the consumers' perceptions of Export Light either as a beer or as a soft drink. Concerning the product's usage, the study found that Export Light was known to be promoted for its beer taste and to be for beer drinkers who, for reasons of driving or perhaps of health, did not want to drink a regular beer.

But with regard to technical product identity, there was a far more uncertain perception of Export Light. Some participants knew it to have some alcohol content and to be, therefore, a beer. "Others, however, regard it as being non-alcohol and/or are vert conscious of the (brewed) soft drink tag used in labelling and advertising. These people regard it as a soft drink in the technical sense."

The researchers found also that introduction of Swan Light Special Light into the picture complicated matters:

> As Swan is known to be a brewery (compare with Export Light's "unknown" origins), the labelling is strongly "beer" and quotes its alcohol content, and the advertising features "lager," there is no doubt that Special Light is a beer in composition, taste and positioning.

"Now that the two products are available," the study reported, "and one is known to be made by a recognized brewery, drinkers are encouraged to look at the side of the Export Light can to see who makes it." The only maker identification found on Export Light was the name "Tarax," a Schweppes soft drink subsidiary. Accordingly, the researchers found, expectations of Export Light's taste were low, and expectations of Special Light's taste were high, so that in "open" tasting, where the brands were identified, Special Light was preferred over Export Light. However, in blind tasting, "both products were judged to be fairly equal in appeal. In fact, they were regarded as very acceptable beers—probably light beer rather than regular beer, but very drinkable beers nevertheless."

The study concluded that the primary reason for drinking either Export Light or Swan Light was the beer taste, and the dominant reason for having one of these in order to satisfy the taste for beer related to driving. A second, "not uncommon" reason was related to diet or health, while a third category of reasons had to do with avoiding alcohol at lunch when returning to work, or when engaging in sports, or when socializing with beer drinkers. The latter reason was found to be "very strong" among women drinkers, who would drink Export Light while male company had their usual beers. (The focus-group study encountered "no single instance of people drinking Export Light for the avoidance of alcohol per se, i.e., anti-alcohol.")

Exhibit 1 excerpts portions of the focus-group report on results of the projective exercises concerning the two beers, and dealing with perceptions of women consumers, perceptions of price and labelling, and some conclusions about Swan's marketing strength. These results showed a tendency on the part of women, who might be more inclined to buy a "soft drink" rather than a "beer," to expect their husbands to buy the household's beers (from licensed outlets); a consensus that the main price competition was versus regular beer and not among the low-alcohol brands; and the conclusion that "Swan Light is about to carve a very significant niche for itself in the Sydney market."

Trends

As Export Light was about to enter into competition in its home territory with the new Swan Special Light, Daryl MacGraw wondered about the implications of recent sales-performance figures for Export Light. Although the short time that Export Light had been on the market, along with the seasonality of beer sales, made it difficult to draw a completely firm conclusion, it appeared that Export Light sales were softening, particularly in the route trade channel. Nielsen figures for the Sydney area showed that Export Light had gained a larger share of a market that was now smaller than it had been in January–February of 1984.

---

[13] In Australia, "drink drivers" is used synonymously with the U.S. expression "drunk drivers."

EXHIBIT I Selected Results of Focus Group Discussion Held with Sydney Beer Drinkers on July 30–31, 1984

The structure of the groups was follows:

1. Current Export Light Drinkers (mainly drink Export Light, but also consume other Light beers and/or regular beers), Males, aged 25–40 years.
2. Current Light Beer Drinkers (excluding Export Light Drinkers), Males aged 25–40 years.
3. Current Light Beer drinkers (including Export Light drinkers), Females aged 25–40 years.
4. Current Regular Beer drinkers (current non-users of Light Beer), Males aged 25–40 years.

As well as conventional discussion arrangements, several semi-projective techniques were included in the sessions (cartoons and sentence completion). Such exercises were completed on an individual basis. Both Export Light and Swan Special Light were tasted during the sessions.

AWARENESS OF EXPORT LIGHT AND SWAN SPECIAL LIGHT

Awareness of Export Light and Special Light and their advertising appeals appears to be particularly sound. Both products have clearly established a presence in the marketplace.

Details of the Export Light T.V. commercials are well recalled:

- Brewed soft drink
- Drink twelve in an hour
- Avoidance of D.U.I., the car keys
- A very masculine pub setting

> It's that ad in the pub with all the blokes singing and you see the car keys. You can drink it all night is a line I think. It's all to do with drink driving. But why does it say soft drink. It does have some alcohol doesn't it?

The Marsh brothers are also well recalled for Swan Special Light. The combination is a good one, the more gentlemanly Graham and "larrikiin" Rod. The elements most recalled are:

- Spending time with the family.
- The lager taste.
- That the product is really Swan lagers with the alcohol taken out.

> Graham and Rod Marsh. You'd expect them both to be drinkers especially Rod and its Swan. It's a beer, new light beer. Says something about spending time with the family. There was an ad in the paper today. It had car keys and was heavy on lager taste.

SWAN SPECIAL LIGHT OR EXPORT LIGHT?

There is a clear preference for the Swan product. This was evidenced from the discussion itself and also from the semi-projective tests which were used.

1. In a cartoon where a barman asked a drinker which he preferred and the drinker replied one way or the other, respondents tended to support or endorse the choice of the Swan product (e.g., "I'll have the same") while they tended to be critical of an Export Light choice (e.g., "Try the Swan instead").
2. In a sentence completion exercise where one product was said to be preferred over the other, most who had the "I'd prefer the Export Light" sentence opted to say the "I" was not them personally but a third

(Continued)

person and that such a preference was for taste or because the third person wanted a soft drink. Those who had the "I'd prefer the Swan Special Light" sentence said they were the "I" and gave reasons such as:

   a known respected brewer

   taste expectations

   actual taste

   can looked like a real beer

   wanted more than a soft drink

3. When asked to complete a sentence which stated one brand was selling better than the other, those who had Export Light as the better seller almost exclusively said it was because it had been around longer, that it had (currently) a bigger user base. Those who had the "Swan Special Light is selling better" sentence gave reasons such as:

   taste

   taste expectations

   the Swan brand

   the advertising

   the authentic beer label

WOMEN AND EXPORT LIGHT

Women drinkers of Export Light mainly drink it when socializing with (male) beer drinkers, either with a group of males or at home. An Export Light allows them to join in and not feel out of it.

Women seem not to buy beer or Export Light for themselves. Most reported that it was bought for them by men when they (the men) bought their beer at licensed outlets (bottle shops).

> I think I've bought it once at a supermarket. But my husband buys the drink, so I usually just tell him to get something for me. Yes, I just don't buy it. I suppose there's no reason why I shouldn't, but drinks are a man's job.

Export Light had been introduced successfully and had driven other low-alcohol beers to cover, leaving only Northern Light (11 percent of the Sydney sales volume in dollars), Birrell (6 percent), Amber (5 percent), and A.S.A. (5 percent) with measurable shares. But in view of the overall market trends, the changing results within Export Light's distribution channels, and the results of the focus-group study, MacGraw was not at all sure that Schweppes had achieved a success that could be sustained.

Final Considerations

Several questions occurred again to MacGraw as he put his papers aside and prepared to draft a new strategy for Export Light. He was struck by some of the contradictions in the situation, starting with the basic paradox of a "brewed soft drink" that was also a "low-alcohol beer." If Schweppes moved Export Light even closer to the supermarket/soft drink alternative, what if anything would that imply for their pricing strategy and what should it mean for their advertising budget? Or MacGraw could try to change

Export Light's position altogether, in which case he wondered where changes would best be made.

If the entire market was declining, why? Would it still decline when Swan Special Light was fully distributed in New South Wales? If Export Light was positioned as a brewed soft drink, would consumers remain confused about its identity, and could there conceivably even be a backlash against presenting a "beer" under the guise of a "soft drink? Already an executive at Swan had suggested to the press that Swan would have wanted to prevent the sale of Special Light in corner stores and unlicensed restaurants, since he said, "We don't want children to acquire a taste for beer on this product."[14]

The latter remark reinforced MacGraw's decision to eliminate the first of three radio ads slated for testing by the agency (see Exhibit 2).

Swan's wrangle with the NSW government had been resolved so that the brewery could indeed now market Special Light as "beer." At the same time, other legislative news might favor Export Light, as a brewed soft drink, since the NSW government had decided that *any* beverage labelled "beer," whatever its alcohol content, could not be sold in supermarkets. There were advantages, MacGraw thought, to being a "soft drink." On the other hand, selling beer to beer drinkers also had obvious advantages. In either case, MacGraw wondered if the product could justify further major media support. He paused and tried not to think for a moment, as he prepared to answer his own questions and develop a strategy for Export Light.

---

[14] *National Times*, October 28, 1983.

EXHIBIT 2 Export Light Radio Advertisements

EXPORT LIGHT—JIMMY

Sound of refrigerator opening, and a drink being poured.

Mother:	Jimmy, where did you get that beer from?
Jimmy:	Dad gave it to me Mum.
Mother:	Oh, did he now? Frank, what do you think you're doing giving Jimmy a beer? He's only six.
Dad:	(Laugh) Now, honey, it's all right, it's not really a beer, it's . . . it's . . . it's a . . .
Mother:	What do you mean it's not a beer? Look, Export Light. Sometimes I just don't know what gets into you.
Dad:	Now really, look honey it's all right, it's really a soft drink. Export Light. Look, see it looks like a beer and tastes like a beer, but it's only a soft drink.
Mother:	What?
Dad:	I bought a whole cart at the shopping market . . . like a drink?
Mother:	But it wasn't on the shopping list!
Voice Over:	Export Light. A great way for everyone to enjoy the taste of beer and keep their head.

(Continued)

EXPORT LIGHT—DRINKING CONTEST

Sounds of a cheering crowd and of a glass hitting a counter.

V1: 22!

V2: What on earth is he doing?

V1: Ah, it's this new Export Light. See, Jim reckons it takes thirty-six minis of this beer to put you over the point limit. And he's going to prove it.

Jim: Ah, 23.

V2: Export Light?

V1: Yeah. He reckons it's really just a soft drink. And you can buy it just about anywhere, even supermarkets. But, I tell you, it tastes just like beer.

V2: Export Light, eh? So you can still enjoy a beer and keep your license.

Jim: Ah, 24.

EXPORT LIGHT—DECLARING WAR

(Sound of ambulance siren under first statement)

DJ: Last Easter twenty-four people were killed on New South Wales roads. We are declaring war on twenty-four. (Music begins and continues under the rest of spot). 2WS and Export Light have joined together in an attempt to reduce the road toll this Easter.

So drink, Export Light it's the full-brewer taste you'll really enjoy, and with Export Light you can drink a dozen an hour and still stay under the limit.

Join us in declaring war on twenty-four this Easter.

And share a few cold Export Lights with your mates without a worry in the world.

Case 24: Ulker Biscuits, Inc.

On November 4, 1983, at 10:00 a.m. Ali Korkmaz, marketing director of Ulker Biscuits, Inc., was meeting with Hasan Beyaz, manager of the company's Export Department in Istanbul. They were discussing a report on the prosperous trading relationship that was developing between Turkey and a number of her Middle Eastern neighbors. Korkmaz thought Ulker could market its biscuit and candy products in these foreign markets; but, before he made decisions, he wanted information that could help the company identify the most lucrative markets in the Middle East for these products. He also wanted Beyaz to prepare a tentative operational plan for

This case is printed here with the permission of the author, Erdener Kaynak of Pennsylvania State University at Harrisburg.

penetrating these foreign markets. Korkmaz knew that the key to success lay in efficient distribution, which he thought could be achieved in one of two ways. On the one hand, he thought, adopting a distribution system in which the regional distributors were controlled by the company and worked for the long-term benefit of the company would be the best method to achieve success. In this system, the control mechanism would be achieved by the joint ownership of the newly built automated plant by the company and its regional distributors. Beyaz realized, however, that to persuade foreign regional distributors to enter a joint venture arrangement with the company would involve a great deal of development work. On the other hand, he also considered a diversification strategy by which the company would appoint regional distributors rapidly in a number of selected foreign markets without requiring their participation in a joint venture. This would lead to much faster market penetration although the risk of lower motivation on the part of foreign distributors could be a problem. Another advantage of this strategy would be that the company could be in the most lucrative foreign markets before some of its main competitors followed it to those markets. Korkmaz and Beyaz agreed to meet on November 18 to finalize the operational plan.

Now Beyaz wondered which one of the following market entry strategy options and operating decisions would maximize their potential for success:

a. Straight extension into the three countries (Libya, Saudi Arabia, and Cyprus) to which they had exported their products in the past.
b. Forming a joint venture with a local company in one of the key countries of the region.
c. Market penetration strategy using import agents and regional distributors.
d. Other strategies

Company Background

Ulker, a family-owned business, was founded in Istanbul (the largest Turkish city) in 1948. For a long time, biscuits and other candies had been prepared with human labor in flat trays. Over the last fifteen years, however, new machinery had been brought in that essentially eliminated the manual labor component of production. There were many reasons for this development. For example, technological progress had resulted in the reduction of production costs, the national income had risen, and population was growing rapidly, necessitating modern production methods. According to Korkmaz new ways were needed to meet the increasing demand in the industry. To meet this growing demand, Ulker had opened a second automated facility in Ankara, the capital of Turkey, three years ago. Shareholders in the new plant were a number of regional distributors to Ulker's owners.

These regional distributors owned the majority of the equity of the Ankara plant. Top management of the company had made this gesture to demonstrate its interest in its regional distributors and hence to help assure their aggressive promotion of Ulker products across the country.

Ulker's major competitors were other large biscuit manufacturers, Eti, Ari, and Besler, although there were smaller biscuit manufacturers in the market also. However, these did not present any imminent danger to Ulker's competitive position in its domestic market. At present, Ulker was the clear leader of the industry in terms of sales volume and profits earned. Ulker maintained a 60 percent market share, compared to Eti's and Ari's 30 percent, and 10 percent shared by Besler and the smaller manufacturers (mostly regional). Ulker had the capacity to produce between 300 to 340 tons of biscuit, biscuit combination, and candies per day. Ari and Eti could produce only 100 to 140 tons a day, which put them in second and third place in the country, respectively.

Ulker's Distribution System

The company owned approximately 30 trailers, 100 large trucks, 20 minibuses and 300 to 400 service trucks to fulfill its transportation needs.

The regional distributors could either use the company's transportation vehicles or their own means to deliver the goods to their warehouses in their respective regions. Some of the bigger regional distributors had their own transportation fleets; all of the regional distributors owned their own warehouses and used their own personnel. The selling functions these regional distributors performed were the backbone of the entire distribution function of the firm. The distribution channel structure for Ulker's products is depicted in Figure 1.

The regional distributors were Ulker's exclusive dealers under contract through special agreements. They were not allowed to handle any other biscuit and/or candy lines. In return, Ulker did not deal with wholesalers and retailers directly in any region except in Istanbul and Ankara where the company's two plants were located. Outside of these two cities Ulker had agreed not to perform any selling activities without the consent of the regional distributors. So far, Ulker had never tried to bypass this agreement. The regional distributors worked on a fixed commission, which was 5 percent of sales plus bonus. Generally, the company depended exclusively on its distributors to distribute its goods throughout the country. Without these distributors, Ulker could encounter distribution difficulties.

The regional distributors carried the goods to warehouses in their respective locations with their own fleets. The distributors as well as the company did not believe in stocking more than a day's demand for the goods. They operated and stocked according to orders from their respective wholesalers and retailers. The company produced according to the orders taken from its regional distributors on a daily basis. From the regional distribution centers, the goods were distributed through the channel as shown in Figure 2. The regional distributor used his own sales agents and his own service vehicles for the distribution in two ways:

1. Sales agents were assigned to specific sales areas in the region. These agents paid visits to their respective areas covering retail grocery stores and other outlets such as canteens. They solicited orders from different retail outlets as well as institutional buyers. Sales agents came back with a list of sales orders. The distributor then sent a truck-full of the combination of goods that had been ordered.
2. Another type of sales agents, similar to drop shipper with a truck-full of goods, covered their respective areas and sold Ulker products only. These sales agents did not accept orders from retailers and other outlets. They delivered goods to their customers at least once a week.

Both types of sales agents worked for a salary plus a bonus for sales above a specified quota. These sales agents were trained by the regional distributor and they reported only to him. In most cases, their training was accomplished in a very primitive way.

FIGURE 1

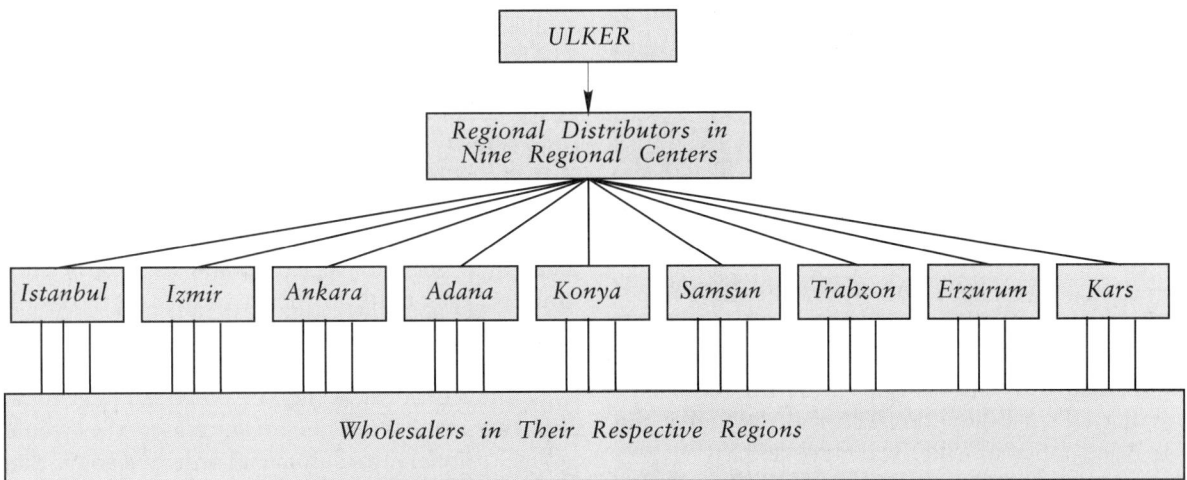

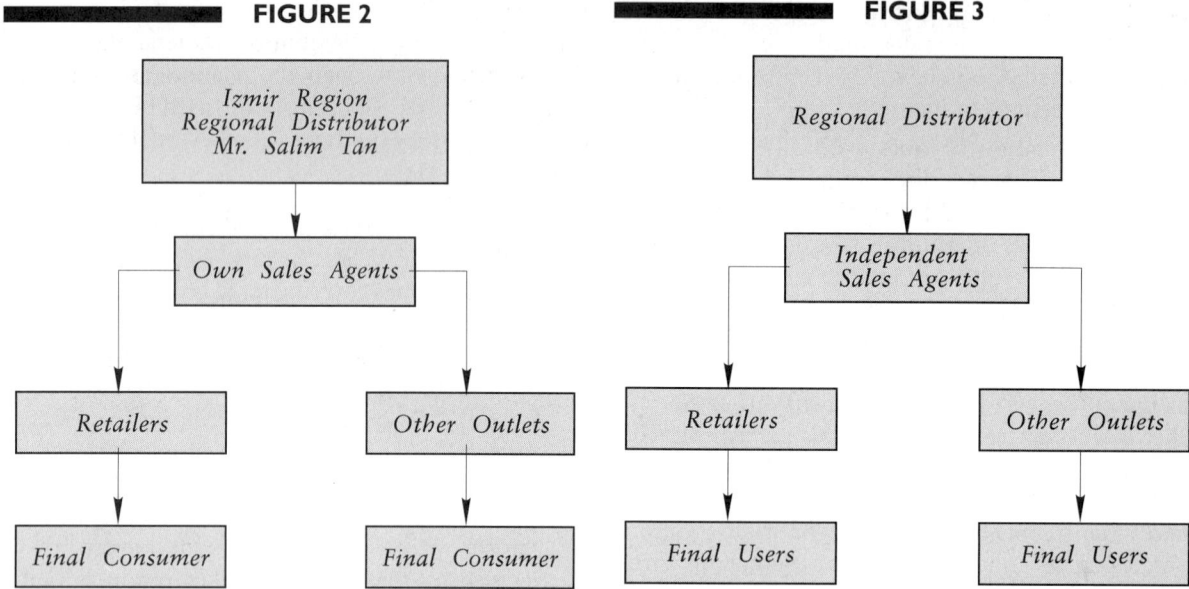

FIGURE 2

FIGURE 3

Salim Tan, regional distributor for Izmir, was quoted as saying, "A new sales agent will go around selling with an experienced salesman for about ten days; then he will be on his own. That is it. . . ."

As shown in Figure 3, there were also independent sales agents who owned their own service trucks and employed their own personnel to push Ulker's goods at their own expense. These independent sales agents sold only Ulker's goods for a commission from the regional distributor. In general, they were in competition with other companies' salesmen as well as with the regional distributors' own selling agents. Different types of independent agents competed with each other on the basis of service rendered and credit facilities provided. Ulker, as a company policy, promoted one price policy for everyone. The only exception to this rule was that the price could be different at the retail level where the company could not maintain standard prices because of severe price competition from other firms. At times, the regional distributors' own inspectors would go around asking retailers how much they paid for different Ulker products. That is how they controlled whether the one-price policy of Ulker was respected.

Another supplier in the distribution channel was the secondary vendor who bought only from the regional distributor, not directly from Ulker. These agencies like BAKSAN and AYKER would, in turn, sell to grocery stores, canteens, and buffets as they wished. They used their own service trucks and personnel to do the selling job. These agencies bought merchandise in larger quantities and thus obtained price discounts from the distributor. These agencies were not tied exclusively to Ulker, and therefore were not required to carry only Ulker's goods. As a result, they carried not only company products, but also other, often competing firms' products. They were completely independent agencies.

Regional distributors also dealt with wholesalers in their own regions (Figure 4). These wholesalers were more or less secondary vendors except that they were more passive participants. As such, they would order and stock a particular line of goods. They would sit back in their offices and wait for the retailers to come to them. These wholesalers were in competition with other wholesalers, Ulker's own sales agents, independent agents, or other sales agents in their own areas. When demand increased, they would call the regional distributors and order the goods that were needed. These wholesalers would get discounts

FIGURE 4

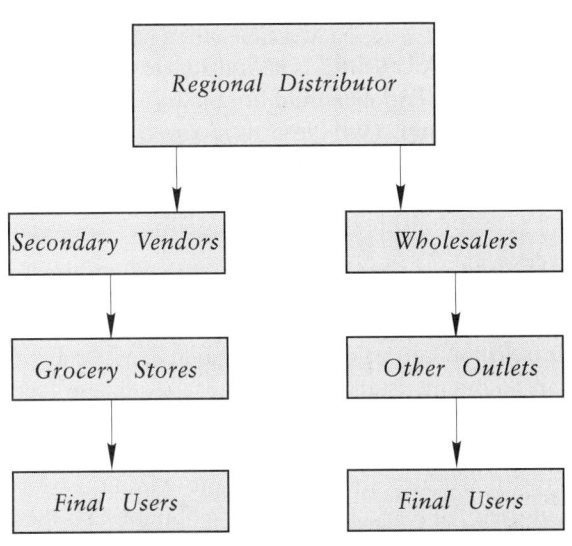

when they bought in large quantities and/or in cash. They could only charge what Ulker had suggested for each type of product. They were not allowed to charge the grocer more than the suggested wholesale selling price. This form of distribution is illustrated in Figure 5.

Before the regional distributors were established in Eastern Turkey, the wholesalers played an extremely important role in the distribution of Ulker products. The wholesalers were used to buying directly from the firm as the regional distributors do today except that they did not have the same exclusive deal with the company. Ulker used its own trucks to deliver goods to that part of the country. Ulker maintained regional wholesalers in Erzurum and Kars who could sell Ulker's goods to the wholesalers. Ulker, in most cases, was unwilling to deal directly with the wholesalers because of the agreement signed between Ulker and its regional distributors. Ulker used its own sales personnel for selling its products in Ankara and Istanbul. These salesmen worked for the company, and were trained and paid by the company. They did the same type of selling and distribution as did the regional distributors' own salesmen.

Foreign Market Survey

In a recent Economic Intelligence Unit Country Survey on Turkey it was stated that the country's dealings with the Arab world and Iran presented a much more stable picture. Trade links with countries such as Jordan and Egypt, which had been somewhat tenuous in the past, had now strengthened. The relationship with Iran was particularly intriguing as that country was about as much the antitheses (under its

FIGURE 5

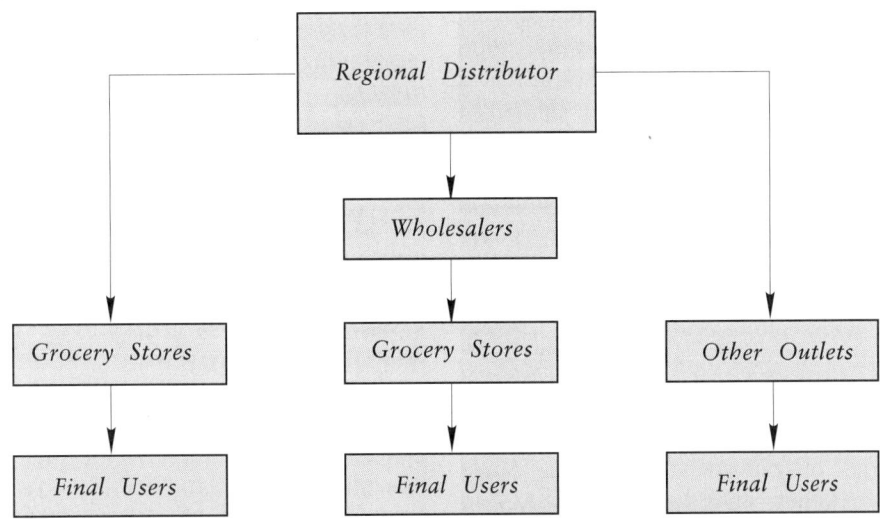

present leadership) of Kemalist secularism as it was possible to imagine. However, it now seemed that Iran was leaning heavily on Turkey for provisions and possibly some political mediation.

In 1983, Turkey continues to expand its trade with both Iran and Iraq, and seems to have become Iran's major supplier. On February 19, 1983, an economic treaty was signed in Ankara that included work on a new railway bridge over the Euphrates at Habur to make railway connections possible between Turkey and Iraq, bypassing Syria. Apart from construction services, Iraq is now a major purchaser of Turkish cement, sugar, foodstuffs, vehicles, and machinery. Two years ago, it replaced West Germany as Turkey's main trading partner. However, it was removed from that position in 1982 by Iran. Turkey also signed an important economic protocol with Iran on April 21, 1983. This was the latest in a series of economic negotiations with that country. According to Kemal Canturk, Turkey's Minister of Trade, Turkey and Iran could do as much as $2.5 billion in trade in 1983. The latest trade agreement covers products like foods, wheat, sugar, barley, dairy products, machinery, ploughs, tractors, chemicals, and 600,000 tons of iron and steel. Turkey is also to expand its infrastructural links and create some joint banking services with Iran. Similar to the proposal for a Turkish-Iraqui bank, Turkey has managed to get Iran to agree that Turkish trucks will have the sole right to transport Turkish exports to Iran and will also undertake freight tasks for Iran. The strength of the agreement, coming at a time when Iran is turning its back on the U.S.S.R., is politically very interesting; but, whether Turkey would be able to hang on to its advantage if the Gulf War were to end is another question. There must also be doubts as to whether present and future supply of foods stocks in Turkey will permit exports to stay indefinitely at the present levels.

In the last few years, Ulker has exported biscuits and candy products, on a piecemeal basis, to some of the selected countries of the Middle East from its warehouses in Istanbul (see Figure 6). These were unsolicited orders from foreign import agents. Because of the socioeconomic and cultural similarities between Turkey and most of the Middle eastern countries. Ali Korkmaz was of the opinion that there were vast market opportunities for Ulker's biscuit, candy, and combination products in these growth markets.

In reviewing all this relevant information, Korkmaz realized that he would have to prepare a very dynamic analysis of the marketing variables he and Beyaz would have to address during their next meeting. Since time was critical, he wondered what the order should be in setting down his lists of things to be done.

FIGURE 6

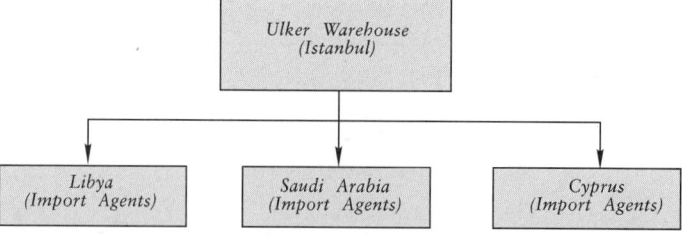

Case 25: TOYS "R" US

In 1989, Toys "R" Us entered into a joint venture with McDonald's Co. (Japan) Ltd. to establish a chain of toy stores in Japan. Pending completion of necessary legal formalities and approval from local authorities, Toys "R" Us soon needed to take some hard decisions to implement their long cherished goal—gaining a foothold in Japan by setting up 5 to 6 stores before the end of 1991. If this approval came through, for which the company was quite hopeful, Toys "R" Us would be the first American retailer to penetrate into the 5 billion dollar Japanese toy market.

Meanwhile, the top management of the international division had to resolve a number of issues. What were ideal location points in Japan for the kind of innovative format the company had introduced in the United States? How should the company adapt its retailing strategy to ensure a smooth transition into the diverse Japanese culture? Should it have its merchandise assortment as broad and deep in Japan as in the U.S. stores? Was there a need for changing the store layout? Most of all, the management was worried about the approach Toys "R" Us should take so that its stores would be able to operate with minimal friction and resentment among local retailers. The company was afraid its operations might cause disruption in the age-old channel structure that supports the Japanese toy industry. The company wanted to play a safe game and could not afford to create any ill-will among local toy retailers.

Toys "R" Us was founded by Charles P. Lazarus in 1948 when he opened a children's furniture store in his father's bicycle repair shop in Washington, D.C. Four years later, in 1952, he added toys and named the store as "Baby Furniture & Toy Supermarket." The store was still in its formative stage. Mr. Lazarus was trying to evolve a new business concept for retailing toys and games in the U.S. market. Influenced by the merchandising practices of discounters like E.J. Korvettes, he began thinking how to blend discounting with self-service and apply this blend in the business of toy retailing.

This case is printed here with the permission of the author, Madhar P. Kacker, visiting professor, Texas Graduate School of International Management.

Retail Philosophy:

The concept finally took a concrete shape in 1958 when Mr. Lazarus set up a 25,000 sq.ft. supermarket type store selling "everything for babies" under the name "Toys "R" Us." The store carried a broad and deep assortment and priced its merchandise 20 to 50 percent below the prices charged by a conventional toy store. Consumers were offered a wide selection of toys, games, furniture, children's wear, etc., at every day low prices, and enjoyed one-stop shopping. The retail philosophy of this company could be described in three key words: selection, stock, and price; in other words, ample inventory of the widest selection of merchandise offered at the best prices.

The stores that were established later had much larger area, about 45,000 sq.ft. of floor and storage space. A typical Toys "R" Us was located away from a busy shopping center on a free standing site and rarely staged a sale. All stores had an identical layout so that customers could find what they wanted without wasting time and with minimal sales help. The ambience created within a store was such that it encouraged a lot of impulse buying.

Lazarus thus came pretty close to his mission: a national toy discount supermarket where shopping is fun. He always said his ambition was to run the largest toy chain in the world. And he did it. Toys "R" Us is today the largest chain of toy stores in the world. To Wall Street analysts, it is considered to be the savviest trend spotter in the toy industry. As shown in Table A, the chain operated 404 toy stores in the U.S. and 74 in foreign countries in 1990 fiscal year. In addition, it operated 137 clothing stores under the name Kids "R" Us. The sales revenues and net income of this company amounted to $4788 million and $321 million respectively during 1990 fiscal (Table B). Its major competitors in the U.S. market, Lionel, Child World, and Kay-Bee, all had sales under one billion dollars.

TABLE A Expansion of Stores In Domestic and Overseas Markets

YEAR Fiscal	Number of Stores Domestic	Number of New Stores	Number of Stores in Foreign Countries	Number of Dist. Centers and Warehouses
1990	404	46	74	21*
1989	358	45	52	21
1988	313	42	37	20
1987	271	38	24	18
1986	233	35	13	14
1085	198	29	5	14
1984	169	25	0	13
1983	144	24	0	12
1982	120	19	0	11
1981	101	16	0	10

Source: Toys "R" Us, Annual Reports for various years
* 16 owned and 5 leased centers/warehouses

TABLE B Financial Performance of Toys "R" Us

YEAR Fiscal	Sales	Net Income	Earnings p/s	Market Share
1990	$4788	$321	1.64	33
1989	4000	268	1.36	25
1988	3137	204	1.04	20
1987	2445	152	0.78	n/a
1986	1976	120	0.62	15.5
1085	1702	111	0.58	14
1984	1320	92	0.48	12
1983	1042	64	0.35	11
1982	783	49	0.28	9
1981	597	29	0.17	7.5

Source: Financial Statements and Annual Reports, Toys "R" Us, Standard NYSE Stock Reports for various years)
N.A. = Not Available

Key Elements of Business Strategy:

Merchandising Strategy: The primary objective of the Toys "R" Us merchandising strategy was to develop a strong consumer recognition through mass media and to increase frequency of customer buying at the store.

A typical Toys "R" Us store featured name brand merchandise at everyday low prices. It carried an extensive selection of toys year round, so much so that the customer was assured of an exchange even after a busy Christmas season. Some merchandise categories made seasonal appeal in spring and summer by displaying items such as juvenile furniture, bicycles, gym sets, and family pools.

The fundamental strategy was to capitalize not only on birthdays and main holiday seasons, but on all special occasions like Valentine's Day, Easter, Halloween, and back-to-school.

The company employed a computer inventory system which constantly monitored current activity and inventory in each region and each store. The system enabled management to allocate the proper amount of merchandise to each store and keep each store adequately stocked at all times.

Other logistical support included 21 warehouse/distribution centers and a large fleet of tractors and trailers which were used to service its 358 domestic stores. Toys "R" Us employed a concept of regionally clustered expansion, which meant entry into a specified market area with a network of stores and warehouse/distribution center. This concept ensured that pre-existing distribution facilities were not overburdened by sporadic and unplanned start of new stores.

Toys "R" Us emphasized stable relationship with over 1,000 manufacturers/suppliers. For most of these suppliers and with respect to a large majority of inventory items, the company was the largest customer and was able to influence business decisions on product design, pricing, and promotion. It controlled nearly one-third of the $13 billion toy market in the U.S. To many small manufacturers, Toys "R" Us was an indispensable business support, as it provided them an assurance of business the year round through a unique blending of inventory planning, merchandising and promotional strategy.

Competition:

Toy retailing in the United States is dominated by four or five major specialty chains led by Toys "R" Us. Other large retailers included The Lionel Corporation, Child World, Kay-Bee Toy & Hobby Shops (Melville Corporation), and Greenman Bros. The U.S. toy market also had a number of smaller chains such as F.A.O. Schwartz, The Enchanted Village, Child's Play, Fun 'N Games, Toys & Treasures International. The Lionel Corporation operated under the names Lionel Kiddie City, Lionel Playworld, and Lionel Toy Warehouse. In addition, a significant business was done by toy departments located within traditional department stores, discount stores, and drug stores all over the country.

It is estimated that approximately 57,000 retail outlets sold toys and games in the United States. In recent years, however, toy sales in department stores registered a steady decline whereas sales in specialty toy stores and discount stores witnessed a remarkable increase (see Table C).

TABLE C Market Share

Category of Retail Outlet	% of Total Sales				
	1984	1985	1986	1987	1988
Discount Store	31	31	33	35	36
Toy Store	22	24	27	30	30
Department Store	15	15	12	9	9
Catalog Showroom	7	7	6	5	5
Variety Store	5	4	4	3	3
Others	20	19	18	18	17
	100	100	100	100	100

Source: Toy Market Index, NPD Group as Published in Playthings, January 1990

The 1989 data for leading specialty chains are given below:

	Number of Stores	Net Sales (Million $)
Toys "R" Us and Kids "R" Us	522	4,000.2
Child World	177	830.3
Lionel	84	408.9
Kay-Bee	727	n/a

Source: Fairchild's Financial Manual of Retail Stores, 1989–1990
N.A.= Not Available

Toys "R" Us, Child World, and Lionel are major competitors in toy retailing in the U.S. All of them have adopted almost a similar strategy of locating stores in proximity to major shopping centers in free-standing buildings along important highways. Kay-Bee shops, Greenman Bros., and other small store chains, on the other hand, prefer locations in shopping malls. The merchandising strategy of F.A.O. Schwartz has emphasized top of the line specialty toys in the premium price range. Lionel and Kay-Bee are smaller retail outlets which offer a narrower range of selection at relatively higher prices. Enchanted Village seems to have a different concept. This small chain sells kits, wooden trains, and prize-winning children's books and puzzles. For a modest hourly fee, it provides baby-sitting service, child-rearing classes for adults, and computer classes.

The Industry Profile:

The domestic toy industry in the U.S. has not been showing encouraging growth in recent years, due presumably to several factors: rising labor costs, modest growth in the child population between the ages of 1 and 14 (see Table D), and a strong import competition (see Table E). Dollar value of shipments of dolls, toys, and games by domestic manufacturers to retailers stood at $3.7 billion in 1989, compared to $3.78 billion in 1988 and $3.71 billion in 1987.

None of the new product entries in recent years was able to create the craze that Cabbage Patch dolls did in the mid-1980s. Electronic video games were the top selling toy in 1989, having found their way into one-fourth of 90 million households in the U.S. According to data published by the U.S. Department of Commerce, total retail sales of electronic games reached $3.5 billion by the end of 1989. Nintendo has been the top selling toy for two seasons in a row. With an annual sales of $1.7 billion in 1988, this company captured between 70 percent and 80 percent of the U.S. video game market.

Imports, especially from the Far East, have gone a long way toward meeting the domestic demand of toys, dolls, and games in the U.S. Leading supplier countries are Japan, China, and Taiwan. In addition, many domestic toy manufacturers have also moved to off-shore production sites in Hong Kong, South Korea, and Taiwan to take advantage of lower labor costs. The share of imports in total retail sales has thus increased significantly. Value of imports of all categories of toys rose from $4.04 million in 1987 to $4.67 million in 1988, a 15.5 percent increase. Imports of games and toys in particular registered a more significant rise. Their value rose from $2.57 million in 1987 to $3.45 million in 1988 and $4.83 million in 1989, about 88 percent increase in two years.

Expansion Within the U.S.:

Toys "R" Us had expanded into four stores within the Washington, D.C. area by 1966 with a combined annual sales of $12 million. At that time, Lazarus decided to sell the chain to Interstate Stores with a view to enhancing its capital base. He remained with the company and continued to manage the operations of the toy division, which had grown into 47 stores with an annual turnover of $130 million by 1973.

Faced with a severe financial problem, Interstate Stores filed for bankruptcy in 1974. In 1978, the reorganization phase was over and the new company emerged under the leadership of Charles Lazarus. The chain had grown into 72 stores by that year. It expanded steadfastly since 1979, growing at the rate of 30 stores per year. As of January 1990, the company had a network of 404 toy stores in 41 states and

TABLE D U.S. Resident Population by Age (in millions)

Year	Under 5 years	5–9 years	10–14 years
1970	17.1	19.9	20.8
1980	16.3	16.7	18.2
1985	18.0	16.8	17.1
1986	18.1	17.2	16.5
1987	18.2	17.6	16.4
1988	18.4	18.0	16.6
Projections	Under 5 years		5–17 years
1990	18.4		45.6
2000	16.8		48.8

Source: Statistical Abstract of the United States 1990, page 18

TABLE E Imports of Toys, Games and Sporting Goods into United States

1980–1988 (In million dollars)			
1980	$1836	1985	$4075
1981	2075	1986	4520
1982	2698	1987	5772
1983	2412	1988	6492
1984	3189		

(Source: Statistical Abstract of the United States 1990, General Imports by Selected Commodity Groups, page 814)

Puerto Rico and 74 stores internationally, in addition to 112 children's clothing stores under the name Kids "R" Us. The company ranked 9th on the list of big builders in retail industry with an estimated investment of $325 million on capital expenditure in 1989.

In 1989, the company had nearly gained a 25 percent market share in the $13 billion U.S. retail toy market. It is predicted that its market share will rise to 40 percent by 1997.

The International Division:

The international division was created in 1983 with Joseph Baczko as its president. The company took this important decision in order to sustain and enhance growth when the domestic market was experiencing a sluggish population growth, especially in the lower level age groups.

In 1984, Toys "R" Us set up four stores in Canada and one in Singapore. Three more stores were added in 1985 in Canada and entry was made in the United Kingdom with five more stores that same year. The pace has since been maintained. Since 1985, 61 more stores have been brought into operation covering many new countries such as Germany, France, Italy, Hong Kong, Malaysia, and Taiwan. During the fiscal year 1989–1990, the company opened 22 new stores in overseas markets, and planned to enter Italy, Spain, and Japan in 1991 and Australia and the Benelux countries in 1992. It had seven regional subsidiaries based in the U.K., Canada, Singapore, West Germany, Hong Kong, France, Taiwan, and Italy. Table F shows the financial performance of foreign operators of the company.

The overseas stores are very similar in size and layout to their counterparts in the U.S. (see Figure 1). They are usually in freestanding warehouse-like buildings, filled with a wide range of merchandise offered at consistently low prices. All stores carry 18,000 to 20,000 items on an average. Adaptations are made to local preferences, though 80 percent of the merchandise sold overseas is the same as sold in U.S. stores. As in domestic stores, the infant care items are discounted heavily in foreign stores to generate traffic of first-time buyers. Once attained, the loyalty of these customers continues to remain a good source of future business throughout the toy purchasing age of children.

Decision to Enter Japan:

The company had considered Japan as a potential market back in 1984 when it was formulating its strategy of international expansion. The toy market in Japan was believed to have a potential of $4.8 billion (see Table G).

In late 1989, the top management in the international division took the decision to enter into Japan and set up five large warehouse-type outlets by 1991, with a long-term goal of at least 100 Japanese outlets. The company decided to have a joint venture with MacDonald's Co.(Japan) Ltd. to implement this expansion program in Japan.

TABLE F Financial Performance of Foreign Operations of Toys "R" Us (Million)

	1990	1989	1988	1987
Sales	$533	$368	$210	$101
Operating Profit	48	27.3	7.6	4.1
Op. Profit as a % of Sales	9	7.4	3.6	4.1

Source: Toys "R" Us, Annual reports

TABLE G Expenditure on Toys per Child in Selected Countries

(Based on Population under 14 years)	
Germany	$252
Italy	160
U.S.A.	244
Entire Europe	179
Netherlands	160
Spain	134
Japan	500

* Based on 1985 Sales
Source: Frost & Sullivan extracted from Playthings, June, 1990, p. 29

FIGURE 1 Store Layout

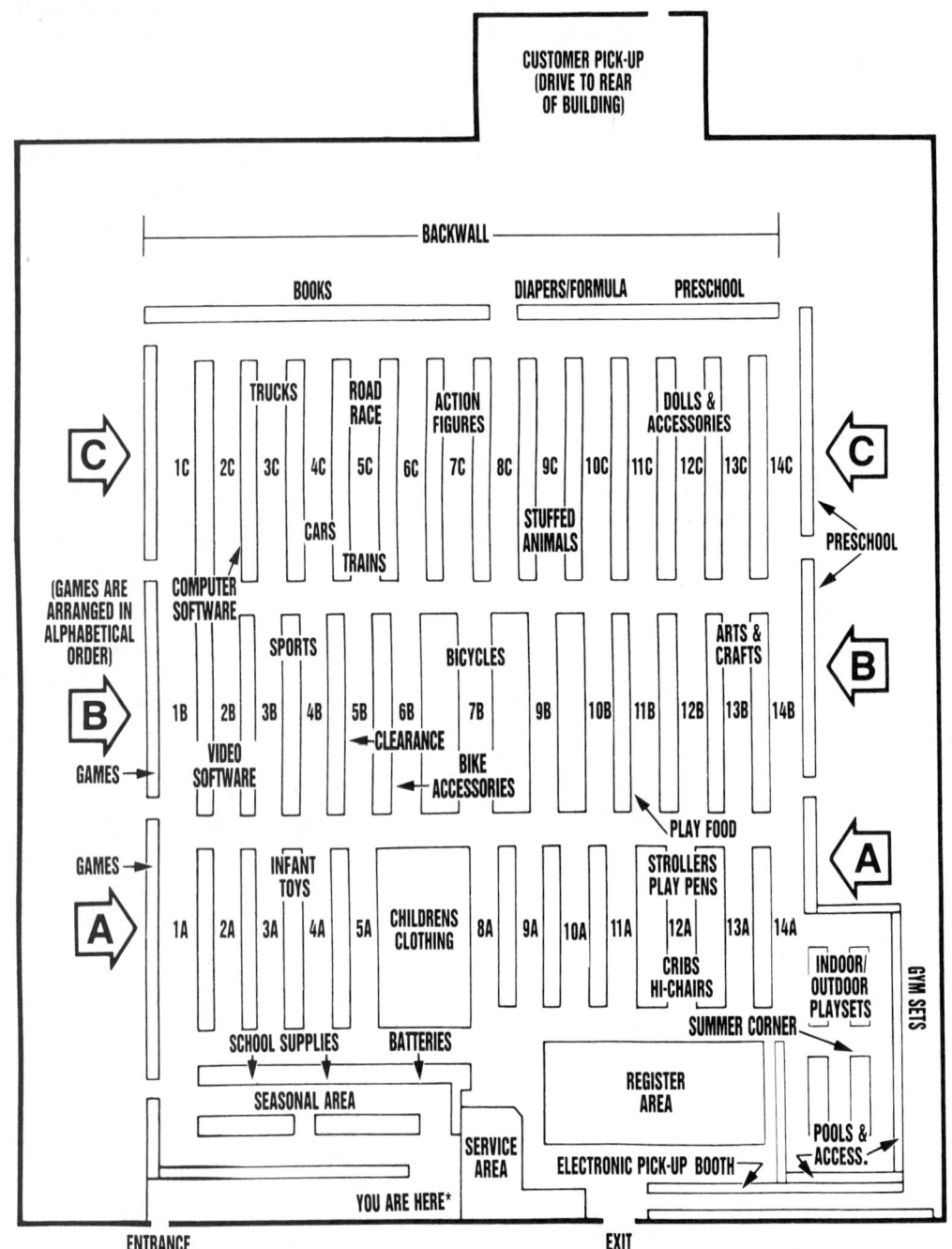

A major hurdle in the way of Japanese expansion was the large-scale retail law in Japan which required large retailers proposing to open stores with a selling area of more than 500 sq. meters to apply for a permit. The process of granting this permit by local authorities was very time consuming, as it required the approval from local merchants who could always veto a grant decision. In the past, opposition from local merchants had blocked the entry of a large retailer for as long as 10 years. Table H furnishes information on retail trade in Japan.

Toys "R" Us, however, was very optimistic that it would ultimately get the approval of local authorities. One of the sites chosen in Japan was Niigata City, 200 miles north of Tokyo, where the company was planning to open a 54,000 sq.ft. store. One reason for the company's optimism was the progress made at the structural impediment initiative (SII) talks in Washington, D.C. In the course of these talks held in April, 1990, Prime Minister Kaifu promised to relax Japanese laws against big retail stores. The Ministry of International Trade and Industry in Japan (MITI) had agreed that it would set a limit of two years within which the local authorities had to act on a permit application from a large retail store.

Such environmental restraints are not unique to the Japanese market. The company had to encounter similar restraints when it entered West Germany in 1986. There, it had to deal with zoning requirements, the power of labor unions, and a negative rate of population growth. In Germany and even other European countries, employees' work week is restricted to a limited number of hours (38.5 hours in Germany), stores have to close early in the afternoon every Saturday, and no Sunday opening is permitted. The population of West Germany was around sixty million when the company entered this market in 1986, but it was heading toward a decline and was expected to fall to forty-eight million by the year 2030.

On the other hand, there were some positive signs of growth in the European environment. The 1992 program of European integration was one aspect that made the entry of Toys "R" Us into Europe a very worthwhile move. And who could have forecast even one year back that the two German nations would integrate and merge as one nation politically and economically, heralding an era of fresh business opportunity in this region?

TABLE H Retail Trade In Japan (Sporting goods, toys, amusement goods & musicals)

	1982	1985
Number of Stores	46,708	43,138
Persons engaged (000)	138	132
Value of annual sales (Billion yen)	1936	2051
Valur of Commodity stocks (Billion Yen)	453	465

Source: Research & Statistics Dept., Ministry of International Trade and Industry

Case 26: The Kellogg Company

In 1990, Peter A. Horekens, marketing director for Kellogg Company, was faced with the problem of developing a market for ready-to-eat cereals in the Latin American region. Although Kellogg had no competition in the ready-to-eat cereal market in this region, they also had no market. Latin Americans did not eat breakfast as the Americans did. This problem was especially prominent in Brazil. To create a market and increase sales in this region, Horekens had to create a nutritious breakfast habit among the Brazilians.

Company Background

Kellogg Company, headquartered in Battlecreek, Michigan, was founded in 1906 by W.K. Kellogg to "help people help themselves." This focus had remained intact throughout the company's history. The company continued to operate successfully with sales in 1990 amounting to $3,215 million.

Scope of Business

The Kellogg Company manufactured and marketed a wide variety of convenience foods with ready-to-eat cereals topping the list. Other products included frozen and fresh baked pies, toaster pastries, soups, soup bases, seasonings, tea, frozen waffles, dessert mixes, and snack items. The company's products were manufactured in eighteen countries and distributed in 130 countries.

Kellogg subsidiaries included Mrs. Smith's Frozen Foods, Inc., Salada Company, and Fearn International Inc. Mrs. Smith's was a leader in the frozen food industry, and the product line included pies, desserts, entrees, and frozen waffles sold under the Eggo brand. Salada Company sold tea bags and other tea products. Fearn International produced quality food service items marketed under the brand name LeGout. The company also produced products for school service and health care markets. In addition, efforts had been concentrated on expansion into delicatessens and restaurant chains. Kellogg engaged in a variety of supporting activities, including grain milling and carton printing.

Distribution of products was handled through brokers and distributors, as well as through its own sales force. Jobbers—independent and chain store warehouses—made Kellogg products available in retail stores, restaurants, and feeding institutions worldwide. Ready-to-eat cereals were sold principally to the grocery trade for sale to consumers.

Kellogg faced intense competition in each of the consumer food areas in which it was engaged from manufacturers who offered products similar in nature or a variety of alternatives.

Kellogg research and development objectives were designed to generate new and improved products, processing methods, and packaging to keep ahead of the competition. Research and development budgeting allowed for this stress on innovation and new product development. Existing and new products were supported through increased budgets for advertising and promotion. Budgets were also increased to modernize and expand production facilities to meet the increased demand for Kellogg products and to keep costs down.

Kellogg had spent heavily and continued to increase its spending to stay at the top of its primary market—the ready-to-eat cereal market. But competition in the domestic market had led Kellogg to seek new markets. Among these, Latin America was at the top of the list. The primary market within Latin America was Brazil.

International Market

In 1990, Kellogg International operations accounted for 42 percent of Kellogg Company's sales of more than $3 billion. International operations were divided into four segments: Canada, the United Kingdom and Europe, Afro-Australasia, and Latin America. Among the products sold overseas were ready-to-eat cereals, frozen pizzas, drink products, entrees, snacks, desserts, and pharmaceuticals. The ready-to-eat cereal sales made up the majority of international sales.

In most of these foreign markets, Kellogg controlled more than half of the ready-to-eat cereal market. The United Kingdom was by far Kellogg's largest market. Internationally, sales in the ready-to-eat cereal market continued to increase, although in the past few years the competition also had increased. But in Latin America, consumption of ready-to-eat cereals was negligible.

The Latin American Market

The Latin American market, mainly Mexico and Brazil, showed great potential as a Kellogg's ready-to-eat cereal market. The demographics fit the ready-to-eat market; the only problem was Latin Americans did not eat the traditional American-style breakfast.

The Latin American market included a growing number of families with children. The population mix was becoming younger. The developing economy enabled consumers to spend more of their income on food. Kellogg wanted to increase sales in this Latin American region, especially Brazil, but consumers had turned their backs on the American-style breakfast. How was Kellogg to create a nutritious breakfast habit among the Brazilians?

The company asked J. Walter Thompson, Kellogg's advertising agency, to help instill the breakfast habit in Brazil. According to Horekens, "In general, Brazilians do what people in *novelas* do." *Novelas* are Brazilian soap operas. J. Walter Thompson tried to advertize Kellogg ready-to-eat cereal and instill the breakfast habit by advertising within a soap opera. The first experience of advertising within a soap opera failed; the advertisement portrayed a boy eating the cereal out of a package.

Kellogg wanted to teach the Brazilians how to eat a complete, nutritious breakfast, not just Kellogg's cereal. The commercial did not work because it made Kellogg ready-to-eat cereal seem more like a snack than a major part of a complete breakfast. Thus, they needed the cereal to be eaten in a bowl with milk along with other foods to make a complete breakfast.

The company believed that the growing population in this region would reinforce the importance of grains as a basic food source. The 1990 population in Brazil was 165 million, which made it the sixth most populated country in the world. The population was estimated to grow to 210 million by 2000. Within this population growth was an increase in the number of women of childbearing age, which further supported Kellogg's potential for a successful cereal market. The structure of the population in Brazil in 1990 was:

- Thirty-seven percent of population under age 15
- Forty-eight percent of population under age 20
- Twelve percent of population over age 50
- Six percent of population over age 60

These figures showed that the population of Brazil better fit the market for a ready-to-eat cereal, with the increasing number of children and elderly people as the two largest cereal-consuming segments.

The "cult of the family" continued to be the most important institution in the formation of the Brazilian society. This cultural ideal was reflected in the ways they conceptualized and evaluated the range of personal and social relations. This seemed to be the way Kellogg would have to demonstrate the importance of a nutritional breakfast—by playing up the family and its importance.

Through the use of the *novelas*, Kellogg made a second attempt to teach the Brazilians the importance of breakfast. Most Brazilian families watched these soap operas, composed mostly of family scenes. In their commercials, Kellogg opted for scenes that showed the family at the breakfast table. One member of the family, usually the father, took the cereal box, poured the cereal, and then added milk. This scene represented a complete "Kellogg" breakfast in a way that Brazilians could relate to. The advertisement focused first on nutrition, then on flavor, and finally on ease of preparation. As a result of this campaign, sales in Brazil increased. Kellogg controlled 99.5 percent of the ready-to-eat cereal market in Brazil; however, per capita cereal consumption was less than one ounce or several spoonfuls per Brazilian annually, even after advertising.

Although Kellogg controlled the market, there was not much of a market to control. Brazilians had begun to eat breakfast, but Horekens was not sure whether sales would continue to increase.

How can Kellogg further convince the Brazilians of the importance of eating a nutritious breakfast in order to establish a long-term market?

Case 27: Avon Products, S.A. de C.V.

In 1990, Philip Evans, marketing manager in the international division of Avon Products, Inc., met with his colleagues to consider long-range marketing strategy for Latin America, especially Mexico. A decidedly profitable market, Mexico and the rest of Latin America accounted for almost 15 percent of Avon's worldwide sales. The problem confronting Avon executives was how to sustain the growth rate it had generated in the past.

Company Background

Avon Products, Inc., a diversified company, included the Avon Division, Mallinckrodt, Inc., Tiffany & Co., and a direct-mail division.

The Avon division was the world's largest direct-selling business. Its two principal industry segments were the manufacture and sale of cosmetics, fragrances, and toiletries; and of fashion jewelry and accessories. Avon Products, Inc., sales in 1989 amounted to $4 billion, of which over 42 percent were from operations outside the United States. Operating profits from international business in 1989 amounted to about 53 percent. Net sales in 1989 from Latin American operations were $545.6 million. Of the total corporate-wide operating profits of $600 million in 1989, $81.6 million were generated in Latin America.

Avon's international division was formed in 1949 when the company expanded the distribution and salesforce to Canada. By late 1954, the company expanded its operations to include Puerto Rico and Venezuela. During the ensuing years, international operations flew at a rapid pace, first to Europe and Latin America and then to the far East and Africa.

In Mexico, the company had a wholly owned subsidiary under the name of Avon Products, S.A. de C.V., headquartered in Mexico City. The Mexican subsidiary had three manufacturing laboratories and five distribution branches covering Mexico and the rest of Latin America.

Avon had captured its largest international market share in Latin America, where competition had been less fierce than in other markets. In Mexico, the results had been truly phenomenal, largely because Latin hospitality blended well with the Avon approach. The Latins were much more apt to invite Avon representatives into their homes. Whereas U.S. representatives, on an average in each two-week campaign, won orders from fewer than thirty customers, Mexican representatives, in each three-week campaign, averaged fifty-four customers.

Products

The two principal businesses of Avon Products, S.A. de C.V., were the manufacture and sale of (1) cosmetics, fragrances, and toiletries, and (2) fashion jewelry and accessories. The products were sold directly to customers in their homes by Avon representatives, following the method used since Avon's founding in the United States in 1886. The company sold more than 650 products. Although the range of products sold in foreign countries was not as extensive as that sold in the United States, most of the products were substantially the same as those marketed domestically. The products marketed in Mexico were categorized as follows:

Fragrance and bath products for women. These products consisted of perfumes, colognes, sachets, fragrance candles, pomanders, lotions, soaps, and powders. They were marketed in a number of fragrance lines, each based on a particular scent and packaging theme.

Makeup, skin-care, and other products for women. These products included makeup items such as lipsticks, mascaras, and eye shadows; skin-care products; nail and hand-care items; and hair-care products such as shampoos, conditioners, and brushes.

Men's toiletry products. Men's toiletries included colognes, after-shave lotions, shaving creams, talc, and soaps marketed in a number of fragrance lines, each based on a particular scent and packaging theme.

Daily need, children's and teen products. Daily need items included deodorants, antiperspirants, oral hygiene products, and household products such as room sprays. Children's and teen products included fragrance products and novelty products for young children.

Fashion jewelry and accessories. The line included rings, earrings, bracelets, and necklaces for women, men, and children. Women's items accounted for most of the sales.

In Mexico, Avon cosmetics were affordable, medium-priced products that appealed to both women at home and the small number of women who worked outside the home.

Avon packaging consisted of glass and chrome bottles and ceramic jars tailored to meet the tastes of its primary market, the vast middle class.

Product Distribution

In Mexico and elsewhere in Latin America, Avon's cosmetics, fragrances, and toiletries were sold by a sizeable salesforce. The salesforce consisted of women known as representatives de Avon (Avon representatives). They served as independent dealers, and not as agents or employees of the company. They purchased products directly from the company and sold them directly to the residents of their communities.

With some exceptions in rural areas, each representative was responsible for one territory. Unlike U.S. sales territories, in Mexico there were 200 homes in an average territory. But like in the United States, Mexican representatives called on homes in their territories, selling primarily through the use of brochures highlighting new products and specially priced items for each three-week sales campaign. Product samples, demonstration products, makeup color charts, and complete sales catalogs were also used. The representatives forwarded orders every three weeks to a distribution center located just outside Mexico City. Each representative's orders were processed and assembled by Avon and delivered to her home using local delivery services.

Over the long term, Avon S.A. had planned for a 10 percent growth in its salesforce—a key determinant in keeping earnings growing at a healthy pace. The company's main method of building a salesforce was to shrink the size of sales territories once an area was covered. This tactic served to intensify sales efforts.

Avon's long-term prospect for recruiting representatives looked particularly bright in Mexico, since neighborhoods were receptive to door-to-door selling. Both personal contacts and local advertising were used to recruit representatives.

As a local manager noted:

> Avon's coverage in Mexico was excellent. We were in every small town and village, as well as in the big cities. Sixty-five percent of Mexico's population is under the age of 25. We are a very young people and a very young country. As the younger generation's buying power increases, we will have many opportunities to create new products that are attractive to them.

Product Promotion

Avon directed its sales promotion and sales development activities toward giving direct-selling assistance to its representatives. This was done by making available such aids as product samples and demonstration products, as well as the Avon brochure. Avon sought to motivate its representatives through the use of special prize programs that reward superior sales performance. Periodic sales meetings were conducted by the district manager to which representatives were invited. The meetings were designed to keep representatives alert to the product line changes, to explain sales techniques, and to give recognition to representatives' superior performance. Mexican representatives took particular pride in receiving recognition for sales achievements, and because of that, management favored an increase in promotional activities in developing future strategy.

An additional promotional tool was introduced in Mexico in 1988—a program called "Opportunity Unlimited." Under this program, top-performing representatives, who qualified as group sales leaders, had the opportunity to earn commissions by stimulating sales increases in their groups or representatives. Representatives could continue to earn commissions as group sales leaders as long as they stimulated sales increases. This program anticipated that group sales leaders would increase group sales by such methods as searching for new representatives, training new representatives, and motivating and assisting established representatives. Mexico was a testing ground for "Opportunity Unlimited." If the program proved successful there, the company planned to introduce it in other foreign markets.

Product Manufacture

Avon S.A. manufactured and packaged almost all of its cosmetics, fragrances, and toiletries products. Although most of the Mexican products were based on U.S. products, Avon S.A. developed several of its own fragrances based on Mexican tastes. Packages, consisting of containers and packaging components, were designed by U.S.-based Avon and manufactured in Mexico.

The fashion jewelry line was generally developed by Avon's U.S. staff and manufactured in Puerto Rico and Ireland or by several independent manufacturers in the United States and shipped to the Mexican distribution center.

Mexican Cosmetics Market

The cosmetics market in Mexico was segmented by product and by final user. Men, women, and children used different products. Similarly, Mexicans of Indian heritage required different products than did those of Spanish descent. However, in both the groups, most products were purchased by women. So the focus of the industry was on women between the ages of 18 and 65. On an average, women spent $35 per capita annually on cosmetics for themselves and their families.

As Mexican society became more liberal, it was anticipated that teenagers (16-18) would become frequent users of a limited number of cosmetics. Avon had produced a line of cosmetics for U.S. teenagers caller "Color World," which was promoted as "not your mother's makeup." Test marketing was being done with this age group in Mexico to survey the acceptance of the line.

Mexican men, especially in the cities, tended to purchase more colognes and after-shave lotions than their U.S. counterparts. They preferred products with a musky, masculine scent. Avon believed that this segment would continue to grow annually throughout the 1990s.

Competition

Avon faced competition from two sources: Max Factor, a U.S. firm with a subsidiary located in Mexico City, and Bella, a Mexican firm also based in Mexico City. Unlike Avon, these companies concentrated their retail distribution through supermarkets, department stores, and pharmacies. Of the two competitors, Bella concerned Avon the most.

Bella manufactured and marketed a full line of products in the medium-level price range. Its highly segmented and differentiated products were aimed at women with either light or dark complexions. Bella sales concentrated in the larger cities, such as Mexico City, Mazatlán, Veracruz, and Oaxaca. The large-city market was estimated to be about $424 million in 1989 and was expected to grow 12 percent annually in coming years.

Promotion was aimed at "La Bella Mujer Mexican"—the beautiful Mexican woman. Focused on ethnic pride, Bella maintained that their line of cosmetics was custom-made for the different complexions of Mexican women. As an attack on Avon's direct selling, Bella incorporated the use of catalog sales. A large number of households were mailed a seasonal catalog displaying the full line of products. Consumers placed their orders with a central distribution center, but the orders were delivered in person by a sales representative, who could then solicit additional orders. In the long run, Avon S.A. saw this as a threat to their door-to-door method.

Issues Confronting Management

Despite its healthy incursion into Mexico, the prospects for long-term growth for Avon, SA. de C.V., appeared hazy, largely because the company faced a major turning point in the years ahead. Its expansion was derived primarily from its ability to move into, and then saturate, vacant territories in its sales network. As mentioned previously, once a territory was covered, Avon simply divided it into smaller areas and added new representatives to canvass customers on a more concentrated basis.

Such so-called downsizing had been occurring since the late 1950s when Mexican representatives were supposed to cover some 400 to 500 households. Naturally, very few managed to do this, so when the company started reducing the territories to 250 to 300, there was little impact on representatives' earnings potential. The impact on the company's earnings, however, was tremendous. This strategy allowed Avon S.A. to more than triple its salesforce over a fifteen-year period.

By 1992, Avon S.A. expected to have completed a planned conversion to 100-home territories in Mexico, from a then current level of 150-home territories. Once this was accomplished, Avon S.A. was unsure about going lower. It became apparent that if Avon S.A. wanted to grow with the population and keep ahead of the rate of inflation, it must find other ways to build sales.

One alternative was to add new lines of products, particularly those that could be tailor-made to the Mexican market. But U.S.-based Avon executives were afraid that these new products would hurt existing products. Evans and his colleagues realized that planning was needed if Avon S.A. was to sustain growth and maintain profits in the future.

Case 28: Connecticut Corporation (Japan)

In late 1988, John Lindstrom, director of marketing for the International Beverage Division of Connecticut Corporation (CC), was faced with deciding what action should be taken to increase the market share for Bleinheau Vodka in Japan. Three strategies were open to him:

1. Increase promotional efforts on behalf of Bleinheau in Japan, and streamline distribution
2. License Suntory, Japan's largest liquor producer, to manufacture, label, and sell Bleinheau in Japan
3. Remove Bleinheau from the Japanese market

Connecticut Corporation entered the market in Japan in 1981 by licensing out Black Velvet Whiskey to the Suntory Company. In this arrangement, CC gave Suntory the rights to produce, label, and sell Black Velvet in return for 10 percent of the profits. In 1985, however, CC opened up branch headquarters in Tokyo to export Bleinheau and other CC beverage products, such as Black and White Scotch, Wild Turkey, Club Cocktails, Grand Marnier cognac, and United Vintners wines from the United States and distribute them in Japan.

Because vodka was not yet popular in the Japanese spirit market, Bleinheau had not yet been able to gain the distribution and market share it wanted. Mr. Lindstrom believed that with the increasing popularity of Western-style drinks, vodka would soon gain the acceptance of the Japanese public.

Corporate Background

Connecticut Corporation is a multinational corporation, headquartered in Springfield, Massachusetts. In 1987, the firm's worldwide sales of $1,921,879,000 were divided among three categories. The following table shows the approximate percentage of sales attributed to each:

Category of Business	Percentage of Sales
Beverage operations	57%
Food operations	24
International operations	19
Total	100%

Connecticut International was responsible for the overseas manufacture and export, as well as the marketing, of all products sold by CC outside the United States. Those products included the ones that were part of the Food Group, both owned and franchised operations of Southern Fried Chicken, A-1

Steak Sauce, Ortega Taco Sauce and Taco Shells, and the ones that were part of the Beverage Operations, such as Bleinheau Vodka, Yukon Jack Whiskey, Black Velvet Whiskey, Irish Mist Liqueur, Arrow Brand Liquors, Lancer Wines, Inglenook Wines, and Club Cocktails.

Connecticut International's beverage operations were divided into two parts: Connecticut de Brazil, which included only the manufacturing, exporting/importing, and marketing in Brazil, and the Connecticut International Beverage Group, which housed, among others, Connecticut in Japan.

Marketing Environment

A study done by Steven Young, marketing research manager for Connecticut in Japan, showed the following facts about the environment the company faced in Japan:

- The overall spirits market environment in Japan is attractive. Although GNP will grow at a slower rate than it has in the past thirty years, it will outstrip the United States and other major industrialized nations. This should mean substantial discretionary income. This coupled with increased urbanization should contribute to the growth of quality spirits. Besides, the post-World War II population has been drinking more in the Western fashion, suggesting that vodka should gain in popularity.
- Because economic activity is contracting, unemployment is at the highest levels since 1946.
- Competition is strengthening. This is especially true of the domestic competition such as Suntory.
- The percentage of the population on the high and upper-middle income segments has increased.
- The consumer economy is relatively healthy as both disposable income and personal consumption expenditures are attractive to other countries. Also, recent trends in household expenditures favor increased consumption of services and nondurable goods at the expense of durable goods.
- Per capita alcoholic beverage consumption continues to increase rapidly along with disposable income, yet is still far from saturation in comparison with other developed/underdeveloped countries.
- Media costs are the highest in the world and increasing.
- Domestic competitors such as Suntory tend to ignore profitability to achieve market share. This attitude fosters dumping. An example is the market for Scotch, which had a reputation as an expensive, high-quality item. Suntory began dumping, and now Scotch is no longer part of the high-quality market for gift giving and other such occasions for which Scotch traditionally has been used.

In summary, because of the size of its population, its stability, and its track record, Japan represented an attractive, although challenging, market with long-term economic prospects. In keeping with Japan's growth-oriented economy and tradition of following America, it would be reasonable to expect that the alcoholic beverage market, particularly the quality spirits market, would experience continued real growth in the foreseeable future, perhaps at a somewhat slower pace.

Advertising and Promotion

Whereas United States laws prohibited the advertising of hard liquor on television, it was not so in Japan. Therefore, a large part of Connecticut's advertising for Bleinheau in Japan was done through television and cinema media. Other forms of advertising media used by Connecticut Japan included posters and billboards, which showed different drinks that could be made with Connecticut products (including Bleinheau) and explained how to make them. In addition, the company provided various freestanding point-of-purchase displays for use in distribution centers where liquor was sold.

The copy used in all advertising centered around the idea of Bleinheau having "world popularity," especially of being "big in the United States," because anything considered popular in the United States has great appeal to the Japanese, especially the younger generation.

In addition to advertising, there were several types of promotion for Bleinheau.

1. Merchandise giveaways were directed at the dealers who supplied the bars and other types of

wholesalers.
2. Bleinheau was directed to the general public through "Bleinheau Nights" in local night clubs and bars. On these nights, Bleinheau offered discounts on all drinks made with Bleinheau vodka. The company also had giveaways such as T-shirts and glasses with "Bleinheau" printed on them.
3. Tie-ins with other products were used. A tie-in was done with Canada Dry. In areas where Canada Dry had a strong market share, consumers would buy a six-pack of Canada Dry and get a bottle of Bleinheau at a very low price. In markets where Bleinheau held a strong position, the purchase of a bottle of Bleinheau entitled the consumer to a free bottle of Canada Dry.

Distribution

The distribution system in Japan was much different from that in the United States. To distribute their products in Japan, Connecticut had to work through a complicated multitiered distribution system. This system had been in a gradual state of change for years because overlapping and the sheer size of the distribution system had resulted in a profit squeeze, with some middle levels being forced to accept lower margins and even being bypassed in some case. This trend was expected to continue in the 1990s.

Connecticut at that time had approximately 20 percent distribution in Japan. This had been achieved through five major wholesalers and seventeen secondary wholesalers. The problem lay in the fact that, while wholesalers were ultimately credited for every sale, they aggressively sold only their proprietary brands.

Competition

Connecticut's competition came not only from other rivals in the vodka market, but from all spirits marketers. For example, Scotch whiskey was very popular in Japan, holding over 75 percent of the spirits market through 1987. Vodka, on the other hand, had not yet become a popular drink in Japan.

In both the spirits market as a whole and the vodka market by itself, Connecticut's major competition came from the Suntory Company. In the vodka market, Nikka was Connecticut's second-biggest competitor.

Suntory Company

Suntory was the largest producer and seller of domestic spirits in Japan, as well as a major importer of whiskey into Japan. Suntory held the number one position in national whiskeys and had entries in all the spirits categories. Further, Suntory held the number one position in vodka with a 57 percent market share (mostly through licensing from companies outside Japan). Suntory's strategy, however, was not aimed at this market, but instead at putting all its resources into maintaining its market share in whiskey.

Nikka

Nikka provided the only other strong competition in the vodka market in Japan, with an 18 percent market share. Assuming the anticipated activity in white spirits materialized, Nikka was expected to be second in market share in the domestic field, behind Suntory.

Other Brands

Of the remaining 25 percent of the market, Connecticut's Bleinheau held 18 percent and the other 17 percent belonged to several domestic and imported brands.

Japanese Consumer

Alcoholic beverage consumption was well accepted in Japan, but usage, penetration, and frequency (especially in regard to wine) were still low. For example, the Japanese rarely drank during the day. Central to this was the increased consumption of Western spirits occasioned by Westernization after World War II. Just as with products, traditions, and fashion, what was popular in the United States often was very attractive to the Japanese. Examples included blue jeans, golf, and tennis. The popularity of Westernized bars and nightclubs also was increasing. The incidence of alcoholic beverage consumption ("drank last week") was increasing among women but stable among men, as the following table shows:

Drinking Population					
	1979	**1981**	**1983**	**1985**	**1987**
Male	26.8%	25.2%	26.5%	26.2%	25.8%
Female	8.0	9.0	10.5	11.5	11.8
Total	34.8	34.2	37.0	37.7	37.6

Except for a few imported brands, the Japanese had little brand familiarity and/or loyalty with respect to alcoholic beverages. The Japanese consumer, however, was responsive to advertising and its creation of "in-ness," as shown with the growth of gin in 1981–1982 when it was heavily advertised and its subsequent deterioration when advertising support was pulled. The trendsetters in Japan were a small group of the post-World War II generation who were the most traveled, best educated, and affluent. The following table summarizes trends in liquor consumption in Japan:

Trends in Served Market in Japan (in Thousands of Cases)			
	1980	**1987**	**1994†**
Scotch Whiskey	199	2,719	4,792
Vodka	25	43	320
Cognac	56	237	651
Others*	198	377	1,251
Total served market	478	3,376	7,014

*Including gin, rum, tequila, bourbon, and Canadian whiskey
†Projected

PART · 6

Planning and Control

CHAPTER 18

Organization and Control in International Marketing

CHAPTER FOCUS

After studying this chapter, you should be able to:

■ Describe alternative organizational designs for international marketing

■ Specify criteria for choosing an appropriate organization structure

■ Examine delegation of authority to subsidiaries for marketing decisions

■ Identify performance evaluation measures

■ Examine conflicts and their resolution between parent and subsidiaries

Markets across national boundaries offer many opportunities for growth and expansion. In taking advantage of such opportunities, international marketers formulate diverse strategies to fit the various different markets and successfully compete in them. A basic requirement for the effective implementation of any strategy is appropriate organizational structure.

Theoretically, the structure of an organization should be commensurate to its task, technology, and external environment. In the context of international business, however, this concept is difficult to put into practice since a multinational firm is faced with diverse external environments with various environmental constraints. Managers, for example, may follow a decision process of global coordination and integration. However, the political demands of a particular host country may require a more diverse and locally responsive decision process. These simultaneous pressures for greater integration and greater diversity create strain in structuring the organization. Thus, the matter of choosing an ideal structure that fits the international marketing strategy and responds to international market demands is an important and complex issue.

This chapter reviews alternative organizational designs that companies use to manage their complex, far-flung operations effectively. The criteria for choosing an appropriate organization structure are examined. Conditions that require organizational changes are analyzed. The question of delegating authority to foreign affiliates is discussed. Finally, different ways of controlling foreign operations and measuring their profitability are considered.

Alternative Organizational Designs

There are several ways to organize a multinational firm. This section discusses distinctive features of alternative organizational designs, relative advantages and disadvantages of each alternative, and the variables that influence the choice of a specific design.

Essentially, there are four organizational structure archetypes: (1) international division structure, (2) geographic structure, (3) product structure, and (4) matrix structure. A fifth type, the functional organization, is not considered because few multinationals adopt this structure. Its biggest disadvantage is too much centralization. This makes coordination of functional decisions difficult and equal interdependence between products and areas rare.

The company's selection of its organizational form has enormous implications for the marketing function. For example, if it is a matrix structure (discussed later), the director of international advertising may have dotted-line responsibility for all the country's advertising managers, who also must report to a local managing director. The director may not find this preferable, but will have to take this as a given. The point is that the MNC is quite unlikely to say everything (finance, production, etc.) is organized on a geographic basis except for marketing, an area that can choose whatever structure it desires.

Factors Affecting Organizational Structure

An MNC must choose an organizational structure that maximizes decentralization while still providing for the coordination of independent activities. The structure is mainly determined by the following factors.

Quality of Management The decentralization of authority to the local level can become quite a problem because the quality of management varies from country to country. However, authoritative committees either at the corporate or regional level with majority control can be used to offset this potential problem.

Diversity of Product Lines Most firms with a high degree of product diversity decentralize on a product basis, rather than on an area basis. Firms producing a few similar products will not decentralize on product basis, because of the high degree of interdependence among these products. However, complete standardization is usually not practical or desirable for marketing decisions because of different market characteristics and consumers.

Size of Firm Firms that derive a substantial portion of business from foreign operations usually drop the international division structure in favor of a product or geographic structure, which facilitates growth. As long as its international business is small, a firm can operate effectively with an international structure.

Location of Subsidiaries and Their Characteristics A company that emphasizes local and regional variations will lean toward the geographic structure because specific geographic variations must be specifically catered to. On the other hand, a company whose subsidiaries are similar to those of the home country is unlikely to favor a geographic structure because a good degree of standardization can be used in promoting products. For example, the U.S. and Canadian markets are quite similar.

Economic Blocs Companies operating within a regional economic bloc usually integrate their subsidiaries within the bloc area to deal better with trade barriers and oversee these operations by establishing special regional organizational units. Such a design makes it feasible to provide adequate responses to the unique economic characteristics of the bloc arrangement.

The ultimate decision on a firm's international organizational structure is based on specific factors unique to that company's operating environment. Hence, no two firms, even in the same industry, will exhibit exactly similar structures. In the computer industry, for example, IBM, Apple, and Digital Equipment all use different organizational structures. Digital Equipment operates with a product structure because of a diversified product line, while IBM, because of its large size, has an area organization. Apple's product line and international business have not expanded to the point where more decentralized decision making is necessary and can thus operate effectively with a functional structure.

International Division Organization

The international division form of organizational design is depicted in Figure 18.1. Under this structure, the firm's activities are separated into two units—one domestic and the other international. The main function of such an international division is a company's deliberate attempt to draw a distinction between its domestic and international business. Companies in a developmental stage favor this structure because they may not have enough trained executives to staff a worldwide organization effectively.

FIGURE 18.1 International Division Organization Concept

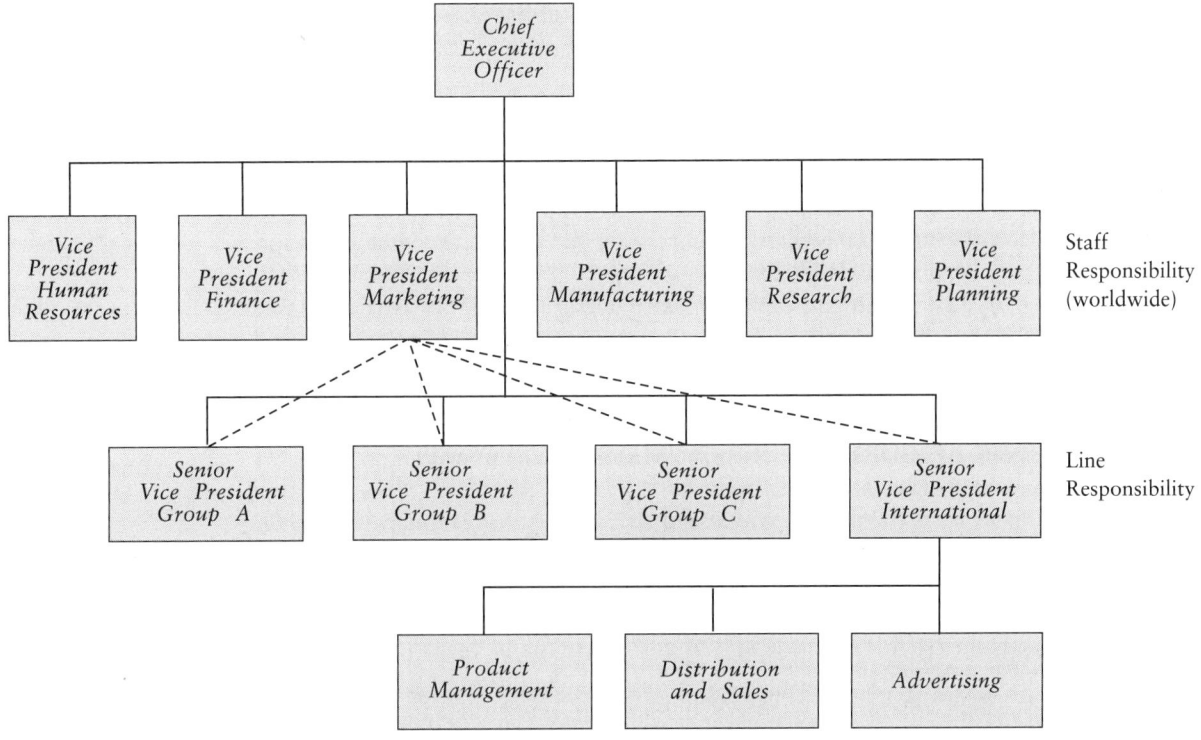

Top management can thus be freed from foreign operations to work on domestic business (see International Marketing Highlight 18.1)

International Marketing Highlight 18.1

Organizing for International Success

Loctite, the engineering adhesives and sealants company, has consolidated all overseas activities under an International Group president based at corporate headquarters in Newington, Connecticut. Within the international group, operations are organized into three overseas regions, managed by a vice president and a secretary; Latin America is managed by the country manager of Brazil. Loctite allows its country managers to determine the product mix and design marketing programs, and to set pricing policy within the context of an annual business plan approved by headquarters.

Source: Winning in the World Market (New York: American Business Conference, Inc., 1989), p. 32.

The drawback to this design is that a firm can easily grow too diverse for this particular structure. Further, corporate planning can become awkward because of the two autonomous units. The isolation of top management, which initially seems like a blessing, can become a curse. Conflicts may occur as operations abroad expand and business overseas grows. Thus, when the perspective of business enlarges, the international division structure becomes ineffective. Another inherent problem with this structure is that R&D cannot be easily decentralized, and, therefore, it tends to be domestically oriented. With the basic research domestically centered, R&D for overseas is usually diminished to only product modification.

Geographic Organization

A worldwide geographic structure can overcome the problems associated with the international division structure. Foreign and domestic operations are not isolated, but are integrated as if foreign boundaries did not exist (see Figure 18.2). Worldwide markets are segregated into geographic areas. Operational responsibility goes to area line managers, while corporate headquarters maintains responsibility for worldwide planning and control.

Companies that operate under a geographic structure usually share the following characteristics:[1]

1. Their product lines are less diverse.

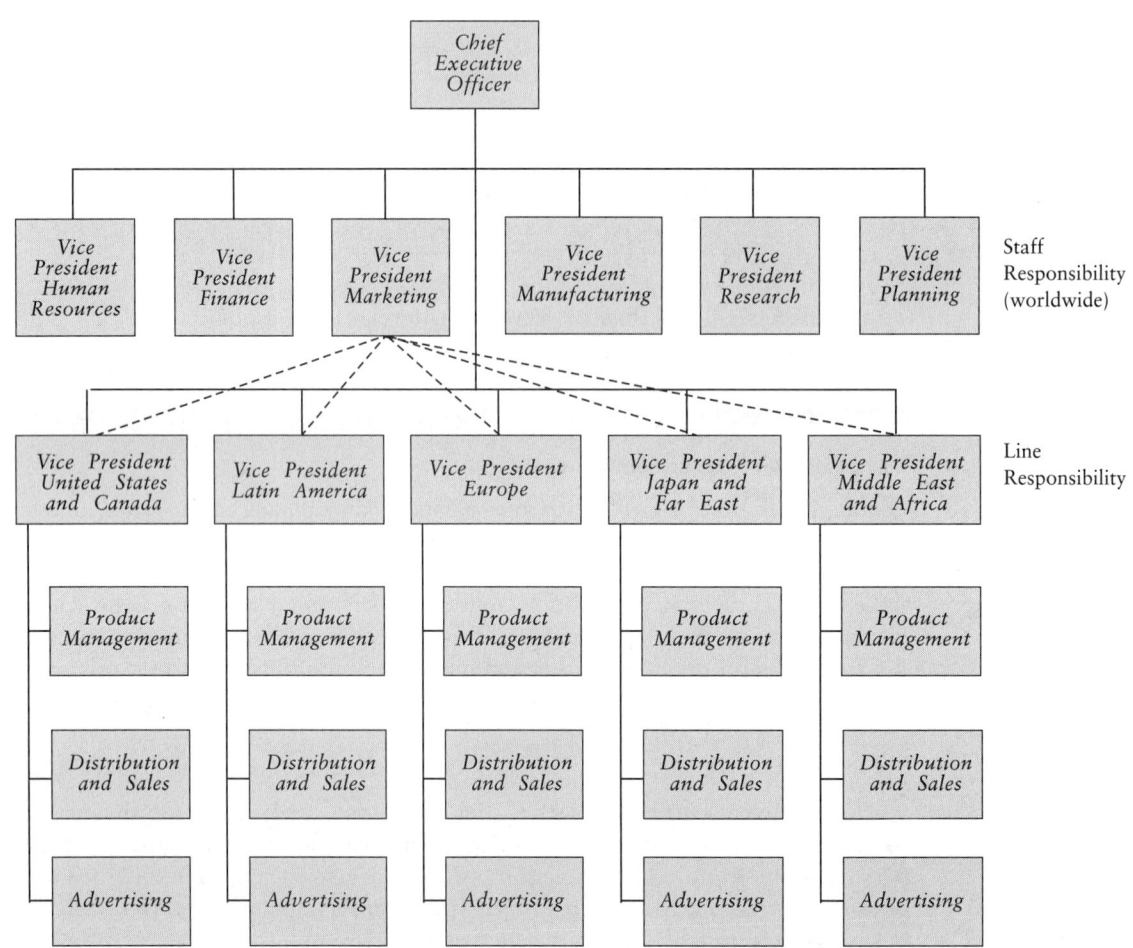

FIGURE 18.2 Geographic Organization Concept

2. Their products are sold to end-users.
3. Marketing is the critical variable.
4. All of their products are marketed through similar channels.
5. Products are changed for local consumer needs.

Geographic organization has many advantages. Delegation of line authority and responsibility is explicit. Coordination of product sales and manufacturing is enhanced, and overall there is a pooling of experience in problem areas. A significant disadvantage of this structure is that a large number of "super" executives are needed to run the organization effectively. Another drawback is that individual products may suffer because there is no single executive responsible for the specific product activities. The use of product managers at corporate headquarters can alleviate this problem by ensuring that each product line has proper penetration in world markets.

Product Organization

The third structure assigns worldwide responsibility to product group executives at the line management level. The coordination of activities in a geographical areas is handled through specialists at the corporate staff level. As shown in Figure 18.3, emphasis is placed on the product line rather than on geographic differences. The firm is segregated along product lines; each division is a separate profit center with the division head directly accountable for profitability. Decentralization is critical in this structure. More decisions are likely to be left to the local manager, who is then usually more highly motivated.

Corporations that operate within the structure usually share the following characteristics:

1. They have a variety of end-users.
2. Their product lines are highly diversified and employ a high level of technological capability.
3. Shipping costs, tariffs, and other specific cost considerations dictate local manufacturing.

Decentralization of authority is a prime advantage of this structure. The motivation of division heads is high. New products can be added and old ones dropped with only marginal effect on overall operations. Another advantage of this structure is that the control of a product through the product life cycle can be managed more readily. Furthermore, MNCs do not have to abandon worldwide product division structure when the size of the foreign operations becomes large.[2]

A drawback of this structure is that coordination problems among various product divisions can arise. Product divisions must constantly be kept in check by top management. Also, division heads promoted to headquarters are likely to be biased in favor of their former product area. The possibility of neglect of certain product areas exists. Many companies employ area specialists who are assigned the responsibility for overcoming that problem.[3]

Matrix Organization

One of the recent developments in organization design is the matrix structure. This structure, which first achieved prominence in the 1960s, has been adopted by many MNCs. The matrix structure offers greater flexibility than the single-line-of-command structures already discussed and reconciles this flexibility with coordination and

FIGURE 18.3 Product Organization Concept

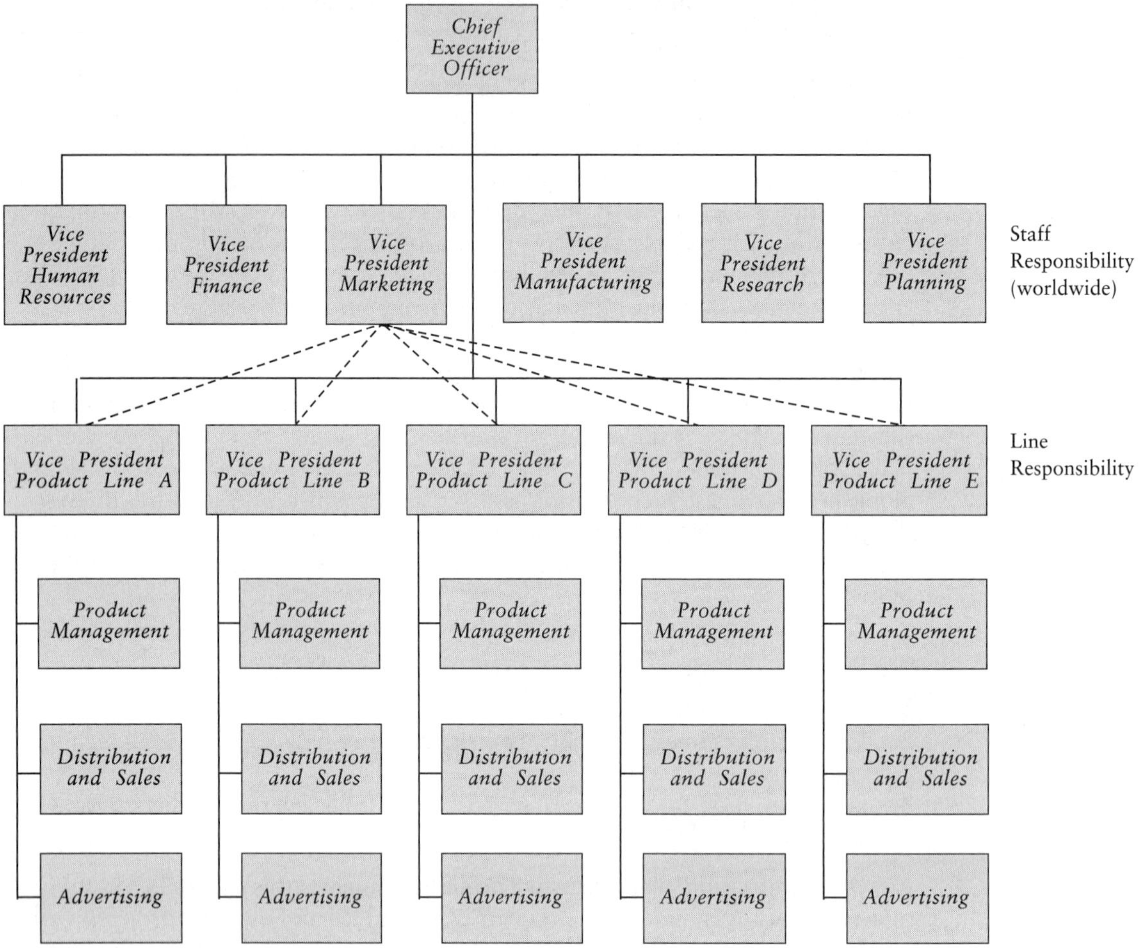

economies of scale—the strength of large organizations. The main identifying feature of the matrix organization is that certain managers report to two bosses rather than to the traditional single boss; there is a dual rather than a single chain of command. Firms tend to adopt matrix forms when it is absolutely essential to be highly responsive to two sectors such as product and geography; when uncertainties generate very high information processing requirements; and when there are strong constraints on financial and/or human resources.[4]

For the multinational firm, the matrix organization is a solution to the problem of responding to economic and political environments. A matrix organization can have both geographic and product management components. The product management component would have worldwide responsibility for a given product line; the geographic management component would be responsible for all product lines in a national setting. Because the responsibilities overlap at the national product/market level, both are brought into play for major decisions. A national subsidiary product division must be able to relate to both in order to operate adequately.[5]

In designing a matrix system, one has to be aware of its typical problems. Power struggles are a constant problem when the system is first applied. These struggles result from the dual command system, which has a tendency to create an imbalance of power as each side determines the limits of its influence. Besides tight control over the budgeting and evaluation systems, balance can be maintained by means of pay levels, job titles, and other means of increasing the status of the weaker side.[6]

Another problem is the mistaken belief that matrix management is group decision making. It is not. Each matrix boss and his or her parallel in the other arm have separate functions that should seldom conflict. Their subordinates should work around any conflicting demands, coming to both bosses only as a last resort. The two bosses should rarely have to meet for decision making.[7]

In conclusion, the matrix system is of great benefit to firms that have to react quickly to the environment Corporations generally evolve into matrix forms rather than starting with them from scratch. Besides geographic and product matrices, there can be geographic and functional, or functional and product, matrix systems. Figure 18.4 shows an example of how the matrix structure of a multinational corporation may look.

Empirical Evidence

Empirical work on organizational structures of multinational enterprises by Halman shows that most firms have complex structures with some sort of matrix structure with product/market on one axis and geography on the other.[8] In most cases the international division, and/or regional office, serves as a buffer between top management and host country management. This tendency can be explained by the fact that top management cannot take the time and energy to deal with the great diversity of operations abroad and the wide variety of laws, cultures, customs, and other international factors. Nor can operating subsidiaries or branches abroad be exposed for long to the monolithic perceptions and policies of top corporate officers. Thus, international divisions are created to translate and buffer the communication between foreign operations and headquarters policy.

Organization Within Smaller Firms

Depending on the size of the firm, the responsibility for international marketing may be held by the president of the firm, be delegated to a line executive (for example, the vice president of sales), or be given to a staff person, like a marketing researcher or a strategic planner, as an additional duty. Occasionally, however, one person is appointed or hired to manage international operations in its entirety.

To illustrate the point, a chemical pump manufacturer in Ohio with annual sales of about $15 million handled its export business of about $3 million through the president's office. A high-technology firm in Boston (annual sales $16 million) with 50 percent of its business originating in Western Europe had a vice president of exports on par with the vice president of marketing (for domestic business). A precision instruments company in Connecticut traditionally filled export orders as received through the domestic sales organization. After a while, the company decided to expand aggressively overseas. It hired an MBA for this purpose who reported to the president.

FIGURE 18.4 Matrix Organization Concept

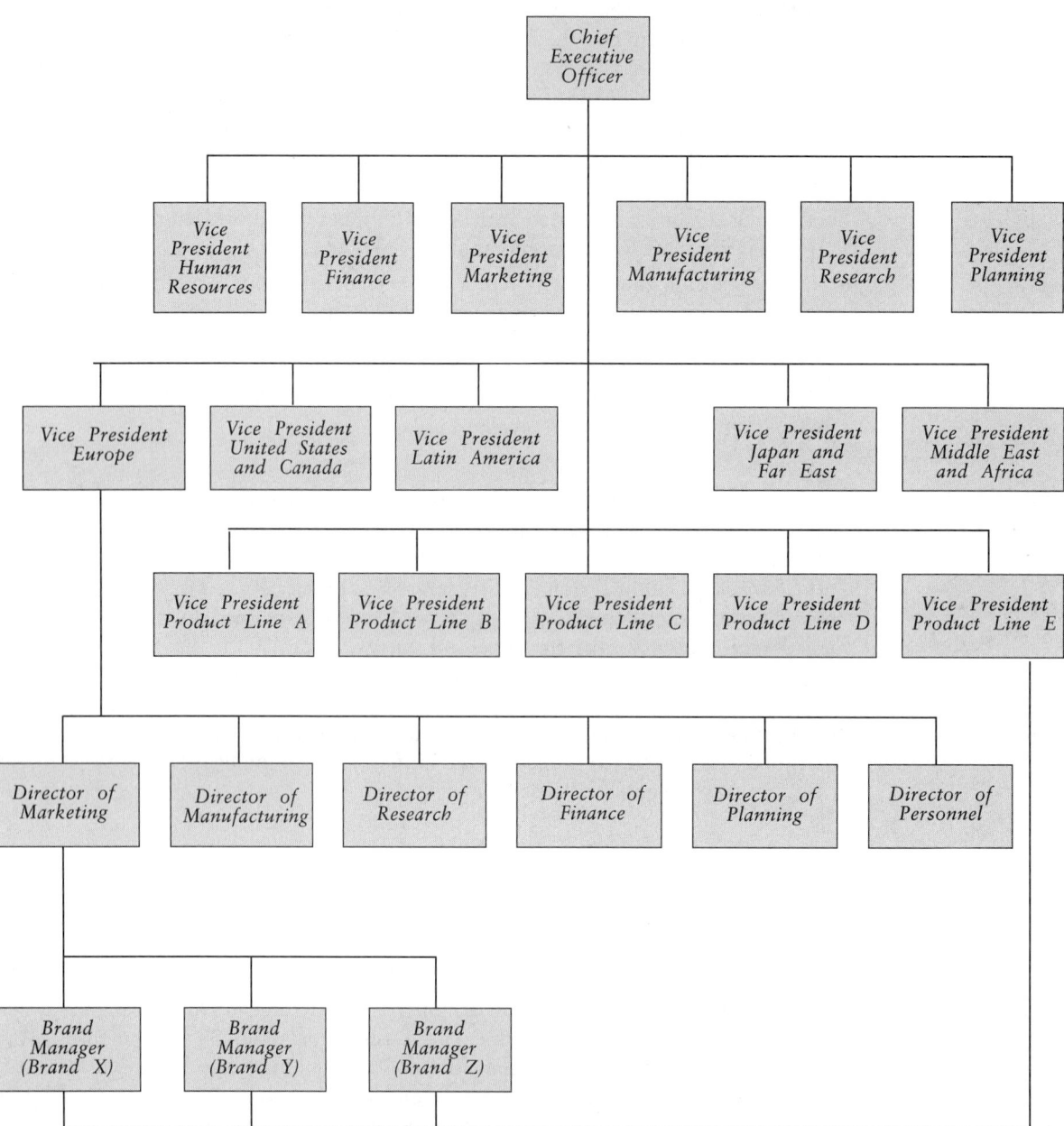

Clearly, the organization of international marketing activity within a small firm depends on the extent of one's involvement in and commitment to overseas markets. Generally, initial international marketing activity is handled through the existing organization. As the interest in overseas business enlarges, a specific office is established for that purpose. That office may expand as the scope of business increases. It must be noted, however, that even one individual, if sufficiently committed and backed by top management, can make important strides in successfully launching or expanding a company's place in the international marketplace.

Choosing an Appropriate Organizational Structure

The organizing goal of international marketing is a structure that helps the company to respond to differences in international market environments and at the same time enables it to extend valuable corporate knowledge, experience, and know-how from the home market to the entire corporate system. In other words, the structure must be compatible with the organization's task and technology and the relevant conditions of the external environment.[9] Obviously, no one structure will meet the requirements of all corporations. The choice of an appropriate form of organization should be based on several criteria.[10]

Foreign Markets Versus Domestic Markets

If a firm does a substantial proportion of business overseas, greater emphasis needs to be given in organizing foreign operations. If the major markets are at home, the foreign part of the business may simply be organized through an export department. For example, a company like Nestlé, which does over 90 percent of its business outside its home market of Switzerland, needs a global organization structure. However, the major thrust of companies like Hershey Foods is on the domestic market; therefore, they would not attach the same importance to foreign markets as does Nestlé.

Evolution of Corporate Organization Structure

When an organization first expands to foreign markets, its foreign affiliates and/or subsidiaries report directly to the company president, or his or her delegate, without assistance from a headquarters/staff group. As international business grows, however, the complexity of coordination and direction will extend beyond the scope of a single person. Assembling a staff group to take responsibility for growing international activities will become necessary. This evolutionary process dictates the choice of structure at any given point in time.

The Nature of a Business and Its Related Strategy

A company with minimum product diversity in different markets (both domestic and international) may effectively organize itself functionally. In other words, when the same products are sold worldwide for similar end-users, through similar channels of distribution and advertising themes, the functional domestic setup may be extended overseas as well. Where product lines are diverse, and/or where local expertise is requisite to adequately serving the market, a geographic organizational structure may be more appropriate.

Management's Orientation

The cultural attitudes and orientation of a company's management toward different aspects of doing business overseas is another factor that affects the choice of an organization's structure.[11] These aspects include such considerations as management's attitudes toward foreigners and overseas environments, management's willingness to take risks and seek growth in unfamiliar circumstances, and management's ability to make compromises to accommodate foreign perspective. Three primary orientations identified among international executives are ethnocentric, or home country oriented; polycentric, or host country oriented; or geocentric, or world oriented.

An ethnocentric orientation considers home nationals more trustworthy and more reliable. Consequently, this orientation requires that home country methods and outlook be accepted overseas without question. The polycentric orientation acknowledges that host country cultures are different and believes that their people are difficult to understand. In line with this is the idea that local people know what is best for themselves and therefore local organizations should have local identities insofar as possible. The geocentric orientation views worldwide markets on an equal basis. Executives who subscribe to this global orientation seek the best personnel for key positions worldwide. The overseas affiliates, under this orientation, are considered an integral part of the corporation, rather than just satellites. The focus is on an amalgamation of worldwide objectives from local objectives with each part making its unique contribution from its particular competence. An organization operating with a world orientation is more complex and interdependent than it would be under either of the other two orientations.

Availability of Qualified Managers

The final criterion that determines the choice of organizational structure is the availability of internationally trained executives. If an adequate number of trained managers is not available, a company may be forced to accept a different structure for the short run than the one considered appropriate. In the long run, however, managers could be trained and the organization appropriately restructured. However, the investment needed for developing internationally trained executives would have to be justified in terms of future potential and foreign business expansion plans.

To evaluate a company's justifiable long-run development of management talent, it is helpful to consider the different conditions under which each of the four organization designs (international division, product division, area division, and matrix organization) appear to be suitable. The scheme presented in Table 18.1 provides a generic framework for figuring out an appropriate organization for an international corporation. Particular schemes, however, may have to be modified to accommodate company-specific factors.

Seeking Organizational Changes

Organizations operate in dynamic environments. Thus, no organizational structure can remain static. As the environment undergoes changes, appropriate changes must be made in the strategy, and structure follows strategy.

Need for Reorganization

Essentially, reorganization becomes warranted as a result of one or more of the following four factors: (1) sales growth, (2) adverse financial performance, (3) new products, and (4) changes in the external environment (for example, political upheaval in the country). Consider a company that has recently entered international markets

TABLE 18.1 Suitability of Basic MNC Organizational Structures to Corporate Concerns

Area of Corporate Concern	Level of Suitability			
	International Division	Worldwide Product Division	Area Division	Matrix
Rapid growth	Medium	High	Medium	High
Diversity of products	Low	High	Low	High
High technology	Medium	High	Low	High
Few experienced managers	High	Medium	Low	Low
Close corporate control	Medium	High	Low	High
Close government relations	Medium	Low	High	Medium
Resource allocation				
Product considerations should dominate	Low	High	Low	Medium
Geographic considerations should dominate	Medium	Low	High	Medium
Functional considerations should dominate	Low	Medium	Low	High
Relative cost	Medium	Medium	Low	High

Source: Reprinted by permission of *Harvard Business Review*. An exhibit from "Reorganizing Your Worldwide Business" by J. William Widing, Jr., May–June 1973, p. 159. Copyright © 1973 by the President and Fellows of Harvard College; all rights reserved.

through filling infrequent export orders. The work involved has amounted to clerical functions handled by an experienced clerk in the sales department. Over the years, as sales grew, the nature of the foreign business changed, requiring a variety of managerial decisions. This triggered a structural reorganization. An international division was established that handled all matters related to business outside the U.S.

Management of Reorganization

Reorganization changes the status quo and established patterns of doing things. People within the organization may not have the capacity and/or willingness to adjust to structural changes. They may, therefore, resist changes. Such resistance can lead to disruption of intergroup and intragroup working relationships. For example, the domestic organization may neglect work strictly meant for international business. Resistance especially becomes a problem when reorganization calls for dilution of the responsibility and authority of an executive or group that hitherto wielded great influence and performed well.

To ensure organizational harmony, the change must be gradual and not brought about in a revolutionary fashion.[12] Nor can structural change be imposed unilaterally. More people than just those likely to be affected should be consulted before finalizing the reorganization; for example, it may be necessary to persuade senior management of the need for reorganization.

New Perspectives on Organization: Corporate Networking

As MNCs become ever larger through foreign acquisitions, joint ventures, or direct investments overseas, the traditional ways of organizing just do not work for them, and no amount of tinkering can change that fact.[13] These companies tend to be technology oriented; they need to stay flexible, respond quickly to technological advances, and become or remain product innovators.

Such companies have decided that the only way they can accommodate their needs is to adopt a radical system of organizing people and work, called corporate networking. This can best be characterized as an "anti-organization" approach, in that its designers are consciously seeking to break through the constraints imposed by all the conventional organizational structures.

In a networked company, employees around the globe create, produce, and sell the firm's products through a carefully cultivated system of interrelationships. Middle-level managers from R&D, marketing, distribution, and other functions discuss common problems and try to accommodate one another. To foster flexibility rather than conformity, information does not necessarily travel along present organizational routes or chains of command as it does in other organization systems.

Thus, marketing people in France would speak directly to manufacturing people in Singapore without going through the home office in, say, the U.S. According to proponents of the network approach, lateral relationships spur innovation, new product development, and better quality control. They believe it is the only way a company can be truly innovative in today's bureaucratic world. Networking puts greater decision-making responsibility in the hands of middle managers, who are not required to clear every detail and event with higher-ups. The idea is to substitute cooperation and coordination, which are in everyone's interest, for strict control and supervision.

Corporate networks require the various groups to stay in close contact with each other. Their success hinges on fast, reliable communication. It is no coincidence that networks have become popular at a time when electronic mail, facsimiles, teleconferencing, and other advanced telecommunications techniques have become accessible, inexpensive, and increasingly recognized as extremely valuable management tools.[14]

Pioneering work on network organization has been done by Bartlett and Ghoshal.[15] They classify companies involved in foreign business into four categories: multinational, global, international, and transnational. The first three categories represent traditional organization, while transnational refers to networking organization. Key characteristics of each type of traditional organization are:

- *Multinational:* Strong local presence through sensitivity and responsiveness to national differences
- *Global:* Cost advantages through centralized global-scale operations
- *International:* Use of parent company knowledge and capabilities through worldwide diffusion and adaptation

The multinational organization is decentralized. Control from headquarters is informal and personal, overlaid with simple financial controls. Top executives consider overseas operations independent profit centers that are part of the parent company's portfolio. This structure allows local organizations to tailor products to their home markets and helps firms avoid trade barriers. Multinational firms are sensitive and responsive to national differences. Local responsiveness gives the firm advantages over competitors, but it has drawbacks. Because the multinational organization is so decentralized, knowledge developed within each unit rarely reaches the rest of the company. Efficiency also suffers since duplication is inherent in the structure and economies of scale are not fully exploited.

The multinational model was frequently adopted by companies prior to World War II, when communications technology was in its infancy and national markets varied dramatically. Overseas operations incapable of operating independently of the home office were not effective in that environment. In some cases, World War II actually forced companies to use a multinational structure when overseas subsidiaries were cut off from the parent company.

The global organization model is almost a mirror image of the multinational model. Highly centralized, the global organization considers overseas operations delivery pipelines to the global market. The corporate headquarters is a central hub maintaining tight controls over decision resources and information. Global companies consider the world one global market. They centralize production and operations. Centralization allows them to capture economies of scale and gain cost advantages. On the other hand, centralization makes firms less responsive to local needs and makes them more susceptible to tariffs and trade barriers.

The global organization model is typical of many Japanese companies. *Group behavior* and *interpersonal harmony* are strongly emphasized in Japanese culture. These cultural characteristics contributed to the adoption of the global organization model by many Japanese firms.

The international organization represents a "coordinated federation." Assets, resources, and responsibilities are decentralized, but headquarters still coordinates many activities. Formal planning and control systems allow central management to coordinate overseas operations.

The control inherent in this system facilitates the transfer of knowledge and skills from the parent company to overseas divisions. Transferred knowledge can be adapted to meet local market needs. Decentralization with tight controls allows the international organization to capture some of the advantages of both the global and multinational models without the disadvantages. However, the international organization does not fully gain the advantages of global-scale economies or responsiveness that the other two models respectively have.

The international model often is adopted by companies with strong domestic positions. These companies move into overseas markets and produce miniature models of the home organization. Overseas operations are given flexibility to adapt to local markets but strong control and coordination is maintained by headquarters.

Bartlett and Ghoshal argue that until recently, most worldwide industries presented relative one-dimensional strategic requirement. In each industry, either responsiveness, or efficiency, or knowledge transfer was crucial, and companies that possessed the matching structure were rewarded. Thus, if the strategic requirement of the industry was *responsiveness* (e.g., branded packaged products), a company following the multinational model found a good fit. Similarly, for companies in industries requiring strategic efficiency (e.g., consumer electronics), the global model was appropriate, while the international model was suitable for companies in industries where transfer of knowledge was a dominant strategic requirement (e.g., telecommunications switching).

In the 1980s, success in global industries depended not just on one dimension (responsiveness or efficiency or leveraging of parent company knowledge and competencies), but on all three at the same time. This need led to a new model of organization, the transnational structure. The transnational model, or network organization, draws on the strengths of the three traditional models as a means to achieve global competitiveness. Instead of making a blanket centralization or decentralization decision, the transnational organization makes selective decisions. Some operations and resources are centralized while others are decentralized. These decisions are made so that the entire company gains from the proper spread of resources and control. The structure relies on interdependencies to integrate all company units while allowing them to concentrate on their strengths and maintain the independence necessary for responsiveness. For example, if Division X has a strength in precision manufacturing technology, that will be its focus. Other divisions will depend on Division X for its expertise. However, precision manufacturing will not be monopolized by Division X.

The transnational configuration develops its strengths from three fundamental characteristics: dispersion, specialization, and interdependencies. New consumer trends, technological advances, and competitive strategies can develop anywhere in the world. The ability to sense and respond to these changes provides a competitive advantage, which is achieved through dispersed assets. Specialization of national operations allows the transnational company to capture minimum-scale efficiencies while retaining a dispersed structure. The current world competitive situation demands that company units engage in collaborative information sharing and problem solving, cooperative resource sharing, and collective implementation. That is, a transnational organization must employ relationships built on interdependencies.

The transnational organization requires highly flexible coordination processes to cope with both short-term shifts in specific role assignments and long-term realignments of basic responsibilities and reporting relationships. Furthermore, it must be capable of modifying roles and relationships on a decision-by-decision basis (see International Marketing Highlight 18.2).

Delegating Decision-Making Authority to Foreign Subsidiaries

Organizations are seldom totally centralized or decentralized. Complete centralization is not economical in most instances because of the administrative impossibility of making *all* of the tremendous number of decisions that would have to be made at the top management level. On the other hand, complete decentralization implies a collection of completely separate businesses, which is also undesirable. Subunits should be more than isolated investments. They should contribute not only to the success of the corporation but also to each other's success as well.

Determining the optimal degree of delegation amounts to an art. There are always trade-offs between control and delegation. Ideally, top management tries to choose a degree of decentralization that maximizes benefits over costs. However, in practice, it may not be feasible to quantify either benefits or costs.

International Marketing Highlight 18.2

Imperial Chemical Industries: A Network Corporation

The archaic name is entirely appropriate: The sun never sets on ICI's far-flung nerve centers, and the company has probably moved as near as any to being truly global. The world's 38th-largest industrial corporation, ICI sells $21 billion a year of pharmaceuticals, film, polymers, agricultural chemicals, explosives, and other products.

In 1983, ICI began to abandon its traditional country-by-country organization and establish worldwide business units. The company concentrated its resources on its strongest ones. Within each, it focused activity where the most strength lay. Four of the nine new business units are headquartered outside Britain. Two are in Wilmington, Delaware—ICI is growing 20 percent a year in the U.S. but only 2 percent to 3 percent at home. A factory in Britain or Brazil producing advanced materials or specialty chemicals answers to a boss in Wilmington.

To avoid overlapping research around the world, labs were given lead roles near the most important markets. Advanced materials research went to Phoenix to be near clients in defense industries, while leather dye research went to the south of France, the heart of the market.

The strategic shift created wrenching changes. ICI reduced its manufacturing jobs in Britain by 10,000 to 55,000; other people were transferred or taken off pet projects. It's hard on people who have built national empires and now don't have such freedom. The company is asking people to be less nationalistic and more concerned with what happens outside their country. The upheaval has been especially worrisome to British employees, since ICI's stronger growth rate elsewhere attracts more resources.

The payoff is better decision making. Before, each territory would work up projects and have warring factions competing in London for the same money. Now with one person responsible for a global product line, it becomes immaterial where a project is located. The profits will be the same. When you start operating in this manner, it takes a lot of steam out of the defense of fiefdoms. In pharmaceuticals, for example, better—and quicker—decision making has helped ICI reduce the time lag in introducing new drugs to different markets from half a dozen years to one or two. ICI hopes eventually to make the introductions simultaneous.

A global company needs a world view at the top. Until 1982, ICI's 16-person board was all British. Now it includes two Americans, a Canadian, a Japanese, and a German. Among the 180 top people in the company, 35 percent are non-British.

British or non-British, they may go anywhere. The new chairman of ICI Americas Inc. is an Australian who also has worked for ICI in Britain and Canada. He quickly learned that a common language is no insurance against cultural shocks. When he went to England, he couldn't get any respect with his direct Australian manner, so he learned the oblique ways of the English. For example, he says, if an English boss reacts to a pet project by saying, "Perhaps you ought to think about this a little more," what he really means is "You must be mad. Forget it." In the U.S., he had to unlearn the lesson. He told a manager, "Perhaps you ought to think about this a little more." The manager took him literally. Asked why he had gone ahead, the man replied, "Well, I thought about it, like you said, and the idea got better."

Source: Jeremy Main, "How to Go Global—And Why," *Fortune*, August 28, 1989, p. 70. © 1989 Time Inc. All rights reserved.

Factors That Affect Delegation

The extent and pattern of decentralization of authority in overseas affiliates varies from situation to situation. Empirical work on the subject, however, has indicated that ordinarily the degree of delegation rests on the following factors: the type of decision, the relative importance of international business and the size of the affiliates, the location of the MNC's home base, and the nature of the industry.

Type of Decision Marketing is a polycentric function that is deeply affected by local factors. Primary authority for international marketing decisions is, therefore, decentralized in favor of host country management. Aylmer's study of what kinds of decisions are made by whom provides some insights. This study involved the local management of the Western European operations of nine major U.S.-based consumer durable goods companies. Aylmer found that local management was responsible for 86 percent of the advertising decisions, 74 percent of the pricing decisions, and 61 percent of the channel decisions. Even where other organization levels were involved, local management often retained a strong voice in the final outcome of these decisions. As far as product design was concerned, decisions primarily rested with the parent organization.[16]

A similar study by Brandt and Hulbert generally substantiates Aylmer's findings. Their study was conducted among 63 U.S., European, Canadian, and Japanese subsidiaries located in Brazil. They concluded that, of the three major marketing areas—product, promotion, and pricing—product-related decisions sustained the most intervention from headquarters. Forty-five percent of the 63 subsidiaries involved replied that they received home office guidance regarding product design specifications. Forty-seven percent received help in making brand-name decisions. These two areas require extensive financial investment. For this reason the home office exercised greater control in any decisions made. Decisions concerning price guidelines received a minimal amount of assistance. Greater autonomy to the subsidiary was permitted because it was recognized that local management has a better knowledge of the competitive situation in the area and is more in tune with how customers and the local market will react to price changes[17] (see International Marketing Highlight 18.3).

Relative Importance of International Business and Size of Affiliates The relative importance of the firm's international operations and that of the local affiliates' position within the firm are two important organizational forces that affect the delegation of authority.[18] The frequency of higher management participation in local decision making is affected by the firm's international sales as a percentage of total sales—the higher the sales, the greater the frequency of high management participation in local decision making. For example, in Aylmer's research in one company with 50 percent international sales, top management was directly involved with the major marketing decisions. By contrast, the policy decisions of another company, where international sales accounted for less than 10 percent of total sales, were delegated to local management. The size of an affiliate also affects the delegation of authority. The larger the affiliate, the greater the authority shared with local management. In the case of smaller affiliates, parent company management more often imposes decisions on local management.[19]

International Marketing Highlight 18.3

Managing a Global Business

Cray Research's organizational approach is designed to suit its product line. The supercomputer industry that it has pioneered epitomizes global business in its purest form, much like the large commercial airframe industry in which Boeing is the world leader. Worldwide installations and clients number in the low hundreds at most. The price tag on a supercomputer is high, averaging $12 million to $15 million. Each sale is a discrete event that moves through a complex and time-consuming cycle lasting anywhere from one and one-half to four years. And each purchase decision commits the buyer for a long period of time.

The focal point of the operation is Chippewa Falls, Wisconsin, the site of the company's research and development and manufacturing facilities, which Cray invites customers to visit. It sets prices centrally, and each sales contract is signed directly by Cray U.S. and the individual customer, regardless of location.

Cray's country organizations handle marketing, sales, and service functions and derive a commission on sales and revenues from service contracts. Sensitive, however, to the value that country managers can add, Cray allows them room for decisions in some areas. For example, the country manager has greater control over the marketing of used equipment in his territory, can determine trade-in credit for upgrades, and sets service fees.

In addition, Cray recognizes that country managers are key frontline players in dealing with customers. To enhance their status, it has the managers of six leading country subsidiaries report to internal boards of directors, which include their peers from various functions and U.S. regions and are chaired by executive vice presidents. This reporting relationship encourages collaborative behavior. Country managers also have direct access to Cray's CEO. Country managers are, however, expected to meet specific financial and technical criteria, both set centrally.

Source: *Winning in the World Market* (New York: American Business Conference, Inc., 1987), pp. 34–35.

Location of MNC's Home Base The delegation of decision-making authority to subsidiaries varies among MNCs of different nations.[20] According to Picard, U.S. subsidiaries of European corporations enjoy more autonomy than subsidiaries of U.S. corporations in Europe for several reasons (see International Marketing Highlight 18.4).

> Many European companies are understaffed at the top executive level relative to U.S. companies; therefore, not enough managerial attention and time can be given to the subsidiaries.
>
> Before modern telecommunications were developed, many European companies were already exporting a large portion of their production and were establishing sales subsidiaries overseas because their own local markets were too small. Lack of rapid telecommunications caused most decisions to be made at the local level.
>
> The American multinational corporations' tendency to control may stem from the fact that when they expanded after World War II, the overseas markets were very small compared to the domestic market.[21]

━━━━━━━━━━ **International Marketing Highlight 18.4** ━━━━━━━━━━

How Japanese Firms Delegate

According to a white paper on Japanese international trade, the widest range of autonomy allowed by Japanese parent companies to their local operations is in decisions on promotion and performance rating systems (in line with adjustment of personnel management to local cultures), supply sources for raw materials and parts, production and inventory volumes, and marketing strategy. The authority most zealously guarded by Japanese corporate headquarters was in the appointment of officers and in decisions on corporate finances (e.g., dividend payouts, long-term fund raising, capital expansions), research and development plans, and plant and equipment investments or expansions.

However, the imperative for centralized management among Japanese companies becomes truly apparent when compared with the management of foreign-affiliated enterprises operating in Japan. While overseas parents still control over half of decisions regarding the appointment of officers and long-term funding, their local subsidiaries in Japan seem to exercise far more control over determination of production and inventory volume, sourcing, sales price and marketing, personnel management, and even R&D. The comparison also reveals that relatively more control over marketing and pricing is held by Japanese corporate headquarters than by non-Japanese firms: About 60 percent of decisions on marketing strategy and selling prices could be made by local subsidiaries of Japanese firms, while over 80 percent of subsidiaries (even in joint ventures) of foreign firms could do so.

Source: H. Aoki, "The White Paper on International Trade 1989—Rapid Progress in Structural Adjustment," *Journal of Japanese Trade and Industry*, September 1, 1989.

Nature of the Industry The degree of delegation is affected also by the nature of the industry. For example, high centralization is more likely to occur among the firms in nonfood categories than among firms in the food category. In general, the nature of a company's products has an important influence on the delegation of authority to overseas affiliates. Consider the following:

> Food products ... are generally perceived to be ... "culture-bound"; this means they often become part of a national culture and their use pattern and meaning to consumers vary considerably from one country to the other. Coffee is an old product—350 years old in Europe, so local patterns and traditions surrounding coffee have been built up over many years. As a result, local taste preferences vary considerably from country to country, and even within a country; the café au lait of France and Switzerland, the thin slightly acid taste of Americans, the strong expresso in the small cup in Italy, coffee as a strong milk modifier in England and Australia, the smooth rich acidic taste of the Germans and the Scandinavians.[22]

Where highly culture-bound products require extensive custom-tailoring or marketing programs to meet local conditions, subsidiary management tends to play a dominant role in the process of marketing decision making.

Integration of Multinational Marketing Activities A key problem of MNCs is how to tie the business activities of the subsidiaries together.[23] There are different ways to integrate subsidiary operations, one of which is centralization. However, centralization has limits. For example, there are products that are relatively culture-bound and require local adaptation. In such cases, the tailoring of marketing programs to local conditions requires that authority be transferred to subsidiaries. When sufficient centralization is not feasible, there are three other methods for integrating corporate activities: corporate acculturation, system transfer, and people transfer.

The process of subsidiary acculturation involves assimilating corporate management's criteria for decision making into subsidiary management thinking. Through this process, subsidiary managers can manage the company's overseas operations with relatively little interference from headquarters.

Systems transfer refers to the use of a uniform framework for marketing planning and budgeting. This can serve to educate managers toward a disciplined analysis of business, provide headquarters with comparable data from all subsidiaries, standardize the process of decision making throughout the organization, and facilitate communication between headquarters and subsidiaries and among subsidiaries in different countries.

People transfer refers to the establishment of personal contact across borders among headquarters and subsidiary personnel. This includes long-term assignment of managers abroad, and short-term meetings between headquarters and subsidiary executives and among personnel from different foreign subsidiaries. People transfer can help to smooth out the differences of viewpoint that exist in a multinational organization.

Increasingly, to operate near key customers and tough rivals in fast-changing markets, companies are transferring world headquarters of important units abroad. Often, companies put a non-American as the chief executive of the operation. This type of organizational shift requires risking a loss of control. Yet, companies have come to accept that they cannot rule the world from one single location any longer.

As an example, American Telephone & Telegraph Co. moved the headquarters of its traditional corded telephone business to France from New Jersey.[24] It marked the first overseas move by a unit of AT&T, whose ranks of non-U.S. workers have jumped to 50,000 from 50 in 1984. The corded-telephone business had scant international sales until 1990. Its approximately 2,000 employees around the globe now report to a Frenchman.

Similarly, Du Pont Co. has shifted its worldwide electronics operation from U.S. to Tokyo, nearer its big base of Asian customers. Du Pont already manages its global agricultural products operations from Geneva, Switzerland.

Performance Evaluation and Control of Foreign Operations

Every company must have a performance evaluation and a control system to measure different operations. This need is particularly acute in the management of far-flung, hard-to-assess operations in different national markets. Broadly speaking, performance evaluation measures can be categorized as either financial or nonfinancial techniques. Nonfinancial techniques are measurements that range from personnel development to the building of long-term profitability. Financial techniques involve financial measurements against established standards, budget, previous performance, and other subsidiaries of present operations. The financial techniques can be further split into two groups:

measurements against budgets and balance sheet ratios. All measures have their relative merits and demerits. Whatever performance measures are selected, the system should be kept as simple as possible; it should not burden managers with endless paperwork.

Further, measurements must preserve a proper balance between immediate results and long-term objectives. A higher rate of return in Brazil may be desirable in light of the economic and political instability threatening foreign investment in that country. However, such a target may be unrealistic because of foreign-exchange losses, import restrictions, and other impediments. Many companies temper a poor performance in the present with expectations for future profitability dependent upon a continued presence in the market.

Controlling Multinational Operations

Controls are defined as checkpoints and are used to verify performance progress by comparison with some standard often defined by top management in the planning process. However, as a corporation's size increases, the distance between top management and marketing operations grows, making the control and analysis process more difficult. At that point, effective controls have to be maintained. In a changing environment, information must come swiftly to ensure quick action in response to any success or failure. This timing factor has led to a trend toward tighter controls of foreign subsidiaries by U.S. corporations. It has been held, for example, that if Union Carbide Corp. had maintained tighter control over its Indian subsidiary, the Bhopal tragedy would not have happened.[25]

A second factor favoring stricter controls is the completion of the European Union's 1992 internal market program. Under this program, EU countries will represent a single market without any barriers. As a consequence, U.S. firms have wisely relocated plants and reorganized distribution and marketing functions to include these countries. However, control must go hand in hand with expansion. Tight control should ensure consistency in product and marketing performance.

The third reason for adoption of strict controls is the correction of unsatisfactory performance by subsidiaries. Frequently, such failure is caused by a subsidiary manager's incompetence. For whatever reason, control over subsidiaries should improve, as well as provide, standards for achievement.

Further, since an MNC typically has several foreign subsidiaries in different parts of the world, a good control system is important to ensure that these subsidiaries move together toward a common goal, spelled out by the corporate strategic plan. On the other hand, a poor control system can make the task of evaluation and adjustment a very cumbersome one. General Motors Corp., for example, operates in 17 European countries. Its European operations have been hurt by the corporation's lack of a coherent strategy and strong management. Its Adam Opel subsidiary in West Germany often has been pitted against its Vauxhall Motors Ltd. unit in Britain. In the absence of proper controls, both companies lost money. Thus, in early 1986, GM decided to overhaul the organization and impose new control procedures in Europe.[26]

A good control system is also vital in evaluating the performance of top management in each subsidiary. Since the environmental conditions surrounding each subsidiary differ, it is impossible to use a completely standard system of evaluation. Some managers are forced to operate under far more severe conditions (cultural, economic, political) than others. A good control system allows for consideration of these variant

Financial Measures of Performance

A number of financial measures of performance are available and relied upon by MNCs. Some of the more popular measures are income or profit contributions, cash flow, and performance relative to a budget. There is a consensus that no single measure of performance is adequate in and of itself. An ideal measure of the true economic benefit of a subsidiary would be arrived at by comparing the performance of the entire MNC with and without that subsidiary. This is difficult, if not impossible, to accomplish operationally, particularly when there are many interrelated subsidiaries in the multinational network. As a practical alternative, corporations rely on a combination of different measures to assess the performance of their operations, both domestic and overseas.

Budgets as Indicators of Performance Companies rely heavily on budgets to compare forecasts of the unit's results with actual results. The variance between the two is then analyzed to evaluate performance and to determine areas in need of improvement. A major problem in the use of budgets for performance evaluation is the setting of realistic, attainable numerical goals.

Income of Profit Contribution Accounting-based net income of a foreign operation is a logical and readily available index of performance. However, it can be an inaccurate measure of performance because profits can be manipulated, especially in the short run. For example, elimination of such staff functions as research may improve the profit picture for the purpose of performance evaluation. However, in the long run, such cuts can also hurt profit performance. Further, net income is not a useful measure for evaluating managerial performance because it typically reflects allocation of corporate headquarters' costs, which are beyond the control of the foreign manager.

Profit contribution is a better measure of managerial success than net income. Profit contribution is unit operating revenues less all expenses directly traceable to the unit, and this figure is more likely to include items under the manager's control. The major limitation of profit contribution is that it omits the unit's share of headquarters' costs. Both net income and profit contribution neglect the investment base required to generate earnings.

Return on Investment (ROI) Evaluation by return on investment is frequently used since it is believed that the ultimate test of performance is the relationship of profit to invested capital. *ROI* is computed by dividing the net income by the net assets. There is a good deal of controversy about what items should be included in the profits (numerator) and the investment base (denominator), and how they should be measured.

As far as marketing is concerned, different factors affect ROI differently. Empirical work by Douglas and Craig provides interesting insights on this issue.[27] Overall they found that, at least in the short run, increased expenditure on marketing mix variables depressed levels of ROI. However, in European markets, high price in conjunction with new product development and expenditure on advertising was positively related to ROI, while salesforce and other marketing type expenditures were negatively related to ROI.

In other foreign markets, the authors found little effect of marketing mix variables on ROI, and that only superior-quality products could be related to ROI. They argue that the consequent ambiguity can be explained by the fact that the effectiveness of different types of promotional activity may vary from one market to another.

Douglas and Craig's work failed to reinforce the opinion popularly held in the U. S. that overseas market share leads to profitability, as little correlation was found between market shares and ROI in European or other foreign markets. This result, however, may be due to manipulation of transfer pricing, where creative accounting is used to show losses in high-tax countries and profits in low-tax areas. In addition, the level of investment (joint venture, wholly owned subsidiary) may serve to obscure any relationship between ROI and marketing strategy.

Residual Income   *Residual income* is equal to a foreign operation's net income less an investment carrying charge equal to the unit's investment base multiplied by the cost of capital. A benefit of this approach is that it relates income to the investment costs of producing that income. Also, suboptimal decisions are not made with regard to investments, as may happen with ROI. Residual income, however, is subject to the same measurement problems associated with ROI.

Cash Flow   *Cash flow* is depreciation plus net income (after taxes). Benefits of the cash flow approach as a measure of profitability and performance are its familiarity to executives as a method and its compatibility with a capital budgeting framework. When figuring the items to be included in the cash flow computation for the foreign subsidiary, it is vital to include the returns to the rest of the corporate system rendered by the activities of the foreign operation. In addition, differential taxes levied on the foreign subsidiary, the cost of transferring funds back to the parent, and funds that can be repatriated to the parent should be included in the derivation.

Nonfinancial Measures

Concern for long-range profitability makes companies focus their concentration not only on the figures in the budget, but also on what lies behind the figures. Measuring foreign subsidiary performance is intimately connected with evaluating a wide range of nonfinancial aspects, some quantifiable, some not. It is these underlying factors that ultimately affect profits, although they may not show up in short-term profit statements.

Nonfinancial measures can cover any aspect of running a business. To be effective, they should be defined as clear and precise objectives with definite times of completion. For example, if a subsidiary plans to introduce in November a new product that has been successful elsewhere, a nonfinancial objective for that product might state that by April a market study of specific dimensions must be completed.

There can be any number of nonfinancial measures of performance. Management should develop a checklist of meaningful measures that it intends to use to rate the relative performance of affiliates.

From marketing's standpoint, one of the most important nonfinancial measures is market penetration. For many products, particularly for consumer products, many companies use market penetration as a yardstick to measure how well business is doing in a given market. A given percentage of the market is required to support the necessary level of promotion for a product to sell effectively and generally obtain a high enough level of visibility to make an overall impression on the consumer. Measuring market penetration can best be done by comparing company sales with the market as a whole. After the size of the potential market has been estimated, the percentage of available business actually captured by the subsidiary should be calculated for total sales and for sales by product. When compared with forecast sales, these figures will give a good measure of how aggressive local management has been and where weak spots in the product line are holding back the overall effort. However, market penetration should be appropriately qualified by the impact of other factors including degree of competition, local and foreign; impact of substitute products; treatment of export sales in view of local laws or incentives, production costs, or tariff position; weighting of captive sales to the total sales effort; and level of the sales effort (wholesale, retail, ultimate consumer).[28]

Evaluation of promotional effort must be basically qualitative, since it is difficult to establish a valid relationship between advertising and promotion expenses, and sales performance. Further, the suitability of promotional effort to the local market is most often the prime factor in evaluating effectiveness. Suitability of the product to the market may also have a significant effect on the marketing effort. Consumer preference evaluation, as well as social and cultural acceptance of the product, is especially important in areas where these factors may differ considerably from American norms. The subsidiary's staff is responsible for recommending and marketing the product that will best suit the local market.

Development of new products is closely linked to product suitability since the subsidiary must make recommendations from field experience as to product development trends in the market. An evaluation measure used by some firms is the frequency and quality of new product suggestions from the field subsidiaries to the parent R&D department and of new promotion and sales techniques.

Distribution and service evaluation may be combined, since the distributor is often responsible for after-sale servicing. The most frequently listed factors for evaluation in this area are most effective use of channels of distribution; attitudes of distributors, retailers, consumers; distributor performance; quality of after-sale servicing; and promptness in filling orders.

In all these areas, a long-term judgment question should always be present: Have actions been taken during the period under analysis that will help or hinder sales performance in subsequent periods?

Conflicts and Their Resolution

As is conceivable in any organizational setup, conflicts are bound to arise between different groups. In the context of international marketing such conflicts usually emerge from differing parent corporation and subsidiary points of view.

Certain problems severely block relationships between management in U.S. corporations and their foreign subsidiaries. For the following reasons, problems often arise in the control of foreign operations.

One of the biggest problems subsidiaries encounter in the control process is that corporate decisions are made too slowly. Delays in receiving important and urgent decisions from headquarters cause companies to miss out on many opportunities.

Subsidiary managers also find that too many reports have to be sent to headquarters. In most cases, they feel nobody reads these reports and that the importance of the information tends to be minimized. The result is that headquarters management often relies on information not from the subsidiary but from superficially formed impressions.

Another aspect of the control problem is attributed to low levels of credibility in both headquarters and the subsidiary management. Corporate executives tend to disregard the local manager's recommendations. As a result, in highly centralized and controlled companies, local managers must resort to persuasion to get their ideas accepted at headquarters. On the other hand, local managers tend to disregard headquarters' directives and doubt the soundness of its decisions because local managers often are uninformed about the reasons for the decisions or they cannot accept that a corporate executive is better informed or better qualified to make decisions. Thus, each distrusts the other's judgments and abilities.

Finally, one of the biggest problems in the control relationship is headquarters' lack of knowledge about conditions abroad. Most U.S. companies with foreign subsidiaries underestimate the importance of social, cultural, economic, and political conditions with which foreign subsidiaries must deal. Many companies are just not well informed about such conditions (see International Marketing Highlight 18.5).

■ International Marketing Highlight 18.5 ■

A Question of Culture

Bosses in France tend to be Napoleonic. Graduates as a rule of one of the elite Grandes Écoles, they are expected to be brilliant technical planners, equally adept at industry, finance, and government. They can be vulnerable to surprise when troops below fail to respond to orders from on high. Stiff hierarchies in big firms discourage informal relations and reinforce a sense of "them" and "us."

Managers in Italy tend to be more flexible. Firms' rules and regulations (where they exist) are often ignored. Informal networks of friends and family contacts matter instead. Decision making tends to be more secretive than elsewhere, and what goes on in a meeting is often less important than what happens before and after.

This can shock Germans, who on the whole prefer to go by the book. Board members tend to have years of technical training and higher degrees. Rarely will a German manager move out of his special field before reaching board-level. This is in sharp contrast to Britain, where tomorrow's top managers tend to be spotted young and then sent rapidly through every department in the firm, giving them a broad, but not always thorough, overview of its operations. To avoid clashes between these strongly flavored national cultures, some European companies prefer Swedish or Swiss chief executives, who, it seems, are better blenders.

Source: *The Economist,* December 7, 1991, p. 64.

An empirical investigation by Wiechmann and Pringle provides interesting insights into the problems that concern marketing executives of large U.S. and European multinationals and their subsidiaries worldwide.[29] In a nutshell, it is not primarily competition, political and legal pressure, nonavailability of channels, and differing social and cultural outlooks that bother marketing executives in corporate headquarters and their foreign subsidiaries. The worst problems are internal, those emerging from friction between two groups. For example, marketing executives at the headquarters may charge marketing managers in foreign subsidiaries with failure to formulate long-term strategy, while subsidiary managers are bothered by the parent company's overemphasis on short-term financial performance.

Summarized below are the major concerns of corporate marketing executives as well as those of subsidiary managers.

A) Problems identified by headquarters' executives:
- Lack of qualified international personnel
- Lack of strategic thinking and long-range planning at the subsidiary level
- Lack of marketing expertise at the subsidiary level
- Too little relevant communications between headquarters and the subsidiaries
- Insufficient utilization of multinational marketing experience
- Restricted headquarters control of the subsidiaries

B) Subsidiaries' concerns:
- Excessive headquarters control procedures
- Excessive financial and marketing constraints
- Insufficient participation of subsidiaries in product decisions
- Insensitivity of headquarters to local market differences
- Shortage of useful information from headquarters
- Lack of multinational orientation at headquarters

Naturally, some conflict is inevitable, simply because the orientation of the two groups is different. The corporate people want detailed information on subsidiary operations to enable them to unify and integrate their far-flung operations. Subsidiary executives prefer less control and more authority and want to be treated as autonomous units. Some conflict and tension may be desirable to help avert obsolete approaches to management and to encourage continual dialogue between the parties. However, some problems need to be eliminated, including such common areas of concern as deficiencies in the communication process, overemphasis on short-term issues, and failure to utilize fully the corporation's experience overseas.

To resolve shortcomings, the first step is to articulate the problems. Then, the causes of conflict should be established. For example, a subsidiary's short-term perspective may be related to unique competitive conditions in its market area. Finally, an appropriate solution should be found. The remedy for each cause will be different. The solution may range from open discussion between the corporation and its subsidiary to organizational changes. In any event, as a lasting solution to conflict resolution, foreign subsidiaries must be adequately involved in both strategy formulation and implementation processes.

Bartlett and Ghoshal note:

When Procter & Gamble launched Pampers in Europe, it directed the marketing strategy from European headquarters. The result: a big failure. The reason: P&G failed to take advantage of particular strengths of national units; country managers, bypassed in the planning, had no stake in the outcome.

The failure led P&G to rethink the way it used local subsidiaries and to form the highly successful "Eurobrand teams," made up of line and staff officers of key national subsidiaries. Shouldering the load in marketing development with product configurations, advertising themes, and packaging, Europbrand teams successfully introduced Vizir, a liquid detergent, in six countries within a year.

In pushing new strategies like this, P&G and other successful MNCs diverge from traditional hierarchical structures in which the top formulates—and the national subunit simply implements—strategy and planning. By cooperating and co-opting capabilities, the parent's sales and market share get a big boost from the country unit's technical expertise, market knowledge, and competitive awareness—all without losing boundary-crossing benefits like scale economies.[30]

Summary

As the scope of a firm's international business changes, its organizational structure must be adequately modified in accordance with its tasks and technology and the external environment. There are four main ways of structuring an international organization: international division structure, geographic structure, product structure, and matrix structure. The organizational structure is affected by such factors as quality of management, diversity of product line, size of firm, subsidiaries' locations and their characteristics, and existence of regional blocks within the market. Each of the different structures has relative merits and demerits. An empirical study of international organizations shows that most firms, however, follow a complex structure along the lines of the matrix organization. Added to that, firms have the international division or regional office to serve as a buffer between the corporate and host country management.

The choice of an appropriate organizational form for international marketing activities is dictated by such considerations as the relative importance of foreign markets vis-à-vis domestic markets, the evolutionary pattern of the firm's organizational structure, the nature of business and its related strategy, management's orientation (home country versus host country versus world orientation), and availability of qualified managers.

Business is conducted in a dynamic environment. As the environment undergoes change, there should be appropriate responsive change in the structure. Change is triggered by such factors as sales growth, adverse performance, introduction of new products, and changes in the external environment. The need for reorganization becomes noticeable as these causes articulate themselves in the form of specific indicators of organizational malaise, for example, conflict among divisions or duplication of administrative services, among many other signs of trouble. The change should be managed in such a way that organizational harmony continues to be maintained. Thus, consultations with people likely to be affected by the change and gradual introduction of change would be in order.

An important decision for international marketing executives to make at the headquarters level is how much decision-making authority will be delegated to subsidiary management. To the extent that marketing is a *polycentric* function subject to influence by local factors, the primary responsibility for marketing decisions is delegated to local management. However, product-related decisions remain largely the prerogative of the parent corporation's management with subsidiary management dominating in decisions of price, promotion, and distribution. The extent of authority delegation differs also according to parent corporation national identity. For example, U.S. multinationals as a group prefer greater centralization than do European or Japanese multinationals. Similarly, the nature of a product also influences authority delegation decisions.

Performance evaluation and control of foreign operations are linked with organizational structure. There are two types of performance evaluation measures, financial and nonfinancial. Financial techniques include measurements against budgets and balance sheet ratios. Nonfinancial measures include market penetration, affiliate export sales results, salesforce workload appraisals, and the general attitudes of distributors, dealers, and large customers toward the company.

Organizational conflicts are inevitable between corporate executives and subsidiary management. One empirical study on the subject showed that the worst problems are internal, emerging from friction between the two groups. For example, both groups charge each other with pursuing short-term orientations. While some of the conflicts can be expected and tolerated because of the different perspectives of their work situations, efforts by and large must be made to eliminate the underlying causes of conflicts with improvements in the organizational structure to smooth the way.

Review Questions

1. What factors affect an organization structure in the context of international marketing?
2. What factors lead a company to opt for the matrix form of organization?
3. What criteria may a firm employ to determine an appropriate organization for structuring international business?
4. Differentiate between ethnocentric, polycentric, and geocentric orientations of international executives. How does each orientation affect organization structure?
5. What factors necessitate change in organizational design to accommodate international marketing?
6. To what extent are marketing decisions delegated to overseas subsidiaries' managers? What insights do empirical findings provide on this issue?
7. What different ways are there to integrate multinational marketing activities?
8. Discuss market penetration as a measure of performance evaluation in international marketing.

Creative Questions

1. Traditionally, subsidiaries have played a secondary role doing what the headquarter desired. Illustrate, with the help of an example, how subsidiaries could become a significant partner in global growth of the parent corporation.

2. What is relationship marketing? How could this concept work in international marketing? Illustrate with an example.

Endnotes

1. Arvind V. Phatak, *International Dimensions of Management* (Boston: Kent Publishing Company, 1983), pp. 65–89.

2. *See* William G. Egelhoff, "Strategy and Structure in Multinational Corporations: A Revision of the Stopford and Wells Model," *Strategic Management Journal*, Vol. 9 (1988), pp. 1–14.

3. William H. Davidson and Philippe Haspeslagh, "Shaping a Global Product Organization," *Harvard Business Review*, July–August 1982, pp. 125–32.

4. Paul R. Lawrence, Harvey F. Kilodny, and Stanley M. David, "The Human Side of the Matrix," *Organizational Dynamics*, Summer 1979, pp. 43–47. *Also see* William C. Goggin, "How the Multinational Structure Works at Dow Corning," *Harvard Business Review*, January–February 1974, pp. 64–65.

5. Y. L. Doz, *Power Systems and Telecommunications Equipment: Government Control and Multinational Strategic Management* (New York: Praeger, 1979), p. 237.

6. Paul R. Lawrence et al., "The Human Side of the Matrix," *Organizational Dynamics*, Summer 1979, p. 47.

7. Stanley M. David and Paul R. Lawrence, "Problems of Matrix Organization," *Harvard Business Review*, May–June 1978, pp. 134–36.

8. Milton G. Halman, "Organization and Staffing of Foreign Operations of Multinational Corporations," a paper presented at the Academy of International Business Meeting, New Orleans, October 25, 1980.

9. *See* S. Samuel Craig, Susan P. Douglas, and Srinivas K. Reddy, "Market Structure, Performance and Strategy: A Comparison of U.S. and European Markets," in S. Tamer Cavusgil, ed., *Advances in International Marketing* (Greenwich, CT: Jai Press, Inc., 1987), pp. 1–22.

10. Stefan H. Robock, Kenneth Simmons, and Jack Zwick, *International Business and Multinational Enterprise*, 4th ed. (Homewood, IL: Irwin, 1989), pp. 270–72. *Also see* Gunnar Hedlund, "Organization In-between: The Evaluation of the Mother-Daughter Structure of Managing Foreign Subsidiaries in Swedish Multinational Corporations," *Journal of International Business Studies*, Fall 1984, pp. 109–24.

11. *See* David K. Tse, Kam-hon Lee, Lean Vertinsky, and Donald A. Wehrung, "Does Culture Matter? A Cross-Cultural Study of Executives' Choice, Decisiveness, and Risk Adjustment in International Marketing," *Journal of Marketing*, October 1988, pp. 81–95. *Also see* Lane Kelley, Arthur Whatley, and Reginald Worthley, "Assessing the Effects of Culture on Managerial Attitudes: A Three-Culture Test," *Journal of International Business Studies*, Summer 1987, pp. 17–32.

12. *See* Christopher A. Bartlett, "MNCs: Get Off the Organization Merry-Go-Round," *Harvard Business Review*, March–April 1983, pp. 138–46.

13. *See* Subhash C. Jain, *Marketing Planning and Strategy*, 3rd ed. (Cincinnati, OH:South-Western Publishing Co., 1993), Ch. 11.

14. *See* Jeremy Main, "How to Go Gloabl—And Why," *Fortune*, August 28, 1989, p. 70.

15. Christopher A. Bartlett and Sumantra Ghoshal, *Managing Across Borders: The Transnational Solution* (Boston: Harvard Business School Press, 1989).

16. R. J. Aylmer, "Who Makes Marketing Decisions in the Multinational Firm?" *Journal of Marketing*, October 1970, pp. 25–30. *Also see* Donna G. Goehle, *Decision Making in Multinational Corporations* (Ann Arbor, MI: University Research Press, 1980); and J. Michael Geringer and Louis Hebert, "Control and Performance of International Joint Ventures," *Journal of International Business Studies*, Summer 1989, pp. 235–54.

17. William K. Brandt and James M. Hulbert, "Headquarters Guidance in Marketing Strategy in the Multinational Subsidiary," *Columbia Journal of World Business*, Winter 1977, pp. 7–14. *Also see* Zada L. Martinez and David A. Ricks, "Multinational Parent Companies' Influence Over Human Resource Decisions of Affiliates: U.S. Firms in Mexico," *Journal of International Business Studies*, Fall 1989, pp. 465–88.

18. *See* Saeed Samiee, "Pricing in Marketing Strategies of U.S. and Foreign-Based Companies," *Journal of Business Research*, Vol. 15 (1987), pp. 17–30.

19. R. J. Aylmer, "Who Makes Marketing Decisions in the Multinational Firm?" *Journal of Marketing*, October 1970, pp. 25–30.

20. Stephen R. Gates and William G. Egelhoff, "Centralization in Headquarters—Subsidiary Relationships," *Journal of International Business Studies*, Summer 1986, pp. 71–92.

21. Jacques Picard, "How European Companies Control Marketing Decisions Abroad," *Columbia Journal of World Business*, Summer 1977, p. 120. *Also see* Hans Jansson, *Interfirm Linkages in a Developing Economy: The Case of Swedish Firms in India* (Uppsala, Sweden: Uppsala University, 1982); Charles Y. Young, "Demystifying Japanese Management Practices," *Harvard Business Review*, November–December 1984, p. 172.

22. Ulrich Wiechmann, "Integrating Multinational Marketing Activities," *Columbia Journal of World Business*, Winter 1974, p. 12.

23. *See* Norman Blackwell, Jean-Pierre Bizet, Peter Child, and David Hensley, "Shaping A Pan-European Organization," *The McKinsey Quarterly*, No. 2, 1991, pp. 94–111.

24. Joann S. Lublin, "Firms Ship Unit Headquarters Abroad," *The Wall Street Journal*, December 9, 1992, p. B1.

25. Thomas M. Gladwin and Ingo Walter, "Bhopal and the Multinational," *The Wall Street Journal*, January 16, 1985, p. 28.

26. "General Motors' Big European Overhaul," *Business Week*, February 10, 1986, p. 42.

27. Susan P. Douglas and C. Samuel Craig, "Examining Performance of U.S. Multinationals in Foreign Markets," *Journal of International Business Studies*, Winter 1983, pp. 51–62.

28. David Norburn, Sue Birley, Mark Dunn, and Adrian Payne, "A Four-Nation Study of the Relationship Between Marketing Effectiveness, Corporate Culture, Corporate Values, and Market Orientation," *Journal of International Business Studies*, Third Quarter 1990, pp. 451–68.

29. Ulrich E. Wiechmann and Lewis G. Pringle, "Problems that Plague Multinational Marketers," *Harvard Business Review*, July–August 1979, pp. 118–24.

30. Christopher A. Bartlett and Sumantra Ghoshal, "Tap Your Subsidiaries for Global Reach," *Harvard Business Review*, November–December 1986, p. ES26.

CHAPTER 19

Marketing Planning and Strategy for International Business

CHAPTER FOCUS

After studying this chapter, you should be able to:

- Describe perspectives of marketing planning at the corporate and subsidiary levels
- Examine the steps in achieving planning effectiveness
- Discuss the current and future role of the U.S. in light of emerging changes
- List strategic changes that MNCs are likely to face in the latter half of the 1990s

The essence of international marketing management is the development of appropriate objectives, strategies, and plans that culminate in the successful realization of foreign market opportunities. The world marketplace is marked by accelerating change requiring explicit statements of objectives and strategies.

Business across national boundaries became a dominant factor in world commerce after World War II. Today, for a number of U.S. companies, as well as for many non-U.S. multinationals, sales and/or revenues from overseas exceed domestic business. The international marketplace is changing fast. In the 1960s, U.S. corporations had an edge in many ways, but no longer. In such markets as automobiles, steel, watches, textile goods, and electronic equipment, there is fierce competition. In addition to multinational enterprises from Europe and Japan, corporations belonging to developing nations, such as South Korea, China, Taiwan, Brazil, and India, are increasingly participating in world markets, giving rise to new forms of competition.

Currently, MNCs are expanding at a rate of more than 10 percent a year, or twice the growth rate for gross world product. The prospect is that these business organizations will become even more important in the future. According to the projections of knowledgeable economists based on present trends, in the year 2000, the economy of the world will be more than half internationalized.

Although markets overseas are changing and the competition increasing, international markets offer attractive opportunities. As a matter of fact, markets across national boundaries frequently offer higher rates of return than domestic markets. However, to make a mark in the international arena, a company needs to define its objectives clearly, choosing appropriate strategies, and develop adequate plans to implement the chosen strategies.

The purpose of this chapter is fourfold. First, perspectives of international marketing planning and strategy are examined. This analysis is followed by a discussion of a short-term operations marketing plan. Next, concepts and procedures for developing and formulating international marketing strategy are studied. Finally, the unfolding environment likely to have an impact on international marketing in the rest of this century is probed. This final section highlights the challenges that lie ahead for international marketing executives.

Dimensions of International Planning and Strategy

Planning practices for multinational markets are far behind those for domestic markets. This is particularly true of strategic planning. Theoretically, international marketing planning and strategy should involve both subsidiary and headquarters management. Further planning should focus on operational matters as well as strategic issues. Currently, however, most marketing planning among MNCs is operational and short term. In a great many corporations, the effort amounts to a set of financial figures extrapolated for the next four to six quarters. In some cases, the plan is put together by the headquarters staff with meager inputs from the subsidiary. In some corporations, however, the planning task is entirely delegated to subsidiary management. In the latter case, the headquarters' review is skimpy and only ritualistic.

The challenge of successfully competing n the international field in the future will force corporations to become more systematic in planning efforts. Every industry must look ahead—1 year, 5 years, 10 years—and plan for: (a) the future political, social, and economic environment; (b) the evolution of that particular industry; and (c) how the industry must change to meet the problems and opportunities it judges it will face.

Essentially, marketing planning at the subsidiary level is short-term planning related to the next 12 to 15 months and not strategic planning, which usually has a long-run focus. A subsidiary's planning efforts should be duly coordinated with those at headquarters. Characteristically, it should be from the bottom up and should take into account the environmental realities surrounding its products/markets. In this effort, the parent corporation plays two roles. The first role involves facilitating linkage between corporate and subsidiary perspectives. This amounts to providing corporate-wide perspectives relative to its overall mission and direction, both generally and with reference to the subsidiary/country market. The second role includes establishing a worldwide planning system. Such a system is achieved by developing planning procedures and communicating them to subsidiaries. An additional role that corporate headquarters must perform is to serve as a catalyst in creating a planning culture among the subsidiary executives.

At headquarters, marketing planning focuses on coordination and approval of plans submitted by subsidiaries, as well as formulation of corporate-wide strategy. The strategy formulation in international business reflects not only the domestic experience of the company, but also management's orientation toward multinational business. Three management orientations were discussed in the previous chapter: ethnocentrism, polycentrism, and geocentrism. A company with a geocentric perspective tends to look at world markets as a whole, with no demarcation between domestic and international business. Its strategic focus is global. However, an executive with an ethnocentric orientation views international business as secondary, a place to dispose of "surplus" products left over after fulfilling domestic demand. The differences in these approaches have been illustrated by choices of branding policy.

- *Ethnocentric approach.* Branding policy in overseas companies stresses the parent company as a unifying feature, but not necessarily the origin of the parent company.

- *Polycentric approach.* Each local company brands products on an independent basis, consistent with local country criteria.

- *Geocentric approach.* A worldwide branding policy exists only for those brands that are acceptable worldwide.

Planning at a Subsidiary Level

Presumably, an overseas subsidiary would undertake both short-term marketing planning as well as strategic planning. The following section examines conceptual designs for formulating subsidiary plans. Also addressed are the problems that hinder the planning process. Finally, suggestions are made to resolve the problem.

Short-Term Planning

A short-term marketing plan constitutes the core of an overseas subsidiary's planning effort. It is operationally, not strategically, oriented. The plan covers marketing operations usually for about a year.

The complexity of planning varies among companies. In some cases, it may amount to simple preparation of sales budgets. In more globally-oriented firms, however, planning would involve multiple considerations to consolidate mutual interdependence between different overseas affiliates and the parent corporation.

The process of short-term marketing planning is depicted in Figure 19.1 The inputs for triggering the planning process are partly received from the parent corporation and partly generated within the subsidiary. The corporate headquarters shares with the subsidiary the perspectives of its mission and objective. This input helps the subsidiary to define its overall goals and specific marketing objectives. Headquarters, in order to establish homogeneity among different subsidiaries' plans, may prescribe a standard procedure for conducting the planning process. For example, a standard format may be required for sales forecasts/budgets. Additionally, the parent organization would provide the subsidiary an analysis of the shape of things to come in the environment. The planning inputs gathered at the subsidiary level consist of external and internal factors. External factors are the emerging trends in the product/market environment (for example, competition, legislation to be enacted, demands shifts, and the like). Internal factors include past sales data and the scope of activities in other functional areas of business.

Equipped with the above inputs, planning starts with a review of past sales and their extrapolation into the future. The extrapolated forecasts are duly revised in light of the planning inputs. For example, sales forecasts may need to be revised downward because of a newly established plant by a domestic competitor. Similarly, sales forecasts for a product/market may be increased if the subsidiary's production facilities expect to be able to manufacture an improved version of the product.

The final sales forecasts form the basis for generating action strategies and developing budget. Action strategies refer to the perspective to be pursued in different areas of the marketing mix—product, price, promotion, and distribution. The budget would include sales revenues, gross margin, full details of selling and administrative expenses, promotional allocations, and other overheads. The budget may include data from the past one or two years to permit historical comparisons. The budget should be prepared in local currency as well as in U.S. dollars.

The marketing budget must be reviewed by the subsidiary management to add to and accommodate the company-wide outlook. For example, the subsidiary's controller office would supply the cash-flow analysis. Similarly, the finance function would reflect the likely impact of the fluctuations in local currency value. Likewise, the budget would have appended a capital-expenditure and working-capital plan. In brief, the marketing budget does not constitute a complete budget. A variety of other financial information must be included before it is ready for submission to the corporate management.

Once the subsidiary review is complete, the short-term marketing plan emerges. This is submitted to the parent corporation for examination together with the subsidiary budget and other related information. Usually, the subsidiary plan and budget are presented to a corporate team in person. The meeting usually is held in the U.S. so the

706   **19   Marketing Planning and Strategy for International Business**

FIGURE 19.1   Framework for Short-Term Marketing Planning by Overseas Subsidiary

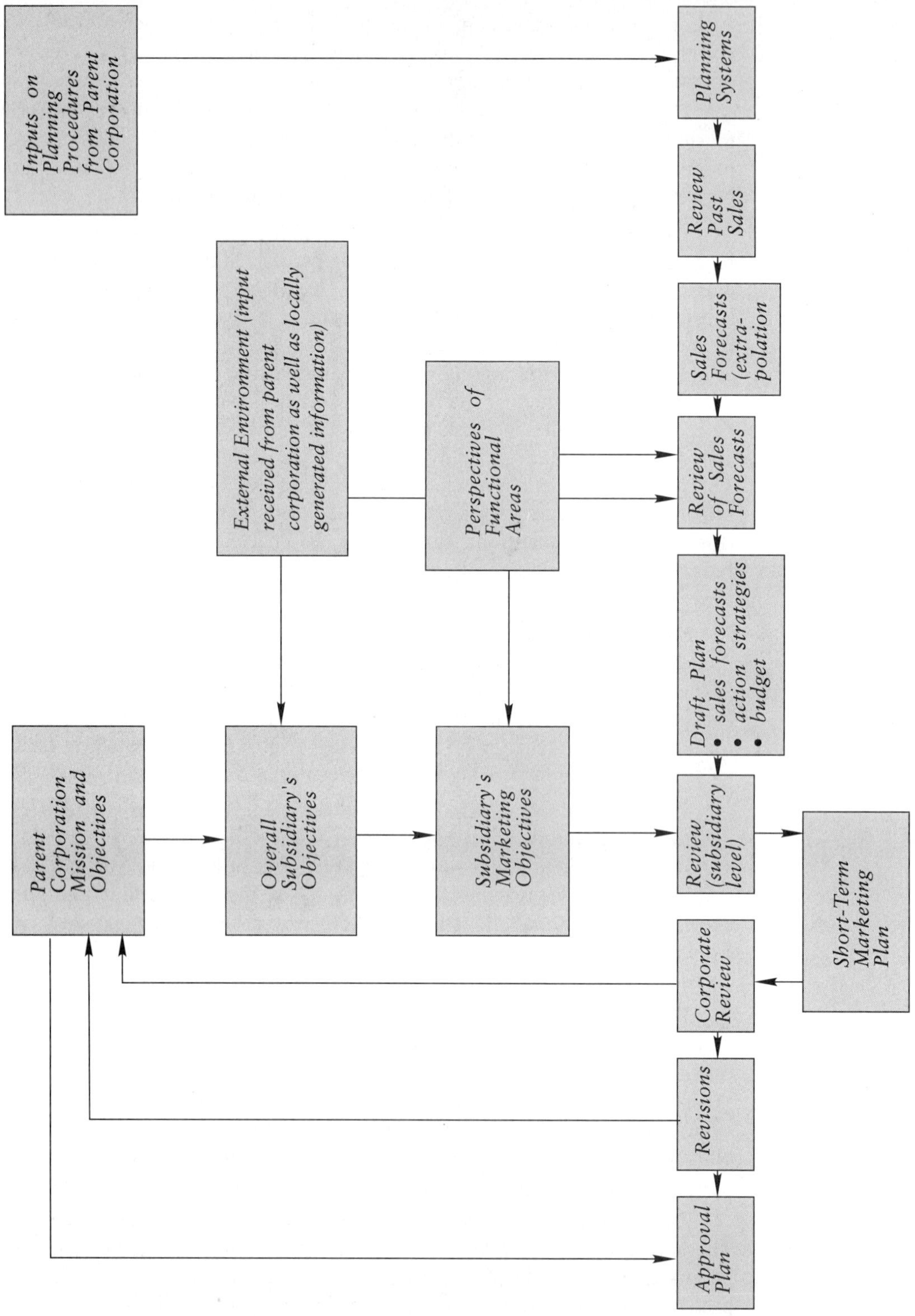

subsidiary executives have a chance to meet different corporate officers and visit various plants and facilities.

If the corporation is regionally organized, the subsidiary may present its plan and budget to the regional management. The regional management then assimilates all the plans within the region and makes a region-wide presentation to the corporate management.

Revisions may be demanded in the marketing plan and/or the accompanying budget. The subsidiary management can accept the revisions or defend their position through supplying appropriate information and arguments. Once a compromise is reached, the parent corporation approves the plan, and it becomes the basis for the subsidiary's operations in the next year.

Ideally, the short-term marketing plan should be initiated by the subsidiary management. Further, it should bear a close relation to the subsidiary's strategic plan, which presumably would be appropriately linked to overall corporate strategy. In practice, however, it would be naive to expect such a systematic effort, for two reasons. First, the state of the art may not permit drawing plans in a smooth, sequential manner. Second, lack of necessary data and of proper management orientation impede adherence to a conceptually sound system. For example, corporate management with an ethnocentric orientation would want the corporate way of planning adopted without consideration of the local environment.

Strategic Planning Very few subsidiaries practice strategic market planning. As a matter of fact, anything beyond short-term planning mainly consists of longer-term extrapolations of the same plan. Such a perspective can be explained by two factors. First, the art of strategic planning is still emerging, and its articulation at the subsidiary level can be difficult. Second, many MNCs consider strategic planning to be the prerogative of the corporation and discourage subsidiary involvement. While centralization of strategic planning at headquarters may appear attractive, there is one crucial problem. Centrally developed strategic plans tend to consider the entire world to be similar, and thus, standardized strategies are formulated for all markets. Unfortunately, such an assumption cannot hold true. Markets outside the U.S. differ in many dimensions, and appropriate strategies to serve these markets cannot be formulated centrally.

Process of Strategic Market Planning Two basic factors of strategic planning are markets and competition. Surrounding these factors are sociocultural, technological, political, and regulatory concerns, unique to each market. Strategic market planning should begin wit customer analysis and end with differential marketing programs tailored to meet buyer needs, giving due consideration to environmental influences.

After a thorough analysis of buyer needs and expectations, R & D should be approached for development of a customized product as necessary. Strategic directions for introducing new products and penetrating new markets should be developed. The customization may simply involve adaptation of package design/size or may require an entirely new version of the product. The remaining ingredients of the marketing mix should be custom designed similarly. Once the strategy is approved by the parent corporation, implementation of the program begins. The implementation of a strategy may take years, and in the process several go/no-go decisions would be made.

In the development of different market-related strategies, the impact of emerging environmental trends ought to be incorporated. For example, traditional wage rates in Germany rose proportionally to productivity increases. This discipline has been one of the strengths of the German economy. However, in 1991 and 1992 wage rates increased by an average of 12 percent each year.[1] Since productivity increases accounted for less than half this amount, how much could be realized in substantial price increases? Naturally, a complete study of competitive conditions would be required to make this decision.

Problems of Strategic Market Planning A variety of problems hinders a subsidiary's planning process. The first problem concerns the availability of adequate information. Both the subsidiary and the parent corporation can be blamed for this problem. Subsidiaries often lack the knowledge and resources to scan the environment systematically and gather adequate information from the external environment. Further, internal information may not be adequately organized. Not the least problem is that available information on national trends and so on is often outdated, particularly in such emerging countries as Brazil and South Korea, which are changing fast.

As far as headquarters is concerned, there may not even be a worldwide marketing information system in place. Thus, information at headquarters from different subsidiaries and different groups is not adequately collected, nor is the gathered information properly disseminated.

Furthermore, sometimes information is poorly coordinated. Thus, while there might be an abundance of information, the right information may be nowhere to be found. Conceivably, headquarters could request information from a subsidiary that headquarters itself had made available.

Lack of an established planning system is another problem. Emphasis on day-to-day matters by headquarters discourages strategic planning at the subsidiary level. In some cases, the planning system is too complex and unnecessarily cumbersome. Thus, a major portion of marketing managers' time in subsidiary companies is spent on responding to the needs of the parent corporation.

Another problem concerns the scarcity of trained managers. Subsidiaries often lack trained personnel to undertake planning. This problem can, however, be mitigated through training arranged by the parent corporation. Finally, if the plan is adhered to as a rigid instrument of control, it could lead to intracompany fighting and manipulations to ensure meeting cost and revenue projections. Such fighting leads to rivalries, which are obviously counterproductive. Manipulations result in a distorted picture of performance.

Seeking Planning Effectiveness

Effective planning at the subsidiary level should be encouraged through the setting of objectives, the training of planning professionals, the development of planning and communications systems and a cordial, collaborative attitude among all the people involved. The core of these measures is cooperation between the subsidiary and the parent corporation (see International Marketing Highlight 9.1).

Objective Setting The subsidiary's objectives must not be directives from the home office, nor be defined solely by the subsidiary itself in isolation from corporate direction.

Rather, the objectives should be jointly set so that both corporate-wide perspectives and conditions peculiar to the subsidiary environment are weighed in arriving at the subsidiary objectives.

Cadre of Planning Professionals The corporation should develop a cadre of international strategic planning professionals. Such professionals should have awareness and insight into the country or region whose planning they coordinate. In other words, marketing planning at headquarters should not be entrusted to finance people who examine strictly in terms of set formulas and cut-off points. The planners at headquarters should be sensitive to the varying environment of each subsidiary before passing judgment on its financial performance.

Planning and Communication Systems Traditionally, MNCs have pursued standardized strategies worldwide. For example, if a corporate decision is made to increase market share for a particular product, that decision must be carried out globally. Standardization, however, ignores the realities of the marketplace in subsidiaries. The problem may be solved in two ways: (1) through overhauling the planning system to take into account the marketing environment of each subsidiary and (2) by developing appropriate databases through effective communication between the subsidiary and the home office.

International Marketing Highlight 19.1

Planning Activities at the Subsidiary Level

Grand Metropolitan monitors the effectiveness of subsidiary marketing programs annually, but evaluation is conducted at the sector level more frequently, and at the local level sales and marketing activity is often measured on a monthly basis.

At the start of each company year, long-term (i.e., four-year) objectives are updated and agreed upon and short-term objectives reviewed. (Long-term overall objectives are set by the individual sectors working in conjunction with representatives from the corporate planning department, but specific marketing tasks remain the exclusive province of the relevant sector managers.) Short-term marketing performance is judged by reference to these short- and long-term goals at regular intervals by local management and by sector management, both of which formally review progress at the end of each quarter.

In the autumn, each sector reviews its strategy and, if necessary, revises it. This review is finalized at the corporate center in December. Local marketing decisions are then amended in the light of any changes that have been agreed to. The review at this time is concerned with strategic concepts rather than specific quantified business objectives. These issues are settled at the subsequent set of meetings that take place in the spring, at which quantified objectives are agreed for actions consequent upon previously agreed strategies. The final step in the process is the submission and agreement of annual plans at local, sector, and corporate levels. This takes place in August/September.

Source: *Marketing Strategies for Global Growth and Competitiveness* (New York: Business International, no date), p. 74.

Collaborative Attitudes Both the subsidiary and the parent corporation should develop an attitude of cordiality toward each other. Neither can do an adequate job of marketing planning on its own. They should collaborate with each other, with the parent playing the staff role and the subsidiary assuming the line responsibility for marketing planning. This way, headquarters would be able to bring its systems capability to the planning, while the subsidiary would contribute its deep knowledge of the marketplace.

Marketing Planning at the Corporate Level

Corporate management mainly plays two planning-related roles. First, it provides various informational inputs to the subsidiaries and reviews and approves their plans. Second, it develops a corporate-wide strategic plan, which may be either one global strategic plan covering both domestic and international markets or two separate strategic plans, one each for domestic and international business. Presumably, companies with an ethnocentric or polycentric orientation would follow the latter course. Geocentrically-oriented firms, however, would consider global markets as one market and would not make a distinction between domestic and international business.

Corporate headquarters' role in the planning efforts of subsidiaries has been examined in the previous section. Studied in this section are different aspects of an MNC's strategic planning activity. Strategic planning among corporations became popular in the 1970s. Initial efforts at strategic planning, as might be expected, were limited to domestic business. Strategic planning in international business is still in the developmental state. Thus, overall experience in strategic planning for worldwide business is limited.

Strategic marketing planning constitutes only a part of the corporate strategic plan. *The true role of strategic marketing planning is to influence the behavior of the competitors and the evolution of the market to the advantage of the corporation.* Stated differently, *marketing strategy is the concept of changing the competitive environment.* Thus, a marketing strategy statement includes a description of the new competitive equilibrium to be created, the cause-and-effect relationships that will bring it about, and the logical steps to support the course direction. A strategic marketing plan specifies that sequence and timing of the steps that will alter competitive status. Against today's background of mounting labor costs, sluggish growth in home markets, shifting exchange rates, and rising import barriers abroad, international strategy becomes increasingly significant (see International Marketing Highlight 19.2).

Shrinking profit margins from domestic operations impel MNCs more strongly than ever to make explicit strategy statements. Marketing figures prominently in these statements.[2]

Two related developments appear to signal the continued importance of strategic planning for international business. First, companies that derive a major portion of their sales and profit from overseas activities and look at markets abroad for future growth must depend on a well-prepared strategy to pursue appropriate paths. Second, giving the changing patterns of competition, strategic planning is a critical factor for maintaining leverage in overseas markets.

Marketing Planning at the Corporate Level

International Marketing Highlight 19.2

Singapore Airlines—The Flying Beauty

It may be the world's 15th largest carrier, but Singapore Airlines is consistently the most profitable. In the year ending March 31, 1991, it made a net profit of S$913 million($513 million) on sales of S$4.9 billion. Its balance sheet shows a mere S$438 million in long-term debt and a cool S$2.1 billion in cash. The carrier has the youngest fleet of any big airline—the average age of its 46 aircraft is under 5 years. It is also the winner of countless awards for service.

The contrast with American and European airlines, many of which began to hemorrhage cash during the Gulf War and have yet to recover, could hardly be starker. This raises two intriguing questions: How has a tiny city-state with a population of under three million, and thus no automatic reservoir of passengers for its national carrier, managed to create a global airline? And can Singapore Airlines maintain its edge?

The recipe for success as described by Joseph Pillay, the airline's chairman since its formation in 1972, looks deceptively simple: "Our mission remains inviolable: offer the customer the best service that we are capable of providing; cut our costs to the bone; and generate a surplus to continue the unending process of renewal."

What has saved this from becoming just another empty mission statement is Singapore Airlines' relentless investment. The most important are 747-400s, which carry more people and fly farther than earlier versions of the jumbo. They also use 35 percent less fuel. Lower running costs and the ability to fly nonstop, a key factor in attracting high-yield business travelers, create bigger profits. These enable Singapore Airlines to pay cash for its aircraft. Another benefit of this virtuous circle is that aircraft can be sold before they are too old.

Source: The Economist, December 14, 1991, p. 74.

Planning Process The process for international strategic planning is depicted in Figure 19.2. The process consists of sequential steps to be followed. These steps are basic to strategic planning, irrespective of management's attitudinal orientation (see International Marketing Highlight 19.3).

FIGURE 19.2 Process of Strategic Marketing Planning at the Corporate Level

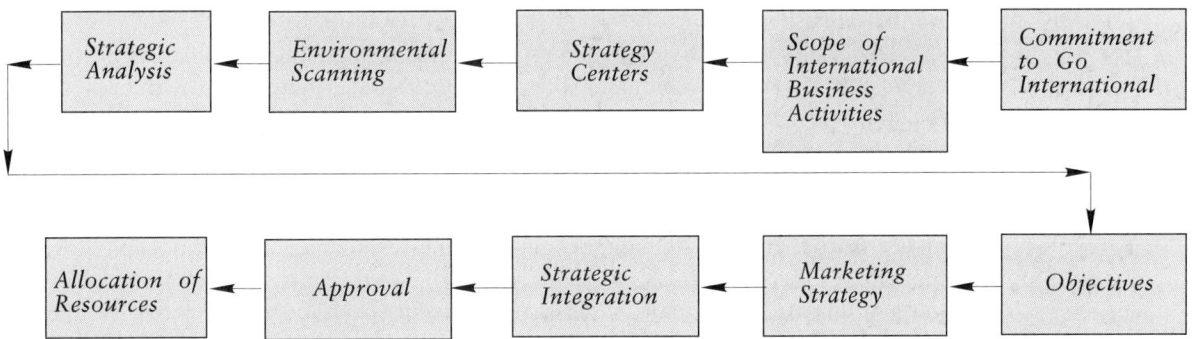

International Marketing Highlight 19.3

How IBM Approaches Global Strategic Planning

IBM has developed an approach to global strategic planning that takes into account the divergence between headquarters and regions. The approach revolves around its unique needs and corporate culture. These include parallel planning process, the ability to direct and leverage the immense resources of the organization worldwide, the ability of corporate planners to promote cultural cross-fertilization and act as "broker" of creative ideas, and the use of global models to promote common goals.

The core of IBM's strategic planning process resides within the divisions. Each geographic and functional division generates its own strategic plan on an annual cycle, coordinated by the corporate planning office. The cycle culminates in "commitment plans," which comprise a five-year strategic plan and a two-year detailed business plan. The plans represent both a blueprint for the division's response to regional market needs and opportunities and a financial commitment to the corporation. There's a qualitative and a quantitative dimension and the latter becomes the measurement for the following year.

Concurrent with the commitment plan cycle, a "top-down" planning mechanism provides direction from senior management. A series of strategic planning conferences is attended by 20 top executives. The strategies emerging from these conferences are often far-reaching in their implications for the organization. An example is the company's commitment to the concept of "market-driven quality" in the late 1980s. Although the concept sounds general, it has had implications for every part of the vast organization. It has affected not only the marketing and production techniques, but the very way in which IBM measures its own progress. This sets the overall framework, defines the business, and establishes a long-range intent.

A third critical dimension to the planning process is product planning. Within IBM, there is a separate framework for technology-driven planning of new products and service concepts, where the time frame may be as long as a decade. A continual exchange takes place between the technological research function and the corporate and divisional strategies, providing input on customer needs or "systems imperatives" on the one hand and defining the "art of the doable" on the other. The technology community provides major input to the corporate and divisional planning processes.

Source: Business International, May 28, 1990, pp. 169–70.

The process begins with the firm's commitment to go international. A corporation enters overseas markets to pursue long-term profitable growth. As growth prospects in the domestic market diminish, international markets provide a strategic alternative. On the other hand, companies frequently opt for international business in response to an invitation by a foreign interest. The decision to go, or not to go, international must be based on such considerations as corporate mission and objectives, long-term opportunity potential, analysis of strengths and weaknesses, management philosophy, opportunities at home, and financial implications of foreign entry.[3] The decision to enter international markets may be an open decision, or it may be relative to specific countries. The decision should be based on a complete examination of the economic, cultural, political, and business environment of the host countries.[4] It would be an arduous task to analyze a vast amount of data (assuming it is available) pertaining to different countries. As a shortcut, therefore, companies often choose countries that satisfy basic criteria such as GNP per capita, growth rate, and market size. Chapter 6, on economic environment, presents a framework for selecting international markets for making investments. This same framework is relevant in the strategic decision process.

Strategic Business Units

After overseas product/market matches are established, the next step is to reorganize different parts of the business that would be involved internationally into strategy centers or strategic business units. *Strategic business units* (*SBUs*) are self-contained businesses that meet three criteria: (1) they have a set of clearly defined external competitors, (2) their managers are responsible for developing and implementing their own strategies, and (3) their profitability can be measured in real income, rather than in artificial dollars posted as transfer payments between divisions. Once SBUs are identified, appointments of SBU heads should be made.

The steps discussed so far are the purview of top management. Such work should be undertaken at the highest level with analytical support provided by corporate staff. It should be strongly emphasized that SBUs do not replace the traditional organizational lines. The operations continue to be planned and implemented as in the past. Over and above the traditional organization, however, SBU structure is created for determining strategy. Thus, an SBU may be established around products/markets in different divisions in different countries. For example, a company may manufacture color TVs in a country, while in another country radios and stereos are manufactured as a part of the home entertainment division. For strategy development purposes, TVs, radios, and stereo equipment may be pulled together in an SBU.

Further strategic planning analysis henceforth is undertaken at the SBU level. In a large multiproduct, multimarket company, strategy cannot be developed at the top management level because it would be too complex a task for one office to examine the perspectives of all products/markets. Each SBU conducts opportunity analysis of the different products/markets under its control. This analysis can be accomplished by the product portfolio approach popularized by the Boston Consulting Group (BCG).

Product Portfolio Approach—The BCG Framework

The BCG framework is based on the assumption that the firm with the highest market share relative to its competitors should be able to produce at the lowest cost. Conversely, firms with a low market share relative to competition will be high-cost producers. By comparing relative market share positions (high/low) with market growth rates (high/low), the firm can position its different businesses on a two-by-two matrix.

Using the two dimensions discussed above, growth and market share, businesses can then be classified into four categories: stars, cash cows, question marks, and dogs. Businesses in each category exhibit different financial characteristics and offer different strategic choices.[5]

Stars High-growth market leaders are called *stars*. They generate large amounts of cash, but the cash they generate from earnings and depreciation is more than offset by the cash that must be put back into these businesses in the form of capital expenditures and increased working capital. Such heavy reinvestment is necessary to fund the capacity increases and inventory and receivable investment that go along with market share gains. Thus, star products represent probably the best profit opportunity available to a company, and their competitive position must be maintained.

Cash Cows   *Cash cows* are characterized by low growth and high market share. They are net providers of cash. Their high earnings coupled with their depreciation represent high cash inflows, while they need very little in the way of reinvestment. Thus, these products generate large cash surpluses, which help to pay dividends and interest, provide debt capacity, supply funds for R&D, meet overheads, and also make cash available for investment in other products.

Question Marks   Products that are in growth markets but have a low share are categorized as *question marks*. Because of growth, these products require more cash than they are able to generate on their own, since they have a low share of the market. If nothing is done to change its market share, the question mark will simply absorb large amounts of cash in the short run and later, as growth slows down, will become a dog. Thus, unless something is done to change its future outlook, a question mark remains a cash loser throughout its existence and ultimately becomes a "cash trap."

What can be done to make a question mark more viable? One alternative is to gain market share increases for it. Since the business is growing, it can be funded to dominance so that it may become a star, and later a cash cow when growth slows down. The other strategy is to divest the business. Outright sale is more desireable

Dogs   Products with low market share and in a low growth position are called *dogs*. Their poor competitive position condemns them to poor profits. Because growth is low, there is little potential for gaining sufficient share to achieve a viable cost position. Therefore, further investment in the business is rigorously avoided. An alternative is to convert dogs into cash, if there is an opportunity to do so.

The usage of the BCG framework for performing opportunity analysis in the context of international business is illustrated in Figure 19.3.[6] The top half of the figure shows product/market portfolios of competitors A and B. Competitor A is a market leader. In the U.S. and Canada, its business has reached maturity, while in Europe it has a solid position. The cash cow position in the U.S. and Canada should generate extra cash for investment in the star markets of Europe. Competitor A has an insignificant position in Brazil and no entry in the Japanese market. On the other hand, B is a smaller competitor, but it occupies a dominant position in the two fast-growing and potentially large markets of Japan and Brazil. It is quite conceivable that in the future, B may generate more total units sales than A, and thus seek lower costs through greater scale effects. The cost leadership may make B more competitive also even in mature markets (the U.S. and Canada), which currently are A's stronghold. In brief, if competitor A does not take adequate strategic measures in its illustrated position, in five years its position is quite likely to be as depicted as in the bottom half of Figure 19.3.

Following the BCG approach, a company may conduct an opportunity analysis by (1) analyzing its current international product/market portfolios, (2) analyzing the competitors' current international product/market portfolio, and (3) projecting its own and the competitors' future international product/market portfolios. The analysis may then be used to define objectives of each product/market. For example, competitor A in Figure 19.3 may set an objective to enter the Japanese market. Likewise, objective(s) may be set to make a major commitment to the Brazilian market. Essentially, a product/market objective should be stated either in terms of growth rate, market share, or profitability.

Once objectives have been specified, alternative strategy options are generated. The preferred strategy will usually have a focus on one of the areas of the marketing mix, product, price, promotion, or distribution. For example, the preferred strategy may be to reduce prices to maintain market share. Here the emphasis of the strategy is on pricing. Thus, pricing would be labeled as the core strategy, the area of primary concern. However, in order to make an integrated marketing decision, appropriate changes may have to be made in the product, promotion, and distribution areas. The strategic perspective in these areas can be called *supporting strategies*.

The strategic perspectives of each product/market will be consolidated into an SBU strategic plan. It is quite conceivable that in some cases an SBU consists of just one product/market. In that case, the product/market would represent the plan of the SBU. The strategic plans of worldwide SBUs are reviewed at the corporate level for the purpose of integration and to develop a corporate-wide posture to achieve synergies and realize trade-offs. Here again, the Boston Consulting Group portfolio framework can be used. Different SBUs can be positioned in the matrix. Based on the matrix position, the role of each SBU can be determined and resources allocated accordingly. For example, an SBU positioned as a cash cow may be expected to generate surplus cash. No new investments would be planned for such an SBU. On the other hand, a question mark SBU may be designated for conversion into a star, which would qualify it for new investments. Once that is accomplished, different SBU plans are approved, and a corporate-wide strategic plan is formulated, after which resources are allocated.

Figure 19.4 illustrates the Ford Motor Company's international matrix.[7] This matrix has two dimensions, "country attractiveness" and "competitive strengths," that have been based on a variety of factors. It is this multifactor characteristic that differentiates this approach from the one just discussed.

Country attractiveness was determined based on market size, market growth, government regulation, and economic and political stability. These factors were combined using a single linear scale as follows:

Country attractiveness = *market size + 2 x market growth + (0.5 x price control/regulation + 0.25 x homologation requirements + 0.25 x local content and compensatory export requirements) + (0.35 x inflation + 0.35 x trade balance + 0.3 x political factors)*

The weights were based on Ford's strategic planning perspective. Another company may use different weights.

Competitive strength also was computed using four factors (market share, product fit, contribution margin, and market support) in the following manner:

Competitive strength = *(0.5 x absolute market share + 0.5 industry position) x 2 + product fit + (0.5 x profit per unit + 0.5 x profit percentage of net deal cost) + market support*

FIGURE 19.3 Strategic Analysis Using the Product Portfolio Approach

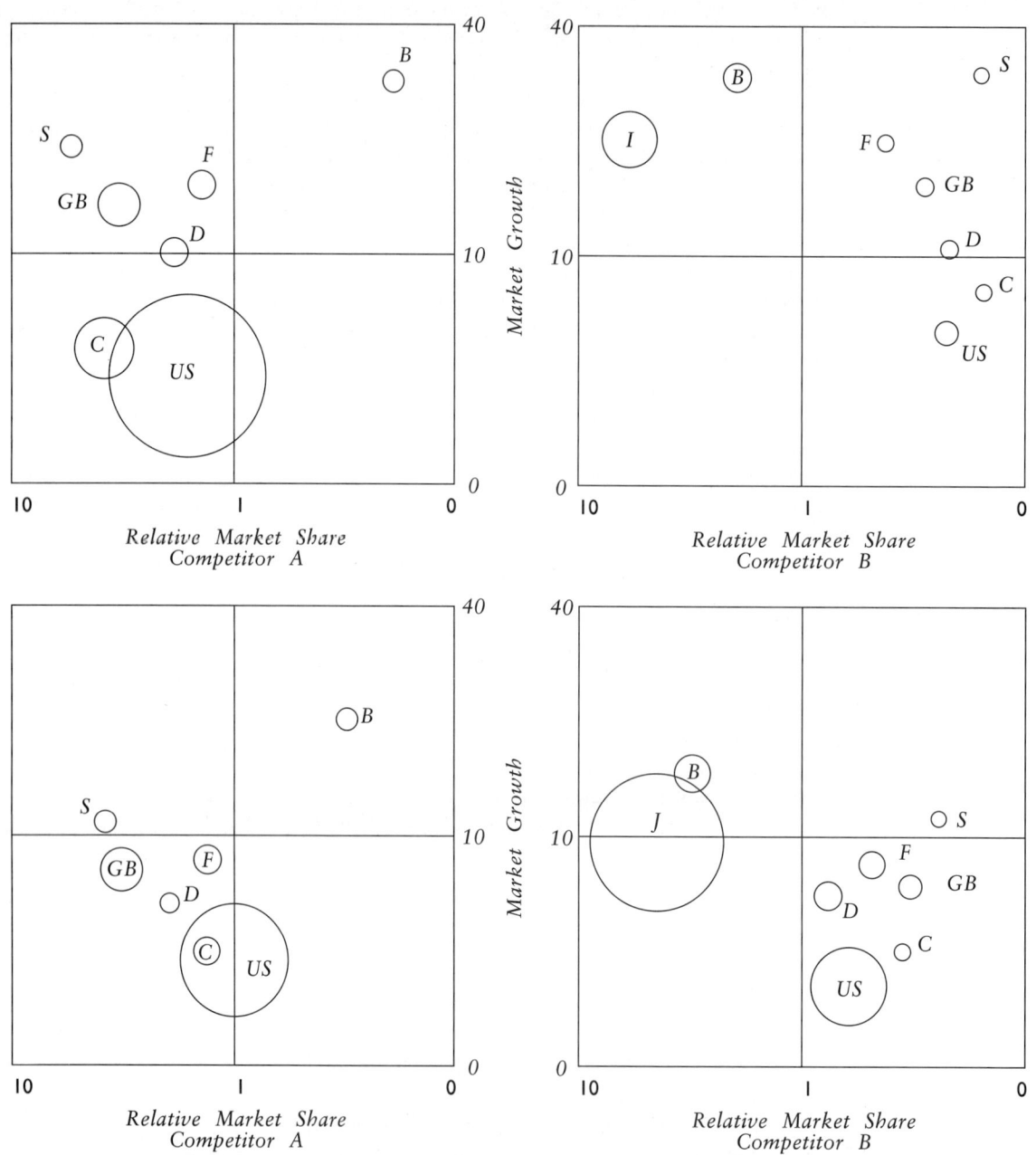

(B = Brazil, C = Canada, D = Germany, F = France, GB = Great Britain, J = Japan, S = Spain, US = United States)

Source: Jean-Claude Larréché, "The International Product-Market Portfolio," in Subhash C. Jain, ed., *Research Frontiers in Marketing: Dialogues and Direction*, Educators' Conference Proceedings (Chicago: American Marketing Association, 1978), p. 278

FIGURE 19.4 Matrix for Plotting Products

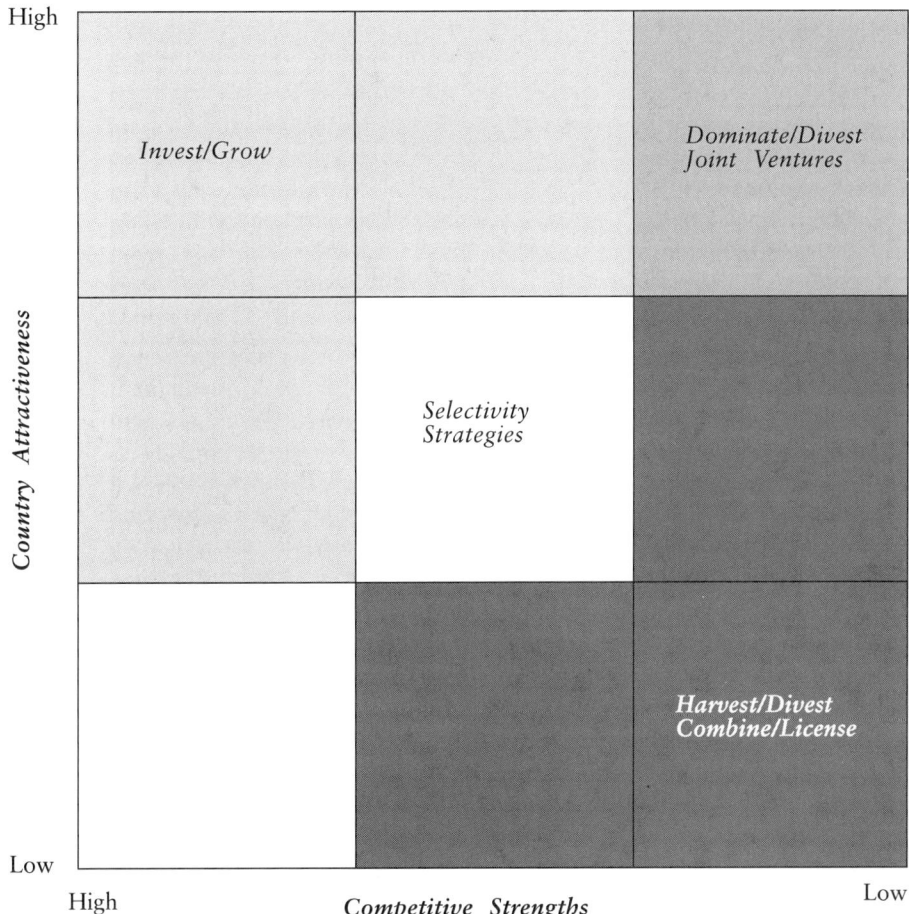

Figure 19.5 shows the position of different countries on the matrix developed using the ratings that were computed based on country attractiveness and competitive strength scores. The invest/grow countries indicate where the company must make a strong commitment. The harvest/divest position refers to countries where harvesting profits or selling the business may be generally appropriate. The dominate/divest joint venture position represents a difficult strategic choice because the firm is competitively weak but the market is appealing. The final decision demands a careful analysis of investment requirements and other available options.

Essentially, as is done with the BCG approach, the multifactor matrix approach offers guidelines for strategy formulation in international market environments. A company may position its products or country markets on the matrix to study their present standing. The future direction of different countries also can be developed, assuming no changes are made in the strategy. The future perspective may be compared with the corporate mission to identify gaps between what is desired and what may be

FIGURE 19.5 European Matrix

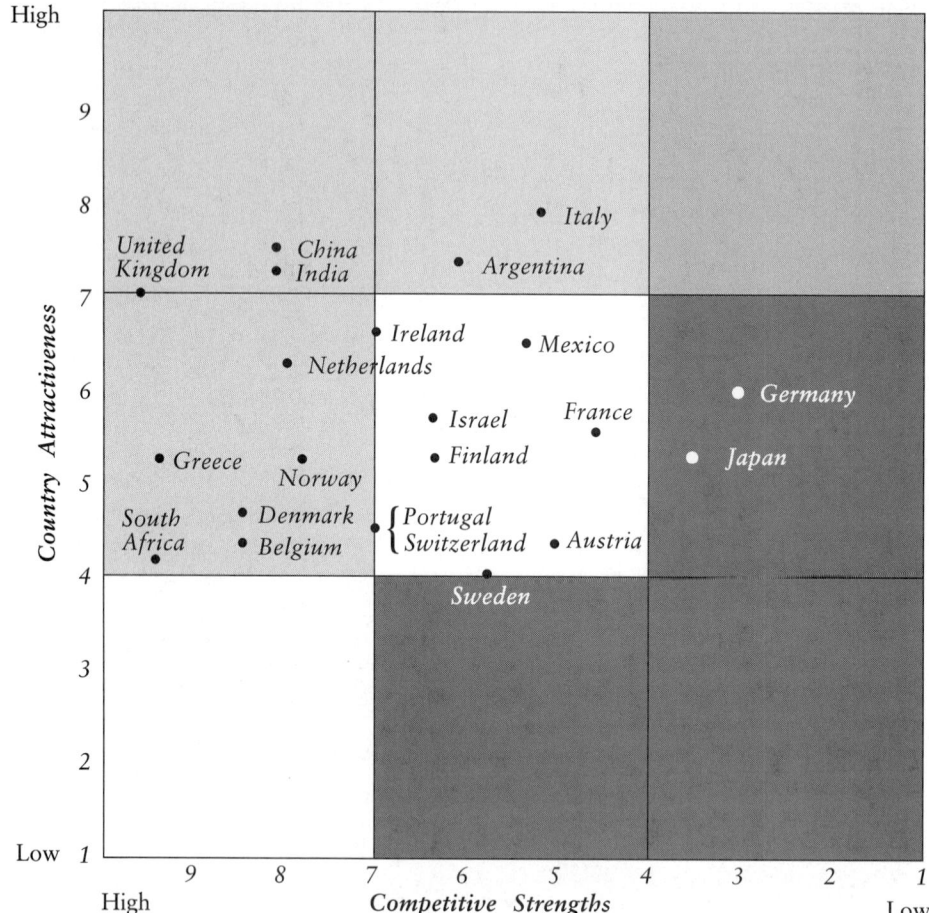

expected if no measures are taken now. Filling these gaps will require making strategic moves for different countries. Once strategic alternatives for an individual country have been identified, the final choice of a strategy will be based on the scope of the overall corporation vis-à-vis the matrix. For example, a country's prospects along the diagonal may appear good, but business in this country cannot be funded in preference to a business in the "high-high" cell.[8]

The strategic planning process just discussed is equally relevant to smaller companies. For example, a small company mainly involved overseas through exporting may use the BCG framework to strategically choose markets where it should lay greater emphasis. Similarly, it may position its overseas distributor on the matrix to determine their relative importance and decide the amount of headquarters support that should be allocated to each.

Information Scanning and Monitoring

MNCs, today more than ever before, are profoundly sensitive to social, economic, political, and technological changes. Each company must scan and monitor relevant changes in the environment to meet these challenges. The scanned information must be analyzed for its impact on marketing strategy. Finally, the impact should be absorbed through appropriate changes in marketing strategy.

The scanning system ought to be comprehensive and include monitoring in several different areas: political, governmental, economic, social, demographic, technological, markets, and resources. Many people will be necessary for whatever monitoring system is developed, because the results must be assessed systematically. Issues considered to be most vital to a company should be followed by action plans stating what the firm is going to do in each area: nothing, gather more data, change product lines, go into new business opportunities, build a defense, or whatever. The monitoring system must be custom-designed for the particular needs of a company.

The development of a system for monitoring diverse and critical areas is an important management task that requires not only the assembly of information, but also the translation of information into whatever meaning it has for the company —opportunities to be grasped or threats to be averted.[9] The resultant system may simply be an organized way for a group of assigned monitors to abstract and process information in cross-disciplinary modes and define the meanings for the company; or the system may involve the use of some of the many new techniques available (for example, Delphi and cross-impact studies).

There are many organizations (for example, Business International Corporation, The Futures Group, and SRI International) and a variety of published sources with information on different areas that is pertinent to monitoring the international business scene. Some of these sources of information have been mentioned in previous chapters. For example, Chapter 10 on marketing research discussed data sources appropriate for demographic monitoring. Chapter 11 on market segmentation identified different ways of classifying market segments, a valuable tool for monitoring. Chapter 8 on political environments noted organizations active in rating countries as political risks.

Achieving Planning Effectiveness

A previous section examined the problems that hinder effective marketing planning at the subsidiary level—similar problems complicate the planning effort at the parent level.

These problems can be categorized as the *management type* (poor definition of planning roles, unclear expectations from planning, short-run perspective, insensitivity to foreign conditions, resistance to headquarters direction, cultural bias against forward planning, local market myopia, and "doctoring" of data), and the *planning type* (oversophistication for subsidiary, overformalization, standardized criteria for evaluation, insufficient data support for subsidiary, scarce market data, unreliable or outdated information, inadequate information system, and unskilled planners).

The problem may exist either at headquarters or at the foreign subsidiary. The geneses of these problems are unwillingness to change, lack of adequate and timely information, and poor communications. While some problems must be tolerated as constraints because of complexity of planning in MNCs, some difficulties can be solved, or at least minimized, by streamlining the system and encouraging mutual understanding of others' roles and viewpoints. The planners at headquarters can play a unique role in smoothing the functioning of the planning activity.

In order for planning professionals at headquarters to be effective, they should serve as agents for bringing corporate direction and subsidiary goals together. For example, the headquarters planners should provide information about techniques and factual data related to international decisions to top management. Planners should find ways of reconciling corporate needs and host country requirements.

Epilogue

This section concludes not only this chapter but also this book, and therefore it seems appropriate to include an overview of American business and trade across national boundaries. A projection of things to come indicates many challenges for international marketers in future years.

For much of the WWII postwar period, international trade and finance occupied only a minor role in the U.S. economy. Exports and imports were a small percentage of U.S. gross national product as compared with the significant, and sometimes dominant, role played by foreign trade in most other industrial economies. Since the driving forces behind the U.S. economy were primarily domestic, policy initiatives by governments of other countries were thought to have only a small impact on the course of this country's economic growth and prosperity.

In addition, during the same period, the U.S. trading position was believed strong, particularly in capital goods, transportation, scientific equipment, and other high-technology industries. Concern among Europeans focused on fears of a growing and perhaps permanent "technological gap" between themselves and the U.S. U.S. direct investment abroad was increasing continuously and rapidly, accounting for a significant portion of the world's production and exports and giving rise to large-scale development of the world's production and distribution systems to serve world markets. The U.S. dollar was the key international reserve currency, and although the U.S. balance-of-payments deficits were becoming a permanent feature of the postwar period, their size generally was not thought to cause major disequilibrating problems for the world economy. Indeed, the main issue was how best to mange aid, trade, and investment without straining the absorbing capabilities of foreign economies.

The U.S. was the dominant force in the world economy at the end of World War II and for approximately two decades thereafter. It took the lead in restructuring the world's economic and political systems and in fostering the postwar trend toward greater international economic and political integration through both its domestic and foreign policies and programs. Its active participation in the United Nations, the International Monetary Fund, the International Bank for Reconstruction and Development (World Bank), the General Agreement on Tariffs and Trade (GATT), and other postwar international organizations has shown the U.S. leadership and its commitment to global cooperation. Although U.S. foreign sector activities in the past have had relatively little effect on the U.S. economy, its trade, investment, and monetary policies and programs were essential to the economic and political interests of the free world.

New International Realities

The current situation presents a market contrast. The issues and problems confronting the world economy have grown in number, size, and complexity, with profound implications for U.S. international competitiveness. Although both the rate of economic growth and the domestic and international economic policies and programs of the U.S. continue to exert a strong influence on the economies of the industrialized and the developing world, U.S. economic prosperity now is inexorably linked with economic and political developments occurring in other countries.

U.S. exports and imports as a percentage of GNP and as a proportion of the total output of goods rose markedly in the 1970s and early 1980s and will continue to rise in relation to greater international interdependence. For some U.S. industries, exports and imports constitute a considerable percentage of total domestic output, and for a growing number of industries, changes in merchandise trade patterns can result in a significant number of gains or losses in domestic employment opportunities. For example, in 1992, (1) one out of every five jobs in the manufacturing sector depended on exports; (2) for each of those jobs an additional one was created in a supporting industry; (3) over 10.5 million domestic jobs depended on U.S. exports; (4) approximately 60 percent of U.S. imports were either essential minerals (for example, chromium, manganese, cobalt, and tin) or products that could not be readily produced domestically; and (5) one out of every three dollars of U.S. corporate profits was derived from international activities.[10]

Although U.S. technological gains have been impressive, the technological accomplishments of its main trading partners—particularly Japan, the Federal Republic of Germany, and the United Kingdom—and the high-technology manufacturing capabilities of the advanced developing countries—South Korea, India, Brazil, and Taiwan—have resulted in both a consistent narrowing of the so-called technological gap and greater competition among manufacturers of high-technology products.[11]

Record-setting United States balance-of-payment deficits have led to declines in the value of the U.S. dollar, whether measured as severe in relation to key foreign currencies or as moderate on a trade-weighted basis. As a result, concern developed, both at home and abroad, that the U.S. economy would no longer be competitive in world markets and that the stability of the world monetary arrangements had been severely and perhaps permanently affected. The depreciated U.S. dollar and persistent trade deficits with certain industrialized countries showed the United States that it was no longer free to pursue economic policies with internal rather than external considerations in mind. Indeed, they were symptomatic of a need for the United States to coordinate economic policies with those of other large industrialized countries.[12]

These examples show not only that U.S. policies and programs have profound effects on other countries, but also that the U.S. has become more vulnerable to developments in other countries. Clearly, the world is becoming increasingly interdependent, economically and politically. An important feature of this growing economic interdependence—and a measure of it—is the degree to which economic developments in one country (particularly those of the U.S.) are increasingly transmitted via market forces, or spillover, into other countries. In turn, this leads to foreign trade (and other) feedback effects that have an impact on U.S. domestic economic activity (see International Marketing Highlight 19.4).

International Marketing Highlight 19.4

How Do You Compete with Mexican Workers?

Dario Sanchez Delgado	Michael Schultz
26, married, two children	36, married, one child
Work: Welder at Chrysler plant in Toluca, Mexico	*Work:* Welder at Chrysler's Sterling Heights, Michigan, plant
Seniority: 5 years	*Seniority:* 17 years
Pay: $1.75 an hour	*Pay:* $16 an hour
Benefits: Mandated profit-sharing, extra vacation pay, one month's bonus at Christmas, a one-cent lunch	*Benefits:* Paid vacation, full health care, income protection for layoffs
Education: Junior High School	*Education:* High School, working on an associate's degree

Source: *Business Week*, March 16, 1992, p. 100.

The Current and the Future U.S. Role

As the foregoing discussion indicates, the U.S. has an enormous stake in economic and political interdependence. On the one hand, the U.S. is no longer insulated from international market developments with regard to terms of trade, price, availability of energy, fulfillment of raw materials requirements, and other relevant factors. On the other hand, the U.S. is the largest exporter and importer of goods and services, and the world's largest foreign investor. In addition, it is becoming the world's greatest host for foreign direct and portfolio investment and is a significant developer and exporter of high technology. The extent of U.S. leadership in restructuring the world's international economic system is likely to be a function of its perceptions of its current and future competitive strength. The central questions are what is the current international competitive position of U.S. industries and how can U.S. competitiveness be improved through public and private policies.

U.S. corporations face a strategic challenge. Competition from Europe, Japan, and elsewhere is becoming insurmountable. As the global market adapts and evolves, competition will further intensify. To cope with worldwide competition, U.S. companies must place renewed emphasis on marketing strategy. At the same time, the U.S. government should adopt policies that enhance, not hinder, corporate efforts in their struggle against foreign competition.[13]

Strategic Challenges for Multinational Corporations

The following review considers some of the important factors affecting the competitive position of U.S. multinationals in world markets and suggests positive courses of action for MNCs.[14]

Management of Foreign-Dominated Liquid Assets MNCs conduct business in a number of foreign currencies. The exchange rates of these currencies are subject to great upheavals with far-reaching consequences for earnings. These changes result from disturbances in international, social, political, and economic environments. Thus, in addition to protecting their business from competitive inroads, the management of foreign funds carries impact (for example, the decision on the best currency mix to maintain on a short-term basis).

Expansion or Growth Policies Traditionally, U.S. corporations have pursued expansion or growth overseas as an important corporate objective. Growth per se, however, may be problematic. The trade deficits of many countries (both among industrialized and developing nations) and a common desire among nations for self-sufficiency may render achievement of perpetual growth in foreign markets difficult. Even where opportunities abound, an entry should be clearly earmarked with the possibility of retrenchment and/or exit forced through economic nationalism or other political reasons. For example, it may become virtually impossible to raise capital in a host country, the traditional source of long-term funding, and that would certainly block growth.

Decentralization of the Production Process For both political and economic reasons, more and more industries may follow the strategic lead of the electronics industry and seek component specialization over product specialization. If not all components of a product can be efficiently manufactured by an MNC in one host country, the MNC may opt for specialization in a few components while depending on other sources for others. The decentralization of the production process is attractive to host nations because local involvement in the manufacture of the product would be encouraged.

Automation of Assembly Lines In advanced countries especially, many routine tasks on the assembly line might be performed by robots, Japan is way ahead in this area. The U.S. will probably move in the same direction in the coming years. Such automation of assembly lines should result in substantial cost reductions and uniformity in product quality, which in turn should affect favorably the U.S. competitive position in the world markets. [15]

Corporate-Labor Relationships The developing nations' MNCs, with the abundance of cheap labor in their factories, may emerge as a newly significant competitive force. This is likely to have a far-reaching impact on corporate-labor relationships in the industrialized countries. A new form of understanding and harmony between the traditional adversaries will become necessary for mutual survival. The change in labor-management agreements for the U.S. auto industry bears testimony to the emergence of this trend.

Globalization of Consumer Tastes Another interesting phenomenon concerns the development of a common worldwide preference for a variety of consumer goods. The global craze for designer jeans and fast foods illustrates the point.[16] However, the commonality of demand does not mean that the same marketing mix strategies will be effective in every overseas market. The marketing strategies must be appropriately customized to the local customs and traditions.

The world marketplace, as the end of the century approaches, will be quite different from what it was in, say, the 1960s, the 1970s, or even the late 1980s. While opportunities should abound, international marketers will need new strategic perspectives to capitalize successfully on these opportunities. The big growth and profits may not come from traditional policies and strategies. Corporations will need to develop new marketing strategies that not only enhance their competitiveness but also fit the needs of the future.[17]

Businesses as Citizens Environmental issues such as waste disposal and pollution are becoming ever more important. Businesses will be expected to play an important role in solving these problems (see International Marketing Highlight 19.5). In addition, improvement in the quality of education will be another significant social issue affecting the organizations. It is commonly felt that business can make a very useful contribution to basic literacy skills.[18]

International Marketing Highlight 19.5

Enlightened Capitalism

The London-based Body Shop, with 14 outlets in the U.S., puts environmental concerns at its core and in the process finds its way to the green in the customers' pockets. The skin- and hair care stores display literature on ozone depletion next to sunscreens and fill their windows with information on issues like global warming. Every employee is assigned to spend half a day each week on activist work. Customers get discounts if they bring their old bottles back to the store for recycling. In 1988, the chain collected over a million signatures in Britain on a petition asking Brazil's president to save the rain forests. In 13 years, the Body Shop has opened 420 stores in 38 countries.

Source: Fortune, February 12, 1990, p. 50.

People Power In the 1990s, a dramatic convergence of demographic, technological, competitive, and global forces is likely to shift power from employers to employees, from the board room to the workplace, where value is added and wealth is created.[19] Throughout North America, Europe, and Asia, these forces will converge in a strikingly similar manner—the power of the 1990s will be people power.

Summary

Effective global marketing calls for a systematic planning effort and an explicit statement of strategy. The need for a planned perspective has never been greater than in the past few years. The world marketplace is highly competitive and changing. The favorable conditions that American business once faced are no longer descriptive of the current situation. The economic turbulence during the 1970s and 1980s shifted the balance so that the simple extension of domestic business overseas could not suffice. The future has never held promises that the past will return. Thus, adequate strategic planning is essential to business success abroad.

Planning in the area of marketing must be undertaken both at the subsidiary and headquarters levels. An overseas subsidiary should engage in both short-term and strategic planning, Essentially, short-term planning involves reviewing past performance, making sales forecasts, and developing/revising marketing strategies to achieve the objectives. The next step is a budget, itemizing the various programs in the marketing strategy in monetary terms. The plan is then submitted to the corporation for approval. Usually the chief executive of the subsidiary presents the plan to the corporation at a meeting held in the U.S. Plan approval follows after revisions recommended by the corporation have been incorporated. Often the planning activity is conducted according to systems and procedures spelled out by corporate headquarters to foster homogeneity in the planning efforts of different subsidiaries.

Strategic planning is usually an exercise in long-term projections of sales and related matters. Both parent corporation and subsidiary share the blame for poor strategic planning. While the parent company may consider strategy development to be its prerogative, the subsidiary fails if it too does not take initiative in this direction. Various problems hinder effective planning at the subsidiary level, and some methods can improve a subsidiary's planning activities.

At the corporate level, the major emphasis is on strategic planning. In addition, the corporation reviews and approves the plans of subsidiaries. The corporate-level strategic planning process begins with a commitment to international business. This commitment is followed by a delineation of the scope of its overseas business and the identification of strategy centers and/or strategic business units. A strategic business unit may be defined as a stand-alone business with identifiable independence from other businesses of the corporation in terms of competition, prices, substitutability of product, style/quality, and impact of product withdrawal.

Strategy development efforts center on an SBU with a review of the environment and an analysis of the business' strategic role. Objectives of the SBU are set, and appropriate marketing strategies outlined. Strategies of different SBUs are reviewed and incorporated by the corporate people. Once the SBU plans have been approved, resources are allocated and the strategic plan becomes the guideline for direction and decision making.

The concept of product portfolio was introduced to determine an appropriate role for each business and to review and integrate SBU perspectives at the corporate level.

Worldwide strategic planning development is still rudimentary. This may be attributed in part to the relatively new development of the art of strategic planning. Strategic planners, however, can play a key role in improving the planning perspectives of their corporations. Suggestions have been made for planners to strive for improvements in strategic planning.

The chapter ended with an overview of the emerging environment—a summary of the shape of things to come— as identified and examined in previous chapters. Finally, eight strategic challenges (management of foreign-dominated liquid assets, expansion or growth policies, decentralization of the production process, automation of assembly lines, reevaluation of corporate-labor relationships, globalization of consumer tastes, the role of businesses as citizens, and the shift of power from employers to employees) that MNCs will likely face in coming years were summarized, and their implications for marketers were examined.

Review Questions

1. What type of planning is mainly conducted by overseas subsidiaries? What input does the parent corporation supposedly provide in their planning effort?
2. Why do many foreign subsidiaries *not* undertake strategic planning? Discuss.
3. What problems hinder a good planning job at the subsidiary level?
4. Examine the reasons that make strategic planning an important activity for the MNC.
5. How can a product portfolio framework apply in the international strategic planning process?
6. What role can strategic planners play in streamlining the planning activity? How?
7. Briefly list the environments/areas that MNCs should scan. Why is such scanning necessary?
8. Summarize the strategic challenges that MNCs are likely to face in the future years.

Creative Questions

1. Traditionally, strategic planning has been the purview of the parent corporation while subsidiaries concentrated on short-term planning. However, since subsidiaries have a better knowledge of local conditions, should they not be doing the strategic planning for their future? Discuss the pros and cons of the transfer of strategic planning responsibility to subsidiaries.
2. There are three billion people in Asia. Half of them are under age 25. Examine how such demographic changes are likely to open new opportunities in Asia.

Endnotes

1. "Ready To Take on the World," *The Economist*, January 15, 1994, p. 65.

2. Bronislaw J. Verhage and Eric Waarts, "Marketing Planning for Improved Performance: A Comparative Analysis," *International Marketing Review*, Summer 1988, pp. 20–30. Also see Martin Van Mesdag, "Winning It in Foreign Markets," *Harvard Business Review*, January–February 1987, pp. 71–74.

3. See Robert J. Mockler, "Strategic Planning for Multinational Operations: The Decision Marketing Process Involved," *Working Paper*, Business Research Institute, St. John's University, 1990.

4. See Leslie M. Dawson, "Multinational Strategic Planning for Third World Markets," *Journal of Global Marketing*, Spring 1988, pp. 29–50.

5. Subhash C. Jain, *Marketing Planning and Strategy*, 2nd ed. (Cincinnati, OH: South-Western Publishing Company, 1993), pp. 260–70.

6. Jean-Claude Larréché,"The International Product-Market Portfolio," in Subhash C. Jain, ed., *Research Frontiers in Marketing: Dialogues and Directions*, Educators' Conference Proceedings (Chicago: American Marketing Association, 1978), pp. 276–81.

7. Gilbert D. Harrell and Richard O. Kiefer, "Multinational Market Portfolio in Global Strategy Development," *International Marketing Review*, Vol. 10, No.1, 1993, pp. 60–72. Also see Subhash C. Jain, *Op. Cit*, pp. 271–80.

8. Susan P. Douglas and Dong Kee Rhee, "Examining Generic Competitive Strategy Types in U.S. and European Markets," *Journal of International Business Studies*, Fall 1985, pp. 437–64.

9. Sumantra Goshal, "Environmental Scanning in Korean Firms: Organizational Isomorphism in Action," *Journal of International Business Studies*, Spring 1988, pp. 69–86.

10. "U.S. Trade Facts," *Business America*, April 1994, p. 40.

11. Norihiko Shirouzu, "Korean Auto Makers Seeking to Tiptoe into Japan's Market," *Asian Wall Street Journal Weekly*, October 3, 1988, p.4.

12. Peter Nulty, "How the World Will Change," *Fortune*, January 15, 1990, p. 44.

13. Brian Toyne, Jeffrey S. Arpan, Andy H. Barnett, and David A. Ricks, "The International Competitiveness of U.S. Textile Mill Products Industry: Corporate Strategies for the Future," *Journal of International Business Studies*, Winter 1984, p. 160. *Also see* David A. Rickes et al., "Global Changes and Strategies for Increasing the International Competitiveness of the U.S. Man-Made Fibers Industry," *Columbia Journal of World Business*, Summer 1986, pp. 75–84.

14. William Lazer, "Changing Dimensions of International Marketing Management—The New Realities," *Journal of International Marketing*, Vol. 1, No. 3, 1993, pp. 93–103.

15. "The Responsive Factory," *Business Week*, Enterprise 1993, p. 48. *Also see* Keichi Ohmae, *Triad Power* (New York: The Free Press, 1985), Chapter 2.

16. Hajo Riesenbeck and Anthony Freeling, "How Global Are Global Brands?" *The McKinsey Quarterly*, No. 4, 1991, pp. 3–18.

17. William U. Lewis and Marvin Harris, "Why Globalization Must Prevail," *The McKinsey Quarterly*, No. 2, 1992, pp. 114–31. *Also see* Benjamin R. Barber, "Jihad *vs.* McWorld," *The Atlantic*, March, 1992, pp. 53–55, 58–63.

18. See Rosabeth Moss Kanter, "Transcending Business Boundaries: 12,000 World Managers View Change," *Harvard Business Review*, May–June 1991, pp. 151–64. *Also see* "Summit to Save the World," *Time*, June 1, 1992, p. 42.

19. "MNCs of Year 2000: Corporate Strategies for Success," *Crossborder Monitor*, March 23, 1994, p. 1.

PART 6

Cases

Case 29: Logitech

Early in the spring of 1990, Pierluigi Zappacosta, CEO of Logitech, reflected on the changing market conditions in North America and Europe and wondered what would be required to maintain and expand Logitech's position in the computer peripherals marketplace. Logitech had become one of three companies that dominated the global market for pointing devices for computers. While Logitech had captured a large unit share of the OEM (Original Equipment Manufacturer) mouse market, Microsoft was the clear leader in terms of industry standards and dollar share of the retail market, and KYE (Genius), having a strong retail presence in Europe, was poised to compete aggressively in North America.

Zappacosta recognized that Logitech had been slow to react to changes in market conditions, such as the 1987 introduction of Microsoft's "white mouse", a shapely design that had developed considerable consumer appeal. This, combined with eroding margins on the OEM mouse business, had left Zappacosta wondering whether Logitech could maintain a leadership position in the pointing device market. Logitech had been successful in developing leadership positions in other niches, such as scanners, and other opportunities existed. Committed to their mission of "connecting the computer to the world" by giving it "senses", Zappacosta wondered what direction(s) the company should take and what the priorities should be.

Company Background

Logitech SA was founded in October 1981 by Mr. Zappacosta and Daniel Borel in Switzerland after Bobst Graphics, the company with which the two had been developing a European word-processing/DTP package, was sold and the new owners did not want to continue the project. Zappacosta had met Borel at Stanford University, while they were completing their MS (Computer Science) degrees. After an initial attempt to bring US technology to Europe with their own software company, Borel, and then Zappacosta, had joined Bobst to gain industry contacts. They had then formed their own software company with Bobst as the major client. Giacomo Marini, a software manager at Olivetti and a friend of Zappacosta's from the time when they had both worked in Pisa, Italy, joined in founding Logitech together with a group of young engineers.

This case was prepared by Brock Smith under the supervision of Professor Adrian B. Ryans, for the sole purpose of providing material for class discussion at the Western Business School. Certain names and other identifying information may have disguised to protect confidentiality. It is not intended to illustrate either effective or ineffective handling of a managerial situation. Copyright © 1992 The University of Western Ontario. This material is not covered under authorization from CanCopy or any reproduction rights organization. Any form of reproduction, storage or transmittal of this material is prohibited without written permission from Western Business School, The University of Western Ontario, London, Canada N6A 3K7. Reprinted with permission, Western Business School.

Two contracts set the stage for the initial growth and development of the organization. First, they won a $1 million contract with Ricoh to develop hardware and software for use with Ricoh printers and scanners. Shortly thereafter, Logitech won a contract with Swiss Timing to develop hardware and software for use at the Olympic Games. Wanting to be close to Ricoh and developments in Silicon Valley, Zappacosta, and later Borel, and then Marini, moved to Palo Alto, California and created Logitech Inc. In March 1982, Logitech Inc. learned of a Swiss watch company, Depraz, that had developed a mouse. Recognizing the advantages of the mouse relative to other pointing devices such as cursor keys, light pens, and touch screens, Logitech secured the rights to market the Depraz mouse in the U.S. and packaged it with software for the operation of text and graphics programs.

A major turning point in the strategic direction of the organization came after Logitech secured a contract with Hewlett-Packard to supply 25,000 mice under an OEM contract. It quickly became evident that Hewlett-Packard's price and quality requirements could not be met by Logitech's initial strategy of contracting out manufacturing to Depraz. Adhering to a philosophy of having direct control of the critical elements of the business, Logitech bought the rights to manufacture and market a mouse designed by CC Corp. With help from Hewlett-Packard, Logitech redesigned the mouse for mass production and set up a manufacturing operation in Redwood City, California in 1984. Production was moved to Fremont, California in 1987 to a facility across the street from Logitech's U.S. headquarters.

Control over manufacturing and a commitment to quality led to rapid growth in the OEM mouse market with contracts from Apollo, Olivetti, AT&T, and other key computer manufacturers. However, Apple and IBM were wary of Logitech's manufacturing expertise and continued to buy most of their mice from Alps, a Japanese company operating in California, which had purchased Apple's keyboard and mouse facility and was the exclusive supplier to Microsoft.

In 1986 two events took place that would help solidify Logitech's future in the mouse market. First, due to slow growth in OEM sales, Logitech entered the retail market with the Series 7 mouse, a product that had been successful in the OEM market. Then, to win a piece of the Apple business and to satisfy the demands of OEM customers for Logitech to lower the cost of mice, Logitech set up a manufacturing base in Hsinchu, Taiwan, with an initial production capacity of 1 million mice per year, but potentially expandable to ten times that volume. In retrospect, Zappacosta thought they had been a bit lucky. For a $300,000 investment, they had secured a high volume, state-of-the-art, manufacturing plant in Taiwan's "Silicon Valley" just before Taiwan became a leader in manufacturing technology and a hot-bed of design creativity, and just as the mouse industry took off under the combined forces of Apple's Macintosh, desktop publishing, Microsoft's Windows, and other applications using graphical user interfaces.

In 1988, anticipating a unified Europe in 1992, and wanting to be close to Apple and potential customers such as IBM and Compaq in Europe, Logitech opened another manufacturing facility in Cork, Ireland, which had a capacity, similar to that of the Fremont plant, of about 1.5 million mice per year. At the same time, they broadened their product line with the introduction of a hand-held scanner, a product that shared some technological features with the mouse, that capitalized on Logitech's experience in software development, and that could be marketed through established retail channels.

By the end of 1989, Logitech had reached sales of over $100 million, employed about 1000 people, had manufacturing facilities on three continents, and had sales offices in England, Germany, Italy, France, Japan, Sweden, Switzerland, the United States, and Taiwan.

Culture

The culture at Logitech reflected the global nature and operations of the organization. Because employees had varied life and educational experiences from around the globe, they were appreciative and accepting of differences in backgrounds, perspectives, and styles. As Fabio Righi, Vice President Sales and Marketing, put it: "our greatest strength as well as our biggest challenge is that Logitech is an international company. It is difficult to be international and local at the same time. Local flavour affects/impacts everything."

Deeply rooted in the Logitech culture was a strong product/technical orientation. Employees gained considerable job satisfaction from being on the leading edge and working on bold, exciting projects. Fabio Righi, for example, talked of the elusive "atomic mouse" like a Grail that helps define the common purpose of the employees. As senior executives admitted, employees tended to be quite internally focused and did not make a great effort to have their beliefs validated before launching a new product into the marketplace. As Ron McClure, Vice President Strategic Marketing, put it: "We are the most critical users of our products. Customer need recognition is limited by their understanding of technology—they don't know what is possible!"

Related to this technical orientation was a strong design and production orientation. According to Chip Smith, Production Manager in Fremont, "Everything evolves around production. The floor, receiving and shipping, traffic, and order processing are key processes by which we satisfy consumers." Therefore, manufacturing was seen as a key marketing success factor.

There was also a strong spiritual component to the culture at Logitech. This was supported in part by the personal philosophies of the founders, but also by the shared vision that employees had for shaping the future. For example, aesthetics were a high priority, not only in the products, but also in the workplace itself. One might infer that if there was a Logitech company handbook, it would probably be *Zen and the Art of Motorcycle Maintenance*.

Working relationships at Logitech tended to be very informal, flexible, open, and close. Employees were genuinely excited to be on the leading edge and found their jobs and the "family" atmosphere fun. This "family" atmosphere was reinforced by Logitech's policy of hiring talented young professionals from around the world and relocating them to enrich their own and other's perspectives. Dislocated from their own families and culture, employees often relied on each other for social, emotional, and cultural support.

Consistent with the informal, close working relationships, there were few formal procedures and structures within Logitech. Executive decisions were generally made by consensus after seeking employee input. Worldwide interaction of management and staff was maintained on a daily basis by an electronic mail system.

Business Strategy

Pierluigi Zappacosta explained the long-term Logitech vision by saying: "Only if the computer becomes a little more human will it become an effective tool for the mind. And evolution of our own brain through computers is our long-term vision. Our more immediate mission is to connect the computer with the world by giving it "senses", humanize the interface to the computer, and help people turn data into meaningful information. Our goals are to maintain/attain the number one position in whatever markets we play in by redefining and continually changing the products and markets we compete in. We want to have a Logitech product on every computer desk."

To achieve their mission and objectives, Logitech's business strategy was to recognize major trends and technologies early, move fast in bringing quality products to market (forming alliances if necessary), develop in-house expertise for product extensions, become effective and efficient manufacturers, have the best sales force and channels to sell the products, and keep ahead of the competition by an accelerated pace of innovation.

Logitech competed aggressively in both the OEM and retail sides of the personal computer accessory business. On the OEM side of the business, they competed using innovation and skill in manufacturing and design that allowed them to bring new technology to market at very competitive prices (see estimated manufacturing costs in Table 1). Toward this end, Logitech had achieved an experience curve in mouse manufacturing of about 70%. On the retail side of the business, Logitech focused on image management. They wanted to be perceived in the marketplace as innovators that develop neat products that were fun to use and were easy to sell.

TABLE I Estimated Manufacturing Costs and Selling Prices

Mouse	Estimated Manufacturing Cost (Jan 1990)	Estimated Average Selling Price to Channel
Logitech S9	$25.00	$60.00
Microsoft Mouse	27.00	75.00
Pilot Mouse	17.40	33.00
Dexxa	16.30	19.50
Logitech OEM	15.20	22.00
Taiwanese OEM	13.10	16.50
Ergonomic (corded)	19.60	Not on the market
Ergonomic (cordless)	64.30	Not on the market

Source: Company records

About 60% of Logitech's unit sales were in the OEM segment but more than 60% of their revenue came from the retail segment. In both the OEM and retail markets, Logitech's financial success (see Exhibit 1) had been, and would continue to be, tied to the development and growth of the PC marketplace and recognition of the need to "humanize" the computer.

Product Development

Product development at Logitech involved finding or developing technologies that required Logitech's skills in design, mass manufacturing, and distribution to bring them to market. Logitech had three basic development strategies: start from scratch, evolve current in-house technology, or buy required technology at an advanced development stage from others. Starting from scratch added about a year to the product development process since employees had to learn about a technology, decide what to develop, and test product concepts. Building on current expertise to extend or develop new generations of products was the most common approach taken. If required technology was not available internally, then Logitech would buy it, make minor adjustments to bring it to market, then develop internally the skills required for product evolution.

Decisions on product development were usually based on consensus among senior managers and tended to be emotional and based on "gut feel" rather than extensive analysis and research. Some of the decision criteria that were considered, however, included licensing or development costs, manufacturing cost, margins, a six-month payback, whether it was going to be fun to work on, and whether the product could gain a 40% share of its market. Focus groups were sometimes used late in the process to validate the "gut feelings". However, Pierluigi Zappacosta recognized that more effort was needed to get qualitative feedback at earlier stages of the product development cycle.

At any given time there were 20–40 official projects in various stages of development, as well as others that were "unofficial". The major projects were managed by multi-functional new product teams. Currently, there was no central authority on any particular project, but Zappacosta recognized the need to have someone who knew how the whole picture was coming together. Logitech was spending over 7% of sales on R&D and money could be found for important projects. Zappacosta thought the biggest problem that Logitech faced in new product development was not getting caught up in "the fun of it."

Personal Computer Industry

After five years of rapid growth, the PC industry was in turmoil in early 1990. The initial standards established by IBM's Micro-Channel, EISA (the Micro-Channel alternative offered by Compaq and six other major vendors), RISC (various versions of reduced instruction set computing used primarily by engineering/scientific work-stations running under the Unix operating system), and Apple's Macintosh. Confusing matters even more were competing operating systems such as DOS, OS/2, and Unix and competing graphical user interfaces such as Microsoft's Windows (version 2), IBM's Presentation Manager, the Open Systems Foundation's "X", AT&T's Unix System 5, and Nest's "NestStep." All of these competing oper-

Case 29: Logitech

EXHIBIT 1 Selected Financial Data

Logitech International SA, Apples (In Swiss Francs)

Full Year Ending	3/31/87	3/31/88	3/31/89	Projected 3/31/90
Consolidated Revenue	33,543,351	62,806,740	124,110,684	180,000,000
Net Income after Tax	1,459,888	7,032,066	11,206,922	14,000,000
% of Revenues	4.35%	11.20%	9.03%	7.78%
Cash Flow	2,136,959	9,413,623	14,290,273	17,500,000
% of Revenues	6.37%	14.99%	11.51%	9.72%
Earnings per Bearer Share	—	54	76	96
Dividend per Bearer Share	—	—	12	16
Engineering, Research & Development Expenses	2,579,023	4,663,430	8,396,799	13,700,000
% of Revenues	7.69%	7.43%	6.77%	7.61%
Number of personnel	240	442	731	1,000

	3/31/87	3/31/88	3/31/89	3/31/90
Current Assets	12,117,422	27,026,936	75,526,814	108,000,000
Property, Plant & Equipment Gross	6,212,338	8,843,297	22,421,727	30,600,000
less Accumulated Depreciation	(1,412,316)	(2,139,330)	(5,222,681)	(8,500,000)
Property, Plant & Equipment Net	4,800,022	6,703,967	17,199,046	22,100,000
Other Non-Current Assets	328,775	2,273,945	1,184,542	3,900,000
Goodwill	0	14,214,241	13,093,605	11,200,000
Total Assets	17,246,219	50,219,089	107,004,007	145,200,000
Current Liabilities	8,945,618	18,701,970	36,775,490	37,200,000
Long-Term Debt & Deferred Taxes	3,858,044	5,517,119	10,541,326	43,500,000
Stockholders' Equity	4,442,557	26,000,000	59,687,191	69,500,000
Total Liabilities & Stockholders' Equity	17,246,219	50,219,089	107,004,007	145,200,000

Logitech International SA, Apples (In Swiss Francs)

	1988	1989
Net Sales	62,806,740	124,110,684
Cost of Goods Sold	30,921,004	71,493,833
Gross Profit	31,885,736	52,616,851
Operating Expenses		
Marketing, Sales and Support	10,070,523	21,081,432
General and Administration	5,553,719	10,276,622
Research, Development and Engineering	4,663,430	8,396,799
	20,287,672	39,754,853
Income from Operations	11,598,064	12,861,998
Other Expenses, Net	191,569	59,656
Income Before Income Taxes	11,406,495	12,802,342
Provision for Taxes on Income	4,374,429	1,594,420
Net Income	7,032,066	11,206,922

ating system and user interfaces, however, used mice or another pointing device to control the operating environment. While it was expected that graphical user interfaces would be adopted on most, if not all, systems, the rate of adoption would depend heavily on the success of Microsoft's newly announced Windows 3.0 for DOS and IBM's OS/2.

The industry itself exhibited characteristics of the maturity phase of the product life cycle. Competition was intense and a shake-out of the market was underway, which affected even some relatively large companies. Consumers were becoming more sophisticated and knowledgeable and did not require the same level of support and sales assistance that they had a few years earlier. Consequently, manufacturers were beginning to make inroads through alternative channels such as mail order, price clubs, and superstores, while traditional full-service retailers such as ComputerLand and Business Land were refocusing their efforts on organizations using outbound direct sales forces. Personal computers themselves were quickly becoming commodity items as limited product differentiation, short technology life-cycles, and steep experience curves combined to put substantial downward pressure on prices. With the early mystique of computers wearing off, users, and in particular corporations, were beginning to question and evaluate the impact of computer technology on employee productivity, health, and other aspects of organizational life. Stress injuries, for example, were gaining prominence and were being linked to workplace computer operation. One of these was carpal tunnel syndrome, which involved painful damage to the nerve that runs through the arm as a result of repetitive strain from the use of typewriters, computers, and other arm- or hand-operated equipment.

Carpal tunnel syndrome had received considerable media attention (see example in Exhibit 2) and a recent ordinance in California required corporations to take measures to reduce this type of workplace injury. Other concerns were also being raised about cathode ray tubes in terms of possible harmful emissions from computer screens and in terms of eye strain. Thus, while unit growth in the PC industry was expected to be in the 10–15% range, profits were eroding and consumers were becoming more critical and discerning.

The Mouse Marketplace

In the computer sense, "mice" were handheld mobile devices that used a combination of hardware and software to translate physical movement into digital signals that controlled cursor movement on a computer screen and executed commands. Named for their basic shape, mice (and trackballs) were more precise and flexible than other pointing devices such as light pens, touch screens, and cursor keys and were generally more intuitive and easier to use. While the first mice developed in the 1960s were mechanical in design and were used predominantly by engineers, mice were now mostly opto-mechanical in technology and were used by a wide variety of users, including children, for a variety of applications ranging from drawing to interacting with most business software.

Market Development

In December 1985, Logitech entered the retail mouse market, first in North America and then in Europe with the Logitech mouse, a retail version of their successful Series 7 OEM mouse. Adopting a penetration strategy for the more knowledgeable and price-

TABLE 2 Estimated World Retail Sales (in thousands of units)

Calendar Year	Logitech	Microsoft	Mouse Systems	Other	Total Retail	Percentage of Total Market
1988	577	803	630	361	2371	35
1989	883	1321	554	400	3158	40

Source: Company records

EXHIBIT 2 Carpal Tunnel Syndrome

"Repetitive Strain Repetitive Pain: Carpal Tunnel Becomes Major Workplace Hazard" Himanee Gupta, The Seattle Times, Vol. 112, Iss: 223, September 19, 1989, Section F, Page 1.

... Throughout the country and in Puget Sound, companies are realizing the painful, often crippling condition [carpal tunnel syndrome] has grown into a major workplace hazard. No one's sure just when and how hard it will hit, but any worker who types at computers, works with electronic scanners or regularly performs other repetitive tasks on automated equipment is at risk.

Carpal tunnel syndrome, one of several ailments known as repetitive strain injuries, occurs when constant bending of the hands, wrists and arms inflames tendons that squeeze the main nerve that runs through the arm ... The problems start with swelling, tingling and discomfort, and can wind up causing numbness, severe pain and paralysis. Treatment often means slow, painful therapy or surgery followed by therapy. And in terms of treatment, therapy and disability claims, the costs for employers can be enormous ...

In 1988, the state Department of Labor and Industries paid $6.5 million for 1,910 workers' compensation claims filed for carpal tunnel syndrome. That compares with 1,228 claims in 1986 and 123 in 1979.

"Pressing for New Ways to Type", Ronald Roel, Newsday, Vol. 50 #50, October 22, 1989, Section 1, Page 71.

... Hodges is one of a handful of iconoclasts promoting radical alternatives to today's conventional keyboard designs. Their devices, which so far have been roundly rejected by the big U.S. keyboard makers, range from variations on Hodges' split keyboard to keys that are moved much like a computer mouse. Like Hodges, most keyboard inventors say their passion for change has been spurred, in part, by an interest in reducing hand and wrist injuries, known as repetitive strain injuries, or RSI, experienced by thousands of computer users each year. Some medical experts believe that conventional flat keyboard designs may contribute to RSI....

IBM and other major manufacturers say they have no plans to radically change the keyboards used by 25 million office workers. If big changes are made within the next decade, it will probably be to eliminate the keyboard altogether, substituting them with other inputting devices that convert handwriting or human speech directly to computer print, says Maryann Karinch, a spokeswoman for the Computer and Business Equipment Manufacturers' Association, a Washington D.C.-based trade group.

---

sensitive North American market, Logitech priced the Logitech mouse at $99 U.S., about half the suggested price of both the Microsoft mouse and the mouse offered by Mouse Systems Corporation (the first into the U.S. market). Targeting the computer "techies", Logitech initially sold the Logitech mouse directly to consumers by soliciting phone and mail orders in trade publications. Initial success generated sufficient market pull to enable Logitech to establish a dealer network and increase the price of their mouse by 10–20%. In the less sophisticated European market, Logitech followed Microsoft's lead and used a skimming price strategy, charging about 30% more than it did in the U.S. Instead of using mail-order for distribution, Logitech developed relationships with a strong dealer network in Europe, who were able to support higher prices and margins by meeting the full-service needs of customers with high quality and prestige image products. In 1987, Microsoft launched its new ergonomic "white mouse", for $200 in the

U.S., but $350 in Europe. Logitech was slow to react and did not bring out their Microsoft-compatible Series 9 mouse until 1988. This new mouse was priced about 20% below Microsoft in North America and Europe. At this time, Logitech also introduced a "low-end" mouse under the Dexxa brand name to compete against the more than 20 Taiwanese manufacturers, who were pricing their mice in the $20–$35 range. These Taiwanese manufacturers had captured about 40% unit market share, compared to the 30% unit shares of both Logitech and Microsoft in the U.S. and Europe.

Supporting their R&D efforts from their high margins in Europe, both Logitech and Microsoft were slow to react to changes in the increasingly sophisticated and price-conscious European market. KYE (Genius), the largest of the Taiwanese manufacturers, had introduced a high quality mouse at $50 in mid-1988 and had captured a major share of the European market. In response, Microsoft and Logitech lowered their prices to $200 and $180, respectively, and Logitech began developing a new mouse at a price of $50–$60. This new "Pilot Mouse" was introduced in Europe at the end of 1989. Microsoft had unbundled their "paint" software from their mouse in the U.S., and had lowered the price to within 20% of Logitech's. KYE (Genius) had just bought Mouse Systems Corporation and were poised to bring their "Genius" product into the U.S. under the Mouse Systems brand name, which had a strong user recognition despite its decreasing market share.

The positioning of the major mouse vendors in Europe and North America in early 1990 is shown in Exhibit 3. Worldwide dollar market shares were approximately 40–45% for Microsoft, 20% for Logitech, and 20% for KYE/Mouse Systems. Demand for mice was expected to grow about 50% in 1990 and only slightly less in the foreseeable future due to trends towards graphical user interfaces. Sales of portables and laptops were expected to grow 22% in 1990 to 1.2 million units (14% of the PC market) and were expected to account for almost half of PC sales within a few years. Manufacturers of these computers would have to offer a built-in pointing device. Mice or trackballs seemed to be the logical choice for these pointing devices, but other technologies involving track pens and pen-based computing would likely play an increased role. Moreover, there would be increasing retail demand for replacement products and upgrades. Industry observers expected KYE/Mouse Systems to experience unit sales growth of 60% in 1990. Microsoft was expected to experience 50% growth and Logitech was expected to experience slightly lower growth. Logitech's retail sales were expected to remain at 40% of total unit sales in 1990. Previous years' unit sales are presented in Table 2.

Buyer Behavior

The mouse marketplace could be segmented into home/personal users, home/business users, corporate and educational users. Home/personal buyers, who accounted for about 48% of Logotech retail sales, were thought to be more price-sensitive than other segments and were less concerned about compatibility with software that they did not yet own. These consumers tended to buy from discount houses or no frills dealers and would choose among the alternative mice available at the most convenient location. Home/business buyers, representing about 26% of Logitech's retail sales, were thought to be value-and brand-conscious, but less concerned about compatibility than corporate users. These consumers were thought to be influenced by articles in *PC World*, *Byte* and other trade magazines, and to a lesser extent, advertisements in those magazines. Word-of-mouth and sales representative recommendations were thought to have the most influence of all. Finally, corporate buyers, representing 25% of Logitech's retail sales but 50% of Microsoft's, were thought to be more concerned with the brand name of a mouse and its likely compatibility with future hardware and software products. If use of the mouse was "mission critical" in the sense of being tied to productivity or used extensively, corporate buyers tended to play it safe and bought Microsoft.

While the profile of the Logitech mouse buyer was not completely understood, Logitech did keep track of who their retail customers were. Some 82% were desktop users and 48% of buyers were also the users. For 60%, the Logitech mouse was the second mouse they had purchased and 27% bought the mouse "bundled" with a paint program. Some 50% purchased the product at a retail store, 26% at a super-store, and 13% through mail order. Forty percent made the brand decision at the store. In terms of demographics, 80% were male, 55% were aged 30–45, and over 60% had 5 or more years of computer experience.

Competition

On the retail end of the business, the major competitors were Microsoft, Logitech, and KYE/Mouse Systems. Microsoft was positioned as the compatibility leader for both hardware and software and marketed its product to the premium, brand-conscious segment. It used its software reputation to help sell mice, and often bundled its mouse with Microsoft programs that required one. The second major competitor, Mouse Systems, was a bit of an enigma. It traditionally competed aggressively on price and promotions, but had limited resources and product quality was not believed to be as high as Logitech's or Microsoft's. However, with KYE's purchase of Mouse Systems, KYE was now claiming to be the largest mouse producer in the world (in terms of units) and was expected to become a force in North America.

On the OEM end of the business, Logitech's main competitors were: Alps and Mitsumi , (the two Japanese companies that supplied Microsoft), KYE/Mouse Systems, Z-nix, Truedox, Primax and Silitec (Taiwanese manufacturers). Primax and Silitec were suppliers to Packard Bell, the fourth largest PC vendor. All these competitors competed aggressively on price, resulting in low margins and profits. While Logitech felt it had a superior product both technically and in terms of quality, new users often could not tell the difference and most products met their basic needs.

Logitech's Positioning and Marketing Strategy

Logitech's overall mouse strategy was to compress technology life cycles and give consumers more options for increasing productivity. They competed by developing innovative designs and technologies, producing high quality products, and pricing the products to deliver good customer value. They aggressively managed their costs and tried to maintain strong relationships with their distributors. Traditionally, their products had been positioned to attract the serious and technically oriented user, but were now also attracting creative and aesthetically oriented users looking for fun, form, and function. This overall strategy had led to an increase in unit sales of over 74% in 1989, but because the average selling price had decreased 22%, revenues increased at only about half the rate of unit sales.

Product Strategy

Logitech's product strategy was to develop products that were consistent with, but not obvious extensions of, current offerings. The image they were attempting to develop was that Logitech offered neat products which were fun to use. Marketed under the theme "tools for the imagination", Logitech's current retail product offering included: the Logitech (Series 9) Mouse (in Europe only), the Dexxa brand muse, Trackman (a trackball pointing device), ScanMan (a hand-held scanner); and utility software (desktop publishing, a DOS unbundled or bundled with popular software such as Microsoft's Windows. On the OEM side, they offered the Series 9 Mouse (a 3-button Microsoft-compatible mouse), the Series 14 Mouse (a uniquely shaped 2-button, Microsoft-compatible mouse that was expected to be very popular), and the new Series 15 mouse.

Pricing Strategy

Logitech's pricing strategy was to support a street price $10–20 below Microsoft by differential channel pricing. This involved starting with a target street price and working back to the manufacturer's selling price using the margins expected by different channels. This was particularly tricky since different channels had very different expectations. Electronic superstores and price clubs worked with 8–25 percent margins, while traditional dealers and department stores worked with 30–40 percent margins and stores would carry the Logitech product, only if they could

EXHIBIT 3 Positioning of Products in the Retail Market in January 1990

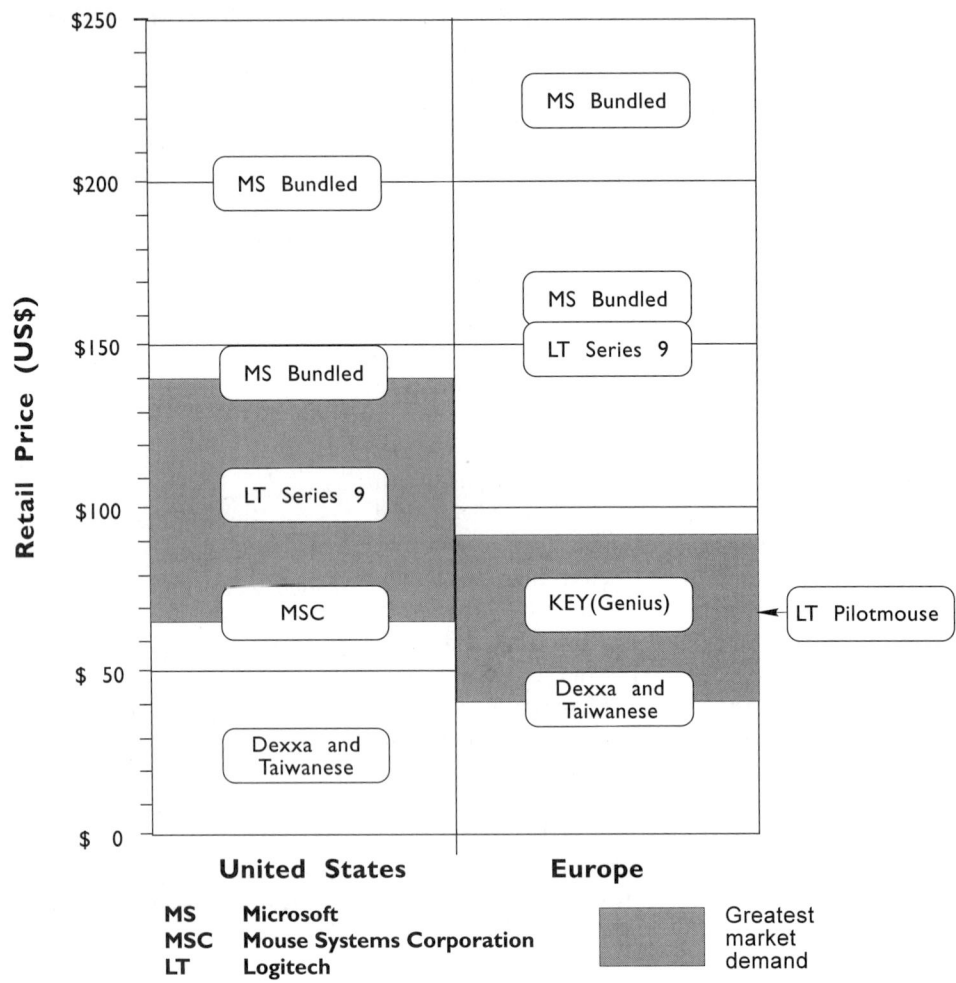

get their margin. Pricing was further complicated by grey marketing and cross-channel ownership. The former would arise if differential pricing in different countries created opportunities for the product to be bought by distributors in one market to be sold at a profit in another. The latter arose if a holding company owned more than one type of Logitech distributor and was able to supply a super store, for example, with a product bought for a full-service dealers. Estimated average wholesale prices for Logitech's and Microsoft's mice products are presented in Table 1.

Distribution and Sales Strategy

Logitech used a mix of direct sales, telemarketing, and distributors to achieve their objective of intensive distribution. Six OEM sales reps backed by 11 support staff managed ongoing relationships with key customers. On the retail side, Logitech had four retail channel groups: major retail and corporate accounts, education/government, international corporate accounts, and other retail chains or independents. While traditionally, Logitech's sales force had focused on developing channel relationships, management had increasing concerns about the lack of inroads made into corporate markets. Where Microsoft marketed directly to major corporations, Logitech had tried to reach the corporations through dealers.

Logitech's distribution goals were to be everywhere they could be, to have as many stock-keeping units (skus) as possible in each store to maximize their shelf space, and to maintain strong distributor relationships. This required utilizing a mix of wholesaling intermediaries and retailers ranging from small independent computer stores to major international chains. Logitech believed they had successfully covered 98% of the market with their distributing strategy and led the industry with 50% coverage in the rapidly growing channel of consumer electronic superstores. However, they actively sought alternative channels of distribution, such as mail-order and telemarketing, as the industry matured and evolved towards commodity products.

Communication Strategy

Logitech's communication strategy had traditionally been a no-nonsense cognitive feature-function-benefit approach designed to present solutions to customer needs. Wanting to develop an upscale image and develop greater affective appeal, Logitech created a new avant-garde visual identity and logo in January 1989. Although Logitech wanted to create an image of being a market leader in design and quality, and to communicate core product benefits of fun, creative freedom, and solution uniqueness, change was not achieved overnight. By the spring of 1990, some Logitech executives were concerned that they had not yet achieved a consistent feeling with their communication strategy. They had used a wide variety of communication media to spread their messages, but relied heavily on print advertising in trade magazines as well as point of purchase materials and packaging. Logitech also paid particular attention to co-operative advertising and special channel programs to motivate and support distributors.

The Situation in Early 1990

While Pierluigi Zappacosta was happy with the performance of Logitech, he was concerned with Logitech's ability to maintain margins in the mouse marketplace and wondered how he could maintain the current rate of growth and profitability into the 1990s. The Series 9 mouse had been a success, but it had been a quick response to Microsoft's sleek redesign and was not perceived internally as leading edge. As most mice now provided the same level of productivity, Zappacosta felt that a move towards ergonomic differentiation might be appropriate. Shortly after the launch of the Series 9 mouse, Logitech had begun developing two versions of a new ergonomic mouse based on the technology of the Series 9. One of these was designed specifically for right-handed users and the other for left-handed users. These new designs were shaped to fit the curve of the hand at rest and would help reduce repetitive stress problems, such as carpal tunnel syndrome. Prototypes of the ergonomic mouse had been completed and had been received well in focus groups. In a second mouse development, Logitech engineers had developed a radio "cordless" mouse that could be used to control a computer without the impediment of a cord and without the line-of-sight requirement of an infrared mouse. This technology could be packaged in the Series 9 mouse shape or the new ergonomic mouse shape at a price about $100 higher than a corded mouse. Finally, Logitech had developed technology for a 3-dimensional mouse that showed promise for high-end CAD/CAM and design applications.

Zappacosta had to decide whether to launch one, two or all of these new products, and if so, how. The cordless mouse and the 3-D mouse were "neat" from a technological perspective and had generated some excitement among the engineers. The ergonomic mouse was not particularly exciting from a technological perspective, but it might help differentiate the Logitech product in the marketplace. In addition, it might provide a "foot in the door" for attracting corporate business. However, from a strategic perspective, not everyone was comfortable with the right- and left-handed approach. Ron McClure, Vice President Strategic Marketing, had expressed concerns about the potential reception for the product among corporate customers and resellers. Corporate buyers would probably not know whether the user would be left-handed or right-handed and many mice would be shared by multiple users. It was not clear, for example, how a purchaser for a school lab would decide how many right-handed versions and how many left-handed versions to buy. Corporate users also might not have much input into the purchase decision to specify brand preference. The "safe" corporate strategy would be to buy a generic "one size fits all" mouse. Ron had a similar concern about OEM customers. An OEM usually bundled the Logitech mouse with the OEM's software or hardware and would probably not want to package left-handed and right-handed versions. Resistance to the new ergonomic mouse was also based on three other factors. Distributor representatives said it could be a sku nightmare for resellers if they had to carry left- and right-handed, corded and cordless mice as well as the current bus, serial port, mouseport, serial and mouseport, IBM and Apple versions, bundled or unbundled. Many employees were concerned that it would be the first Logitech product launched that was not based purely on a technological innovation/advantage. Finally, for many of the reasons outlined above, Logitech SA did not think they would want to launch the product in Europe.

While Logitech had been built on mouse technology, there were other directions that seemed to have great long-term potential. Scanner technology was similar to mouse technology and Logitech's hand-held Scanman had been a great success in terms of market share, margins and product image. Driven by increased demand for desktop publishing and multi-media solution, the scanner market was expected to grow 25–30% per year and opportunities existed to produce better grey-scale or even color scanners. Another opportunity related to scanners would be to develop a digital camera that captured black and white images and downloaded them to a computer. Finally, the interactive gloves developed for computer games might be improved upon to use with computers.

There were lots of neat products to develop but Zappacosta knew he needed to act strategically. Personally, he was a strong champion of the new ergonomic mouse, but he recognized that it might be risky. The product was ready to launch and he could not put off the decision much longer. He wondered, if they did launch, how it should be done. Would this be an addition to the line or a replacement? How could Europe be convinced to carry the product? Should the cordless mouse be launched as part of the new ergonomic product line, or separately, or not at all? How should the products be priced? How would Microsoft react? Would pursuit of other opportunities be a better use of resources? Zappacosta thought the best place to start looking for answers and directions was in their mission statement and long-term vision. He wondered whether "humanizing the computer" by giving senses to the computer adequately reflected their current and potential operation.

Case 30: Barossa Winery

Mr. George Steen, marketing manager for the Barossa Winery, had just been given an interesting assignment: to evaluate the feasibility of launching a major export drive. The Barossa Winery, an Australian producer of quality table wines, had experienced rapid growth in the early 1980s, but in 1986 and 1987 sales and profits had slowed considerably. At a strategy meeting held in early July 1988, the senior management group, which included Mr. Steen, decided that a growth opportunity existed in export markets and Mr. Steen agreed to prepare a feasibility study for the next strategy meeting.

As Mr. Steen sat in his office, Mr. Tony Clark, the general manager, came in and they began discussing the assignment. Mr. Steen said, "There will never be a better opportunity for us to get into foreign

This case is printed here with the permission of the author, Gordon H. G. McDougall of Wilfrid Laurier University, Canada.

markets in a big way. The world has now heard of Australia because of Crocodile Dundee and the Bicentennial Celebration, we've got a very favorable exchange rate, and we produce great wines." Mr. Clark replied, "I agree, it's a good opportunity for growth and we've got the capacity of doing it and making a profit. I know our wines are as good and, in some instances, better than comparable European wines, but the consumer doesn't know that." Mr. Steen replied, "That's true, but we only need a small share of any one of a number of markets to sell a large volume of wine. I think it's a matter of selecting one or two markets and going after them." Mr. Clark responded, "You are probably right, but I'm more cautious. I'll be very interested in hearing what you recommend. Our future growth may depend on your report."

The Company

The Barossa Winery, located in the Barossa Valley of South Australia, was started in the early 1960s by a winemaker, Mr. Rolf Mann, who had obtained a degree in viticulture from a well-regarded French school and emigrated to Australia. Since 1970, the firm had captured numerous awards every year at national and regional wine shows for both its red and white wines. By 1980, the company had established a solid reputation in Australia as a consistent producer of high-quality premium table wines.

The company was also known for its marketing skills. Mr. Steen, who joined the company in 1976, instituted various marketing initiatives including a series of labels that were regarded by many industry analysts as exceptional in terms of communicating the quality of the wines and "standing out" among the many competitive brands. As well, Mr. Steen established a distribution system that resulted in the prominent display of the company's products in many retail outlets. Finally, many of the advertising campaigns prepared for the Barossa Winery were judged as innovative and had contributed to the recognition and acceptance of the company's brands.

These efforts had resulted in rapid growth for the company. Between 1980 and 1985 sales increased from $18,500,000 to $33,900,000 and profits before tax from $1,600,000 to $3,100,000 (Exhibit 1).[1]

However, in 1986 and 1987 sales grew more slowly and profits were unchanged. Company officials felt that recent results were due, in part, to a slowdown in the growth of both the overall market and the table wine market (Exhibit 2). As well, increased competition in the quality premium bottled table wine market had led to price discounting by some wineries. As a policy, the Barossa Winery did not engage in price discounting.

With respect to export activity up to now the company could best be described as a passive exporter. While George Steen had made one overseas trip in the past two years (the trip covered stops in the United States, Canada, and the United Kingdom) to "drum up" some business with wine importers, no explicit export strategy had been established. In fact, the company's export sales had been generated by wine importers who had approached the Barossa Winery.

The interest of those wine importers (primarily from the United Kingdom) in Barossa Winery products was due to the increasing recognition by many knowledgeable buyers of the quality of Australian and the company's wines. In the early 1980s, wine experts from the United Kingdom visited Australia and sampled numerous wines. Upon their return home, many wrote glowing reports on the quality of these wines, including Barossa Winery's products.

In 1987, the company exported 37,400 cases of wine valued at $2,094,400, an increase of 42 percent in volume and 70 percent in dollar value compared to 1986 (Exhibit 1). In fact, 1987 was the first year the company received the same average price for its wine in both the domestic and export markets. In prior years it was estimated (no records had been kept) that export sales generated a price per case of approximately 15 percent less than the average price received in the domestic market.

The Australian Wine Industry

In many ways, the Australian wine industry is similar to other world wine markets. The first requirement for producing good wines was to have the appropriate

---

[1] All figures in this case are quoted in Australian dollars, unless otherwise noted. At the time of the case, $1.00 Australian = $0.99 Canadian.

EXHIBIT 1 Barossa Winery—Selected Company Statistics (1980 to 1987)

	1980	1981	1982	1983	1984	1985	1986	1987
Profit and loss statement (in $000,000)								
Sales	17.5	20.6	23.6	26.8	30.5	33.9	35.3	36.8
Cost of goods sold	11.7	13.8	15.6	17.9	20.8	23.2	24.4	25.7
Gross margin	5.8	6.8	8.0	8.9	9.7	10.7	10.9	11.1
Marketing expenses	3.0	3.5	3.9	4.5	4.8	5.5	5.7	5.8
Net margin	2.8	3.3	4.1	4.4	4.9	5.2	5.2	5.3
Administration and overheads	1.2	1.5	1.7	1.8	2.0	2.1	2.2	2.2
Profit before tax	1.6	1.8	2.4	2.6	2.9	6.1	3.0	3.1
Sales by Volume								
(000 litres)	4,120	4,520	4,830	4,950	5,210	5,680	5,800	5,900
(000 cases)[a]	468	502	537	550	579	631	644	656
Average selling price per case ($)	37.40	41.00	44.00	48.70	52.70	53.70	54.80	56.10
Export statistics								
Export sales (000 litres)	84.2	122.0	115.9	158.4	187.6	215.8	237.8	336.3
Export sales (000 cases)	9.4	13.6	12.9	17.6	20.8	24.0	26.4	37.4
Average selling price/case ($)[b]	31.80	34.90	37.40	41.40	44.80	45.60	46.60	56.00
Export sales ($000)[c]	298.9	474.6	482.5	728.6	931.8	1094.4	1230.2	2094.4
Consumer Price Index	100.0	109.8	120.8	135.5	148.7	160.9	176.7	186.0

[a] One case equals 9 L (12 bottles containing 750 mL each).
[b] Up to 1987 detailed sales records on prices were not kept. Company officials estimated that between 1980 and 1986 the average selling price per case was approximately 15% less than the domestic price per case.
[c] It was estimated that marketing expenses and administration and overheads amounted to 3% of sales for export sales versus around 8% for domestic sales.
Source: Company records.

climate and soil conditions. Many regions of Australia had these conditions and produced wine grapes including such classics as Cabernet Sauvignon, Grenache, and Pinot Noir for red wines, and Clare, Rhine Riesling, and Traminer for white wines. Most medium- and large-sized wineries in Australia made a complete range of wines, each with their own individuality. The Barossa Winery made six different white wines with two brands, Barossa Chardonnay and Barossa Rhine Riesling, making up over 80 percent of the company's white wine sales. The company produced five different red wines and, again, two brands, Barossa Cabernet Sauvignon and Barossa Hermitage, accounted for the majority of sales. Dry white wines accounted for 85 percent of total company sales.

A second requirement for producing good wines was to have a skilled winemaker. Mr. Mann had quickly established a reputation throughout Australia for producing high-quality wines on a consistent basis. He was renowned for his ability to purchase the finest grapes (the company did not own any vineyards, but instead purchased its grapes from among the over 4,000 grape growers in Australia), and he used the latest technology in producing many award-winning wines.

The third requirement was the ability to market the company's wines. Few, if any, product categories offered the consumer as wide a choice of varieties and brands as the wine category. For example, one of the large wholesalers of beer, wine, and spirits in Australia listed 577 brands of bottled table wines, including 256 red wines and 273 white wines. Most of these listed wines would be supplied by the fifty medium to large wineries in Australia.

Retail liquor outlets would not carry the complete range of wines offered by a wholesaler, but a typical outlet would handle at least 100 different brands of red and white bottled table wines. This large selection meant that marketing was critical in getting a brand known and recognized by consumers. While wine connoisseurs understood the differences between the varieties and brands of wines, these consumers constituted a very small percentage of the wine buying public. A second group, who knew a reasonable amount about wines and could identify the major and some minor brands, tended to purchase the majority of the bottled table wines.

In terms of quantity, most table wine in Australia was sold in two- or four-liter casks to consumers who were relatively price sensitive. Retail liquor outlets in Australia could advertise and offer beer, wine, and spirits at any price. A consumer could purchase a four-liter cask of average-quality Riesling for about $7.00 on sale (regular price $10.00) or a 750 mL bottle of slightly higher quality Riesling for $3.50 on sale (regular price of $6.50). As shown in Exhibit 2, soft pack or cask sales of table wine constituted about 61 percent of total table wine sales, while bottled table wines constituted about 24 percent of total table wine sales by volume.

A further indication of the price sensitivity of the market was the impact of government taxation policies on the level of wine consumption. In late 1984, a

EXHIBIT 2 Australian Wine Market—Selected Statistics (1980 to 1987) (000 liters)

	1980	1981	1982	1983	1984	1985	1986	1987
Total wine sales	245,040	262,872	278,595	293,582	305,802	320,478	325,183	329,952
Table	160,867	179,278	197,904	216,948	227,805	245,400	253,045	258,231
Fortified[a]	45,587	45,868	45,189	43,027	42,587	38,617	36,819	36,246
Sparkling[b]	29,915	29,577	27,749	27,022	29,021	31,277	30,413	30,098
All other[c]	8,671	8,158	7,753	6,585	6,389	5,182	4,907	5,378
Table wine sales by variety								
Dry white	121,093	138,016	155,310	172,334	175,341	179,286	171,780	176,227
Sweet white	3,497	3,912	4,529	4,929	10,060	20,840	36,936	34,657
Red Rose	27,667	29,258	30,362	31,856	34,480	37,805	37,188	40,192
Rose	8,610	8,091	7,706	7,830	7,924	7,466	7,140	7,155
Table wine sales by package								
Soft pack—white	51,148	69,525	84,680	103,585	111,486	137,675	140,788	138,787
Bottled—white	34,300	36,709	39,368	38,644	36,278	39,559	38,851	41,743
Soft pack—red	7,451	8,871	11,263	12,787	14,425	16,191	16,927	17,659
Bottled—red	11,507	12,455	12,252	12,657	14,058	16,779	16,838	19,004
All other[d]	56,461	51,718	50,341	49,275	51,558	35,196	39,641	41,038

[a] Includes sherry and dessert wines.
[b] Includes champagne and carbonated wines.
[c] Includes flavored and vermouth.
[d] Includes white, red, and rose sold in bulk and in bottles over one litre in size.
Source: Australian Wine and Brandy Corporation.

10 percent tax was placed on wines, and in 1985 the tax was increased to 20 percent. As shown in Exhibit 2, the total market growth rate, which averaged 5 percent between 1980 and 1984 declined to 1.5 percent in 1985.

On a broader scale, the consumption of wine in Australia appeared to have peaked in 1985 at twenty-one liters per capita. This compared to per capita consumption of nine liters in 1970, twelve liters in 1975, and seventeen liters in 1980.

Against this backdrop, the Barossa Winery competed in the bottled table wine markets. Its target market was the relatively sophisticated wine drinker who was somewhat knowledgeable about wines and was likely to drink wine with his or her evening meal two or more times a week. Within this target market, the Barossa Winery competed with virtually all the wineries in Australia as this was the most profitable segment. However, only a few companies, such as Wolf Blass and Leasingham had been as successful as the Barossa Winery within this segment. While no market data were available, some industry observers felt that Wolf Blass and Leasingham were increasing their share of the market at a faster rate than the Barossa Winery.

The World Wine Industry

On a worldwide basis, the wine market was dominated by the European Community (EC) and within the community, by three countries, France, Italy, and Spain. The EC vineyards accounted for approximately 27 percent of the total area of the world under vines, 38 percent of the world's grapes, and 60 percent of the world's production of wines. Because of price supports within the EC for the wine industry in the past, the EC countries typically produced more wine than could be consumed within the EC. Consequently, there was considerable pressure to export wine. Due to declining consumption within the EC countries and revised price support policies, in recent years the production of wine by EC nations had declined (Exhibit 3). However, a surplus of wine was still produced within the EC, and the countries collec-

EXHIBIT 3 World Wine Market—Selected Data (000,000 liters)

	Production			Exports	Imports	Per Capita Consumption (liters)	
	1983–84	1984–85	1985–86	1985	1985	1983	1985
France	6,855	6,436	7,015	1,189	701	85	80
Italy	8,228	7,090	6,258	1,803	n/a	91	85
Spain	3,247	3,625	3,277	731	n/a	57	48
Portugal	845	850	855	152	n/a	89	87
West Germany	1,340	889	540	292	962	27	26
Greece	525	503	478	140	n/a	44	43
United Kingdom	—	—	—	—	580	9	10
Total EC	21,040	19,393	18,423	4,307	2,243		
Europe—All others (incl. U.S.S.R.)	7,031	6,692	5,804	—	—	—	—
United States	1,476	1,670	1,810	—	519	8	9
Australia	396	451	480	11	8	20	21
Canada	47	50	50	—	140	9	10
Africa, Latin America, and South Africa	3,312	2,931	3,124	—	—	—	—
All others	1,002	918	981	—	—	—	—
Total	34,304	32,105	30,672	4,318	2,910		

Source: Australian Wine and Brandy Corporation.

tively exported over four billion liters of wine annually. Exporting of wine was encouraged by governments as the EC provided export refunds and subsidies for table wine exported outside the EC.

Australian Wine Imports and Exports

Between 1980 and 1985 only a small portion (about 3 percent) of Australia's total wine production was exported. In the 1985–86 period exports increased to 11 million liters, and in 1986–87 exports rose to 21 million liters (Exhibit 4). This was due primarily to a more favorable exchange rate as the Australian dollar had fallen sharply against most foreign currencies (Exhibit 5). Two other factors also contributed to this increase. First, the Chernobyl nuclear incident (nuclear reactor exploded in Ukraine in 1986 and nuclear waste was spread across Europe) had raised concern in a number of countries (particularly in Scandinavia) about contamination of European grapes. Second, there was a growing awareness in many countries of the quality of Australian wines.

The vast majority of Australian wine exports were table wines and most of these exports went to seven countries with the United States, the United Kingdom, and Canada being three of the largest markets. The value per liter of export sales varied considerably by country. At the lower end, Sweden purchased wine in bulk (it was shipped from Australia in large containers) at a value per liter of $1.01. The wine was bottled and sold by the Swedish liquor control board. At the upper end, all of the wine exported to the United States was in bottle form at an average price to the exporter of $3.59 per liter.

The Export Decision

In preparing the report, Mr. Steen first considered the possible countries where the Barossa Winery could achieve significant sales. Based on a preliminary screening, he decided to limit his investigation to the three countries that he felt offered a good potential for the company's products: Canada, the United States, and the United Kingdom.

Canada

Canada was an attractive market because the domestic wine industry was not well developed and was not recognized as producing quality wines (Exhibit 6). The marketing of wine and spirits in Canada was strictly controlled by the ten provincial governments, and most sales were made through government liquor stores. In March 1988, the Australian Wine and Brandy Corporation sponsored a tour of the listing agents for the ten liquor control boards of Canada. The agents visited the major wine-growing areas and sampled many of the wines available for export. The main objective of the tour was to acquaint the agents with the quality, variety, and availability of Australian wines.

The two major drawbacks to the Canadian market were the difficulties in getting a general listing and the restrictions placed on marketing activities. Australian wines would compete against all other wine-producing countries for listings. It was estimated that up to 1,000 listing requests were received by each of the ten boards every year and a selection committee might list seventy-five new wines. Chances of acceptance were improved by a personal visit to present the listing application. Primarily, it was felt that price (within a given quality range) was the dominant criterion in getting accepted on the list. Government restrictions placed on marketing activities (for example, no price discounting, restrictions as to the amount and type of advertising, no point-of-purchase displays) made it difficult to develop brand awareness and trial by consumers.

In preparing his report Mr. Steen obtained information on the largest Australian wine exporter's operations in Canada (Hardy's Wines). It was rumored that Hardy's held somewhat over 40 percent share of the Canadian table wine market for Australian wines. As well, Hardy's was thought to have about a 50 percent share of the "All Other" wines category. It had achieved this position by spending approximately $200,000 each year in Canada. Hardy's had two full-time employees, one in Ontario and one in Québec (total costs for both employees including salaries, office space, cars, and expenses were $100,000) and the company spent about $100,000 on all types of promotions, including visits by the Aus-

EXHIBIT 4 Australian Wine Imports and Exports, 1986–1987

	Imports			Exports		
	Liters (000)	Value ($000)	Value/Liter ($)	Liters (000)	Value ($000)	Value/Liter ($)
Champagne	1,134	19,628	17.31	370	1,484	4.01
Table wine	4,852	17,084	3.52	18,627	37,967	2.04
All others	1,573	4,899	3.11	2,326	5,170	2.22
Total	7,559	41,611	5.50	21,323	44,621	2.09

Exports From Australia by Destination (000 Liters or $000)

	Champagne		Table Wine		All Others		Total		Value/liter
	L	Value	L	Value	L	Value	L	Value	
United States	36	$ 171	2,455	$ 9,029	422	$1,255	2,913	$10,455	$3.59
United Kingdom	34	122	2,190	6,775	96	352	2,320	7,249	3.12
Sweden	—	—	5,223	5,257	—	—	5,223	5,257	1.01
New Zealand	183	611	1,054	3,397	177	540	1,414	4,548	3.22
Canada	—	—	1,228	3,017	791	1,283	2,019	4,300	2.13
Hong Kong	28	149	527	1,009	108	246	663	1,404	2.12
Fiji	14	67	230	426	72	136	316	629	1.99
All Other	75	364	5,720	9,057	660	1,358	6,455	10,779	1.67
Total	370	$1,484	18,627	$37,967	2,326	$5,170	21,323	$44,621	$2.09

*Largest imports (in 1000 L) come from Italy (2,714), France (1,981), and Portugal (777).

EXHIBIT 5 Exchange Rates (units of foreign currency per $ Australian)

June	United States Dollar	Canadian Dollar	U.K. Pound Sterling	West German Mark	French Franc	Italian Lira	Trade Weighted Index[*]
1984	0.86	1.14	0.64	2.40	7.36	1,477.13	79.2
1985	0.67	0.91	0.51	2.03	6.19	1,294.40	65.0
1986	0.68	0.94	0.44	1.48	4.73	1,019.90	56.3
1987	0.72	0.96	0.45	1.31	4.40	955.48	56.6
1988	0.81	0.99	0.44	0.99	3.97	1,099.32	56.8

*Trade-weighted index of average value of the Australian dollars vis-à-vis currencies of Australia's trading partners. May 1970 index 100.
Source: Reserve Bank of Australia, Bulletin, Publication No. NBP 4521

tralian export manager. The two employees spent the majority of their time making regular calls on the liquor board head offices, checking stocks, and calling on individual liquor stores to ensure that the product was available. As well, the employees would have the product on hand at any wine tastings within the provinces. A further important duty was to encourage Canadian wine writers for newspapers and magazines to write about Hardy's Wines. Hardy's also employed agents in Alberta and British Columbia who received

EXHIBIT 6 Fact Sheet on Canada

- Canadian consumption of wine, particularly imported wine, is increasing despite severe marketing restrictions. The import and retailing of all alcoholic beverages is controlled by individual provincial monopolies, as are all aspects of product marketing (for example, advertising, sampling).
- Import licensing as such is not required. However, distribution is controlled by the provincial government liquor monopolies who will only list a brand if convinced it will achieve the required sales volume.
- Import duties are $12 Canadian per imperial gallon (one imperial gallon equals 4.546 liters). Excise taxes are $.35 Canadian per liter. Federal sales taxes are 12 percent on the landed duty and excise paid value. As of June 1988, import duties in Australian dollars would be $2.64 per liter, excise duties would be $0.35 per liter, and federal sales tax would be $1.14 per liter.
- No major difficulties in terms of certification, packaging, etc. However, with respect to labels, the label information must be in English and French.
- Canada produces less than one-half of its wine requirements and Canada's climate is not conducive to grape growing.
- Prices to the provincial monopolies should be quoted in Canadian dollars CIF (cost, insurance, freight). Each province arbitrarily sets the retail price of a product by applying a fixed markup to the landed cost (C$CIF). For example, Alberta has a markup of 55 percent; British Columbia has a markup of 50 percent on B.C.-produced table wines, 110 percent on other Canadian-produced table wines, and 120 percent on imported wines; Ontario has a markup of 58 percent on Ontario-produced table wines, 98 percent on other Canadian-produced table wines, and 123 percent on imported wines; Québec has a markup of 80 percent on Québec-produced table wines, 114 percent on other Canadian-produced table wines, and 120 percent on imported table wines.
- Distribution of all wine and spirits sold in Canada is controlled by government monopolies and/or liquor boards. Each of the ten provinces has its own liquor board. Since each province will stock a limited range of wines out of the hundreds of different types and brands available, it establishes a price list giving the names of those wines available for sale. However, even when a wine is listed, it will probably not be available in every store.
- The majority of Canada's 26 million people reside in Ontario, Québec, British Columbia, and Alberta.

Primary source: Australian Wine and Brandy Corporation, *Export Market Grid*.

a 10 percent commission plus up to 5 percent more for expenses.

Most Australian wine producers who exported to Canada used agents to perform the marketing function. The agents worked on a commission basis (usually 10 percent of the landed cost in Canada) and their prime role was to obtain product exposure. This could be done by convincing restaurants and hotels to include the product on wine lists, by conducting tastings, and by obtaining good press for the product. Agents could be valuable because the need for personal selling was considerable in Canada. Wine consumption in Canada had been increasing and per capita consumption had risen from 6.3 liters per year in 1976 to 10 liters in 1985. Over 50 percent of the wine sold in Canada was imported and over 80 percent of that came from the wine-producing countries of the EC. Some well-known European brands such as Blue Nun, Black Tower, and Mateus had substantial sales in Canada. Of the 140,000,000 liters of wine imported to Canada in 1985, 90 percent were table wines.

United States

By Australian standards, the magnitude of the U.S. market was staggering (Exhibit 7). Imports of table wine alone were about 313 million liters in 1986, most of it coming from Italy (48 percent), France (30 percent), and West Germany (11 percent). The Italian wine imports tended to be lower-priced ($1.52/liter

EXHIBIT 7   Fact Sheet on the United States

- The United States consumption of wine, both domestic and imported, has been increasing and the absolute size of the market is one of the most attractive in the world. Estimated sales for 1988 are 2 billion liters.
- Import licenses may only be held by U.S. citizens.
- Import duties on table wines are $0.375 per U.S. gallon (one U.S. gallon = 3.785 liters). Excise taxes are $0.17 U.S. per U.S. gallon. As of June 1988, import duties in Australian dollars would be $0.12 per liter and excise taxes would be $0.06 per liter.
- No major difficulties in terms of certification, packaging, labeling, etc.
- Seventy-two percent of the table wine sold in the U.S. was produced in California, 24 percent was imported, and 4 percent was produced by other states in 1986.
- The US. market, because of its size and complexity, should be treated on a state-by-state basis. The sale of alcoholic beverages is controlled by state organizations, the degree of authority ranging from minimal licensing requirements to complete control of retail outlets. There are eighteen "monopoly" states that operate in a similar manner to Canada. Most of the larger states, including California and New York, are nonmonopoly states. The nonmonopoly states operate in a similar manner to the Australian system. In these states, the product can only enter the U.S. through a licensed importer, who, in turn, can only then sell to a wholesaler. A direct sale to the retailer or consumer level is not permitted. Importers' or agents' margins range from 10 percent to 25 percent of landed cost, wholesalers' around 15 percent to 30 percent and retailers' 30 percent to 40 percent.
- In 1968, the majority of table wines sold in the U.S. retailed in Australian dollars between $3.40 and $5.25 (69 percent). $5.26 and $7.10 (15 percent), and $7.11 and $9.26 (9 percent).

on average), while the French imports were relatively high-priced ($4.43/liter). The German imports ($2.89/liter) were close to the average of all imports ($3.09/liter).[2] In 1986, the Australian share of the U.S. table wine market was estimated at 0.06 percent.

The top-selling import brands in the U.S. market included Riunite from Italy (8,500,000 cases), Blue Nun from Germany (1,000,000 cases), and Mateus from Portugal (800,000 cases). It was estimated that the wholesale prices per case for these brands were: Riunite $19.35 ($2.15/liter), Blue Nun $33.12 ($3.68/liter), and Mateus $21.30 ($2.37/liter). Promotion expenditures for many of the imported wines were extensive, and while total expenditures were not available it was estimated that Riunite spent over $12,000,000 in television advertising and Blue Nun spent approximately $2,400,000 in radio advertising.

With respect to markets, the top ten markets for table wine in the United States accounted for 65 percent of all sales. The New York metropolitan area had sales of 5.9 million cases of imported table wine, and Detroit (ninth-ranked) had sales of 550,000 cases in 1986.

Selection of an agent or importer was obviously an important consideration. Numerous spirit agents were available ranging from small companies that specialized in a few product lines in one area of the country to national distributors that had a vast product line and covered the entire country.

Marketing activities for wine companies, particularly in the nonmonopoly states, could be extensive and include advertising, in-store promotions, and price specials. Many United States wine producers, particularly from California, had established well-known brand names and were recognized as producing quality wines.

United Kingdom

The third market under consideration was the United Kingdom (Exhibit 8). In the past few years, per capita wine consumption in the United Kingdom had increased and stood at ten liters in 1985. A review of

Value at foreign export port exclusive of shipping costs and taxes.

EXHIBIT 8 Fact Sheet on the United Kingdom

- The U.K. consumption of wine has been increasing and all wine consumed in the U.K. is imported. The U.K. is a member of the EC.
- Import licenses can be easily obtained although there are major difficulties in complying with various EC requirements for import.
- Import duties on table wines entering the EC are £8.58 per hundred liters. It should be noted that wines entering the EC must exceed a minimum threshold price. Excise taxes in the U.K. are £0.980/liter on table wine. As well, a value added tax of 15 percent is placed on all products. As of June 1988, import duties in Australian dollars would be $0.20 per liter, excise taxes would be $2.23 per liter, and the value added tax would be $1.34 per liter.
- Considerable efforts are required to comply with EC standards with respect to certification, packaging, and labeling. In particular, an EC analysis certificate that describes the wine' characteristics including actual alcohol strength, total dry extract, total acidity, and residual sugar must be completed (the analysis can be done in Australia) and meet EC requirements.
- In 1985, the United Kingdom imported 580 million liters of wine, most of it from member countries of the EC.

Primary source: Australian Wine and Brandy Corporation, *Export Market Grid*.

the U.K. wine market in 1986 noted that Australia had less than 2 percent of the table wine market.

The U.K. market was very competitive and extensive advertising, point-of-purchase displays, and price specials were used at the retail level to promote individual brands.

The major drawback for any exporter in developing the U.K. market was the potential threat that import regulations for wines might be changed. In the past France had engaged in certain activities that "changed the rules" resulting in a new set of regulations that disrupted the marketing activities of exporters to the EC.

Most of the larger and some of the medium-sized Australian wine producers had entered the export market by focusing first on the United Kingdom. For example, one of the largest Australian producers, Orlando Wines, had been very active in the United Kingdom. Orlando regarded the U.K. as an important market. As one executive of Orlando stated: "If you can be successful in the U.K., it will stand you in good stead in other export markets." Orlando had established its own company in the U.K. and the subsidiary performed the role of the importer. The export marketing manager visited the U.K. four times a year, spending two weeks on each visit. His main activities were to motivate the distributor of the company's brands and to discuss the brands with wine writers, if possible. The distributor was a medium-sized wholesaler who sold to retail liquor chains, primarily in the London area. While no figures were available on Orlando's export sales it was estimated that in 1988, its sales into the U.K. market would be approximately 40,000 cases.

Orlando did some advertising in both consumer and trade magazines in the United Kingdom. In a recent issue of *Decanter* (a consumer magazine targeted at wine buffs) Orlando had a full-page ad emphasizing the quality of its brands and stated, "They [the two brands] compare beautifully with similar wines from France, yet only cost around half as much."

Another company that was actively involved in export marketing was Wolf Blass, a well-known medium-size producer of quality wines. In 1985, it set up distributorships with agents in both the United States and the United Kingdom. Wolf Blass was one of the few companies that received the same price of wine in both the domestic and export markets (in 1987, the average price received was approximately $65 per case). In selecting the distributors in both the U.S. and the U.K., Wolf Blass had decided on large agents to give them access to the markets they wanted. In 1987, Wolf Blass had sold a total of 50,000 cases in the export market, but it was not clear whether it had made any profits. Some experts felt that the money Wolf Blass invested to develop the export markets (estimated annual marketing expenditures for both major markets were $600,000) had been substantial and that no profits would be obtained for at least four years.

Preliminary Cost Data

Mr. Steen prepared some rough calculations on the costs of getting a case of wine to each of the three markets and what it might sell for at retail (Exhibit 9). With respect to costs of production, Mr. Steen had read a recent newspaper article on the costs of wine and was surprised at how close those costs were to those of the Barossa Winery. As shown in Exhibit 10, the production cost for a 750 mL bottle of good-quality Chardonnay was $3.02. By the time the consumer purchased it, the price was $11.08. While the cost of grapes for some of the other varieties of wines could be considerably less (for example, $600 per metric ton for Semillon), most of the price of a bottle of wine ($8.06 per the example) was made up of margins and taxes.

Mr. Steen also worked out some preliminary estimates of what it would cost to actively enter all three export markets. In terms of personnel, the cost of an export sales manager was about $60,000 and if the manager made six overseas trips a year, this expense would be about $100,000. One or two sales clerks might be required at a cost of $30,000 each. Preparation of custom requirements including documentation, obtaining label approvals, and sending samples could cost up to $30,000. Promotion costs were difficult to estimate, but they could exceed $100,000 for expenditures on wine tastings and shows for both the public and the trade, advertising expenditures for consumers and the trade, and public relations.

EXHIBIT 9 Estimated Retail Price of a Case of Barossa Wine in the Three Markets

	United Kingdom	United States	Canada
Barossa Winery price	$ 56.00	$ 56.00	$ 56.00
Transport to destination[1]	2.55	2.85	2.85
Landed cost	58.55	58.85	58.85
Import duties and excise tax[2]	21.90	1.60	26.90
Other taxes[2]	12.05	—	10.30
Landed cost with duties/taxes	92.50	60.45	96.05
Importer/agent margin[3]	27.75	9.10	9.60
Importer price	120.25	69.55	105.65
Wholesale margin[4]	—	13.90	—
Wholesale price	120.25	83.45	105.65
Retail margin[5]	60.15	29.20	64.75
Retail price	180.40	112.65	170.40
Bottle price (750 mL)	$ 15.00	$ 9.40	$ 14.20

Assumptions:
[1] It costs $347 to ship a container from the Barossa Valley to Port Adelaide. On average, a container holds 1,000 cases. One case contains 9 L or 12 bottles (750 mL) Port Adelaide to U.K. is $2,200 per container; to U.S. or Canada, approximately $2,500.

Based on information in fact sheets.

Importer margin in U.K. ranges from 25% to 40% of landed cost (assume 30% for estimation purposes); in U.S. range is 10% to 25% (assume 15%); in Canada agents average 10%.

Wholesale margins in U.S. range from 15% to 30% (assume 20%).

Retail margins in U.K. are about 50%; in U.S. from 30% to 40% (assume 35%); in Canada, range from 55% to 123% of landed cost (assume 110%).

A portion of these expenditures could be recovered from the federal government through the Export Market Development Grant. Firms engaged in export marketing were eligible (for the first five years) to receive up to 70 percent of certain export costs including printing of special labels, preparation and printing of point-of-sale material, a portion of the cost of any personnel who were located in the export market, air travel, and a portion of accommodation expenses for managers visiting the export markets, samples, and expenses related to wine trade shows. While it was difficult to estimate the precise proportion of costs that would be recovered, depending on the type of expenditure, Barossa Winery could receive up to $100,000 each year.

Although the Barossa Winery had not aggressively pursued the export market, Mr. Steen was quick to capitalize on any export opportunity that was presented. For example, if a British importer expressed interest in any of the company's products, Mr. Steen, or a member of the marketing group, would provide free samples, information on the wines, and product availability. If an importer placed an order, Mr. Steen ensured that the order was shipped as quickly as possible with proper documentation. As Mr. Steen once joked to a colleague, "We may not go after the export business, but if anybody comes to us, we'll offer better service and support than any other winery in Australia."

EXHIBIT 10 Typical Cost Structure of a Bottle/Case of Wine

	Per Bottle	Per Case
Product*	$ 1.61	
Packaging	1.07	
Bottling	.22	
Transportation	.12	
Total production cost	3.02	$ 36.24
Manufacturer margin (50% of costs)	1.50	
Price to wholesaler	4.52	54.24
Wholesaler margin (25%)	1.13	
Wholesaler price before taxes	5.65	
Federal tax (20%)	1.13	
Wholesaler price after federal tax	6.78	
State tax (9%)	.61	
Wholesaler price after taxes	7.39	88.68
Retailer margin (50%)	3.69	
Retail price	11.08	132.96

*Based on premium Chardonnay fruit at a price per metric ton of $1,200. One metric ton will produce 744 bottles of 750 mL wine. A case contains 12 bottles (9 L).

Mr. Steen was pleased with the growth of exports in the past few years, but he was concerned about the tenuous nature of the business. While the export business had experienced steady growth, the source of sales often changed substantially on a yearly basis. For example, sales to the United Kingdom had been made through two different U.K. importers in the past three years. Between 1981 and 1984, Star Importers, a U.K. importer who specialized in Australian wines, had purchased up to 10,000 cases of Barossa Wines in a given year. In late 1984, Star Importers switched their major buying from Barossa to a competitive winery in New South Wales. In 1985, the Reid Company, another U.K. importer, began buying Barossa Wines and in 1987 purchased 18,000 cases for the U.K. market.

Similarly, the company had been approached in the past five years by six different United States importers. The Barossa Winery had conducted business with all six (sales in a given year to any one of the importers ranged from 400 to 4,500 cases) over the years and in 1987 sold a total 9,000 cases through four importers to the U.S. market. Two sales agents in Canada (who have been importing the product for about four years) had generated sales of about 800 cases in Ontario and Alberta. As well, the company had sold about 10,000 cases to the "rest of the world" through two Australian exporters. These two firms approached Australian wine producers and obtained products that they would sell to distributors at the wholesale or retail level in other countries. As far as Mr. Steen could tell the two exporters who sold Barossa Wines had most of their sales in New Zealand, Micronesia, and the Far East (for example, Japan, Taiwan, Thailand, Hong Kong).

Mr. Steen realized that the Barossa Winery did not have strong links with these importers or exporters in that no formal contracts were signed with any of them in terms of an exclusive agreement. In all cases, both parties were free to buy from or sell to anyone. Further, the company had little expertise in exporting as most of the work and all of the marketing was done by the importer or exporter. In the final analysis, Mr. Steen felt that the company's success to date had been a combination of good service, good prices, and good-quality wine.

The Decision

Having gathered the preliminary data, Mr. Steen began thinking about the report. He was not certain what he should recommend. On the one hand, export sales were growing with little effort and expense on the company's part. Possibly with a little more effort, sales could be increased without going "full speed ahead" into exporting. On the other hand, the tenuous nature of the company's relationship with its exporters suggested that some action should be taken.

Mr. Steen knew that the senior management group was expecting a report that contained specific recommendations including whether the Barossa Winery should aggressively enter the export market and, if so, how many markets to enter. As well, the group would expect to receive details of the proposed strategy Mr. Steen would pursue for the next three years in the export area. With these thoughts in mind, Mr. Steen began writing the report.

Case 31: Federal Express Goes Global

Federal Express has always been known as the company started by a man who received a "C" at Yale University in the 1960s on an overdue economics paper proposing a new business concept. Undeterred, Frederick W. Smith went on to build the first private American company to report $1 billion in revenues within ten years of being launched (without the benefit of any merger or acquisition). Operations began in April 1973; in fiscal year 1992, company revenues hit $7.55 billion. Employees numbered more than 93,000 worldwide, making some 300,000 daily calls (pick-up or drop-off). Four hundred and fifty-four aircraft and 31,000 vehicles serviced an average daily package volume in 1993 of 1.7 million worldwide.

For years Chairman Fred Smith had been saying that Federal Express (Federal) would have to become a global player if it was to survive in the year 2000. Then in 1989, Fred Smith made an audacious move to stride onto the world stage. Federal acquired Tiger International (Tiger), owner of the "Flying Tigers" name, for $895 million.

Only three years later, on May 1, 1992, the company announced a decisive and massive retreat from most of its disastrous European operations where it had piled up a total of $1.2 billion in debt.

That year, the company reported a first-time pre-tax loss of $147 million. Fred Smith admitted that a full recovery from the international debacle was not likely "any time soon." Industry commentators alleged that Federal paid too much for Tiger, moved too quickly, over-estimated market growth, and fundamentally overreached itself in trying to go global all at once.

Company Background

The term "Triad markets" was coined by Kenichi Ohmae in his 1990 book entitled *The Borderless World*. It denotes North America, Western Europe, and Japan. Ohmae is a widely published Japanese management consultant who has argued consistently that companies must develop strength and presence in the three major markets if they are to be considered truly global players. When Fred Smith decided to purchase Tiger International, he obtained for Federal an immediate entry into the Japanese market. Other acquisitions both preceded and followed the Tiger purchase in order to build a company-owned network of ground and air services. Exhibit 1 lists the acquisitions made by Federal Express during 1984–90. The goal was for Federal to become world leader and be the first company to offer an overnight delivery service that would span the world, serving a mega market of some 700 million consumers.

This case is printed here with the permission of the authors, Lyn S. Amine of St. Louis University, and M. G. Mostafa Khan of the University of Bahrain.

EXHIBIT I Acquisitions by Federal Express Corporation

	Company Purchased	Country(s) Served	Closing Date
1.	Gelco Express Int'l Ltd. & Gelco Express Int'l N.V.	(Worldwide courier service–84 countries)	Jan. 1984
2.	Jean Dandois Transports SPRL	Belgium	Oct. 1985
3.	Lex Wilkinson, Ltd.	United Kingdom	Jan. 1986
4.	Lex Systemline Lt.d	England	Mar. 1986
5.	Cansica Ltd.	Canada	Feb. 1987
6.	Williames Transport	Nothern Ireland & Rep. of Ireland	Apr. 1987
7.	Island Couriers	Latin America	Dec. 1987
8.	SIAMEX	Italy	Apr. 1988
9.	East-West Courier Ltd.	Canada	Jul. 1988
10.	Binghalib Group	United Arab Emirates	Dec. 1988
11.	Winchmore Development Ltd.	England (London)	Dec. 1988
12.	Daisei Companies	Japan	Dec. 1988
13.	Home Delivery Service Ltd.	United Kingdom	Dec. 1988
14.	Elbe Transport GmbH	Germany	Dec. 1988
15.	Transport Group Alvracht	Holland	Feb. 1989
16.	Flying Tigers	Worldwide	Feb. 1989
17.	Yuill Couriers Ltd. &	Canada	Feb. 1989
18.	Blue Jay Couriers Ltd.		
19.	Rainers Customs & Transport Pty Ltd. Service (Express Shipping Division)	Australia	May 1989
20.	Transports Transvendeens Chronoservice	France	June 1990
21.	Aeroenvios S.A. de C.V.	Mexico	June 1990

Source: Company records

Federal Express defined its business as "the time-definite transportation and distribution of goods and documents throughout the world." It became familiar to consumers in America through the fast-talking TV spokesperson who recommended Federal for any package that "absolutely, positively has to be there overnight." The company's mission aimed at an absolute commitment to creating the most capable, extensive, and reliable express transportation company in the world.

Federal Express is committed to our People-Service-Profit philosophy. We will produce outstanding financial returns by providing totally reliable, competitively superior air-ground transportation of high priority goods and documents that require rapid, time-certain delivery. Equally important, positive control of each package will be maintained utilizing real time electronic tracking and tracing systems. A complete record of each shipment and delivery will be presented with our request for payment. We will be helpful, courteous, and professional to each other and the public. We will strive to have a satisfied customer at the end of each transaction. (Company Mission Statement, 1992)

This mission statement was backed up by a Five Point Strategy:

1. Continuously improve quality to achieve 100% on-time deliveries, 100% information accuracy, and 100% customer satisfaction after every contact with Federal Express.
2. Lower costs and prices.
3. Make International profitable and the world's leading express system.
4. Get closer to our customers.
5. Continue to focus on People-Service-Profit issues.

The company's emphasis on quality service led to its receiving the Malcolm Baldrige National Quality Award in 1990.

In pursuing its goals for growth, the company diversified not only its market coverage but also its product lines, aiming to balance slower growth rates in one sector against faster growth elsewhere. In 1990 immediately after the acquisition of Tiger, Federal was operating in 127 countries and offered 12 different products. By 1993, Federal was operating in 180 countries.

Market Coverage

The acquisition of Tiger International, Inc. on August 7, 1989 gave Federal strategic air routes, an expanded fleet of aircraft, additional ground facilities, and valuable distribution experience in the heavyweight air cargo business. Prior to the acquisition, Federal used a "hub and spokes" type of market coverage in the U.S., with Memphis (TN) serving as a central sorting facility. Other sorting centers were added in Newark (NJ) and Oakland (CA), along with a second national hub in Indianapolis (IN). In 1989, Anchorage (AL) became the site for a new transcontinental sorting facility; two regional Metroplexes were added for sorting in Chicago and Los Angeles.

The Anchorage site was a trans-loading facility for flights eastward and westward from the U.S. along polar routes to Europe and the Pacific Rim. Anchorage was the first destination and customs clearing point for international express packages inbound from the Pacific Rim to cities in the U.S.

Federal Express carried three main types of goods: documents and light parcels; packages under 150 pounds (boxes); and heavyweight air freight (unlimited size and weight). It offered a range of shipment schedules from overnight with morning (10:00 a.m.) or afternoon (3:00 p.m.) deliveries, to second, third, fourth business day deliveries. Customers were able to choose the speed of delivery for their shipments both at home and overseas, based on a range of prices and options for customs clearance services, pick-up, and delivery. Federal built its business on the guarantee of absolute reliability and convenience—a service for which it consistently sought to maintain a premium price. This policy produced an average revenue per express package of $5.30–$5.50, while heavyweight package revenues reached only $1.12–$1.17, as shown in Exhibit 2.

Performance

During the period from 1983 to 1992, Federal achieved remarkable, sustained growth. Fred Smith commented on these results in 1992:

> When we entered the European market, in the mid-1980s, we did so with the belief that Europe would one day rival North America in the express transportation industry. With its huge population and high volume of economic activity, we believed that Europe would embrace the concept of overnight delivery just as the United States and Canada had done in the 1970s. The promise of a tightly woven European Community after 1992 only heightened our optimism. Events, however, have simply not supported our beliefs. (Annual Report, 1992)

Exhibit 3 gives details on operations in domestic and international markets from 1988 to 1992. Exhibit 4 presents consolidated statements of operations for the period 1990–1992, and Exhibit 5 shows consolidated balance sheets for 1991 and 1992.

Industry Background

The express shipment business has always been essentially a commodity business. It suffers from a lack of differentiation in the same way as the airline industry, which basically offers the rental of an airline seat from one location to another. In the express shipment industry, lack of differentiation is even more acute because the customer does not have any way of experiencing the service personally. By contrast, an airline

EXHIBIT 2 Selected Consolidated Financial Data

Years ended May 31. In thousands except per share data and Other Operating Data	1992	1991	1990	1989	1988	1987	1986	1985	1984	1983
OPERATING RESULTS										
Revenues	$7,550,060	$7,688,296	$7,015,069	$5,166,967	$3,882,817	$3,178,308	$2,573,229	$2,015,920	$1,436,305	$1,008,087
Operating Income	22,967	252,126	387,355	414,787	379,452	364,743	344,021	258,617	188,752	150,737
Income (loss) before income taxes	(146,828)	40,942	218,423	298,332	302,328	311,885	305,085	212,272	176,804	150,216
Income (loss) from continuing operations	(113,782)	5,898	115,764	166,451	187,716	166,952	192,671	138,740	125,431	88,933
Net income (loss)	$(113,782)	$ 5,898	$ 115,764	$ 184,551	$ 187,716	$ (65,571)	$ 131,839	$ 76,077	$ 115,430	$ 88,933
PER SHARE DATA										
Earnings (loss) per share										
Continuing operations	$ (2.11)	$ .11	$ 2.18	$ 3.18	$ 3.56	$ 3.21	$ 3.86	$ 2.94	$ 2.74	$ 2.03
Discontinued operations	—	—	—	—	—	(4.48)	(1.22)	(1.33)	(.22)	—
Cumulative effect of change in accounting for income taxes	—	—	—	.35	—	—	—	—	—	—
Net earnings (loss) per share	$ (2.11)	$ .11	$ 2.18	$ 3.53	$ 3.56	$ (1.27)	$ 2.64	$ 1.61	$ 2.52	$ 2.03
Average shares outstanding	53,961	53,350	53,161	52,272	52,670	51,905	49,840	46,970	45,448	43,316
Cash dividends	—	—	—	—	—	—	—	—	—	—
FINANCIAL POSITION										
Property and equipment, net	$3,411,297	$3,624,026	$3,566,321	$3,341,814	$2,231,875	$1,861,432	$1,551,845	$1,346,023	$1,112,639	$ 596,392
Total assets	5,463,186	5,672,461	5,675,073	5,293,422	3,008,549	2,499,511	2,276,362	1,899,506	1,525,805	991,717
Long-term debt	1,797,844	1,826,781	2,148,142	2,138,940	838,730	744,914	561,716	607,508	435,158	247,424
Common stockholder's investment	1,579,722	1,668,620	1,649,187	1,493,524	1,330,679	1,078,920	1,091,714	812,267	717,721	503,794
OTHER OPERATING DATA										
Express package:										
Average daily package volume	1,470,520	1,309,973	1,233,628	1,059,882	877,543	704,392	550,306	406,049	263,385	166,428
Average pounds per package	5.5	5.5	5.3	5.4	5.3	5.1	5.3	5.6	5.5	5.8
Average revenue per pound	$ 2.95	$ 3.11	$ 3.14	$ 3.04	$ 3.10	$ 3.33	$ 3.40	$ 3.45	$ 3.80	$ 4.02
Average revenue per package	$ 16.08	$ 17.08	$ 16.53	$ 16.28	$ 16.32	$ 16.97	$ 17.92	$ 19.19	$ 21.03	$ 23.42
Airfreight:										
Average daily pounds	2,654,646	2,880,106	3,310,494	4,019,353	—	—	—	—	—	—
Average revenue per pound	$ 1.16	$ 1.17	$ 1.12	$ 1.06	—	—	—	—	—	—
Aircraft fleet at end of year:										
Boeing 747s	13	18	19	21	—	—	—	—	—	—
McDonnell Douglas MD-11s	4	1	—	—	—	—	—	—	—	—
McDonnell Douglas DC-10s	28	27	26	24	21	19	15	11	10	6
McDonnell Douglas DC-8s	—	—	6	6	—	—	—	—	—	—
Boeing 727s	151	149	130	106	68	60	53	53	47	38
Cessna 208s	216	193	184	147	109	66	34	9	—	—
Fokker F-27s	32	26	19	7	5	—	—	—	—	—
Dassault Falcons	—	—	—	—	—	—	—	—	—	32
Vehicle fleet at end of year	34,000	32,800	31,000	28,900	21,000	18,700	14,500	12,300	9,000	5,000
Average number employees (based on a std full-time workweek)	84,162	81,711	75,102	58,136	48,556	41,047	31,582	26,495	18,368	12,507

EXHIBIT 3 Consolidated Statement of Operations

Year ending May 31 In thousands, except per share amounts	1992	1991	1990
REVENUES	$ 7,550,060	$ 7,688,296	$ 7,015,069
OPERATING EXPENSES			
Salaries and employee benefits	3,637,080	3,438,391	3,045,250
Rentals and landing fees	672,341	650,001	657,995
Fuel	508,386	663,327	521,256
Depreciation and amortization	577,157	562,207	505,412
Maintenance and repairs	404,311	449,394	424,923
Restructure charges	254,000	121,000	—
Other	1,473,818	1,551,850	1,472,878
	7,527,093	7,436,170	6,627,714
OPERATING INCOME	22,967	252,126	387,355
OTHER INCOME (EXPENSES)			
Interest, net	(164,315)	(181,880)	(188,109)
Gain on disposition of aircraft and related equip	2,832	11,375	13,791
Other, net	(8,312)	(8,679)	5,386
Payroll tax loss	–	(32,000)	—
	(169,795)	(211,184)	(168,932)
INCOME (LOSS) BEFORE INCOME TAX	(146,828)	40,942	218,423
PROVISION (CREDIT) FOR INCOME TAX	(33,046)	35,044	102,659
NET INCOME (LOSS)	$ (113,782)	$ 5,898	$ 115,764
EARNINGS (LOSS) PER SHARE	$ (2.11)	$ .11	$ 2.18
AVERAGE SHARES OUTSTANDING	53,961	53,350	53,161

Source: Annual Report 1992

passenger can evaluate different airlines on the basis of the enjoyment of a flight or a meal, or the friendliness of a cabin attendant, or an on-time arrival. In the case of express shipment, the customer only comes into direct contact with company personnel at the time of pick-up or delivery.

For these reasons, competition for customers in the express shipment industry has focused on proxy measures of performance that the customer can use as criteria for choosing an express carrier. Proxy measures popular in the late 1980s and early 1990s included reliability and guarantees of on-time performance records; package tracking information, in-house computer terminals and company-supplied software; a range of price points; availability of volume discounts; total number and location of destinations; and frequency of pick-ups and deliveries. If the customer was satisfied with one or more of these proxy measures of performance, then repeat purchasing might be expected to turn into brand loyalty to a particular express carrier.

In order to reinforce customer loyalty and differentiate itself from the competition, Federal invested heavily in leading-edge technology. During the late

EXHIBIT 4 Consolidated Balance Sheets

Year ending May 31 In thousands	1992	1991
ASSETS		
CURRENT ASSETS		
Cash and cash equivalents	$ 78,177	$ 117,692
Receivables less allowance for doubtful accounts of $32,074 and $37,694	899,773	924,773
Spare parts, supplies, and fuel	158,062	154,941
Prepaid expenses and other	69,994	85,441
Total current assests	1,206,006	1,282,847
PROPERTY AND EQUIPMENT, AT COST		
Flight equipment	2,540,350	2,394,326
Package handling and ground support equipment	1,352,659	1,296,706
Computer and electronic equipment	851,686	756,638
Other	1,433,212	1,447,501
	6,177,907	5,895,171
Less accumulated depreciation and amortization	2,766,610	2,271,145
Net property and equipment	3,411,297	3,624,026
OTHER ASSETS:		
Goodwill	487,780	521,079
Equipment deposits and other assets	358,103	244,509
Total other assets	845,883	765,588
	$ 5,463,186	$ 5,672,461
LIABILITIES AND STOCKHOLDER'S EQUITY		
CURRENT LIABILITIES:		
Current portion of long-term debt	$ 155,257	$ 202,653
Accounts payable	430,130	533,621
Accrued expenses	799,468	687,498
Total current liabilities	1,384,855	1,423,772
LONG-TERM DEBT, LESS CURRENT PORTION	1,797,844	1,826,781
DEFERRED INCOME TAXES	123,715	217,436
OTHER LIABILITIES	577,050	535,852
COMMITMENTS AND CONTINGENCIES		
COMMON STOCKHOLDERS' INVESTMENT		
Common stock, $ .10 par value; 100,000 shares authorized, 54,100 and 53,632 shares issued	5,410	5,363
Additional paid-in capital	672,727	652,045
Retained earnings	906,555	1,015,205
	1,584,692	1,672,613
Less treasury stock and deferred compensation related to stock plans	4,970	3,993
Total common stockholders' investment	1,579,722	1,668,620
	$ 5,463,186	$ 5,672,461

Source: Annual Report 1992

EXHIBIT 5 Summary of Selected Financial Information for Domestic and International Operations for the Years ending 31 March, 1988–1992

In thousands $	U.S. Domestic	International	Total Worldwide
Revenue			
1992	5,194,684	2,355,376	7,550,060
1991	5,057,831	2,630,465	7,688,296
1990	4,784,887	2,230,182	7,015,069
1989	4,144,827	1,022,140	5,166,967
1988	3,459,427	423,390	3,882,817
Operating Income (loss)			
1992	635,872	(612,905)	22,967
1991	671,186	(419,060)	252,126
1990	608,089	(220,734)	387,355
1989	467,143	(42,708)	424,435
1988	409,977	(30,525)	379,452
Identifiable Assets			
1992	3,941,022	1,522,164	5,463,186
1991	4,032,361	1,640,100	5,672,461
1990	3,798,364	1,876,709	5,675,073

Source: Compiled from various issues of Annual Reports of Federal Express

1980s and early 1990s, Federal installed more than 11,000 POWERSHIP computer terminals in the offices of large corporate users. These allowed customers to prepare their own packages for delivery, then track them electronically from point of shipment to final destination. Within the company, Federal used it COSMOS (Customer Operations Service Master On-Line System) network to track shipments worldwide. This was complemented in 1989 with Tiger's KIAC (Key Information Air Cargo) computerized system, designed specifically for heavyweight cargo. In the early 1990s a new information service, EXPRESSCLEAR was launched to provide customers with customs information electronically, in advance of a freight shipment. This allowed faster clearance of customs when a shipment reached a gateway airport.

Ground service couriers who picked up packages from customers' offices were dispatched by DADS (Digitally Assisted Dispatch System). Each courier carried a SuperTracker with which to record details of the pick-up by scanning a computerized code on the air-bill. About the size of a candy bar, this small computer recorded information about the package, figured out the best way to route the package through the Federal Express system, and displayed a specific routing code.

The nature of the express shipment business, with its primary emphasis on time sensitivity and complete market coverage, rendered decisions on company growth very difficult. Incremental, market-by-market expansion could take a long time to implement, due to the need for complex, overlapping networks of pick-up, shipping, and delivery routes. Fred Smith's preference for a faster option is seen in his comment to shareholders in 1990: "To extend our service capabilities outside the U.S., acquisitions have proven more expedient in entering new markets than creating 'de novo' ventures."

Federal's purchase of Tiger presented a way of avoiding the incremental growth option. However, Federal inherited major problems as well as the expected benefits of immediate access to new markets. The two combined companies' debt totaled $2.1 billion in 1989, almost two and a half times Federal's current level at the time. Federal's workforce of 65,000 non-union employees was expanded to include Tiger's 6,500 unionized workers. Integrating the two teams of pilots, 1,000 from Federal and 970 from Tiger, proved difficult and expensive. Before a joint seniority list could be established, many lower-paid Tiger pilots were left to sit around during 1989 while Federal pilots took home huge paychecks after working extensive overtime hours.

The Tiger acquisition was an important element of Federal's decision to "go global" in 1989. This decision required the company to set up three new types of operation: inbound into new national markets; outbound from each market back to the U.S.; and intra-country transportation services within a geographic region. It also required implementation at two levels, ground and air. Ground services were needed to guarantee the customer benefit of flexible pick-up and drop-off services. Air services were needed to link together the many nations across the Triad markets. Federal succeeded in implementing most of these activities in most of their markets, but not all of them as planned.

The Japanese Market

With the acquisition of Tiger International, Fred Smith acquired three key assets: their routes, their fleet, and their landing rights in Japan. Saul Steinberg, a financier who held a 16.5% stake in Tiger International, had approached Federal in late 1988 and offered the company for sale. Three weeks later, Federal bought the company.

One reason for haste may have been a fear that arch-rivals in the U.S. market would jump at the offer. United Postal Service (UPS) said later that it had looked at Tiger a number of times and decided to pass. Chairman John W. Rogers commented in 1989 that his company had "shied away from Tiger out of fear that differences in corporate culture and union squabbles might outweigh any advantages." Earlier during a period in 1987–1988, Rogers had negotiated to buy DHL Worldwide Express (DHL) but nothing came of it. Rogers then went on to acquire several operations in Europe as a means of progressively building a ground service and expanding air coverage in Europe.

As Federal discovered to their cost, Tiger's fleet needed immediate repairs for corrosion and structural problems to meet Federal Aviation Administration (FAA) maintenance deadlines. Still, the addition of Tiger's 39 cargo jets pushed Federal's fleet to 151 aircraft, increasing significantly its cargo-carrying capacity.

Key to the acquisition were Tiger's landing rights for inbound and outbound flights. Before acquiring Tiger, Federal had five foreign airport landing and take-off slots: Montreal, Toronto, Brussels, London, and Tokyo. But its Tokyo slot was limited due to Japanese government regulation; it could not be used as a springboard to other destinations in Asia to support intra-regional services. As a result Federal had in the past relied on other commercial airlines to carry shipments further into the heart of Asia. This reliance on other companies jeopardized their ability to ensure reliable performance and guarantee on-time arrivals. Federal executives felt that access to the landing rights alone amply justified the cost of the Tiger acquisition.

Federal now had principal centers of operation spanning the Pacific Rim from Australia and New Zealand to Hong Kong, Thailand, Singapore, the Philippines, Taiwan, and Japan (Osaka and Narita). Leading competitors in these markets for heavy air cargo were Japan Airlines, Nippon Cargo Airlines, DHL, and an Australian company, TNT Ltd. (TNT).

The European Market

An early effort to expand outside North America led Federal to acquire Gelco Express International in 1984. This was a worldwide, on-board courier service with offices in London, Amsterdam, Paris, Brussels, Hong Kong, Tokyo, and Singapore. Other acquisitions of local couriers followed, in order to complete Federal's ground network in Europe for pick-ups and deliveries. Federal's goal in Europe was to replicate its U.S. mode of operations by achieving complete ground and air coverage.

Two key players in the European market were DHL, headquartered in Brussels, and TNT. In the late 1980s TNT extended its presence in Europe through acquisitions in Spain and Italy. At that time DHL controlled 40 percent of Europe's express traffic and 60 percent of all U.S.-bound express packages. By 1990, DHL had become the world market leader for air express delivery of small packages, serving 188 countries with 190 aircraft. In response to Federal's purchase of Tiger, DHL made an agreement with Lufthansa and Japan Airlines that the two companies would each purchase 5 percent of DHL with an option to buy another 25 percent. This deal had two benefits: access to cargo space onboard the two airlines, and an infusion of cash that would allow DHL to face off with Federal.

The Middle Eastern Market

In 1993, DHL strengthened its position in the Middle East in the heavy cargo market by opening new facilities in Bahrain, a small island in the Arabian Gulf. $60 million would be invested there over four years, beginning with $12 million in 1993. This investment would allow DHL to more than double its current handling capacity. To support this initiative, DHL took over 15 acres of land formerly occupied by Federal at Brussels airport in Europe. DHL's Middle East sales development manager, Mike Wood, said that there had been a dramatic upsurge in heavy-weight cargo shipped by air in recent years.

> This is particularly true [in the Gulf] where nearly everything has to be brought in from other parts of the world.... In the past, using conventional airfreight would take four weeks or more... to transport, clear, and collect heavyweight dutiable items. But with the new service launched, the duration of the delivery will be cut down to just a few days, door-to-door. (Manama, Bahrain, June 21, 1993)

The new service was promoted in print media across the world with ads in *Business Week* in the U.S. and *The Economist* in Europe during 1993 and 1994, showing on-time deliveries being made in remote locations.

Other competitors in the Gulf included commercial airlines from across the Triad including Northwest Cargo, Cathay Pacific Cargo, and Federal's Flying Tigers. Cathay Pacific, like DHL, was planning to expand its cargo operations with flights to London, Frankfurt, and Hong Kong. In contrast to most airlines whose cargo revenue was only about 10 percent of total revenue, Cathay's cargo revenue stood at about 22–25 percent. Facing an over-supply of cargo service in Dubai (United Arab Emirates) in the Gulf, Cathay was seeking to diversify its market coverage by expanding its operations into Bahrain.

The North American Market

Federal's competition in North America, particularly in the U.S., was fierce and varied. Competitors included: other express shippers (such as UPS, Airborne Express, and in earlier years Emery Air Freight and Purolator Courier); the U.S. Post Office; commercial airlines; and freight forwarders. To varying degrees, Federal encountered a similar mix of competitors in the other two Triad markets, requiring vigilant monitoring of competitive moves worldwide.

Purolator Courier and Emery Air Freight

Throughout the 1980s, Federal had faced low-price competition from Purolator Courier, whose slogan was "overnight, not over-priced." Emery Air Freight had been one of the largest air carriers of express heavy cargo with a strong presence in international markets. By 1989, however, neither could compete with the four true heavyweights of the business, Federal, UPS, Airborne, and the U.S. Post Office. By 1992, market shares for the major U.S. competitors were: Federal, 43.3 percent; UPS, 25.2 percent; Airborne, 14.3 percent; and the U.S. Post Office, 7.6 percent.

UPS

Like Federal, UPS also intended to expand its international business. It acquired Seaborne European Express Parcels based in Brussels. In 1989, UPS increased the number of countries it served from 41 to 150. This expansion was complemented by plans to develop a pan-European trucking business to provide ground transportation, using a network of alliances rather than wholly owned acquisitions.

In 1990, UPS followed Federal into the Japanese market by obtaining rights to fly into Tokyo six times a week. Print ads in the business press promoting UPS' international express service emphasized its long-established familiarity to U.S. customers and its enviable record for efficiency. In the early 1990s, one UPS ad layout showed a simple image of one of the company's brown vans, accompanied by the slogan "We run the tightest ship in the shipping business." U.S. television commercials also reinforced the theme of dependability, showing vans on location in unfamiliar and exotic locales. In 1993 the brown van ad was updated, drawing attention to a new message painted on the side of re-styled company vans: "Worldwide Delivery Service 1-800-PICK-UPS." The headline proclaimed the new world service, saying, "Soon every UPS vehicle will come with a map of its delivery route."

In sheer number of total packages carried, UPS was rivaled only by the U.S. Post Office, earning the company nicknames in the business press such as a "behemoth" and a "titan." Traditionally, UPS had competed in the domestic U.S. market using a fixed schedule of pick-up and drop-off services. In order to compete more effectively against Federal's flexible, customer-oriented service, UPS installed some 11,500 next-day letter boxes in office buildings and opened 15 full-service air-express counters. Federal at that time had 12,000 drop-boxes in the U.S., 165 drive-through centers, and 371 storefront locations. In 1989, UPS introduced a new "on call" service in Dallas and Philadelphia. Finally, after many years of reliance on a fixed-price policy, UPS decided to match Federal's use of price reductions and volume discounts, backed up by a guarantee of "insured" performance.

UPS was a long-established, conservative company (85 years old in 1993), known for the strict discipline demanded of its drivers. Until Federal's purchase of Tiger, UPS had used Tiger's services for its own overseas cargo trade. Like Federal, "Big Brown" lost money in its 180 international markets due to the combined costs of expansion of the air fleet, acquisition of foreign couriers, and introduction of computerized tracking systems. UPS expected to turn its first profit in Europe by 1994. As one industry analyst commented, "UPS moves slowly, but when it moves, it's the 900-pound gorilla."

U.S. Postal Service

The U.S. Postal Service had two characteristics in common with UPS, longevity and regularly scheduled pick-ups. However, as a government agency, it was not allowed to participate in overseas markets sending inbound express deliveries into the U.S. Its great advantage in the U.S. for outbound international shipments was its customers' long-standing familiarity with Post Office locations, hours, and even the staff at their local office.

In 1993, the U.S. Postal Service stepped up its competitive position in the outbound market by focusing on price in its print ads. Federal responded by offering money-back guarantees of on-time delivery, thereby side-stepping the need to cut prices.

Competition from Airlines and Freight Forwarders

Traditionally, all types of mail and packages have been carried as cargo by commercial airlines. Express shipment companies relied on foreign airlines to cover smaller, more distant markets, but rapidly built up their own fleets and routes to reduce this dependency. Express shipment companies also put in place their own infrastructure on the ground to support door-to-door service. Airline carriers, in contrast, only serve their customers from airport to airport. The airlines' greatest strength is their ability to compete on price for cargo shipments by using passenger traffic revenues as a contribution toward the fixed costs of flying each route.

Freight forwarders are professional service companies that take over where the airlines leave off. They specialize in customs clearance procedures, packing and labeling requirements, insurance, transportation options, rates and discounts, and local ground delivery arrangements.

With the purchase of Tiger, Federal's EXPRESS-freighter service for heavy air cargo found itself in competition in the Pacific Rim with many of its own customers who were also freight forwarders. Initially, managers at Federal feared that they would lose these customers. However, seasonal demand for air cargo space for inbound U.S. shipments far outstripped supply on Asian routes in the peak period of September–December. This meant that freight forwarders who did not book cargo space early in the season might not find space available later in the year. The same constraints on space did not apply, however, to cargo outbound from the U.S. headed toward the Pacific Rim.

In Europe the competitive scene was quite different. Over-capacity for express air shipments resulted in heavy price competition from freight forwarders that was difficult for Federal to handle. After acquiring Tiger, Federal had to cut its cargo space on EXPRESSfreighter flights between 15–20 percent on European routes outbound to the U.S. In 1993, Federal fought back by challenging European freight forwarders in their role as customs brokers. A new service, FedEx International Priority Broker Selection Option was introduced, allowing customers to combine the services of their own broker with the reliability of FedEx's express shipment service.

The European Debacle

Managers at Federal over-estimated growth rates for the European market. As Thomas Oliver, VP for international operations admitted in 1990:

> We didn't make money in the U.S. until we were over 25,000 pieces in 1976. None of our regions outside the U.S. has come close to that number yet, and in a nutshell that is why they lose money. Europeans think that three-day delivery is very reasonable.

By 1992, European express package shipments had stalled at only 150,000 per night, a mere 5 percent of the U.S. market. As Fred Smith said,

> We ultimately concluded that the intra-European and intra-country market potential did not justify our remaining in these segments.

Domestic businesses in Italy, Germany, France, and the United Kingdom, as well as the intra-European service, were discontinued on May 4, 1992. Federal offered service to and from, but not within Europe. Fred Smith had originally forecast that the European market would eventually rival the U.S. market in size, with its nearly 3 million daily shipments. It was this expectation that was used to justify the creation of the costly hub and spokes air network centered on Brussels.

With regard to heavyweight shipments by Federal's EXPRESSfreighter service, return cargo flights from Europe to the U.S. were usually less than full, just like the flights outbound from the U.S. to the pacific Rim. Yet in 1992, Federal's EXPRESSfreighter service was the only overnight service from Europe guaranteeing delivery by 10:30 a.m. throughout North America. (A similar guarantee applied to next-day shipments from Asia back to North America.) Federal would have much preferred to fill its European and Asian flights with high-yielding, time-sensitive documents and small packages, rather than with heavy cargo that generated only a third of the revenue per pound.

Evolution of the Market

In the 1980s, a dramatic new type of competition hit the time-sensitive document segment of Federal's market—the fax machine. In the early days when fax transmission was still an exciting innovation in the business world, Federal had tried single-handedly to create its own fax network, called Zapmail. But poor transmission quality, the rapid proliferation of cheap office and home fax machines, and Federal's own high prices (initially $35 per 10-page document) undermined the appeal of Zapmail. It was discontinued in 1986 after having piled up losses of $350 million.

In 1990, annual growth rates for overnight letters in the U.S. market slowed to around 10 percent, down from 25 percent in 1988 and a high of 58 percent in 1984. Industry analysts predicted that fax machines alone would eventually displace 30 percent of Federal's overnight letter business in the U.S.

In 1992, Fred Smith talked of the company's future in these terms:

> The express network we have created in Asia and the Pacific positions Federal Express well to serve the explosive growth this region is expected to experience

throughout the 1990s and into the 21st century.... Our comprehensive service and numerous competitive advantages will position us well in serving the new engine of the world's economy.

A dynamic new growth market for Federal emerged in the early 1990s: logistics management.

> Companies in the fashion trade race to stay ahead of the trends by getting the latest designs from the factory floor to the retail store faster than the competition. High-tech equipment manufacturers scramble to market in an attempt to avoid being leapfrogged by a competitor. Service companies strive for global coverage and shorter response times. (Annual Report, 1992)

Federal successfully built a presence in the logistics management market through its Business Logistics Service (BLS). BLS's regional headquarters were set up in Singapore and the U.S. (Memphis), with regional offices in the U.K., Germany, and the Netherlands. New BLS contracts in 1992 included a major agreement with Laura Ashley Company in the U.K. BLS undertook to manage Laura Ashley's worldwide logistics operation, providing worldwide inventory and transportation management services. After its launch in 1988, BLS's business grew to over 200 clients in 1993.

"Retreat Does Not Mean Surrender"

Fred Smith always had a penchant for military imagery. His first management group in the 1970s was nicknamed "Ho Chi Minh's Guerrillas." He used to reward outstanding achievement with Bravo Zulu stickers—from the Navy signal flags meaning "job well done." In 1992, some commentators felt that Smith's "take no prisoners" approach to going international backfired badly. Others felt that it was just a question of time. Building volume and improving productivity were considered critical to success in this high fixed-cost industry. Once optimal volumes were reached, then substantial earnings leverage could be achieved.

Productivity increases were expected to benefit the company in the 1990s, following large-scale investments in new aircraft. In May 1992, Federal took delivery of four of thirteen new MD-11s, with final delivery slated for September 1993. Immediate savings were achieved. On a single run from Hong Kong to Anchorage, the smaller widebody jets saved $40,000 over the costs of flying an older 747. Over one year on that route alone, savings added up to nearly $12 million. New aircraft were introduced into the domestic market in 1994 with the first of 25 Airbus A300–600 freighters. One A300–600 with two pilots and two engines carries the same amount of cargo as nearly two and a half 727–100s with their seven pilots and seven engines. In 1992 Federal reduced its 727–100s to only four, from eight in 1991 and nine in 1990.

Outlook for the Nineties

Fred Smith's intentions to go on fighting to become a global leader were apparently undeterred by the bumpy ride after the Tiger acquisition. In 1990 he quickly became impatient with his critics, saying,

> They were all there in the Seventies, and they're back today. We stayed the course then and made it to the promised land. We're going to stay the course again now.

In 1992 Fred Smith affirmed once more the same determination:

> What I can say is that we're moving down the road with what I believe is absolutely the right strategy.

For 1993 he expressed this hope:

> In fiscal 1993, we will continue to confront the issue of declining yields through increased productivity, lowered costs and our on-going commitment to incorporate total quality improvement methods into the very fabric of the Company.... We remain committed to our goal of making Federal Express the premier provider of express and logistics services throughout the world.

Industry analysts were not so sanguine. Big questions remained in many people's minds about Federal's ability to handle the diverse challenges of the 1990s. These include a maturing market in the U.S., intense global competition, over-capacity in international markets, rapid growth of information technologies, and the persistent effects of different cultural attitudes toward the role of time in business transactions. It became clear that not all business people in Federal's target markets considered speed to be a prerequisite for business transactions—at least not in Europe. The advent of e-mail (instantaneous worldwide communications by means of personal computers) poses a further challenge to Federal's basic business of shipping documents. In 1994, the company was given a new look with an abbreviated company name and logo, "FedEx." This reflected the public's familiarity with the company and its services. As stated in the promotional print ad campaign: "Isn't that what you call us anyway?"

Case 32: Mubarak Dairies Limited

Mubarak—An Innovative Company

Mubarak Dairies Limited (MDL) is established in Jhang, with its head office in Lahore, Pakistan. MDL aims to become a market leader in the production and distribution of prepacked milk. MDL plans to innovate at the level of packaging and distribution. In order to test the viability of its creative ideas, a consumer market survey was commissioned. Students at Punjab University in Lahore and Quaid-e-Azam University in Islamabad carried out the field work under the direction of Mohammad Khan, a marketing executive from MDL. When the results of the survey were presented to the chief executive officer, decisions had to be made about critical aspects of the marketing mix.

This case is printed here with the permission of the authors, Lyn S. Amine of St. Louis University and Mohammad Ishaq Khan.

FIGURE 1

The Market Environment of Pakistan

Pakistan is the seventh-largest country in Asia. It is bounded to the west by Iran, to the north by Afghanistan and the former Soviet States, to the northeast by China, to the east and southeast by India, and to the south by the Arabian Sea (Figure 1). The population in 1985 was estimated at some 100 million inhabitants, with an annual growth rate of 2.7 percent. Forty-five percent of the population is under 15 years old. Urdu is the official language. Ninety-seven percent of the population are Muslims, and there are Christians and a small number of other minorities.

Although only 28 percent of the population is urban, the influx of rural migrants to Pakistan's few and crowded cities causes housing shortages and overburdens transportation. Islamabad, the capital, had a population in the early 1980s of 201,000; Karachi, 5.1 million; and Lahore, 2.9 million.

Pakistan has a developing mixed economy based largely on agriculture, light industries, and services. GNP totaled U.S. $35 billion in 1983, and the GNP per capita was $370. The overall literacy rate is 26 percent, but for women the rate is only 16 percent. Television is therefore the most important communications medium, and the government radio broadcasts in more than twenty languages.

Competition in the Dairy Industry

The Gawallas

Dairy products include milk, yogurt, and butter. Milk is used as a main ingredient for tea-making, and is an important element in the diet of infants and small children. Butter is used for baking and for breakfast. Yogurt is served at home with meals, and is used for making "Lassi." Lassi is diluted yogurt churned with added sugar. It is made at home or purchased from specialized retail outlets.

Traditionally, fresh milk with 5 percent to 7 percent full fat has been delivered door-to-door to consumers by the Gawallas. The Gawallas bring the milk in a big can of their own and carry a measure, with which to ladle milk into each customer's jug. Typically, the Gawallas will spend five to seven minutes at each door, and will seek feedback from the customer on the level of satisfaction with the milk delivered each day.

The Gawallas are local people who own small dairy farms, ranging from a couple of cows to as many as one hundred. All their methods of production are manual, and milk is delivered by horse-drawn carts or bicycles, and just occasionally by small motorcycles or lightweight trucks. The milk provided by the Gawallas is fresh, not processed in any way, and does not contain any preservatives. It is delivered to each customer's door twice a day, between 6 and 9 A.M. and 2:30 and 6:30 P.M., in time for breakfast and evening tea preparation. The tradition of home delivery is long-established and carried on from one generation to the next.

Prepacked Milk

Prepacked milk was introduced into Pakistan by the Milkpak Company, under the brand name TetraPak some ten to fifteen years ago. Originally, it was bought from small retail stores by occasional customers who needed to buy milk between the hours of the delivery by the Gawallas, that is, between 9:30 A.M. and 1:30 P.M., and late at night.

Gradually, occasional users became regular users and now represent some 23 percent of the total consumer milk market. Of the remaining 77 percent, 74 percent are now occasional buyers of prepacked milk.

Since the introduction of prepacked milk by Milkpak, other suppliers have entered the market, namely Haleeb and Greens. The Milkpak Company has a production capacity of 150,000 liters/day, and the other two producers can provide 100,000 liters/day. None of these plants has ever operated at full capacity. Currently, Milkpak has a national market share in the prepacked segment of 35 percent while Haleeb has 30 percent. The remaining 35 percent is divided among eight producers, some of whom serve only local markets.

Finding a Niche in the Prepacked Milk Market

Mubarak Dairies Ltd. (MDL) believed that it could compete against the Gawallas and the other milk packers by emphasizing two key competitive advantages: packaging in plastic pouches and home delivery. In order to test the strength of these two features, the market survey was commissioned. Two objectives were identified: to study current buying behavior among households and to analyze potential demand for a new prepacked milk product.

On the basis of survey results, a market launch strategy would be developed.

The Consumer Survey

A consumer sample of 1,000 households and a trade sample of 200 grocers were designed, based on three major cities. Sample organization was designed as follows:

City	No. of Consumers	No. of Grocers	No. of City Zones
Lahore	500	100	5
Rawalpindi	250	50	3
Islamabad	250	50	2
Total	1,000	200	10

The research budget was estimated at about 25,000 rupees (Rs) (U.S., $1.00: Rs 17.50). Key results from the consumer survey are presented in Tables 1 through 8.

Additional Results

Respondents were asked which size pack they prefer. In Rawalpindi and Islamabad, 72 percent prefer a 500 milliliter pack, 27 percent a 1 liter pack, and the rest a 250 milliliter pack. In contrast, in Lahore, preferences were 20 percent for 250 milliliter, 50 percent for 500 milliliter, and 40 percent for 1 liter.

Respondents also identified inconvenient features of present milk packages. Ninety-five percent of respondents in Rawalpindi and Islamabad and 85 percent in Lahore favor a change in packaging. The major complaint focused on the problem of storing the angular TetraPak, a reinforced paper container with four triangular sides. To open a TetraPak, typically a corner is cut off and used as a pouring spout. Spillage occurs easily if the pack is not handled carefully.

Developing a Market Plan for MDL

The management at MDL considered that the survey results indicated at least two significant findings:

1. Consumers were familiar with prepacked milk and valued its features.
2. Consumers were dissatisfied with current brand offering of prepacked milk. The pointed Tetra-Pak, in particular, tended to tear plastic shopping bags during the trip home.

Therefore, the following market plan was developed.

Marketing Objective

- Market penetration

Sales Goal

- 10,000 liters/day in each of the three target cities by the end of the three months

Market Share Goal

- 10 percent of the prepacked milk market after three months

Product Policy

- Produce better-quality milk than Milkpak or Haleeb, the two largest competitors

TABLE I Sources of Milk Purchases in Rawalpindi and Islamabad

Zone	Gawallas	Prepacked Supplier (regular)%	Prepacked Supplier (occasional)%
I	97	3	69
II	88	8	72
III	80	8	87
IV	79	20	82
V	70	28	58

Note: percentages do not total 100 due to multiple answers.

- Use a family brand name for milk and extend this later to butter and yogurt
- Introduce the new plastic pouch for prepacked milk; emphasize the convenience features as a special advantage
- Produce three sizes of pack: 250 milliliters, 500 milliliters, and 1 liter, with emphasis on the 250 milliliter pack in order to satisfy the preferences of occasional buyers
- Develop a special milk for children

Pricing Policy

- Meet major competitors' retail prices at Rs. 6.00/liter
- Squeeze out smaller suppliers by increasing retailers' commissions to Rs. 0.80/liter from Rs. 0.50
- Sell direct to institutional buyers at Rs. 5.40/liter for a minimum order of 50 liters/day (known as "bulk sales")

TABLE 2 Monthly Household Income by Zone—Rawalpindi and Islamabad

Zone	1000–2500 Rs. %	2501–4000 Rs. %	4001–5500 Rs. %	Above 5501 Rs. %
I	32	30	19	19
II	32	27	15	26
III	17	20	18	45
IV	21	48	18	13
V	2	17	17	64

Note: Percentages total 100 reading across the columns. One U.S. dollar equals 17.50 rupees.

TABLE 3 Monthly Household Income by Zone—Lahore

Zone	1000–2500 Rs. %	2501–4000 Rs. %	4001–5500 Rs. %	Above 5501 Rs. %
I	16	49	19	16
II	21	27	24	28
III	43	21	16	20
IV	4	26	23	47
V	7	19	25	49

Note: Percentages total 100 reading across the columns. One U.S. dollar equals 17.50 rupees.

TABLE 4 Sources of Milk Purchases—Lahore

Zone	Gawallas %	Retail Stores %
I	75	25
II	69	31
III	70	30
IV	62	38
V	56	44

TABLE 5 Reasons Why Consumers Prefer to Buy from Gawallas

City/Zone	Availability %	Low Price %	Freshness %	Purity %	Credit Facility %	Home Delivery %
Rawalpindi and Islamabad						
I	25	3	28	21	6	17
II	22	1	28	20	6	23
III	25	4	26	26	8	11
IV	15	4	31	26	4	20
V	19	8	30	22	0	21
Lahore						
I	22	9	20	13	13	23
II	25	11	20	12	9	23
III	24	11	23	16	3	23
IV	24	7	19	15	7	28
V	20	8	24	13	7	28

Note: Percentages total 100 reading across the columns. Only the major reason was solicited.

TABLE 6 Reasons Why Consumers Buy Prepacked Milk

City/Zone	Availability %	Low Price %	Freshness %	Hygiene* %	Ease of Storage %	Quality %	Status %	Other %
Rawalpindi and Islamabad								
I	21	2	15	18	15	10	0	19
II	20	5	22	28	10	14	0	1
III	21	5	20	23	9	18	1	3
IV	27	1	23	26	6	12	0	5
V	12	1	22	28	14	20	1	2
Lahore								
I	28	5	18	17	13	13	1	5
II	28	0	17	11	14	17	3	10
III	27	3	18	16	8	10	1	17
IV	36	3	16	12	12	10	1	10
V	28	3	13	26	9	7	0	14

Note: Percentages total 100 reading across the columns. Only the major reason was solicited.
*Pasteurized and homogenized at 3.0% fat.

TABLE 7 Major Decision Maker for the Purchase of Prepacked Milk

City	Male Head %	Children %	Housewife %	Servant's Discretion %
Rawalpindi and Islamabad	28	14	54	4
Lahore	32	15	50	3

TABLE 8 Actual Purchaser of Prepacked Milk

City	Male Head %	Children %	Housewife %	Servant %
Rawalpindi and Islamabad	39	34	10	17
Lahore	25	40	11	24

Note: Percentage responses by city zone have been averaged.

Promotional Policy

- Advertising would be used at a later stage to support the new flavors of milk
- A "push" strategy as the main promotional strategy, based on increased retail commissions

Distribution Policy

- MDL prepacked milk to be home-delivered and credit facilities to be offered, as a means of competing directly with the Gawallas
- MDL also to be distributed to retailers such as general grocery stores and bakeries

During the research survey, it was ascertained that consumers preferred the Gawallas as a source of milk due to the facility of home delivery. MDL saw this as a major opportunity and identified a creative means of distributing the new brand of milk.

Home Delivery—A Key Competitive Weapon

School children are transported to school in vans. Primary education is free, and enrollment is about 80 percent for boys but only 30 percent for girls. Children are transported twice a day, with about thirty in each van. During the rest of the day, the drivers are unoccupied. The same is true for Friday, the day of prayer, and for vacations, which run from June to mid-August.

MDL believed that these drivers had both the knowledge of the community, the time available, and the motivation to deliver milk during their quiet times. Most drivers own their own vans. MDL believed that these drivers could use their contacts with the thirty families they each already knew to identify another forty families who would like to buy home-delivered, prepacked milk. MDL had set a goal of distributing 200 liters of milk each day to seventy families, a rate of consumption documented in the consumer survey.

MDl proposed to pay the van drivers the higher retail commission of Rs. 0.80/liter, or Rs. 160.00 daily. It was estimated that a driver would be able to sell 200 liters a day in a forty-mile radius, and expenses were estimated at Rs. 30.00 and Rs. 20.00 respectively. Total daily earnings for each driver would be, therefore, about Rs. 100.00 (Rs. 160.00 − Rs. 50.00).

Thus, home delivery promised to be a cost-effective means of distribution, as well as a way of achieving high levels of customer satisfaction.

Case 33: MacDermid, Inc.

In 1990, Buzz Fanning, technical liaison for MacDermid, Inc., was sent to Korea to investigate MacDermid's loss of market share in the Korean market. MacDermid was an international specialty chemical company that supplied the metal finishing, printed circuit board, and microelectronics industries. The majority of sales in the Far East were for the printed circuit board (PC) market. In a two-year period, MacDermid had gone from a 30 percent to 50 percent market share to a 10 percent market share in the Korean PC market. Fanning was charged with regaining MacDermid's market share and its leadership position in Korea.

Background of the Company

MacDermid, Inc., was founded on February 2, 1922, in Waterbury, Connecticut, by Archie J. MacDermid, a Scottish immigrant. MacDermid's first product was Metex Metal Cleaner #1 for the metal finishing industry. Metex was an alkaline metal soak and electrolytic cleaner that was used to clean brass and other metals. The thriving brass industry in Connecticut provided a large market for MacDermid. In 1930 MacDermid moved its manufacturing facilities to a new location in Waterbury. This plant still serves as MacDermid's primary manufacturing facility in the U.S.

In 1938 Harold Leever joined MacDermid as a research chemist. Leever later served as the second of only three MacDermid presidents and subsequently as chairman of the board. It was Leever's innovative and insightful ideas that led MacDermid to be a world leader in specialty chemicals for the metal finishing, printed circuit board, and microelectronics industries.

Leever began changing the company when he developed Anodex, a reverse-current alkaline cleaner. Anodex could be used to clean steel and this opened the automotive market to MacDermid. With this, MacDermid became a national marketer.

Leever also developed the philosophy of "sales and service." This philosophy merged research and sales by requiring that research conducted in Waterbury start from and serve the customer's needs. This philosophy still works at MacDermid today.

During the 1940s and 1950s, MacDermid introduced some industry firsts. Cyanide bright copper addition agents eliminated dull finishes and the need for buffing procedures. Dry acid salt replaced the more hazardous liquid acids thus providing environmental improvements. Metal strippers allowed customers to salvage scrapped electroplated parts. Metex Acid Salt M-629 was a refinement of the original salt and provided a longer life and a better adhesion of plated metals. Chromate conversion coatings improved corrosion resistance and appearance. The 1950s also saw the construction of another MacDermid manufacturing facility located in Ferndale, Michigan. MacDermid had emerged as an innovator and market leader in the metal finishing industry. This reputation would help propel the company into new markets.

By 1954, Leever had earned the position of president of MacDermid. Archie MacDermid remained active in the company until 1959 when he retired. With $3 million in sales, seventy-five employees, and fifty products, Archie offered ownership of the company to the employees. The employees bought 29,000 of Archie's shares for $961,640. This allowed control of the company to remain with those who had helped make it successful.

Leever introduced the concept of "Complete Cycle Responsibility," which then became company policy. This policy stated that every MacDermid representative will accept responsibility for satisfactory operation of a complete processing cycle.

In the 1960s MacDermid began to develop and market chemicals for a new industry that was very significant in size—the electronics industry. Printed circuit boards are an essential component of this market. Chemicals are used to clean, coat, etch, strip, and protect printed circuit boards. MacDermid's first product in this market was alkaline etchant. This eliminated the need for hazardous chromic acids and ferric chloride and thus improved working conditions and worker safety.

In 1966 a public stock offering of 20 percent of the 510,456 outstanding shares was made. By this time, MacDermid had also begun to compete internationally, with $200,000 in overseas sales. A 50/50 joint venture with Occidental Petroleum Corporation was formed and called MOSA. MOSA was responsible for worldwide manufacturing and distribution of proprietary chemicals. This agreement was terminated in 1983.

In 1977, MacDermid had $42 million in sales, 440 employees, and 500 specialty chemicals. There were manufacturing plants in Connecticut, Michigan, California, Missouri, England, and Spain, and a research facility in Tel Aviv, Israel. There were sales and service operations throughout the world. It was in this growing environment that Arthur J. LoVetere was made the third and current president of MacDermid. LoVetere joined MacDermid when he was eighteen as a summer worker. He continued his association with MacDermid as he earned his BS in chemical engineering and his MBA. In 1963, after receiving his MBA, LoVetere began as a technical sales representative for the mid-Atlantic. By 1966, LoVetere was the company's youngest regional sales manager at age 27. In 1973 he became vice president of marketing and by 1975 he was vice president and chief operating officer. In 1977 he was made president and chief executive officer. LoVetere believed in management by participation. Although LoVetere was now responsible for daily operations, Leever remained as an active participant in the company and chairman of the board.

Under LoVetere, the company continued to expand its operations by acquisitions and entry into international markets. In 1978 MacDermid had 6,000 customers in the U.S. and Canada. Products were marketed in Europe by twenty-five sales representatives located throughout England, Germany, the Netherlands, Spain, and Switzerland. Proprietary products were manufactured and sold in Australia, Italy, and on a limited basis in Japan. MacDermid purchased the Plating Systems Division of 3M. This acquisition provided manufacturing, distribution networks, and a basis for overseas business that were extremely valuable, especially in the Far East.

In 1980, the Employee Stock Ownership Plan was instituted, continuing the tradition of employee ownership. Employee ownership was now 40 percent with retirees, friends, and families of employees constituting another 25 percent.

By 1990, MacDermid had $106 million in sales, 800 employees, 1,000 products, and served twenty-three countries. The company was still characterized as an innovator and industry leader. There was no rigid organizational chart and the "MacDermid Spirit" was evident to anyone who came in contact with a MacDermid employee. In 1986, a 2,500-square-foot manufacturing plant was built in Taiwan.

Products—PC Market

MacDermid had a full line of products to service the PC industry. Products included Metex activators, accelerators, acid cleaners and acid salts, electrocleaners, strippers, antitarnish coating, circuit board tapes, polymer thick films, solder pastes, resists and masks, and etch resists and inks. These products are used in such applications as communication systems, television, video and sound recorders, compact discs, microwaves, radios, industrial automation and robotics, computer system electronics, navigation electronics, and medical instrumentation and monitoring devices. MacDermid was considered one of the major competitors in this market. It was the only specialty chemical company with direct operations in every major market in the world.

Competition

Shiplee Corporation of Germany was MacDermid's major competitor. Shiplee was privately owned and had a significant market share. Their claim to success was consistent quality. Shiplee competed with MacDermid in most major markets in the world.

Korean Market

MacDermid was well established in Japan, Korea, Singapore, Hong Kong, and Taiwan. MacDermid had its own manufacturing facility in Taiwan and used contract manufacturers in Japan. For thirteen years, the Korean market had been served by MacDermid out of its Japanese division. The Japanese fully controlled the market. The Korean market had become significantly large due to the government's commitment to the electronics industry. However, because of the loss of one major account, MacDermid's market share had dropped to 10 percent. There was considerable animosity between the Koreans and the Japanese. A brief history lesson highlights the fact that the Japanese invaded Korea during World War II. In addition, the cultural, political, and economic differences between the two nations further increased the friction.

The Korean market was serviced by Japanese salesmen. There was no local representation. The price charged by the Japanese division was twice that available in the U.S. This was primarily due to the strength of the yen. In 1990, the Korean sales volume was $40,000 per year.

The Korea government had recently mandated a balance of trade. Currently, there was an excess of imports from Japan and an excess of exports to the United States and Hong Kong. The Korean customers were requesting to deal directly with the U.S. division, which would result in a better balance with the United States and Japan (i.e., fewer imports from Japan and more imports from the United States). MacDermid's Japanese employees furiously fought this option. They would lose a large percentage of sales if they lost the Korean market. Buzz was challenged with finding a solution to this complicated international problem.

Case 34: American Express International, Inc.

In January 1984, Seoul branch executive of American Express International, Inc., Mr. Steve Lowe, was considering the marketing strategy for the American Express Card's introduction to Korea with a local advertising agency, ORICOM. They were reviewing whether to enter the Korean market and, if so, what marketing strategy to adopt.

Company Background

American Express Company, founded in 1850, is a diversified financial and travel services company. Through its four principal operating units—American Express Travel Related Services, IDS Financial Services, Shearson Lehman Hutton, and American Express Bank—the company is one of the leaders in payment systems, travel, asset management, investment banking, international banking, etc.

American Express Travel Related Services (TRS), the largest operating unit, markets the American Express Card along with Gold Card, Corporate Card, American Express travelers checks, and American Express money orders. The company's network of over 1,400 travel offices serves millions of people around the world each year. Internationally, Japan, Brazil, Germany, Hong Kong, Italy, and Spain are expected to experience sharp gains in American Express Cards in force. Asia, Korea, India, and China are expected to be the next target markets for the cards.

Korean Operation

As an initial stage to launch the American Express Card in Korea, a branch of American Express International, Inc., was installed in Seoul in 1983. Branch director Steve Lowe, assisted by a small staff of local MBAs, was primarily responsible for the successful preparation of its introduction. As soon as the decision to enter the Korean market was made, the branch was expanded with more staff and local networks established across the country.

Product

By the end of 1983, over 20 million American Express Cards were in force worldwide; this figure was expected to reach over 30 million in 1990. The card

---

This case was prepared by Kwangsu Kim, a graduate student at the University of Connecticut, under the supervision of the author.

offers a wide range of financial services to cardholders such as credit line, insurance, and online cash services.

The basic operation of the card is similar worldwide. Cardholders pay an annual fee for the American Express Card, and are supposed to pay for their purchases within a certain period of time. The card to be offered in Korea would provide the same services. Monthly balance can be paid in won (Korean currency) or U.S. dollars.

Competition

There are generally two major categories to classify various credit cards available in Korea: (1) bank cards: National, Visa, Bank Credit, long-term bank, and (2) charge cards: both American Express and Diners Club cards were expected to be available soon.

A bank card did not require any fee for card membership; if a person had an account with a bank, he or she could get the bank card without any annual and initial application charge. In contrast, a charge card such as the American Express or Diners Club required both application and annual fees, which could discourage some people from holding charge cards.

In addition to the competition of bank cards, it was expected that a charge card would be introduced in Korea by Diners Club in spring 1984. If both American Express and Diners Club were to launch their cards, there should be direct competition between the two to maintain the market share.

Exhibit 1 shows the comparative features of different cards. There are relative advantages and disadvantages associated with various cards. The American Express Card would charge substantial annual fees whereas National Bank, Bank Credit, and long-term bank cards would charge nothing (while they require a transaction fee upon opening the account, the amount is minimal).

Further, the banks have branches across the country while American Express did not have branch network in Korea, resulting in inconvenience for the cardholders. But the American Express Card has its own strengths. First, the card can provide services abroad and permits purchase of airplane tickets. Second, it provides substantially more cash loan than the bank cards.

Market

Since a department store credit card was introduced in 1969 in Korea, there have been several other department store cards issued. But the era of the credit card was initiated in 1982, when eight banks formed an association to introduce Bank Credit card. The same year Visa card was also introduced for use in foreign countries as well as in the domestic market.

Exhibits 2 and 3 shows the market-related information.

In 1983, the ad agency, at the request of American Express International, Inc. conducted a study to predict the potential market for the charge card. The

EXHIBIT 1 Comparative Features of Different Cards

Name	Transaction Fee	Annual Fee	Purchase Limit	Interest Rate (yr)	Cash Loan Limit	Insurance Limit
National card	$1	None	$500	19%	$300	$2000
Bank credit card	$1	None	$500	19%	$300	$2000
Visa	$5	None	$1500	19%	$500	Unlimited
Long-term bank card	$1	None	$1000	19%	$500	$2000
American Express	None	$45	No limit	12.9%	$1500	Unlimited
Diners Club	None	$45	No limit	3%/month	$1000	Unlimited

Source: Company records.

number of subjects sampled was 1,500. They were over 25 years old and lived in cities such as Seoul, Pusan, and Kwangjoo. In addition, their average annual incomes were above 8 million won (U.S. $13,700). The results of the study are shown in Exhibit 4.

Based on the consumer survey, the target market has a strong level of awareness of the charge card. It was encouraging that the awareness level of the American Express Card reached 22 percent even before its launch. According to the consumer survey, the target market should be businesspeople who travel frequently and often organize business receptions.

Marketing Strategy

The ad agency proposed the following marketing strategy:

a. *Marketing Goal*
Launch the American Express Card in won (Korean currency).
Obtain 8,000 cardholders by the end of 1984.
Obtain 2,850 service establishments who would accept the card by the end of 1984.

b. *Strategy Thrust*
Increase awareness of the card through advertising and direct marketing.

c. *Advertising Strategy*
Advertising goal: increase awareness/establish brand image as a quality card.
Primary target market: more than 35 years old; income more than U.S. $10,000; businesspeople.
Additional target market: more than 25 years old; income more than U.S. $10,000; businesspeople

Brand positioning: The American Express Card is a high-quality card, which can be used in foreign countries as well as domestically. It is convenient for traveling and business entertaining. In particular, it symbolizes business success.

Prelaunch advertising: in major daily newspapers to increase the expectation of the launch; to counterattack the launch of such competitive cards as Diners Club.

d. *Direct Marketing Strategy*
Direct mailings will be sent to the following: (1) Passport holders (those who have passports evidently travel abroad).

EXHIBIT 2 Size of the Market Provided by the Advertising Agency

Number of households in the country	7,971,147
Number of households in 6 metropolitan cities	3,409,371
Number of households whose annual income is greater than 7 million won (U.S. $12,000)	477,000
Number of cardholders	850,000

Source: Company records.

EXHIBIT 3 Market Position of Select Cards

Name	Number Of Cardholders	Service Establishments
National	470,000	25,000
Visa	38,000	7,000
Bank Credit	300,000	16,000

Source: Company records.

EXHIBIT 4 Highlights of Consumer Survey

Awareness of American Express Card	22%
Awareness of Diners Club Card	6%
Awareness of National Card	58%
Percent of National Bank Card members	15%
Percent of Bank Credit Card members	6%
Foreign travel in last 2 years	12% (average 2–3 times)
Purpose of foreign travel	business (84%)
Domestic travel in last 2 years	78% (average 6 times)
Purpose of domestic travel	business (57%)
Business reception* in last month	51% (4–5 times)

*Business reception refers to the occasions when business partners entertain each other to promote mutual relationship and interests.
Source: Company records.

(2) List of car owners (in Korea those who own autos are thought to be rich).

(3) Lists of golf-club memberships (high-income people).

e. *Promotion*
A trade show will be held to celebrate and promote the card's launch. At the show, application forms will be distributed.

f. *Distribution Efforts*
Application forms should be available in travel agencies, banks, service establishments, etc.

Based on the above information, the branch executive had to decide whether the American Express Card should be launched in Korea and, if so, when and how the card could be introduced. The decision to enter the market seemed obvious in that the country has been economically strong and was expected to grow constantly in the future. Further, after the Summer Olympic Games scheduled to be held in Seoul in 1984, the country was expected to experience further economic growth.

However, Mr. Lowe wondered if the proposed marketing strategy by the local agency emphasized too much advertising. He felt greater emphasis should be placed on direct marketing. For example, travel agents could be included as one of the target markets since they might persuade travelers to apply for the American Express Card.

Further, since there were anti-American demonstrations recently among the university students, he thought that the older segments of the population should be targeted. He also believed advertising in major daily newspapers would be appropriate.

As Mr. Lowe left the office, he planned to think the problems over.

Subject Index

Accounting, international, 134–139
Achievers, 387
Ad valorem duty, 40
Administrative entry procedures, 41
Advance pricing agreement (APA), 502
Advertising, 4, 52, 229–230, 240
  agencies, 578–579
  goals, 571–572
  international, 548–582
  media for, 566–570
  regulation and, 575–578
Aesthetics, importance of, 7
Africa, 153, 335
Afro-Malagasy Economic Union, 45, 46, 142–143, 146–147, 153
Agency for International Development (AID), 348–349
Agent/Distributor Service (A/DS), 530, 617
Agriculture Department, U.S., 287
Aircraft industry, 9, 142, 315
Airlines industry, 36, 711
Algeria, 253, 536
Altered marketplace competition, 200
American Arbitration Association (AAA), 296
American Institute of CPAs (AICPA), 136
American Trading Company (ATC), 517
Andean Common Market, 154
Animism, 384
Antiboycott laws, 285
Antibribery provisions, 283
Antidumping practices, 41, 278–279
Anti-private-sect attitude, 260–261
Antitrust certification provisions, 620
Antitrust laws, 282–283, 489–490
Apparel. *See* Textiles
Arab Common Market (ACM), 155
"Arbitrage support points," 104
Arbitration, 295–297

Architecture industry, 184–185
Argentina
  advertising expenditures in, 551
  consuming capacities of, 190
  expropriations in, 253
  GNP of, 20
  retailing in, 536
  telephones in, 356
Asia
  business climate in, 250
  economic cooperation in, 154–155
  shopping mall in, 539
  tariff reduction programs of, 47
  television advertising in, 550
Asia-Pacific Economic Cooperation (APEC), 155
Assembly lines, automation of, 723
Assimilation approach, 231
Association of South East Asian Nations (ASEAN), 154–155
Athletic equipment, 563
Audio-visual services, 46
Austria
  advertising expenditures in, 551
  European Free Trade Association, 144, 152
  GNP of, 20
  wholesaling in, 534
Australia
  advertising expenditures in, 551
  consuming capacities of, 190
  food consumption, 193
  marketing research industry in, 335
  retailing in, 536
Automated Information Transfer System (AITS), 616
Automobile industry, 370, 459
  business adaptation problem dealing with, 236–237
  in China, 165–166
  culture as it affects purchases, 228
  exchange rates affecting, 112

  foreign competition, 8–9, 32, 45, 247, 282–283
  import licensing in, 279
  Japanese imports and exports, 197–198, 281
  people-per-car ratio by country, 11

Baby food, 367, 462
Bahrain, advertising expenditures in, 551
Balance of payments, 113–117, 120, 607, 721
Balance of trade, 607
Balance sheet, 134
Bank guarantees, 287
Bank of America, 349
Banks, 349–350, 613, 619–620, 635
Bargaining power, 267–268
Barter, 634–636
Beer industry, 6, 227
Belgium
  advertising expenditures in, 551
  consuming capacities of, 190
  consumption expenditures, 192
  European Coal and Steel Community, 143
  European Union, 146
  food consumption, 193
  gift-giving in, 226
  wholesaling in, 534
Benin, taboos in, 230
Bicycle industry, 5
"Big Emerging Markets" (BEMs), 375
Bill of lading, 630
Blocked currency, 43
Bolivia, advertising expenditures in, 551
Boltin International, 356
Booking contract, 631
Border tax adjustment, 41
Boston Consulting Group (BCG) product portfolio approach, 713–718

777

"Botique" marketing system, 528, 627
Boycott, 255
Brand names, 288, 466–472, 489, 564
Brazil
 advertising expenditures in, 551
 antidumping laws in, 279
 bargaining power of multinational corporations in, 268
 culture of, 222
 economy of, 198–199
 consuming capacities of, 190
 gift-giving in, 226
  International Monetary Fund assistance, 107
 market size of, 376
 material life in, 217
 political risk index of, 265
 postal system, 356
 retailing in, 536
 wholesaling in, 534
Breakthrough product, 195
Bretton Woods Conference, 104
Bribery, 283
Britain. *See* United Kingdom
British Market Research Bureau, 352
Brussels Tariff Nomenclature (BTN). *See* Customs Cooperation Council Nomenclature
Buddhism, 385
Bulgaria, 152, 230
Buyback barter, 635
Buying proposal, 561

Canada
 architecture industry in, 184–185
 automobile purchasing, 226
 cigarette purchases, 227
 consuming capacities of, 190
 consumption expenditures, 192
 dual cultures in, 216
 food consumption, 193
  Free Trade Agreement with United States, 155–157
 global brands in, 369
 Louvre Agreements, 108
 market, size of, 376
 marketing research industry in, 335
  North American Free Trade Agreement, 157–158
 Canadian-American Commercial Arbitration Commission (CACAC), The, 296
Capitalist economic systems, 194

Caribbean Community Common Market, 154
Cartel, producer, 159
Cash cows, market share and, 714
Cash flow, 694
Cash in advance, 631
Catalog, overseas, 617
Central American Common Market, 153
Certificate of origin, 629
Channel alternatives, establishing, 525–527
Channel members, international, 514–525
Channel theory, 509–511
Channel management of distribution, 525–533, 544
Channel research, 343
Chewing gum, 281
Chile, 251, 253, 534
China. *See* Peoples Republic of China
Christianity, 385
Cigarettes. *See* Tobacco industry
Clearing agreement, 634
Clothing. *See* Textiles
Coal, 143
Cobalt, 35
Code law, 275, 290, 297
Coffee, 23, 227, 456, 553
Colombia, 20, 551
Colors, cultural norms and, 230
Commerce. *See* Trade
Commerce Department, U.S., 614–618, 620
Commercial invoice, 629
Commissaries, 518–519
Commission agents, 517
Commodity agreement, 159
Commodity tax, 247
Common agricultural policy (CAP), 147
Common law, 275, 290, 297
Common market, 145
Commonwealth of Independent States (CIS), 146, 159
Commonwealth of Nations, 146, 159
Communist governments, 257
Comparative advantage, theory of, 30–36, 53
Comparative costs, 31
Comparison shopping, 617
Compatibility of new product, 463–464
Compensation for sales personnel, 594
Competition, 449–450, 487–488

 foreign, 8–10
 marketing agreement change, 142
 sources of, 195–196
Competitive advantage, 196–198
Competitive product, 195
Computer simulation models, 6
Competitive strength, 715–716
Complexity of product, 464
Computers, personal, 228
Confiscation, 253
Conflicts and their resolution, 695–698
Congo, Republic of, languages spoken in, 357
Consignment sales, 632
Conspiracy, 250
Consular invoice, 629
Consulates, 349
Consulting firms, 349
Consumer behavior, cross-cultural analysis of, 232
Consumer protection, U.N. guidelines on, 293–294
Consumer tastes, globalization of, 723–724
Consumption, 189–193
Continuous innovations, 464
Contractual agreements, 22–23
Cooperative retailing, 539–540
Cooperative exporter, 518
Coproduction agreement, 22
Copy development and testing, 573
Copy machine industry, 8
Copyrights, 46, 261, 290–291
Corporate-labor relationships, 723
Corporate networking, 683–686
Cost analysis, 485–486
Cost approach, 490–491, 493, 505
Cost-benefit criteria analysis, 200–201
Cost-benefit relationship, 448–449, 561
Cost, insurance, and freight (CIF) price, 497
Costa Rica, advertising expenditures in, 551
Council for Mutual Economic Assistance (CMEA), 152
Council of Mutual Economic Cooperation (COMECON), 152
Counterfeiters, 289
Counterpurchase, 634
Countervailing duties, 41
Country-controlled buying agent, 517
Country of origin, identifying, 470–471
Coupons, 597

Creeping expropriation, 253
Critical mass, 623
Cross-checking, 340
Cuba, 253
Culture, 240–241
 assessment of, 231–233
 concept of, 215–217
 field for understanding, 217–222
 Hall's map of, 233–235
 influences on advertising, 560
 management differences due to, 696
 marketing and, 222–227, 385–386
 popular, 608
Cultural adaptation, 234–238
Cultural change, 238–240
Cultural environment, 202, 214–244
Cultural diversity, 221
Cultural training, 593
Currency, 40–43, 100–110, 103, 493, 505
Customer demand, 488–489
Customer innovativeness, 464
Customization of products, 447–451
Customs and administrative entry procedures, 41
Customs Cooperation Council (CCC), 354
Customs Cooperation Council Nomenclature (CCCN), 354
Customs duty, 40, 278
Customs union, 145, 146
Cyprus, advertising expenditures in, 551
Czech Republic
 European Union and, 152
 investment rating of, 266
 taboos in, 230

Debt crisis and International Monetary Fund, 105–107
Decentralization of production process, 723
Decisions, foreign subsidiarie's authority to make, 686–691
Deficit, balance-of-trade, 6, 8
Deficit Reduction Act of 1984, 614
Delivered duty-paid price, 497
Delphi technique, 264
Democratic government, 257
Denmark
 advertising expenditures in, 551
 consuming capacities of, 190

European Free Trade Association, 143–144, 152
European Union, 146
 food consumption, 193
 GNP of, 20
 taboos in, 230
Department of Agriculture, U.S., 349
Department of Commerce, U.S., 282, 348, 362, 530
Depreciation, accelerated, 280
Desired position, 445
Detergents, 460–461
Developing world, opportunities in, 210–211, 373–375
Differential exchange rate, 43
Differential versus uniform pricing, 483–484
Dictatorships, 257
Diffusion, impact on new products, 465
Direct distribution channel, 514
Direct effects, 250
Direct mail, 352
Directories, 356
Disclosures, 135
Discontinuous innovations, 464
Discount houses, 538
Discretionary product adaptation, 453
Distribution, 228–229, 343, 695
 through agents, 520
 alternative channels of, 508–547
 company-owned, 522–523
 indirect channel, 514–517
 internal channels of, 508–547
  through merchant intermediaries, 520–522
 research, 343
 requirements, 473
Distributorships, 274
Diversification, 465–467
Dividend policy, international, 130
Divisibility, 464
Dock receipt, 630
Documentation requirements, 41
Dogs, 714
Dollar, U.S., 103, 111
Dolls, 228
Domestic assistance programs, 41
Domestic industry, 13, 285
Domestic international sales corporations (DISCs), 613–614
Domestic markets versus foreign markets, 681
Domestication, 253–254

Dominican Republic, advertising expenditures in, 551
Dumping, 46, 278–279, 501–503, 506
Duties, 40–41
Duty-free zones, 633
Dynamically continuous innovations, 464

East Africa Customs Union, 153
Economic ability, 465
Economic assistance programs, 5
Economic blocs, 674
Economic Community of West African States (ECOWAS), 153
Economic dependence, 195
Economic environments, 188–213
 analysis of, 200–210
 impact of domestic, 200
 marketing strategy and, 198–200
Economic integration, regional, 143–144
 cooperation, 144
Economic philosophy, 257
Economic status grouping of countries, 381–382
Economic systems, 194
Economic Union (EU), 47, 145–146, 152, 274
Economics, 217
Economies of scale, 268
Economist Intelligence Unit (EIU), 264
Ecuador
 advertising expenditures in, 551
 consuming capacities in, 190
Education, 217–218, 240, 724
Egypt, 146, 356, 534, 536
Elasticity of demand, 489
Electronics industry, 9, 12, 344, 379
Embargoes, 41
Embassies, 349, 352
Engel's law, 192
England. *See* United Kingdom
Entry of product, 458
Entry strategies into foreign markets, 21–25
Environmental factors, 343, 724
 advertising and, 557–561
 channel agreements and, 532–533
 internal, 17
 affecting international marketing, 187–211
 affecting price, 450, 489

Subject Index

Environmental laws, trade barriers and, 621
Eternal values, 469
Ethics, 222, 485, 498
Ethnocentric approach, 231, 682, 704
Eurobrand, 388
Eurodollars, 117–118, 120
Europe 1992 program, 149–150
European Coal and Steel Community (ECSC), 143
European Common Market. *See* European Union
European Currency Unit (ECU), 151
European Economic Area (EEA), 152
European Economic Community (EEC), 143
European Free Trade Association (EFTA), 47, 144–146, 152
European Union (EU), 141, 146–152, 160, 287, 383
  antitrust laws of, 490
  internal market program in, 532, 692
  as marketing agreement, 294–295
Evaluation, 458
Exchange, government approval to secure, 43
Exchange control, 254
Exchange rate, 43, 104, 107–108, 110–111
Ex-factory price, 497
Existing demand, 195
Expansion policies, 723
Expatriates, 584–586
Experience effect, 487
Expert opinion, 264
Export Administration Act, 618
Export broker, 520
Export-Import Bank, U.S., 48, 287, 505, 613, 635
Export Contact List Services, 616–617
Export distributor, 520–521
Export documents, collecting, 629–630
Export drafts, 632
Export duty, 278
Export jobber, 521
Export licensing, 279, 627–629
Export management, 622
Export Management Company (EMC), 514–516
Export market, 34, 146, 346–347
Export marketing, 605–638
Export merchant, 518
Export packing list, 630

Export pricing, 493–497, 505
Export procedure, 627–632
Export restraints, voluntary, 42, 281
Export strategy, 626–627
Export tax, 40
Export subsidies, 41
Export Trading Company Act (ETC) of 1982, 48, 517, 613, 619–620, 636
Export vendor, 518
Export Yellow Pages, The, 616
Exporter, 14
Exporters Licensing services, 618
Exporting, 21
Expropriation, 252–253
External environment facts, 17

Faith. *See* Religion
Faking, 469
Farm equipment, 379
Fast-food industry, 26, 452, 470, 538
Federal Reserve Board (FRB), 620
Fees, 41
Fieldwork, 231
Fifth world, 382
Finance, international, 122–134
Financial Accounting Standards Board (FASB), 136
Financial indicators, 445
Financial management, multinational, 125–130
  financial objectives, 127–128
  money management, 128–129
  repatriation of funds, 130
Finland
  advertising expenditures in, 551
  automobile purchasing, 228
  European Free Trade Association and, 152
First world, 382
Fixed cost, 485–486
Fixed exchange rates, 107–108
"Flexible" exchange rates, 107
Flexible strategy, 130
Floating exchange rates, 107–108
Food, 193, 224–227, 277, 282, 285
  industry, 42, 287, 374, 461–462
Food and Drug Administration, 282
Foreign aid, 12, 49
Foreign buyer program, 617
Foreign Corrupt Practices Act (FCPA) of 1977, 48, 282–283, 621
Foreign direct investment (FDI), foreign exchange, 108–112

  meaning of, 108–109
  risk, 130
  transactions, 111
Foreign freight forwarder, 516, 631
Foreign investment regulations, 279–280
Foreign retailers, 521
Foreign Sales Corporations (FSCs), 613–614
Foreign Trade Index (FTI), 616
Foreign-trade zones, 633
Formalization, 532
Forward deal, 111
Foundation for Transportation Development (FTD), 237
Fourth World countries classification, 382
France
  advertising in, 228, 230, 551
  consumption in, 190, 192–193, 227, 356
  ethics of managers in, 222
  European Coal and Steel Community and, 143
  European Union and, 146, 158
  foreign investment in, 247–248
  government in, 257
  Louvre Agreements, 108
  market size of, 376
  political conflict in, 250
  public-sector enterprise, 261
Franchising, international, 540–541
Free-along-side-ship (F.A.S.) price, 497
Free-on-board (F.O.B.) price, 497
Free trade area (FTA) market agreement, 141, 145
Free-trade zones, 633

General Agreement on Tariffs and Trade (GATT), 43, 45, 47, 105
  agreement on trade in civil aircraft, 315
  DISC program and, 613
  Omnibus Trade and Competitiveness Act of 1988 and, 620
  market agreements under, 159
  regional cooperation, 12, 159
  ruling of, 621
Geocentric management orientation, 682, 704
Geography, market segmentation, 382–383, 676–677
Germany, Federal Republic of

Subject Index

advertising in, 228, 230, 551
consuming capacities of, 190, 227
European Coal and Steel Community and, 143
European Union and, 146, 158
ethics of managers in, 222
gift-giving in, 225
labor in, 256
market size of, 376
attitudes toward punctuality in, 219
"round-tripping" in, 280
Ghana
  business climate in, 250,
  retailing in, 536
Gift-giving, 225–226
Global Scan, 387
Gold bullion standard, 115
Gold exchange standard, 115
Gold standard, 110
Governments, role of, 44–47, 252, 258–262, 351
Grand tour, 264
Gray market, 523–525
Great Britain. *See* United Kingdom
Greece, 20, 146, 158, 551
Gross national product (GNP), 3, 20, 189, 191
Group of Seven, 155
Guatemala, 219, 536, 551
Guinea, political intervention in, 251

Hall's map of culture, 233–235, 238–239
Hard currencies, 110
Harmonized Commodity Description and Coding System, 353–354
Health clubs, 338
Hinduism, 385
Holland. *See* Netherlands, the
Hong Kong, 230, 277–278, 336–337, 551
Host country
  inducements of, 268
  laws, 276–281
  requirements, 618
Hungary, 152, 221, 226, 266
Hypermarkets, 538

Iceland, European Free Trade Association and, 152
Image-building, pricing and, 485
Imitation, 469
Imports

challenge, meeting, 503
charges on, 41, 45
credit discriminations, 42
duty, 278
licensing, 279
restrictions, 254–255
share of U.S. market occupied by, 612
valuation of, 41
Improved product, 195
Incipient demand, 195
Inconvertible currencies, 110
Income, population and, 189–190
Income statement, 134
India
  advertising expenditures in, 551
  Bhopal disaster in, 25, 276
  business climate in, 250, 266–268
  consumption in, 11, 190, 192
  culture of, 221, 357
  government in, 257
  host-country currency, 129
  import licensing requirements in, 279
  joint venture in, 247
  marketing in, 335, 357, 373, 376
  retailing in, 536
  wholesaling in, 534
Indonesia
  advertising expenditures in, 551
  business climate in, 250, 265–266, 268
  marketing research in, 337
  tobacco consumption in, 7
Inducements of host country, 268
Information scanning and monitoring, 719
Insider trading, 135
Inspection certificate, 629
Insurance certificate, 630
Insurance industry, 288
Inter-American Commercial Arbitration Commission, 296
Inter-American Convention, 290
Intergovernmental acceptance of testing methods, 41
Intermarket segmentation, 386–388
Intermediaries, 522, 528–531, 544–545
Internal environment factors, 17
Internal Revenue Service (IRS), 282, 506
International Accounting Standards Committee (IASC), 135, 138
International Bureau for the Protection of Industrial Property, 290

International business, 5–14. *See also* Multinational Corporations
  dividend policy, 130
  franchising, 540–541
  organization of, 674–676
International Chamber of Commerce (ICC), 296
Internal Market Program of the European Community, 149
International Center for Settlement of Investment Disputes (ICSID), The, 295–296
International Civil Aviation Organization (ICAO), 291
International Claims Commission (ICC), 297
International Congress of Accountants (ICA), 135
International Convention on the Harmonized Commodity Description and Coding System, 293
International Coordination Committee for the Accounting Profession (ICCAP), 135
International Country Risk Guide (ICRG), 264
International Court of Justice (ICJ), 296–297
International Information Services Ltd. (IIS), 351
International Labor Organization (ILO), 291
International marketers, information requirements of, 341–345
International marketing
  aspects of, 2–28
  definition of, 15–16
  framework of, 17–18
  growing importance of, 13–17
  research, 335–364
International Monetary Fund (IMF), 104–107, 118–119, 159
  Articles of Agreement, 107
  debt crisis and, 105–107
  as source of secondary data, 345
International Standards Organization (ISO), 292
International Telecommunications Satellite Consortium (INTEL-SAT), 292
International Telecommunications Union (ITU), 291

International Trade Administration (ITA), 614–618
International Trade Commission, 279
Internalization theory, 38–39
Inventory management, 542
Investments
  direct, 6
  incentives for, 280
  international, 131–133, 260, 269, 279–280
  proposals, 131–132
"Invisibles," 607
Invoices, 629
Iran
  international stance of government in, 260
  religion and economic systems in, 194, 220–221, 262
  retailing in, 536
Iraq, expropriations in, 253
Ireland
  advertising expenditures in, 551
  Economic Union and, 146
  food consumption, 193
  wholesaling in, 534
Iron ore, 143
Islam, 194, 216, 220, 262, 357, 372, 385. See also Muslims
Israel
  advertising expenditures in, 551
  Arab boycott of, 285
  consuming capacities, 190
  market control in, 255
  retailing in, 536
  wholesaling in, 534
Italy
  advertising expenditures in, 551
  automobile purchasing, 228
  consuming capacities of, 190, 193, 227–228, 356
  European Coal and Steel Community, 143
  European Union, 146
  government in, 257
  Louvre Agreements, 108
  market size of, 376
  retailing industry, 4
  wholesaling in, 534

Japan
  advertising in, 229–230, 551
  attitude toward foreign investment in, 260, 268

automobile industry in, 197–198, 287
customer service in, 513
consumer attitude surveys in, 344
consuming capacities of, 15, 23, 190, 227, 457, 529
consumption expenditures, 192–193, 228
culture of, 221–222
delegation in firms, 690
distribution channels in, 511–513
dumping accusations toward, 279
export market, 34, 281, 285
fast food industry in, 26
gift-giving in, 225
Louvre Agreements, 108
market size in, 376
marketing in, 335–337, 493
mail-order business in, 538
music industry in, 611
pricing structure in, 487, 499
privacy concerns in, 357–358
attitudes toward punctuality in, 219
retailing in, 536, 538
steel industry, 35–36, 279
tariffs in, 15, 42, 47
tobacco monopolies in, 248
trade policy of, 277, 288
trading companies in, 521–522
U.S. pressure to reduce trade barriers in, 619
wholesaling in, 534
Johnson, Lyndon, administration
  dollar valuation, 111
Joint ventures, 23–25, 253, 283, 447
Jordan
  government in, 258
  state-controlled markets in, 526
Judaism, 385
Justice Department, U.S., 283

Kelly's Manufacturers and Merchants Directory, 356
Kenya
  bargaining power of multinational corporations in, 268
  retailing in, 536
  tobacco consumption in, 7
  taboos in, 230
Knowledge, 217
Korea
  brewery, 8
  coffee consumption, 227
  culture of, 222

consumption expenditures, 192
taboos in, 230

Labeling, 41, 473–474
Labor, 35, 13, 142, 256, 723
Labor restrictions, 256
Language, 218–219, 592
Latent demand, 195
Latin America
  economic cooperation in, 153–154
  expropriations in, 253
  Inter-American Convention, 290
  labor unions in, 256
  market opportunities in, 372
  marketing research industry in, 335
  nonresponse by interviewees, 357
  tariff reduction programs, 47
Latin American Free Trade Area (LAFTA), 145, 153, 383
Latin American Integration Association, 153
Laws, 273–295
  host country, 276–281
  international, 288–295
  restricting trading, 281
Leasing, 504–506
Less-developed countries (LDCs), 6, 15–16, 118
Letter of credit, 632
Levies, variable, 42
Libya, expropriations in, 253
Licensing, 22–23, 41, 282, 447, 627–629
Liechtenstein, European Free Trade Association and, 152
Liquid assets, management of foreign dominated, 722–723
Localized advertising, 553–563
Location research, 343
Lome Convention of 1975, 146
London Court of Arbitration, 296
London Stock Exchange, 136
Louvre Agreements (1987), 108, 109
Luxembourg, 143, 146

Macroeconomic environment, 189–190, 198–199
Madrid Arrangement for International Registration of Trademarks, 290, 470
Magazines, 563–566, 569
Maghreb Economic Community, 153
Mail order, 352, 538

Subject Index

Malaysia, retailing in, 536
"Managed trade," 45
Management contracts, 22
Managerial know how, 36
Managers, attitude toward foreign, 260
Manufacturer's export agent (MEA), 516
Market, dimensions of global, 375–377
  segmenting global, 377–380
Market approach to price setting, 491–493, 505
Market access, control of, 268
Market agreements, regional, 140–161
  effect on marketing, 141–143
    in Asia, 154–155
    in Europe, 146–153
    in Latin America, 153–154
    North American Free Trade Agreement, 157–158
    U.S.-Canada Free Trade Agreement, 155–157
  types of, 144–146
Market characteristics of new products, 464–465
Market conditions, 450–451
Market control, 255
Market development, 448
Market Groups, 294
Market penetration, 694–695
Market potential, 342
Market promotion program, 287
Market research, 342, 359
Market saturation, 7–8
Market segmentation, 377–378, 380
Markets/marketing
  agreements, 42, 141–143, 283
  cultural influence on, 222–227
  customers, locating, 627
  domestic versus international, 16–17
  environmental factors affecting international, 187
  financial decisions affecting, 123–125
  information system, international, 336, 359–362
  intelligence, 336, 359
  international, 2–28, 97, 333–364, 441–480, 456
  mix variables, 336
  performance research, 342
  plans, 207–210
  politics and, 246–248
  research, 335–364

  analysis, interpretation, and report preparation, 340
  data collection, 340
  framework for, 338–340
    identifying alternative information sources, 339–340
  meaning of, 336–337
  organization for, 358–359, 672–701
  planning and strategy, 702–727
  types of, 341
  share, 342
  social, 539
  standards, 41
  strategy, 198–200, 204–207, 540–541
  structure, 338
  testing, 458
Markets
  multinational corporations and world, 49–54
  selecting national, 203–204
  emergence of new, 10–11
  choosing export, 622–627
Marketplace, global, 365–439
Marking. *See* Labeling
Marshall Aid Program, 5, 143
Maslow's hierarchy of needs, 238
Matchmaker Trade Delegations, 618
Matrix organization, 677–680
Maastricht Treaty, 151
Media, 560–561, 563–570, 573–574
Medical equipent industry, 288
Mercado Comun del Sur (Mercosur), 154
Merchant intermediaries, 517–527
Metric system regulations, 618
Mexico
  consumption in, 190, 192
  foreign investment in, 247, 268
  gift-giving in, 226
  government in, 257
  market size of, 376
  North American Free Trade Agreement, 157–158, 265
  political risk index of, 265
  purchase behavior, 228
  retailing in, 536
Microeconomic environment, 195–198
Minimal product adaptation, 453
Minimum import price limits, 41
Monarchy, 258
Monetary system, international, 102–121
Money management, 128–129

Monopoly, 487
Mores, importance of, 222, 226
Morocco, retailing in, 536
Most-favored-nation clause, 47
Multilateral Development Banks (MDBs), 105
Multilateral Trade Organization, 47
Multinational corporations (MNCs), 14, 18–26, 378, 519
  challenges for, 722–724
  conflicts and their resolution, 695–698
  consolidation of accounts, 136–137
  control within, 691–693
  bargaining power of, 267–268
  as agents of change, 239–240
  dimension of, 19–20
  entry strategies into foreign markets for, 21–25
  evaluation and control of foreign markets, 691–695
  financial measures of performance of, 693–694
  as instruments of foreign policy, 284
  home base location of, 689
  internalization theory and, 39
  marketing integration in, 690–691
  marketing planning and strategy for, 702–727
  organizational designs of, 673–681
  political perspectives affecting, 256–263
  sales management of, 583–604
  from the Third World, 21
  world markets and, 49–54
Music industry, 611
Muslims, 218, 457. *See* also Islam
Mutual economic dependence, 195

National Bureau of Standards (NBS). *See* National Institute of Standards and Technology
National Center for Standards and Certification Information (NCSCI), 618
National Export Strategy (1994), 613, 621, 636
National Federation of Coffee Growers of Colombia, 553
National Institute of Standards and Technology (NIST), 292
Nationalization, 253
Natives, 584
Need perception, 464–465

Negotiating, 597–598
Netherlands, the, 4, 143, 146, 190, 193
 automobile purchasing in, 228
Networking, corporate, 683–686
New International Economic Order (NIEO), 144
New Product Information Service (NPIS), 616
New York Stock Exchange, 135
New Zealand, 20, 190, 335, 536
Newspapers, 563–566, 569
Niche market, 379
Nigeria, 257, 536
Nontariff barriers, 41–43, 148, 281
North American Free Trade Agreement (NAFTA), 48–49, 157–158, 265
Norway, 144, 152, 193

O-analysis, 386
Objective setting, 708–709
Obligatory product adaptation, 453
"Offshore market," 117
Oil, 35, 106, 118–119, 486
Oligopolistic competition, 487
Omnibus Trade and Competitiveness Act of 1988, 48, 282, 284, 292, 612, 620–621, 636
Open account, 631–632
Orderly marketing agreements, 42
Organization for Economic Cooperation and Development (OECD), 105, 382
Organization for European Economic Cooperation (OEEC), 143
Organization of Petroleum Exporting Countries (OPEC), 6, 118
Organizational designs of multinational firms, 673–686
Orientation for foreign sales personnel, 592–593
Overseas military market representatives, 518–519
Overseas Private Investment Corporation (OPIC), 49, 618–619, 635–636

Pacific Basin Economic Council, 154
Pacific Rim countries, 369–370
Packaging
 international, 472–474
 labeling, and marketing standards, 41
Packing and marking, 472–473, 630–631
Pakistan, 217, 236–237, 335, 536

Paper industry, 21
Paper gold, 105
Par of exchange, 110
Paraguay, consuming capacities of, 190
Parent company's home government, multinational corporations relationship with, 260
Paris Convention, 470
Patent licensing agreement, 22
Patents, 46, 288
Payment, receiving, 631–632
Peoples Republic of China
 automobile industry in, 165–166
 as a market, 11, 97–98, 373, 376
 tariff reduction programs of, 47
 trial of a salesman in, 277–278
Performance evaluation and control of foreign operations, 691–695
Perfume, 554
Permanent Court of Arbitration (PCA), 297
Personal selling, 343, 549, 584–590
Personnel
 policy guidelines, 590–594
 sales, 584–590
Peru, 190, 251, 253, 268
Philanthropy, global, 602
Photography market, 456
Physical distribution (PD), 541–544
Piggybacking, 518
Piracy (brand piracy), 469–470, 611
Planning and strategy
 control and, 671–701
 achieving effectiveness, 708–710, 719–720
 international, 703–710
 process, 711–713
 professionals, 709
 short-term, 705–707
 strategic, 707–708
Pluralistic model of national politics, 263
Poland
 European Free Trade Association, 144
 European Union and, 152
 investment rating of, 266
Polycentric approach to marketing, 682, 699, 704
Pharmaceuticals, 378
Philippines
 consumption in, 190, 192
 political conflict in, 250
Political conflict, 250–251

Political environment, 202, 245–272
 intervention, 251–256
 market segmentation and, 383–384
 perspectives of a nation, 256–263
 sources of problems in, 248–251
Political grouping of countries, 383–384
Political model systems, 262–263
Political risk assessment (PRA), 250, 263–266
Political sovereignty, 249
Political union, 145–146
Politics and marketing, 246–248
Pooled strategy, 130
Popular culture, 608
Population
 income and, 189–190, 194
 world, 366
Portugal
 European Free Trade Association and, 152
 European Union and, 146, 158
Post exchanges (PXs), 518
Postal system, 356
Postcommunist countries, 370–372
Predicasts, 349
Preferred relationship, 145
Price/pricing, 230–231, 255–256, 343
 control, 255–256
 destination, 493, 505
 escalation, 495–496, 505
 factors of, 485–490
 governments and, 489–490
 international, 481–509
 objective, 485
 orientation, 490–493
 responsibility for, 484–485
 transfer, 123, 498–501
 uniform versus differentiated, 483–484
Pride/prejudice, importance of, 221–222
Price sensitive industry, 486
Primacy of host country approach, 231
Primary data, 339, 347, 355–358
Primary message systems, 233
Prior import deposit requirements, 41
Private branding for foreign markets, 471–472
Private safety net, 119
Privileged position, 487–488
Procurement policies, 41
Producer cartel, 159

Product(s), 237
  adaptation and diffusion of, 453, 462–465
  characteristics of, 560
  commoditization of, 469
  complexity of, 464
  concept, 338
  design strategy, 447–453, 476
  development process, 453–462, 476, 695
  differentiation, 268
  diversification, 465–467
  elimination, 461–462
  introducing to host country, 455–458
  life cycle model, 36–37, 447, 454
  meaning of, 443–444, 476
  nature of, 448, 493–495, 505
  objectives, 445
  organization, 677–678
  patterns, 560
  planning, 442–480
  portfolio approach, 713–718
  proliferation, 469
  research, 342
  specialization, 624–626, 674
Production indicators, 194
Production process, decentralization of, 723
Production sharing, 37–38
Productivity, 34
Profit performance, comparison of, 137
Promotion, 229–230, 549
  research, 342–343
Property, protection of, 288–291
Protectionism, 40, 44–45, 48, 148
Prototype product, 458
Public relations overseas, 601–602
Punctuality, attitudes toward, 219
Purchasing agents, 520

Question marks, market share and, 714
Questionnaires, use of, 357
Quotas, 41–43, 285

Radio, 567–569
Razor market, 452, 529, 556
Recession, 13
Reciprocal Trade Agreement Act of 1934, 47
Reciprocity, 532
Reconstruction after World War II, 103–104

Regional Cooperation for Development (RCD), 155
Regional exporter, 14
Religion, 194, 216, 220–221, 384–385
Repatriation and reassignment of sales personnel, 130, 594–597
Research and development (R&D), overseas, 459–461, 476–477
Research information, general, 344
Research institutes, 351
Residents, 113
Residual income, 694
Retailing, 4, 535–540
Return on investment (ROI), 693–694
Revenue Act of 1971, 613
Risk, 24, 264
Risk/reward criteria analysis, 202
Robinson-Patman Act, 489, 501
Romania
  European Union and, 152
  attitudes toward punctuality in, 219
Rome Treaty of 1957, 146
"Round-tripping," 280
Russia
  Coca Cola's agreement with, 283–284
  Commonwealth of Independent States, 159
  Council for Mutual Economic Assistance and, 152
  market size in, 371–372, 376
  wholesaling in, 534

Sales forcasts, 342
Sales generation, 584
Sales negotiations, international, 597–598
Sales promotion, 549, 599–601
  foreign, 583–604
Sales representative, 520
Sales support, 584
Sampling, use of, 355–366
Sanctions, 249
Saudia Arabia
  aircraft purchase by, 49
  copyright law in, 291
  government in, 258, 262
  marketing research industry in, 335
  retailing in, 536
Screening, 458
Second World countries classification, 382
Secondary marketing research data, 339, 345–355

Service industries development program, 618
Services, 7, 695
  international, 474–475, 489
  tariff reduction programs, 46
Self-reference criterion (SRC), 236
Sheltered businesses, 34
Shipper requirements, 473
Shipper's export declaration, 629
Shipping, 631
Shoe industry, 5
Simulation models, computerized, 26
Singapore, 20, 279, 281, 338, 536
Single Administrative Document, 150
Single-column tariff, 40
Single Europe Act (1986), 151
Social/cultural factors, economic environment and, 202
Social interactions, importance of, 217–218
Social roles, 218
Socialization, 253
Soft currencies, 110
Soft drink market, 11, 337, 443–444, 454, 456
South Africa, 190, 536
South America, marketing research industry in, 335
South Asian Association for Regional Cooperation (SAARC), 155
South Korea
  culture of, 221
  government in, 257
  retailing in, 536
  subsidy in, 278
  tobacco monopolies in, 248
  trade policy in, 276–277
  wholesaling in, 534
Soviet Union. See Russia
Space, occupation of, 220
Spain
  Economic Union and, 146, 158
  food consumption in, 193
  market control in, 268
  retailing industry in, 4
Special drawing rights (SDRs), 105, 120
Specialization, 34–36
Specific duty, 40
Sri Lanka, 192, 282, 335
Stabilized competition, 487–488
Stakeholder's interests, 445
Standard disparities, 41
Standardization, 447–451, 532

in advertising, 553–563
Standards (nontariff barriers), 41
Staple Food Control Act, 277
Stars, market share and, 713–714
State-centric model of international politics, 263
"Stateless money," 117
State-owned (Marxist) systems, 194
Steel industry, 7, 143, 279, 369
 in Japan, 35, 36
 pricing of, 283
 subsidies for, 42, 278
Stock ownership, 6
Strategic alliances, 25
Strategic business units (SBUs), 713, 715, 725
Strategic market planning, 707–708, 710–712, 725
Strategic response to political risk, 266–269
Strivers, 387
Subsidiaries, 674
 decision making authority of foreign, 686–691
 planning at level of, 704–710
Subsidies, 42, 46, 278
Supermarkets, 538
Sweden
 consumption expenditures in, 192–193
 European Free Trade Association and, 144, 152
 GNP of, 20
 wholesaling in, 534
Switch-trading arrangement, 634
Switzerland
 consuming capacities of, 190, 193
 European Free Trade Association and, 144, 152
 GNP of, 20
 languages spoken in, 357
 television advertising in, 4
Syria, 146, 526
System of National Accounts (SNA), 354–355

Taboos around the world, 230
Taxes
 border, 41
 commodity, 247
 on foreign interest payments, 129
 holiday, 280
 international dividend policy, 130

laws to eliminate loopholes, 286
Teenage market, 559
Television, 570
Trade-policy, 45
 value-added, 247
Taiwan, 230, 248, 261, 276
Tanzania
 political intervention in, 251
 retailing, 536
Target Group Index (TGI) 1990 survey, 352
Target market for advertising campaign, 559
Tariff(s), 40, 145, 278, 283
 barriers, 377
 classifications, 41
 in Japanese markets, 15
 reduction programs, 43–47
Tariff Schedules of the United States Annotated (TSUSA) and Schedule B, 354
Tax control, 255
Tax havens, 285
Tax incentives, 13
Tax treaties, 286–287
Tax Reform Act of 1976, 285
Taxes
 border, 41
 commodity, 247
 on foreign interest payments, 129
 holiday, 280
 international dividentd policy, 130
 laws to eliminate loopholes, 286
Tea, 282, 357
Technology, 36, 247–248, 377
Teenage market, 388
Telecommunications industry, 288, 292
Telephones, 356
Television advertising, 4, 550, 566–569, 576–578
Terrorism, 251
Testing methods, intergovernmental acceptance of, 41
Textile industry, 626
 advertising for, 554
 foreign competition in U.S., 8
 import restrictions, 45, 282, 285
 quotas, 43
 tariff reduction programs, 46
Thailand
 advertising in, 229–230
 consuming capacities, 190
 investment rating of, 265

milk-based products in, 338–339
 retailing in, 536
 tobacco imports, 577
 taboos in, 230
 tobacco monopoly in, 248
Third country nationals, 584, 587–590
Third World countries, 11, 382
Tire industry, 282
Tobacco industry, 7, 227, 229, 247, 248, 577
Toiletries, 10, 230
Trade, 6
 barriers, 39–47, 621
 economic rationale of multination, 29–56
 fairs, overseas, 617
 history of, 30
 laws affecting foreign, 282–283
 liberalization of United States, 47–49
 liberation, 39, 47–49
 limitation on, 41
 managed, 45
 missions, overseas, 617
 policy taxes, 45
 product life cycle and international, 36–37
 protection, 45
 specialization of, 35–36
Trade Act of 1974, 48, 279
Trade and Tariff Act of 1984, 618
Trade associations, 351
Trade Expansion Act of 1962, 48
Trade Opportunities Program (TOP), 616
Trade quotas, 283
Trademark Registration Treaty, The, 290
Trademarks, 46, 275, 288, 468–469
Trading companies, 521–522
Training, 592–593
Transactions, 113
Transfer pricing, 123, 498–501, 506
Transferability analysis, 561–562
Transit tariff, 40
Transnational politics model, 263
Transnational structure, 686
Treaty of Montevideo, 154
Triad market, 367–369
Turkey, 146, 190, 356, 534
Turnkey operation, 22

Uganda, 190, 260
UNESCO (the United Nations Educational Scientific and Cultural Organization), 519
UNICEF (the United Nations Children's Fund), 519
Uniform pricing, differentiated pricing versus, 483–484
United Kingdom (UK)
  consumption in, 190, 192–193, 227, 356
  economic cooperation in, 144
  European Free Trade Association and, 143–144, 152
  European Union and, 146, 158
  gift-giving in, 226
  government in, 257–258
  Louvre Agreements, 108
  market size of, 376
  milk-based products in, 338–339
  public-sector enterprise in, 261
  retailing industry in, 4
  wholesaling in, 534
United Nations (UN), 291–294, 345, 350, 519
United States
  automobile market in, 8, 197–198, 278–279, 281, 285
  balance of payments accounts (1993) of, 114
  business overseas, perspectives of, 5–7, 9–11
  consumption in, 190, 192–193
  ethics of managers in, 222
  exports of, 3, 6, 8, 49, 256, 606–622, 721
  multinational corporations as instruments of foreign policy, 284
  government involvement in business, 257, 287, 489–490
  imports in, 3, 6, 279, 282, 609, 612, 721
  Inter-American Convention and, 290
  laws of, 282–288
  international monetary system and, 103, 108
  market size of, 376
  market and role of internationally, 722
  marketing research industry in, 335
  North American Free Trade Agreement and, 157–158
  retailing in, 536
  secondary data gathered in, 345–350
  tariffs in, 47, 283
  trade policies, 47–49, 288
  wholesaling in, 534
U.S. and Foreign Commercial Services (US/FCS), 614–615
U.S.-Canada Free Trade Agreement, 48, 155–157
U.S. Securities and Exchange Commission, 135
U.S.-Taiwan Friendship, Commerce and Navigation Treaty of 1948, 261
Universal Postal Union, 291
Universal products, 17
Urbanization, 366–367
Uruguay Round Agreement. *See* GATT

Valuation of imports, 41
Value-added tax, 247
Variable clusters (V-clusters), 386
Variable costs, 486
Variable levies, 42
Verbraucher markte, 538
Video-catalog shows, 617

Video games, 279
Vietnam, 248, 262
Vitamins, 15–16
Volume sensitive industry, 486
Voluntary export restraints, 42
Voluntary product adaptation, 453

Warehouse receipt, 630
Warehousing, 542
Warranties, international, 474–475, 489
Watch industry, 16
Webb-Pomerene Association, 516
West African Economic Community (WAEC), 153
West Germany (former), 108
  consumption expenditures, 192
  food consumption, 193
Wholesalers, 533–535
Wholly owned subsidiaries, 6
Wine, 227, 274, 356, 459
World Bank, 159, 345
World Development Report, The, 345
World Federation of Stock Exchanges, 136
World Health Organization, 291
World Information Services, 349
World Traders Data Reports (WTDRs), 617
World Trading Organization (WTO), 47

Yemen, political union of, 146
Yugoslavia, wholesaling in, 534

Zaire, mineral trade in, 35
Zambia, 35, 251
Zimbabwe, retailing in, 536

Name and Company Index

A & P (Great Atlantic and Pacific Tea Co), 6
A & W Brands Inc., 6
A. T. Cross Pencil, 554
Abrahams, Eric Anthony, 284
Aeritalia, 311
AHV Lifts, 81
Airbus, 9, 12, 142, 301–317
Ajinomoto, 457
Akhter, Humayun, 252
Alcoa, 602
Alfax, 230
All-Shave Company, 330–32
Allaire, Paul, 57, 72
American Express, 602, 773–776
American Motors, 392
American Standard, 19
American Telephone & Telegraph, 691
Amine, Lyn S., 429, 753, 765
Anderson-Clayton, 224
Anheuser-Busch, 6
Aoki, H., 690
Apple Computer, Inc, 15, 195, 246–247
ASEA Brown Boveri (Holding) Ltd., 6, 10
Au Printemps, 539
Autlan, 21
Avon Products, S.A. de C.V., 664–667
Avon Products, 19, 229, 373, 538, 664

Bahl, Amit, 416
Bahl, Raj, 416
Banks, Michael, 177
Bar Maisse, 85
Barossa Winery, 740–753
Bavishi, Vinod, 180
Beaupre, Phillipe, 85
Benetton, 3
Berg Steel Pipe Co., 633

Berne Manufacturing, 82
Bic Pen Corporation, 6
Birds Eye Wall, Ltd., 193
Birkigt, Holger U., 324
Birla Group, 21
Black & Decker, 19
Blackwell, Roger D., 232
BMW, 6, 197
Body Shop, 724
Boeing, 9, 12, 49, 301–317, 474, 585
Boston Consulting Group (BCG), 713, 715
Boyd, Alan, 317
Bradley, David G., 253
Braun AG, 282, 456
Bristol-Myers, 267, 378
British Airways, 562
British American Tobacco Company, 467
Brooke Bond Tea Company, 456
Brooks, Mitch, 182
Brown Boveri, 266
Bruce, Grady D., 410
Bull Groupe, 248
Burger King, 287
Business International Corporation, 351

C. Itoh & Company, 522
Cadbury Schweppes PLC, 6
Cadbury-Schweppes Pty. Ltd., 639
California Foods Corporation, 433–437
Campbell Soup Co., 287, 373, 388, 450, 454, 461, 467
Canadian Tire, 81
Canon, 59, 62, 65, 70–72, 493
Cantina Sociale di Foggia, 274
Carlsberg, 230

Carlson, Chester, 59
Cartier, 470
Caspar, Christian, 112
Caterpillar, 19
Cavusgil, S. Tamer, 347, 495
Cereal Partners Worldwide (CPW), 324, 326
Chesbrough-Pond, 25, 466
Chivaly International, 437–439
Chrysler Corporation, 195, 388
Ciba-Geigy, 453
Cincinnati Milacron, 10
Clark Equipment Company, 504
Clinton, William, 49
Clondike Works, The, 328–330
Coca-Cola Co. 11, 19, 23, 219, 250, 283, 285, 443, 447, 454, 466, 600
Colgate-Palmolive Company, 19, 230, 454, 593
Combustion Engineering Inc., 6
Compagnie International pour L'Informatique, 267
Compaq, 457
Conklin, David W., 169
Connecticut Corporation (Japan), 667–670
Coors Brewing Co., 8
Copyer, 62
CPC International, 266
Cray Research, 689
Currency Concepts International, 410
Curtis Automotive Hoist, 80–87
Curtis, Mark, 80

Dairy Queen, 541
Data Research Inc., 361
Datsun, 9
Deere & Company, 379, 554, 562
Del Monte, 287

789

Dell Computers, 195
Denny's, 541
Disney, 8
Domino's Pizza, 450
Dow Chemical, 19, 596
Dunn, Herbert, 251
Drefuss, Joel, 486
Drucker, Peter, 37, 38, 54
duPont, 266, 602, 691

Eiteman, David K., 252
El Norte Chemicals, Ltd., 317–323
Engel, James F., 192, 232
EQ Bank, 177–179
Estee Lauder, Inc., 388

Farris, Paul W., 639
Federal Express, 753–765
Federated Department Stores, 538
Fieldcrest Mills, 528
Firestone, 81
Florio, James, 316
Foote, Arnold, Jr., 284
Ford Motor Company, 3, 9, 13, 141, 197, 247, 268, 379, 474, 600
Fuji Photo Film, 60
Fuji Xerox, 57–79
Fujitsu Ltd., 499

G. D. Searle & Co., 360
Gagnon, Pierre, 80
Gallup Research, 351
Gandhi, Rajiv, 250
Gardner, Ian, 224
GE Mintel Ltd., 193
General Electric, 9, 311, 448, 613, 635
General Foods, 23, 562
General Mills, 324
General Motors Corporation, 20, 23, 195, 280, 370, 556, 692
Gerber Products Co., 6, 7, 11, 367, 462, 498
Gergacz, Joseph, 177
Gillette Co., 10, 19, 49–53, 195, 282, 451, 452, 456, 529, 555, 556
Glavin, William, 72
Gloria Vanderbilt, 12
Gomes-Cassers, Benjamin, 57
Goodyear, 81
Graham, John F., 416
Grey Advertising, 554
Gucci, 3, 12
Gulf Oil, 456

H.J. Heinz Co., 19, 472, 602

Hall, Edward T., 233, 234, 238
Haloid Corporation, 59
Harrari, Ehud, 588
Hassan, Salah S., 389
Hatfield Graphics, Inc., 94–98
Helene Curtis, 195
Henley, Donald S., 488
Hershey Foods, 287, 681
Hertz, 219
Hertzell, Staffan, 112
Hewlett-Packard, 13, 19, 602
Hicks, Wayland, 67
Hillebrand Estates Winery Limited, 169–176
Hitachi Ltd. 289
Hogan, Paul, 225
Honda Motors, 9, 195
Honeywell Bull, 267, 461
Honeywell Inc., 267,, 288, 461
Hoover Company, 465, 600
Human Relations Area Files Inc., 386
Hunt, Mark, 94,

IBH Holding AG of Mainz, 280
IBM, 19, 23, 65, 67, 142, 195, 247–248, 266, 268, 456, 579, 602, 712
Idéale Imprimerie, 429–433
Impecina, 87–91
Imperial Chemicals Industries, 468, 687
Intel, 13
International Harvester Company, 379
International Machine Corporation (IMC), 180–181
International Playtex, Inc., 554, 562
ITT, 13, 19, 268, 456, 461

J. C. Penney, 472, 538
J. Walter Thompson, 358
Jinro, 8
Johansson, Johny K., 344
Johnson & Johnson, 19, 195

K-Mart Corporation, 538
Kaihatsu, Hideki, 60
Kanter, Rosabeth Moss, 231
Katsanis, Lea Prevel, 389
Kaynak, Erdener, 649
Kearns, David, 63, 67, 68, 70
Kellogg Co., 193, 324–327, 373, 662–663
Kennard, Jeff, 59, 63
Kentucky Fried Chicken, 224, 227, 251, 541, 556
Khan, Mohammad Ishaq, 753, 765

Kirkland, Richard L., Jr., 625
Kitasei, Hilary Hinds, 513
Knowlton, Thomas A., 324
Kobayashi, Setsutaro, 60
Kobayashi, Yotaro (Tony), 57, 59, 62, 63
Kodak, 65, 450, 543
Kollat, David T., 232
Konica, 62
Kraft, 535

Langbo, Arnold G., 324
Larréché, Jean-Claude, 716
Law, Thomas, 60
Lee, James A., 236
Lego System, 290
Lever Brothers, 6, 593
Levi Strauss & Co., 289, 468, 559
Levien, Roger, 77
Levitt, Theodore, 12
Li, Hang, 163
Linear Technology, 379
Lippman, John, 576
Lockheed Corporation, 309, 373
Loctite, 675
Logitech, 729–740
LTV, 7
Lusch, Robert F., 252

M&M Mars, 287
MacDermid, Inc., 771–773
MacLennan, John, 182
Main, Jeremy, 50, 687
Malespin, Carlos, 395
Malik, Leena, 416
Marcona Mining, 268
Marks and Spencer, Ltd., 92–94
Martre, Henri, 317
Marubeni Corporation, 522
Maslow, Abraham H., 238
Massy-Ferguson Ltd., 379
Matsushita Electric Industrial Co., 6, 23
Mattel Toys, 228
Maxwell House, 23
Maytag Corporation, 445
MCA, 6
McCollough, Peter, 61, 67
McCullough, James, 218
McDonald's, 3, 4, 26, 227, 287, 373, 452, 470, 541
McDonnell Douglas, 9, 49, 301–317
McIlhenny Company: Japan, 395–410
McIlhenny, Edmund, 395
McIlhenny, Walter S., 395

Name and Company Index

McQuade, Krista, 57
Mead Corporation, 222
Mead, Nelson, 222
Mercedes-Benz, 12, 387
Meredith, Bob, 68
Metro Corporation, 87–91
Meyer, Herbert E., 528
Mill, John Stuart, 30
Minnesota Mining and Manufacturing, 468
Minolta Camera Co., 288, 472
Mishel, Boris, 314
Mitsubishi, 9
Mitsubishi Corporation, 522
Mitsui & Company, 522
Mitsui, 634
Mitterrand, Francois, 246
Modha, Ash, 416
Modha, Prashant, 416
Mondetta Everywear, 416–429
Moriarty, R., 308
Morita, Akio, 344
Motorola, Inc., 289
Mountain Dew, 224
Mubarak Dairies Limited, 765–770

N&N Contact Lens International Inc., 615
Nabisco, 287
Nasar Car Company, 22
National Semiconductor, 13
National Tank Inc., 88
NCH Promotional Services, 599
Neor, David M., 590
Nestlé S.A., 6, 23, 260, 266, 324, 447, 467, 562, 681
Network Backer Spielvogel Bates Worldwide Inc., 387
Newhouse, John, 304
Nike, 554, 563
Nintendo, 12
Nissho-Iwai Company, 522
Nixon, Richard, 255
Nonaka, Ikujiro, 344
NTT, 288

Ocean Spray Cranberries, 287
Ogawa, Yoichi, 61
Ogilvy & Mather, 579
Ohbora, Tatsuo, 457
Ohmae, Kenichi, 753
Ohta, Takeshi, 109

Parsons, Andrew, 457

PepsiCo Inc., 11, 224, 247
Pepsodent, 230
Perkins, Stuart, 125
Philip Morris, Inc., 562
Philips Company, 448
Pierson, Jean, 301
Pillay, Joseph, 711
Plummer, Joseph T. 226
Pohorly, Joseph, 169
Polaroid Corporation, 12, 448, 456, 472
Predicasts, 351, 361
Price Waterhouse, 358
Printemps, 92
Procter & Gamble (P&G), 195–196, 211, 230, 373, 460, 469, 562, 573, 593
Prudhomme, Paul, 397

Quaker Oats, 287

R. J. Reynolds, 224
Rank Xerox, 59–77
Rao, C. P., 163
RCA, 9
Reagan, Ronald, 48, 316
Reardon, Jim, 183
Reebok, 563
Renault, 228
Ricardo, David, 30, 31
Rickitt & Colman, 224
Ricoh, 59, 62
Riesenbeck, Hajo, 457
Rimmel Ltd., 456
Riunite, 274
Rizkallah, Elias G., 390
Robichaux, Mark, 615
Robock, Stefan H., 234, 235
Roetman, Orvil, 316
Rokeach, M., 231, 233
Root, Franklin R., 40
Ryans, Adrian B., 729

Saatchi & Saatchi, 562
Sadat, Anwar, 250
Safeway Corporation, 538
Sakamoto, Moto, 61
Salinas de Gortari, Carlos, 265
Sandoz AG, 6
Schick, 529
Schweppes Drinks, 639–649
Sears, Roebuck, 228, 538
Seiko, 529
Seiko Epson, 494

Sensortron Technology Ltd., 457
Shanghai Aviation Industry Corporation, 312
Shanghai Volkswagen Corp., 163–168
Shawinigan Chemical of Canada, 456
Shawky, Hany A., 180
Shell Oil, 468
Shono, Nobuo, 62
Shrontz, Frank, 301
Sieff, J. Edward, 92
Simmons, Kenneth, 234, 235
Simmons, Ned, 396
Singapore Airlines, 711
Skenazy, Lenore, 229
Smith, Adam, 30
Smith, Brock, 729
Smith, David K., Jr., 317
Smith, Fred, 753
Smith, Theodore F., 163
Sony, 3, 12, 344
Sorensen, George, 169–176
Sperry, Drew, 182
Sperry/MacLennan, 182–186
Sperry Rand Corporation, 201
Sperry, Sheila, 182,
Squibb, 378
Srinivasulu, S. L., 125
Stonehill, Authur I., 252
Sumitomo Shoji, 522
Swan, John, 169

Takara, 228
Tan, Tiong Chin, 218
TAW Company, 504
Taylor, Sir Edward, 216
Terada, Matazo, 62
Thomson, 9
Timex Co., 373, 633
Toyota, 9, 12, 459
Toys "R" Us, 539, 655–661
Tyco, 290

Ulker Biscuits, Inc., 649–654
Underberg, Emil, 170, 176
Unilever, 224, 466, 468, 554, 573
Union Carbide Corporation, 25, 276, 456, 596, 692
United Airlines, 225
United Brands, 490
United Laboratories, 21
United Technologies Corporation, 613
USX, 7

Valentine, Charles F., 193, 259, 338

Van Doren, William, 639
Vayle, Eric J. 301
Vernon, Raymond, 54
Volkswagen (VW), 9 124–25, 163–168, 195, 279, 392, 448, 461

W.R. Grace, 19
Wal-Mart, 539
Warner-Lambert Company, 229, 452
Welch's, 287
Wells, Louis, 54
Wessel, David, 54
Western Electric 268, 619
Westinghouse Electric Corp., 6, 360, 373, 590
Whitman, Daniel, 177
Whittaker Corporation, 22

Xerox, 8, 19, 57–79, 493

Yoffie, David B. 301
Young & Rubicam, 284
Yves St. Laurent, 12

Zeeman, John R., 225
Zeira, Yoram, 588
Zeming, Jiang, 168